Praise for

STEVE GOODMAN
Facing the Music

Definitive.
DAVE HOEKSTRA, *CHICAGO SUN-TIMES*,
JEFF TAMARKIN, *HARP* MAGAZINE,
BURT CONSTABLE, *DAILY HERALD*, CHICAGO

Goodman's charisma and good-time energy
shine through in hundreds of anecdotes.
PETER FENIAK, *THE GLOBE AND MAIL*

Sensationally researched and lovingly written.
TOM SHEA, *THE REPUBLICAN*,
SPRINGFIELD, MASSACHUSETTS

What a cool book about a cool guy.
CHRIS SPECTOR, *THE MIDWESTERN RECORD*

A shadow history of the '70s mainstream.
MARK ATHITAKIS, *CITYPAPER*, WASHINGTON, D.C.

Towering. ... The author's attention to detail,
journalist's experience and storyteller's ear
come to the fore.
GARY WHITEHOUSE, *GREEN MAN REVIEW*

Stunning scholarship. ... As deep and expansive as
Goodman's music. ... Does justice to one of the
greatest singer/songwriters this country has known.
PAUL ZOLLO, *AMERICAN SONGWRITER*
MAGAZINE

Likely to go down in the history of music journalism
as one of the most comprehensive tomes ever
written about a performer. ... If it was the only book
to be found on a desert island, it would keep
its discoverer thoroughly engrossed
until the rescue boat had arrived.
DOUGLAS HESELGROVE, *THE MUSIC BOX*

Thoroughly researched? Engagingly written? Covers
all the bases? I'd say yes on all counts and more! ...
Eals' grist-laden biography relates the story of this
musician in Wide Screen Technicolor complete
with Surround Sound. ... Eals' work is way beyond
exceptional and has set the biographical bar at a
whole new level.
ARTHUR WOOD, *FOLKWAX*

Exhilarating and enlightening.
MICHAEL TEARSON, *SINGOUT!* MAGAZINE

Excellent ... a sweet valentine. ...
with intelligence and compassion.
PAUL DEMKO, *CITY PAPER*, MINNEAPOLIS

Hundreds of rare and moving photographs ...
(an) insightful, well-researched exploration.
MICHAEL PARRISH, *DIRTY LINEN* MAGAZINE

It excels. ... Not to be taken lightly.
ARI DAVIDOV, *THE KLEZMER SHACK*

It's quite something. It's celebrity-packed.
STEVE COCHRAN, WGN-AM, CHICAGO

An astonishing compendium.
DIANA BREMENT, *JTNEWS*, SEATTLE

Fascinating ... wonderful, brilliant.
BILL HAHN, WFDU-FM, TEANECK, NEW JERSEY

A treasure trove. .... If you were unfamiliar with
Steve before reading this book, by the time you
work your way through he will be
forever engraved into your memory.
RICHARD MARCUS, *BLOGCRITICS.ORG*

STEVE GOODMAN
Facing the Music

A Biography by CLAY EALS

ECW Press

The front-cover photo is by Gina Jett of Largo, Florida. She captured Steve basking in applause before a trio of spotlights on Dec. 7, 1980, at the Rainbow Music Hall in Denver.

The back-cover photo is by Jim Shea of Hanalei, Hawaii. In the late spring of 1984, Shea drove Steve northeast of Los Angeles to El Mirage Lake Bed, positioned him on a board above the mosaic of clay and captured him while the sun set. This was among several potential cover images for Steve's "Santa Ana Winds" LP.

The title-page photo, by Eugene Vigil of Lynden, Washington, came by way of Jim DiOrio and was taken July 5-6, 1976, at Summerfest in Milwaukee, Wisconsin.

ECW PRESS
ecwpress.com

Library and Archives Canada Cataloguing in Publication

Eals, Clay   Steve Goodman: facing the music / Clay Eals.

ISBN 978-1-55022-732-1

1. Goodman, Steve. 2. Composers — United States — Biography. 3. Singers — United States — Biography. I. Title.

ML410.G653E12 2007

782.42164'092

C2006-906795-3

Printed in the United States

Second printing, February 2008

What's inside

THE AUTHOR

Clay Eals, 2005

(Photo by Ian Woofenden)

Clay Eals lives in Seattle, Washington, and has devoted his adult life to writing and publications. He worked 15 years as an editor, reporter and photographer for four Pacific Northwest newspapers, two years as a journalism teacher and 13 years as a curriculum writer and publications editor for Fred Hutchinson Cancer Research Center.

He is doing research for a biography of the namesake of baseball's Hutch Award, Fred Hutchinson, who was named Seattle's Athlete of the 20th Century.

His volunteer work has included community history projects, such as leading the preservation of a 1942 movie theater, on behalf of the Southwest Seattle Historical Society and playing Santa for the American Heart Association.

Clay, 56, is married to former journalist Meg Eals. His daughter, son-in-law and granddaughter — Karey, Jesse and Ronia Emma Bacon — live in Chicago.

OTHER BOOKS BY CLAY EALS

◆ Author and designer of the biography *Every Time a Bell Rings: The Wonderful Life of Karolyn Grimes*, © 1996, Pastime Press, Seattle, Washington, USA, 248 pages, ISBN 0-9654984-2-5.

◆ Editor, project manager and contributor, *West Side Story*, the history of West Seattle and White Center, Washington, © 1987, Robinson Newspapers, Seattle, Washington, USA, 288 pages.

◆ Designer and contributor, *Rain Check: Baseball in the Pacific Northwest*, edited by Mark Armour, photos from the David Eskenazi Collection, © 2006, Society for American Baseball Research, Cleveland, Ohio, USA, 128 pages, ISBN 1-933599-02-2.

AUTHOR'S NOTE FOR SECOND PRINTING

For this 800-page biography to merit a second printing just nine months after its initial publication in May 2007 is a dream come true. Not only does it reflect significant interest in the book's subject, but it also allows me to fix typos and other minor errors and incorporate clarifications, new anecdotes and quotes, discography listings, acknowledgments and index entries (as well as 30 new photos, for a revised overall total of 575) that surfaced since the first printing.

If you discover items in this edition that you feel need correcting, please contact me via **http://www.clayeals.com**. Fixes will be noted at the site.

The site also is where to find details on the myriad reading/music events from coast to coast that have and continue to spread word about this tome. I am grateful beyond words to the musicians, venues, media, hosts and others who have insured the success of these events. It all has proven what I've long known deep in my heart: Goodman people are everywhere. ♪

Clay Eals

'In his last days, dying, he was more alive than ever'

**Come and show me another city
with lifted head singing so proud to be
alive and coarse and strong and cunning.
CARL SANDBURG
FROM "CHICAGO," 1916**

Studs Terkel, shown in 2002.
(Photo by Stephen Anzaldi
of Northwestern University)

Steve Goodman had all of "it." The "it" is a compote of all sorts of ingredients that make a whole artist. First of all, he had the natural giftedness of a brilliant lyricist and music man. Consider the songs he composed that have become classics. The "City Of New Orleans" becomes the train of hope and joy for the human species. The others — and there are so many — add to the richness of all our lives. They evoke the laugh and the cry.

The other hallmark of this Chicago original is his generosity of heart. I have lost count of the celebrated singers whom he has brought forth to public acclaim. The wondrous John Prine comes to mind. Steve always shared; it never occurred to him to act otherwise. In knowing Steve, we loved him not only for his talents, but also for his gallantry. In his last days, dying, he was more alive than ever.

I'll never say Steve Goodman was. No, Steve Goodman is. 𝄞

Studs Terkel

'There was nothing phony about Steve Goodman'

No one wants to believe consciously that they're going to have a short life. The most brilliant people in the world are going to deal with that kind of news or suspicion with some regret. It's just your body chemistry, the most basic part of being a human being.

At some point or other, I think everyone really knows. Whether they want to know it or have a chance to know it consciously or not, I don't know. I'm not an expert in this stuff. But I have a sneaking suspicion that you really do know how long it's going to take you to fulfill the mission of your life, and I felt that in Steve Goodman.

I felt that he knew at some point, with a typical sadness that was not debilitating, that actually energized him in such a way that he could deal with things by writing songs that are deeper — or in some cases even funnier — than normal people would want to go. That kind of instinct opens up doors and allows you to be more real because you've got nothing to lose.

I sense it in people like Goodman, who, when you look into their eyes, are just taking it all in. They aren't afraid of anything. They're fearless. That kind of living gives you abilities that most people are in fear of because they recognize that those abilities come hand in hand with destiny. So most people will not take the abilities, even if you offered it to them.

You don't get that stuff, generally, until you're very old and you've worked through all the issues of life. I see it in a lot of older people. They're fearless. However, that fearlessness at the old-age home is not the same as having it onstage when you're 20-something or 30-something years old.

I met Steve Goodman maybe four or five times in my whole life face-to-face. But since the first day, I felt like I knew him. I felt like we were friends on a deeper level than just a passing, chance meeting. I felt I had a real sort of kinship, and I know he felt the same way.

I felt he had a real respect for me, and I had a tremendous respect for him. It was not a mutual admiration society. It was deeper than that. I'm sure he had that effect on other people because he just was that kind of guy.

He was just a real guy. I like real people. There was nothing phony about Steve Goodman. 🎵 **Arlo Guthrie**

> I have a sneaking suspicion that you really do know how long it's going to take you to fulfill the mission of your life, and I felt that in Steve Goodman.

(Opposite page) While performing at the 2005 Kerrville (Texas) Folk Festival, Arlo Guthrie tells a story illustrating how "one person can make a difference."
(Photo by Jim Dirden)

'You offer your love and goodness to the world'

"He was an incurable romantic. He was a little guy who never tried to make out that he was bigger. He was as engaging a performer as they come. And he was unabashedly old-fashioned."

That was the opening for a combined obituary/tribute for Steve Goodman that I wrote in September 1984 for a Seattle newspaper. I had enjoyed Steve's recorded music for more than a dozen years. But what I held more dear was twice sharing time and place with him as he performed in concert — both times in Eugene, Oregon, where he opened for Randy Newman in a basketball arena in 1977 and played a solo show in a more intimate hall in 1981. I knew that Steve wasn't a star, and it really didn't matter.

Emmylou Harris, among the last of my more than 1,000 interviewees for this book, hit it on the button when she told me, "There are a lot of great people out there that are not household words, and you know what? It's not a bad thing. Someone like Steve really touched you in a way that music is supposed to touch you, and the people who are fans of Steve Goodman will be fans till death. That's really the best success you could have as an artist."

Till death. In many ways, that's what this book is all about.

One might think the book is about Steve Goodman's music — the magical, ephemeral tunes that glow in the warmest of memories, songs so potent that I used them to woo my wife. One might think it's about the Chicago folk scene — a cacophonous cauldron of talent and spirit, a saga woefully unsung on a national scale. One might think it's about a writerly challenge — of vividly capturing a contagious life in the confines of a book. Though all of these endeavors are present, at its core this book is about living in the face of death.

Most of us seem to live as if oblivious to our mortality. Not Steve, whose leukemia struck when he was just 20. That he pushed himself to survive nearly 16 more years is remarkable. That he achieved so much in that time is a marvel.

Leukemia intensified Steve's quest for a full life, but there is no question that Steve was Steve long before his diagnosis. From his earliest days, he was driven. No one has ever tried harder to leave his stamp on the world.

Yet Steve's heightened drive shared the stage with a deepened humility that understood that we all vanish like the gold dust in "The Treasure of the Sierra

The people who are fans of Steve Goodman will be fans till death. That's really the best success you could have as an artist.
EMMYLOU HARRIS

(Opposite page) At Northwestern University's Cahn Auditorium in Evanston, Illinois, Steve performs on Feb. 5, 1977, nine months before the author first saw him in concert.
(Photo by Charles Seton)

John Hartford, shown in 1989, had a Steve-like sensibility about visions of legacy: "The first thing you do when you start having those thoughts," he said, "is go get you a book about European history that tells about all the beheadings. ..."
(Photo by Art Thieme)

Madre." One of his homilies was: "A hundred years, all new people." Kindred spirits included John Hartford, who, like Steve, lived with cancer for more than 15 years and who, seven months prior to his own death, delivered an explicit lecture that Steve may have laughed about many a time. It was about legacy.

"The first thing you do when you start having those thoughts," Hartford told me, "is go get you a book about European history that tells about all the beheadings. Then if you're still having those thoughts, you go get you a book about dinosaurs. Then if you're still feeling blue because you don't feel consequential, go get you a book on outer space. If that don't work, I don't know what the hell to tell you. Y'know, I always think about the mosquito floating down the river on his back with a hard-on, hollering, 'Open the drawbridge!' "

Though Steve was well aware of the fleeting nature of human existence, he also had the grounding, the intellect, the altruistic tenor of his turbulent times, perhaps even the spiritual ken, to understand that his life held a purpose that only he could give shape. Another of Steve's musical contemporaries, Corky Siegel, catches this point: "When you get up onstage, you realize it's not about the music. It's about something much bigger. The music is merely the medium we're working from. The work of art is small compared to what you're putting into it, the energy that's going out. You offer your love and goodness to the world, and that becomes part of the world. It never goes away."

Steve had that effect on me — among tens of millions mesmerized by his songwriting, singing, guitar playing and overall stagecraft. As I wrote in 1984, "Steve Goodman inspired a lot of what I'd like to believe is my better self. ... He brought those who knew his music a genuine zest for life." He also ruined me for any other musician. No one else has been able to quite measure up.

Our natural tendency when we revere someone is to twist perceptions into myths, to turn heroes into saints. At root, however, I am a journalist, and in writing this biography I have aimed to heed the mantles of fairness, completeness and accuracy. After all, he was Steve Goodman, not Steve Perfectman, and more than a few sources exhorted me, "Tell the truth. That's what Stevie would have wanted." I have aimed to do just that, especially when legendary impressions and accounts revealed themselves to be apocryphal. And I've tried to do it in language that is by turns gentle and crude, articulate and down-to-earth — a reflection of Steve's own varying forms of expression.

With Steve gone and his journey so far-reaching, the task was formidable. In more than eight years of research, I amassed thousands of news clippings, concert tapes, photos and myriad other physical items. But the linchpin of my work was eliciting stories and insights, told anew, from those who had significant experiences with Steve. A symphony of sources, their memories burnished to a reflective glow, responded eagerly with time and materials. Only a few, including Steve's widow, mother and brother, declined to participate. Whatever may be their reasons, I have respected and continue to respect their decisions.

Sources I interviewed and assumed to be living at the time of publication are given present-tense attribution in the text. Sources who have died since I interviewed them are given past-tense attribution. In the latter category falls Justin Devereaux, who said at the close of our encounter in his tiny apartment in Greenwich Village, "Write fast. I have cancer." Mimi Fariña, too, knew her time on Earth was short when she granted me an hour by phone. They and many others enjoyed reflecting about Steve in the moment, trusting that their comments had value even if they themselves would not live to see them in print. That was the case with Steve Burgh, also no longer living. "You've caused a reunion," Burgh told me. "It's part of the vibe of what's happened. It gave us all a lot to talk about. I went through a period where all that stuff faded away, but everybody's sort of drawn back together."

Gracing these pages are the fresh reflections of celebrities from Steve Martin to Hillary Clinton whose willingness to be interviewed drew on their affection for Steve Goodman. Their insights are key. While they feel that Steve deserved more fame than he received, they also grasp implicitly that fame is a misleading measure of greatness — and that, as Steve exhibited, there is greatness in us all.

That lesson emerges in Steve's relentless gratitude. Though some friends and fans rail and weep at what didn't happen for him professionally, Steve's own assurances paint him as no victim. A year before his death, with no support from a major record company and no indication that any song of his, as performed by him, would ever be a hit, he still could summon a charming barroom analogy in saying he had been "grievously overserved."

I feel much the same about the opportunity to write this book. Foremost in my gratitude is the incalculable appreciation I hold for my wife, Meg, whose steadfast love remains the strongest evidence to me that I have lived. Jack David, owner of ECW Press, also deserves enormous credit for seeing potential in a subject that other publishers dismissed and for assuring me of the nobility of the quest. I'll thank the seemingly endless list of others, many of whom welcomed me into their homes and lives, in acknowledgments that appear in the back of the book.

Researching, writing and laying out a biography is like a trip down Alice's rabbit hole. It's hard to know when to stop. Sage words came to me from one of Steve's closest friends, John Prine, who has had similar experience in seeking perfection in a record album or CD. "I get to a point where I'm double-guessin' my double-guessin'," Prine told me. "I repeatedly run into, not dead ends, but tryin' to better it, and it doesn't go any better. It goes sideways and goes nowhere, and it leaves what's there already lookin' really good. That's when I kinda know that it's the end."

From the beginning, I knew that this book would be a tangible way to heed the advice of Steve Goodman, embodied on the last LP that he put together, in the title of its last song, "You Better Get It While You Can." The title fit its author and over time has settled easily into its true meaning: Get it, folks. Understand. Live as if we comprehend and embrace the ultimate truth spelled out in Steve's lyrics — that death is always on our shoulder.

"If you wait too long, it'll all be gone." ♪   **Clay Eals**

Steve Burgh, shown in 1973 while backing Steve at the Philadelphia Folk Festival, said that reminiscing about his friend helped reconnect him with a fulfilling past: "I went through a period where all that stuff faded away, but everybody's sort of drawn back together."
(Photo by Barry Sagotsky)

Maple Byrne, who had logged several hundred shows as the road manager for Steve Goodman, including Steve's openers for Steve Martin, put extra effort into creating this freehand, red-and-blue poster for Steve's May 21, 1984, show at Parody Hall in Kansas City, Byrne's home base at the time.

(Poster courtesy Maple Byrne)

'Glad you're alive — spread it around'

Death will take center stage tonight.

The audience knows it. So does the entertainer. Both may hint at it, but no one plans to admit it outright.

For despite its eerie unpredictability, this death will rattle with joy, see nearly everything with wit and breathe life into mortality.

Or so everyone hopes.

* * *

The sun — the world's unforgiving timekeeper — is setting on the day's 82-degree swelter. Dozens of 30-somethings eat the last bites of their restaurant dinners in the bustling, historic Westport district, climb into their cars and drive 10 blocks west to join scores of others from all over Kansas City for an 8 o'clock show.

Cruising through mostly residential Midtown, along the West 39th thoroughfare, less than a block past the busy, six-lane Southwest Trafficway, they pass the Nichols Lunch truck stop, a corner liquor store, a 24-hour escort service and the Stooges Three bar. They pull into an insurance-company parking lot on the north side of 39th, across the street from a dilapidated, 1930s-era building. Once a movie theater, the edifice sports a second floor that has evolved from a ballroom to a dinner theater and, finally, to a music club named Parody Hall.

An outpost to the hipper Westport, the club is close enough to share some of its traffic, yet removed enough to feel down-home. The top of its façade bears gentle, serpentine curves, peaking at the midpoint. Just below the roofline, inset in a faded, yellow brick face, a pair of steel-framed casement windows and a large picture window, all painted dark, look out over 39th. At street level, to the left of the entrance to a beauty school on the first floor, stands a wooden door. Topped by the address numbers "811" and a striped awning, a backlighted "Parody Hall" sign beckons like a glowing lampshade in the hazy dusk.

Inside, concertgoers climb a narrow, carpeted stairway patched with frayed duct tape. On the second-story landing, they pay the $8 cover fee and step through a curtained door into a room that has the comfy feel of a pair of shabby slippers. To the right, they see 14 rows of worn church pews positioned in front

> Once a movie theater, the edifice sports a second floor that has evolved from a ballroom to a dinner theater and, finally, to a music club named Parody Hall.

9

of bass speaker cabinets that support a slightly elevated stage. Before finding seats, they step left around a few scattered wooden chairs to the bar to place orders for bottles of Busch chilling in yellow, plastic, 40-gallon barrels of ice or imported brews in grey, 10-gallon ice buckets. Other fare includes draught beer, wine and liquor, along with paper bowls of stale popcorn and beer nuts.

Ceiling fans rotate to keep the muggy air moving, while two yardstick-sized blowers, mounted in window openings on the wall opposite the stage, loom motionless and silent, poised to vent smoke and heat.

The legal capacity of the room is about 130, and at times it draws twice that number (along with the local fire marshal). On this night, a standing-room-only crowd of 200 quickly fills all the available seats, setting drinks on the narrow shelves provided by the pew backs. Some have shown up merely for an enjoyable evening of music, but many others comprehend the ephemeral, even precious nature of the moment.

It's Monday night, May 21, 1984, in a time-beaten, character-filled, upstairs club in the geographical heart of America. [1] Backstage and unseen by the crowd, with as many as 2,000 concerts behind him, sits the headliner, a balding, 35-year-old Chicago native who hasn't played a show in Kansas City in two years and who quietly sips from a green bottle of Heineken.

Shortly before 8, some in the crowd notice the presence of singer/songwriter Beth Scalet, a 34-year-old local folk favorite who was enlisted just a few hours earlier to be the opening act. She walks into the wings and, unseen by the audience, asks the headliner if it's OK if she sings his song "Lookin' for Trouble" in her set.

"Well, that'd be really cool," he tells her. "I'd like to hear it."

John Hughes, music writer for the *Kansas City Star*, peeks backstage to chat with the headliner, who allows that he's a little tired.

"But I'm here," he adds, "so you can't beat that."

Moments later, as Scalet takes the stage with her guitar and the audience focuses its attention on her bluesy, low-voiced 40-minute solo set, the headliner slips inconspicuously into the room, walks past the bar and leans on the back wall to watch and hear her perform. Before Scalet ends her closing song and the house lights come up for a 20-minute break, he steps back into the wings.

About 9:10, the lights dim, and the audience hushes, expecting a live performer, the main act, to appear onstage. Instead, however, a film starts to flicker on a 9-feet-wide, 6-feet-high white screen.

"Welcome to where you are right now," intones the image of the mustachioed film and TV actor and novelty songwriter Martin Mull.

Dressed in a dark-blue coat, light-blue shirt and red tie, Mull sits at a desk in his Los Angeles home, an ashtray to his right and a rubber duck to his left. The Parody Hall audience snickers as he assumes the role of a cinematic master of ceremonies:

"Tonight, you'll be joining me in enjoying some of the finest music ever to be made in the United States of America: the music, the words, the laughter,

Welcome to where you are right now.
MARTIN MULL

1: The detailed description of Parody Hall in spring 1984 comes largely from its proprietor at the time, Tracy Leonard.

the fun of Mister" — he pauses to read from a 4-by-6 card in his hands — "Steve Goodman."

The crowd roars with cackles and hoots at Mull, his voice saturated with the smarmy enthusiasm of a game-show host.

Mull backhandedly alludes to Goodman's lack of a recording contract despite having generated two Buddah LPs and five for Asylum, and his decision to issue a pair of current albums on a newly born, home-grown label.

"I know, as happens with so many people," Mull says, "that at the end of tonight's performance your hearts will be so filled with that music, you're going to say, 'Gosh, I wish I could take it home with me. Why doesn't he have a record available?' Well," he says, punching the air with his left index finger and winking his left eye, "I've got good news for you. He does."

The crowd continues to howl, and Mull, a smirk planted on his face, presses on.

"If you're sitting here, in a concert hall more than likely, that record is available immediately after the performance, in the lobby. If you're in a nightclub, perhaps you might want to ask your waiter person, 'Where's the darn record?' Or, if you're in a gym, again very likely, I'll bet the coach knows where it is."

More bursts of laughter.

"It's a wonderful record. I've heard it and loved it many, many times," Mull says. "But why take my word for it? Hell, I'm a comedian, not a singer. Let's ask some people who are actually, really performing artists, people like Jimmy Buffett and Bonnie Raitt."

The film cuts to the two popular singers, who often shared the stage with Goodman and, in Buffett's case, wrote half a dozen songs with him. Raitt, in a short haircut and a short-sleeved sweater, and Buffett, in sunglasses and a blue baseball jacket, sit on an outdoor stairway at Hollywood's SIR Rehearsal Studios, in muted discussion of how Steve has secured their celluloid appearance.

"Is he paying you anything to do this?" Buffett asks.

"He said he would," Raitt responds. "He said he'd be delighted."

"How much?"

"Well, it's hard to tell whether, with Steve —"

"No, I want to know how much, because I know what he offered me. I want to know what he offered you."

"I told him to call my agent."

Back to Mull at his desk, where a filter cigarette smolders in the ashtray. He invokes another Goodman compatriot, singer/songwriter Jackson Browne, whose shorthaired, confused visage looks to either side in his studio loft in downtown Los Angeles and turns to the camera, saying only:

"Steve Goodman — who's that?"

More laughter. The film cuts to the poker face of the "Wild and Crazy Guy" with whom Goodman performed more than 200 shows, Steve Martin. In a tan shirt and white sweater vest, the grey-haired comedian sits calmly, his hands folded atop a desk in his office.

**Steve Goodman —
who's that?
JACKSON BROWNE**

"I knew Steve Goodman," Martin deadpans, "when he was a tall woman."

The house erupts as Mull introduces comedian and movie actor/director Carl Reiner, shown in a black sweater, light shirt and tie and sitting at the same desk. Reiner, who has just wrapped work with Steve Martin on the film "The Man with Two Brains," had incorporated a Goodman song in his previous Martin movie, "Dead Men Don't Wear Plaid." He looks exasperated.

"Hold it, hold it, hold it! There's sound out there. We're shooting in here!" Reiner shouts with irritation at someone off-screen. He turns to the camera, brightens to a brassy smile and says:

"Steve Goodman was the first Muppet to make it on his own."

More howls.

Mull announces, "Jacqueline Onassis." He glances to his right. A look of surprise fills his face. "No? OK," he says.

Steve Martin reappears on the screen.

"A lot can happen in three years," he says. "Steve Goodman used to open my show for me when I was on the road. Now I'm a big movie star, and Steve is headlining at this dump."

Laughter ripples again as the film cuts back to Mull.

"Well, there you have it. They said it better than I could. And I know what you're probably thinking. You're thinking, 'Martin's only doing this because he's got a piece of the action.' Don't be silly. If you think 48 cents an album is a piece of the action, 52 in Canada, you're crazy. I'm doing this because I love Steve's music and always have.

"In fact, hey, let's quit talkin' here," he says, thrusting an outstretched thumb off-screen like a hitchhiker, "and let's get him onstage. Let's go get Steve right now, get him out there and perform. See you later."

Gales of laughter, cheers, shouts of "Yee-hah!" and applause wash through the room. A spotlight switches on. With a huge guitar strapped around his 5-foot-2 frame and perspiration beading on his deeply dimpled forehead, Steve walks onstage and up to the single microphone, strumming a couple of chords. Once again, as on a hundred other nights over the past year, the 2-minute-and-19-second video "testimonial" has done its job. The film's faint praise — truth layered within the jest — certainly fits this performer. Over the years, he has galvanized audiences from the dozens to the tens of thousands, but somehow he hasn't reached the status of a household word.

Without a spoken greeting, Steve launches into the song that put him on the nation's musical map, the one with the "Good mornin', America, how are ya" chorus that everyone knows, the train tune called "City of New Orleans." And from the first chords, more than a few sense that something is different. The song's tempo is half a beat slower than Steve usually plays it, and he omits his customary instrumental break between the second and third verses. More striking, the diminutive minstrel himself looks gaunt, and an unusual, shiny bump pokes out high on his forehead from beneath a receded hairline.

But the audience pays little heed to those factors as Steve flawlessly perse-

I knew Steve Goodman when he was a tall woman.
STEVE MARTIN

veres through his signature tune. The lyrics' fond, symbolic lament holds sway, and those packing the club eagerly give the anthemic "City of New Orleans" a ringing ovation, some rising from their seats as it bounces to a close.

"Yeah, yeah," Steve says amid cheers, whistles, shouts and sustained applause. "Thank you. Appreciate it. Thank you. Bless your hearts. Thank you for coming out here."

Years before, Steve didn't open his shows with "City of New Orleans." The song, one of the first he had written, routinely came partway through his set, often near the end, almost always with spoken thanks to Arlo Guthrie, whose spare, accordion-laced, gospel-tinged recording emblazoned it in the public consciousness in 1972.

This night, however, its placement at the outset and with no introduction imbues the show with singularity. The tiny troubadour — wracked his entire adult life with a fatal disease but not going public about it until a relapse forced him to do so nearly two years ago, and on this night looking thinner than ever — seems to be up to something definitive, perhaps a career synopsis.

The reason for this perception lurks partly in an irony. Steve has written, recorded and performed with easily a hundred musicians far better known than he. He also has defined his persona, in part, by inviting onstage and jamming with many of those same vocalists and instrumentalists on tunes from the faded to the familiar to the fresh.

Yet on this evening, Steve is solo — the way so many believe he's at his best. He's collaborating not with other musicians, but with an adoring club audience that's the perfect size for his one-man band of styles and mastery of dynamics and pacing. And for this agreeable group of club patrons, some of whom learned the details of Steve's leukemia the previous fall by reading a first-person story in *People Weekly* or watching a profile of him on the NBC-TV magazine show "First Camera," it feels on this night as if he's embarking on encapsulation of his musical legacy.

But Steve throws 'em a curve. With his energy ratcheted up by the crowd's response to "City of New Orleans," his fingers begin to pick a slinky blues lick as he dives into a song that he wrote just seven weeks ago and that no one in the audience has heard before, "Hot Tub Refugee."

Wielding wacky rhymes and puns, the first-person tune exuberantly skewers the Hollywood hot-tubbing culture that Steve began to encounter four years prior when he moved his family from the Chicago suburb of Evanston to the Los Angeles suburb of Seal Beach. Steve sums up its theme for the audience:

"That's 'Tom Petty, eat your heart out,' right?"

The crowd cheers as Steve sings each slightly off-color reason for shunning the liquid pastime, such as, "My onions mean too much to me." They hoot as he introduces a guitar solo with "Soak it, now," and they chuckle as he pops his lips to imitate a Lawrence Welk bubble machine.

"The title for that came from Kansas City's own Maple Byrne," he says, injecting a genuinely local reference amid approving applause. Byrne, Steve's

> **Thank you. Appreciate it. Thank you. Bless your hearts. Thank you for coming out here.**
> **STEVE GOODMAN**

road manager, has worked with him since Steve Martin and Goodman teamed up for a series of continental concert tours by bus that began in 1978.

"I figured we'd do all the normal songs first, right?" Steve continues, with self-deprecating sarcasm. "Well, here's a song I made up with John Prine about nine months ago."

The allusion to Prine, the quirky and celebrated lyricist who has been Steve's closest musical collaborator since their early performing days in Chicago, draws respectful applause. Steve's use of the phrase "a song I made up" typically plays down the process and carefully crafted results of his own songwriting.

"We made this up after I had been overserved with tequila in a saloon," Steve says. Rapidly and rhythmically thumping the bass string of his guitar, he adds, "I heard this noise in my skull for three days."

A throwaway called "How Much Tequila Did I Drink Last Night?," the song strings together a succession of exaggerated predicaments resulting from an alcohol-induced blackout, including an inability to remember whose house he has awakened in and "the names of all the people sleeping in this bed."

The song plays well to the throng of beer drinkers, who laugh, holler and whoop throughout. But the heat of the evening and the upstairs sultriness have taken their toll. Ceiling fans notwithstanding, Steve continues to sweat. He moves on, however, segueing with the dependable excuse of mock musical laziness.

"I have one other in A minor, so I might as well do it," he says. "Put the capo on, so that I won't even recognize it."

He tunes the guitar briefly. "Pretty close, gee. Won't mess with that," he says, drawing laughs from those in the audience familiar with Steve's more usual, lengthy bouts with tuning. He introduces another newer song, known to only a few in the crowd, "about a fellow who falls asleep with his television set on," to the approval of three guys in the audience who shout, "Yeah!"

Like the "Tequila" song, "Vegematic" capitalizes on a litany — in this case, the intrinsically outrageous names of the cheap products advertised on late-night TV. Fueled by Steve's own bursts of midsong laughter, the crowd cheers the satiric horror of the tune, in which the protagonist inadvertently orders all the items by phone while dreaming and discovers that "when I awoke, it was no joke, 'cause all that shit was here."

As an unintended extension, however, a hint of real-life horror emerges. While Steve's guitar playing is undeterred during the song, afterward he strums a minor chord over and over and mentions in self-taunting manner that his hands are not feeling right.

"Did'ja ever try to play 'Harlem Nocturne' on the kazoo?" he quips, referring to the minor chord. "That's what it felt like there. Where did the fingers go?"

The crowd laughs with him at the comment, apparently dismissing it as a leftover joke from the era of drugged-out hippie humor.

"Well," Steve persists, "those last two are on this little LP that we made. May

> **I figured we'd do all the normal songs first, right?**
> **STEVE GOODMAN**

as well do a couple more from that one, and then we'll move on to some other stuff."

"What was the little LP?" a guy in the audience asks.

"The little LP? Well, they've got a couple of them over there. This is the one with me standing with all the porcelain statues in the Mexican parking lot," a reference to the cover photo on "Affordable Art," whose visual pun of a smiling Steve standing stiffly amid scores of inexpensive, inanimate sculptures is not lost on several in the crowd.

The tone ventures further into the morbid as Steve introduces "Watching Joey Glow."

"This is a song about a post-nuclear, nuclear family — mother, father, sister, brother and little Joey, the human hot plate," he says to peals of laughter. "Wrote this with a guy, he still works as one of the editors of the *National Lampoon*, and his name is Sean Kelly. He and I were sitting up one night. We were a little disgusted with how much hype the end of the world has been getting," a reference to two movies from the previous year about nuclear annihilation, "Testament" and "The Day After."

From the wings, Byrne, the road manager, tosses Steve a cloth to wipe sweat from his brow. Without missing a beat, Steve interprets the move with mordant wordplay.

"The road manager just threw in the towel," he says. "It's all over."

"How about a fallout?" a guy in the audience shouts.

"Yeah, y'know, they have a film, a made-for-TV movie, a couple of books. 'Film at 11,' right? So here it is, a song about this little kid that they didn't get into the shelter on time."

Notwithstanding its grim focus, nearly every black-humor line of "Watching Joey Glow" — which describes how the irradiated boy turns bread into toast by touching it, heats up coffee with his toe and serves as a naturally illuminated Christmas tree — breaks up the audience.

"Yeah, appreciate it," Steve says to the end-of-song applause. Buying a few seconds, he piggybacks on a reference in the lyrics, absently picking on his guitar a quiet instrumental chorus to "We Wish You a Merry Christmas" while considering what to play next.

The decision is pivotal. He opts to pull out one of his most recent creations. It's a song that he debuted less than five months earlier, shortly after 4 a.m. on New Year's Day on Chicago's "Midnight Special" show on WFMT-FM. A song that soon he will position as the last cut on what will become his final album. A song that, despite its purported purpose as a tribute to someone else, turns out to be Steve's most fundamentally autobiographical composition.

"Well, tell you what," he says. "Here's a song about a 73-year-old guy at the time of his death. His name was Carl Martin, and he played in a string band, Martin, Bogan & Armstrong. They're, y'know, not the most notorious group in history, but Carl started playing with them in 1923, and he played with them until his death in 1979."

> **The road manager just threw in the towel. It's all over.**
> **STEVE GOODMAN**

He pauses, filling five seconds of silence with a couple of slight guitar licks, before dealing a punch line:

"So they had the arrangements pretty much together by the time —"

The crowd's raucous laughter drowns him out in midsentence.

"I used to drive these guys to folk festivals in the East. We'd pick up the fiddler, Armstrong, in Detroit, where he lived, and we'd head for points unknown. And they used to try to keep me awake. They were sure their death was going to come at my hands behind the wheel."

Steve quotes his favorite Howard Armstrong homily: "Steve, always remember, just like Socrates told Plato: When thine opus becomes thine onus, thou art out on thine anus."

Again, peals of laughter ring from the crowd.

"Words to live by," he follows up. "So, I really appreciated these guys."

Lowering his usual stage voice, in a gentler, more intimate tone, Steve says in a half-whisper, "They played just *every*thing."

The half-spoken, half-sung masterpiece that follows is "You Better Get It While You Can (The Ballad of Carl Martin)." Its quiet lyrics and bouncy, infectious rhythm both belie and enhance the song's dead-serious message: "From the cradle to the crypt, it's a mighty short trip. ... If you wait too long, it'll all be gone." Its lesson rings clear: Live — and comprehend ("get") — life to the fullest in the face of death, "while you can."

The message may have originated from the life experience of ex-highway asphalter Carl Martin, as the song states. But for Steve, who will not end up living half as long as the mentor whom the song memorializes, the message has become his own. By performing the tune in his precarious state of health, Steve embodies a profound mixture of performer and content, literally living the message.

He ends the song with a five-bar guitar solo that abruptly halts on a splayed chord, like a minor car crash, but the song's words have brought the audience to a hush, and somehow it all works.

"Thank you, folks," he says to cheers and loud, reverent applause. "Thank you so much."

On a roll, Steve sticks with the formula of fatality as he selects yet another just-written song that no one present has heard.

"Well, let's see here," he says. "All right, I got a dead-girl song. I never had one before."

The comment breaks the serious mood and shakes more laughter from the audience.

"That's a horseshit introduction," Steve comes back. "This was going to be a serious song. I don't know if I'm gonna be able to get through it now."

But he does. The song, a pulsing ballad called "Fourteen Days," tells the story of heartbroken, estranged lovers who ultimately remain so. It uses a device often used by Goodman, that of a woman who wrongs a man, and twists it. From out of town, the woman writes the man a letter asking his forgiveness but

When thine opus becomes thine onus, thou art out on thine anus.
HOWARD ARMSTRONG

threatening suicide if he doesn't meet her at the local airport in two weeks (the 14 days of the title). The man, out of spite, doesn't open and read the letter until, coincidentally, a few hours after the woman is to have arrived at the airport. He rushes to meet her, but she's gone, and the next day a newspaper reports that she has taken her life.

The song contains a blatant reference to Steve's imminent fate to which the audience is oblivious. The woman's letter is postmarked "Seattle, just 1,000 miles away," where Steve himself is slated to fly in less than three months for a bone-marrow transplant that offers his final hope for survival.

As the song proceeds, the crowd titters at what initially sounds like one melodramatic development after another. But with the passing of each verse, the gravity of the story unfolds, and during the song's final two lines, the laughter recedes completely. At the end, amid giggles and enthusiastic applause, Steve acknowledges the song's sneaky intention.

"You laugh now," he says, as if issuing a warning. "I bet someone that no one would be able to tell if that was a sad song or a funny song. I think I might win the bet."

"You win it," a guy shouts.

"It is on the edge, yeah," Steve says. "Well, I haven't had one of those in awhile, so every now and then you just gotta take a chance."

"What's the answer?" another guy shouts, confirming the song's edge, to which Steve can only snort.

By this time, following "City of New Orleans," Steve has played six consecutive newer songs, and the audience, antsy to hear something more familiar, starts calling out requests.

"I Don't Know Where I'm Goin'!" one guy shouts, indicating one of Steve's earliest songs, and certainly the one with the longest title: "The I Don't Know Where I'm Goin' but I'm Goin' Nowhere in a Hurry Blues."

"California Promises!" shouts another, referring to a more recent Goodman tune.

A third shouts the name of the early Bob Dylan classic, "Blowin' in the Wind."

"Yeah. Hey, Bob," Steve responds dryly, acknowledging the folk and rock legend who recorded two songs with him a dozen years prior. He tunes his guitar to the strains of one of his better-known mid-1970s songs, "Banana Republics," an intricate commentary on the fate of well-heeled but lonely Americans who can't find happiness stateside and opt to look for it south of the border.

"Well, I made up this song a few years back about Central America, and I hate like hell to see it come true," he tells the audience. "This was originally just for the square-grouper fishermen down there. That's what Jim Buffett called the runners."

While Steve talks, he tunes. Dissatisfied, he tunes some more. He breaks the repetitive strumming by telling a time-tested joke on himself:

> I bet someone that no one would be able to tell if that was a sad song or a funny song.
> **STEVE GOODMAN**

"It's my delicate, birdlike technique that keeps the strings in tune."

Guffaws rise and fall, as Steve further adjusts the pegs on the guitar neck, searching for the right blend. He pitches another favorite gag:

"What I do is get the one that's the worst, and I tune the other five to it. Takes a little longer, but it's worth it."

More laughter ensues. Finally pleased with the tuning, Steve begins the familiar instrumental opening to "Banana Republics," prompting cries of recognition. The song's contemporary content, delicate melody, bittersweet chord changes and at times whispered presentation quickly transform the audience's mood to somber. It's no wonder, as the tune's metaphorical hook, "Give me some words I can dance to, and a melody that rhymes," perfectly undergirds its characters' melancholy — not unlike the feelings that some in the audience may have tried to leave behind for the evening by coming to the show. The song draws both respectful and resounding applause.

In a shrewd move of nonverbal pacing, Steve pops onto his head a bright blue Chicago Cubs hat, with the red letter "C" on the crown, drawing cheers from those who remember the deep love he's long held for his native North Side big-league baseball team.

> **If you grew up in Chicago, you knew everything there was to know about pain by the time you were 10 years old.**
> **STEVE GOODMAN**

"These guys are trying to make me look bad," he says in sardonic reference to the Cubbies, launching into an update on the team's sizzling status in the East Division of the National League. "They're in first place by a game. They've managed to lose a couple of pitchers in the last week, though, so they might change. They lost (Scott) Sanderson and (Dick) Ruthven, and they're hot for awhile, and no one knows when they'll be back. Went out for a beer."

The mocking comments about the team's meteoric, early-season success point directly to the song Steve is about to introduce, "A Dying Cub Fan's Last Request," his instantly consummate 1981 valentine to the seemingly cursed Cubs, who, in their "ivy-covered burial ground" of Wrigley Field have served as "the doormat of the National League" for most of the previous four decades.

"If you grew up in Chicago, you knew everything there was to know about pain by the time you were 10 years old," he tells the doubled-over audience as he tunes again. "That's why there aren't so many psychiatrists in Chicago, because we have the Cubs. If you can learn to forgive your parents and the Cubs, you can save yourself $25,000. They're liable to screw it up and win it, just to fix it so I can't sing this song."

As earlier in describing Martin, Bogan & Armstrong, his voice shifts to a quieter, slightly lower register for another moment of intimacy.

"I'd be there to cheer for 'em," he coos while softly strumming and picking the song's rhythm pattern. "I admit I like baseball as much as I like music, and that's a hell of an admission."

But he bounces back, louder, with a local wisecrack.

"And I sure am happy to let you have Willie Wilson back," he says, eliciting a round of cheers and groans.

Five days earlier, Wilson, the Kansas City Royals' star outfielder, resumed active status after he and two other players served nearly three months at the federal penitentiary at Fort Worth, Texas. The three pleaded guilty in federal court the previous November for attempted possession of cocaine — the so-called 1980s "drug of choice" — and were suspended by the commissioner of baseball for a full year. But in April, an arbitrator ruled that Wilson could return to action in mid-May.

Steve sarcastically likens Wilson's preferential treatment to that of the 59-year-old former sports-car maker John DeLorean, who, using an entrapment defense, soon is to be acquitted on federal drug charges even though police videotaped him in 1982 closing a cocaine deal worth $24 million.

"What a crock of shit that is, ain't it?" Steve says. "I don't want to preach, but you know John DeLorean's gonna walk, don't you? What a lotta shit. He had a big suitcase full of it. He's gonna walk. He won't do day one, guaranteed. You can go to the bank on that."

"Wilson tried to find some. Three months," he says pointedly, to the audience's wild laughter. "Yeah-h-h."

Steve performs his six-minute Cubs epic, which depicts, in unquestionably autobiographical spirit, the title character planning his funeral at Wrigley. The scenario brims with details, including umpires who "bark me out at every base" and a bonfire of baseball bats at home plate into which his coffin is thrown so that his ashes "blow in a beautiful snow" over the left-field wall to nearby Waveland Avenue.

Ever the editor of his own work, Steve skips over a couple of lines from the original third verse that revive Hall-of-Famer Ernie Banks' fabled phrase "Let's play two" and that beg departed broadcaster Jack Brickhouse to conduct a final interview. He also updates the song by throwing in a reference to the Cubs' recently hired broadcaster, Harry Caray. By the end of the mostly talking blues, he has the crowd whooping and whistling.

In a role reversal after the song ends, a guy in the audience yells to Steve, "Thank you!"

"Yeah, any old time," Steve replies. "So, how we doing?" he asks while peering at a clock on the wall and tuning again. "Oh, we got plenty of time."

A slurred voice in the crowd shouts, "Elvis Presley!" Many in the audience don't realize it, but the shout constitutes a request for Steve's "Elvis Imitators," which Jimmy Buffett, calling himself Freddie and the Fishsticks, recorded in 1981 and which Goodman performed with showy aplomb in 1982 on PBS-TV's "Austin City Limits" fund-raising special, "Down Home Country Music."

"You want that? My kids like that one," Steve says, referring to his grade-school daughters Jessie, Sarah and Rosanna. He mimics his girls' 8 o'clock Sunday morning whine: "Pop, do the one about the Elvis imitator! C'mon, dad!"

"If Elvis imitators could ever get a union, this could be their song," he adds, drawing laughs as he strikes an Elvis pose and asks the soundboard operator to turn up the "slap," or echo, from the speakers.

With a reasonable facsimile of Presley's voice, Steve launches into the affec-

Pop, do the one about the Elvis imitator! C'mon, dad!
STEVE GOODMAN
quoting his daughters

tionate rockabilly parody of Elvis impersonators from their own point of view. His presentation comes complete with pouty facial mannerisms, a laundry list of Presley song and movie titles and a chorus that drives home the message: "Imitation Elvis may not be The King, but baby, I'm the next best thing."

The surreal tour de force, packed into a performance not even two minutes long, draws hearty, sustained applause from the audience. Mopping his brow, Steve again imitates his daughters: "C'mon, dad!"

"Well," he says, applying another layer of self-effacing sarcasm, "while we're doing all the sensitive stuff —"

But as a beer bottle clinks on the floor, the hyped-up horde again pelts Steve with song titles.

"Sin to Tell a Lie!" shouts one man.

"Talk Backwards," yells a woman.

"I'm My Own Grandpa," offers another guy.

I know there aren't enough songs about biker chicks.
STEVE GOODMAN

Opting for "Talk Backwards," Steve sends his fingers racing over the guitar frets as he propels himself faster than usual through his 1980 collaboration with Michael Smith (best known for writing "The Dutchman," which Steve recorded memorably a dozen years before). In "Talk Backwards," Steve assumes the role of mock huckster, promoting a fictional "new sensation" of pronouncing words and phrases as if their letters appear in reversed order. The audience marvels and whistles at his pell-mell enunciation of the tune's inverted sentences and phrases ("I love you" becomes "You, oh evil eye").

As the two-minute novelty song ends and the applause and hollers die down, Steve holds up a magazine to introduce another just-written tune that no one in the audience has heard, "Queen of the Road."

"This is *Easy Rider*. It's sort of a cross between *Hustler* and *Road & Track*. And I know there aren't enough songs about biker chicks," he says, to whoops and belly laughs. "So I wrote this song about this young lady — this old lady, old Oyl — and her bro', right?"

Adding to the intrigue, he throws out another hook:

"I'm not Pete Seeger, y'know," he says, referring to the folk-music legend with whom he has recorded and shared the stage, and to Seeger's enthusiastic ability to lead sing-alongs. "This has a little part for you in it, but you're going to have to figure it out."

The crowd roars its approval as Steve pounds his bass string with a speedy, double-timed, rock 'n' roll beat. To the audience's delight, he also buzzes his lips to approximate the thunderous revving of a motorcycle "hog" and launches into the song, a sympathetic character study of a woman with a "roadhouse reputation" whom "nothing can stop." The song's opportunity for audience participation comes in the chorus, in a repeated, syncopated ditty: "Putt-putt." The crowd joins in readily and clamors for more of the same rowdy material when the tune ends.

Pacing is on Steve's mind again, however. Nearly an hour has passed since he stepped onstage. Pausing a few seconds, slowing his breathing and searching his memory, he summons a request shouted half an hour earlier for a composition inspired by the coastal L.A. suburb he's called home for the past four years.

"This is a song for a couple who meet by the Seal Beach Pier in Seal Beach, California, right before the wind comes and destroys the pier. She says, 'I'll be right back.' "

In the quiet, sad little tune, "California Promises," the woman never does return. On this night, it produces pin-drop silence, then, at the end, booming applause.

"Appreciate you letting me sing that," Steve says.

After an instant of calm, the requests tumble forth, overlapping each other.

"Learn to Dance!" a man shouts, a reference to one of Steve's first songs, which Jackie DeShannon recorded in 1972, the touching "Would You Like to Learn to Dance?"

"Video Tape," yells another.

"Oh yeah, so —" Steve begins, but the requests keep pouring in.

"Do You Want to Learn to Dance!"

"Blue Umbrella!"

"The Oldest Baby!"

"Oldest Baby?" Steve responds. "That's John Prine's."

"This Old Hotel!" another guy calls out, intending Goodman's "This Hotel Room."

Steve rolls his eyes for a moment.

"I missed a few of 'em, huh?" he says.

"Yeah," says a guy in the front row.

"I tried to sing a couple of the new ones tonight. I hope I didn't screw up."

"No, not at all," the guy says.

"I'll get the other ones next time," he says, injecting an extra inflection of sarcasm. "I obviously didn't know the new ones real well. Have to learn 'em sometime."

"They're great," the guy says.

"Didn't mean to do it at your expense," Steve says. In another glancing reference to the fatigue lurking beneath his enthusiasm, he adds, "I've been looking for my left hand for an hour now. So, anyhow, oh, I know what I wanted to sing. This is an a cappella song —"

Several in the crowd whoop at the prospect of Steve performing the only composition that he has written and recorded for unaccompanied voice, "The Ballad of Penny Evans," a strident anti-war song from 1972 that is told from the viewpoint of the 21-year-old widow of a Vietnam War soldier. The power of the song derives not just from its lyrics, but also from its presentation without instrumentation, and by a male voice, no less.

But that isn't the song Steve has started to introduce.

"OK, I guess we'll do two a cappella songs," he says, to clue in the audience that eventually he will sing "Penny Evans."

He resumes his introduction of another voice-only song, a biting sendup

> **I tried to sing a couple of the new ones tonight. I hope I didn't screw up.**
> **STEVE GOODMAN**

that borrows the format of the traditional Scottish "Oh, come all ye" ballads. No one in the room has heard it before. Few anywhere have ever heard it.

"I woke up in Ottawa, Ontario, a couple of years ago after playing a club there that's about half the size of this and twice as warm temperature-wise, and full of a certain kind of smoke and haze, and then I went upstairs. Y'know, it was a good gig, but it was draining somehow, right? So I drained a bottle of brandy about that far (halfway) down, right? And I woke up in this place the next morning. I should have known better when it said, 'The room comes with the gig,' right?

"I was in the motel where the bar was, and the place had been furnished in 1947 and had a lot of Formica all over it and a TV from not long after that, which I had left on where I had passed out.

"And in French and English was the cable news for Ontario, and in French and English the first story I saw was the sad tale of a William Kemp of Sudbury, Ontario, a mining town, filthy town. William Kemp, 61 years old, had fallen asleep in a dumpster behind a bar, and the coroner's verdict was death by compacting. That was the first thing I saw, and my head's like, 'Ohhh shit!' So here's the song."

Steve picks a note on his guitar, hums briefly to match its pitch and, in a sonorous, almost nasal brogue, sings his "Ballad of William Kemp." In three verses, he details the demise of the foul-smelling drunkard, building the audience up for a wicked, culminating punch line: "Mark well the saga of William Kemp, a hopeless Sudbury rube / who began his life as a perfect square and ended as a cube."

Whether the name William Kemp is that of a real person or a clever reference to the founder of English morris dancing, the precursor of American square dancing (and thus "a perfect square"), is a question lost on the audience.

But the listeners recognize the song's dark humor, in which all death — even that of a hapless vagrant — becomes the ultimate joke. With each progression of Kemp's story, they cheer, and when Steve irresistibly approaches the closing geometric wordplay, they anticipate it with howls and laughs, followed by boisterous applause.

Amid the hubbub, a bartender, taking note of the late-evening mugginess and Steve's feverish appearance, flips the switch for one of the huge wall fans.

"We turned on the air, Steve," he shouts.

"Oh, good, now I'll catch pneumonia," Steve shoots back. "Good. Great. Don't leave it on too long. I'm a little damp up here, OK?"

A guy in the crowd yells out one of his previous requests:

"I Don't Know Where I'm Goin'!"

"Yeah," Steve says, a laugh under his breath. "Join the club."

The retort — saturated with double meaning — breaks up the crowd.

"I know what bus I'm taking," Steve says. With a nod to 19th-century songwriter Stephen Foster, whose short life span paralleled Steve's, he adds, "Doo-dah, doo-dah."

Oh, good, now I'll catch pneumonia.
STEVE GOODMAN

He introduces, as promised, "The Ballad of Penny Evans," once again downplaying the deftness of his songwriting:

"Here's a song that was recited to me without the rhyme by a young woman in Rochester, New York, in 1972, and all I did was make the last line of whatever she said rhyme with the next line. That's all I did."

The audience, of course, knows better, and just two lines into the unaccompanied, bitterly emotional plaint, once again Steve's presentation brings the crowd to an awed silence that endures through its remainder. After its pointed final line, "They say the war is over, but I think it's just begun," the Reagan-era crowd erupts in unison with 15 seconds of nonstop applause.

Under the din, however, the torrent of forced air from the wall fan shakes Steve. He seeks to catch the bartender's eye.

"I'm starting to melt up here. Can you keep it off me?" he asks.

Again, after the applause dies down, he addresses the bartender.

"It's blowing right on me. Is it OK if we turn it off for just a minute? It's blowing right on me. Can't even — "

Finally, Steve pulls off his drenched shirt, stripping to a T-shirt, accompanied by hoots from the crowd.

"Snappy, huh?" he says.

"Go, Steve!" a guy in the audience yells.

"Yeah, really," Steve replies. "Take it all off."

Another man in the audience prompts a scant exchange of intimacy.

"We love you!" he shouts.

"Love you guys," Steve answers.

He pauses for the split second wherein the emotion hangs, then moves forward in ingratiating fashion.

"Well, I promised someone this song. It actually made it to the flip side of a Rodney Crowell single. The Nitty Gritty Dirt Band recorded a song by Rodney, called 'It's a Long Hard Road,' good song. If you buy it, you get the Dirt Band's version of this song."

The B-side song, from 1977, is "Video Tape," possibly Steve's best-crafted composition, which displays all of Goodman's quintessential songwriting talents. With its sturdy and efficient tripod of verses, the song comically yet matter-of-factly explores the fantasies of changing the past and predicting the future, including the ability to dodge the "grim reaper." It finally settles upon a romantic embrace of life's realities: "I know it will all make sense, if you love me in the present tense."

After singing the sobering song, Steve keeps strumming with the same rhythm and in the same key. To transform the mood once again, he turns to well-honed shtick to introduce his staple of a closer.

"Well, does anybody have a cowboy hat, so I can sing this song here?" he asks, assuring the uninitiated, "I'll give it right back, I promise."

One man passes his hat forward to Steve. Another takes a hat off the head of a friend. Someone shouts, "Give him the hat!" The second hat comes forward.

Does anybody have a cowboy hat, so I can sing this song here? I'll give it right back, I promise.
STEVE GOODMAN

"I'll give it right back, I promise," Steve repeats.

He holds up and looks over the two hats.

"Hey, man," a guy in the front row says. "We'll A/B 'em. We could A/B 'em, if you like," a reference to the audience ranking them as A and B.

Steve nods and says, "We'll size up the situation."

He places on his head the larger and more elaborate of the two hats, to wild cheers from the audience. Though he can barely see out from beneath it, he declares it the winner.

"No fucking contest!" he says.

He passes the other hat back and, for a moment, strikes a play-acting cowboy's pose.

"You see a one-armed man count his change?" he asks, waiting for the delayed reaction to the quip.

"No? Well, anyhow, this song here, John Prine and I made up one night, and we tried to put into one song anything that had ever been in any of the country songs we'd ever heard."

The audience cheers and whoops in anticipation of the country parody "You Never Even Call Me by My Name," written in 1971 and made a country hit by David Allan Coe in 1975.

Before starting the song, however, Steve signals that it is indeed his closer.

"This hat is perfect. And so are you guys. And thank you very much, OK, for coming out tonight. And thanks to Beth for playing so good."

Bursts of "Thank you!" come back at Steve from the crowd. One guy shouts, "Welcome to K.C.!"

"Nice to be here," Steve answers. With no hint of irony, he adds, "I hope it ain't two years again." He pauses, to more cheers, and says dryly, "I'll come back when I know my new songs, I promise."

He widens his stance and tilts forward, explaining, "Country bands always lean into the mike at a 45-degree angle." The crowd roars as Steve adds a geometric point: "This is hipper for people in the wings."

As he plays the opening bars, cries of "Yee-hah!" come from the crowd. The song lampoons every aspect of country-western music, from its simple, three-chord structure and mournful lyrics to the harmonica, fiddle and pedal steel that are the targets for Steve's incisive vocal and physical mimicry.

Throughout the song, the borrowed, oversized hat keeps falling over Steve's brow. "It's a good thing I have ears," he jokes between verses.

Near the end, he throws in other asides. At the song's reference to his savior calling him home, Steve calls out, "Bring in those sheaves!" Preacher-like, he shouts, "Heal!" Summoning a medical metaphor for the tune so far (which doubles as an in-joke for the last-ditch treatment he faces in three months), he says, "Well, the operation was a big success." Many howl at each line.

The song's capper comes when Steve tells the listeners he's about to throw together in the final verse a ridiculously long list of prototypically country elements: prison, farms, Mother, trains, trucks, Christmas, dead dogs and getting

Well, the operation was a big success.
STEVE GOODMAN

drunk. On this night, though, perhaps inspired by the crowd and a devil-may-care sense of challenge, he adds two more items: bullwhips and CB radios.

"I appear to have dug myself a hole," he says, before pressing on with the last four lines, in which he tells how a farm dog gets drunk and dies while Mother bullwhips a guard, breaks out of prison on Christmas and drives a CB-equipped truck into a train.

The outrageous logic and Steve's lyrical dexterity bring the crowd to its feet, as he broadly tips the cowboy hat, passes it back to the audience and leaves the stage. The throng cheers, chants and stomps for an encore, and Steve returns, soaked and visibly exhausted, yet wearing the huge Goodman grin.

"It's a big treat for me," he says, "taking in O_2 and lettin' out CO_2."

The crowd clamors for more.

"Now, here's a song —" he says, but the shouted requests nearly drown him out.

"Door Number Three!" one guy yells.

"Yeah, 'Door Number Three'!" another calls out.

"Here's a song," Steve begins again, "called 'The One—'"

"Yeah, do 'The One That Got Away'!" a man shouts.

"Good guess," Steve answers.

He starts strumming the tune's opening chords, when yet another guy shouts a phrase that is both a lyric and an admonition:

"Stay all night! Play a little longer!"

From his mental songbook, Steve responds instantly and instrumentally, noodling on his guitar to the chorus of the shouted phrase from an old Bob Wills swing song. He shifts to tuning again. After a few seconds, a guy in the front row nods his assent that the strings are in sync.

"Finally, huh?" Steve says.

"Just in time," the man says.

"Don't screw it up and tune, right?" Steve says.

Moving on to introduce the song, he pays tribute to a smooth-voiced pop crooner who died two decades prior.

"I just wish Sam Cooke was alive, so that he could sing this," Steve says. "I was born too late to get this one to him."

It's an irresistible entrée for a fan in the audience, who triggers an exchange that sums up both the evening and Steve himself.

"We're glad you're alive," the guy calls out.

"Me, too," Steve answers, to cheers. "Glad you're alive. Spread it around. Might as well have some fun while we're here, right?"

In prescient fashion, "The One That Got Away," which Steve released in 1979 with a harmony vocal by Nicolette Larson, is the perfect follow-up. The tender story — of a pair of men and a pair of women reveling in their past, would-be romantic glories — leads seamlessly to the song's advice, which is to not "run around saying 'I love you' with your fingers crossed."

When Steve reaches the next line of the song, "It's too late to go back now /

I just wish Sam Cooke was alive, so that he could sing this.
STEVE GOODMAN

That's just about as good as it gets," he laughs to himself, letting slip another reference to the transplant looming for him in Seattle.

The song draws rapt attention throughout and warm applause at the end, after which Steve puts down his guitar and picks up a larger, rounded, stringed relative called a mandola.

"I forgot to play this," he says as he starts tuning it. But he notices a pool of his sweat beneath his feet.

"Well, good," he says, returning to sarcasm. "Let's step in the puddle, then touch the microphone. All right."

Strumming a hypnotic riff on the mandola, Steve once more introduces a song that no one in the room has heard. This time, though, it's an instrumental, and as Steve plays it, he explains its offbeat background.

"Someone actually told me this joke right before I made this melody up, so I'll pass it on to you. The title of this song is 'Your Monkey's Ball's in My Beer.' See, there was this organ grinder standing out in front of a bar in New Orleans, where they have huge, hurricane glasses, about as big as my arm. A fellow walked out with one full of beer. The monkey leaped off the organ and sat on the edge of the beer glass. The guy looked at the organ grinder and said, 'Hey, your monkey's ball's in my beer.' The organ grinder played this."

The attempted joke elicits a few titters, but its point remains elusive. So Steve quickly segues to a second instrumental, "If Jethro Were Here," a tune that Steve released the previous year and named for his elder, frequent partner over the previous decade, Jethro Burns, the mandolinist of Homer & Jethro fame.

"OK, now, this song here is dedicated to Jethro Burns, one of the finest musicians of this century, who deserves a better intro than the one I gave him. And if he was here, he'd show us all how to play these things.

"Which is what my road manager did. He told me that this (the mandola) was the bottom four strings of the guitar backwards. So if you have dyslexia and you can play the guitar, there's no secret to this thing," he says, siphoning more laughs from the audience.

The fast-paced instrumental barrels along with periodic bursts of syncopation that draw whoops from the crowd and a loud ovation at the end.

"Thank you," Steve says. "Here's our swan song. This is a song I learned off a Burl Ives record when I was a kid."

"Who?" asks a guy in the front row.

"Burl Ives. Remember him?"

"Oh yeah!" several say. "Yeah."

Steve catches a signal from the wings and says, "I've been told to announce that I'm going to change my shirt and then come back over there, and if you bought one of our discs, I'll be glad to sign it for you."

"We'll buy two!" a man shouts.

"Sounds like some of you have 'em already, for which I'm eternally grateful, OK?" he says. "This is one of the few towns where they actually ended up in the

This song here is dedicated to Jethro Burns, one of the finest musicians of this century.
STEVE GOODMAN

stores, OK? It's amazing. I owe that to Maple Byrne and your local merchants."

He strums the mandola a few more times.

"OK, this song that I learned off the Burl Ives record has some verses that Burl didn't sing."

Some in the crowd guffaw.

"Seriously," he says, "I found them in a fake book, y'know, one of those things with a thousand songs, and it was then that I learned that this is an old hobo song, written by some of those pinko hobos — all right, pink and purple, right? So here's the song, and thanks again."

It has been an evening during which Steve, while enduring obvious illness, has shared some of his finest songs and risked showcasing an equal number of newer, mostly unheard efforts. More than half the night's selections have centered — poignantly, uproariously or both — on living in the face of doom and demise.

So his choice of a traditional standard sung and adapted by many others, "The Big Rock Candy Mountain," seems an inspired ending for a nonstop, 90-minute performance by a little guy who routinely has championed the talents of his musical peers and scoffed at claims of his own.

Perhaps the song — with its indulgent vision of endless food and drink, and idle pleasures — points to a world that the weary Steve longs for:

> *I'm headed for the land that's far away*
> *Beside the crystal fountain*
> *Where I'll see you all this coming fall*
> *In the big rock candy mountain*

Picturing a world where "they hung the jerk who invented work," the lyrics hint at fantasies harbored by the "freight yards full of old black men" that Steve summoned in "City of New Orleans":

> *Oh, the buzzin' of the bees in the cigarette trees*
> *By the sody-water fountain*
> *Where the lemonade springs and the bluebird sings*
> *In the big rock candy mountain*

The song proves satisfying to many of the concert-goers, who briefly turn their thoughts away from mortality and focus instead on the tune's affectionate humor, along with Steve's easygoing rhythm and hushed vocal.

At the end, Steve tacks on an instrumental reprise of the chorus, landing upon a gentle chord.

"Well, thank you," he says to reverberating applause. "I hope to get to play for you again some night." ♫

This is an old hobo song, written by some of those pinko hobos.
STEVE GOODMAN

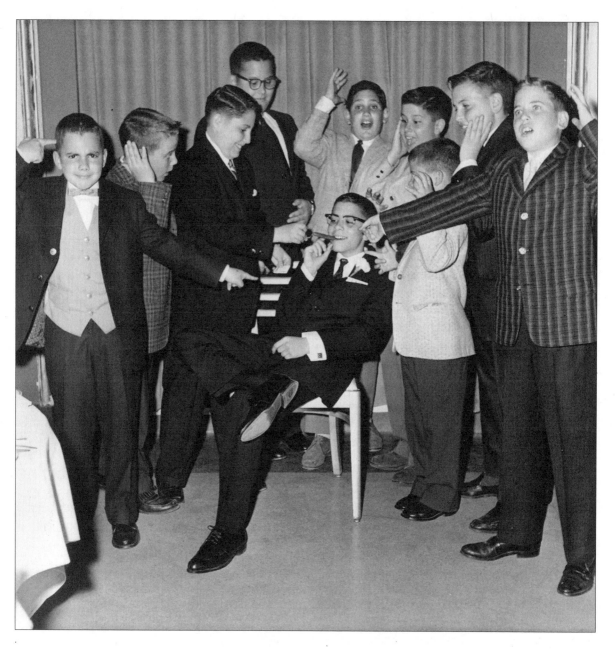

Thirteen-year-old Temple Beth Israel youth-choir standout Barry Ellegant, seated, jokingly tries out the "adult" mannerism of cigar smoking on May 13, 1960, following the traditional Jewish rite of passage, his bar mitzvah. But it was 11-year-old Steve Goodman (left) who best spoofed the incongruity of it all. Others (circling Ellegant from left, after Steve) were Mark Shapiro, Ned Fishkin, Danny Simon, Marvin Siskind, Steve Benjamin, Bruce Benjamin, Jeffrey Platt and Larry Gomberg.

(Photo courtesy of Benyomin Ellegant)

A voice that 'brought you to the music'

Beneath an arch at the podium of the cavernous sanctuary in the oldest synagogue on the North Side of Chicago, a 13-year-old stood nervously awaiting his formal passage into manhood. He read from the Torah and delivered a memorized bar-mitzvah speech. The rabbi's hands touched the teen's head to bless him. Then, as a chord sounded from the temple organ, scores of family and friends lifted their attention two floors up to the choir loft to focus on a high-pitched, musical prayer caressing their ears via the solitary voice of a tiny, 10-year-old boy:

> *This child we dedicate to Thee*
> *Oh, God of grace and purity*
> *Shield him from sin and threatening wrong*
> *And let Thy love his life prolong* [1]

The prayer, slow and powerful. The voice, a clear, rich soprano. The singer, Steven Benjamin Goodman.

Draped in a blue cotton robe, the cherubic, brown-eyed soloist sang the *Union Hymnal* verse with a solemnity that moistened eyes and stilled the air. "There wasn't a sound in the synagogue while he sang this," recalled choir mate Sue Ellen Schwartz, daughter of then-Rabbi Ernst Lorge. "He was just a little guy, and people were amazed at what would come out of him," says another in the choir, Barry Ellegant. "He had a voice like an angel," remembers Stuart Gordon, a would-be choir member. And as Steve stood in front of a microphone, perched above an audience of 200 or more, he knew no fear, only praise. "He understood the moment and enhanced it," says Eudice Lorge, widow of Rabbi Lorge. "The people who were there always congratulated him, told him how great he was, gave him a lot of strokes. The family was proud. Even the rabbi told him how proud he was."

In an era in which Americans soared into the space race, on Saturday mornings Steve joined 10 other boys and 20 girls in some climbing of their own — up the narrow back stairs of Temple Beth Israel to the choir loft. There, they donned robes, sat in three rows and waited to sing in both Hebrew and English during back-to-back bar-mitzvah services prompted by the postwar baby boom.

There wasn't a sound in the synagogue while he sang this.
SUE ELLEN LORGE SCHWARTZ

1: This is the first of two verses from "Blessing the Child," written in Germany by Cantor Jacob Singer and translated into English by Sam Gilman. It is song 240 in the *Union Hymnal (Songs and Prayers for Jewish Worship)*, copyright 1932, as published by the Central Conference of American Rabbis, third edition revised and enlarged, 1940.

29

The Goodman home at 5116 North Monticello Avenue. Shown in 2001, it is largely unchanged from when it was built in 1956.

(Photo by Clay Eals)

2: "Black Metropolis" was the name for the "city within a city" of prominent Chicago businesses started by African Americans who migrated from the South in the early 20th century. Later, it became known as Bronzeville.

3: The Army Air Forces was a new name in 1941 for the outfit known for the previous 15 years as the Army Air Corps, the appellation used by Steve in his 1977 song, "My Old Man." Immediately after World War II, Bud Goodman developed an aversion to fruit, vegetables and milk. A diet of K-rations had prompted his yearnings for fresh foods as he flew back to Chicago from Burma. On a layover in Hawaii, he gorged himself on pineapples, tomatoes and milk and spent the next 18 hours of his flight in the toilet. "He never ate any of those again," said Steve's steel-guitar accompanist, Winnie Winston. The most that Bud would indulge in such foods would be "a bowl of cereal with milk once a year on his birthday."

A decade earlier, on Sunday, July 25, 1948, at Chicago's Michael Reese Hospital, in the "Black Metropolis" [2] alongside the railroad tracks that parallel Lake Shore Drive and about 25 blocks south of the Loop, Steve was born into that generation. He was the first child of 30-year-old Joseph Bayer Goodman and 21-year-old Minnette Erenburg Goodman.

Steve's dad, known as "Bud," was born May 23, 1918, in Indianapolis, Indiana, but Bud's family soon moved to Chicago's then-Jewish West Side (some called it the Zest Side), where he grew up as what Steve described as a street kid. Bud, who dropped out of Marshall High School after just one year, later followed the lead of a brother and joined the Army Air Forces in time for World War II. In the military, he exaggerated his educational record and, said Steve, studied "all night long in the john" to learn trigonometry and become a pilot. As Steve later wrote in a song about him, Bud flew combat cargo in the China-Burma-India Theater, then served as a general's staff pilot. [3]

After the war, Bud came back to Chicago and became an auto salesman, but not without regrets. "He was always thankful to the United States Army for having given him something to do with his life that he was proud of," Steve recalled in a 1980 interview.

Bud soon met young Minnette Erenburg, a Chicago West Side native and only child, who had been born May 22, 1927. The 28- and 19-year-old were married by Rabbi Norbert L. Rosenthal on Aug. 29, 1946. When Steve was born two summers later, they were living in Chicago's Uptown neighborhood, about 15 blocks north of Wrigley Field. After giving birth on Aug. 27, 1952, to a second son, David, they moved another 20 blocks northwest to a brick four-plex on West Farragut Street in the Budlong Woods neighborhood near the Chicago River's man-made north channel.

The summer of 1956 found the Goodmans moving yet another 15 blocks west to a more idyllic setting: a brand new home just inside the city limits at 5116 N. Monticello Ave., just south of the stretch of busy Foster Avenue that borders Bohemian National Cemetery and crosses the snaking north branch of the Chicago River. The Goodmans' small, rectangular, tan brick structure held just 1,200 square feet on its ground floor — along with a similar-sized basement, the only finished one on the block — and sat along a quiet, one-block street that ended at its intersection with the river. From the front, the house looked to be part of any relatively new 1950s neighborhood, with two dozen modest homes, virtually indistinguishable from each other, lining both sides of Monticello.

But outside the back doors and fenced yards of the Goodmans' and other homes on the west side of the street lay a young boy's version of paradise: the northern triangle of Eugene Field Park, with a huge baseball diamond and backstop. Just beyond left field was Foster Avenue and the cemetery. Right and center field (which doubled as a football field) abutted the homes' back fences, so if a lefty batter really smacked one, he could hit it into the Goodmans' backyard.

BEST WISHES FOR A

Merry Christmas

STEVE, MINNETTE AND BUD GOODMAN

This Christmas card (left), sent by the Goodmans in 1950 or 1951, illustrates the dichotomy of raising a Jewish family and staying connected to a world dominated by Christian and secular holiday observances. Above, Steve is shown at 5 and 6 in class photos from Budlong Woods School in fall 1953 (left) and fall 1954.
(Card courtesy of Michael Litt, school photos courtesy of Linda Wolf Pepper)

The ballfield wasn't the only attraction, however. Just a few dozen paces in back of home plate, a rickety, wooden footbridge crossed the Chicago River to the larger, southern portion of Eugene Field Park and its imposing, 1928-era, two-floor fieldhouse. The footbridge also served as a gateway to the blue-collar, lower-to-middle-class Albany Park neighborhood, with which Steve and his family associated. There, spread out over a dozen square blocks, were three-story Alessandro Volta Elementary School, which Steve attended through eighth-grade graduation; Lawrence Avenue, the area's east-west commercial spine with its delicatessens, hobby shops and candy stores; and the northern end of the Ravenswood line of "the El," the city's elevated/subway train. Dotted among the 1910-1930-era bungalows and two- and three-story flats were Temple Beth Israel, two other synagogues and a pair of associated youth centers, the touchstones of a mostly multiple-family residential district that was almost entirely Democratic and nearly 100 percent Jewish.

"It was pretty homogeneous," says Gary Mechanic, one of Steve's childhood friends who grew up in the neighborhood. "You had to speak Yiddish to do business in at least half of the stores on Lawrence Avenue, and each year the signs commemorating the Holocaust were in every store window."

In some homes, the Holocaust hung as an unspoken backdrop of angst, says Jo Ann Stepan (now Simich), another of Steve's friends who, as a European-American Serb, was one of the handful of non-Jews in the neighborhood. "Some of these three-bedroom apartments had just one bed and a table with two unmatched chairs," she says. More than a few families had come directly to Chicago from the World War II concentration camps and housed aunts, uncles, other relatives and long-term boarders. "There was relief to be in America, but there was such a heaviness, and their kids didn't take life lightly. They didn't talk about their experiences in the war, but they were proud to be Jews."

Three-story Volta Elementary School, shown in 2001, was a potent presence to Holocaust survivors in 1950s Albany Park, says one of Steve's classmates, Jo Ann Stepan: "Education was everything to those people – everything."
(Photo by Clay Eals)

4: The Holocaust backdrop was not so overbearing as to preclude wicked humor. Steve learned – and later incorporated in his shows – an off-color World War II parody to the tune of the "Colonel Bogey March": "Hitler has only got one ball / Goering has two but they're real small / Himmler's are somewhat similar / and Dr. Goebbels has no balls at all."

"It was the kind of thing that people, if they spoke at all, would speak in hushes," says Cary Lerman, another friend. "It was shrouded in mystery. There were no classes or lectures on it like today. People wouldn't openly talk about it. There was a dark shadow about it, almost as if there was a shame associated with it."

While their bodies had escaped the camps' horrors, the survivors' minds and hearts were deeply scarred, Stepan says. Among the losses they grieved were one-of-a-kind heirlooms and family diaries, similar to the well-known writings of Anne Frank. "They lost their written history," Stepan says, "so theirs was an oral history, and everything was through stories and songs. It was revered if you had a talent. Education was everything to those people — everything." [4]

The neighborhood's center of education, of course, was Volta Elementary, which "would as much as shut down on Jewish holidays," adds Scott Berman, another of Goodman's classmates. "It didn't, of course, because it was a public school, but when a Jewish holiday occurred, this school of 1,000 kids wound up with only 10 kids coming to school. Many of the teachers were Jewish. So the 10 kids went to the auditorium and watched movies on Jewish holidays."

Berman, who works as a community organizer in his boyhood neighborhood, says Albany Park played a big role in the migration of Jews within segregated Chicago. "All the larger, three- to-four-story buildings in Albany Park were built for proximity to the El," he says. "The El came out here in 1907, and teeming thousands of Jews from the West Side said, 'Oh, the promised land! We can go north.' There were more Jews moving to Rogers Park farther east and north, but Albany Park was also booming with two-flats and three-flats. The owner usually lived in one of the units and rented the rest to Jewish relatives and friends."

After the Great Depression hit, Berman says, "the banks usually allowed each Jewish family to keep the building they lived in, but not necessarily their holdings. So, through the Depression and the war, nothing got built at all. Boom came the postwar. Not only did we have new highways and veterans with money to buy homes and people moving to the suburbs, but Jews said to themselves, 'We've got this nice neighborhood that we're living in, but there's this huge area to the north, across the river.' " Some families moved to Skokie or even farther to Highland Park, Deerfield and Northbrook, but for others the move was mere blocks.

One destination was Monticello Avenue, the sparkling, dead-end lane on which the Goodmans lived. It literally embodied the baby boom. "You opened the door at night, in the evening after dinner, and all the kids poured into the street," says Laura Freedman (now White), who also grew up with Steve on Monticello. "You knew everybody. The sidewalk was meaningless. There were a few cars parked, but you played in the street and on the front lawns of most of the houses. We could hear the Good Humor truck coming on the other side of the river, and we'd run home and get money, because we knew how many minutes it would be till he got to our part of Monticello."

As the $25,000 dwellings took shape on Monticello's formerly wooded lots, neighborhood children played on their unfinished foundations. "We called them the new houses," Berman says. The homes' status as new among Albany Park kids didn't last long, for although the Goodmans and others on the street were geographically partitioned from the rest of the neighborhood by the river, Steve's friends pedaled their bikes across the footbridge to his house countless times. For many neighborhood kids, the homes on Monticello were "like Richie Rich," says Linda Black, a childhood friend. "It was a delineation. The closer you lived to Foster, people owned things. It was unheard of. He lived across the footbridge, are you kidding? Across Eugene Field? Oh! Houses? Nobody! Everybody lived in apartments. To have a house? Oh!"

The Goodmans' home sported "clean lines" and was modern, light and pleasant, says Jo Ann Stepan. Its large, square windows contrasted with those south of the footbridge in the neighborhood's multi-family walk-ups: "the wood ones that you had to put a Coke bottle in to keep them open, and you were lucky if you had a screen."

What Steve's friends found when they visited his home was "a middle-class family, as normal as you can get," he recalled in a later interview. But a normal family to Steve was extraordinary to others. "Steve had the coolest parents," says Linda Black. "It was a neighborhood where everybody's mother usually wore their father's undershirt to dress up in. But Steve's parents used to go out to drink. They went on dates. They went downtown, to Rush Street. They were the littlest people you ever saw, and we considered them so socially advanced. Other parents would meet with the relatives, and if they went out, they went someplace in the neighborhood. But his parents were so sophisticated."

Even so, Steve's parents' disparate schedules and temperaments could not have been entirely harmonious.

His dad was "a friendly, outgoing guy," "always up and jovial, anything to make you happy," remember two of Steve's childhood friends, Stuart Gordon and Ken Kruss. Bud was an attentive Eisenhower-era father, telling countless stories about piloting planes during the war, shooting home movies of his sons and the rest of the family and showing off new Chevrolets for the neighborhood from the Z Frank and Keystone dealerships at which he worked. Once, Bud drove home a "gorgeous" white Corvette from 1953 or 1954, the make's first years of production, says another of Steve's friends, Rodney Zolt. Kids gathered from all around, their mouths agape, and Bud treated them to rides around the block. [5]

Still, Steve's cousin on his mother's side, Mark Erenburg, picked up disquieting undercurrents from within the family. "There was something palpable that Bud was different," he says. "It wasn't direct and nasty, but it was always in the tone of a misfit relationship. It was always, 'He's the odd person out.' I thought he was the nicest guy in the whole world, but as a kid, you could feel it, that he was the strange one."

Aiming to be a "good provider," Bud often was away from the house, work-

> **Steve's parents used to go out to drink. They went on dates. They went downtown, to Rush Street. They were the littlest people you ever saw, and we considered them so socially advanced.**
> **LINDA BLACK**

5: "The Goodman family seemed to have a variety of cars, all Chevies, of course," says Linda Wolf (now Pepper), an early grade-school friend. "I got my one and only ride in the teeny-tiny back of a Corvette when they took me along to see the Clydesdale horses."

ing on weekdays, evenings and weekends, achieving moderate financial success at the auto-sales trade. He told his son that he worked at "Sharkskin Alley," as Steve put it in a 1979 concert in Cincinnati. "More double-knit suits down there than anywhere else. He had purple double-knit suits. Had to tell everybody the green one was blue — a special job being a car salesman."

Though Minnette's first cousin, Shirley Litt, recalls Bud as "loud and pushy," the memories of another of Minnette's first cousins, Josephine "Joey" Sage, who with her husband Gene bought two cars from Bud, are more kind. "Buddy was a charming guy," she says. "He would come across as very sincere, like good salesmen do. You think that they've got your best interests at heart, that all they care about is pleasing you. He was very good at that, very good at gab."

Measured in his assessment, Bert Brodsky, a fellow salesman and later supervisor, characterizes Bud as "a real nice guy" who "had the ability to talk to people and convince them that he was straight and honest," an asset in an era when auto salesmen were seen as "scum of the earth." At the same time, he says, Bud had a Little Caesar-like "overrated opinion of himself" and "weaseled" his way into higher salary and status by playing bridge and dining with dealership owners. "He wouldn't make you any money," Brodsky says. "If you wanted a fixture in the place, he was wonderful, but talent-wise, ability, aggressive, hungry, he laughed it off. He was a hang-around guy. That's how he made his money. The house threw him deals, and they took care of him." Phil Slavin, owner of Keystone, made Bud "some kind of a manager, gave him a title," Brodsky says. "Bud was very impressed with that title business."

In contrast, Minnette (whom Bud called Minnie) was a fastidious, full-time homemaker who swathed the interior of the Goodman house in aqua and pink. She swept the sidewalk daily while doting on her two boys and keeping track of a collie with failing eyesight named Duchess. Stuart Gordon says that his mother was bowled over whenever she drove over there to pick him up. "I'd walk in, and the place would be spotless," Gordon's mom would tell Stuart later. "Minnette would always be dressed impeccably, perfectly, she would have something fabulous smelling on the stove, and she'd be so nice. I could never figure out how that woman managed to do it all."

Minnette's devotion to her home and brood, along with the values of loyalty and generosity, ran deep in her ancestors, say members of the Erenburg family. Her grandfather, machinist Solomon Erenburg, and his wife, Ruth, emigrated to the United States from Ukraine, a future Soviet Republic, at the turn of the century, looking for a better life and perhaps to avoid decades-long conscription in the czar's army. Solomon was "the kindest man you could imagine" and more interested in family than in financial stature, says his daughter-in-law and Minnette's aunt, Pat Erenburg. "He was a very unusual person," she says. "He wasn't interested in making a lot of money. I don't even think it's practical to be like him." His wife, Ruth, was more of a religious person, making sure their daughter and two sons attended synagogue and Sunday school. "They were all very close, and they would do almost anything for a member of their family."

Buddy was a charming guy. He would come across as very sincere, like good salesmen do. You think that they've got your best interests at heart.
JOSEPHINE 'JOEY' SAGE

One son of Solomon and Ruth, Morris Erenburg, who ran the Chelsea Hotel restaurant on Chicago's North Side and became Minnette's father, "always had a gift" for family members young and old, says Shirley Litt. "He was very warm and full of fun," adds Pat Erenburg, "one of the sweetest, kindest human beings you ever met."

Pat Erenburg says that when her husband (Morris' brother) was overseas in the Army during World War II and she was living in Los Angeles, Morris sent her a box of a dozen chocolate bars every week without fail. "Nobody," she says, "could get chocolate during the war because it was sent to the soldiers, but somehow Morris did." She recalls a revealing exchange by phone with her brother-in-law after his first shipment:

"Look, I can't eat all these chocolate bars," she told him. "I can't use these."

"You know," he replied, "when anybody does something for you, you can tip them with a chocolate bar or two because they're more valuable than money."

Pat Erenburg shakes her head in astonishment at the memory. "I could have asked him probably for the moon," she says. "If he could have gotten it, he would have."

Steve's grandfather on his mother's side, Morris "Ziss" Erenburg, poses in the early 1950s with his ever-present cigar and his nephews (Steve's second cousins) Steve, center, and Mark Erenburg. Ziss figured prominently in a 1977 Steve Goodman song, "Old Smoothies."
(Photo courtesy of Michael Litt)

The cigar-chomping Morris, who along with his wife, Mary, later owned a luggage store, showed a similar allegiance to his nephews, nieces and grandchildren (including Steve), giving them baseballs and mitts and taking them out for sodas and to Cubs games. One of the nephews, Mark Erenburg, fondly recalls Morris spoiling him and his brother and admonishing their father. "Don't be hard on them. Don't yell at them. They're nice kids."

Known by kids in the family as "Ziss" or "Zissie" (because Shirley Litt, as a child, couldn't pronounce his real first name), Morris made an indelible impression on young Steve. For a 1975 concert audience, Steve fondly recalled that his grandfather's cigars were made of "horse shit and splinters — Perfecto Garcia Blotz." At later shows, introducing his "Old Smoothies," Steve said that when he was young Mary and Ziss often joined 10,000 others in flocking to Chicago Stadium to see the Ice Capades, Holiday on Ice, Ice Follies and Blackhawks hockey "because my grandfather was Russian, and he would go to anything involving skates. He used to close the store and drive from Chicago to Detroit to see people play hockey. ... I think my grandfather wanted us to remember how cold it was in the Ukraine when he was a child." Until he suffered several strokes, including one that left him paralyzed and in a nursing home, Morris joined Mary for frequent visits to the Goodman home on Monticello. After his death in late 1959, Mary worked part-time at a nephew's restaurant, lived with her daughter and became a strong presence in the Goodman household.

Decades later, upon meeting "Grandma Mary" Erenburg, Steve's musical colleagues said to themselves, "That's where Steve Goodman came from." One was singer/songwriter Chris Farrell. "She had the eyes, the smile, the same bouncy, joyful energy that Steve had," he says. "You see a lot in Minnette and David, the same look, very friendly, generous, but they don't bounce around like Steve and Grandma Mary did. The energy is Grandma Mary, those eyes lighting up."

Eight-year-old Steve sits in the front row for his 1956 Volta Elementary School class photo.
(Class photo courtesy of Janette Ferdinand Woods)

Another who was on the scene, publicist Liz Danzig (now Derry), says Mary served as "everybody's grandmother."

Friends who gathered at the Goodman home in Steve's grade-school days recall Minnette's welcoming personality. Jo Ann Stepan, as tall for her age as Steve was short, remembers Minnette's touch. "She would put her hand on my shoulder, look me in the eyes and say, 'It's nice to see you, Jo Ann. Are you having a good time? Steve's so happy to have this party.' "

But perhaps the biggest impression that Minnette left in the Albany Park neighborhood was her physical appearance. "She was really small, tiny and absolutely striking, absolutely beautiful," says Stuart Gordon. "When she showed up at PTA meetings, all the moms were jealous." He and others remember Minnette's long, dark-brown hair that she wore in a ponytail or braid down to the back of her knees and that swung back and forth as she walked. "The ponytail wasn't 'in,' but she didn't care," says another of Steve's classmates, Barb Nicker (now Stewart). "She was like a movie star," says Anita Gold, an across-the-street neighbor who was about six years younger than Minnette. Steve's cousin, Mark Erenburg, likened her to a tiny Audrey Hepburn with a "sweet, kind, soft, flexible" personality.

With Bud away at work so often, Mark Erenburg saw Steve as mostly a "mother's boy." Assisted by her own mother, Minnette instilled her sensibilities in young Steve, who was known in his grade-school years — as he was in his adult life — by the affectionate moniker of "Stevie."

"Stevie was one of my favorite people, and he was very, very, very well kept," says Anita Gold. "He was always dressed immaculately. I never saw his clothes dirty or disarrayed. He was perfect. And he had the manners of a sophisticate. He was so sophisticated for his young age. He was a very kind person. He never had a cruel word to say to anybody. His parents raised both their sons to be gentlemen, and Stevie was the epitome of a gentleman."

Gold says she was both surprised and delighted as a result. "He was really held down at his parents' request. He would always keep his dark hair combed perfect, and he had perfect haircuts. I never, ever saw a hair out of place. I don't think the wind could blow it. He didn't wear spray; it was just very well kept. He was immaculately clean. Usually you see a boy with dirty hands. Not him."

Parents in the neighborhood enjoyed having young Steve as a playmate for their kids, says Arlynn Gottlieb, a Volta classmate who lived down an alley from the Goodmans and who, in the summer of 1956, several times had Steve over to her home, where, in the basement, the two 8-year-olds created plays for her lion and tiger hand puppets. Arlynn sat and typed on a typewriter with Steve standing next to her while the scripts took shape. "We practiced them," she says. "I had a wooden toy chest, and we used that for the stage. He was more sensitive and easy for a girl to talk to and play with than the other boys."

He also was more educated. "Books were highly valued in his house," says Norm Kanter, another Volta classmate, who says Steve's bedroom had a library of 40 orange-bound biographies of George and Martha Washington, Abraham

Lincoln and other historical figures. "I went to the library to get these books, but Steve had a lot of them at home."

Steve's gentlemanly and cultivated appearance and demeanor extended to his role as an older brother. Laura Freedman says that, one time, Steve's brother David had done something to hurt her feelings, and it was Steve who was enlisted, probably by his mother, to walk David across the street to her house to apologize. She recalls Steve standing in her front doorway and saying, "David has something to tell you."

Years later, those close to Steve perceived a self-assurance that stemmed from his early upbringing. "There wasn't a lot of worrying about credit in reference to him because he came from a household where much was made of him already," says singer/songwriter Michael Smith, whose "The Dutchman" became one of Steve's signature tunes. "He had a very good foundation from the parents. His mom is obviously a very bright and careful woman. I just got the feeling he was very secure."

Still, as an undersized child of undersized parents (Bud stood about 5-foot-3, and Minnette was less than 5 feet), Steve could not rely on physical stature to carve his way through a preteen's formative years. As well, he carried a roly-poly build that he didn't shed until well into his adulthood. So he honed his personality instead, showing early signs of the warmth, self-deprecation and hamminess that were to define his character years later.

While his dad nicknamed him "Stove" and "the Crisco Kid" because he was short and squat, Janette Ferdinand (now Woods), a Volta classmate, says that Steve's moniker among friends was "Piggy," given that "his nose looked like a pig nose because it was kind of squashed upward." She treasures a childhood autograph book in which Steve inscribed not only "Good luck, Steven Goodman" but also, scrawled across two pages in huge capital letters, "PIGGY." "He wasn't one who made fun of me," Ferdinand says. "He didn't make fun of other people. He was just a nice guy."

Steve's "tremendous amount of internal energy" sticks in Gary Mechanic's mind. "Instead of seeming flabby and unathletic, he always seemed like he was ready to explode from extreme enthusiasm. He just looked like he was chubby from packing too much energy inside, like he was going to blow up."

Rick Eisenstaedt, bar-mitzvahed on the same day as Steve at Temple Beth Israel, remembers him as "sweet and good-natured and serious, all the wrong traits to have to be successful in Albany Park as a kid. You had to be a good athlete, you had to be big, to be among the socially elite."

But not all his peers saw drawbacks in Steve's stature. As the shortest boy in his Volta classes, his stock rose during fire drills. "We were the two most petite people," says classmate Linda Black, "and in fire drills you had to go by height, so we were the captains and always the last ones out. I used to call him Captain Goodman."

"The thing about Steve when he was young was how cute he was," adds Gordon, who was seated in alphabetical order behind Steve in Volta classrooms.

In this December 1958 Volta school photo, Steve poses with neighborhood friend Arlynn Gottlieb. The two had created plays with animal hand puppets in Gottlieb's basement.
(Class photo courtesy of Arlynn Gottlieb)

Twelve-year-old Steve poses in the front row of his 1960 Volta Elementary School class photo.
(Class photo courtesy of Janette Ferdinand Woods)

"He was this little, round, cute kid. He looked younger than he was, so everybody thought he was adorable, and all the girls were nuts about him because they thought he was the cutest thing on two legs. I was jealous of him. We used to kid him a lot about his baby face and about how he could get away with murder. All the teachers loved him, too. So if the two of us were talking, I would always get blamed for it. Steve was always teacher's pet."

In fourth grade, Steve's teacher, Donna Wender, often had him read aloud in front of the class because he was the best reader. Classmate Norm Kanter recalls her praising Steve's ability to simultaneously read a paragraph and scan the next one. One summer vacation, Steve even took the unusual step of inviting Wender home for a visit. Wender says that Minnette, who was "absolutely adorable," prepared a delicious lunch, and afterward the two played board games in the living room. Wender was flattered by the attention and confirms Steve was a "star" in class. "Everybody loved him. He was kind, intelligent and very, very popular, and he deserved to be popular because he was a fine person and a lot of fun."

Two years later, Steve furthered his good will in an incident treasured by Volta counselor Maggie Ratchford. His teacher had become momentarily ill, and Steve left the classroom, hurried to a janitor's closet and returned with a pail so that the teacher could vomit. "No one else in that room thought of that," Ratchford says. "The teacher was rather embarrassed about it, but it was very kind. That really showed compassion."

Like many Chicago Public Schools students in the 1950s, Steve originally was part of a class that entered Volta in February instead of in September, as part of a two-tiered cycle. But the district soon annualized its timetable so that all students would attend on a September-to-June schedule. So Steve and many others were "triple-tracked," given three semesters of instruction in two semesters' time (plus summer school during seventh grade) and thus were boosted by half a year by the time they graduated from eighth grade. The promotion posed no academic challenge for Steve, known as one of the school's more intelligent students, other than making him even younger for his grade level than his size already made him appear.

Ever more gregarious as he grew toward his teen years, Steve found many places in his safe, insular neighborhood to rub shoulders with other families and gather with kids of all ages. "We would come home from school, maybe get something to eat, then we were gone, parents not really knowing where we were, but not worrying about the fact that they didn't know where we were," says Volta classmate Cary Lerman. "At night, during the summer, it was always too hot to be inside, so everyone would be downstairs, men and women out in lawn chairs, sitting outside talking. We didn't feel anonymous at all, didn't have a feeling of alienation. We were very much connected in friendship, activities and family, and we felt we were really part of the community."

The focal point for kids, of course, was Eugene Field Park, right outside Steve's back door. "From 3 to 10 at night, you were there," says TV broadcaster

Bob Sirott, a friend two years younger than Steve. "The park was a total magnet," says Hart Weichselbaum, another of Steve's classmates. "After school, summers, weekends, there was all kinds of stuff going on there, and it was wonderful for us because we all lived so close. With the river flowing through, it was just a great place to play."

Besides the ballfield and fieldhouse, the park sported swing sets, a basketball court, a covered play area and, in the winter, a long, rectangular ice rink. Routinely, Steve popped out his back door and hustled past the ballfield and over the footbridge to meet with 20 to 30 others on the benches next to a concrete pond fed by a tall fountain outside the fieldhouse. Sometimes, the activity was a simple sidewalk game like 1-2-3 American Eagle, Olevio, Kick the Can, Red Rover or What Time Is It, Mr. Fox? (a form of Simon Says). Sometimes, the group worked on befriending the Eugene Field staff and teachers, shooting hoops in the fieldhouse gym or helping clear stones from the softball diamond's infield.

Boys hung out and talked warily of a tubercular sanitarium north of Foster and a nearby home for unwed mothers, both of which their parents had declared off-limits. Occasionally, the action took on an edgier feel. Older kids goaded each other to scare younger ones into the cemetery across Foster, and once in a while, members of the group took turns grasping the electrical cable beneath the footbridge and pulling themselves hand over hand across the riverbed without falling into the mucky, occasionally sewage-laden water. "That old bridge had a Mark Twain kind of feeling if you were hanging around it," says Berman. "We played Tarzan by dangling on that wire above the water. Kids used to say, 'The bloodsuckers are gonna get you,' and we knew that we should fear them and that they probably would kill us."

In cold weather, the boys often retreated to the Goodmans' finished basement to sit on a couch and watch TV or sit at tables and play board games such as Photo-Electric Football, which consisted of a cardboard box with a light bulb underneath to illuminate a vibrating football field on which teams of plastic players moved rather erratically. On Saturday afternoons, the kids' hot spot shifted to Lawrence Avenue, [6] where they could buy Italian ices, and the Terminal Theater, [7] named for its proximity to the end of the Ravenswood El line. There, the draw was the 25-cent matinee double-feature (the 1958 Steve McQueen feature "The Blob" was a big hit), with popcorn and a Coke costing just another quarter. "It was just a melee," Weichselbaum says. "It was too noisy to watch the movie, and the floor was sticky with all the crap that kids spilled."

In spring and summertime, though, when the weather was sunny and warm, the thoughts of Steve and other boys in the neighborhood turned to baseball. "Baseball was a religion," Steve recalled in a 1983 interview for the NBC-TV "First Camera" magazine show. "Wrigley Field was a shrine. It was a place of worship." And in Albany Park, says Bob Sirott, "Organized sports to us was: Open your window, stick your head out and yell, 'Hey, anybody want to go to the park and choose up a game?' "

6: Another hot spot on Lawrence Avenue was Maury's Hot Dogs, a 20-by-24-foot storefront with three tables, a counter with revolving stools and three pinball machines. "This neighborhood, there was nothing like it," Maury Andes reminisced in the March 31, 1978, *Chicago Reader*. "You never had to worry. There were always people around, always different organizations to inspire kids. They made kids into doers and leaders." Sydney Lieberman, writer of the article, added that in Albany Park, "Life was as warm and safe as your parents' bed when you crawled in early in the morning. The people, food and holidays were familiar. Places were known to you, and you were known in those places. ... Cross out of the boundaries, and you were in enemy territory. But there was no need to step out. Everything we wanted was in Albany Park!"

7: Steve fondly recalled being in the balcony of the Terminal Theater and singing Dion DiMucci's "Runaround Sue" when it was a #1 hit in 1961. But with his adult backdrop of leukemia, the theater's name became a bugaboo when Steve looked up and saw it on signs during countless airline trips. As recalled by steel-guitarist Julian "Winnie" Winston and others, Steve often said, "Terminal — what a terrible thing to call something at an airport. It scares me every time I have to go to the terminal. Y'know, they could use another word."

If only three guys were available, the game was line ball, played in streets that were framed by cottonwood and elm trees and drew only a smattering of parked and moving vehicles. "One guy bats, one guy pitches, one guy fields, and you hit it in a straight line," Weichselbaum says. "It was better in the street," adds Mechanic, "because you had less chance of breaking house windows." Gordon remembers that they used a 16-inch-circumference ball, too big for a mitt, called a Chicago softball, with the brand name of Clincher. "It was almost like a pillow, so if it hit a car, it wouldn't break the windshield." Of course, as they crafted batting stances, the boys pretended to "be" Ernie Banks, Billy Williams, Ron Santo or other favorite Chicago Cubs. Sirott says the popularity of the North Side big-league team was so strong that kids even sought to "be" Al Sheuneman, the team trainer.

If the turnout was in double digits, the get-up game was full-fledged softball at Volta or in Eugene Field Park, at either the large diamond behind Steve's house or a smaller version just outside his backyard. "He had the perfect location," says Stuart Gordon. "You literally would go through his gate, and you'd be in the middle of the diamond." Steve's position? In both informal and Little League games, it was behind the plate. "He had the full catcher's regalia: the padding, the knee guards and the whole works, because he was the right build for a catcher," Gordon says. He also had an earnest desire to play, and, fortunately for him, the catcher's equipment ensured his participation. As another Volta classmate, Alan Rosenfeld, put it, "Steve couldn't hit for nothing."

Fittingly, the love of baseball — and of the hapless Chicago Cubs — was inculcated early in Steve's childhood by good-natured parents and "well-meaning older relatives" who introduced him to Wrigley insiders and taught him to love jokes, "practical and otherwise." Years later, in 1981, Steve told *Chicago Tribune* reporter Bill Jauss that when he was just 5, his great-uncle, Harry Romanoff, the legendary *Chicago American* night city editor, got Steve's family into games gratis, courtesy of usher Tates "Whitey" Johnson, who stood watch at the leftfield pass gate. Steve's grandfather, "Ziss" Erenburg, fueled the youngster's interest by buying him entire boxes of baseball cards (although not before removing, at Minnette's insistence, the pink, tooth-rotting gum tucked inside each pack). Ziss was the one, Steve fondly told WGN-AM's Roy Leonard in 1981, who taunted him more than once with a punster's prank.

Steve would bound through the door, and, in an excited voice, Ziss would say, "Hey, Steve! Cubs won!"

Taking the bait, Steve instantly would respond, "Great!"

Ziss, knowing he'd caught Steve on the "won/one" homonym, would follow up with "Dodgers seven!"

Similarly, during concerts in 1983 and 1984, Steve related another, decidedly mordant illustration of his youthful diamond psyche. When the White Sox of the South Side, home to many Albany Park parents in their youth, defeated the Cleveland Indians to clinch the American League pennant late the night of Sept. 22, 1959 (the first time since the ignominious Black Sox did so 40 years earlier), play-by-play broadcaster Bob Elson barked "Sox win! Sox win! Sox win!" into his WCFL-AM radio microphone. Meanwhile, Chicago Fire Commissioner Robert J. Quinn ordered the city's air-raid sirens to howl citywide for a full five minutes. The wail alarmed tens of thousands of unfathoming Chicagoans, many of whom rushed to the streets or led their kids to shelter. In the Goodman home, Steve and his 7-year-old brother, David, thought the sirens signified a real attack, so the two dropped and cowered beneath a table. "My brother later said something to the effect of 'Perfect — a Chicago team wins something, and it's the end of the fucking world.' I always appreciated my brother's view of that." [8]

As Steve grew to be 11 or 12 years old, he began to ride the El to Wrigley dozens of times each summer with neighborhood friends. "We sat in the bleachers," Gordon says. "We moved around, but we mostly were in center field. And Steve was a great heckler. Of course, we never heckled the Cubs. We were always getting on the other team. We knew we'd scored if the guy looked back at us. And then we'd yell at him, 'Hey, watch the game!' We ate popcorn, hot dogs, the whole works. It was a great way to spend the day, one of the best things you could do."

No matter the grip that baseball had on Steve, an equally compelling thread in his youthful life was musical performance, beginning with his voice. He harmonized with classmates on the Volta playground on the Tokens' "The Lion Sleeps Tonight" and other top-40 songs he'd heard at night on a transistor radio stashed under his pillow, and he had the musical instruction typical for grade-schoolers. This included talent shows in which he sang "Sixteen Tons," "Kisses Sweeter than Wine" and "Love and Marriage" and assemblies during which entire classrooms of students trooped to the auditorium stage to sing "The Star-Spangled Banner," "Swanee River," Christmas carols and an obligatory Hanukkah song. "Steven would be the one we could hear singing," classmate Arlynn Gottlieb says. "I liked to stand next to him," adds classmate Tony Mackin, "because I didn't have to do anything."

But more than his schoolteachers, Steve's musical pathfinders were the disc jockeys of Chicago radio. [9] "You could spin the AM dial and get darn near anything," he recalled in a February 1984 interview with New York deejay Pete Fornatale. "(W)CFL had country music, and (W)VON had all the R&B — for blues, you could catch Big Bill Hill and the Shopping Bag show on the way to school, right? — and there was just a ton of pop radio with good deejays, and it made me listen."

In a 1972 *Chicago Daily News* interview, Steve traced how he bounded out of Volta in 1957, bouncing along Lawrence Avenue and thinking about his dad's desire for him eventually to find a better job than as a car salesman and to prepare for a career in medicine.

"I'm going to be a doctor," the 9-year-old Steve said to himself as he reached into his coat pocket, pulled out a transistor radio, tuned it to WLS, held it to his ear and heard the rollicking beat of "School Days."

You could spin the AM dial and get darn near anything.
STEVE GOODMAN

8: In some concerts, Steve attributed this quote to himself instead of his brother. Received uproariously by audiences, the quote may have been merely Steve's fanciful creation.

9: Steve later told New York radio host Oscar Brand, "Chicago's a great melting pot for traditional songs. You get all the music, white and black, that came up from the South after World War II, and I guess that's where I learned all those Jimmie Rodgers songs, and the Muddy Waters ones."

The stained-glass windows of Temple Beth Israel included icons of American life as well as Judaism. (Photos by Clay Eals)

10: Temple Beth Israel sold its Albany Park building in December 1980 to the First Korean United Methodist Church and opened a new temple in a bank building in Skokie in July 1981. While the Korean church still uses the Albany Park structure, its stained-glass windows survive intact and, under a covenant, remain in the ownership of Temple Beth Israel.

"Doctor, schmoctor," Steve thought. "This is Chuck Berry!"

All day long you've wanted to dance! ...

"Dance! Yeah, and sing, too!"
Steve rotated the dial to another station.

I'm all shook up! ...

"Elvis! Cool!" He listened further.

Whole lotta shakin' goin' on! ...

"Jerry Lee rockabilly!"

That'll be the day! ...

"Oh, man, Buddy Holly!"
Steve's intrigue was palpable, he told interviewer Marshall Rosenthal. "I just wanted to be all those people." The only person he could be at the time, however, was a kid in Albany Park, and because of his neighborhood's day-to-day religious and cultural focus, the place he spent most of his time other than at home and Volta was at synagogue. Of course, Temple Beth Israel wasn't exactly a prep academy for early rock 'n' roll. But it was the only Reform congregation in Albany Park (two other nearby shuls were of the Conservative branch), and as it placed a premium on music and its presentation, Steve jumped in headfirst.

Constructed at the southwest corner of North Bernard Avenue and West Ainslee Street as a one-floor synagogue between 1917 and 1921, and expanded upward by two floors in the early 1950s, Temple Beth Israel provided a marvelous physical setting for music performed before a large audience. For the High Holidays each fall, the main sanctuary and balcony on the second and third floors accommodated a full house of 900 adults (not an atypical turnout for a congregation of 725 member families). At the same time, an equal number of youths packed the multi-purpose auditorium on the ground floor. Saturday-morning services, bar mitzvahs and youth-choir concerts typically drew a smaller but formidable gathering of 200 to 300 people in the main sanctuary.

What greeted the attendees when they arrived was a visual representation of the liberality of an urban, Reform congregation. As members of the shul walked down the center aisle to take their seats, light streamed in on each side of the sanctuary through two imposing, colorful stained-glass windows. Twenty feet high, the vertical arrangements of 16 large and 32 smaller panes elaborately depicted religious and secular symbols and stories, ranging from Noah's Ark and Moses leading Israelites out of Egypt to the Liberty Bell and the Statue of Liberty. [10] Similarly, on one side of the sanctuary stood a pole with an Israeli flag, while a pole on the other side flew an American flag. "The purpose of all this was not only Judaism but also American life, so that the presentation wouldn't be so heavily religious," says Scott Berman. "It's about wanting to be a part of the nation that you're in."

Straight ahead of the seats and two steps up was a wide, carpeted stage that led to an arch in the middle that stood 25 feet high. On each side of the arch, inset in the high walls above sections of richly paneled wood, sat two horizontal lofts. The one on the right sheltered the shul's Hammond organ and organist, and the one on the left housed the 30-member youth choir.

The blue-robed choir reflected a Reform shul that invested deeply in the musical realm. "It wasn't grandiose," said Rick Eisenstaedt, "but they obviously paid attention to the music and always had a more lush production than you would expect in a synagogue." This tone and direction flowed from the shul's rabbi, Ernst Lorge, considered a strong Zionist and knowledgeable, thoughtful and commanding leader who dedicated himself to teaching, as well as from its cantor and choral director, Irving Zummer.

Zummer, steeped in the Conservative branch, selected music with a traditional bent, but he also faced the challenge of shaping a group of antsy youngsters into a cohesive chorus. In his favor, he possessed a sonorous singing ability that young Steve later likened to that of one of his radio idols, Buddy Holly. To try out for youth choir was considered a tough task, and it was an honor, among parents as well as peers, to be selected for it. Zummer labored to get the youngsters to open their mouths in certain ways to produce "ahh" and "ayy" tones, to take breaths unobtrusively and to learn the nuances of dynamics. He also devoted ample time to correct pronunciation, for while a few of the songs borrowed from Christian style and were translated into English from German for the Reform audience, many lyrics were in Hebrew.

"They were an extraordinary group," Zummer says. "You're talking about really young kids, and they were able to do three- and four-part harmony. But they were also very devoted to the choir. They practiced frequently after school, sometimes more if we had a program going on, and we did some remarkable stuff."

The vocal abilities of two members of the choir stood out above the rest — Steve Goodman, a soprano, and Barry (now Benyomin) Ellegant, an alto. "Steve and I were kind of the untouchables," Ellegant says. Their skills, which lent prestige to the temple, merited individualized instruction from Zummer, so that they could be called upon to sing solos. As Beth Cohn (now Sair), then-president of the temple youth group, puts it, "This was the mentality where they needed boys to sing the prayers. It didn't matter how many girls you had. You needed the cantor image. You needed a boy."

Ellegant remembers well the lessons from Zummer, who endeavored to produce in him and in Steve what is known as a trained voice. The cantor encouraged the two to sing from their diaphragms and thereby produce powerfully resonant "head tones" so that they would not strain when singing Hebrew prayers in the upper registers. "I couldn't fully figure out what Zummer was trying to teach me," Ellegant says, "but I thought he was an excellent coach, especially for Steve," whose voice took on a timbre richer than the fragile, "thin" quality that people associate with boy sopranos of the renowned Vienna Boys Choir.

They were an extraordinary group. You're talking about really young kids, and they were able to do three- and four-part harmony.
IRVING ZUMMER

Such coaching gave Steve a stature in contrast to his size, bolstering his motivation to improve his Hebrew and participate in other synagogue activities. His family belonged to the temple, and Minnette sang in the adult choir for awhile, served on the parent-teacher board and even supervised a shul fashion show. But the Goodmans were not to-the-letter devout and treated holidays mainly as family gatherings. Steve's motivation to get more involved than attending Sabbath School for an hour and a half each Saturday morning was more social than spiritual. "I had to ask to go to (weekday-afternoon) Hebrew school," he said in a 1975 interview. "My pals were going, and they were all laughing at me because I wasn't going. So it was peer pressure. It was important to go to Hebrew school, I guess. Pure peer pressure." (He added with typical wit: "Sounds like a rock band: Pure Peer Pressure.")

> Jew church music is some hip stuff. It's got some rhythm things going on.
> STEVE GOODMAN

The social obligations of Hebrew school and music rooted themselves so deeply that Steve drew from them in his adult songwriting. In a 1973 interview in *Zoo World*, for example, Steve noted, "When I was a kid, we sang 'Hava Nagila' (which means 'Come, let's enjoy ourselves'). We didn't sing, 'I'm So Lonesome I Could Cry.' " The inspiration was direct in his Alex Haley-influenced composition "Family Tree." In 1981, he said the song stemmed, in part, from his youthful participation in the school's annual "Plant a Tree in Israel" drive by filling a poster with evidence of financial generosity. "When I was a boy," he said, "I used to have to buy stamps to put on this (illustrated) tree, and as soon as we got $5 worth of stamps, they would plant this tree in Israel."

The temple milieu amounted to a near-daily immersion, says another of Steve's synagogue friends, Jeff Gordon (no relation to Stuart Gordon). "It was our life, and we spent a lot of time with each other," he says. "We were just bound together. There was an umbilical cord to temple."

That cord extended to scouting activities, including overnight trips to summer camps in the southern Wisconsin towns of Oconomowoc and Baraboo, where youth groups played Capture the Flag, sang and told stories around evening campfires and slept in cabins. At Camp CHI in Baraboo, Steve impishly kidded Marla Bovar (now Boarini) because she had an overbite. "Kiss me, Bucky, my tonsils itch," he taunted her.

"Everybody knew each other, we all went to shul, we observed all the Jewish holidays, went to all the different services," says Scott Berman. "The temple for us was not only a religious place, but it also was our social center. We were constantly going to temple, probably four or five days a week."

Often as not, this congregation heard Steve sing. Many looked forward to it, a few with apprehension. "I was his age," says choir mate Gary Klott, "and I felt the jealousy of 'How do I get that good?' " What's more, Steve found enjoyment in the task. "Jew church music is some hip stuff," he reflected in a 1977 interview for *Come for to Sing* magazine. "It's got some rhythm things going on," he said. "That's what appealed to me, not the intellectual side of it, but the rhythm thing." On WGN's "Roy Leonard Show" in 1983, he also noted his affection for the songs' minor-key melodies, which "made me crazy."

Even as Steve turned 11 and his voice dropped into the tenor range, he sustained his standout status, thriving in this milieu of religious and emotional expression. It was not without strong encouragement — if not pressure — from his mother, Minnette, who years later told one of Steve's college friends that she had hoped Steve someday would become a cantor.

Steve's singing roles at Temple Beth Israel swelled accordingly. At the adult services for Yom Kippur and with a blue and white striped, fringed prayer shawl draped over his head, he sang Kol Nidre, the ancient, pensive opening prayer declaring the annulment of personal vows made to God in the preceding year. For the teen group, he was the soloist for all 20 to 30 songs for the High Holy Days, and he entertained for junior youth-group parties. (The temple bulletin, reporting on a "wonderful" December 1959 gathering, noted repetitively, "What with dancing, some new games, dancing, Stevie Goodman's singing, refreshments and dancing, the evening went by smoothly and happily.") Every March, he performed for the Purim Festival cantata. At services the rest of the year, he routinely sang the sh'ma, the liturgical watchword of the Jewish faith ("Hear, oh Israel, the Lord our God, the Lord our God is One"), and Ein Kamocha, the solo signaling the taking of the Torah from the Ark. And every Saturday morning, he soloed at bar-mitzvahs.

"Steve was known to everyone because of his mellifluous voice," says Oscar Miller, principal of the temple's Sabbath School: "He was able to learn and sing these songs very quickly. He was a model student in many ways, a good young man. When he'd sing in the choir loft, he was this little guy with this tremendously beautiful voice."

"He had a wonderful smile, those deep, beautiful, friendly eyes and a great personality that came across in his singing," says Steve Westman, who, three years older than Steve, occasionally played piano from the floor of the sanctuary for Steve's solos. "You wanted to hear him sing. It wasn't 'Oh, God, we have to hear this obnoxious kid again.' It was just the opposite. He was charming, he was right on the money with the music, he was the star of the choir, and he seemed like everybody's little baby brother. What more could you want? He had it all."

Despite the seriousness of the religious ceremonies, from Steve's viewpoint high above the sanctuary in the choir loft, not all was solemnity. Sitting in metal folding chairs on three stair-stepped levels, the 30 choir members were partly shielded from the congregation by see-through, diagonal-mesh panels on either side of the loft opening. As a service progressed below, the kids squirmed in their seats, trying not to screech their chairs. Scott Berman says he and Steve sat mostly hidden in the upper left corner of the loft, whispering to each other and playing tic-tac-toe, battleship and other paper-and-pencil games during speeches.

When it came time for a solo by Steve, however, the other kids made room as he crept down to the loft's front-row center, between the decorative screens. The nearest choir member lowered the microphone to accommodate Steve's

You wanted to hear him sing. It wasn't 'Oh, God, we have to hear this obnoxious kid again.'
STEVE WESTMAN

height, often drawing a snicker or two. And when the mike was clicked "on," so was Steve. Week after week, year after year, his temple soloing became routine and gave him an on-stage comfort and energy that he embraced throughout his adult musical career.

"It was a really moving experience, most of all musically," says Gary Klott, who followed Steve as a temple youth soloist. "We had a huge sanctuary and large crowds, and at times the temple was full. It was quite something to know that you're singing before that number of people. It gets you into the frame of mind that 'This is really something, performing up here.' Everybody's in suits and dresses, and everybody's waiting on every word. Everything's really focused on you. You have an organ playing, and while you're singing a solo, you've got a whole choir behind you, too.

"It was a big deal because only a couple of kids at any one time were singing solos, and they were essentially playing cantor. It's got to give you self-confidence. It's like being an all-star baseball player on a Little League team. It was quite a thing to be singing emotional songs, regardless of whether you knew what they meant. They're naturally very strong songs, and to do that in front of that large group with all ears on you is a pretty powerful experience."

That power, say all who knew Steve then, happily did not translate into arrogance. "He knew that he was talented and sang better than we common kids did," Scott Berman says, "but he was not snooty or stuck up." Adds Gary Klott, "He was always a gentleman, always had a little smile on his face."

As Steve entered the transition from child to teenager, that distinctive smile, an expression of joy and impish glee (what temple friend Ken Kruss labeled an "angelic and devilish look all in one"), merged with deep, brown eyes inherited from his mom to play a role in the next step he took in learning the art of performance — comedy sketches. His mentor was classmate Stuart Gordon, who was one year older and at least that much farther down the road in his thinking about the world's ironies and absurdities. "Stuart," Steve recalled bluntly in a 1972 interview, "was nuts."

Steve's friendship with Gordon took root at Volta, where in the primary grades the two excelled in English, history and art more than in math and science. But their relationship really blossomed in their seventh- and eighth-grade years from 1959 through 1961, when the wacky and sophisticated humor of Ernie Kovacs, Stan Freberg, Spike Jones and Tom Lehrer had taken hold on radio and TV stations nationwide.

For Steve, it led to a double life, of sorts. During the school day in those years, he forged a role as a leader, serving on Volta's Student Council and Service Group, even joining a cadre of kids in planting tulips in front of the school. By contrast, and as an antidote to the seriousness of the synagogue services, Gordon and Steve — along with neighborhood friends Gary Mechanic, Hart Weichselbaum and Ron Giannetti — gathered at each other's houses after school to share goofy songs and sketches they'd heard and seen on radio and TV and on the street. Among their favorites was a slightly off-color children's rhyme, sung to "Humoresque," the first line of which 10 years later became part of Steve's best-known song:

> *Passengers will please refrain*
> *From flushing toilets while the train*
> *Is in the station. Darling, I love you!*
>
> *We encourage constipation*
> *While the train is in the station*
> *Moonlight always makes me think of you. ...*

Another "offbeat and kind of sick" favorite, Gordon says, was Lehrer's 1953 parody "The Irish Ballad (Rickety Tickety Tin)," which depicted a maiden who, unhappy with her father, mother, sister and two brothers, "did everyone of them in" and confessed to police about the crimes because "lying, she knew, was a sin." The sly, sardonic "Poor Jud Is Dead" from the 1943 musical "Oklahoma!" and the 1954 Danny Kaye tongue twister "Triplets" ("And what is more, we hate each other very much") fell in the same category. Gordon, Steve and others played the LPs of these songs over and over and wrote down the words until they were able to sing them themselves for talent shows at Volta.

It didn't take long for this self-described group of "oddball comedians" to start dreaming up their own songs and sketches, a step up from the hand-puppet shows Steve earlier created with Arlynn Gottlieb in her basement. Gary Mechanic recalls a sixth-grade skit in which the group parodied Walter Cronkite's "You Are There" TV show for extra credit in history. "Steve played Socrates in a really extensive death scene," Mechanic says. "He was the ultimate ham, dying three times: 'One last word: Ahhh! And another thing: Ahhhuhh!' "

During the lazy summer days of 1960, the group sought even more offbeat fun. In his backyard, Stuart Gordon hosted marathon games of the then-new

Steve played Socrates in a really extensive death scene. He was the ultimate ham, dying three times.
GARY MECHANIC

Stuart Gordon, shown in 1962, and Steve led the Albany Park clique of grade-school "oddballs." Each had his specialty, says Gordon: "I may have introduced Steve to Tom Lehrer, but Steve introduced me to Chuck Berry."

(Photo courtesy of Marc and Susan Miller Schneider)

11: For Al Rudis of the *Chicago Sun-Times*, Steve later revealed the rationale for his childhood admiration for Berry. "He was the first guy to say something intelligent on top of that beat, past 'Ooh, baby, baby.' He told stories. That's what always knocked me out. 'Maybellene' is about a guy trying to catch a girl in a car. 'Memphis' is about a guy trying to patch up his family. 'Johnny B. Goode' is about a kid who lived in the hills and became a guitar player, fairly autobiographical. 'Nadine' is about a guy looking for a girl, chasing her all over town. 'School Days' describes what that guy does at school and when he gets out. 'Roll Over Beethoven' is something else again."

board game Risk that lasted three to four days. "We formed alliances in Risk and would almost get into fights when somebody broke an alliance," Mechanic says. The group also staged parties in which lights were turned off and Gordon played LPs backward to create ghoulish sounds. "He had bags of peeled grapes and spaghetti, and we put our hands in it to describe what it was, and he'd say they were goats' eyes and brains," says Jo Ann Stepan. In a technological nod to the space race triggered by the 1957 Soviet launch of Sputnik, the group also made rockets out of carbon-dioxide cartridges, Mechanic says. "We put little fins on them and took them down to the park to try to shoot airplanes out of the sky."

Sometimes, the group used Freberg-style voices to play practical jokes on people by telephone. "We wrote out elaborate scripts where we got people to believe that they were on a call-in radio show and that they were going for prizes by answering questions," Mechanic says. "People would get excited when we'd tell them their Amana freezer was on the way."

"We were a gang, and we just hung out and came up with crazy things to do," Gordon says. "It wasn't like we were doing it to get people ticked off. We were doing it because we thought it was funny."

"We were the oddballs who didn't fit in," Mechanic adds. "There was a hip group of 'in' kids who were into status, but that wasn't us. We stood out as a little weirdo clique."

The force within the clique was the imagination of Stuart Gordon, whose mother was an English teacher at nearby Roosevelt High and whose father was a show-business attorney. As an adult, Gordon went on to write and produce plays and films both beloved ("Bleacher Bums" and the "Honey, I Shrunk the Kids" movie series) and provocative (a nude version of "Peter Pan," the futuristic "Warp" and a string of horror and sci-fi films, including "Re-Animator"). "Stuart was the one who drew us into the arts," says Giannetti. "Everybody knew that Stuart was going to be famous," Mechanic says. "It was common for people to say to him, 'I can say I knew you when.' I don't think anybody had that sense about Steve until much later."

The youthful chemistry between Gordon and Steve, however, was potent. "The two of us were trying to lead, and neither one of us was a follower," Gordon says. "We were a good combo. We spurred each other on. I may have introduced Steve to Tom Lehrer, but Steve introduced me to Chuck Berry." [11]

Gordon characteristically took the lead in the spring of 1961, after Weichselbaum's mother treated the group to a grammar-school graduation gift in Chicago's Old Town that fit their zaniness — a performance at the locally popular then-two-year-old Second City club, which at the time featured the comic talents of Jack Burns and Avery Schreiber, David Steinberg, Nina Kolb and Del Close and later spawned much of the talent of TV's "Saturday Night Live." "That was our first exposure to live, onstage, satirical, improvisational comedy," Mechanic says, and it inspired Gordon to later write a musical-comedy revue, "Critique," which the youth group presented at the temple.

Twelve-year-old Steve, meanwhile, got a glimpse of folk music when Harry Romanoff, the great-uncle who got him into Cubs games for free, drove him to downtown's Rush Street district one night to see Bob Gibson sing and play his 12-string guitar at the trendy Gate of Horn. "I thought he was terrific," Steve recalled a dozen years later. [12]

Steve's bent toward the musical hits of the day led him to attend a concert at the Regal Theater on the South Side in the spring of 1961 with another Volta classmate, Alan Rosenfeld. It was a rock 'n' roll revue whose touring troupe of headliners included the Jarmels, an African-American vocal group whose "Little Bit of Soap" spent 10 weeks on the top-40 charts that year and peaked at #12. The Jarmels threw tiny chips of soap into the audience as they performed, but even more memorable to Rosenfeld was that throughout the revue "Steve sang every single word to every single song that was there. He was way ahead of the rest of us. He knew who these people were. He knew everything about them."

As creative as Steve's involvement was with the Stuart Gordon crowd, and as knowledgeable as he was about the musical world outside Albany Park, other facets of Jewish neighborhood life reached out to embrace him with conformity. Though they still attended classes at Volta school, seventh- and eighth-grade boys held a special status in the neighborhood, signified by their eligibility for junior membership in temple-based, invitation-only "social athletic clubs" run by high-schoolers. The physical proof of that status was the club jacket.

Emblazoned on the back of each baseball-style jacket was the name of the club — Anacondas, Funny Fellows, Originals, Jovens, Epsilons, Top Hats, Aristocrats, Cobegos, Vampires, Condors, Torpedoes, Centurions — along with the initials SAC. Some members had their individual names sewn on the front, and Steve's jacket bore his nickname "Piggy," says Rodney Zolt. New members procured jackets as hand-me-downs from departing high-school grads or purchased them new at Ned Singer's apparel shop on Lawrence Avenue.

"You had to buy a jacket, which wasn't cheap, plus shorts and jerseys," says Scott Berman. "The clubs were an outgrowth of the tough-guy old days on the West Side, where each of the ethnic groups was fighting with each other. When the Jews moved to Albany Park and looked around and saw they were all Jews anyway, they said to themselves, 'We don't have anybody to fight with, so we're not really a gang, more of a club.' "

The boys played penny-ante poker on Friday nights at club members' homes. "Steve usually lost, so we always invited him," Zolt says. "He was the kid when you didn't want to do something, you kind of cornered him, and he relented into doing it." Once a week, the clubs met at Steve's house or others' homes to prepare for football, basketball or softball (16-inch circumference) league play at the two local Jewish community centers, Deborah Boys Club and Max Strauss Center, both of which had gyms, locker rooms and outdoor playfields. Sometimes, the community centers hosted club overnights. Boys played basketball, ordered in pizza and hot dogs, watched movies such as "Blackboard Jungle," spread sleeping bags on the gym floor and, in the dark of the night, engaged in

Steve sang every single word to every single song that was there. He was way ahead of the rest of us.
ALAN ROSENFELD

12: Fourteen years later, for Mary Cliff of WETA-FM in Washington, D.C., Steve put into context his early exposure to Bob Gibson and other folkies: "I was impressed by things that were called folk songs and by people who were called folksingers. But I think they were, for the most part, just people who were tryin' to entertain other folks with music." Within perhaps days of Steve's visit to the Gate of Horn, Gibson and Hamilton Camp recorded their classic live LP at the trendy nightclub. Gibson became a pivotal influence for the adult Steve. "Steve's need to play the guitar, and not just write songs and strum along, came out of the passion and spectacular style that Gibson invented," says a later friend, Paula Ballan. "Steve very much emulated that. Gibson was a monster performer, and the 12-string was his instrument. Nobody played it like him."

sexual "whack-off" contests, "claiming how high they were going," says Cary Lerman, a Centurions member who adds with a laugh that "it was part of youthful male bonding."

The clubs also hosted adult-supervised "mixers" for the important task of getting together with those of the opposite sex, who themselves had clubs, such as the Acralons, Lammedolas and Vakitas. "We'd bring records and learn to dance," says Bob Green, who belonged to the Jovens. "The girls liked you if you were in a club. That was a prestige thing." A few lucky girls wore boyfriends' jackets as a sign of going steady.

Rick Eisenstaedt, who with Steve joined the Centurions, remembers that much like college fraternities, the clubs carried distinct identities. "There was a pretty defined class or caste system to it all that was largely athletically defined, and there was a close link between athletic prowess and social prowess. The more athletic clubs held the cache, were top tier."

Steve's stint with the Centurions, a "middle-tier" club, was short-lived, Eisenstaedt says. "He was too serious for the other kids in that group. He was the secretary of the club briefly and tried to take notes and keep things organized. But people just weren't interested, were goofing around and thought the whole idea of meetings and minutes was a big joke. They were focused on ballgames or the socials with the girls' clubs."

Girls undoubtedly were on Steve's mind in the summer of 1961 after his graduation from Volta. In fact, his own backyard became the site of boy-girl parties and rites-of-passage games such as Spin the Bottle, and Minnette rented two rooms of a motel and its swimming pool as the site for a boy-girl party to celebrate Steve's 13th birthday. But while his bar mitzvah a month and a half later cemented his status as a teenager, Steve's short stature and cherubic face gave him the appearance of a younger, still-elementary-grade boy when he entered nearby Roosevelt High School that fall as a freshman.

The stage was set, however, for the next major step into what became Steve Goodman's adult persona. As a veteran singer at Temple Beth Israel, he had the voice and more than a taste of performing for large audiences. His association with Stuart Gordon and other friends had tapped into the warm irreverence of his upbringing and introduced him to the creation of original material. And as he later recalled fondly, the rock and rockabilly music that he heard on the radio "drove me crazy" with inspiration. The only remaining element to incorporate in his ensemble of readiness was an instrument.

Instrumental musicianship did not flourish in Steve's family. In 1984, Steve told radio host Pete Fornatale with characteristic wit, "No one in the house played. My dad played the record player. We had a Harry Belafonte record and a Noel Coward record." Steve's great aunt, Pat Erenburg, was a practiced violinist, but her love was chamber music, and she had little contact with the Goodmans. In 1977, Steve said in *Guitar Player* magazine that his mother once knew piano, but he didn't find that out until he was an adult and acquired an upright that he never learned to play. One day, he said, "Mom sat down at it and played 'Summertime' not bad, bouncing her left hand." "How come you never did that before?" Steve asked her. "We never had a piano before," she answered. Likewise, Steve also didn't discover until he was an adult that his grandfather, Ziss Erenburg, had been a fair stride-piano player. "I found out he played after he was dead," he told an interviewer, adding sardonically, "He was a brilliant decomposer."

So it made sense that Steve's first tangible exposure to learning an instrument came not from home, but via Roosevelt High. It was embodied in a classmate whom Steve later remembered as "the neighborhood juvenile delinquent," Jack Decker. [13] Steve's physical opposite, Decker was skinny as a rail and stood six feet tall, with a manly, know-it-all countenance. His main interest was science, but he entered Roosevelt from Jensen Park south of Lawrence Avenue with a fearsome reputation.

"I was a troublemaker," says Decker, whose high-school years were marked by nefarious incidents. "I had a motorcycle two years before I had a driver's license and rode it through the high school. I was suspended for throwing a pound of potassium permanganate in the swimming pool and dyeing it purple. I took worms from the biology lab and put them on a kid's sandwich in the lunchroom. Halfway through lunch, I told him about it, and he got pretty sick. They had their hands full with me. They didn't know what to do with me."

In contrast, Decker says, Steve was "very nice, easy, outgoing, mellow. No such thing as conflict with him."

The two — one among the tallest students in the school, and the other, at not even 5-feet, clearly the shortest — befriended each other "like Heckle and

No one in the house played. My dad played the record player.
STEVE GOODMAN

13: Pinning down Steve's first guitar exposure is a tad iffy. In a November 1977 interview with Evanston Township High School student interviewer Vicky Newberry (now Costakis) and her friend Lynne Bryan, Steve said, "I think I was 7 or 8 and tried to play the guitar for about two weeks." In his *Come for to Sing* interview, in July 1977, Steve said he first strummed a guitar at age 12, when his dad was hospitalized and a nurse let him try out her Harmony Classic. "I scratched it," he said, "but she never said anything." In Steve's pre-teen years, said his mother, Minnette, in an Oct. 29, 2006, interview with Sue Kessell on "The Folk Show" for WNUR-FM in Evanston, she and Bud rented a guitar for Steve's use for two weeks. However, in two other mid-1970s interviews, Steve asserted that his genuine introduction to guitar came via Jack Decker.

In the robe of the Roosevelt High symphonic choir, Steve poses for a yearbook photo along with ...
(Choir photo courtesy of
Flora Schwartz Chamberlain)

Jeckle" that fall. What brought them together, Decker says, was the clichéd attraction of opposites. "Roosevelt had a lot of people like myself who were wild animals. We hung out on a corner. We weren't bad kids. It wasn't like today. If you got into a gang fight, somebody would get a bloody nose, and that was it. Heaven forbid if somebody showed up with a baseball bat. But behind my facade, deep down inside, there was a soft spot, and as a friend, Steve fit into that soft spot. He was a genuine person. He was mature in ways that a lot of the other kids weren't."

The pair would ride downtown on the El, check out the Art Institute of Chicago and the Museum of Science and Industry and walk along Lake Michigan. Decker often used the time to complain about Hebrew school, but the pair also verbally dissected the songs they were hearing on top-40 radio, from Dee Clark's "Raindrops" to Del Shannon's "Runaway." "I don't believe he was interested in girls yet. His love," Decker says unequivocally, "was music."

Steve got nervous, even panicky, about some of Decker's more untoward antics on these trips, telling him after one prank that Decker is still too ashamed to describe publicly, "I'm going. I'm leaving right now. I'll have no part of this." On another occasion, Decker bought an inexpensive Japanese electric guitar at the Maxwell Street open-air market, drilled it with holes, filled them with phony rhinestones, glued on a metal Rickenbacker label (made famous by the Beatles) and tried to sell the doctored instrument, passing it off as the real thing. "That'll never, ever, ever work," Steve told him. "Finally," Decker says, "I found someone who bought the guitar."

At Roosevelt, the intimidating Decker quickly took on the role of Steve's protector, which came in handy for the diminutive freshman when the two enrolled in school's co-ed, symphonic choir.

"There was a kid who always used to bully him," Decker says. "I was going to knock the hell out of the kid because I really liked Steve, and Steve wasn't a fighter. He never started with anybody. He was just a real mellow, easygoing, nice guy. When this other character was picking on him, I had him take old shirts and pants and draw and cut out 100 'ooblecks' (a greenish substance depicted in a Dr. Seuss children's book), characters that could be no more than three-quarters of an inch high. I told him if he didn't, I'd light him on fire or run over him with my motorcycle. I was bluffing, but he cut out the ooblecks, and he left Steve alone."

Symphonic choir, in Helen Johnson's room, became a musical catalyst for Steve, for in that class he and Decker teamed up and entered as the only freshmen in a 10- to 12-act talent show for the entire, 2,000-member student body. But what would they perform? Decker had bought a cheap, six-string guitar (Steve said in a later interview that Decker had stolen it) and had learned four basic chords that allowed him to play Pete Seeger's and Joe Hickerson's "Where Have All the Flowers Gone?" and the traditional "Michael, Row the Boat Ashore," folk songs made popular by the Brothers Four and the Kingston Trio. Knowing that Steve had "a really neat little voice," Decker thought the two of

them would make a good singing/guitar duo, and they told Mrs. Johnson that most likely Steve would be the guitarist.

Within a week, Steve had persuaded his grandmother, Mary Erenburg, to spring for a $30 acoustic Harmony Sovereign guitar at Sears, complete with steel strings and a pickup. "I was sure this was the answer," he recalled in the 1977 *Come for to Sing* interview. "It's called being a dumbbell and buying a gimmick." Steve's friend Jeff Gordon recalls Steve proudly showing the six-string guitar to him the day it was given to him: "We walked into his house, said hello to his grandmother, bypassed their blind collie and went to his bedroom. He pulled out the guitar, put it on his knee, put his arm around it and started strumming." Steve looked up with his broad grin and said, "Look what I got!"

Steve turned up at Decker's house with the guitar and asked him for help. With the only four chords he knew, Decker gave Steve his first crude lessons.

"I tried for a week or two to show him the chords," Decker says. "We were sitting there with guitars every day after school for two-three hours, at his house, my house. We went back and forth. I had mastered my four chords, but Steve had little, stubby fingers, and he had a lot of trouble hitting the frets on the guitar neck. He was excited about the talent show, but he was moody. Sometimes, I'd get pissed at him because he couldn't play the chords, and he'd get pissed at me for getting pissed at him. But after some milk and cookies, we both were fine afterwards."

Two days before the show, Decker took charge, telling Steve, "Y'know what? Your fingers are too small. You'd better take up a different instrument. You're not going to be able to play the guitar. I'll play the guitar, and we'll both sing."

Which is what they did. In the show, the two stood before microphones and performed two songs ("Flowers Gone" and "Michael") on the same program

... 82 other Roosevelt High choir members. Steve is in the front row, second from left. Jack Decker, also in the choir, says he routinely avoided being photographed and thus is not present.
(Choir photo courtesy of Flora Schwartz Chamberlain)

with older students who had more polished acts, including the nucleus of the rock band the Buckinghams, which five years later charted nationally with "Kind of a Drag" and a half-dozen other hits. Steve sang high melody, Decker played guitar and sang low harmony, and both whistled at times. "The low parts I got better, and the high parts he got better, so we went with that," Decker says. "I let him orchestrate it. He already had a feel for it. I had my four chords down pat, but everything else he did."

Their appearance proceeded without a hitch and even drew a standing ovation, but what Decker had said two days prior stuck with Steve like a burr. Years later, Steve recalled that Decker hadn't just told him that he shouldn't try to perform on guitar at the talent show. "He told me I would *never* be able to play," Steve said in a 1975 interview. And Decker confirms it: "He had no future in guitar, according to me."

"So I got pissed and learned a couple of chords just for spite," Steve said in a 1973 *Rolling Stone* interview. Decker clearly remembers Steve's fury: "If he would have had to have taken a pliers and pulled his fingers each night for an hour till he stretched them, if that's what it would have taken to play the guitar, he was going to play the guitar and show me."

That determination eventually paid off in many ways, including emotionally, Steve reflected in his *Come for to Sing* interview. "I'd spent all this time wantin' to be a punk (because) it was a way of sayin' something," he said. "How fortunate that you get to turn the motivation around at a certain point, because it starts from such an ugly place."

Steve recalled that he "didn't really do anything" with the guitar chords he learned until months later. But what Steve did do during his freshman days at Roosevelt, Decker says, was develop a thicker skin about his height.

"He was nice, and he was sensitive, but he didn't hesitate to speak his mind. When he had strong feelings about something, he followed through with them," Decker says. "One of the big bullies would start with him, and he'd turn around and tell him, 'Kiss my ass.' Oddly enough, you could push him and push him and push him and push him with nothing happening, and he'd hit a breaking point where he'd turn around and say things that would get him in trouble. But there really was no justification for picking on him. He was a freshie."

Besides encountering such hostility at school, Steve may have been sensing the beginnings of discord between his parents, who did, in fact, divorce 10 years later. Decker, who holds a doctorate degree in psychology, looks back on the freshman time that he and Steve shared and reflects that while the issues were never a topic of conversation, Steve appeared to "carry a lot of pain around inside him. He came from a nice home, but I guess there was some conflict there, and I came from a nuthouse, where there was always conflict. So we shared a camaraderie and sensitivity.

"Steve was a guy who was really hurting inside, and I was a guy who was really hurting inside, and that was the bond we had as friends. Never spoke about it, never elaborated, never complained about it, always held it inside, but

> If he would have had to have taken a pliers and pulled his fingers each night for an hour till he stretched them, if that's what it would have taken to play the guitar, he was going to play the guitar and show me.
> **JACK DECKER**

we could talk to each other on a certain level where you could feel the pain and feel that you had something in common that was unpleasant to go home to."

In that same fall of 1961, Steve connected with another kindred spirit across the street from his family's home, Anita Gold. Her husband, Seymour "Sy" Gold, was a promoter of rock records on Atlantic, Vee-Jay and other labels. The trunk of Sy's light-yellow Impala sedan — purchased from Bud Goodman at Keystone Chevrolet — invariably was filled with promotional copies of 45s that were popular with teenagers. "Kids were always hanging around his car the minute he came on the block," Anita says. "They would run out like crazy, like God-knows-what, and he'd give them all promotional records. All the kids on this block adored my husband. He was like a pied piper."

To Steve, a precocious singer who loved the songs he heard on the radio and had only lightly scratched the surface of performing music of his own choice, Sy Gold represented even more. He was a direct pipeline to slake Steve's thirst for musical knowledge. Steve recalled in a 1984 interview, "I used to make a list for the guy of the stuff I'd heard." And Sy Gold would tell him, "Well, Steve, any 45s that you want, I'll see if I can trade out for some."

Sy's job often took Sy backstage when the musicians whose records he promoted came to Chicago to perform. "Stevie wanted to go with my husband to those concerts more than anything," Anita Gold says, "but his parents wouldn't let him because people were smoking pot, and his parents were afraid he would get caught up in their world. I don't know how many of the rock stars my husband promoted were smoking pot, but pot was very prevalent, and if you went with any of these people, they passed you the weed."

Through his contact with Sy Gold, Steve came to know the songwriting talents of Anita, a seasoned Top-40 tunesmith. Her best-known work eventually included "Come Back, Little Girl," recorded by Ronnie Rice of Chicago as an answer song to "Go Away, Little Girl" written by Gerry Goffin and Carole King in 1962 and popularized by Steve Lawrence a year later.

For a few months, Steve and Anita became a musical match. The 13-year-old high-school freshman with the trained voice and an eagerness to learn was a perfect complement for the 28-year-old songwriter with ready material. Day after day, Steve brought his guitar across the street to Anita's house, and the two sat on the floor, where they spread out the music and lyric sheets to Anita's songs and set up Anita's bulky Webcor tape recorder. By trial and error, Steve learned the chords to the songs as he sang the melodies. Anita occasionally sang backup, and the two became fast friends.

"He thought that I was like the moon, which you could understand," Anita says. "If you were a young boy and wanted to do music, and a songwriter and record promoter lived across the street and were very nice to you, how would you feel? It wasn't that he was hypnotized or anything, but he was drawn to us."

"When Stevie walked into my house, it was like magic took over. We were both transported to another place. It wasn't my front room anymore. It seemed like we were on the stage. We used to close the drapes so nobody could look in

When Stevie walked into my house, it was like magic took over. We were both transported to another place.
ANITA GOLD

the window and want to come in. We would fool around like we were big singers. We'd kid around with songs and music and lyrics. Sometimes, we'd look at something and Stevie would write a song about it. He was like a little flower budding. He was just really getting into it.

"Sometimes, we would sing together, and I would try to get in harmony with him, but I was no singer. Once I told him, 'I wish I could sing like you,' and he broke out laughing. But it was most enjoyable."

One song that Anita wrote captured Steve's fancy. Though she can't recall its title, it was about a boy seeking a lost love. The opening verse set the scene:

> *I put a message in the personal*
> *To ask anybody if they'd seen my girl*
> *She had big blue eyes and long blond hair*
> *But no one ever seemed to see her anywhere*

Anita says Steve enjoyed singing the chorus — "Woo, I gotta find her. Woo woo woo woo, I got to find her" — and vowed to record the song someday. "He sang that song fabulously," Anita says. "You really felt it right down to your toes. He didn't only sing the song. He performed the song. You could just picture this guy looking for his girl."

More than her songwriting skills, Anita offered Steve sincere support. Sometimes they stopped between songs and solemnly discussed his future.

"You're going to be a big star," Anita told him. "You're gonna see. They'll know you all over the world."

Steve looked at her and replied, "I want to. Do you really think so?"

"I don't really think so," she said. "I know so."

Anita's affection for Steve arose from his personal qualities as much as his musicianship. "He wasn't the pushy kind of person," she says. "He wasn't a braggart or anything like that. This boy just literally glowed. He was so sophisticated, especially at his age. There was nobody like him. He wasn't the kind of boy who would do anything to upset anybody. He would never try to come across as 'I'm better than you are.' He wasn't like that. He was Stevie."

Soon, however, Albany Park was to lose that youthful persona to another neighborhood, eight miles northwest, where the burgeoning communities of Niles, Morton Grove and Des Plaines and well-established Park Ridge converged. Like many other parents of baby boomers in early 1960s Chicago, Bud and Minnette Goodman chose in the spring of Steve's freshman year to move their family to the suburbs.

Those who experienced the moves differ over whether they were a manifestation of white flight. Scott Berman, who was sad to see the changes, says, "It was more that the suburbs were new and up and coming, and people thought that was the way to better themselves." From the perspective of the teen on the street in Albany Park, the suburbs were "another world," says Cary Lerman. "That's a world of money and privilege that few of us could dream of."

But another Albany Park teen who knew Steve through the social athletic

The suburbs were new and up and coming, and people thought that was the way to better themselves.
SCOTT BERMAN

clubs, and whose family moved out of Albany Park to roughly the same suburb as did the Goodmans, sees the trend otherwise.

"Parents thought the neighborhood was changing," Bob Green says. "Everything was starting to go. A lot of new ethnic groups were coming in from the South Side, and our parents wanted something better for us. It was just a movement, changing from neighborhood to neighborhood. Everyone was moving. If you had more money, you moved out to the suburbs. Besides, I was starting to hang out with people who weren't the best type to hang around with, attitude-wise, so my parents thought, 'Let's get him out now, so he can develop.' It was good. It made me grow."

As warm as was Steve's upbringing in Albany Park, he apparently wasn't heartbroken to depart, says his Roosevelt High friend Jack Decker. "Steve and I made a lot of plans that never happened, but even with me, when he left, he left quietly," he says. "There was no explanation. I got the impression that he felt 'good riddance,' at least for Roosevelt, where two or three kids kept picking on him and made it really uncomfortable for him."

In a sense, some in Albany Park already had left Steve. His friends Stuart Gordon, Gary Mechanic and Ron Giannetti were enrolled not at Roosevelt, considered the neighborhood high school, but at the nearby, all-North Side, 5,000-boy Lane Tech, known as the Harvard of Chicago high schools. Given his aptitude, Steve may have fit better at the more exclusive Lane, whose curriculum featured music and art along with science, math, engineering and architecture. But if Bud and Minnette anticipated leaving Albany Park before it was time for Steve to sign up for high school, they may have steered him away from Lane, feeling it would be easier to depart midyear from Roosevelt.

Whatever the case, the impression Steve left among his friends as he left Albany Park was not one of impending fame. "He was a very sweet guy and very sincere and very unpretentious, obviously confident, self-assured, but he was kind of a geeky kid like I was," says Rick Eisenstaedt. "Really smart, great with music, but he lacked the currency that made you attractive in any other way. I can't remember him ever being with a girl, but few of us were doing very well in that department. He was easy to smile and upbeat and perceptive, but I never foresaw the charisma or offbeat perspective."

Decker, however, had a glimmer of Steve's promise, and it lay in his friend's aural impact. "Steve could do something with his voice that I couldn't do. There was a slight reverberation in there, like a warble," says Decker, who conducts neurobehavioral research and teaches police how to release endorphins. "Steve's voice did something to change people's neurochemistry. Very few vocalists can do that. Gregorian chants can do that. Steve's voice was a mood-changer, an attention-getter. You know how some speakers give lectures and everybody gets bored right away? Other speakers talk on the same subject and everybody's really entranced with them? Steve had a male voice that did that. It got your attention. It brought you to the music, it brought you to what he was singing, and that was very, very unique."

He was easy to smile and upbeat and perceptive, but I never foresaw the charisma or offbeat perspective.
RICK EISENSTAEDT

The national popularity of folk music swept Maine East High School in 1964, and Steve Goodman's versatility and gregariousness put him in the center of it all. Entertaining a group of students sitting at their feet while posing for the "Activities" section of the Maine East yearbook in a room off the school's auditorium are, from left, Vicki Marti, Geoff Harpham, Jackie Anderson (now Griesemer), Jim Waddington, Steve (with 12-string guitar), Bill Hagerup, Chip Rollins, Tom Griesemer and Earl Runde.

(Photo for *The Lens* yearbook by Steve Holton)

'He was just infectious — the entire world was his clique'

Faint static buzzed through the tinny speakers of countertop radios in the suburban neighborhoods two miles north and east of O'Hare International Airport until, precisely at noon, the hum evaporated to make way for a pair of teenage male voices.

* * *

"This is WMTH, the voice of Maine Township, signing on at 88.5 on your FM dial, serving Park Ridge, Des Plaines, Niles, Morton Grove and Glenview. Good morning, I'm Robin Pendergrast, and —"

"Uh, Robin, don't you mean 'Good afternoon'?"

"That's right, we're coming to you just as it's turning afternoon on this chilly Monday, November 5, 1962."

"Well, it's tryin' to snow while we're recording this, before school starts, but by noon it may warm up to a balmy 39 degrees."

[Laughter] "Folks, I should introduce you to my partner, the one with the big guitar on his lap, the one you can hear strumming in the background, my classmate here at Maine East High School, Steve Goodman."

"Thanks, Robin."

"And we're serving the communities of both Maine East and Maine West high schools from our 16-watt transmitter that sits on the roof above this tiny, first-floor control room, right across from the auditorium here at Maine East. We're here for the next 15 minutes to bring you some news about what's happening at the schools and maybe a song or two."

"You gonna tell 'em how we got in here at 6 o'clock this morning?"

"Ah, I think I'd rather tell 'em about last Saturday's football game."

"Oh, you mean how the Blue Demons turned cold blue again?"

"Code blue?"

"No, cold blue. You were there. Man, it was near-freezing. None of 'em could hold onto a pass. Had to run a ground game. The defense had a strong line, but as they say in 'da big city,' it wasn't enough. The defense fell apart in the secondary, Downers Grove scored 22 points, and we came up with a goose egg. Once again, Maine East snatched defeat from the jaws of victory."

> Once again, Maine East snatched defeat from the jaws of victory.
> **STEVE GOODMAN**
> from re-created radio broadcast

[Laughter] "Where'd you learn that phrase?"

"Paul Christman, when he came here to be interviewed on the air last month. Remember, he's not just the sports guy on Channel 7. He was an All-American quarterback, played for St. Louis and Chicago. And he gave me that phrase when you were out of the room: 'We snatched defeat from the jaws of victory.' "

"That sounds like the Maine East theme song."

"Did you know that guy once had five fumbles in one game?"

"Now, how'd you get that information?"

"Looked it up. That's what Casey Stengel says: 'You could look it up.' Actually, I read it in the *Trib*. It happened when the Chicago Cardinals were playin' Green Bay. Anyway, Christman lives in Park Ridge, and we're proud to have him here."

"We sure are. Folks, we get pretty amazed being able to interview such celebrities as Paul Christman here in our WMTH studio. Other than New Trier, I think we're the only high school in Chicagoland to have our own radio station."

"Yep, in these palatial surroundings, how could we go wrong? And it's just us, the two crewcuts — me, a sophomore in a white cardigan sweater, and you, a senior in black, horn-rim glasses. Of course, you're the brains of the outfit."

"Well, it takes a lot of brains to play guitar the way you do."

"I'm lucky they let me sneak it in here."

"You gonna play anything for us now?"

"I've been workin' on that song about mashed potatoes in the lunchroom, the one we were talkin' about last week." [He strums and sings.]

> *We get mashed potatoes with gravy, and toasted cheese*
> *And applesauce, too, so we're on our knees.*
> *This stuff is so good that it's oh, so clear*
> *That the food and forks and plates are gonna disappear.*

[Uproarious laughter] "Oh, man —"

"That'll be just right for our 'Music to Eat By' segment."

"Man, how are we gonna live that down? That's something we can truly say, 'You heard it here first.' "

"Well, I'll keep going here. Maybe I can come up with something all of us heard somewhere else first." [He keeps strumming.] "OK, yeah, I got one."

> *If I had a hammer ...* [1]

*   *   *

Steve Goodman couldn't have hammered out a more fertile or challenging place than Maine East High School to find an audience during his last three-plus years of high school.

One of the largest in the Midwest, the enormous school 15 miles northwest

---

That'll be just right for our 'Music to Eat By' segment.
STEVE GOODMAN
from re-created radio broadcast

1: The radio script opening this chapter is a re-creation of the kind of programs that Robin Pendergrast and Steve Goodman recorded and that were aired on WMTH-FM during the 1962-63 school year, as recalled by Pendergrast. "If I Had a Hammer" is the classic folk song written by Pete Seeger and Lee Hays.

of downtown Chicago resembled a college campus in its design, girth and numbers. Built in 1929 on 90 acres of cornfields and patterned after UCLA's Royce Hall, the three-floor, ivy-covered educational institution reflected the dichotomy of the communities it served: the stability of the upper-crust, bedrock suburb of Park Ridge to the south and the rapid, post-World War II/Korean War growth of Niles and parts of Morton Grove, Glenview and Des Plaines to the north. The number of students in each of the school's four grade levels dwarfed the populations of entire high schools elsewhere in the Chicago area. Despite the addition of a new high school (Maine West) for the township in 1959, by the early 1960s Maine East teemed with more than 4,100 students.

The size held advantages. As the school newspaper, *The Pioneer*, noted, "The schools in southern Illinois, where the average enrollment is about 300, offer about one-third as many courses as Maine." Full-blown extracurricular activities flourished in every corner of the school (even an "underground" newspaper called the *Pterodactyl*), and teachers and students alike built and enjoyed a reputation for academic excellence.

Immensity bore a price, however, particularly for a newcomer trying to get to know others and not become lost in the crowd. In Steve Goodman's years as a Mainite, the student body was so vast that it sported 37 sets of twins. Noting that 6 percent of Maine girls were named Susan and 7 percent of boys went by Bob, *The Pioneer* giddily suggested that students having trouble remembering classmates' names could try playing the odds: "One can always ask a girl if she is one-and-three-tenths in a hundred. If she gaily answers, 'Of course!' her name must be Sharon."

Classes ran between 7:30 a.m. and 4:30 or 5:30 p.m., and there were 11 periods a day. Between classes, hallways strained with students. A senior cheerleader and honor student complained in a profile in *The Pioneer*, "I just can't stand having books jabbed in my back all the time!" In a droll editorial, the paper pleaded for student courtesy in a mock obituary: "Deceased, a Maine student. Authorities report death was due to continual exposure to pushing and shoving crowds. Charges are being pressed against the other 4,099 students."

"They had to make so many accommodations to having so many students," says Sue Moestue (now Bradford-Smith), a member of Steve's class. "Lunch periods were very brief. Study halls were very large. Congestion was great. I found that a very, very stressful way to go to high school."

Stress didn't arise solely from the numbers, though. To attend Maine East was to be thrust into a cauldron of class and ethnic differences stirred by economics and the baby boom.

Within Maine East's south reach lay Park Ridge, a premier Chicago suburb settled and built up by Germans, Scandinavians and others in the first half of the century. By the early 1960s, the commuter-rail hamlet had become a posh, politically conservative and entrenched bastion of stately, upper-income brick homes and Protestantism by covenant. Its high-school-age population dominated Maine East until the postwar era, when vast produce farms and nurseries

Its three-floor main building patterned after UCLA's Royce Hall, Maine East High School resembled the girth of a college campus, inspiring a deadpan observation in The Pioneer, *the student newspaper: "Deceased, a Maine student. Authorities report death was due to continual exposure to pushing and shoving crowds. Charges are being pressed against the other 4,099 students."*
(Photo from *The Lens*, 1965)

on the school's north flank (like those in fictional High Prairie in *So Big*, the 1924 Pulitzer Prize-winning novel by Edna Ferber) gave way to tract housing and commercial strips. Filling the new homes were liberal and working-class Italian, Irish and Jewish families headed by Depression-raised parents who left Chicago and obtained GI Bill mortgages ($500 down on a $17,000 home), seeking better lives and education for their children. Maine East, its quality founded and bolstered by Park Ridge, was a potent draw for the big-city émigrés.

The resulting change was clear to the eyes of math teacher Bob Craddock, who'd begun teaching at Maine East in 1957. "You'd go down the hall, and they were all blond-head, Scandinavian-looking students," he says. "Then as the years went by, the hair color started to get darker."

What Steve Goodman entered in April 1962, therefore, was "a real, honest-to-God preppie school — it might as well have been a private school," says Howard Berkman, a Jewish classmate of Steve's who figured greatly in his musical development. The school fronted on Dempster Street, the east-west arterial that divided Park Ridge from the newer neighborhoods of Niles, Morton Grove and Glenview to the north. Because the recently built subdivision to which the Goodmans moved lay about a mile and a half north of Dempster, straddling Niles and Glenview, Steve instantly joined the budding ranks of Mainites who felt they lived on the proverbial wrong side of the tracks. The perception only deepened years later as the public became aware of an emerging string of non-ethnic celebrities who had attended Maine East, including actors Harrison Ford, Karen Black and Carrie Snodgrass and, from Steve's class, U.S. Senator, former first lady and 2008 presidential candidate Hillary Rodham Clinton, all of whom hailed from Park Ridge.

The blunt-spoken Berkman says only half in jest that Park Ridge parents thought it was a mistake that he, Steve and other Jews were enrolled at Maine East. "These people in their palatial homes and huge lawns and servants around the house didn't realize that we were in their school district," he says. "Somebody had sold off farms and put big housing developments on them, and they were selling the houses to Jews. These people were quite shocked by this, that there were actually Jews going to schools with their kids."

"We were outsiders," confirms Jerry Needelman, Jewish resident of Morton Grove who was one year ahead of Steve at Maine East. He notes that because school boundaries did not conform to the borders of the burgeoning communities, many Jewish students whose families lived nearby attended other high schools. While Needelman doesn't recall "overt anti-Semitism" among his Maine East classmates from Park Ridge, "You just wondered under the surface. We weren't excluded, but we weren't included, either."

The near-exclusion extended to African-Americans as well, so much that, but for a fleeting exception that only one student can recall, no blacks attended Maine East, and they showed up in Park Ridge only as domestics. "My mom used to call it the land of nickel millionaires," says Eileen Alonso (now Stratton), a classmate of Steve's who lived in Park Ridge. "It was a great place to grow up,

> **These people were quite shocked by this, that there were actually Jews going to schools with their kids.**
> **HOWARD BERKMAN**

a safe community, but there was a lot of bigotry. Blacks were not allowed in Park Ridge before 6 in the morning and had to be out at 6 at night if they worked there."

Not that Park Ridge — a bulwark of Republicanism, in which no alcohol was sold, and only one in every 1,000 residents was non-white — paraded its exclusive stance. "It was very suburban, very genteel, very Christian but lacking in the sectarian spirit," offers Geoff Harpham, a Park Ridge resident who was one year ahead of Steve's class at Maine East. "Park Ridge was not a Bible-belt community."

Begging to differ, however, is Hardye Simons (now Moel), a Jewish class-mate of Steve's from Morton Grove. "Park Ridge *was* kind of a Bible-belt com-munity. They won't admit it, but they were," she says. "Segregation really was an issue. It was subtle, but it was there in the environment." [2]

"It couldn't have been more completely apolitical," adds George Scarola, a non-Jewish classmate of Steve's who lived in Glenview. "People didn't talk poli-tics. Race was something you read about in the papers. It just had no bearing on our lives. It wasn't part of what you did with your life. It was bad form to talk about politics. That was private information." [3]

More often, WASP-ish divisiveness went underground. Maine East girls from Park Ridge recall parents prohibiting them from accepting dates with Jews from their school. Slurs such as "hebe" were shared in hushed tones. One Jewish classmate two grades older than Steve, Neal Pollack, ruefully remembers being told that the Oreo cookies he was eating were called "sheeny wheels."

Simons and others estimate that only 1 percent of Maine East's enrollment — perhaps 40 students — was Jewish, and the solution for some of those, including Steve and herself, was to ignore the bigotry and jump into leadership roles and after-school activities.

"It was a hard ladder to climb," she says, "and we always felt like if we did push forward and make new friends, some of the kids we left behind were resentful. I had girlfriends who pleaded with their parents at some point to move to Park Ridge so that they would feel better about themselves. There was always this undercurrent of not being good enough or not fitting into the main-stream."

With a last name that classmates instantly identified as Jewish, Steve em-barked upon fitting in at Maine East with two months left in his freshman year. Art Curtis, a classmate from Park Ridge, says that during the waning days of freshman PE, Steve invoked something akin to the then-#1 hit by Chubby Checker, "The Twist."

"We were doing dancing in gym class, and one of my next-door neighbors was just totally disgusted by Steve's dancing," Curtis says. "Steve was dancing in a very uninhibited fashion, a new or extemporized step that most Park Ridgeans, including me, would have been too uptight to do. He was very friendly and outgoing, but I'm sure he turned some people off. Park Ridge was very Victo-rian, and if you're Victorian, you don't show your emotions, you're always polite

It was very suburban, very genteel, very Christian but lacking in the sectarian spirit.
GEOFF HARPHAM

2: Harpham reflects further that "there was, as far as I know, no conscious effort of exclusion or segregation. Total cluelessness is more like it." Harpham adds that he didn't know that Steve and Simons were Jews until he left high school. "When I did learn it, the fact meant nothing to me at all," he says. "It was just neutral information."

3: Political discussion wasn't entirely absent from Park Ridge, says Jim Dernehl, a Maine East student two years older than Steve. On Friday nights, Dernehl's father, a sales executive and a liberal, hosted all-ages discussions at his home, fueled by Meister Brau beer. Steve attended and was of like mind, while conservative stances were represented by future Republican gubernatorial candidate Jack Roeser, as well as the young Hillary Rodham, who lived across the street.

Standing at the right end of the second row, Steve poses in June 1962 with his Temple Beth Israel confirmation class in Albany Park.

(Photo courtesy of Marc and Susan Miller Schneider)

and restrained, and you don't have your heart on your sleeve, so he was very different to us."

With that wary reception from many in his midst, Steve naturally retained an affection for many of the friends and activities he'd left back in Albany Park. Besides, his old neighborhood was beckoning him.

In late May, one month after Steve enrolled at Maine East near the end of his freshman year, the Chicago Board of Rabbis notified him he had won first prize in the high-school division among northwest Chicago temples for his entry in a composition contest. He had written the 800-word piece five months earlier for his confirmation at Temple Beth Israel, selecting its serious subject — "Torah and Israel: The Role of the Land of Israel in Judaism" — from a list of topics approved by the temple.

While the essay recounted a huge swath of Jewish history, from biblical times through the Holocaust and the United Nations' establishment of a Jewish homeland in 1947, its writing style was more dramatic than academic. With visceral vocabulary ("This fraud left such a deep scar ..." "... homeless and beaten..."), Steve told a story of suspense and resolve, invoking vocal rhythms as would a seasoned orator or TV script. Nowhere was this more evident than in the essay's opening lines:

> *A dream. A vision and a hope of Jews everywhere for thousands of years. A force so strong that oppression after oppression and tribulation after tribulation could not daunt it or the people who held fast to it. Yes, this was the dream that there might be a Jewish homeland in Israel someday.*

The temple newsletter proudly deemed the essay "brilliant" when publishing it in late July. Just as confirmation symbolized Steve's religious-school graduation, the writing award indirectly signaled the end of his singing in the youth choir. "Soon enough," he reflected cryptically in a 1975 interview, "I was just greasy enough that it wasn't for me. I just sort of drifted away from it." But even though he had moved to the suburbs, that summer Steve found another way to entertain the Temple Beth Israel congregation — by reconnecting with the wacky creativity of his friend, Stuart Gordon.

Gordon, Steve and the other Albany Park cut-ups knew that a live show provided its own rewards, but its appeal was fleeting. So that summer, the group switched to celluloid. Inspired by the TV zaniness of Ernie Kovacs and a chance viewing of the witty, obscure, 1956 Peter Sellers ("Goon Show") film "The Case of the Mukkinese Battle Horn," Gordon directed a cast of seven boys, whom he later dubbed the Human Race, in a 10-minute mostly silent film produced on 8mm stock. The trenchant title: "Mental Illness for Fun and Profit."

With slapstick and sight gags, the boys hammered their way through episodes involving a bicycle-riding newspaper carrier getting whacked by a paper thrown from a block away, and a shopping-cart race that ended with a fiery crash. The troupe also fashioned a dummy out of stuffed clothes and a handmade latex face mask, took it to a gangway that ran between the second floors of a pair of walk-ups, noisily thrashed the dummy and shoved it over the railing to the ground while unsuspecting girls walked by and screamed. Other pieces involved aborted attempts at human flight and an underwater drama in which plastic battleships were set afire. To top it off, Gordon threw in a stop-motion anima-tion routine in which, to the accompaniment of the "Blue Danube Waltz," a line of Dixie cups "danced" with each other before one was crushed by a human hand and shunned by the others.

The uncontested highlight of "Mental Illness," however, was also the only segment in which Steve Goodman appeared in front of the camera. The near-14-year-old was both its star and foil. Filmed by Gordon compatriot Michael Waitsman near Gordon's house at the southwest corner of North Keystone Av-enue and West Ainslie Street, the black-and-white episode, running a minute and a half, played like a Keystone Kops adventure.

At the outset, a barely 5-foot-tall Steve ambles toward the camera, his atten-tion fixed on a newspaper in his hands. Suddenly, he stops, looks up in horror as he sees five much taller boys — labeled "morons" in the credits — in front of him, each with an expression of menace. One of the morons, played by Gary Mechanic, holds a can of black paint and a brush. For a moment, the five stare at Steve, who fearfully fidgets with the paper. As a unit, the morons bolt toward him. Steve drops the paper and runs away. With the morons in close pursuit, the frenetic chase is on. The camera stays in one place, panning from left to right as it follows Steve and the morons racing in a huge circle behind houses and three-flats and back to close range, where the morons catch up with and surround their target. For several seconds, they appear to be pummeling him. They back away, out of the frame, leaving Steve, who, facing away from the camera, staggers as if punch-drunk. But as he turns around, it becomes appar-ent that the only thing that the morons have done to him is to paint onto his face an oversized, black mustache. End of segment.

With a musical score that featured the classical theme from Prokofiev's "Lieu-tenant Kije" suite, the completed "Mental Illness" premiered that fall on the

In his segment for "Mental Illness for Fun and Profit," Steve walks down the sidewalk in his Albany Park neighborhood when a surprise stops him in his tracks. The rest of the segment is depicted on the following page.

(Still courtesy of Stuart Gordon)

In his segment of Stuart Gordon's film "Mental Illness for Fun and Profit," Steve is shocked by the appearance of "morons" who chase him around Albany Park, surround him and paint an Ernie Kovacs-style mustache on his face.

(Stills courtesy of Stuart Gordon)

outdoor wall of an Albany Park burger and coffee shop and later played at temple youth-group carnivals. Friends, family and temple members showed up at each screening, greeting the film with gales of laughter.

"It was a summer's worth of fun," says Mechanic. "Stuart played director and producer and was really the sparkplug, like John Lennon's role with the Beatles." In contrast, Mechanic says, Steve was just one of the gang. "He was just a nice guy. I don't think any of us would have done the film on our own. But everybody got into it: 'Let's do this!' 'Yeah!' We all learned to throw in shtick as we went along. It was a creative group effort."

It also was one of the last times his Albany Park friends saw Steve, for he and his family were settling into the suburbs. A step toward promise and away from the hard edges of the city, the Goodmans' new neighborhood on the northern edge of Niles burst with unpaved cul-de-sacs (dubbed "ovals") instead of perpendicular streets, and with barren, dirt lots and fledgling lawns instead of sturdy trees and greenery. Unlike the boxy house on Monticello, the family's newly built home at 9929 North Warren Oval — just three miles from Maine East High — boasted a trendy, split-level Chesterfield design, with hints of elegance throughout, from a fountain in the interior entryway to the letter "G" embedded in the master-bathroom shower door upstairs. Its four bedrooms accommodated Bud and Minnette, Steve, David and Minnette's mother, Mary Erenburg, who lived with the Goodmans. Befitting a sociable family, the house teemed with gathering places: a family room, dining room, living room and backyard patio, as well as a basement rec room, complete with pool table, and a driveway with a basketball hoop, where Steve practiced long hot-shots.

While Bud maintained long hours away from home, Minnette kept the new house in spotless condition, says Rita Matulef, who, one week after the Goodmans' arrival, moved with her husband and three young children into the oval's only other completed home. "She was the most fastidious woman," Matulef says. "She was crazy clean. Every week, even in below-zero weather, she scrubbed her garage door. My kids would come up to talk to her, and she'd say, 'Don't touch the windows!' She never had a weed in her yard. She was just fanatic, even about her lawn. She was out there mowing. It had to be perfect."

Steve's own quest in the suburbs was to nourish his increasingly outgoing personality and the performing skills he had discovered and launched back in Albany Park. In the summer of 1962, three weeks before his 14th birthday, he joined a friend from his old neighborhood, Ken Kruss, in deciding to take lessons in guitar. Their instruments in tow, they climbed aboard the El, heading south, got off at the Sedgwick station and walked two blocks to an old meeting hall at 333 West North Ave. There, on the second floor, resided the now-legendary Old Town School of Folk Music.

Founded by locally renowned folksinger Win Stracke, guitar instructor Frank Hamilton and administrative "mother" Dawn Greening, the school boasted the premise that "music is accessible, divergent, not an exclusive club, available to all walks of life." [4] In just five years, the informal, "anti-university" methods of

Gary Mechanic, shown in 1961, says the "Mental Illness" film "was a summer's worth of fun." It also was Steve's last hurrah with his Albany Park friends. (From Volta graduation photo, courtesy of Janette Ferdinand Woods)

4: Hamilton says the school built upon a model forged in Boston and Los Angeles by folklorist Beth Lomax Hawes. In Groening's Oak Park living room in 1957, Hamilton and Stracke concluded that "Chicago needs a school to bring the various ethnic elements together. Folk music was the catalyst because it was the simplest and had the most direct feeling. It could have been the Old Town School of Popular Music or the Old Town School of Rock 'n' Roll, but we wouldn't have reached as many people as we had if we had done that."

Jack Coombe, faculty adviser for WMTH, immediately saw talent in Steve's early sports broadcasts: "We used to get a lot of people call us and didn't know who he was. They'd say, 'Hey, that boy who did the color was very, very good.'"
(Photo from *The Lens*, 1963)

the school had undergirded the careers of Chicagoans Bob Gibson and Roger (Jim) McGuinn and drawn Big Bill Broonzy, Pete Seeger, Fleming Brown, George Armstrong, Mahalia Jackson and Doc Watson as guest teachers and performers. A surviving registration card, in Steve's own hand, shows that "Steven Goodman" signed up for an "Adv. Beginning Guitar" class on Monday, July 2, 1962.

"It was a fluke," says Kruss. "We were looking for something to do, and he said, 'Let's start playing guitar,' so that's when we signed up. We both began from scratch. He enjoyed singing. I figured, 'OK, he can sing, I can accompany him.' I soon realized it really wasn't me, but it was just a natural extension for him. He took to guitar like a fish to water. He was a natural." Though Old Town, with its bars and run-down buildings, was "not the best neighborhood for two Jewish kids with guitars to be walking," Kruss says their El trips to the school were "kind of a thrill. No one in the (Albany Park) neighborhood was doing this. It was our own thing."

Over two weeks' time, Steve attended four or five classes at the Old Town School, but as summer gave way to fall, he turned his attention to his first full year at Maine East High, as a sophomore. There, his parents hoped, he would amass a record to propel him to college and into a career as a doctor. "That was a thing you could get a lot of respect for doing and make a lot of money at the same time," Steve said in a 1980 *Chicago Tribune* profile.

But while Steve might have been labeled in today's parlance as academically gifted, studying didn't rule his thoughts. Over the next three years, he scored at or near the top in standardized tests and enrolled in advanced classes, but he hit the books only sporadically, earning decent but not stellar grades. What fueled Steve instead, both in and out of school, was a kaleidoscope of activities, some feeding his affection for sports and nearly all embodying his fascination with music and performance. Each pursuit may not have appeared extraordinary in isolation, but the aggregate was audacious. They were the steps of a young man boldly preparing himself for a life of inspired connections, both one-on-one and from a stage.

In fall 1962, Steve joined the 30-member student staff of WMTH-FM, Maine East's "Family Listening Station." He teamed with senior Robin Pendergrast to anchor the school's varsity football and basketball games and to produce and star in new daytime talk shows interspersed with broadcasts of news reports and assemblies. Just three years old and one of the most prominent examples of the school's girth and wealth, WMTH not only educated students in the art of the airwaves, giving them academic credit in drama, but also served as a public-relations pipeline to homes within five miles of the school. "It was aimed primarily at the parents and the community," says Jack Coombe, faculty program director for WMTH. "It was to give the community an idea of what was going on in the school and its activities, plus uncovering and encouraging talent."

Among the more talented students were Pendergrast and Steve, who made WMTH their sanctum and enjoyed taping their 15- to 30-minute morning shows that were aired in the afternoons. A voiceover artist today, Pendergrast says that

in most of his shows with Steve, the two dissected the previous weekend's games, sometimes aiming barbs at the coaches and team. Steve, who stored his six-string guitar at the station, constantly cradled and strummed the instrument with stubby fingers callused from constant practice. With his engaging voice, he made up musical recipes to chide the cafeteria food and played folk songs he had "picked up immediately by ear," says Pendergrast — tunes popularized by groups such as Peter, Paul & Mary, who were just snaring the national limelight — and analyzed them.

"I would perpetually kid Steve, tongue-in-cheek, for plagiarizing," Pendergrast says, "and he would always say, 'Y'know, in two or three years I'll be writing my own music.' But Mr. Coombe didn't buy a lot of what we did. Talk shows were unusual at the time, and he was very conservative. He was afraid of what we might do because he was responsible for the license. High-school radio stations were brand new, and it was an adventure to have students at age 14, 15 or 16 on the air saying stuff that could influence a lot of people, which was scary to the school board."

If their taped talk shows were an adventure, Pendergrast says the two "really had a field day" live each Friday night as they recounted the foibles of the Maine East football team, with the quick-witted Steve as the color man to Pendergrast's play-by-play. Steve stood out, he says, because while he was a "little, squatty guy" who couldn't compete in sports and weathered the taunts of those who could, he nevertheless knew the uniform numbers and statistics of every player. Chiming in is Ron Davitt, one of the school's two public-address announcers who sat in the press box with Steve and Pendergrast during games and says the two did a speedier job calling plays than he did. "We'd always try to beat the kids on the radio," Davitt says, "but they were quick. They had their information." About Steve, Coombe says, "We used to get a lot of people call us and didn't know who he was. They'd say, 'Hey, that boy who did the color was very, very good.' "

Pendergrast became close to his broadcast partner that year, delighting in Steve's gregarious, "always smiling" personality. The two were considered

(Left photo) During his sophomore year at Maine East High, Steve, standing third from left, poses with other student broadcasters for the school's WMTH-FM. The staff included two of Steve's friends, Neal Pollock, sitting at far left, and Richard Stock, standing fourth from right, as well as (above) Steve's talk-show partner, Robin Pendergrast.

(Photos from *The Lens*, 1963)

"preppies," "collegiates" or "skinheads," as opposed to tough-guy athletes who were "rocks" or "greasers." But Pendergrast also fumed at how some students treated Steve's religious background. "I really took great issue with those who called him the little Jew, mostly behind his back, and there was a lot more. I had confrontations with greasers over this, but Steve was too laid-back. He took a lot of this anti-Semitic stuff with a grain of salt. I know that it affected him. I'd say to him, 'How can you put up with all this bullshit?' And he just smiled. He just wasn't going to be affected by it.

"He really knew what his mission was. Obviously, he was blessed with a talent to carry on that mission. A kid of that age at that time — talk about being unique. Even when he was a sophomore, dragging his oversize guitar case around on his 5-foot frame, he had a mission."

The teacher in charge of WMTH perceived that mission as well, recalling that Steve "came to life" with a guitar in his hands. "He wanted to become a sportscaster in the worst way, and he wanted to know about the colleges where he could study radio and do top games, but I kept discouraging him," says Coombe, a former radio announcer, TV writer and percussionist with the Artie Shaw and Louis Bellson big bands. "I knew right away that he had talent. I told him, 'Steve, forget sports. There's all kinds of sportscasters around. You might go places as a sportscaster, but I really feel you have a talent that should be exploited. You should go into show business.' He got annoyed at me a couple of times, but I'd say, 'Steve, pick up that guitar and start singing some of your compositions,' and he began to realize that he had this talent."

Coombe wasn't the only one that year who was encouraging Steve on the guitar. Family members arranged for Steve to sing and play songs at gatherings, including his second cousin Nancy Sage's confirmation party. Initially, the 14-year-old Sage was dubious. "He came out, did the niceties, and we rolled our eyes," she says. "Then he got his guitar out, and he played. He was wonderful. Talk about learning not to have preconceived ideas."

Steve also began to make music-minded friends in his class, such as Brad Ellis, who often hung out on the front stairs and in the family room of Steve's home, nuzzled by Duchess, the collie, and added harmony while Steve sang and strummed Kingston Trio and Chad Mitchell Trio songs. The guitar seemed "enormous" in the lap of his diminutive friend, Ellis says. "That's one of the reasons he sat on the stairs, because it was easy for him to rest the guitar rather than use the carry strap. He knew a little bit about how to play it, but he really was not proficient at all." But then, Ellis says, he introduced Steve to another "natural talent" in his class, Howard Berkman.

Like Ellis and Steve, Berkman was Jewish, and while that connection may have helped trigger their meeting, music cemented the bond. Berkman, "a brain" who had been known in grade school for his visual art, was a year older than Steve and had performed for money since age 10. A prodigy, he learned guitar from his father, Marv Berkman, who for three-plus decades was the house entertainer at the swanky Riccardo's restaurant beneath the *Chicago Sun-Times*

He took a lot of this anti-Semitic stuff with a grain of salt. I know that it affected him. I'd say to him, 'How can you put up with all this bullshit?' And he just smiled.
ROBIN PENDERGRAST

and *Chicago Tribune* buildings and around the corner from the Billy Goat Pub (later made famous by "Saturday Night Live") at the end of Rush Street, just north of the Loop. Marv, whose father, Ralph, had been a noted Russian singer in Chicago, was a self-described gypsy or saloon guitarist who knew thousands of songs and strolled through the three-room Italian eatery with hunchback accordionist Roberto "Bobby" Rossi and headwaiter Bruno Pacini, singing and playing Flamenco, Greek and Italian folk songs, operatic arias, blues, show tunes and other customer requests.

Riccardo's had a liquor license letting it stay open until 4 a.m., and Howard Berkman essentially grew up there, emulating the late-night performances of his father, who wore a shiny red patent shirt, sometimes unbuttoned to halfway down his torso, and smoked the slim, harsh Italian Parodi cigars later popularized by film actor Clint Eastwood. Howard also soaked up the ambience of Rush Street, a hangout for journalists and the arts crowd, as it was Chicago's glitziest concentration of restaurants, bars and nightclubs.

By the time Howard was 14 and met Steve at Maine East, he was steeped in renowned Chicago writer and poet Carl Sandburg's 1950 book, *The New American Songbag*, had become adept at Dixieland guitar and had moved on to the instrumental rock 'n' roll tunes of the Ventures ("Walk, Don't Run"), the Surfaris ("Wipe Out") and twangy Duane Eddy.

In a sense, Steve's parents already were seeking Howard. Bud and Minnette, who regularly drank at Riccardo's, asked Marv Berkman to give guitar lessons to their son. Marv told them, "I don't know anything Steve's going to want to know. Why don't you send him to my kid Howard?"

In Howard Berkman, Steve found his first true musical mentor. Certainly Berkman believed it. "I thought I knew everything," he says. The two began sleeping overnight at each other's houses, staying up late and sitting across from each other playing guitar. Howard also was Steve's entrée into ensemble work, as Howard had put together a four-piece band, the Jesters, that played bar mitzvahs and Sweet Sixteen parties in backyards and VFW halls all over the North Side and had even recorded an instrumental 45 called "Side Track." In the Jesters, Berkman played lead guitar, and Steve would soon be the band's fifth member, on rhythm guitar.

Steve later said that from his handful of classes at the Old Town School, he knew five or six chords and could play a few folk and rock songs, so he quit the school because he thought he "knew everything ... and then some." But when he heard Berkman play him the haunting chord melody of Errol Garner's "Misty" (a Johnny Mathis hit), "that scared the shit out of me. I didn't know there was such a thing, and I was hooked — crushed on one end and hooked."

Berkman taught him the blues progressions of "St. James Infirmary," the finger-picking styles in George Gershwin's "Summertime," the Lonnie Johnson solo in "Goin' to Chicago Blues" and the half-tone octave line of "Deep Purple," all of which his dad had taught him and were reinforced by guitarists Berkman had studied on TV's "Lawrence Welk Show" (Neil Levang) and "The Adven-

Smoking a Parodi cigar, Marv Berkman, shown in the early 1970s, strolls and entertains late-night diners at swanky Riccardo's restaurant, which became a training ground in guitar for his son, Howard — and soon Steve as well.

(Photo courtesy of Marv Berkman)

Howard Berkman poses with the future Hillary Rodham Clinton for a photo of 23 Maine East sophomore contributors to a class newspaper, The Ghost Writer. *Berkman found Steve's memory stunning. "He had total access to all the music in his head at all times," he says. "He was like a vacuum cleaner. He sucked up everything anyone could show him as fast as it could be shown."*

(Photo from *The Lens*, 1963)

tures of Ozzie and Harriet" (James Burton, the rockabilly lead for Ricky Nelson). From "Jamaica Farewell" and "Railroad Bill" to "Basin Street Blues" and "Sweet Georgia Brown," Steve soaked up all of it like a sponge.

Steve's response to Berkman's versions of "Misty" and the rest didn't surprise Berkman. "When you're a young, budding guitarist, to see a guy who can play chord melody on a guitar with a flatpick without having to sing and not backing something else up, that's very impressive to you," he says. "Steve really was knocked out that you could get so much out of a guitar, because most of the guys who were playing were just strumming."

The two hung out at Riccardo's so that Steve could learn licks from Berkman's dad. But Steve's proficiency, honed by years of synagogue singing, along with what later co-writer Sean Kelly would call a phonographic memory, soon became irritating, even maddening, to Berkman. "Steve had such good ears that he very quickly got very far past me in a lot of respects," he says. "That was what was so disgusting about him. He'd say, 'Show me something,' and I did, and it would be gone. You would have struggled for years learning these things, but boom, he would have it. I was so jealous. But, of course, I was so young.

"He was one of those kids who could just hear everything. Once he knew a chord, he knew where it belonged, even if it was in a different musical situation. He had total access to all the music in his head at all times. He amazed me. He was like a vacuum cleaner. He sucked up everything anyone could show him as fast as it could be shown."

Steve later confirmed this. "I guess I was sort of like a walking tape recorder," he said. "I'd hear something, I'd like it, and I'd try and learn how to play it, and it really didn't matter what the hell it was." He characterized his high-school persona as "an amateur musicologist."

Berkman, with long, dexterous fingers, was all the more annoyed — and impressed — because somehow Steve overcame the disadvantage of his "little fat, square fingers. I'd look at him and think, 'How could he make all this delicate music out of these fingers? They look like bananas or little king shrimps.'"

Other differences between Berkman and Steve emerged as well. Steve's connection to Berkman netted him a "free pass" to Berkman's group of friends, who dressed and postured in "continental" fashion. "We wore tight, sharkskin slacks, black socks and pointed-toe shoes, Gant or Hathaway shirts with tabs, mohair sweaters and ID bracelets that you could wrap around your knuckle," Berkman says. "We hung together with the Italian kids and had that ethos. We were ethnic, and we had a chip on our shoulder." In contrast, he says, Steve was considered one of the finicky "dupers" or "skinheads" who wore ironed and starched pinstripe or madras Oxford button-down shirts, white or wheat-colored Levi's and shiny penny loafers.

"He had a crewcut, and he was real preppy. He had really big eyes and long eyelashes. His eyes always looked like he was wearing mascara. He was a very pretty boy," Berkman says. "Steve was always like Ivy League. He always fit in with those people, and I wasn't able to put up with that kind of shit. I was militant. If somebody had made a half-joking anti-Semitic comment, I would have been all over them in a minute. But Steve could understand, could see the bigger picture."

Besides music, the two had in common a routine and image that was less than wholesome, hanging out, smoking cigarettes, playing cards for money and shooting pool in the basement rec room of Steve's house while Bud and Minnette were away at cocktail parties or taking in the Old Town and Rush Street nightlife.

"All the young guys in our little Mafia would go over to Steve's house," Berkman says. "As a pool shooter, he had a great stroke. When he pulled the cue into his side, he twisted his palm up and put a real twist on the cue so that his shot came out with heavy English, like a rifle bullet with incredible sideways spin. And he was a real competitor. When you were making your stroke, he wasn't above sneezing or lighting a cigarette or any of the little moves. When you played cards with him, he'd keep those cards pasted to his chest like W.C. Fields. He was playing for keeps. You weren't going to re-divide the money because you lost and you were only 14 years old. You were playing cards."

With a cigarette as a prop, Steve did "old Jewish man routines," imitating George Burns and Groucho Marx and holding his cigarettes Russian style, with the lit tip facing his palm, Berkman says. "His mom used to give us packs of Camel cigarettes so we wouldn't steal them in the store, so I started smoking Camels. Steve started smoking Pall Malls, which my Aunt Hattie smoked, because his folks smoked Camels. You never wanted to smoke what your folks smoked." Gesturing with a cigarette to his receding hairline, Steve would tell Berkman, "Lookadis, lookadis! Damn, I'm an old man!"

Notwithstanding Steve's preppy look and genial personality, Berkman also found that at times his friend turned hard-line. "He could get real arrogant and real tough, not nice," he says. "He could use his fists and his hands. He could push you around." Once, he saw Steve confront a friend — early Jesters guitarist Sam Siegel — who came to Steve's house dressed like what Steve considered "a slob." Steve slapped Siegel and said, "You should show more respect for my mother. Don't ever come to my house like this!"

Like the Flock, Little Boy Blues and countless other bands of mostly Jewish kids from Chicago's north and west suburbs, the Jesters (a reference to Marv Berkman's collection of medieval-style armaments) carved out a youthful appeal. Steve, Berkman, rhythm guitarist Richard Stock, drummers Gene Lubin (preceded by Perry Johnson) and stoic Miles Davis devotee and trumpeter Steve Debs, along with Steve, all were 14 and 15, except Lubin, who was three years older and hosted the band's rehearsals at his house in Skokie. Berkman designed silver-colored business cards for the group and hired an agent, Harry Oppenheimer, to book and transport the band to its gigs. "He picked us up at our parents' homes, we'd put our guitars and little amplifiers in his trunk, he'd drive us out north to play lawn parties or motel ballrooms, then he'd drive us home," Berkman says. "We were little boys."

One formative engagement, Berkman says, was for wealthy but mentally

> You should show more respect for my mother. Don't ever come to my house like this!
> STEVE GOODMAN

challenged eccentrics at the Hotel Moraine on the Lake, formerly a posh resort in the north suburb of Highland Park. Older women in negligees flashed the band members, "and we didn't know what was going on. Nobody told us that we were playing at a place like 'King of Hearts.' " Lubin, the drummer, says, "All these adults are drinking and carousing and talking money, and they're being entertained by kids, but they're not looking at you as kids. They're looking at you as professional entertainers."

Steve's stint with the Jesters, which lasted more than a year, gave him his first, hands-on life in a musical group — one with a charismatic and bossy "front man." Berkman instituted the group's look: black sharkskin slacks, skinny string ties and collarless, avocado green, rayon cardigan jackets with large, white pearl buttons. ("We looked 'sharp,' " Steve joked 12 years later.) Berkman also decreed a largely nonverbal repertoire of more than a dozen songs that included dance selections by the Ventures and Duane Eddy, Dixieland tunes, cha-chas, "Temptation," "Perfidia," "Heart & Soul," "Hall of the Mountain King," and one vocal, "Summertime." At gigs, Berkman called out the songs' chords, occasionally barking an order ("Jam in the key of C"), and the rest followed. So when he recruited Steve as a backup guitarist, Berkman found it natural to think, "I'll grow this rhythm player. I'll tell him what to do, and he'll do it."

Berkman's dress code didn't faze Steve, but Steve sought to inject rowdier vocals into the mix and sing them himself. In addition to his bent toward Kingston Trio tunes such as "Tom Dooley" and "M.T.A.," Steve promoted the raucous Chuck Berry and Little Richard songs from the transistor radio that had energized him as a grade-schooler. This fried Berkman. "I was too cool for that," he says. "We were an instrumental band, and I said, 'Oh, no, we can't do that. Oh, no, no, no.' I was not the easiest guy to get along with."

Steve's equipment, and how he acquired it, also irritated Berkman, who had a rocky home life, had to scrounge funds to buy a pickup for an old Epiphone Triumph and used bar-mitzvah cash to acquire a nicer Gibson SG electric. In contrast, Berkman says, Steve quickly graduated from his inexpensive Harmony Sovereign to a top-of-the-line reddish brown Gibson Hummingbird (Steve called it "the Bird") and an equally prestigious, "batwing"-style Epiphone electric guitar, both of which his parents purchased for him. (Bud and Minnette also hosted the Jesters to entertain at their home on Bud's 45th birthday.)

"Steve was always more. He had things planned," Berkman says. "He wasn't the sleeping-on-the-floor, no-money-in-his-pocket kind of guy. He came from a little different class of people, and he always had a couple of bucks in his pocket. He always had the support of his family."

Quickly, those who knew the two sized up the dynamics between the tall, aloof Berkman and the cherubic, soulful-looking Steve. Whereas Berkman was more of an improviser, Steve memorized licks and meticulously prepared guitar solos. Berkman's occasional vocals were raw, while Steve's singing voice, reflecting his temple days, were vaguely operatic, at least initially. Both exuded intensity and craved audience attention. Neither wanted to be upstaged.

Howard was always full of rebellion and passion, and his excitement was a truly volatile thing. Steve's passions were different. He had a spiritual aura about him and a more joyful feeling.
MARV BERKMAN

"Howard was always full of rebellion and passion, and his excitement was a truly volatile thing," says his father, Marv Berkman. "Steve's passions were different. He had a spiritual aura about him and a more joyful feeling. He was much more of a poet. They did not belong in the same organization."

Girls were an integral part of the Jesters equation for Berkman, who says he never lacked for female companionship and was "heavily involved in necking, petting and doing everything but having straight sex." Not so for Steve, whom Berkman never knew to have a girlfriend in high school. Music alone filled Steve's soul.

"Steve was concerned about playing and singing, and that was it," says Stock, the Jesters' second rhythm guitarist. "He wasn't concerned about identifying himself with a group to do what teenagers need to do. Steve got his warm fuzzies from people who gathered around and listened to him sing. Even though he was a modest, embarrassed kid, he ate up the applause. Howard couldn't get that at home, so he needed to be the spotlight, and that's how he got girls, typical high-school stuff. But I never got that feeling from Steve. His guitar playing was his identity. If he lost his fingers, I don't know what would have happened to him. Howard saw his guitar as a babe magnet, but singing and guitar playing was just who Steve was."

"Berkman was a precocious, talented, extroverted 15-year-old, the kind of kid that other kids secretly wanted to be," adds Lubin, the drummer. "You just knew he would be the first to get laid, and it would probably be with a gal twice his age. But not Steve. He had a kind of quiet urgency about him, as if he knew who he was and what he wanted, had it all planned out. He talked lovingly about folk music and his guitar the way the rest of us talked about meeting girls at the next gig. Playing music or being part of a group of musicians was an extremely proud thing for him. He wasn't just having fun like the rest of us. It was some deep, private feeling he had about it. He had a calling, and he knew it.

"It seemed like the rest of the guys in the band were dysfunctional in some way, but Steve seemed to be a normal guy from a normal family. He didn't have any gripes or grievances against the world, whereas the rest of us had some beef or something to prove.

"He and Howie were alike, the way that garlic and cream custard can be said to be alike — each unique, distinctive, unforgettable in his own way. Both of these guys seemed graced with an ineluctable sense of self."

Inevitably, Berkman and Steve parted ways. Stock says the break came in the Goodmans' living room during the May 1963 birthday party for Bud. "There was a lot of tension that night. When it came time for a solo, Steve went for it, and Howard exploded. There could only be one fast gun in town at the time, and it had to be Howard. In that verbal scuffle, it was pretty obvious that Steve wouldn't be playing with the Jesters much longer. Steve just said, 'Enough of this. I don't have the interest for negative stuff,' so one day he was no longer part of the group."

For several months afterward, as he moved to his junior year, Steve played

Richard Stock, second rhythm guitarist for the Jesters, says that in contrast to Howard Berkman, for whom performing was a means to meet girls, Steve's attraction to music was more primal: "Singing and guitar playing was just who Steve was."

(Photo from *The Lens*, 1965)

Sweet Sixteen gigs on his own, with Stock as backup. Because of a family move, Berkman left Maine East High for nearby Niles East and carved a path in stark contrast to Steve's. He drifted into the "English invasion" music of the Beatles, Rolling Stones, Kinks and the Who, as well as radical politics and the drug culture. He also formed a hard-edged, proto-punk suburban band, the Knaves, whose original songs bore hostile lyrics and whose stage manner amounted to an aural assault on audiences.

At Maine East, Steve stayed immersed in WMTH, played for class parties and sang in the school's senior choir. Such activity along with his stint with the Jesters helped launch him to the school's auditorium stage — in a series of dramatic productions and talent shows tailor-made for his exuberance and individuality, with casts in the hundreds and appreciative mainstream audiences that numbered in the thousands.

His first such foray had come in May 1963, the spring of his sophomore year, when he won the role of Marcellus Washburn in the MEHS production of Meredith Willson's "The Music Man." The sidekick part, played by portly Buddy Hackett in the film of the play one year prior, fit Steve's talents and personality, particularly in the songs "The Sadder but Wiser Girl for Me" and "Shipoopi." More than 200 students were involved in the mammoth musical, and the school's 1,480-seat auditorium filled up for each of its three shows. The school was so big that parts were double-cast, and Steve alternated in the part with classmate Roger Voegele. Steve also doubled as one of the 13 traveling salesmen in the play's opening scene.

A year later, Steve, as a junior, played a similarly showy and stocky role in the school's production of Lerner and Lowe's "My Fair Lady," portraying Alfred P. Doolittle, the rambunctious, drunken father of the title character. Randy Lamson, a classmate who played a dustman, says Steve slid into his part seamlessly. "Everybody else's Cockney accents were slightly weak, still needed a lot of work," he says, "but Steve had a great ear, and he had the accent down before tryouts were even held." Again, he alternated with Voegele, and their performance of Doolittle's two songs "steals the show," opined the school newspaper, *The Pioneer*. The paper praised the "bouncy, carefree attitude" of "With a Little Bit of Luck" and pronounced "Get Me to the Church on Time" "the best scene in the show." (*The Pioneer* also noted, "Keep in mind that even though it appears that way, no beer has been allowed backstage.") The production, mounted five months before the movie version was released with Stanley Holloway playing Doolittle, sold out every seat in the MEHS auditorium for its three-night run.

Between the two musicals, Steve's stage stature ballooned and matured, thanks to the blockbuster "Mainspring" variety show (or V-show, as it was dubbed) put on by Maine East students each February. Stemming back to 1929, when it was called the Winter Carnival, V-show was the school's all-out annual musical and theatrical gift to Niles, Glenview, Morton Grove and Park Ridge. Its quality, the caliber of good community theater, drew people of all ages, not just relatives of the 200-plus students in the cast.

> **Everybody else's Cockney accents were slightly weak, still needed a lot of work, but Steve had a great ear, and he had the accent down before tryouts were even held.**
> **RANDY LAMSON**

The V-show that ran Thursday through Saturday, Feb. 20 to 22, 1964, adopted the theme of "Showboat," based on the 1926 Edna Ferber novel and subsequent multiple Broadway and Hollywood incarnations of the same name. Set in 1840 on a Mississippi riverboat that paddled from St. Louis to New Orleans, the MEHS production boasted 35 songs performed by "jugglers, dancers, gamblers, folk singers, minstrels and puppeteers," as well as "adventurers, pioneers, rivermen, roustabouts, gamblers and fancy ladies." Scenes took place in a gambling house, a carnival and a parade through Mardi Gras, all before the eye-popping backdrop of a smoke-plumed, two-deck, 26-foot-long riverboat (complete with a large, revolving paddlewheel) that engulfed the stage.

While many of the show's highlights and climactic episodes were elaborate set pieces with scores of student dancers, singers and actors taking the stage, the scene that left the deepest and most lasting imprint was the show's first vocalizing and simplest segment. It featured just one student — Steve Goodman. In bib overalls and straw hat, perched on a hay bale and bathed in a solitary spotlight, he intoned the resonant spiritual "Old Man River."

It was an audacious choice for Steve when he had auditioned after school for the show the previous December. Sung indelibly in decades past by legendary African-American singers Paul Robeson and William Warfield, "Old Man River" expressed both the hopelessness and the faith that a black dockworker felt when confronted by the symbolic force and indifference of the nation's most famous waterway. The song had embedded itself in U.S. culture as one to be sung by a physically imposing black man with the deepest of bass voices. Yet at all-white Maine East, the diminutive Steve, one of the school's few Jews, turned out to be an inspired interpreter.

Preserved on a two-LP recording of the show that was sold to raise funds for future productions, Steve's performance of "Old Man River" radiated power and presence. After a lively overture and backed gently by a 19-student orchestra, Steve plunged into the song's profound lyrics, surging faultlessly to the culminating chorus that proclaims that the river "just keeps rollin' along." The resonance of his voice hinted at Al Jolson in his prime and drew ringing applause.

Taking immediate notice of Steve's rendition of "Old Man River" was a classmate who later rocketed to international prominence as the nation's first lady and a U.S. senator from New York — Hillary Rodham Clinton. "It was a singular moment," says Clinton, who had a minor role in the show as a dancer. "When Steve performed, he had kind of a glimmer in his eye, almost a wink like 'This is gonna be fun.' But this was a really serious song, a beautiful, moving song, and he just knocked it out of the park. He wanted to connect with people, he loved communicating through music, and he felt the emotional content of music." [5] She speculates that the song's Mississippi River motif may have been part of his later inspiration to write the similarly themed "City of New Orleans," which became his best-known tune.

"Old Man River" surprisingly matched Steve's skills, says classmate Sue

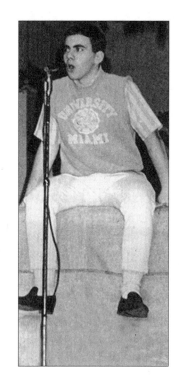

Perched atop bales of hay befitting the "Showboat" theme, Steve rehearses "Old Man River" for the Mainspring variety show in spring 1964.
(Photo from Mainspring '64 program, courtesy of Barb Pritchard Robbins)

5: Clinton says it was remarkable how well "Old Man River" turned out in performance, given how much of a "cut-up" Steve and other boys were in rehearsals. "Here we were trying to put on this serious variety show in a very large auditorium," she says, "and it was all the girls trying to get the boys to take it seriously."

The double album produced as a fund-raiser for Maine East High (cover above) contained most of the music performed in Mainspring '64. It became Steve's first appearance on an LP, and his solo version of "Old Man River" was later played on the "Midnight Special" show on Chicago's WFMT-FM.

(LP courtesy of Ellen Press Murdoch)

6: Steve tweaked a line from "Old Man River" in 1981 while autographing his "Words We Can Dance To" LP for Roger Jones. An Uptown Theatre employee, Jones volunteered to squire Steve and John Prine in his 1966 Cadillac Coupe DeVille to the Kansas City airport after their dual billing at the Uptown. Steve handed Jones a $20 bill and inscribed the album, "To Roger, Pad that voucher. Lift that bale. Steve Goodman."

Moestue. "This was a man's song that went to the core of American music, and Steve's beautifully mature baritone voice had a timbre and emotional sophistication that was very unusual for a young, high-school singer," Moestue says. "Steve was not merely singing the notes or words. He was treating it as the aria that it is. He did not have that low of a voice, but it didn't matter because of his passion."

Passions of a different sort stirred at the time of rehearsals, when the V-show crew weighed whether some numbers, including Steve's "Old Man River," would be performed in blackface. The rationale was that the popular 19th century custom — in which white (and, later, black) performers assumed a stilted African-American persona by wearing burned cork on their faces and painting their lips pure white — would be true to the minstrel milieu of "Showboat."

Enough students and staff objected to the outdated practice, however, for a compromise to be invoked. With blackface cartoons painted on the undersides of circular skirts that their wearers sashayed in dance numbers, and with glow-in-the-dark makeup painted onto hands and facial features for other songs, the show's costumers and technicians approximated an authentic result.

"It all was meant to give the blackface effect because of the way it was lit," says Lynn Pankau (now Miller), the show's student art director: "It was in evening-glow light, with highlighted makeup — sophisticated, like light flashing off the river."

The result, unfortunately, bespoke white suburban naivete, circa 1964. "We were all quite offended that anybody could think that we were racist," says Geoff Harpham, who played Mr. Interlocutor (master of ceremonies) for the show's minstrel routines, "but little did we know. We had no clue about blackface musicians and certainly had no sensitivity to how these things might be offensive to other people." Steve Holton, yearbook and newspaper photographer in Steve's class, sums it up as "tradition butting heads against the beginnings of activism."

Tickets for the show ranged from $1.25 to $1.75, and every seat for every show was filled. Steve was part of the seven-student Mainspring writing staff, and with six other students near the end of the show he sang the upbeat song "Three to Make Ready." But it was his performance of "Old Man River" that rooted itself in the audience's collective memory. [6]

"He just took the house down," says classmate John Benda.

"The song has range, and top to bottom he got 'em all," says Steve Horelick, who knew Steve in Albany Park and was a year ahead of him at Maine East.

"People cried when they heard it," says V-show assistant choreographer Hardye Simons.

"Right then, I just thought, 'This guy is really special,' " adds classmate and V-show usher Barb Pritchard Robbins.

"That's when he made his grand entrance, so to speak," says Roger Voegele, Steve's "Music Man" and "My Fair Lady" double. "That's when everybody got to know him in the whole school."

By this time, mid-junior year, Steve stood out in many ways, recall his classmates. Cathy Lind (now Edler) recalls a loving, gentle approach. "He always had a smile on his face and wanted to share something," she says. "Anytime that Steve pulled you aside, you felt close to him because it was always a one-on-one. He was focused on you. He just wanted to share. He was like a magnet, and everybody was there for him." Adds Betsy Ebeling, "His piercing, button eyes just glowed through you." Brad Ellis intensifies the description, calling him a "live wire" (coincidentally, the title of a Goodman concert CD released in 2000). "He was the third rail on the Chicago El, the one that's electrically charged, and if you step on it, you die," Ellis says. "This was a guy nobody didn't like. He always made you feel good. It mattered to him what was going on in your life, and it energized you."

Neal Pollack, self-described as "pissed, angry and hostile" in high school, likens Steve at the time to a koala bear. "He was a roly-poly little kid with a nice smile, good attitude, a lot of personality," he says. "Little rosy cheeks — the guy could have been a Jewish Santa Claus, man. He was a genuinely sweet guy."

But also emerging was a caustic surface humor that some misunderstood. "It was premature for a lot of people," says fellow guitarist Mike Nilles. "He had a way of saying something that sounded sarcastic but wasn't intended to be at all, and at times he would rub people the wrong way. People sometimes said he was an obnoxious little kid who thought he had the world by the balls. I don't think he was trying to be eccentric or obnoxious or arrogant, but people didn't appreciate his humor. In hindsight, it was actually very funny."

His popularity, high profile and immersion in high-school activities paralleled the course of classmate Hillary Rodham, yet their personas were quite different. "Hillary was multi-talented. She was extremely bright, personable and attractive. She could do no wrong," says Joel Platt, a friend of Steve's and a student politician. "Steve could be a little abrasive, and although he was bright, you couldn't always tell."

"Steve was very friendly, very high-spirited, a very happy figure," adds fellow folksinging guitarist and V-show performer Geoff Harpham. "I never saw him in a neutral mood. He had a lot of juice and was a good guy to be around. It was a very democratic quality. Hillary would have been very conscious of who was where on the totem pole, and even though you had 1,000 people in your class, there still would have been a range from zero to 1,000, whereas Steve played a different game. He was a popular guy, but he was not a Popular Guy."

In her own reflections, Hillary Rodham Clinton agrees. "Steve crossed all lines, got along with everybody, attracted people, had a smile on his face, always wanted to be where the action is," she says. "He was someone who you wanted to know, you were drawn to. I loved kidding around with him, talking with him, being with him, having a chance to kid him and be kidded back. Because of his talents musically, he could move from group to group and talk to anybody.

"I admired him because he was so upbeat and positive, and he used his

Steve "was someone you wanted to know," says classmate Hillary Rodham Clinton. "He used his talents to really make people happy, make them laugh. Y'know, you were always glad to see Steve comin' down the hall."
(Photo from *The Lens*, 1964)

Sue Moestue, who interacted with Steve on student council, recalls his "powerball" persona: "He took up a lot of what you might call oral space."

(Photo, *The Lens*, 1965)

7: Steve's hometown was rife with musical influences, he reflected in a June 1979 interview with Rob Patterson of the *Daily Herald* of suburban Chicago: "Everything passes through Chicago. Chicago's big industry has always been transportation, and just about everything comes through Chicago at one point or another. Chicago is more of a Tin Pan Alley than anyone realizes. ... As I found out more about people like Blind Blake, Blind Willie McTell and Big Bill Broonzy, I started hearing all kinds of other instruments being played in my music."

talents to really make people happy, make them laugh. Y'know, you were always glad to see Steve comin' down the hall."

· Many attribute Steve's outgoing nature to a need to compensate for his lack of height. Nearly every boy and girl at Maine East was taller than Steve, so he became a "powerball," says Sue Moestue. "He was full of energy, very bright-eyed, very quick in his movements. He took up a lot of what you might call oral space." Ever talkative, he enjoyed telling stories and embellishing them to sustain interest, says Howard Primer, a close friend of Steve's at the time. "Steve had a way of making stories be the stories he wanted them to be," he says. "Many times Steve would take a story that I was a part of and tell it to somebody else, and the story was changed in significant ways to make the story better. In fact, one thing that turned people off to Steve was his storytelling because Steve's stories were a little far-fetched at times."

The most effective way for Steve to compensate, his classmates recall, was through music. So it was no surprise that a guitar served as his constant talisman, at V-show rehearsals, in impromptu cafeteria sessions and anywhere students gathered. He even became the focal point for a large Steve Holton photo, captioned "Enthusiasm," that straddled the two pages that opened the activities section in *The Lens*, the Maine East yearbook. Staged in the school auditorium, the photo depicted Steve, seven other guitarists and one banjo player performing for more than a dozen seated students in hootenanny style, mirroring the Saturday night TV show of the same name.

Wherever he went, Steve's hands were in perpetual motion as he strummed and picked chords and melodies to songs popular on AM radio and even those, such as Billie Holiday's version of "Strange Fruit" and Josh White's "One Meat Ball," aired on the eclectic "Midnight Special" on WFMT-FM on Saturday nights. [7] "We were really big Josh White fans," says classmate Bob Berg, part of the folkie Colony Men. "He was the only black blues guy that we knew of. Steve and I were very into him because he knew how to bend strings, to force a string into a higher note by increasing the tension and back down again."

Steve also plucked new licks to silly compositions that he made up on the spot, such as one inspired by Chicago's nasty winters and remembered by classmate Brad Ellis:

> *It's cold, it's cold, it's cold, it's cold*
> *It's colder than the foam on a champagne glass*
> *It's colder than a hair on a polar bear's ass*
> *It's colder than a nipple on a witch's tit*
> *It's colder than a hunk of penguin shit*

As well, Steve sought and played gigs at area coffeehouses. Accompanied by his year-older Maine East friend and bongo-drum player Willie Riser, Steve entertained at The Hut, a dance club and former church across from a burger place called the Choo Choo in next-door Des Plaines. Sunday evenings, Steve's dad, Bud, also dropped him off for hootenannies (or "hoots") at It's Here, a lakeside teen hangout on Chicago's Sheridan Road, where youths sat on overstuffed pillows instead of chairs.

And in Morton Grove, he played Scot's Cellar, a dark, 12-table sanctuary squatting in a basement beneath a Dempster Street drive-in for greasers and bikers with custom cars varooming in the parking lot while trains rumbled by on nearby tracks. "Friday night was Corvette Night, and Saturday night was '57 Chevy Night," says musical satirist Larry Rand, who attended Niles East High and also played Scot's. There, he says, a high-strung Steve earned $17 a night for singing "Greenback Dollar" and a half-dozen other songs by the Kingston Trio, Bob Dylan, Leon Bibb and Peter, Paul & Mary while opening for the house act, a fledgling 20-year-old Pete Seeger protégé named Fred Holstein, who was "a workshop every night" and a few years later became Steve's musical mentor in Old Town. "I wasn't real enamored of Steve," Holstein recalled decades later, "but he came on pretty strong. He did a lot of other people's songs and jumped around."

Back at Maine East, having upgraded to a 12-string guitar, Steve also jammed with other bands, including the Saharas, a well-established Park Ridge rock group that played at basketball half-times, and the Port Calm Trio, an all-girl threesome also based in Park Ridge that performed traditional and popular folk songs. Mike Nilles, of the Saharas, says Steve intently took mental notes while playing with the band. "He was really focused on wanting to do music," he says. "Steve had that wild grin. It was almost demonic at times, like he was thinking, 'I'm going to master this.' "

While Steve declined an offer by the Saharas to join them, he subtly sought to become a guitarist for Port Calm. The trio didn't give him the chance, however. "Steve was so good, but we decided we just wanted to be the girls," says Kathy Rogers (now Burgess). "We thought that it made a difference, that we should be on our own. The fellows who had gotten together and were playing were doing different things and going into the city to perform. We were not in that league at all. In fact, I don't think we were in much of a league." Art Curtis, a classmate, suspects that unspoken social boundaries also were a factor: "Here were three very popular WASP-ish girls from Park Ridge, and he was this short Jewish guy."

The band that appealed most to Steve was the Impalas, Maine East High's other rock group, which played established hits and whose members were one to two years younger than Steve. They sought another lead vocalist, but unlike Howard Berkman with the Jesters, embraced folk-oriented Steve in that role.

"He brought us a dimension we didn't have," says Kent Cerrone, lead guitarist for the group, named after the make of his parents' car. "Steve had lead capabilities and a broader sense of music and the industry than we did. Everybody looked up to him because he was older and brought musical experience of his own and was from a different genre than what we were doing."

Twice-weekly practice sessions for the group, which also included guitarist and lead vocalist Casey Kenzel, organist Paul Gryglas, bassist Doug Martens

Here were three very popular WASP-ish girls from Park Ridge, and he was this short Jewish guy.
ART CURTIS

Phillis "Toxie" Wirtz, who dated Steve occasionally, says he was self-conscious about his height: "I don't think he felt awkward with me, but the relationship we had was mainly because I was short and he was short."
(Photo from *The Lens*, 1965)

and drummer Frank Guignon, led to gigs every other week or so. The Impalas played birthday parties, YMCA gatherings, proms, after-game dances, a local teen Coca-Cola rock bar called the Green Gorilla and even a downtown New Year's Eve bash. Sporting a two-tiered look, they wore purple shirts, skinny black ties, Edwardian coats and grey slacks for the first half of a show, then, in a nod to beach music, changed into purple surfer shirts and white Levi's.

The lead guitarist for a rival band, the Tokens, looked at Steve with admiration. "He never made you feel as though you had to measure up," says Dennis Holton, a classmate two years younger who stopped by the Impalas' rehearsals in front of Martens' garage and drank sodas with Steve. "He was always there with a helping hand or a good piece of critique. He could warm you up no matter who you were. It was a shame we didn't understand better, because of a lack of maturity, what we were really dealing with — somebody who really stood out from the crowd, big time."

Enjoying once again the prominence of membership in a band, Steve went out with girls occasionally and yearned for a relationship, but despite his musical appeal, his height disqualified him in the eyes of most prospects.

"Nobody really wanted to dance with him because he was shorter," says Phillis "Toxie" Wirtz (now Witwicki), a classmate whom Steve took to a homecoming dance and on two other dates. She agreed, not because she felt sorry for him. "Steve was a really nice guy, but he was self-conscious about his height. You could tell. I don't think he felt awkward with me, but the relationship we had was mainly because I was short and he was short."

Wirtz also was the only non-Jew in her subdivision in Morton Grove, one of the Maine East feeder communities that were considered the "wrong side of the tracks" from Park Ridge. "It was amazing how those people looked at you. It was horrible. If you were Jewish and came from Morton Grove or Niles, or just the fact that you came from Morton Grove or Niles, they thought you were from the low class."

Most Park Ridge girls, Wirtz says, saw Steve as more of a brother than a potential boyfriend.

One of those was Kathy Rogers of the Port Calm Trio. She adored the twinkle in Steve's eye and his interest in others. But she already had a boyfriend, so, instead, in long talks she became Steve's romantic confidante. Rogers recalls an afternoon the two spent sitting in her red Chevy Impala convertible while it was parked top-down in her driveway, she in the driver's seat and Steve with a guitar on his lap. "We talked about everything in the world for hours and hours as he was strumming," she says. Topics included baseball, music and girls he had crushes on. "Some of the girls who were most popular were these real tall, lanky blondes with long ponytails. We'd talk about 'What do you think of this one? What do you think of that one?' At the same time, he'd be strumming and saying, 'Think of how this would sound. Maybe you should try something like this. Or maybe this. No, wait a minute.' He'd get ideas like it was a nervous habit."

It was as if Steve, unable to attract a girlfriend, found a means of loving expression by embracing the guitar and sharing the musical possibilities that it let him explore. "It was like angel music," Rogers says. "During our conversations, he'd be picking away. It was very light. He'd think of something and say, 'Wait a minute. That sounds great.' And then on his 12-string, he would pound away and bop on the side to make a rhythm, then bring it back down to angel plucking. You got so used to it, you wouldn't even bat an eye."

Frequent audiences for such noodling were the parents of Steve's friends, including Rogers. "He'd stop by my house, and my mother would look like, 'Oh, no, another guitar in the house,' but then she heard him play. My parents couldn't believe how wonderful he was."

Twice, Steve showed up on a weekend night at the home of Willie Riser, and, aided by Riser on bongos, serenaded Riser's older sister and widowed mother in their living room. "Steve had this sparkle," says Riser's sister, Virginia Scott. "My mother, who was a Latin teacher and a woman of great warmth but had conservative musical styles, was charmed by him. He didn't seem to be self-conscious or scornful in the presence of older people. It was that seminal audience, just two women in a living room. He was so winning so early."

One of Steve's closer friends during their junior year, Les Detterbeck, became one with whom Steve spent social time instead of with a girl. Similar to Steve, Detterbeck had grown up in Chicago until his family moved to Park Ridge when he was 10. He joined Steve at solo gigs and at times was pressed into service as a second singer. "He and I double-dated a few times, but the girls were just someone that you needed to have to go out on a date," Detterbeck says. "There wasn't any special attraction (from girls) for him or me. We used to joke about it, but neither of us was too worried."

Prompted by his parents, who had joined a local Reform congregation called B'nai Jehoshua Beth Elohim, Steve found an avenue to meet a larger circle of Jewish girls than could be found at Maine East. He joined the Morton Grove chapter of AZA (Aleph Zadek Aleph), a B'nai B'rith fraternity for teenage Jewish boys sponsored by the Northwest Suburban Jewish Congregation. Beyond the religious connection, AZA was a social club that held twice-monthly, chaperoned get-togethers with Chicago-area chapters of a Jewish teen sorority called BBG (B'nai B'rith Girls) and held male-only "smokers" at which they screened stag films. To aid in assembling a quorum, Detterbeck sometimes accompanied Steve to AZA meetings, where, during their junior year, Steve was elected by his peers to serve as chapter president and, later, co-vice-president.

At the mixers with BBG, often held in the Rogers Park neighborhood, Steve didn't make many female connections. "We hated those girls," fellow classmate and AZA member Jerry Needelman says with a laugh. "We grew up with them, so we didn't want anything to do with them. Besides, we were both short, Steve a little shorter than I, so a lot of time we were competing for the same girls. When we first looked at a girl, if she was too tall, we weren't even going to talk to her."

> **He didn't seem to be self-conscious or scornful in the presence of older people. It was that seminal audience, just two women in a living room. He was so winning so early.**
> **VIRGINIA SCOTT**

As in other settings, Steve fell back on music, bringing his guitar to play familiar songs and improvise others. "He was a great presence," Needelman says. "We all wanted him to play." Another AZA member, Brad Ellis, says Steve made up a chant for the group reflecting that the teen boys had shed any pretense of reverence for the Jewish faith:

Izzy, Ikie, Jakie, Sam
We're the boys that eat no ham
"Matzo, matzo," is our cry
"Matzo, matzo," do or die

A more serious note soon emerged from Steve, however. Each spring, the regional AZA held a jamboree, and members were invited to compete in talent contests. In the spring of 1964, Sam Siegel, another of Steve's classmates and an AZA member, collaborated with Steve and six others to present a skit to mark the recent assassination of President John F. Kennedy. Each teen boy recited a portion of a Kennedy speech, and at the end, accompanying himself on guitar, Steve sang "The Summer of His Years," the hymn written by Herbert Kretzmer of BBC-TV's "That Was the Year That Was" and popularized in America in early 1964 by Connie Francis and the Chad Mitchell Trio. The somber song, with its famous line, "No one guessed that a man so blessed would perish by the gun," hearkened back to the drama of Steve's version of "Old Man River" and his synagogue singing in childhood.

Their skit snagged first place in the Morton Grove chapter and at the northwest suburban regional level, and the group headed for a citywide competition before an audience of 1,000 at McCormick Place south of downtown Chicago. But Steve had an unshakable family commitment that night, so he sang and played the song into a Webcor tape recorder and convinced a "terrified" Siegel to wield his guitar and lip-sync to the tape during the show. Without Steve in the flesh, the skit merited second or third place, Siegel says, and though it didn't win the top city honor, "everybody was really happy about it."

Electoral politics were the talk of Maine East in the late spring of 1964 and became the province of Steve and the Impalas as well. In the school's mock presidential election, bedrock Republican U.S. Sen. Barry Goldwater, touted by Hillary Rodham in student debates, won unsurprisingly over incumbent Democrat Lyndon Johnson, a reversal of the eventual national results. The 1964 presidential race also was the backdrop for the satirical Chad Mitchell Trio song "Barry's Boys," which Steve quickly worked into his repertoire.

Meanwhile, the annual student elections at Maine East took on double significance because rapid growth of the northwest suburbs had prompted construction of a high school to the south in Park Ridge. That fall, nearly half of Maine East's students were to move to brand-new Maine South High School. This meant students were to elect two sets of officers for the coming year. The Impalas played during the student-election skits in the Maine East cafeteria, with Steve leading the group in a parody of Eddie Cochran's "Summertime

He was a great presence. We all wanted him to play.
BRAD ELLIS

Blues" on behalf of the candidacy of his friend Les Detterbeck, who was running for Maine East student-body president. Detterbeck lost to another of Steve's friends, Joel Platt, but the impression left by the Impalas was indelible. "When Steve played the guitar in the cafeteria, he just blew everybody away," says classmate Tom Riesenmy.

The power of the skits and of Steve's campaigning ability was not lost on Hillary Rodham, who failed in her bid for the student-body presidency at the new Maine South. "Steve was somebody who you always wanted to be on your side because he would lead, like a pied piper, through the aisles," she says. "He would compose funny songs and lead people in singing. He was great on singalongs, even if you didn't know what he was singing, so he kept people entertained and made politics more entertaining."

With summer came more independence and exposure. Turning 16, Steve secured a driver's license and was able — with a phone book under his bottom — to drive used cars that his dad brought home from dealerships. Besides freeing him to drive to practices and help transport his Impalas mates to occasional gigs, the license let Steve take on more remote jobs than the babysitting, lawn mowing and snow shoveling he had been doing for neighbors in Warren Oval.

In Niles, he shagged golf balls at Fink's Links driving range and tuned guitars at Pearson's Music & Art Shop in the Golf Mill Shopping Center. He also delivered evening phone-in orders for the Park Ridge branch of a four-outlet chain called Broasted Chicken Royale, to which Steve brought his acoustic guitar, says Bill Travis, who worked the counter. Travis says that on slow nights when the owner was away, and while chicken, fish and fries cooked in the seven-minute pressure broasters, Steve sat on a couch in the lobby, strummed and picked guitar and made up ditties about the greasy chicken that may have later inspired his "Chicken Cordon Bleus." He came away with more than just a $2.25 hourly wage and tips because the lyrics that he liked best he wrote down in a small, spiral notebook.

When the weather turned sunny, Steve stole time from the jobs to drive east with friends to Skokie, hop the Skokie Swift train to Howard Street, transfer to the El and ride to Wrigley Field to see the Cubs. Steve habitually kept score and stayed till the end of each game, even if it was a blowout. "We were both aspiring athletes that really loved this stuff, even though we both knew we were never going to be major-leaguers," says Les Detterbeck, who sat with Steve in the $1 left-field bleachers as they talked about baseball, girls and jobs. Brad Ellis, too, along with classmates Jeff Rubin and Henry Brenghause, took in dozens of games in the left-field bleachers that summer with Steve. "I used to beat him up over it all the time. I said, 'You know, they're never going to win,' and he'd say, 'Yeah, I know.' "

Ellis says Steve maintained a running joke with a roving vendor: "Steve yelled at him, 'Hey, do you serve beer to minors?' And the guy turned around and said, 'Yeah, coal miners!' " Once, Ernie Banks, the Cubs' beloved shortstop and future Hall of Famer, hit a homer that zoomed directly toward Ellis and Steve.

> Steve was somebody who you always wanted to be on your side because he would lead, like a pied piper, through the aisles. ... He kept people entertained and made politics more entertaining.
> **HILLARY RODHAM CLINTON**

Jim Brewer, shown singing at the No Exit coffeehouse, was one of Steve's earliest in-person influences. "He'd look up with those blind eyes and say, 'Yass, yass.' He was the real thing," says Howard Berkman. Steve later incorporated in his shows Brewer's enriched lyrics to the spiritual, "I'll Fly Away."

(Photo courtesy of Sue & Brian Kozin)

"I got up to catch it, and it went right through my hands and landed on my seat and bounced to a guy a couple rows behind me," Ellis says. "I was heartbroken, but I'll never forget the look Steve gave me, like 'You incompetent so-and-so. You're supposed to have good hands!' He never said anything. It was just the look." Such quips and mugging drew friends to Steve's side, Ellis says. "People just naturally gravitated to him. He was an electric, magnetic personality."

Occasionally that summer, the freedom that a car provided had a price. Detterbeck and Steve pulled up at the North Side branch of Moishe Pippic's, a hole-in-the-wall eatery known for its combo of Vienna hot dogs and French fries for just 30 cents. "We went in and both ordered a hot dog and fries," Detterbeck says, "and we could see in the back, and the guy who was working had to go get fries and put 'em in the deep fryer. He whipped out his thing and took a pee on the box of fries, and then he proceeded to pick them up and put 'em in the deep fryer." Of course, the two didn't eat the fries. "But from that day forward, if there were French fries on his plate, Steve would break out in hives. You would see the bumps."

In nearby Evanston, the 65-seat No Exit coffeehouse, which Howard Berkman had introduced to Steve, also became a destination. Steve appreciated its name, a reference to hell and to the existential play by Jean-Paul Sartre, and its clever juxtaposition with a bookstore across the street by the name of Great Expectations (both a Charles Dickens novel and a literary allusion to heaven). "The coffeehouse was open at night, and the bookstore was open during the day, and most people didn't get the joke," says owner Joe Moore, who regularly hired Steve for pass-the-hat shows. "He was so polished, it was almost a turn-off because he was too young to be authentic," Moore says. "It didn't seem right for a kid not to be nervous, to have presence, to put on the big finish, wave the guitar around and so forth, shaking the last note out of the guitar, and his voice, the whole routine. And here was a 16-year-old kid doing it."

At the Exit, as it was known, Steve met a nearly blind African-American guitarist who inspired and shaped his later performance style — bluesman Jim Brewer. Originally from Brookhaven, Mississippi, Brewer had honed his act at the South Side's famed, rag-tag Maxwell Street Market. Discovered there by a No Exit customer, Brewer passed an audition at the coffeehouse and became the house regular on Wednesday nights, each week making his way or being driven from his South Side apartment to the far North Side. "We all just loved that guy," says Howard Berkman. "He'd look up with those blind eyes and say, 'Yass, yass.' He was the real thing. Learning about Jim was learning about what's really going down. That's how Jim would impress you, with story songs about real people doing stupid things. It wasn't all cut and dried like white music."

Brewer's repertoire ranged from "Poor Kelly Blues," whose protagonist shot and killed his "mean mistreater" of a wife, to standards such as "St. James Infirmary," "Nobody Knows You When You're Down and Out" and "Goin' to Chicago Blues." But it was an Alfred E. Brumley hymn about the afterlife called "I'll Fly Away" that became Brewer's signature tune. When Moore, the No Exit's

owner, wanted Brewer to end his set, he called out, "Fly away, Jim, fly away," and Brewer closed with the song. Years later, "I'll Fly Away" became a crucial part of Steve's act. Like Brewer, Steve played it on slide guitar and sang the words in a near-whisper, complete with a double-time verse in the middle that Brewer himself had written.

Steve also played Sunday afternoon open-mike sessions at the Fickle Pickle, a coffee-and-pastries venue across Chicago's hip Rush Street from the Gate of Horn, which had been lionized as the setting for a popular 1961 live LP by Bob Gibson and Hamilton Camp. Greg Trafidlo, a fellow Fickle Pickle performer, says that not only did Steve hone his craft there, but he also rubbed shoulders with its headliners, including Josh White, as well as with acts that wandered over from the Gate, such as Chad Mitchell, the Limeliters and Judy Henske. "That," Trafidlo says, "was a real plus."

As Steve began his senior year in the fall of 1964, Maine East High shrank from 4,100 students to a more manageable group of 2,600 enrollees, many of them former social also-rans in the eyes of the academically and athletically stronger students from Park Ridge at the new Maine South. Those torn away from friends by the move mourned the split, but a trimmer enrollment enhanced the Maine East school spirit and let Steve shine even more brightly.

Surprising no one, the standardized tests for college resulted in top marks for Steve, who earned a nearly perfect ACT score and later membership in the National Honor Society. He often helped students with homework, in one case pilfering and sharing the answers to a major chemistry test. But of more importance to Steve than academics that fall was sports.

As a radio announcer, he had been restricted to observing games on the sidelines in street clothes. Going into his senior year, however, he shed the microphone and applied for and became manager of the school's football team, an incongruous position. As lineman and honorary captain Herb Johnson puts it, "Here's this 5-foot-2 Jewish guy who you could never picture in gym shorts and a shirt, running around with buckets and towels and footballs as the manager. But he liked it so much."

Steve, far right in front row, poses for the 1965 Maine East High yearbook in his letterman jacket, earned for serving as manager (equipment assistant) for the school's 1964 football team. Jim Freitag, fourth from right in middle row, figured in Steve's life several years later. Below, Steve helps coach Robert Schildgen on the field. (Photos for *The Lens* (above) and *The Pioneer* by Steve Holton)

Proudly displaying his electric guitar, Steve gathers in 1965 around a vintage car in the Maine East parking lot with 10 classmates, including Howard Primer (left, pointing), Joel Platt (in passenger seat, with trumpet), Ralph Furmanski (above Platt), Les Detterbeck (in driver's seat, next to Platt), Jay Peterson (sitting on car, with trumpet) and Bill Blodgett (next to Steve).

(Photo by Steve Holton, for *The Lens*)

Decimated by the departure of its star players to Maine South and fielding a squad with 18 boys who had never played organized football, the Maine East Blue Demons finished last in the conference and won just one of eight games. Moreover, the coach, Robert Schildgen, was a stern, Marine-like taskmaster who chewed out Steve for staying in his advanced-placement biology class at the end of the school day instead of skipping it for practices. The manager's job — hauling water, sweeping the workout area, keeping records and tracking equipment — was essentially thankless.

Still, the job netted Steve the perks (if not the status) of an athlete, including a coveted letterman's jacket, reminiscent of the social athletic club jackets from his days in Albany Park. "He probably wore that letter jacket every minute after he got it," says classmate Katie Webb (now Hartwell). Brad Ellis, manager for the basketball team, says that he and Steve joked about the "MGR" qualifier on their jackets. "When anybody asked, we said it stood for Maine's Greatest Runner."

The football manager's job also threw Steve into contact with the team's rowdy players, many of whom became close friends and appealed to his warmth and earthiness. Each athlete had a nickname based on initials or family connections (JL for Jeff Lind, CH for Herb Johnson's dad's name, Padelick for Chuck Branick's stepdad's name), abbreviations (Potts for Bob Pottinger) or other crude characteristics (Chicken Man for delivery driver Dave Spaulding, Baldy for Dennis Scharlau, Pork Chop for Tom Heston). Steve's moniker, originated by Lind and adopted by the others, was less innocent — the Little Hebe. It wasn't intended as a religious slur, says Pottinger. "None of us was the slightest bit religious in any way," he says, "and if Jeff hadn't called him Little Hebe, it would never have crossed my mind that he was Jewish. That wasn't an issue at all, zero. I don't think Steve liked it, but he bore it with fortitude."

As typical of football players, this was not a sedate bunch. Off the field, they drank beer at each other's houses or drove around the suburbs getting, as Lind puts it, "into one predicament after another." The musician of the gang, Steve brought along and played his guitar. But while engaging in the group's shenanigans — shaving each other's heads, cutting classes to join a minuscule crowd at a Cubs weekday game, racing cars and thrusting their rear ends out the side windows to "moon" passers-by — he was more follower than leader.

Their gatherings, in the basements of their parents' split-level homes, were unlike the tame, chaperoned, snacks-and-soda, "American Bandstand" style dance parties they had enjoyed a few years prior. "It was always a big deal about who was responsible for getting the beer, and where was the party going to be," says Chuck Branick. "Usually, somebody's parents were on vacation, usually there was alcohol and a band involved, and usually there was a certain amount of riotous behavior the parents wouldn't allow. It was some guy who's a junior thinking he can drink a lot of beers, and he's on his third one, and he pukes all over himself. Or somebody drives his car through the neighbor's bushes or throws somebody into the pool."

Steve, says Branick, "wasn't a goody two-shoes, was certainly willing to test the envelope," and Steve's house on Warren Oval often was the setting. "His parents went away enough times," Johnson says. "Steve was very gracious, because if you invite a lot of kids that age, things can go wrong, but nothing ever did at his house. He'd go through the house, playing guitar for people in the basement, then go to the living room and do the same thing. We always respected the house because we knew Steve's parents. These parties weren't 20 guys coming over, smoking cigars and throwing beer cans. They were, 'Hey, bring a girl. We can drink some beer. You can make out on the couch.' "

Fueling the parties were Steve's parents. "His dad let us drink," Lind says. "The beer was in the refrigerator in the laundry room." At other times, when the party had been held at another house and Steve's friends were dropping him off late at night, they came inside to the Goodmans' kitchen, where Bud, Minnette and Minnette's mom, "Grandma Mary," shared lox and bagels.

Understandably, the football gang liked Bud and Minnette, who treated them with respect. "It was nice to go over to somebody's house where you know you probably did things wrong, smashed up the car, spilled beer or got caught having a party at your house, but you were still treated nice," Johnson says. "They were warm people — friendly, kind, fun people to be around," says Branick. "They took an interest in what was going on, the issues kids face." Bud's long work hours, until 9 p.m. at Spradlin Chevrolet in Park Ridge, made an impression on the group, as did Minnette's beauty and sensitivity. "She always cared about the things we did and the things that we were open enough to talk to her about," Johnson says. "When she walked into the room, we didn't have to worry that 'Oh, my God, here's Steve's mom. Let's shut up. We can't

These parties weren't 20 guys coming over, smoking cigars and throwing beer cans. They were, 'Hey, bring a girl. We can drink some beer. You can make out on the couch.'
HERB JOHNSON

talk about this.' Not that she was a surrogate mom, but she listened a lot more than most of our parents, and she knew the impact a kind word would have."

Bud — "Everybody referred to Steve's dad as Bud. Nobody called him Mr. Goodman," says Branick — had a fireplug physique and a mischievous, fun-loving bent that let Steve's friends see him as a "normal guy." It was a disposition that came out in jovial, late-night advice that Bud had for Steve's friend Willie Riser, an avid Christian at the time.

"You know, you're a little fixated on this crucifixion stuff," Bud told Riser with a chuckle. "You don't have to dwell on the nails and hands and feet and how the soldiers pierced his side and all this suffering and sorrow and sad stuff. Sure, it's sad. A lot of people get murdered. We lost 6 million of 'em over there. But even with what Hitler has done to us, you gotta get up and go to work. The real wisdom is just to seize every day and be a good human being, and the afterlife will take care of itself. If there is one, it'll be fine. Just act as an ethical human being right now."

Ethics naturally came into play in some of the gang's escapades. One night, Johnson and Steve drove the group in two cars to a tiny eatery in the northeast suburb of Evanston. A second bunch of guys there gave Steve's group a funny look, and when Steve's group left the restaurant and drove away along an arterial, the second bunch followed. Johnson decided to stop his car, Tom Heston opened a back door to get out, and the second bunch sped forward, ripped the door off Johnson's car, screeched to a halt, zoomed back in reverse, rammed the front grille of Johnson's car, then floored it down the road.

Jeff Lind, in the back of Steve's car, shouted, "Let's go get 'em!"

But Steve, his hands in the 10-and-2 position on the steering wheel, poked along at 35 mph.

"Goodman, get on the goddamn gas, would ya?" Lind screamed. "Move!"

"JL," Steve said, "I'm not gonna speed!"

"Fuck you! Let's get this guy."

The gang eventually caught up with the second bunch, not through a chase but by turning in the car's license number at an Evanston police station.

Another night, a half dozen members of the football gang left a pizza parlor, drove to Maine South and spray-painted the new school with "Maine East Rules," an act that later prompted a retaliatory burning of a Maine South emblem on the Maine East football field. "The biggest joke wasn't the vandalism, but that Steve Goodman was along when it was done," Johnson says. The whole time, Steve, a "nervous wreck," sputtered, "Where are we going? We're doing what? I'm not sure we can do that."

"Steve was right there with us, and a lot of times he didn't want to because he knew that we were up to something," Lind says. "He would say, 'Ohhh, why am I with you guys?' "

The answer, of course, was obvious. "Steve tempered things," Johnson says. "He was always under control. He was stabilizing. He was focused. He was the sense of reason. He was quiet. We weren't oddities to him. We didn't do drugs

Even with what Hitler has done to us, you gotta get up and go to work. The real wisdom is just to seize every day and be a good human being, and the afterlife will take care of itself.
JOSEPH 'BUD' GOODMAN

or carry guns. We were fun guys, so he liked being around us. He just wasn't the wild and crazy drinking hooligans we were."

Nevertheless, the group's pranks influenced Steve to initiate some of his own. One afternoon, after Roger Miller's "Chug-a-Lug" topped the national radio charts in September 1964, Steve walked the hallways of Maine East with his guitar, singing the paean to teenage alcohol binges while leading a long line of students who rhythmically shook gravel-filled, empty beer cans.

Later, as a lark on an afternoon during the cold of winter, in the honors study hall that was linked to his AP biology class, Steve opened a rear window and climbed out onto a narrow, snow-covered, second-floor ledge. "As soon as he stepped out there," says classmate Elliott Yablun, "we slammed the window shut, locked it and threw down the shade." Steve started banging on the window, teacher Leila Baas walked in, heard the ruckus and discovered it was Steve when she lifted the shade and opened the window to let him back in. The stunt became notorious school-wide, and years later Steve told the self-deprecating story to friends, saying that while out on the ledge he felt like the Human Fly.

"The remarkable thing was that not only was Steve not put on probation, but none of us was," says classmate Roy Ritzmann. "They didn't even take the honor study hall away because he talked his and our way out of it by a fast-thinking mix of contrition and reason, with the silver tongue that only Steve had. 'We certainly deserved to lose this. You trusted us.' It was total bullshit. The guy could sell ice cubes to Eskimos."

His senior year reflected Steve's serious side as well. Elected by his class to serve on Student Council, he helped pass a long-sought proposal to install in the school's athletic trophy room a fruit dispenser to counter the school's ubiquitous candy machines. Along the way, his "radiant" demeanor left a deep impression with at least one other council member. The academically gifted but shy Sue Moestue, appointed to the council by the faculty, says Steve warmly welcomed and sat next to her during the weekly sessions. His simple gestures — smiling, saying hello and talking with her — "made that experience less painful," Moestue says. "It went beyond gregarious. There was an underscore of kindness. I did not see myself reflected as an outsider from him, and he was the only one. The others just ignored me."

Steve tried not to ignore academics that year, becoming one of 38 Maine East senior winners of an Illinois State Scholarship. Also, he took first place in a U.S. Constitution contest sponsored by the Park Ridge post of the American Legion, besting 65 students on an objective test and 10 finalists in a 15-minute oral exam consisting of five questions posed by a panel of seven Legionnaires. The prize was an expense-paid, two-week "history on wheels" trip to Gettysburg, Williamsburg, Washington, D.C., and Boston, plus $75 spending money, to take place the coming summer with Maine South students. [8] Steve also entered a mid-year, district-wide speech contest in nearby Elmwood Park, competing in the category of after-dinner speaking.

The school's musicals lured Steve back to the stage in his senior year. Besides

Herb Johnson, one of the football-team "hooligans" Steve hung out with, says Steve was a stabilizer: "He was focused. He was the sense of reason."
(Photo from *The Lens*, 1965)

8: Throughout the trip, Steve played guitar, including the novelty hit "Jolly Green Giant," recalls classmate Judith Maute. His roommate for the excursion, classmate John Heenan, adds, "Neither of us got any sleep on the trip because we would stay up all night trying to stump Steve with a song that he couldn't play and sing note for note, chapter and verse. I had considered myself an authority on all types of music, but I never could come up with a song, no matter how obscure, or what genre, that Steve didn't know all the parts and all the words."

Steve snags a kiss and strums his acoustic guitar during rehearsals for Maine East's spring 1965 variety show, "Music to Fight By."

(Photos from Mainspring '64 program courtesy Barb Pritchard Robbins)

Forming a sexually tinged circle with his left forefinger, Steve plays a bootlegger in the 1965 Maine East variety show.

(Photo by Steve Holton for *The Lens*)

singing in the concert choir for the spring production of the well-known "Carousel," he anchored and helped write that year's V-show as its assistant student director. The original revue, "Music to Fight By," was a time-travel farce exploring the battle of the sexes in five stages, from cave life in 1000 B.C. to election of the first female U.S. president. In skits that emphasized comedy, Steve appeared as a page in King Arthur's court, a Roaring Twenties gangster drinking Seagram's 7 whiskey and a soloist singing the signature tune of the famed African-American vaudevillian Bert Williams, "Nobody." Its melancholy litany — "Who soothes my thumping, bumping brain? ... Who says, 'Come in and have a beer'? ... Who says, 'Look at that handsome man?' ... Who hands to me a glowing kiss?" — was answered at every turn by the song's one-word title. "Steve was on an empty stage," says Art Curtis, "and he did it very well."

Steve's immersion in the persona of a black entertainer was not an anomaly. On weekend nights about twice a month for more than a year, he and close Jewish friend Howard Primer had sneaked away to a section of Chicago that many of their suburban classmates had never experienced, to partake in an activity that would have shocked everyone they knew. On these evenings, the two told their parents they were going to one of the neighborhood hangouts — Booby's drive-in on Milwaukee Avenue or Big Boy's burgers on Dempster Street. Instead, however, at Steve's behest, they drove 15 to 20 miles to the South Side to see, hear, smell, taste and devour the music and atmosphere of the renowned Regal Theater as well as dozens of tiny, cramped and stuffy blues clubs. "If the kids in our school had known what we were doing, they would have thought we were absolutely crazy," Primer says, "and we went every chance we got."

With names such as Peppers and the Blue Flame, the clubs were the exclusive hangouts for adult African-Americans, but Steve and Primer, underage and white, were allowed entrée, and for both of them the clubs became night school. The teachers were Muddy Waters, Howlin' Wolf and Willie Dixon, unknowns to the white mainstream, as well as black acts such as the Miracles with Smokey

Robinson, the Temptations and B.B. King, who was emerging from obscurity thanks to a live LP recorded in November 1964 at the Regal. (Twenty-five blocks north of the Regal on South Michigan Avenue, many of these entertainers were being launched on vinyl in legendary Studio A of Chess Records.)

Primer, who lived near Steve in Morton Grove, teamed with him partly because they both had grown up Jewish and shared an appreciation for musical lyricism. Plus, both generally were dateless. "Neither of us had girlfriends, and neither of us wanted to date somebody just for the sake of dating somebody," Primer says, "so we joked about the fact that we were each other's date."

Showy acts at the Regal left a deep impression on Steve, who referenced them in later interviews and included their songs (notably "My Girl" by the Temptations, "La La Means I Love You" by the Delfonics and what he called "that 'Soul Train' stuff") in future performances. But it was the musicians in the hole-in-the-wall corner clubs that Primer says were seminal to Steve's blues-oriented songwriting and stage persona as an adult.

Getting to the clubs was no easy feat. Steve usually drove one of the used cars from his dad's lot, the frigid night air frosting the windshield. "We were driving cars of the 1950s, it'd be 20 below, and the defrosters didn't work, so we could only look through little peepholes, and our side windows would be open to get air into the car," Primer says. "The radio would be blaring loud because it was never very good, and Steve was a terrible driver. He wasn't paying attention because we were listening to AM music, and he was in a conversation, and the driving was incidental. It was always a disaster, but it was a fun time." [9]

Steve had the clubs' locations down, and, from his record collection and listening to the radio, he knew which performer he wanted to see at each one. So as he careened through the back streets of dilapidated walk-ups, the two never got lost. "We'd park and walk to the door, little Steve would joke and handle his way in, and everybody would laugh at us and welcome us because we were the odd white people," he says. "It was sort of refreshing for them to see these preppy kids from the North Side coming in and being a part of that." The air inside was anything but refreshing, however. "It would smell just terrible, the smoking, the beer and everything else," Primer says. "Winter or summer, the place would always be stuffy. But it would be packed with 50 to 60 people — men, women, some together, some not together, some drinking heavily, some just there for the music — and there would always be somebody playing up front, with no amplifiers, sometimes with a microphone, sometimes not."

The two sat at tiny tables, and while Steve joked with others, Primer stayed quiet. Steve also smoked heavily and drank beer, while Primer refrained. "Steve was much more comfortable getting into the dynamics of the culture," he says. If Steve's academic performance at Maine East was erratic, he was wholeheartedly studious at the blues clubs, absorbing lyrics and learning guitar chords. "He'd sit there staring and fingering an invisible guitar," Primer says. "His left hand would be in the air, and his fingers would be moving, and his right hand would be moving, and then he'd be jotting words down on napkins." On the

Howard Primer, Steve's cohort in trolling Chicago blues clubs.
(Photo from *The Lens*, 1965)

9: An older Steve endured jabs about his lack of ability behind a steering wheel. "The rumor is that you shouldn't let me drive," he said on "Austin City Limits" on Sept. 8, 1977. "I haven't had an attention span in so long, it's just hard to do it." But at times his poor driving had a bright side. Jim Post says that after a 1970s show at Amazingrace in Evanston, Steve backed his car into the front of another. He wrote a note ("Hi, my name is Steve Goodman. I backed into your car. Sorry. Here's my phone number.") and put it under the windshield wiper. The next day, Steve's phone rang. "Are you Steve Goodman?" "Yeah." "*The* Steve Goodman?" "Yeah." "You play the guitar and sing songs?" "Yeah, why?" "You backed into my car." "Oh, yeah, man, I'm really sorry. I'll take care of it." "Oh, no, no. I'm not gonna take that scratch out of my car, but if you'll come over and play guitar with my kid, we'll call it even." The deal was struck. "You gotta realize," Post says, "he was God in Chicago."

way back home, Primer drove while Steve cradled his guitar and played the songs he had just learned.

Primer, who grew up seeing his parents lock their car doors when driving through black neighborhoods, says the recurring jaunts to the blues clubs galvanized him politically. "This very deep immersion was my introduction to the depths of society," he says. "For me, the lyrics were poetry, they had a message, and I loved the message. The blues music brought me into the sorrows of being black, of being Negroes and of racism that I didn't know existed. I feel that everything thereafter that changed my life started there." Primer later marched with Martin Luther King Jr. in Birmingham and worked for Robert Kennedy's presidential campaign. He believes the South Side trips were similarly profound for Steve.

> All the way home we were talking about how shallow our lives were, how much we regretted our lack of understanding what the real world was all about. Of course, we then went back to our lily-white suburban high school.
> **HOWARD PRIMER**

"I was the only person he would ever tell what was going on in this part of his life," Primer says. "We knew our folks would kill us if they found out. But he had a hunger to be near that music, and I had a hunger to learn about it as well. All of everything we both became came out of those nights — sitting in those clubs with the only two white faces in the crowd and just grooving into the rhythm of R&B and listening to the tunes and lyrics, finding ourselves lost in the sorrow associated with it." One night, the two were emotionally overwhelmed by the powerful performance of a female singer. "She had Steve and I both crying, and all the way home we were talking about how shallow our lives were, how much we regretted our lack of understanding what the real world was all about. Of course, we then went back to our lily-white suburban high school, and it seemed so superficial."

During spring vacation of senior year, Steve took a longer trip with a much different purpose. He was the only Jew among 80 Maine East and Maine South seniors to travel in two chartered buses to Miami for a week of spiritual gatherings and fun on the beach sponsored by a Christian group called Young Life.

Primer, who was drawn to philosophical conversations, had led Steve to join Young Life, and during their senior year Steve served improbably as its president. The position meant that he presided over weekly meetings on Tuesday evenings that drew 20 to 40 students and were held in the living rooms of members. The purpose of the meetings "was simply to help kids get a fresh glimpse of who Jesus Christ was, and so we didn't talk about church much. We just talked about Him," says staff leader Doug Barram.

Steve, Barram says, was "an absolute delight," typically opening meetings by standing up, brandishing a toilet plunger and announcing, Ed McMahon-style, "Heeere's Doug!" quickly followed by "Don't believe a damn word he says." The meetings proceeded with skits, singing and a message, the air thick and blue with cigarette smoke. Barram loved the off-the-wall tone of Steve's introductions. "It told me that Steve, as a boy of Jewish heritage, was respectful of me as a friend and Christian. He knew well how much I also enjoyed and respected him. He understood that our message was not about Christianity the religion, but rather about Jesus Christ."

The message of the one-week Young Life trip to Miami, however, was more social than serious, particularly as it reunited a class that had been split apart a year prior by the opening of Maine South. "There were no religious overtones on that trip whatever," says classmate Bill MacKay. "It was strictly an excuse to get out of the state of Illinois and party." The life of the party on the 27-hour bus ride each way was Steve, who was the only one to bring a guitar and who played folk songs such as "500 Miles" seemingly continuously — a feat rivaled in the collective memory only by a handstand stunt on a skateboard down a freeway off-ramp by classmate Gary Ryan during a bus breakdown in Nashville. "He was like a jukebox," Ryan says of Steve. "He'd hit two or three notes of a song and be right there automatically."

In rare moments on the bus when he wasn't playing guitar, Steve talked with classmate and Saharas guitarist Tom Griesemer and Griesemer's girlfriend (and future wife) Jackie Anderson about religion. "It was not proselytizing," says Griesemer. "It was more question-answer." Anderson says Steve was genuinely interested in Christianity, asking her, "Why is this important to you? What does it mean to you? What does it do for you? How's it benefit you?" She says Steve also was shocked to learn that Christians studied the Old Testament of the Bible, which is the basis for the Jewish faith. "Why do you learn that stuff?" he asked her. "It was incredibly gutsy for Steve to come on the trip, because he knew he was going to hear evangelical messages every night. But he really was a seeker of truth. He wasn't into 'I'm right, and you're wrong.' He wanted to know."

> **It was incredibly gutsy for Steve to come on the trip, because he knew he was going to hear evangelical messages every night. But he really was a seeker of truth.**
> **JACKIE ANDERSON**

Upon reaching Miami, the chaperoned group stayed in the inexpensive six-floor Biltmore Terrace Hotel. Rooming with Les Detterbeck, Steve joined in the one-hour morning and evening fellowship sessions. But the seniors also had a lot of free time, and they swam in the hotel pool, drove rented mopeds along the strip and walked barefoot on the beach, unwittingly sunburning their feet. Steve spent time smoking English Oval cigarettes while shooting pool in the hotel lounge with classmate Paul Niesen, drinking beer that had been iced in the bathtub of MacKay's hotel room and playing his guitar at evening campfires on the beach.

It's also possible that Steve lost his virginity on the trip. "Steve was into women by then," says Bill MacKay. "The guys were on one floor of the hotel, and the girls were on another floor, and the chaperones were strict about not having girls in guys' rooms and vice versa. So that just forced us outside, and the beach was the place to be. We yanked blankets off the hotel beds at night and took them down to the beach. That's where we bedded the girls down, getting sand in places you really don't want to have sand." Nearly two decades later, Steve co-wrote and performed an uptempo beach song with the same theme: "Don't Get Sand in It."

After his return from Miami, and as the end of the school year approached, Steve and the Impalas again came to the aid of a Maine East student election campaign. At an all-school assembly, they performed on behalf of secretary

Steve (right photo) leads the Impalas in a spring 1965 Maine East cafeteria show while campaigning for student-body secretary candidate Nancy Telesnicki, then (left) leads students in a parade on behalf of Telesnicki, who won her race.
(Photos by Steve Holton for *The Lens*)

candidate Nancy Telesnicki, who eventually won the vote. Steve led students in a continuation of the rally as they carried "Vote for Nancy" and "Nancy Will Help Us" signs around the school gym.

The Impalas' stature rose further when they won a Saturday-night "battle of the bands" contest at the Lincoln Junior High gym in Park Ridge. The prize was a two-hour recording session at a "two-bit," two-microphone studio in the rec room of the promoter's nearby house, resulting in what became Steve's second recording (after "Old Man River"), a 45-rpm single of two songs: the traditional "House of the Rising Sun," a hit for the Animals in the summer of 1964, backed by a hornless version of "Shotgun," which Junior Walker and the All-Stars charted in early 1965. The record, which survives today, includes a gospel-tinged, high harmony vocal by Steve on "Rising Sun."

"We all had aspirations that the recording session was going to be a break-through and we were going to move on to the next level, but that obviously never happened," says lead guitarist Kent Cerrone. The promoter pressed just six copies of the record and gave them to the band. "We thought we'd run around with the 45 and see if we could get somebody interested in it and get a contract going," says drummer Frank Guignon, "but we played it for different people, and more or less they had a good laugh at it. It never went anywhere."

Shortly afterward came two senior proms, for Maine East and Maine South, and while Steve had no regular girlfriend, he squired a girl to each. On his Maine South prom date, Steve and Vicki Marti, singer/guitarist in the Port Calm Trio, spent time on a boat on Lake Michigan. Though Marti regarded Steve as more of a brother, at one point he sweetly reached over and held her hand. Though it was a romantic gesture, all Marti could think of was the small size of his hands. "He played a huge, 12-string guitar, but his hands were smaller than mine, and I was thinking, 'How can he play so well?' "

To the Maine East prom at a country club in nearby Wheeling, Steve took Katie Webb, who wore flats to better view his "cute brown eyes" while dancing and not to "tower over him too much" at 5-foot-4. She accompanied Steve on a four-hour class trip by train early the next morning to a ski resort in Galena, near the Illinois/Iowa state line. When the 200 couples lined up for a ski-lift ride over the snowless Chestnut Hill overlooking the Mississippi River, the lewd joke was about which couple would be number 69 to hop onto the lift. It turned out to be Steve and Katie.

One night later, Steve underscored such sexual silliness onstage at the 1965 Maine East commencement ceremony, which honored 610 graduates, 355 of whom were college-bound. Accepting his diploma with one hand, Steve signaled the audience with the other by making a circle with his forefinger and thumb. It was a common risqué gesture among boys, and whoever saw it was supposed to put a finger in the hole. "Steve kept it very subtle down at his side," says Charlotte Webb, then a junior, "but everybody who knew him caught on. It was a perfect stage opportunity."

Given his packed and varied years at Maine East, it wasn't surprising that out of 42 "senior superlative awards" voted on by his class, Steve won three ("class wit," "best musician" and "most versatile") and tied for two others (with Howard Primer for "best gift of gab" and with Herb Johnson for "most likely to be remembered"). His "last will" in *The Pioneer* was a droll nod to the window-lockout stunt and his musicianship: "I, Steve Goodman, being of sound body and demented mind, will to all aspiring physics students one window ledge strewn with broken guitar strings."

For all of Steve's facetiousness, however, life for him still boiled down to values of integrity and decency. Art Curtis discovered this when he read what Steve inscribed in his edition of *The Lens* yearbook: "It will be very easy for me to tell you how I feel, 'cause I mean it. You have to be one of the nicest guys I have ever met. You never let your great mental capacity use itself to belittle other people. It is a pleasure to have met a fellow who is smart enough to be nice." In signing it, though, Steve couldn't resist a final opportunity for self-deprecation: "Best of luck always, Steve (WINDOW-LEDGE) Goodman." [10]

Herb Johnson perhaps best captures Steve's appeal at the close of his high-school years: "He was just infectious. He wasn't the isolated guy who happened to play the guitar and that was his clique. The people he affected were so different. It wasn't like one class of people. The entire world was his clique."

While college was on the horizon, music was on his mind and in his heart. So where was that heart headed? A clue lay in *The Pioneer*, which in Steve's senior year ran an article on "one of the nation's most intriguing sections, Old Town." The story mentioned the district's offbeat pawnshops, art houses and espresso cafés. "At several of these coffeehouses," the article said, "one can hear original poetry and songs recited and perhaps join in the entertainment himself." ♪

**You have to be one of the nicest guys I have ever met. You never let your great mental capacity use itself to belittle other people.
STEVE GOODMAN**

10: Steve's yearbook inscriptions also could be crass. Three years before Dick Martin of TV's "Laugh-In" cracked endless variations on the joke, Steve wrote in former band mate Richard Stock's edition of *The Lens*: "Best of luck to a great guy, and may the bluebird of happiness crap all over your college career and your future life."

On Sept. 24, 1967, at the opening of fall quarter at idyllic Lake Forest College, Steve Goodman — in white shirt and tie and sporting a mustache and the beginning of a beard — serenades male students in front of the student union, with Lily Reid Holt Memorial Chapel in the distance. To Steve's left are, from left, Jon Rose, Neil Tolciss and Steve Cantor.

(Photo by Ron Pownall)

'He was a fireball of energy – he just exuded happiness'

T om Paxton's wanderlust was calling:

If you see me passing by,
and you sit and you wonder why
and you wish that you were a rambler, too

Nail your shoes to the kitchen floor
lace 'em up and bar the door
Thank your stars for the roof that's over you [1]

A Chicago native, Paxton achieved his singing and songwriting reputation in New York City by way of Oklahoma. So as these closing words to his "I Can't Help but Wonder (Where I'm Bound)" spilled out in Steve Goodman's performances during the summer of 1965, they were saturated with irony. Despite their literal advice to stay put, this and other Paxton tunes, popularized by the Kingston Trio and Peter, Paul & Mary, carried a tone that encouraged youths — including college-bound high-school graduates like Steve — to ramble, to roam, to find themselves. Like the song's "do as I say, not as I do" protagonist, Steve was headed out the door, although not down an uncertain road but to the mammoth University of Illinois and a conventional, professional path designed to help him build a roof over his head.

Still, given his ardor for music, Steve sensed that his eventual destination lay elsewhere. For the indefinite future, his was to be a restless quest.

To Jane Kamman (now Galler), the Paxton song, particularly the "nail your shoes to the kitchen floor" line, was the best in Steve's repertoire. "It was my absolute favorite," says Steve's first real girlfriend, who shared his personal journey firsthand that summer. Two years younger and three grade levels lower than Steve at Maine East, Kamman had admired his performances at pep rallies and student-election skits.

Once, the gregarious girl had told him, "I loved hearing you play, it was wonderful," and thereafter they had waved "hi" to each other when they passed in the halls. But the two soon met more memorably in a way neither probably would have chosen, while Steve was joyriding in Park Ridge with his football-

I loved hearing you play,
it was wonderful.
JANE KAMMAN

1: The final verse of "I Can't Help but Wonder (Where I'm Bound)" by Tom Paxton, copyright 1963, Cherry Lane Music, is reprinted by permission.

Jane Kamman, shown in 1965, found Steve's shows "magnetic." (Photo from The Lens)

2: Staples of Steve's repertoire at the Y Coffeehouse included "Chicago Cops," a song from the "Gibson & Camp at the Gate of Horn" LP that skewered police who solicited payoffs from speeding motorists. Filling out Steve's Y sets, which continued for three years, were "Summertime," Tom Paxton's "Daily News," about the famed New York tabloid's right-wing bias, and jokes about Mayor Richard Daley. The Y's assistant manager, Mark Nowakowski, recalls Steve's fledgling beard ("a young person's sort of fuzzy thing, like an undernourished caterpillar") and Steve's admonition to "Be kind to your waiter, because if you don't remember him, he's going to remember you."

team buddies six blocks from the high school along Birch Lane, where Jane lived.

"I was walking home, and here comes this car whizzing by with arms and butts all over the place, and there's this big fanny hanging out of the window of the car," Kamman says. "I look over, my mouth is like, 'Oh, my God!' And then the fanny goes down, and a little head pops up, and it was Steve Goodman. I recognized him, and he recognized me, and I laughed so hard the rest of the way home." The next day, at school, Steve told her, "I am so sorry, I'm so embarrassed. We were just out having fun, mooning people." "I was just a dumb freshman," she says with a laugh. "I didn't even know what mooning was. But from then on, it was more than hi."

The pretty, petite teen with long bangs and a shoulder-length bob hung out with Steve and others when he played guitar and sang on the steps of the Maine East gym. A fledgling guitarist herself and an admirer of Joan Baez and the Beatles' George Harrison, Kamman learned Goebel Reeves' "Hobo's Lullaby" and other folk songs from Steve during those after-school sessions. Their shared musical interest and their height — she, too, was 5-foot-2 — made them a good match. That summer, Steve asked Kamman to accompany him to Chicago coffeehouses such as the Loft in Old Town, the Y Coffeehouse next to Wright Junior College on the northwest side and the teen hangout on Sheridan Road called It's Here, where he had begun to play at unpaid "open mike" sessions. [2] "I can't believe my mom would let me go in a car downtown," Kamman says, "but she did."

In the car, the constant topic was music. Steve asked what she thought of songs he'd learned, and they sang "all the way downtown." At the teen clubs, the two sipped fancy coffees with whipped cream while waiting for Steve's turn to perform. "It was like being with a star," Kamman says.

"He was magnetic, and he had the most beautiful brown eyes. He could do the whole finger-pickin' thing, play the melody and the chords behind it all at the same time. I was infatuated with how great he could play, and he wasn't afraid to get up and do it. He'd talk to the audience, the songs he sang were wonderful, and the whole room came alive. It wasn't that he had a great voice — it was a bit gravelly, soulful, earthy — but he just had such enthusiasm, and he didn't bore people like a lot of those guys in those shows at that time. They'd do these long ballads, and it's like, 'C'mon.' But when Steve got up there, there was electricity and excitement, and everybody had a great time. He was wonderful, he was fabulous, I was with him, and it was like, 'Oh, my gosh, I'm on cloud nine.' It was awesome."

One song Steve performed that Kamman says "brought down the house" wherever he played was "The Kretchma," a mock Russian tune by Gene Raskin (who later wrote "Those Were the Days") that Steve had learned from a 1959 recording by Theodore Bikel played on WFMT's "Midnight Special." Its racy verses were set-ups for an upbeat "Hi di di" sing-along line and a catchy chorus: "Come to the Kretchma, that's where you'll catch ma (or more), making whoopee every night." The sentiment wasn't lost on Steve, who had romance on his mind with Kamman, dating her all summer and even bringing her home to meet his parents. "He was a great kisser," she allows. But Kamman wasn't similarly inclined.

For one thing, Kamman was a Lutheran (years later she converted to Judaism), "and his parents were probably thinking, 'This is not what we'd hoped for our Stevie.'" Also, she had just finished her freshman year at Maine East, while Steve was headed for the U of I. "I was such a baby, such a kid," she says. "I wanted to play guitar like him and be like him. I adored him, but it wasn't a romantic thing at all."

Fortunately for Steve, other activities and friends, particularly his Maine East football buddies, turned his attention from would-be romance. With Steve, they hung out on the picnic tables at Booby's drive-in late at night after the place closed, saw the Cubs at Wrigley in the heyday of Ernie Banks, Ron Santo and Billy Williams and sneaked into taverns such as Ray's Bleachers after the games. "Poor Steve, he always had a car, so I'd make him drive us anywhere," says Jeff Lind. "I dragged him into a lot of situations he probably didn't want to be involved with." Mixed in was beer — a lot of it, and consumed underage, although Steve wasn't as rowdy a drinker as his friends — and a big measure of "goofiness," Lind says. "We'd go to double-headers and try to drink a beer an inning and then drive home," he says. "I always sat in the back seat. We'd be going down the expressway, and I'd cover his eyes, just till I thought we might get hit. He'd be screaming. We were always doing stuff like that."

One postgame ride was particularly raucous, Lind says. Several guys had squeezed into a two-door Corvair that Steve was driving. "We were all drunk, and Steve threatened to throw us out of the car," Lind says. "The traffic was backed up, so we all got out, and we were running down the street. I don't know why, but I ran up to the porch of a house that had a big vase with a plant and dirt in it, and I grabbed it and ran and jumped in his car and dumped dirt all over. He was all mad. We were laughing, and we finally made him laugh, but we picked on Steve a lot because he was small."

Another incident that summer started in the evening at Steve's parents' house and revealed the notoriously corrupt side of Chicago-area police, as well as Steve's compassionate side in the face of his friends' revelry. Bud and Minnette were on their way out the door, to fly to San Francisco, and Bud's last words to Lind were, "JL, there'll be no parties over here," Lind says. "They no sooner got out of the cul-de-sac before everybody piled in over to Steve's house with all the beer."

Late that night, Steve, Lind, Bob Pottinger and Dave Spaulding hopped into Lind's car, all drinking from open six-packs of beer. With Lind at the wheel and heading to Pottinger's home to drop him off, they were followed for a couple of miles by an unmarked Cook County Sheriff's car. Just as Lind pulled the car into Pottinger's driveway, the deputies activated their dashboard flasher. Lind stopped the car. Steve, who was in the front passenger seat, told Lind,

We'd go to double-headers and try to drink a beer an inning and then drive home.
JEFF LIND

"Switch seats with me, Jeff," and the two did so. Oblivious, the officers got out of their car and, because it was his home, led Pottinger to the front door, which his father, groggy and clad only in his underwear, answered in a funk. One deputy told him, "I want $200, or your son here is going to jail." Pottinger's dad replied, "Throw him in jail," closed the door and went back upstairs to bed. "The cops just looked at each other and left almost immediately because they knew they weren't getting any money out of it," Pottinger says. "All they wanted was to solicit bribes from us, so Steve never even got a ticket."

Lind and Steve returned to the Goodman house, and Lind stayed overnight. When Steve's parents returned from San Francisco, Bud asked Lind, "Well, did you guys stay out of trouble?" Lind deadpanned, "Yeah, but boy, does your bed squeak." It became a standing joke between Steve's friends and the Goodmans.

The friends, of course, were loyal to Steve's early performances, says Herb Johnson. Prompted by a call from Steve or Bud ("Herb, I need a favor — I need the guys again"), they inflated his opening-night appearances to impress coffee-house owners. "Ten or 12 of us," says Pottinger, "would pile in the cars and go down and listen, to fill the chairs for him." Johnson says, "The owner would think, 'This guy draws pretty good,' and afterwards he'd sign Steve to a week or more. Then nobody showed up, but Steve had his week gig, and eventually more people turned out. We didn't have to do that many more times before Steve was able to do it on his own, because he did draw. But like anybody, he needed a little break."

To pay for coffeehouse drinks, Cub games and car upkeep, as well as save for college expenses, Steve needed a summer job. What better place for a would-be showman than the three-and-a-half-year-old Golf Mill Theater, which anchored the Golf Mill Shopping Center less than a dozen blocks south of his home in Niles. [3] Lee Stein, whose father owned the 1,800-seat, single-screen moviehouse, says Bud Goodman asked Lee's dad if Steve could work as an usher that summer. Stein, Steve and other teens toiled more than 40 mostly evening hours a week, wearing red suit coats and black pants and taking turns to speak over a microphone to hawk the featured film and provide updates such as "Seating available in the first five rows only!" Stein says that Steve, "always the enter-tainer," jazzed up the announcements with a spiel: "It's a great movie, very funny. Don't worry about sitting up close. You'll have a great time. Come right in."

That summer, the moviehouse drew crowd-pleasers ranging from "The Monkey's Uncle" for the kids to the adult-oriented "How to Murder Your Wife" and reissued "Dr. No" and "From Russia with Love." Throngs queued up from noon to midnight. The theater also sported a large TV lounge with free coffee and hot pizza delivered by a local eatery. "It wasn't unusual on Saturday night, when the 8 o'clock show was sold out, that people would be perfectly content to wait two hours to see the next showing," Stein says. "Steve would just go up and talk to the people. If they were asking, 'Should we wait two hours?' he'd be the guy to say, 'Listen, this is a really great movie that people have been coming out

---

Like anybody, he needed a little break.
HERB JOHNSON

3: In Niles, Steve also briefly held another summer job (exactly which summer is unclear), on the bakery assembly line at massive Salerno Biscuit. Drawing from a burgeoning suburban work force, the 300,000 square-foot factory was built in 1954 and churned out huge quantities of processed cookies. "I started out in receiving," Steve told Mary Cliff of WETA-FM in 1975. "I threw my back out loadin' 100-pound sacks of corn flour, so they moved me down to the other end where the cookies came out at the other end. My favorites were always Royal Stripes. These Royal Stripes would come off, and they let you eat as many as you wanted, and after the first day I hoped I'd never see another Royal Striped cookie as long as I lived." The Salerno facility later sold to Sunshine Bakery, then Nabisco, which became Kraft. In 2004, the plant was closed, and nearly 400 workers lost their jobs.

for. They love it. I've seen it. Two hours is going to go by real fast. We've got some coffee, we've got some pizza coming in, and there's a great show on TV in the lounge. You can stay.' And people would just listen to him. He was a very good promoter, just the friendliest person I ever met." Ron Blumenfeld, 15 at the time, says Steve roved the line, making up songs to "whatever people yelled out."

Steve didn't forget his guitar, either, playing and improvising songs for ushers on breaks in the back room, but not while on duty. "He told us he was going to be a famous folk singer," Stein says. "Of course, as teenagers, we just gave him shit about it."

One thing that Steve and other high-school grads had to take seriously during the summer of 1965, however, was the country's deepening military involvement in Vietnam. Though he would not turn 18 and be eligible for the draft until a year later, Steve was aware that President Johnson already had sent combat troops into the southern half of the divided Southeast Asian country, and monthly draft calls that summer had doubled to 35,000 nationwide. While protesters were snaring media attention by burning their draft cards, Johnson signed a bill that threatened five years in prison and a $1,000 fine for precisely that act. For many young males, avoiding the draft had become an unavoidable thought, and the most palatable vehicle was a student deferment via higher education.

"There was peer pressure to go to college. Everybody was going to go, even the worst students," says Steve's friend, Dave Spaulding. "Even though Vietnam was going full tilt, we weren't thinking about it because we were saying, 'We're going to college. We don't have to worry about it because in four years it'll be over with.' That was the mindset."

So despite Steve's intensifying immersion in folk music that questioned the status quo, the twin threats of Vietnam and the draft gave him ample motivation to proceed along the path that conformed to his parents' desire for him to become a doctor — a college education.

With his Illinois State Scholarship in hand as summer turned to fall, Steve's sights turned 140 miles south, to the twin towns of Champaign and Urbana, a small metropolitan area surrounded by Midwest farmland and holding not even 2 percent of the population of greater Chicago. There lay the stately, 97-year-old University of Illinois.

One of 355 Maine East graduates heading to college, and one of 28 enrolling that fall at U of I, Steve knew that the sprawling, 27,941-student, land-grant school had a reputation for political conservatism and tough academic standards. He had heard that the school sent home more than half of freshmen before they had a chance to become sophomores. But Steve also recognized that, in the face of Vietnam and the growing civil-rights and anti-war protests, still thriving at Illinois were the decades-old traditions of Greek life: scholastic competition, social cohesion, wild parties, a reverence for sports and the lure of quality food. With 57 fraternities and 24 sororities, the university was the nation's

> **Even though Vietnam was going full tilt, we weren't thinking about it because we were saying, 'We're going to college. We don't have to worry about it because in four years it'll be over with.'**
> **DAVE SPAULDING**

Steve as a freshman pledge at Sigma Alpha Mu (the "Sammy" house), one of eight Jewish fraternities at the University of Illinois, Champaign/Urbana, poses as part of a group photo.
(Photo courtesy of Sigma Alpha Mu)

4: Steve also was selected for the exclusive Freshman Seminar, an extracurricular leadership club sponsored by the Student Senate that held occasional meetings with professionals. The guest speakers included University of Illinois graduate Roger Ebert, who was writing sports for the Champaign/ Urbana *News-Gazette* and was two years away from the beginning of his career as film critic for the *Chicago Sun-Times*.

most "Greek-crazy" campus. Its eight Jewish fraternities were particularly attractive for students of Steve's background.

His close friend from Maine East, Les Detterbeck, says that Steve "didn't want to be stereotyped as just another Jewish guy in a Jewish fraternity house." So Steve first sought acceptance at Sigma Chi, a non-Jewish house that bore a white cross as an emblem and that Detterbeck and several others from Maine East and Maine South had pledged. But the diminutive Steve was turned down, and the "rush" process in the Jewish fraternities was no easier. "It was a horrible experience," says another Maine East friend, Joel Platt, who pledged at Zeta Beta Tau, considered one of the top Jewish houses, which also rejected Steve.

Steve ended up president of an unusually large, 29-member pledge class of freshmen and sophomores that provided an infusion of new blood for a so-called mid-level Jewish fraternity called Sigma Alpha Mu, or, for short, the Sammy house. There, says Barry Lewison, who pledged it at the same time, Steve found a desirable home. "The feeling was that with 80 guys, they'll get to know you real well," he says. "In this big sea of students, you've got a bunch of buddies." While all the Sammy house members were Jewish, the environment was only marginally religious. "In that sea of a Gentile world, culturally we were all Jewish, but observantly, no," Lewison says. Thus, Steve fit in. Sealing the deal was his personality.

"You met him, and you just said, 'What a nice kid.' A light went on, an infectious smile," says Sammy house member Jerry Bernstein. "When he smiled at you, you just had to smile right back. It was instantaneous, 'I like this guy.'" Ron Weindruch, in Steve's Sammy pledge class, agrees. "He had that sparkle in his eyes," he says. "Everybody was a buddy to him, and he would suck people right in. He was like a little pixie."

Steve's high test scores and ranking in the top 10 percent of his Maine East class also were helpful factors, for if the Sammy house had a singular reputation, it was as "a little bit more nerdy," and the expectation was that members would go to graduate school, Bernstein says. Steve brought with him two advanced-placement credits in trigonometry, and as fall quarter began he declared a pre-med major in the College of Liberal Arts and Sciences. With others in his pledge class, he enrolled in a rhetoric class for "superior students," and he signed up for American history, biology, handball and beginning French, a switch from the German he took at Maine East, amassing a full course load. "It should be pretty good, if I work," Steve wrote at 3 in the morning on Sunday, Sept. 19, in the first of a series of handwritten letters to his summertime girlfriend, Jane Kamman. 4

But academics were not to become Steve's hallmark at the U of I. His practice of skating by at Maine East didn't fly, and he habitually skipped classes. While he tried to be optimistic in his letters to Kamman, he gradually watched most of his grades fall to the "C" level. "Studying here is hard," he wrote on Sept. 25. "At first, I thought college would be like a glorified high school, but it isn't. It's something else." On Oct. 10: "I can't type, and since much of my work must be type-written, I've been getting some help from my pledge brothers." And on Oct. 24: "Grades are hard to come by down here. I didn't believe it when anybody told me, but take it from me, Janie: Laugh it up in high school, 'cause college is really work."

Instead of scholastics, in a laid-back, sometimes annoying, sometimes charismatic manner, it was the passion of Steve's music that held sway in Champaign/Urbana. "Steve always had a guitar, from the minute I first saw that guy," says Lewison, echoing a dozen Sammy members and other U of I students who say he constantly lugged a guitar case and pulled out his six-string to play — daytimes at the student union and on the way to classes, evenings and late nights in the Sammy dining room downstairs, and at all hours in the third-floor dormitory crammed with bunk beds where the pledges slept. Sometimes, he even performed in the shower.

"It was part of his being," Lewison says, noting that some Sammy members thought he was immature, if not obsessed. "Up in the dormitory, he'd be playing, and some guys would yell at him, 'Shut up!' and 'Put it away!' They gave him static, especially the sophomores, and he'd either move to the other side of the room or stop playing. But if you'd come back the next day, if Steve wasn't in class, he'd be up there in bed with the guitar. It got to the point that he was a one-trick pony. It became almost too much of a good thing. The deal with Steve Goodman was, he was the guitar. That was him. Most people like music, but you can't do it 24 hours a day."

It didn't take long for Steve to discover other musically inclined Sammy members and organize a house band. Scrambling to assemble instruments and borrow an amp, by three weeks into the first semester the Juicy Fruits — Steve on lead guitar and vocals, Ron Banion on rhythm guitar, Howie Hartman on bass and Elliot Engelhart (now Abbott) and, later, Joel Hagedorn on drums — had formed and played its first house mixer.

The band, the Sammy house's first in at least two years, drew its name from Engelhart's father's job as a producer of commercials for Wrigley chewing gum. Through his dad, Engelhart snagged a "Juicy Fruit" logo to affix on the front of his bass drum. But it was clear, Engelhart says, that Steve, with his Les Paul-style solid-body Gibson electric guitar, was the band's leader. "He was the only lead anything," he says. "He was the only one with any talent. We were so bad, and he was so good. It'd be like playing basketball with Michael Jordan."

Playing sorority mixers and other dances on the first-floor indoor terrace of the Sammy house but also drawing paying gigs at men's residence halls and dance clubs, the Juicy Fruits specialized in rock hits. Its repertoire ran the gamut of songs by Chuck Berry, Rick Nelson, the Beatles, the Rolling Stones, the Dave Clark Five, the Animals and the Byrds, including "Sweet Little Sixteen," "Hello, Mary Lou," "Satisfaction," "Get Off My Cloud," "House of the Rising Sun," "We Gotta Get Out of This Place" and "Feel a Whole Lot Better." The band's theme song and Steve's signature tune was "Johnny B. Goode," with Steve doing an exuberant, Berry-style duck walk.

> Grades are hard to come by down here. I didn't believe it when anybody told me, but take it from me, Janie: Laugh it up in high school, 'cause college is really work.
> **STEVE GOODMAN**

Between gigs, Steve wanted the rest of the Juicy Fruits to rehearse with him, but often they begged off. In that event, Banion says, "he would look for people to play with, and if it wasn't in another house, it was in the dorms, and if it wasn't in the dorms, it was in a private apartment someplace." It was not so much a betrayal as a compulsion, Banion says. The Juicy Fruits' lack of practice didn't hurt the band's performance, he says, because "Steve had a photographic ear. If he could hear the song, he could play it. It was easy to do backup for him because he told you what key we were playing in, and he knew all the words."

Steve dazzled student audiences with his musicianship, emulating players such as James Burton, lead guitarist for Rick Nelson in episodes of TV's "Adventures of Ozzie and Harriet." But for all of Steve's talent, he sometimes revealed musical insecurities. "His fingers were just loaded with blisters and no fingernails, and he would say to me, 'My hands are too small, my hands are too small,' because he had to do things that people with normal-sized hands didn't have to do when they played the guitar," Weindruch says. "He also wasn't convinced that he was a singer. He'd say, 'I can tell a story, but I'll fake it as a singer.' He never thought he could carry tunes that well." Weindruch didn't agree, though. "The edge in his voice was like the sparkle in his eye. He just had a way of telling the story. It wasn't like he was an opera singer, but he was a communicator."

That skill, says Mal Klugman, a Sammy member a year and a half older than Steve, brought uniqueness to the Juicy Fruits that other fraternity-house bands lacked. "What made him a little bit different, even then, was what made him special later on, in that he would often talk between songs. He wouldn't just stand up there and do one song and then say, 'The next one is going to be the Beatles' "Twist and Shout." ' Instead of it being boring or dull and you couldn't wait for the next song to start, he had interesting raps and stories, some of which had to do with the music and some that didn't." [5]

Just as the Juicy Fruits enhanced the social stature of the Sammy house, they also cemented Steve's visibility within it. But while music made him distinctive, Steve didn't differ in other ways from his 80 Sammy brothers. In dress and grooming, "he was as straight as they come," says Larry Ross, from the same pledge class. Steve willingly endured hazing rituals, from carrying a raw egg around all day to being forced to eat unknown foods while blindfolded. Like others, he freely drank beer, was a heavy smoker and enjoyed playing hearts, bridge and other card games until the wee hours. "He was not into studying," says Ross. "He loved talking and chatting, and he was generally warm. But whatever he was doing, he would always be picking up the guitar and strumming."

He quickly became a known quantity by teasing house members with impromptu, sarcastic parodies in the juvenile, rhymed style of Allan Sherman, who two decades earlier had belonged to the same U of I fraternity and had risen to national fame with his 1963 summer-camp ditty "Hello Muddah, Hello Faddah." Steve's goofy writing also extended to a skit for a dance to which a

The edge in his voice was like the sparkle in his eye. He just had a way of telling the story. It wasn't like he was an opera singer, but he was a communicator.
RON WEINDRUCH

5: The 6-foot-4, 280-pound Klugman, who had a massive music library, says that he became a Mutt & Jeff-type confidant for Steve, who shared a premonition that his life would be truncated by disease. Klugman distinctly recalls Steve telling him, "I'm going to have a short life, so I need to hurry up." He says Steve told him to keep it a secret because "I couldn't stay in the house if people were all feeling sorry for me and treated me differently." Klugman in contact with Steve only during the 1965-66 school year, so his memory cannot be from a later time. Of more than a dozen other Sammy members, only one recalls Steve baring a similar omen. Larry Cohen says it came during the 1966-67 year: "He was terribly depressed about a medical diagnosis."

Jewish sorority, Phi Sigma Sigma, was invited, Ross says. Playing upon the sorority's nickname, the medieval skit called for a Sammy to say to a Phi Sig Sig, "Fie on you, fie on you, pig, pig, pig!"

Steve's dramatic flair also emerged in unstaged incidents, such as late one night when a pledge brother — another study-phobic, inveterate card player — had been arrested and held in town overnight on a drunk and disorderly charge. Larry Cohen, a sophomore Sammy, recalls that after the arrestee returned to the house to sleep off the incident, Steve perched next to him on a cot and woke him up by playing the Elvis Presley hit, "Jailhouse Rock."

The joke played well, but what had to be less than amusing to Steve was attention to his height, or lack thereof. Sammy members quickly dubbed him "Shorty" because of his 5-foot-2 frame. "Whenever he got up to stand and say something in front of people, we always yelled out, 'Stand up, Steve,'" says Ross. "We were pretty cruel people." In the same vein, another Sammy brother, Allan Lieberman, says inches, not inability, foiled Steve's audition to be the rhythm guitarist for the most popular band on campus, the One-Eyed Jacks of Sigma Alpha Epsilon, a precursor to the 1970s rock band REO Speedwagon. "They liked the way he played, but he was too short," Lieberman says. "Barry Fasman, their bass player, was about the same height, and they didn't want two short guys in the same band."

Height-related rejection was tougher for Steve to take when the same, often unspoken jab came from women — including, perhaps ironically, those who were his size. An example was tiny Arlynn Gottlieb, his playmate from Albany Park days, who also attended U of I. When she ran into Steve in the basement of the student union, he asked her on a date. "I turned him down because short boys always asked me out, and I was pretty sure at the time that they only asked me out because I was short, not because they were interested in me," she says. "So I didn't want to go out with him because I figured that was why he asked me out."

His Sammy brothers don't recall Steve ever having a girlfriend ("A ladies man he was not," says Bernstein), but it wasn't for his lack of trying. He sent 10 wooing letters to the diminutive Jane Kamman back in Park Ridge. In one, he wrote her the guitar chords to the Beatles' hit "Yesterday," and in another, he offered advice on stagecraft: "You shouldn't be afraid to play your guitar in public. When you play just remember to smile at the audience, but other than that try to concentrate more on what you're playing. You'll do alright." He asked after Maine East's football team and Kamman's plum role as a sophomore on the school's "really sweet" pompon squad. He tried to arrange dates with her during his three visits home that fall, and, at one point, he wrote her an apology for assuming she would be available: "I guess I didn't think that you have a mind of your own and can go wherever you wish. I've got no strings on you, and I should have remembered that." Still, he signed most of his letters with "Love Steve."

Kamman agreed to see him once while he was home, on Nov. 6, a chilly

> **I turned him down because short boys always asked me out, and I was pretty sure at the time that they only asked me out because I was short, not because they were interested in me.**
> **ARLYNN GOTTLIEB**

From the U of I, Steve offered optimistic advice to Jane Kamman back at Maine East High School, as with this excerpt from an October 1965 letter, but his romantic intentions were unrequited.
(Letter courtesy of Jane Kamman Galler)

You shouldn't be afraid to play your guitar in public. When you play just remember to smile at the audience, but other than that try to concentrate more on what you're playing. You'll do alright.
Love Steve

Saturday night. After Steve picked her up in one of his dad's sedans, he drove to a park at the end of her street, pulled over, told her he'd been initiated into his fraternity and started to fasten a Sammy pin to her sweater. "He was very nervous, his hands were shaking, and he actually put the pin on me," she says, "but I don't think I'd even heard of being pinned." She told him, "Steve, I just don't think I can do this. You're down in Champaign, and I'm up here, and I don't think this is a good idea." Covering his hurt, he replied, "Well, you're probably right," and he backed off. "He was really good at that," she says.

Steve soon asked Kamman to travel south to visit her sister at the U of I and join him at a Dec. 11 Sammy pledge dance. "It's really gonna be quite a bash. ... It's an important thing to me, and I'd really like to have you there," he wrote. "I don't know who else I'd like to ask. It's almost like a prom, and I would really have to start lookin' around shortly if you can't make it." But Kamman declined, and the intensity of Steve's letters evaporated, as did his pursuit of her. "I'm surprised he was interested in me at all," she reflects. "I was so young, and I was a very busy girl. He did care for me, and it's almost like I used him, and I feel so bad about that, but I didn't have the same romantic feeling for him. I just loved to hear him play." [6]

Over that first year at U of I, Steve's academic record proved as rocky as his romantic life. While he barely earned a "C" average during his first semester, in the second he improved to "B" work in history and rhetoric while posting a "C" in biology and flunking French, which he was "done in by," says Larry Ross. Fifteen years later, Steve co-wrote "Talk Backwards," a song partly inspired by his difficulty dealing with instructional tapes in the university's language lab. [7]

Weindruch, a pledge brother with whom Steve "did almost everything," didn't like the trend. On frequent jaunts to the student union, he says, "Steve would take a guitar and find people to talk to, and I'd play pool. Neither of us got that good a grade the first semester. Second semester, I said to myself, 'This is bullshit,' and I went to the barber and had my head shaved, so I would look in the mirror every morning and say, 'Hey, dummy, you'd better study.' I tried to talk Steve into it, too, but I couldn't get him to do it. So I studied the second semester and did fine, and he continued to go to the student union."

6: Some 14 years later, Kamman had a brief, awkward conversation with Steve when she worked as a bartender and Steve was headlining at the Harry Hope's club in Cary, Illinois. She later married a Jew and converted to Judaism. Today she directs the youth choir and Sunday school at her temple in Florida. "I learn Jewish songs and teach 'em to the kids," she says, "but I still love the folk songs. I did a wedding not too long ago, and they wanted all the old songs. That was fun."

7: Though Steve told a concert crowd in 1975 of his troubles with French at U of I and said that he had been "sleeping with the instructor," Ross doubts that that was the case, particularly for a 5-foot-2, 17-year-old freshman. Ross does say, however, that it was known in the house that another Sammy brother had an affair with a U of I language teacher, which could have been the inspiration for Steve's concert tale.

Sometimes Steve took his guitar to clubs and apartments in local African-American neighborhoods, says Steve Sher, a Sammy junior who shared a chest of drawers with Steve and accompanied the freshman on such jaunts. "He'd go out at night to blues and jazz places and played with a lot of the black musicians in Champaign," Sher says. "He would just light up, he would get excited and play and play and play." Occasionally, Steve's wandering was more solitary. He recalled in a 1980 profile in the *Chicago Tribune*, "I used to go up to the rare-book room at the library and read these 400-year-old books on King Charles and sort of drift off to Mars." [8]

Steve's grades dipped so low by the end of the school year that in mid-June 1966 he was placed on academic probation, no doubt disappointing his parents along with his Sammy brothers. Feeling increasingly like an outcast, he prepared to leave the house — a decision that was no surprise to fellow house members steeped in the demands of the scholastically competitive university. "It was his own doing," says Lewison. "It came from within. It wasn't like somebody went down the road and took him drinking all night every night." "He knew he was screwing up," adds Banion, his Juicy Fruits rhythm guitarist. "Every once in a while, if it got too late or if he was getting melancholy, he would talk about how he knew he had to get his act in gear or lose his scholarship." Steve naturally grew more distant from his Sammy brothers. "Once you didn't make grades, you separated yourself from everyone," Ross says. "You moved in your own direction."

Looking back, during the 1980 *Tribune* interview, Steve shook his head at his fraternity involvement. "I don't know why that interested me at the time," he said, adding cryptically, "I found meeting those fellows very gratifying but being in the fraternity very unsatisfying. I was undoubtedly asking it to do something it had no business doing."

During his summer back home in Niles, Steve twice rehearsed with the Juicy Fruits at Howie Hartman's parents' home in Lincolnwood, but Steve's refuge from college became his old Maine East friends. Their fuel was alcohol, and the settings, their parents' houses, were equally familiar. "It was a party mode for all of us," Bill MacKay says. "We were still underage but very much into drinking beer, and we were spreading our wings into the ladies of the world." The gatherings centered on "getting unbelievably drunk" by tapping quarter- and half-barrels of Budweiser from ice-filled, galvanized steel buckets, MacKay says. One gathering at Steve's parents' house resulted in an automotive altercation with police and late-night jail visits for several of Steve's friends. "Generally speaking, we were good guys. We had fun, but we didn't cause so much trouble. Most of the time, we would have parties when the parents weren't home, but the parents knew about the parties. It wasn't like we were pulling the wool over their eyes."

One marathon bash, on the Fourth of July at MacKay's house, was a "blowout," MacKay says. His parents, who'd left for the day, had said, "Just make sure the door is facing the street when you're done." With volleyball in the front

8: In the rare-book room, Steve might have come across an 1889 hardcover, book-length travelogue by Carter H. Harrison, then-mayor of Chicago, and titled *Race with the Sun* (G.P. Putnam's Sons, New York, and W.E. Dibble & Co., Chicago). The words of the title would take on a haunting meaning for Steve more than three years later and be part of the lyrics of his first serious song.

*Steve smiles with Bonnie Johnson,
then flips off the photographer
while Pat Chaffee hugs Jeff Lind
during a between-semester party in
Chicago in 1966. Gatherings with
high-school friends buoyed Steve
while he wrestled with dropping out
of the University of Illinois.*
(Photos courtesy of Bill MacKay)

yard and croquet in the back, and fueled by picnic food and barrels of beer beneath the breezeway, Steve and friends caroused, leaving motorcycle tracks in the garden, vomiting on antique furniture and watching Jeff Lind hijack a Good Humor truck from its distracted driver. The highlight, however, emerged on the back porch in the evening when Steve brought out his guitar and led the group and neighbors in a lengthy stream of rhymed verses to the Kal Mann and Dave Appell sing-along "Loddy Lo," which Chubby Checker had popularized three summers earlier. "Steve was cracking us up all night," MacKay says. "We all came up with stanzas, and some of them were off-the-wall ridiculous."

That summer, Steve also honed his performance skills by snagging sporadic gigs, hanging out a couple of blocks from his childhood home in Albany Park in the cafeteria of Northeastern Illinois University, showing up at open-mike auditions and doing musical favors for friends in Chicago and environs. To help the recruiting efforts of the Sammy house, he and his old high-school band, the Impalas, entertained at a pledge party at Devonshire Cultural Center in Skokie, and he played at his Sammy brother Jeff Rochman's sister's Sweet Sixteen party in Lincolnwood, declining payment from her dad. Steve's father, Bud, even organized a Monday-night solo show for Steve at a live drama venue called Country Club Theater in Mount Prospect. The father of Hardye Simons, a former Maine East classmate who had moved to upscale Highland Park, owned and made the theater available gratis. That evening, Simons, home from Boston University, filled it with her friends.

Via the radio, the South Side blues clubs and the emerging North Side folk scene into which he was making inroads, Steve that summer also sought to forge "a musical identity in the midst of everybody else's stuff," as he put it in a later interview. "One thing led to another," he added with a laugh. "Got in over my head."

One summertime gig illustrated his willingness to risk such a reach. Steve and the Impalas drove 30 miles north, just across the state line, to play rock 'n' roll for a dance at Carthage College in Kenosha, Wisconsin. "It was the first time we had played on a stage with a curtain," says Kent Cerrone, lead guitarist. "A bunch of college kids were in the audience, and we were setting up behind the curtain." Steve picked up his acoustic guitar.

"I'm gonna go out there," he told Cerrone.

"All right," Cerrone said. "Knock yourself out. We'll finish setting up."

Steve parted the curtain and launched into Jesse Fuller's jubilant lament, "San Francisco Bay Blues," which Peter, Paul & Mary had recorded the previous year. It turned out to be the perfect warm-up.

"All of a sudden, everyone quiets down, and they start listening to him," Cerrone says. "Little pixie Steve with his chubby fingers is just chunking away, they start clapping in rhythm, and he gets the whole audience going. He was so charismatic, and he just gave it a go. It wasn't the style of music we were playing at all, but it was what he was doing at the time. When he was through with the song, we opened the curtains and got back into some rock 'n' roll, and the evening went pretty well."

Recharged for another try at college and having turned 18 and therefore eligible for the draft, Steve returned to the U of I in the fall as a sophomore and moved into a 13-floor dormitory named Bromley Hall. Normally, at the Greek-dominated university, to step from a fraternity to a dorm would have seemed regressive. But among non-Greek facilities, the pricey, brand-new Bromley was considered the Ritz, boasting suites, free laundry facilities, a snack bar, mini-libraries, music-listening rooms and an indoor swimming pool, along with a co-ed atmosphere fostered by allowing men and women students to live in the building, albeit on separate floors. "It was the ultimate, high-class private dorm," says Michael Bender, one of Steve's older Sammy brothers. [9]

But Steve's move to Bromley was less a choice than his only alternative to fraternity life because the U of I made it nearly impossible for students to live off campus. What's more, under the supervision of graduate advisers on each floor, Bromley residents had a strict curfew, in contrast to the lax rules at his ex-fraternity. "Most people were trying to get out of the dorm," says Cary Lerman, an Albany Park buddy of Steve's who attended U of I, "but the university had spent a lot of money building dorms, and they were going to make damn sure that people filled them up. If you weren't in a fraternity and you weren't married, you had to be in the dorm. You had no option."

His new digs that fall may have had a temporarily salutary effect on Steve's academic standing. Again that semester, he flunked French, but his other grades improved, as he earned a "B" in English literature and math and even an "A" in principles of political science. But soon, as he recalled years later, "this guy who used to be a decent student was starting to air-ball everything." As his sophomore year progressed, Steve spent little spare time studying or at Bromley Hall, preferring to seek out captive musical audiences.

Such chances were fewer in the nation's rural breadbasket than in liberal college towns elsewhere in the nation. But one ray of hope at the university was

> **Little pixie Steve with his chubby fingers is just chunking away, they start clapping in rhythm, and he gets the whole audience going.**
> **KENT CERRONE**

9: Another feature of Bromley Hall was musical entertainment in the dining room every Friday night. "Most of us were pretty blown away by his talent," recalls MaryAnne Erde (now Spinner), who also lived at Bromley. "There was no real stage. Steve would just push a couple of tables away, pull up a chair, plug in the microphone, and start singing and playing. We heard a lot of amateurish musicians on those Fridays, some so bad that people would sit at tables as far away from the performer as possible. But Steve always drew a big crowd, and sometimes after dinner, when the dining room finally closed and they kicked us out, his concerts would continue on in the lobby near the fireplace, and we'd turn the TV off."

In Steve's hand, the back of a reel-to-reel tape box lists the nine songs that he, vocalist Lycurgus "Larry" Mitchell and bassist Bill Wencel recorded in Steve's parents' basement in the winter of 1966-67.
(Tape box courtesy of Bill Wencel)

10: Back home during Chicago's legendary blizzard of early 1967, such a chance arose with a gig that Steve snagged at the It's Here coffeehouse on Sheridan. The audience was slim, however. He played an hour for just two people – his former Sammy brother Steve Trachtman and a date.

11: When Steve and Cohen posted bail, Champaign police wouldn't count the pop-machine change, so when Steve, Cohen and Mitchell went to an all-night diner for breakfast, they paid for the meal with the quarters. Johnson recalls that Steve kept a written record of each source of the bail money and that with help from his dad, Bud, Steve was able to reimburse all the contributors. "Steve was a loyal person," Johnson says, "very caring."

the Campus Folk Song Club, which on Friday nights drew crowds of 300 to 400 to hootenannies, billed as "folksings," that featured nine to 12 performers at Lincoln and Gregory halls and other auditoriums. Steve belonged to the club and attended at least a couple of these informal sessions, says Andy Cohen, a club member and U of I student. The club's faculty adviser, however, was folklorist Archie Green, known for touting the traditional, Appalachian-style bluegrass and old-time music of performers such as Doc Watson and Sleepy John Estes. Green insisted that the "fakelore" of Peter, Paul & Mary and the Chad Mitchell Trio was "cutting the guts out of folk music and turning it into pabulum and mass culture."

Steve, particularly given his fraternity stint, "must have had a sense that his future lay in the popularization of folk music" and therefore did not become a force in the club, Green says. "The fraternity boys were square and conformist and had their eye on the mainstream," he says. Despite the club's admitted snobbishness, the "folksings" were run democratically. "We said that anyone could sing who could carry a guitar and get up on the stage for three songs, and the audience would tell them whether they were succeeding," Green says. Still, while Steve no doubt benefited from the sessions, Green is sure that Steve found greater satisfaction elsewhere. [10]

Creating such an opportunity, Steve set up and rehearsed a folk-duo act with an African American singer, Lycurgus "Larry" Mitchell, of Urbana. Tall, with close-cropped hair and a resemblance to actor Sidney Poitier, Mitchell possessed a vocal dynamism equal to Steve's but also bore a penchant for trouble with the law. On Saturday night, Jan. 7, 1967, Mitchell was one of 14 arrested by city and state narcotics agents who raided a Champaign apartment. Seized, says Steve's ex-Sammy brother, Larry Cohen, was enough marijuana to be termed the largest drug bust in Champaign County history.

Steve secured Cohen's help late that night in scouring the campus to raise the $501 needed to bail out Mitchell. They also received help from Steve's former Maine East classmates Herb Johnson and Jeff Lind, who happened to be visiting that weekend. "We had to go through the dorms all night long," Johnson says. "Steve would ask, 'You got five bucks? You got 10 bucks?' " From the pop machine at the Sammy house, the group sprang countless quarters, and Steve ran upstairs, waking up his former frat brothers by shouting, "We gotta get Larry out! They'll fry him!" One of those awakened, Jeff Rochman, says, "We were all laughing at him, but he was serious. ... We ignored him, rolled over and went back to sleep."

Undaunted, Steve and Cohen completed the quest by heading one mile north "across the tracks" to a popular barbecue and Polish sausage shop called Po' Boys in the African-American sector of Champaign. There, they persuaded owner Arnie Yarber — a friend of Cohen's older brother who had catered the Sammy house's Shipwreck parties — to add a final $135 toward Mitchell's release. "Race relations were strained," Cohen says, "but here was a bunch of white guys going to bail out a black guy, and Arnie gave us the money." [11]

The same winter, Steve and Mitchell joined U of I student and Bromley resident Bill Wencel to record a demonstration tape in Steve's parents' basement. Wencel, who had thumped string bass with Steve at Maine East High, supplied a rudder, and Steve strummed acoustic guitar while he and Mitchell traded vocals on nine classics that would have been the envy of any lefty musical group. The tape, which survives today, ranged from rousers such as the Limeliters' "There's a Meeting Here Tonight" and the Rev. Gary Davis' "If I Had My Way" to softer material such as Ewan McColl's "The First Time Ever I Saw Your Face" and Charlie McCoy's "Cherry Berry Wine." The session — invigorated by the vocal blend of Steve and Mitchell and the unpolished spark of recording as an ensemble in single takes — was food for Steve's soul.

"He was not happy in school," says Wencel, who had commiserated with Steve several times in the Bromley Hall snack bar. "He wanted to pursue a musical career. I said, 'Steve, you have the talent. You should just do it.' But he didn't need my recommendation. He already knew what he wanted."

One portion of the demo tape, a two-song medley, was conspicuous given Steve's high-school performance of "Old Man River" and what would become his best-known original composition. The trio melded a wistful Roy Rogers and Dale Evans meditation, "Wagon Wheels," with an uptempo New Christy Minstrels tune, "Mighty Mississippi," that followed the legendary river's course via its nearby cities, from Greenville, Vicksburg and Natchez, Mississippi, to Louisiana's Baton Rouge and New Orleans "down to the Gulf of Mexico."

Steve found ready listeners along that very route during his U of I years — aboard the fabled train that would not be fabled if not for Steve, the City of New Orleans. The Chicago-based line, named for its southern hub, served the length of Illinois and thereafter generally followed the course of the Mississippi River, providing a passenger link for prairie and riverfront burgs and towns along the way.

In the mid-1960s, five years before Steve completed the song that would enshrine the vanishing vehicle in popular culture, the all-coach City of New Orleans, inaugurated in 1947, was just one among a collection of lines making up the Illinois Central Railroad, which got its start in 1851 and had dubbed itself the "Main Line of Mid-America."

Two other IC lines, the cushier, overnight, all-Pullman (sleeper-car) Panama Limited, which largely paralleled the City of New Orleans' route, and the City of Miami, which continued on to south Florida, carried a higher-class clientele and received more ink in promotional ads, which labeled them "mid-America's two great trains." Other IC lines and spurs with more fanciful, even exotic names — the Green Diamond, the Land o' Corn, the Southern Express, the Louisiane and the Creole — also plied the Midwestern tracks through cornfields and meadows and along riverbanks.

In the years prior to the early-1970s completion of the Chicago-to-Champaign/Urbana segment of Interstate 57, many University of Illinois students often chose the comfort and speed of the train over more tedious bus and

The cover of the timetable for the Illinois Central Railroad, dated April 24, 1966, lists the system's trains, including the City of New Orleans.

CHICAGO—MEMPHIS—NEW ORLEANS
Main Line of Mid-America

READ DOWN — Table A — READ UP

	3 The Louisiane	+5 Panama Limited	1 City of New Orleans	25 Southern Express	Station	8 The Creole	4 The Louisiane	+6 Panama Limited	2 City of New Orleans	
....	7.15PM	4.30PM	7.45AM	11.00PM	Lv ...CHICAGO, ILL... Ar	6.40PM	7.00AM	8.00AM	11.40PM	....
....	9.55PM	6.30PM	9.55AM	2.20AM	Lv ...CHAMPAIGN, ILL... Ar	3.30PM	4.10AM	5.48AM	9.30PM	....
....	12.25AM	8.15PM	11.48AM	5.55AM	Lv ...CENTRALIA, ILL... Ar	12.55PM	1.45AM	3.50AM	7.28PM	....
	15	**105**	**101**			**108**	**16**	**102**		
....	11.55PM	6.45PM	10.20AM		Lv ...ST. LOUIS, MO... Ar	2.30PM		7.15AM	8.50PM	....
....	2.10AM	8.40PM	12.15PM		Ar ...CARBONDALE, ILL... Lv	12.30PM		4.40AM	6.50PM	....
....	2.00AM	9.21PM	12.55PM	7.45AM	Lv ...CARBONDALE, ILL... Ar	11.20AM	12.25AM	2.48AM	6.22PM	....
....	3.17AM	10.34PM	1.58PM	9.17AM	Lv ...NORTH CAIRO, ILL... Ar	10.13AM	11.11PM	1.38AM	5.11PM	....
....	4.20AM	11.31PM	2.57PM	10.40AM	Lv ...FULTON, KY... Ar	9.10AM	10.05PM	12.35AM	4.10PM	....
....	6.50AM	1.40AM	5.00PM	1.15PM	Ar} ...MEMPHIS, TENN... {Lv	6.45AM	7.30PM	10.30PM	2.00PM	....
....	7.50AM	1.50AM	5.15PM	9.00PM	Lv} ...MEMPHIS, TENN... {Ar	5.45AM	6.55PM	10.15PM	1.50PM	....
....	12.20PM	5.40AM	9.10PM	2.15AM	Lv ...JACKSON, MISS... Ar	12.45AM	2.45PM	6.30PM	10.10AM	....
....	4.15PM	9.00AM	12.25AM	6.45AM	Ar ...NEW ORLEANS, LA... Lv	9.15PM	11.35AM	3.30PM	7.10AM	....

(Vertical annotations in table: "All Pullman Streamliner" and "All Coach Streamliner")

The Illinois Central schedule offered several options for student travel between Champaign/Urbana and Chicago. The Creole had the most appealing northbound times, and the Louisiane and Panama Limited supplied the best runs southbound. Ironically, the City of New Orleans had the least convenient schedule for University of Illinois students.

12: The IC also had a train not on the printed schedule that ran between Chicago and Carbondale, called the Campus Special. "It usually ran from Carbondale on Friday afternoon," recalls U of I classmate Jim Videbeck, "got into Champaign about 4 or 5 p.m. and arrived in Chicago about 7 to 7:30 p.m. Then it left Chicago late Sunday afternoon and went back to Carbondale. Since it only transported college kids, not real people who tipped the porters, it needed no publicity." Students whose first class Mondays started at 1 p.m. could catch the Special that morning in Chicago and arrive at 11 in Champaign. Rowdiness often prevailed, Videbeck says. "Pyramids of empty beer cans in the windows were not unusual."

car travel on two-lane highways through dozens of tiny towns. "If you took the car, it took four, four-and-a-half hours," says Cary Lerman. "It was a real schlep, a real trek." By contrast, the train ride lasted as little as two hours, and the round-trip fare was $7.05, eminently affordable, particularly for students who didn't own a car. "Your parents drove you some of the time, but some of the time they didn't," says Les Detterbeck. "For most of us, it was about half the time with the parents and half the time with the train, and the train was a pretty normal thing."

But perhaps surprisingly, given its later familiarity via song, the City of New Orleans was not the IC line of choice for U of I students whose homes were in the Chicago area, mainly because of its schedule.

The City was primarily a daylight train, known for making the Chicago-to-New Orleans run (or the reverse) in just under 16 hours. This resulted in a timetable that bypassed the needs of many U of I students bound for home on weekends or holidays to visit family. The City headed north from Champaign at the late hour of 9:30 p.m., arriving at Illinois Central Station in Chicago 20 minutes before midnight, far later than most parents wanted to pick up their students. And it headed south from Chicago at 7:45 a.m., arriving in Champaign at 9:55, quite early to return to school on a Sunday and too late to make most morning classes on a Monday. So when they were heading home, students often climbed aboard the IC's Creole instead, leaving its Champaign station at 3:30 p.m. and arriving in Chicago at 6:40. Heading back to school, students could take the IC's Louisiane, which departed Chicago at 7:15 p.m., reaching Champaign at 9:55, or the Panama Limited (round-trip Pullman fare of $8.80), leaving Chicago at 4:30 p.m. and hitting Champaign at 6:30. [12]

No matter the line, however, weekend runs were understandably the most popular and packed. "The train never seemed to have quite enough cars, kids would be sitting in the aisles, and it didn't have heat," says Steve's childhood friend Norm Kanter. "The people who ran the train must have thought, 'Well, they're only students, so they really don't count, so we'll pack as many in as we can, and they'll create their own heat.' " Lerman adds, "The trains were almost

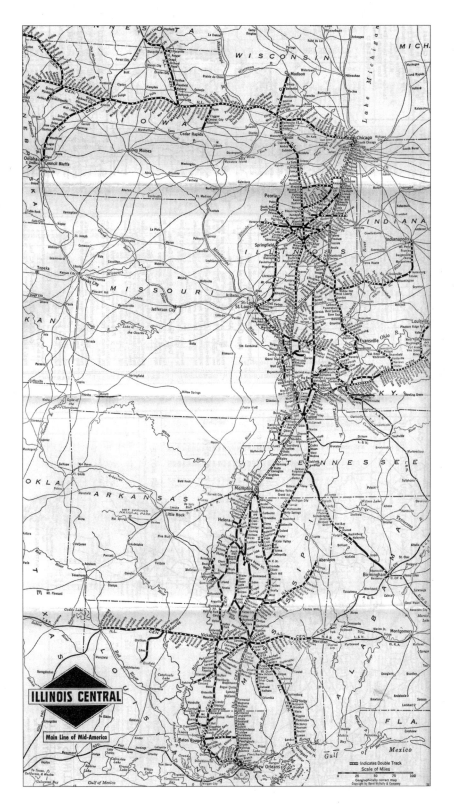

The Illinois Central Railroad system map left no doubt that its matrix of trains and stops constituted the "Main Line of Mid-America."

The trains were almost always late, almost always steamy inside. The temperature was never right. It was very bumpy. But still the trains were still adventuresome for us. There was a magnetism about it.
CARY LERMAN

always late, almost always steamy inside. The temperature was never right. It was very bumpy. But still the trains were still adventuresome for us. There was a magnetism about it."

Students from Southern Illinois University, 200 miles south in Carbondale — some of whom had grown up with Steve in Albany Park or Niles — added to the mix of riders, and the atmosphere inside the coaches was anything but staid, in part because of Steve's music-making. One of Steve's classmates likened the ambience to the free-flowing train scenes in "A Hard Day's Night," the Beatles' hit movie that was fresh in students' minds from two years prior. "A whole gang of students would take up half a car on the train, and Steve would sit there and play the guitar," says Frank Guignon, the drummer in Steve's high-school band, the Impalas. Guignon says his girlfriend told him, "Sometimes, it was a lot of fun, and other times you just wanted to choke Steve because he wouldn't stop playing, and all you wanted to do was sleep. He'd just keep playing and singing, and I'd be thinking, 'Oh, Steve, shut up!' "

Given Steve's class skipping, it wasn't unusual for him to board a south-bound train in Chicago, skip the Champaign stop, ride three hours more to Carbondale, hang out with friends there, then hop a northbound train and head back to Champaign. "A lot of the time, it was a big party going and coming," says Bill MacKay, a U of I student who also visited friends at SIU and whose parents alternated with Steve's in picking up or dropping off Steve and MacKay in Chicago. "So Steve could easily have stayed on to Carbondale and never had to pay another ticket because the conductors couldn't keep track of which school all the kids were going to."

Of course, there was the added temptation for students to remain on the train past Carbondale and ride it all the way south to the gulf. "You always wanted to know what was beyond," Lerman says. "Most of us got off at school, went to our classes, did what we were supposed to do and grew up and became lawyers and such, but there were those who stayed on the train to see and experience what those who got off in their hearts wanted to do." Late in his freshman year, Steve was one of those who seized the mystique.

"One Sunday night," recalls Steve's Sammy brother Jerry Bernstein, "we both had been home for the weekend, we'd met at the Illinois Central Station, and we were riding the train back to Champaign. I knew his grades weren't going that well. When we got to Champaign, he announced to me that he was going to stay on the train and take it down to New Orleans. I kind of bawled him out. He said, 'I only have a class on Monday, maybe just a class on Tuesday.' Wednesday night he showed back up at the fraternity. I was pissed at him, in a way."

Steve did the same thing at least once more, in February of his sophomore year, to experience Mardi Gras. Shortly afterward, a realization had taken root — the inspiration for a serious song of his own.

This became clear when, during spring break in mid-March, Steve reunited one weekday evening in Chicago with his Maine East friend Howard Primer, his compatriot in secretly exploring the city's black blues clubs. "We were trying

> **Sometimes, it was a lot of fun, and other times you just wanted to choke Steve because he wouldn't stop playing, and all you wanted to do was sleep.**
> **FRANK GUIGNON**

to recapture what we did in high school," says Primer, who also was home on break from the University of Iowa. But instead of the South Side, where Primer says that "the white/black divide had started getting hot," the two drove to Old Town. There, they sneaked into an open-mike night at a downstairs bar.

Steve had brought his guitar, hoping to get a chance to perform a couple of songs. That opportunity didn't materialize, but during a break, sitting at a round table two tables back from the corner stage, he started telling Primer about his 1,700-mile journey from Chicago to New Orleans and back north to Champaign/Urbana. "He was really proud of the fact that he just took off, took the train all the way down there by himself, did the scene and came back," Primer says. Steve became most animated, Primer says, when talking about the return trip, when he had drifted off and fallen asleep. "He said that when he woke up, it was like he was in a surreal world: the sound of the train, the rhythm of the train, the swaying of the train, looking out the windows at the misty morning on the delta country. And he was talking about 'Good morning, America.' "

As they had done at the blues clubs during high school, the two scribbled out lyrics on a napkin. They crafted the song's opening, and Primer helped with the "native son" line of its chorus. "That came out of seeing ourselves as the true sons of America, the true representation of what America stands for," Primer says. "This is anti-establishment time, and we saw ourselves as the native sons.

"Steve did all the writing. I would reach over and scratch out something and write something next to it. He'd say, 'Hey, man, that's neat.' That's how it developed. We struggled with some lyrics, and I had a real interesting time seeing his vision. I wasn't on the train, I didn't ever make that trip, so all the images I have of it are by virtue of his sharing with me what he had experienced on his own."

Previously, Steve's songcrafting amounted to silly parodies that built upon his ability to summon descriptive detail, improvise stories and rhyme almost anything. But this early draft that gave a human voice to a train — a song that eventually would take on the actual name of an Illinois Central train, the "City of New Orleans" — was a signal. It meant that he was entering a profound realm, a world of lyrics and tone and meaning that up until now he had only been able to emulate. However partial the initial result, it was a bolt of serious creativity. Steve recognized it as such, and it didn't take long for him to decide that he was never going to look back.

A couple of weeks after his reunion with Primer, and after playing a Chicago club date with bassist Bill Wencel, Steve fired an admission letter to a smaller, more liberal and certainly looser private school north of Chicago, the exclusive Lake Forest College. In the application, received at LFC on March 30, the major that Steve listed was not pre-medicine, as he had forecast to the U of I nearly two years prior, but instead "government or history." His written reason for wanting to transfer to LFC bitingly reflected his discontent and agitation:

"After two years at the University of Illinois, I have found the very 'rat race' I went to college to avoid *is* the system at Illinois. Grades at Urbana seem to be at far more of a premium than knowledge. Illinois is not a school; it's a machine

He said that when he woke up, it was like he was in a surreal world: the sound of the train, the rhythm of the train, the swaying of the train, looking out the windows at the misty morning on the delta country. And he was talking about 'Good morning, America.'
HOWARD PRIMER

for turning out careers. It's a *great* machine, but not a good school. I am hoping to find a small college program to be more suited to academic endeavor in the liberal arts."

The most revealing portion of Steve's application to Lake Forest lay in his answer to the question "What vocation, occupation, or profession might you consider after graduation?"

Steve's answer: "Education or professional musician's career."

Whether he told his parents of his Lake Forest application is unclear. But after formally withdrawing from the University of Illinois on Thursday, April 20, Steve hatched a more drastic plan. That weekend, he showed up at his parents' home in Niles and shocked them with the news that he had dropped out. The next step that Steve planned was certain, his mother Minnette recalled in a 1983 interview for NBC-TV's "First Camera" show: "He was going to New York to play his guitar."

Quitting school was one thing, but fixing sights on the Big Apple deepened the impact considerably. New York City — in particular, Greenwich Village — had become Mecca for folksingers, and everyone in America knew it. For several years, TV programs and splashy spreads in *Life* and *Time* magazines had traced the Village's evolving coffeehouse scene, which had fueled the careers of elders Woody Guthrie, Pete Seeger and Josh White as well as hundreds of more recent folk celebrities such as Bob Dylan, Judy Collins, the Kingston Trio and Simon & Garfunkel. The cover of the first Peter, Paul & Mary LP, an icon of its time, showed the trio in front of the famed, dark-red brick wall of the Bitter End, one of the Village's more popular clubs.

Of course, the Beatles had "invaded" from England and upended the course of American popular music, Dylan had shocked the folk world by electrifying his sound, and the coming "Summer of Love," acid rock and the fledgling hippie lifestyle were beckoning from the West Coast. But for a young man with a voice and a guitar, not to mention a solid grounding in the best of the era's personal and political songwriting, Greenwich Village was still the primal destination, the first place to go, to see, to experience, to soak up, to embrace.

Bud and Minnette Goodman knew this, and they also had supported Steve's musical endeavors, but only to a point. As Minnette stated carefully in 1983, "I don't think I ever knew that Steve was *going* to be a musician. I think Steve thought he *wanted* to be a musician, and that opportunity was available to him." In his own way, Bud, who didn't finish high school much less attempt college, felt the same and wanted his son to stay grounded in conventional reality: "You have your avocation and your vocation," Bud would say. "Music's great, but you've gotta make a living, and you've gotta have a job."

The two parents had invested money, time and emotion in their vision of Steve finishing college and embarking upon a doctor's career. To think that he was going to throw that away, even temporarily, left them bewildered and furious. As with countless other "generation gap" arguments of the time, "there was a scene and a little noise," Minnette recalled. But in a burst of grudging, paren-

> **I don't think I ever knew that Steve was going to be a musician. I think Steve thought he wanted to be a musician, and that opportunity was available to him.**
> **MINNETTE GOODMAN**

tal pride, she and Bud summoned a modicum of acceptance: "We put a couple of hundred bucks in his pocket, and we convinced his father to drive him to the airport and told him that no one we love eats crow. He should go and do it and be successful, and if he didn't, come on home. And off he went."

For his longtime friends, Steve's decision to suspend college and pursue music was an eye-opener but no surprise. "He always went in that direction," says Bill MacKay. "He knew how hard it was to get involved in music, and so did the rest of us. There were a lot of people wanting to be onstage and strumming a guitar and singing, and the competition was murder. But he kept going back to it. You could tell that that's where his love was." Another Maine East classmate, Paul Niesen, who marveled at Steve's ability to talk himself and his underage friends into bars in Old Town, recalls thinking that the best place for Steve was not at a university. "His classroom was the world," he says.

After tangling with his parents and being dropped at O'Hare International Airport to board a New York-bound flight, Steve encountered an inspiring symbol of his independence. It was witnessed by Bob Berg, a guitarist who had been a friend of Steve's at Maine East and hadn't seen him for a year or two. On a lark, Berg and another friend had decided to visit the airport, smoke marijuana in a restroom and watch jets take off. While Berg and the friend sat stoned on the floor, Steve walked by, his guitar in tow as carry-on luggage. Berg called out to him, Steve sat down, and the two passed the guitar back and forth, swapping songs. "Screw it," he told Berg. "I'm done with being a doctor. I'm gonna be a folksinger." Suddenly, Steve looked up and sputtered, "Holy shit!" Walking by was an entourage, and leading the way was the world's heavyweight boxing champion, Muhammad Ali.

While Steve may have wanted to conquer New York, he knew that first he needed to pay his dues, or, in the parlance, "get his chops." Upon reaching Manhattan, somehow he found a couch to sleep on in a tiny apartment in the West 90s and secured a part-time job in the accounting department of Columbia-Presbyterian Medical Center. In his spare hours, he rode the southbound subway with his guitar and began to try his hand — and voice — at busking beneath the best-known emblem of Greenwich Village's bohemian spirit, the arch in Washington Square Park. There, he met another musician, veteran busker Justin Devereaux, who Steve described in a 1973 *Rolling Stone* interview as a "wonderful maniac" who was the key to his endurance: "He showed me how to panhandle in the park with my guitar."

Six years older than Steve, Devereaux himself was a study in Village survival. "All I had in those days was me and my guitar," he said. "I didn't stay long in any one spot. I would play in the park and stay up until 4 in the morning, go over to the Cube Steak and grab breakfast and then flop in one of the cheap, little hotels. Or if I had enough money, I'd go up to the Y because that was a lot cleaner, and they had TV." In the afternoons around the fountain beneath the arch, 10 to 12 musicians at any one time drew small circles of onlookers, each player fortunate to earn $5 to $6 a day in coins tossed into their guitar cases.

Justin Devereaux, shown in 1967, instructed Steve that summer in how to panhandle in Washington Square Park in Greenwich Village.
(Photo courtesy of Lee Robinson)

Late that spring in the park, before he headed to Cape Cod for the summer, Devereaux met Steve, who — unlike hundreds of others who "wanted to try the waters of the Village" — left an indelibly incongruous visual and aural impression. Clean-cut, and wearing "preppy" duds, the 18-year-old from Illinois was playing the gut-level songs he had learned on his sojourns with Howard Primer to Chicago's South Side. "He just didn't look like somebody who would sing those kind of blues," Devereaux said. "He was terrific at it, but he wasn't making anything in the park. New York City really didn't need another young, white, Jewish blues singer because we had all the originals. Besides, it wasn't what people were looking for."

Devereaux instructed Steve that the influx of tourists lured to the Village did not have the blues on their minds. "They wanted to hear the lighter stuff, the folkier stuff. They were looking for 'clap your hands' and 'row the boat ashore' and 'working in the mines' and 'save the planet' and 'study war no more.' Civil rights was very big back then, too." He told Steve, "You've gotta go out in the park and do numbers about what people want to hear about. If you sing long enough and hit your guitar long enough, you can gather a crowd, but you've got to know your audience and give them what they're looking for, or they're not going to come to you. Basically, if you know your audience and you can play to them, then you'll be OK."

Steve took the advice to heart, said Devereaux and others, and it informed his music the rest of his life. Certainly, it altered his repertoire in the park. It also shadowed him as the sun set each day, to nearby Bleecker and Macdougal streets, into a world that was a step up from street or subway singing — the basket houses, so named because the sole payment for performers materialized when a basket made its way around the room.

Faithful to the Village's personality, the basket houses were known by hip names: the Basement, the Id, the Third Side, the Café Wha?, the Underground and the Freudian Slip. Penny Simon, with her husband Ed, operated one of the more popular ones, the Four Winds, on West Third Street, just off Macdougal — and, more than he did with Devereaux, Steve left a vivid imprint on her, emotionally as well as musically.

"He was the cutest thing," Simon recalled more than 30 years later. "To me, he was like a kid, a little boy," said Simon, who was nine years older than Steve and always tucked $5 from her personal funds into his basket. "He was so sweet and adorable and jolly. He had this kind, round face, and he mesmerized you in a lot of ways. He played only a few chords and a few songs, but he'd get up on the stage and play with all his heart. You were fascinated by him, and he was a real showman. People absolutely loved him, and all the musicians loved him, but he just was an innocent."

Steve later shook his head at his naïveté. "I knew four or five Theodore Bikel songs and some Kingston Trio numbers, and I thought I was gonna cut it in New York," he said with self-deprecation and honesty during a 1975 interview for a British magazine, *Omaha Rainbow*. "I was a classic. Everybody else was turning into hippies, and there I was with my suit and tie, going down to the Four Winds and passing the hat."

Relentlessly, Simon and others kidded Steve about his suburban sheen, which clashed with the faded, ragged T-shirt and jeans worn by more seasoned male performers. "He wore his white shirt and jacket and dress pants and a pair of shoes, and the other kids and I made fun of him because it looked like he'd gotten all dressed up to play in the Village," Simon said. "Finally, one day he comes in, and, I'll be damned, he has on a pair of sneakers. Whoa! Wow, Steve! The next time he comes in, he doesn't have a tie on, and he has a white shirt, sport jacket and jeans. That was what became his outfit. He really still was halfway in and halfway out. You couldn't get him out of his upbringing, but he got into it."

Steve soon learned from Simon, Devereaux and others the mechanics of the scene, which was both colorful and nerve-wracking. Hired "draggers" outside each club beckoned tourists inside, saying, "Come on in, don't be afraid. This is what you've been reading and hearing about!" For a cover charge of $1 and perhaps two non-alcoholic drinks, tourists flooded into the tiny, low-ceilinged, 20- to 100-seat venues, watching a cycle of four singers perform for 20 minutes each. Remuneration was inconsistent, based on the whims of the audience.

"You'd run from one club to the next to get your 20 minutes at each one," Devereaux said. "Many times, I'd play one club, then I'd play another, and by the time I hit the third club, I'd have my first audience from the first club back. They'd say, 'Wait, didn't we just see you at the other club?'" Within the cycle of four performers, the fourth was called the clearing or turnover act, "someone who is so bad that they would chase the audience away to make way for the next guy up, who had to rebuild the house again. The best spot to be was number three," Devereaux said. "It was all very political. If you played down at the Raffio and the Dragon's Den, you couldn't play at the Basement or the Four Winds. If you played at those, you couldn't play at the Café Bazaar or the Champagne Gallery. Some people who ran these places were snappy and wouldn't let you play sometimes, and other times you had to kiss butt to play. Oh, God, the coffeehouse politics were amazing."

Equally amazing to Steve was the rest of the Village scene. By his presence and participation, he was like a sponge in the deep end of the pool. He became immersed in the phalanx of other paying clubs such as the Gaslight, the renowned Bitter End, the Fat Black Pussycat and Gerdes Folk City, as well as watering holes like the White Horse and the Kettle of Fish, along with a virtual sea of impressive musicians.

Some, like Phil Ochs, Dave Van Ronk, Peter Tork and Tom Rush, already had made national names for themselves. ("I saw Doc Watson in New York and went nuts," Steve recalled in a 1971 interview. "He was the epitome of singing and picking.") Some, like Sonny Terry and Brownie McGhee, Sleepy John Estes, Yank Rachel and John Lee Hooker, epitomized African-American blues. Others, like Emmylou Harris, David Bromberg, Fred Neil, Paul Siebel, Loudon

David Bromberg — shown in the studio of WBAI-FM, New York, in 1968 — was among the many up-and-coming musicians playing the clubs of Greenwich Village when Steve showed up there after he dropped out of the University of Illinois in 1967.
(Photo by Ron Rosoff)

Mark Ross (above) and Len Chandler crossed paths with Steve in 1967 in Greenwich Village.

(Photo above courtesy of Mark Ross, photo below by Joe Alper, courtesy of Len Chandler)

Wainwright III, Carly Simon, John Sebastian and Maria Muldaur, soon would achieve prominence. Still others, such as Karen Dalton, Roger and Wendy Becket, Jay and Lynn Ungar, John Bassette, Jo Mapes, Paul Geremia, Mark Ross, Tom Ghent, Len Chandler and Susan Martin (now Robbins), while prominent at times and respected by club owners and peers, never became true celebrities.

All of them, in one way or another, were vying with each other, grasping for the elusive success that record-company staffers, ever present in the Village, were dangling — and many of these musicians crossed paths significantly with Steve.

◆ Geremia, a Big Bill Broonzy fan and early expert at bottleneck blues guitar, played the Four Winds with Steve and identified with his duds. "We looked like a couple of Amish with our grey sport coats and dark-colored blue jeans," he says. Steve's voice and sense of humor drew Geremia's admiration, but what stood out most were Steve's skills on rhythm guitar. "That's not a little accomplishment," he says, "because there aren't very many good rhythm guitars in folk music." But Geremia initially laughed off Steve's potential for stardom, primarily because of Steve's affection for "The Kretchma," which Geremia considered "the most ridiculous song I'd ever heard." One evening at the apartment of a friend of Geremia's, the friend said, "That guy's going to make it. I think he's going to be famous." Geremia replied, "Really? Why? You think 'Come to the Kretchma' is going to be a big-selling song?" The friend, he says, "caught something about Steve's approach to music that I didn't see."

◆ Ross, who had grown up in the borough of Queens and sported skills on the harmonica in addition to guitar, felt lucky to amass $5 playing three or four sets a night in the Village and wound up sleeping on friends' floors or in the subway. Two years younger than Steve, Ross was a turnover act, vulnerable to the competition Steve provided. "It was a sink-or-swim situation, and I was terrible," he says. "Goodman would show up on the weekends, and I'd get fired. He was so dynamic. He had such incredible energy that the audience would focus on him."

◆ Chandler fit the "urban folk" mold. Steve watched and listened to the African-American folksinger whose style influenced that of Richie Havens, another Village regular, and Steve learned the ringing, life-affirming, prejudice-be-damned "To Be a Man," the title cut from Chandler's first album on Columbia Records. It became Penny Simon's favorite in Steve's repertoire. "He got into it almost like Richie Havens," she said. "He had that style at the time, that hard strumming, because he only had a few chords."

◆ Ghent, who was struck by that energy and booked Steve at the bottom end of hoot nights on Tuesdays at the Gaslight, liked the promising, "bright-eyed, wide-faced, smiling kid." But he found that, like Devereaux, he had to counsel Steve away from the blues, telling him, "Steve, it's a pretty bad avenue to take because there's 14 million 16- to 20-year-old urban kids who think they're going to be blues singers, and unfortunately, there's about 9,000 78-year-old black guys who have been doing this all their lives and who *are* the blues. If that's what you're going to do, you're dooming yourself to failure." Steve resented the advice, Ghent says, "but he started bringing out songs he was writing, more like what was accepted as urban folk," and Ghent started moving him up in the hoot-night lineups.

◆ Martin, a more offbeat guitarist because she focused on fingerpicking blues and ragtime, befriended Steve and recalls both his charming onstage presence and offstage affability. "There was a warmth about him that came across interpersonally, one on one, and also when he was onstage, a real genuineness," she says. "He was just the sweetest person."

While singing and playing in the Village matured Steve and enhanced his confidence, the coins and dollar bills in the baskets and in his guitar case didn't come close to paying the bills. "I was really inspired then, but I wasn't making any money," he reflected in 1971. By summer, he scavenged for out-of-town opportunities for sustenance.

Along with Roger and Wendy Becket and Susan Martin, Steve traveled to upstate New York to perform clothed at a riverside nudist camp. "We were real uncomfortable looking to see who was going to be the first one to undress," Martin says. "That's something you didn't do among friends, not in public, anyway." Steve also joined other musicians in a jaunt to Rhode Island for the 1967 Newport Folk Festival, where he worked briefly as a security guard.

Then, as noted in the 1980 *Chicago Tribune* profile, a friend from Detroit whom Steve had met at a convention of his high-school B'nai B'rith fraternity showed up in the Village with another friend. The three cooked up a scheme to leave Manhattan and get jobs two-and-a-half hours west at Indian Head Camp in the tiny town of Lookout in the northeastern corner of Pennsylvania. The three counselors enjoyed modern cabins complete with plumbing and electricity. For Steve, with memories of the Wisconsin camps of his youth, the eight-week camp was a familiar setting in which he could flourish, as his singing and guitar licks were a boon to evening campfires. [13]

But there, isolated from urban life in the aptly named Endless Mountains, the national divisiveness over the Vietnam War nevertheless bared itself, as the trio of young men decided to set a peaceful example for the enrollees by refusing to salute the American flag during camp ceremonies. Somehow, the three held onto their jobs, but only until Steve's Detroit-based friend had a physical altercation with one of the larger campers. Though the boy who was struck "asked for it," as Steve put it, the incident marked the end of the trio's camp employment. Outside Steve's cabin the night before he left, he shared a smoke break with camper Bruce Brookoff, who says that Steve "seemed like a very sweet guy with a case of the blues."

No wonder. From news reports, it was clear that draft inductions were escalating. There even was serious talk of ditching the "oldest man first" rule and instituting a lottery to choose draftees, as had been done in World War II. Eligible males once again were reminded of the attractiveness of the deferment for college students. So while Steve and his guitar sneaked into campfire song

Tom Ghent, shown in 1967, steered Steve away from the blues.
(Photo by Carolyn Giliberto, courtesy of Tom Ghent)

Susan Martin, shown in 1969, recalls Steve's sweetness in 1967.
(Photo by Ron Rosoff)

13: The Indian Head Camp stint reverberated a decade later when Steve recalled it for compatriot David Amram. "He talked about how that was a way to tie people together," Amram says. "He talked about the ancestral vibration that every person and culture has, and how America makes you change that part of yourself … for an uptight, rigid, semi-sarcastic, soulless, cold, supposedly sophisticated way of being a more deadened person. Steve always wanted to be engaged in life."

sessions at the seventh annual Philadelphia Folk Festival after leaving Indian Head Camp, he had mentally abandoned his five-month musical adventure in the East and, in time for fall classes, headed back to Illinois. He moved back into his parents' home in Niles, and in September became one of the few students commuting 17 miles north to Lake Forest College. [14]

Steve's return no doubt relieved Bud and Minnette, but it also served his own purposes. Not only did it keep him out of the armed forces and the war, but it also realigned him on a track of legitimate academic progress while returning him to familiar musical turf. Invigorated by his stint in the Village, he felt more than ever the urgency and allure of performance, and by re-rooting himself in Chicago with a reliable roof over his head, he could answer that call without the shiver of financial desperation.

In fact, even before attending his first class at Lake Forest, Steve walked into the No Exit coffeehouse, which had just moved from Evanston to a 125-seat site in the Rogers Park neighborhood, and he played the first of what became eight weekend dates there that fall. In addition, just before college classes started, his ex-Sammy house brother and Juicy Fruits band mate Ron Banion and Steve coincidentally showed up together at a short-lived coffeehouse on North Avenue for an open-mike audition that became the reason Banion stopped playing guitar. "I had just played a set and didn't get the gig, obviously, but Steve came up, he borrowed my guitar, and he played a set. He had just come back from New York, and he was so polished and had broadened himself so much. Before, he had kind of a nothing voice and good guitar, but that night he had a richer voice, and his guitar technique was so much better. Still, he didn't get the gig, either. I figured if he wasn't going to get a job at this, I sure as hell wasn't, so I gave it up."

Steve did land a periodic gig at the no-alcohol coffeehouse on Sheridan Road called It's Here, to which two years prior he had taken Jane Kamman. Just north of the giant Granada movie palace, the unusual teen nightspot featured three cycles of four acts a night with a $1.50 cover charge, and routinely drew many more youths to its pillows-on-the-floor seating than its stated capacity of 65. "A bizarre club," says 12-string guitarist Richard Wedler. "You'd come out and play and watch teenagers make out." While the underage audience ordered from a "dry" menu, the Hungarian proprietor, Eddie Gunger, downed a bottle of Crown Royal whiskey behind the scenes most nights. Gunger, volatile to the extreme, banged on his light board routinely with a machete, blinded his audiences with strobe lights, cursed his local warm-up acts and ran one of them — singer/ guitarist Norm Siegel — off with a blast from a Beretta .32 shotgun in the middle of his set.

One Sunday night that fall at It's Here, while playing an open-mike session with his reddish brown Hummingbird guitar, Steve closed a set of rock classics with an affectionate take on the teen tragedy, "Tell Laura I Love Her." But Siegel says that in the final chorus of the musical melodrama, instead of the title line Steve had the hero wail, "Tell Laura — screw you!" The crowd loved it, but

You don't talk like that in my club. Go somewhere else!
EDDIE GUNGER

14: Steve's admission to Lake Forest College had been confirmed by letter on May 1, 1967, a little more than a week after he had bolted for Greenwich Village.

Gunger, his ears beet red, boiled. "You don't talk like that in my club," he roared at Steve. "Go somewhere else!" Eventually, Gunger let him return. "Gunger fired people all the time," says Larry Rand, another frequent It's Here act. "It was his way of saying hi."

Such performing invigorated Steve's return to college, and with its quirky mixture of progressiveness and provincialism, Lake Forest and Steve came to embrace each other in the fall of 1967 and throughout 1968. The exclusive private school, founded in 1856 and sporting an enrollment of just 1,000, lured creative activists and pampered overachievers, many of whom were "dumped" there by affluent, upper-crust families from the East, say Steve's LFC classmates. "Too many of the people who went there were basically preppy, not especially imaginative and full of attitude," says Jon Rose, of New York. Few, adds Gayle Pemberton, had grown much beyond the protections of their youth. "I didn't think they were expansive," says Pemberton, an African American from Chicago and Kansas City. "Steve was an expanded personality. He had charisma, and there was a light there. I can imagine he thought, 'I'm caught in a black hole here. There's no energy coming back.' "

Steve found such stimulation at LFC, however, in policies that were ahead of their time and in younger faculty who aimed to befriend as well as teach. Students at Lake Forest took only three courses a term for three terms a year. There were no traditional grades or grade point averages. Students either passed or failed their classes, and exceptional performance merited "high pass" or "honors" marks. Men and women had separate dormitories, but they could visit each other's rooms. Curfews had evaporated.

"Our college president, Dr. (William Graham) Cole, was always a couple steps ahead of us and brought out changes before we knew to ask for them or demand them, so life on Lake Forest's campus was more harmonious than a lot of campuses we were hearing about," says Sidney James (now Kistin). "It left us with an ability to discuss and deal with more important issues than whether women had to sign in by 10 p.m." Professors, she says, insisted on being addressed by their first names. "We were in an environment in which there was a lot of accessibility to faculty and a freedom to really feel that anything we wanted to ask or have an opinion about would be heard."

Heeding that freedom, Steve, who contemplated a teaching career, became a political-science major, finally having found college courses that spoke to his soul and to the news of the day. With the equivalent of one full year of completed course work from the University of Illinois under his belt, Steve signed up for such traditional, required classes at LFC as narrative writing and American history. But he also chose courses that related to raging, front-page concerns: "Political Philosophy," "Urban Political Administration," "Development of Modern Europe," "Comparative Totalitarian Government" and "World Politics." Leavening these weighty topics were classes in modern drama, theater production and "The Art of the Actor." For most of his courses, he earned grades of "high pass."

> **We were in an environment in which there was a lot of accessibility to faculty and a freedom to really feel that anything we wanted to ask or have an opinion about would be heard.**
> **SIDNEY JAMES**

"He liked the professors as much as anything else," says William Benz, who taught totalitarian government. "His sense of humor was pretty wild, and he liked to kid." Adds Kenneth Bennett, Steve's theater professor, "He was never a complete academic type but a wonderful spirit and very pleasant person to deal with, certainly alive to the possibilities of drama." Modern Europe professor Ed Hawes says Steve was "an articulate, engaged, intrigued guy, a shining light" who "wouldn't have responded to the stuff in European history if he weren't looking at what things were going on. They weren't abstract words on a page. He could get something out of them." Steve also expressed himself well in writing, Hawes says. "He was someone I looked forward to reading his paper. There are not many of them."

Hawes worried about bestowing too much attention on Steve, who was "head and shoulders" more mature and conversant than his course's 20 or so other students. "He had wonderfully bright, wide-open eyes, and he brought that approach to the class," he says. "He wasn't all closed up like most of the students. But I had to be pretty careful not to talk to him, as I was supposed to be teaching a whole bunch of people. It wasn't an insurmountable difficulty, but you want to draw out the most interesting people because they have something to say. Certainly, he was that person in that class."

Other than trips to Wrigley to see the Cubs from coveted upper-deck seats above home plate and an occasional out-of-town foray — such as a weekend caravan with 10 of his Maine East drinking friends to Oktoberfest in LaCrosse, Wisconsin, during which Steve got a speeding ticket and later dragged an intoxicated young African-American woman named Charlie out of a bar's restroom and sat with her on the sidewalk for hours while she sobered up — Steve was earnest about his LFC coursework.

> **You got this urgency from him that there wasn't any time to waste, and he was not to be bothered trivializing about people or engaging in the usual social game.**
> **JON ROSE**

"He had an independent thrust, but he was hungry, passionate about discourse and about knowledge, events and people understanding each other," Rose says. "You got this urgency from him that there wasn't any time to waste, and he was not to be bothered trivializing about people or engaging in the usual social game. If we had disagreements, he was so staunch and articulate about how he felt that he was never offensive."

Getting to and from campus could have been a challenge if not for fellow commuter Jim Dernehl, who lived across the street from Hillary Rodham's family home in Park Ridge. For the first few months, Dernehl drove Steve, who split his time in the car between guitar strumming and last-minute studying. Later, Steve's dad bought him a used, blue Karmann Ghia, the first stick-shift car he had driven. John Posniak, another friend and Lake Forest student, taught Steve how to synchronize the clutch — not a smooth procedure, given that Bud had arranged for kids' tricycle blocks to be installed on the pedals so that Steve's legs could reach them.

Typically, Steve just joked about such an obvious compensation for his height. "He was a fireball of positive energy," Posniak says. "He just exuded happiness." Moreover, adds Rose, "When you were his friend, it was not to be taken lightly.

There was always a warmth, always a greeting and always some good conversation. He did not put on airs." A telling tendency, says James, was the loving way Steve spoke about his family, in contrast to "kids in college who try to create a façade that doesn't include any of their roots."

Some friends gave him the nickname Hobbit, a reference to the short, chubby, imaginary being with a sociable, peace-loving nature created by novelist J.R.R. Tolkien. Carrying his guitar everywhere and wearing his hair cut short and an ironed, button-down shirt and sport jacket, Steve almost looked more like an instructor than a student. "It was a very unglossy combination of academic and folk Bohemian," Rose says.

Terry Pearl taught Steve a road song, "Southwind Train," during their Lake Forest College years. (Photo courtesy of Terry and Lenora Pearl)

His appearance only enhanced his personal appeal as he sought out others for exchanging musical licks. One such encounter was with Lake Forest classmate and guitarist Ward "Terry" Pearl, who lived at his parents' home near the campus. Steve brought over his Martin D-28 guitar, and the two sat in Pearl's bedroom trading songs, including one that Pearl had written in 1963 called "Southwind Train," a ballad inspired by a rail trip Pearl had made to Fort Lauderdale to take an entrance exam for a private high school. Steve undoubtedly tucked the song's chorus ("From the sunshine to snow and rain / I don't know whether I'll be comin' back / because I'm traveling on a southwind train") into the mental file cabinet where he had stored the early draft of his "City of New Orleans."

That day, Steve also picked up the germ of an affectionate country-western parody he wrote a couple of years later, "You Never Even Call Me by My Name," which became one of Steve's best-known show-stoppers. "We talked about how every country song has to have a train, a dog run over and an unfaithful wife," Pearl says.

While in Pearl's bedroom, Steve also revealed a homophobic streak typical of the times. Pearl had picked up a decal that played on the ubiquitous slogan of Tareyton cigarettes. The decal read, "I'd rather swish than fight." Steve saw it stuck on Pearl's guitar case and blanched.

"Wait a minute," Steve said. "Hold on, buddy. If you're like that, I'm not staying."

"No, that's just a joke, Steve," Pearl said. "Relax."

Afternoons on campus, Steve often drew onlookers as he picked chords and songs while kneeling on the grass beneath old, sturdy campus trees or as he jotted down trial lyrics at a table inside Lake Forest's indoor commons. "He exuded a sense of guiding the moment," Rose says. "You knew that he was doing something interesting, and you sat with him out of a sense of great respect." "He had such a respect for other people and could always learn something," says James, a close friend who might have become a lover if she hadn't already been attached to a boyfriend. "He was always interested in talking to someone. He was a real mensch. He just wanted to absorb the world, curious and optimistic. I really admired him, especially in the gloomy times that were the end of the 1960s."

With the Vietnam War looming over that era, there perhaps was irony in Steve earning money from a part-time job with the government agency that was delivering draft notices — the U.S. Postal Service. After enrolling at Lake Forest in September 1967, he applied for a postal assistant's job at the Park Ridge station, getting hired Oct. 6 and beginning work Nov. 7. Earning $2.44 an hour (later boosted to $2.59), he worked 16 hours a week — Thursday afternoons and full-time shifts on Saturdays and early-morning Sundays — unloading trucks and sorting mail.

The job lasted just three months, however. "I had to learn all the routes by heart so I could chuck the mail in the right cubbyholes," he told *Rolling Stone* six years later. "Guess what? I got bored." Steve told his postmaster that the work was taking too much from his studies, and he resigned on Feb. 9, 1968, just as a series of events began to pile up and crush the spirit of a generation.

As with many students, the war half a world away dominated Steve's thoughts and conversations. He cautioned an old Maine East classmate, Kathy Rogers (now Burgess) about taking a job as a flight attendant for 21 airlines that were chartering troops across the Pacific to and from Vietnam. "Are you scared to death?" he asked her. "You don't know what's happening." Steve was right to question her, she says, for as she found out on the job, "Everywhere out there, the war was everywhere around you." In Chicago's Old Town, Steve bumped into another Maine East classmate, Bob Berg, whose head was freshly shaved because he was soon to depart for Vietnam. "Call me," Steve implored him. "You don't want to do that. You gotta talk to me." Berg never called him, served his hitch and, fortunately, returned unscathed. "I didn't get hurt, and I didn't hurt anybody," he says.

> **What's anybody doing to really build from this? Has anyone learned the lessons that Martin Luther King was trying to teach?**
> **STEVE GOODMAN**

Another seeming war, a domestic one triggered by assassination, affected Steve as well. One day after the Rev. Martin Luther King Jr. was shot dead on Thursday, April 4, in Memphis, riots broke out in the largely black neighborhoods on the West Side and South Side of Chicago. Mobs looted stores, fired shots and set fires that lasted through the weekend, and the outbreak fanned racial tensions at Lake Forest. "I had very good friends who were black suddenly deciding they couldn't be my friends anymore," says Sidney James. Soon after the riots, in the LFC English building, Jon Rose says, he ran into Steve, who was shaken by the close-to-home violence. His eyes wide and shaking his head, he pelted Rose with a series of unanswerable questions: "What have they done? Where is this going? What does it result in but people's homes and lives being reduced to nothing? And what's anybody doing to really build from this? Has anyone learned the lessons that Martin Luther King was trying to teach?"

Steve's plaint reflected his "extremely independent way of being very Jewish without being religious," Rose says. "He had a traditional sense of civil liberties and striving for openness and humanism and progress of people that is the Jewish tradition in Chicago and New York and other big cities in this country and in Europe. He came from middle-class suburbia, but it was adjacent enough to city life that he knew of the tradition of working people who look out for one another and open up to people from different backgrounds. He also saw the other side, which never failed to sadden him, but in a way that didn't make him cynical or reconciled. He was the kind of person who would wear his peace button with the greatest pride, and he did."

Heightening the anxiety of Steve and countless others in the following months was the June 6 assassination in Los Angeles of Democratic presidential hopeful Robert Kennedy. Those feelings were compounded less than three months later by the infamous, televised police beatings and tear-gassing of war protesters in Chicago's Lincoln and Grant Parks outside the Democratic National Convention, presaging Richard Nixon's victory in the fall. Steve did witness some of these altercations firsthand, and Mayor Richard J. Daley's sanction of them became a crucial part of a song that Steve wrote nine years later upon the death of Hizzoner da Mare.

Change was churning literally on the home front, as well. Steve's younger brother, David, was making a name for himself at Maine East as a wrestler and weightlifter when he wasn't practicing drums in the basement of the family home in Niles. And in September, the number of "sons" in the Goodman household suddenly grew by two: a high-school exchange student named Eduardo from Punta Arenas on the southern tip of Chile, and a former Maine East classmate of Steve's whose parents had died recently, Jim Freitag. Minnette had invited Freitag to live there rent-free, and he was given a bedroom of his own, as was the Chilean student, while Steve and David moved into a third and Minnette's mother, Mary, moved out.

The generosity left Freitag flabbergasted. "What can you say about people who let you move into their house, give you your own room, double their kids up, include you in everything and treat you like you're their own?" he said. "This was a Jewish family that never had a Christmas tree in their life, but with two Gentiles in the house, they had a Christmas tree that year. They were strong and decisive. If somebody needed help, they were there for them, and not the type to ask for anything in return. They weren't butt-inskis, either. You got support from them, whatever your decision was."

Throughout this turmoil and activity, from the political to the personal, Steve drew energy and comfort from his lifeblood — finding an audience and putting on a show. It served both as his mode of expression and a refuge.

◆ He found an audience during orientation week at Lake Forest, when jug player Jon Rose organized a welcome-back concert for students with a bill of a half-dozen acts at Hixon Hall recreation center. Steve sang Theodore Bikel and Clancy Brothers songs, and the Russian take-off "The Kretchma" was his closer. "He sat on a chair in the middle of the floor and did 20 minutes or so, and he just dazzled us," Rose says. "It was as though he was an old, familiar voice."

◆ He found an audience when Gayle Pemberton, a rudimentary guitarist, volunteered to manage in the same hall an eight-table coffeehouse that she named the Dangling Conversation, after the Paul Simon song. With doughnuts and cider along with folk music on Friday and Saturday nights, it was "the

A recipient of the Goodmans' generosity was Jim Freitag. "What can you say about people who let you move into their house, give you your own room, double their kids up, include you in everything and treat you like you're their own?"
(Photo courtesy of Herb Johnson)

Gayle Pemberton, a Lake Forest College classmate of Steve's, managed an eight-table campus coffeehouse at which Steve performed: "You could not believe what he could do on the guitar with such stubby, little fingers."
(Photo courtesy of Gayle Pemberton)

15: Not long before she died in 1999, Gerry Armstrong related this anecdote to her daughter, Rebecca Armstrong.

only show in town" for students who lived on campus and decided not to leave the isolated campus. Several times, Steve brought in his "really lovely voice" and sang in mock homage the infectious hits of Chuck Berry, Jan & Dean and Bill Haley, Pemberton says. "You could not believe what he could do on the guitar with such stubby, little fingers," says Pemberton, who says his appearance was as intriguing as his sound. "He had that receding forehead that you knew in time was going to leave him pretty much without any hair, and big, round, brown eyes that told you that he was taking in the world without being threatening, and taking you in along with it."

◆ He found an audience at several mid-1968 parties hosted in the northern suburb of Wilmette by the legendary folk duo of George and Gerry Armstrong. Steve brought his "razzle-dazzle guitar stuff," but Gerry wanted to hear the lyrics more clearly and told him so. "It would really improve your performance if you focus more attention on how you deliver the song," she said. Steve, momentarily speechless, drank in the storied advice. [15]

◆ He found an audience by hanging out and picking at the new home of the Old Town School of Folk Music, which in 1968 had just moved about a block from the El stop on West Armitage Street inside the ornate edifice of a two-story 1896 building. Called the Aldine, the former bar and boardinghouse sported a large performance space that was dedicated to the legendary Big Bill Broonzy, who had died 10 years prior. (Eight years later, Steve paid tribute to Broonzy by recording the bluesman's signature tune, "The Glory of Love.")

◆ Obliquely, he found an audience the very night following Robert Kennedy's killing, when Steve finished his first year of LFC classes and capped his theater-production course. He directed, as part of the climax of a three-day student drama series, a pair of existential one-act plays by Tennessee Williams, "The Long Good-Bye" ("Because that's what life is," the main character sobs at the end) and "Lord Byron's Love Letter."

The place that Steve's passion for music and performance took hold most deeply during his Lake Forest years, in a way that gripped and came to define him, was not at the college but in the Old Town section of Chicago. On the dingy first floor of an old brick building just two doors from the busy intersection of North Avenue and Wells Street, a pub was making a name for itself as a folk-music haven. It was the Earl of Old Town.

Old Town, of course, was hardly unfamiliar territory to Steve. The trendy district anchored the southeast corner of the city's notorious 43rd Ward, which had been enshrined in song by longtime Chicago folkie Win Stracke and represented for years by a corrupt North Avenue bar owner and city alderman, Mathias "Paddy" Bauler, who locals held in affable esteem for his brassy proclamation that "Chicago ain't ready for reform!"

Nor was the Earl of Old Town foreign to Steve, given that he had sneaked in while on breaks from the University of Illinois. Positioned across Wells Street from the Second City comedy club and measuring just 2,000 square feet, the elongated saloon with 85 seats (standing-room capacity of 125) and a homey

entrance (25-foot storefront, a stoop and two steps) had built a loyal clientele ever since its opening on March 14, 1962. With a liquor license allowing it to stay open until 4 a.m. instead of 2, as was the case with many other booze establishments, it had become an after-hours hangout for the hip, artistic crowd (including other club owners) and the journalists who reported on it. Not coincidentally, from the likes of fledgling film critic Roger Ebert, other newspapermen and long-established WFMT-FM raconteur Studs Terkel, as well as the station's "Midnight Special" co-host Ray Nordstrand, the Earl netted more than its share of squibs and on-air asides.

Integral to the appeal of the Earl of Old Town was its namesake owner, Earl J.J. (Jesse James) Pionke, a loud, brash, tall, stringy-haired, bearded bear of a Polish man whose brand of crude bravado and hearty generosity would lead anyone to believe — and not question — that he was viscerally connected with the Chicago mob scene, or to believe that if he wasn't, he was doing a good job at acting the part and reveling in it. Pionke himself and his saloon both were known by all, reverentially, almost royally, as "The Earl," nomenclature that he never discouraged on either score.

Orphaned at age 5 and growing up on the tough South Side, Pionke was both a reader and a fighter, articulate and profane. "I was a combination, and the nuns couldn't figure it out," he says. "They couldn't put together the ruffian and the smarts." When he bought the former antique shop that became the Earl in 1962, he had run a liquor store for 10 years, and all he had in mind was a bar. "I wasn't dreaming of music at the time because in Old Town all you needed was an old-looking place, maybe with a fireplace, maybe without, no jukebox. Old, just look old. It was my dream."

Eventually, Pionke changed his tune. As the 1960s progressed, he bar-hopped with friend and future employee George Spink at area musical venues such as the landmark Gate of Horn, Mother Blues, Le Montmartre, Poor Richard's (predecessor of the Quiet Knight), the Yellow Unicorn, the Old Town Pump and the Blind Pig. At first, Pionke contemplated hosting blues at the Earl, but he came to suspect that for the sake of his business (and, he would say, his soul),

(Left photo) Two Chicago legends – author and radio host Studs Terkel (left), holding his portable Nagra tape recorder, and songster and Old Town School of Folk Music co-founder Win Stracke, with guitar and everpresent cigar – quickly became a part of Steve's circle as he sought out musical audiences in the late 1960s. (Right photo) A third Chicago legend, Earl Pionke, shown in 1972, ran the Old Town club that became a regular haunt for the likes of Terkel, Stracke – and soon Steve.
(Left photo by Art Thieme, right photo by P. Michael O'Sullivan)

The Earl of Old Town — the left building in the larger photo in 1965, one year before Earl Pionke began hosting folk music, and, in the smaller photos, the club's exterior and interior in the late 1960s.
(Large photo by George Spink, smaller photos by David Maenza, ©DMaenza, chicagostockphotos.com)

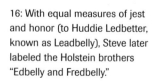

16: With equal measures of jest and honor (to Huddie Ledbetter, known as Leadbelly), Steve later labeled the Holstein brothers "Edbelly and Fredbelly."

the key to his success would be folk music. By late 1966, however, folk had taken a distinct back seat to electric music at local clubs.

This didn't dissuade Pionke, who, despite contrary advice (*Chicago Tribune* columnist Will Leonard said Pionke "might as well try to bring back the buggy whip"), plunked down $450 in cash for an Allied Radio sound system, mounted its two vertical speakers on the bar's south brick wall and on Nov. 1 of that year launched folk music at the Earl. Venerable baritone interpreter Fred Holstein opened for Maxine Sellers the opening week, and the cover charge was just 50 cents. He followed with Ginni Clemmens (known for her version of Ida Cox's "Wild Women Don't Have the Blues"), gospel-tinged Willie Wright (a Josh White protégé) and the frenetic, high-voiced Jim Post and his wife Kathy (who two years later with the stage name Friend & Lover hit nationally with "Reach Out of the Darkness"). Holstein became a regular headliner, and soon, to Pionke's lasting satisfaction, the Earl became Chicago's premier haven — what Roger Ebert called "the epicenter" — of folk music.

"I love it, I perpetuated it, I thank God I did, and I still perpetuate it as much as I can," Pionke reflects, characteristically leaving behind modesty and decorum. "I'm the patriarch, the guardian angel and every other fuckin' thing. I learned a long time ago, always pass along greatness, and I've been great forever. I pass it on forever. I lost my humility. I got no fuckin' powers. I got my fuckin' benevolent heart."

Into this milieu plunged Steve Goodman. Anchored by a raft of regular performers, from Ed Holstein (Fred's songwriter/comedian brother) [16] to the jangling 12-string guitar of will o' the wisp Bob Gibson, the Earl enveloped the underage Steve. It stirred in him a desire to move from a riveted member of the audience to the one making music from the pub's tiny, six-inch-high stage. [17] His chance came on a weeknight in the fall of 1967, some sources say near Christmas, when the New Wine Singers were the headliners.

It was an eye-opening evening that extended nearly till dawn, says Lake Forest College friend Sidney James, who accompanied Steve to the tryout session for walk-ons. (Steve later joked that on such nights, "The star of the show is Open Mike.") As Steve and James strolled through Old Town prior to Steve's tryout at the groggy hour of 2 a.m., they were stopped by a young woman, "a homeless, hippie type," who asked them, "Woah, have you guys seen my old man? He, like, is wearing pink pants, and he's got earrings." Later, James, who didn't understand that the woman was looking for her boyfriend, asked Steve, "Can you imagine if your father looked like that?" Steve, she says, "didn't roll his eyes or laugh. He just said, 'Welcome to the city.' "

Once inside the Earl, says James, "We were trying desperately to stay awake for this bizarre audition time, but it was so fun to be there with him and the two other drunk people who were there listening. He was nervous, which surprised me, because he so clearly was terrific."

Sharing her assessment that night was tall, flat-topped Gus Johns, a high-school buddy of Pionke's who worked at the Earl as bartender, doorman, bouncer, booker and fill-in manager and who had plugged Steve into the red-eye slot. "I just liked him. I instinctively liked him, and that was that," Johns says. "He was a nice kid, school kid. No phoniness with him, and he worked his ass off. The more he got into it, the more intense he got, and everything came together."

Steve showed up again soon for another open-mike night at the Earl, and while he was standing by the telephone near the back room (Pionke labeled it his "Star Cave" for a large, crooked star hanging over the doorway), Johns was at the microphone, announcing the rest of the week's program. "Wednesday through Sunday, I had to have paid acts," Johns says, "and I forgot that I had not hired someone for one of the nights, and I'm announcing, and I'm thinking, 'Oh, my God, I forgot Wednesday night.' So I said, 'And appearing will be Steve Goodman.' "

At once, Steve looked up and beamed, having just secured his first paid gig at the Earl, a weeknight spot as an opening act, for the not-insignificant sum of $30.

Not long afterward, Steve showed up on a weekday evening and pulled Johns out of another jam — a dreadful performance by a Dixieland band — by hopping onstage and putting on an energetic show. "In a sense, he saved Gus' life," says Ed Holstein. "It was a tough crowd, very rowdy, and those people were going crazy. They wanted to hang the doorman because the band was so bad."

By playing the Earl two weeknights some weeks and with his short-lived job at the Park Ridge post office, Steve was making $100 a week. [18] "The reason I really liked him a lot was he would never say no to you," Johns says. "You'd ask

Lake Forest College classmate Sidney James accompanied Steve to his early-morning audition at the Earl of Old Town in late 1967.
(Photo courtesy of Sidney James Kistin)

17: Over the years, Pionke loved retelling how musicians kept asking for a raise and how he responded by impishly announcing that he had built the stage a couple of inches higher.

18: When Pionke first hired Steve as a billed act, Pionke hilariously misidentified him in Will Leonard's Jan. 14, 1968, *Chicago Tribune* column with the name of film star Steve McQueen. Steve's mom, Minnette, called Pionke to seek a correction, which Pionke made. Pionke and Steve laughed about the story often in later years, with Steve telling a Chicago TV audience in 1982 that his mother didn't realize that he had changed his last name to McQueen "for income-tax purposes."

him for a favor, and, boy, he was right there. Sometimes somebody wouldn't show up or walk in stoned out. I could call him from wherever he was playing. 'Come on over for the late one, Stevie. I've got $15 for you,' or whatever I could afford to give him, and he would do it. This guy had nerve. He had chutzpah. He had balls as big as watermelons."

Before long, Pionke himself got a glimpse of Steve in performance. "Funny, fun, impish, great stage performance, right a-fuckin'-way," Pionke says, recalling a particularly biting satirical blues that Steve sang about North Vietnamese Communist leader and guerrilla-warfare expert Ho Chi Minh. By September 1968, showcasing such rousers as Terry Gilkyson's "Fast Freight" (popularized by the Kingston Trio) and "Tear Down the Walls" by Fred Neil, Steve had landed not only regular midweek slots but also occasional billings on Friday and Saturday nights. It was prime exposure to influential audiences and a heady atmosphere for a 19-year-old.

It also served as a street-smarts version of college for Steve — and the required course was Loyalty 101, says Steve's Maine East friend and guitar mentor, Howard Berkman. "If you were one of Earl's boys, he pretty much kept you working," he says. "You'd have at least two-three nights a week. He'd find room for you. And you could always go in and eat for free, and bring your girlfriend, and she would eat for free. It was gracious, gangster Chicago style, where they would never dream of bringing you a check or making you sign a check or even saying, 'Don't look at the expensive side of the menu.' It was strictly, 'You're working for the Earl, you can eat the Earl's food anytime. You can drink the Earl's beer anytime.' "

In return, Pionke not so subtly persuaded Steve and other young charges to forgo long-running gigs at competing venues. Berkman recalls how Pionke wooed him away from the No Exit, where he was paid by the passing of a hat. "Is that nice, when I'm paying you money?" Pionke asked him. "Well, no, that's not nice," Berkman replied. "Well, Howie," Pionke said, "if you want to work for me, maybe you should think about that."

Of course, playing in what some would call a seedy bar full of smoke and noise — the phone and cash register ringing, the Mixmaster making Harvey Wallbangers, the toilet flushing, the back door slamming — was as much a challenge as an opportunity. Steve himself smoked unfiltered Camels while performing at the Earl, but even he was affected by the haze. Typically, during sets on frigid winter nights, he asked Johns for a shot of DeKuyper's blackberry brandy to soothe his throat, Berkman says. "Gus," Steve would say from the stage, "bring me the grape." It was an example of how informality permeated the place. "The Earl was a dump," says Johns, "but that's why you felt good in it. You didn't have to walk in there with suit and tie. You could walk in there with jeans. As long as you didn't have your wiener hanging out, you were welcome, and sometimes you'd see that."

Johns was only one in an eccentric cast of characters who worked the Earl. The cooks, who endlessly pumped out cheeseburgers, were Henry "Duke"

It was gracious, gangster Chicago style. ... It was strictly, 'You're working for the Earl, you can eat the Earl's food anytime. You can drink the Earl's beer anytime.'
HOWARD BERKMAN

Nathaus and an elderly German named Anton who had prepared food for Adolf Hitler at the Ritz in Berlin and was known for his steak sandwiches. Bouncers with the names of Vince, Vito and Pete patrolled the Earl to quash rowdy behavior so that the music could be heard. Sometimes, the enforcement became as obtrusive as the original distraction. Berkman recalls a two-step system used by Vito, who first would lean down and quietly warn a heckler, "Hey, excuse me, sir, but the people here paid a cover charge to hear the singer sing his songs, and obviously you don't want to hear him sing his songs, and nobody else can hear it, so we'd appreciate it if you would help all the people here." If the warning didn't work, Vito would return and say, "Excuse me, we're covering your tab. You've got to leave now." Vince or Gus would open the front door, and Vito would pull the heckler out of his seat and propel him outdoors into the adjacent parking meters or the middle of traffic on Wells Street.

Such protection pleased the musicians, but no staff could fully quell the tendency for boozy patrons to socialize. Lake Forest College friend Lucy Wells recalls going with Gayle Pemberton to one of Steve's budding shows at the Earl and being riveted by his performance while Steve struggled to snare the attention of others. "That's where Steve seemed to get better and better," Wells says. "That's where he really learned to work a crowd, in that environment."

Sometimes the Earl milieu supplied real surprises. Lake Forest classmate Terry Pearl says that one day Steve sat down next to him in the LFC student union and told him, "You'll never guess what happened." He told Pearl that in the audience at the Earl the previous night, visiting Chicago in the middle of her eight-year string of more than 2,800 performances of "Hello Dolly!" on Broadway, was none other than Carol Channing. She came up to Steve afterward with a brief, unequivocal message. "You have a future," she told him. "He was bouncing around in the chair, he was so excited," Pearl says.

Just a few months after his Earl debut came a night when Steve finally "got his guts" in the saloon's rough-and-tumble climate. "He was always letting audiences run over him," Johns fondly recalled in a 1986 interview in the *Chicago Sun-Times*. "But that night, all of a sudden, he just chewed out everybody's ass. And then he did the best set you ever saw. Nobody could stop him after that."

Four blocks north of the Earl on Wells Street was the apartment of blond folksinger Jo Mapes, a frequent performer in 1963-64 on ABC-TV's "Hootenanny," who had dropped out of the Greenwich Village scene and moved to Chicago to raise two daughters and a son. In addition to snagging an occasional gig at the Earl, Mapes had secured a position as entertainment critic for the *Chicago Sun-Times*.

Ringing Mapes' doorbell one day in 1968 was Steve, who came inside and picked her brain about the repertoires and guitar skills of those in the local music scene. "It's almost as though he was saying, 'I've got to check out the competition here.' I told him, 'Just people,' and he kind of laughed and said, 'Oh, well, then there's no problem.' " Eight years older than Steve, Mapes detected in him a "tender boy" filled with restlessness. "He was an intense charge

You have a future.
CAROL CHANNING

By late 1968, Steve had become the regular opener for Bonnie Koloc, the newcomer whose clear and powerful voice arrested audiences at the Earl of Old Town.
(Photo by Ron Rosoff)

of electricity and energy," she says. "His eyes — snapping, dark eyes — his manner, his laughter, it all was intense. It was as though there was a determination to live and succeed, all packed into this incredible package of pure energy."

This "package" by late 1968 had earned a regular spot at the Earl to open for a talented contemporary, 25-year-old Bonnie Koloc. Physically in the mold of Buffy Sainte-Marie and Joan Baez, with long, straight, brown hair and piercing, searching brown eyes, along with a voice of arresting clarity and range, the Iowa-bred Koloc was seemingly born to embody a folk/pop/blues/jazz diva. With a repertoire ranging from the Beatles and Joni Mitchell to her own compositions, Koloc had arrived in Chicago during the summer's Democratic convention, and her persona emerged and evolved as she worked the Earl, the old Quiet Knight and other clubs. Drawing rapt crowds, she, by all accounts, was a star in the making.

Koloc's accompanist, Ron Buffington, recalls Steve as a "ball of fire" whose performances "knocked everybody out" and nearly pulled the rug from under Koloc. "It made it difficult for Bonnie, but she enjoyed it, too."

By this time, Steve had become such a fixture at the Earl that his dual life as folksinger and college student became cause for public curiosity, if not concern. Will Leonard, who in the Sept. 1 edition of his "On the Town" column for the *Chicago Tribune* described Steve as "a little guy with a big voice that carries conviction," posed a pertinent question in an Oct. 20 installment. "We can't help wondering how Steve Goodman is doing in his studies at Lake Forest College," Leonard wrote. "He was singing folk songs at the Earl of Old Town until 4 a.m., then making an 8:30 class in world history at the campus about 30 miles from Wells Street. Now, however, he sings only Fridays, Saturdays and Tuesdays because he has no class on Wednesday mornings or weekends. His performance improves all the time, so how can his work as a political science major be getting enough attention?"

Complicating the situation was something the *Tribune* may have implied but didn't mention: Steve's worsening health.

To Lake Forest classmate and guitarist John Bowen, Steve was just "chronically sleepy." Fatigue, shortness of breath, a pale complexion, joint aches and not being able to bounce back quickly from bruises or cuts — to Steve and others, these all seemed to be merely the logical result of his hard-hitting lifestyle. So as 1968 drew to a close, it was not unexpected that Steve began missing classes at LFC.

Fellow students and his professors — many of whom were huge fans of his performances and of folk music in general — tried to help by keeping him posted by phone and delivering course materials to his parents' house in Niles. "You wanted to pay special attention to him," says William Benz, political science professor. "He was trying to keep up, but he was trying to do too many things at once. We ended up giving him all kinds of ways of getting the work done. We kept him going."

Steve didn't let on that his absence from classes was due to anything other than his late nights at the Earl. But there were unspoken clues. "Obviously, there were things going on in his life that he didn't share with us," Benz says. "There was a lot of stuff there. That was evident."

Before long, Steve, suffering from what he thought was a bad cold or possibly pneumonia or mononucleosis, knew that a trip to the doctor was imminent. The trigger came when his dad suffered a heart attack. When Steve visited him at Weiss Memorial Hospital on North Lake Shore Drive, several cousins told Steve that he looked worse than his father. A visit to his family's physician triggered extensive blood tests. It also led to an aggravating confrontation later in the day, says Terry Pearl.

With memories fresh from the beatings of protesters during the Democratic National Convention a few months earlier, Steve came up to Pearl at Lake Forest and angrily spat out, "Damn Chicago police!" Steve described what had just happened to him. "He was walking down the street with his guitar," Pearl says, "and he got stopped by the police, just for general principles. His sleeves were rolled up, and he had something like five needle punctures on his arms. They took him down to the station, and they searched him. He said, 'Call the hospital.' They did, and they found out it was legitimate, so they let him go."

Pearl didn't ask Steve what the blood tests were for. "I figured it was none of my business."

Steve didn't know what the test results would bring, but he was hoping for the best. The resulting diagnosis, however, was just the opposite. Steve had leukemia. 🎵

Damn Chicago police!
STEVE GOODMAN

'This was the time to do it — either do it or don't'

Stomping into the two-bed hospital room, he huffed into bed and closeted himself behind a curtain. He told nurses he wanted no visitors. He insisted he would talk only to doctors. He screamed at aides who tried to make his bed. He threw a lunch tray on the floor.

"He was one very, very angry, small man," says Jack Goldberg, who shared the room with Steve Goodman on the eighth floor of the James Ewing wing of Memorial Sloan-Kettering Cancer Center on the Upper East Side of New York City.

In the nearby lounge, oncologists had just told Steve that over the past week their tests had corroborated his Chicago doctor's diagnosis of terminal illness. It enraged Steve, and his livid behavior persisted unrelentingly for another week and a half.

But one day, after lunch had been brought to the room, Steve climbed out of bed, pulled open the curtains, hopped back onto the bed, looked at Goldberg and broke his long, uncomfortable silence.

"Hey, what're you having?" he said.

"Well, I don't know," Goldberg replied. "I guess I'm having the chicken."

"Oh, I don't care for the chicken. They serve it too much. But I've asked 'em to make me a hamburger."

Finally, thought Goldberg, some conversation. Also finally, Steve was able to hold his lunch down. Chemotherapy had made throwing up almost a routine, not to mention cramps and fever. But it wasn't the physical side effects that had infuriated Steve. It was the diagnosis that he was the bearer of a fatal disease — acute lymphoblastic leukemia — as well as the prospect that he might not survive another year, that perhaps his demise was just a few months away.

The disease and its implications, even the magnitude of its acronym of ALL, consumed Steve. How and when and why had he contracted leukemia? No one could say. What would an immediate death sentence mean to a vibrant, gregarious and talented 20-year-old? Steve was about to find out.

None of Steve's doctors at Sloan-Kettering would borrow from the movies and tell him, "You have X months or years to live." The possibility he would live for three years, they knew, was perhaps 10 to 15 percent. They talked in

> **He was one very, very angry, small man.**
> **JACK GOLDBERG**

(Opposite page) Steve poses for roommate Ron Rosoff on a sunny morning in August 1969 next door to his apartment on Southport Avenue.

(Photo by Ron Rosoff)

terms of hope, of similar case studies, of trial drugs and transfusions that held potential for keeping his disease at bay while they searched for answers. In early 1969, the treatment of leukemia was in its infancy. Assurances or even optimistic odds of a permanent remedy did not exist.

"We were just beginning to crack acute leukemia," says one of Steve's oncologists at Sloan-Kettering, Dr. Monroe Dowling. "Most of the people with leukemia were going to be dead in six months. We didn't have cures, and we were just beginning to really understand it. We had a lot of drugs that we could do things with, but we didn't know necessarily the best way to use them, so we were learning about that. It was essentially a disease in which you did experimental work."

Since his 1967 foray into the Greenwich Village music scene, Steve had imagined coming back to Manhattan, but certainly not for medical reasons. The road to his return resulted, in part, from a tangled family connection.

It began with tests of Steve's blood ordered in December 1968, just prior to the Lake Forest College winter break, by the Goodmans' compassionate family physician at Weiss hospital, Dr. Gene Handelman, who had grown up with Bud Goodman on Chicago's West Side. Once Handelman suspected leukemia, he consulted with another of Bud's friends, Chicago urologist Dr. Herb Sohn, who had bought his first car, a Corvair, from Bud at Keystone Chevrolet and had received a replacement from him after windows in the first one repeatedly imploded. Bud, it turned out, also had been seeing Sohn's wife on the side. Sohn's father had been treated for colon cancer at Sloan-Kettering, and Sohn says he urged Handelman to send Steve there because "they don't give up on anybody." Handelman's thoughts also shot to another young man from Niles with leukemia, Scott Murphy, a friend of Steve's younger brother, David, and whom Handelman had referred to the same place. "It was considered the top cancer center in the country," says Handelman's widow, Natalie. It became the immediate destination for Steve.

Before leaving Chicago, however, Steve had to face dropping out of college for the second time in less than two years. During exam week in December, Steve had worn a button stating "I Really Didn't Want to Go to College Anyway." But a decision to leave school, mirroring his departure from the University of Illinois two years earlier, was particularly wrenching because he had embraced Lake Forest's left-leaning slate of political-science courses — so much that he had agreed to help design a new one. Steve and Lucy Wells, both juniors, and other students were working with a half-dozen younger faculty to initiate an interdisciplinary course on colonialism with a Chicago think tank called the Adlai Stevenson Institute, named for the former governor and two-time Democratic presidential nominee. The course, set for winter term 1969, called for a dozen visiting scholars to lecture on topics related to the Vietnam War era. Each student, including Steve, was to focus on one speaker and write a culminating paper.

The course faculty included Ed Hawes, associate professor of history, in

It was essentially a disease in which you did experimental work.
DR. MONROE DOWLING

whose fall 1968 class, "Development of Modern Europe," Steve had earned the highest possible grade, an "honors" mark. One afternoon in early January, just prior to winter term, Wells dropped by Hawes' tiny, two-floor, minimally furnished rental cottage, which stood across the street from Lake Forest, to consult with him about the Stevenson course. There, she found Hawes and Steve sitting cross-legged on the living-room floor, classical music playing on the stereo, the atmosphere sad but the tone matter-of-fact.

Wells sat on a mattress as Steve told Hawes that over winter break he had seen Handelman several times, that he probably had a rare form of leukemia with an uncertain prognosis and that he was headed to New York. Steve said his doctor had told him he was doing too much and handed him a choice: Give up music or college. "He was paying his way through college by doing music," Wells says, "so his choice was clear to him. He couldn't do college without music, so he was going to leave college."

"I figured I was a time bomb," Steve told Jack Hurst of the *Chicago Tribune* in 1983. "I said, 'What do I really like to do?' I decided it was to play music, write songs and listen to other people play and sing. I just liked music and wanted to be a part of it somehow."

Steve could have made the decision without telling anyone. But he felt he had to face Hawes because of his commitment to those who had worked on the Stevenson course. "It was also because he always needed an audience, whether one person or a roomful or a convention hall full," Wells says. "Steve had those big eyes that would look you right in the face, catch your eye, and there was no unhooking from that. He was a personality who did his best with an audience, so if he had your attention, you were his audience, and he was very good at getting your attention in a very positive way."

His approach to the immediate topic, though, was one-to-one and low-key. While "he asked that we not talk a lot about his leukemia," word spread quietly, Wells says. "Everybody knew. We just didn't hold press conferences. We all knew."

As Wells listened to Steve's chat with Hawes, her shock and bewilderment presaged the feelings that Steve's countless friends encountered as they learned of his diagnosis. For many, it became their first in-person experience with the prospect of youthful mortality.

"I had lost people that I had known, but no one who had been really close to me," Wells says. "I had never witnessed someone who was dying of a disease that would leave them wasted over a period of time. I didn't really have a handle, at 20 years old, on what this meant. To really grab hold of what he was trying to grab hold of was difficult for me and not something that I wanted to dwell on."

Nor did Steve, but he had no alternative. He spent a few more days informing friends, including Maine East football buddy Paul Niesen. Over dinner at Niesen's house, he announced that he was heading to New York for treatment. Steve already had grasped what his role would be at Sloan-Kettering, telling Niesen and his parents, "I'm going to be a guinea pig." Niesen, who knew the

I figured I was a time bomb.
STEVE GOODMAN

One evening during Steve's first stint of leukemia treatment at Sloan-Kettering in New York, he signed himself out to attend a concert by Tom Paxton, many of whose songs Steve knew and later performed.

(Photo by Ron Rosoff)

1: The James Ewing wing, named for an early cancer researcher, later was renamed for a major donor, Marie Schwartz.

ramifications, having experienced the loss of the child of a family friend to leukemia, was stunned. "We were 20 years old, and we thought we were invincible, that nothing could happen to us," he says. "We had proved that over and over by chugging cases of beer and partying all night, so how could this happen?"

Another visit Steve made was to his carpooling Lake Forest classmate, Jim Dernehl, who had moved to nearby Riverside. "He was very down," Dernehl says. "What could I say to a guy like that, other than 'You never know what's going to happen.' " Steve had brought along a bottle of wine and asked Dernehl to save it so later they could drink it together. Dernehl sensed Steve was feeling that, "If he placed enough little things like that around, he'd last forever."

Steve formally withdrew from Lake Forest on Friday, Jan. 17, 1969, the last day his name would appear in the Earl of Old Town listing in the *Chicago Tribune* entertainment pages for the next eight months. Shortly afterward, he flew to New York, where, for the rest of the winter and spring, Sloan-Kettering became his campus for an unwelcome but necessary new curriculum in leukemic cancer.

Leukemia had been seen since the 19th century as a disease that produces abnormal white blood cells. But it wasn't until after the United States' use of atomic weapons on Hiroshima and Nagasaki triggered Japan's surrender during World War II and ballooned leukemia rates that the first chemotherapy drugs were developed in the 1950s to fight the disease, primarily in children. But the drugs did not eradicate leukemia. They only suppressed it, normalizing blood-cell counts for a span of time — months, perhaps years — in a stage called remission. Today, in part because of genetic research, chemotherapy drugs are more refined, and bone-marrow and stem-cell transplantation is the state-of-the-art treatment, producing cure rates of 70 to 90 percent for many leukemic strains. But in 1969, transplants had been effective in only a few children and were unproven in adults. Oncologists still were casting about for proper combinations of drugs such as prednisone (a steroid), vincristine and asparaginase to keep patients alive long enough to attend a family reunion or high-school prom.

"This was really the Dark Ages for leukemia treatment," says Dr. Isabel "Bonnie" Cunningham, an oncologist and stem-cell transplantation expert who later became one of Steve's doctors. When he was admitted to Sloan-Kettering, however, she was less than a year older than Steve, held a bachelor's degree in French and religion and worked as the record-keeper for the center's experimental leukemia treatment service on Ewing 8. [1]

"Those were the very, very first years that there was any progress being made at all for adults with leukemia," Cunningham says. "It was really a bleak overall prognosis, in the single digits of chance of cure. In fact, people never talked about cure in 1969. But certainly there were remissions. You could get a string of drugs for, say, four or five months — hard, more than normal in terms of duration — and make the disease go away and go back to your life for a few months, then bounce back and go back and forth."

Cunningham played Girl Friday to the oncologists on Ewing 8, who, besides Dowling, included Drs. Timothy Gee (Steve's lead physician) and Phillip Salem and the service's head, Bayard "Barney" Clarkson. She likened them all to youthful, energetic cowboys on a mission to tame a little-known wilderness — a medical quagmire whose tragedies were exploited and exaggerated by such popular novels and films as Erich Segal's weepy *Love Story*.

"They were very optimistic doctors, with a lot of laboratory proof that this disease could be successfully treated, and we just had to work out how to do it," she says. "It was like a M*A*S*H unit. It was a new, more aggressive approach, rather than sitting back. They were young and fun and interested in getting this disease brought under control. The idea was that they would knock down the leukemia so that it seemed to disappear. I think of it like spraying for roaches in your kitchen. When you spray for roaches, they're gone, but you know that they're going to be back, right? Then if you're wise, you say, 'Well, look, I'm sick of waiting for them to come back. I'm going to spray every month with a different kind of a spray in hopes that they will never come back,' rather than sit around your house and wait for the bugs to come back. It is exactly the same principle."

Steve was one of the first patients to undergo such intravenous, multi-drug treatment, Cunningham says. Not only did it disrupt his digestive system and prompt temporary hair loss, it also meant that he needed to stay at Sloan-Kettering for frequent observation and regular bone-marrow draws, as well as blood transfusions that would help him fight infections invited by the lowered resistance that the chemo drugs brought on. "We were following a protocol, trying to understand the disease and the effect of the drugs," she says. "You're not going to know if somebody goes into remission or comes out of it unless you're following them all the time. Just like the bugs around your sink, when the first bugs come back is when you want to attack them again. You don't want to wait until your kitchen is overcome with bugs."

Occasionally, Steve left the hospital for a few hours, often for a malted across the street at the Acropolis luncheonette, operated by Nick "the Greek" and Pete Papadatos, brothers who ran up tabs for Sloan-Kettering patients and looked after their relatives' kids. One evening, Steve signed himself out to attend a concert by one of his musical heroes, Tom Paxton. Other times, Steve took leave of the hospital for an overnight or a weekend. "We were a little relaxed about letting people out," Cunningham says, "and Steve always had friends. He was always living on somebody's (living-room) floor." But for his first several months of treatment, his home was primarily the rooms, lavatories, halls and lounge of Ewing 8 at Sloan-Kettering.

Ewing 8 didn't lack for people Steve's age. About a dozen other patients in their late teens and early 20s were on the floor because Sloan-Kettering was one of only a handful of referral centers in the country (whereas today leukemia is treated at hundreds of community hospitals nationwide). One such patient was Eric Lund, a Norwalk, Connecticut, teenager whose rambunctious but losing

It was like a M*A*S*H unit. It was a new, more aggressive approach, rather than sitting back. They were young and fun and interested in getting this disease brought under control.
DR. ISABEL 'BONNIE' CUNNINGHAM

battle with leukemia became the focus of a poignant, best-selling memoir, *Eric*, by his mother, Doris, in 1974. (Less than two years later, CBS aired a Hallmark TV movie based on her book, starring Patricia Neal, Claude Akins, Mark Hamill and, in the title role, John Savage.) Another Ewing 8 patient was Steve's roommate, Jack Goldberg.

Two years younger than Steve, Goldberg, a self-described "happy-go-lucky hippie type" from Brooklyn, had been diagnosed five years earlier with Hodgkin's disease. He quickly tried to befriend Steve, "but I tried too hard and had very little savvy when it came to respecting other people's boundaries." A nurse named Mary Lou called Goldberg to the nurses' station to tell him, "Steve really needs some space. I know what you're doing is well-intended, and Steve will probably appreciate having more of a peer to talk to, but it has to be on his terms and on his time."

So Goldberg waited. He assumed that Steve played guitar because one was propped up against the wall near Steve's bed, but it remained untouched until a couple of days after Steve ended his isolation and chatted with Goldberg about lunch. Their treatments had disrupted their patterns of rest, prompting them to nap during the day, so they'd gotten into the habit of staying up late. One night, neither could sleep, so Steve grabbed his guitar and told Goldberg, "Hey, c'mon with me down to the end of the hall." Daytimes, the lounge was busy with patients and visitors watching TV and smoking cigarettes, but on this night it was empty, except for the two of them. For the first time since he'd arrived at Sloan-Kettering, Steve eased the guitar onto his lap and started playing — and playing, and playing.

> **He would stay alive and healthy, and I would stay alive and healthy and not relapse, and it was like we had to hold each other to that.**
> **JACK GOLDBERG**

"The nurses brought us a can of apple juice and some cups and ice, and we just sang song after song together," Goldberg says. "He could play anything I would name, any song that I happened to like: 'Hey, how about that Beatles song?' He was like an entire songbook." Equally impressive to Goldberg as the Manhattan darkness turned to dawn was the affecting timbre of Steve's singing. "He had a lovely voice, and it emoted sensitivity and, at the same time, humor. We stayed up all night, and it was wonderful."

In all, Steve and Goldberg shared the same room for a month and a half, baring hopes and fears. "It started out as sort of a cat fight, two young men at each other's throats, keeping their distance and not liking one another at all," Goldberg says, "but after six weeks, we had come to love one another, and we were very, very close." Goldberg confided his own substance abuse to Steve, and the two made a pact: "He would stay alive and healthy, and I would stay alive and healthy and not relapse, and it was like we had to hold each other to that."

As Steve felt more at home at Sloan-Kettering, he welcomed visitors, including his brokenhearted family. His dad, Bud, came to see him once, but the most dedicated caller, at first, was his mother, Minnette, who was faced at the time with an unenviable choice. In her home in Niles, she was looking after not only her other son, David, a junior at Maine East High, but also a Chilean exchange student and Steve's 21-year-old friend, Jim Freitag. More wearing, however, was the deteriorating bond with her husband, Bud, who had begun a romantic relationship with Dr. Herb Sohn's wife and who had just suffered a major heart attack. Should Minnette stay at home and take care of her recuperating but straying husband and the rest of her household, or should she go to New York and shepherd the treatment of her just-diagnosed son? In the winter and spring of 1969, Minnette chose the latter course almost exclusively.

The mood in the Goodman house at the time was "pretty down," Freitag said, adding that Minnette's trips to visit Steve did not bolster her ties with Bud. "It strained their relationship a lot, with Minnette being gone all the time, and Minnette being such a strong person and Bud being equally as strong." Once, in a helpful gesture, Freitag even traveled to New York to spell Minnette and see Steve himself.

Another early visitor for Steve was a woman who became a trusted friend and lifelong champion — a folk-music insider, guitarist and Jewish raconteur named Paula Ballan. Blessed with the gift of articulate gab and a razor wit, the short, rotund, chain-smoking woman with long, brown hair and saucer glasses had grown up in working-class South Bronx and made it her business to affiliate herself with as many Greenwich Village musicians as possible. Since 1966, she also had been on the program committee of the Philadelphia Folk Festival and had just landed the job of booking the prestigious annual event. In January 1969, Ballan had recently moved into a compact, $78-a-month, two-bedroom apartment at the top of an aging, five-floor walk-up on East 67th Street, one-half block west of Sloan-Kettering.

Three years older than Steve, Ballan met him in a roundabout way, via the Philly festival, where Steve had picked up one of only 100 "Member Haynes Family" buttons that honored the behind-the-scenes role that Bert and Judy Haynes had played at the event since 1963. Wearing the button while walking down a Manhattan street to Sloan-Kettering, Steve bumped into actress Harriette Segal, a Haynes family friend. Segal spotted the button, stopped and talked with Steve and alerted Bert Haynes, who contacted African-American folksinger John Bassette, who had shared club stages with Steve in 1967 in the Village. Bassette called Ballan and told her, "Listen, a real good friend of mine is in the hospital right down the block, and could you go visit him?" Ballan walked over, introduced herself and realized that she'd crossed paths with Steve in the Village and at the Philly festival.

Soon, Ballan's dingy brownstone apartment, with its bunk beds and fold-out couch, became Steve's gratis getaway from Sloan-Kettering, a refuge where he could rest — and throw up, when necessary — in relative privacy. "We nursed him, we kept people away from him, we kept the blinds down, and if he had to go somewhere and couldn't get there himself, we took him there," recalled Ballan's then-boyfriend, Paul Hecht. "His treatments were terrible, just gluppy. We'd have to put new sheets on the floor."

The privacy also gave Steve the chance to smoke pot whenever he wished. While he had been exposed to marijuana in college years, particularly during

John Bassette, shown in the mid-1960s, connected Steve to Manhattan resident and Philadelphia Folk Festival booker Paula Ballan after Haynes family friend Harriette Segal alerted Bassette after seing Steve wearing a "Haynes Family" button (below).
(Top photo courtesy of Paula Ballan, bottom photo by Clay Eals)

Paula Ballan, shown with her dog, Woody Guthrie, on the steps of her brownstone in 1968, became an informal nurse for Steve, given that her apartment was a half block from Sloan-Kettering. "He was scarfing down food because I was bringing him as much hash as he wanted to smoke, and he was developing the munchies and keeping his weight up."

(Photo by Ron Rosoff)

2: Dr. Barney Clarkson, head of the oncology service, says the National Institutes of Health eventually issued Sloan-Kettering a supply of cannabis, which was kept in a safe. "The nurses would go crazy because they introduced all these restrictions," he says. "It was much more tightly controlled than the morphine and the other narcotics. It was sort of ridiculous."

1967 in Greenwich Village, as a Sloan-Kettering patient he used it, in part, to combat treatment-induced nausea. "The doctors became confounded when other people who were getting the same red-death chemo that Steve was getting were just puking while Steve was scarfing down the food," Ballan says. "He was scarfing down food because I was bringing him as much hash as he wanted to smoke, and he was developing the munchies and keeping his weight up."

Cunningham confirms that the Sloan-Kettering oncologists didn't know of marijuana's palliative effect on vomiting. "We did not have the strong pills and medicines to prevent nausea. That was before the doctors realized that marijuana was a very good anti-emetic." She says that it didn't take long, however, for Ewing 8's young patients to be found regularly sneaking tokes of grass in the floor's restroom. "We knew nothing about it," adds Dowling, "and we didn't *want* to know anything about it." [2]

Ballan also looked after Steve in other ways, loaning him countless pairs of gloves to protect his hands and bringing him six-packs of Coca Cola to settle his stomach and combat his greenish pallor. It also was at Ballan's apartment where Steve received a distressing call from a young, slender, blond waitress and single mother who had been his girlfriend in Chicago and whose plane trip to New York Minnette apparently had financed in an attempt to comfort her son. The overnight visit quickly turned sour, Ballan says, because within hours of her arrival the woman broke off the relationship, saying she couldn't cope with Steve's disease.

Beyond proximity to Sloan-Kettering, privacy, rest and marijuana, what drew Steve to Ballan and her apartment was their mutual passion for music. "I'd had music and on-the-road musicians and their girlfriends and entourages in my apartments from the time I moved out of my parents' home," she says, "and because I was already involved with programming festivals, I was regularly courted by performer wannabes." Her Upper East Side flat rapidly became a way station for hungry, itinerant singers and instrumentalists of all stripes within the counterculture. At one point, more than 30 copies of Ballan's apartment key floated among musicians around the country. Her connections were so expansive and her door so revolving that New York bluegrass guitarist and psychotherapist Gene Yellin says that Ballan was to the Manhattan folk world what Washington, D.C., millionaire and hostess Perle Mesta (of "Call Me Madam" fame) had been to the previous generation's political arena.

One of Ballan's frequent guests, Philadelphia folksinger Mike Miller, became fast friends with Steve. While Miller was a mountain of a man compared to Steve, each possessed a pudginess and wicked sense of humor that led to their participation in the mythical Fat Folksingers of America. "Some scurrilous guy nominated me for membership, which pissed me off, so I nominated Goodman," Miller says. The club's symbolic handshake included a wiggling of the belly, and its purported induction procedure was a nasty insult. "The initiation was, there's good news and there's bad news," Miller says. "The good news is that Odetta has been elected to membership in the FFA, and the bad news is you've gotta tell her." Miller and Steve also shared a love of limericks, engaging in "Can you top this?" exchanges of lewd lyrics for hours at Ballan's apartment — one night continuing the contest by spouting ever bawdier versions while each coupled with a woman on separate levels of Ballan's bunk bed.

What Ballan knew instinctively, if not consciously, was that music and its adherents could fuel Steve's recovery. "We were all musicians," she says. "We all filled our non-working hours with playing, either alone or with anyone else who could either keep up or show us something new."

Freitag, who met Ballan when he visited Steve at Sloan-Kettering, confirms music's essential role in his friend's struggle: "It gave him someplace to bury himself, totally immerse himself in and put what was happening out of his mind, so that he wasn't just welling in self-pity."

Fortunately for Steve, impromptu picking parties sprang up at Ballan's at all times of day and night. Sometimes 10 to 15 musicians with instruments squeezed into the cramped quarters. "You wouldn't believe the number of people who were there and the music that went on," says Steve Mandell, the banjoist who two years later hit big as a performer on the instrumental "Dueling Banjos," featured in the film "Deliverance." "It was astounding. Five floors up we would trudge. Every once in a while, someone would even come up with a string bass. You never knew who you would meet there."

Ray Frank helped Steve shape a fledgling song about his race with the sun. "It just kind of poured out of me," Steve said.
(Photo by Ricky Pearl Smith, courtesy of Ray Frank)

The musicians got to know Steve either at the apartment or, at Ballan's behest, by seeing him on Ewing 8, where he tinkered with his fledgling "City of New Orleans" chorus and other lyrical scraps. One visitor was college student and seasoned accompanist Ray Frank, who took his guitar to Sloan-Kettering several times to trade licks with Steve. Each time Frank visited, he slipped off his shoes and climbed onto Steve's bed, where they sat cross-legged, facing each other and playing their guitars as Steve's intravenous chemotherapy line swayed to the beat of the music. One week, Steve's upper lip bore a mustache, Frank says, but the next week the mustache was gone. "It doesn't work with chemo and throwing up," Steve told him. "It doesn't smell too good when the food is passing back up."

One of their picking sessions became more than just trading other people's tunes. Intimacy gripped the two as Steve opened up a notebook of lyrical fragments and shared with Frank a fledgling composition.

"I wrote this song," he told Frank. "It just kind of poured out of me."

In contrast to the whimsical, rhyme-heavy ditties of Steve's younger days, this was a serious musical poem, stunningly slow and desolate. By turns literal and metaphorical, its words spoke of feeling unwound and weary, of risking participation in a race and of suspecting a rigged outcome. Nowhere did the word "leukemia" or anything like it appear, but an omen of ultimate failure saturated the allegory. The key phrase was a question, unanswered: Why bother to compete with the "treacherous pace" of the sun?

The song's emotional honesty stunned Frank. "Wow, my God, man. You just said what it's like to be where you are," he told Steve.

"There was a sense of desperation in him," Frank says. "He was doing music nonstop, holding onto what he thought would allow him to leave something behind. He felt that he had very little time to leave his mark. At the moment, I represented his lifeline."

While Steve had the words and melody down, with Frank he struggled with the chords. Over and over, Frank listened to Steve's lyrics — the sun, normally an upbeat symbol, in this song equating to merciless mortality — and he played along. By chance, Frank had been working up an unusual arrangement of the "Porgy and Bess" standard, "Summertime." Inspiration struck, and he summoned its haunting, minor-key patterns for Steve.

"How about these?" Frank said, strumming the yearning Gershwin chords.

"What was that?" Steve blurted out, mimicking them on his guitar. "Great! I like that!"

The two tinkered some more, and soon the words and music had the fit and feel of a bittersweet embrace. One aspect of the song, its voice, gave it a tone of mystery. Steve had elected to tell the song's existential story in the third person, so that the character pondering the race with the sun was "he" and "David," not "I." Further, he titled the composition "Song for David."

"Who's David?" Frank asked him.

"Well," said Steve, "he's my brother, but ..."

> **There was a sense of desperation in him. He was doing music nonstop, holding onto what he thought would allow him to leave something behind.**
> **RAY FRANK**

The third-person approach was certainly oblique. Like cloaking an open wound, it betrayed the source of the song's intimacy, sealing Steve's plight and anguish from any of the song's potential listeners and stealing a significant portion of its power. In using this approach, however, Steve achieved what he saw as a greater and more sophisticated good, says Ballan, who, like Frank, heard the song in its early stages. While its lyrics made David the subject of the song, Ballan emphasizes that its title made David its primary audience and beneficiary.

"Steve was mostly trying to explain to his brother his own fear and anxiety over his disease," Ballan says. But noting that their mother, Minnette, had made several trips to New York and was "focused entirely on Steve" because of the leukemia, Ballan also interprets the song as an apology. "Steve cared about his brother in such a way that he would have understood how abandoned David must have felt, and this was a song to reach out as a brother and say, 'I'm sorry all this focus is on me. I didn't intend for this to happen, and I'm dedicating this song to you so that you understand that it isn't about anything you've done. It's about what's happening to me, and I'm sorry.'"

Steve never publicly clarified the true meaning of the song. Perhaps the closest he came to doing so was in an August 1976 interview for the London music magazine *Omaha Rainbow*, in which he identified David as "my younger brother, who went through some difficult times." As Steve tried to elaborate, his vagueness compounded. "I don't know the thing about families and siblings," he said. "The song's about a particular time in my brother's life, one of the few times that I could honestly say I was getting to know the guy. He was my

Bonnie Koloc, shown performing with accompanist Ron Scroggin, couldn't believe her eyes when she visited Steve at Sloan-Kettering. "There he was in the lobby with his guitar singing to other patients, and he really wasn't very well himself. He got better by helping others to get better."
(Photo courtesy of Gib Foster)

brother, I lived with him long enough, so I was just trying to address myself to a specific thing there. If there's anything universal in it, that was an accident, and it happened later."

Frank felt at the time that Steve shared it with him that "Song for David" reflected an astonishing maturity — particularly as it was the first solemn song that the 20-year-old had completed. "He was able to expose the emotions that he felt but we can't speak, and, to me, that's always been the real value of music, that it's a different language than English," he says. "English does not have good and easy ways of dealing with emotional stuff, but music is that language. It is the language of emotion. So he was saying the things that he couldn't say in English in music."

The third-person approach of "Song for David" also signaled a hallmark of Steve's future songwriting. It was the first of many songs in which he dealt with death, but at a distance.

"One of the things he did so successfully after he became ill was he built around him walls of protection against his own raw emotions about what he was going through," Frank reflects. "The protections were his abilities to tell stories and write songs, and when you tell stories and write songs, you create a whole mythos, an alternate reality that becomes a real reality."

The reality expressed in "Song for David" soon was to spread, thanks to Frank and his Earl of Old Town colleague from Chicago, Bonnie Koloc. That winter of 1969, Koloc had traveled to New York City to record a demo tape, was seeking a new accompanist and, at Ballan's behest, met Frank in Paula Ballan's apartment. Voice and guitar blended like buttered bread, and Koloc invited Frank to fly to Chicago as her sideman for a six-week run at the Earl of Old Town that spring.

Meanwhile, Koloc, no stranger to Steve's increasingly compelling shows at the Earl, got a call from him at Ballan's and soon visited him at Sloan-Kettering.

She'd been shocked by Steve's leukemia diagnosis, but what she saw on Ewing 8 moved her indelibly. "I couldn't believe my eyes," she told the *Chicago Tribune* in 1985. "There he was in the lobby with his guitar singing to other patients, and he really wasn't very well himself. He got better by helping others to get better." Koloc made several visits to Steve at the hospital, one time bringing a reel-to-reel tape recorder to preserve his words and music. "We spent hours," she said, "singing together in that lobby."

The resulting tape, which survive, was "quite depressing," says Gib Foster, a graphic designer and friend of Koloc's who sobbed as he later listened to the recording. "They just let it go and sat and talked and sang these very down songs. It was a real outlet for Steve. He was going through some real realization that he was going to die, and he was letting it out in his music."

On the tape, Steve twice played and sang "Song for David," and Koloc was taken with its context and immediacy. Harvesting the only completed song of a composer whom she knew might not live long enough to perform it for audiences himself, Koloc carried it back to Chicago, incorporating it in her sets with Frank on April 16-20 and April 23-27 at the Earl. The song's stark, somber tone repeatedly brought the saloon's chatty audiences to aching silence. "We probably played it every night," Frank says.

In the early evening of Saturday, April 19, Koloc and Frank dropped by WFMT-FM to play half a dozen songs — including "Song for David" and Bob Dylan's "Just Like a Woman" — for Ray Nordstrand, manager of the station and co-host of its weekly, free-form "Midnight Special." [3] Nordstrand taped the session and played a few songs from it, including "Song for David," later that night on the 10:15 p.m. show. That evening, after Koloc and Frank had left the station, Nordstrand confided to a University of Illinois history major, protégé Rich Warren, the urgency behind "Song for David." Nordstrand told him, "Bonnie said it's written by this guy named Steve Goodman. He's dying, he's in a hospital in New York, he's got three days left to live." Following Nordstrand's lead, Warren took a copy of the Koloc-Frank tape with him back to the University of Illinois in Champaign/Urbana, where on the campus radio station, WPGU-FM, he hosted a folk program, "Changes." Warren played the tape a week later, on April 26, on the show.

In this manner, through the voice and guitar of others, via radio stations that reached audiences in his native city and the site of his first years in college, and while he fought stomach-wrenching chemotherapy from the bed of a cancer clinic more than 800 miles away, the music of the adult Steve Goodman first hit the public airwaves. [4]

As spring waned, Steve responded serviceably to his treatment. "This was tough chemo, it was tough going, it was depressing, but his manner of handling it was to fight back with his personality," Cunningham says. The prospect of Steve returning to Chicago gradually became more real, but undeniable as well was the fact that for the rest of his uncertain life, he would need to return regularly for checkups and transfusions. Manhattan and the Village scene, par-

---

Bonnie (Koloc) said it's written by this guy named Steve Goodman. He's dying, he's in a hospital in New York, he's got three days left to live.
RAY NORDSTRAND

3: The program's other co-host was Norm Pellegrini, WFMT program director who originated the folk-music show in the early 1950s, added Mike Nichols, an announcer from the South Side (who later broke away as a famed film director), and with Nichols expanded the fare to show tunes and farce and — triggered by the signature song of the local Willow Singers, led by banjoist Fleming Brown — gave the program its title.

4: A recording of Bonnie Koloc, backed by Ray Frank, performing "Song for David" on April 19, 1969, survives in the WFMT-FM archives and was aired more than once in later years during the station's tributes to Steve Goodman.

ticularly as it wove its way through Ballan's apartment, would become his home away from home. It was not an unappealing prospect, given that it built upon the musical connections he had made two years earlier with the likes of Four Winds coffeehouse owner Penny Simon.

On a weekend visit to Simon's home in New Jersey late that spring, Steve sat on the floor, picked up her husband's Style 18 Martin guitar and played and sang songs for her infant son, Eddie. "The baby was fascinated, climbed upon Steve's knee and just stared in his face," Simon recalled. "He was mesmerized by him, and Steve was really into it." The topic of leukemia was brief but potent. "He told me he was sick for three weeks, he'd feel good for one week, and then it was time for more treatment, and he'd feel lousy for three weeks and then good for a week, over and over," she said. "He was devastated, but he really didn't talk much about it. He was taking it one step at a time. He didn't know how long he had, but he had no reason to go to college anymore. He just took it as a sign to do what he wanted to do. This was the time to do it — either do it or don't."

Steve was uninsured,[5] so financing his stay and treatment at Sloan-Kettering loomed as a challenge. But the heritage and generous mission of the cancer center eased the burden considerably. "Nobody paid cash," Cunningham says. "We had huge funding from the National Institutes of Health, and insurance paid some, but we were a little liberal with the use of (that). I don't think money was the primary objective, and I'm sure Memorial lost a lot. Everybody was determined to do everything they could to wipe out this disease." Part of Sloan-Kettering's approach, she says, stemmed from the young age of many of the leukemia patients. "They were kids, and none of them had any money. We weren't fast and loose, but the money was there, so we just put 'em in the beds. It just wasn't an issue."

Confronting Steve and his family as he underwent treatment in New York was persistent talk of an unusually high number of childhood leukemia cases stemming from Niles, where he had lived for most of the past seven years, as had his brother's friend and fellow Sloan-Kettering leukemia patient Scott Murphy. Naturally, evidence of a pattern would have helped answer "Why me?" questions, and such talk indeed had basis in fact. The federal Communicable Disease Center (predecessor of today's Centers for Disease Control) in 1961 had sent Epidemic Intelligence Service officers to the fledgling Illinois suburb to investigate a rare, so-called "cancer cluster." Eight Niles children had been diagnosed with leukemia between 1957 and 1960, including four in a three-month period, and seven had died from it. Three had attended the same Catholic school, four were preschool-age siblings, and one who was unaffiliated lived a block away. As well, three adults who belonged to the parish at the time also had leukemia.

After a one-year study, Dr. Clark Heath of the CDC (whose work was cited in Jonathan Harr's 1995 best-selling legal/environmental thriller *A Civil Action*) wrote in the *American Journal of Medicine* in 1963 that he found no hereditary

They were kids, and none of them had any money. We weren't fast and loose, but the money was there, so we just put 'em in the beds.
DR. ISABEL 'BONNIE' CUNNINGHAM

5: Though other sources indicate Steve was uninsured, his mother, Minnette, told a tribute audience of 250 on Nov. 19, 2007, at Lake Forest College that a health-insurance policy that Steve had procured from the college provided at least some coverage of Steve's medical costs throughout the rest of his life.

The cheery nature of Minnette Goodman, shown in summer 1969, was repeatedly tested when she had to explain to those who hadn't heard that her son, Steve, had leukemia.
(Photo by Ron Rosoff)

factor in the Niles cases. But he also said they could not be chalked up to coincidence. "These cases constitute a clearly defined micro-epidemic," he wrote, in findings that received prominent media coverage. But sadly, no cause could be proved. Years later, the only similarity that Heath and others saw between the Niles cluster and a handful of other similar ones was that they occurred in relatively newly settled communities, making for nothing more than an inconclusive hypothesis.

Without answers to "why," Steve was left with "what" and "how." The trick to gaining longer freedom from the hospital was for his blood-cell counts to respond to treatment. Periodically, to assess progress, Sloan-Kettering staff used a large syringe to draw marrow from the bone in his hip, a painful procedure whose discomfort lasted days. Once Steve's blood counts returned to acceptable levels and he, in the parlance, "entered a remission," the doctors cleared him to fly to Chicago that summer. He did so, attending the June 20 wedding of his friend Jim Freitag. Awaiting Steve at home in the weeks ahead were the burgeoning clubs of the folk scene and myriad friends to update on his condition.

When he bumped into Ron Isaacson, a Temple Beth Israel friend from Albany Park days, Steve talked more about music than about his disease. "He didn't go full-blown into it, but physically you could tell he was having problems," Isaacson says. "He was just real tired, withdrawn. There was something going on physically that he didn't have the bubbly energy. But fairly early on, he made the decision that he was just not going to let it get to him and just threw himself more into the music."

With high-school friend Cathy Lind, Steve delivered the leukemia message musically, stopping by with his guitar at her home in Park Ridge, pulling her aside, sitting her down in a corner of the living room and playing "Song for David." "I felt it as a serenade," she says, "but it was very different."

Howard Berkman, Steve's high-school guitar mentor, says he and others initially greeted news of Steve's diagnosis with suspicion. "I didn't believe it," says Berkman, who heard about it via Earl Pionke. "I really thought Steve was just making up a story to get the gig, to make people feel sorry for him, because he had that real theatrical, schmaltzed-out, emotional nature." After he found out the leukemia was real, Berkman saw immediate changes in his high-school competitor. "It made Steve honest," he says. "He stopped lying about himself and telling stories, which he did a lot of. Steve was a white liar, a fibber, mostly to not hurt other people's feelings. But that (leukemia) gave him a different perspective."

Some, such as Ron Weindruch, of Steve's 1965 Sammy pledge class at the University of Illinois, got word of the disease indirectly. Steve's mom, Minnette, telephoned Champaign/Urbana to ask Weindruch if he could host a weekend visit by Steve's brother, David.

"Sure," said Weindruch, who hadn't talked with Steve for about a year. "How's Steve doing?"

"Steve," Minnette replied, "has leukemia."

"You've gotta be kidding."

"A mother doesn't kid about that."

Steve himself also didn't kid anyone about his disease, but the topic wasn't always the first out of his mouth, particularly with the Vietnam War raging under the newly elected Nixon administration. His high-school football friend Herb Johnson says while most in their Maine East gang thought the war "must be right" because "the government can't do anything wrong," Steve's view was the opposite. "This is a stupid thing," Steve told Johnson. "What are we doing there? These people won't even fight for themselves. We're there fighting for them and dying for them." That July, however, when Johnson married, Steve's present to the wedding couple was a symbol of the government, a U.S. savings bond. "I was very touched that he hadn't totally given up on the system," Johnson says. "He was just against this policy."

Eager to get back on the stage in his home city, Steve once again snagged a gig at the no-alcohol coffeehouse It's Here. He landed the third spot on a four-act weekend bill. Larry Rand, who had met Steve in their high-school days when both performed at suburban Scot's Cellar, was the opener. Rand, a Northwestern University student in nearby Evanston, had just completed a two-year hitch in the Army and hadn't seen Steve in years. Steve's improvements in repertoire, dexterity and poise had left Rand slack-jawed.

"What are you doing?" he asked Steve as the two stood and talked on the sidewalk between sets. "You look like you've really grown as a performer."

"Oh, thanks. I've been working a lot."

"Where's that?"

"Oh, places like the Earl downtown."

"Whoa!"

"Man, once you're done with school for the year, we can hang out, and I can introduce you to people," Steve said.

Bowled over, Rand brushed past the genuine offer.

"Man, you're doing so well," Rand said. "It's great, you've got it made —"

Impatient, Steve looked Rand in the eye.

"And I've got leukemia."

The word sent Rand reeling. It spelled death, a notion brought home to him viscerally as a soldier in Chicago the year before, when he was on the South Side, driving north along Lake Shore Drive to deliver Army documents to an armory, and was hailed by the rifle fire of a sniper. Rand wanted to know more from Steve.

"You've got *what*?"

"I don't want to talk about it," Steve said. "I'm in the middle of a gig. I want to focus on my gig. I don't want to get all worked up talking about this."

Steve paused, held the gaze, then added:

"Let's go back inside, and let's work."

Steve's work resumed almost furiously, as he knocked on familiar club doors and re-established the weekly slots he'd had at the Earl of Old Town before his

Upon reconnecting with Steve, comic songwriter Larry Rand, shown in 1970, was awed by how Steve had improved as an entertainer, but he also was shocked to learn that he'd been diagnosed with leukemia.

(Photo by Dave Wohl, courtesy of Larry Rand)

The mesmerizing medleys and stagecraft of Terry Callier, shown in 1976, inspired Steve to impersonate him during the summer of 1969.

(Photo by Art Thieme)

diagnosis. Because the drugs his oncologists had prescribed weren't conducive to driving, Freitag or Steve's dad, mom or brother had to escort him from Niles to the Earl. Once there, however, he became a super-ball, his disease invisible. In fact, the Earl was a perfect venue for him, says Jeff Rochman, former Sammy brother at U of I. "Steve was small, and everyone was close in there," he says. "So much of him was his eyes. His eyes were so wide and dark, and they took you in and darted around. You felt real close to him."

Like a sponge, Steve absorbed the songs and styles of other musicians, including a mesmerizing, bearded, 24-year-old African-American singer, Terry Callier. The main act at It's Here and in other Chicago clubs, Callier was known for stringing together poignant folk songs into seemingly endless 20-minute medleys suffused with strummed mantras. In his hands, compositions such as Leonard Cohen's "Suzanne" grew to twice their original length, extended into other drawn-out songs and echoed in reprise without a break. As Callier puts it, "I was trying to be open onstage, trying to communicate more, to be introspective but not so much a navel-starer. I could play for a minute, minute and a half before I even sang a word." It was an approach he had picked up from New York folksinger Odetta and one that had influenced Richie Havens.

Callier's stagecraft was so irresistible that Steve "went through the entire summer doing an impersonation" of it at the Earl, says Larry Rand. In fact, he says, a 15-minute medley that Steve incorporated in his act — the Lennon-McCartney lament "Eleanor Rigby," the weary "I'm a Drifter" by Travis Edmonson and the taunting Jefferson Airplane hit "Somebody to Love" — was a "straight steal" from Callier's style. No matter, as Steve used an insistent voice and driving guitar to distinguish it as his own. It was an intense lyrical/musical exploration of loneliness, and it became a vibrant set closer that staggered audiences, including an unwitting Rich Warren.

In Chicago during his summer break from the University of Illinois, Warren dropped by the Earl one Wednesday night in early July. (Pionke routinely let him in at Ray Nordstrand's behest, even though Warren was two years shy of the legal drinking age of 21.) Warren found himself riveted to the act onstage, especially when he heard the performer sing, word for word, "Song for David," the same tune that he had broadcast three months earlier at the U of I, in Bonnie Koloc's voice. At the end of the set, Warren approached the singer and introduced himself.

"Y'know, it's amazing, you know Steve Goodman songs, too," Warren said.

"Yeah, I *am* Steve Goodman."

Warren's eyes widened to pies.

"Yeah, I know, I know," Steve said. "I'm not dead, I'm not dead. I'm here. I got this incredible remission. They tried a new drug on me, and it worked."

His mental wheels spinning, Warren blinked and drew in a breath.

"Mr. Goodman, can I tape you?"

"You want to tape *me*?"

"Yeah."

"Sure, come on over anytime, if it's OK with Earl."

The two set the session on a weekday evening. So on Thursday, July 17, 1969, three nights before Neil Armstrong walked on the moon and one month before hundreds of thousands of youths thronged to upstate New York for the first Woodstock Music & Art Fair, Warren hauled into the Earl of Old Town a carload of recording equipment from the Audio Consultants stereo store where he worked as a salesman in Evanston. Steve, just eight days shy of his 21st birthday, also had come prepared, with good reason. Not only was it a chance to be captured on tape that might be aired later throughout Chicago, but it also was a chance to preserve for posterity what he felt he did best — while he was still alive to do it.

In three sets, before a talky audience varying from one to two dozen, including two of Warren's acquaintances who lived in the apartment above the stereo store, Steve played 22 songs, including the "Eleanor Rigby" / "I'm a Drifter" / "Somebody to Love" medley, filling two and a quarter hours of Warren's tape.

From melancholy to playful, from grave to impudent, Steve's selections blanketed the emotional map. His overall performance, his voice still hinting at the operatic tone of his temple singing, revealed glimpses of the galvanizing and self-deprecating stage persona he was to develop, along with signs of immaturity that he eventually would shed. Occasionally, he berated the audience with petulant sarcasm ("Don't everybody talk all at once," he said at one point), and three times, emulating a Fred Holstein mannerism, he brought momentum to a halt to light a cigarette for himself. "You notice how professional all this is," he deadpanned mid-show, "how, y'know, together I got the whole act — every move rehearsed for hours in front of a mirror. I couldn't bring the whips, though."

By turns strident and ponderous, Steve tore into some of the most earnest, socially conscious folk songs of the era's top writers, including "To Be a Man" by Len Chandler, "Both Sides Now" by Joni Mitchell (and made a hit by Judy Collins), "Bird on the Wire" by Leonard Cohen (recorded by Collins) and "That's the Way It's Gonna Be" by Phil Ochs and Bob Gibson (known via its Chad Mitchell Trio version), along with a haunting chestnut by Hoagy Carmichael, "Baltimore Oriole" — each, in Steve's hands and with Callier's style, drawn out to more than six minutes. In a hint of his future bent for story songs, Steve identified the biting civil-rights ballad "The Lonesome Death of Hattie Carroll" as his favorite Bob Dylan song and performed a nine-minute version.

Two more songs — Eric Andersen's energetic "Rollin' Home" and the heartfelt "Early Mornin' Rain" by Gordon Lightfoot — had reached the pop mainstream, dooming their hipness in the eyes of some in the folk elite, but Steve would have none of that sentiment, saying of the Lightfoot tune, "Folksingers don't sing it too much anymore. That's 'cause Peter, Paul & Mary made a record of it, and so now all folksingers think that it's a bunch of commercial crap that they don't have to be bothered with. If Lightfoot wrote no other song, this one would have been enough." Steve also selected a pair of bleak, third-person portraits: Tom Paxton's "The Hooker," which painted a graphic image of a prosti-

> **You notice how professional all this is, how, y'know, together I got the whole act — every move rehearsed for hours in front of a mirror. I couldn't bring the whips, though.**
> **STEVE GOODMAN**

tute and heroin addict, and "Nashville 40" by Paul Geremia and Frank Wakefield, which depicted a "long, lonesome boy" who hitchhikes east from Nashville to Kingsport, Tennessee, and "just can't keep from cryin'."

Wanting the tape to reflect audience engagement, Steve trotted out a pair of Paxton classics known for their Chad Mitchell Trio and Kingston Trio versions and easy, sing-along choruses, "I Can't Help but Wonder (Where I'm Bound)" and "Ramblin' Boy." But he soon lost his patience, repeatedly and ineffectively rebuking the handful of Earl patrons for their half-hearted vocalizing: "You gotta be kiddin' me. ... See, it's supposed to sound like I'm gettin' you excited. You get the picture? ... Let's do it again, OK? Whaddya say? Like you meant it. ... God, that was awful."

But Steve leavened his upbraiding with doses of fun. Stretching back more than a decade to vintage rock and rockabilly, he launched into Chuck Berry's "Carol," preceding it with "Blue Jean Bop," calling it Gene Vincent's greatest song and reveling in its line "C'mon, baby, bop with Gene." "Oh, man, I can't stand it when he does that," Steve said. "I just crack up."

Also lightening the proceedings was an extended and bitter joke, spoken to strummed Mexican chords, in which Steve took on the persona of "Juan," a Puerto Rican thief and radio repairman whom Steve claimed had been his neighbor in Manhattan's Spanish Harlem. Mirroring a Lenny Bruce routine, Steve had "Juan" pleading for peace among the "brothers" of a litany of races and nationalities, ending with "We should stand together as brothers, marching down the aisle of liberty as brothers, arm in arm and hand in hand as brothers, all for one and one for all as brothers — and kick the shit out of the Greeks!"

Steve also used humor to poke at fundamentalist religion, stringing together "Heavily into Jesus" by a Second City comedy troupe that evolved into the Chicago folk-rock group Wilderness Road and the standard "Plastic Jesus (on the Dashboard of My Car)." He laced the two musical gags with three spoken bits in the voice of a "Revival Hour" radio host who pitches for "the Pink and Pleasant Plastic Icon Company of Del Rio, Texas — amen to God, hallelujah."

More remarkable than Steve's palette of others' tunes were several of his own. In the six months since first arriving at Sloan-Kettering with a death sentence, his songwriting labor had yielded multiple births — not one of which was upbeat. He performed "Song for David," which he said was "probably the only reason the machine's in here." (Of the song's façade, his only comment was: "I wrote it for my brother, for whatever that's worth.")

The other two originals, further reflecting the desperation his illness had induced, were passionate but grim yearnings for romance. "Song for Sally" briskly tracked the confident walk of a mysterious, attention-getting "young girl" who "doesn't have a care" but whose eyes say that she "hates to walk alone" and whose smile at day's end turns "quiet blue." And "Climb the Hills to Dale" was a spare lament about the narrator's failed courtship of a woman in Denver with whom he had walked mountain paths and shared "dreams to last forever." [6]

Mindful of the need for a strong finish, Steve drew on two songs by country

---

See, it's supposed to sound like I'm gettin' you excited. ... God, that was awful.
STEVE GOODMAN

6: Two years earlier, about the time Steve left Illinois for Greenwich Village, he talked feverishly to Maine East and U of I classmate Bill MacKay about "chasing some girl out West" to a university she attended in Colorado or Utah. "He was hot on her," MacKay says, "and he had to go after her post haste." Whether Steve made the trip, as implied in "Climb the Hills to Dale," is an open question.

artist Billy Edd Wheeler that came from a failed Broadway show about coal mining and had been popularized in concert recordings by Judy Collins. [7] The first, "Coal Tattoo," which the Chad Mitchell and Kingston trios had recorded, exalted hard-bitten labor and an afterlife of singing "with the angel band," while the second, "High Flyin' Bird," was in the voice of a disabled, out-of-work miner with "a case of them sit down, I can't fly, oh Lord, I'm gonna die blues." Bookends, the songs brimmed with despair, yet Steve's ringing guitar and full-bodied, edgy voice transformed them into anthems for the dispossessed and easily won the loudest applause of the night from the scattered patrons. [8]

As they packed their equipment and prepared to leave the Earl, both Warren and Steve knew they had created an important set of tapes, each for his own purposes. Warren invited Steve to his acquaintances' upstairs apartment in Evanston so the group could listen to the recordings right away. Little more than an hour later, Warren, Steve and the couple sat in the apartment, all but Warren smoking marijuana and "getting stoned out of their minds." As the tapes played, Steve grew dissatisfied. He could hear that he was "too out of it" and not connecting with the audience. He also decided that he had regretted his chemical preparation.

"Y'know," he told the group, "it's a lot of fun to listen to the music stoned, but I've learned a lesson tonight. You don't perform stoned. I don't sound as good as I could when I perform stoned. I can hear these mistakes, and I'm slipping. I'm sloppy when I'm stoned."

Warren understood. "Steve was right," he says. "He was singing all these gorgeous songs, but he wasn't there. But the irony was that even if Steve was 'out of it,' he was still better than 80 percent of the performers around." With that in mind, two nights later, on July 19, Warren took the tapes to WFMT and played them for Ray Nordstrand, who hadn't heard Steve's voice before.

"You've got to play this guy on the air," Warren said. "He's really good."

"Yeah, he's good, but the crowd wasn't paying much attention, were they?"

"Well, it's still good stuff."

Nordstrand agreed, and he played "Song for Sally" and "Climb the Hills to Dale" on that night's "Midnight Special," the first time any of Steve's songs hit the airwaves in his own voice.

Two weeks after the recorded Earl of Old Town session, as Warren worked at the Evanston stereo store, a tiny, balding, middle-aged man walked up to him.

"I understand you taped my son," he said.

"Who's your son?"

"I'm Bud Goodman," said Steve's dad, extending his hand. "Nice to meet you."

"Yeah, I taped Steve," Warren said. "He's really good. You should be proud of him."

Bud drew closer.

"Listen, I want to ask you a favor," he said. "Steve's not going to be around very long, and I'd really do anything for a copy of those tapes."

Even if Steve was 'out of it,' he was still better than 80 percent of the performers around.
RICH WARREN

7: Judy Collins is not surprised that much of Steve's early repertoire came from songs she popularized. "They are very seminal," she says. "They were primers for me on writing and on American music, and people were very attracted by that. I knew a lot of these people, I listened to them sing, I went to their concerts, and I fell in love with their songs. There's something very organically right about the Americana tone of those songs, Canadian as well as American, that continental American flavor."

8: Steve's July 17, 1969, recording at the Earl of Old Town has not been released officially. Only one of the songs that Steve performed that night, his "Song for David," appeared on a later Goodman LP, but the version of "Song for Sally" from the night has been aired during WFMT tributes to Steve.

Steve's dad, Bud Goodman, shown in the summer of 1969, was eager to hear tapes of his son's July 17 sets at the Earl of Old Town. "Listen," the car salesman told WFMT-FM protégé Rich Warren, "I want to ask you a favor. Steve's not going to be around very long, and I'd really do anything for a copy of those tapes."

(Photo by Ron Rosoff)

Warren gladly obliged. A couple days later when Bud returned to pick up the copies, his sales personality emerged. In words honed by years of practice, he told Warren, "Now, I manage a car dealership, and any time you need a car, you come and see Bud Goodman. I'll take good care of you." Four years later, Warren did just that.

Besides booking gigs and otherwise immersing himself in the Chicago folk scene, Steve found another way to take care of himself that summer. He left his parents' home in Niles and moved to Chicago's North Side, into a ground-floor, two-bedroom flat in an older building at 2336 N. Southport Ave., 10 blocks west of the fledgling Lincoln Avenue club district and less than two miles northwest of the Earl. This not only truncated his "commute" to key venues but also gave him greater freedom to keep late-night "musicians' hours" and partake of drugs and the pre-AIDS sexual revolution. It was his first real step toward setting down adult roots in the city.

As a new renter, Steve quickly found himself hosting a 27-year-old guest, by way of his Manhattan friend, Paula Ballan. Photographer and former singer/guitarist Ron Rosoff, wrestling with a heroin habit, had fled New York, and Ballan had advised him to stay in Chicago with transplanted folksinger Jo Mapes. However, upon his arrival, Rosoff found that Mapes, a single mother of three, couldn't welcome a new boarder. By phone, Ballan quickly suggested he ask Steve.

Well after midnight on the rainy night of Wednesday, July 16, a soaked Rosoff walked into a near-empty Earl of Old Town with a rucksack and camera bag and found Steve playing to a couple who sat at a table a few feet from the performer. The pair, Evanston residents Jim and Linda Trattner, had just learned of Steve's leukemia and were transfixed. "What caught me," Rosoff wrote later in a journal, "was the look of sadness, morbidity, death, mixed with a loyalty on both sad faces, especially the man's." Rosoff introduced himself to Steve and the Trattners, and, starting that night, he had a home on Steve's living-room couch.

Ten days later, the night after Steve's 21st birthday, the Trattners took Steve out for a celebratory dinner, at which the two gave Steve a deeply felt gift that Linda had made — a cloth-covered book whose rectangular pages contained the words for "Song for David" in script and were joined by red ribbons, opening like an accordion and stretching as long as a yardstick.

Rosoff looked after Steve's apartment over the next three weeks while Steve returned to New York for cancer treatment. Struggling to abort his own drug habit and reverting to mescaline and other hallucinogens, Rosoff appreciated the stability of even so transient a bunk as Steve's couch. But it was in the center of the apartment's foot traffic and next to Steve's portable record player, which sat atop two bricks and a plank, a juxtaposition that became vexing when Steve returned to Chicago.

Having heard the Buddy Black/Leroy Van Dyke novelty song "The Auctioneer" in New York, Steve had brought home the 1962 Van Dyke LP "Walk on By." For several days in a row, with pen, notebook and guitar in hand, Steve awoke at 8 or 9 a.m., sat in a chair next to his tiny turntable in the living room. He listened to "The Auctioneer" over and over at 16 rpm (half speed) and scribbled down its comically breakneck double-talk. Rosoff, a night owl, found it hard to endure Steve's seemingly endless practicing of tongue-twisting lines such as:

Steve's determination to absorb "The Auctioneer" was annoying for temporary roommate Ron Rosoff. "I thought it was a cute and catchy song," Rosoff says, "but just having witnessed him learning it all those hundreds of times when I was just waking up in the morning was the killer. It was grim."

(Photo courtesy of Ron Rosoff)

> *25 dollar bidder now 30 dollar 30 will you*
> *give me 30 make it 30 bid 'em up all at 30 dollars*
> *will you give me 30 who will bid it at a 30 dollar bid?* [9]

"He was teaching himself the song with this dedication, almost an obsession," Rosoff says. "About the 40th or 50th time, I began to get fed up with it, and I came to hate it. I thought it was a cute and catchy song, but just having witnessed him learning it all those hundreds of times when I was just waking up in the morning was the killer. It was grim."

About the same time, at 2 a.m. a few days after Steve had spent a night at the flat of a young woman, he startled a sleeping Rosoff, who slowly arose from the couch. Steve was agitated.

"Ron, are you awake?"

"What, Steve?"

"I was just scratching the scabs on my stomach."

"Yeah?"

"One of 'em just moved."

Steve "totally lost it" when Rosoff told him that this was his first run-in with venereal disease, or "the crabs." Rosoff, "an old hand at this," tried to calm Steve's panic, telling him to wash all his clothing and offering reassurance: "Don't worry, it doesn't hurt bad." Later that morning, Rosoff walked to a pharmacy and bought Steve "a bottle of anti-crab shit," satisfied in the role of big brother.

9: This verse from "The Auctioneer" by Buddy Black and Leroy Van Dyke, copyright 1956, is reprinted by permission.

The poses in Ron Rosoff's promo-photo session with Steve in August 1969 ranged from commanding to pensive and even included a playful encounter with two children from the same block of Southport Avenue.

(Photos by Ron Rosoff)

The professional photo skills of Rosoff came into play one sunny August morning when he asked Steve to be the subject of an outdoor shoot. Rosoff positioned Steve on a porch rail one door south where, as his hands cradled his reddish brown Hummingbird guitar and his bare feet perched on a black guitar case, he stared intently at the camera.

Rosoff also posed Steve sitting on the narrow cement walkway between the brick walk-ups and standing behind the leaves of short trees. The purpose of the photos was to promote Steve's fledgling career. The resulting 36 frames portrayed him, with beatnik-style mustache and short beard, as an earnest artist with a serious message and only a hint of mischievousness — a countenance broken in two shots when a grinning Steve strummed for two tots who happened by.

"A powerful imp" emerged in the photos, says Rosoff, who gave Steve 20 copies of the best porch print. "It says: working man, middle class, humble, normal little home, average, everyday," Rosoff says. But none of the images was ever published. "They reflect," Rosoff says, "a moment in time when we both agreed that he was wonderful and wanted to capture it."

Rosoff genuinely liked Steve and admired his musicianship, though Steve's intensity was "a little spooky sometimes." As he wrestled with his own drug-related demons, Rosoff also grew impatient with Steve's bouts of despondency over leukemia: "People around him were feeding into that, saying, 'Oh, you poor genius. We love you because you're dying.' My attitude was 'You're alive and a genius. That's all I'm concerned with.' Unfortunately, I was extremely blunt and undiplomatic."

The two grew distant, and Rosoff's brashness and volatility didn't help. One evening in late September, Rosoff blurted out, "If all I've got to do is watch you die, fuck you, I'll leave right now." Shortly afterward, he did.

Steve's life that fall settled into a pattern of gigs at the Earl and other clubs and return trips to New York every few weeks for treatment. Along the way, he stopped at the annual Philadelphia Folk Festival, gaining entry and free food as a volunteer. He was "on a truck, collecting trash or collecting cans and bottles," says Gene Shay, the festival's longtime emcee.

His days in Chicago were spiced with outings to touchstones from his childhood — Wrigley Field to see the first-place but ultimately collapsing Cubs, and the now-razed Chicago Stadium to see the Ringling Brothers and Barnum & Bailey circus. Another circus buff, No Exit owner Joe Moore, visiting the big top for the third time in a week, "went early to feed the elephants, and there was Stevie in back. It was his fifth time there." Both were fans of the blond, bare-chested German billed as the world's greatest animal trainer, Gunther Gebel-Williams. "We were awesomely impressed with Williams, an unbelievable showman," Moore says. "I liked everything about circuses, and so did Steve."

Moore was part of a growing coterie of friends and musical contacts in Chicago and New York who knew of Steve's leukemia and felt honor-bound to stay mum. "He didn't want to play on it. He just wanted to get on with whatever life

People around him were feeding into that, saying, 'Oh, you poor genius. We love you because you're dying.' My attitude was 'You're alive and a genius. That's all I'm concerned with.' Unfortunately, I was extremely blunt and undiplomatic.
RON ROSOFF

he was going to have," says Paula Ballan, "but hundreds of people knew, and it was like a social contract that if you were really a friend of his, this is something that you keep among yourselves."

The unspoken pact, Ballan says, also meant that leukemia was not to be the prime topic in his presence. "When he was feeling shitty, you would ask him 'How are you feeling?' and he would tell you how shitty he was feeling. But he would also give you the signal that your presence there and whatever way you could divert him from feeling rotten was why he was hanging with you and why he wasn't sitting and feeling sorry for himself."

"He didn't want sympathy," says Larry Rand. "He wanted respect, and we all really respected that. He didn't want to be known as 'Oh, this is my friend Stevie with leukemia.' He wanted his art to be judged pure, which tells you how serious he was about it."

Steve's musical drive diverted his friends' attention, if only temporarily, from his impending mortality. But feelings of compassion were inescapable.

"It actually made it easier for me to be around him," Rand says. "When I first met him, he was wound so tight, that energy thing was just cranked up so high, that he made me anxious. He was just as in a hurry before he had the disease, and it would drive me crazy, like 'Why don't you calm down a little, you pipsqueak?' I don't think (leukemia) changed his behavior all that much, but it allowed me to like him a lot better. All this urgency and 'I've gotta have it yesterday,' all of a sudden I could forgive that. It made me a lot more relaxed around him."

While his urgency propelled Steve musically, leukemia tempered his career's liftoff in the latter half of 1969, even at times when his disease was invisible. Thirty miles south of Chicago in the suburb of Richton Park, for example, Steve played three 45-minute sets at the Twelfth of Never, a five-year-old, 125-seat, no-alcohol listening room with frills ranging from tablecloths and tiny candle lamps to strobe lights and echo effects. Between Steve's sets, co-owner Ed Zuckerman, a daytime reporter for the *Gary Post-Tribune* across the nearby Illinois-Indiana border, buttonholed him in the back-room coffee bar.

"In all the years I've been hanging around this place, you are hands down the finest performer who's ever appeared here," the 25-year-old Zuckerman told Steve. "I'm wired into the whole publicity game. Maybe I can help you get an appearance on the Johnny Carson show. I can write letters, I can call people, and if there's anything I can do to help you, let me know. You're really going somewhere."

"Thanks," Steve replied, "but I'm not going anywhere."

"What?"

"I'm not going anywhere. I can't book anything a year in advance. My days are numbered. I've only got a short time to live."

The statement, Zuckerman says, wasn't sarcastic or angry. "He was nice about it, it was just matter of fact, but to me it was like being hit in the head with a two-by-four. It was the last thing I was prepared to hear." [10]

It allowed me to like him a lot better. All this urgency and 'I've gotta have it yesterday,' all of a sudden I could forgive that.
LARRY RAND

10: Earlier in the year, when Zuckerman's partner, Volmar "Chip" Franz, learned of Steve's leukemia, Franz told a friend that he had mailed Steve a sympathy card. The response of Franz' friend, a Chicago emergency-room physician, was "You should have sent him a coffin."

Even when opportunities for Steve walked through the doors of the Earl, leukemia played a central role in their evaporation. One such case was Keith Christianson, a Minneapolis-based promoter who trolled for talent to be inserted as opening acts for one-hit headliners on regional tours of college campuses. He had represented two singers linked with the influential Chad Mitchell Trio: its namesake founder and a later member, Michael Johnson. In Chicago in mid-1969, the 32-year-old Christianson dropped in several times a week at the Earl, where another promising musician, Frank Hall, had referred Christianson to Steve.

Christianson had mixed feelings about the Earl. "It was a lower-class place. Toilet would be a great word," he said. "It was a place where you could hear folk people who were just starting out, even though you wouldn't want to eat the food. You'd certainly clean the glass before you drank out of it." About Steve, however, Christianson's regard was unqualified. "He was a great performer, and you don't see that very often," he said. "You see talent, but you don't see a performer. There's a lot of difference. He was great onstage, even though he was covering songs by others."

One evening, Christianson sat at the bar with Steve, alerting him to a tour coming up in eight months. Steve, intrigued by an insider connected to musicians he revered, said he was eager to participate, "but I think you ought to know that I have cancer, and there's a possibility I might not be here." Christianson reluctantly opted not to extend Steve an offer. The prospect of Steve's early demise, he said, "was the only reason."

Leukemia also altered Steve's relationships with women, usually intensifying them. Such was the case with Jeany Walker, a singer and freeform dancer who was three years older than Steve and exactly his height and lived one block west of the Earl. The two had met at the Earl and known each other for more than a year. Walker harmonized with him, played straight man to his endless jokes and plotted with him the formation of a rock band. "He was really fun to be around," she says. "He was honest, and when he teased you, he wasn't mean about it. He knew how to touch my heart, and that's what he did in his performances. We'd be laughing hysterically, and the next minute you're just about crying. That was, I thought, the gift that he had, of really touching inside people."

She adored Steve, and the feeling apparently was mutual, but the two never went beyond close friendship because of bad timing. "Every couple of weeks or months we would call each other when we broke up with someone, only to find that the other person had just gotten together with somebody," Walker says. "It was a standing joke between us: How are we ever going to get together when we're always falling in love with somebody else at the wrong moment? It was like one of these silly songs. That was our song. It was a bittersweet thing, humorous and yet very sad."

During Steve's first months at Sloan-Kettering, Walker and Steve corresponded almost every day. "He wrote me really romantic letters, so I knew it was serious. He didn't write me romantic letters before, so I just wrote him

Ed Zuckerman, co-owner of the Twelfth of Never coffeehouse in Richton Park, was convinced that Steve was "really going somewhere" and told him so. Steve replied, "I'm not going anywhere."

(Photo courtesy of Ed Zuckerman)

romantic letters back, saying how much I loved him. The letters were probably true, but when you have something like that (leukemia) going on, it's really good if you have someone you love, and so it was me, that's all. It gives you some other way to be than just afraid, and you can think about that person. The love between us really culminated with that time, but instead of it turning out to be boyfriend and girlfriend, it was support. We were just totally buddies."

Characteristically, when Steve returned to Chicago wearing a hat to cover his bare head, "he showed me how he lost all his hair and made a whole bunch of jokes about it," Walker says. "He wasn't moaning and groaning about it. He had to make a funny comment that would make me laugh."

A haphazard encounter at the Earl with a different woman soon had a far more enduring impact on Steve's life. It took place on a weekend evening in September after he had finished a set. The 5-foot-2 performer was about to leave the stage and head for the backroom "Star Cave" at the same time as a striking, slender and shapely, long-haired, 5-foot-9-1/2 waitress was bustling between tables with a tray of drinks. She was used to attention, and was "hit on more times than a baseball at a Cubs game," says bartender Roger Surbaugh. But she seriously attended to her work.

> **Steve just looked up at her with those big, brown eyes and a big smile on his face, just as innocent as a choirboy, and said, 'Would you like to learn to dance?' Everybody in the room just cracked up.**
> **ROGER SURBAUGH**

As she whirled around, Steve stepped off the 8-by-5-foot stage, and — as he told folksinger Jim Post and others in later years — he "walked into her abundance." Surbaugh, who witnessed the collision, says, "This could have been a terribly embarrassing moment for both of them, for everybody. But Steve just looked up at her with those big, brown eyes and a big smile on his face, just as innocent as a choirboy, and said, 'Would you like to learn to dance?' Everybody in the room just cracked up."

The waitress was Nancy Pruter, and the quick, bold wit of their meeting fit the chemistry that sizzled between them. "They hit it right off," Howard Berkman says, intending no pun.

Nearly two years older than Steve, Nancy, the middle child and only girl in a household of five children, had grown up since age 4-1/2 in Berwyn, a western Chicago suburb. Born 16 miles from the Canadian border in the remote town of Jackman in northwestern Maine, she was the daughter of a Congregational minister. Like Steve, she was intelligent, an academic achiever at Proviso East High School.

By age 17, Nancy had left her male-dominated home to work toward a dream she had held since she was a young girl — to become a nurse. First, she majored in math at Roosevelt University in the Chicago Loop (later using those skills as an insurance company statistician), then enrolled in the College of Nursing at the University of Illinois at Chicago on the West Side.

When she met Steve, the 23-year-old, blue-eyed student/waitress lived in an Italian neighborhood near the UIC campus, in a basement apartment in the same brick building on Flournoy Street as did a friend of Berkman. "She was a beautiful, nice, kind-hearted, good sense-of-humor, take-care-of-business kind of girl," Berkman says. "She was lithe and what we would call perky." Her blue eyes and expression often bespoke cheer. "I always called her Nancy with the Smiling Face," says Volmar "Chip" Franz, co-owner of the Twelfth of Never and a frequent customer at the Earl. "She was real friendly, very sweet, but she wasn't a pushover," says Surbaugh, the barkeep. "She was a strong woman but not overbearing or pushy. She was a straight shooter. You knew pretty much where you stood."

Differences between Steve and Nancy were less severe than their Mutt-and-Jeff stature might suggest. While Steve was a Jew and Nancy had been raised in her father's church, observant practice of a faith was not important to either. And while at times Nancy was more reserved than Steve, she could hold her own in one-upping others with "demonic" conversational zingers. It took guts for Steve to pair up with a woman who towered over him physically, but finally he had found someone with whom he could connect seriously and humorously and build a home — and who also wasn't put off by his own compact frame.

Nancy Pruter, shown in 1972, immediately sensed Steve's strength in coping with leukemia in late 1969. "From the time I met him," she said 14 years later, "I felt a confidence that he had about being able to get through this and live a life." (Photo by P. Michael O'Sullivan)

Perhaps most surprising, music was not a strongly shared interest, says Nancy's next older brother, Robert Pruter, a Chicago writer and an authority on the blues who worked as an encyclopedia editor. Nancy was a fan of folk priestess Joan Baez and enjoyed R&B, particularly the early work of Junior Wells, joining her brother in visits to the city's South Side blues clubs. But she was not waiting tables at the Earl to get close to folk music. "It was a gig. It was no groupie-type thing," Pruter says. Her attraction to Steve "had nothing to do with him being a musician, not at all. He could have been a plumber if she was working in a plumbing store."

In fact, the chauvinistic attitude toward women in the down-and-dirty music world could have worked against Nancy's regard for Steve. "She was a very bright person, got all A's and all that, and probably was brighter than Steve," Pruter says. "Steve and his folkie friends had no respect for a woman's independence, so they never really appreciated my sister's intelligence. She had to keep that suppressed in that type of music culture."

If not the music itself, the passion that Steve held for it was central to his appeal to Nancy. For interviewer Win Stracke, she later cited Steve's ability to personalize and transform the songs of others. "When Steve first learns a song from a record, he always sounds exactly like the person who sang it, but after he's sung the song a few times, it becomes his own," she said. "It's just Steve to me, except it's everybody that he's ever heard."

Moreover, as the two got to know each other, Steve's leukemia — and his determination to immerse himself in music despite it — also captivated Nancy. "One of the things that attracted me to him was that incredible drive to be alive and to be something and to make the most of his life," she said in a 1983 interview for a profile of Steve by the NBC-TV "First Camera" magazine show. "From the time I met him, I felt a confidence that he had about being able to get through this and live a life. I don't know that he would say that he felt it at that time, but that had a lot to do with why he was such a good fighter."

Steve's desire to build a family of his own also was a factor, illustrated by a

Robert Pruter, shown in 1970, says Steve was not a typical fiancé for his sister, Nancy, to bring home to meet the family: "He was just someone who played in clubs and hardly was the ideal husband material that a mother envisions."

(Photo courtesy of Robert Pruter)

segment in the NBC interview in which Nancy turned to Steve and addressed him: "I think, in the beginning, (the leukemia) made you more aggressive. A lot of the decisions that you made or the way you went after things, your wanting to get married and have kids, was 'I may not have the chance in five years. I want it now.' It made things more immediate."

Marrying Steve appealed to Nancy partly because of her longing to be a nurse, says Robert Pruter, who observes that women who marry severely ill men often are in or join the medical field. "She already had an interest," he says, "but I think (Steve's leukemia) just accentuated it."

One evening late that fall, Steve and Nancy drove to the North Side home of Nancy's mother to announce their engagement to her and two of Nancy's brothers, including Robert Pruter. The prospective groom — a folksinger with leukemia — was hardly a conventional choice, and the discussion was strained. "He had no career, he had no record label or anything," Pruter says. "He was just someone who played in clubs and hardly was the ideal husband material that a mother envisions, where someone has an establishment job and just got a new desk at IBM."

After the two left, Nancy's mother sat down and shook her head.

"Oh, dear," she said.

"You don't have anything to worry about," her son, Robert, replied coldly. "He's going to die in two or three years." (Of his bluntness, Pruter explains: "Us Pruters, we don't mince our words.")

Divulging their intentions to friends was easier for Steve and Nancy, and it was usually accomplished between sets and around a table at the Earl. One such chat involved a talented multi-instrumentalist who had begun accompanying Steve at club gigs, Bob Hoban. During a joking exchange, Nancy suddenly pressed the serious point that marriage wasn't what it used to be, repeating the question, "How many families do you really know?"

Jumping to Hoban's mind was the "Tenement Symphony" from the Marx Brothers' film "The Big Store." He began to sing lustily: "Well, there's the Cohens and the Kellys, —"

"— the Campbells and Vermicellis," Steve chimed in.

Nancy erupted in laughter, endearing herself to Hoban. "After the light had dawned on her what a ridiculous remark she had made, she was able to laugh," he says. "It's a rare quality to realize what you've done and catch it, instead of trying to cover it up with another line."

Hoban at once sized up the two as a delightful match. "She was no wallflower or subservient, and she had an air of life about her that was wondrous," he says. "Steve was very lucky. There would be no reason not to love her. She just found something in Steve. She always had a twinkle in her eye, and there was a lot of bubbly fun, but also a great kindness about her, an incredible thoughtfulness."

Soon, Steve's friend Jeany Walker received an excited phone call.

"I finally found her," Steve said.

"Oh, Goodman, I can't believe it," she replied with a laugh. "Here we go again. I was just going to call you. It isn't fair!"

"Walker, we just don't have our timing right."

Steve invited his friend to dinner at a German restaurant in the Loop so that she could meet Nancy. "It was clear," Walker says. "He knew Nancy was the one, and he was meant to marry her."

"The romance, this was fast," says a Lake Forest College friend, Carol Laciny. "It was as simple as falling off a log. At the time, people were getting it on with everybody. It was really very free. There was a lot of sexual liberation going on. So being in love had to be pretty special because you could be with anybody you wanted to. But these two clearly had fallen for each other."

Another evening that fall, Steve invited three or four Lake Forest friends, including Lucy Wells, to his Southport flat to meet Nancy. Over a dinner of wine and pizza, Steve sang songs popularized by Elvis Presley and Johnny Cash, as well as a few of his own, stopping at one point to say, "What do you think of this woman here? She knows I'm sick, she knows I could die, and she wants to marry me." Wells says that she and her friends "were mostly shocked that any-one our age was getting married." Nancy, meanwhile, was quietly "making sure our wine glasses were full" and said little. "You could see in her face how much she enjoyed watching him perform — and performing was who he was."

Folksinger and columnist Jo Mapes, shown performing at the Fifth Peg in 1969, saw "a calmness and a belongingness" in Nancy Pruter and Steve.
(Photo by Ron Rosoff)

Each time Steve and Nancy walked into the Earl and greeted friends, Steve "had a smile that was so welcoming," says folksinger and *Chicago Sun-Times* critic Jo Mapes. "It was tall, slim Nancy and short Steve, whose face was just a flesh-colored, radiant light bulb encased in dark hair. There was certainly that difference between the two, but there was a calmness and a belongingness to them. They fit. They just absolutely fit."

Though there was no way to prove it, the euphoria of being with Nancy and their plan to marry had to have a salutary effect on Steve's health. It also took his mind off the discord that he increasingly perceived between his parents, who separated in early October when Minnette moved out of the home in Niles and to a lakeside apartment in the city near Lincoln Park.

Possibly motivated by a perception that his remission was stabilizing, by echoes of his parents' long-held desires for him to complete a college degree and by his affection for his year and a half at Lake Forest College, Steve made an optimistic decision. On Nov. 3, he formally applied for readmission to LFC, effective winter term 1970. "My physical condition is sound enough to permit me to resume my studies on a part-time basis," he wrote Francis "Spike" Gummere, admissions director. If he were to be reinstated, he would continue work on his political-science degree as a mid-year junior.

Oddly, he received encouragement on this plan from one of his biggest musical champions. "You ought to go back to school," Paula Ballan told him. "I figure it's going to break your heart to try to break into this hopeless, thankless (mu-sic) business when you've got this thing that you're dealing with. At least if you go back to school, you can put a sort of normal life together."

That fall, Steve booked a slate of shows all over Chicagoland, as if to prepare for a 1970 hibernation in which to re-focus himself on studying. He again played the No Exit in Rogers Park, where Howard Berkman noted that Steve's longer but receding hair gave him an uncanny resemblance to the equally short Paul Simon. In addition, for an unusually high payment of $100 a night, Steve played a weekend at the Twelfth of Never. [11] And in the north suburb of Skokie, Bud Goodman rented the Old Orchard Theater and summoned his automotive acquaintances to a concert by his son and opener Bonnie Koloc. "Steve just tore the place up," said his friend, Jim Freitag.

Seemingly every evening was a blur of activity: if not a booked gig, an impromptu musical endeavor. To record a demo tape of promising material, he booked time at Universal Recording Studio near Rush Street. There, accompanied by piano, bass and drums, he laid down one-take tracks on "Song for David," "Climb the Hills to Dale," the breakneck Paul Geremia and Frank Wakefield ditty "Nashville 40" and a metaphoric waltz with advice that fit Steve's — and anyone's — mortality, "Sands of Time":

> *If by some trick, you can make the grains stick*
> *And glue one or two to your mind*
> *Then you won't have to worry about time on your hands*
> *Have your hands on some time* [12]

Throughout October, on Armitage Street across from the Old Town School of Folk Music, Steve attended hoots at the 65-seat Fifth Peg. There and at the nearby Saddle Club, he and other folkies joined the school's staff and students on Thursdays for open-mike sessions lasting well past midnight. "He looked like a little kid, like he was 13, so young and so tiny," says Oak Park record store owner Val Camiletti. Steve's presence at these gatherings paved his entrée into the daytime world of so-called commercial music — known informally as jingles.

Steve's first jingle work had come after he was billed at the Earl with a group called the Banjo Rascals, headed by Fifth Peg regular and Old Town School instructor John Carbo. One of Carbo's band members worked for the Foote, Cone & Belding ad agency and talked Steve into a tryout for singing a brief tune for Dial deodorant soap for an initial fee of $60. Wearing worn overalls, a Mackinaw shirt and open-toed sandals and carrying "a dilapidated guitar," Steve rode the El to the Magnificent Mile north of the Loop, walked east toward Navy Pier, stepped into the one-year-old, curvilinear, 70-story Lake Point Tower (at the time the tallest residential building in the world), rode to its 48th floor and about 11 a.m. strode into the office of Nuance Productions, run by a jazz musician who was one of a handful of Chicago jingle producers, Dick Boyell.

"Advertising agencies were very strict, and most jingle singers had the same voice and the same style," says Boyell, who was eager to try out new, young performers. "For this job, the agency wanted something a little more authentic, a folksinger," he says. Within minutes, Steve learned a tune Boyell had sketched out, sang it for him and got the gig. "He did a wonderful job," says Boyell, who

---

He looked like a little kid, like he was 13, so young and so tiny.
VAL CAMILETTI

11: Without warning, Steve brought bluesman Jim Brewer to the Twelfth of Never, fibbing to co-owner Ed Zuckerman, "I found him on the sidewalk playin' for tips. Can he play for you here?" Zuckerman assented and later invited Brewer back, hiring him as a paid performer.

12: The author of "Sands of Time" is unknown.

Steve later credited with giving him "my first real help in the music business."

Completing the Dial spot at a tiny studio in the Loop called Audio Finishers — the first time he set foot in a recording studio — only whetted Steve's appetite. His contact with Carbo and others at the Thursday-night open-mike sessions put Steve in touch with a gifted guitar teacher and Fifth Peg co-owner who was working his way up the Old Town School's administrative ladder, Ray Tate. An experienced jingle producer, Tate brought Steve into Paragon Studios on Ontario Street just north of the Loop to sing on a radio spot Tate had composed for Mateus Rosé wine. "Steve had that real nice sparkly, upbeat voice, and even though he was ill, he delivered," Tate says.

Chicago served as a hub for mega-ad agencies, Tate says, and 30- and 60-second jingles were studios' bread and butter. For the performer, however, the price of entry for such piecework — which required membership in the American Federation of Television and Radio Artists and the Screen Actors Guild — was high, and competition was stiff. Still, Steve's voice and guitar skills netted him additional spots for Schlitz Malt Liquor, Pabst Blue Ribbon and Texas-based Pearl beer, an ice-cream company, a Minnesota savings and loan, Red Ball Jets tennis shoes, John Deere snowmobiles ("Nothing runs like a Deere") and — eventually most memorably for Steve — Maybelline Blushing Eye Shadow.

"I just had to hum it," Steve said of the Maybelline spot, in a 1979 interview with Steve North of WLIR-FM on Long Island. "All I had to do was go 'Ba-da-da, ba-da-da,' and a girl named Kelly who was dating some football player opened her eyes real wide, and they had eye shadow all over 'em, and the eye shadow kept changing colors, and then Frank from Frank's Drum Shop did 'Dddddrrrrrring!' on the tinkle bells."

Fred Breitberg, a veteran producer who began his career assisting on Steve's jingles, says Steve's voice snugly fit the material: "For Maybelline, Steve had such a rich, resonant tenor, bridging toward the baritone, that they probably thought it was sexy, and for John Deere, Steve sounded like every cool, macho farmer on Earth. Steve could do anything anybody asked him to. He could take your concept and make it better by doing exactly it."

Steve's adaptability was as political as it was musical, illustrated by spots he did for the U.S. Navy. Aurally, at least, the military branch had shed its clean-cut persona by fashioning jingles that imitated the hip styles of The Band [13], Joe Cocker, Crosby, Stills, Nash & Young, Dionne Warwick, Burt Bacharach, Harry Nilsson and Blood, Sweat & Tears. Included on a Navy promo LP called "Something Special," the jingles that Steve recorded under Boyell's production didn't mimic other hit artists. But in Steve's gentle voice, along with mellow guitar accompaniment, the nation's war-making apparatus sounded sweetly benign. In spots to be aired in 1970 and aimed at high-school seniors, he intoned:

> *Thinkin' back to what used to be*
> *Hoping I can see*
> *Just what life has got for me*

For Maybelline, Steve had such a rich, resonant tenor ... that they probably thought it was sexy, and for John Deere, Steve sounded like every cool, macho farmer on Earth.
FRED BREITBERG

13: The vocalist for spots imitating The Band was singer/songwriter Jim Post, who says at first he recorded a jingle with the refrain, "Flying high in the sky with the Navy." But an admiral caught on to the drug pun, and Post came back to the studio to sing on an ad with unambiguous meaning — to urge college grads to "be someone" as a Navy officer instead of joining a private firm. In a track mimicking "The Weight," an underground hit, Post sang of a scenario so sour that it would prompt listeners to enlist: "Poundin' the streets, knock on doors, you went lookin' for a place to work / The man with a grin said, 'Come on in, gonna start you as a clerk / Steel desk and a pencil, you get a phone in a year or two / Gonna start out small till you learn it all and we know what you can do.' " Post says, "I think I got paid $50 for that."

The words "U.S. Navy" were absent from the cover of the LP of 30- and 60-second jingles that was sent to radio stations. Steve's vocal contributions were listed on the labels below.

(Images courtesy of Chris DeJohn)

Thinkin' back to what used to be
Now I know that I can see
Something there
Gonna find out what it can mean — to me

Steve also sang a polished pair of appeals to enlistment-age teens of both genders. The lure for boys was ethereal:

There's a very special sea, a very special sky
A very special world, for a very special guy
It's the Naay-vee, the Naay-vee ...

But for girls, the attraction was more earthbound (and implicitly sexist):

There's a very special world, with some very special guys
And a very special place, for the nurse who's aiming high
It's the Naay-vee, the Naay-vee, the Naay-vee ...

More like the military than the club milieu, the jingle world was rigid and precise — some said emotionless — especially for someone like Steve. "It was very sophisticated work, especially for television, where you've got cues at certain points to match up with what's going on film," Tate says. "He's gotta go in there and perform in front of these agency and creative people, and they're real nitpicky, screening every word he sings for accuracy, so it was a real challenge."

The sessions, Steve said later, were rote: "The client says, 'I want this,' or 'I want that.' " He modestly said he "kidded around" and took the work lightly because of the anonymity of the result. "I figured it didn't count," he said.

But Tate saw ample proof of Steve's spontaneity, memory and ability to accompany himself — key traits since Steve couldn't read music. "We'd just sing it to him, and he'd pick it up right away," Tate says. "He also was a very good improviser, so we gave him a little freedom. I wouldn't ask him to sing every note as written, so it always came out as if he'd just done it for the first time."

The city's jingle performers ranged from Old Town School co-founder Win Stracke, valued for his low crooning for the *Chicago Today* newspaper and Maurice Lenell cookies (with Steve chiming in with "Say, can I have one?"), to Bonnie Koloc, whose clear voice lent warmth to spots for United Airlines (using John Denver's "Leaving, on a Jet Plane," popularized by Peter, Paul & Mary), Kellogg's Pop Tarts, Miller High Life beer, Vick's Vapo-Rub and Dial soap ("Aren't you glad you use Dial?"). Jingles also attracted Steve's accompanist Bob Hoban, who played on Sears ads with alternate versions targeted to whites and blacks.

Occasionally, a jingle went national, which the performer would learn by checking the mailbox for residual payments. "For it to run the first 13 weeks, you would get paid maybe $65 or $70," Hoban says, "but 13 weeks and one day later, in the mail would come 32 checks, if this was national play, for anywhere from $50 to $400 apiece." In the life of a successful national spot, a performer could earn $10,000, a coveted jackpot. But the more common reality was that residuals were meager, so that performers such as Steve needed to land a steady stream of jingle jobs to pay the rent and maintain their more creative nightlife.

Just a year older than Steve, Hoban helped him reach a creative high point when the two paired up for the middle position in a downstate evening concert that also featured opener Fred Holstein and closer Bonnie Koloc. The show, ensconced by Rich Warren in the acoustically sublime University of Illinois Auditorium in Urbana on Nov. 10, was a significant out-of-city booking, attended by Steve's parents and Earl Pionke. The Monday-night concert was heavily publicized by the sponsoring graduate student association, but because of midterm exams that week it drew only 100 people, well shy of the building's 1,750-seat capacity.

Even so, Steve's 70-minute set, accompanied by Hoban and preserved on tape by Warren, was a revelation in its range, dynamics and pacing. Steve's onstage dismissal — "We start out kind of slowly and over the course of the set we die out altogether, OK, until we just sort of slither away at the end, and no one is any the wiser" — was self-deprecating to the point of inaccuracy.

Steve opened by charging into Willie Dixon's "You Can't Tell a Book by the Cover" and dropping in a minuscule snipe by Tom Paxton, "The Ballad of Spiro Agnew," before launching into an eight-minute, mostly spoken blues. It detailed a bizarre scenario in which the narrator finds his "baby" in the arms and bed of his roommate, trains a pair of .38-caliber pistols at them both and relents only when the woman sheds a tear and pleads, "Did you ever wake up with bullfrogs on your mind?" He showcased Hoban's bass on Terry Gilkyson's train song "Fast Freight" and Hoban's fiddle on Bob Dylan's just-released "Country Pie," sandwiching them around a pair of traditional British a cappella tunes, "Byker Hill" and "John Barleycorn." Two country standards were next, Merle Haggard's "Mama Tried" and Terry Fell's "Truck Drivin' Man," followed by the first Michael Smith song Steve had learned, an amphetamine-paced ditty stuffed with racy rhymes and pointed puns, "The Wonderful World of Sex."

Smith was to become a major songwriting influence on Steve as well as a direct collaborator, but "Sex" came to Steve circuitously.

The Florida-based Smith had written the novelty come-on years earlier as an imitation Roger Miller tune, and singer/guitarists George Blackwell and Michael Johnson had learned it at the Flick Coffeehouse in South Miami from a tape Smith had made. The two joined New Christy Minstrels bandleader Randy Sparks as part of a "New Society" tour of Asia, during which Johnson performed Smith's "Sex" with a few changes, modifying "tailored suit" to "Hong Kong suit" to appeal to Vietnam soldiers familiar with the phrase. A year after their return, Johnson became part of an off-Broadway touring company of the hit stage musical "Jacques Brel Is Alive and Well and Living in Paris," which started a 40-week run at Chicago's Happy Medium theater in the summer of 1969. During off nights, Johnson frequented the Earl of Old Town, where Steve met him and learned Johnson's version of Smith's "Sex." Steve didn't meet Smith in person until a year later.

Not a single song in Steve's U of I show was a repeat from the fare that

We start out kind of slowly and over the course of the set we die out altogether, OK, until we just sort of slither away at the end, and no one is any the wiser.
STEVE GOODMAN

The psychedelic cover of Chad Mitchell's 1969 LP "Chad," on Bell Records, reflected the singer's esoteric, post-Trio identity as he moved into the headliner's role as a soloist at Punchinello's, where Steve and Bob Hoban opened for him.

(LP by permission of Chad Mitchell)

Warren had recorded at the Earl in July, except for the medley of "Eleanor Rigby" / "I'm a Drifter" / "Somebody to Love," and Steve even modified that for this occasion. At the outset of the pastiche, he appended a new song of his own, "Where Are You Goin' Mister?," which starkly depicted the heroin scene on the sidewalks surrounding the Earl. "Here's a song about the junkies on Wells Street," Steve said in his intro, "the just plain folks who are part of the everyday makeup." The overall piece was a 19-minute meditation on loneliness that rang with drama and despair. As if to counter this, he topped off the show with the zany double-talk tune he had meticulously transcribed four months earlier in front of a bleary-eyed Ron Rosoff, "The Auctioneer."

Besides its versatility and power, Steve's set displayed his repartee with Hoban and supplied an audacious preview of the duo's next booking — an indefinite run beginning Dec. 1 at Punchinello's East, formerly the Chez Paree, the lavish, 1,200-seat nightspot at Ontario and McClurg known for shows by legends from Frank Sinatra to Jimmy Durante. A leap upward in prestige from the Wells Street club scene, Punchinello's drew Shriners, other conventioneers and theatergoers to the Rush Street nightclub district along the Magnificent Mile. Enhancing the privilege was that Steve and Hoban would be opening for one of Steve's early musical heroes — Chad Mitchell.

The Chad Mitchell Trio's careful mix of topical songs (Woody Guthrie's "The Great Historical Bum") and humor (Michael Brown's "Lizzie Borden") had bridged relevance and fluff in the early 1960s, and its popularity rivaled that of the Kingston Trio and Peter, Paul & Mary. From its best-selling live LPs, Steve had learned many of the trademark songs of the trio, which had continued with new personnel, including a then-little-known John Denver, after Mitchell left the group in 1965 to pursue a solo career.

A transplanted Chicagoan, Mitchell had made the rounds of the city's folk-club scene in the late 1960s. To be billed and directly linked with the nationally known Mitchell was, for Steve, a musical honor.

Icing the cake 10 days before the Punchinello's gig, Lake Forest sent Steve an enthusiastic letter approving his application to re-enter the college as a part-time, degree-seeking student. "If you wish to discuss full-time study, we shall be happy to do so," wrote LFC's Gummere. "May I say that we have enjoyed working with you and look forward to having you with us in January." So on Monday evening, Dec. 1, as he began his Punchinello's run, replacing comic Ronny Graham as Mitchell's opening act, Steve's outlook was buoyant.

To step down into the below-street-level Punchinello's was to enter a swanky world that felt like Las Vegas tinged with the Hotsy Totsy Club and the Mafia. "The only thing missing was the showgirls," Hoban says. "In fact, we wondered where the showgirls were." The shows ran seven nights a week, at 8:30 and 11 p.m. Sundays through Thursdays, and at 9 and 11 p.m. and 2 a.m. Fridays and Saturdays. Most customers were twice the age of Steve and Hoban, and from Fridays through Mondays the place teemed with out-of-towners.

Though Chad Mitchell's name was the main draw, his act and image had

To be booked for an indefinite stint at swanky Punchinello's East to open for national star Chad Mitchell — as depicted in this Dec. 7, 1969, newspaper ad — was a huge step for Steve and his partner, Bob Hoban, "the human parsley."

morphed from his close-cropped "Mighty Day on Campus" incarnation of 10 years prior. With longer hair and wearing no tie, he fronted an eclectic band of five bell-bottomed musicians that produced a heavy electric sound while Mitchell sang a more melodic and esoteric repertoire than the protest rousers from his trio days. Mitchell says he was trying to model himself after Jacques Brel, the Belgian-born sensation from France whose music had fueled the popular road show playing a few blocks from Punchinello's at the Happy Medium.

"In the midst of the Beatles and the acid-rock rush, I was trying to be a French chanteur in America," Mitchell says, adding ruefully, "What a strange desire. It was as self-destructive as you could get. I was just dying. I thought, 'Oh, my God, why am I doing this?' This was not a high point of my career."

To set up Mitchell's 40-minute set required an act that woke up the alcohol-sodden audience and crudely kicked it in the pants — and Steve and Hoban did their animated best. (Hoban, of course, downplays his second-banana role. "I was the human parsley," he says.) Their act, which commenced after a short set by the Dave Shipp Trio, was to run just 12 minutes. The nightclub's announcer, a former roommate of playwright Neil Simon, introduced the two with "Ladies and gentlemen, please welcome our own Kuklapolitan Players," because their faces vaguely resembled the famed children's puppet from TV's "Kukla, Fran and Ollie."

Backed by Hoban's bouncy bass, Steve roared into a speedy opener, Buck Owens' 1968 tune "I'm Coming Back Home to Stay" or Fred Neil's "Everybody's Talkin'," the theme song of the year's hottest movie, "Midnight Cowboy." Then came three minutes of improvised, sarcastic nonsense with Hoban embellishing at the piano or stomping and whining in a frenzied fiddle break, often followed by a serious song, if time allowed. A deadpan send-up of the Jay & the Americans hit "Come a Little Bit Closer" was the closer, complete with sound effects and props for the melodramatic story of the narrator's sensual dance in a Mexican cantina with a temptress whose boyfriend José arrives in time to thwart the tryst. Mid-tune, Steve and Hoban segued into a risqué frat-house trifle: "Was it you who did the pushin'/ Put the stains upon the cushion / Footprints on the dashboard upside down?" The medley ended with slapstick, usually the smashing of a sugar glass with a baseball bat.

"It was supper club, pure hell," Hoban says. "One night, we were arguing during a song, after a solo. Both of us had misheard each other, and snot flew out of our noses. When the act didn't work, there was no way we could recoup, but (owner) Dave Silver never said a word to us to change anything. He liked the ad-libbing."

Mitchell, then 33, found Steve deferential ("there was a kind of 'Hey, Mr. Mitchell' aura about him") and his act with Hoban clever and offbeat. He also saw in 21-year-old Steve similarities to the singer who had replaced him in the trio that had made him famous: John Denver. "Steve was young, he really liked being onstage, and he exuded that real optimistic sense of what he was doing there. He was charming and funny. Denver also had that boyish quality, but Denver eventually got much more of a command, as opposed to the raw enthusiasm that was there in Steve."

The Punchinello's engagement, far more goofy than serious, was a stark contrast to contentious political and social headlines that were snaring the city's attention. The nationally notorious trial of the Chicago Seven, demonstrators who allegedly had conspired to riot at the previous year's infamous Democratic National Convention, was in full swing, and city police had just raided a West Side stronghold of members of the Illinois Black Panther Party, killing two.

Amid such strife and the drumbeat of the Vietnam War, Steve and Hoban began to build a following. On Monday nights, they became regular, on-location guests for the radio show of Jack Eigen, a notoriously abrasive announcer for WMAQ-AM, who broadcast inane, live conversations with celebrities that became known as "America's most imitated interviews." The duo's show also rated a rave from Jo Mapes in the *Chicago Sun-Times*. Her Dec. 12 column, while lauding Mitchell's sensitive voice, lamented that the headliner's material and sound were a "jolt" and that his set was not entirely "together." But Mapes rated Steve with unqualified praise:

"Goodman is a Wells Street coffeehouse graduate singing folk and funny songs to people who, for the most part, think they hate it, and he's proving them wrong. With an almost frantic insistence, Goodman zeroes in with a heavy rhythmic guitar and a taut, persuasive voice. Unhindered by the slick art of being a pro, Goodman comes off a good 10 notches above amateur, presenting a pretty disciplined, tight show. For someone who hasn't been told you just can't sing 'those kinds of songs at a place like this,' Goodman is doing a fine job of doing just that."

Daytimes, Steve hustled to sublet his apartment on Southport so that he could move with Lake Forest College friends John Bowen and Carol Laciny to a flat on North Sedgwick Street, two blocks west of the Earl of Old Town. Living temporarily with his grandmother, Mary Erenburg, he bought paint and spruced up the place that soon became his more logically located home.

For someone who hasn't been told you just can't sing 'those kinds of songs at a place like this,' Goodman is doing a fine job of doing just that.
JO MAPES
CHICAGO SUN-TIMES

At night, however, Steve's focus was stylish Punchinello's, and with Chicago's sub-freezing temperatures and chill wind, Steve began to go high fashion. Larry Rand sat with Ed Holstein at the bar of the Earl one afternoon, waiting for Pionke to treat his musicians to a free dinner out, when Steve strolled in wearing an immaculate, camel-hair coat.

"Where did you get the money for a coat like that?" Holstein said, nearly foaming at the mouth. "You've got a relationship. You've got rent to pay."

"Eat your heart out," Steve said with a grin.

"No, really," Holstein persisted.

"Hey, 36 bucks, boys department, Marshall Field's. The same coat in the men's store, $200."

At Punchinello's, Steve and Hoban clicked with Mitchell and went over so well with conventioneers that they even did a 45-minute fill-in set one Saturday evening when Mitchell had to appear across town on "The Marty Faye Show," live and low-rent on WLS-TV. "We did a lot of jokes and ad libs, and we killed," Hoban says. "Chad came back and found the audience had given us a standing O, and he wanted to see what we had done, so he suggested that we headline the second show, but management said no."

The compatible pair ("The most fun I've had in music at one point or another I've had with Bob Hoban," Steve said seven years later) got a couple of nights off the weekend after Christmas, when Steve played a scheduled gig at the Twelfth of Never coffeehouse, but they were back at Punchinello's for yeoman duty with Mitchell on New Year's Eve, for $10-per-head shows at 10 p.m., midnight and 2 a.m.

Art Thieme, a traditional folksinger known as "the Burl Ives of Chicago" and who caught their act that night, says Steve used a wry, fill-in-the-blank technique on the Marty Robbins classic, "El Paso." Steve sang each line in full except for its final word, for instance: "Out in the west Texas town of El Paso / I fell in love with a Mexican __," or "Nighttime would find me in Rosa's cantina / Music would play and Felina would __." The real final words were "girl" and "whirl," but with Steve's eyebrows arched, other text easily came to mind. "People thought it was hilarious, because it left it to the audience to fill in," Thieme says. "It made a real dirty, fun song out of it."

As Steve helped ring in 1970 at the downtown nightclub, his leukemia loomed large, but his engagement to Nancy, his plan to move to an Old Town apartment, the prospect of returning to college and his upscale billing with Chad Mitchell fueled his spirit. In fact, the Punchinello's experience gave Steve musical legs he didn't know he had.

"It was seminal for him," Hoban says. "It was his first gig with a mainstream audience, and he could do it. He just had balls. Most performers are afraid to make an ass of themselves, but he was respected by those people. He was realizing the relevance of it. He saw the light. It woke him up to lots of music, and Steve wanted to be part of everybody's music."

Before long, everybody across the nation would want to be part of his. ♪

Art Thieme, shown in 1963, marveled at how Steve, playing to the Punchinello's crowd in 1969, turned "El Paso" into a "real dirty, fun song."

(Photo courtesy of Art Thieme)

In March 1971 on Chicago's North Side, Steve plays the Quiet Knight, the site that spring of his launch to prominence.
(Photo by John Bowen)

'His genius and humility were the magnets'

I was standing on top of a volcano looking down at this beautiful island paradise, holding hands with Nancy, and asking myself, 'Why is she here?'
STEVE GOODMAN

On the clear, balmy evening of Thursday, Jan. 22, 1970, while standing 9,740 feet above sea level at the top of Mount Haleakala on the Hawaiian island of Maui and gazing at a setting sun, a rising full moon and a brilliant rainbow in-between, what was Steve Goodman thinking?

He wasn't contemplating his latest gig 5,000 miles away in Chicago, opening for Chad Mitchell at Punchinello's East, whose owner had just suffered a heart attack and whose new manager had first dropped Steve and accompanist Bob Hoban from its newspaper ads and then fired them when they asked to work under a contract.

He wasn't mulling over his final decision not to return to Lake Forest College, whose admissions director he had telephoned Jan. 7 to say that he couldn't re-enroll because he wasn't feeling well and was planning to return to New York for further leukemia treatment.

He wasn't critiquing a Jan. 14 show he had done with African-American folksinger and artist-in-residence John Bassette at Oberlin College near Cleveland.

No, Steve's thoughts were solely on one individual — the woman whose hand was clasped in his.

The afternoon prior, he had opened an envelope containing a whopping $1,500 in residuals from the airing of a jingle he had sung the previous September for Maybelline Blushing Eye Shadow. [1] "I had never seen anything like that before," he later said. Steve's response was instantaneous. He jumped into his car, drove to Nancy Pruter's apartment and whisked her to O'Hare International Airport, where the two boarded a plane for Los Angeles and Maui by way of Honolulu. "The next day," Steve later told Lake Forest friend John Bowen, "I was standing on top of a volcano looking down at this beautiful island paradise, holding hands with Nancy, and asking myself, 'Why is she here?' "

The folksinger and the nursing student/waitress clearly were in love, and their engagement to be married was real. Still, the Waikiki whirlwind that Steve had instigated was as boggling as it was invigorating.

"He surprised himself a little bit by becoming so attached to Nancy," Bowen says. "He was living such a life full of travel, and yet here was somebody who

1: The Maybelline radio spot ended up running more than two years, paying Steve dividends totaling some $9,000. "It paid my rent until I was fortunate enough to make my first album," he told Steve North of WLIR-FM on Long Island in 1979. "It saved my rear end ... got me out of hock."

*John Bowen plays guitar near
the front window in the
Sedgwick Street apartment that
he shared with Carol Laciny,
Steve and Steve's fiancée,
Nancy Pruter, in early 1970.*
(Photo by Robert Pruter)

was maybe an anchor for him that he could come back to. He asked himself, 'Why did I bring her to Hawaii? Why is she important to me?' The importance of that relationship sort of snuck up on him."

Steve and Nancy "spent every dime" of the $1,500 on the two-week Hawaii trip, then returned to Chicago to get married. "We had our honeymoon first," Steve noted with a grin.

The two already were spending nights together, often at the first-floor apartment that Steve had moved into early that month, just north of Mama De Luca's Italian restaurant at 1626 North Sedgwick Street. There, Steve had claimed the smallest of the apartment's three bedrooms, in back and off the kitchen, saying that for him to have one of the larger bedrooms, given his frequent traveling, would be unfair. He wasted no time filling his space, however. On a weekend drive that he and Nancy took through Michigan, they bought an enormous bed that, when reassembled, filled two-thirds of the back bedroom, its polished brass frame shining brightly into the nearby kitchen. "It was beautiful but out of place," says then-roommate John Bowen, "like a rose in a cornfield."

Their bed stretched beneath the bedroom window, which looked out to a busy alley. On the windowsill sat a sample of Steve's drollery. There, he had placed a triangular, wooden wedge, likely pocketed from the teller's station of a bank. Its message, with an arrow pointing left toward the building to the north, faced the alley and addressed potential burglars: "NEXT WINDOW PLEASE."

Besides Bowen, a Lake Forest graduate and classical guitarist, and Steve, the apartment's third dweller was Carol Laciny, a St. Louis native and Lake Forest student who 10 months earlier had been diagnosed with multiple sclerosis. Laciny was an unlikely roommate, given Steve's engagement to Nancy. But Steve and Laciny were no more than "just friends," bonded by their medical conditions. During a chance meeting a few months earlier near the Lake Forest campus, the two had discovered their commonality.

"Haven't seen you for a long time," Steve told her. "I dropped out of school. I'm playing at the Earl of Old Town."

"Oh, cool," she replied. "I'm about to drop out of school, too."

Laciny, whose MS stabilized in the years ahead, says that during the conversation "our different illnesses came up, and it was like, 'Yeah, what's the point of going to school?' "

While Steve wanted to live close to the Earl and needed roommates to share expenses, his beckoning to Laciny as a lodger amounted to a favor. "I was still getting used to the idea of having this illness that nobody could tell me much about," she says. "I didn't know if I was going to die. I had basically no information, and I was very confused. Steve helped me out by being contact with reality for a kid from St. Louis who wanted to live somewhere and make life so complicated that I didn't think about my illness.

"It was well understood that both of us had faced our mortality, that it was really fun to be around to appreciate what life is offering, that it's definitely true that one needs to seize the time that one has. He shared a lot of the same attitude toward 'What do you do when your body wants to give out?' You push it as far as it will go. It was a general understanding that we shared: What do you do? What can you do? You do what you can."

The apartment — with its unfinished brick interior wall along the south side of the living room echoing that of the Bitter End in Greenwich Village, not to mention the Earl — teemed with activity at all hours. In addition to Nancy, Steve often brought musicians to the flat, where Bowen experimented with a banjo and Laciny learned guitar. Laciny, an interviewer for the Institute for Juvenile Research at the University of Chicago, also frequently brought to the apartment homeless street people. "It became a crash pad, became kind of crazy, but it was a crazy time," Laciny says.

"Steve was so explosively talented and loving," she says. "He just loved life. His enthusiasm was infectious, his talent was bottomless, infinite, and there was always live music in the house. He was always going, 'Listen to this!' " One day, she said, Steve came home, said "Listen to this," and launched into Taj Mahal's train song, "She Caught the Katy and Left Me a Mule to Ride."

The gregarious mite also had not shed his high-school bent for lowbrow parody. That winter, set to "Mr. Bojangles," [2] the popular paean to an impoverished and imprisoned dancer, Steve made up "Mr. Abromovitz." It skewered Jewish stereotypes, depicting an Old World peddler of used clothing: "I knew a man, Abromovitz, he'd sell to you worn-out shoes. ... He would start out real high, and then he'd lightly come down." The final line was as crude as it was pointed: "Mr. Abromovitz, Mr. Abromovitz, die!" Several times Steve sang it at the Earl until one night a woman in the audience told him sarcastically, "That was very, very funny. I'll have to tell my uncle about it." She then disclosed that "Abromovitz" was her uncle's last name. "She was really frosty," Bowen says. "Steve sat down with her and talked her into a good humor. He was able to let her know that it was a joke and that he was Jewish himself and apologized for hurting her feelings." Still, says Bowen, the spoof "was pretty funny."

Because of the closeness that Steve and Laciny derived from their illnesses, the Sedgwick flat resembled a refuge for the unwell. "It wasn't like a love relationship," says Bob Gross, a Lake Forest friend. "They both thought they were going to die. It was like a hospice." Dan Jaffe, Laciny's boyfriend at the time, adds, "There was some synergy there that was quite wonderful." Jon Rose, another LFC friend, noting that Laciny seemed to be "fading rather quickly," says that she and Steve had an unspoken covenant fueled by Steve's magnetism. "He had this thing with women, and it wasn't a groupie scene," Rose says. "It was a very personal attraction for women. He had a feeling for them. It was the warmth. He had a way of capturing you. It was like a sunrise when he said hello to you."

Laciny says that Steve talked about her teasingly in front of Nancy upon occasion, but there was never any question where his true intentions lay. This was confirmed when Steve and Nancy applied for a Cook County marriage license on Monday, Feb. 2, 1970. The two were married on the chilly afternoon of Friday, Feb. 6, in a religious ceremony at Temple Jeremiah in the north sub-

Having been diagnosed with multiple sclerosis, Carol Laciny, shown in about 1970, found a kindred spirit in Steve while serving as his roommate: "It was well understood that both of us had faced our mortality."
(Photo courtesy of Carol Laciny)

2: Notwithstanding his parody, Steve admired "Mr. Bojangles." Its author, Jerry Jeff Walker, views it as a "folk-story philosophy song" that digs below the surface. "Through a story, you get a little sense of a bigger thing going on outside of life," Walker says. "It's like hearing tales of your great-great-grandfather coming from someplace and starting with nothing and doing this or doing that. And you think, 'Wow, boy, we think things are weird,' but they went through the Depression or the Dust Bowl things, and you hear stories of human struggle and survival." Into the same category Walker places the song that became Steve's best-known: "City of New Orleans."

urb of Winnetka by Allan Tarshish, founding rabbi of the liberal Reform congregation. The occasion was not without lighter moments, owing to the couple's difference in height. As Steve and Nancy faced Tarshish, the rabbi asked them to stand "arm in arm and shoulder to shoulder." Each looked at the other and dissolved in laughter.

That evening, the reception site was no surprise, nor was its music. While the temperature outside dropped more than 10 degrees below freezing, family and friends warmed up the Earl of Old Town, sharing champagne, eating wedding cake and seeing and hearing a performance by Steve. Clean-shaven, with tousled hair and mutton-chop sideburns and wearing a brown suit, light-blue shirt and a tie with diagonal swaths of gold, brown and black, formal duds uncharacteristic for him at the Earl, Steve nonetheless felt right at home. In front of a brick wall adorned with posters bearing nearly life-size portraits of Bonnie Koloc and Fred Holstein alongside leftover Christmas fliers and thick, faded, brown 1966-vintage wreaths, one of which encircled a tiny mug shot of Dean Martin, Steve sang and strummed the reddish brown Hummingbird guitar his parents had given him in 1963.

Nancy, in a dark blue, short-sleeved dress, beamed throughout the night but was quiet and shy while immersed in the cacophony, says Cathy Lind (now Edler), a Maine East High friend. In contrast, Lind says, Steve was ebullient. "He was so excited that we came to see him perform and to share in his joy."

For about a dozen weeks following their wedding, Steve and Nancy lived mostly with Bowen and Laciny at the Sedgwick apartment, savoring its proximity to the Earl and rough-hewn charm. But the 1,100-square-foot dwelling also bore its share of challenges. While a pair of fan-driven, gas-fired space heaters kept rooms sporadically comfortable, Chicago's winter chill seeped into gaps in the tuck-point and through two large windows that were covered with plastic film instead of glass, the frosty clime particularly palpable when the absentee landlord failed to pay the gas bill.

The trio of renters complained of the chill to no avail, but a less-than-innocent phone call by Steve finally spurred action. One afternoon, he telephoned the landlord's home to seek the return of a blanket the landlord had borrowed for an assignation in the vacant third-floor apartment. The landlord's wife answered the phone, and Steve stumbled through an explanation of why the landlord had needed a blanket. That evening, Steve, Bowen and Laciny heard shouts upstairs and giddily watched out their front window as the landlord's shoes and clothes fell to the snowy street.

As the thaw of spring approached, the lure of finding privacy in a place of their own proved strong for the newlyweds. When Nancy's brother, Robert Pruter, agreed to take their place in the Sedgwick apartment, Steve and Nancy moved two miles north to a $90/month unit on the seventh floor of a high-rise at 515 West Briar Place. Though farther away from the Earl of Old Town, the new residence placed Steve and Nancy just one block east of the Broadway business district, three blocks west of Belmont Harbor and the shore of Lake

He was so excited that we came to see him perform and to share in his joy.
CATHY LIND

Michigan, six blocks east of the burgeoning night life of Clark and Belmont and only one mile — an easy walk — from Wrigley Field.

Their move produced annoyances quelled by the zest of courtship. Bowen noticed Steve carrying boxes to Nancy's Volkswagen bug while wearing a pair of then-unfashionable high-topped black sneakers. "Oh, yeah," Steve told Bowen with an ironic grin. "They're great! Great for basketball and for steppin' in dog shit!" For emphasis, he scraped the sole of a soiled shoe across the edge of the curb. "See?" Another time during the move, Bowen saw the couple try to squeeze Nancy's bug into a tight parking space. With Nancy at the wheel and depending upon Steve, on the passenger side, to lean out his open door and look to the rear to see if the back wheel was close enough to the curb, Nancy backed the passenger door into a fire hydrant. The crumpled door never again latched correctly and had to be tied shut with a length of rope. Not long afterward, because of the greater congestion of their new neighborhood, they got rid of the car.

Within days of their move, Steve showed up at a Chicago hotel to compete with scores of other musicians for openings in the New Christy Minstrels, the co-ed choral folk group popular in the early 1960s ("Green Green") that nearly a decade later had fallen out of favor. Terry Tiz, the only musician chosen from the Chicago "cattle call," says one of the group's staff told him later that Steve had been impressive in his tryout, but leukemia proved the foil. "We were going to hire him," the staffer told Tiz in so many words, "but he has this health problem, and we're going to be going overseas during the year, so we can't hire him."

Such a professional dead end could have demoralized Steve but for the support of his new wife. "Saved my ass, man, Nancy Goodman did," Steve told Al Rudis of the *Chicago Sun-Times* five years later, in reflecting on her steadying early presence. While he didn't reveal his leukemia during the interview, it was a strong subtext for his expressed gratitude.

"I had nothing going for me when I met her," Steve told Rudis. "I was busted, I was out of school, broke, no dope, no prospects. They broke the mold after they made her. She's a sucker."

"Was she a pusher?" Rudis asked.

"No. She was just there. You could take one look at her face and tell you'd done something right or you had screwed up. She's just strong, is all. Not a pushy woman."

"Was she the type to get you off your ass and do something?"

"I had enough of my own motivation," Steve said. "But through all of this, when I could have gotten depressed about what was happening and packed it in, all I had to do was talk to Nancy for a while, and it would become very clear to me that everything was all right.

"She never once allowed me to feel sorry for myself, especially in the midst of getting away with actually doing nothing but play a guitar for a living. I mean, all you've got to do is read a newspaper and find out how many people

> **Through all of this, when I could have gotten depressed about what was happening and packed it in, all I had to do was talk to Nancy for a while, and it would become very clear to me that everything was all right.**
> **STEVE GOODMAN**

are unemployed to know what a joke that one is. ... She never let me get away with that bullshit, the 'Oh, the world is doing this or doing that' crap. She made me be as good a musician as I could be and as good an entertainer as I could be."

While Steve already had made invaluable inroads and built a musical foundation before meeting Nancy, it was following his marriage to her that his milestones snowballed. The first of these came that spring, when Nancy unintentionally prompted a defining moment in Steve's career. What started out as a routine visit to a relative who lived downstate became a trip that has since been etched into folk-music lore and burnished to a warm glow.

Early one cold Monday morning in April 1970, Steve — carrying a Martin D-28 guitar he had acquired from John Bassette a year or two prior — and Nancy made their way through the Loop to the south end of lakeside Grant Park. There, they entered an all-brick, 10-story, Romanesque building topped by a lofty clock tower, the 77-year-old Illinois Central Station. After walking through the deteriorating, red-roofed landmark, each paid $11 for a round-trip ticket, and the two boarded one of 14 cars of a chocolate- and orange-colored train shortly before its 8 a.m. departure. It was their first railroad ride together. Their destination, three hours south, was Mattoon, where they would visit Nancy's "90-and-change" grandmother a few miles northwest on the campus of the Illinois Masonic Home near the tiny town of Sullivan. The purpose of the day trip was to introduce Nancy's grandmother to the man her granddaughter had just married. The train, barely a year older than Steve himself, was the City of New Orleans.

The resulting tale was one that Steve told interviewers and others hundreds of times, likely more often than any other story during his life.

"We had to get up pretty early because the train left at 8, and Nancy was sleeping in the seat next to me," he said in one of his lengthier recitations. "I just took out a sketchpad, and I looked out the window and wrote down everything I saw: junkyards, little towns that didn't even have a sign to say what they were. Just out of Chicago, there was a bunch of old men standing around tin cans, warming themselves and waving. Nancy was still asleep after about an hour and a half, so I went down to the club car and ended up playing cards with a couple of old men."

Repeatedly, Steve insisted in interviews that the words on his sketchpad assembled themselves into the thematic whole that became Steve's fifth or sixth serious musical composition — a folk/country anthem with a title matching the name of the train: "City of New Orleans." [3]

"I don't know, I just wrote it, and it was starting to turn into something, and I got the chorus," he told WXRT-FM's John Platt in 1975 in Chicago. "I mean, it just was there. I was visited by the muse. I don't feel like I did anything. The whole thing took about 35 minutes. ... It was just one of those things, (seemingly) in the dark in the middle of the night, that happened."

"It was an accident. It just tumbled out," he said in 1976 for the London

---

It just was there. I was visited by the muse. I don't feel like I did anything. The whole thing took about 35 minutes.
STEVE GOODMAN

3: An early draft of "City of New Orleans," written in Steve's hand on lined notebook paper, shows refinements he made while drafting the song's first verse and chorus. He changed the number of "restless riders" from 50 to 15, making the interior picture of the coach emptier and more poignant. He altered "I'm the Illinois Central City of New Orleans" to "I'm the train they call the City of New Orleans," eliminating repetition of a first-verse reference and giving the line a more mythic and down-to-earth feel. In the chorus, he halved the trip's length, perhaps realizing that 1,000 miles exaggerated the actual 921-mile route and tracing the fewer miles the train covered in daylight hours. The draft was displayed on a booklet in the 1994 2-CD anthology "No Big Surprise."

magazine *Omaha Rainbow*. "I don't want to make it out as anything more than it was."

But Steve was doing just that. He consistently failed to mention that he had begun to draft it three years prior with his Maine East High friend Howard Primer — including the opening line of "Riding on the City of New Orleans," the key chorus greeting of "Good morning, America" and the phrase "native son." The lyrics may have jelled on his 1970 ride to Mattoon with Nancy, but their genesis lay in a solitary 1967 college-skipping trip to New Orleans on the same train, followed by a collaboration on a napkin with a high-school buddy in a Chicago club.

Twice, during shows in 1972 and 1975, Steve disclosed having ridden the train to its southern terminus during his University of Illinois years. Similarly, he told an interviewer he'd lyrically charted the train's nighttime route "strictly from memory" because he figured he "couldn't write a song about a train that went 900 miles through the center of the country and stop the song in Mattoon because I was getting off." But in dozens of other documented and prominent retellings, Steve left the unambiguous impression that the song simply materialized during his trip with Nancy.

Why did Steve rarely bring out the college experiences that triggered the tune's true birth? The answer is easy, says Primer. "The college chapter of his life was not as romantic as the chapter with his wife," he says. "He was a storyteller. Everything about Steve's music was telling a story, so it was not unreasonable for him to weave that into his natural life as well. The moral of the story wasn't the important thing. What was important was that the story hung together and that you could get yourself into it and see yourself in it. You really didn't know how much of it was real and how much of it was fabricated."

While Steve's claim that he was "visited by the muse" while Nancy napped next to him on the train was partly fabricated, the remainder of his recounting of the song's origin was real. Upon returning from his train trip with Nancy to Mattoon, Steve hurried back to his haven, the Earl of Old Town, to share his musical news. His song had two verses that evoked the bittersweet path of an Illinois Central train and a ringing chorus that personified a locomotive and summoned nostalgic souls to face "the disappearin' railroad blues."

Steve knew the tune held potential. The Earl's house act and resident mentor, Fred Holstein, later recalled the honor of being the first musician to hear the fledgling lyrics.

"What do you think of this?" Steve said.

"Oh, God," replied the brash Holstein, who was known for his musical taste and interpretation of others' work, "an American folk-song classic."

"You think I should finish this thing?"

"Abso-fuckin'-lutely."

Heartened, Steve also sought counsel from the lead guitarist for Bonnie Koloc's backup band, Richard Wedler. Steve was enamored of Wedler's 12-string technique, a cross between mandolin and guitar picking, and the two had become

> **What was important was that the story hung together and that you could get yourself into it and see yourself in it. You really didn't know how much of it was real and how much of it was fabricated.**
> **HOWARD PRIMER**

Upon hearing two verses of "City of New Orleans," Richard Wedler, shown in 1970, told Steve, "You can do better. ... Work on something different than just the train. What happened on it? Why don't you do more of a Steinbeck?"

(Photo by Jim Chambers, courtesy of Richard Wedler)

compatriots during Steve's frequent stints as Koloc's opening act at the Earl.

During a break, in the Earl's back-room Star Cave, past a meat locker and surrounded by beer kegs, a liquor cabinet, stacked booze boxes, a safe, a hand truck, a deep freeze, office supplies, cluttered shelves and an overstuffed coat rack, Steve perched on Pionke's tiny desk with his foot on a chair and played his early version of "City of New Orleans" for Wedler.

There, Steve's oft-told tale continued with Wedler's response: "He said I had looked out of the window pretty good and had described the disappearing railroad blues and the cars changing late at night and all."

But then, Steve said, Wedler asked him, "What else happened on the train itself?"

"Well, there was a low-calorie gin rummy game going on," Steve replied.

"Why don't you talk about what happened on the train?" he said Wedler told him. "Then you'll have it."

"Sure," Steve said.

"And so I wrote the (middle) verse about the sleeping people and the card games and the brown bag. The whole thing at that stage took 10 minutes. I wrote it at Earl's desk at the back of the bar, and that was it."

Wedler confirms Steve's version of their encounter, but he says his tutelage had a sharper edge.

"You gotta hear this, you gotta hear this," Wedler recalls Steve telling him.

When Steve played him the song, "the guitar was really humming along," Wedler says. "He was playing flatpick style. It sounded pretty good. It sounded like it really had some form." Still, Wedler, who had come to Chicago as a solo act and was "carrying a bit of an attitude" because he had settled into the lesser role of Koloc's accompanist, says that he'd had "a shitty night at the club" and was growing irritated.

"Well, that's cool," Wedler recalls telling Steve, "but you can do better than that. (Gordon) Lightfoot already wrote a hell of a train song, 'Canadian Railroad Trilogy.' Work on something different than just the train. What happened on it? Why don't you do more of a Steinbeck?"

Regardless of whose recollections of the exchange are more precise, there's no question that Wedler's probing prodded Steve to produce the verse with the song's most enduring images — "penny a point" card games, wheels "grumblin' 'neath the floor," mothers rocking babies to "the rhythm of the rails" — and to give it a timeless context with a visual metaphor of the railroad as a "magic carpet made of steam." The overall result was a true-to-life movie that could play in the listener's mind.

"To me," Wedler says, "folk music was very much like (John) Steinbeck's writing. It was about very common things and life experiences, more journalistic than just fiction, and you could believe the stories. They were possible. They were human. That's what I was trying to get across to Steve. I'm not sure exactly why. Something in what he already had triggered me to that type of feel about it."

Wedler says he intended his advice about the song to be useful. "I wasn't trying to tear it down, because it was a well-constructed piece already, but it didn't break new ground, and I've always been a stickler for that," he says. "I was pretty ardent about it. In fact, I remember a touch of needling to it because I used to think that Steve played off other people's ideas until I realized that, wow, this guy is just incubating, his ideas are really jelling, and as confidence came, so did his creativity."

Upon reflection, Steve saw the value of his song's concrete detail, in the second verse especially, while also backhandedly acknowledging his craft.

"Everything in the song happened," Steve told WGN-AM morning host Roy Leonard in March 1972. "I wish I'd made it up, y'know, but I'm not good at makin' up songs. I guess I'm not too good at fiction. I guess I can surround real events with some fiction every now and then to dress 'em up, but I don't come up with fictional situations too often. I kind of have to see it first."

With the sensibilities of a language-arts teacher, Steve both pinpointed and denigrated his feat in an interview, also in May 1972, on "FolkScene," a Los Angeles radio show helmed by producer Roz Larman and host Howard Larman.

"It's just using your eyes, really," he said. "My big trouble is that I don't use 'em well enough, because I usually filter what I see through my own set of experiences and stuff like that too much. It's very hard for anybody around to take an objective view of anything — y'know, just describe it. Sometimes what you think is the best poetry in the world is just somebody using their eyes right and just tryin' to describe what they saw rather than what they felt about what they saw. Then it makes the listener or the reader of the poetry do the work. ... The good poets use the kinds of words that will help you paint the picture in your own head."

Wedler allows that "City of New Orleans" might not have had a future without the sensory description of its second verse. "It had a very positive effect," he reflects. "Talk about the guy holding the bottle in the bag, and 'penny a point and no one's keeping score' — that's pretty profound stuff. It paints a picture that really makes you feel like you're there. It makes it all very acceptable, very American and historical. You can just see these old guys playing there, and they've got nothing else to do but ride on the train, and they're just passing the time. It's a lot more like a well-written short story than just another train song. That's what I was trying to get across to him, but I hadn't any idea what he'd do with it."

Ironically, Wedler didn't wait around that night to hear the second verse and soon left Chicago for California. After Steve finished the verse and embedded it in his memory in the Star Cave, he couldn't wait to play the full song for others. The first time he had a chance later that night at the Earl, the completed "City of New Orleans" had its debut.

The song sadly reflected the nation's transition from manufacturing to a service economy, and its message was unmistakable for listeners who were aware of the decline of the railways. The signs were everywhere. The U.S. Postal Service's

In Clifton, 75 miles south of Chicago, the Illinois Central tracks run through town in 2001. Steve said the key to his song about the train was having seen what he was writing about: "Sometimes what you think is the best poetry in the world is just somebody using their eyes right and just tryin' to describe what they saw rather than what they felt about what they saw."

(Photo by Clay Eals)

Gordon Lightfoot, shown in 1970, found that Steve's "City of New Orleans" resonated with him: "It's just the feel and the melody and the imagery, describing the movement of human beings fulfilling their destiny, looking after business matters, visiting their people."

(Reprise photo, courtesy of Valerie Magee)

4: In Steve's hometown seven years after Steve wrote the song, Lightfoot gave it a wry seal of approval. As longtime Lightfoot fans Jim Brankin and John LaCloche recall, during the second half of an April 9, 1977, concert at the Auditorium Theatre in the Chicago Loop, Lightfoot recognized Steve in the audience. Lightfoot, not one to speak much between songs, told the crowd, "My friend, Steve Goodman, is out there somewhere, and we're going out afterward to paint the town. He wrote the second-best train song ever written." Steve stood to acknowledge a standing ovation, after which Lightfoot played his own "Canadian Railroad Trilogy."

introduction of ZIP codes in 1966 had led to the closure of downtown sorting centers next to railway stations, which spurred a devastating switch to trucks and planes for mail transport. Completion of the interstate highway system also was imminent, and air travel was soaring in popularity, reducing several-day journeys to just a few hours. Chicago, which poet Carl Sandburg had characterized in 1916 as a "Player with Railroads" and the "City of the Big Shoulders," was keenly feeling the decay. So at the Earl, Steve's song held instant resonance.

One of the saloon's late-night regulars, *Chicago Sun-Times* film critic Roger Ebert, embraced the song instantly. "I told Steve that it was like a standard," he says. "You hear it for the first time, and you think you've been hearing it all your life. It's one of those songs where the material and the music fall together into such inevitable, perfect kind of unity."

Toronto-based Gordon Lightfoot, who around this time played a triple bill at the Earl with Steve and Bob Gibson, likened the north-south reach of Steve's "City of New Orleans" to the east-west scope of his "Canadian Railroad Trilogy." But he also appreciated that the "City" theme extended to the interior lives of its riders.

"It's just the feel and the melody and the imagery, describing the movement of human beings fulfilling their destiny, looking after business matters, visiting their people," Lightfoot says. "It was a very charming time for a certain while, when everything was sort of calmed down. It sort of fits into that 1940s, 1950s time, and you get the feeling that you want to look back, think about hotels and shoeshine parlors and bars." 4

The song also arrested the attention of the Earl's namesake, whom Steve had come to revere. ("He's like a father who doesn't want me to be a doctor," Steve said in a December 1971 *Chicago Daily News* interview.)

"Steve, you've got a winner," Pionke told Steve soon after hearing "City of New Orleans." "I'm not an agent, I don't intend to be one, that's not my business. But you have to get yourself an agent like the good guys do. I give you two days."

"What are you talkin' about?" Steve replied.

"You've got a fuckin' hit," Pionke said, goading Steve with typical crudity. "You've got a classic. It's topical. The trains are dying. Fuck the trains. It's all airplanes. This is it, man. You've got it all. You gotta get that copyrighted, patented, I don't know the official term, but so nobody can steal that song from you. I give you two days. If you don't have that fuckin' thing copyrighted, whatever you call it, I'll kick your fuckin' ass and drag you down there. You understand that?"

"OK, Yarns, I understand." ("Yarns" was one of Steve's two nicknames for Pionke. "I'm a bullshit artist, weaving yarns," explains Pionke, whose other nickname was "Disappearo," because "I disappear at all opportune times, when most people don't expect it.")

The next day, Steve returned to the Earl, buttonholing Pionke at the bar.

"Guess what," Steve said.

"You got the thing done," Pionke shot back.

"How'd you know?"

"Because I know you're a smart fuck, and you listen to one even smarter than you, you prick — me — and you went and did it."

"Yeah, it's all done."

"Good, let's have a fuckin' cheeseburger and a fuckin' beer."

"Cheeseburger and a beer? Fuck you. I want champagne."

"We don't sell champagne here. You want a cheeseburger and beer or not?"

"OK, let's have one."

What Steve had done was seek out Dick Boyell, the jingle producer who had given Steve his first commercial work the previous fall. Steve walked in with his guitar and told Boyell, "Hey, I want you to hear this tune." After Steve played it through, Boyell was hooked. "I was stationed in New Orleans during the war (World War II), and I took the train back and forth to Chicago," Boyell says, "so when he started describing all those things, the whole thing rang a bell with me."

Boyell wrote out the melody and chords on a lead sheet so the song could be sent to the U.S. Copyright Office (which Boyell did as its publisher, under his firm's name, Nuance Productions, on May 25). He asked Steve, "Why don't you make a demo tape of it?" Within days, Boyell sandwiched the project between jingles at Universal Recording Co. on East Ohio Street along the Magnificent Mile. Boyell had written "a little rhythm background, a funky thing," for the piece. Boyell paid for the session, bringing in a bass guitarist, a drummer, three violinists and Old Town School of Folk Music teacher Ray Tate on lead guitar. On piano was Boyell himself. The group, with Steve singing vocals only, recorded the song without overdubs.

Tate clearly recalls the session and how the song struck him. "I loved it," he says. "It was fun to play. It had a nice swing to it. It had a great chorus. I saw it as an historical piece and a celebration of America."

Boyell made 50 vinyl copies of the demo 45. Hoping more than one record company would snag the tune, "we sent them to everybody that I knew and he (Steve) ever heard of," Boyell says. "The result was nothing. The rejections were unbelievable. One company even sent it back — not only did they not open it, but it was warped from sitting on the radiator or something." No copies of the demo apparently survive today.

Making "City of New Orleans" a regular part of his repertoire, Steve began telling audiences and interviewers not just how — but also why — he wrote the song. His answer drew partly from the temper of the political times, including the April 30 expansion of the Vietnam War to Cambodia, which led to the May 4 National Guard shooting of student demonstrators at Kent State University, which triggered the May 21 recording of the Crosby, Stills, Nash & Young plaint "Ohio." Though "City of New Orleans" had nothing to do with Vietnam, and Steve had none of the fame necessary to storm the national airwaves, he knew that invoking vivid images to undergird a phrase he had coined — "the

Dick Boyell, shown in the studio in 1969-70, helped Steve to copyright "City of New Orleans" and supervised the recording of a demo 45-rpm single. "The result was nothing," Boyell says. "The rejections were unbelievable. One company even sent it back — not only did they not open it, but it was warped from sitting on the radiator or something."
(Photo by Murray Allen, courtesy of Dick Boyell)

disappearin' railroad blues" — constituted his own musical call to action.

As he featured "City" in sets at the Earl and elsewhere, Steve said he wrote it because of news reports that Illinois Central was planning to take the dilapidated train off its line. He also tried to point out the environmental benefits of railroads. "It's a proven fact," he told listeners at the Earl one night, "that trains don't screw up the air the way airplanes do and cars and stuff like that — just steam, for God's sake. Pretty good way to travel." In addition, trains' role in the settling of the West and the industrial revolution in the late 19th century appealed to Steve's reverence for the past. He noted in an interview, "The railroad was so responsible for so much of American history that the good features of it should have been retained."

What Steve may not have realized was how effectively "City of New Orleans" could tap the impending nostalgia craze fueled by the younger generation and soon to be validated by a *Life* magazine cover. The song was a way to embrace something old without swallowing the excesses of an older generation that seemed bent on destroying, with plasticized progress, the charming, venerable icons of the romantic past.

Steve allowed that his "City of New Orleans" was influenced by the rich heritage of train songs that preceded him, from rollicking versions of "Casey Jones," which detailed an April 30, 1900, wreck along the same Illinois Central line, to Goebel Reeves' plaintive 1961 "Hobo's Lullaby." The lineage included the 1929 classic "Waiting for a Train" by one of Steve's musical heroes, the first solo singing star in country music, the frail but grinning Jimmie Rodgers, who succumbed to tuberculosis at age 35. Steve said in his 1971 *Chicago Daily News* interview that before he penned "City of New Orleans," he was "writing some songs, but nothing that I liked hearing." That appraisal changed with "City of New Orleans," he said. "I knew then that I had written something I'd like to hear. 'City' is like a Jimmie Rodgers song — it's even about trains!"

The feeling, however, wasn't universal. That spring, while opening for the locally popular Righteous Bluegrass Band at the Earl, Steve called its members into the back-room Star Cave, said, "I've got a great song for you guys," and played "City of New Orleans" for them. "The band didn't hear it as a bluegrass song," says the band's manager, Michael Aisner, "and never worked it up."

Despite that cold shoulder, "City of New Orleans" caught on fast at the Earl, with Bonnie Koloc and Fred Holstein incorporating it in their sets. "Everybody was singing it, and all of a sudden I'm a songwriter," said Steve, who credited Holstein's "huge baritone voice" with popularizing the song at the Earl. "The first guy that ever learned anything I wrote was Fred Holstein," Steve told "FolkScene" in March 1972. "He sang the devil out of it, and it was my excuse for workin' in Chicago for about a year."

Work he did, both in and out of town, and in the midst of visits to Sloan-Kettering every few weeks for leukemia checkups and treatment (getting "cooked," he told friends), the pace of his musical life quickened. In the spring and summer of 1970, Steve embarked on his first tour, a chancy endeavor by bus and train in which he played small clubs in Louisville and four cities in Georgia — his first immersion in the Deep South. "I put myself on the road," Steve said in a 1972 interview. "It was a kind of telephone circuit. If I did well in a club and the owner liked me, I'd ask him if he knew anyone else, and the guy would phone ahead to another club."

An impromptu gig that helped trigger the tour was Steve's performance on April 26 at the Raven Gallery in the Detroit suburb of Southfield. The billed act was Miami-based Bittersweet, consisting of Don Dunaway and George Corrochano. It was a slow Sunday night, and the Raven's owner, Herb Cohen, told the duo that Steve had just hitchhiked from Chicago and asked if they would mind if he did a guest set. They acceded.

"We didn't know what to expect," says Dunaway (now Oja-Dunaway). "He wasn't the biggest man I'd ever seen, and I was looking at his little hands." Steve closed a strong set in timely fashion, singing Joni Mitchell's "Woodstock," the hit version of which had just hit the airwaves that spring from the Crosby, Stills, Nash & Young "Déjà vu" LP and was the title cut from the festival's three-hour documentary film that had just opened in Detroit. "He blew us off the stage, and we were devastated," Dunaway says. "We didn't know how we were going to get back on. He just got up there, and boom, pyrotechnics were going on with his guitar, his singing, his stage presence."

After the show, the duo invited Steve to their room at the Royal Oak Motel, and the three stayed up talking half the night. Pressed about his future, Steve rolled up his sleeves to display scars on his forearms, evidence of the blood work forced by his leukemia. He said bluntly, "I'll be dead in a year."

"We were freaking out," Dunaway says. "George and I said, 'Man, we've got to do something. This guy is one of the most incredible people we've ever seen, and then to be dealing with this?' "

As they headed back south, by phone Dunaway and Corrochano sang Steve's praises to their manager, Tom Hayward, who helped secure bookings for him at the Bistro clubs in Atlanta and Augusta and the Last Resort in Athens, [5] and Dunaway later pushed for Steve's booking in Florida. Steve spent another spring stop in Georgia, for two weeks in coastal Savannah in early June and with Nancy in tow. The booking let Steve indulge his passion for baseball, as the couple took in home games of the Savannah Indians, the AA farm club of the Cleveland Indians, but it also sharpened his cunning creativity.

In sizzling Savannah, the fully bearded Steve, in bib overalls, opened for two groups: the Sandalwood Castle, a folk duo from Charlotte, North Carolina, and a pioneering bluegrass band from northern Kentucky called the Cumberlands. Their venue was the aptly named Other End, a bar owned by a "retired" Mafioso and located in the basement of another riverfront eatery, the Boar's Head. "They had a boar's head up over the fireplace in the restaurant upstairs, and they had the boar's ass and tail hangin' up over the stage in the Other End," Steve recalled in a 1975 interview on Long Island's WLIR-FM. The "beef and reef" club fronted on River Street, 30 feet from the bank of the

Don Dunaway, half of the duo Bittersweet, was blindsided by the impact of the unscheduled appearance of Steve at the Raven Gallery near Detroit. "We didn't know how we were going to get back on," Dunaway says. "He just got up there, and boom, pyrotechnics were going on with his guitar, his singing, his stage presence."

(Photo by Bob Patterson)

5: The Last Resort was "the first place where I was ever really a draw" away from home, Steve said. "I have no idea why I went over in Athens, Georgia, but outside of Chicago, that was my town, a place where everything worked."

Savannah River, where ocean-going ships anchored. The seafaring crews made up a big part of the Other End's audiences, and the bar catered to them, from the red bow tied on the curly tail of the boar to the men's restroom, which Steve discovered was sexually stocked and which he decided to immortalize in song.

"In the men's room," Steve said, "there were all these machines up over the urinals with a deck of playin' cards the size of your thumb with pictures of your sister on the back, and all these salves you could rub on your body to make it last longer. Great trade names: Delay, Prolong, right? I don't know who thinks up this stuff, but this is in the classiest restaurant in town, so I couldn't wait to go to a gas station and see the hardcore stuff."

In these surroundings, Steve became inspired. "I wasn't necessarily sheltered about stuff like this (the restroom machines), but it surprised me to see it in a restaurant," he told *Omaha Rainbow* in 1976. "I just went in and thought, 'This is a funny place. I bet there's $20,000 in there,' so I made up the song."

It was a whimsical "outlaw ballad," as he called it. Focusing on an imaginary highway bandit, "Turnpike Tom" soon became one of Steve's most requested tunes. In it, a driver picks up the hitchhiker (whose alternate alliterative nicknames, Steve said, were "Entrance Ramp Ernie" and "Freeway Fritz"), who promises that "$20,000 in unmarked green" from a 1942 bank robbery is hidden in a condom dispenser hanging on the men's room wall of "Rusty's Roadside Cabaret" in Greensboro, Tennessee. Tom gives a key for the dispenser to the driver, who motors on to Rusty's, opens the dispenser and finds a note: "You've just been had in a sanitary way by Turnpike Tom, the outlaw with the fastest sense of humor." Cleverly capping the song was a moral: "You only fall for lies and stories when you really want to."

Steve milked the song's punning possibilities, saying during one performance that it was "just off the wall enough, as it were." [6] More important, the song gave him the chance to convey — and embellish on — the lengthy tale of its origin, a harbinger of the onstage storytelling that became one of his hallmarks. For "Turnpike Tom," he appended a deceptively simple joke that commented on the art of embellishment itself. "The song's really about the difference between bullshit and lying," he would say. "The difference is that a liar usually believes his own bullshit."

From Monday through Saturday in three sets a night at the Other End, Steve performed a sweeping array of songs. They included Jimmy Driftwood's "Long Chain On" (1960), Chuck Berry's "Johnny B. Goode" (1958), the 1930s' "Walkin' Blues" by Robert Johnson and "This Land Is Your Land" by Woody Guthrie, Irving Berlin's "I'll See You in C-U-B-A" (1920), the traditional "Pallet on the Floor" and James Taylor's new "Steamroller Blues."

It was Steve's rendition of another Taylor song that particularly moved Gerry Dionne, who with Dick Lewis made up the headlining Sandalwood Castle. Steve and Nancy had built a friendship with the duo, showing up in their trailer one night to make a dinner of spaghetti and red wine. On another night, standing in line inside a White Castle eatery to buy 25-cent mini-burgers, the four

---

I just went in and thought, 'This is a funny place. I bet there's $20,000 in there,' so I made up the song.
STEVE GOODMAN

6: Thirteen years later, for Barry Hansen ("Dr. Demento"), Steve explained the "trick" behind such twisted tunes: "It's to take something that you see every day and stretch it out to its most ridiculous extreme and actually pretend that it's music."

became an impromptu quartet singing at the top of their lungs a medley of country tunes.

At the Other End, Steve took Dionne into a closet near the stage to practice a song or two. There, Dionne asked Steve his long-term plans.

"I don't make long-term plans," Steve replied. "I have leukemia. If I didn't have Nancy in my life, I'd be a standup comic."

Steve switched the subject. "Do you know James Taylor's music?" he asked, before playing Taylor's "Sweet Baby James." When he got to the phrase "But singing works just fine for me," Dionne, still reeling from the leukemia comment, started crying.

"We were about the same age, but he was an old soul with a deep, deep wisdom," Dionne says. "He could play the dogshit out of a guitar, and he sang well enough, but the power lay in his eyes. They looked past the ephemera down to your soul. Even a tipsy crowd of rednecks felt it at some level. The sad songs were happy; the happy songs, sad."

Savannah provided Steve with one of his earliest opportunities to broaden the geographical appeal for his happy/sad epic, "City of New Orleans." [7] He trotted it out with a burst of geography and advice. "It's train #1 out of Chicago," he said, "and runs every day at 8 o'clock in the morning from the 12th Street and Michigan Avenue station in Chicago down through most of central Illinois, starting with the Chicago suburb of Homewood-Flossmoor and moving on to Kankakee, Rantoul, Champaign/Urbana, Mattoon, Effingham, Carbondale, the west end of Tennessee, Memphis, through Mississippi, Jackson and Brookhaven, down into New Orleans, 955 miles. Trip takes about 17-and-a-half hours, which is why most people fly to New Orleans, or anyplace else that's 955 miles away from them. The next time you have a middle-distance trip, I think it'd be a good idea if you took the train. I say that every night, but I mean it. Passenger trains are dyin' out, and you may as well get on 'em while you can. Might even be able to save some of 'em if you rode 'em long enough."

Guitarist Harold Thom and banjo player and "train nut" Jim Smoak of the Cumberlands were taken with the tune, and Steve encouraged the group to record it. "We happened to have a recording session in Nashville two weeks

7: The first edition of Charlie Gillett's landmark rock history, *The Sound of the City*, was published in July 1970 and concluded with an unwitting reference to "City of New Orleans." Lamenting the end of true development of rock and the beginning of "singing writers" such as Carole King and James Taylor, the book ended with a brief sentence: "Goodnight America."

after the gig in Savannah," Thom says. "We tried to talk the producer into letting us record the song, but the producer didn't like it." With words he later may have regretted, the producer told the group, "It's a good song, but it's just not a commercial song." [8]

Steve's penchant for endless adjustment of his strings onstage was on full display on his last evening in Savannah: "Posterity will record that on Saturday night, the 13th of June, at 26 after 9 (p.m.), Goodman cussed and drank a glass of water and made a vain attempt to tune this goddamn guitar."

He also strained to impart a congenial assessment of the South. "It's been a pleasure to be here, really," he told the crowd near the end of his final set at the Other End. "I had all kinds of weird hang-ups about comin' south and stuff, and it's all bullshit, and I just wanted to thank you folks for makin' this two weeks pretty nice." Steve added an affectionate jab at the region's staple food of grits, calling it "Southern caviar." But he also revealed a cynical side while introducing his closing song, a version of Dino Valenti's "Get Together," which became a top-10 hit for the Youngbloods folk-rock band in 1969, triggered by its use in a public-service TV spot for National Brotherhood Week. Steve cracked, "That's the week when you say, 'Well, when we call 'em niggers, we mean somethin' else.' "

Steve's sarcasm undercut what apparently was his sincere belief that "Get Together" ("C'mon, people now, smile on each other ...") could rightly become the new national anthem. "The Star-Spangled Banner," he said, had "too many rockets, bombs and guns in it to be very relevant to anything that this country should be tryin' to do in the last years of this century, and in the next century, if any." To goad the club crowd into joining him on "Get Together," Steve said, "You're gonna have to sing this song at football games and school assemblies the rest of your lives, so you may as well learn it right now." Reflecting the turmoil of the still-raging Vietnam War, Steve even inserted a few choruses of John Lennon's one-year-old hit "Give Peace a Chance." But while urging the audience to sing along on the Lennon chant, he couldn't resist a skeptical dig: "Yeah, a chance of an iceberg in hell."

A retired Southern colonel witnessing the show was so irked by Steve's putdown of "The Star-Spangled Banner" that he threatened Steve with physical violence. But Steve departed Savannah unscathed. Following his "telephone circuit" tour, plus a weekend gig at the Gaslight in Greenwich Village with Janis Ian, [9] Steve returned home.

Flush with new material, written by himself and others, Steve ventured to one of the more unusual venues of his life. Earl Pionke had booked Steve and brothers Ed and Fred Holstein two hours northwest of Chicago in Madison, Wisconsin, for what they assumed would be a college crowd. When they arrived at the venue, a hotel, they discovered instead that the audience was 3,000 drunken bankers attending a late-summer University of Wisconsin seminar on accounting.

"It was brutal," Ed Holstein says. "We had to follow go-go girls and a strip-

---

That's the week when you say, 'Well, when we call 'em niggers, we mean somethin' else.'
STEVE GOODMAN

8: The Cumberlands eventually put "City of New Orleans" on a self-produced live album that they recorded Dec. 9, 1978, at the Cumberland Gap Lounge in Louisville. "It has gone on to be one of the most requested songs we do," Harold Thom says, "especially when I precede the song with the story of Steve."

9: Early on, Steve impressed Janis Ian ("Society's Child," "At Seventeen") with his kindness. "You didn't see a lot of graciousness in the folk world in those days," she says. "We weren't brought up to it. Artists by nature are very full of themselves, and Steve certainly had an artist's ego, but he was gracious about it, and that's something most of the rest of us have really had to learn with time. He came by it pretty naturally."

per. Freddie made a good go of it. He actually completed a song. I did a verse or two onstage. But these guys all had short, cropped hair and were ready to throw shit at us. Then Steve sang 'The Auctioneer,' and he got 'em. Then he sang 'Detroit City' (a train song), and they were in tears. He just knew how to get this audience. It was amazing. It was when I realized that this was what he was supposed to do in his life, was perform in front of people. Goodman really felt these were great songs. He happened to know them, and he knew this crowd would want 'em, and he knew how to connect to 'em. He could read a crowd."

Steve got the opportunity to read a larger, outdoor crowd at summer's end during the 1970 edition of the Philadelphia Folk Festival. The previous winter, Steve had chauffeured Chicago bluesman Jim Brewer to the monthly meeting of the organization's board, where the shy blues singer aced an audition for the festival's bill. That summer, Steve drove Brewer to the three-day gathering on the Old Pool Farm in Schwenksville, ostensibly to assist during Brewer's performance on Aug. 28. But the lure of the main stage was potent, and Steve angled for an opening, using the comic Michael Smith tune, "The Wonderful World of Sex," as bait. "He sang it backstage for us, and everybody flipped out," says longtime host Gene Shay. "People said it was a real hit song up in the (festival) campgrounds, and they said, 'Can we invite him onstage as a filler if we have a spare five minutes to fill?' We did, and the song was a big hit." [10]

The festival was fertile ground for Steve to absorb dozens of songs — including complex traditional tunes — to add to his repertoire, says his New York friend Paula Ballan, who booked the event and marveled at Steve's nearly photographic memory. "He could listen to a ballad that had 15 or 20 verses and sing it back to you. But he sang it back to you not verbatim, but better than the original, because in his not-quite remembering, his rewrites usually made the verses more succinct and really ended up better than the originals," Ballan says. "In fact, that's what traditional music is, anyway. That's the folk cycle."

From a three-member British folk group called the Young Tradition, Steve gleaned "Knight William and the Shepherd's Daughter," a lengthy, centuries-old tale (#110 of the Francis J. Child Ballads) about drunkenness, rape and robbery. Most versions have 14 to 16 verses, but some have more than 60. Steve soon converted it to an a cappella farce by impersonating all four of the song's characters, invoking a roaring, raspy voice for the king and a nasal voice for the daughter. Further spicing it up, he explained that "Falal all diddle all day," the phrase repeated with each stanza, "is Middle English for 'Stay out of the wheat fields, grandma, or you'll get reaped.' "

"If you saw him do it when he did all the parts by himself, where he'd bang the mike stand to make the sound of the horses' hooves or the pounding on the door, he started out looking like the shortest man in the whole world, but by the end of the song, he was this gigantic, huge presence," says New York friend and journalist Leslie Berman. "It was literally breathtaking. You cried, you laughed, you peed your pants, you cried again, you laughed some more. By the end of the song, you could not hold yourself, it hurt so much."

You cried, you laughed, you peed your pants.
LESLIE BERMAN

10: Near the end of "Sex," Steve inserted – and thus gave the tinge of sexual bondage to – a line lifted from the Coasters' "Along Came Jones" novelty hit that referenced old-time hero/villain/damsel/buzzsaw melodrama: "And then he tied her up. 'Help! He's tyin' me up!' " Steve added the same reference to his recording of Greg Hildebrand's "Chicago Bust Rag." (See pages 200-201.) For the 1970 Philly crowd, Steve also debuted "City of New Orleans," identifying the train as one of three "famous" lines of the Illinois Central, the others being the Panama Limited and a South Shore commuter express "affectionately called the Vomit Comet." His tempo was fast, his strumming insistent and his mood ebullient. He inserted "buddy" in the lyrics three times, introduced an instrumental break with "Here comes that train now" and ended with a fadeout imitating a locomotive barreling down the track.

But laughter was not always on Steve's mind in the early fall of 1970. Illness and perhaps his extended time on the road figured in a new and quiet composition that rivaled "Song for David" in its melancholy. It debuted back in Chicago during a spaghetti dinner with Fred Holstein, guitarist Jack McGann and Ron Buffington, accompanist for Bonnie Koloc, at Holstein's girlfriend's house. Buffington says Steve slipped into a bedroom with his guitar and emerged later, saying, "Here's a new one." It was called "Eight Ball Blues." [11]

In it, the song's protagonist, drunk in a tavern, listed his failings in the form of universally unrealized desires — from money, travel, education and fame to the ability to attract the attention of a woman. During a show the next year, he sardonically called it "an I-wish-I-was song, third person once removed, subtitled, 'You're outta here.' " Three years later, he told audiences he came up with the lament after reading German psychologist Frederick S. Perls' book *Gestalt Therapy Verbatim*. Steve dedicated the song to "all the barflies in the world. It could be called 'The Singles Bar Blues.' " Even though he had been married for half a year, it's clear that the tune was originally autobiographical. The lyrics speak of knowing "the worst" in life, and its most poignant line, given Steve's leukemia, was "I wish I had the common sense to be satisfied with me."

Steve's wish to become a better-known entertainer was bolstered that fall, when he found himself on another telephone tour. This one stretched to the southernmost part of the continental United States — to a former silent-movie parlor on Ponce de Leon Boulevard that hugged the University of Miami. The ice-cream parlor and coffeehouse, with its interior décor of dark red, flocked wallpaper and Tiffany lamps that hung over marble-topped, two-seat tables, was known for a bright-red exterior sign that radiated the club's name, "THE FLICK." (Wags noted that the capital letters were positioned so closely that, in the nighttime, from nearby U.S. Highway 1, the second and third letters appeared to join in a "U" to form a wholly different word. They also laughed at the result when bulbs in the "F" would burn out.)

To say it was a privilege to play the Flick was an understatement, given the array of talent that flowed through the 100-seat club, says the house act, the talented guitarist Ron Kickasola. Performers ranged from Jerry Jeff Walker ("Mr. Bojangles") and Fred Neil ("Everybody's Talkin' ") to the Serendipity Singers' breakout storytelling guitarist Gamble Rogers and the "big, fat, Russian teddy bear," David Crosby. The Flick's owner, Max Launer, was notorious for his ever-present cigar and idiosyncratic tastes in booking, says Peter Neff, singer/guitarist. Launer favored the quiet comedian Gabe Kaplan (soon to be the star of TV's "Welcome Back, Kotter") but refused to hire José Feliciano because "No one wants to look at a blind man onstage with a dog." He also infamously implored Joni Mitchell to sing pop and folk standards such as "They Call the Wind Mariah" by Lerner and Loewe and the Seeger-Hickerson "Where Have All the Flowers Gone?" instead of her brilliant original compositions.

To this milieu, Steve brought a unique persona, Kickasola says. "He had a very muscular, powerful voice, a sense of whimsy and a self-deprecating sense of

His shtick was different. It was a Northern kind of sound. It was aggressive without being abrasive. It was both humorous and deep.
RON KICKASOLA

11: In various recorded and performed versions, Steve also listed this song as "Eight-Ball," "Eight-Ball (Neurotica)" and "Behind the 8 Ball Blues."

humor," he says. "His shtick was different. It was a Northern kind of sound. It was aggressive without being abrasive. It was both humorous and deep. It had roots that were not part of the Southern tradition, and he looked like a man who was comfortable in his own bones."

In his 25-minute sets at the Flick, Steve unfurled a cornucopia of compositions, including a hunting tune, "The Innocent Hare," and a bawdy medieval yarn, "Chastity Belt," both of which he'd recently learned in Philadelphia from the Young Tradition. He added Tom Paxton's strident anti-war elegy, "Jimmy Newman," a spare version of Joni Mitchell's wistful surrender to the seasons, "Urge for Going" (recorded two years earlier by Tom Rush), and sprinkled a melodramatic parody of J. Curly Putman's country-tinged "Green, Green Grass of Home" (a Tom Jones hit) with crude lines: "Pretty girl, but her legs are hairy … There's the old oak tree I used to pee on … For there's a guard, and there's a sad old padre / Arm in arm, they sure are gay." He ended each verse with an obvious drug joke: "It's good to smoke the green, green grass of home." [12]

Not surprisingly, Steve's own "City of New Orleans" left his deepest impression at the Flick — especially upon Kickasola, a self-described "train freak" who had grown up at the southern tip of Illinois in tiny Metropolis, along the Ohio River near its confluence with the Mississippi. "When the train went through my home town and blew the whistle, my granny said, 'There goes the City of New Orleans.' She was a train freak, too." The intricacies of river trestles and the re-routing of trains inside huge roundhouses had fascinated him. "When I heard that song, I thought, 'God almighty, it's like being a little kid again.' It evoked all sorts of Illinois Midwestern farm-belt memories."

Moreover, the warning posed by the song's imagery tugged at childhood heartstrings both specific and universal. "As a kid, the train is big," Kickasola says. "It goes places, just the idea of going to mysterious places. You could eat there and play cards, all that stuff. Just the idea of going is exciting. I had never been to New Orleans before. It seemed to me the most exotic place on earth. Big River, the Mississippi, all of that, and here is this thing that conveys people to places of wonder and amazement. But in the song, it's only 15 people on 15 cars. Something's wrong. Something precious and beautiful is vanishing from the world. There's the feeling that we need to not let this happen."

The song's broad appeal, Kickasola says, was enhanced by the lively, clickety-clack tempo that Steve chose. (In one Flick performance of "City," Steve sped along so quickly that when he couldn't contain a guitar lick in the time he'd given it, he jabbed himself with an aside, "Catch up, Steve.") "It was a ripping good tune," Kickasola says. "It was exciting, it moved. It was smooth and gliding, almost lighter than air but connected to the earth."

From Kickasola, Steve not only drew admiration but also soaked up more of the songwriting of Michael Smith, whose "The Wonderful World of Sex" Steve had learned from Michael Johnson the year before. Smith, a longtime Miamian, ex-comedian and free spirit, along with his wife, Barbara Barrow, and Kickasola, had formed a band called Juarez and moved to Los Angeles, where the group

For Ron Kickasola, Steve's "City of New Orleans" summoned childhood dreams and present-day gloom. "In the song, it's only 15 people on 15 cars," he says. "Something's wrong."
(Photo by Bob Patterson)

12: Another ditty in Steve's repertoire, taught to him by Greenwich Village singer Erik Frandsen, was the 1947 Lonzo & Oscar hit "I'm My Own Grandpa," which traced the tortuous route to an unlikely set of family relationships. Singer/songwriter James Durst, who learned the tune from Steve at singer/songwriter Gamble Rogers' home in Coconut Grove, appreciated Steve's "impeccable judgment to allow the song to unfold verse by verse before revealing the ultimate punchline refrain."

"The Dutchman" author Michael Smith says Steve's familiarity made him nervous.
(Photography ©1973 Evan Soldinger)

13: Masters' "Spoon River Anthology" was adapted by Charles Aidman and Naomi Caryl Hirshhorn as a musical that ran on Broadway for 111 performances in the fall of 1963. One of its songs was called "Spoon River," and like Smith's song, it was a waltz. But its lyrics, with the refrain "Spoon River is calling me home," are wholly different.

14: Staying in an upstairs apartment at the Bistro, Steve found a marijuana connection in guitarist and stagehand Reuben "Flash" Morgan. "Flash, you need to go down to the strip for me," Steve told him. "Here's $20 or $40." The deepest impression Steve left with Morgan, however, was his Cheshire-cat smile. "When he was amused," Morgan says, "he would smile from ear to ear."

played the hip Ice House in Pasadena and recorded a quirky, self-titled (and low-selling) 1969 album for Decca. Kickasola soon left the group and returned to Miami, where he taught Steve several Smith tunes. "Steve was blown away by them, as all of us were," he says. Two were a haunting, post-Civil War waltz, "Spoon River," based on Chicagoan Edgar Lee Masters' 1915 anthology of 244 free-verse "epitaphs" from voices in a rural Illinois graveyard,[13] and "Crazy Mary," which paid melancholy tribute to a lonely woman derided by neighborhood kids. Most gripping, though, was "The Dutchman," Smith's elegant ode to the love between an aged and failing former tugboat worker and his loyal wife.

"The Dutchman" started out three years earlier in Smith's mind as a nostalgia piece set in high-school days in his hometown of Little Falls, New Jersey. It focused on his sister, Margaret, and a boy she dated whose nickname was Dutch. When Smith imagined its first line — "The Dutchman's not the kind of man who keeps his thumb jammed in the dam that holds his dreams in" — the song took off. "I knew when I wrote it that this was a big song," Smith says. "It was almost like, 'Don't fuck this up, Michael.' That first line is a gift." With the emergence of the second line — "That's a secret that only Margaret knows" — came an intuitive flash. "Up to the second line, these were teenagers," he says. "The song was saying to me, 'Go someplace else.' " He switched the protagonists to an elderly couple but infused a yearning for spent youth.

Smith also gave the song an otherworldly setting by culling details of Amsterdam from the writings of Dutch novelist and playwright Jan de Hartog. Borrowing melodic ideas from the Kingston Trio's performances of Will Holt's "Raspberries, Strawberries" and Jacques Brel's "Old Folks" and "Seasons in the Sun," with a touch of John Hartford's "Gentle on My Mind," Smith finished crafting what became his musical masterwork.

In Kickasola's sets at the Flick, the song was a stunner. "I got more requests for 'The Dutchman' than almost anything else I did," he says. One night, a devoted fan of the song — a man in his late 50s who was starting a new marriage and "enjoying an epiphany in life" — led Kickasola to his car and opened its trunk, revealing an expensive and immaculate Guild guitar. The fan told him, "This is for you, in appreciation."

Clearly, "The Dutchman" could arouse emotions. In Steve's hands and voice, it eventually would find its definitive version. And at one of several other Southern stops on his autumn telephone tour, at the Bistro in north Atlanta,[14] where Smith's Juarez band was playing the night before Steve's cycle, Steve met the song's 29-year-old author. With his quick memory, Steve already was trying out versions of "The Dutchman" and "Spoon River," but neither musician could envision the fruit that would flower from the convergence of their talents.

"He knew who I was," says Smith, who allows that his own standoffish disposition stood in sharp contrast to Steve's. "He was very personable and outgoing. He made you like him right away, but he seemed more willing to put out conversationally than I was. He made me nervous because he was so familiar. He was willing to let you into his family right away, and I wasn't the kind of person who bought that from people. Nonetheless, I liked him a lot." The two were not to communicate again for two years, but their association would resonate indelibly throughout their professional lives.

A similarly strong but more puckish connection arose for Steve when he returned to Chicago that fall. He stopped by a late-night hoot at the tiny club across West Armitage Avenue from the Old Town School of Folk Music called the Fifth Peg and heard the fledgling performances of a mailman and ex-Army draftee with a thin, nasal and scratchy voice by the name of John Prine. Nearly two years older than Steve, Prine had grown up in the western suburb of Maywood, was a high-school gymnast and, as coincidence would have it, because of the spelling of his last name, had sat in front of — and ogled — Steve's wife Nancy in their homeroom. At the Fifth Peg, despite Prine's less than smooth vocals ("he sings like a duck," Steve opined), Steve admired Prine's affecting compositions. They included the story of a heroin-addicted Vietnam veteran, "Sam Stone"; a plea for communication with neglected elders, "Hello in There"; a tale of loneliness and sexual self-gratification, "Donald and Lydia"; and a lament over strip-mining in a Kentucky coal town, "Paradise." But the two did not meet that evening.

Prine was aware of Steve, but only aurally. Several times, he had listened to and been impressed by Steve's songs on WFMT's "Midnight Special." The 5-foot-8 Prine conjured "a real good picture in my mind" of what Steve looked like, right down to the "little bitty beard" of a stereotypical collegian. "I figured he was this fella about 6-foot-2 and had a suit on from, like, Robert Hall's and a long, drawn-out face," Prine reminisced on PBS-TV's "Austin City Limits" in 1986. "Y'know, he would have fit right into the Chad Mitchell Trio."

Their actual meeting, in the back-room Star Cave during one of Prine's first appearances at the Earl of Old Town, dispelled Prine's mental image. "I was sittin' on top of the deep freeze, and they said Steve Goodman was comin' back to meet me," Prine said. "This little guy came back with a big, chunky face, and he acted like Edward G. Robinson — y'know, he was always pointin' at people and everything. He said, 'Are you John Prine?' And I said, 'Yeah.' And he said, 'I'm Steve Goodman.' And my jaw dropped, and I didn't know what to think of this guy." Soon they sealed a brotherly bond that became more consequential than either could have predicted.

That fall, Steve played benefits for the Twelfth of Never coffeehouse in Richton Park and the private Francis Parker School in Old Town, a dozen blocks south of his apartment. In the latter show, on Nov. 7, his selections included an upbeat version of the traditional "I Bid You Goodnight," with which the Grateful Dead had closed its influential two-LP set "Live/Dead" the year before, and another comical Michael Smith song, "Everybody's High" ("but me," the lyrics said). Between gigs, day and night, those who associated with Steve rarely saw him without his guitar.

"Steve must have played 18 hours a day," said Fred Holstein. "I think he played in his sleep." To feed the obsession, he said, Steve found a three-quarter-

> This little guy came back with a big, chunky face, and he acted like Edward G. Robinson — y'know, he was always pointin' at people and everything. He said, 'Are you John Prine?' And I said, 'Yeah.' And he said, 'I'm Steve Goodman.' And my jaw dropped.
>
> **JOHN PRINE**

size Gibson guitar to carry with him everywhere. Holstein said when Steve visited his apartment, he'd tell Steve, "Hey, put it away. I'm tired of it. Let's talk about pussy or something. Leave me alone, man." He even quoted a famous Groucho Marx line to Steve: "I like my cigar, but I take it out of my mouth once in a while." Holstein shook his head at the memory. "He drove me fuckin' crazy with the guitar, but that's what you've got to do."

Wherever Steve encountered music of any style, he devoured it. During a visit to the apartment of Nancy's brother, Robert Pruter, Steve dove into Pruter's collection of blues LPs. "He started pulling out records and playing them like crazy," Pruter says. "He would just listen, fascinated."

Steve's embrace and eventual mastery of an eclectic mix of songs and genres had begun to cement his place in the Chicago folk scene, and by power of personality he slowly and seemingly without premeditation moved ever closer to serving as its hub. While Fred Holstein had become the Earl's house act and was seen as the cocky expert on good songs and stagecraft, Steve increasingly came to be viewed by musicians and friends as no less than a musical encyclopedia.

He could give you an anthology, a master's class on Jimmie Rodgers or Blind Lemon Jefferson or Mahalia Jackson or Leadbelly, just like that.
BRIAN GILL

"He could give you an anthology, a master's class on Jimmie Rodgers or Blind Lemon Jefferson or Mahalia Jackson or Leadbelly, just like that," says Brian Gill, who grew up in Kankakee, spent 20 years in Chicago as a folksinger and was two years Steve's junior. "We were all coming out of a Woody Guthrie, Pete Seeger, Peter, Paul & Mary bag, and he was coming out of left field, doing stuff like 'Goody Goody' and 'Lady Be Good.' He also really wanted to know what song you were learning. He was just like a laser beam, man."

"He was very fast in terms of retention and learning," says Fred's brother, Ed Holstein, who sat in Steve's apartment and watched him summon and play, seemingly out of the blue, "Inchworm," a children's tune he'd learned from the Danny Kaye soundtrack LP for the 1952 movie "Hans Christian Andersen." "It was really odd. Everybody's got songs they don't like, but I don't think there was a song he didn't like." [15]

One night, Steve, Ed Holstein and Pionke left the Earl, crossed the street and walked a few doors north to have a drink at a go-go saloon called the Midas Touch. While Holstein and Pionke sat at the bar, Steve walked up to the front window, where a female dancer gyrated to the music of singles she was playing on a tiny, portable record player at her feet. Trying not to be obtrusive, Steve pawed through the dancer's stack of records, and between songs he pulled out a 45. "Hey," he shouted to Holstein, "she's got Mary Wells' 'You Beat Me to the Punch'!" [16]

"He was so positive all the time," Holstein says, "and I like to be a little negative once in a while, so he would drive me nuts. There would be some kid onstage who was really terrible, singing some dismal song, and Steve would say something nice about him. He'd find something good to say about the song or that the kid changed his strings or had a nice shirt."

"Steve, he stinks," Holstein would say.

15: Dan Johnston, owner of Orphans on Lincoln Avenue, says Steve's wide tastes let him tailor songs to a crowd. At a Tuesday-night open stage, Johnston says, Steve was performing when a rowdy group of conventioneers came in. "He looked down and started playing 'Truck Drivin' Man,' and the guys froze. He was into their culture. It wasn't 'Kumbaya.' He sensed the audience, went right to their heart."

16: Steve, the Holsteins, Earl Pionke and others formed somewhat of a social clique, Ed Holstein says. "We went out to dinner a lot and clowned around a lot. We were like the folk 'Goodfellas,' without the crime."

"Well, yeah, but he's trying," Steve would reply.

"The guy's depressing me."

"Well, he'll get better."

Steve's ebullience, accompanied by a vise-grip handshake, also made for long, inopportune conversations, Holstein says: "When you walked out of a room with him because you were going somewhere, he'd never leave. He was a shorter, Jewish version of Franklin Roosevelt. He could have been a great politician. He really enjoyed being around people and talking to people. There wasn't a time we were leaving a room where I wouldn't say something like, 'Steve, y'know, I'd really like to go. I've gotta get home.' But he never would go."

Much of Steve's talk that fall centered on his "City of New Orleans," particularly after October, when Congress tried to revive the country's failing train lines by approving the Rail Passenger Service Act, which President Nixon signed into law the day before Halloween. The act created Railpax, a subsidized private company that starting in spring 1971 was to manage a newly networked national passenger-train system. Cutbacks on lines such as the aging City of New Orleans became a foregone assumption.

Steve broadened the reach of "City of New Orleans" one Saturday evening by dropping in unannounced during WFMT's "Midnight Special" show and playing the song for co-host Ray Nordstrand, who had been impressed with Steve's songs via Bonnie Koloc and by tape the previous year.

"I did the show for 40 years, but the highlight certainly was the night that Steve walked in and said he had this song he had written on the train, and he wanted me to hear it during the show," Nordstrand said. It was unusual for musicians to perform live on the regular, weekly installments of the program, he said, "but I had so much respect for him that I didn't question it. He took out his guitar, and we set up a microphone in the control room. He sang it, and I knew instantly that it was a winner."

Nordstrand not only aired the performance live but also recorded it and played it at the end of that night's show — and during many later shows. What distinguished "City of New Orleans" from other songs, Nordstrand said, was its specificity. "It had a lot of information that rings so true," he said. "It did a perfectly credible job of evoking that train ride and that life."

The version that Nordstrand aired — which survives today in an audition tape that Steve assembled soon thereafter — was gentle and spare, with placid sections in which he softened his strumming and even halted it momentarily, in contrast to the consistently driving guitar of his later records and performances. The chords at the end of verse lines were tame, there was no break for an instrumental solo, and Steve didn't push the melodic line of "Good morning, America" to the rousing high note ("a-MER-ica") of his future versions. Retaining a hint of the operatic quality from his youth, his voice was restrained. He also carefully chose correct grammar ("the steel rail hasn't heard the news" instead of "ain't"). Overall, the recording wanted for urgency, but the power of the song's narrative imagery was undeniable.

Ed Holstein, shown in 1969, says Steve's positiveness and congeniality made him like "a shorter, Jewish version of Franklin Roosevelt."

(Photo by Ron Rosoff)

Greg Hildebrand, shown in the 1970s, says his "Officer Rigoni" song, made more prominent by Steve's recording (called "Chicago Bust Rag"), was based on a true incident when he lived in Chicago in 1966.

(Photo by Christine Broderick, courtesy of Greg Hildebrand)

17: In concert, Steve sardonically invoked the sun metaphor between songs. One evening in the early 1970s, while introducing "The Dutchman" at Chicago's Quiet Knight club, he took note of a sunset streaming through the bar's second-floor windows. "Ah, the magic lighting effects here at the Quiet Knight," he said. "The showbiz comes to Belmont Avenue. Jesus Christ, it's beautiful, I like it, but I sure didn't expect it. It's sorta like a great voice in the sky saying, 'All right, Steve, take it down.' That's all it ever says, other than 'You piss me off!' "

18: Stanza of "Chicago Bust Rag" by Greg Hildebrand, copyright 1966, reprinted by permission.

Train songs had emerged as an integral part of Steve's persona, which he admitted sheepishly in a half-minute intro on the audition tape, which, besides the WFMT studio recording of "City of New Orleans," consisted of live material captured by Rich Warren at the Earl. "The tape is top-heavy on train songs, but other than that, it's fairly representative, I guess," a tentative, solicitous Steve said on the recording. But his intro slightly exaggerated the contents, as only three of the seven songs, taking up just half of the tape's 27 minutes, dealt with railroading. The other two train songs were Terry Gilkyson's "Fast Freight" and a frenetic, commanding take on the traditional "Mobile Line" ("Hey Lordy mama mama, hey Lordy papa papa").

Of the four non-railroad tunes, "The Wonderful World of Sex" and "The Auctioneer" had become staples in his repertoire, but two were intriguing newer entries. One, likely entitled "Ball of Fire," was a peaceful, mid-tempo, philosophical tune that may have been written by Steve, because it amounted to a more optimistic update of "Song for David," even using the same metaphor — his relentless "race" with the sun and mortality. Comparing himself to "a ball of fire rollin' on a tightrope wire," the song's narrator said that he "can't stop this ramblin', heaven knows," a clear nod to Tom Paxton. "You're judged by the part of you that's free," said one verse, an oblique reference to his leukemia. "Only time will tell if there's a change in me." [17]

The other new song may have been an inspiration for Steve to write "Turnpike Tom" and other witty parables. With words set by Greg Hildebrand to the traditional "Stagger Lee," the tune was known as "Chicago Bust Rag," but Hildebrand's unwieldy title for it was (and still is) "Officer Rigoni to the Rescue, or How the People of the State of Illinois Saved Me from Myself." An autobiographical drug ditty from 1966, it described Hildebrand arriving home and finding four "great big old ugly" Chicago police waiting inside to arrest him after discovering his roommate's supply of hash, LSD and "roaches, clips and papers on the floor." The narrator dealt with the confrontation with aplomb, slipping out of trouble with a lie:

> *Officer, I don't know what you're talkin' about*
> *Besides, you're in such a rush*
> *I never set foot in this house before*
> *Would you like to buy a Fuller brush?* [18]

In truth, Hildebrand, then 28, did walk in on the drug bust of his roommate, who bore the iconic name of Davy Jones. But instead of talking his way out of it, Hildebrand was arrested for possession of prescription sedatives he had procured from his girlfriend's father, a physician. "While out on bail, I got to thinking that I should write a song about all this," says Hildebrand, who has lived in Australia for decades. Within an hour he had finished the song, complete with references to narcotics Lt. Anthony Rigoni and Chicago's election-year, drug-war politics. Hildebrand sang the song several times at Poor Richard's, an Old Town bar in a former synagogue on Sedgwick Street, but he left Chicago in mid-1966 and never met Steve. Jones, Hildebrand's roommate, who also was a musician, had taped Hildebrand performing the song in their kitchen, and the tape was passed around the folk scene, eventually making its way to Steve, who interpreted it affectionately, invoking a distinctive, near-falsetto rendering of the line, "PO-lice! It's the PO-lice!"

As a whole, Steve's audition tape, assembled at Universal Recording, is a fascinating, early glimpse of how he tried to portray and sell himself. Arranged like a concert set, the seven songs darted between fast and slow, serious and funny. "Mobile Line" was an invigorating opener, and "City of New Orleans" sat in the penultimate position as if it were the closer. The final piece, "Fast Freight," became a six-and-a-half-minute, tour de force encore that started slowly and quietly, building tempo and volume to the ringing climax of "If you go, well, then, you can't come back, can't come back, can't come back, can't come back. No, you can't come back, buddy. You will never come ba-a-a-a-ck!" — the prototypical big finish.

It was no accident that Steve showcased himself in mostly live performance instead of perfecting his musical business card in a studio. By late 1970, onstage he was commanding, confident and comfortable, some said fearless. No question, what he wanted to do most was to win over an audience. "He bathed in it," says Linda Morrison, who waitressed at the Earl. "That was his warm tub."

For Liz Danzig (now Derry), who worked for Earl Pionke as a press agent for $400 a month, Steve's drive to please a crowd made life easy. "If you bring a newspaper person to a club, you want a performer that's going to live up to what you're representing," she says, "and Steve never failed to deliver. He couldn't. He didn't have that ability to not perform. It was in his soul, everything he did. Everything was looking for approval."

"With that uncontrolled energy, he was trying to sell everything," says satirist Larry Rand. "He was the son of a salesman, and he just didn't know any other way. I was real shy and conflicted about performing, and here's a guy who just looked like he came out of the womb doing it. When I stood next to him offstage, I was amazed at how small he was, but onstage he didn't work small."

Steve's desire to perform approached the level of compulsion, like a newspaper reporter who can't take a day off when a story is breaking.

"He was just on fire," recalled folksinger Ginni Clemmens. "He would not pass up a chance. He'd go home, and he'd write a song, and he'd find out who was singing where, and he'd come in and sing on their set. Automatically, of course, we loved to see him coming." [19]

"He really was a gunslinger when it came to playing music onstage with other people," says bassist Simeon "Wally" Pillich. "He was like, 'I'm going to show you what I can do. Look out!' And he would. He would take over. He was all bravado, but he always managed to back it up with action."

Late one night when Rand was performing a set at the Earl, Steve popped in the door at 1:30 a.m. and typically sidled up between songs.

"Would you mind if I did a few tunes?" he asked Rand.

He didn't have that ability to not perform. It was in his soul, everything he did. Everything was looking for approval.
LIZ DANZIG

19: Steve's ability to jump on a stage and perform a long set at any provocation came in handy a year or two later when "outlaw" songwriter Billy Joe Shaver played the Quiet Knight in Chicago. Shaver called Steve to the stage, then walked out of the club, leaving Steve to finish the set. For the perpetually drunk Shaver, the stunt was typical. "I used to unload on everybody," he says. "I was known for that, and they didn't know until it was done. Actually, they got a treat, because he (Steve) was a whole lot better than me, and he'd be hard to beat. I wouldn't get nobody up there unless they was real good. That way, nobody felt cheated. They felt like they got a little extra."

Jim Post, shown in 1973, coped with Steve's impromptu appearances by bidding him onstage, where the two goaded each other to improvise songs lasting 10 minutes or more. "We had almost a sibling competition," says Post, writer and co-singer (as part of Friend and Lover) of "Reach Out of the Darkness," a 1968 hit.
(Photo by Mitch Gawlik)

20: Five years before his death at age 61 in 2004, Fred Holstein reiterated the "whole show" ethic. "I am not here to save the world for folk music. A lot of it is boring and self-indulgent like anything else, but us guys in Chicago knew how to entertain people. When I walk on that stage, I get paid to perform, whether I stand on my head, jerk up with my feet or spit wooden nickels. The gig is I want that audience to love me. I want to entertain them. I happen to use folk music as my medium to do that with, but the primary thing is to entertain people."

"Well-l-l, sure, Steve. Go ahead," Rand replied out of professional courtesy but knowing that because Steve was asking, it would mean an hour or more.

The brash Jim Post ("Reach Out of the Darkness," top-10 *Billboard* hit in 1968) headlined on other nights at the Earl when Steve happened along. When Post bid Steve to perform, however, Post ignored protocol and didn't vacate the stage. Instead, the two goaded each other into concocting songs with ideas shouted by the audience. "Steve would start the first verse, and I'd sing the chorus to his verse, then I'd start the next verse," Post says. "One of my favorite things was to think about where he was takin' the song and change it. Some of those songs went 10-15 minutes. They became epics until they just drove into nothing, but everyone was so drunk they thought we were fantastic."

A competitive edge also figured in an agonizing experience recalled by Fred Holstein. Late on a Wednesday night at the Earl, with only two dozen in the audience, Steve walked up in the middle of Holstein's set and asked, "Fred, can I do a couple?" True to custom, Holstein yielded the stage. "So he gets up there, and after the third song, he's kickin' ass, and I'm supposed to go back up there and follow him? I'm thinkin', 'You little motherfucker, man. I'm on the scrap heap.'" Holstein finally looked up, his palms extended, a pained expression on his face, wordlessly pleading to Steve for help. "He looked down at me, and he started into a slow, dragged-out version of 'The Water Is Wide,' a beautiful arrangement, and he just brought it right back down." As Holstein returned to the stage, he told Steve, "Thanks, babe."

Rand knew that in these instances Steve didn't aim merely to try out a song or two. "He wanted to do a set, because that's what he was really rehearsing. He wanted to see how the pieces of the puzzle fit together."

Instead of being devious about his requests, Steve admitted the compulsion. "This is what I do. I have to do it every day," Steve told Rand. "Now, I can go home and go to sleep. But if I haven't performed today, I haven't done my job. I have to do it every day, or I don't feel like I've put my day in."

Much of this ethic came straight from Fred Holstein, the Pete Seeger protégé who forged an informal compact for Steve and other homegrown and immigrating folksingers. "Fred was like the gym instructor," Rand says. "He was like Coach Holstein. Somebody would do a show, and Fred would casually come up afterwards and say, 'You know, that was a bunch of bullshit that you did. You could do much better than that.' And nobody wanted to square off. It was 'OK, what would I have done different?' And you'd talk about it. The feedback was immediate."

Blunt assessments of pacing and presence became both a universal standard and goal. "The word that would get used over and over again," Rand says, "was vaudeville. Like, 'Oh, sure, you play guitar, you write interesting songs, but you don't have a show.' People would be scrupulously honest with one another and say, 'The songs are great, but you're looking at the ceiling because you're scared of the audience. Look people in the eye. Smile at 'em. Do a show.' There was this peer pressure that it had to be a total entertainment package." [20]

Some fledgling artists took offense at such frankness. "When you said, 'Oh, c'mon, man, your guitar was out of tune,' that was like accusing someone of being a right-wing Republican," Rand says. But the critique prevailed. A typical exchange included the line "I'm another musician, asshole. I have to listen to you, night after night." Tempers simmered and sometimes flared, Rand says. "Some couldn't handle that openness. They just weren't used to that Chicago, in-your-face, this-is-how-it-is."

But Steve thrived on it. In fact, Rand says, Holstein's hounding of Steve about his guitar playing "pissed Steve off to the point where Goodman was 'Not only am I going to play better guitar, I'm going to play rings around you, you asshole.' He got that type-A thing cooking, and his guitar playing became not only better but also completely unlike anybody else's." [21]

Steve's fixation on performing allowed him, like a woodworker, to sand his shows to smoothness. This gave him the confidence to spontaneously insert friends' names in songs and the aplomb to gloss over instrumental errors with no apparent effort. Richard Wedler, who prompted him to flesh out "City of New Orleans," had been an attentive witness. "Sometimes, he'd give that little, funny look, like 'Whoops. You'll forgive me, won't you?' Of course, everybody always did. It was charming. You have to work off your mistakes, and that's where the fearlessness comes in: 'OK, I did that wrong. I'll do it twice, and it'll sound like I meant it.' But with Steve there also was a coyness where he'd give this little look like, 'Y'know what I mean?' He was a very natural person onstage. There was no attitude. It was 'Hey, I'm just like you, and this is what I do.' "

Part of the reason "City of New Orleans" didn't jump out more on Steve's audition tape was precisely because it was not an onstage recording. Realizing this, Steve began to hone his intros to the song, leavening them with humor. For a while, he reached to his younger days to resuscitate a pun he learned in college: In it, the conductor for the northbound City of New Orleans train typically draws out the names of small-town stops: "Ar-cola! Tus-cola!" A passenger shouts, "What's next, Pepsi-Cola or Coca-Cola?" The conductor replies — and Steve spoke the punchline in his best alcoholic W.C. Fields imitation — "Nope, Champaign!"

It didn't take long for Steve to devise gags of his own for "City of New Orleans." One poked geographical fun: "They don't have trains in California," he said at an Evanston show. "They have trains that run there like the Zephyr and the Santa Fe Super Chief and all that, but they don't have any within the state itself. They were outlawed, along with buses, subways, anything other than cars. There are more cars in that goddamn state. Next year, they're gonna outlaw legs."

Earl Pionke, whose bar was burgeoning as a middle-of-the-night drop-in spot for out-of-town performers, thought so much of "City of New Orleans" and Steve's ever-improving act in late 1970 that for the first time he booked Steve for the saloon's New Year's Eve show. The opener was blues singer Ginni Clemmens, one of the Earl's first musicians in 1966, who had recently returned

Fred Holstein, shown in 1973, became the Chicago folk "coach" in the early 1970s.
(Photo by Mitch Gawlik)

21: Guesting on "The Mike Douglas Show" in 1975, Steve downplayed the caustic critiques of the Chicago folk scene. "Sort of an innkeeper's delight" is how he labeled the process for Douglas. "We all go to a bar and take it apart, and sometimes songs come out of it, and sometimes they don't. Somebody's ego and heart is on the line with somethin' they wrote, somethin' they're really proud of or somethin' like that, so criticism isn't really the word for it. But you can kid a guy into changing somethin' if it needs it. You have to be close with someone, though, before you can do something like that."

from California and revered Steve almost at first sight. "He had sparkly eyes, he loved what he was doing, and he was just on fire with writing," Clemmens recalled. That night also was the first time that Steve left the Earl in the sleepy, early-morning hours to play on the live, all-night, New Year's Day broadcast of the "Midnight Special," at WFMT's studio along the Magnificent Mile.

If the New Year's Eve gig was a heady step, Steve drank in the reality of his rough-and-tumble milieu 24 hours later, when he again played the Earl. Always bordering on the raucous, the saloon hosted a memorable escalation on the night of New Year's Day, says Norm Siegel, a string-bass player who had accompanied Steve and Clemmens on New Year's Eve and was backing up Steve on this night. During Steve's third or fourth set, at about 3 a.m., in walked Pionke and Fred and Ed Holstein, heavily lubricated with alcohol, followed a few minutes later by three loud drunks who sat behind Pionke and the Holsteins. Pionke soon told the group to shut up, and a long fight ensued, with the muscular Pionke brandishing chairs to bloody the noisy trio and knock them to the ground. Siegel stood onstage kicking the intruders, but Steve said, "I'm gettin' outta here," and scooted to the front windows, away from the action. "He grabbed his guitar," Siegel says, "and held that thing dear to him like a woman."

He grabbed his guitar and held that thing dear to him like a woman.
NORM 'MAD DOG' SIEGEL

When Chicago police arrived, they identified the drunken trio as off-duty officers. They asked a roughed-up Pionke, "What happened here?" "A couple of them fell down a lot," Pionke replied. The arriving officers just laughed and left with their beaten and besotted brethren. (For his efforts in the brawl, Siegel earned from Fred Holstein the nickname "Mad Dog.")

Steve played the Earl often in the first weeks of 1971, and Pionke constantly poked at him to do more to promote "City of New Orleans" and make it a success. "They were like the Bickersons," Rand says.

"It's just a train song," Steve told Earl one night. "I tried writin' a Johnny Cash song. Get over it."

"That's a hit," Pionke retorted. "That song is a hit."

"Earl, have another cognac," Steve said.

Pionke's instincts began to be verified with the onset of spring when Steve and Nancy took in an evening concert just six blocks west of their Briar Place apartment at the Quiet Knight. The show eventually would have an impact on the couple that was monumental.

Run by Pionke's friendly competitor, Richard Harding, the Quiet Knight sprawled atop a set of 23 steps above street level on the second floor of a ruddy, red brick building abutting an El stop, at the southeast corner of Belmont and Sheffield avenues. The focus of its décor was a full-size suit of knight's armor looming inside a large picture frame that hung behind the stage. Harding recently had moved the Quiet Knight (the name inspired by the Silent Night club in San Francisco) from a 65-seat bar a few doors up Wells Street from the Earl, having previously run Poor Richard's in Old Town. Harding himself was a late-night denizen and "party animal" who frequented the Earl and other bars after his own establishment's 2 a.m. closing time. His much larger Belmont

Richard Harding, shown in 1979, was determined in March 1971 that Steve play his "City of New Orleans" for Arlo Guthrie. "The word was out that Steve had leukemia," Harding says. "I wanted him before he died to have a major hit, whether he was singing it or not."

(Photo by Art Thieme)

location, with its square room and 340 seats, became a home for touring musicians of national stature.

The performer whom Steve and Nancy went to see at the Quiet Knight was the son of American folk music's most revered icon. Then 23, just one year older than Steve, Arlo Guthrie had emblazoned his identity in the country's consciousness, transcending his status as the child of his famous dad, Woody Guthrie. In 1967, he had released an LP for Warner Brothers Reprise that featured the popular, 18-minute and 20-second, anti-establishment musical shaggy-dog story, "Alice's Restaurant," and in 1969 he had starred in an offbeat feature film of the same name. [22] His profile had risen further with a spacey bit in "Woodstock," the 1970 wide-screen documentary of the landmark 1969 rock festival held in upstate New York.

A big-enough draw to play larger venues, Guthrie was working the Quiet Knight as a favor to Harding, a longtime friend. The show that Steve attended was the March 20 closer of a four-night run. [23] After Guthrie had finished the last of three sets and the audience filed down the stairs into the sub-freezing night air, Guthrie ambled with his guitar to Harding's back-room office to say goodbye. Awaiting him was Steve, who had been corralled by Harding and knew that a meeting with Guthrie was about to materialize.

Tipsy and tired, Guthrie wanted to return to his hotel. Harding, too, was inebriated, but he had a mission. Hearing Steve perform "City of New Orleans" at the Earl had reminded Harding of youthful railroading days in the late 1940s when he had ridden the Twentieth Century Limited and the Rock Island Line. "I wanted somebody to record it that would make it a hit because the word was out that Steve had leukemia," Harding says. "I wanted him before he died to have a major hit, whether he was singing it or not."

Guthrie had been primed for the meeting by Harding, who also had told him of Steve's medical plight. It was an instant parallel because Guthrie's father had suffered starting in his early 40s from the relentlessly debilitating Huntington's Chorea (which became known by the plainer title of Woody Guthrie's disease) and died from it in 1967 at age 55. The genetic chance that his

22: As an album, Guthrie's "Alice's Restaurant" fared well, riding the *Billboard* LP chart for 99 weeks and peaking at #17.

23: Media listings indicate that Guthrie also played the Quiet Knight two months earlier, in late January, but the March run is the more likely scenario for this show.

Arlo Guthrie, shown in 1972, says that when Richard Harding introduced him to Steve in the back room of the Quiet Knight in early 1971, Steve "just looked like a little guy. There's a thousand little guys everywhere with songs."

(Photo by Dennis O'Neill, courtesy of Peter Weisz)

24: In a July 1976 interview with Wim Bloemendaal on radio VARA in The Netherlands, Steve said Harding had "corralled" him and Guthrie "and embarrassed me to death. Arlo was polite enough to sit there and listen to the song, even though I didn't really want to play it for him. I wanted to run out of the room, and the owner kept grabbing both of us, and Arlo finally said, 'Play the song.' "

father's fatal nervous-system disorder eventually would befall Guthrie was perceived to be 50 percent. "I was under the same gun," Guthrie says, "even though nobody knew anything definitive."

After Guthrie ambled into Harding's office (with his bass player and co-producer John Pilla), Harding picked up Guthrie's guitar and handed it to Steve. As overheard by WFMT's Rich Warren, who happened to be standing outside the office door, Harding bellowed at Steve, "Sing him the goddamn train song! Play the goddamn train song!"

Harding also backed Guthrie into a corner of the office, Steve noted in a 1975 interview, and told him, "Now, Arlo, you've gotta take this song down to Nashville and give it to John Cash because it's about trains." Cash had built much of his musical identity upon railroad tunes.

Both Steve and Guthrie felt they were being thrown together unceremoniously. As Steve noted during a 1973 show in Miami, "Arlo was trying to get out of the room as politely as he could, and so was I."

Guthrie, in the comic version of the story that he has told from the stage for decades, has characterized himself as responding to Harding like a "butthead." For instance, he told a 1996 pub audience in Ireland that he shot back to Harding, "I don't want to hear no songs. I hate songs. I don't even like my songs. Why should I listen to other people's songs, man?"

In contrast, however, Steve observed that Guthrie acted graciously. "He just didn't tell everybody where to go and walk out of the room," Steve said.

And Guthrie allows that his stage story is an exaggeration. "I wasn't really in the mood to hear a song from anyone," Guthrie says, "but he (Steve) just looked like a little guy. There's a thousand little guys everywhere with songs, y'know? I didn't have a policy about it." The fact that Steve was a friend of Harding's made the prospect more palatable. "I probably didn't hesitate to say yes," Guthrie says, "even though in my story I make it seem like I really wasn't that interested." [24]

Harding says Guthrie told him, "I'll listen to the song, Rich, if you say so, but he's got to buy me a beer." In his more colorful stage yarn, Guthrie says that he told Steve, "OK, tell you what. Buy me a beer, I'll sit here and drink it, and as long as it lasts, you can do whatever you want."

So while Harding furnished the beer, Steve proceeded to perform "City of New Orleans" for Guthrie, who afterward asked Steve for a lead sheet and a tape of the tune, both of which Steve supplied. "I put those in my suitcase and thought no more of them until I got home, whenever that was, it might have been days or weeks later," Guthrie says. "When I got home, I put the sheet music on the piano, and it stayed there for months. I didn't think anything of it. I was just busy doing other things."

Of course, Guthrie ends his stage story otherwise, playing off the beer reference. While Guthrie wouldn't realize or state it until two years later, his punchline was: "It turned out to be one of the finer beers of my life."

Steve also said later, with keen directness, that the night "changed my life."

Exactly how would not be revealed to him — or anyone else — right away.

A beloved celebrity whose appeal veered more to the mainstream also stood ready to offer Steve a life-altering opportunity, not so much because of Steve's music as because of his malady. Slapstick comic Red Skelton, whose popular TV variety show was nearing the end of its 20th and final year, somehow had gotten wind of Steve's leukemia, the same disease that had killed Skelton's son Richie in 1958.

"Steve got a personal call, which he wasn't there to take," says Bob Hoban, Steve's frequent accompanist. "But he almost hid from this call. He refused to talk to Skelton because he felt it would be the smarmiest thing in the world to take advantage of Skelton's sadness and capitalize on it. He just couldn't do it."

Instead, Steve quickly immersed himself in an ambitious task entirely new to him — recording for an LP. It was not an album of his own, but a Chicago folk sampler that was the brainchild of Earl Pionke. The title, naturally, was "Gathering at the Earl of Old Town." Produced by Jim Post at Paragon Studios on the Magnificent Mile, the project brought together Steve and other regulars from the ragged but increasingly fashionable watering hole: Ginni Clemmens, Fred and Ed Holstein, local folk-rock group Aliotta Haynes Jeremiah (whose national hit "Lake Shore Drive" summoned the druggy LSD pun) and the energetic Post.

The only artists honored to perform as many as three of the project's 13 cuts were Steve and Fred Holstein. [25] Steve's contributions — all recorded with Jack McGann on second guitar and Jim Atlas on bass from 10 p.m. to 1 a.m. the night of Tuesday, March 23 — were "Eight Ball Blues" (on which Steve overdubbed his own harmony vocal), Greg Hildebrand's Arlo-esque "Chicago Bust Rag" (in which Steve substituted "Spumoni" for the last name of narcotics cop Tony Rigoni, to avoid a lawsuit) and, of course, a low-key version of "City of New Orleans," which prestigiously closed the LP. As with the other musicians, he was paid a union wage of $90.

Initially, just 1,349 copies were pressed, on the Dunwich label owned by Bill Traut, a producer Post brought in who was known for launching a hit version of Van Morrison's "Gloria" by the Chicago rock band Shadows of Knight. For his role in "Gathering," Traut obtained part of the publishing royalty for Steve's "City of New Orleans" and financed half the LP's production. [26] A vanity project for Pionke, who put up the other half, the album was sold only at the Earl of Old Town once it was released later in the spring. It amounted to a clever aural invitation to the saloon, despite packaging that was drab. The album's background color was a bland tan that nearly camouflaged a charming cover sketch by John Craig depicting the bricked Earl building and its inviting array of neon signs ("Folk Music/Char Burgers/Irish Coffee") and ragged posters ("Matinee Sundays/Folkarama/Continuous Shows/Day & Nite/All Ages Welcome").

Far more visually effective was the album's interior. The cover symbolically opened to a sepia gatefold photo showing an inside view of the Earl, albeit spotless and devoid of people. Positioned vertically in one of 14 wooden swivel

Matinee Sundays
Folkarama
Continuous Shows
Day & Nite
All Ages Welcome
EARL OF OLD TOWN
window signs

25: Post says he allocated Steve three tracks because he didn't think Steve would live long enough to have his own LP. For a different reason, Post slotted Fred Holstein three tracks. He says Holstein was unlikely to secure an album of his own in the near future because he was solely an interpreter, and record companies were favoring singer/songwriters.

26: In an admittedly "slimy" move, Traut says he tried to elevate the stature of "City of New Orleans" by paying unknown guitarists to play the tune in the dressing rooms of name artists playing Chicago, New York and Los Angeles. He was disappointed that his attempt at subliminal persuasion didn't work. "I owned 13 publishing companies," he says, "and as a publisher I thought the song was accessible enough for somebody to make a standard out of it."

*Spanish Civil War veteran and
Chicago folk-scene mainstay
Eddie Balchowsky, shown in
1967, became the focus of a
song on the "Gathering at the
Earl of Old Town" LP – the first
album on which Steve played.*
(Photo by Art Thieme)

chairs at the bar, and thereby anchoring the Earl's claim as the hub of the Chicago folk scene, was an icon on loan from the Old Town School of Folk Music. It was an acoustic guitar that had belonged to a revered Chicago bluesman who had died 13 years earlier, Big Bill Broonzy.

Liner notes by WFMT's Ray Nordstrand hailed the album as "high art" from "some of the best singers and composers the Midwest has developed," the result of a "creative vitality" thriving in Chicago because "there are fewer rules than on the Coasts." He praised Pionke for his "boundless enthusiasm and loyalty for his performers" and for the cheerful and casual "vibe" of his saloon. "No one is hassled or hustled, and most of the customers really listen to the words and the music." He singled out Steve for his "sharp wit and keen eye."

Those who played the "Gathering" LP heard an emotional portrait of the youthful left, from anti-war themes ("Prepare for Invasion" by Post and Tom Paxton's "Jimmy Newman" by Fred Holstein) to sexual abandon and even narcissism (Ida Cox's "Wild Women Don't Have the Blues" by Clemmens and "Fat Stuff" and "Jazzman" by Ed Holstein). The album also had its touching moments, anchored by Skip Haynes' "For Eddie," a gentle tribute to a flamboyant and strung-out character revered by Steve and everyone, Eddie Balchowsky, who had lost an arm while fighting as part of the Abraham Lincoln Brigade in the Spanish Civil War in the late 1930s and routinely played solitary piano with his good arm at the Quiet Knight and the Earl of Old Town after closing time.

With spare production — a bass here, a harmonica there — that displayed to good advantage its exuberant performances (along with its re-issuance and wider distribution with a brighter-colored cover five years later on the Wisconsin-based Mountain Railroad label), "Gathering" eventually found a national folk audience that persists to this day. Other than an affectionate but lukewarm review by Marshall Rosenthal of the *Chicago Daily News* and the depiction of the LP's cover in a Will Leonard column in the *Chicago Tribune*, the project never drew press attention. But for some listeners over the years, the album has become their only exposure to recordings of several Chicago-based artists. It also holds special status as Steve Goodman's earliest commercially available recording.

It was invigorating for Steve to finally appear on vinyl, but just six days after he laid down his tracks for the "Gathering" LP, the deepening chasm between his parents became more formal and hit him like a sledgehammer. On Monday, March 29, his mother, Minnette, angry that for two years Bud had been seeing another woman, filed suit in Cook County Circuit Court for a divorce from her husband of nearly a quarter century. "That was very hard for Steve," says Lake Forest College friend Lucy Wells. "He couldn't understand it."

Neither could others who thought they knew the family, including Jim Freitag, who had lived in the Goodmans' Niles home during the 1968-69 school year. "I was the most shocked person in the world," he said. "Far as I was concerned, those two were what you looked for in a married couple. They communicated. They were always happy, upbeat, and I never, ever heard them argue.

Then all of a sudden, out of the clear blue sky, they're getting a divorce."

If there were any hope of reconciliation, it was quashed in a succession of bitter court documents. In her initial missive, Minnette cited Bud's "vicious temperament, bad habits and abusive manners" and said she had been forced to move to an apartment the previous October because Bud had said he no longer loved her and wanted her to move out, and she feared physical injury. Bud's written answer, filed a month after Minnette's complaint, claimed that he had been a "good, true, kind and affectionate husband" but that he had suffered from harassment, belittling and financial complaints, all of which had contributed to his heart attack two years prior and was requiring him to take medicine to prevent another. What hung in the balance was not whether the two would reunite but rather how a judge would divide the assets. Four months later, on Sept. 15, Judge Robert Hunter sided with Minnette, declaring Bud "guilty of extreme and repeated mental cruelty" and requiring him to forfeit the lion's share of proceeds from the sale of their house and to funnel funds to Steve's medical care.

In the face of this familial maelstrom, Steve chose in early 1971 to focus on music. Playing the Earl late one spring night, Steve encountered a quartet of industry types in the audience: Neil Bogart, the president of New York-based Buddah Records, Buddah promo staffers Jerry Sharell and Jack Hakim and Chicago's hottest rock deejay, Kris Erik Stevens of WLS-AM. The liquor was flowing, and chatter of the four got increasingly loud. Finally, Steve stopped mid-song and addressed the group with a mix of pluck and poignancy: "Excuse me, all of you radio and record folks, some of the people here came to hear me sing, so could you give me a break? I'm nobody, so you can't hurt me." An impression was left. A seed was planted.

With Steve's deepening association with Richard Harding came regular employment — encouraged by Earl Pionke — as a warm-up act at Harding's club, the Quiet Knight. "It was your typical low-bread, second-act gig, but I thought it was great," Steve later told *Rolling Stone*. The first such engagement, which paid a total of $125, came Friday through Sunday, April 23-25, when Steve served as the opener for 28-year-old William C. "Buzzy" Linhart, an animated, frizzy-haired folk-rocker who soon would earn fame as the writer of the Bette Midler hit "Friends." Under contract to Buddah/Kama Sutra Records, Linhart was making his first Chicago appearance, but his lack of cachet soon became obvious to Steve. "I was more of a national act," Linhart says, "but I wasn't getting paid enough to even rent a hotel room, and at sound check it became apparent. Steve said, 'Man, you could stay at my place.' Just the sweetest, nicest guy I ever met."

The headliner also was taken with Steve's talent. When Linhart talked with Steve after the sound check, Steve gave him a copy of the "Gathering at the Earl of Old Town" LP. "If there's any chance you can move this up a notch," Steve said, "I sure would appreciate the help." That night before the show, Linhart talked up Steve to a Buddah promo man named Andy who had flown to Chi-

Buzzy Linhart, for whom Steve opened at the Quiet Knight, found himself without enough money to rent a hotel room, so Steve offered his apartment. "Just the sweetest, nicest guy I ever met," says Linhart, who also was so taken with Steve's talent that he planted a seed with a Buddah Records promo man about Steve's "genius."
(Photo courtesy of Buzzy Linhart)

In the dramatic lighting of the Quiet Knight, Steve opened for Kris Kristofferson, leading to a fateful overnight breakfast.
(Photo by John Bowen)

cago from New York to see how Linhart would do. But with only eight people in the audience for the first set, the promo man wasn't initially excited. Linhart pressed on. "Look," he said of Steve, "this guy's a genius. He's a bridge between folk and country and rock and doing this incredible stuff like Ogden Nash with his lyrics." After hearing more of Steve's set, the promo man relented and eventually placed a call to the New York office of Buddah chief Neil Bogart to crow about a "discovery." The seed was starting to sprout.

Steve continued in the same role at the Quiet Knight the following week, opening from April 28 through May 2 for a country-tinged songwriting sensation — Kris Kristofferson. For these gigs, Steve derived fresh patter from the newspapers, as the federal government announced April 28 that it would change the name of its national passenger-train network from Railpax to a friendlier, easier-to-understand moniker, Amtrak, on its first day of operation, May 1. Also effective May 1, the Illinois Central took a decisive step toward consolidation, scuttling its nighttime sleeper-car train, the Panama Limited, while retaining the cheaper and more popular daytime coach train, the City of New Orleans.

The move kept the name of Steve's song alive despite the tune's lyrical premonition of the train's disappearance. But Steve remained skeptical while introducing "City of New Orleans" during one of his Kristofferson dates. "I may as well tell you this song is an anachronism," he said. "Last spring, when I wrote the song, they were thinkin' of taking the City of New Orleans off the line. In fact, they did that with a lot of passenger trains. They cut the service by 60 percent when the Railpax went into effect. But you know that the City of New Orleans is still on the line. That's one damn train that they didn't cut back. But they took the Panama Limited, and I've been tryin' all week to get the words changed, to find something like, 'I'm the train they call the Panama Limited.' Doesn't make sense, y'know. Can't get anything to rhyme with that." The joke played well, despite the fact that in his song, the words "City of New Orleans" were positioned such that they didn't need to rhyme with anything.

Steve's career soon would be profoundly transformed by his openers for Kristofferson. The Rhodes scholar and onetime Nashville janitor had soared to fame because rock/blues belter Janis Joplin, who had died of a heroin overdose just seven months earlier, had recorded a road ballad he had co-written, "Me and Bobby McGee." The key line of Joplin's posthumous single ("Freedom's just another word for nothin' left to lose") was inescapable in early 1971, as was the Joplin LP on which it appeared, "Pearl," which topped sales charts for nine straight weeks. At the same time, sultry country singer Jewel Fay "Sammi" Smith's version of Kristofferson's ode to a one-night stand, "Help Me Make It Through the Night," had reached the top of the country charts and was settling in as a top-10 pop staple.

Kris Kristofferson, shown in the early 1970s, was in prime position to transform Steve's career. "All of a sudden, Kris was hot everywhere," Steve said. "It didn't matter which market you were talking about, everybody was cuttin' his stuff, and for good reason."

(Photo courtesy of Paul Colby)

These hits capped a 12-month period during which Kristofferson, who had just one album to his credit on the independent Monument label, received country star Johnny Cash's blessing on national TV as "the finest young songwriter today," and *The New York Times* tagged him as personifying "the new Nashville sound." The career of the handsome, rough-voiced 35-year-old as a large-venue musical performer and the romantic lead of big box-office films was yet to come, but the semi-autobiographical songs that he already had penned and that had been recorded by others, including the award-winning "For the Good Times" (Ray Price) and "Sunday Mornin' Comin' Down" (Cash), were formidable.

A dozen years older than Steve, Kristofferson was a songwriter to emulate, not just for his craftsmanship ("He's the king of iambic pentameter — everything scans," Steve said) but also for his commercial success. As Steve reflected later, "All of a sudden, Kris was hot everywhere. It didn't matter which market you were talking about, everybody was cuttin' his stuff, and for good reason."

Even so, Kristofferson's ragged and alcohol-soaked performances at the Quiet Knight that week left much to be desired. More often than he bared his boyish smile, he gazed at the stage floor or turned his back on the club's crowd — and it didn't help that he poorly enunciated his well-crafted lyrics and that his voice resembled that of a fatigued frog. Members of Kristofferson's band, as well as his female traveling companion at the time, 31-year-old British film actress Samantha Eggar ("Walk, Don't Run," "Doctor Doolittle"), both endured and lamented his success-driven malaise.

"Kris was very uncomfortable," Eggar says. "He found it difficult to face the audience, even at the end of his songs. His songs were so brilliant, but I don't think people even got them at that time. They just heard this sort of mumbling person." Adds Terry Paul, Kristofferson's bass player and road manager, "It was a rough period. Kris had walking pneumonia, and he was an alcoholic. He was not feeling well most of the time. He would wake up every morning with diarrhea and throwing up." Stephen Bruton, Kristofferson's guitarist, attributed the toll to a roller-coaster, 18-month touring schedule. "It just did not stop," he says. "You'd be, like, two pages from the end of your itinerary, and you'd get another itinerary." Kristofferson himself confirms that he was "really in rough shape. We had been working forever. As tired and hung over and sick as I was, I'd sleep and then get up and barely make it out."

Kristofferson's condition made it remarkable that he managed to sit through one of Steve's entire opening sets, much less take the time to meet him afterward. "Hey, you've gotta see this guy who's playing in front of us," Paul, the bass player, told him. "He's really good. He's a special, special person." Reluctantly, Kristofferson relented. "I swear to God, I would never have watched him, I was so damned tired and so sick at the time," Kristofferson says. But then he saw Steve's act. "I was knocked out," he says. Kristofferson and his band had been told about Steve's leukemia, but Kristofferson says that wasn't a factor in his assessment.

"City of New Orleans" impressed Kristofferson, but so did a song that Steve said he'd completed just a week before, a quiet tribute to tentative courtship, "Would You Like to Learn to Dance?" [27] Ostensibly, the title was the line that Steve improvised when he first bumped into his taller wife-to-be a year and a half earlier at the Earl. But Steve later said he wrote the song to cheer himself up, "to rationalize what I was doing even standing there." The tune's sentiments — a gentle progression of learning to "dance," "sing" and "love" — reminded Kristofferson of country songwriter Mickey Newbury's best work. "The emotion was right there," Kristofferson says. "It was one of those things where the words and the music go perfect, and the performance was perfect, and I didn't want to hear anybody else even do it."

"I didn't think the song was any good until Kris did," Steve reflected in typical self-deprecation during his 1976 *Omaha Rainbow* interview. "I thought it was a nice-enough ballad, but I didn't think it was saying anything to anyone apart from me. The night when Kris heard it at the Quiet Night, I sang it because I couldn't think of anything else to sing. It was pure luck. I couldn't remember all the words to 'California Blues.' I was feeling a little low, and I thought I'd buy myself three minutes."

As compelling as "Learn to Dance?" was, to Kristofferson the true stunner in Steve's set was his rendition of John Prine's "Sam Stone," whose stark chorus image of heroin addiction ("There's a hole in daddy's arm where all the money goes") complemented Kristofferson's own anti-war and world-weary imagery.

"Goddamn, that's a great song," he told Steve.

"You gotta hear the guy that wrote it," Steve replied.

The emotion was right there. It was one of those things where the words and the music go perfect, and the performance was perfect, and I didn't want to hear anybody else even do it.
KRIS KRISTOFFERSON

27: An early recording of Steve's indicates that "Would You Like to Learn to Dance?" originally was titled "Do You Want to Learn to Dance?" In that version, the three verses each began with the "Do you want" phrase. The change to "Would you like" suggested a more tender approach.

Kristofferson's first emotion was dread because he had become accustomed to song pitches by "the local guy," a recurrence that he felt had begun to stunt his own creativity. But as the five-day run progressed, Kristofferson and his troupe grew more attached to Steve, and Kristofferson allowed that he might be willing to meet and listen to Prine. "We'll do it the last night when I'm not working the next day," Kristofferson told him. Then, on the penultimate night, Saturday, May 1, into the Quiet Knight walked a mystical show-biz opportunity — in the unlikely form of ex-teeny-bop heartthrob Paul Anka.

The Canadian-born writer and performer of the late-1950s hits "Diana," "Lonely Boy," "Put Your Head on My Shoulder" and "Puppy Love," Anka had embraced the pop mainstream in the 1960s, writing the theme for TV's "The Tonight Show" and penning Frank Sinatra's 1968 signature tune, "My Way." By 1971, with 50 major-hit copyrights and 350 self-penned songs under his belt, the 29-year-old Anka had shed his teen chubbiness and was sporting hip, longer locks (one writer called it "Julius Caesar hair") that drew attention away from a receding hairline. But while he no longer projected the image of a boy wonder, he remained ensconced in a Las Vegas persona that the leftist youth culture found alien.

The tuxedoed Paul Anka was a welcome sight when Kris Kristofferson invited him to the Quiet Knight stage to sing "Help Me Make It Through the Night" with Kristofferson's band. "Oh, it was great," Kristofferson says. "Paul Anka was a songwriter when I was just thinking about being one."
(Photo by Bob Gruen)

Having just signed with Buddah Records after 15 years on the Riviera and RCA labels, Anka was in town the week of Kristofferson's Quiet Knight gig to play the green and gold, high-French-style Empire Room of the majestic, 1,600-room Palmer House hotel in the heart of the Loop. Huge newspaper ads trumpeted his "first time on a nightclub stage in Chicago."

Kristofferson and Anka had never met prior to their chance encounter the previous weekend on their flight to Chicago. There, Anka told Kristofferson he had incorporated "Help Me Make It Through the Night" in his act. Late the night of May 1, after finishing his own performance downtown, a still-tuxedoed Anka bounded up the steep stairway of the Quiet Knight during Kristofferson's closing set and, as a gesture of professional thanks to the author of the song, found himself on the club stage crooning it with Kristofferson's band. Anka's audacity floored the shaggy headliner. "Oh, it was great," Kristofferson says. "Paul Anka was a songwriter when I was just thinking about being one."

The camaraderie didn't end at the Quiet Knight. After the show ended and the patrons had filed out, Anka invited Kristofferson and his troupe, including Samantha Eggar, keyboardist Donnie Fritts and Steve, to his plush suite at the Palmer House for a middle-of-the-night gathering over gourmet breakfast and drinks. A more eclectic bunch of entertainers would have been hard to assemble. Anka's entourage included Lola Falana, the 29-year-old singer and dancer, who was performing with Danny Thomas at Chicago's Mill Run Theater, and Melvin Van Peebles, 40, a South Side native who was in town to promote the premiere of the first movie he had written, produced, directed and starred in, the X-rated "Sweet Sweetback's Baad Asssss Song," which came to be known as the first "blaxploitation" film.

To Charlene Bos, who owned an antique shop near the Quiet Knight and

Film actress Samantha Eggar, Kris Kristofferson's companion who was present for the early-morning breakfast with Paul Anka, says Steve's "discovery" emerged honestly. "The success of his music came to him because of his purity," she says. "He didn't have to go out and sell himself in some crass, awful manner that a lot of people do nowadays or throughout all time."

(Photo courtesy of Samantha Eggar)

was a friend of Kristofferson and Terry Paul and therefore along for the ride, it felt like a scene from TV's "Playboy after Dark" or a Fellini film. Steve felt likewise. "I felt hopelessly out of place," he later recalled for WGN-AM's Roy Leonard. "It's a situation that had nothing in common with anything I had experienced, before or since," he told the *Omaha Rainbow.*

In this setting, as the hour neared 5 a.m., Terry Paul asked Steve to play for Anka a couple of original songs. Kristofferson got even more specific: "Take out your axe and sing 'Would You Like to Learn to Dance?' "

Steve did so, quieting those in the suite to pin-drop silence. The tune moved Anka. "It just totally knocked him out," Kristofferson said. And by all accounts, including Steve's recollections, Anka had a singular response, much like the question of the song's title:

"How'd you like a plane ticket to New York?"

The offer was redolent with implications — that the setting for commercial success was not Chicago, and notably that Anka would open the door for exposure to Manhattan-based record-company execs. This was the break, the chance, the fleeting instant to seize, and Steve knew it. Anka's Palmer House suite became a parallel to Schwab's Drug Store in Hollywood, and Steve later called this his "Lana Turner moment." ("I must've shown my legs right at the bus stop or something," he said.) Steve's inspired reply to Anka — also a question — broke up the room:

"How'd you like to see the short, fat Jewish kid dive into a vat of Chicken Kiev?"

The crack, as unpretentious as it was eager, both fit and enhanced what was an easy atmosphere. Eggar, who sometimes hosted Steve during his later trips to Los Angeles and became a lifelong friend, says, "It wasn't checking each other like animals stalking around and looking at each other and sizing each other up, whether an actor, whether a musician, whether somebody's famous or they're not famous. Steve was just enjoying it."

Van Peebles, the maverick filmmaker, recalls it as a magic moment. "There was such a supportiveness," he says. "Everybody there was just cheering each other on, just relaxed. Everybody had a little bit of a name by that time — well, most of us did — but we were just there havin' a good time. It was early, early in the morning, but it was nice. It was just nice."

It was a moment that came to Steve honestly, Eggar says. In retrospect, the lyrics of "Would You Like to Learn to Dance?" can be seen as a calculated sales call — a metaphorical audition wrapped up in a single song. But in that gathering in Anka's suite, as Eggar points out, the solicitation fittingly emerged from someone other than Steve.

"The star power that night for Steve was, I'm sure, tremendously exhilarating," Eggar says. "The success of his music came to him because of his purity. He didn't have to go out and sell himself in some crass, awful manner that a lot of people do nowadays or throughout all time. His genius and his humility were the magnets that brought this success to him. I don't remember any nerves at all. Maybe there were nerves inside, but as he sat and played, this extraordinary persona, this teddy bear, just oozed kindness.

"He was so completely different from the spirit it took to be a musician and singer/songwriter at the time. I had seen the lifestyle and the drinking and the tension of being a writer who composes from nothing. But Steve was a relief to me from that slightly strange world. Steve was so easy and so warm and so dear, and so open and funny and approachable and gentle. You only needed to meet him once for him to make a mark on your soul."

The most extraordinary aspect of the overnight breakfast was yet to come, however.

Steve simply could have expressed his gratitude, accepted the offer and raced home to his apartment buzzing with excitement to convey to his wife. "Man, I was so excited," he told the *Chicago Daily News* seven months later. "I couldn't even remember our phone number in order to call Nancy and tell her about it."

But Steve's upbringing and the experiences of his nearly 23 years, including a looming mortality, wouldn't let him leave the situation as it was. At an hour that usually produces bleary-eyed, foggy thinking, Steve's first impulse was strikingly clear-headed. He made a magnanimous decision he would never regret. He implored Anka to give a listen to a friend.

"I'll go with you," Steve said, "but if you like what I'm doing, there's something else you ought to do before you leave town. You've got to see my pal, John Prine."

Steve told radio host Roy Leonard nearly a year later, "I know I stuttered a lot, and I figured, well, since the gravy train was in town, I'd take everybody over to the Earl of Old Town to see John Prine, who I thought was pretty much the best lyric writer I'd ever heard."

Prine two months earlier had graduated from the tiny Fifth Peg to the Earl. His obscurity was reflected by his first Earl billing in the March 5 edition of the *Chicago Tribune*, as "John Pine." On March 14, he was listed as a "folk star" at the Earl, and by March 28, he was holding down the Thursday-through-Sunday slot "until further notice," being paid a not insignificant $1,000 a week. The folk-rock group Aliotta Haynes Jeremiah shared the bill with Prine through the month of April, and his booking had become so regular that Prine resigned his job as a mail carrier.

"When I quit the post office, a job with benefits, that was a huge move," Prine says. "It meant not only that I was makin' a living as a musician, but it also meant, obviously, to me, that that's what I wanted to do."

Though he had garnered only a minuscule reputation, Prine already had encountered industry reps who salivated over his songs and made offers, including one tendered at the Fifth Peg by an unlikely source, the manager of pop singer Peggy Lee, and another by Roy Silver, the infamous manager of Bill Cosby and Tiny Tim. But the scruffy singer rejected those opportunities.

"I was really both scared and adamant at the time about not wantin' to move," Prine says. "I was real gun shy, to tell you the truth. I hadn't really ever

> I figured, well, since the gravy train was in town, I'd take everybody over to the Earl of Old Town to see John Prine, who I thought was pretty much the best lyric writer I'd ever heard.
> **STEVE GOODMAN**

thought that I could make any kind of a livin' in the music business. I just thought that people that made records or were on TV were from a whole different land. I was knocked out that somebody'd give me 20 bucks or 40 bucks because I came down and sang, because I'd just be doing that alone in my room anyway. So I didn't really have any long-range plans."

In this state of mind, Prine got a phone call from Steve to report on his startling overnight breakfast with Kristofferson and Anka. Steve told Prine to stick around after his last set at the Earl of Old Town that night because the luminaries wanted to meet him. To Prine, the stunner in Steve's message was the name of Kristofferson, his musical idol, in the same league as Johnny Cash and Bob Dylan. Earlier in the week, Prine had slipped away between sets at the Earl to see Kristofferson perform at the Quiet Knight. He knew Kristofferson's every song. "He was the real deal," Prine says.

Well past midnight on Sunday, May 2, after Anka finished at the Palmer House and Kristofferson closed his 11 p.m. show at the Quiet Knight, two groups assembled. Kristofferson, Samantha Eggar, Terry Paul, Charlene Bos and Steve piled into Kristofferson's two rented station wagons. Meanwhile, Anka, his guitar player and a bodyguard hopped into a limo. The vehicles converged in Old Town, which, Kristofferson later wrote, "was nothing but empty streets and dark windows." Fred Holstein, one of the few people lingering at the Earl, where most of the chairs were sitting upside down on tables, recalled that it was about 2:30 or 3 a.m. when the motley bunch walked in. Shortly before, just to make sure, Steve had urgently telephoned Holstein, saying, "Freddie, keep John there. Keep him there."

Prine was indeed present. "I was waitin' around to be paid, and I was in no hurry," he says. "I was just chattin' with the bartender." Kristofferson says that when they arrived, Prine unpacked his guitar and stumbled to the stage, while the entourage flipped a few chairs right-side up and took seats at a table in front of the microphone.

To Prine, the tiny audience was surreal. "When Steve brought Kris down to see me, he (Kristofferson) could have had the Cowardly Lion and the Tin Man with him, for all I cared," Prine says. The presence of Anka, he says, didn't register at all. "I couldn't have cared if it was Paul Anka or Bugs Bunny. To me, Anka was just one more show-biz guy."

Kristofferson says he initially was embarrassed at inducing a bedraggled local singer to "perform for the so-called stars," and he started drowning his reticence with bourbon. But then Prine began to sing. With a sandpaper voice and rudimentary strumming, the ex-mailman delivered half a dozen original compositions from his "A" list and left Kristofferson in a daze.

"I was tryin' my darndest to impress him so he wouldn't get up and walk out," Prine says. "I didn't know that he was just absolutely in love with everything I sang."

"He proceeded to just destroy us, song by song," Kristofferson says. "He started with 'Donald and Lydia,' and every one of those songs was great, like

'Hello in There.' I felt like we were at something like when somebody might have stumbled on Bob Dylan. John Prine just scalded my brain that night. He was the best damned songwriter I'd ever seen."

After Prine was through, he sat down and had a beer with the group. Kristofferson quickly told Prine, "Start right over and sing every one you sang and any other one you want to sing for us."

"So I got back up and sang every song that I ever wrote," Prine says, "even parts of songs."

At some point between tunes, Kristofferson leaned over and said to a nodding Anka, "I guess you're buying two plane tickets."

With reassurances by both Kristofferson and Anka — "Can I help you out?," "Come hang," "Come see me," "You guys are great," "You should be out makin' records, both of you" — Steve and Prine fairly floated out of the Earl close to the crack of dawn.

Later that Monday, Steve again called Prine, reminding him that although Kristofferson was leaving town, Anka was still playing the Palmer House through the following Monday. "He's really interested in talkin' to us some more," Steve said.

"Why?" a dubious Prine asked. "What for?"

"Well," Steve said, "he's talking about maybe us going to New York to make some demos."

"You're kiddin' me."

"No, he is, and he wants us to come down to see his show and bring our wives."

Steve and Nancy, plus Prine with his wife Ann Carole, caught Anka's Empire Room production — and what a production. The crooner was backed by a 27-piece orchestra, including horn and sax sections, 14 strings and a rhythm core that featured Afro-Cuban drummer extraordinaire Chano Pozo on bongos. The ensemble swept through a repertoire of others' hits ("Help Me Make It Through the Night," "Let It Be") and Anka originals, both early ("Diana") and contemporary ("She's a Lady," "My Way"), closing with the previous winter's chart-topper by ex-Beatle George Harrison, "My Sweet Lord." Anka's slick shtick had little in common with Steve's and Prine's more austere styles. But Steve fondly noted that Anka was willing to engage in self-parody, twisting his teen hit "Put Your Head on My Shoulder" into "Put Your Legs on My Shoulders."

Afterward, the foursome joined Anka in his suite, where he touched on record-industry topics and confirmed what he'd told Steve — that he wanted the two Chicagoans to come to New York to make demos (initial recordings) at the Record Plant. Supervising the sessions would be Phil Ramone, the already legendary engineer and producer of scores of prominent acts ranging from jazz (Stan Getz and Quincy Jones) to pop (Burt Bacharach and Harry Nilsson) to folk (Arlo Guthrie and Peter, Paul & Mary) to rock (The Band and the Rolling Stones).

Engineering behind-the-scenes deals for singer/songwriters was nothing new

I guess you're buying two plane tickets.
KRIS KRISTOFFERSON

for Anka, who had assisted artists ranging from David Clayton-Thomas, lead singer for Blood, Sweat & Tears, to country hitmaker Jimmy Dean ("Big Bad John"). "I had a track record of helping people through my publishing company and with record contracts," Anka says. "This was just kind of part of my M.O." Steve and Prine, he says, fell into the same pattern. "I was really very taken by both of them as talents," he says. "John was more eclectically rooted with social relevance, in terms of his observation from Vietnam to relationships in a very different way — Dylan-esque, I guess, would be the word. And Steve was just a good songwriter and had very good tone to his voice."

But Anka's pitch failed to dislodge Prine's reticence. "I didn't know if I wanted to take a jump, whether it was Paul Anka or not — no reflection on Anka, but anybody like that," Prine says. "If it had been Kristofferson, it would have been a different thing to me, a different offer. Kris would have just gone, 'Hey, man, grab your guitar. Let's go.' But Anka was discussing business already, and that scared me. Kris was just totally unselfish, whereas Anka wanted to get in on the action right away. Kris wanted to help us as much as possible, but he didn't want any business part. Kris didn't want to take us to his publisher or his record company, which I always thought was really grand, especially after being in show business for so long — somebody that comes along to help you and doesn't cut themselves in or anybody that they know.

"I couldn't believe things were movin' as fast as they were. I had the feeling that I had my feet in further than I thought. That's when I had to stop and think, 'Well, what is it you're lookin' for?' I still didn't know. All I knew is that I really enjoyed the fact that I was singin' my own songs and makin' a livin' at it. But I was very wary of signin' anything or gettin' wrapped up with anybody."

A day later, Steve and Prine talked again. "I just don't know," Prine said.

Steve was incredulous. "Have you ever been to New York City?"

"No," Prine said.

"Well, let's go!" Steve burst out. "What's the matter with you? The guy's payin' your plane ticket."

Prine hedged a bit more, mulling it in his mind. "I just thought, 'Well, you don't get nothin' for free in this life.' I was suspicious right from the get-go."

But Steve wouldn't let up. "You've never been to New York before," he told Prine. "Here's your chance!"

What finally persuaded Prine was his compatriot's enthusiasm and profound act of friendship.

"Stevie was well situated in the folk scene long before I came into it, from the time when he probably had to tap people on the shoulder and wait in line to get out there to do one song," Prine says. "Here comes his time for his spotlight to hit him, and all he wants to do is talk about his buddy and 'Wait'll you hear these songs.' He had been lookin' for a break, but when his break came, he wanted to include me. To this day, I just think — especially when I see how hard it is these days for people to get noticed or to get a record deal, they have to have a manager and almost have a video made and everything else goin' for

---

I had a track record of helping people through my publishing company and with record contracts. This was just kind of part of my M.O.
PAUL ANKA

'em before they can even get in the door — that what a great thing it was for me, more than a lucky break. If there's anything like fate, it was me meetin' Steve Goodman and then Steve and I meetin' Kris. I couldn't have bumped into two better guys."

The ebullience of Steve was not lost on Kristofferson and Anka. While Prine's lyrical brilliance impressed the influential listeners, Steve's more outgoing and engaging nature — along with his complete package of showmanship — engendered their respect.

"I always liked Steve," Anka says. "He was a very decent guy and had a lot of courage." Steve's support for Prine also impressed Anka, who found it "gracious" and emblematic of an era that was less cutthroat.

Kristofferson, who later worked onstage and in the studio with Steve, was particularly enamored. "Steve was a perfect performer of his art, of the stuff that he wrote and the emotions that he felt," Kristofferson reflects. "To me, he was like a candle that burned steadily and brilliantly onstage. His guitar work and his charm, his elfin personality, were so winning to so many people. He just absolutely won everybody's heart, I guess with a mixture of sincerity and the knowledge — that we all stuff — of living with a death sentence."

Kristofferson came to find deep satisfaction in his role as a catalyst for the careers of both Steve and Prine. "It was really a magical time, when things like that could happen," he says. "You would see something that was worth succeeding, and you could help it succeed, and it worked."

As a result, Steve and his buddy soon were headed to the Big Apple for something that transcended yet another treatment to stave off leukemia. ♪

> **Steve was a perfect performer of his art. ... He just absolutely won everybody's heart, I guess with a mixture of sincerity and the knowledge — that we all stuff — of living with a death sentence.**
> **KRIS KRISTOFFERSON**

Standing next to a grinning Carly Simon, Steve looks on as John Prine gets an enthusiastic greeting from the Bitter End's Paul Colby, on Nov. 3, 1971, the opening night of the first twin billing of Goodman/ Prine at the famed Greenwich Village club. That night (right), before the iconic brick wall, Steve and Prine launched a tradition for their co-billed shows by playing a dual encore. Steve had triggered Prine's rise to prominence but felt like Jingles to Prine's Wild Bill Hickock.

(Top photo by Bob Gruen,

bottom photo by Mark Chester)

'It wasn't about ego or attitude
— it was just this hunger'

From the time Steve Goodman was 3 until he was 10, he and tens of millions of other youthful North American baby boomers gazed wide-eyed while 113 installments of "The Adventures of Wild Bill Hickok" raced across their black-and-white TV screens. In each show, the gallant Guy Madison took on countless bad guys, solemnly announcing upon his arrival, "James Butler Hickok, mister." Then came 300-pound Andy Devine, playing comic sidekick Jingles P. Jones, who added in a shrill, raspy voice, "That's Wild Bill Hickok, mister — the bravest, strongest, fighting-est U.S. marshal in the whole West!" In the opening credits of every episode, riding his horse, Buckshot, Madison galloped away with guns ablaze. Straddling a slower steed named Joker, Devine wheezed after him: "Hey, Wild Bill, wait for me!"

Some 20 years later, the reedy John Prine and the pudgy Steve Goodman were not the stars of a children's TV show. But in Steve's mind, from the moment that Kris Kristofferson and Paul Anka first heard Prine sing at the Earl of Old Town late on the night of May 2, 1971, a visceral resemblance to the pair of Western characters materialized — and it persisted three weeks later when they flew east to enter the musical Big Time.

"For a while, John was gettin' all the attention," Steve told John Tobler in a lengthy 1976 interview with the British-based *Omaha Rainbow*. "I felt like Andy Devine to John's Wild Bill."

The admission was revealing. There was no question it was based in truth. But because it bordered on a complaint, reflecting a feeling of having been slighted, it also was atypical of Steve's usual insistence that he and Prine were each other's biggest champions.

Tobler, the interviewer, pointed out to Steve the irony that he was the one whom Kristofferson and Anka had "discovered" first, and yet the singer/songwriter whom Steve had served up to them — Prine — was receiving more acclaim.

"Well, shit, it's not a question of that. I would do it again in that situation for anybody," Steve replied, backpedaling into generosity. "It was such a good thing for him to get out (of Chicago) and be that strong. I thought it was great. I'd do it again in a minute." [1]

> For a while, John was gettin' all the attention. I felt like Andy Devine to John's Wild Bill.
> **STEVE GOODMAN**

1: Steve expressed the same offhand sentiment for Howard Larman of the "FolkScene" radio program in 1972: "Anybody could have done that," he said of leading Kristofferson and Anka to Prine. "I just happened to be around, is all. That wasn't no big thing."

The Bitter End, shown in 1999, much as it looked in 1971.

(Photo by Clay Eals)

Exactly how Prine was outpacing Steve unfolded shortly after their plane touched the ground in New York City on Sunday evening, May 23, and it shaped the two folksingers' relationship and fate for years to come.

While they had traveled to the Big Apple at Anka's behest and on Anka's dime, again it was Kristofferson who emerged as Steve's and Prine's true catalyst — and an initially unwitting one at that.

The two Chicagoans were anticipating their stay that night at the landmark Roosevelt Hotel in Midtown and their demo session with Phil Ramone at noon the next day, both paid for by Anka. "We picked up a *Village Voice* at LaGuardia, and I was thumbin' through it while we were waitin' for our bags," Prine says. "I see 'Kristofferson,' and I went, 'Wow,' because I thought (it meant that) he was comin' soon to New York, and then we looked at the date, and he was playin' that very night at the Bitter End."

Excited, Steve and Prine hopped a cab to the Roosevelt to drop off their bags, then took another cab to Greenwich Village. They pulled up at the club just as Kristofferson's first show had ended. As fans were lining up outside for the second show, Kristofferson and his band were filing out during the break to get a drink next door at a bar called the Dugout.

"Hey Kris!" Steve called out, as he and Prine followed them.

Kristofferson turned and brightened in surprised recognition.

"Steve Goodman, man!" he said.

The two talked for a few moments. Kristofferson asked, "Where's that buddy of yours from Chicago?"

Prine, who says he "would try and be a fly on the wall no matter where I was," was standing right next to Steve. "I couldn't have been closer to him," he says.

"He's right here," Steve said, gesturing to Prine.

"Hey, man," Kristofferson said, "you guys need to get up and play."

"Yeah," chimed in Donnie Fritts, Kristofferson's keyboard player, "that's what you guys ought to do."

Soon, the group hustled back into the Bitter End, with Kristofferson bearing a command: "Put these guys up onstage!"

Kristofferson's admonition was directed at Paul Colby, manager of the 200-seat, no-alcohol club, whose red brick wall had become a folk icon. Its aural fare — music transformed by social activism — had earned the Bitter End a reputation over the past decade as the hippest listening room in the Village and probably the nation. Colby says he had "fallen in love with" Kristofferson's earthy and sensual songwriting. But the impresario's enthusiasm also was financial, because at Kristofferson's previous two Bitter End bookings, crowds had queued up around the block to see him, fueled by laudatory spreads in *The New York Times.*

That night, the second to last of Kristofferson's 12-night gig at the club, sizzled with anticipation, as the *Times* had just gushed over the relatively new face of Carly Simon. The previous month, Simon had recorded a debut LP on

Elektra Records, with the single "That's the Way I Always Heard It Should Be" already on the radio, and she was opening for Kristofferson for the last four nights of his Bitter End run.

Colby was a happy man because the second show audience that night was bulging with press and record-company executives and their families and friends. But he wasn't prepared for Kristofferson's impromptu request to give stage time to a pair of Chicago unknowns.

"I got two kids I want to put on as a guest set," Kristofferson told him.

Worried about turning off his crowd of music-industry insiders, Colby balked.

"Kris, I can't do two kids tonight," Colby replied. "I'll tell you what. Put one guy, pick one, whoever you want to go on first. Otherwise, it'll kill the show for me, because you've got to give 'em at least 20 minutes or a half hour each."

Kristofferson stared at Colby. "I want these two guys," he said.

A moment passed.

"Fuck it," Colby said. "Put 'em both on."

"I could never refuse Kris," Colby says. "If I hadn't cared about him, I would never have put two guys on. Somebody else, I would have turned them down, but Kris and I were close. He was my friend, and I respected him and loved him." Besides, Colby says, the Bitter End thrived on unpredictability. "That's what the club's all about — magic. How do you say no?"

Sitting at a back table were brothers Harry and Tom Chapin, who had been the core of a five-member Crosby, Stills & Nash-style rock group, including their brother Steve, called the Chapins. The band, managed by Colby, had been the Bitter End's house opening act during 1969 and 1970 but otherwise remained obscure. On this night, one year before Harry's classic story song, "Taxi," inundated the country's airwaves, Harry and Tom had stopped in merely to witness what Harry called the "super cooled-out" appeal of Kristofferson. Prior to the second show, the brothers glimpsed Simon and Kristofferson making out in the club's back room, but their even more memorable discovery came during the show itself.

Before Kristofferson took the stage, Steve and Prine were giddy and nervous. As Steve recalled years later, Kristofferson told them, "You're in the big city now. Couth up." Midway through his first set, Kristofferson introduced the two visitors in the same order that he'd encountered them several weeks prior.

"I was just in Chicago," Kristofferson said with a drawl, "and this guy played us the best damn train song I ever heard in my life. Please welcome, from the windy city, Steve Goodman."

Steve strode to the mike with a borrowed guitar and sang "City of New Orleans" and a couple of other songs. Riveted, Tom and Harry Chapin turned to each other, smiled and said, "Oh, my God." [2]

In the second and traditionally more important spot, Kristofferson brought to the stage "a guy who's been a mailman." Prine came to the stage and performed a trio of tunes, including "Sam Stone." Afterward, Harry Chapin looked

Tom Chapin, shown in 1971, and his brother Harry were incredulous upon hearing the dual guest set of Steve and John Prine at the Bitter End.

(Photo courtesy of Tom Chapin)

2: On later reflection, Tom Chapin realized that "City of New Orleans" was more than a train song. "It's very much about the death of something," he says. "It's full of life but also the awareness of death at the end, that it's coming around the corner. "

at Tom, shook his head and said, "What are they smokin' in Chicago?"

Both Steve and Prine "went over terrific," Kristofferson says.

"I fell in love with the kids," adds Colby. "It was a very exciting night."

And for the Chapin brothers, the night "was just astonishing," Tom Chapin says. "We were trying to be singer/songwriters, and here were two guys we'd never heard of who had two of the best songs I'd ever heard in my life. That was a very formative night for both of us, and what a way to be introduced to the magic."

The Chapins' incredulity reflected the buzz in the room, and the newcomers found it pleasantly disorienting. "We were living in a dream," Steve said in the *Omaha Rainbow* interview. "We didn't know what was happening."

Missing from the audience was Paul Anka, who was playing his own week-and-a-half engagement at New York's most elegant and best-known hotel, the 1,245-room Waldorf-Astoria in Midtown. But attending from Buddah Records — which had signed Anka, hoping to revive his hit-making — was the firm's vice president in charge of artist relations, Ron Weisner.

Fritts, from Kristofferson's band, had invited a friend of his own to the club that night. He was Jerry Wexler, producer and executive vice president for Atlantic Records, a longtime industry-leading label rooted in rhythm and blues (Ray Charles, Aretha Franklin, Wilson Pickett) and more recently in pop and rock (Young Rascals, Dusty Springfield, Crosby, Stills & Nash, Led Zeppelin). Fritts wanted Wexler to meet Kristofferson, but Wexler asked Fritts, "Who in the world is this kid?" The reference was to Prine. Fritts made the introduction, and the courtship was quick. Wexler extended Prine an offer and bid him to his office two mornings later, at 10 a.m. Tuesday, to sign a contract.

No similar offer surfaced that night for Steve. The Buddah brass were intrigued but didn't pounce. Nor did Wexler, who told Prine that it would be difficult for one record company to "do a big splash and separate you guys."

Wexler says he considered signing Steve with Prine, and he still muses over whether he should have gone through with it. "I was super-impressed with both of them, but I knew I had to make a decision," Wexler says. "It was a logistical question. I just couldn't see signing two of the same genre at one time. We were not a folk label. The roster just wouldn't fit, y'know. Maybe it would have. I don't know." Why did he opt for Prine instead of Steve? "That's an imponderable," he says. "Who the hell knows? Maybe his songs were richer at the time. I don't know."

Steve and Prine were reeling as they returned that night to the Roosevelt and their "little bitty" shared room, which Prine later told a radio deejay was "a little bit larger than your turntable." Prine put a smattering of beer cans on ice in the tub in the adjacent bathroom, a practice that he adopted in later hotel stays with Steve and that Steve "always got a kick out of." But when Steve asked him, "What are we supposed to do if I want to take a bath?" Prine replied, "Well, go get a room. Man, this is to ice down the beer."

The next day, after the two recorded demos with Phil Ramone ("He just let

We were trying to be singer/songwriters, and here were two guys we'd never heard of who had two of the best songs I'd ever heard in my life.
TOM CHAPIN

us roll with our guitars and told Stevie and me to sing everything that we ever had"), Prine walked around Manhattan rubbernecking. "I felt like Stevie Wonder," he says with a laugh. But the tall buildings held little solace for Steve. While he enjoyed the rush of activity and felt happy for his friend's reward, looming was a lack of similar recognition for him.

Fortunately, an ultimately beneficial diversion awaited both Steve and Prine that night. Anka had invited the pair to watch his Vegas-style revue just five blocks north of the Roosevelt, in a two-story, 300-seat cabaret adorning the Waldorf-Astoria's main floor that bore the same name as the hall in which they'd seen him perform three weeks before in Chicago, the Empire Room. "I wasn't nuts about goin' to see the show again," Prine says. Nor was Steve, who said later, "Levi Strauss is my tailor, and I wasn't dressed for the Waldorf."

Out of deference, however, the two took in Anka's extravaganza, arriving at the Empire Room a few minutes late. As they observed the set, Steve sat agape. He had taken pride in polishing the structure of his own concerts, but the resulting enchantment that his audiences were feeling stemmed from an impression that much of it was thrown together impromptu. Anka's performances were clearly anything but. Partway into Anka's second show, Steve discerned this, and he later regaled audiences with his insight.

"I figured it out," Steve said. "There's a script for the show. Everything stays the same. Nothing changes, including the order of the songs, the lines he says exactly before the songs. Everything was written down, it was in the book: the light cues, the way he held the mike at certain points, the way he cued the band. Every bead of sweat, man, every gesture of his arm was in the script. He's got a tight act. It's great. It's like seeing a Broadway play. It was perfect.

"I could appreciate how hard Paul Anka worked. That's probably why he made $18 million. He knows what's good, and he sticks with it. He don't fuck around. They don't gamble, and I don't blame him. I don't hold that against anybody."

By the third song of Anka's second show, Steve had stomached all that he could. He said he told Prine, "It's like being at the movies, and this is where I came in, because I just saw this. I could probably see it again tomorrow night, I really like it, but I couldn't see it again tonight, so why don't we go?" So began the wackiest story of how a Steve Goodman song — one of his best known and most highly regarded — came to be written.

Anka, as Steve often told the story, had invited him and Prine to make use of Room 1079 of the Waldorf, a 420-square-foot, one-bedroom suite that doubled as Anka's dressing room. Anka offered them gratis use of room service because, Prine says, Anka said the Waldorf would pay for it. The two rode the elevator up 10 floors, found the suite and, once inside, picked up the phone and "ordered everything on the menu," Steve said, including strip-steak dinners, a plate of cold crab meat, a trio of desserts — chocolate mousse, Baked Alaska and Cherries Jubilee — along with a platter of assorted canapés. "Whenever I'm in a joint like that, the first thing I do is get the assorted canapés," Steve said with

> **I could appreciate how hard Paul Anka worked. That's probably why he made $18 million. He knows what's good, and he sticks with it.**
> **STEVE GOODMAN**

an impish gleam. "I didn't want to be called a cheapskate, so I wrote 'Add 20 percent' for the tip on that check, right under where I signed Anka's name."

But Steve claimed that the food was just the beginning. Steve said they also ordered four bottles of Jack Daniels Old #7 Tennessee Whiskey (which he called "redneck LSD"), three bottles of Remy Martin champagne cognac ("which will set you free, if you give it the chance") and a case of "rude, impolite" Rheingold beer, "which was extracted with a vise by squeezing the kidneys of the last remaining buffalo in the state of New York." (Steve added, "I spent a month thinking up a neat way to say buffalo piss.")

"We made bourbon brandy beer boilermakers in the sink — that's what you call it when you pour it all in the same glass," Steve said. "We floated a couple of paper cups in there and proceeded to get rat-fuck, shitfaced, commode-hugging drunk. We spent most of the night in the next room kneelin' and prayin' at the porcelain altar, drivin' the porcelain bus, anything you care to call it. John and I are deacons in that church, by the way. You get ambitious when you're that drunk. See, it was the 10th floor, and John convinced me that I could not fly."

So then and there, "by accident," Steve said, they began to write a song that "had 48 verses once, but the maid came in and wiped all but four off the wall before we could wake up."

Prine says Steve's account was accurate until he got to the booze. "That's where Steve started takin' his poetic license," he says. "That's where stuff that he'd pick up on the road different times we partied, it would become part of his stage story. Whatever worked, that's what he'd say."

In contrast to Steve's outrageously alcohol-fueled yarn, Prine's version is less flamboyant and tinged with Steve's melancholy. He says that after their room-service meal in Anka's Waldorf suite, he decided to head back to the Village for a few beers and to "see what was goin' on" for a few hours while Steve remained in the suite. "When I came back," Prine says, "he was over in the corner sittin' at the desk, hunched over a piece of Waldorf stationery, right under one of those fancy, shiny, green-glass desk lamps, and that was all that was lit. The whole rest of the room was dark. I looked over his shoulder and saw, 'It was all that I could do to keep from crying. Sometimes it seems so useless to remain.' And he meant it as a really sad song."

Feeling his beer, Prine decided not to put up with the mournfulness of Steve's lyrics and started teasing him. "I jumped up on the bed like I had an imaginary violin, like I was a weeper, and I was standin' on the bed playin' it, and I went, 'You don't have to call me darlin', darlin', but you never even call me by my name.' And we both laughed and hooted and beat on the walls and thought it was the funniest thing. And then we made a total shambles of it, just wrote corny jokes, the worst dreck."

Prine contributed two other lines to the song — "You're the one who always tried to change me, and that is why I'll always stay the same," and "I heard my name a few times in the phone book, and on the neon sign above the bar I used

> We floated a couple of paper cups in there and proceeded to get rat-fuck, shitfaced, commode-hugging drunk. We spent most of the night in the next room kneelin' and prayin' at the porcelain altar, drivin' the porcelain bus, anything you care to call it.
> **STEVE GOODMAN**

to own" — and surmised that it would get no further than the Waldorf suite. "I just totally disowned it," he says. "I was trying to keep him from writin' this awful, sad stuff, and it was just a one-joke song. It never went anywhere. To me, it just kept goin' back to 'you never even call me by my name,' but Stevie thought that was what made the song. I was really surprised when he told me that he considered it was a song and was gonna continue workin' on it."

Part of Prine's distaste for the song stemmed from the country-music roots of his family and upbringing. "I thought country music had enough of a bad rap from people in rock music who didn't like it, that they didn't need another song makin' fun of it." Steve insisted, however, that the composition was a keeper. "I told him, 'The hell with you,' and I copyrighted it in the vain hope that Porter Waggoner would do a cover version," Steve impishly said to a Chicago audience six months later.

It was a milestone — the first writing collaboration of Steve and Prine. From its three-chord structure to its invocation of big names such as Merle Haggard and Charley Pride, the composition became a letter- and note-perfect send-up of country-western lyrics and music that eventually became "You Never Even Call Me by My Name." [3] Steve zipped down to the 14-year-old Folklore Center at 110 MacDougal Street in Greenwich Village to show it off. "Man, we just wrote a song," he told Paula Ballan, who also was at the Folklore Center to see a concert that night by Bruce "Utah" Phillips. At an informal gathering afterward, Steve played the tune and told a boozy story of its origin. "That's the first time I heard him say they were praying at the porcelain altar," Ballan says. "We all just roared."

On their second morning in New York, Prine walked into Jerry Wexler's office to find a contract on Wexler's desk awaiting Prine's signature. It called for Prine to record 10 albums, with 10 original songs on each one, for a payment of $25,000. The proposal floored Prine because it was based on Wexler having heard just three of his songs, and "I'd never heard of $25,000 in my life." But Prine didn't grab the pen. "I didn't feel like I should go ahead and sign the paper without tellin' Anka about it because Anka had paid for the plane ticket," Prine says. Anka, he says, was determined to play the middleman. When Prine told Anka about Wexler's offer, Anka brought in a lawyer to negotiate the deal. "If Anka would have had his way, he would have taken both of us to Buddah because he was linked with them," Prine says. But Wexler's tangible offer was on the table, and Anka backed it, so the deal was struck.

Prine was understandably excited that week, but Steve's state of mind needed a lift. At one point, as the two walked through Greenwich Village, "I caught him in a bad mood," Prine says.

"Steve," Prine asked, "what are you up to?"

"Ah, I'm goin' back to the hotel and check out. I'm goin' back to Chicago."

"No way," Prine said. "What for?"

"Man, they don't want me," Steve said. "They just want you."

Prine looked at him for a moment. "Steve," he said, "that's not like you."

> **Man, they don't want me. They just want you.**
> **STEVE GOODMAN**

3: A year later, Steve explained to the British *Record Mirror* his rationale for creating a parody of U.S. country music: "We have an expression, 'If you give something a kick up the butt every now and then, it's good for it.' I hate to see country music gettin' stodgy. I appreciate the music for its basic honesty, but people were writing such contrived songs ... so I figured that I would contrive one to counteract contrivance."

Steve "kinda agreed with me that it wasn't," Prine says. "I guess he was just feelin' just a little sorry for himself."

Prine quickly learned what underlay Steve's angst. Rooming for a week with Prine in New York and needing to take tests at Sloan-Kettering, Steve couldn't help disclosing his disease, which was a shock to Prine but also helped Prine understand Steve's mood swings. "I didn't know hardly anything about leukemia," Prine says, "but neither did the medical world a whole lot, because from what Steve told me, everything he was doing was pretty primal. They were shooting chemo straight into his veins, and he told me how few of the people were left from the original volunteers that went in there and did chemo that way, just to kind of underline for me where he was at with it." Prine didn't detect self-pity, however. "Other than joking," he says, "I never, ever heard Steve talk about havin' any limited time."

By week's end, Prine flew back to Chicago with his Atlantic Records contract in hand and hired "the best, most expensive music lawyer I could get." Steve, meanwhile, stayed behind, determined to be available for whatever deal that might be in the offing.

Grateful for Anka's hospitality ("He was beautiful that whole week — he bought everything"), Steve needed other Manhattan digs to settle into for an extended stretch. He alighted in various places, in a rented room and with Paula Ballan, Penny Simon and Steve Mandell, one night traveling with Mandell to Mount Vernon, north of the Bronx, for dinner at Mandell's parents' home. There, for an hour Steve played songs, including "City of New Orleans," for Mandell's mother. "He insisted on helping wash dishes, which was unusual for a guy in those times," Mandell says. "My mother loved him to death."

In Midtown Manhattan, meanwhile, on the 21st floor of an office building three short blocks south of Carnegie Hall, wheels were turning on Steve's behalf in the headquarters of four-year-old Buddah Records.

Linked to Kama Sutra Records (a label built on the success of eight hits by the folk-rock Lovin' Spoonful in the mid-1960s) and the distributor of a dozen smaller imprints (including Curtis Mayfield's Curtom, based in Chicago), Buddah, born in 1967, had an idiosyncratic identity. At the dawn of the 1970s, the label with the misspelled name ("Buddha" is correct) and clashing logo (a Shiva Indian statue, not a Buddha) was known to the record-buying public primarily as a fount of popular AM radio singles with stubbornly lingering musical "hooks" that appealed mostly to pre-teens — a genre of silly songs known as bubblegum. From "Chewy Chewy" and "Yummy Yummy Yummy" by the Ohio Express to "1-2-3 Red Light" by the 1910 Fruitgum Company, Buddah developed a reputation for superficiality in an era of passionate social upheaval. The charismatic, hands-on, 28-year-old president of Buddah, Neil Bogart (originally Bogatz), initially defined the niche as "pure entertainment ... about sunshine and going places and falling in love and dancing for the fun of it." For reasons both personal and economic, however, by 1971 it was a pigeonhole that he desperately wanted to escape.

From what Steve told me, everything he was doing was pretty primal. They were shooting chemo straight into his veins.
JOHN PRINE

"Those bubblegum records sold so many copies, but they were the laughingstock of the business," says Jude Lyons, who worked in Buddah's production and advertising departments at the time. Bogart, she says, "was trying real hard to go from a bubblegum company to being respected as an album-selling company, not only for the respect of it, but they needed to do it financially because the singles didn't make a lot of money, even though Buddah was selling millions of them."

The term "album selling" referred to artists who could promote their product via media interviews and record-store appearances while touring big cities and whose music would find favor on "progressive" or "underground" FM stations that aimed for a more left-leaning, young-adult market. Bogart's forays in that direction splayed all over the musical map. "Neil was a great gambler," says Buddah executive Lewis Merenstein. "Neil rolled all the dice all the time."

Bogart's gambits encompassed his signings of the eclectic Frank Zappa compatriot Don Van Vliet, whose stage name was Captain Beefheart; the New York ensemble Elephant's Memory, whose songs graced the film "Midnight Cowboy" and which later recorded with John Lennon and Yoko Ono; the R&B group Stairsteps, known for their hit "Ooh Child"; folk-rockers Brewer & Shipley ("One Toke over the Line"); so-called flower child Melanie (last name: Safka), who found fans with "Beautiful People" and "What Have They Done to My Song, Ma" after her appearance at the 1969 Woodstock festival; gospel groups Ocean ("Put Your Hand in the Hand") and the Edwin Hawkins Singers, known for "Oh, Happy Day" and backing Melanie on "Lay Down (Candles in the Rain)"; Richard Nixon mimic David Frye; the 1950s nostalgia group in a greaser get-up, Sha Na Na; and former teen idols James Darren, Bill Haley, Freddy Cannon, Gene Vincent, Chubby Checker and — yes — Paul Anka.

"We were notorious," says Ron Weisner, the Buddah artist-relations VP who in later years independently managed superstars Michael Jackson, Madonna, Steve Winwood, John Mellencamp and Paul McCartney. "We were the rebel company at that time. We would do things that nobody else would think of, in terms of signing people that nobody had any idea. We'd start from scratch, or we'd sign people that were absolutely dead to the world and bring 'em back. It was a David and Goliath story. We were the small company that would be up against all the big ones."

Would Steve Goodman fit into this diverse milieu? The outlook among Buddah brass was favorable, but not based on a spur-of-the-moment hunch. Anka had "passed the baton" to the label, Weisner says, and the deliberation over Steve's future with Buddah took time. As Weisner puts it, "It was a great team. Everybody contributed in a lot of ways to making things happen." The execs already had heard Buzzy Linhart's endorsement via the Quiet Knight. They also asked the advice of Mike Brewer and Tom Shipley (Brewer & Shipley), who had seen Steve in the spring at Chicago's Earl of Old Town. "Naturally, we thought he was great," Brewer says. Even the Bitter End manager, Paul Colby, got into the act, lobbying for Steve.

Neil Bogart was desperate to shed Buddah's bubblegum image when he considered signing Steve in mid-1971.

(Photo courtesy of John Rook)

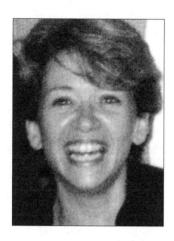

Buddah staffer Jude Lyons says the personas of Steve and John Prine were distinct: "Prine was more compared to Dylan. You would never put that to Stevie, even though his lyrics might have been as good. Stevie was more like Burl Ives. He almost was too cute sometimes."

(Photo courtesy of Jude Lyons)

4: In a later meeting with Neil Bogart and Buddah co-founder Art Kass, in which Steve and his manager Al Bunetta tried unsuccessfully to wrest the publishing royalty from Buddah, Steve uttered a memorable line: "Guys, allow me to change my pants before you pick my pockets."

One thing in Steve's favor, Lyons says, was a "fierce competition" developing between Buddah and Atlantic, fueled by the quick signing of Prine. (Intensifying the labels' rivalry a few months later, she says, was Atlantic's snaring of the up-and-coming Bette Midler, after Buddah "went crazy" to sign her. Not coincidentally, Midler recorded Prine's "Hello in There" on her debut Atlantic LP, released in 1972.) But the Buddah team wasn't necessarily sorry to lose Prine to Atlantic over Steve.

"Everybody (at Buddah) felt stronger about Steve," Weisner says. "Part of it was just him as a person. John was a little bit harder — talented but harder. Steve was a very soft, personable kind of person. They were both great, but they were completely different, and all of us collectively felt that Steve was the guy. And he had a different kind of hunger. Steve just wanted this vehicle to get his music out there, and it wasn't about an ego, and it wasn't about an attitude. It was just this hunger."

Steve's warmer personality along with his drive added up to a marketer's dream, Lyons says, because he would be able to "play the circuit, get the airplay, get the interviews and the audience and, consequently, get the sales." But she says Steve's hearty nature also had a down side: "Stevie could go a little overboard and not be as respected a musician. He almost went into comedy. John Prine was more compared to (Bob) Dylan. You would never put that to Stevie, even though his lyrics might have been as good. Stevie was more like Burl Ives. He almost was too cute sometimes. I have nothing but praise for him, but he almost bordered on being corny. That's why John Prine got more respect."

"People thought Prine was deeper and sang about Vietnam," adds Larry Harris, Buddah's national director of album promotion and Neil Bogart's cousin, "where Steve was much lighter. His stuff had humor, and it was fun. It wasn't depressing at all, like John's was. John also had the Dylan-esque kind of nasal sound, which people probably thought was cool and hip."

After all the discussion, Bogart offered Steve a contract, probably a standard one- to two-year arrangement, with options for Buddah to pick up at the end of that period. A provision that became contentious years later was that while the deal gave Steve his writing royalty, it ceded to Buddah Steve's publishing royalty. 4

The label, Weisner says, was prepared to give Steve unqualified support. "Our position was, if we really couldn't be aggressive and work it, we didn't want to make commitments to people," he says. "If we believed in somebody, we wanted to sign them, get the product done quickly, put a marketing and promotion campaign together and deliver it. Everybody would put our blinders on and do everything conceivably possible to make sure that that product and that act came through."

When the contract reached Steve, he signed enthusiastically like any first-timer. But compared to Prine's overnight deal, it had been a long wait — well into June, according to a reference in a Buddah press release issued six months later. (After Steve's Bitter End guest set, the release said, "the next three weeks were nervous ones for Goodman as he awaited word on whether he had a shot at an album.")

The anxious wait had an unexpected benefit, however, because it gave Steve the idea for an upbeat, laugh-in-the-face-of-disaster song. The press release said, "He was living in a rented room on the West Side and taking long walks in Central Park when he remembered an old blues line, of which there are a hundred versions and derivations: 'Been losin' so long, it feels like winnin' to me.'" The resulting tune invoked one sorry situation after another as suffered by a fictional Beverly Jones, a secretary with a doctorate in physics; by "my friend Fred," possibly a reference to Chicago singer Fred Holstein, losing $100 on a "hot tip" at the track; and by General George Custer, during his infamous "last stand" against the Sioux Indians.

The song eventually became the lead track on Steve's first LP and the composition with his longest-ever title: "The I Don't Know Where I'm Goin,' but I'm Goin' Nowhere in a Hurry Blues." Lyrically and melodically imaginative, the tune didn't wail like a traditional blues. Rather, it depicted the blues as might a witty journalist. His audiences later made it a frequent request because at the end he kept appending new and timely material. Mocking and mimicking the misfortunes of a growing litany of famous figures from ancient times through the 1970s, Steve rhymed their predicaments with the word "blues":

♦ Cleopatra, "when that asp crawled up her boobs."
♦ Marie Antoinette, "before her head rolled down to her shoes."
♦ Napoleon, "when he met with Wellington at Waterloo."
♦ Fatty Arbuckle, "when he leaned over to tie his shoes."
♦ Adolf Eichmann, "in that courtroom packed full of Jews."
♦ Richard Nixon, "when he turned on the Six O'Clock News" or "on the David Frost interview."
♦ New York City, "when Gerald Ford refused."
♦ Patty Hearst, "when they threw her in the calaboose."
♦ Muhammad Ali, "when Leon Spinks gave him the news."

Upon first hearing the song, those in Steve's circle couldn't help thinking that its comically existential sentiment was a deft autobiographical reference to his leukemia and treatment. Lines such as "I don't know how long the journey will last" and the title itself seemed obvious clues. "Kick me again and I'll come up grinning," says Dr. Isabel "Bonnie" Cunningham, then a record-keeper at Sloan-Kettering, "is about chemotherapy."

But apparently the fatal disease, with an uncertain prognosis of time left to live, was anything but obvious to Buddah. Lyons, Weisner and others insist that no one at the label knew that Steve was sick when Bogart offered him a contract. Certainly, they didn't hear it from Steve, who told Mike Miller, his Philadelphia folksinging friend and occasional boarder at Paula Ballan's apartment, that withholding the information was to his advantage.

"He didn't want anybody to say anything about the leukemia because he said Buddah didn't know about it," Miller says. "His disease was a secret, and

> **His disease was a secret. ... Buddah would not have invested money to promote his first album if they thought he was going to die and there wouldn't be a second one.**
> **MIKE MILLER**

The entrance to Steve and Nancy's apartment building at the corner of Wayne and Grace, shown in 2001, was five short blocks west of Wrigley Field.
(Photo by Clay Eals)

5: At the Earl, Bob Hoban and Steve watched one night as Bonnie Koloc performed Red River Dave McEnery's classic, "Amelia Earhart's Last Flight" while she stood atop a piano stool and waved her arms like a bird. Steve and Hoban laughed so hard that "snot shot out of our noses," Hoban says. Steve told Hoban, "I think I pissed myself" and ducked into the restroom, emerged with his wadded-up underwear and tossed the ball into the trash.

nobody was talking about it because if they had known, Buddah never would have agreed to make the recording. As he explained it, generally, first albums are not where you make your money. First albums are just like build-up things to sell the second album. It's your follow-up albums, when you have built a following, that sell. Buddah would not have invested money to promote his first album if they thought he was going to die and there wouldn't be a second one."

On the heels of Steve's Buddah contract, headlines from his home state provided him a shock. Late in the morning of Thursday, June 10, as the City of New Orleans left Effingham station, the front axle of its rear truck locked up, and as the train barreled south at 90 mph, its wheel-set developed a false flange and slid flat for 40 miles. At 12:30 p.m., when it was three miles north of Salem and passing the whistle stop of Tonti, the train derailed. Of the 211 passengers riding in its 13 coaches, 11 died and 163 were injured. It was the first fatal wreck for the barely one-month-old, consolidated and federally subsidized Amtrak. As graphic photos spread across the nation, it became an embarrassing blow. The tragedy also infused Steve's song about the "disappearin' railroad blues" with an unintentionally dreary and deadly serious meaning.

Steve's personal euphoria over the Buddah contract also was nagged by a mystery — when, where and with whom the recording session for his first LP would take place. No one at Buddah seemed motivated or able to find Steve a producer, which reflected an early indication of professional neglect by Paul Anka, who was busy performing and preparing to record an album of his own the next month at the Record Plant.

Back in Chicago, Steve and Nancy had moved to a $145/month apartment in a brick building at 3759 North Wayne Avenue, five short blocks west of Wrigley Field. In preparation for recording, Steve polished a handful of songs and tried them out on audiences for two weeks at the Earl of Old Town.[5] There, he also continued to build friendships with touring musicians such as Indianapolis-based Bill Swofford, who under his middle name of Oliver had notched the 1969 hits "Good Morning Starshine" (#3 in *Billboard*) and the million-selling "Jean" (#2) and had switched to a folk-rock persona.

Steve also encountered a hometown hero's welcome similar to the one recently accorded Prine. "We felt like they might as well have thrown a tickertape parade, at least in the folk community," says Prine, who was fully aware of their unusual status. "There were people in Chicago for years on the edge of havin' a recording contract, and they all had to leave — I mean, totally leave, not just leave overnight or for a week — and make their home in L.A. or New York. I'm talkin' about people that were always drawing in clubs in Chicago and were names in Chicago, and they still couldn't get arrested as far as a record contract. To get an actual record deal and be livin' in Chicago was pretty much unheard of. The fact that Steve and I had kinda overnight gone to New York and came back with these record contracts, it was the talk of the town, man."

The success story helped Steve retrieve the publishing royalty for "City of New Orleans," which Chicagoans Dick Boyell and Bill Traut returned to him free of charge so that he could cede it to Buddah. "I was glad for him and that I had helped him a little bit," Traut says. "We were very happy about Steve getting that kind of break."

But without a producer, how would Steve move forward with a recording? The solution emerged when Steve traveled to Washington, D.C., to open for Kris Kristofferson the week of July 4-10 at the 200-seat Cellar Door. As with later such double bills, Steve "blew me off the stage," Kristofferson says. "The guy had only 35 or 45 minutes to shoot all his ammunition. I mean, can you imagine following that little son of a bitch? I had to have more courage than sense." Between sets, Steve sought advice from his musical mentor because "nobody else would produce the record. Nobody else had any ideas as to what to do," Steve told *Omaha Rainbow*.

"Hey, man, I hate to do this to you," Steve told Kristofferson. "You've already done everything else, but do you know any record producers by name who you could call up and talk them into taking this one?"

The query reflected Steve's willingness to tie his musical identity to the blurred lines between genres embodied by the popular Kristofferson. New York had been the Mecca for folk, and Nashville had played the same role for country-western, but Kristofferson (as with Bob Dylan and his 1969 "Nashville Skyline" LP) was one of the main forces in fusing the two. Though Steve publicly disavowed musical pigeonholes, if pressed he would have had to classify himself, at heart, as a folkie. Still, the songs he performed and wrote embraced all categories, from country to R&B, from rock to Tin Pan Alley pop. Turning to the similarly genre-blind Kristofferson was less an act of desperation than a step of symbolism.

Steve's request also tapped into Kristofferson's intimate knowledge of Nashville's elite, including bassist and R&B/soul aficionado Norbert Putnam, who had earned industry fame as part of the Muscle Shoals studio rhythm section in northwest Alabama. Putnam had rescued Kristofferson earlier in 1971 by filling in as producer for Joan Baez' two-LP set "Blessed Are," which featured her hit version of The Band's "The Night They Drove Old Dixie Down." Kristofferson had been announced as producer for the Baez project, but only a few hours into it he felt inadequate for the job and asked the help of Putnam, who with David Briggs had just opened Quadrafonic Sound Studios and was turning it into Nashville's latest hip locale for record-making. It was to be the setting for the recording of Steve's first album for Buddah.

"Here's the thing," Kristofferson told Steve. "I've never done one, but I'll do it. I've got three days in August, and we'll do it with Norbert because he knows the studios and the players, and between the two of us, we'll get something."

Steve's gratitude to Kristofferson was immeasurable. "It wasn't going to happen at all," he told *Omaha Rainbow*. "Shit, he saved it." For WGN-AM's Roy Leonard in 1972, Steve called the involvement of Kristofferson and Putnam a "lucky break" that gave him "an air of legitimacy" that he was "sorely lacking." It also helped him catch up with Prine, who already had started studio work.

The guy had only 35 or 45 minutes to shoot all his ammunition. I mean, can you imagine following that little son of a bitch? I had to have more courage than sense.
KRIS KRISTOFFERSON

Atlantic Records served up veteran R&B and jazz producer Arif Mardin to helm Prine's first album for sessions in July with some of Elvis Presley's accompanists at Memphis-based American Recording Studios. Steve, who witnessed the sessions, said 10 years later that Prine's "one-take wonder" on his old-people's lament "Hello in There" was "the best record session I ever saw." Dissatisfied with the track for one of his signature songs, the anti-strip-mining broadside "Paradise," Prine and Mardin returned to New York later that month and booked time to re-record it at A&R Studios. There, while Prine's older brother Dave provided backup fiddle, Steve sang high harmony and played guitar for the song and added an acoustic-guitar solo to "Flashback Blues."

Anka, while focused on his own music, wasn't out of the picture. The week that Steve and the two Prines were re-cutting "Paradise" in Manhattan, Anka played the expansive host, inviting the trio and other musicians to a late-night gathering at his two-floor, four-bedroom Upper East Side townhouse, 20 blocks north of Sloan-Kettering. Inside, a huge crystal chandelier hung over a winding staircase that connected a lemon-yellow dining room, a living room filled with French furniture and a den with a Steinway spinet, fur rugs, a tufted sofa and a wall that showcased 18 gold records. The surroundings were startlingly luxurious to the scruffy guests.

> It was a night of all kinds of contradictions — conversations, just us bein' dressed as we were and Anka's swanky apartment. We were seein' how odd it was to be aligned-up with Paul Anka.
> **JOHN PRINE**

"My brother had a bottle of Jack (Daniel's) hangin' out his back pocket and a fiddle in his other hand," John Prine says. "We all looked like we should come in the service entrance. It was a night of all kinds of contradictions — conversations, just us bein' dressed as we were and Anka's swanky apartment. We were seein' how odd it was to be aligned up with Paul Anka."

The party's setting and goings-on were so opulent (including trendy Goldberg's Pizza that a maid served on gold plates and cutlery) that Steve took mischievous delight in recounting the event in concerts in coming years. Curiously, he noted, Anka's party focused on a form of entertainment different from the one that tied the crowd together — the movies.

"One wall of his living room became a screen, and out came these two 35mm projectors," Steve said. First up were clips from Anka's early, abortive film career, including "The Longest Day," the star-studded D-Day epic from 1962 in which he had a minor role and for which he co-wrote a song. (Steve also incorrectly stated that Anka ran clips from a 1958 film that Anka made with Annette Funicello. No such film was produced, so it's possible Anka screened excerpts from his films "Girls Town" or "The Private Lives of Adam and Eve," released in 1959 and 1960, and in which the featured female was Mamie Van Doren.)

Switching gears, Anka "made us watch stag movies until 5:30 in the morning," Steve said. In time for this portion of the party, Anka's doorbell rang. Donnie Fritts answered it to find a "great-looking gal," two bodyguards and the sexually charged pop singer Tom Jones, whose version of Anka's "She's a Lady" was flooding the AM radio dial. The juxtaposition of guest and activity did not escape Steve's sardonic eye. "Live and learn," Steve told a 1972 audience at the Cambridge (England) Folk Festival. "I would have thought the one fellow in the whole world who doesn't have to watch stroke-and-jerk movies would be Tom Jones. He was breakin' an illusion I had." [6]

The Nashville milieu would prove to be a similar eye-opener for Steve the following month. Likewise, Music City studio regulars such as the 29-year-old Norbert Putnam knew next to nothing about Steve. Because Kristofferson had brought Putnam success with Baez' version of "The Night They Drove Old Dixie Down," Putnam says he "couldn't say no" to Steve's project. Besides, Kristofferson provided Putnam a blanket reassurance about Steve: "He's one of the real guys. He can do it. Just get those guys."

"Those guys" were an aggregation of musicians known informally by a geographical moniker: Area Code 615. Needing little rehearsal and ready at a moment's notice to back up and enhance the recordings of any performer from any category, the group — including guitarists Grady Martin, Billy Sanford and Pete Wade, harmonica player Charlie McCoy and Kenny Buttrey on drums, along with Briggs on piano — had acquired a mythical prestige in music circles.

So in the first days of August 1971, Steve, who had just turned 23, flew to Nashville and received entrée to a country-based world that was to shape his initial image to the record-buying public nationwide. This physical world, however, was hardly vast. Quadrafonic was simply a converted 1905 house. "The control room was on the porch," Putnam says. "Steve was in the living room, where there was a grand piano, electric guitars, a bass. The kitchen was for the drums, separated by a glass window. It was an innovative place because it had the first isolated drum booth."

The atmosphere was rather homey as well. "We did the son of a bitch in three and a half days, just non-stop, and the whole damn thing was a party," Steve told *Omaha Rainbow*. "I don't think there was anybody who wasn't high for under 35 to 40 seconds of the entire record. I didn't have the slightest clue what to do. I just said, 'Great, you mean I go in there, and I sing out loud? Outasight.' They were trying to figure out what the hell I was doing. I gotta thank them for that 'cause I must have appeared so off-the-wall to those cats. It wasn't like Dylan coming down with a real concept of what he wanted to do when he made that first Nashville album. I stumbled in there. ... I'd just written half the fuckin' songs that I was going to cut. I didn't know what they were supposed to sound like or anything. I just figured, though, that if you don't go do it, you'll never find out."

Kristofferson, who says he was constantly drinking cheap wine that week, confirms the party atmosphere, but Nashville's intense, "in and out" work ethic was also at full bore. "If you didn't get three songs in three hours, you felt like you were not up to speed," he says. "It was a party, but you could get stuff done."

Quite a few of Kristofferson's friends and other singers and songwriters showed up for the sessions. Some, like Mickey Newbury and Sammi Smith, came to observe, while others, like Joan Baez, Bill Swofford, Bucky Wilkin, Tom Ghent (recording an album of his own), Linda Hargrove, sisters Mary and Ginger

> **I don't think there was anybody who wasn't high for under 35 to 40 seconds of the entire record. I didn't have the slightest clue what to do. I just said, 'Great, you mean I go in there, and I sing out loud? Outasight.'**
> **STEVE GOODMAN**

6: When Steve saw Tom Jones' stage act a year later, he marveled: "His whole thing is, he walks out onstage and, I mean, challenges you, right? He looks right at you and says, 'I don't know about you fuckheads, but I get mine.' It's the attitude, man. He sweats that, y'know? He actually cops an attitude about it. It's really somethin' to see."

Norbert Putnam, co-producer of Steve's first LP, knew Steve would find performing for Nashville's god-like session musicians stressful: "They'd take his tunes, just turn them inside out."

(Photo courtesy of Norbert Putnam)

7: Two songs that Steve chose not to record at the Nashville session were "Lincoln Park Pirates" and "Paul Powell," both of which he had just written late that summer. At the time, he believed their lyrics were too tied to Chicago and Illinois to appeal to a national audience. See the next two chapters for details.

8: In an attempted comeback after battling drug addiction, Bob Gibson had recorded a six-minute version of "Sam Stone" on a self-titled album on Capitol Records in 1970. But after it drew increasing airplay, Prine's label, Atlantic, went to court and enjoined Gibson's LP to keep it from eclipsing Prine's version, released in late 1971.

Holiday and even Prine, hung out to chime in with backup vocals. Of the milieu, Prine says, "Me and Goodman, we were the kids with our heads under the circus tent lookin' into the whole thing." With such a constant flow of visitors and a tight timeline and budget (about $45,000, including $2,000 a day for the studio alone), a lot of the project's outcome depended upon the steerage of Putnam and Kristofferson.

Kristofferson says he never had illusions about what he contributed. "I got my name on it, but I wasn't really a producer," he says. "I've always felt a little guilty about any of the production part, but for some reason my name would get things going in those days. Putnam knew what he was doing. He did all the real work. I would do stuff like talk to the singers." Putnam, who directed proceedings while wearing headphones and playing bass inside the control room, plays up Kristofferson's role. "Kris offered his ideas throughout," he says. "I knew how to record properly from a technical standpoint, but he knew how to talk to the musicians. He had wonderful musical instincts."

Putnam and Kristofferson both credit Steve himself for supplying the sessions an emotional rudder. "Steve was a sweet, loveable, warm little guy," Putnam says. "He was infectious and put everybody at ease. It was very pleasant for me, and he helped make it that way. I'm sure that underneath his skin, he was experiencing quite a bit of stress. These players are very intimidating because they're like gods. They'd take his tunes, just turn them inside out, and Steve went, 'Oh, my goodness.' It really was something to become comfortable with. Very few artists can do it the first time. But by the second day, he was having the time of his life."

"He was quite humble, but totally charming," Kristofferson adds. "He was such a funny guy to be around and such a bright spirit. He was so alive, I'd never even think about the fact that he had leukemia."

Word of Steve's disease was whispered around the Quad studio, but "he looked the picture of health," Putnam says. "We all knew leukemia could be fatal, but I don't remember anybody treating him with kid gloves. He was always joking. He was jovial. He was funny, witty."

The wit, of course, flowed from the gentle humor inherent in several songs that Steve brought along to record, [7] including his shaggy-dog story, "Turnpike Tom"; the country parody he wrote with John Prine, "You Never Even Call Me by My Name"; and the existentially comic tune whose title alone could summon smiles, "The I Don't Know Where I'm Goin' but I'm Goin' Nowhere in a Hurry Blues."

Sly grins in the studio also greeted "Donald and Lydia," the Prine-written fantasy romance between two outcasts who had never met but "made love" with each other via simultaneous sexual self-gratification. "I wanted to cut one of his, and it could have been any of them," Steve told *Omaha Rainbow*. "I didn't think anybody else would have the nerve to cut that one. I figured there'd be about four million covers of 'Sam Stone' [8] and a couple of others. ... He told me he didn't think anyone else would cut 'Donald and Lydia,' so I said, 'This one is special.' " As if winking at the subject of the song, Kristofferson and his current paramour, Baez, supplied background harmonies ("the sublime and the ridiculous together," Kristofferson says), with Baez' hummed vibrato unmistakably permeating the third verse.

Turning again to Chicago for another selection, Steve honored his relationship with the Holstein brothers by recording Ed Holstein's "Jazzman," a tongue-in-cheek (and everywhere else) glorification of the easy sex that a self-absorbed performer seeks from fawning females. Filled with double entendres, the racy ditty also had just been covered by Tom Rush and Bonnie Koloc.

Steve tackled three more renditions of others' songs during the sessions, including one that served as a tangible expression of appreciation to Kristofferson. "Rainbow Road," a rags-to-riches-to-prison yarn penned by Kristofferson's organist, Donnie Fritts, and Dan Penn, featured Fritts on organ. "I was wondering how I could thank Kris and all those people for everything they'd done, and I didn't know how he would feel about producing one of his own songs with me singin' it," Steve told *Omaha Rainbow*. "I loved all the guys, and Kris was singing 'Rainbow Road' in his set and kept saying how nice it would be if someone had a hit with Donnie Fritts' good tune." [9]

> **The only reason we did it country, shit, we're in Nashville, let's see what it sounds like country.**
> **STEVE GOODMAN**

The two other songs of others that Steve recorded were direct nods to Nashville. In a live-in-the-studio rendition, he took on a 1949 tune by country legend Hank Williams, "Mind Your Own Business," whose message held personal appeal to Steve in trying to deflect questions about his leukemia. He also reached into what he called his "bar band background" to sing a twangy version of Johnny Otis' "So Fine," an R&B and pop hit in 1959 for a black vocal-harmony group, the Fiestas. "The only reason we did it country, shit, we're in Nashville, let's see what it sounds like country."

The showpiece of the sessions was the song Steve had written 16 months earlier, "City of New Orleans," but its recording was steeped in incongruity. Literally, "City" was a clarion call to save the country's failing railroads and, metaphorically, the nation itself. But in its Nashville incarnation, the song instead exuded an air of celebration. Backed by a bouncy beat to approximate the "rhythm of the rails" found in the lyric and accompanied by the nostalgic wails of Charlie McCoy's harmonica, Steve's voice radiated contentment, as did the chorus of indistinguishable vocals on the repeated line of "Good morning, America, how are ya?"

Compounding the vocal irony was one that was wholly instrumental. The recording of "City" featured four guitarists — Stephen Bruton and Pete Wade on rhythm, Bucky Wilkin on 12-string and Billy Sanford (revered for his intro on Roy Orbison's "Oh Pretty Woman") on lead — but not Steve. "We couldn't get it with me playing rhythm guitar," Steve told *Omaha Rainbow*. "That happens sometimes, and I went for a walk around the block. When I got back, they played me a real good-sounding track, and I went in and sang on it." Steve told Putnam he thought he could play a better lead line than Sanford's, and Putnam offered him a chance. "All the musicians left the studio," says Tom Ghent. "They

9: Inspired by Steve's version, Baez recorded "Rainbow Road" on an LP of her own, "Come from the Shadows," in the following year.

sat Steve down, and he tried it for about 10 minutes, and he finally said, 'No, I think that Billy got it better.' But Steve took a shot at it, and I don't blame him.''

For this album, Steve avoided his bleaker material, including "Song for David," "Climb the Hills to Dale," "Song for Sally" and "Where Are You Goin' Mister?" Of these, the only song he eventually put on vinyl was his cryptic meditation on facing leukemia, "Song for David," delaying its official debut until his second LP, where it could hide among showier tunes.

Steve didn't spare the Nashville project a few somber compositions, however. One was his "Eight Ball Blues" whose introspective lyrics had been revealed more quietly and sensitively on the "Gathering" LP earlier in the year but were belied by the full-bore, instrument-laden presentation it received at Quad. "That's got nothing but busting hump guitar on it, and Buttrey smashing on the drums," Steve said. "I could have said no and done it acoustic, and Kris would have let me." Steve later regretted the heavy-handed approach to the song. "There was about 30 musicians in the studio," he told Howard Larman of L.A.'s "FolkScene" radio show, "and the track sounded so good when they were playin' it ... that if I'd had another set of lyrics for it, we probably could have had a rock 'n' roll smash record, 'cause that's a great track, man, but it sure don't fit 'Eight Ball Blues.' " At the time, however, Steve bowed to his benefactors.

Another contemplative contribution, "Would You Like to Learn to Dance?" drew an arrangement that differed startlingly from the loud ones. Perhaps because it was Kristofferson's favorite, the song was given a delicate treatment, including a classical-guitar solo by Grady Martin, the gruff-looking but gentle picker who had anchored countless country sessions while sipping Jack Daniel's whiskey from a swiveling easy chair parked in the corner of the studio. Martin, who had played on three Baez albums, dropped by the sessions to see her, ended up intrigued with Steve and played on three of Steve's cuts.

Steve's fatal disease gripped the emotions of the Buddha-like Martin, who Putnam says looked at Steve as if he were thinking, "You poor kid, you're going to be dead." At one point, Steve admired Martin's handmade Spanish guitar, worth more than $5,000 and identical to one played by famed classical guitarist Andres Segovia, and Martin simply gave it to him. "I want you to have it. It's yours," Martin said. (Months later, Martin had second thoughts. "It was his favorite acoustic guitar, and he got to feeling bad about it," Kristofferson says. When Martin telephoned Steve to ask for its return, Steve bought the guitar a plane ticket and put it on a plane back to Nashville.)

Picking on gut strings, made from the small intestines of sheep, Martin supplied a warm hue to another quiet piece that dangled a series of questions — "Yellow Coat," a tender, lost-love song that Steve had composed in Paula Ballan's apartment that summer. Though written as only one end of a conversation, the lyrics vividly convey the complete picture of a wistful young man trying to reconnect with his taciturn former lover by reminiscing about their experiences and dreams, including the repeated line, "Tell me how you've been. Did you ever get to buy that yellow coat?" Semi-autobiographical, the song may have

> **The track sounded so good when they were playin' it ... that if I'd had another set of lyrics for it, we probably could have had a rock 'n' roll smash record, 'cause that's a great track, man, but it sure don't fit 'Eight Ball Blues.'**
> **STEVE GOODMAN**

been an attempt by Steve to put his previous relationships with women behind him. It apparently threaded into a coherent whole the scraps of experiences with several significant females in Steve's life, including the one who had flown in from Chicago to briefly visit him at Paula Ballan's apartment shortly after his leukemia treatment began and perhaps Jeany Walker, who indeed owned a bright yellow, woolen coat.

In later years, Steve discussed only vaguely the realities behind "Yellow Coat." When Philadelphia radio host Gene Shay asked him in 1974, "Is that a true story?" Steve had a self-mocking reply: "Yeah, it is, sorta, but on account of situations I had to change some of the facts to protect the innocent. Only the facts have changed. Just the fiction, ma'am, just the fiction." Two years later, he said, "I've met that person again. A few minor structural details happened and keep happening." [10]

More important than its veracity was that the song was one of Steve's best uses of specifics to paint a sentiment to which anyone could relate. "When you see someone after a long time and neither of you have anything to say, it's just a shame to see a situation we've all experienced and see it completely empty," Steve told *Omaha Rainbow*. "It hits me that it's the most universal song that I've ever written, because that's just the way it goes. When it's there, it's wonderful, and when it isn't, phew! You can see ice cubes in the air. It's like emptying a big ice cube tray all over the place." [11]

A week after the sessions, Putnam and engineers Gene Eichelberger and Gene Hazen folded in overdubs and mixed the tracks. Putnam says his approach to the project, and all others, was to create musical "wallpaper" behind a singer. "We sell emotion," he says, "and people who buy records are emotionally moved by the timbre of the voice of the singer." But there is no question that during the recording of Steve's album, the wallpaper threatened to steal center stage from the solo performer. From a brassy, Dixieland opening for "Nowhere in a Hurry Blues," to the walls of sound in "Eight Ball Blues," "Jazzman" and horn-heavy "Rainbow Road," it was often a strain to detect and absorb Steve's oral and instrumental "voice." Even the quiet "Yellow Coat" was nagged by a persistent harmonica whine. Using kind terms in later years, Steve acknowledged such overproduction.

"The feeling on it is great," Steve told Al Rudis of the *Chicago Sun-Times* while reflecting on the LP in 1975, "but it ain't necessarily what my music is. But that's OK because at that time, I didn't necessarily have all that great an idea of what the hell I was, either. They make good sounding records in Nashville, so the sound quality on it was wonderful. I was basically pretty happy with it, for where I was at the time."

Kristofferson put it much more bluntly when he later crossed paths with Steve: "Sorry, man, about fuckin' up your album."

Others refute such self-deprecation. Ghent, a friend of Kristofferson who had known Steve since their Greenwich Village days in 1967, insists that the sole factor that kept the LP from descending to a faceless formula was

10: Carrie Ann Warner of Evergreen, Colorado, says that her late mother, an intelligent, flamboyant Chicago club waitress named Cathy Szajko, had claimed to be the inspiration for "Yellow Coat." Warner recalls childhood years when her mom repeatedly pointed out a yellow, patchwork, vinyl coat in the window of a secondhand store near the Quiet Knight on Belmont near Sheffield. Warner says that when she was 11 and attending the 1981 Chicago Fest, she asked Steve if her mother's assertion was true and that Steve confirmed it.

11: When Fred Holstein first heard "Yellow Coat," he had a question for Steve. Holstein, whose yen for folk music stemmed from its breadth of topics that rose above the ubiquitous, one-note laments over failed relationships, asked Steve, "How come there are so many songs about unrequited love?" Steve cracked, "Freddie, if your relationship is working out, you don't have time to write songs." Steve later worked the quip into his onstage routine.

The team of Larry Rand (left) and Rich Markow, shown in 1981, got "the ultimate compliment" from Steve in August 1971 — the admonition to sing one of his songs.

(Photo by Art Thieme)

12: Markow and Rand later "fooled around" with the song but felt they couldn't do it justice. "Steve, you're working all over town," Rand said. "What's going to be useful about it? We can't do it any better than you doing it. We tried, and it's just not as good." But Rand says Steve was not pleased. "He wanted us to do it."

13: Carl Martin's gift to Steve's wife, Nancy, on their return trip from Philadelphia also drew Steve's admiration. "We stopped at a Stuckey's in Michigan," Steve said, "and he bought a present of a key chain for my wife. On the key chain, it had one of those little telescope things that you look through with a picture at the end of it. There were two women eating each other." Steve said Martin told Nancy, "You don't think there's anything wrong with that, do you?" The story became a constant in Steve's later concerts.

Kristofferson. "People listened when Kris talked to them," Ghent says. "He would stop everything and take Norbert aside and say, 'Well, I don't think you've got this quite right.' A lot of the expertise in putting the record together had to do with Norbert and the entire studio band, because those guys made records day in and day out, but the fact that the record conveyed Steve Goodman as well as it did was due to Kris."

Upon his return to Chicago, Steve was flush with intensity from the heady experience, and his friends' reception was triumphal. At a late-night gathering with friends, Steve proudly played the LP's rough tapes over and over. Steve also stormed into the Earl of Old Town and encountered Larry Rand, who by that time was billed with fellow satirist Rich Markow as a comedy duo. Sitting at a table with Rand, Steve pulled out a few of the bar's blank guest checks, scribbled out the lyrics to "Nowhere in a Hurry Blues" and slammed them on the table.

"When are you guys going to start doing this?" he demanded.

"What do you mean?" Rand said.

"I've listened to you two, I've wanted to write a song like you guys do, so here it is. Now, do it."

Rand grins at the memory. "It was the ultimate compliment," he said. [12]

While awaiting the release of his LP, however, Steve didn't stick around Chicago. "I was out on the road," he told Al Rudis. "I was crazy like that before the record." Late that summer and early fall of 1971, he returned to the telephone circuit, picking up $200 to $300 a week at clubs in the Georgia cities of Atlanta, Savannah and Athens, as well as in Louisville and Miami. Steve also made what was becoming a traditional pilgrimage to the Philadelphia Folk Festival. This time, he drove a station wagon 950 miles east with Nancy and what he termed "a whole car full of old-timer musicians": bluesman Jim Brewer and a Chicago-based, African-American string-band trio for which Steve had signed on as a devoted champion: Martin, Bogan & Armstrong.

Carl Martin (mandolin and guitar), 65, Ted Bogan (guitar), 61, and Howard Armstrong (fiddle and mandolin), 62, had performed in roadhouses, bordellos and speakeasies as part of such "race" groups as the Tennessee Chocolate Drops, the Four Keys String Band and the Four Aces in the late 1920s and 1930s. For decades, they had gone separate ways, with Martin working as a Chicago street asphalter and Armstrong building cars in Detroit, but Armstrong's retirement from Chrysler earlier in 1971 triggered the trio's reunion. Thanks to Steve, those attending the Philly festival's Friday and Saturday sets (and overnight motel jam sessions) received their first earful of the inexhaustible group's upbeat repertoire of pop standards, rags, blues, jigs, polkas, spirituals, international songs and show tunes. "They've been turnin' everybody's head around," Steve told a Sunday workshop. "Musicians have just been pourin' into the room to take notes on what these cats are puttin' down."

Steve became particularly close to Carl Martin, [13] in part because of his admiration for Martin's tune, "The Barnyard Dance" (also known as "The Vegetable Song"), a frothy romp that humanized a group of peas, cabbage, beans, beets and other farm-grown foods that made their own music and strutted their stuff at a late-night "spree." Steve enjoyed its playful rhymes, such as "little tomato, agitator" and "old man garlic dropped dead of the colic," and soon adopted the song as a staple of his own act.

As arresting as Martin, Bogan & Armstrong were at the Friday mainstage show, Steve was equally impressed by an earlier act that night, flatpicker and finger-stylist Doc Watson, who performed with his son Merle. At an earlier Philly festival, sitting next to Laura Haynes (now Aiken) of the festival's backbone family during a Watson set, Steve had revealed his deep regard for the master guitarist. "I'll never be that good," he had told Haynes, adding as he gestured to his guitar, "I'll never play this again." [14]

His self-mocking vow, of course, proved untrue at the 1971 festival. Fresh from his Nashville recording session, Steve left a deep impression, personally as well as professionally. Dulcimer player and workshop leader Chuck Klein, who had a medical background and whose father was in a long remission from leukemia, was taken by Steve's fortitude. "Given that he would be in constant treatment and had no clue about life expectancy, the logical lifestyle wasn't going to involve scraping a living as a traveling musician on the road all the time," Klein says. "But here was a guy who was so driven to have the life that he wanted, and so talented that he could actually pull it off. It was amazing."

Steve's Saturday night set, just four songs, was his first billed appearance at Philly. As he took the mainstage with an unrehearsed trio of backing guitarists — Steve Burgh, Jack McGann and David Bromberg, who all would figure prominently in his future recordings — he leapt at the chance to showcase "City of New Orleans." ("It's gonna do a lot for me," Steve told bluesman Paul Geremia during the festival. "People really like it, and I think it's gonna make all the difference in the world.") Steve also revealed a confidence bordering on cockiness. Bounding through "City," Steve threw in new lyrics: "shootin' craps," "nine's my point," "the bag that holds the Tequila" and a biting change, in the final verse, replacing "I'm your native son" with "I'm your bastard son."

The brashness persisted as Steve gave a sharp read to the weary Bobby Bare/ Billy Joe Shaver anti-war elegy, "Good Christian Soldier," which Kristofferson had just recorded on his "The Silver Tongued Devil and I" LP. Then Steve turned pointedly to Prine's "Donald & Lydia": "Here's one that's a little bit crazy. This one's about masturbation, the only song I ever heard on the subject that was anywhere near sensitive. This ain't no joke. This is actually a song, my friends." As if to counter any shock he'd just induced, Steve closed with the Hank Williams admonition he had just recorded, "Mind Your Own Business."

Steve wasn't finished with indignity, however. The next afternoon, he delved more deeply at a bawdy-songs workshop led by 61-year-old Oscar Brand, host of WNYC-AM's weekly "Folksong Festival" since 1945. Because of heavy rains and mud, the workshop shifted from a remote, ground-level side stage to the festival's elevated mainstage. There, at about 3:45 p.m. and with Brand's help, Steve goaded an audience of 5,000 to join him in singing what *Crawdaddy*

Steve introduced a uniquely entertaining African-American string-band trio at the 1971 Philly festival: from left, Howard Armstrong, Carl Martin and Ted Bogan (above, at the Earl of Old Town in Chicago, backed on bass by Armstrong's son, Tom "Rap" Armstrong).
(Photo by P. Michael O'Sullivan)

14: Doc Watson had his own fondness for Steve. Watson made Steve a tape, at Steve's request, of a 1963 LP, "Koto & Flute," featuring Kimio Eto, a blind Japanese man, on koto and Bud Shank on flute. Watson especially liked Steve's "City of New Orleans" because "it tells it like it is. He had a way of telling a story in a song that left you thinking and thinking and thinking about it. You realized just what all the song says. You're on that train. It's real."

Paula Ballan, a fellow performer in the notorious bawdy-songs workshop at the Philadelphia Folk Festival in 1971, recalls that Steve had "full audience participation from five on down" when he sang "The Twelve Days of Syphilis."

(Photo courtesy of Paula Ballan)

magazine later called "a thoroughly filthy, absolutely delightful" Christmas-carol parody dubbed "The Twelve Days of Syphilis." Steve said he'd learned the ditty six years earlier in what he termed the "provincial" environment of the University of Illinois, where the state's 1947 Clabaugh Act, a McCarthy-esque law overturned in 1968, had eliminated "subversive" speeches. "They don't let Socialist speakers speak there, but they let you sing these songs," Steve said. The lyrics swelled with lines for which no one ever would likely claim authorship:

Twelve tons of Vaseline
eleven lesbians licking
ten twats a-twitching
nine nipples dripping
eight gaping assholes
seven scrotums swinging
six sacks of shit
five motherfuckers!

Four cocksuckers
three French ticklers
two brass balls
and a hand job in a hair tree

Another workshop performer, Paula Ballan, notes that Steve had "full audience participation from five on down." Because the workshop employed the mainstage's better-amplified sound system, the profanity carried to nearby farmhouses, whose residents responded with a campaign to exile the festival from its rural site. The neighbors filed suit against the festival but relented after leaders agreed to stricter conditions starting in 1972, including a decibel cap, a maximum audience of 15,000 and a provision that Steve would confront five years later — a midnight curfew on the Sunday closing night.

Nearly four months after the 1971 festival, on a late December night in Chicago after he had just returned from the road, Steve risked performing "The Twelve Days of Syphilis" again. With saucer eyes, Steve told Ed and Fred Holstein in the Star Cave of the Earl, "I just learned the grossest song I ever heard. You guys are gonna love it. This song is so awful." When he sang it to them, Ed Holstein and his brother found it "grim," but because a full house was waiting, the two goaded Steve to do it for the crowd.

"Nah, I don't think it'd be appropriate," Steve told them. "It's two days before Christmas."

"Steve, it's your room, your night, go ahead," Ed said. "These are your people. You've gotta do the song."

"You think so?"

Taking the bait, Steve took the stage and got three or four verses into the profane parody. But the listeners groaned, scooted their chairs and wrinkled their faces into scowls. "It felt like it might be his last day in show business," Ed says with a laugh. Recognizing his blunder, Steve halted the tune, muttered, "You get the idea," and broke into "City of New Orleans." Afterward, the Holsteins roared at him as he told Ed in mock fury, "You put me up to it. I'm not gonna talk to you for a month, you motherfucker."

Steve's initial instincts had collided with his penchant for risk-taking, and the audience's reaction had proven his instincts correct. "Guys like the locker-room stuff, but it wasn't appropriate," Ed Holstein says. The bawdy song would have worked "maybe at 3 o'clock in the morning when all the lowlifes were there, but this was prime time."

In the fall of 1971, awaiting his LP release, Steve found other ways to pursue the elusive goal of national prime time. Steve's newfound friend, Bill "Oliver" Swofford, bid him back to Nashville to assist during two days of sessions at the studio of Fred Carter Jr., known for his guitar intro for the Simon & Garfunkel hit "The Boxer."

There, Steve sat in the control room with Scott Turner (the veteran producer of Slim Whitman, Vicki Carr and the early Harry Nilsson) while Swofford and a Nashville rhythm section laid down a dozen delightful tracks. The output included four Swofford originals, two John Prine songs and Steve's "Eight Ball Blues." On several tunes, Steve supplied harmony vocals, including a low-pitched "My baby tells me so" on "So Fine." During Swofford's recording of Prine's cryptic ode to marijuana, "Illegal Smile," Steve suggested the flatulent sound of a tuba to underscore the song's whimsy. Oddly enough, multi-instrumentalist Charlie McCoy happened to have a tuba in the trunk of his car, and Steve's proposal quickly became reality. But the tapes, which survive in Turner's library, never reached commercial release.

Another entertainer with national stature, whose breakthrough song had just topped the pop charts, also beckoned Steve that fall — John Denver.

Denver's "Take Me Home, Country Roads," written mainly by backup duo Fat City (Bill Danoff and Taffy Nivert) with a dash of Denver's help, had burst onto the radio the previous spring. Its warm, singable chorus was both inescapable and irresistible as it rose to #2 in *Billboard*. Denver (a stage name to replace his birth name of Deutschendorf) had briefly led a group that succeeded the Chad Mitchell Trio after Mitchell's departure, and Denver had earned prominence for having penned Peter, Paul & Mary's million-selling 1969 #1 single, "Leaving, on a Jet Plane." But "Country Roads" provided the bespectacled, boyish blond his first entrée into America's mainstream, and sales for the single — and, correspondingly, his fourth RCA album, "Poems, Prayers and Promises" — sizzled at 1.3 million copies. As RCA punned in a full-page *Billboard* ad, "It seems today all roads are leading to Denver."

Scavenging follow-up hit material became Denver's primary pursuit. (Keith Christianson, who had managed Denver, said that when "Country Roads" took off, Denver told him, "I never thought about it. Now I've got to have another one, and then I've got to have another one.") One artist Denver looked to was the late Buddy Holly, and in June, Denver had recorded a slowed-down version

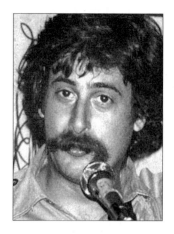

Ed Holstein, shown at the mike of the Earl of Old Town, goaded Steve to perform his bawdy "Twelve Days of Syphilis" parody in December 1971, knowing full well that it would bomb during "prime time" at the club. "Guys like the locker-room stuff, but it wasn't appropriate," Holstein says.
(Photo by Mitch Gawlik)

John Denver, shown in 1973, wanted to record "City of New Orleans" in the fall of 1971 but alerted Steve that he wanted to make alterations: "I don't think it is commercial the way it is, and I want to rewrite the last verse because I think I can say something with it."

(Photo by Clay Eals)

of Holly's joyful 1958 ode to new love, "Everyday." Holly was in vogue because Don McLean's epic "American Pie" was rising on the charts and had anchored its narrative on "the day the music died," a reference to the 1959 plane crash that killed popular rockers Holly, Richie Valens and the Big Bopper.

In the first week in September, when Denver and Fat City were playing the Troubadour in Hollywood, another hit candidate fell into Denver's lap. Sitting next to the rooftop swimming pool of the Continental Hyatt House hotel (featured 30 years later in the film "Almost Famous"), Denver encountered Arlo Guthrie. "He was telling John how much he liked the 'Country Roads' song, and he said he had this song that John ought to hear," says Bill Danoff, the "Country Roads" co-writer. "Arlo said that it'd be a great follow-up because it had that kind of Americana theme to it."

The song, of course, was "City of New Orleans." Guthrie says he then played it for Denver in the back room of the Troubadour, much the same way that he had learned it from Steve on March 20 in the back room of the Quiet Knight in Chicago. Guthrie "suggested I might want to record it," Denver told the *Los Angeles Free Press* a year later. But Guthrie recalls that he told Denver, "Don't record this song because I'm doing it now myself."

Denver apparently liked the song so much that he opted to record it regardless of Guthrie's wishes. But Denver also "felt like the song needed something," says Mike Taylor, Denver's lead guitarist. So Denver called Steve, telling him he would be in New York that month to finish work on his next album and asking Steve to mail him a tape of "City" so that he could figure out how to alter it. "I dug it, but I felt it wasn't quite right for me the way it was," Denver told the *Free Press.* Taylor says that Steve, knowing he was due for chemo at Sloan-Kettering, replied, "Well, I'm goin' to New York, too, and I'll see you there."

Steve's ardor for a meeting with such a famous pop performer not even five years his senior was natural. If he felt any wariness about a revision of "City of New Orleans," he apparently didn't let on to anyone, and he showed up at the room that Denver was sharing with Taylor at the posh Warwick Hotel in Midtown. While Taylor tried to take a nap, Steve and Denver talked for an hour, Steve confiding in the musicians about his leukemia. "He told us that he had a rare blood disease and didn't expect to live out the year," Taylor says. "He was laying out this thing in great detail about how he's got only eight months to live or whatever, and that it was wonderful that John was going to do the song, and it would be some money for his wife."

Denver outlined for Steve his proposal for "City of New Orleans," which was to model its structure on the formula of "Country Roads," also a song of travel and yearning. Steve's "City" had three verses and a chorus, but "Country Roads" had two verses, a chorus and what is called a bridge — a separate verse with a different, transitional melody and chords.

Steve recalled five years later in his *Omaha Rainbow* interview that Denver told him, "Steve, I really want to record this, but I don't think it is commercial the way it is, and I want to rewrite the last verse because I think I can say something with it." Steve had no objection and said he replied, "Go ahead."

"He just wanted a musical bridge to end the song," Taylor says of Denver. "It had nothing to do with what the song had to say or anything like that. There wasn't that kind of depth of thought. It was just very straightforward: 'This would be more interesting if it had a musical bridge. Sit down, and let's see what we can do.' They sat there right in front of me and rewrote a verse."

The result indicated that they — or, afterward, Denver himself — did much more than that. The last half of the song's second verse was replaced, with phrases describing mothers rocking their babies to the "rhythm of the rails" tossed out in favor of an awkward and less visual line: "The days are full of restless, and the dreams are full of memories, and the echoes of the freight train's whistle's squeal." So that the third verse could serve as a bridge, it was given a more transitory melody, and its eight lines were sliced to just four. In two of the remaining lines, "nighttime" was changed to "twilight," and references to Memphis and the Mississippi River were dislodged by the phrases "Talk about your pocket full of friends" and "With no tomorrow waitin' 'round the bend." Lopped off were the verse's final four lines, which had supplied the song's most overt and powerful social statement, a declaration of the train's "disappearin' railroad blues." Finally, in the culminating, double repeat of the chorus, the line "Good night, America, how are you?" was altered to "Good night, America, I love you."

Vivid description and commentary had been sacrificed for softer, cloying, emotional language — the type of "commercial" lyrics that middle-of-the-road America was beginning to buy in the persona of the fresh-faced, seemingly squeaky-clean (if long-haired) Denver. As Danoff bluntly puts it, the rewrite turned a good song into "mush."

Nonetheless, the hotel-room collaboration between Steve and Denver appeared satisfying to both, says Taylor. "Steve was very happy with it," he insists, adding that when the two amicably parted, Denver invited Steve to visit RCA's studio in Manhattan an evening or two later to meet producer Milt Okun. "Steve said he might be able to do that," Taylor says, "but that what he was doing medically affected him and he didn't know if he could, but he was going to try — and he did show up at RCA."

There, Steve listened to a recording that Denver and his band had made of the revised "City of New Orleans." At this point, it became clear to Steve that a further lyrical modification — to just one word — apparently had arisen at the studio. It was the slightest of all the changes but perhaps the most provocative because it addressed a question of race: Should a descriptive reference to skin color be stripped from a song if it could be viewed as degrading? In the first verse of Steve's version of "City of New Orleans," the train passed "freight yards full of old black men." But as Steve recalled in the *Omaha Rainbow* interview, "There was a black engineer at RCA who was offended by the line 'old black men.' That's why Denver changed it to 'old grey men' on the record(ing)."

Danoff, who did not witness Denver's conversations with Steve, assumes that Denver, given his eagerness to sing civil-rights songs in his Mitchell Trio

> **There was a black engineer at RCA who was offended by the line 'old black men.' That's why Denver changed it to 'old grey men.'**
> **STEVE GOODMAN**

days, was just trying to be open-minded. "It wasn't any sort of a prejudice thing," Danoff says. "(It was) probably the sense that you didn't have to be black to be an old guy hanging around a railroad yard."

But for Steve, the change to "old grey men" apparently was the last straw. He was offended by what he saw as an accusation of racism. In the 1976 interview, Steve said he confronted Denver,[15] telling him, "You've got to be kidding me. No one will ever be able to accuse me of consciously coming on like that. If I make a mistake because I'm stupid, all right, you call me on it. But cut that out. Don't ever call me on something like that, especially in the stuff that I'm writing, the one part of me that I want to last."

Though Steve may have developed such hard feelings that evening in the studio, it makes sense that he might have deferred to Denver and chosen to veil his outrage later. Taylor says Steve "seemed perfectly happy" that evening upon hearing the recording — and after meeting with Okun to discuss terms for a split of songwriting royalties. "Steve was excited because he felt that John was really on his way up, which John was at that time. 'Country Roads' had come out, John was a commercial success, and Steve knew he was going to make a lot of money." More bluntly, Taylor told the *Los Angeles Free Press* in 1972, "Goodman wasn't very well known, and he probably would have been happy to let John rewrite the whole fucking thing except for the chorus, as long as he knew that it was going to be recorded and might become a hit."

It was at this point, however, that Steve let on to friends that his feelings had soured. Before going to RCA that evening, Steve breathlessly called Paula Ballan's apartment and talked with Philadelphia singer/guitarist Mike Miller. "You've gotta get down here right away," he told Miller, who couldn't misconstrue the excitement. "Steve was kveln (a Yiddish term), swelling with pride, happy as a lark, man," Miller says. "He's about to become rich because John Denver, for Christ's sake, is going to record his song." But when Ballan and Miller arrived at RCA an hour or two later, it was after Steve had heard the recording, talked further with Denver and met Okun — and by then, Steve's ebullience had evaporated. There, Miller says, Steve told them, outside of Denver's earshot, that he had been offered only a 50 percent share of the songwriting royalty for the revised song and that Denver had handed him an ultimatum: "No changes, no recording."

"He was destroyed, wrecked," Miller says. "He was, like, in tears. You could see the money and the creative thing flying away. He wanted the recognition, and he was afraid, you have to remember, because he didn't know if he was going to die the next day. But he talked himself into it. He wanted that shot, so he had to agree, and he finally decided that half of a John Denver thing is better than nothing."[16] Ballan adds, "It pissed Steve off that John had the chutzpah to do this, but there's no way Steve would have refused what was going on. Professionally, he couldn't."

The notion that Steve faced an ultimatum on the song's lyrics does not ring true to Taylor. "Steve agreed to this before he even showed up in New York,"

> **He finally decided that half of a John Denver thing is better than nothing.**
> **MIKE MILLER**

15: At this point in the 1976 *Omaha Rainbow* interview, in recounting how he vented his ire over the word change from "black" to "grey," the words Steve used were, "I called the guy." It isn't clear whether by "called" he meant telephoned or confronted, but the latter is likely, given the way Steve used the word "called" later in the quote. It also isn't clear from the context or sources whether "the guy" was Denver or the black recording engineer. But given that Steve recently had spent an hour working with Denver on "City of New Orleans" in Denver's hotel room, it's more likely that he was communicating his outrage directly to Denver.

16: Steve later related the same sentiment to singer/songwriter James Lee Stanley: "I had 100 percent of nothing. Fifty percent of a Denver hit is better than 100 percent of nothing."

Taylor says. "It wasn't like he came to the hotel room and John said, 'This is what's going to happen or I'm not going to record the song.' It wasn't anything like that." Both Taylor and Okun also dismiss the claim that Steve was induced to forgo half of the song's writing royalty. "I can guarantee that it wasn't any 50-50 split," Taylor says. "With Milt, you sat down and counted words and counted bars (measures of music). I would be surprised if John had 10 percent of that song." Okun says no paperwork was signed but says that, "if anything," Denver's share amounted to 10 percent.

At some point during his time with Denver at the RCA studio, Steve (and Paula Ballan) felt comfortable enough to join 16 other voices in overdubbing the anthemic chorus to "Friends with You," an upbeat Danoff-Nivert paean to fellowship that was recorded during the same New York sessions. (In the credits for the song that appeared on the resulting Denver LP, Steve was given the cryptic label of "Turnpike Tom.")

Regardless of what transpired among Steve, Denver and Okun, there is no question that the sequence of events — which resulted in severe changes to a song that Steve regarded as one of his best — amounted to an ego bruise. Still, in an industry heralded for artistry but steeped in compromise, it was an indication that Steve was making headway.

Buddah sought to continue that progress, laboring behind the scenes that fall to boost Steve's stature and the company's fortunes by pitching his material to other artists. The consensus, says Eddie O'Laughlin, a "song plugger" for Buddah, was that "City of New Orleans" was Steve's most marketable tune. Buddah's Neil Bogart and Bob Reno sent O'Laughlin, 25, on a sales trip to Nashville, and, as Bill Traut had endeavored to do the previous year, O'Laughlin's job was to "create some heat" and get a rough tape of the tune into the hands of those who could give it a prominent cover version. O'Laughlin was aware that John Denver had just recorded a rewritten "City," but he says, "I was told to get covers on something that had nothing to do with John Denver, and they (the covers) were going to fight and duke it out a little bit. They were trying to establish Steve Goodman without this John Denver connection."

The "top producers of the day" in Nashville — Owen Bradley, Billy Sherrill, Glenn Sutton and Ricci Mareno — had visits from O'Laughlin, but their reaction was puzzling given that Steve had just recorded "City" with Area Code 615. "Nobody would take it," O'Laughlin says. "They were actually offended and would stop the song halfway and would say, 'That's not country, boy.' They were really not nice about it. They were almost like, 'How dare you even come down here?' I was friendly and everything, but they didn't want anybody from the North. I went home dejected after four and a half days. I loved that song, and I was so hurt."

Back in Chicago, Steve was given a chance to showcase "City of New Orleans" for the influential ears of the grass-roots movement to end the continued U.S. involvement in the Vietnam War. On the evening of Friday, Oct. 1, more than 2,300 people, paying from $3 to $25 a seat, filled Chicago's Orchestra Hall,

They were actually offended and would stop the song halfway and would say, 'That's not country, boy.'
EDDIE O'LAUGHLIN

Joan Baez, shown in 1977, had promised Steve that she would accompany him on a song during the 1971 Business Executives Move for Vietnam Peace rally in Chicago. "I just thought she was bein' sweet, sayin' that she would sing with me," Steve said later, "(but) she knew damn well I was going to be in trouble."

(Photo by Richard McCaffrey)

across South Michigan Avenue from Grant Park, the site of televised police beatings of protesters just three years earlier during the Democratic National Convention, for a four-hour rally put on by a group called Business Executives Move for Vietnam Peace. In what *The New York Times* dubbed "a kind of Academy Awards for Peace," honors were to be given 15 activists ranging from Oregon's outspoken Wayne Morse, one of two U.S. senators to vote against the war-expanding Gulf of Tonkin resolution in 1964, and Dr. Benjamin Spock, famed infant expert and draft protester, to Daniel Ellsberg, who earlier in the year had leaked the U.S. Defense Department's so-called Pentagon Papers, and a young John Kerry, the leader of Vietnam Veterans Against the War and future U.S. senator and Democratic presidential nominee.

Also to receive a "peace Oscar" was Joan Baez, and the musical interlude after her receipt of the award was to be provided by Steve.

He'd been asked to sing "City of New Orleans," marginally popular in Chicago but unknown to the many national figures present. But just as he had done in responding to Paul Anka's offer five months earlier, Steve also tried to shine light on his songwriting compatriot. As Steve recounted to "FolkScene" the following March, he told the organizers, "Sure, I wouldn't mind doing that, but why don't you call up my friend John Prine and have him sing his songs, since I think they're a little bit more relevant, a couple of 'em, anyhow, than that song about the train." Steve said the group — made up of business figures "who for some reason or other want the war to end now, where they never had any interest in anything like that prior" — decided to stick with him. But following Baez proved formidable.

Civil-rights activist and former Attorney General Ramsey Clark, along with a Vietnam veteran who wore cut-off fatigues, called Baez to the stage to receive her award. But she refused it with impudence, telling the crowd, "First of all, don't you think it's a little bit premature to be giving these things out? Two, this veteran here deserves it a lot more than me, so I'm going to give it back to him." She handed back the award, walked to both sides of the stage, pulled American flags out of their stands, laid them on the stage, came back to the microphone and said, "These flags are an obscenity. They are not sacred. Our lives are sacred ... We've always known how to defend a piece of property or a piece of cloth but never how to defend a human life, and it's about time that we learned defense." She walked off to applause and a few shouts for the flags to be replaced — what Steve termed "loud, mixed reaction."

"And now," an announcer's voice said, "a friend of Miss Baez, Steve Goodman, is going to sing for you." Steve warily came on, sang a couple of songs while the audience buzzed about the flags, then gladly re-welcomed Baez. "Joan had promised me earlier that she'd come out and sing one with me and bail me out," Steve said. "She knew what she was gonna do, even though I didn't. I just thought she was bein' sweet, sayin' that she would sing with me, (but) she knew damn well I was going to be in trouble."

Steve elected to sing a perfectly titled song to complement the flag stunt.

With Baez on harmony, Steve eschewed "City of New Orleans" in favor of a pointed, blasphemous tune of Prine's, in which "the man at the pearly gates" speaks the title line, "Your Flag Decal Won't Get You into Heaven Anymore."

Downstairs, waiting for his turn, a fuming Wayne Morse eyed the proceedings on TV monitors and told two aides that he would not appear onstage until the American flags were replaced in their holders. So, during "Flag Decal," two of his aides, who didn't realize that Morse, the final awardee, wasn't scheduled to be on for 45 minutes, rushed onto the stage and set the flags back up.

Baez, however, was undeterred. "I look over at Joan, and she ain't there," Steve said. "It's in the middle of the second verse, and I'm just strummin' away and singin', and all of a sudden there's no harmony. Joan is back, laying the flags back down on their sides." When Baez returned to the mike and finished the song with Steve, the two drew a raucous response. "I figure about half the folks liked it and about half the folks might not have, but everybody was standing," Steve said. "We walked off together arm in arm, and I was trembling. So was she." (Later, Clark and U.S. Rep. Pete McCloskey stood the flags up again prior to McCloskey's introduction of Ellsberg.)

Steve insisted that the Morse aides' mid-song flag replacement didn't bother him, because, even though he didn't know it at the time, the gesture had been ordered by Morse, an early war critic. "I respect the heck out of the guy for having the, uh, testicles to speak his mind when it was needed and bein' the only guy in the Senate to do it at the time," he told "FolkScene."

What impressed Steve even more was Baez' courage. "I didn't know what a brave woman she was until I was forced into a situation where I had to muster up that much all by myself," he said. "That's not like standing in the park and gettin' hit over the head, (and) you're just angry. There she was, just downright confronting 2,500 screaming businessmen for peace." [17]

Baez' regard for Steve was so strong that she affixed to him an alliterative nickname that endured for decades, Chicago Shorty. Steve, however, preferred an insider moniker that capitalized on a pun between his disease and a 1967 Paul Newman movie: Cool Hand Leuk.

Buddah couldn't be accused of "a failure to communicate" about its fledgling recording artist that fall. The label prepared a sizable splash for the release of Steve's first LP — and Atlantic was doing the same with John Prine. More evidence of the tandem approach, instigated by Anka ("We tried to make it a joint effort: two Chicago boys"), was a dual booking Nov. 3-8 at the site of their New York debut the previous May, the Bitter End. [18] To herald the double billing, Buddah and Atlantic took out ads in the *Village Voice* — a half page for Prine, a quarter page for Steve — that hatched their differing public personas in a manner that didn't stray far from the truth.

For Prine, the image was that of a cerebral loner: "He writes songs. Probably the most intelligent and well-written songs you've heard in a long time. He writes soft songs about his country childhood memories. And hard songs condemning the wrongs of the city ... songs which poetically examine our unpo-

I didn't know what a brave woman she was until I was forced into a situation where I had to muster up that much all by myself.
STEVE GOODMAN

17: Unwittingly or not, in recounting the incident Steve doubled the actual size of the 1,200-person crowd.

18: As with his first billing at the Earl of Old Town the previous March, Prine's unknown status in New York resulted in an advertising typo. In a Bitter End ad in the Nov. 4 *Village Voice*, his last name was misspelled "Prime."

etic, everyday lives and expose the irony, humor and pathos of them." In contrast, while the ad for Steve quickly noted his songwriting, it mainly sent a message of sociability and down-to-earth appeal. Dropping the names of Buzzy Linhart, Brewer & Shipley, Paul Anka, Kris Kristofferson and Area Code 615, the text concluded, "The Buddah/Kama Sutra secretaries and mailroom boys have already picked this album as their favorite, and that's always a good sign."

Despite their different record companies, the pair's album covers bore striking similarities. Both were self-titled, in fashionably unpretentious lower-case lettering ("john prine" and "steve goodman"), and both were shown staring into the camera with supposedly hip Mona Lisa expressions.

But parts of both covers were puzzling. Instead of communicating the intellect of his lyrics, the photo of Prine played upon the rural roots of his parents and the setting for one of his songs, "Paradise," by showing a full-bodied Prine sitting on baled hay, his guitar nearly invisible off to one side. Instead of representing the urban analyst of most of his repertoire, the photo portrayed him more like a youngish good ol' boy. In contrast, Steve's cover photo, by Bob Cato, was a close-in head shot, his shoulder-length hair diverting attention from a receding hairline and framing his riveting brown eyes in the middle of a face puffed up by prednisone. The arresting image suffered, however, from a fuzzy focus. As if to compensate, a smaller head shot on the back cover, in which Steve looked down with a big grin, was sharp and conveyed a reassuring sense of his buoyant personality.

Thrilled to have his first album in hand, Steve soon found a practical use for it. Trying to cash his first royalty check at a Manhattan bank, he discovered he didn't have adequate identification, so he walked to Paula Ballan's apartment, grabbed a copy of the LP and brought it back to the bank. "Have you got some ID, young man?" the teller asked. Holding the album level with his face, he told the teller, "See?" The teller called out a supervisor for verification and eventually cashed the check. "She kept the album," Steve said later.

To bolster their songwriting identities, the record companies included printed lyrics with both LPs, Steve's more expensively in a gatefold and Prine's on an insert. The accompanying liner notes reinforced the artists' Wild Bill/Jingles disparity. On Prine's album, Kristofferson described how Steve had introduced him and his band to Prine in Chicago the previous spring. His mini-essay included an endorsement of Prine often cited by writers in the years ahead: "Twenty-four years old and writes like he's two-hundred and twenty." Steve, too, could have sought a written seal of approval from Kristofferson or another luminary. Instead — again, deferring to his friend — he chose Prine, who recounted meeting "short, stout" Steve at the Earl of Old Town. Fortunately for Steve, Prine's prose included an equally quotable accolade for "City of New Orleans" (borrowed from Kristofferson's introduction of it at the Bitter End back in May): "the best damn train song I ever heard."

Steve acknowledged a long list of musicians and others in his credits, dedicating the LP to his wife, Nancy, and brother, David. But those who knew of

Steve's leukemia also found a message that was mysterious to the masses. Poking fun at the legal custom of recognizing the help of those who "appear courtesy of" other musical labels, Steve wrote, "Steve Goodman appears courtesy of Barney, Tim, Phillip, Monroe, Gene and the rest of the memorial magicians." The reference, of course, was to his doctors (Clarkson, Gee, Salem, Dowling and his family's physician, Handelman) and the staff at Memorial Sloan-Kettering Cancer Center. (It probably was no accident that the photos on the cover showed Steve with dark chest hair peeking out from low-buttoned shirts — a clear symbol of vitality.)

By this point, no one at Buddah could have been mistaken about Steve's disease. But his cheerful disposition had helped transcend commercial fears and drawn the label's execs to his corner. "I was more concerned personally than I was business-wise," says Ron Weisner. "It wasn't as if we were making this big investment and we were worried about what's going to happen to our investment. The consensus from everybody was, 'What's going to happen with Steve?' That's what was more upsetting, because everybody felt totally helpless."

Steve had become adept at timing his chemo at Sloan-Kettering so that his sickly recovery periods didn't coincide with his scheduled shows. As a result, his energetic performances in support of the LP on Nov. 3-8 at the Bitter End were an immense help in calming Buddah's concerns.

The afternoon before the opening night, however, presented some titillating anxiety for Steve. At a party in Carly Simon's Manhattan apartment came Steve's introduction to the nation's most prominent folk/rock trailblazer, the reclusive Bob Dylan. Simon and Kristofferson had invited Steve and Prine, who didn't know until they arrived that Dylan soon would show up. When he did, the group passed around Simon's guitar and took turns playing songs, a session known as a "guitar pull." The songs included Prine's "Donald and Lydia," which Dylan praised, and "City of New Orleans." Simon was the only one who shunned a turn. "Carly wouldn't sing anything she wrote," Steve later told Al Rudis. "I was a little pissed off about that because everybody else was forced to contribute in the presence of 'God.' " [19]

Steve admitted to angst over the quasi-audition with Dylan. "There I was, face-to-face with the greatest musical influence in the past 20 years, and I was nervous," he told the *Chicago Daily News*' Marshall Rosenthal. "The only reason I was nervous is because Kristofferson was nervous, and he knew the guy," Steve added in his interview with Rudis. "He (Kristofferson) was the interpreter, the organizer of this little gathering. He felt a responsibility to make sure that John got to sing a couple of his songs and I got to sing a couple and we'd all have a good time, just to make sure that Dylan didn't get pissed off and split before he heard some of the tunes."

Prine was both intimidated and wowed during the gathering. "I was scared out of my gourd," he says. "I couldn't believe that Bob Dylan was actually there. I thought he lived on another planet." Prine was stunned that Dylan had learned a couple of his songs (including "Far from Me") from an advance copy of his

> **The consensus from everybody was, 'What's going to happen with Steve?' That's what was more upsetting, because everybody felt totally helpless.**
> **RON WEISNER**

19: Of Simon's reluctance to sing one of her songs, Prine takes note of her well-known stage fright, adding, "I guess that carries into apartment fright."

first LP and even sang along on them. Even more impressive to Prine, however, was Kristofferson. "Kris wanted to show off Steve and me," Prine says. "Kris probably hadn't asked Bob Dylan for one favor, and he decides to use his big favor by calling him up and tellin' him to come on over and listen to these guys."

But Dylan was not merely a sounding board for others' compositions. He sang and played a pair of tunes he had just written: the gentle "Wallflower," which appeared more than a year later on a Doug Sahm LP, and an imminent release, "George Jackson," a rant to protest the black-rights author's recent killing at San Quentin prison. It was then that Dylan got a stinging review from the unlikeliest of sources. Prine says that "Goodman looked him dead in the eye and took the guitar from him, and he said, 'Well, ain't no "Masters of War," Bob.' "

For Steve to offer such instant criticism ("Masters of War," from Dylan's second LP in 1963, was a classically vicious tirade against corporate militarism) seems inconceivable given that this was Steve's first meeting with the legend. But Prine insists that it took place as he recalls it. How could Steve summon such effrontery? "I don't know," Prine says, "but it was not unlike Steve to say that. But sayin' that to Bob Dylan at the time I thought was hilarious." [20]

The marketplace soon bore out Steve's slam. "George Jackson" didn't succeed critically or commercially. But on that afternoon in Carly Simon's apartment, Steve's crack could have created a lasting schism. Fortunately for Steve, Dylan perhaps saw truth in the remark. "He was taken aback, but I don't think he was mad," Prine says. "I don't think he held it against him. He took it all in." In fact, the gathering ended congenially. "We were all able to just sit around like four pickers and run through some Hank Williams tunes," Steve said later.

As the sun set on that November afternoon, Steve made a further connection with Dylan. "Steve was gonna go down to the Village to go to a guitar shop, and Dylan offered him a ride," Prine says, "so Steve took off with Dylan on his motorcycle at the end of the thing." It was a connection that Dylan would later renew.

Three days before his co-billing with Prine, Steve had recruited two veteran sidemen — lead guitarist Marc Horowitz, who Steve had encountered two years earlier at Paula Ballan's apartment, and bassist Patrick O'Connor, an Englishman who Steve had met in Chicago when O'Connor played with the Chad Mitchell Trio. Horowitz was stunned to discover a surge in Steve's guitar technique. "He had evolved this very intricate flat-picking style, playing rhythm and lead at the same time," he says. "It was really startling. He just became a monster, a very idiosyncratic but intense guitar player. The guitar went from just being accompaniment to being half the act." Horowitz found that Steve's animated ability made accompanying him a challenge. "I had to be careful not to step on his leads," he says, "because he had a real love of sticking in quotations, quoting other songs in his guitar leads. He was just a humorous player and facile after he developed that cross-picking style." [21]

Goodman looked him dead in the eye and took the guitar from him, and he said, 'Well, ain't no "Masters of War," Bob.'
JOHN PRINE

20: While Prine and others close to Steve delight in retelling the story of Steve's rebuke of Dylan, Steve himself apparently never aired it, at least not in public.

21: Steve's dexterity on guitar was in full view during all-night song-trading sessions in the early 1970s with Mark Ross, Paul Siebel, Saul Broudy and Erik Frandsen at the Kettle of Fish in Greenwich Village. Once, Ross said Ramblin' Jack Elliott was adapting a song to a minor key. "Goodman had never done the song in a minor key, but he came up with an incredible arrangement," Ross says. "He knew where all the chords were. It's like the old-time typesetters who didn't have to look at what they were doing. It was just automatic. It's ear memory, which is better than sight training."

Their stone faces perhaps unintentionally reflecting the unlikelihood of their association, Paul Anka, center, embraces John Prine and Steve at the pair's first billing at the Bitter End on Nov. 3, 1971.

(Photo by Bob Gruen)

Steve's Bitter End shows scored raves in both an industry publication, *Billboard*, and a national music magazine, *Crawdaddy*. The *Billboard* review, with the mistaken "Tom Prine" in the headline, noted Prine's "exceptional" songs but called him "an essentially functional singer who throws away his songs in a deceptively offhand, head-scratching manner." More glowingly, it credited Steve's "fresh writing mind" and humor, noting that he "is more outgoing than his partner and talks a lot more between songs."

Crawdaddy's Linda Solomon focused almost entirely on Steve, and her long piece, titled "He's Good, Man," set the tone for hundreds of reviewers to come: "He is a natural performer with a fine, expressive, deep-toned voice: a flashing, satiric (sometimes satanic) sense of humor and irony, and a disarming, literally charming manner. Both hip and straight audiences dig him. ... When he comes on-stage, he often puts his audience at ease by comically referring to himself as 'the human thumb.' They laugh because Steve is not very tall, but by the close of his set, he seems to have grown. The audience hangs on to his every word, every slow smile. He tells them stories through his songs. They don't know quite what to expect from number to number, but they listen intently to every thought from stanza to chorus, from tuning quips to quasi-serious song intros."

This gregarious quality served Steve well in dealing with the phalanx of stars and others whom Buddah and Atlantic had coaxed to show up for opening night of the six-day Bitter End engagement — and not just those with direct connections such as Anka and Kristofferson. Also present were Carly Simon, José Feliciano, Bette Midler (whom Steve and Prine had known as an opening act at Mr. Kelly's nightclub in Chicago), Mary Travers (of Peter, Paul & Mary), John Hartford (writer of "Gentle on My Mind") and Bob Dylan. Besides doctors and staff from Sloan-Kettering who came to show moral support, Steve also was pleased to see in the crowd Chicagoans Bonnie Koloc and her friend Gib Foster, as well as Steve's and Prine's benefactor, Earl Pionke, who had fronted $150 for Steve's airfare and, as a surprise, had flown in others as well, including Steve's wife, Nancy.

"It was 'introduce the kids to New York shot' night," Steve told the *Chicago Sun-Times'* Al Rudis eight months later. "Here are these two people from the woods. They don't realize that Chicago is a city out there."

Steve played off the celebrity crowd, honing in on Anka by playing a medley of the crooner's teen hits and copying Anka's "Put Your Legs on My Shoulders" lampoon. Anka took the kidding well, joining Steve in a jam at the end along with Prine and Hartford. [22]

Soon after the successful opening, Steve renewed his link to Carly Simon, acting as a quasi-agent for Chicago friend Ed Holstein. Already planning to fly in that day for the Steve-Prine Bitter End show, Holstein got a call the night before from Steve, who said Simon was impressed with Holstein's "Jazzman" and wanted to meet him. That night, Steve brought Holstein to Simon's apartment for another song swap, witnessed by Prine and Kristofferson.

In a gathering that Simon taped on a home recorder, Holstein sang "Jazzman" and another song that celebrated easy sex, "Fat Stuff." But lest Simon get the impression Holstein had a one-track mind, Steve himself played her Holstein's "Victoria's Morning," more of a highbrow metaphorical romance, "so she gets pitched a good tune." Steve also ran through Tex Ritter's "Bandit of Brazil" and a lengthy talking version of "Stagger Lee" before unveiling a new composition of his own called "Don't Do Me Any Favors Anymore." On the surface, "Favors" was merely a rant about betrayed confidences, but to insiders it was a veiled plea for those in the know to stop spreading word of his leukemia. Simon even sang harmony on its chorus.

Simon told Holstein his "Fat Stuff" was "terrific," but she didn't end up recording any of his work. Nor did she record any of Steve's. But from the Bitter End stage and in the two song swaps in her apartment that had spanned just 36 hours, Steve left a deep impression. "What a great guy and a great musician," she says today. "I so loved Steve. He was sheer talent pouring out all over." And in an interview published in *Rock* magazine in March 1972, she had singular praise for Steve's first album. "One of the few records that I heard that was just love the first time I heard it was Steve Goodman's," she said. "I just thought it was absolutely fabulous."

Released in the first week of November in New York and in later weeks in the rest of the country, the debut albums of Steve and Prine needed to crack a strong sweep of product by more prominent singer/songwriters. The competition included Carly Simon's "Anticipation," Wings' (Paul McCartney) "Wild Life," Harry Nilsson's "Nilsson Schmilsson," Carole King's long-running "Tapestry" and new "Music," plus a much-hyped three-disc live recording of two fund-raising "Concerts for Bangladesh" held the previous Aug. 1 at Madison

22: The jam fortified a notion stirring in Steve's mind, he told the British paper *Sounds* the following May: "I've got a pipe dream, which is to give concerts by myself but during the show to bring people out of the woodwork, as it were."

Square Garden, headlined by George Harrison and featuring Dylan. It would have been easy for the initial efforts of two folkies to vanish from sight, particularly two folkies shepherded by a distant, Vegas-style entertainer who was focused on his own career.

Hands-on help arrived during the week of their Bitter End gig in the persona of 29-year-old booking agent Al Bunetta. An Italian high-school dropout from New Jersey whose father had been a TV producer, Bunetta had driven trucks and managed equipment for the Rascals pop/rock band. He was working in New York for Creative Management Associates, the firm contracted by Paul Anka to provide agents to book gigs for Steve and Prine. While other CMA agents represented acts ranging from Tom Jones and Engelbert Humperdinck to the Manhattan Transfer and the Byrds, Bunetta had signed up as an agent for Prine. A co-worker, Vince Romeo, had elected to be Steve's agent but found Steve "a pain in the neck," so Bunetta — a go-getter himself — said he would give Steve a try.

Hailing a cab to an afternoon sound check at the Bitter End, Bunetta spotted Steve and his "big, round, brown eyes" outside the club and was struck by an uncanny physical resemblance. "He could have been my brother, a very young version of me," Bunetta says. "I just fell in love with him instantly. Something clicked. I just instantly knew we would spend our lives together. From that moment on, I kind of took responsibility for Steve as an agent."

Similarly enthusiastic attention came from the press as well. [23] Though Steve and Prine worked for different record companies, they often were paired in the public eye, which aided the fortunes of both — in Steve's case, quite literally and accidentally as word of the two rippled from one coast's entertainment capital to another.

With two months left in 1971, Ira Mayer of the New York-based *Village Voice* jumped the gun and anointed Prine and his LP as new performer and album of the year. The snowball continued on Nov. 21 when Robert Hilburn, music critic for the *Los Angeles Times*, termed Prine's album a "genuine classic" in an assessment that topped the front page of the *Times*' Sunday entertainment tabloid, just two days before Prine was to begin a six-day run as the opener for Brewer & Shipley at the Troubadour in Hollywood. Prine, however, took ill at the last minute and was hospitalized for a week near his home in Melrose Park west of Chicago. "I thought it was ulcers," Prine says. "It'd been diagnosed as several things. It was just a bad case of nerves. I don't mean stage fright. Everything had caught up with me. My stomach got tied up in a knot, and I could hardly breathe."

Rushing in to fill Prine's slot — and benefiting from his buzz — was Steve. Though he apologized to the audience for his role as a last-minute replacement, Steve had nothing to apologize for, wrote *Times* critic Michael Ross, who witnessed his opening night and labeled him "indisputably a performer of the first rank," quoting lyrics from "Yellow Coat," "Turnpike Tom" and the crowd-pleasing "Nowhere in a Hurry Blues." [24] Nine days later, Hilburn chimed in with a

He could have been my brother, a very young version of me. I just fell in love with him instantly. Something clicked. I just instantly knew we would spend our lives together.
AL BUNETTA

23: The *Chicago Reader*, the alternative weekly that had debuted two months prior, compiled a "year in review" in its Dec. 17 edition, identifying Steve as the city's "tall, dark and handsome pop star of the year."

24: In *New University*, the student newspaper at UC Irvine, David L. Wilson cited Steve's rapport with the Troubadour crowd: "While many performers make a habit of distancing themselves from their audience, Goodman appears ready to invite their participation. ... Sometimes, his music has an almost distressing lack of self-consciousness."

"special merit" review of Steve's LP, classifying him as "an excellent entertainer with a marvelously accessible manner and attitude and who has a sense of humor about his work." Steve, he wrote, "is moving up fast."

One of the world's most prominent and revered concert venues, Carnegie Hall, soon became proof of that. Opening for Brewer & Shipley's Dec. 3 stop on a tour to promote a fourth album, Steve again impressed writers, despite playing to a "papered" house that was less than half full, including hundreds who had been given free tickets on the street. Bob Glassenberg of *Billboard* compared Steve to "the early Bob Gibson" and cited Steve's "flow, with-it attitude and graceful showmanship." Anne Tan of the *Village Voice* focused on Steve's guitar skills: "Goodman stood on the stage like a candle, with a big smile on his face, managing to fill in the sounds of all rhythm and bass on one acoustic guitar. ... (He) gave a little tour de force of pace, variety and all the different sounds you can make with an acoustic guitar and five very supple fingers." Fred Kirby of *Variety*, despite an unintentionally diverting headline typo ("Steve Godman"), called Steve "excellent" and "particularly effective."

The *Variety* squib also noted that Steve "had a slight run-in with a youth in a box in front of the audience right speaker. Goodman did not realize he was not being heard properly. Goodman apologized, explaining he had no control over the sound and had actually rehearsed earlier in the day with different microphones."

The incident was much more caustic, however, say friends who were present. The youth was "screaming for Brewer & Shipley songs," says Leslie Berman. "Steve had not been going down incredibly well with this audience. They were lager louts. This was not an audience that listened to lyrics. He was having a lot of trouble, the sound was bad, and it was hard for him to hear himself." The heckler persisted, and "Steve asked him to cool it a couple of times," says Jack Goldberg, Steve's former Sloan-Kettering roommate, who also was at the show. But Steve's entreaties didn't work. Finally, his frustration turned to fury.

"I promised my wife that when I got to Carnegie Hall, I'd play this song for her," Steve said, as he was about to sing "Would You Like to Learn to Dance?" Glaring at the guy in the box, he added, "And I don't kick the shovel out of your hands when you're working — motherfucker."

It was as if Steve had ignited a flash fire. "The audience, on the word 'motherfucker,' stood up in a body, screaming and cheering for him," Berman says. "They were not his audience, and then suddenly they were." The embarrassed heckler didn't spout another word the rest of the night.

Steve's crack wasn't out of character, for he was accustomed to matching rudeness with crudeness. ("You all can do me a favor, and shut the hell up, thank you," he'd told one table of rowdy talkers at the Quiet Knight earlier in the year.) [25] The zinger also made sense to the friends who had come to see him make his Carnegie Hall debut. "It was very indicative of Steve's type of sarcasm and humor," Goldberg says. "You're talking about this huge, formal symphonic hall, and this little guy with a guitar, all alone onstage. It was something that

---

The audience, on the word 'motherfucker,' stood up in a body, screaming and cheering for him. They were not his audience, and then suddenly they were.
LESLIE BERMAN

25: Steve also could silence a rowdy crowd with silence, particularly in a small club, says guitarist Trevor Veitch. "He would walk away from the microphone and go somewhere on the side of the stage, no amplification or anything, and just by sheer force of will make them shut the fuck up and listen, which I thought was a very brave thing to do."

most anybody could have found intimidating, but Steve was just as comfortable as all hell about it."

Berman found the retort audacious and was so stunned by it that she scribbled it in a notebook that she carried. "I've seen a lot of people stop hecklers before, but I'd never seen anything that received such a positive, enormous, overwhelming approval," she says. "That he would be so quick on his feet to say to this guy, 'Be nice to me,' is a difficult thing to do when you want to sing for your wife for the first time you play this important place."

Still, the brash profanity that punctuated the "shovel" line may have ill suited the prestigious venue and Steve's own sensibilities for his debut there. It also could have reflected — consciously or not — internal tension over what was fast becoming Steve's signature song. While Buddah was doing its best to promote him and he was getting good press, several things nagged at Steve. First, in response to the tragic crash of the previous June, Amtrak developed cold feet about the name of the train that traversed the country's north-south spine. On Nov. 14, the agency dropped the name of City of New Orleans, resurrected the Panama Limited label for the same run and switched the train to an overnight instead of daylight schedule. [26] The move conformed to the "disappearin' railroad blues" presaged in Steve's song, but without a bona fide train to give credibility to the threat, prospects for the tune's commercial viability seemed to match the "bad dream" of its lyrics.

What's more, in December, just as Steve was receiving his first significant ink and his debut album was heading to record stores nationwide, RCA released John Denver's fifth LP, "Aerie." The title referenced the nest of an eagle — a lofty, incorruptible symbol — and the album's photos depicted Denver in his recently adopted homeland, atop one of the Rocky Mountains of Colorado, an eagle perched on his arm. On the record inside was a mix of a dozen original songs and covers, including a John Prine song, "Spanish Pipedream" (which, with Prine's permission, Denver had re-titled "Blow Up Your TV," from the tune's chorus) along with the rewritten version of "City of New Orleans" that Denver had recorded three months earlier. The LP's first single, "Friends with You," with "Starwood in Aspen" on the B side, had been issued more than a month prior to the album, breaking into the *Billboard* pop chart on Nov. 6 at #90, and topping out at #47 (Dec. 25) during an 11-week run. But "Friends with You" was not the expected blockbuster follow-up to "Country Roads." "It was a real failure," says producer Milt Okun. "After a giant hit, you'd expect better than that. It wasn't."

The release of "Aerie" triggered a variety of questions for Steve. Would Denver's "City of New Orleans" become the LP's next single? If so, would it compete with or enhance sales of Steve's own version that Buddah planned to issue as a single after the first of the year? Would the public rally to Denver's schmaltzy lyrical alterations to "City"? Would it become a John Denver song in the public's mind? Or would RCA bypass it and choose another track to release as a single? Or did the success of singles really matter, given that Steve had

> You're talking about this huge, formal symphonic hall, and this little guy with a guitar, all alone on stage. It was something that most anybody could have found intimidating, but Steve was just as comfortable as all hell about it.
> **JACK GOLDBERG**

26: In early 1972, the Illinois Central trains vacated Chicago's Central Station and gradually shed their chocolate-and-orange locomotives and Pullman-built painted-steel cars.

aligned himself with Buddah, a company that was reshaping its image and sales focus into albums and away from pop hits?

Steve had heard that Mary Travers of the disbanded Peter, Paul & Mary also had recorded an unreleased version of "City," and he knew that Arlo Guthrie had been performing the song in concert and was planning for it to be part of his next album. But these were down-the-road prospects. The Denver version of "City" was a reality — and an icy one to Steve, given its presentation. When he first picked up a copy of Denver's "Aerie" and flipped it over, the fourth track of side one leaped off the back cover: "City of New Orleans by Steve Goodman and John Denver."

No matter that Denver had instigated and participated in the rewrite. No matter that Denver's name was listed second. The shared credit came as a blow to Steve, and he had to have been further dismayed by reviews of "Aerie" that — understandably, given Denver's celebrity — seemed to put Steve in a subordinate position. On Dec. 15, a blurb about Denver's LP in *Variety* gave passing notice to the song, "which he wrote with Steve Goodman." Three months later, *Rolling Stone* critic Alec Dubro all but sealed the implication as fact:

"Denver is a quite capable songwriter, within limits. His forte is, of course, sentiment, which he demonstrates fine and good on 'City of New Orleans,' which he co-wrote with Steve Goodman. The City of New Orleans is an ol' freight train, and John's in the back with the hoboes, passing around the bottle, dealing cards and singin' about America in the finest dusty boots tradition. Like his last hit, 'Country Roads,' this has a very catchy melody and is sung with John's clearest of clear voices. ... It's plain, rural nostalgia without any pretensions to reality, and it's good."

The double credit on the LP apparently shook up Denver as well, [27] enough for him to pick up the telephone and reach out to Steve. Johnniy Morris, a Scottish storyteller Steve had befriended at the Philadelphia Folk Festival and who was visiting Chicago and staying with Steve and Nancy, clearly remembers a call that Denver made to their apartment. In the conversation, audible over a speakerphone, Denver — who had just embarked on his first European tour — tried to sound contrite.

"Big problem," Denver said, "big problem."

"What?" Steve replied.

"Oh, the album's been released, and there's a printer's error."

It was clear from Steve's expression, Morris says, that Steve didn't believe Denver's explanation.

"Oops, you better phone Al," Steve replied, referring to his agent, Bunetta.

"Would three-quarters be OK?" Denver asked.

"Well, it's OK," Steve said, "but you better get in touch with Al."

The conversation over, Steve hung up the phone, and Morris asked him, "What's three quarters?"

"Three quarters of a million," Steve replied.

Okun says that Denver — who died in October 1997 in the crash of an

---

The City of New Orleans is an ol' freight train, and John's in the back with the hoboes, passing around the bottle, dealing cards and singin' about America in the finest dusty boots tradition.
ALEC DUBRO
ROLLING STONE

27: In an apparent bid to clarify the double credit that appeared on the "Aerie" LP, the crediting for Denver's version of "City of New Orleans" was altered slightly in the "Aerie" sheet-music songbook, released after the album. The songbook credit stated, "Words and Music by Steve Goodman / Additional Lyric by John Denver."

experimental plane he was flying over California's Monterey Bay — could have been referring to $750,000 only if he were assuming that his version of "City of New Orleans" would become as big a hit as "Country Roads."

"I don't think John was too aware of all these technicalities of all these details," Okun says. "I don't think he knew what he was talking about. If the song went on to do what 'Country Roads' did, Steve would have made it to three quarters of a million. So it's very possible that John was just talking off the top of his head, because 'Country Roads' by then was just a monster. But who knows what these guys were talking about? John was kind of ignorant, and Steve was ignorant squared."

Okun, an arranger, conductor and composer who produced prominent folk acts from Tom Paxton to Peter, Paul & Mary, played key roles in more than 75 gold and platinum records and founded the Cherry Lane music publishing firm, assumes today that the double credit for "City of New Orleans" on Denver's LP "was just a mistake. Someone just assumed that. Everyone knew that John worked on the song, (but) it was never documented or written down or anything."

If Denver slighted Steve, Okun says, it was unintentional and out of character. He says he had to coach Denver not to just hand credits out as gifts. "He is by far the most gracious and fairest person I ever worked with," Okun says. "John would go out of his way to give other people reasons to make money. He was kind of dumb about certain things."

"Hell, I didn't care one way or the other whether I had writing credit," Denver told the *Free Press*, "but my producer, Milt Okun, wanted me to. He phoned Steve's publishing company and, as far as I know, Steve agreed to the split."

The double credit left Steve — and those he talked with afterward — with a nasty taste. Soon after Denver's phone call to Steve's home, John Prine and his older brother, Dave, an old-time banjo and fiddle player, stopped in at the Earl of Old Town and ran into Steve, who was livid. "I don't think I would have wanted to cross him," Dave Prine says. "Steve was blowing steam and smoke out his ears. I'd never seen him so pissed. He was about two feet off the ground, and if he could have gotten his hand on Denver, he probably would have throttled him. I had never really seen him upset, and I thought to myself, 'Gee, that's really tacky — you, the guy that's a big name, that's got money coming out his ears, you'd think you could give a struggling songwriter proper credit. I mean, geez. You've gotta have it all, I guess.' "

Denver told the *Free Press* that he soon got wind of Steve's ire. At some point, he said, "I find that Steve is pissed with me, and people are saying I ripped off his song." Not long afterward, Denver and his accompanists, Mike Taylor and Dick Kniss, along with Denver's opener, Chicago folksinger Megan McDonough, [28] were performing at a showcase for record distributors and radio execs in Philadelphia, and Steve showed up backstage. In the middle of the show, while Denver performed a few songs by himself, Taylor greeted Steve.

"I wish I had done a better job for you on that song," Taylor said, referring

> **Steve was blowing steam and smoke out his ears. I'd never seen him so pissed. He was about two feet off the ground, and if he could have gotten his hand on Denver, he probably would have throttled him.**
> **DAVE PRINE**

28: McDonough, who changed the spelling of her first name to Megon in the 1990s, says Steve's legendary warmth "came from a real fire. He was just on fire for the song. His whole aura just sparked. He was a sparkin' guy. He had sparks coming off his heels."

to his dobro playing on Denver's version of "City," which he thought could have been better.

"No," Steve spat out, "the only one who owes me an apology is John." Taylor says that Steve continued his rant by accusing Denver and his management of "stealing" his song.

"Well, wait a minute, y'know," Taylor said. "Y'all sat there and rewrote and all."

"I didn't know it was gonna be like that," Steve said.

McDonough, just 17, had finished her set and was watching Denver when she felt "this heat, this energy, right at my shoulder." She turned around, and it was Steve. "He was so angry he was seething," says McDonough, who was familiar with Steve and his club work in Chicago. "The guy was obviously not to be crossed," she says. Steve briefly related to her his gripe over Denver, ending with an epithet:

"That bastard."

After the end of the show, Taylor says, Steve and Denver sat down and talked with each other. Later, as they were packing up, Taylor approached Steve again.

"Did you get it all worked out?"

"Yeah," Steve replied. "I can't stay mad at the guy." [29]

Someone who could and did, however, was the shaggy-haired musician who nearly a year prior in the back room of the Quiet Knight in Chicago learned "City of New Orleans" from Steve and six months later in the back room of the Troubadour in Hollywood had taught the song to Denver — Arlo Guthrie. His reaction upon seeing the song and its crediting on Denver's "Aerie" LP was instantaneous.

> I went ballistic. I went what could only be described as letters that are not part of the alphabet. I went crazy.
> **ARLO GUTHRIE**

"I went ballistic," he says. "I went what could only be described as letters that are not part of the alphabet. I went crazy. I didn't understand it."

It was not just that Denver had ignored Guthrie's admonition and recorded and released the song before Guthrie had. It also was that it appeared that Denver had significantly changed the song and had induced the disease-threatened Steve to accept only partial credit for it.

"That was the thing that in folk music you didn't do," Guthrie says. "They did that in rock 'n' roll, where they pressured writers to take part of their money." He cites a phone call that his father's manager, Harold Leventhal, once received from Elvis Presley's management indicating that Presley wanted to record and release his own version of "This Land Is Your Land." The catch was that Presley wanted to claim 50 percent of the songwriting royalty. Leventhal rejected the offer.

"They don't do that in folk music, especially with a good guy like John Denver, who really was a good guy," says Guthrie, who had known Denver since the blond singer was performing Guthrie's dad's songs as the replacement for the namesake of the Chad Mitchell Trio. "But I was angry. I was just mad at him. I was so burnt, I didn't know what to do. I felt personally betrayed, and every time the guy's name would come up, I would go nuts."

29: One of Steve's few public criticisms of Denver's version of "City of New Orleans" — perhaps the only one — came in March 1972, when he told Howard Larman of the L.A. "FolkScene" radio show with self-deprecation: "I felt kind of stupid that I let him change the last verse."

Guthrie's ire was rooted in not only the music that drew him and Steve together but also the craft attitudes of an industry that often appeared more cutthroat than honorable.

"If somebody wants to add stuff to a song, that's fine," Guthrie says. "The only thing I have a problem with is when people change it and the motivation is not guided by the artistic integrity of the work itself. I mean, should I change 'God Bless America' or the national anthem? Should I change a few words so I can say I wrote it, too? I mean, where does it end? At some point, the creative process requires that you pay tribute to the person or persons through whom these images become reality. They're the ones responsible."

Today, Guthrie allows that as part of the folk process he has made changes to even his father's classic songs, but he insists that he has never claimed credit. "My heart of hearts will not allow me to adjust the creative work of somebody else for me to profit by. I just can't do it," he says. "But the very guys that do that stuff, those guys are the thieves of the heart. They steal what's good in creative people all over the world. I hate those guys. I don't care who they are. Even the friends of mine, who I love dearly, who have done this, I can't forgive. I would love to. I just can't do it. That's not in my being to do it. I will still love them, but there's a place that I have to withhold. I know people who are very dear to me who have done this kind of thing, and if ever I've done it, there's a part of me that I can't forgive because it's just not right.

"I don't always know the difference. I know the difference between right and wrong, but I try to skip by on a few things from time to time. I'm not a perfect human being or nothin'. But the 1960s was a time of change, and one of the changes that should have been made for all time was to put these guys out of business. It's one of the failures of our generation. We succeeded in a lot of other things. We stopped nuclear power, we made people all be able to vote, brought women into the workplace, did all kinds of wonderful things in the world. But one of the things that somebody needs to succeed in sometime is stopping these thieves from stealing what's not theirs.

"What does it hurt to give somebody credit when it's due? How big a pain is that? How much money is it worth? Y'know, there's a lot of guys like this. I know them. These are wonderful people, for the most part. They all love their kids. They may do philanthropic things that benefit the whole world. But they're still thieves. They're nice thieves. At some point, you want to stop the pain in the world from being so prevalent, and the only way to do that is to be more generous than greedy."

Eventually, both Steve and Denver would hear directly from Guthrie, who made changes of his own to "City of New Orleans" — and, unlike Denver, did so without consulting or collaborating with the author. Instead of appearing to engage in thievery, however, Guthrie got the train back on track. ♪

At some point, you want to stop the pain in the world from being so prevalent, and the only way to do that is to be more generous than greedy.
ARLO GUTHRIE

Steve performs during a sound check at a suburban Chicago venue in January 1972, looking the same as he did on "The David Frost Show" and acknowledging applause with typical sheepishness.

(Photo ©2007, Richard Stock, Steve's Maine East High classmate and bandmate)

'That's what it's like when you're not in it for the chips'

With a studied gleam, David Frost welcomed cherubic Steve Goodman and his guitar to one of the orange swivel armchairs on the interviewer's platform. The appearance, aired on Jan. 3, the first weekday of 1972, was part of Frost's 90-minute, syndicated TV show, which was taped in a Manhattan studio and aired five days a week on stations throughout the United States. It was a soaring leap from Steve's previous peaks of broadcast prominence: a few non-mainstream shots on Chicago television ("The Marty Faye Show") and radio ("The Midnight Special").

That the Frost show amounted to national exposure didn't escape Steve. But the 23-year-old couldn't keep from placing his tongue firmly in cheek. His shoulder-length hair swaying to the rhythm of his guitar, Steve had just performed his train song, "City of New Orleans," and Frost, the famed, 32-year-old British satirist and interviewer, was curious.

"Smashing song!" Frost said. "And you really are a train nut, are you?"

Steve paused for a split second. ("I figured, what the hell," he told a Club Passim audience in Cambridge, Massachusetts, more than three years later.)

"I don't subscribe to all the, uh, railroad publications or anything like that," Steve said, "but I know most of the local schedules out of Chicago."

"Really? Really?" said Frost. "I mean, you'd know — how would you get from Chicago to Des Moines by train?"

Once more, Steve hesitated for an instant. ("I don't know if you have to *walk* to Des Moines," he admitted to the Passim crowd.)

"Uh, Northwestern has got a line," Steve said uncertainly.

"What time would you have to leave?"

"It's a morning train," Steve replied. "It's in the morning, about 10 in the morning."

Watching at home in Chicago, the Holstein brothers and Earl Pionke were aghast. "Stevie!" they yelled at the TV. "Don't bullshit him! He's smarter than you!"

Indeed, Frost had caught on. "Very good," Frost said, as the audience laughed. "You could be making it up, and I wouldn't know."

To divert Frost's focus, Steve shifted the topic slightly. "There's very little

> Very good. You could be making it up, and I wouldn't know.
> **DAVID FROST**

David Frost offered formidable banter during the first of Steve's three appearances on the British satirist's syndicated TV show in 1972.

(Photofest photo)

1: Twice more, Steve appeared on the Frost show. In a March 1, 1972, episode, Steve guested with pop star Stevie Wonder, education expert Haim Ginott and comic Steve Landesberg, and he performed "Eight Ball Blues" and "Yellow Coat." Frost also had Steve on his June 28, 1972, show with folksinger Don McLean, *Ms.* magazine editor Gloria Steinem and President Nixon's daughter, Julie Eisenhower.

major rail service left in the United States," he said. "It's just about 21 lines."

But Steve's ploy didn't work. "That's why you know it all," Frost returned.

"Doesn't take much," Steve said.

"It gets easier every week."

"Right."

"It gets easier every year," Frost said. Then he bored in again. "Did you come by train to New York?"

"No," said a grinning Steve. The jig was up. "I flew from Los Angeles."

"You deserter," Frost said with a laugh and pointing a finger. "It's because of people like you that they're cutting down the trains."

"It's actually cheaper to fly from Los Angeles," Steve said. "One of the reasons why passenger trains are disappearing is that I think the railroad companies have just made it almost impossible for people to ride them, y'know, efficiently and comfortably."

"It's a shame, really," Frost chimed in, "because I think train travel — I agree with you, rail travel is a delightful way to —"

Interrupting and tossing the ball back to Frost, Steve said, "I guess in Europe they've done a much better job of keeping their trains than we have here."

"Oh, I don't know," said Frost, his own expertise kicking in. "I think in England they're in decline, too. I think the trains — yes, they appoint people to run the railways with the express job of closing stations."

"Well," Steve said, "that was the case with the City of New Orleans. Made its last run in November."

The banter impressed the host, who invited Steve to return to the show two months later. [1] Steve's appearance on the Frost show (along with circus lion trainer Mary Chipperfield, commentator Rod MacLeish, the Staple Singers and Ed Sanders, author of a book on killer Charles Manson) was just one of myriad manifestations of Buddah's promotion of its newly recorded artist. A debut LP meant introducing not just Steve's music but the musician himself — getting his face and personality before the public so that the first album would sell and a potential second LP would have a base of recognition from which to grow.

That meant media exposure, starting at home with a lengthy cover story by Marshall Rosenthal in the Panorama section of the New Year's Day edition of the *Chicago Daily News*. Placing Steve "at the top" of the city's singer/songwriters who had gained or were seen as destined for cross-country recognition, the article noted Mayor Richard J. Daley's proclamation of December as Chicago Songwriters' Month and called Steve and John Prine "national stars."

"Ain't it ridiculous," Steve said with a self-deprecation that was becoming his trademark. "But maybe that's what it's like when you're not in it for the chips, but for the love of the music."

Such sentimentality was reflected in Buddah's promo photos of Steve, which showed him shirt-sleeved and paddling a canoe in a pond, and in a jacket and tie and quietly strumming on his guitar while sitting on a white, wrought-iron filigree armchair in what could pass for an English garden. But in its publicity,

STEVE GOODMAN

"Country boy from Chicago," is what they call short (5'2"), stocky, solid, twenty-four-year-old Steve Goodman. Girls flip over him because "he's so cute—just like my own kid brother!" But most kid brothers aren't quite so talented! Steve writes gentle, country songs which reveal a strong strain of Jimmie Rodgers and are loaded with down-home wit and wisdom. Steve is a good friend of John Prine—and nothing would please them more if both made it big. Steve calls himself "the human thumb," but he's already got a firm grip with both hands on the superstardom ladder.   (BUDDAH)
·—Art Unger

The April 1972 edition of Ingenue, *whose audience was teenage girls, included Steve among nine "Rock Superstars '72" and said his appeal lay partly in his unthreatening appearance: "Girls flip over him because 'he's so cute — just like my own kid brother!' But most kid brothers aren't quite so talented!"*

Buddah also couldn't resist hearkening to its bubblegum roots, engineering Steve's inclusion among nine "Rock Superstars '72," a feature eventually printed in the April edition of the teen-girl monthly magazine, *Ingenue*. Vignettes by Art Unger and accompanying photos hyped "the super-troubadours — the new rock stars who we predict may make it to superstardom": Emitt Rhodes, Livingston Taylor, Marc Bolan, Loudon Wainwright III, John Prine, Jonathan Edwards, Jeremy Storch, Randy Newman and Steve, in that order.

The only Buddah artist of the bunch, Steve was tagged as a "stocky, solid," 5-foot-2 "country boy from Chicago" whose appeal lay in his unthreatening appearance and association with Prine as much as his music: "Girls flip over him because 'he's so cute — just like my own kid brother!' But most kid brothers aren't quite so talented! Steve writes gentle, country songs which reveal a strong strain of Jimmie Rodgers and are loaded with down-home wit and wisdom. Steve is a good friend of John Prine — and nothing would please them more if both made it big. Steve calls himself 'the human thumb,' but he's already got a firm grip with both hands on the superstardom ladder."

The country appellation, which ignored his urban/suburban roots, obviously stemmed from the Nashville sound of his self-titled LP. But Steve himself had come to embrace the persona, both in dress (bib overalls and cowboy boots) and speech (dropping the "g" from most every word that ended in "ing" and invoking grammar errors that belied his intelligence). Friends from high-school days who saw him perform in Chicago spotted the disorienting difference.

"Steve had developed this cracker accent like Kris Kristofferson: 'Well, I'll tell ya, Hoss.' Why does this guy talk like this? Is this part of becoming famous? In high school, he was a roly-poly Jewish kid," says Neal Pollack. "Steve was writing the good tunes, but he wasn't Kristofferson. 'Take the ribbons from your hair' — that sounds like a guy talking to chicks. I can relate to that. But Goodman didn't sound like a guy that talked to chicks. He was talking to the public at large, with love for humanity, and I thought it was a little Pollyanna-esque. Truth be told, we made fun of him but never wished him ill. The guys on the street were referring to him as the Jewish ham, but it was with affection."

The Nashville affectation was viewed with something less than amusement by others. It drove a wedge of distance, for instance, between Howard Primer and his blues-loving high-school friend. "Before I knew it, Steve was talking country and western to me," he says. "Here was a guy who grew up on the north side of Chicago and never was around a country-western anything, and all of a sudden I'd be talkin' to hee-im, ay-und he'd bay-ee talkin' to me lahk thee-is." Once, Steve called Primer to alert him to a show: "How-ahd, Ah'm gonna be pu-foh-min'. Whah don'tcha come see me?" Primer hung up the phone, scratched his head and told himself, "I can't believe that's Steve." More puzzling to Primer was that Steve's accented diction came during a private phone conversation, "not something he was doing on the stage for effect." Primer, who had plunged into the civil-rights and anti-war movements, was disappointed. "We were so close all through high school, but our gears were not meshing."

While "City of New Orleans" helped summon a country image for Steve, one of the comic highlights of his album, "You Never Even Call Me by My Name," explicitly reinforced it. But after he played it at the Orphans club in Chicago, songwriter Albert Williams "kept hittin' on me," Steve later recalled. Just as Richard Wedler had offered with Steve's fledgling version of "City of New Orleans," Williams furnished a key observation about Steve's country song.

"Man, you missed everything important in that," Williams told Steve.

"Well, what you want me to do?"

"Dope, Dallas, divorce, dogs — there must be 100 things that you've missed."

Steve acknowledged the omissions and later confessed, "I'm kind of mad at myself. This song stops where it's supposed to start." But he didn't want to throw out the entire composition. What he settled for was altering its ending. On his album, the song had finished with a serviceable coda ("It's not her heart, Lord, it's her mind. She didn't mean to be unkind.") followed by a kiss-off ("Bye, baby"). Prodded by Williams, however, Steve shed that ending and put together a new verse. For a moment, he hedged because he thought it might be too sappy. But Williams would have none of it. "You're nuts," Williams admonished him. "Add that in there because that's gonna be the hook. That's gonna really make it." The new verse capped the song and enabled the parody to eventually become a classic.[2]

The earliest evidence of the new verse came in Marshall Rosenthal's article about Steve's mid-December 1971 gig at a branch bar that Earl Pionke had just opened at 4343 North Harlem Avenue, in the northwestern corner of Chicago. Near the end of the song, before singing the freshly written segment and while continuing to strum the song's chords, Steve told his Earl on Harlem audience how, after he and Prine had created the tune, he decided to take it further.

"When we got through writing this all-country country song, some friends realized we'd left out 'mother,' 'truck,' 'train,' 'prison' and 'farm.' Well, here's the verse I added."

Then he sang it. Eliciting howls at its daring and economic use of all five words, the verse had the narrator's farm-based mother gain her release from prison and crash her pickup truck into a train.

You're nuts. Add that in there because that's gonna be the hook. That's gonna really make it.
ALBERT WILLIAMS

2: The inspired new ending to "You Never Even Call Me by My Name" had an earlier conception, in 1967-68 in Steve's conversation with Lake Forest classmate Terry Pearl (see page 127). Steve's high-school guitar mentor, Howard Berkman, recalls a similar session in the summer of 1969 in Steve's Southport Avenue apartment. Berkman says that while they sat with guitars "playing our new stuff for each other," Steve tried out a similar lyric and told him, "Y'know, a country song needs this. ..."

The augmented version of "You Never Even Call Me by My Name" evolved into Steve's crowd-pleasing closer, and he enhanced its appeal by adding visual and aural shtick, honing it to hilarious effect. First, as if conducting a light-hearted test, he would focus the attention of audiences by saying beforehand, "We tried to put everything into one song that's ever been in any of the other country and western songs that we ever heard." Then, he would tip his torso forward and explain: "Country bands always lean into the mike at a 45-degree angle." ("I don't even know how they do that," he said at one show. "I can't do that for a whole set. I think there's a weight in the hat that keeps 'em up.")

Occasionally, Steve would note with crudity that a country song typically slows down as it closes: "They have a retard ending. There's a reason why they call it that." Several times during the song, he would move his strumming hand up the guitar neck à la Ernest Tubb, and for the tune's instrumental solo, his mouth and hands would offer a spot-on, imitation steel-guitar whine, with flashes of violin and harmonica pantomime (and eye-rolling) mixed in.

The prelude that Steve devised for the song became its literally crowning touch. He had noticed that in many of his audiences, at least one person had come wearing a cowboy hat, so before launching into the song, he would ask for anyone with a hat — preferably a cowboy hat — to pass it forward and up to the stage so that he could wear it for the duration of the song. "The guy who gave up the hat would feel instantly, absolutely bonded," says Paula Ballan, who says the maneuver exemplified how Steve could make listeners feel that he was speaking or singing solely to them.

"Many people who really didn't know him felt that they really knew him," Ballan says. "It was a magical quality he had. Some of it was eye-to-eye, and some of it was a way in which he fed a punch line to an individual, to create some little moment of intimacy, making them feel like he had shared something very special or funny with them and not with anybody else. It wasn't fake at all. It was the way he operated. It was like the class clown who can't say it out loud, so he says it to the guy sitting next to him, and that guy feels privileged that he was the one."

Therein lay the true key to Steve's emerging appeal, not a spin or perception that he was "country" or any other category. So the problem with Buddah pushing — and Steve welcoming — a country image was that while he revered the legendary figures and traditions of the genre, Steve really wasn't a country songwriter, musician or performer. A folksinger at heart, he wove a variety of styles into his compositions and shows, flitting between pigeonholes. So in January 1972, as Steve embarked on a series of club dates that began with a four-day run opening for Buddah artist Bill Withers ("Ain't No Sunshine") at the 200-seat, no-alcohol Main Point coffeehouse next to Bryn Mawr College outside of Philadelphia, [3] Steve embodied a challenge. Despite obvious talent and a riveting stage personality, his eclectic interests — in addition to his less than movie-matinee-idol looks — made him difficult to market.

Standing in the shadow of Prine's acclaimed songwriting (validated by

The guy who gave up the hat would feel instantly, absolutely bonded.
PAULA BALLAN

3: While in Philadelphia, Steve appeared on the TV show of broadcast pioneer Jerry "Geator with the Heater" Blavat.

Kristofferson and others who performed his songs in concert [4]) and the vaunted "Woodstock" image of Prine's label posed further barriers. "I was very annoyed because they seemed to have such a huge budget at Atlantic," says Nancy Lewis, Buddah publicist. "They were doing a huge push, and Buddah was just a little company. (Radio program directors) would say, 'We're not going to play Steve Goodman. We're playing John Prine.' It always bothered me. I thought John Prine was good, but I just thought Steve Goodman was amazing."

The disparity was evident in concert fees as well. "John started off at $1,000 a night, and Stevie was like $500, maybe," recalls his manager, Al Bunetta. "Stevie had to earn everything, and boy, he did."

Steve wasn't beyond chewing out Prine on this point. Chet Hanson, who booked shows for Steve starting in 1972, recalls the sting of such a rebuke.

"This is no big deal, this life we have, the fact that we make a living singing," Hanson recalls Prine saying while the three sat at Hollywood's Troubadour.

"Man, this is the greatest life," Steve countered. "Do you realize how many people would love to make a living singing? You never had to struggle with it. One day, you were not a singer, and the next day you sang in front of some people, and bing, it all happened for you. Most people, it doesn't happen that way. They've got to work, and they've got to work, and they've got to work. God gave you this great talent that you can write these incredibly sensitive songs. So just because it came easy to you, don't take it for granted. This is a great, great, great gift that you've been given." [5]

Steve and Prine initially appeared often on the same bill, but Bunetta tried to improve the fortunes of each by separating them. "Some people thought we were a duo, that we just followed each other around," Prine says, "and it was only Bunetta that figured out after awhile that it'd be good to not book us together, so we'd have separate personalities." Inevitably, however, came unavoidable requests for the two to be paired, and Bunetta acceded.

While Prine's record sales were higher, Prine also says his own performing limitations led to a formula in which Steve opened for Prine and returned to the stage at the end of shows to accompany him on a half-dozen Prine songs and country standards. Steve never was billed above Prine, and Prine never returned the favor and accompanied Steve on songs that Steve had written. Ironically, a key factor was Steve's stage prowess.

"I'm not a very good harmony singer, and I'm not a guitar picker where I can just get up and pick on anybody's song," Prine says. "Steve, though, was just the opposite. He could jump in the middle of any of my songs and sing the lead or the harmony or play the lead or background. If we could have figured a way for me to pick on Steve's songs, we would have just done the whole thing as one show. But I wasn't then and I'm not now that dexterous, and Steve always put a couple of really hard chords in his stuff. I didn't write such simple melodies on purpose, like that's all I knew, but Steve knew all the old standards like 'Lady, Be Good' and what I'd call nine-fingered chords, where you need nine fingers to hold 'em down. I didn't know those things, so Steve would be the helper."

Steve knew all the old standards like 'Lady, Be Good' and what I'd call nine-fingered chords, where you need nine fingers to hold 'em down. I didn't know those things, so Steve would be the helper.
JOHN PRINE

4: Prine was floored by how Kristofferson plugged his songs. "Everything was happening for him," Prine says. "Anytime I was around Kris, open one door, and there'd be 12 press people in there. There'd be somebody from *Life* magazine followin' him around for three weeks, and he'd answer about three questions and go, 'Here, interview this kid from Chicago. Don't interview me.' You couldn't begin to get press like that. It was like B.C. and A.D. for me. After Kristofferson, it was a whole new world."

5: Prine doesn't recall the lengthy exchange, but he adds, "I can imagine Steve readin' me out about somethin.'"

Despite such obstacles to Steve's instant commercial success, Buddah considered him a boon, says Jude Lyons, a production and advertising exec for the firm. "He got a lot of attention from us," she says. "Everybody liked him, everybody worked real hard for him, and we all had a great time." The gist of that satisfaction was that Steve and his guitar easily conformed to the relatively inexpensive promo formula of club dates and FM interviews and airplay that Buddah pursued for album sales in metro areas such as New York, Boston, Los Angeles, San Francisco, Chicago and Philadelphia, "where the bulk of the sales were," Lyons says. "I'm sure he sold no records in Dayton, if you know what I mean."

Still, despite the big-city push, Steve's LP never entered the top 200 on the *Billboard* album chart. "We didn't get the kind of sales that we thought we were going to get," recalls Joe Fields, Buddah sales manager. "It didn't sell a ton, but it sold very, very steady." In the face of 100,000 sales for Prine's debut album (which spent three weeks in the top 200, peaking in March at #154), Steve later claimed 50,000 copies of his own LP were sold. But Larry Harris, Buddah's national director of album promotion and the cousin of Buddah chief Neil Bogart, says that the LP sold "no higher than" 30,000 copies. The discrepancy is understandable, says song plugger Eddie O'Laughlin. "There was no way of knowing" the actual sales for Steve's LP, he says, "because Neil Bogart was so talented at cosmetically making something look more successful than a project may have been."

Of course, the LP's prime asset was "City of New Orleans." "Everybody knew that was the strength," Lyons says. But Steve was not perceived as a "singles act," she says, and Bogart "badly wanted to sell albums because as the bubblegum king he was never respected. Single acts would sell to kids. The emphasis was really on album airplay." Furthermore, she says, a hit single was not the aim of many "album acts" at the time. "They almost didn't want to have a hit single. It was like they were selling out if they did."

In that vein, when Buddah launched Steve's "City of New Orleans" as a single in late January, Steve quickly incorporated the release in his act in a manner that was affectionately sarcastic. He told his Earl on Harlem audience a month earlier, "The record company called me and said, 'Steve, we picked a song off the album for a single that the kids can dance to.' Imagine me lip-synching this song on the Dick Clark show ('American Bandstand'). Jimmie Rodgers'd shoot me!"

Steve's "City" single never cracked the *Billboard* top 100, "bubbling under" for two weeks and peaking Feb. 5 at just #113. "Nobody was duly upset," Lyons says. "We tried very hard to make 'City of New Orleans' a hit," adds Harris, who says that Steve's recording may have been too upbeat or "nice" for the hip audience to which Buddah was aiming him. "I got him a ton of airplay on progressive radio, but we just couldn't pull it off." [6]

The failure could not be laid at the feet of competition from John Denver. While Denver's "Aerie" reached a high of #75 during a 16-week run on the *Billboard* LP chart, his version of "City of New Orleans" was not a driving

Imagine me lip-synching this song on the Dick Clark show. Jimmie Rodgers'd shoot me!
STEVE GOODMAN

6: Five months later, Steve only half-jokingly laid the blame for low sales in Chicago of the Buddah 45 of his "City of New Orleans" on Ray Nordstrand and Norm Pellegrini, hosts of WFMT-FM's "Midnight Special" show, on which Steve's earlier, unreleased version of the song had been airing since late 1970: "Christ, one of the reasons 'City of New Orleans' didn't become a million-seller, so to speak, in Chicago was because everyone assumed it was an oldie but goodie by the time the record came out."

factor. Nor did RCA want it to be. Instead of releasing "City" as the follow-up single to "Friends with You," the company chose Denver's rendition of the Buddy Holly hit "Everyday," placing "City" on its flip (or "B") side. The Feb. 12 edition of *Billboard* listed the 45 in its "Top 60 Pop Spotlight," hyping it as "strong material ... a sure topper for his recent 'Friends with You,' " and *Variety* listed it in its "Top Singles" column of Feb. 23, noting that the B side "is a big number by Steve Goodman and Denver."

But "Everyday" flopped. The 45 spent only three weeks on the *Billboard* top 100 singles chart, peaking at only #81. Milt Okun, Denver's producer, originally wanted "City" to be the follow-up single to "Friends with You," but RCA's executives, whom he labels "idiots," were not happy with making "City" an A side. "At that point, even though we had had one monster hit ('Country Roads'), I didn't feel that I had the muscle to insist, and I didn't realize I could have insisted," Okun says. "So it was sort of a compromise to put it on the B side."

Even on the B side, there was hope for Denver's "City," Okun says. "In those days, B sides happened occasionally," he says. "About a quarter of the time, the B side started getting played." But Denver's version of "City" did not succeed, and the song sat buried on an album that never had a breakout single. Denver, a far more commercial artist than Steve would ever become, had to record another LP and wait till the end of 1972 before a single of his would again achieve hit status and etch his persona into stone, "Rocky Mountain High."

"City of New Orleans" — Steve's version, Denver's version or both — did gain enough airplay to land him a pair of unusual bookings that winter, one in the 5-degree bite of central Minnesota and the other in balmy Florida.

The federal men's prison in Sandstone, a tiny town between Minneapolis and Duluth, was the site of the former show, for a crowd of 200 inmates eyeing him as he entertained in front of a "Land of Sky Blue Waters" mural backdrop, depicting deer sipping from a babbling stream. It was Steve's first experience playing for prisoners, "scary dudes" who ranged "from Indians from the reservation who were truant to white-collar criminals to dopers to draft protesters," recalls Suzanne Weil, who organized the show. Steve teamed with John Prine, and not long into his opening set, Steve heard a cry from the audience: "Shorty, blues me or lose me!" The challenge was momentarily unnerving. "God, I was scared shitless," Steve said later. "I played every blues song I knew — about five, but I played 'em long."

"It's a tough audience, and you don't want to be patronizing," says Weil, who persuaded artists to do free concerts at Sandstone after playing paid gigs the night before at Walker Arts Center, where she directed performing arts. At first, she was skeptical about bringing Steve to Sandstone, thinking, "Oh, God, the last thing that these guys want is a little Jew from Chicago." But he "won them over brilliantly," she says. "Steve had such an honest patter that was so ingratiating without trying to be ingratiating. There was something vulnerable and confident all at the same time. Just from the way he took the stage, there was no artifice, and those guys (the inmates) can tell in a minute."

> **Steve had such an honest patter that was so ingratiating without trying to be ingratiating. There was something vulnerable and confident all at the same time.**
> **SUZANNE WEIL**

Less threatening but more revealing for Steve was his stint as a hired musician for the campaign of the Lincoln-esque front-runner for the Democratic presidential nomination, Sen. Edmund S. Muskie.

Steve didn't seek the gig, but neither did he spurn it. The Muskie campaign had cooked up the "Sunshine Special," paying Amtrak $5,852.50 to rent a six-car Seaboard Coast Line diesel train for an eight-city, 407-mile, southbound zigzag journey through the Florida panhandle, as an echo of President Harry S Truman's fabled 30,000-mile, nationwide whistle-stop tour of 1948. The Feb. 18-19 trip from Jacksonville to Miami was intended to shore up support prior to Florida's first-ever presidential primary on March 14 and deflect attention from Muskie's rivals: Sen. Hubert Humphrey, Muskie's 1968 running mate; renegade Alabama Gov. George Wallace, who ended up winning the primary; and Sen. George McGovern, the longest-running war critic and eventual party nominee. The idea was to bolster the centrist Muskie's image as the Democrat to beat in the fall. To fill out the whistle-stop tour's nostalgic railroad theme, the Muskie brass sought a musician who could sing about trains, and Steve's "City of New Orleans" had come to their attention. Contacted to find out if Steve could be available for the trip, Buddah chief Neil Bogart asked Steve if he was game. He replied with an agreeable shrug.

"Steve didn't believe there were political solutions to life's problems," wrote Steve's wife, Nancy, more than 20 years later. In liner notes to a 1994 Goodman anthology, she said that Steve bestowed upon politicians "the irreverent admiration he always showed for desperados, con artists and pitchmen." So when the Muskie gig arose, Steve consented, less as an endorsement of a candidate than for the chance to partake of the balmy, near-spring Florida weather and observe a national campaign firsthand.

It wasn't the first presidential opportunity for Steve, who had sung "at all kinds of benefits for McGovern and (John) Lindsay," he said. "I sang for Lindsay until I talked to a couple of New Yorkers who told me that Lindsay was a wonderful idealist but probably the worst administrator in the history of the city, and he'd screwed things up pretty bad, so I said, 'All right,' and I started singin' for McGovern and all these (other) guys." [7]

Tying his image to a mainstream Democrat such as Muskie didn't bother him. "Reputation?" Steve reflected for a later audience. "I would have sung for Strom Thurmond (South Carolina's conservative Democratic senator) for the chance to meet him. It didn't matter to me. ... The hell with it, I'd just show up. I figure, you never get to meet U.S. senators anyhow. ... I like trains, it was the dead of winter up there (in Chicago), it was colder than shit, and I figured, 'All right.' "

With an eye to Florida's diverse population, Muskie staffers also had hired two African-American entertainers for the train ride: O.B. McClinton, the self-described "black Irishman of country music," and the better-known Roosevelt "Rosey" Grier, the 6-foot-6, 340-pound singer, actor and ex-NFL linebacker and tackle who had gained political renown when, as a bodyguard to Robert

---

I would have sung for Strom Thurmond for the chance to meet him. It didn't matter to me. ... The hell with it, I'd just show up.
STEVE GOODMAN

7: One McGovern benefit that Steve and Ed and Fred Holstein played was at the University of Colorado in Boulder, where Steve and John Prine were booked at Tulagi's. "Broke my fuckin' heart," recalled Fred Holstein, who said only 80 students showed up, many of them high. "I couldn't believe it. Out of the 80 kids who were there, 40 of them were wired for sound. They glowed in the dark."

Campaigning for the Democratic presidential nomination, U.S. Sen. Edmund S. Muskie greets Miami voters Feb. 19, 1972, at the end of his whistle-stop tour of Florida, aided by a trio of tunesmiths, from left: Steve, the massive Rosey Grier and, in a leopard-skin suit, O.B. McClinton. The entertainers' diversity, Muskie told crowds, "helps us to recognize the mistakes we have made in the past in dealing with each other, young and old, black and white."
(Photo by Emil Fray)

Kennedy, he subdued the presidential candidate's assassin, Sirhan Sirhan, late the night of June 5, 1968.

The campaign year of 1968, which also had included the killing of the Rev. Martin Luther King, Jr., the disastrous riots during the Democratic convention in Chicago and the hair's breadth November victory of Richard Nixon over Humphrey, hovered heavily in the minds of the 100-plus friends, politicians, journalists and several wives of Vietnam prisoners of war who rode with Steve on the 1972 Muskie train. With the Vietnam War raging, Muskie's relatively late switch to favoring a pullout — and his regret that he didn't do so earlier — was painfully evident to the 70 journalists aboard. (Four newsmen aboard the train composed a parody called "Indecisive Choo-Choo.") Scribes ranged from reporters for all three TV networks and big-name national veterans to drugged-out "gonzo" writer Hunter S. Thompson, who derided the Florida tour in meandering dispatches for bi-weekly *Rolling Stone* that were compiled in his 1973 book *Fear and Loathing: On the Campaign Trail '72*. Thompson, who had reported on Nixon's 1968 successful run, slammed "Muskie and his goddamn silly train," noting that "It came as a definite shock to find that hanging around Florida with Ed Muskie was even duller and more depressing than traveling with Evil Dick himself."

Not surprisingly, a formulaic agenda played out at each stop: Whipped up (and paid, Thompson claimed) by advance staff, festive local audiences of 250 to 1,500, ranging from high-school students to union workers, assembled at the appointed towns' ordinarily neglected railroad stations. As the train rolled in, bearing the words "Sunshine Special" painted on the side and sounding a full-throated whistle, it halted briefly to let camera crews disembark and scurry forward a few hundred yards to set up equipment along the tracks. Then it pulled up to let the crowd gather around the caboose, which was draped with a wrap-around "Ed Muskie for President" sign. With all the elements in place, the show — anchored by Steve's guitar — began.

As if to offset his shoulder-length hair, Steve had clothed himself for the occasion, wearing a sport coat, open-necked white shirt and dress shoes. "City of New Orleans" and the Leadbelly train song "Rock Island Line" were to be his regular contributions, [8] but after the first stop in Jacksonville he came down with "a really bad cold" and "couldn't sing a note." Steve still could play guitar, and he did so while McClinton, outfitted in a leopard-skin suit, sang Muskie's praises to the tune of the Wrigley's Doublemint Gum jingle ("he's gonna double your pleasure"). McClinton also performed Merle Haggard's "Daddy Frank (The Guitar Man)" and Charley Pride's "I'm Just Me" before crooning the railroad song, "This Train Is Bound for Glory," written by Big Bill Broonzy and popularized by Woody Guthrie — but with words McClinton had altered for the occasion:

> *This train is the Muskie train, this train*
> *This train is the Muskie train, this train*
> *This is the Muskie train*
> *This train carries the man from Maine*
> *This train is the Muskie train, this train*

Next up was the massive Grier. With spectacles, mustache and goatee and wearing an open-necked paisley shirt and vest, he lumbered onto the caboose platform, stepped up to a mike and welcomed the contrived horde. Steve stood at Grier's side, strumming a strong rhythm as Grier began a crusading rendition of "Let the Sunshine In," the mantra-like Fifth Dimension hit from "Hair," the 1968 anti-war Broadway musical. ("Me and Roosevelt Grier, one of God's better Mutt and Jeff acts," Steve quipped. "He was big. I came up to his tits.")

Following this 10-minute musical fanfare came the man from Maine himself, in shirtsleeves, delivering a 15-minute stump speech that Hunter Thompson wearily reported as never failing to include some variation on the line, "It's time for the good people of America to get together behind somebody they can trust." (While Muskie was hardly an electrifying presence, his use of the word "trust" was prescient, as the Republicans' infamous Watergate burglary was just five months off.) At the end of each oration, Muskie invited Steve and the rest of the musicians back onto the platform for a rousing reprise of "Let the Sunshine In." While the candidate leaned over the railing to autograph pamphlets, signs and straw hats, the crowd cheered as the train slowly pulled away from the station — a scene straight out of Frank Capra's "Mr. Deeds Goes to Town."

Muskie capitalized on the symbolism supplied by the entertainers' ethnicity,

It's time for the good people of America to get together behind somebody they can trust.
SEN. EDMUND MUSKIE

8: Steve also sang an improvised song with the words "We're gonna ride the Sunshine Special, down the Florida line," according to a UPI report in the Feb. 19, 1972, edition of the *Times-Union* of Jacksonville.

reported the *DeLand Sun News*. "It shows that we try to strike accord between us," he said while speaking to 1,500 high-school and university students and others at the DeLand stop. "It helps us to recognize the mistakes we have made in the past in dealing with each other, young and old, black and white." Throughout the tour, Muskie lent his praise to folk music itself. "These songs have been written for thousands of years. ... Thousands of years of human life come out to you, come out to me, in these words," he said. "This is why I like to have Rosie and O.B. and Steve with me, because in the words of these songs, they manage to say better than I can say what it is that we all yearn for in our country."

While the "Sunshine Special" plied the tracks between stops, Steve occasionally serenaded Muskie[9] and strolled through the rest of the air-conditioned rail cars. But when the train left the fourth stop of Winter Haven, Steve — fortunately accompanied by Grier — remained on the rear platform of the caboose. As the train sped up to 60 mph and whipped around a bend, Steve (115 pounds "on a good day") somehow lost his footing. "I went over the side, I mean, I flew, and all I saw was bushes and gravel coming up at me, and I knew I'd bought it," he said. "This big hand went 'Unnh!' and hauled me in and put me back down on the platform." It was the hand of Grier. "He saved my life," Steve said. More than three decades later, Grier does not recall the incident but says he had made it his practice to befriend "all little guys."

Even more mythic than Steve's dramatic rescue was an episode during the tour's fifth stop, and its setting was the train station in a tiny inland town east of Tampa named Sebring, population 7,223. Whatever happened there in the heat of the afternoon inspired a story that became rollicking for Steve's later concert audiences but impossible to fully verify today.

Steve said he hadn't known it at the time, but Muskie planned a longer-than-usual speech in Sebring "because he got out all the voting records from four years back and eight years back and 12 years back, and put 'em into his computer. The computer comes out with this answer that says that Sebring, Florida, is the most right-wing county in the United States and that he's in a lot of trouble in Sebring, that there's parts of Sebring that make Mississippi look like Sweden, that in 1968 in Sebring, Florida, 418 people voted for George Wallace, 246 people voted for Richard Nixon, seven people voted for Hubert Humphrey, and 5,324 voted for (the late Nazi military leader) Hermann Goering, the heavy write-in favorite."

Beset by stomach cramps that resulted from recent chemotherapy, his cold and what Nancy described as "an ill-advised Mexican meal the night before," Steve played his instrumental portion of the rear-platform show for a Sebring crowd of 400 senior citizens and others, then bolted for the bathroom during Muskie's speech, which focused on growth, jobs and Vietnam. After relieving himself, Steve eyed a sign that had become so familiar during his college-era rail trips in Illinois that he had quoted from it in "City of New Orleans": "Passengers will refrain from flushing the toilet while the train is in the station." He thought it best to heed the sign.

> I went over the side,
> I mean, I flew, and all
> I saw was bushes and
> gravel coming up at me,
> and I knew I'd bought it.
> **STEVE GOODMAN**

9: An on-board photo by Burton Berinsky — showing Steve perched cross-legged on a chair and picking a tune on his guitar and Muskie and Grier listening intently from a facing seat — has been printed often enough that some written summaries of Steve's life state incorrectly that he was inspired to write "City of New Orleans" while traveling on Muskie's campaign train.

"I didn't want to be rude to whoever else might have to use those facilities later," he said, "so I figured I'd sit it out, it's a five-minute speech, the train pulls out, I hit the chain, I get up.

"Well, about 35-40 minutes go by (the *Sebring News* said the speech was just 15 minutes long), and he's still talking. I was thinkin' to myself, 'Steve, when you wake up tomorrow morning, you're gonna have to shoot a whole lot of Preparation H unless you get up right now.' I figured the hell with it, I'm gettin' up. I'll hit the chain, it all goes out on the tracks, and no one is any of the wiser until we're out of town."

Steve pulled the cord and wandered back to the lounge behind the rear platform to wait for Muskie to finish his address, unaware that his waste had not simply fallen to the tracks. Instead, he said, "there's a goddamn vacuum pump that blows it out of the back of the train with a great force."

At the exact moment that this occurred, Steve — in a portion of his story that surely was a contrivance — said Muskie had just told the crowd, "My friends, I know what the voters of this county want, and I can deliver it!"

"The senator," Steve said, "couldn't have timed it any better if he wanted to."

This sequence of events, Steve said, didn't become clear to him until 10 minutes later while he sat in the lounge. With Muskie still speechifying, press secretary Dick Stewart (who was on the train but today doesn't recall the incident) rushed through the lounge, horrified but not knowing that Steve had executed the fateful flush.

"Steve, a terrible thing's happened out there!" Stewart said.

"Yeah, what?" Steve replied.

"A lot of people got covered in *shit* out there, boy!"

"Man, I didn't think *you* thought so," Steve said. "C'mon, man, you work for the guy!"

Steve insisted to his audiences that the story was true, and in an interview with freelance journalist Steve Weitzman he claimed that his effluent had splashed a UPI photographer and an Amtrak official. "I hit specific people," Steve said. But a campaign tape recording of the proceedings at Sebring, stored at the Edmund S. Muskie Archives and Special Collections Library in Lewiston, Maine, yields no hint of such a fecal disruption.

Authentic or apocryphal, Steve's tale foretold the failing fortunes of the Muskie campaign. Days later, memories of Muskie's train trip were eclipsed by Nixon's unprecedented visit to the People's Republic of China. Three weeks after the whistle-stop tour, Muskie's so-called crying scene on a flatbed truck in front of the Manchester, New Hampshire, *Union Leader* signaled his campaign's freefall. Three more weeks later, following his brutal trio of primary defeats in Florida, Wisconsin and Pennsylvania, the man from Maine pulled out of the race.

The crowning anti-political touch of the whistle-stop tour for Steve came when the train hit Miami. There, Steve reconnected with "one of my neurotic friends from New York," the manic Jerry Rubin, 33-year-old co-founder of the

> I figured the hell with it, I'm gettin' up. I'll hit the chain, it all goes out on the tracks, and no one is any of the wiser until we're out of town.
> **STEVE GOODMAN**

irreverent Youth International Party (the "Yippies") and a defendant in the 1969-70 federal trial of the Chicago Seven activists who were accused of conspiracy to incite a riot during the 1968 Democratic National Convention. While awaiting the ruling of a federal appeals court (which eight months later reversed his conviction), the zany Rubin was in Miami to prepare protests during the Democratic and Republican conventions to be held there later in the year.

Rubin had used press credentials to board the train in West Palm Beach, and Rubin heckled Muskie about Vietnam during his speech in Miami, drawing a testy scolding from the candidate. Steve, however, saw in Rubin an engaging and insightful personality. "He's one of the three or four most intelligent men I've ever met," Steve said. "His life is a lot different than his act. It's fantastic, incredibly together. He knew just what he was doing all along, for all those years. Beautiful to see him get away with all that, right? Because all he did was stand around and tell everybody what they already knew, that it was OK to act like an asshole, because everybody else was doing it. And it didn't matter what kind of asshole you were. Assholes are assholes, that's what his whole message was. It was great."

If Steve retained a belief in the political process from his studies at Lake Forest College, his experience on the Muskie train and his encounter with Rubin started to dissolve it. With the "Sunshine Special" and the waffling war posture of its candidate fresh in mind, Steve soon found reason to create what some consider the most moving anti-war song of the era.

One week after joining John Prine, Bob Gibson, Ed and Fred Holstein and Jackson Browne on the stage of Chicago's Arie Crown Theater to back Joni Mitchell on the chorus of her encore, "The Circle Game," Steve headed east for a Feb. 28-March 5 gig in cold, snowy Rochester, New York. One afternoon there, Buddah slated a promo appearance downtown in which Steve played songs while sitting in a chair atop a cabinet behind a glass counter at Sibley's Department Store. On another morning, as a favor to local folkie/teacher Bob Schwartz, Steve sang and played a handful of songs — and explained the meanings behind the cultural references in Don McLean's hit "American Pie" — for Schwartz' fifth-grade students at St. Theodore's church school.

Evenings that week he spent south of Rochester, performing at the Nugget Pizza Palace, an eatery decorated in barn wood and flocked wallpaper whose raucous din — customers' order numbers flashing on display screens, the ding-ding-ding of pinball machines and the smack of balls on a nearby pool table — resembled that of the Earl of Old Town.

There, he opened for the New York Rock Ensemble, led by Michael Kamen, who later composed film scores for "Lethal Weapon," "Die Hard" and "Robin Hood: Prince of Thieves." Offstage, Kamen, whose parents had introduced him at a young age to the Seeger family and immersed him in folk music, enjoyed bouncing traditional songs back and forth with Steve. At one point, he sang to Steve the first verse of a traditional union tune, "My Old Man Was a Man Like Lincoln," whereupon Steve sang to Kamen the remainder of the

All he did was stand around and tell everybody what they already knew, that it was OK to act like an asshole, because everybody else was doing it.
STEVE GOODMAN

lyrics. "He knew very much about the historic nature of politics in American folk music," Kamen said. One night midweek, Steve summoned a newer tradition, borrowing an electric guitar and joining Kamen's group for a jam on Paul Anka's "Diana," Bobby Day's "Rockin' Robin" and other oldies. "We should have opened for him," Kamen joked.

But that week at the pizzeria was to become most notable for Steve because of someone else he met — a short, slender woman whose recent experience he transformed overnight into a memorable anthem of anger and affirmation.

Her name was Penny Evans, or so he said. She sought Steve's ear, so the two went out for coffee with four others after one night's show. The encounter started off as one that Steve was finding increasingly typical. "When you do what I do and travel around the country, people think you really do understand," he told Howard Larman that spring on the L.A.-based "FolkScene" program. "I don't know why that is, but they feel that you have some grip on reality that they're lookin' for because you can sing about it. But what they don't understand is that I'm singin' about it because I don't understand it. So people always come up to you and tell you their life story."

As Steve listened to the woman, however, a riveting narrative emerged. She told him that she was a 21-year-old single mother of two daughters — one 3 years old, the other 9 months — and that she was working daytimes as a computer operator while her mother took care of the kids. "I started thinking this has got to be the bravest woman alive," Steve said. "She's the picture of what you call the average, middle-class, young married woman, only the situations of life have hit her in the nose rather abruptly. ... Here she was with no particular political connections, just a typical God-fearing American." Her husband of three years, a soldier, had recently died in Vietnam, and she had become so furious about the war that when the federal widows-and-orphans benefit checks came to her in the mail, she was ripping them up and sending them back to the government.

"She was crying on his shoulder," recalls Lee Grills, the Nugget's owner. "She was really goofy, kind of a little girl and kind of pretty, a little spacey."

But the woman's circumstances deeply touched Steve, particularly the combination of protest, pride and despair reflected in her refusal to take money from a system that she felt had sentenced her spouse to die. It was, he told Al Rudis of the *Chicago Sun-Times* four months later, the most honest, self-sacrificing thing he'd heard anyone do in the name of integrity.

After the woman related her story, the two fell silent for a moment. Steve finally spoke.

"Don't give me any more details," he said. "I'm gonna write a song."

"I'd be flattered," she replied quietly.

Trying to move on, Steve decided to change the subject.

"What do you know about music?" he asked her.

"I know 'Chopsticks' and 'Heart and Soul' on the piano," she said.

"Well," Steve said, "it takes two people to play 'Heart and Soul.' "

Lee Grills, owner of the Nugget Pizza Palace in Rochester, found the young woman talking with Steve about her Vietnam war widowhood "really goofy, kind of a little girl and kind of pretty, a little spacey."

(Photo by Eleanor Grills)

Tears welled in the woman's eyes.

"Yeah, I know," she said between sobs.

Her story reminded Steve of the words to a Civil War ballad, "Cruel War" ("The cruel war is raging / Johnny has to fight"). "There's something constant about that, and I saw a 20th century example of it, and I wanted to catch it before I lost it," Steve said.

After hustling back to his hotel, Steve organized the story's fine points and found himself humming a tune he had heard sung at the Philadelphia Folk Festival by both traditional songster Louis Killen and the British folk group Young Tradition — a sea chantey that reached back to the 1820s called "The Flying Cloud." The a cappella ballad, whose author is unknown, is told in the voice of an Irishman, an only child whose future spelled "good fortune" but who instead grew up to become a thief, torturer and murderer while working aboard an American slaving and pirate ship named in the song's title. The musical tale ends with the narrator and the rest of the crew succumbing to an attack by a British vessel and languishing under a death sentence in London's Newgate prison.

"It's a broadside about a young man who's drawn into bad things and pays the price," says Killen, who had learned it as a youth from a 1952 recording by Ewan McColl and others and pared its 56 verses down to about a dozen after consulting the 1938 Joanna Colcord folklore textbook, *Songs of American Sailormen*. The final verse, in which the Irishman tells his love, "I'll never kiss your cheek again nor hold your hand no more," helped inspire Steve to compose an inverted version by telling Penny Evans' home-front story in her own narrative voice.

"Nobody writes about anybody that's left at home," Steve told *Omaha Rainbow* magazine in 1976. Plus, he discovered that the six-verse song that he was putting together "scanned" (possessed meter and rhyme) like the 150-year-old chantey. "So I decided that rather than making something up that wouldn't be half as appropriate, it sounded like that kind of time." Thus, in just 30 minutes in a Rochester hotel room, with a solitary chord alteration, was born "The Ballad of Penny Evans."

In many ways, it quickly became a distinctive, iconographic work, both of its era and for the ages. It addressed unblinkingly the notion of a life lost young, a serious theme that Steve, with his leukemia, already understood and had explored but which was not commonplace in popular music. It also revealed — in individual, humanizing fashion — the devastating home-front effects of the war that was dominating that year's presidential election. In that sense, it was a bookend to Prine's "Sam Stone," which, while written in third person, was told from the fatalistic viewpoint of its battle-scarred, heroin-saddled protagonist. Steve's song went further, however, closing with a suspended tension that reflected the agony — and challenge — of all conflict: "They say the war is over, but I think it's just begun."

Because Steve had heard the story straight from the source and believed its authenticity (including the woman's innocent assertion that Bill, her husband, was "the only boy I slept with and the only one I will"), it summoned journalistic instincts, letting him mine the story's imagery and make it accessible, a characteristic that was becoming typical of Steve's work. Listeners could "see" Penny playing the left-hand part of "Heart and Soul" on her father's grand piano while Bill played the right-hand part — a vivid set-up for a line later in the song that conveyed the war's devastation by referencing "50,000 'Heart and Souls' being played with just one hand." As with "City of New Orleans," the specificity allowed the song to break through to the universal.

From its very first word, the song was told from a personal, identifiable and therefore undeniable point of view, but what gave it unusual authority was that it was a woman's story told by a man. This was not uncommon in traditional English music, but it was rare in songs designed for the American mainstream of 1972. Steve may have taken a cue from Prine, who had used the same technique the year prior in "Angel from Montgomery," although the bitter character in Prine's song was "an old woman," not a 21-year-old. The move was audacious in its courage and humility, akin in today's world to a straight male playing the part of a gay man. Killen says it reflected Steve's mature understanding that the power of a story could transcend the identity of the singer. "It's not, 'Listen to me sing this song.' It's that the story is so important that the singer gets behind it, and what you see is the story when you're listening. You don't see the singer."

Ingeniously, though, Steve as the song's messenger gained stature and an aura of sensitivity by singing with a masculine timbre the tale of a woman whose voice society might stereotypically expect to be weaker and whose plight might otherwise have gone untold.

The song's most drastic departure from Steve's repertoire — and from the musical mainstream — was his decision to stick with an a cappella presentation. For years, the Persuasions and other doo-wop groups had carved out this style, but their harmonies approximated the missing instrumentation. In 1971, Judy Collins tried a voice-only approach on her recording of "Farewell to Tarwathie" but relied on the moans of humpback whales for counterpoint. In many shows (enshrined famously in the 1970 film "Woodstock"), Joan Baez sang sans guitar on "Swing Low, Sweet Chariot," but the focus was on her supple soprano, and the familiarity of the spiritual sapped any suspense over the song's content. Steve's "Ballad of Penny Evans" offered his resonant voice, an original allegory and nothing else. As such, it carried a singular narrative punch.

"That very act gives incredible power," says Killen, who felt honored by Steve's adaptation of "The Flying Cloud" and its a cappella form. "Sung with a rhythmic accompaniment like a guitar, words are forced into a mode, whereas singing a cappella actually allows you to tell a story, as if he was talking to you, or as if Penny Evans were talking. He saw the power in the way that I sang 'The Flying Cloud' and the effect that had on audiences, and he thought, 'This fits what I want to say.' "

Louis Killen, shown in 1977, whose "The Flying Cloud" helped inspire Steve to write "The Ballad of Penny Evans," says the female voice of Steve's song reflected maturity: "It's not, 'Listen to me sing this song.' It's that the story is so important that the singer gets behind it, and what you see is the story when you're listening. You don't see the singer."
(Photo by Art Thieme)

Perhaps the underlying key to why Steve gave the song a female viewpoint and a solitary vocal arrangement was that it allowed him to deliver a strident message but at the same time distance himself from it. "I just want folks to have a good time," he often said, adding in reference to "Penny Evans" in one interview, "One of the things I'm really trying to avoid is preaching."

But Steve mostly shunned such analysis in describing "Penny Evans" and reverted to self-deprecation. "Oh, for God's sake, I didn't write that song," Steve told Howard Larman. "The tune is an old, traditional sea chantey, and the words, except that I made 'em rhyme, are hers, basically. ... It got filtered through me." Steve told Robert Brinton of the British *Disc* music magazine, "Here was a case where I felt I simply wouldn't be doing my job if I didn't use what she'd told me." He said to Rudis, "I just wanted to tell that story because I thought it should be told, and she told it to me. If she told it to somebody else, maybe they would have written it. I called Prine and said, 'Hey John, let me sing this to you, and when I get done, tell me if you wrote this,' because it's certainly out of touch with what I usually do." [10] The song, Steve insisted, "was an accident. It was a one-shot item."

But as he soon found, the "accident" gave Steve a spellbinding tool to rivet an audience's attention. Back home on Tuesday, March 7, just two days after finishing his run in Rochester, Steve was one of nine local folk, comedy, blues and classical acts entertaining at a four-hour "Salute to the Nominees" put on at the O'Hare Marriott by the Chicago chapter of the National Academy of Recording Arts and Sciences one week before the national Grammy Awards. The industry audience of 400, including soul luminaries Jerry Butler and Smokey Robinson, heard performers ranging from Prine, Kris Kristofferson and (via taped message) Rod Stewart to Muddy Waters, Howlin' Wolf and B.B. King. Just as he did with the Business Executives Move rally the previous fall with Joan Baez, Steve immersed himself in singing an anti-war song, but this time it was his own: "Penny Evans." His guitar gamely slung over his shoulder, he stepped to the microphone — just as he had done with Saturday morning musical prayers a dozen years prior at Temple Beth Israel — and summoned a commanding voice and a balanced tone of melancholy and anger to launch into the ballad, providing what Steve Metalitz of the *Chicago Reader* called the evening's "most electrifying moment."

"In the hands of a lesser performer," Metalitz wrote, "it wouldn't have worked. The anachronistic style was a gamble. The theme ran the risk of mawkishness. But Goodman brought it off just right, with a sob in his voice but always in control. The audience, lulled into drowsiness by Kristofferson's mellow guitar and soporific baritone, woke up, took notice and applauded long and loud. This disconcerted Goodman a bit, but Kristofferson was like a proud papa at his son's bar mitzvah. It pays to have friends like that."

In performances of "Penny Evans" later that year, Steve galvanized audiences and instantly won lifelong fans. [11] David Schulman, a student at Stanford University who was troubled by the moral issues inherent in registering for the

---

The anachronistic style was a gamble. The theme ran the risk of mawkishness. But Goodman brought it off just right.
STEVE METALITZ
CHICAGO READER

10: Steve often called friends in the middle of the night to play them a newly composed tune. "There were a whole bunch of people he would do that with, depending on the genre of the song," says Paula Ballan.

11: "Ballad of Penny Evans" had its detractors, as when Steve performed it on a local Saturday night staple, "The Marty Faye Show" on WLS-TV. "It was a surprise to him," Steve later told interviewer Win Stracke. "It went on the air because we were live, but I don't think he was real pleased." Steve also performed "Penny Evans" for his June 28, 1972, appearance on the "David Frost Show," but it was cut.

draft, says the song endeared him to Steve by taking a "pre-feminist feminist" approach that indirectly bucked the macho sexism that had permeated the anti-war and civil-rights movements. "It was a song about the war, but it wasn't 'One, two, three, four. We don't want your fucking war.' It was a humane statement of suffering without beating you up about it," says Schulman, who later became Los Angeles' (and the nation's) first municipal AIDS anti-discrimination attorney.

The song also fiercely appealed to Rand Smith, a graduate student at the University of Michigan in Ann Arbor, where, while sitting on the floor at The Ark coffeehouse [12] in 1972, he first heard Steve sing the song in a set that lasted until 2 a.m. Smith, who went on to be a political-science professor at Steve's former school, Lake Forest College, teaches a course there on the Vietnam War. Though he doesn't possess Steve's vocal range or natural vibrato, Smith sings the song for his students, telling them it's the best broadside of its era. "It tells a story and draws you into a person," Smith says. "It pushed the envelope. It's not some student agitprop stuff. He met this character."

Six months later, Steve met her again, when she called and told him she would be in Chicago, and they arranged to connect at the Earl of Old Town. Steve had been talking as if he were "ready to take care of her for the rest of her life," recalls his manager, Al Bunetta. "We were all built up for Penny Evans. He made her sound like a little girl who had lost everything." But when she walked into the Earl, Steve said later, he sensed something was not quite right. Her appearance and the way she carried herself were no longer innocent. Wearing hot pants, white go-go boots and red lipstick, to Steve she looked like a *Playboy* bunny. Instantly, he recognized his "blind spot," as the woman he had initially encountered as Penny Evans told him that she had left her girls home with their grandmother and was managing a Buffalo-based rock band, traveling the country with its six male members.

"I'm not denyin' that that might be a very good thing for her to do," Steve said as he related his unsettling discovery a year and a half later to an audience in Portland, Oregon. "I'm just sayin' this is probably not the same person I wrote the song about. What I mean is, I bought a bill of goods. I'm pretty gullible. I'm a mark. I mean, people sell me encyclopedias. I'll buy anything once, and I bought this story."

Speechless while the woman continued talking to him at the Earl, Steve extricated himself from the conversation, sidled up to the bar and whispered to fellow singer/songwriter Bob Gibson: "That's Penny Evans."

"If that's Penny Evans, we ought to fix her up with Sam Stone," the acerbic Gibson shot back with a laugh, referencing the self-destructive Vietnam veteran invented by John Prine. "I'd really like to see the two of them go out on a date," Gibson added. "They could cheer each other up, because she doesn't look anything like that song." [13]

For several years, Steve told audiences this part of the story — an extended joke on himself — to great comic effect. [14] But he also hastened to add that he

12: The Ark, a three-story house, was operated by David and Linda Siglin. There, Steve and David played catch on the front lawn and argued baseball for hours. Steve, says David Siglin, "was really proud of the fact that he could snap off a curve ball."

13: In mid-2007, someone writing as "Penny Evans" e-mailed the author saying that when she saw Steve at the Earl she was merely "with my girlfriends and their husbands, who were in a band" and that she didn't manage the band or wear hot pants and go-go boots. "If you really knew Steve," she wrote, "you would know he was a kidder." She also said she worked most of her life "for the government," was four months' pregnant when she first met Steve and soon gave birth to a boy. She said her son never served in the military. Her elder daughter died in 2006, she said, and her younger daughter is married with two sons. "I had a hard life, but the children and I did OK," she wrote. "(We're) just normal people with normal lives." The woman did not answer requests to talk by phone or in person. Meanwhile, a Boston-area man, David Curran, posted to a blog identifying himself as the son-in-law of Penny Evans, who he says lived in Spain and now lives west of Boston. Separately, he said his mother-in-law doesn't wish further communication about her life or to verify her identity.

14: Steve's admission that the woman's story was suspect "gave the song a hugely more complex and powerful setting and context," notes Flawn Williams, co-founder of the Amazingrace concert-producing co-op in Evanston, and now an engineer for National Public Radio in Washington D.C.

Paul Powell's shoebox stash made him a target of ridicule for Steve and others, including an Illinois native with the unusual name of Seth! Leary. The Kirkland, Washington, resident caricatured Powell for an Internet site on geocaching (high-tech treasure hunting), a hobby in which the prize is usually the size of a shoebox.
(Image © Seth! Leary)

15: While Steve consistently referred to a total of $750,000, the 1999 book *Paul Powell of Illinois: A Lifelong Democrat*, by Robert E. Harley, indicates that the total actually approximated $800,000.

felt the song was still worth singing because "there might be somebody out there somewhere" whom it matched. Then, in his August 1976 interview with *Omaha Rainbow*, Steve disclosed that the woman had remarried and was living in Boston. "At one point, I wasn't sure that she'd been telling me all the facts, or she might have made up some of it or imagined it before she even told it to me," he said. "But I guess that wasn't the case, and it turns out it was all pretty much the way it was told to me. I've since met a couple of people who were in the same situation, so I guess that's who the song's for."

"Penny Evans" wasn't Steve's only musical foray into politics in early 1972. Inspired by his stint on the Muskie train, he penned a timely, two-minute ditty called "Election Year Rag." Its words of cynicism set to a bouncy beat of celebration, the song outlined a metaphorical dance ("Take two steps to the left, and two steps to the right / Stand in the middle and you hang on tight") and tendered the conclusion that in a presidential race, "It's nobody's choice, and it's anybody's guess." Like any good satire, the tune walked the fine line between a call for change and an invitation to apathy.

Steve also had begun performing a rant about a corrupt Illinois official that was every bit as remote in its subject and preachy in its approach as "Penny Evans" was not. This more conventionally structured diatribe, which Steve had written the previous summer, took on the late Paul Taylor Powell, a longtime racetrack investor and Democratic officeholder and party leader. When Powell, then secretary of state, was felled by an Oct. 10, 1970, heart attack at age 68 in Rochester, Minnesota, he was said to have left behind in the closet of his apartment at the St. Nicholas Hotel in the state capital of Springfield an astonishing stash. Several metal strong boxes, a leather briefcase, loose envelopes and one notorious Marshall Field & Co. shoebox reportedly overflowed with a total of $750,000 in cash. [15] Questions proliferated after the story broke on Dec. 30, 1970, but official investigations and exposés by *Chicago Daily News* columnist Mike Royko and others in 1971 produced few firm answers. The motives of associates who discovered and disclosed the stockpile were suspect, and no conclusive proof surfaced about the source of the money or whether Powell was the one who had left it in the hotel closet.

Even so, rumors were rife, and the Democrat Powell was an easy and fascinating target for Steve to pillory at a time when the ire of youth was directed mostly at President Nixon and other Republicans. ("Avarice is a bipartisan proposition, and it's not limited to federal situations," he told audiences. "You can be in on it.") The young, former political-science student facing his own mortality found a compelling subject in the old pol who engendered enmity upon his demise. With biting lyrics ("You're a thief and a bum / Where's the money, and how come?"), accompanied by scathing intros in concerts, Steve's song — never given a title but known as "Paul Powell" — gave the deathbed discovery of Powell's riches a new life.

"I don't usually write songs about dead people, because you never know when they're going to come back and fuck around with you, but this guy had earned it," Steve said of Powell in October 1973 at Bubba's in South Miami. "Dying was probably the smartest thing he ever did. It kept him out of jail. It wasn't like these scandals that you see on TV. The guy was dead. They couldn't do anything to him." He added in February 1974 at a Portland, Oregon, show, "I don't think people were so mad at the guy because he took the money. Everybody does that where I live. But they were really mad that he had the good fortune to die before they could do anything about it. He had the big out."

With theatrical flair, Steve injected litanies and exaggeration to enliven his sardonic blast. In his portrayal, the $750,000 in cash that Powell "robbed" from the public was augmented by $400,000 in negotiable racetrack stocks and $300,000 more in July oats, September soybeans and pork-belly futures on the Illinois commodity exchange. The solitary shoebox that apparently contained a portion of the Powell money grew, in Steve's elucidation, to countless shoeboxes accompanied by "459 pairs of Thom McAn Romas." In a Philadelphia show, Steve added, "He was the first guy to combine fraud with fetish. That's what I liked about him. Not every day you can find a guy who's not only a pervert but a crook, too."

The song's lyrics equated Powell's stature with that of other "mighty men" in Illinois' past, from gangsters (John Dillinger and Al Capone) to politicians (Govs. William Stratton and John Peter Altgeld, State Auditor Orville Hodge and native-son President Abraham Lincoln). The length and outrageousness of the song's so-called titles drew chuckles: "These $750,000 Shoes, They Hurt My Feet, Lord, Lord, and I Ain't Gonna Be Treated This-a-Way," "When It's Coupon Clippin' Time at the Racetrack, Baby, Baby, I'll Come Shoeboxing Back to You," and "Don't Blame Desenex, for He Died with His Shoeboxes On."

Politics on an even more local level laced another song that had become popular in Steve's repertoire since early 1972. The tune skewered Lincoln Towing, a firm on Chicago's North Side that for years had thwarted the law and public decency by picking up autos from legal parking spots, recklessly breaking into and damaging the vehicles, impounding them for exorbitant prices and sicking goons and vicious dogs on the vehicles' unsuspecting owners.

"It was really intense to watch," says Kate Ertel Bowers, a club waitress who witnessed the nightly ritual from her apartment across from a North Side supermarket lot. "They looked like ex-cons, big, burly men with flattop crewcuts," she says. "They bruised in with these giant chains, and it was like a tag team. They would wait for the time to expire, and they came in with these big trucks and had a vehicle up and gone in about a minute. People would see them and come and try to talk them out of it, but no, they would never release them back to the owners once they had them."

Mike Royko's columns had pilloried Lincoln Towing since 1967, but not until early 1971 did the city's papers explode with reams of copy about the firm and its crass, rotund owner, Ross Cascio. Triggering the coverage was Dick Simpson, a candidate for alderman in the 44th Ward encompassing the Lakeview neighborhood who filed a class-action suit against Cascio's firm. Simpson, a

Dick Simpson, Chicago alderman candidate, filed a class-action suit against the unscrupulous Lincoln Towing, triggering public outrage that led to Steve researching the controversy in Simpson's city office and writing the biting "Lincoln Park Pirates."
(Photo by William J. Mahin, courtesy of Dick Simpson)

political-science professor and a favorite of Chicago's folkies, won office in large part by exploiting the horror stories of Cascio's thuggery.

Across the street from the Earl of Old Town, the Second City comedy troupe had gotten into the act, improvising routines about Cascio by audience request, says Jim Staahl of the resident company. "The city was abuzz with how Lincoln Towing was taking people's cars away, and people were getting into fights," Staahl says. In one sketch, set in a jail, a chat among inmates zeroed in on the point:

"What are you in for?" one asked.

"Murder."

"Bank robbery."

"I tow cars."

"You!" the first inmate shot back. "Disgusting! Can't find a place to park! Criminals like you are making things bad for all of us!"

One of Steve's friends had told him about a grisly Lincoln Towing incident in mid-1971 and "asked me if I could do something about it," Steve told WGN's Roy Leonard two years later. "I went to Alderman Simpson's office and got out this file that he had ... full of stuff, including bits from the state's attorney's office and all kinds of photographs and everything there, and he built up a whole case. I figured if the state's attorney was in on it, that it merited a song."

But how would he set up the lyrics? He already had penned a straight-on broadside with "Paul Powell." The story of Lincoln Towing, which had aroused the ire — and drained the wallets — of countless "little guys" from Rush Street to Wrigley Field, deserved a more accessible touch. Steve found his inspiration while watching late-night TV. He had just viewed Walt Disney's first live-action feature, the 1950 film of Robert Louis Stevenson's *Treasure Island*, which starred British box-office star Robert Newton as the sneering pirate captain Long John Silver. Steve had found the model for an anti-hero, and using a tone of whimsical ridicule, he began writing a song that put Cascio, 44, into the nefarious role.

As he was to do a few months later with "Penny Evans," Steve built the tune from a sea chantey. He had the Cascio character bellow a sing-along "Way-hey, tow 'em away" refrain in a minor-key waltz melody drawn from the traditional "Blow the Man Down." [16] He stuffed the song with local references, and with each verse, Cascio and his bandits kept hauling more cars until, insatiable, they started towing away the boats in Belmont Harbor and the planes at Chicago's three airports. The song's title became a natural: "Lincoln Park Pirates."

When Steve sang it to WFMT's Ray Nordstrand over the phone, Nordstrand wondered if the song's slanderous specificity — including the line "Cascio's countin' the cars" and the narrator's boast that his drivers were "recent graduates of the charm school (state prison) in Joliet" — would land Steve in court. Nordstrand telephoned Cascio's lawyer, a good friend of Nordstrand's named Herbert Barsy, who assured him that Cascio wouldn't sue anyone over the song. "In fact," Nordstrand said, "the lawyer was convinced that Ross Cascio would be very flattered."

I went to Alderman Simpson's office and got out this file that he had ... I figured if the state's attorney was in on it, that it merited a song.
STEVE GOODMAN

16: In writing "Lincoln Park Pirates," Steve also may have drawn from an early 1800s sea chantey, "Haul Away Joe," in whose chorus was the repeated line, "Way haul away, we'll haul away, Joe." In the late 1950s, idiosyncratic Chicagoan Joe Klee wrote and performed a work song for garbage collectors, employing the same tune.

Early on, Steve used crude wordplay to present the song in his act. Once, he gave it the facetious title of "Even Though the Price of a Hooker in Chicago Varies from Avenue to Avenue, a Tow Job is $25." Another time, he described a parking-lot sign as saying, "90-Minute Parking/The Owner of the Car Will Be Violated at the Driver's Expense." But he soon found that brutal anecdotes also made for a riveting intro. "Once a fellow had his car towed away by them," Steve said during a Long Island radio show. "He was at the supermarket, where they had his car up on the blocks, had it up on the jack there, and he came out of the supermarket and said, 'I'm sorry I'm late, but I'm here now, and there was a long line in the eight-items-or-less line there, and I couldn't get out too fast, and I wish you'd put my car back down, and I'll just drive away.' And they knifed him."

Capitalizing on the song's pirate connection, Steve eventually added to his stage intro a note-perfect distillation of the buccaneer brogue of the actor Newton. "It was Newton who invented the word, 'aarrgghh,' a-a-r-r-g-g-h-h — I don't know how that damn thing's spelled, but that's the word he thunk up," Steve told a 1974 crowd. "All through that movie, he goes, 'Aarrgghh, there be eight million in doubloons out there, and the only thing twixt it and we is a wee slip of a boy, and his name is Jamie Hawkins, aarrgghh!'"

Elaborating for effect, Steve noted that Newton, who died in 1956 of alcohol-related causes, was a notorious drunk. But Steve, sounding giddily high himself, couldn't resist adding vulgar embellishments of dubious veracity. One anecdote credited a besotted Newton for sending "the world's greatest telegram" to actor John Barrymore, another frequent inebriate, from Venice, Italy. The missive read: "Streets full of water. Advise." Another story was cruel if unsubstantiated. "Newton used to take his characters out in the street with him and live them," Steve said. "He was a little kinky. He'd walk up to people in Los Angeles and go, 'Aarrgghh, and sure wouldn't you be bendin' over for the old captain now? Aarrgghh, be grabbin' your ankles, too, and wouldn't you be takin' a wee bite outta me crank?' "[17]

Stage levity gave way at times to outrage at Cascio, particularly after anonymous threats to "back off or we'll rough you up" reached Steve by phone.[18] "Boy, I wish I could say I felt sorry for the guy," Steve told a crowd in January

Ross Cascio's notorious Lincoln Towing signs and trucks became a fearsome sight in Chicago because of Steve's wicked seafaring lampoon, "Lincoln Park Pirates."

(Photo of early 1970s Lincoln Towing sign by Rich Seafield, tow-truck photo courtesy of Bill Nestos, Lincoln Towing)

17: Steve's characterization of actor Robert Newton's sexual exhibitionism is refuted by Susan Ciriello, who runs an extensive Newton site on the Internet at <http://www.mooncove.com>. "From everything I know about Robert Newton, this is pure fabrication," she says of Steve's innuendo. At best, Ciriello says, Steve's remarks constituted "highly imaginative parody," but they also unfortunately are insulting to Newton's memory.

18: Alderman Dick Simpson says that his wife also received telephoned threats at home, along the lines of "If you don't lay off Cascio, (your husband) won't live."

Ross Cascio, shown in the 1970s, showed up unbeknown to Steve at one of Steve's Earl of Old Town shows, invited by Earl Pionke. After Steve played "Lincoln Park Pirates," Cascio drew an ovation.

(Photo courtesy of Bill Nestos, Lincoln Towing)

1973 at Amazingrace, an Evanston coffeehouse founded by a collective of a dozen former Northwestern University students. "I don't know, like with malice towards none, with charity for all, right? Fuck him. ... I wish he hadn't ripped so many people off in the process, but I really don't care what happens to him."

When Steve sang "Lincoln Park Pirates" around the city's North Side, it drew cheers, says longtime Chicago newspaperman, author and radio host Rick Kogan, who found that it held much the same appeal as Royko's down-to-earth prose. "There was a simple poetry to Steve's music, as there was to Mike's writing," Kogan says. "There wasn't a person around who didn't get it. It was unbelievably natural and colloquial and in Chicago vernacular."

The vernacular, embodied by the song's narrator/villain, eventually supplied an in-person endorsement. It was at the behest of Earl Pionke, who triggered a visit by Ross Cascio to his club to see Steve perform.

"You gotta come by," Pionke told Cascio while drinking with him at Cascio's late-night hangout, the Seminary Restaurant on Lincoln Avenue.

"Yeah, I heard his fuckin' song," Cascio replied. "What's with this kid?"

"You won't put him in cement shoes, will ya?"

"Ah, fuck you, what are you talkin' about, cement shoes?" Cascio said. "I want to see this fuckin' kid."

Pionke invited Cascio and other Seminary regulars to the Earl as his guest. "Do whatever you want," Pionke said. "Just tip the waitresses."

On the appointed night, Cascio and his associates arrived, the house was full, and the undaunted Steve launched into a stellar set. Midway through, ready to perform "Pirates" and flashing a gleam at the saloonkeeper, Steve paused to introduce the tune:

"And now," he said, "I'm going to dedicate this song to a good friend of the Earl's."

The remark surprised Pionke, who stared daggers back at Steve. "I'm thinking, 'Cement shoes, you prick. You ain't takin' no chances, huh, Goodman?' "

Steve pulled no lyrical punches while making his way through the send-up, and he finished to heavy applause, even from Cascio. Sensing no risk, Steve plunged further and said, "By the way, the gentleman who's the proprietor there, he also was from the charm school, Mr. Ross Cascio." The crowd roared, and Cascio stood up, acknowledging the ovation. "He was lovin' it all," says Pionke, who says that while Cascio and crew racked up a $300 tab for Pionke to pay, he tipped the waitresses and the bartender $50 each.

Cascio's response didn't surprise Fred Holstein, who called the towing villain "a fucking gangster. I was a tough kid, but I looked at these motherfuckers, man, three teeth in their mouth, a million tattoos, whoa. But Steve couldn't hurt Ross. He was a multimillionaire. He didn't give a fuck. The real tough guys, they don't bother with that shit. It's a joke to them."

As the spring of 1972 approached, Buddah seemingly spared no effort in keeping Steve on the road. Al Bunetta filled in for manager Paul Anka, who was booked nearly nonstop from March through September with tours in Japan,

Puerto Rico and Canada, as well as domestic gigs in Las Vegas, Iowa, Cleveland, Buffalo and Connecticut.

With an itinerary spanning the North American continent and then some, Steve returned to the Cellar Door [19] in Washington, D.C., for a well-reviewed weekend stint, co-billed with TV comedienne Lily Tomlin, fresh off a Grammy win for her "Laugh-In"-inspired debut LP, "This Is a Recording." Two weeks later, on March 31, Steve returned to Carnegie Hall for a one-nighter, again paired with Tomlin, but with a result that was demoralizing.

The first choice for an opening act for Tomlin that night was John Prine, says Tomlin's manager, Irene Pinn, but Prine was unavailable and suggested Steve. Tomlin, a "big fan" of both singer/songwriters at the time, admits today that Steve's portion of the show was doomed from the outset because she committed a well-intentioned blunder.

Tomlin, in her New York theater debut, was the advertised attraction, and Steve was the last-minute opener whose billing had not been announced until the day of the show. Tensions were high because Tomlin's performance at the venerated playhouse was to be taped for a future LP. So after long discussion, Tomlin and Pinn decided to try to allay audience anxiety over a surprise opening act by having Tomlin go onstage first for four minutes and warm up the crowd. After a loud ovation and a few jokes, Tomlin announced to the sold-out house, "Here's my friend, Steve Goodman. He's a great folksinger. I brought him along for you to enjoy tonight. I'll be back."

"We wanted to give him the best shot," Pinn says. "We certainly felt that if they didn't really jump into his music, they would at least be polite." Intended as a salve, the move amounted to a tease, and it backfired. "That was a big mistake," Tomlin recalls. "We thought that would be a good idea, but I don't think it worked."

Several of Steve's Manhattan friends — Paula Ballan, guitarist Don Burnham and the Bitter End's Paul Colby — had accompanied him to the show and stood mortified in the wings as they watched it unfold. From Steve's first moments, a murmur of grumbles permeated the hall. Between songs, the crowd, particularly in the upstairs seats, started chants of "Lily! Lily!" and "We want Lily!" Steve persevered, but the insistent naysayers were daunting. Partway into his set, he turned to "Penny Evans," which induced momentary silence, but a mid-song heckler in an upper balcony proffered pro-war catcalls. As he had done nearly four months earlier from the same stage, Steve summoned his "I don't kick the shovel out of your hands" put-down line, [20] and it placated the complainer but only until the song's end, when the chanting resumed.

Pinn and Tomlin watched the crowd's rudeness from backstage, "and we were both going nuts," Pinn says. "They were disgusting."

"You wouldn't think that would happen at Carnegie Hall," says Tomlin, who today remains shocked by the behavior of the evening's crowd. "The audiences were really bad in those days in that regard."

"There was nothing that he could have done," Burnham says. "Those people

19: Meeting with Steve backstage at the Cellar Door, Lake Forest College friend John Posniak heard Steve wickedly reference his leukemia. When Posniak told Steve he was seeking a career direction, Steve said, "So many people just sit around and waste time and have no goal." The two also traded stories about having tried to quit smoking, and Steve, who was smoking a cigarette, referenced a popular TV game show: "You got 'Jeopardy,' and you got 'Double Jeopardy.' "

20: Tomlin says she thought Steve's use of the "shovel" line "was debasing to people who work with a shovel. I understand the point of it, but I wish he had chosen a different (word). I would have liked him to come at it from a different place. I'd rather have him come and say, 'I don't come and kick the stock ticker out,' or something else. None of that works, really. It's better not to do it. It's better to rise above it, but it's pretty hard. Or else it's better to almost be plaintive, throw yourself on the mercy. I don't know what you do at a time like that. But people do like to see it come to a little combat, a little confrontation. It's more theater for them."

Lily Tomlin, shown in the early 1970s, says she was shocked by her 1972 Carnegie Hall audience turning on Steve after she came onstage to warm up the crowd and introduce him.
(Photo by Mary Angela Hight, courtesy of Lily Tomlin)

came to see Lily Tomlin, and they didn't want to be bothered seeing anybody else, especially when she came out and titillated them and got them started and into the groove. Now they're seeing her show, and all of a sudden she pulls the plug and sends out this unknown guy that they don't even care to see. It was a stupid idea to do it, unfair to Steve."

Steve was so shaken by the insolent reception that he walked off the stage sans encore and "lashed out" at Tomlin as she was preparing to go on, Pinn says. "He was justifiably upset, and he got somewhat belligerent. I completely understood. He was totally, emotionally distraught." Still, Pinn says she "had words" with Steve for chastising Tomlin.

Seeking out Colby, Steve embraced him and shed tears on his shoulder. "Stevie, erase this," Colby said. "This doesn't count. Whoever did this made the biggest mistake. That's not your audience. Nobody there wants to see you. Nobody came for you. They wanted to hear jokes from Lily Tomlin. They're from Westchester, New Rochelle and Stamford, Connecticut, and you're from the Village, and never the twain shall meet."

Colby says Steve absorbed and appreciated his message of consolation, telling him it was "like my dad" would have offered. "Let's go get a drink," Colby said, and before Tomlin began her main act, the group left the hall.

The incident had lasting impact on Pinn and Tomlin, who abandoned the "warm up" concept and after that season's tour never had an opener again.

Because of the celebrity of Tomlin's "Laugh-In" characters (the smug telephone operator Ernestine and the spoiled kid Edith Ann), the show snared prominent reviews, and Steve was swept up in the coattails. *Variety,* noting that most in the audience "seemed to dig Goodman's performance, especially his satiric raps and tunes," also acknowledged the "problem" audience: "It's getting tougher for unbilled acts, even good ones." *Billboard* likened Steve to a "demonic imp," and London-based *Sounds* found his performance "infinitely tasteful and relaxed," identifying two songs, "Nowhere in a Hurry Blues" and "You Never Even Call Me by My Name" as exceptional.

One of Steve's most provocative songs, the just-written "Somebody Else's Troubles," also reached the ears of that night's Carnegie crowd. Drenched in the humor that stems from misfortune, the uptempo tune surveyed a series of characters who couldn't be bothered by mishaps because they were happening to other people. Steve disclosed, in a San Francisco concert five years later, that he had come up with the song's title based on advice from his auto-salesman father: "When I was 16 years old, I put together $400, and I asked him to sell me a car, and he told me that all I could afford was a used car, and when you bought a used car, you were buying somebody else's troubles." While the song, in its first incarnation, had a political element, poking fun at "the man from the White House on the TV in the bar," its lyrics mostly focused on how the everyday struggles of individuals — old-time movie slapstick victims, medical patients and factory workers — usually don't matter to anyone except the people who do the struggling.

"At first, I thought I was taking a poke at do-gooders, but it got past that," Steve told Chicago raconteur and radio host Studs Terkel the following year. "I think 'talk-gooders' is what I meant. ... I just figured that when it all boils down to it, everybody takes care of themselves, no matter what they say they're doing at the time. Even if they're taking care of somebody else, it's because they want to, y'know? I just wish people would admit that a little bit."

What elevated "Troubles" to universality, while supplying a nearly transparent hint of the leukemia hanging over Steve's head, was the song's final verse, written in the first person. In it, Steve asked a funeral director how he could laugh in the face of his clients' tears. Displaying a bouquet of flowers that he had received in Steve's name, the undertaker replied, "Steve, business just gets better all the time." It was yet another example of the conflict that Steve faced in wanting to keep his fatal illness a secret and yet feeling compelled to creatively explore it. "Troubles" walked a fine line between disclosure and discretion, but the song's driving rhythm and celebratory tone deftly deflected the passing focus on himself and let listeners laugh at how the words also applied to themselves.

A radically different result of creativity arrived in Steve's life while he was on the road the week after the Tomlin gig at Carnegie Hall. Steve was to fly to Toronto on Tuesday, April 4, to play the first of five nights at the Canadian city's trendy Riverboat club, but he bowed out of the initial show. [21] Instead, he jetted directly back to Chicago to take part in a monumental milestone, to fulfill a dream that he and Nancy had nurtured since their marriage more than two years prior, to add a new and lasting dynamic to their home — a child.

Building a family of their own had loomed as a greater challenge for them than for most other couples because of Steve's leukemia. [22] His doctors had discouraged the two from trying to procreate because the effects of Steve's experimental treatment were unknown. There was no guarantee that Steve would survive the nine months of a pregnancy, and no one wanted him to pass down his disease to a new generation. Isabel "Bonnie" Cunningham, the record-keeper for Steve's unit at Sloan-Kettering, says the oncologists' focus was on more immediate results.

"You have to go back in your mind-set to a time when nobody knew what was going on," says Cunningham, later an oncologist herself. "Everybody (in Steve's leukemia unit) was dying right and left, and so the whole idea of fertility was a nonissue, right? People were saying, 'Can I get to the prom?' 'Can I get to my kid's graduation?' People were measuring their lives in shorter times."

It was natural for the few leukemia patients — such as Steve — who were surviving two or three years to contemplate parenthood, Cunningham says, but the prevailing thought was, "Oh, my God, it'd be so awful. You'd have these deformed children." Accordingly, Lucy Wells, Steve's friend from Lake Forest, recalls that Steve's doctors told him, "Don't even think about it. We don't know what this stuff is doing to your body, never mind a child of yours, your sperm. So don't even try it."

When it all boils down to it, everybody takes care of themselves.
STEVE GOODMAN

21: This cancellation was a rare step for Steve, who took pride in showing up for his scheduled shows in spite of his regular need for leukemia checkups at Sloan-Kettering. In part because he did not want his disease to become public, Steve did not wish to build a reputation as someone who bailed out of gigs at the last minute. When he missed the first night of his Riverboat engagement, Toronto musician Keith McKie replaced him.

22: When Steve and Nancy visited the home of Steve's Maine East friend Les Detterbeck that spring in the Chicago suburb of Arlington Heights, Detterbeck and his wife already had a child. Detterbeck knew about Steve's leukemia, "but when you're in your 20s, everybody's almost immortal. You don't think of people dying. Leukemia? I guess that's like hurting your ankle or something."

Earl Pionke nuzzles 4-month-old Jessie in August 1972 at the Goodman apartment.

(Photo by P. Michael O'Sullivan)

23: Jessie Goodman discovered this information during a search for her biological parents in 1997.

24: The spelling of "Jessie" wavered over the years. It was listed as "Jesse" in the credits for Steve's 1972 LP, "Somebody Else's Troubles," possibly to conform to her namesake. But most printed references have used a feminine spelling, "Jessie," because that is how the name appeared in the title of Steve's 1975 LP, "Jessie's Jig & Other Favorites." Today, Jessie Goodman spells her name without the "i," but for consistency and so as not to disorient the reader, this book uses "Jessie."

Heeding Sloan-Kettering's advice, Steve and Nancy bypassed the genetic risk, but they also trusted that Steve would live long enough to devote significant time as a father. Of course, a potentially quicker alternative to natural conception was available, and to them, the choice had become obvious: They would adopt. Steve, who got his shoulder-length locks cut short to present a picture of responsibility, approached the man who increasingly had become his protective father figure, Earl Pionke.

"Earl, I got to talk to you," Pionke says Steve told him. "Y'know, with my stuff, you don't publicize this disease to the world. I don't know, the doctor says we should wait, but we want a kid. Now, I heard that you got a nice adopted kid for your nephew, legal and proper."

Pionke says he told Steve, "OK, if you want it, I'm buyin'."

"Yeah? I didn't mean to ask you that," Steve said. "I just wanted the particulars."

"I'm buyin'," Pionke repeated firmly. "Whatever it takes."

(Four years later, without disclosing his leukemia, Steve expressed in an interview for *Come for to Sing* his endless gratitude for the sustenance provided by Pionke: "The guy tried to see what I was thinkin', bothered to give me his time, and gave it to me at a time when time was precious. He means so much to me. Bravest guy I know. Biggest, biggest guy.")

That spring of 1972, the Goodmans' family physician, Dr. Gene Handelman, located a prospective adoptee — an infant girl who had just been born at Belmont Community Hospital. Only six days old, she was the daughter of teenagers: a 16-year-old Puerto Rican boy and a 13-year-old Italian girl.[23] Steve arranged to fly home while Nancy and his mother, Minnette, drove to Sears to buy a car seat and blankets and headed for the hospital. When a nurse brought the infant out to the waiting room and to Nancy, the new mother gasped at the beauty in her arms. She looked like "the obvious Gerber baby," as Nancy later described her. The girl's name, Jessica — Jessie for short — was taken from the middle names of her benefactor (Jesse James), and Pionke became her godfather.[24]

Back at the Wayne Avenue apartment, Jessie was placed on display in her car seat atop the kitchen counter. Steve telephoned from an airport and talked with his mom.

"Ten fingers, 10 toes," she said, "and Steve, besides David she's the most gorgeous baby I've ever seen."

Nearby, Minnette's mother, Mary, shouted to Steve that she was whipping up a batch of chicken soup.

"Don't you dare feed my kid chicken soup," Steve said, a grin in his voice.

Exultant as he got back in line to board a plane, Steve passed out the remaining cigarettes from a pack in his pocket and vowed to quit smoking. His life, and that of Nancy, had changed forever. The seriousness of their choice was underscored during their adoption hearing.

The two stood and held hands while the judge for the case cut to the quick: "What are your plans if Steve should not overcome his illness?"

Steve, Nancy and Steve's dad, Bud, all hold the adopted Jessie Goodman during the August 1972 gathering, an album-cover photo session.

(Photos by P. Michael O'Sullivan)

The answer came from Nancy. "Not many people know that they have a limited time," she said, "and we think, because of the limited time, that we can give Jessie even more love." [25]

Steve quickly became a doting dad, in ways that were conspicuous. Liz Danzig (now Derry), then a publicist and host for Chicago folk musicians, says there was no mistaking the father-daughter connection. "She acted like her dad, and she had the same little round face," Danzig says. "Anybody would be hard pressed to call her adopted in any way or form because from day one, she was Steve's little girl."

As an infant, Jessie traveled with Steve and Nancy to out-of-town shows, such as to Cambridge, Massachusetts, where Steve played Club Passim in February 1973. He and Nancy asked his newly married Lake Forest College friend, Sidney Kistin, to babysit while the couple had dinner with Steve's childhood friend, Rick Eisenstaedt, and during the show itself. Kistin says that when she and her husband, Marty, arrived for duty at the Goodmans' hotel, "Steve was so in love with this little baby and was giving us detailed instructions on how to feed her and take care of her, how to warm up the formula. He was showing us where he kept everything and gave us a million phone numbers where he could be reached." The fuss was amusing, given that Kistin was a nurse and Marty was a doctor, but it became charming when, a half hour after Steve and Nancy had

25: With tears in her eyes, Nancy related the story of the adoption hearing to Margaret Swofford (now Southern), then-wife of Bill "Oliver" Swofford.

left the room, Steve realized he'd forgotten several guitars and returned to pick them up for the show. When he departed again, Kistin says, "he was shouting back instructions again about how to warm up the formula. It was adorable."

The same winter, Boulder, Colorado, played host to concerts by Steve and singer/songwriter Tom Rush, who recalls driving back to his hotel in the snow at 2 a.m. and spotting Steve standing on the side of the road hitchhiking. But Steve wasn't alone. He was clutching a stuffed pink rabbit so tall that its ears extended higher than Steve's head. "He'd missed his ride back to the hotel, and it was snowing," Rush says. "He was having trouble getting a ride. People would slow down a little bit, and then they'd hit the gas and go on by." Rush picked him up, drove him to his destination and found out that Steve had just bought the rabbit for Jessie. (Nancy eventually threw out the hare, which towered over Jessie and frightened her.)

Jessie even became a factor in Steve's concerts, such as when he and Nancy brought her along to a performance at Northern Illinois University in DeKalb, 65 miles west of Chicago, in October 1973. The 18-month-old toddler fidgeted and cried a few times mid-show, drawing her dad's attention. "Who's that?" he said in the middle of a "Somebody Else's Troubles" intro. "That who I thought it was? Is she happy?" Steve left the stage and walked over to pick up Jessie from her mother's arms. "All right, for a minute, just a second — hi, babe," he said, drawing the audience's cooing laughter. Twice more his daughter distracted him. "Aw, Jessie," he said as she fussed. "Please, darlin'. Get a little brandy in your milk." He also imparted advice to potential parents in the crowd: "This is a great kid. She knows she's got me wrapped up, and there's nothing I can do about it. She just knows how far she can (go). They're great. I recommend 'em, y'know? If you ever get into a situation where you think that might be a good thing to do, don't wait just 'cause you're broke or something like that."

But while Steve's fondness for fatherhood was evident, so were his contradictions. In fact, life had changed far more for Nancy than it had for Steve. When they adopted Jessie, Nancy (who is still drawn to all infants, says a grown-up Jessie) stopped working and suspended college coursework and progress toward a nursing career to become a full-time mother and wife. Steve, much as he loved Jessie (and Nancy), embraced traditional gender roles and felt it was his rightful place to follow his career whenever and wherever it took him. This was unmistakable in his interview with Al Rudis three months after Jessie arrived.

"I want to be a family pretty bad," he rationalized. "I'm not so sure I want to settle down, not the best thing you can do for a kid. Just give the kid something to be proud of. This is what Daddy does. Daddy doesn't sit around at home all day because he wants to be with Jessie. Daddy's a musician, therefore Daddy goes out on the road and does what Daddy has to do." [26]

So he did. After staying up without sleep through the first 48 hours of Jessie's presence in his household, Steve flew to Toronto to recoup most of his Riverboat gig, arriving with an hour and a half to spare and playing two "honest, up-front sets," reported the bi-weekly *Grapevine* newspaper. "He was a little long in the

---

Daddy doesn't sit around at home all day because he wants to be with Jessie. Daddy's a musician, therefore Daddy goes out on the road and does what Daddy has to do.
STEVE GOODMAN

26: Part of what Daddy Steve did from the road was check in with Nancy. John Coleman, "blown away" after hearing Steve's clever "Nowhere in a Hurry Blues" on Philadelphia's WMMR-FM, booked Steve in 1972 for a mid-week performance at the 75-seat Rhodora Theater coffeehouse at Trenton State College in New Jersey. Coleman took Steve to a pre-show dinner at a nearby Steak and Brew, where they were served by a stunning waitress. Coleman, "being a stupid college kid," whispered to Steve, "Wow, look at this one." Steve replied, "Yeah, she is pretty, but nowhere as beautiful as my wife. I think I'll call her right now." Steve left the table, went to a pay phone, called Nancy and returned with a big smile. "Boy," he said, "do I love that woman."

tooth at times, but after a good night's sleep he'd provide four nights of solid music."

Close-in and far-flung bookings gave Steve a wealth of opportunities to promote the songs on his LP and try out newer ones in the spring of 1972. In Chicago, he played at a benefit for *SingOut!* magazine hosted by radio host Studs Terkel at the Quiet Knight and made his first of many appearances on Roy Leonard's popular WGN-AM morning show. [27]

Meanwhile, Buddah tried to plug Steve in to the adolescent market that had been its forte. While he was back in New York for treatment, Buddah booked Steve as a guest along with NBC "Today" co-host Barbara Walters on a live Saturday morning teen show, a low-budget TV series called "Take a Giant Step." With no host or studio audience, the hourlong April 29 episode on WNBC-TV, Channel 4, focused on a quartet of high-schoolers — a Chinese-American boy, a white boy from New Jersey, an African-American girl and a Latino (labeled Chicano) girl from Texas — who sat in white plastic chairs and talked meanderingly about stereotypes and the difficulties of fitting in. Introduced by the Buddah promo photo showing him paddling a canoe, Steve, wearing a sport jacket and striped shirt, performed two songs that seemed to fit the theme: his "Nowhere in a Hurry Blues" and Hank Williams' "Mind Your Own Business" (with the teens and Walters chiming in on the "mind your own business" echo).

Steve gamely tried to validate the students' feelings, saying that he, too, was confused as a teenager. "You're not alone," he said. "Everyone on the planet feels that way at some time or another." He also turned to humor. When one student fretted aloud about the intimidation of others, Steve tried making a sarcastic joke — "You don't have to worry unless the people who think that their way of living is the *worst* impose it on you" — but it fell flat. He tried another jest, introducing "Mind Your Own Business" by saying, "Hi, there, friends and neighbors. This isn't 'Barn Dance.' This is 'Take a Giant Step.'" He did just that as he strode back to his seat, nearly tripping on a wire. "Walkin'," he quipped, "that's the hard part." The closest he came to direct advice during the broadcast was in explaining the point of "Nowhere in a Hurry Blues" as "sort of like laughing to keep from cryin'." The show faded out partway through Steve's performance of a third song, the traditional "I Bid You Goodnight," an incongruous ending given that the program aired between 11 a.m. and noon. [28]

Blowing into Bozeman, Montana, to play for an older audience of 4,000 Montana State University students at an outdoor festival in mid-May, Steve faced the anger and irreverence fueled by the Vietnam War. One year earlier, the required 38 states, including Montana, had ratified the 26th Amendment to the Constitution lowering the voting age to 18, and students were eager to take part in their first presidential election. President Nixon had just ordered the mining of Haiphong Harbor in North Vietnam and the bombing of strategic targets in that country, and, as Steve said later, the MSU students "were a little ticked off about this."

During his set, Steve looked up to find three airplanes circling in the sky,

You don't have to worry unless the people who think that their way of living is the *worst* impose it on you.
STEVE GOODMAN

27: Interestingly, given Steve's ire over the changes in "City of New Orleans" wrought by John Denver, Steve made several alterations of his own when he performed it for Roy Leonard. For instance, he sang the "paper bag that holds the Tequila" (instead of "the bottle") and "their daddy's (instead of father's) magic carpet." But some 150 concert and radio recordings indicate that in later performances of "City," Steve consistently stuck to his original words.

28: "Take a Giant Step" was a one-season blunder. The July 30, 1972, *New York Times* said it had poor ratings and lost NBC $635,000.

and, as if to mirror the military action a hemisphere away, about 16 members of the MSU Skydiving Club jumped out. After they landed, one diver ran to the stage, grabbed the microphone in front of Steve and led the students in what he said would be a "Fuck Nixon" cheer. Just as most of them had seen throngs do in the 1970 "Woodstock" documentary, many in the crowd called out "F," "U," "C" and "K," and on command they repeatedly shouted out the one-word obscenity. Then the skydiver asked "Who?" Expecting to hear "Nixon," the leader got a different answer: "You!" It was the proverbial tough act to follow. [29]

Two weeks later, reflecting its investment in Steve, Buddah sent him much farther afield than Montana. After opening for electric bluesman Luther Allison at the recently founded Amazingrace coffeehouse in Evanston, Steve boarded a plane headed for London. "The record company I work for sent me to England because they knew I wasn't selling any records here," Steve cracked during later shows back in the States. "They gave me four boxes of records and a one-way ticket to Heathrow Airport."

Steve, who had written and collected enough songs to serve as the nucleus for a second album, actually was looking for a producer, since Kristofferson was busy touring and Steve wanted a more "live," natural sound than Nashville could provide. "I'm getting really excited about coming over and recording," he told Jerry Gilbert of the UK's *Sounds*, for an article printed May 27. Buddah, he said, was talking with a pair of producers in England, including Paul Samwell-Smith, the 29-year-old ex-Yardbirds bassist who had helmed Carly Simon's "Anticipation" LP and had launched what would become a string of hit albums for Cat Stevens. The prospect stirred Steve's soul: "I'm just interested in meeting some English musicians ice cold and recording with them."

The immediate impetus for the trip, however, was a gargantuan gathering like many that had sprouted in the wake of Woodstock nearly three years earlier. Dubbed the Great Western Express Festival and held on a farm near Bardney, 120 miles north and a four-hour drive from London, it straddled the country's spring bank holiday weekend. The May 26-29 event — the largest outdoor pop-music aggregation in Great Britain since the famed Isle of Wight Festival in 1970 — boasted 39 name acts, whose headliners included Joe Cocker and Sha Na Na of "Woodstock" film fame along with Don McLean, the Faces (with Rod Stewart) and the Beach Boys. [30]

With a title referring to a well-known British railway and a locomotive as a logo, the festival was a hand-in-glove fit for Steve, with "City of New Orleans" his strongest promotional card. Nancy Lewis, Buddah publicist, says she had sent Steve's LP to the festival promoter, John Martin, who loved the album (especially Steve's version of Prine's "Donald and Lydia") and offered him a spot — a coup for both Buddah and Steve.

Despite temperatures in the 40s, rain torrents and gale winds that relentlessly transformed the grounds into a muddy mess, British news reports and Steve's own accounts placed the attendance at an astounding 40-45,000. [31] It was a mere one-tenth of the reported crowd at Woodstock but larger than any

---

The record company I work for sent me to England because they knew I wasn't selling any records here. They gave me four boxes of records and a one-way ticket to Heathrow Airport.
STEVE GOODMAN

29: The date of this anecdote is uncertain. Nixon's order came May 8, 1972, and a "Festival of Life" was held in Bozeman May 13, but Steve's appearance there is difficult to verify. Steve told this story at the Cambridge (England) Folk Festival in late July while introducing his song, "The I Don't Know Where I'm Goin' but I'm Goin' Nowhere in a Hurry Blues." Of the cheerleading skydiver, Steve said, "That guy knew what this song was about."

30: The bent of the rock event, emceed by the BBC's John Peel, was clear. Steve observed: "Don McLean and I had the only two acoustic guitars in 300 miles."

31: *Variety* used an attendance figure of 50,000 but, noting a rumored $100,000 deficit, labeled the festival "a peaceful flop."

Steve found himself billed midway down the left column in the poster for the 1972 Great Western Express Festival north of London, England. The Woodstock-like event drew more than 40,000, the largest live audience for which Steve ever performed.

(Poster from http://www.ukrockfestivals.com/.)

other single live, in-person audience for which Steve would ever perform.

Steve, shorn but retaining his mutton-chop sideburns, struggled to keep a large, floppy Stetson from blowing off his head while playing in blustery rain during his Saturday morning set. Though he was sandwiched between the just-formed (and later influential) Hungarian rock quartet Locomotiv G.T. and the debuting British glam band Roxy Music, his performance drew glowing reviews that helped launch in England his just-released single, "Nowhere in a Hurry Blues" backed by "Turnpike Tom." [32]

"It was a strange place for him to play," says Lewis, the Buddah publicist, who joined Steve in England. "It was much more a rock festival. I felt we were sending him out to the lions in a way, just Steve and his guitar, but I thought he

32: Later, in the June 17, 1972, edition of *Sounds*, famed British music journalist (and later Dusty Springfield biographer) Penny Valentine raved about "Nowhere in a Hurry Blues," likening it to Randy Newman's work. "It has that same kind of lovely, tongue-in-cheek, 1930s backup feel and vocal," she wrote. "The song itself has a smile about it that reminds me of a cross between Hoagy Carmichael and John Sebastian."

went down pretty well. I thought it was lovely. They didn't all jump on their feet, but I thought he did a good job of holding his own."

Press reviews of Steve's show weren't so equivocal. "He was so diminutive he probably couldn't have been seen beyond the first 100 yards, but what he lacked in physical appearance, he made up for with sheer personality and vocal strength," wrote Jerry Gilbert in *Sounds*. "He got one of the best receptions of the entire festival when he sang his unaccompanied 'Ballad of Penny Evans,' which is surely the anti-war song to end them all."

Steve "quietly proceeded to demolish the hard-core rock fans with his mixture of musical humor and pathos," added Robert Brinton in the British music publication *Disc*. But with typical self-deprecation, Steve told Brinton that he couldn't move his hands properly in the chill and "felt lucky to get away with my skin, let alone an ovation of any kind."

The other two Buddah bookings of Steve's UK trip [33] were indoors in London and promised to reach 100 times as many Britishers as Steve did at the festival — via the British Broadcasting Corporation.

For the BBC, Steve taped "City of New Orleans" and an interview with "Whispering Bob" Harris for a segment on a pop-music TV program, then just one year old, called "The Old Grey Whistle Test."

More memorably, however, Steve performed on "Country Meets Folk," an hourlong BBC radio program of records and live acts aired Saturdays from London's Playhouse Theatre, with an audience of four million listeners, largely in the English countryside. The appearance supplied Steve with one of his most entertaining tales for U.S. audiences and cemented his persona as an on-stage storyteller.

Part of the story's allure was its absurdity. To fit the show's theme, Steve was to perform his country parody, "You Never Even Call Me by My Name," but he discovered shortly before taking the stage that English law forbade him from doing so because he hadn't secured a work permit. "This was the crusher," he told later audiences. "You need a work permit for everything you do in England. You need a work permit to fart over there. I'm not kidding. If you get paid for it, you need a permit. I could talk, I could be interviewed on the radio, but I could not sing or play the guitar."

The solution lay in a technique familiar to U.S. TV watchers: lip-synching — mouthing the words and moving hands over a guitar while a recording of the song is played. This, however, was radio, not TV. The listeners couldn't see him lip-synching, but the theater audience of 200 could. So Steve pantomimed in front of the mike while sound-booth engineers played the record.

"It really happened," Steve said. "It was Dick Clark taken to its logical extreme. ... I'd never lip-synched anything in my life. It was pretty funny because who cares if you move your lips? I was doing anything but playing this song. The audience was laughing hysterically through the whole thing, and I was having the time of my life." [34]

But the yarn didn't end there. The next performer, Redd Sullivan, 41, and

His unaccompanied 'Ballad of Penny Evans' ... is surely the anti-war song to end them all.
JERRY GILBERT
SOUNDS

33: On a surviving ticket stub, Steve was named as the opener for a Kinks concert on Monday, June 26, at Free Trade Hall in Manchester, England, sponsored by the War on Want charity. But Steve left England to return to Chicago at the end of May and didn't revisit the UK until late July. The cancellation of Steve's set apparently took place after the tickets were printed. The fill-in opening act, listed in a newspaper ad two days before the concert, was Max Merritt and the Meteors.

34: Jim Lloyd, who handled the "News, Views and Interviews" segment for "Country Meets Folk," says Steve was the only performer who ever lip-synched on the program, which ran seven years from the late 1960s to 1972.

emcee Wally Whyton, 42, former street buskers who were elder statesmen in the groundbreaking skiffle style of British music in the 1950s, had something extra in mind for Steve. The 6-foot-4 Sullivan had derived his nickname from his mane of red hair and a red beard — "a solid piece of hedge" jutting out below his mouth, says Louis Killen, who recalls Sullivan as "an anarchist of the first order," known throughout England for his bawdy music-hall songs.

Steve finished his lip-synching and walked offstage, but Sullivan turned him around and dragged him back. [35]

"Now, it's a shame you didn't have a permit to sing," Sullivan told Steve off-mike during the applause, "but you should get to sing as long as you're here, so come out and sing on my song."

"But Redd," Steve protested, "but Redd ..."

"C'mon," Sullivan said. "They're not going to see you sing the chorus of this with me. Just sing. Don't play the guitar, and they won't get ya."

Steve had no idea what to expect. ("I didn't know the song he was going to sing, but I figured there was no one within 4,000 miles who could give a shit, so I went out there. I figured that if you're gonna make a fool of yourself, that's as good a place as any.")

Just then, Whyton announced to the audience and over the air, "And here he is, Redd Sullivan!"

One beat later, Sullivan pulled Whyton and Steve to his side and started to sing a traditional Cockney tune, "The Winkle Song." Sullivan stopped after the first verse, turned to the pair, pulled Steve to his side and said:

"I say, guv'nor, did you hear the one about the man with the wooden leg?"

("By now," Steve said later, "I'm ready to crawl in a hole.")

Steve said, "What?" and Whyton replied, "Why, no, I didn't."

"It's a matter of opinion."

(When Steve told the story later, stony silence greeted this punch line. "That's how the audience felt about it that night," he said. "It's amazing how you duplicated that.")

After punching out the second verse, Sullivan pressed on:

"I say, how do you get milk from a tomcat?"

("I'm trying to get off the stage," Steve said later.)

"I don't know," Steve replied, "how do you get milk from a tomcat?"

"You take away his saucer."

(By now, Steve had figured out he was the foil, the straight man to Sullivan's jokes. "You ever try to dig a hole in wood?" he said later.)

Maintaining his hold on Steve's arm, Sullivan launched into the chorus of the "song":

> *I can't get my winkle out, isn't that a sin?*
> *The more I try to get it out, the further it goes in*
> *I can't get my winkle out, isn't that a doer?*
> *Can't get it out with an old, bent pin, has anybody got a skewer?*

Redd Sullivan, shown in 1971, would not let Steve leave London's Playhouse Theatre stage without engaging him in bawdy riddles and song.

(Photo © Alison Chapman McLean)

35: Relating this story in October 1972 at the Whole Coffeehouse at the University of Minnesota, Steve described in detail how Redd Sullivan was mid-set when he invited Steve back to the stage. In many other versions, however, Steve said Sullivan immediately pulled him back onstage.

(Steve told his later audiences, "A winkle is a kind of shellfish that they have over there." Then, after a beat, "I didn't know that.")

Steve's account of the BBC show ended there, but not his overall story. He said he ran out of the theater and back to his hotel, where he scribbled a note to his British agent ("Be back in three days") and stuffed it into his mailbox. He surprised his Scottish storytelling friend Johnniy Morris with a phone call, boarded a train heading north and spent much of the next 72 hours with Morris and a fellow musician, Bobby Eaglesham, at Sandy Bell's Pub in Edinburgh. At this point, Steve's lengthy narrative [36] became pedestrian, even tedious, centering on a binge of sea-chantey singing that entailed the ingestion of unbelievable quantities of UK alcohol — a plot line that reflected his immersion in the liquor-soaked Chicago club scene and was almost quaint, given the more prevalent marijuana jokes in vogue in the early 1970s, epitomized by Cheech & Chong.

To hear Steve tell it, the point of his story was the potency of the booze that he guzzled at all times of day and night at Sandy Bell's Pub, including McEwen's Ale, Glenlivit Scotch and especially Younger's Tartan Ale. But except for a clever line or two (such as Steve saying that Younger's "will make you do the dance of the seven drunken tourists"), it was a yarn that paled in comparison to his similar but wittier monologue from the year prior that was set in Paul Anka's suite at the New York Waldorf.

More telling were the parts that Steve omitted. They left an impression upon Morris that was inescapably sobering.

Following his exit from the BBC show, Steve had called Morris at 8 p.m. to say that he was lonely, and Morris invited him to visit. Steve took an all-night train (waking Morris at 4 a.m. to say he had reached Newcastle) and arrived at 7 a.m. in Edinburgh, where Morris picked him up and drove him 20 miles east to his home in Haddington, a village of 4,000. After giving him breakfast, Morris drove Steve and his guitar to his office, where during a downstairs board meeting the room's chandelier shook as Steve entertained the upstairs staff. "He got the place bouncing," Morris says. After an evening of drinking and singing at Sandy Bell's Pub, Morris took Steve back home, setting him up in the living room with a bed and a hot-water bag and turning off the electric heater.

"Is it OK if I leave the (electric) fire on all night?" Steve asked.

"No," Morris said, "it's not OK."

"Why not?"

"Well, one, it dries up the room, and you'll wake up with a terrible hangover, and two, it's very expensive. If you want an extra hot-water bag and a blanket, I'll get it to you."

"Fine."

In the morning, Steve asked Morris, "Do you have an electric razor?"

Morris, true to the mean and stingy Scottish stereotype, was quizzical, wondering, "What the hell are these Americans all about?"

"No I don't," he told Steve.

"OK."

Is it OK if I leave the fire on all night?
STEVE GOODMAN

36: With typical self-deprecation, Steve acknowledged the length of this story while introducing "Six Hours Ahead of the Sun" during a March 1974 show in Santa Monica: "I'll shut up and sing the goddamn song now. I disappeared up my own asshole there for a minute, I'm sorry."

The next morning, Morris left on a three-day work trip out of town and let Steve stay at his place. Steve departed a day later, and upon Morris' return, a friend asked him, "Did you know your wee pal's got leukemia?" Suddenly, Steve's actions made sense to him. "The reason he wanted to leave the electric fire on all night was that he couldn't afford to get a cold, and the reason he wanted an electric razor was that he couldn't afford to cut himself."

One thing Morris couldn't fathom, however, was how Steve summoned the energy to forge with others such a deep and sustained personal and musical bond. "The man was unreal," Morris says. "He was a magician." [37]

Returning to London, Steve reconnected with Buddah's Nancy Lewis, and in the lobby of the Churchill Hotel, he played her a song he had just written about his UK experience — the uptempo "Six Hours Ahead of the Sun," a reference to the time difference between London and Chicago (and a reminder of his two previous sun-as-metaphor-for-life compositions, "Song for David" and "Ball of Fire"). With plentiful references to alcohol and the reasons people imbibe, the song's rambling lyrics disdained Steve's own indulgence ("Drinkin' just gives me amnesia ... I can't get all this mud out of my eye") and expressed an Everyman's yearning to leave the land of "someone else's time" and get home.

Steve later joked that the song was a tribute to Younger's Tartan Ale or jet lag. ("Have you ever read *An American Abroad*? Same book.") But Lewis understood otherwise. "He was quite lonesome for Nancy," she says. "I do remember him being homesick. That's what 'Six Hours Ahead of the Sun' was about."

Less than a week long, the British trip held a measure of success. Steve reached a startling number of listeners, both in person and over the TV and radio waves, and with his vigorous performances and articulate gift of gab, he charmed the UK press. [38] "If I could eat my reviews, I'd retire," he quipped. He also managed to keep his leukemia a secret from reporters. For instance, in glossing over why he dropped out of Lake Forest College, he told *Disc*, "It was just natural to go into music full time."

The BBC lip-synching experience held added value as well, inspiring him to fortify a gag he used while introducing "City of New Orleans" in concert. Concise and pointed, it consistently brought laughs: "I had a bad dream that I had to lip-synch this on 'American Bandstand.' It was a nightmare. A kid gave it a 52, said it had a nice beat, but he didn't know what a train was."

The gag soon grew engaging embellishments. In July 1972, in explaining "American Bandstand" to an unknowing folk-festival audience in Cambridge, England, he added, "I don't know how you get graded over here, but 52 sucks a dead banana." In his October 1973 show in DeKalb, he augmented the depiction of his professed bad dream: "Everybody in the peanut gallery was there with Dick Clark. Did you ever hear (of) *The Little Engine That Could* as a kid? I think they did that thing, 'CLEAR-a-sil, CLEAR-a-sil.' "

But the UK excursion was not all smiles. Steve failed to nail down a producer for his next LP, and the exposure didn't stimulate a British run on his first album. His domestic LP sales were disappointing as well, prompting Larry Harris,

> **If I could eat my reviews, I'd retire.**
> **STEVE GOODMAN**

37: Some years later, Morris says that on the day that his wife and daughter had left him and he was "cracking up," Steve telephoned him from the United States and invited Morris to visit. Two days later, in the mail from Steve came a plane ticket to Chicago.

38: British reporters enjoyed quoting Steve's take on his home city. "In some parts of the world, Chicago is still thought of as Al Capone's town," he told the *Record Mirror*. "We're not really gangsters. We haven't beaten anybody up for two or three weeks!" After extolling his musical compatriots in Chicago, he said, "There's something about the Midwest, a kind of sarcasm in the music. ... The further west you go, the more sarcastic people get. They almost have to be, in order to survive. There's all those plains and prairies. ... People in the Midwest are usually very dry, and this shows in John Prine's work. He has a very good grip on the anatomy of America."

Buddah's national director of album promotion, to adopt a strategy that was drastic — and some called disgraceful.

The germ was an elevator ride Harris took with Steve to Buddah's offices in New York. Harris knew of Steve's disease, and while they ascended to the 21st floor, he decided to broach the topic.

"So," he asked Steve, "what is it you want to accomplish?"

Steve's reply cut to the chase: "I just want to live long enough to leave some kind of legacy for my kid."

The exchange gripped Harris. "I was ready to cry," he says.

Within days, Harris, 25, walked into the office of New York's purveyor of progressive music, WNEW-FM, to lobby the station's music director, a 33-year-old former stage crew member for rock impresario Bill Graham, the colorful Mike Klenfner.

It wasn't Harris' first visit to Klenfner, who says he had an eye-rolling affection for the schmoozing promo man and enjoyed teasing him. But Harris was pushing "really horrible" music, including a Buddah act named Exuma that Klenfner called Excema. WNEW, whose playlists ranged from the Bay Area's Jefferson Airplane to British blues rockers Spooky Tooth, was known as "the hippest station in America," Klenfner says. He repeatedly had told Harris that while Steve was "a quality, top-shelf artist," he was "not right" for the station's mix.

The tenacious Harris did not let that deter him. "Larry was nothing else if not dogged," Klenfner says. "He wouldn't stop." Both vividly recall their give-and-take over Harris' ultimate pitch.

"You gotta play this record," Harris said. "You gotta play it like (it's by) a major superstar."

"Why do I have to do that?" asked Klenfner.

"The guy's gonna die, and he's really a good guy," Harris said. "You've gotta try and do this, just so he has something to leave, his legacy to his kid."

For a moment, Klenfner just stared at Harris. He nearly spit in Harris' face. "Larry, you can't use that one," Klenfner said. "That's too terrible. It's just too terrible."

Harris persisted. "The guy's dying of cancer," he said. "You've gotta give him a break so that he hears the record on the radio."

"C'mon, Larry, don't tell me the guy's going to die," Klenfner said. "Don't you have anything better? Why don't you take out hundred-dollar bills and throw 'em?"

The dumbfounded Klenfner turned to black humor: "Larry, are you sure he didn't contract it two years ago and he died from it then, or you wished it on him, and you were selling your soul out beforehand?"

As a final insult, Klenfner added wickedly, "Larry, when he dies, we'll play him."

Over the next few years, Klenfner taunted Harris with "Hah! The guy's not dead yet!" and other jabs. "We had a lot of fun with it, in a sad sort of way,"

Don't tell me the guy's going to die. Don't you have anything better? Why don't you take out hundred-dollar bills and throw 'em?
MIKE KLENFNER

Klenfner says. "I didn't do it in a mean way. I mean, really, who would want to make fun at anyone's expense for dying? But," he says with remorse, "Larry took so much crap." [39]

Harris says he had no qualms invoking Steve's leukemia. "My job was to get the record played any way I could," he says, "and if I had to use the leukemia angle, which I wasn't lying to anybody, any way I could without lying and cheating, I would." Nor did he discuss this approach with Steve. "There was no reason to talk about it with him," Harris says. "I'm sure he probably wouldn't have looked on it that he would be proud to do it that way. I'm sure he would want it done because his music was that good."

But "that good" simply wasn't selling, which left Steve anxious and irritated. "He would cut you off," says Buddah song plugger Eddie O'Laughlin. "He wanted results. It was like talking to a banker as opposed to an artist, and if I didn't have them, he was away from me fast." But after someone told him of Steve's leukemia, O'Laughlin became more forgiving. "It made all the sense in the world to me," he says. "This guy was going to die, and, of course, he's not going to be in a good mood."

Fending off foul feelings as the summer of 1972 approached, Steve enmeshed himself in activity, supplying a major assist in the recording of John Prine's second album, "Diamonds in the Rough." In contrast to Steve, who was still in search of a producer for his second album, Prine was reuniting with the producer of his first, Arif Mardin, who booked a weeklong session at Atlantic Recording Studios in New York in early June.

Befitting the LP's title, Prine and Mardin approached the task as au naturel as possible, arranging the musicians — who, besides Steve, were David Bromberg, Steve Burgh and Prine's older brother Dave — in a circle to perform the songs "live" with little overdubbing. In town for another round of treatment, Steve sang or played on seven of the LP's 13 cuts.

While some of his contributions were minor and merely blended into the whole, Steve's voice and guitar occasionally shone, including low harmony on a song that cemented the sentiment between Steve and Prine, an ode to the fragility of elusive memories called "Souvenirs." Nearly a dozen years later, Steve resurrected the song for an album of his own, and it later became a staple of Prine's concert repertoire, always dedicated to Steve.

The song on the LP evoking the most vivid images for Dave Prine — and the only one not written by his brother — was the album's title cut. It was truncated to one verse and the chorus of a 1929 Carter family tune rich with the biblical notion that those who give their souls to God will find, upon their death, that their "diamonds will be shining, no longer in the rough." The two Prines and Steve sang the song a cappella, and while the finished product was faithful to the original, the session was suffused with raucous laughter.

Straight from Sloan-Kettering, Steve had walked in wearing bib overalls, to which were pinned a large button bearing the face and name of a famed African-American prizefighter who had retired nine years before, Archie Moore.

My job was to get the record played any way I could, and if I had to use the leukemia angle, which I wasn't lying to anybody, any way I could without lying and cheating, I would.
LARRY HARRIS

39: Jonathan Takiff, weekend deejay for Philadelphia's WMMR-FM, got the same "pretty creepy" spiel from Buddah's promo staff. "It might have given some jocks a nudge, but others were turned off by the opportunism or distrusted the reality of the gossip. Nobody at the station repeated this news on the air. Hey, Steve looked good, sounded good, seemed happy. Wouldn't he have been in a sorrier state if he were sick?"

Dave Prine, shown in the mid-1970s, says he couldn't keep from cracking up while singing harmony in the studio with Steve: "All he had to do was twitch an eyebrow, and we were dead. I have never laughed so hard in my life. The only way I could get through it was not look at him."

(Photo by Art Thieme)

40: The trio broke into laughter a final time after they sang the song's last word, "rough," in a drawn-out, modulating chord. Switching on the intercom, Arif Mardin said from the control booth in his Turkish accent, "Fun-TOSS-teek!" Mardin's one-word commendation remains on the LP.

Mardin gathered the three singers closely around a single microphone, and Steve sat on a high stool to raise his mouth to the proper position. The effect — the overalls, the button, the stool, along with Steve's impish eyes — induced repeated giggles in the two brothers, and the song took 48 takes to record.

"He looked like a little doll," Dave Prine says with a laugh. "I could hardly look at him, and I'd start to break up, and he knew it, damn it, so every time I'd look at him, he'd do something, like throw in these one-liners." For instance, when they sang in the chorus, "When Jesus comes to claim us," Steve finished the line with "at the great dry-cleaners in the sky."

"Once that got going," Dave Prine says, "all he had to do was twitch an eyebrow, and we were dead. I have never laughed so hard in my life. The only way I could get through it was not look at him. I said to Arif, 'You got blindfolds?' If I looked at him, we all came apart." [40]

During the Prine sessions, Steve hoped to persuade David Bromberg, who Steve admired as a guitarist and entertainer, to produce his own second LP. Steve had performed with the influential instrumentalist at the 1971 Philadelphia Folk Festival, and he liked Bromberg's production that year of John Hartford's quirky, progressive bluegrass LP, "Aereo-Plain." "I figured we ought to try it, especially since we knew each so well, and he knew pretty much what I wanted," Steve said. "I thought it would be easy and fun." But Bromberg turned him down, citing a busy summer schedule of touring and recording.

Buoying Steve as summer approached were recordings of his own songs by other influential artists.

One came as "really a surprise," Steve said. Recently signed to the same label as Prine and working with Mardin was Jackie DeShannon, the singer/songwriter ("Needles and Pins") who rose to stardom in 1964 by opening for the Beatles on their first U.S. tour and by making top-10 hits of Bacharach/David's "What the World Needs Now Is Love" in 1965 and her own co-write, "Put a Little Love in Your Heart," in 1969. For her 16th LP, titled "Jackie" and released in mid-June, DeShannon recorded Steve's "Would You Like to Learn to Dance?"

With a faster tempo and a full bass/drums rhythm section, her version of the tune left behind much of the song's charm, but its latter half did feature the delicate fills of a harpsichord played by Bee Gees co-producer Albhy Galuten. As sung by DeShannon, the lyrics underwent a slight but intriguing gender reversal. (In the line, "You can lead now if you want to, I don't mind," the last three words were changed to, "You're doin' fine.")

DeShannon learned of "Would You Like to Learn to Dance?" through Mardin, who played her Steve's version, and it made an instant impression. "I thought it was a song that James Dean would have written if he was a songwriter," DeShannon recalls. "It kind of reminded me of when he made tea for Elizabeth Taylor in (the film) 'Giant.' It was just an immediate connection."

The song "passes the test of time," she says. "It reaches all those films that I love, like 'Picnic,' and it really hit a chord with me, being from a small town (Hazel, Kentucky). It's from a man's point of view, it's very vulnerable, and I

always love that in acting and songwriting, where they come up and ask you to dance in a rather shy way, but, of course, you're dying to dance with that person. It's one that's going to be around a really long time. It's a great piece of writing."

In the summer of 1972, however, DeShannon's version of the song was merely an album cut, and her "Jackie" LP reached only #196 on the *Billboard* charts for two weeks in late July. [41]

A different artist's version of another song of Steve's was to meet an astronomically different fate that summer — and Steve got his first tangible signal of this on the other side of the world. 🎵

Jackie DeShannon, shown on the back of her 1972 "Jackie" LP, says Steve's "Would You Like to Learn to Dance?" appealed to her because it portrayed a man who was expressing vulnerability.
(Photo by Barry Feinstein for Camouflage, http://www. barryfeinsteinphotography.com/)

41: From the "Jackie" album, DeShannon's rock-beat version of Prine's "Paradise" was released as a single in September but rated only the #110 slot for two weeks in October before vanishing from the *Billboard* charts. In the chorus phrase, "I'm sorry, my son," the last two words were changed to "my dear" to accommodate the gender switch.

Steve backs up Arlo Guthrie at the Cambridge, England, Folk Festival on Sunday, July 30, 1972, the afternoon that Guthrie showed Steve a copy of Billboard *indicating that Guthrie's version of "City of New Orleans" had entered the Hot 100.*
(Photo by Nigel Luckhurst)

'I'll sing you a medley of Arlo Guthrie's hit record'

In cold black and white, it bears no ambiguity. You're either there or you aren't. Like a stock-market listing to an investor, like a morning-after review to a Broadway producer, like a box score to a baseball player, it stands as a resolute measure of commercial success in the music world. Hidden near the back of the weekly *Billboard* magazine, for those monitoring what the ears of America are hearing and buying it's usually the first place to turn — a complex compilation of national retail sales and radio airplay known as the Hot 100.

The singles on the Hot 100 list for July 29, 1972, conjure up an era. They also encompass songs that today remain popular — even delightfully or irritatingly pervasive — in grocery stores and elevators. Grasping the top four slots were Gilbert O'Sullivan's "Alone Again (Naturally)," "Brandy (You're a Fine Girl)" by Looking Glass, "Too Late to Turn Back Now" by the Cornelius Brothers and Luther Ingram's "If Loving You Is Wrong, I Don't Want to Be Right." In the top 10 and still climbing were "Where Is the Love" by Roberta Flack and Donny Hathaway, Alice Cooper's "School's Out" and "Long Cool Woman" by the Hollies. Not far behind but on their way up were "Coconut" by Harry Nilsson, Al Green's "I'm Still in Love with You" and "The Happiest Girl in the Whole USA" by Donna Fargo. Holding on but starting to drop were Bill Withers' "Lean on Me," "Layla" by Derek and the Dominos, the Eagles' "Take It Easy," Elton John's "Rocket Man" and "Song Sung Blue" by Neil Diamond. Newcomers included "The Guitar Man" by Bread, the Bee Gees' "Run to Me," "In the Quiet Morning" by Joan Baez and Rick Nelson's "Garden Party." Even the novelty instrumental "Popcorn" by Hot Butter was percolating.

Steve Goodman's name was nowhere to be found. But on Sunday morning, July 30, when he gazed at the Hot 100 page while standing 4,400 miles from home in a field at England's Cambridge Folk Festival, no one on the planet could have worn a broader grin. There, in white type, on a black star — a "bullet" indicating brisk upward movement — was the #86 designation for his musical jewel, "The City of New Orleans." [1]

"You could just feel the fog lifting," Steve said two years later of the single's ascendance. "Luckiest thing that ever happened to me."

The name affixed to the song in *Billboard* was that of the artist who had just

> You could just feel the fog lifting. Luckiest thing that ever happened to me.
> **STEVE GOODMAN**

1: On the LP and single sleeves for Arlo Guthrie's recording of "City of New Orleans," the word "The" was inserted at the beginning of the song's title, even though Steve never did so.

shown him the magazine, Arlo Guthrie. "Hey kid," Guthrie said, "look at this."

Guthrie wasn't on the bill that summer at Cambridge. Neither was Steve, who had traveled to the UK once again to chase down a potential producer. This time, the prospect was Bob Johnston, who had shepherded some of the 1960s' most influential albums by Bob Dylan, Simon & Garfunkel, Johnny Cash and Leonard Cohen. Steve's in-name manager, Paul Anka, and Buddah's Neil Bogart had been in touch with the London-based producer, and Steve said before the trip that it "really looks like Johnston is going to do it."

But when Steve and agent Al Bunetta arrived at the hub of England in late July, they waited four days for Johnston to return phone calls. Finally, Bunetta tracked down Johnston, who "acted quite a bit like he didn't want anything to do with it," Steve later told *Omaha Rainbow*. "He was supremely uninterested and had no idea why they were there," adds Richard Flohil, Mariposa Folk Festival publicist who accompanied Steve and Bunetta to England. "They felt that they'd gone over there as almost a done deal that needed an interview and a meeting and a 'let's get on with it.' It turned out the guy didn't know who Steve was."

Johnston "was really dealing with a lot of personal issues," Bunetta says. "He was caught up into who he thought he was, and he didn't think Stevie measured up, didn't think he looked like a star. Boy, I was angry over that. I was mad-mad. I was as mad as a person could get." But Bunetta says he never completely recounted the meeting to Steve. "I just said, 'Y'know, we should just go. This isn't right.' "

Compounding his disappointment over Johnston, Steve said, was that Buddah had purchased an excursion ticket that did not allow him to return immediately to the States. While the irate Bunetta flew on to Rome to cool off, Steve, who had "$30 to my name" and "nothing to do," telephoned the *Sounds* reporter he'd met two months prior, Jerry Gilbert, who "saved my life," Steve said. "You can't go home for another few days anyhow," Gilbert told him. "Go up to Cambridge, and I'll introduce you to Ken Woollard."

The reference was to the eighth annual Cambridge Folk Festival, headed by Woollard, on whose floor Steve slept along with piper Cathal McConnell of Boys of the Lough. The implication in Steve's later recounting was that he hadn't planned to turn up at Cambridge. But Woollard, writing two years later in the book *Ten Years of Folk*, implied otherwise, indicating that Steve and Artie Traum (who was on the bill with his brother Happy) had alerted Guthrie about the festival and encouraged him to attend.

Steve, who showed up at Cambridge and asked if he could "pick somewhere," wowed Woollard from the outset. "After we gave him a half-hour spot on the main stage, he didn't stop picking for 48 hours," Woollard wrote. "The festival followed him around. He had a crowd wherever he went." Woollard attributed this in part to "an abrasive quality" that carried Steve over an obstacle that other American artists faced, of being "too smooth for Cambridge." [2]

Indeed, Steve's festival performances were laced with his story of the Mon-

---

He didn't think Stevie measured up, didn't think he looked like a star. Boy, I was angry over that. I was mad-mad. I was as mad as a person could get.
AL BUNETTA

2: Woollard also laid the favorable "abrasive" tag on John Prine, who Steve incessantly promoted at Cambridge, even spelling out his last name for one audience. "You're going to hear a lot about him," Steve said. "This kid is the best songwriter in the United States. ... There's about 15 other guys over there who write almost as good as he does. Who can tell who's the best writer? That's all a matter of taste, but John's got about 40 of the best songs I ever heard in my life, not just five or six that you really like and the rest are pretty good. ... He's so prolific I'd like to break his brains."

Above, Steve guests with Happy (left) and Artie Traum at the 1972 Cambridge, England, Folk Festival. Left, between sets he gets a light for a cigarette, while Loudon Wainwright III, right, talks with a fan.

(Top photo by Joe Gedrych, courtesy of fROOTS magazine; photo at left by Peter Weisz/Dennis O'Neill)

tana State University "Fuck Nixon" cheer and other crudity. At one solo show, intermittent police messages mistakenly squawked through the sound system, interrupting his set. To the audience's delight, Steve answered the garbled words with, "There's trouble about 40 miles from here, and that car's going to go get it, Roger Wilco, 10-4." Then, testily, "That's right." Then, with a chuckle, "Hey, fuck you — not fuck me, fuck you!"

Guesting with Happy and Artie Traum and Isaac Guillory, Steve faced similar interference while singing "Would You Like to Learn to Dance?" and handled them with gritty charm. The amplified voice of a warbling female singer at the nearby mainstage intruded, so Steve halted his song to tell of his English travails. When quiet returned, he resumed "Dance" and made it nearly to the final

Cambridge Folk Festival-goers gather in a field on Sunday afternoon, July 29, 1972, the last day of the event, to hear the unbilled Arlo Guthrie, center, jam with Steve and other musicians. Steve's head and hairline can be seen at left, just right and in the gaze of the young woman in right profile.
(Photo by Peter Weisz/Dennis O'Neill)

3: Indiana University folklore student Peter Weisz – who while dueting with Dennis O'Neill played folk and country and led a festival workshop on Merle Travis-style finger picking – later poetically summed up Steve's visual impact at Cambridge: "a matzoh ball in bib overalls."

line when the loud woofs of a nearby dog broke the spell. Instantly, Steve jettisoned the word "lovin' " and ended the tune with, "We could try a little barkin', I don't mind." The resulting ovation seemed endless.

In the environs of "introverted" and "grimy" England, Steve left a buoyant impression, says Ralph McTell, whose own "Streets of London" had become a British folk anthem. "He was a little, roundy man with big, blue, bib-and-brace overalls, and he just radiated good times," says McTell, who met Steve at the festival. "He was just beaming and happy and spontaneous. There was no hint of any kind of self-promotion, yet his enthusiasm just bubbled over." [3]

Steve later said his Cambridge success brought him great relief. "I ended up playing six sets and had the time of my life," he said. "I was so ready to have a good time doing anything, because everything else seemed to have fallen through."

Guthrie turned up at Cambridge on Sunday, the festival's final day, and by the time organizers had decided how to invite him to perform without appearing to "hustle" him, "Arlo and Steve Goodman were playing to a small crowd, growing bigger every minute, in the middle of the field," Woollard wrote. Finally, famed Scottish folksinger Alex Campbell, who had offered to approach Guthrie, fibbed that a mainstage act was AWOL and asked Guthrie to fill "a big, embarrassing gap of about half an hour." Guthrie acceded and, carrying a banjo and guitar, walked onstage with three other festival musicians. Also joining Guthrie was Steve. "We have an unbelievable stroke of luck — or mass, as it were," emcee Derek Brimstone told the Cambridge crowd. "The place," wrote Woollard, "erupted."

Part of the ovation had grown from the buildup Steve had provided by play-ing at earlier slots for some 10,000 festival-goers, many of whom were intrigued to hear "City of New Orleans" as performed by the artist whose version was hitting the radio and as simultaneously backed by its author. [4] In introducing his own performances of the song that weekend, Steve had been saying that Guthrie was "paying my rent" — a line that soon became an enduring part of his act. Steve further underscored Guthrie's persona as "City of New Orleans" hit-maker by telling a joke that appealed to both general audiences and the festival's traditionalists. "The record company released my version of it in the States, and it sold two copies," he told one Cambridge crowd. "My mother bought one of 'em, and I bought the other, and I sold it to a friend for three times what the record cost. I took the label off and told him it was a Mississippi John Hurt record."

While July 29, 1972, marked the first appearance of Guthrie's rendition of "City of New Orleans" on the Hot 100 singles chart, its emergence that week-end was not entirely a surprise to Steve. Branded a "pick single" by *Billboard* nearly a month earlier, on July 1, it "bubbled under" the Hot 100 list at #106 on July 15 and at #101 on July 22. The Guthrie album on which it appeared had been released in late May, just before Steve's first England trip, with *Variety* labeling it a "click." *Billboard* reported June 3 that the LP was getting airplay on FM stations, and it entered the publication's album chart on June 10 at #152, rising by the Cambridge weekend to the #116 slot.

Steve's awareness of Guthrie's version predated the release of Guthrie's re-cording, however. After the lead sheet that Steve had given him in March 1971 at the Quiet Knight languished for months on the piano at Guthrie's western Massachusetts home, Guthrie finally noticed it. "One day, just out of the blue, I walked over to the piano, sat down and looked at the song, tried to remember how it went," he says. "I thought, 'Y'know, this is really a nice song.' " He started performing it in concerts, including one in Chicago, in the fall of 1971 and early 1972. "I didn't change hardly anything," he says. "There was some phrasing and some words that I thought needed a little help, but barely any-thing."

The deep resonance of "City of New Orleans" had impressed Guthrie from the moment Steve first played it for him. "It builds on the legends of an era, and it talks about an America that's disappearing, and it becomes symbolic," Guthrie says. "It becomes much bigger than what it is, because it's talking in myth and symbols and reaching people on levels that are incredible."

But what Guthrie added to the song was much more than "barely anything." To begin with, he altered words in five verse lines. In his rendition, "trains," not "towns," had no name, "cards" became "card games," and the wheels were "rumblin' " through the floor, not "grumblin'." Also, Steve's rhyming phrases "their father's magic carpet made of steam" and "the rhythm of the rails is all they dream" ended in Guthrie's version with "steel" and "feel." [5]

Far more significant than the lyrical differences, however, were two key

4: The 1972 Cambridge festival was the first of only three times that Steve and Guthrie shared the same stage. The other two instances were Nov. 11, 1974, at WTTW-TV in Chicago, and Oct. 5, 1975, in Worthington, Massachusetts.

5: Guthrie today disputes that he changed "steam" to "steel." He says the version of the song that Steve gave him at the Quiet Knight contained the phrase "magic carpet made of steel." He says he saw that the corresponding line ended with "dream," so he changed "dream" to "feel" so that the lines would rhyme. He insists that if "steam" had been in Steve's version, he would not have changed "dream" to "feel." Guthrie can't verify what was on the lead sheet Steve gave him. But in 150-plus recordings that survive of Steve singing "City of New Orleans," including two made before he gave Guthrie the lead sheet, Steve sang "steam," never "steel." When other lyrical differences are pointed out to him, Guthrie says he did not intend to change the words from Steve's lead sheet. Reflecting on the differences, however, particularly Steve's "towns" vs. his "trains" that "have no name," Guthrie allows that he may have made the changes inadvertently.

musical changes to the chorus. First was an immediate emphasis, after "native son," on the word "I'm" in the phrase, "*I'm* the train." This hammered home the commonality that a listener could share with the personified, failing railroad. Second was a shift of melody and chording in the line, "I'll be gone 500 miles when the day is done." In Steve's version, the melody traveled down a major-chord scale on the words "I'll be gone." Guthrie, instead, lifted the phrase to an ear-pleasing, flatted seventh chord on the word "gone," giving the chorus a more plaintive impact and what is known in the industry as a "hook" — a musical trigger that delights the listener's mind and persists in the memory.

"That's me," Guthrie says of the melodic alteration. "I don't know where it came from. That's just how I felt like it ought to be. That was my one big musical contribution, one chord out of a zillion." [6]

When Guthrie began performing his version of "City" in concert, he chose to accompany himself on piano, not guitar, and the song had a hard-edged, rock 'n' roll tempo. Guthrie's bassist, John Pilla, saw potential in the composition and asked Lenny Waronker, Guthrie's producer at Warner Brothers, to hear it played to a live audience. Waronker, who was juggling recording sessions that he was producing for Gordon Lightfoot, Ry Cooder and Randy Newman, hopped a flight from Los Angeles to San Jose, where Guthrie was performing. The plane was late, and Waronker walked into the concert when Guthrie had just started the song. It had immediate impact.

"You could easily recognize it as a very unique and beautiful song," Waronker later told Dan Daley of *The Mix*. "It was almost like watching a movie, it was so cinematic. The three verses were a play in three acts, united by the soaring chorus." The rock arrangement, however, was less thrilling. "My sense was, the way the song was laid out, it probably needed a different kind of approach," Waronker says, "but when you have a song like that, it's just a matter of finding the right way to do it."

Guthrie had been contemplating a live album but opted instead to cut another studio effort. When he, Pilla and Waronker entered Sun West Studios in Hollywood to record basic tracks, "City of New Orleans" emerged as an obvious focus. There, Guthrie recorded his piano-based rock arrangement, backed by an electric guitar. But Pilla and Waronker, often compatriots in nudging Guthrie in new directions, remained dissatisfied.

"It short-circuited the song and didn't make a lot of sense," Waronker says. "There was such beauty in that song, a vast, Americana quality that seemed lost in the rock version."

Understandably, Guthrie was heading in the direction of rock, in part to separate himself from his father's legacy, [7] but Pilla and Waronker imagined "City" with a sound that was less aggressive, not more. "John (Pilla) and I were really into the idea of trying to take it more like Johnny Cash, to get the beauty of the song out," Waronker says. "Arlo was adamant at the time. He didn't want it to be like Goodman's own version of the song, which was folkier, the kind of thing he was trying to get away from. But Arlo also liked a good argument. He

---

Arlo was adamant at the time. He didn't want it to be like Goodman's own version of the song, which was folkier, the kind of thing he was trying to get away from. But Arlo also liked a good argument.
LENNY WARONKER

6: Jim Dickinson, who eventually played keyboards on Arlo's recording of "City," says the chord change grew organically from the melody. "The chord is there. I just don't think Steve played it," he says. "Mental closure plays the chord in your head. I just don't think it was being articulated in Steve's version."

7: Little known today is Guthrie's rock version of "Alice's Restaurant," called "Alice's Rock 'n' Roll Restaurant," from December 1969. The song, 14 minutes shorter than his 18:20 folkie version two years prior, grazed the *Billboard* Hot 100 for just two weeks, topping out at #97.

knew we were trying to finesse him on the song to see it our way, and that just made him dig in harder about it. He is a great guy with a big heart, but he did like to take part in a benign conflict."

At another studio, Amigo in North Hollywood, Guthrie finished his recordings for the LP, to be named "Hobo's Lullaby" after the classic Goebel Reeves song by that name. It was at Amigo that Guthrie bent to the wishes of Waronker and Pilla. For several weeks, with guitarist Ry Cooder, bassist Chris Ethridge, drummer Jim Keltner and pianist Jim Dickinson, Guthrie experimented with giving "City of New Orleans" a variety of styles. "I tried it bluegrass, I tried it orchestrated," Guthrie says. "We recorded it seven different times from scratch, seven different ideas, speeds, moods. I didn't like any of it."

Finally, about midnight at one session after everyone was exhausted and Guthrie's resistance had ebbed, the group recorded a simpler, uncluttered arrangement with a laid-back rhythm that everyone seemed to like. The next day, however, Waronker found it depressingly slow. "We had rushed to get it done before it got too late, but we didn't really think it out in terms of tempo," he says. The next day, engineer Donn Landee accelerated the track slightly to a rhythm that elevated everything by a fraction of a tone and infused an indefinable charm. "Once we were able to get the tempo right, it was fine," Waronker says. "We had to speed it up, and the more we sped it up, the more rickety it sounded, and ultimately it almost sounded like a train."

Overdubs ensued at the modified speed. Ace multi-instrumentalist Nick DeCaro added a warm but slightly mournful concertina. A chorus of gospel voices — from three African-American women called the Blackberries and four white barbershop-style singers, including Thurl Ravenscroft (the voice of Tony the Tiger in Kellogg's commercials and famed for his basso rendition of "You're a Mean One, Mr. Grinch" in TV's animated special, "The Grinch Who Stole Christmas") — chimed in on the chorus. "We wanted an angelic sound, but not too much church," Waronker says.

"We started to add little touches here and there, and everything about it was train-like," he says. "I wanted to keep trying because it was fun to add stuff. But I remember finally thinking, 'Don't push too hard. Stay the hell out of the way of a great song.' It was a great thing to come upon as a record producer, knowing when to back off and not be afraid of the space. Once we got to that place of, 'Oh yeah, we can see that train,' we knew we were on the right track. It became much more visual. That's the most fun part of making a record, is when you can actually listen and imagine."

When Waronker and Pilla were done tinkering, Guthrie shed his reticence. "We fought really hard to get the version that we got," Waronker says. "Once Arlo got into it, it was over with. He really understood."

Especially crucial to Guthrie was the tempo, which, despite the studio magic that had speeded it up, was still more languid than Steve's rendition — a pace that Guthrie thought was a better match for the message of the song. "I thought Goodman's version was a little too happy for his own lyrics," he says. [8]

> **Once we were able to get the tempo right, it was fine. We had to speed it up, and the more we sped it up, the more rickety it sounded, and ultimately it almost sounded like a train.**
> **LENNY WARONKER**

8: Singer/songwriter Danny O'Keefe ("Goodtime Charlie's Got the Blues") later agreed with Guthrie. O'Keefe wanted to tell Steve, "Slow it down. Let everybody see just what this is in America. Don't speed it up and make a ragtime tune out of it."

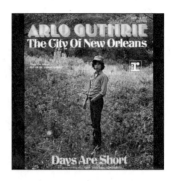

The picture sleeve for Arlo Guthrie's version of "City of New Orleans" replicated the image on the cover of the LP in which it was included, "Hobo's Lullaby." Warner Brothers did not issue the song as a single until after a groundswell of radio airplay starting in Atlanta. The B side was a Guthrie composition, "Days Are Short."

When Guthrie's version reached his ears, Steve wasn't sure that he agreed. Still stung by what he considered the Denver debacle, he felt wary. It took him awhile to embrace Guthrie's interpretation.

"I listened to it, and at first I didn't hear it," Steve told John Platt of Chicago's WXRT-FM three years later. "What he did is, he made it the disappearing railroad blues, or at least that's what I ended up thinking he did. ... It's a beautiful record, a very well-produced record. ... It was just gorgeous, the sounds on the record, and he read the lyrics so well. He slowed it down so that everybody could hear the words."

Indeed, "everybody" did hear it on the AM and FM waves in the summer and fall of 1972. In contrast to many of the other incessant hits of the season, it wasn't a gooey love ditty or a lost-love lament. It was a song of substance and symbolism for the counterculture that was beginning to age and realize that precious, visceral touchstones of their lives were dying before they themselves would. The singable chorus (with Guthrie's new chord), the train-like tempo and production, along with Guthrie's distinctive voice (not to mention his heritage), combined to make it both inviting and inescapable.

But it wasn't the corporate efforts of Guthrie's record company that made possible the hit status for his version of "City." Rather, it was a groundswell that took root at a small station in Marietta, Georgia, just north of Atlanta, WFOM-AM, which operated at just 1,000 watts by day and 250 watts at night. Danny Davenport, Warner Brothers' promotion man in Atlanta, a self-described "very young, very shy, pushin' guy" with "good ears," knew that Arlo's "City" was absent from his home office's priority list and "on the fringe" of what most top-40 hits sounded like. Nonetheless, Davenport spotted its potential. "The song just had something that touched me," he says. He urged it upon Jimmy Davenport (no relation), owner of WFOM, whose weekly tip sheets of "adds" was influential regionally and nationally. At his home on Monday evenings, the station owner held meetings attended by up to 25 label promo men. Each played a new cut he was hyping, and the competitors voted on it. "Instead of animosity, it became a well-organized group and promoted goodwill," Jimmy Davenport says. "We didn't think of breaking records nationally. We just wanted to play good music." [9]

It didn't take long for the listener response to reach Guthrie. "We were gettin' calls from everywhere, from Louisiana, Alabama, Mississippi, all throughout Georgia, South Carolina, North Carolina," he says. "Throughout the South, it was booming. It was rippling out from the South. It didn't come from L.A. or New York."

Consequently, the Warner Brothers brass were late in seeing the promise of the song, waiting a month and a half after the issuance of the "Hobo's Lullaby" LP to release "City" as a single. "The record company was in such disbelief that as the momentum built, they refused to believe that it would go anywhere, and so, if anything, they held it back," Guthrie says. "If they had gone with it from the beginning, it could have gone all the way." Danny Davenport confirms

9: Of WFOM-AM's disc jockeys, the one who played Guthrie's version of "City of New Orleans" most regularly was midday host Bill Huie, who on the side sang bass in gospel groups.

Guthrie's assessment. "When you lost an entire chunk of the country like the Southeast," he says, "you simply couldn't do as well with a record as you could with it all at the same time."

Despite the late entry, Guthrie's single filled the airwaves in the summer and fall of 1972, steadily climbing the *Billboard* Hot 100 list for three months, peaking Oct. 28 at #18 and dropping off the chart three weeks later. [10] A guitarist and later songwriting and producing partner of Steve's, New York-based Steve Burgh, echoed the feelings of many when he witnessed the song's commercial success: "It's a classic American folk song like 'This Land Is Your Land.' It's right up there with Woody Guthrie, so it was fitting that Arlo had the hit. It's right in the tradition. It couldn't have been any better if a fairy tale had come true."

The ubiquity of Guthrie's rendition fit the reach of the song, says London folksinger Ralph McTell, who instantly comprehended its native appeal. "It is what America aspires to in a good morning," he says. "It's like beginning. It's the train that links the states together. Norman Rockwell would have painted that picture if Steve hadn't written the song. And everyone's got their dignity. Even when he managed to talk about 'freight yards full of old black men,' it's an incredibly romantic and positive view of the States, this train that travels across (the country) in a day. It's the way we were sold the idea of America, the American dream personified in actual fact. It's very close to how most Americans view themselves and their aspirations."

Though bewildered about Warner Brothers' initial approach to "City," Guthrie says he held no ill will toward the label. In fact, the song's ascendance via the grass roots "was especially nice," he says. "It was not just nice for me, it was nice for Goodman, because the real people were listening to the song, and they really liked it. There was no hype about it. It was never a song that was hyped. Nobody ever put money into it to promote it. By the time they did, it was too late already. It was already gone.

"In one sense, it was hurtful that the record company didn't want to even support it. It was totally atypical, when it would have been in their interest to sell more records. But they didn't believe in it. That was the most low-key song on the record. Just a piano and guitar and accordion — that's not 'radio.' But it caught the attention of real people who heard in it an American song about a way of life that is passing by, something that was recalling another era. They heard in 'Good night, America' a sort of reminder of who they were. That was the greatness of the song. Didn't have to do with me." [11]

Publicly begging to differ was Steve, who at every juncture earnestly expressed his gratitude to Guthrie and his version of "City." It supplied him with a never-ending stream of revenue from songwriting royalties and, even more important, emblazoned him with an indelible professional identity. Still, he continually leavened his appreciation by poking fun at himself for the prominence of Guthrie's version and the invisibility of his own.

"I'll sing you a medley of Arlo Guthrie's hit record," he told a January 1973 benefit for the United Farm Workers Service Center at ritzy New Trier West

The author of "Streets of London," Ralph McTell, shown in 1976, says "City of New Orleans" is iconic: "Norman Rockwell would have painted that picture if Steve hadn't written the song."
(Photo by Michael Putland / Retna)

10: Not coincidentally, Buddah that fall released Steve's version of "City" as a single (backed by "Mind Your Own Business") in England. Sales were tepid, but James Hamilton of the *Record Mirror*, termed it a "perky ditty" that was "rather less bland than the better-plugged cover version by Arlo Guthrie. Steve wins artistically, especially with the bonus of his faithful Hank Williams re-creation."

11: "You can't stop people from singing it," says a co-founder of the Amazingrace cooperative, Darcie Sanders, of the "City" chorus. "This goes beyond classic into something archetypal that hooks into people so deeply that they're moved, and they join in. That's an incredible test."

Steve told his New Trier West High audience on Jan. 24, 1973, that he was proud that "Woody Guthrie's kid" made "City of New Orleans" into a hit.
(Image courtesy of Matt Sohn)

12: One of Guthrie's face-to-face times with Steve was an afternoon at a Cubs game at Wrigley Field. "The only ball game I ever went to in my entire life, Steve Goodman took me to," he says. "We sat somewhere right down close, and we had a great time, just goofing off, drinking beer. It was just a wasted day, but a wonderful moment of my life."

High School north of Chicago. "That song has been paying my rent, and as long as I'm going around doing benefits, somebody may as well pay my rent, so I'm glad it's this song, and I'm glad that Arlo's doing it because it's Woody Guthrie's kid. I'm going to be serious for 10 seconds. That's sort of an honor. Woody wrote a whole bunch of dustbowl ballads for farmers, so maybe it's fitting that I do a song about a train. Farmers don't get to see too many."

"Folks, I like this song, and I'm going to tune for it," Steve told a first-show audience during a weeklong engagement in October 1973 at Bubba's in Coconut Grove, Florida. "Folks ask me if I'm tired of singing this son of a bitch. Nope. When I get tired of eatin', I'll be tired of singin' this song. ... They can plant this song when they plant me. That's it. I didn't even know I was a train buff. I didn't even know this song was commercial. Shit, every song on the radio is about unrequited love, so how the hell did this song get there? This is a song about a train I once loved, but she left me." (After the quip received scant response, Steve invoked a crack that became a staple of his act: "I just told myself a better joke than I told you.")

During a late-night Bubba's show the same week, Steve introduced "City" by saying, "I know damn well that part of the reason that a lot of you came out was only to hear if I actually sing this song like Arlo Guthrie or not — and I don't, so I better just do it once. It's the only one that I'll repeat, and I'll beg the indulgence of the people who were here first set." One night later at Bubba's, he praised Guthrie's hit and chided his own lack of stardom. "That is the luckiest thing that ever happened to me, and that is the facts," he said. "I used to look up in the sky and wish on 'em, and now I are one, huh? Yeah, bullshit!"

Three weeks later, at Northern Illinois University in DeKalb, Steve again marveled at his fortune. "I could have been doing this in the bathroom, really," he said. "I probably will be sometime in the not-too-distant future."

In February 1974, he alluded to "Arlo cuttin' that song" for a Portland, Oregon, audience. "Someday maybe I can cut something he wrote and pay him back."

The same month, Steve related what he called a "twisted" story for Howard Larman of L.A.'s "FolkScene" show. "Someone called up a place where I was playin' and asked who was there that evening."

"Steve Goodman," the club staffer said.

"Yeah," said the caller, "what'd he do?"

"Well, he's the fellow who wrote that song, 'City of New Orleans.' "

"Oh yeah, him, Woody Goodman's kid."

In spite of — and no doubt because of — such wacky confusion and the levity surrounding it, Steve and Guthrie genuinely liked each other, based on only four or five in-person encounters [12] and what they heard about how each other handled "the song."

"Arlo was beautiful about it, man," Steve told WLIR-FM on Long Island in August 1975. "Everywhere he went, he would say, 'Here's a song Steve Goodman wrote.' Arlo was just so straight about that that there was never really any problem with anybody who was payin' attention, so you can't ask for much more than that."

The success of Guthrie's rendition of "City of New Orleans" had to contribute to Steve's regard for it, particularly since it was no doubt paying for his formidable medical expenses in addition to the "rent" he often cited. But the fact that Guthrie stayed truer than John Denver did to Steve's lyrics also helps explain why Steve was at ease bantering about Guthrie's hit. Steve never performed "City" with any of the changes Guthrie made to it, [13] but Steve also never volunteered — or swallowed the bait offered by interviewers — to state which version he liked better. Instead, he evaded attempts at comparison and slipped into expressions of gratitude.

Steve also publicly tempered any anger he felt for Denver. After Guthrie's version became ubiquitous, Steve never initiated commentary about Denver's failed rendition. The few times he was asked directly about it, Steve took the high road, such as when John Tobler of *Omaha Rainbow* asked him how Denver had significantly changed its words. "I could have told him not to, so it's my fault," Steve said. "It was nice of John to even consider doing the song, but what I'm really happy about is that the version with the right lyrics is the one that caught on."

Guthrie says that when he told Steve how he was offended that Denver had not only made big changes to the song but also claimed partial songwriting credit, Steve shrugged it off. "Don't worry about it," Steve replied. "I'm really happy my songs are gettin' out there." Guthrie shakes his head and says, "I was more pissed off for him than he was for himself."

In private thoughts, Steve may have wanted his own version to become a hit, but there was no denying that he — with the help of Richard Harding at the Quiet Knight — had achieved a significant musical and commercial accomplishment by instigating a popular version of a song from his own pen. John Prine's songs were racking up plenty of recordings that year (two by Denver, "Hello in There" by Bette Midler, "Paradise" by Jackie DeShannon, a version of "Sam Stone" by the soul artist Jerry Williams calling himself Swamp Dogg and promoting anti-drug awareness, and even a rendition of "Pretty Good" by none other than Paul Anka), but none of them came close to being a bona-fide hit.

Of course, Guthrie had his own reasons for gratitude. The frequent airplay for "City of New Orleans" was a welcome first for him, because his marathon "Alice's Restaurant" had stretched out to six times longer than most singles, and his drug-oriented "Comin' into Los Angeles" had been banned by many radio stations. By contrast, as Guthrie noted, "City" was "a normal song," and it expanded his geographic marketability.

"Arlo couldn't buy a gig in the South or Southwest — y'know, anti-Vietnam War, that didn't go over in the heartland, and his father was an Okie, and they called him a lousy Commie," says Richard Harding. "But with 'City of New Orleans,' he became a major star all over the country, and he was a Southern hero. He could go anywhere in the South and play because it was about a train.

> **It was nice of John (Denver) to even consider doing the song, but what I'm really happy about is that the version with the right lyrics is the one that caught on.**
> **STEVE GOODMAN**

13: Wally Podrazik, then-program director at the Northwestern University radio station, WNUR, recalls a concert by Steve on campus at Amazingrace during which a heckler shouted "Yay, Arlo" after Steve played "City." Steve then briefly mocked Guthrie's slower version of the song: "Ri-i-idin' on the Ci-i-ity of New Orle-e-eans."

From the Civil War on, that was the way to go in the South, and there were trains everywhere, just like the coal train in John Prine's song, 'Paradise.' For the agriculture, it was vital to have trains to haul the stuff around."

Guthrie, who grew up singing Jimmie Rodgers train songs, says that to the public "I became a train guy, a guy that sings about trains. I got letters from railroad guys all over the country — still get 'em, who hear that and start cryin'."

Irony lay in the fact that the man whom Americans most identified as a musical "train guy" — Johnny Cash — had passed up the chance to record and release a version of "City of New Orleans" that might have beaten Denver and Guthrie to the punch. Trains provided the backdrop for many of Cash's hits, such as the line "I hear that train a-comin'" from "Folsom Prison Blues." In the 56 episodes of his popular TV show, which ran from June 1969 through March 1971, Cash unfailingly included a "Come Along and Ride This Train" medley. In fact, *Billboard* reported in January 1971 that Cash planned to tape a segment featuring the City of New Orleans train, well before the release of any recordings of Steve's song by the same name.

Harding had asked Guthrie to pass Steve's "City" along to Cash, but the true agent became Kris Kristofferson, who slipped Cash a tape in mid-1971. Cash, however, was focused on preparing for a three-week trip in November to Tel Aviv, Israel, to film scenes for a movie he was producing, scoring and narrating, "The Gospel Road." Cash later admitted that forgoing the chance to be the first major artist to record "City of New Orleans" ranked as one of his biggest regrets. [14]

"He was so bullheaded," Kristofferson says. "He'd decided he'd done too many train songs. He didn't even like trains, and people kept sending him train songs. I even gave him a big train from some big antique place about the same time that I gave him that song."

Cash later became one of a string of musicians to record versions of "City of New Orleans" in the wake of Guthrie's hit, legitimizing it for the country-music establishment. But in the summer of 1972, as Steve turned 24 and "City" had just cracked the Hot 100, Steve had no assurance of the song's national future. He was confident only that in his home city, it was becoming a folkie standard — oddly, a Chicago song without the word "Chicago."

Flying home from his unbilled, ovation-filled sets at the Cambridge festival in England, Steve had to be reflecting on where his 1970 train trip with Nancy had brought him. (Given how memorable "City of New Orleans" became, it's an irony that Nancy's grandmother in Mattoon apparently didn't remember their visit that day. Steve recalled, "Nancy went and saw her about a year and a half later, and she said, 'You must bring this Steve down here so I can meet him.' I must have made a big impression on her.") The obvious questions were the vagaries of fate: What if it was he and not Nancy who had fallen asleep on the train? What if, instead of boarding a train, they had driven a car to Mattoon? Would there ever have been a song of his hummed and sung by tens of millions?

Just as potent, though, were questions about the immediate future: What

---

(Johnny Cash) was so bullheaded. He'd decided he'd done too many train songs. He didn't even like trains.
KRIS KRISTOFFERSON

14: Cash said in December 1980 that his mistake reflected his religious conviction. When Jack Hurst of the *Chicago Tribune* asked him if being born again was a liability, Cash replied, "If your religion is real, you don't care. I expect to give up a lot of worldly things if my Christian witness is effective. Which I have. For instance, I did the movie 'Gospel Road,' and Kristofferson brought me a song and said, 'You gotta record this.' I said, 'I'm not interested in hearing it right now. I'm doing a movie about the life of Christ.' He said, 'OK, you'll be sorry.' I knew he was right because Kris has brought me songs before. But I was going to Israel and didn't have the time to call a session and record a song. When I got back from Israel, I heard the song on the radio by Arlo Guthrie."

songs would be on Steve's next LP? Who would produce it? Would any of his newer compositions match the achievement of "City"? A recent television interview of fellow Buddah artist Bill Withers — which took place after Withers' hit, "Ain't No Sunshine," had faded and before his next smash, "Lean on Me," had broken — had made an impression on Steve, who said later: "They asked him if he thought he was a one-shot artist, and he told them that he used to make toilets for airplanes, and he thought one hit song was great."

Such down-to-earth perspective bolstered Steve. Setting in was an enhanced air of maturity. In a pair of lengthy summertime interviews between gigs in and out of Chicago, an appealing optimism was in full bloom.

Asked by the *Chicago Sun-Times'* Al Rudis about his life aspirations, Steve mentioned his desires to record a second album and for Nancy and Jessie to accompany him on the road. To entertain onstage, however, rated the top slot. "Singin' is my dope," he said. "I like to perform unabashedly. No sense lyin' about that, (claiming) that it's a strain for me to get up onstage and that I'm nervous about it. Shit, I just like to do it. I get a big kick out of it. I don't feel confined in the studio, but I really like folks and to sing for the people. Singin' in the shower sounds good with all that echo on it, but the walls give you hardly any feedback."

When Rudis pushed Steve to explain why he seemed to approach even the most serious topics by "laughing it all off," Steve shared an insight that applied to his leukemia without baring the secret of his disease. "Laughing to keep from crying is just that old blues line, and it's a fact," Steve said. "You can function better when you're laughing, at least from what I've learned. You can go about facing certain situations, both in public and in private, if you can laugh at them a little bit. According to the latest rumors, the sun still comes up in the East every day, and if you keep that in mind, you can laugh at damn near everything."

His upbeat approach, he said, arose in part from coming of age in the hopeful 1960s. "There was a young guy who was president, there was a civil-rights movement, and you really thought that you could do it. There was that kind of optimism about it: 'We can really fix it.' I didn't lose it all, but I got a lot more realistic about it as I watched all those people who said those things I believe in get shot. So it was half out of survival that I decided I was going to laugh because nobody's going to shoot a guy who's laughing. At the same time, I was still going to keep a little bit of that zeal about it. It won't go away.

"The world walks around and kicks everyone in the ass every day. It's like breathing in air. For 45 minutes a night, people can have a chance to have a good time, and if I still get to speak my mind with all that, then I'm shootin' the works. I'm gettin' the best of all possible situations. If I can entertain folks and still speak my mind, then that's a lucky thing." [15]

Prior to a summer "Chicago Night" that featured John Prine, Bonnie Koloc, Bill Quateman and himself at the Ravinia Festival in suburban Highland Park, Steve engaged in an even more articulate chat with *Chicago Tribune* guest re-

In 1972, Al Rudis of the Chicago Sun-Times *conducted the first of three long interviews with Steve, often eliciting Steve's sense of humor. "Singin' in the shower sounds good with all that echo on it," Steve told Rudis, "but the walls give you hardly any feedback."* (Photo courtesy of Al Rudis)

15: Steve also sketched a prophetic vision for the coming MTV generation. "I'd like to do the things that don't get done on TV except on PBS," he told Rudis. "I'd really like to videotape some live concerts with an audience — not with me, but with all my goddamn friends and their friends and folks they know. Not so that people won't come out. Just show them this little half hour to whet the appetite, so that somebody can see if all that is studio magic or a particular band or a particular singer." But Steve qualified his vision in a manner that today seems quaint: "I don't think I would be in a position to go to the TV manufacturers and say, 'Put (in) decent speakers.' That's certainly the drawback."

Graphic artist Gib Foster, shown in 1972, says Steve sought an "old feeling" for the cover of his second LP, as if family and friends were "sitting on the front porch."

(Photo by P. Michael O'Sullivan)

16: Not long after the interview, Stracke was injured in an auto accident, retired from performing, cinched up his belongings and moved to Mexico. Jane Bradbury, Stracke's daughter, says that before leaving, as a way of "passing the torch," her father gave his only guitar, a Martin dreadnought, to Steve. Stracke died of a stroke in 1991.

porter Win Stracke, co-founder of the Old Town School of Folk Music. The two explored further the theme of activism through song. [16]

"I've gotten to the point where I'm not tryin' to change anybody. I'm just tryin' to tell those stories and have people identify with 'em, if they can," Steve said. "I just try to paint the picture, and I trust the intelligence of the audience a little more than I used to. That's because I didn't trust my own intelligence."

The 1970s, Steve said, were witnessing "a much more realistic attitude" toward social change than in the previous decade. "It looks more like folks are looking for a better world in smaller ways," he said, counting his musical peers among those ranks.

"The singers in Chicago don't really try to preach that much because we've learned that the guys who have all the power are just as smart or smarter than a lot of the people in the movement, so to speak, or they wouldn't have all that power," he said. "You can't walk down the street and act like an idiot and expect to impress Mayor Daley, understand what I'm sayin'? You have to meet him on his own terms. You have to be as cunning as he is, as subtle as he is. There's a lot of times when he's as subtle as a truck, but he's a master in making people do what he wants 'em to do. Young folks have to realize that if they want somebody in power to do something, they for the most part have to do it themselves and have to deal with methods that are as sharp and as organized as Daley's."

That translated into serving an audience, Steve said, instead of telling it what to do — particularly if it's a paying audience. "You sing for yourself in the shower or on your front porch, and the second you get paid for it, you're singin' for somebody else," he said. "That keeps it very straight for me."

To let an audience absorb the stories told in songs, Steve told Stracke that he'd learned not to linger in any one mood for too long. "What I like folks to see is that I like to play and sing and that I'm havin' a good time, and maybe they'll have a good time — and if I've got some stories to tell that are not about good times, well, I'll tell 'em. In the course of the whole evening, I can do something that is reflective of life. There are good times, and there are bad times, and I don't want to dwell on the good times or the bad times because I imagine they're so related. You can tell that with babies. Babies cry, and about 30 seconds later they're laughin' outrageously, and that's not because they're manic-depressive. It's because that's the way life is."

Probed by the 64-year-old Stracke, Steve pooh-poohed the notion, advanced by some musicians in the guise of integrity, of drawing lines between traditional compositions and so-called "commercial" songs.

"That all gets very lost for me," he said. "A lot of those songs folks call traditional music were popular songs in their day. ... There would have been no 'City of New Orleans' without Jimmie Rodgers. He wrote so damn many great train songs. And Jimmie Rodgers was not a traditional artist. Yeah, he learned and loved old songs, old-timey country melodies and stuff like that. But Christ, he was a millionaire, drove Cadillacs. Once he started selling records, he was a pop star in the late 1920s and early 1930s, doin' just that in an era when the

Overseen by the outsize personality of Earl Pionke, left, the photo session for Steve's "Somebody Else's Troubles" LP cover included (top photo, from left) Pionke, Steve, John Prine, Jimmy Buffett and Fred and Ed Holstein. After the troupe dined on a roast — prepared by Nancy and sliced by Steve, left, while Pionke held infant daughter Jessie — the shooting began.
(Photos by P. Michael O'Sullivan)

Charleston, the flapper and jazz were catchin' on like crazy, like the rock 'n' roll of today. He was the guy playin' the acoustic guitar who sold records. That's why those definitions break down for me a little bit, because Jimmie Rodgers was not consciously tryin' to work within the limits of the tradition. But he wrote such great train songs that they became part of the tradition. They worked their way in."

Upon his return from England in early August 1972, Steve himself was trying to work his way into a tradition — visually.

Though he hadn't lined up a producer for his second album, Steve had held three meetings in June and July with Gib Foster, the graphic-artist friend of Bonnie Koloc who often frequented the Earl of Old Town, to conceptualize the LP's cover. Steve had liked Foster's designs for Koloc's first two albums on Ovation and told him he wanted his second LP to look like "a Western antique thing" similar to the Civil War motif of the 1970 "Déjà vu" album by Crosby, Stills, Nash & Young. "He wanted that old feeling to it, sitting on the front porch in costumes," Foster says.

To frame such a scenario, Foster acquired from a tannery a large, thin piece of pigskin, mounted it on an illustration board and rubbed it with shoe polish to a textured golden brown. With a wood-burning tool, he etched custom lettering (created by Chicago graphic designer Joe Sundwall) into the pigskin, complete with filigree "stitching," to give it the look of a leathery cattle brand. For the main image, he set aside a horizontal oval, then, to fill it in, hired award-winning Chicago photographer P. Michael O'Sullivan, who six months

Steve, Nancy and infant Jessie anchored the 150 "Western style" images that were shot for Steve's "Somebody Else's Troubles" LP cover. Two dozen of the photos, including this alternate image, also featured a feline, Jerome the Creep.
(Photo by P. Michael O'Sullivan)

17: That year, Chicago-based Follett Publishing Co. released a book of O'Sullivan's "Bloody Sunday" photos, *Patriot Graves, Resistance in Ireland*. The book was the proudest achievement of O'Sullivan, who became severely disabled after a motorcycle crash in 1982 and died in 2004.

18: Frequently, Steve himself cooked up elaborate feasts to share with friends. "He loved wine, and he loved to cook," says Ed Holstein. "We used to go to his place for dinner. He was the first person I knew who cooked beef with wine. He was always cooking some meat dish with wine — and oh, the smells."

19: Sneak Joynt owner Sylvester Klish told the *Chicago Reader* in 1977 that between his sets at the Earl, Steve became a "fanatic" on a Chicago Coin pinball machine, High Score Pool. "He'd wander in about noon and get a roll of quarters and wouldn't leave until 4 a.m.," Klish said. "He worked on it for three months and brought John Prine in and beat him." The feat didn't faze Prine. "I don't play those stupid games," he told Klish.

earlier had photographed the "Bloody Sunday" shootings in Ireland [17] and whose image of the summer 1967 riots in Detroit had made the cover of *Life* magazine ("Negro Revolt: The Flames Spread").

In the meantime, Steve had chosen the cast for the cover photo, and he asked Foster to show up at his Wayne Avenue apartment on Monday afternoon, Aug. 7. "I'm going to have some friends over," Steve told him. "We're just going to take it easy. We're gonna have some drinks, and Nancy's going to cook a roast beef. Just bring Michael over, and we'll go from there." [18] When Foster and O'Sullivan walked in, they found Steve, Nancy and Jessie, and the gathering soon included Steve's dad Bud, Earl Pionke, Ed and Fred Holstein, John Prine — and a recent entry in Chicago's North Side music lineup who was staying on the Goodmans' sofa bed, laid-back Southern singer/songwriter Jimmy Buffett.

"I was a nobody then," says Buffett, who was breaking out of Nashville by landing warm-up gigs in Chicago at the Quiet Knight. "Prine and Goodman were the hot kind of leaders of that folkie scene. I was an up-and-coming guy, just an opening act. Nobody really knew me." Buffett soon embraced Chicago as his favorite city and still does today. At Steve's behest, Buffett started taking in afternoon Cubs games, devouring one of the last visits of the aging Willie Mays. Buffett also gleaned that the "in" musical hangout was the Earl of Old Town, along with a smaller bar and pinball parlor that opened in September 1971 in an old frame house 30 feet outside the Earl's back door called the Sneak Joynt. [19] "I just kind of fell naturally into that scene," Buffett says. "Sitting in a great nest of performers that inhabited Chicago couldn't help but wear off, and we just kind of hit it off."

For Buffett, the relationship with Steve had tangible benefits from the start because it gave him a chance to absorb Steve's stagecraft. "I loved his sense of performing and his sense of humor on the stage, and as a performer I kind of was in the same vein," Buffett says. "We kind of recognized that in each other, and that was probably what established our friendship. He came over and saw my show at the Quiet Knight, and from that point on our friendship was kind of sealed." [20]

Despite the quick rapport, Foster says that Buffett was bashful about being part of Steve's photo. "He didn't know why he was getting involved," Foster says. But Steve liked giving his Chicago peers visual recognition and insisted upon including the newcomer. "I want everybody in," he told Foster. "I want everybody to look like they're having a good time." [21]

In the apartment's living room, Foster arranged the group sitting and standing in front of a barely visible piano, on which, at Steve's request, he placed a framed portrait of one of Steve's grandfathers. As a joke, Foster positioned a small houseplant so that its twin branches appeared to grow out of Buffett's head. Pionke held a tapered glass of cognac, and sitting on a table in front of them was a can of Schlitz. With Nancy at his side and the nearly bald, white-gowned Jessie in his lap, Steve sat in a chair with his bare right foot on the table as O'Sullivan clicked off nearly 150 images of the "half looped" mélange, two dozen of which included an orange-striped cat named Jerome the Creep. (The "creep" moniker stemmed from the jealous cat's habitual urination in Jessie's crib. At one point, Jerome swiped at the infant and sliced the skin under her eye, earning the feline a one-way trip to the animal shelter.)

Foster's finished result indeed was a contemporary urban version of "Déjà vu." In the photo that he selected and bathed in a sepia tone, Jerome the cat was nowhere to be seen. Pionke, Prine, Buffett and the Holsteins bore amiable expressions, Steve and Nancy looked deadly serious, and as the crowning touch, the infant Jessie engaged in a gloriously oblivious yawn. The importance of Jessie's presence in the photo lay in its context. Steve was naming the LP after his song "Somebody Else's Troubles," and Foster says that for Steve, Jessie embodied the concept. "It was never said, but it was always implied that 'somebody else's troubles' was Jessie," Foster says. "He inherited somebody else's troubles — here's Jessie."

When Foster returned to the apartment to show Steve his LP mockup, Steve eyed it silently for a minute or two. Finally, he looked up and said, with a twinkle, "Gib, I knew it'd be good, but I didn't think it'd be this good."

Now came the challenge of recording the music inside. As Steve mulled who would produce it, the Arlo Guthrie version of "City of New Orleans" kept climbing the top 100 chart, landing Arlo an Aug. 17 appearance on late-night TV's "The Tonight Show." Meanwhile, shows in Chicago and on the road kept Steve's attention on the move and stimulated his sense of silliness.

On the last weekend of August, during his regular stop at the Philadelphia Folk Festival, he led workshops in songwriting and rock 'n' roll and performed an evening set. [22] But he also slipped into the photographers' pit on the festival's final night and taunted the closing act, an inebriated John Prine: "John, your

20: Steve cemented the bond with Buffett by driving him to the train station to get to his next gig, in Denver. Buffett asked Steve to loan him $50 for train fare, which Steve did "without hesitation." Otherwise, Buffett says, he "would have hitchhiked" to Colorado.

21: Steve identified Buffett on the album as "Marvin Gardens," from the board game of Monopoly. "As a solo performer, I had the imaginary Coral Reefer Band," Buffett says. "I did a stage bit about the phantom members of the band, and Marvin Gardens was one of them." Buffett Web sites have enlarged the character into a legendary alter ego.

22: At the 1972 Philly festival, Steve's "Penny Evans" induced silence, says Mike Sangiacomo. "There usually was mumbling in the crowd, but when he did that, you could hear the crickets. It was chilling. You could tell he believed in what he was doing." The same weekend, Steve appeared on the WDAS-FM show of African-American deejay "Georgie Woods, the Man with the Goods." Saluting Woods' gift of gab, Steve said, "If bullshit was music, Georgie Woods would be a symphony."

*Steve poses with John Prine
and Bonnie Raitt and leads a
workshop at the 1972
Philadelphia Folk Festival.*

(Photos by Steve Ramm)

zipper's open! Your zipper's open!" ("John didn't hear it," Steve said later. "I just wanted to see what he'd do.")

Opening for Bonnie Koloc at Marquette University in Milwaukee a week later, he stole the show, in part by trotting out a Mike Hunt parody of Pope Paul VI, the "Giovanni Montini Rag," with lines like "No one would ever dare quibble, with a man who is infallibibble." Weeks later, when Steve opened for Prine at Tulagi's club in Boulder, Colorado, the two made up farcical monologues for Prine because "everybody was goin' up to him after his sets and saying, 'Heavy, man.' " The first soliloquy cast Prine as a Swede, in full accent: "My name is Yonny Prine. I come from Chi-cawgo. Everybody thinks I from Kentucky, so I let them. Everybody tells me my songs are deep and heavy, but I know they're good. They make my pockets yingle." In the second one, as an Italian, Prine's identity became "Giuseppe Prinney."

The presidential race also stimulated Steve's sardonic bone, particularly the summer blunder by Democratic nominee George McGovern in selecting fellow Sen. Thomas Eagleton as his running mate and two and a half weeks later forcing the Missourian to withdraw. Eagleton quickly had become a political liability after admitting he had been thrice hospitalized for nervous exhaustion and twice received electric shock therapy for depression, notwithstanding his current clean bill of health. The "Eagleton affair" raised deep doubts about McGovern's judgment, and Maine East High classmate Art Curtis says Steve milked the error that fall from the Earl of Old Town stage. "Boy, we have a great choice this year," Steve said. "We can vote for the crook or the dummy."

In a crude refinement that he used with audiences before and after the November election, Steve tarnished all politicians: "I feel sorry for 'em because they're all crazy. I really believe that there's only one politician in America that has the credentials that say he's sane, and that's Thomas Eagleton. He got certified, he's all right now, he took the cure, and even he blew it. I saw him sayin' on TV, 'I'm not crazy,' and holdin' the paper up and shakin' it."

As fall approached, Steve had amassed enough new songs of his own, plus a few favorites of others, to comprise his second LP, but he still was on a search for a producer. So was his label's president, Neil Bogart. The Buddah boss was wholly aware of the success of the Guthrie version — and the failure of Steve's version — of "City of New Orleans." Bogart also was wavering on his wish to lift his company from its pop-hit pigeonhole to an album-oriented identity. He told *Billboard* that Buddah was developing successful singles for acts that the label previously would have pushed only via their albums. "Our promotion staff has discovered that even traditionally album-oriented stations would rather receive one good cut than an entire new album," he said. "Success, not to mention survival, depends on sensitivity to the marketplace, and we are confident that our sensitivity in this direction will best serve the needs of our artists."

Bogart thought he had the producing answer for Steve in a Big Apple duo that was bringing a commercial bent to modern folk music — Dennis Minogue and Tom Picardo, known by pen names Terry Cashman and Tommy West, or Cashman & West. The 30-year-olds were veteran hit songwriters (Minogue co-wrote "Sunday Will Never Be the Same" for Spanky & Our Gang, in the top 10 during the 1967 "Summer of Love") and performers (1969's "Medicine Man," under the Buchanan Brothers nom de plume). Further, the pair had just scored by producing the debut ABC/Dunhill album of one of Steve's peers, Philadelphia-rooted Jim Croce. "You Don't Mess Around with Jim," released in April, soared impressively as both an LP and to #8 on the Hot 100 as a single. "We were just two Catholic kids who grew up liking folk music and doo-wop and decided to produce records together," Picardo says. "We forged what *Rolling Stone* called a production style of 'Cinerama folk,' which means we used strings."

As they told Steve in 1972, the approach of producers Dennis Minogue (Terry Cashman, top) and Tom Picardo (Tommy West) was: "Every two or three songs we do, we want one of them to get on the radio."
(ABC/Dunhill promo photo, courtesy of Mary Muehleisen Nowak)

In seeking the duo, Bogart was not alone. As Minogue puts it, "The minute that we had success with Jim (Croce), every record company in the business wanted us to produce their resident folk artist." Flush with offers to produce Mary Travers, Eric Andersen and Dion DiMucci, putting together their own material ("American City Suite" and "Only a Woman Like You") and having begun work on Croce's second LP, the two still felt they had time for Steve, partly because of their regard for "City of New Orleans."

But Steve was wary, not just of the reputation of the duo for sticky, hook-driven productions but also of anyone whose approach resembled the heavy-handed Nashville-ization of his first LP. Even so, Steve agreed to talk with the pair on his next trip to New York. The initial encounter came during John Prine's Sept. 6-11 run at the Bitter End. Backstage, Picardo says, he and Minogue explained to Steve and Bunetta their approach to production: "Every two or three songs we do, we want one of them to get on the radio. What the hell, man? If nobody hears what you do, they can't buy it." Their pitch impressed the man who was increasingly assuming the role of Steve's manager. Excited, Bunetta stood up, leaned over Steve, grabbed his shirt and started shaking it.

"Stevie, it's sink or swim!" Bunetta shouted as Steve's eyes became saucers. "You've gotta have something more, sell more records! It's sink or swim!"

The talk continued on the street outside the Bitter End, where Steve sang them "Ballad of Penny Evans" and the foursome talked baseball. [23] For the next step, at least, Steve was hooked.

In the Theater District the following day, Steve walked into the office of Minogue and Picardo with conflicting desires. "Steve, for all intents and purposes, didn't want to be a commercial guy," Picardo says. "He was a little above that." But the two also recall that Steve kept asking their secretary to telephone *Billboard* and Warner Brothers for updates on where Guthrie's rising version of "City" was placing on various charts, "which meant he wanted to sell as many records as anybody else," Picardo says. "There were a lot of people in that bind from the folk era. A lot of people didn't like what we did with Croce because it was a hit. A folksinger, you're supposed to be like a pauper, struggling and anti-establishment."

Steve told Minogue that he objected to what he saw as Croce's self-censorship in pursuit of success. As an example, Steve said that if he were to have written the song "You Don't Mess Around with Jim," he wouldn't have recorded it with the phrase "You don't spit in the wind" because an accurate version would use the word "piss."

"Well," Minogue replied, "that would ensure you of not getting played on the radio."

Despite such friction, Steve recorded a demo tape for Minogue and Picardo on a two-track tape recorder in the duo's office. Accompanying himself on guitar, Steve performed nine of his own unrecorded tunes, plus Carl Martin's "The Barnyard Dance" and Michael Smith's "The Dutchman." [24] Steve's own songs included "Song for David," [25] a countrified version of "Don't Do Me Any Favors Anymore," plus a trifle that was as brief as it was wicked.

"I Ain't Heard You Play No Blues" was a wry insult that clocked in at only a few seconds shy of one minute, and it played well to unsuspecting audiences. In this shortest of short stories, the narrator's girlfriend gave him the choice of whom to rescue from a drowning — her or B.B. King. Reflecting the dominant role of music in Steve's life, the narrator chose the bluesman. Why? The answer lay in the hilarious title line. [26]

Steve later told *Rolling Stone* contributor Steve Weitzman that he drew his inspiration for the ditty from the feared New York Giants and Brooklyn Dodgers pitcher Sal Maglie, whose nickname, "The Barber," derived from his penchant for throwing "chin music." A reporter once asked Maglie, "Would you throw a brush-back pitch at your mother?" Maglie replied with an insult similar to that of the song: "Only if she was crowding the plate."

Though three times he flubbed the "Somebody Else's Troubles" instrumental solo ("I don't got it today, OK?"), Steve's demo tape was impressive enough for Minogue and Picardo to book studio time from noon to 6 p.m. a few days later at the Hit Factory. The pair had brought in a drummer and bass player

23: Minogue had been a minor-league prospect in the Detroit Tigers system. Years later, in 1981 under the name Terry Cashman, he recorded the popular and sentimental tribute, "Willie, Mickey & the Duke (Talkin' Baseball)."

24: Upon hearing "Dutchman," Picardo fell in love with it. "I admire Steve for teaching me the song," he says. Two years later, he and Minogue, under the name Cashman & West, recorded and released a cover version, backed by a string quartet.

25: On the demo tape, Steve was circumspect with "Song for David," ending it not with a repeated reference to David's (his) "race with the sun" but instead with a similarly despondent image: "David opened that bottle and poured out a taste. Then he emptied one glass, and then he emptied another."

26: Five years later, at a June 20, 1977, show at the Main Point in Bryn Mawr, Pennsylvania, Steve inserted the word "sucker" in the girlfriend's ultimatum ("If me and B.B. King were both drowning, sucker, which one would you choose?") intimating that the girlfriend knew what the answer would be all along.

and, based on the demo tape, had sketched out chord sheets. But starting with the first song, "Troubles," things turned sour.

"He started to play it," Picardo says, "and he changed it. So we said, 'OK, we'll change it to this,' and pretty soon the only musical sound you heard was erasers on paper: Cht-cht-cht. 'I don't want that.' Cht-cht-cht. 'I don't want that.' "

It was important to Minogue and Picardo, as producers, to remain flexible. "We never did things that artists didn't want to do," Picardo says. "It was a collaborative kind of thing because we were artists ourselves, and we knew how it felt not to have a producer who was sympathetic. Believe me, we were patient guys. We've worked with some people that would put most people in the loony bin, but there were two of us, and we could smooth over anybody's ruffled feathers."

Except those of Steve, whom Picardo says engaged in "passive aggressiveness, so if you just kind of fuck around and don't do anything, somebody's going to get disgusted. He was very nice and witty and funny, and everybody liked him, but he just wouldn't cooperate. It's a formula, and you go in, and you make it as commercial as you can. That's what Steve feared most, that we would probably corrupt his tunes, because we would try to make them tighter, but he would change the arrangement and wouldn't repeat the chorus where we wanted to repeat the chorus."

After about an hour, Steve and the producing pair decided to part ways. "The chemistry wasn't right," Minogue says. "There were no fights, and it wasn't an ugly situation. It just wasn't going to work." Picardo recalls one of them saying, "Ah, let's just go to a ballgame."

With a tinge of regret four years later, Steve confirmed his professional flirtation with the duo. "I had an impression of what I wanted to do, and they had another impression," Steve told *Omaha Rainbow*. "Undoubtedly, they were right for Jim Croce and make first-rate records, and I'm proud to say I know 'em, but it wasn't happening. I'm sure it was at least as much my fault as anybody's in the long run. I'll take the rap. Shit, maybe we would have had some hits."

Steve finally settled on a producing solution by looking backward. Having pursued four failed scenarios, he concluded that Atlantic's Arif Mardin, who he had known from the Prine sessions and Jackie DeShannon's self-titled LP, was "all that was left." Mardin "had always expressed interest," Steve said. While it was deemed a conflict of interest for a producer to take on a rival label's project, Mardin, who had long been impressed by the "pure Americana" of "City of New Orleans," told Steve, "Have no fear." Mardin secured permission from Atlantic VP Jerry Wexler, who Steve said was "real sweet about the whole thing," and Steve's second album finally got under way. Starting with weekends in late September, Steve said, over four months' time "we sort of fly-by-nighted it."

If the sporadic sessions in New York at Buddah-owned Bell Sound and at the rival Atlantic studio took on a haphazard ambience, they certainly suited Steve, who had told Al Rudis that he didn't want his second LP to have "as

> **They were right for Jim Croce and make first-rate records, and I'm proud to say I know 'em, but it wasn't happening. I'm sure it was at least as much my fault as anybody's.**
> **STEVE GOODMAN**

much twang" as his first. Also important, Steve told *Sounds* writer Jerry Gilbert, was that he wanted it to be "simpler and less arranged," including Steve himself "playing more guitar on it, for better or for worse, because I want to do something that's more representative of what I do onstage."

Far from what might have been expected from a last resort, Mardin fit the task, asking Steve to hire accompanists from his own milieu. Steve chose David Bromberg, with whom he'd played at the Philly festival and on Prine's second album. Bromberg, who had developed a reputation as a "musician's musician," acceded for a time, bringing along his bass player Steve Burgh and others from the Woodstock-Manhattan corridor such as drummer Steve Mosley, who had been recruited by Burgh. Bromberg also played dobro and mandolin on a couple of cuts, but his most memorable contribution came when Steve asked him to provide a pianist.

"Well, there's two guys," Bromberg told him. "The one's Jeff Gutcheon, who's really good, and then there's this other guy, who's really great, but he's not that dependable."

"Call Gutcheon," Steve replied.

But Bromberg cryptically opted instead for the "other guy." The recording session at Atlantic was to begin at 1 p.m. The other musicians — including guitarist Marc Horowitz, who had accompanied Steve at his November week at the Bitter End — showed up on time and began rehearsing material while waiting for the pianist. "We had already run down 'Election Year Rag' three or four times," Steve told *Omaha Rainbow.* "Everybody else knew it and was feeling like they wanted to start taking it, just to see what would happen."

Impatient, Horowitz asked Bromberg, "Where's the piano player?"

"Well, he told me he would be here," Bromberg replied, a hint of significance in his eyes, "so he will."

It was the decisive clue for Steve. "That was when I figured it out," he said. The mystery man was Bob Dylan.

The 31-year-old Dylan in September 1972 was still a reclusive legend whose most recent recordings, both a seeming eternity of two years old, ranged from banal ("Self Portrait") to less than brilliant ("New Morning"). Instead of creating new and original musical testaments, Dylan was re-emerging publicly in small tastes — as a nostalgia merchant (a "Greatest Hits Vol. 2" package with previously unreleased tracks), guest performer (the Bangladesh benefit and an Earl Scruggs show) and sideman (recording with Doug Sahm of the Sir Douglas Quintet).

Bromberg had played on both of Dylan's 1970 LPs, and Dylan had returned the favor for Bromberg's self-titled 1971 debut album for Dylan's label, Columbia. As Burgh put it, Dylan "had an infatuation" for the multi-instrumentalist Bromberg, extending him a portion of his enigmatic aura. But Bromberg may not have been the only reason Dylan assented to play on Steve's second LP. Steve apparently had impressed Dylan during the afternoon jam session at Carly Simon's apartment 10 months prior.

> **I want to do something that's more representative of what I do on stage.**
> **STEVE GOODMAN**

Also, given Dylan's early and heartfelt admiration for Arlo Guthrie's father, the sweeping success of Guthrie's version of "City of New Orleans" may have propelled Dylan to participate. Dylan had admired the song itself during the Philadelphia Folk Festival the previous month. Early-morning jam sessions at the George Washington Motor Inn following the festival's Saturday night show included one room of musicians (not including Steve) who played "City of New Orleans" while Dylan watched. When the tune ended, Dylan said, " 'Graveyards of rusted automobiles' — that's a great line. I wish I could have written that."

Dylan gave Steve an in-person appraisal at the same festival. "A guy told me to go across and meet a friend," Steve told London's *Record Mirror* a year later. "I walked across, and the next thing I knew, I was looking at him. I guess I didn't know what to say, as I was sure that he would have forgotten all about the previous meeting. So I said, 'You may not remember me, but my name's Goodman, and I played some Hank Williams songs with you at Carly Simon's house,' and I got ready to walk away. It was one of those occasions when you couldn't just say hi. You just had to say something else. Anyway, he stopped me and said that he just loved 'City of New Orleans,' especially the line 'disappearin' railroad blues.' That really knocked me out, and I guess I just said the first thing that occurred to me. I started telling him that 'Gypsy gal, the hands of Harlem cannot hold you to its heart' (from Dylan's "Spanish Harlem Incident") wasn't a bad line, either. What could you say to a guy like him?"

Later, back at the motel, Steve took Dylan to his room, awoke his wife, Nancy, and showed him 5-month-old Jessie. "Yeah," Dylan said, "I got four of those."

Whatever triggered Dylan to sit in on Steve's LP session, his presence was seen afterward as a meted-out privilege. Beforehand, however, Horowitz and the other accompanists hadn't been told the identity of the imminent visitor. "C'mon, let's do something," Horowitz told Steve.

"Ahh, we gotta wait for the piano player," Steve said.

"Let him overdub it!"

"No, no, I really want the live sound, y'know. I want him to play with the rhythm section."

The privilege walked through the door about 3 p.m., a cowboy hat pulled over his eyes, a muffler around his neck and a jean jacket and boots covering his thin frame. He was the skinny visage of a prototypical character from a movie western. (In two months, he would be in Durango, Mexico, for the shooting of his debut as a film actor in such a role, in Sam Peckinpah's "Pat Garrett and Billy the Kid.")

"OK, the piano player's here," Steve deadpanned. "We can start now."

The group punched out "Election Year Rag" and "Somebody Else's Troubles" with Dylan banging odd riffs throughout both tunes. "It was a lot of garbage and stuff," says Mosley, the drummer. "He just went clunking around and sounded like a real amateur." Mardin, however, handled the situation adroitly.

> 'Graveyards of rusted automobiles' — that's a great line. I wish I could have written that.
> **BOB DYLAN**

Steve Mosley, drummer and sometime cheeks player for the "Somebody Else's Troubles" LP sessions, says Bob Dylan's piano strains amounted to "clinking around." But overall, Mosley appreciated the atmosphere of spontaneity. "It was pretty happy music, and the songs had some meat to them as far as the lyrics went, so everybody was digging it, having a lot of fun."

(Photo by Jerome Knill)

"You know," he told Dylan at one point within earshot of the others, "I'm not going to use the piano in this part of the song."

Dylan did supply a few keyboard glissandos, most of which were only barely audible in the finished tracks. But the final version of "Somebody Else's Troubles" also featured Dylan's recognizable voice in pleasing, high harmony (particularly on the word "SOME-body") in the chorus.

Burgh noted that, as called for in celebrity protocol, Steve remained "cool" throughout the day's session with Dylan, even contributing a wacky kazoo solo on "Election Year Rag." But Erik Frandsen, who supplied Jew's harp on the track, says that everyone present was feeling, "Hey, I'm in a session with Bob Dylan! Hot shit!" Mosley says that "we young-pup musicians" were "thrilled to death" by Dylan's participation, though it was decidedly low-key. "He didn't say much. He didn't say squat. Just when they wanted him to do something, he would do it, and they were trying to figure out which stuff he would play on."

Hours passed, but seemingly as quickly as he had arrived, Dylan was gone, like a ghost. "He was very quiet, very polite, very shy, very nice. There were no airs, nothing," Mardin said. "He just kind of stealthed in and out," Burgh added. "The only way he could really do these things was to make himself invisible, to turn on his stealth button."

Bromberg, pulled by his own projects and concert dates, soon left the project as well, leaving Burgh to take over as chief instrumental collaborator. It was a welcome promotion in folk-based studio guitar work for the tall, paunchy Burgh, who in various musical configurations by age 21 had opened for the Doors and jammed with Alvin Lee, Jimi Hendrix, Buddy Miles, Johnny Winter, Hot Tuna and the Grateful Dead. A deep friendship soon grew between Steve and Burgh, whom Steve later labeled as "young and impetuous."

The intermittent scheduling of the sessions meant that the "Troubles" LP project would stretch well past the Nov. 7 presidential election, so Buddah decided to rush-release a single of "Election Year Rag" (backed by "Somebody Else's Troubles") in an attempt to snare some timely sales. It was too little, too late, however. Despite Dylan's role as a sideman, "Rag" received scant airplay and little notice: a fine-print mention in *Billboard* and a *Rolling Stone* blurb that ran two months after Election Day. "Rag" became an eye-blink curiosity — and no wonder. Its irreverence stood in stark contrast to the sitting president's impending landslide that disheartened the diehards working for McGovern.

Just two and a half weeks before the election, while playing for 350 students at the Whole Coffeehouse in the basement of Coffman Union at the University of Minnesota in Minneapolis, Steve indirectly acknowledged the disconnect of song and cause. He opened his show with "Election Year Rag" but provided no commentary, as if the song's "What, me worry?" gist needed no context. One song later, he turned to his bipartisan rant, "Paul Powell." Next, he introduced "Turnpike Tom" with his well-honed crack about the difference between bullshitters and liars ("Liars believe their own bullshit") and ladled out more cynicism. "I'm not leavin' myself out of this," he said. "Anybody who does this and gets paid for it is full of shit." Two songs later, he launched into a 10-minute narration of his Muskie train experience.

In this telling, with the election looming, he all but apologized for singing for the senator eight months prior. "You deserve an explanation," he said. "I knew he didn't sound much different than Nixon. Y'know, if I shut my eyes, it was real hard to tell on a lot of issues." But Steve said he had a clear incentive to participate. Typically, he said, campaigning musicians never get to meet the candidate, and if they ask about issues, they receive only canned position papers, "a little frustrating when you want to know who you're singin' for." In contrast, Steve said, the Muskie trip offered in-person access: "I figured I wouldn't blow the chance to unload how I felt about the war and all that crap on Edmund S. Muskie for all the money in the world." Further, he advised the audience to follow suit: "Supposedly they represent us, so if you ever get a chance to meet one of those guys, don't just buck-dance there. Get it off your chest. It's his problem. That's why he took the gig."

But what did Steve actually tell Muskie? And how did Steve feel about the election now? He sidestepped such talk and instead zeroed in on pleasing the Minneapolis crowd with his story about the messy toilet flush.

Near the end of the show, Steve did weigh in against the Vietnam War with his stinging "Ballad of Penny Evans," and afterward he volunteered to donate to a good cause the royalties from his impending recording of the song. "There won't be any (royalties), really, when you think about it. It's something like a penny a record for the writer, right? So they sell 20,000, you get $200 or something like that. So I'll give that to the American Friends Service Committee." (He had headlined a benefit concert for the committee the previous night in Chicago.) Instantly, however, Steve veered back to what he saw as his main job, entertainment: "I'm gonna change the subject before I commit suicide. Yeah, that's really sick. I feel like I'm manic-depressive. What the fuck did I say anyway? I was havin' a good time." He revived the evening's merry mood with his typical closer: "You Never Even Call Me by My Name." [27]

While the remainder of Steve's "Troubles" LP sessions in the fall of 1972 in New York may have lacked the drama of Dylan's brief materialization, they were imbued with spontaneity. "It wasn't one of these uptight kind of recording situations," Mosley says. "It was a living-room scenario. They had the room set up so that everybody was in a big circle. It was pretty happy music, and the songs had some meat to them as far as the lyrics went, so everybody was digging it, having a lot of fun."

Part of the fun lay in Steve's own buoyancy and readiness, which was obvious to a key visitor, Milt Okun, the producer of John Denver's records for RCA. In gestures that erased his lingering bitterness over Denver's version of "City of New Orleans," Steve had visited Okun's studio on 34th Street, played him tapes of a handful of his "Troubles" tracks, asked his advice and invited Okun to one of the "Troubles" sessions at Bell Sound. Okun suggested just a solitary change to the arrangement of a song (he can't remember which one), to which Steve

Supposedly they represent us, so if you ever get a chance to meet one of those guys, don't just buck-dance there. Get it off your chest. It's his problem. That's why he took the gig.
STEVE GOODMAN

27: Steve was in a particularly tasteless mood this evening, evidenced by his intro to the quiet encore song, "Would You Like to Learn to Dance?" He said he'd changed the title because he had become "sick" of other love songs with similar titles, such as "Do You Wanna Dance?" and "Dance with Me, Henry." "There's 100 of 'em," he said. "So I changed this one to, 'I Love You So Fuckin' Much I Can't Shit.' I figure that'll throw off all the folk purists. I figure there ain't nothin' like a straight song with a warped title."

Arif Mardin, who produced Steve's "Somebody Else's Troubles" LP, had a "great time" doing so. "The songs were very strong. What we were doing was a beautiful, artistic album, and we were not even thinking 'Will radio play it?' "

(Photo courtesy of Arif Mardin)

28: Steve's other recently composed, Illinois-based song, "Paul Powell," was not recorded for the LP, and a version of it by him has never been released.

agreed, and came away impressed and delighted. "Steve was kind of up, and I couldn't believe he was sick," Okun says. "He was not only in good shape, but he was also interacting with everybody clearly and very, very positively. He had none of the earmarks of someone who was in trouble. He was much better than he had been on his previous stuff. He sounded energetic, clean, clear."

Setting such a tone at the sessions was Mardin, whose career continued to soar through the decades, including his 21st century productions of jazz/pop singer Norah Jones. Working with Mardin for the first time was therapeutic, says Hugh McDonald, whom Burgh snagged to step in on bass guitar. "A lot of producers produce by intimidation," says McDonald, known today as the bassist for the pop-metal band Bon Jovi, "but Arif could nudge you into the right direction without any sort of animosity. He made you want to please him. Never, ever said anything that made you feel belittled." Mosley adds that Mardin's touch extended to knowing when to quit. "He kept the energy up, and when everybody needed a break, he took us all out to a nice place for dinner."

Mardin insisted he was merely reflecting the kindness and politeness of Steve. "He was just a genuinely good guy," Mardin said. "I remember those kind eyes." The songs and mix of musicians also spelled a more relaxed perspective, Mardin said. "We're talking about an album that didn't have the soup du jour pop commerciality," he said. "The songs were very strong. What we were doing was a beautiful, artistic album, and we were not even thinking 'Will radio play it?' Maybe I was very naïve myself because I was having a great time, musically."

That approach — the pursuit of creativity over formula — spawned a miscellany of moods and flourishes.

On "The Barnyard Dance," Steve sang with a falsetto in one stanza, and Mosley slapped his cheeks throughout to provide goofy, Spike Jones-like percussion. "It was like a tympani drum," Burgh said. For "Don't Do Me Any Favors Anymore," Mardin secured jug-band chanteuse Maria Muldaur for a harmony vocal on the chorus. For "Song for David," which Steve included despite its veiled introspection, Mardin overdubbed an extended Jerry Burnham flute part that was reminiscent of the iconic Bud Shank solo on the Mamas & the Papas' "California Dreamin'," along with Charles McCracken's low-toned, brooding cello.

And for "Lincoln Park Pirates," Mardin enlisted Eddie and David Brigati of the disintegrating Rascals pop group (for which Al Bunetta had roadied) to overdub vocals on the "Way-hey" chants. By trying out the song at shows from Buffalo to Los Angeles, Steve had shed his fears about it being "too local" for a national album. "They tow cars away in every town," he said. "You can write about specific things like that and be on pretty safe ground." [28] (As he had done with narcotics agent Tony Rigoni's name in his recording of "Chicago Bust Rag" in early 1971, Steve edited a name out of "Pirates," omitting from the lyrics the last name of Ross Cascio and replacing it with a three-syllable phrase, "the fat man." The new words softened the song's Chicago focus, but there was no mistaking the reference.)

As he finalized the LP's lineup, Steve toyed with re-recording the spoof from his debut album, "You Never Even Call Me by My Name," so that he could include its consummate (mother-farms-prison-trains-trucks) final verse. He told Jerry Gilbert of *Sounds* that doing so would "be kind of an imposition on the public, but if I put 13 songs on the album, I don't think they'll feel they've been cheated." Perhaps because he already was recording "Don't Do Me Any Favors Anymore" with a country flavor and didn't want to go overboard with "twang," he thought better of the idea.

Steve brought to a later session a song born over Thanksgiving in Paula Ballan's Upper East Side apartment. It would become a standout on the LP and a perennial in his stage shows — a simultaneous lampoon of holier-than-thou vegetarians and their antagonists. Oddly, the song began as a diatribe about someone close to him having been arrested in Illinois for possession of two marijuana joints and was to be called, "You Get No Champagne in the Champaign County Jail." But as Steve noodled with the tune, his thoughts drifted to a California man "who told me how he straightened out his life by eating organically," Steve said later. "He told me he had only two weaknesses: reds and cheesecake. ... It's always nice when somebody tells you that and then passes out while he's telling you." Ballan says Steve kept "carping about all of this crap about granola and health-food shit that he was not down with at all."

"Why don't you call it the 'Cordon Bleus' and spell it like the French?" Ballan asked.

"How about the 'Chicken Cordon Bleus'?" Steve replied.

He conjured the first verse, in which the narrator complained to his girlfriend that she lured him with fancy meat dishes but now was plying him with "seaweed and alfalfa sprouts." Ballan added a complementary second verse, and a friend of Ballan's, Toni Mendell, tossed in verbal garnish. The pun-laden parody, pre-dating Larry Groce's #9 national hit "Junk Food Junkie" by more than three years, cracked a joke in every other line and culminated with the devastatingly vivid image of a street dog grinning because "they let him eat meat."

For the portly Steve, and for overweight guys who heard it later, the song affirmed what it meant to be "a regular fella," made clear in the fadeout: "Y'know, fat is where it's at." [29] But its worship of jellyrolls, cannoli, French pastry, chocolate éclairs and lasagna (and, in later concert references, everything from baklava to a Clark bar) was clearly tongue-in-cheek. [30]

The arrangement of "Chicken Cordon Bleus" underscored its wicked wit. Throughout, Larry Packer, another Burgh recruit, supplied snaky violin (one reviewer termed it "great drunk fiddle"). Mardin brought in Atlantic musicians David "Fathead" Newman for a bouncy tenor-sax solo (preceded by Steve's recorded in-joke appeal: "Now won't you play me them fat licks") and Willie Bridges on bass saxophone for deep honks that sounded like squatty farts.

"That was just wonderfully fun," Burgh said of "Cordon Bleus," allowing that girth such as his own deepened his appreciation. "Steve and Paula were the perfect people to write about food obsession, and that song is so much about

Vocalist Maria Muldaur and fiddler Larry Packer, shown performing at a 1970s festival, were among many contributors to Steve's "Somebody Else's Troubles" LP.

(Photo by Barry Sagotsky)

29: The indulgent attitude toward eating meat in "Chicken Cordon Bleus" flew in the face of Steve's Jewish heritage. Paula Ballan sums up Steve's stance: "Don't put me down, don't beat me up. I am a Jew, and I will not deny that. My father fought in a war to protect us from people who would have taken my life away. I will defend with my life my right to be Jewish. But beyond that, I like my pork chops well done, thank you."

30: In lyrics printed the next year in *The Steve Goodman Song Book*, the song faded out with the phrase: "My shadow disappeared."

Steve's everyday personality and how he dealt with life, because he was battling his weight all those years. It just said it all."

In Mardin's mind, all was proceeding well, but at one point he suspected that Steve was exercising another obsession — an illegal one. While overdubbing vocals one afternoon, Steve abruptly left, saying only, "I have to go." Mardin thought, "Oh, wow, this guy's going somewhere downtown to buy some drugs." After Steve's departure, Mardin quietly pulled Al Bunetta aside.

"So sorry, I feel something," he told Bunetta. "Obviously, he's an addict, and he has to find his fix."

"I'm sorry," Bunetta replied, "I didn't want to tell you, but he's going for his chemo."

Learned in that fashion, the news of Steve's leukemia jolted and embarrassed Mardin. "He was such an unassuming, wonderful person that I felt so ashamed," Mardin said. "Obviously, he was getting his drugs, but it was chemo."

The fragility of life provided the backdrop for what became the musical jewel of the LP sessions — the Michael Smith song that Steve had learned two years earlier in Florida, "The Dutchman." On its face, the tune had little potential to reach the youth market. It merely recounted the daily routine of a couple in their twilight years in Amsterdam: an unnamed man who today would be said to be in the beginning stages of Alzheimer's disease, with his devoted wife, Margaret. Not only were the song's characters elderly, but its setting was also remote. Other than in the chorus, none of the lyrics rhymed. Moreover, as Smith (or his wife, Barbara Barrow) typically performed it, "The Dutchman" had the tempo of a dirge.

To its enduring credit, however, the song's lyrics wrung universal yearnings from its simple story. Swirling from morning to noontime to night, its three verses encased its inviting and deeply moving chorus:

> *Let us go to the banks of the ocean*
> *where the walls rise above the Zuider Zee*
> *Long ago, I used to be a young man*
> *and dear Margaret remembers that for me* [31]

Moreover, while the main character of the two was the male Dutchman, the tune devoted equal time and granted gentle dignity to Margaret — a plus in an era in which the feminist movement was flowering.

To boost the song's appeal and suffuse it with his own spark, Steve sped up its tempo. But in his recording of it, he also risked unconventionality by featuring a distinctive instrument (besides Hugh McDonald's quiet bass and his own tinkling acoustic guitar) that was associated most readily with the Geritol set's Lawrence Welk and polka parties — the accordion.

The actual Hohner accordion used on the track was "finished in mother of toilet seat," Steve said, and its chord buttons didn't work properly. But its sound, more authentic to the folk culture than saccharine strings would have been, blanketed the recording with warmth. Its player was a longtime Chicago com-

---

So sorry, I feel something. Obviously, he's an addict, and he has to find his fix.
ARIF MARDIN

31: Chorus of "The Dutchman" used by permission, Michael Peter Smith, Bird Avenue Publishing, copyright 1969.

patriot who was one of the first to hear Steve's "City of New Orleans" and shared Steve's wit and native intelligence, Jack McGann. On guitar, McGann had accompanied Steve on the "Gathering" LP in early 1971, and by the time he was recording "The Dutchman" with Steve, McGann was only "fiddling" on the accordion with standards such as "Lady of Spain," says former companion Ann Mintz. But just as with Nick DeCaro's concertina in Arlo Guthrie's version of "City of New Orleans," the emotion that McGann somehow squeezed out of the defective instrument lent the tune much of its aural magic. [32]

"The Dutchman" resembled the Guthrie tune in other ways as well. Both songs were slightly longer than usual for top-40 radio (4:18 for "Dutchman," 4:31 for Guthrie's "City"), both had engaging details and a nostalgic air, and both were one singer/songwriter's interpretation of another's composition. Steve's resonant, slight vibrato was as perfectly matched to "Dutchman" as Guthrie's amiable nasality was to "City." In fact, in this recording, Steve's voice — on both melody and overdubbed harmony — embodied poignancy and bitter-sweet bravery as in no other song he would ever perform. It repeatedly brought tears to the eyes of McDonald in the studio, and as Steve himself later reflected, "I'm as happy with that track as anything I've ever recorded."

The potential didn't escape Buddah. One night after the song was finished, over dinner and wine in Arif Mardin's apartment on the Upper West Side, Mardin played it over and over for Neil Bogart, who told Mardin and Steve that "The Dutchman" would be his favorite song on the LP. No doubt Bogart was hoping that it would meet with the same success as Guthrie's version of "City" and become Steve's first self-performed hit. But after the nosedive of "Election Year Rag," there was no desire to issue a second single before the album could be released and build a foundation of FM airplay — and the LP was yet to be completed because Steve had one last song to throw into the mix.

The song was not his own, but for someone whose energy seemingly belied his leukemia, its theme, encapsulated in the title, was irresistible: "The Lovin' of the Game." Steve had first heard it a few years earlier at the Quiet Knight as performed by the couple who wrote it, Pat and Victoria Garvey. It came to his attention again in October when Pat Garvey, recently divorced and living out of a converted Travelall truck, drove to Ann Arbor to see Steve at a weekend gig at The Ark coffeehouse. After Steve's final Sunday-night set, the two gathered around guitars and a piano until daybreak, and Steve became captivated by the song's Tom Paxton-like imagery and wanderlust, particularly its final verse:

> *So long darlin', don't you cry, hope that things pan out for you*
> *All the good times goin' by, got to get ourselves a few*
> *Where I'm goin' has no end, what I'm seekin' has no name*
> *The treasure's not the takin', it's the lovin' of the game* [33]

Two months later, Garvey again met up with Steve at a late-night apartment party following Steve's Dec. 8-9 booking in downstate Urbana in the chapel of the Channing-Murray Foundation as part of a series organized by Rich Warren

Jack McGann, shown in the early 1970s, supplied accordion accompaniment for Steve's version of "The Dutchman," helping make it one of Steve's best-loved recordings.
(Photo by Diana Park, courtesy of Ann Mintz)

32: McGann, who in later years revealed himself as gay, was the plaintiff in a prominent 1988 lawsuit that challenged his Houston employer's reduction in AIDS benefits. He lost a bid for the U.S. Supreme Court to review an appeals-court ruling against him, and he died of the disease in 1991. The Americans with Disabilities Act, which disallows such benefit reductions, took effect the following year.

33: Last verse of "The Lovin' of the Game," words by Pat Garvey, music by Victoria Garvey Armstrong, ©1966 by Ashcroft Music (ASCAP), reprinted by permission.

Pat and Victoria Garvey's "The Lovin' of the Game" became an irresistible addition to Steve's "Troubles" LP, a fact that pleased lyricist Pat Garvey, for whom Steve was "the single most exciting package of entertainment I'd ever heard." (Photos courtesy of Pat Garvey, from the LP "Songs: 1965-1971")

at Steve's former school, the University of Illinois. As Steve and Garvey stood across from each other with guitars in the kitchen, Steve asked him to run through the song. While Steve picked the tune on his guitar, he changed nuances in the melody.

"No, it goes like this," Garvey said.

"Let me do it my way," Steve replied.

Garvey, 41, was more the songwriting veteran, but he had no objection to Steve's alterations. "Steve was so great because he was unique," Garvey says. "He didn't try to sound like anybody else. His voice was his own and very unusual. At the time, everybody was trying to sound like somebody old or putting on the raspy voice. But Steve, when he sang, it sounded like when he talked. He was the single most exciting package of entertainment I'd ever heard. Singing, playing guitar, songwriting, talking, it was all there in abundance and quality."

The opening act for the two-night U of I gig — Al Ierardi, an exuberant but inexperienced folksinger who had improvised an unusual guitar style after damaging his middle two chording fingers in a lawn-mower accident — couldn't have agreed more with Garvey, but only after he saw Steve's first show. Ierardi, two years older than Steve, had been oblivious to the Chicago headliner other than knowing he had written Arlo Guthrie's recent hit. Ierardi failed to recognize Steve at first sight and barked at him as Steve noisily entered the warm-up room. Worse, at the end of his opening set, Ierardi played three encores lasting 20 minutes while a smiling but perturbed Steve glared at him from the wings.

"Only afterwards did I find out from everybody involved that the opening act does not do encores," Ierardi says. "I was so embarrassed." Ierardi apologized to Steve for his gaffe at the post-show party, and Steve graciously invited him to his room in a nearby dorm to drink beer, play guitar and talk. After the second night's show, as the two parted, Steve gave Ierardi a promising verbal send-off.

"You did well down here. I understand it. This is your territory," Steve said, adding with an enigmatic grin, "One of these days, you'll be on my turf, and you'll see what it's like for a Chicago audience."

That opportunity came the following spring when Steve set up for Ierardi a Sunday-afternoon slot at the Earl of Old Town. Steve was there when Ierardi took the stage, and throughout Ierardi's set, the room felt like a tomb. "Nobody was even looking at me," Ierardi says. "People were quietly talking at their tables, and I was playin' my heart out. I pulled every trick out of the book that I could, and nothing — nothing." During the break, a puzzled Ierardi sat in the back-room Star Cave, and in walked Steve.

"Well," Steve said with the same smirk he'd flashed in Urbana, "what do you think of Chicago audiences?"

"Y'know," Ierardi stammered, "I've never played anywhere where I've felt like this. I don't know if I have the guts to get up for a second set."

Steve couldn't hold back the truth. He told Ierardi that he had primed the

Earl crowd by saying, "When this guy gets up here, just kind of be blasé about the whole thing and make him sweat." Steve also reassured Ierardi that he would end the prank by warmly introducing him for the second set — which he did, allowing Ierardi a bona-fide chance to shine in the big city.

"I was blindsided," Ierardi reflects with a laugh. "Steve had set me up in his little devilish way to get a taste of Chicago." Ierardi considered the payback an honor. "As soon as he told me, it was a relief. There was no animosity. It was just, 'I'll get you, but in a fun way' — and it was."

Two weeks after Steve's U of I concerts, just before Christmas 1972 while housesitting for folkie friends Herb and Betty Nudelman in Chicago, Pat Garvey checked his mail at the post office and was thrilled to learn that Steve had recorded his "Lovin' of the Game." Arif Mardin had wanted Steve to return to Atlantic in New York to put down one more track, and Steve had chosen the Garvey tune. Weaving in subtle wah-wahs by David Bromberg on electric guitar, piano fills by Jeff Gutcheon, a peaceful pulse from drummer Steve Mosley and overdubbed harmony by Steve himself, Mardin crafted a charming, genre-straddling track. As with "The Dutchman," Steve had interpreted the song so warmly that, in the parlance, he made it his own.

In fact, Steve came away from the entirety of the "Troubles" recording sessions ebullient. In contrast to the Nashville recordings for his first LP, these tracks possessed a friendly and informal tone that just sounded a lot more like Steve. While the master tapes were pressed into vinyl, covers were printed and other album-release preparation was under way, this was a time to celebrate — and Buddah had just the ticket for its stage-hungry artist: a prestigious, high-profile gig on the other end of the country.

It was a slot as the third artist (after John Prine and jazz saxophonist Sonny Rollins) to be featured on the influential new Sunday-night music series "One of a Kind," produced by KCET, the public-TV station for Los Angeles. In his Dec. 6 taping, Steve reverted to a semi-preppy appearance, wearing a black jacket and brown vest covering a blue T-shirt as he stood in front of a huge, triangular wooden scaffold. With no host, the show relied solely on Steve entertaining a college-age studio audience of about 100.

His one-hour set was rearranged and edited to 30 minutes when it eventually aired the following Feb. 18, but it covered a lot of ground: four songs from his first LP (including "City of New Orleans") and three from the one yet to come. Editing kept any potential indelicacies in check, as Steve's intros were brief to nonexistent. The soft ("Would You Like to Learn to Dance?") and serious ("Penny Evans") material allowed for soulful close-ups. But the funny songs drew the loudest reaction, Steve getting mileage from a profile view of him demonstrating how "country bands always stand at a 45-degree angle and lean in towards the mike." Aimed at a populous market of educated Southern Californians, it was an appealing, down-to-earth performance.

Days after the taping, however, what was under way 238,857 miles away from Earth would give Steve a truly celestial stature. What he had introduced to

Al Ierardi, who overextended his opening set for Steve in Champaign, had a surprise awaiting him a few months later when he accepted Steve's invitation to play the Earl of Old Town in Chicago.

(Photo courtesy of Al Ierardi)

Astronaut and country-music fan Harrison "Jack" Schmitt appreciated the "Good morning, America" wake-up call when he was 238,857 miles away from Earth.

(Photo courtesy of Space Facts, http://www.spacefacts.de)

his "One of a Kind" audience as merely "a song about a defunct Illinois Central train" literally reached the moon.

Apollo 17, the sixth and last Apollo mission in which humans were to walk on the moon's surface, lifted off Dec. 7 from the Kennedy Space Center in Houston, and four days later, on Dec. 11, reaching lunar orbit was the mission's command module, named "America." For their period of rest prior to the lunar landing, astronauts Gene Cernan, Ron Evans (who named the module) and Harrison "Jack" Schmitt (an exploration geologist and the first scientist and non-military-trained pilot in space) had each swallowed a Seconal. While they slept, Houston contemplated what would be the right music to rouse them.

With Arlo Guthrie's hit version of "City of New Orleans" fresh in the minds of those on the night shift in the NASA pressroom, the choice became obvious. What better song to awaken astronauts shepherding a patriotically named space capsule than the popular song whose chorus showcased the phrase, "Good morning, America"?

Once the idea was born, NASA staff scrambled to locate a copy of the tune, and someone scurried home to find one. But instead of the Guthrie version, the one that turned up was John Denver's rendition from his year-old "Aerie" LP. Therefore, at precisely 1 second past 7:38 a.m. Eastern time, into the command and service module flowed Denver's voice, starting with the song's first chorus: "Good mornin' A-MER-ee-ca ..."

Two and a half minutes later, after the end of the song, Joe Allen, the NASA capsule communicator in Houston, reinforced the musical greeting.

"Good morning, America," he said. "How are you?"

"Uh, this is America," replied Evans, the command-module pilot. "That's a good way to wake up."

"Good morning, America. How are you?" Allen repeated. Alluding to the song's "gone 500 miles" phrase, Allen added with playful exaggeration, "You'll be gone a million miles before the mission's done."

Evans laughed, and the two confirmed that their exchange was coming in "loud and clear." A few seconds later, Schmitt, the lunar-module pilot, joined the conversation. A fan of country music from his days growing up in Silver City, New Mexico, Schmitt had a request.

"Let's hear it again, Joe," Schmitt told Allen.

"Are ya serious?" Allen replied from Houston.

"Well, I just got on a headset," Schmitt said with a laugh. "You never had a chance to wake me up before."

"Stand by, here it comes," Allen said. "It's comin' at ya, America."

During the replay of the first chorus, the song inspired Schmitt to imitate the high-pitched, two-toned warble of a country singer: "*AW*-haw!"

"How about that?" Allen asked the crew after Denver's second serenade.

"Thank you, Joe, that's great," said Schmitt, who invoked the title of a number-one Hank Snow classic ("I'm Movin' On") by adding, "We're movin' on."

"Don't you know?" Allen said with a laugh.

Schmitt drawled the first words of the Snow song: "That-a big eight wheeler."

A few moments later, Schmitt asked Allen, "How long are you with us this morning?"

"Oh," Allen replied, "not too many more minutes."

"Hope we didn't keep you up last night," Schmitt said.

"The pleasure was ours, Jack. We devoted our eight hours to selecting your wake-up call this morning and got a little help from the newsroom pool on that suggestion."

"Well, that was a good suggestion," Schmitt said. "I had forgotten all about that song. That's a good one. You ought to find the 'Golden Rocket' for us some morning."

Allen responded with a joke: "You'll wish you hadn't asked."

Schmitt's request was for another Snow song, whose title vehicle, like "City of New Orleans," was a train. But Houston couldn't find or fit into the schedule an airing of "Golden Rocket." Steve's "City" became the only railroad tune the astronauts heard.

Astronauts had played their own music in space since the Mercury days of the 1960s, but Apollo 17 was the first mission in which music was routinely played for wake-up calls. Selections used on the 13-day mission ranged from college fight songs that matched the alma maters of the astronauts to Roberta Flack's "The First Time Ever I Saw Your Face," the Carpenters' "We've Only Just Begun" and the Doors' "Light My Fire."

For Schmitt, who four years after the mission served one term in the U.S. Senate as a Republican from his home state, "City of New Orleans" was the musical highlight of the trip.

"Clearly, the line 'Good morning, America, how are you?' was most appropriate and welcome," he says.

Steve had no idea the Apollo 17 astronauts would hear his signature song — and twice, no less. He considered the event an honor, but he couldn't let it escape his wit. On a Buddah record sleeve, he was quoted, "That's funny, playing a train song to three guys going to the moon."

Later, describing the tune's role as a wake-up call, Steve impishly deadpanned a question that had an obvious answer for its asker: "How would you like to be Reveille?"

> I had forgotten all about that song. That's a good one.
> **HARRISON 'JACK' SCHMITT,** astronaut

'It's a family thing – it makes you feel good that they feel good'

Earl Pionke may have served as a second father to Steve, but he also relished his role as an affable, would-be Mafia don.

"Y'know, Steve," Pionke said in late 1972 as the two nursed drinks across the Earl of Old Town bar, "you got a couple big markers out there with me."

"What're you talkin' about?"

"Markers, like in Vegas. You borrow two G's, you get markers."

"What the fuck you talkin' about? You're tellin' me I owe you?"

"Yeah, man, I want to call in some of the fuckin' markers."

"OK, tell me what they are."

Pionke could have named a litany of his favors: hiring Steve for regular stints starting in 1967, letting Rich Warren record Steve at the Earl in 1969, insisting that Steve copyright "City of New Orleans" in 1970, partially bankrolling the "Gathering" LP in early 1971 and fronting Steve's airfare to his Bitter End debut in New York later that year. In return, of course, Steve's innumerable shows at the Old Town saloon had brought Pionke cash in the till and a measure of fame. But Steve could not contest the overarching favor on the ledger — Pionke's financial and logistical help in the spring of 1972 in the adoption of his daughter, Jessie. For that "marker," Pionke had a plan.

"You're gettin' big, popular," Pionke told Steve. "I want a tradition of New Year's week with you for two nights, or one or three, whatever your schedule calls for."

Steve had played the past two New Year's Eves at the Earl, but Pionke was looking for a lifetime commitment.

"What the fuck? That ain't a marker," Steve said. "You've got that. That's a given."

"OK, but here's what we gotta do, Steve. We get the ticket money, you pay all your musicians and your opening act. Then we take what's left from the tickets, and I'll throw in 20 percent of the gate and the bar, and we'll pick charities, and we'll give the fuckin' money away. But not with checks and all that. I'm talkin' about under the table."

"That's your marker?"

"Yeah."

I want a tradition of New Year's week with you for two nights, or one or three, whatever your schedule calls for.
EARL PIONKE

(Opposite page) David Bromberg, top, and Leo Kottke look on as Steve picks a guitar solo during an early-1970s festival in the St. Louis area.
(Photo by James Black, courtesy of Leo Kottke)

1: "You're like my dad away from
home," Pionke says Steve told him.
"I could call you a prick. You can
call me whatever you want. I can't
do that with my dad or mom."
Pionke also insists, however, that
he didn't replace Bud and
Minnette in Steve's life: "He loved
his parents. There's nothing
hocus-pocus here. But I was his
dad away from home."

"What the fuck? That's great. That ain't a marker. We're on." [1]

Thus, on Dec. 31, 1972, began the formal tradition — no matter what offers that might be dangled for Steve at venues across the country — that Steve would headline every New Year's Eve show at the Earl of Old Town (Steve's "throne," as one musician termed it). The charities, most of which were never disclosed by Steve or Pionke, ranged from social services to needy musicians, and the dollars each year hovered in the low thousands. "We did some fuckin' beautiful things" with the money, Pionke says.

The true gift, however, became the New Year's Eve music itself, generated until the wee hours year after year at the Earl by Steve and an unpredictable assortment of musical "ringers," many of whom visited from Philadelphia, New York and elsewhere, simply for the opportunity. Steve and others dubbed the mélange a Mongolian or Albanian "cluster-fuck."

"The Earl was packed to the rafters for this annual event because all the Chicago luminaries would show up," says Ken Bloom, who moved to Chicago from California in part because of the chance to play clarinet, dobro and other instruments in such a circumstance. "You name it, they'd be there. Sometimes that whole huge band thing was really good, because all the musicians were great. There wasn't a single one who wasn't just absolutely top-notch. So that meant everybody (onstage) was listening. They knew when not to play. Usually, when you have these 'Let's get everybody up for the big final number' it's a big moosh. It rarely works because there's no organization and discipline. But with people Steve picked to play for him, they were all great players and musicians, so they all listened."

The signature tune for the occasion, performed with up to a dozen musicians crowding the postage-stamp stage, became "Mama Don't Allow It." Affectionately impudent, the song was written in the 1920s by Charles "Cow Cow" Davenport, an Alabama-born and Chicago- and Cleveland-based African-American blues pianist who on his many tours no doubt had crossed paths with the string band of Martin, Bogan & Armstrong, from whom Steve likely learned the tune. The song was a jam session that bid instrumentalists and vocalists of all stripes to take turns performing a series of 16- or 32-bar solos. Each solo was preceded by the phrase, "Mama don't allow no _____ playin' in here," and filling the blank was the name of the instrument or singing style. "It was his way of letting people play, and he just loved playing with people, the more the merrier," said Fred Holstein.

"You get up, show off, do the best you can," explained Howard Armstrong, whom *Chicago Sun-Times* film critic Roger Ebert aptly labeled the "showboat" and "peacock" of Martin, Bogan & Armstrong. "So many musicians play in a group, and they feel like they've been overlooked, just being used or misused," Armstrong said. "But when you call them out, even if they don't do but two or three lines, then they feel like they belong, you know? It's kind of like a family thing. You can't play in a group that's one pulling one way and one pulling the other way. And it seems to me, the audience can tell when there's something

Howard Armstrong, taking a fiddle solo at the Earl, says musicians appreciated the dynamic of "Mama Don't Allow It," particularly as led by Steve: "When you call them out, even if they don't do but two or three lines, then they feel like they belong, you know? It's kind of like a family thing." (Photo by P. Michael O'Sullivan)

wrong like that. But when the group seems to be happy, and they're all working together, putting lot of unction into it, well, then they'll start tapping and rockin' and reelin'. And it makes you feel good that they feel good."

With Steve at the helm, the song's intros became a series of rhymed couplets that he made up on the spot, based on the player's name, instrument or other details. The improvisational aspect — a clear influence from the Second City comedy troupe's John Belushi/Bill Murray era across from the Earl — didn't daunt Steve. To the contrary, he thrived on it, says Bloom: "He really loved the energy of having it all sort of explode all at once."

"Mama Don't Allow It" soon became the climax of the tour-de-force shows, which careened from hilarious parodies to dramatically quiet ballads to rowdy rock, blues and country standards for which Steve was the engine, Bloom says. "I can't think of a single person I've known over the years who could walk out on the stage by themselves and generate the kind of energy that he did and have the same emotional range. He really had, by himself up there, total control. There were better technical singers, better technical guitar players, I don't think there were better writers, but with the kind of energy he was able to project onstage, it was always astounding.

"The focus of it was really something to watch. It's the kind of thing you don't often see in the folkie acoustic world. You see it in classical musicians and jazz musicians and people who are serious about playing traditional music. You don't often see it in singer/songwriters. Most of them sing their songs, and sometimes they expect the marvelousness of their writing is going to do it. With Steve, he really was intent that people hear what he said, so he was really intent on engaging in severe acts of communication."

Steve also possessed the fortitude to penetrate noisy New Year's audiences who were feeling no pain, says the *Sun-Times'* Ebert. "Steve loved to sing and for people to have a good time, so he was OK with the fact that half the crowd was drunk out of their minds. He didn't demand total silence and attention. He loved to be leading a raucous party. He could quiet a room and could certainly

*Ray Nordstrand (top) and
Norm Pelligrini, shown in 1981,
helmed WFMT-FM's live,
marathon New Year's Eve
shows, which in the 1970s drew
the informal leadership of
Steve. "He sort of implied that
he was a circus barker,"
Nordstrand said. "He came in
rather modestly and sort of
joined in, and everybody
surrounded him."*

(Photo by Art Thieme)

2: In its Sept. 29, 1972, edition that
proclaimed the city's "Heavy Sixty,"
a fledgling news/arts weekly, the
Chicago Reader, had dubbed Steve
"the balladeer and bard of the
Chicago folk revival."

3: Post, though he had written and
co-performed a top-10 hit ("Reach
Out of the Darkness") for the
folkie Verve Forecast label in 1968
and starting in 1972 recorded a
string of four LPs with Bay Area-
based Fantasy Records, somehow
couldn't crack the commonly cited
"holy trinity" tag used for Steve,
Prine and Koloc.

perform in a concert situation where his music was the point, but on New Year's Eve, he'd be up there onstage having a hell of a good time with everybody else."

Sometimes three or four sets long, the New Year's shows often lasted two or more hours past the 4 a.m. legal closing time, an infraction OK'd by cops who were paid to look the other way. "It's 5:30-6 a.m., the joint's still packed, Goodman's still tryin' to sing songs, and two policemen come in with their big stripes," Pionke says, recalling one New Year's Eve. "They walk through, puttin' the flashlights on all these people." Then an officer addressed Pionke at the bar.

"Hey," Pionke said. "What do you want?"

"What do you mean, what do I want?" the officer shot back. "Y'know what time it is?"

"Yeah," Pionke replied, "it's time for you to wish me Happy New Year."

"Yeah, that's what we're here for," said the officer, not missing a beat.

"Good. By the way, stroll by a couple days from now. I'll be here."

Pionke basks in the memory and says, "Not everybody could do that."

The only extended interruption in the New Year's Eve action came when Steve left the Earl at about 2:30 a.m. for an hour or so to play a few songs with other Chicago folk musicians and Second City sketch comics who gathered at WFMT-FM downtown to perform for the station's distinctive all-night, live "Midnight Special." The unquestioned high point of the broadcast was the appearance by Steve. "He sort of implied that he was a circus barker," said "Special" co-host Ray Nordstrand, the station's president and general manager. "He came in rather modestly and sort of joined in, and everybody surrounded him. He was the catalyst of the whole thing."

The launching of Steve's New Year's shows at the Earl, with his corresponding visits to WFMT, marked the coming of age of the Chicago folk scene, which Kris Kristofferson blessed in 1972 as "today's Greenwich Village." Clearly, a musical golden era for the North Side had begun. [2]

Three artists who had followed in Bob Gibson's footsteps by progressing commercially beyond the city's borders — Steve, John Prine and Bonnie Koloc — were dubbed the scene's "holy trinity." Their example inspired countless youths to take lessons at the Old Town School of Folk Music, their frequent local gigs kept a steady flow of audiences coming to the Earl and scores of other venues, and their reputations lured out-of-towners to Chicago to try their hand and, in many cases, put down roots in fertile ground. Within the trinity, however, Steve stood as first among equals. "The whole folk music scene in Chicago was energized and maybe defined by Steve," Nordstrand said. "It was a very exciting scene for a couple of decades, but really, Steve was at the center of it."

Those taking notice and soon deciding to make their home in Chicago included the acerbic Harry Waller ("Cockroaches on Parade") from Pittsburgh, the swamp-sounding Mike Jordan from the St. Louis suburb of Winfield and vibrato-voiced Chris Farrell from the Philadelphia outpost of Pottsville. Even Jim Post, the wacky, high-pitched, Texas troubadour, returned after several years in San Francisco. [3] Other folkies also poured in:

◆ Homegrown artists Stephen Wade, Bill Quateman, Andrew Calhoun, Corky Siegel, Mick Scott, Tom Dundee, Al Day and Sally Fingerett. [4]

◆ Immigrants Claudia Schmidt, Mike Lieber, Cindy Mangsen, Rich Markow, Anne Hills, Thom Bishop and Jim Tullio. [5]

◆ Frequent and sporadic visitors Saul Broudy, Lew London, Rod MacDonald, Tim O'Brien, Bryan Bowers, Winnie Winston, David Amram, James Lee Stanley, Gamble Rogers and Len Chandler. [6]

"It was like Paris with the Impressionists," says Harry Waller. "Everybody sort of hung out."

Part of the tangible lure was Steve's "Somebody Else's Troubles" album, released in January 1973. [7] From its down-home, textured exterior (with the misleading cover photo implying that John Prine and the emerging Jimmy Buffett were musical contributors) to the 11 offerings inside, Steve's finished LP underscored the good-time aura that outsiders were sensing in Chicago. Neither screeching nor sedate, it drew from a variety of genres. Vitality poured from each cut, and many listeners and critics instantly saw it as a leap forward from Steve's debut LP, a flowering beyond a formula.

Certifying its trendiness were the back-cover credits, which listed as accompanists David Bromberg and a playful pseudonym: "Robert Milkwood Thomas," derived from "Under Milk Wood," the best-known work of poet Dylan Thomas. An explicit clue to the mystery sideman was a line found elsewhere in the credits: "Thanks to Bob Dylan." However, only one of Steve's pair of Dylan-assisted songs, the title cut, made it to the album. Though the record had plenty of room for Steve's two-minute "Election Year Rag," the song, anchored in the just-completed presidential race, was deemed no longer timely. Politics took a further step back as Steve, in the LP's title song, excised a derisive reference to "the man from the White House," replacing the character with that of a factory boss.

But there was nothing apolitical about "The Ballad of Penny Evans," which on the "Troubles" album was as conspicuous for its a cappella presentation as it was for its anti-war message. The unconventional track was positioned at the close of Side Two — to enhance its impact but also to let anyone wanting to avoid a stark song without instruments to hit "reject" on their turntables without missing any other cuts on the side.

International events made "Penny Evans" a compelling cut within days of when the "Troubles" LP hit record stores. The U.S. government announced on Jan. 15 an end of all mining, bombing and other military operations against North Vietnam. It also signed, on Jan. 23 in Paris, a nine-point cease-fire agreement calling for the United States to remove all its forces from South Vietnam, which it did on March 28.

One day after the Paris signing, Steve somberly introduced "Penny Evans" at a farm workers benefit at New Trier West High School north of Chicago, grudgingly noting the war-ending role of the newly elected president, Richard Nixon, amid the unfolding Watergate scandal. "The war is over. ... I certainly believe

4: The parents of 16-year-old Sally Fingerett took her to see Steve perform at Orphans in 1971. "That's when I knew that's what I wanted to do," she says. "I kind of wanted to be Joni Mitchell, but then I really, really wanted to be Steve Goodman." Fingerett later forged a solo career and joined the Four Bitchin' Babes, founded in 1990 by Christine Lavin.

5: Tullio, 22, who had played string bass for Steve in 1971 at the Riverboat in Toronto, moved to Chicago from New Jersey in late 1974 to write music for *Playboy* magazine. He wanted to leave his unwieldy instrument behind, but Steve told him otherwise. "You're not going to sell that bass," said Steve, who wanted Tullio to back him up at Chicago gigs. The *Playboy* job lasted eight months, but Tullio had steady bass work in Chicago for years, which helped launch him as a jingle writer and producer. "Goodman convincing me to bring my bass really enabled me to do that," he says.

6: Chandler taught Steve his pensive anti-war rant, "My Ass Is Mine," which Chandler had sung in the 1972 Vietnam tour film "F.T.A." ("Fuck the Army"), starring Jane Fonda. The song's core was a litany of how the military drafts, drills, breaks, ships and shoots "your ass," with the capper, "They can kiss my ass." Chandler says, "Steve would stand by the stage with a big grin lovin' that song." Steve taught it to others, including singer/songwriter and John Denver sideman Bill Danoff, for whom Steve made a demo tape.

7: Though copyrighted in 1972, the "Troubles" LP didn't reach stores and trigger mentions in the press until mid-January 1973.

Sweat beads on Steve's forehead as he performs on the sweltering weekend of June 8-10, 1973, at the Culpepper festival in Warrenton, Va.

(Photo by Andrew Czernek)

8: After his New Trier West show, Steve delivered a quick lesson to Paul Zollo, a 14-year-old sophomore who boldly stepped backstage and asked Steve to listen to one of his songs. Steve loaned his black acoustic guitar to Zollo, who played for him an abstract composition, "Troubled Winter." Steve listened patiently, then said, "Y'know, that's pretty good, but I could have written that whole song in one line. There's a lot of poetry in there, but how much really means anything? It's harder to come up with a song where people understand what you're talkin' about." The advice "spoke volumes" to Zollo, who today is a musician and journalist. "No one else did that for me. It really meant a lot."

that the agreements were initialed," Steve said. "I don't think any of them tell the truth, man, but I think it's pretty much over. The consequences of lying this time are extreme, not that they weren't before, but this time they'll be extreme domestically on a large scale, I assume, mostly because it's his ass. That's what those guys are good at." [8]

In this context, the prescient last line of "Penny Evans" — "They say the war is over, but I think it's just begun" — took on extraordinary relevance that reverberated in performances that reduced crowds to a palpable hush. When Steve returned to Sandstone prison in Minnesota on May 7, the song commanded the attention of inmates, and by the end, stunned silence filled the auditorium for several uncomfortable seconds. "I think this tune's killing some of those Marines in back," a prisoner whispered. Then the startled group rose to its feet with firm applause, wrote Jon Bream of the *Minnesota Daily* student newspaper. In respectful retort, Steve said, "It's about time somebody understood that song."

The broadside also worked in the wide-open outdoors. On the sweltering weekend of June 8-10 at the Culpepper Music Festival in Warrenton, Virginia, Steve played to 1,500 chattering youths struggling in 90-degree heat not to slide down the thunderstorm-slicked, grassy hill of Lake Whippoorwill's natural amphitheater. Bottles already had been thrown at the stage, reflecting the crowd's mixture of "redneck beer drinkers and weed-smoking hippies," says *Village Voice* writer Ira Mayer, and Steve worried about his precarious post above the lake. But as Steve removed his guitar for "Penny Evans" and got a third of the way into its lyrics, "the crowd started to notice it, and by the end of the song, you could hear a pin drop," says Washington, D.C., journalist and ex-club owner Ed Zuckerman. "It mesmerized that crowd, and he held them for the rest of the set. It was an amazing performance under very difficult circumstances."

"Penny Evans" wasn't the only rallying cry on Steve's "Troubles" LP. While Ross Cascio's ego had enjoyed the anti-hero status that Steve's live performances of "Lincoln Park Pirates" had wrought, the song in recorded form subjected his nefarious business to more intense local governmental scrutiny and public humiliation than ever before. Chicago stations such as WXRT-FM that featured local artists knew that Cascio, as a public figure, was fair game for criticism, and they reveled in the chance to further expose his greed on the airwaves.

With Steve as a guest, Studs Terkel aired "Pirates" during the Jan. 30 edition of his WFMT-FM show, choosing also to recite part of the previous day's column by the *Chicago Daily News'* Mike Royko in which Cascio promised to sue "everybody involved" with the song. Terkel then tweaked Cascio's rough-and-tumble reputation by challenging Steve's off-the-cuff vocabulary.

Explaining why he wrote the song, Steve referenced Alderman Dick Simpson's thick file on Cascio, including memos from the Illinois attorney general: "When I saw that the state's attorney's office had this enormous case against the guy, I said what the heck, I can take a shot."

Terkel jumped in: "Let's just avoid that word 'shot,' if we may, OK?"

"Oh, wrong word, huh?" Steve said. "Well, people shoot dice, too."

"Forgive me," Terkel replied. "I'm thinking of your interests."

"Oh, I understand that, Studs. ... Ross, if you're listening, no offense, OK?" Steve said, adding, "If I see the guy, I'm gonna buy him a drink."

At another Chicago station, however, "Lincoln Park Pirates" wasn't taken so lightly, triggering a snag of corporate censorship.

Bob Johnston, program director and on-air personality at rock station WBBM-FM (and no relation to the London record producer of the same name), wanted to play "Pirates" but ran into static from a risk-shy general manager and ultimately the New York-based attorneys for CBS, the station's parent network. "There was the concern that Ross Cascio would sue anybody," Johnston says, a concern that Steve himself exacerbated in his shows. "Here's a song," Steve told a March 3 crowd at the Bitter End, "that's going to get the Buddah record company of New York City sued to their ass."

Determined to prevail with his station's brass, Johnston forged a middle ground, working with WBBM's music director, Jim Smith, to modify the three spots in the song in which the words "Lincoln Park Pirates" were heard. "Tying Lincoln Park to 'the fat man' was the problem," he says, "so we replaced the words 'Lincoln Park' with an instrumental part of the song. We didn't put a tone in there but actually re-did it with the correct measures and cadence and everything." It was the same treatment WBBM had accorded the song "Lake Shore Drive" by the local folk-rock group Aliotta Haynes Jeremiah in 1971, excising the title's acronym because of its obvious drug reference ("trippin' on down on LSD").

The "Pirates" compromise satisfied Johnston because the station would not have played the song otherwise. "Technically, I thought it was fine, for what it was," he says. The altered version didn't escape columnist Henry Hanson of the *Chicago Daily News*, who tweaked the station's timidity on Feb. 12: "Gee, 'Lincoln Park Pirates' is the name of the song, WBBM." [9]

The "Troubles" LP scored ethically on a more personal level with crediting for "Chicken Cordon Bleus" that included co-writers Paula Ballan and Toni Mendell. It was the first of more than 40 Goodman songs that would carry multiple writing credits. "It's just sort of a question of bouncin' ideas off folks," Steve later told "FolkScene" host Howard Larman. "If they were in the room, I just sort of put their name on it. I just figured it was fair. They were there, they helped, they got credit, that's it."

Steve Burgh was one of many who found Steve's approach refreshing: "Even if one word was thrown in or a mood was set, that person was involved in the writing and got credit. I've sat all night long writing songs with other people who got up at the end of the night and said, 'I'll go send the copyright in on my song now.' Steve was right. It's the right thing to do." Louis Killen, listed in the "Troubles" LP credits for "providing the outline" for "Penny Evans," says Steve's approach assured accuracy for posterity. "People with integrity always give credit," he says. "If you pass on your source, you're keeping the source's memory alive,

The nefarious, sue-happy reputation of Ross Cascio was so potent that the CBS station in Chicago modified Steve's "Lincoln Park Pirates" to remove a direct connection between Lincoln Towing's horror stories and the "fat man" who ran the firm.

(Photo courtesy of Bill Nestos, Lincoln Towing)

9: Following crackdowns from local and state government, Ross Cascio sold his towing business on Jan. 20, 1981, the day Ronald Reagan was inaugurated and U.S. hostages in Iran were released. In 1984, Cascio told *Chicago Sun-Times* columnist Bob Greene that he didn't regret his notoriety. "The more they wrote about me," he said, "the more accounts I got." His reflection on the author of "Lincoln Park Pirates"? "Steve was a good kid," said Cascio, who died three years later on Sept. 30, 1987.

not just the song you sing. You're putting on that chain, that set of links, that tradition."

Other collaborators viewed the finished album with keen interest. Pat Garvey "loved" Steve's version of "The Lovin' of the Game," which was "the first time I'd heard anybody else (record) it." Ray Frank, for whom Steve first played the anguished "Song for David" on a hospital bed at Memorial Sloan-Kettering nearly three years prior, was stunned to see the cut on the LP. "I was surprised simply that it came out at all," he says, "but I realized that the references were oblique enough that they weren't going to get in the way for people who didn't know about his condition."

Vexation, however, was the initial response of another key contributor, Michael Smith, author of "The Dutchman." Smith had moved to Detroit from Miami, and Steve had telephoned him in late 1972 to tell him he had recorded the song. When Smith first obtained the album, he was pleased to see that "Dutchman" was the LP's opening cut, the showcase position. But after he listened to the track, he fumed. "I was so annoyed with him because he got a lot of the words wrong, and he got the melody wrong," Smith says. "It really bothered me."

The alterations to the melody were slight, and the changes that Steve had made to Smith's lyrics — deliberately or unintentionally (Steve never publicly explained which) — resembled the nuanced modifications that Arlo Guthrie had made to Steve's "City of New Orleans." In Steve's version, Amsterdam was golden "in the summer," instead of Smith's "in the morning." Steve's version of the last verse opened with "The winters whirl the windmills 'round," a flip-flop from Smith's original line, "The windmills whirl the winter in." In perhaps the most noticeable change, Steve had Margaret "sing" an old love song and later had her and her husband "sing together in the dark." Smith's verb in both instances was "hum."

While the changes colored the meanings of phrases, their impact was negligible. The song's charm and depth remained unscathed. Smith today admits this and expresses nothing but gratitude: "Now I see that I was just a tense young man and needed to have everything a certain way or I wasn't happy."

Steve's recording of "The Dutchman" transformed Smith's life. [10] Because of Steve's home base, Smith and his wife, Barbara Barrow, began landing frequent gigs at the city's folk clubs. In 1976, they moved from Detroit to an apartment on Chicago's North Side, where they resided for the next 30 years. Smith, the author of more than 300 songs, for decades has been regarded by the folk world as a songwriting genius and stirring performer. But without Steve's recording, Smith says, "I would not have had any work at all. I would be struggling. It was as good a thing for me that he recorded 'The Dutchman' as Arlo Guthrie did 'City of New Orleans' because I got more work and recognition from that recording than any other recording, really. It's my signature song."

In yet another parallel with Guthrie, Steve astonishingly told Smith seven years after the release of his "Troubles" LP that "The Dutchman" was his own

---

I was just a tense young man and needed to have everything a certain way or I wasn't happy.
MICHAEL SMITH

10: "The Dutchman" also changed the life of fledgling Toronto singer/ songwriter Norm Hacking, who in September 1973 snagged a front-row seat for a Steve show at the Riverboat club to learn the tune's chords. Hacking later befriended Michael Smith and placed a recording of the song on his own live album. Before Steve's June 6, 1978, show at Ontario Place, Hacking left the LP backstage. Introducing the song mid-show, Steve said, "Norm, I got the record, wherever you are." Though the two hadn't met, their bond was sealed.

signature song. That notion may have contained more flattery than veracity, given the firm foothold that "City of New Orleans" had assumed in the nation's consciousness, but Smith says that Steve's actual words to him about "The Dutchman" were "This is the one that people talk about when they talk about me."

Even if it was an exaggeration, Steve's sentiment validated the beauty of the recording, which Buddah saw from the beginning. The cut became the "Troubles" LP's first single in early 1973, [11] and, as Steve slyly noted in his gigs, the label asked Steve to perform it at each show. Buddah also sought to give the song an aesthetic dignity. The 45 of "The Dutchman" came encased not in the usual generic wrapper but a more expensive picture sleeve with an intricate, sepia-toned sketch of the tune's elderly characters. As drawn by graphic artist Glen Christensen, the Dutchman's white beard and Margaret's white hair were intertwined and indistinguishable. Closed-eyed and ensconced in a seemingly eternal embrace, the two resembled characters from an ancient frieze. No one could have conjured a more fitting image. It was a classy treatment, verifying Buddah's faith in the song's appeal. [12]

Unlike Guthrie's "City of New Orleans," however, Steve's version of "The Dutchman" never surfaced in *Billboard*. Steve attributed the washout in part to its nearly four-and-a-half-minute length. But that was a mere technical observation that masked disappointment over a recording that he later rated his best.

Despite its commercial failure, "The Dutchman" became an oft-requested pillar of Steve's performances. Early on, he sometimes gave it an indelicate intro, as "the only love song I know that does not grunt," but after the guffaws, the song routinely brought audiences to pin-drop silence and teary-eyed clarity. On occasion, Steve quietly asked audiences to sing along on its chorus, the only song for which he ever did so. To those who knew of Steve's leukemia, the depiction of life's final years in "The Dutchman" was especially poignant because it illustrated an age that Steve would not likely reach.

Its emotional power was emblematic of later reflections about Steve's seemingly innate ability to clasp the collective heart of his listeners — such as an observation by Jimmy Ibbotson of the Nitty Gritty Dirt Band: "Every time you would see Stevie, it was like a wonder. He'd cheated death. The angel of death had fled from us again and left us this little elf, who could take any audience in any place and mesmerize them, and by the time he was done, not only did they love Steve, but they loved their wives more, and they loved their children more, and they laughed more."

Steve's audience of music critics — for whom Steve's leukemia was no factor because most weren't aware of more than vague rumors about it — was equally upbeat about his "Troubles" LP. Reviews in more than a dozen national magazines in 1973 hailed the album as "twice as good as his first" (*SingOut!*), "a brilliant exposition of contemporary folksong" (*High Fidelity*) and "a veritable Maserati by comparison" to his debut LP, which "was pretty much a record with training wheels" (*Rolling Stone*). Eager to pigeonhole artists, *Billboard* labeled

Every time you would see Stevie, it was like a wonder. He'd cheated death. The angel of death had fled from us again and left us this little elf.
JIMMY IBBOTSON

11: The B side of the "Dutchman" single was "Song for David."

12: To encourage radio stations to play "The Dutchman," Buddah issued its promotional staff, including Bruce Shindler, who handled the U.S. northeastern region, distinctive trinkets to give to deejays — tiny pairs of wooden Dutch shoes.

the "Troubles" LP "a tremendously beautiful, progressive country album with vestiges of blues and even bluegrass licks interspersed with pop lyrics and melodies." *The New York Times* called it "a fully rounded portrait of the artist ... (that) has much strength and realism in its simplicity." Added *Cash Box* magazine, "His realism will ultimately make him a legendary songwriter." [13]

Particularly thoughtful was *Crawdaddy* critic Toby Goldstein, who wove into his "Troubles" LP review an echo of Steve's "Good morning, America" chorus from his best-known song. "Goodman knows how to handle all the Americas in the United States — the personal good and bad of individuals relating (and not relating), the dreadful seriousness of the Vietnam aftermath, the whimsical complaint of a meat-lover in the midst of vegetarian consciousness and, on the title track, the absurd sickness we all share of getting along with somebody else's troubles, while never considering that somebody else is getting along with ours. America today, as Goodman is brilliantly aware, is a chronic case of pretense. The dream, as we go along, is that everything will be all right in the end."

The critical praise fortified Steve's hope that the LP would sell well. But as he performed at Amazingrace in Evanston on a sub-freezing night Jan. 5, a few days before the "Troubles" album hit Chicago-area stores, the crowd could detect that Steve had steeled himself for a fall. Introducing a song from his earlier LP, he said sarcastically, "This is one of the smashes off of the first album I recorded for Buddah." The LP itself, he said, was "a rumor everywhere except Chicago. It's great. You don't know how great it feels to walk around and not have to put up with reporters and stuff asking you questions about your first album, other than asking you when it's coming out, right? It's great. Everywhere outside of Chicago, nobody ever heard this one, so it's fantastic. A little bit, but nothing that would cause 200 people to come out on a night like this or anything. It's weird. So I get a clean bill of health, right? I get a clean start with the second one."

Impressive reviews and high hopes notwithstanding, Steve faced competition from new albums by better-known artists on other labels, among them Traffic, Bruce Springsteen (his first), Elton John, Judy Collins, Eric Clapton, Doug Sahm (like Steve, featuring Bob Dylan), Stealer's Wheel, Jerry Jeff Walker and the Mahavishnu Orchestra. Buddah relied on its promotional formula of securing FM airplay — and made some headway. Progressive rock stations in Chicago (WBBM) and New York (WNEW) placed the "Troubles" LP in their top-20 rotation from early to mid-February, and six other stations from Seattle to Hartford gave it "hot action," *Billboard* reported. Nationally, however, the album slipped in at only #216 on the magazine's album chart in early March and stayed there for just three weeks, eking out a peak position of only #214. Over the course of 1973, the record's sales never topped the 30,000-50,000 of Steve's debut album. [14]

Still, Buddah's strategy of shows and interviews reaped rewards, gaining Steve "a fan at a time," as his manager Al Bunetta liked to say. A musical Energizer Bunny, Steve bounded through a relentless itinerary of concert and festival dates

---

America today, as Goodman is brilliantly aware, is a chronic case of pretense.
TOBY GOLDSTEIN
CRAWDADDY

13: A mixed assessment came from *Stereo Review*'s Noel Coppage, who was disappointed by Steve's songs but impressed by "his interesting mind and quantity of apparent talent." On the home front, David Witz of the *Chicago Reader* wrote that the "Troubles" LP was "the album that the hardcore Steve Goodman fans have been waiting for. It's funny, moving, bouncy and tender." In the same review, Witz irreverently dismissed Steve's first LP as "a stack of rabbit farts, and poor Steve was going to have to live with being buried in a record that sounded like the Phil Spector Nashville Sessions."

14: Steve addressed the allegedly tepid "Troubles" LP sales eight years later. "That one did better than they ever told us," he said. "They had some creative accounting there because more people have told me they liked that record than I knew had it."

Steve rehearses with John Prine in Chicago's WTTW-TV studio in March 1973 for an appearance on the special, "They Kept the Faith," aired April 13, 1973. Page C4 has photos of the show's finale.

(Photo by Jon Randolph)

in big cities and college towns during 1973. Some gigs were local (four on Chicago's North Side, two in Elgin and one each in Evanston and Winnetka, plus a high-profile appearance with an Old Town folk phalanx that included Bonnie Koloc and John Prine on WTTW-TV's "They Kept the Faith"). Some were regional (Rockford and Champaign/Urbana). Others were far-flung (a half dozen in New York City and Long Island, three each in the Boston area and Washington, D.C., [15] two each in Toronto, Boulder, Austin, Ann Arbor and the Philadelphia area, and one each in Rochester, Buffalo, Denver, Houston, San Francisco, Los Angeles, Minneapolis, St. Louis and South Miami, as well as Rhode Island, Minnesota, Virginia and Nebraska. He even returned to Europe, taking John Prine to Cambridge and Stockholm.

Along the way, he generated scores of reviews, as well as major profiles in *Rolling Stone*, *Zoo World*, the Toronto-based *Beetle* and the London-based *Record Mirror*, leaving an indelible impression upon countless readers and tens of thousands of concert-goers.

The impression, Steve noted later, was not always savory. With Nancy and Jessie home in Chicago on Tuesday, Feb. 6, the evening of his third wedding anniversary, Steve was 1,000 miles east in Medford, north of Boston, standing in the wings at Tufts University's Cohen Auditorium, where he was the warm-up act for John Hartford. He intended to celebrate the occasion solitarily by pouring two glasses of Paul Masson Cabernet Sauvignon wine (which he termed "California Vino Inferior"), clinking the glasses together and drinking both. But his watch had stopped, he'd lost track of the time, and he was talking with Hartford and gripping the just-opened bottle when 8:30 arrived and the emcee called him to the stage. "I grabbed the pick, and I ran out there with the bottle of wine, and they started cheering because they saw the bottle of wine," Steve said. By the close of his 70-minute opening set, he'd sung a dozen songs while

15: Opening for Ian & Sylvia Tyson Feb. 4, 1973, at the Kennedy Center in Washington, D.C., Steve encountered a sound system that emitted electrical snapping sounds before the amplification cut out completely. Steve walked to the stage front and with a yell — "Let's see how good the acoustics are in here" — finished the set under his own power.

Jim Croce became a cheery compatriot, and his death in 1973 hit Steve hard.

(Photo by paul s wilson/philadelphia)

16: Steve collected risqué gags anywhere he could find them. Jeff Rochman, former Sammy brother from the U of I, recalls Steve telling a joke at the Earl that he'd learned in Boston. Steve had asked a cab driver, "Where can I get scrod?" The driver replied, "I never heard of anyone refer to it in the past pluperfect."

17: One of Steve's Lake Forest College classmates, Gayle Pemberton, shared drinks with him from a pint of bourbon backstage during the Club Passim dates. She found him "bedraggled" after putting on an energetic show. That night, she says, "It was clear to me that things ran deep, that he was intense and deeply caring. He couldn't write the humorous songs he did without having an enormous amount of seriousness and an emotional maturity that just ran the bell curve."

polishing off the wine, to loud applause — but someone else had to tell him later what had happened after his third song, "Chicken Cordon Bleus." "Three-quarters of the way through the fadeout, I just disappeared up my own asshole," he said. "In a puff of smoke, I was gone, and I don't remember a thing that happened to me the rest of the night."

Two mornings later, the *Boston Globe* ran a brief review, captioning an accompanying two-column portrait of Steve with a perhaps intentionally misspelled phrase: "STEVE GOODMAN ... happy enebriation." The paper's Bruce Sylvester wrote that Steve had maintained an intimate mood and that his intoxication "didn't mar his act as it might a lesser performer." In fact, Sylvester noted that someone said of Steve: "He's the only person I know who can swear with flair. Even his lewd is shrewd." [16] Still, the notoriety embarrassed Steve. Two weeks later, with Nancy and Jessie along for the trip, Steve played the nearby Club Passim in Cambridge for four nights, and at each show someone brought him booze. "People would just come in with bottles of whiskey and wine and say, 'Here, drink this.' " [17]

Sans wine bottle, Steve twice reached television viewers outside U.S. borders, first as a guest with George Hamilton IV on the Canadian "Ian Tyson Show." He also anchored a round-robin gathering with Lori Lieberman, co-writer of "Killing Me Softly," and Swedish pop star Tomas Ledin, filmed in the round before 200 people at Capitol Records in Los Angeles. The latter program, later aired in Sweden, was titled "L.A. Sessions." It was the first appearance before an English-speaking audience for the nervous, pre-ABBA Ledin, and he appreciated the presence of Steve, whose banter loosened the proceedings. Steve's versions of Michael Smith's "The Dutchman" and Marty Robbins' "Big Iron," as well as his own "Chicken Cordon Bleus" and "Penny Evans," also drew the most vociferous applause. "I was very impressed by his presence," Ledin says. "It was really his show. He had a very strong stage presence, very comfortable."

Steve also left an astonishing mid-spring impression in Minneapolis during what was to be his first formal pairing with Jim Croce, whose Cashman & West-produced AM radio hits had put the mustachioed singer/songwriter in high demand. Steve and Croce had forged a routine in Croce's early days in which Croce, while playing the Earl of Old Town, would start to play "City of New Orleans," and Steve, acting like a boorish drunk, would taunt him, saying, "You don't know how to play that guitar. I'll show you how it's done." Whereupon Croce would invite Steve to the stage, and the two would finish the song as a duo, delighting patrons. Such shtick made their May 6 co-billing at Guthrie Theater eagerly anticipated, by the performing pair as much as the audience.

Shortly before their double-show booking that night, however, Croce took ill and could not perform. Some fans demanded and received refunds, but half-sized audiences of 700 hung in. With an entertainer's brand of heroism, Steve doubled his set length and performed concerts that ran nearly two hours each, making sure to sing Croce's "You Don't Mess Around with Jim" for each crowd.

Steve was "remarkably relaxed for a performer in his position," wrote Roy M. Close of the Minneapolis-St. Paul *StarTribune*. "He needed only a couple of songs to win the audience completely."

Steve connected with Croce again Aug. 24-26 at the Philadelphia Folk Festival, at which Steve took on a greater presence and responsibility than in past years. He put on a "Chicago: My Home Town" solo show, helped drive a 1950s doo-wop workshop, joined mentor Bob Gibson in a short set, hosted a reunion of Gibson with Hamilton Camp and even served as a reluctant host for the Friday evening concert.

"Uh, I'm supposed to emcee this?" he said with exaggerated disaffection. "Stand up here and tell you all the stuff you already know about people that you paid good money to come and hear? I'm probably not going to be real good at that." The comments were ironic, given Steve's penchant for collaboration with other musicians and promotion of their work, often to the detriment of his own. To the crowd's delight, he retained his humor, humility and raunch. Introducing Breakfast Special, Steve noted that the group was to perform three days hence in New York, "and if you're not there, I guess you'll have to listen to 'em here." Steve also praised overall host Gene Shay, who "knows how to do this emcee shit, and I don't, and if he hadn't been here, I would have fucked up worse than I did."

The 30-year-old Croce, meanwhile, also was conspicuous at the 1973 festival. Though he arrived too late to lead a scheduled early-afternoon workshop titled "There's Certainly No Arguing about Taste," he took part in a later songwriters tune swap led by Patrick Chamberlain and was one of nine artists in the Saturday-evening lineup. Road-weary, Croce at the time was eagerly anticipating free days the following month, so upon learning that Steve was booked Sept. 18-23 at the Castle Creek club in Austin, he planned to show up unannounced and turn the tables on Steve with some good-natured heckling. "It's the least I can do," Croce told autoharpist Heidi Barton. Though a series of shows on five consecutive nights in five states was soon added to Croce's schedule, Sept. 23 remained open, and some say he planned to fly to Austin and surprise Steve on that night.

But it was not to be. Croce's life ended in abrupt violence when at 10:45 p.m. Thursday, Sept. 20, a twin-engine plane carrying him, musical partner Maury Muehleisen and four others hit trees and crashed during a takeoff from Natchitoches, Louisiana, and all aboard perished. Mere hours later, not long after his last Castle Creek set 250 miles west in Austin, Steve learned of Croce's death via the radio in his room at a Holiday Inn. The news hit Steve hard. He wanted to turn to booze, but Austin's liquor laws forbade package sales after 9 p.m., and the bars had closed at midnight.

"He somehow managed to get a cab driver to take him out East Sixth Street and pick up some hooch," says Castle Creek owner Doug Moyes. "When I came back to the club about 10 in the morning, Steve was curled up in front of the door with his head between his legs and was a pretty sorry sight. I didn't

I'm supposed to emcee this? Stand up here and tell you all the stuff you already know about people that you paid good money to come and hear?
STEVE GOODMAN

Idiosyncratic guitarist John Fahey – shown in the mid-1970s at the Queen Elizabeth Theatre in Vancouver, B.C. – was so angered by an assumption he made about Steve at the 1973 Buffalo Folk Festival that 28 years later he expanded it to a bitter screed.
(Photo by Rick McGrath)

know who he was. I came up, and he was fairly looped and just stood up and gave me a big hug and said, 'One of my friends in life died.' So I went out with him, and we had something to eat, and we drank ourselves into oblivion. I joined him just to keep my new friend company. He didn't know anybody in Austin but me, so he was just unloading, lettin' out what he needed to let out."

"Listen," Moyes told Steve, "let me get you on a plane so you can head back. I know you want to be there for the funeral."

"No," Steve replied, "the best thing for me to do is to stay right here. That's what Jim would want, and that's what I do. I'm obligated to stay, and I'm gonna do it."

Worsening the shock of Croce's death was how it was presented on the radio when Steve first heard of it. The deejay, says Steve's manager Al Bunetta, was playing Croce's fall 1972 hit, "Operator (That's Not the Way It Feels)," and dropped between its lyrical phrases his own ridicule: "He's gone! ... That's all, folks! ... He's outahere! ... Bye bye!" The next day, an incredulous Steve telephoned Bunetta and told him, "Holy shit! That's pop radio?" "Stevie was freakin' out," Bunetta says. "He felt so insulted for his buddy." No doubt Steve also momentarily wondered if such insensitive — if not deranged — treatment would greet his own demise.

Eventually, it did. Five days after Steve's would-be teaming with Croce earlier that year in Minneapolis, Steve apparently left a bitter imprint, not upon a deejay but in the warped mind of 34-year-old guitar genius John Fahey. What Fahey took offense at took place after 11 p.m. on Friday, May 11, at the Buffalo Folk Festival, where the final three acts on a lengthy evening bill — blues pianist Roosevelt Sykes, Fahey and Steve, in that order — were still yet to perform. In an acrid account for memoirs published in 2000 just a few months before his own untimely death, Fahey depicted a claustrophobic backstage room in Buffalo in which workers and hangers-on were jammed with weary and irritable festival artists — all except Steve, whom Fahey said had a space elsewhere in which to relax and "feel more important."

Fahey wrote that a staff member walked into the cramped performers' room and approached the 67-year-old Sykes. "Steve Goodman's got an early show tomorrow night back in the City," the staffer said. "He was wondering if you could trade him time slots so he can get out of here earlier." Sykes agreed, and the staff member replied "Great" without offering thanks, and walked away, according to Fahey. "Sykes stays cool. He doesn't seem to care," Fahey wrote. "But I care. And I'm mad."

The root of Fahey's animosity emerged in his narrative when he excoriated Steve as "an aggressively inoffensive, grievously suburban, vividly moderate, tame and 'NICE' entertainer" whose purportedly important and relevant "City of New Orleans" was anything but. "It is an aggressively bland and aggressively consonant song. It is too perfect for my blood. There are no rough edges. It is a smoothie. A song that a person would write exactly the way some stupid book about writing songs said that you should write songs. Inoffensive. Safe."

Fahey mentioned nothing in his account about Steve's leukemia or the possibility that Steve might have been heading to New York for treatment at Sloan-Kettering — factors that were public knowledge and easily discernible in 2000. "Now that he is dead we can talk about him. Har, har, har. I've waited a long time," Fahey viciously wrote. "He thinks he's great. And relevant. And important. Significant. RIP. Har, har, har. RIP." As Fahey fan Matthew Fox stated in a message to an acoustic-guitar e-mail group in 2001, Fahey's Buffalo tale was one of several "paranoiac rants" in an otherwise insightful book by "a profoundly disturbed man." [18]

To most others, Steve was on a roll, unmatched as an in-person entertainer. As a reward, he played a handful of dates with the rhythm section for David Bromberg's band — electric guitarist Steve Burgh, pianist Jeff Gutcheon, Steve Mosley on drums and Hugh McDonald on bass, all of whom had played on Steve's "Troubles" LP. Two days before the Buffalo festival, the opportunity expanded when Steve found himself on the same bill with Bromberg and crew May 9 at the second Nassau Community College Folk Festival on Long Island. There, after playing three songs by himself, he brought out the accompanists for filled-out versions of six more tunes. They included "The Barnyard Dance," during which Mosley played an extended, unaccompanied percussion solo by slapping his cheeks, and, for the encore, a wild version, augmented by Bromberg horn players John Payne and Peter Ecklund, of the James Brown classic, "I Feel Good." [19]

The vibrant Nassau set left the crowd in a "state of ebullient fascination," said *The Vignette*, the college newspaper. Oscar Brand, WNYC-AM's "Folksong Festival" host since 1945, interviewed Steve and recorded the show, and when Brand aired it 11 years later, he called it "one of the most exciting performances I've ever heard and seen by anybody, including Steve." [20]

Gutcheon, the pianist, likened Steve's stage presence to a radiant heat source. "You were defenseless against that kind of innate charm," he says. "I don't know anybody who put out quite as much as Steve. You hear of people saying, 'He gave 110 percent.' Steve was more like 150 or 200. Sometimes he would wail the hell out of his guitar. Sometimes it would come through on his singing. His commitment level at the performance exceeded everything. Sometimes it even exceeded the musical level. But nobody cared. It didn't make any difference because the commitment is what's read."

To Burgh, the success of Steve's full-band approach was no surprise. "When I started playing with Bromberg and then Steve and John Prine, I dedicated myself to get these guys to play with bands rather than be solo artists," he said. "These guys were so much better than the rock singers I'd met. They had so much talent that they should be playing the big world stage, and I felt one way to do it was to have a big sound — not a sound that would get in the way of what they did, just a platform for them to rise from."

Despite a short stature, Steve had the tallest potential, Burgh said. "He was better than everybody else," he said. "He had more charisma. He was funnier.

18: Fahey's book, *How Bluegrass Music Destroyed My Life*, was published by Drag City of Chicago.

19: Steve preceded "I Feel Good" with a wry, unassuming spoken line that he made a standard part of his shtick when introducing a classic that he was going to cover: "Here's a tune I wrote when I was workin' under the name James Brown." When he would cover a different classic, he would use the same line and merely insert the name of its composer.

20: Brand enjoyed Steve's respect for musical roots. In the interview, Brand told Steve that Ira Gershwin — the Pulitzer Prize-winning lyricist who with his brother George had dominated American songwriting in the first half of the 20th century — "didn't think much of the songs of the day." Steve replied, "I'm gonna go out there and sing 'Lady Be Good.' Now, I imagine Ira is still out there somewhere saying that 'City of New Orleans' or (John Prine's) 'Sam Stone' or some of the Beatles things, whatever, that they aren't in the same league with 'It Ain't Necessarily So' and all that stuff that his brother wrote. Well, no accounting for taste, I guess. I like their songs, and if they don't like mine, that's too bad. I figure it's their loss because I sure sing their stuff, and I know where I came from."

His guitar playing was snappy and to the point but primitive at the same time, like a blues guy. He played eloquent, simple stuff, like Muddy Waters. He could get one note going that could blow your mind. He could make the thing speak, and the guitar was singing with him. His voice was simple, raw, compelling, honest, sweet but bittersweet, a little rough, again like a blues man. He was really a people's guy, that salt of the earth. A larger-than-life campfire sing-along guy. Just the way he connected with the audience and the whole thing came together, there was a certain beauty and innocence to him. He was larger than life, but in a beautiful, simple way."

Steve took the same backup group with him to play Chicago (at the Earl) and Washington, D.C., even though the money to support such an endeavor was elusive. "He really couldn't afford a big band, but he wanted one anyhow," said Burgh, who, like the other accompanists, found it impossible to turn Steve down for the tiny tour. "Once you met this guy, you loved this guy, and it was a wonderful honor to be asked. I could never say no to him." [21]

The pace picked up during the same month as the Nassau show. First, Steve and the Burgh/Gutcheon/Mosley/McDonald group helped Brooklyn folksinger Doris Abrahams make demo recordings of four songs, including two, Dolly Parton's "As Long as I Love" and Jonathan Sabin's "I Can't Control Myself," on which Steve sang harmony.

Then, on May 13, Steve reached the trendy overnight audience of New York City's WNEW-FM as the guest of Alison Steele, known as "The Nightbird." In Steele's low, purring voice, Steve couldn't have asked for a more alluring advocate. In just half an hour, she played six songs from his first two albums, lauded his "Troubles" LP as "beautiful" and "lovely" and explored complex, music-related topics with Steve — while interspersing three jarring commercials for the Army Reserve (slogan: "It pays to go to meetings"), two of which she voiced herself.

Steele zeroed in on Bob Dylan's piano and vocals in the song "Somebody Else's Troubles" and intimated that Buddah had erred in not releasing it, instead of "The Dutchman," as the album's first single. Her on-air critique became prescient two months later, when Buddah issued "Somebody Else's Troubles" as the "Troubles" LP's second single.

Steve even chose "Troubles" as one of two songs to sing (as well as "Would You Like to Learn to Dance?") on the 25th installment of the year's groundbreaking, late-night NBC-TV pop-music show, "The Midnight Special." Aired following "The Tonight Show" at 1 a.m. Saturday, July 21, the 90-minute program featured Black Oak Arkansas and Bloodstone before Steve, who was followed by Mimi Fariña, Wilson Pickett and the Pointer Sisters. Host Joan Baez, Fariña's sister, gave Steve an extra boost, plugging him as "a little guy I met in Nashville. He's short on height but long on talent, and he makes very beautiful music. He wrote 'City of New Orleans,' which Arlo Guthrie made into a hit. He's here on the show tonight at my request." Wearing a short-sleeve blue shirt, jeans and boots, Steve — often shown in close-up portraits and framed

---

The way he connected with the audience and the whole thing came together, there was a certain beauty and innocence to him. He was larger than life, but in a beautiful, simple way.
STEVE BURGH

21: At the Earl of Old Town, the band's affection for Steve was clear during a performance of the Johnny Mercer/Matty Malneck standard, "Goody Goody." In the call-response verses, instead of voicing the words of the title, the band sang, "Goody Goodman."

by a kaleidoscope of still images of himself — performed to a large audience that sat on benches and the floor and gave him resounding applause.

Other than that solitary, high-profile TV exposure, the "Somebody Else's Troubles" single had little fanfare and never cracked the *Billboard* Hot 100 chart. Buddah's bubblegum image and marketing formula were limited in serving Steve's recordings, says Steve Begor, promo man for the label from 1972 to 1975 in Atlanta. "Buddah was top-40-oriented, and Steve's singles were not top-40 songs," he says. "Steve got FM play, but not a lot. It was all about radio. We didn't know a lot about alternative ways of breaking records." So the "Troubles" troubles became yet another instance in which sales failed to correspond with raves Steve was receiving at his shows.

The brisk schedule of Steve's concert and club dates was attributable to the dogged work of Al Bunetta, who had taken over the hands-on duties of managing both Steve and Prine, which included connecting them and their road accompanists with the era's pleasures of the road. "Those two guys were his babies, and Al was not like a mother hen, but like a big brother," says percussionist Steve Mosley. "Al was an amazing party animal," added guitarist Steve Burgh. "He's funny, he's charming, he's got eyes that light up, and he's a wise guy. ... He's Italian, with that certain connectivity." [22]

In contrast, Paul Anka, Steve's manager in name (like a "gentleman farmer," says Steve's friend Paula Ballan), was busy with a "new career," as feted in a *Billboard* article that said Anka was producing, directing and developing talent for Caesar's Palace in Las Vegas as well as composing, recording and performing. Bunetta's workload with Steve and Prine had grown to such a degree that in 1973 he took on a full-time assistant, Tom King, to execute the details of shows and tours that Bunetta negotiated. From the outset, King saw that the performing careers of Steve and Prine drew their vitality from his aggressive boss. "An artist's best asset was an Al Bunetta who could fight tooth and nail and represent the artist in the best possible way," King says, "and Al was absolutely a fighter."

Bunetta realized this and even trumpeted it. Recalls guitarist Herbert Scarpelli (stage name Mick Scott), who accompanied Jimmy Buffett, Dion DiMucci and others while bouncing between Miami and Chicago during 1973, Bunetta offered a blunt self-introduction: "Hi, I'm Al Bunetta. I'm an asshole. I'm paid to be an asshole." An unheralded musician known for writing "The Last One of the Night People," Scarpelli caught Bunetta's drift. "Someone's got to go out there and do war," Scarpelli says. "I knew that was exactly what he was talking about." So did Steve, who told a fellow musician, "Look, if Al's an asshole, I want him on my side to fight all the other assholes because Al's a bigger asshole and scumbag than the other guys." [23]

Anka recognized Bunetta's key role by forming a new and separate company, Anka/Bunetta Management. "I knew I was busy and doing my thing," Anka says, "and that's why Bunetta was brought in to make sure that there was some continuity and to take care of them."

Joan Baez, shown in 1974, hosted NBC-TV's "Midnight Special" at 1 a.m. July 21, 1973, saying Steve was a guest on the show at her request.

(Photo by Richard McCaffrey)

22: The definition of Bunetta was "C'mere, y'talkin'? C'mere, c'mere, I wanta talk t'ya. C'mere, c'mere, c'mere, c'mere, c'mere," says Steve's road manager in 1976-77, Steve Cohen. "Goodman loved to do him. He did Bunetta better than anybody did Bunetta."

23: Speaking about Steve, Bunetta readily returns the "compliment," indicating that the word "asshole" was a term of endearment: "I don't want to sainthood this guy, but a stand-up guy. What an asshole, too. I mean, we had so many battles together, but he was my asshole. Y'know, he was my buddy. We could argue better than anybody. We used to argue, slam phones. 'I quit!' 'I quit, too!' 'OK!'"

King credits Anka with giving him and Bunetta free use of a room, desk, phone and file cabinet in Anka's swanky Upper East Side townhouse, which Anka seldom was in town to use — no small contribution, given the high price of business overhead in Manhattan. But in the day-to-day handling of the careers of Steve and Prine, King says, "Al was 99 percent the guy."

Though they shared a songwriting talent, the musical sensibilities and audiences of Anka had little in common with those of Steve and Prine. "It wasn't just another generation," says Paula Ballan. "It was another universe of entertainment."

Anka did endeavor to bridge the universes. In an ad in *Cash Box*, Anka sent a united message to the industry, linking his second Buddah LP, "Jubilation" — showing a tuxedoed Anka in orgiastic grin while playing a double keyboard — with the scruffier images of Steve's "Troubles" album and Prine's "Diamonds in the Rough." To underscore the ad's trio theme, its bold headline, next to a drawing of a white dove bearing an olive branch in its beak, invoked a trendy, three-concept slogan: "Love, joy and peace." The underlying relationship, though, amounted to just the opposite.

This tension surfaced in Anka's occasional referrals of material to record. "Anka would give Steve the most god-awful songs," says Steve's brother-in-law, Robert Pruter, "and Steve was tearing himself up (about it)." Once, Pruter says, Anka forwarded to Steve a tune he had written with the theme of "Please don't be prejudiced against me because of my long hair." Steve rejected the song, telling Pruter, "I'm supposed to be indebted to him, but he wants me to record this awful piece of shit?" Pruter says Steve's resistance to Anka "showed a lot of character, that he could stand up to that." [24]

During shows in early 1973, Steve regarded Anka with cautious praise. "Offstage, he's pretty straight," he said Jan. 5 at Amazingrace in Evanston. "He's the only reason I'm making records. Kristofferson liked it and all that, but Anka's the guy that got me the contract, so I ain't gonna stand here and put him down." Three weeks later, at New Trier West High School north of Chicago, Steve injected slang to describe Anka: "He is a little kinky. That rock 'n' roll stuff from the 1950s and that Vegas thing is a little swift. But he's really a beautiful cat

24: Anka says he may have given to Steve songs that he had written, but he doesn't recall one about prejudice over long hair.

offstage, and I like him a lot." However, after another six months, any remaining blooms had fallen from the rose. Given the chance to comment on Anka in a Sept. 27 *Rolling Stone* profile, Steve labeled him as "a gentleman and a wonderful host when he feels like it."

More troubling than Anka to Steve (and Bunetta and King) as 1973 proceeded was the sinking feeling that Buddah was giving up on the tiny troubadour. Steve had alluded to this in his interview with WNEW's Alison Steele.

"Are you happy with what you're doing?" she asked him. "Do you like the music business as a business?"

Steve paused a moment.

"Uh, I'm not so sure, to tell you the truth, how much I like the music business," he said. "But I like to play and sing so much that I think you have to learn how to do all kinds of things if you want to play and sing in different places."

His vague allusion to "all kinds of things" no doubt included stomaching the vagaries and failures of record promotion. Even Dylan's role in the "Troubles" track, while mentioned in press releases and talked up by Buddah with deejays, carried little weight. "Just having Dylan playing backup, who cares?" says Larry Harris, Buddah's national director of album promotion. "We just used that because it was a wedge. We needed something. We'd grab at straws that people would use to pay attention to a record because, obviously, there are so many of them. The other problem was, he was a short, pudgy little guy, so there was no sex appeal there."

There was no lack of affection for Steve within Buddah, Harris says. "I saw him perform numerous times, and he blew me away every time," he says. "Everybody in the company loved him. Everybody in the company thought he was a great artist. There was nobody in the company who said, 'Oh, this guy, forget about it.' Everybody really wanted to see it happen for him. We tried and tried."

One gambit was a TV news segment filmed aboard an Illinois Central train leaving Chicago at 8 a.m. one snowy morning in early 1973. Though the City of New Orleans name had been eliminated since November 1971, NBC wanted Steve to sing his most famous song as a backdrop for a segment on the decline of passenger service. Steve and his traveling companion for the day, Earl Pionke, almost didn't make the trip, however. Pionke, hailing a cab after his car had broken down, picked Steve up late, and the two hustled to the departing railcar a few minutes after 8. "We actually ran for a moving train," Steve later told a concert audience. "I'd seen that in the movies but never gotten to do it. Now I know why they hire stunt men. It's interesting when you've got one leg up, and it's starting to accelerate, and you're tryin' to grab the guitar. I felt like Audrey Hepburn." Out of breath when they reached the train car containing the NBC crew, they were greeted by a reporter's cry of "Son of a bitch!" Steve said, "I thought it was a hell of a way to say good morning."

The train chase symbolized Steve's pursuit of respect from Buddah. From a musician's perspective, Mosley, the "Troubles" drummer, saw the Steve/Buddah

> **He was a short, pudgy little guy, so there was no sex appeal there.**
> **LARRY HARRIS**

Steve grins onstage at the 1973 Philadelphia Folk Festival. Jude Lyons says of Steve's stint with Buddah, "We made a lot more money from his publishing than from his records."

(Photo by Barry Sagotsky)

25: Johnny Cash also sang "City of New Orleans" while hosting the CBS-TV broadcast of the Country Music Association awards on Oct. 15, 1973. It was "the thrill of my life," Steve said. "I almost forgave him (Cash) for all those goddamn Standard Oil ads." Cash also sang "City" on TV's syndicated "Hee Haw" on April 16, 1974.

26: Strangely, the publication presented Arlo Guthrie's lyric and chord changes to "City of New Orleans" as Steve's own. In 1976, the booklet was merged with a similar songbook for Glen Campbell, bound back to back with a plastic coil spine. When the color cover of one songbook was face up, the other color cover was flipped upside down, so that both songbooks ended in the book's middle. Both the original version and the Goodman/Campbell dual version are long out of print.

picture with bitterness. "He had all kinds of problems with that label," Mosley says. "They wanted a big hit, and I don't think he provided it. He provided a lot of great tunes, but I don't think they handled him properly. If you don't have a big hit for these record companies, you're nobody to them. Suddenly, you're a tax write-off, and they will play it out and ignore you. They won't make sure that your stuff is distributed properly. They won't give any more than a few print ads. There were a lot of ways to promote back in those days, radio spots and the like. But for somebody in that type of music, essentially folk music, if you're not making huge profits, they will treat you like dirt. The people that sign you suddenly can't be bothered to see you. They're just bloodsuckers."

Part of Steve's lifeblood held by Buddah was the financial royalty from his songwriting, called "the publishing," which kept cash rolling into the Buddah coffers from recordings of Steve's songs, including Guthrie's hit with "City of New Orleans," regardless of whether Steve's own albums sold. This became a huge consideration when others — from Jewel Fay "Sammi" Smith and Lynn Anderson to Johnny Cash and the Country Gentlemen, a total of 25 artists — hopped on the "City of New Orleans" bandwagon and put versions of their own on albums issued in 1973-74. [25] Buddah further recognized the commodity of Steve's songs by publishing, via New York-based Cimino Publications Inc., *The Steve Goodman Song Book*, in 1973. The large-format, 80-page paperback contained lead sheets for the 15 Steve-written songs on his first two albums, as well as seven pages of black-and-white photos and a 16-by-19-inch foldout poster of the "Troubles" LP cover. [26]

"Stevie's publishing doubled his value to Buddah," says Jude Lyons, who worked in Buddah's production and ad departments. "We made a lot more money from his publishing than from his records." This, combined with bleak record sales, produced in Steve a growing sense of entrapment.

Like a tightening wrench, the anxiety crystallized in revealing offstage moments, one of which went public in an April 29 article in the *Chicago Tribune*. Stationing himself inside the Earl of Old Town to profile Earl Pionke, reporter Les Bridges witnessed a "roaring, name-calling argument" between Pionke and Steve, who, irked by his low record sales, "had been moping around the place for a week" and spending $10 a night on pinball at Pionke's Sneak Joynt out back.

"You blankety-blank," Goodman was quoted as shouting at Pionke, "I'm not happy with my new album. And I'm overexposed here in Chicago."

"Listen, you S.O.B.," Earl snarled in return, "it happens to be a good album, but that doesn't make any difference. An album is nothing. If you never cut another album, you could stay up there for years because you know hundreds of songs. You're an entertainer."

Pionke, noted the *Tribune* story, proved his point later that evening after Bonnie Koloc's second set earned two encores and "ecstatic" applause. "Listen, you bleep," Pionke told Steve. "It's too bad you don't want to work anymore — especially in Chicago where you're overexposed — 'cause I got an audience out there tonight that won't quit." Five minutes later, Steve was onstage singing a Hank Williams tune, backed by Koloc's band.

Two months later and 2,000 miles west, during a June 26-July 1 stint at the Boarding House club in San Francisco, Steve unmasked his ire before an old friend. Mal Klugman, a Sammy brother in 1965 at the University of Illinois, had moved to the Bay Area and, seeing an ad for Steve in the newspaper, brought his girlfriend to see the show. Afterward, Steve let the pair come backstage. The unsmiling Steve asked Klugman — who in his U of I days was known for his extensive record collection and musical knowledge — what work he was doing. Klugman replied that he was a salesman at KSFX-FM, the top-40 San Francisco ABC affiliate and sister station of the legendary talk-format KGO-AM.

In a peeved tone, Steve burst out with: "Well, if you liked the show, why don't you see if you can get my records played on your station?"

Klugman was taken aback. "I'm not involved in programming, Steve," he replied haltingly. "I sell time, I sell commercials. That's what I do. I don't control what programming does."

But Steve persisted, and the chat ended quickly and sourly. Klugman's girlfriend told him she was stunned, and Klugman just shook his head sadly. "Steve and I had never had any falling out or disagreement or anything of the kind," he said. "I was surprised and disillusioned by the whole thing."

If such turmoil churned inside Steve, he didn't reveal it to audiences. He said later that his road schedule, fueled in large part by Arlo Guthrie's "City of New Orleans" hit, was satisfying in itself. "I was just out there doin' it as if I had made a third album," he told Al Rudis of the *Chicago Sun-Times* two years later.

The "doin' it" included a refreshing return to the site of his walk-on triumph in England the previous summer. This time at the Cambridge Folk Festival, Steve was formally booked, as was John Prine, and the two enjoyed a hero's welcome. The BBC's pop-music TV program, "The Old Grey Whistle Test," invited Steve for a reprise, and the performers and listeners witnessing his stage show for the first time were galvanized. "He was so far ahead of anything we'd seen, in terms of his musical ability, his sheer energy and his passion," says British singer/songwriter Harvey Andrews, author of "Soldier," an underground hit of the day about the Northern Ireland civil war. "You only had to see him work once, and you were just knocked out."

Even the festival poster, featuring what artist John Holder terms "a wacky little trail of stuff," joined in the warm reception for Steve and Prine. Holder sketched into the design a trio of naked, rollerskating women holding a "Prine/Goodman Fan Club" banner. "It was three girls with enormous breasts," Steve said later, "and I had a hell of a time explaining this poster when I got it home."

Back in the States, any anguish churning within Steve over Buddah's neglect lay enmeshed in the gallows humor and sarcasm that were typical of his stage patter, lending his jokes a stronger bite. The topic of the day — the Watergate scandal — offered ample fuel for bitterness and cynicism, and Steve exploited it whenever he had the opportunity. [27]

This portion of John Holder's 1973 Cambridge Folk Festival poster gave Steve pause: "I had a hell of a time explaining this poster when I got it home."
(Detail courtesy of John Holder)

27: Steve's Watergate fascination was clear to Jack Watters, Old Town School of Folk Music teacher and later board member. Hanging out at the school in 1973, Watters told Steve he'd heard that U.S. Rep. William Hungate, a Missouri Democrat, had written a satirical, two-minute waltz, "Down at the Old Watergate," and put it on a telephone recording. Steve bolted to a phone and dialed the number. "He insisted on calling back a couple times so he could write down the words," Watters says. There is no evidence that Steve ever performed the tune, but Hungate released it in 1973 as a single on Perception Records.

One chance came days after the televised Watergate hearings began, at the third annual *SingOut!* magazine benefit on May 28 at the Quiet Knight in Chicago. "This hasn't been a good year for crooks," Steve said. "They're gettin' 'em."

"Not yet," a man in the audience shot back.

"Oh, y'know," Steve replied, "you can lead an elephant to Watergate, but you can't make him remember anything."

Visiting Chicago over the summer, Scottish storyteller Johnniy Morris found it a challenge to digest the voluminous news reports about the Watergate break-in and if or how it could be traced to then-President Nixon.

"What's it all about?" Morris finally asked Steve.

"Hell," Steve said, "it's just thieves interrogatin' thieves."

Playing Charlotte's Web in Rockford northwest of Chicago on the weekend of Sept. 28-30, Steve told another Nixon joke, this time tying it to a 1972 porno film that had become a household word:

"Did you hear about Dick Nixon? He saw 'Deep Throat' three times and still couldn't get it down Pat!"

The next month at Northern Illinois University in DeKalb, one week after Nixon nominated Gerald Ford to replace the resigned Spiro Agnew as vice president, and on the very evening that Nixon's firing of Special Prosecutor Archibald Cox triggered what became known as Watergate's "Saturday Night Massacre," Steve shared a blunt assessment.

"I don't think they should have let Nixon pick the new vice president," Steve said. "He screwed up everything he picked. Let somebody else take a shot at pickin' something, just for the heck of it." [28]

Later in the show, Steve kept the tone light, however, while strapping onto his instrument a capo — a small clamp that changes the pitch of the strings. Steve supplied an outrageous description of its function:

"Cuts the nuts off of the guitar and raises its voice."

Steve couldn't resist sustaining a high pitch of irreverence throughout his Oct. 1-6 stint as the headliner at a 145-seat south Florida bar and restaurant called Bubba's. Performing two sets a night at the Coconut Grove club, and remembering the warmth of his gigs two and three years prior at the Flick just two miles away, Steve spent nearly as much stage time as a storyteller and comic as he did performing songs, his and others'.

His sweeping repertoire seemed to expand by the minute, as he carved a swath from serious love songs (Richard Rodgers & Lorenz Hart's "My Funny Valentine" and a Hank Snow hit, Bill Trader's "A Fool Such as I") to oldie hits ("Dorsey Burnette's "It's Late," popularized by Ricky Nelson, and Dion DiMucci's "Drip Drop" and "Runaround Sue," with DiMucci in the audience) to the blues (Willie Dixon's "Playhouse Blues," the Holy Modal Rounders' off-the-wall "Blues in a Bottle" and Robert Johnson's "Sweet Home Chicago"). But relentlessly leavening the proceedings was his levity. In "Sweet Home Chicago," after the line "If the river was whiskey, and I was a duck," [29] Steve squawked like

---

Did you hear about Dick Nixon? He saw 'Deep Throat' three times and still couldn't get it down Pat!
STEVE GOODMAN

28: More seriously, Steve told journalist Steve Weitzman in December 1973, "The whole sad part about all these elections, man, is that you can't find anybody who voted for Nixon now. They've disappeared — 60.8 percent of the popular vote disappeared."

29: Steve also used the whiskey/duck line in a song he wrote and performed starting in 1974 called "East St. Louis Tweedle-Dee" (also known as "The Consumption Blues"), a tune notable mainly for its naming of cities bordering the Mississippi River. However, in at least one instance, his fourth wedding anniversary on Feb. 6, 1974, when he was called to the stage of Chicago's Quiet Knight by Tom Rush, Steve deviated geographically by substituting "Kansas City" for "East St. Lou-ee."

a drunken Donald Duck. Singing Randy Sparks' sarcastic "Saturday Night in Toledo, Ohio," he adopted an Elmer Fudd affectation, "So wiv and wet wiv, wet this be our motto." And he had a tough time maintaining the slow-building anguish of Roy Orbison's "Crying" with a straight face. "It's a bitch," he said, "to laugh through this whole goddamn song."

Likewise, one-liners and other jokes permeated his Bubba's sets, among the loosest of his career. [30] Bumping his head on the mike stand, he said, "I'd like to thank my choreographer, Mr. Jim Beam." Vamping later, he said, "This dance here is a multiple choice. Everybody dance with the person on his left."

Steve also reveled in oft-repeated anecdotes about Ross Cascio, his Muskie train trip and his first trip to England, as well as silly and crude story-jokes that often ran longer than his songs.

One he told because he knew he would be singing "Chattanooga Choo Choo" as a train-themed prelude to "City of New Orleans." In the tale, a mountain lion sneaked into cowboy singer Roy Rogers' house and used its fierce jaws and teeth to rip up his just-bought, shiny, beaded boots. His wife Dale Evans, his horse Trigger and his dog Bullet jumped into Nelly Belle, the Jeep, and drove off to find the beast. After shooting the lion, they hauled it back to display it for Rogers, singing the musical pun, "Pardon me, Roy, is this the cat that chewed the new shoes?"

Undeterred by the audience's groans, Steve replied, "Get the hook! Oh, Christ!" then told another yarn in which NBC-TV newsman Garrick Utley asked a Canadian game hunter by the rhyming name of Jacques Lecoq to describe his unique method to track moose. Lecoq's reply let Steve fashion an exaggerated French accent and periodically emit a high howl:

"In the winter, I take ze gun with the dum-dum bullets and the camping equipment, and I get into the Jeep, and I go up into the farthest reaches of the Yukon, and I wait. And in the spring, I take the gun with the dum-dum bullets, and I go into the bush, and I wait, and I give my now-famous moose holl-air. Ah-ooo! Ah-ooo! The mating call of ze female moose to the male moose in the spring, and I am calling to him. I am his lover, and I am calling to him. Ah-ooo! Ah-ooo!

"And I wait in the bush, always I am waiting with the gun with the dum-dum bullets. Ah-ooo! And soon, I see him. He is two miles away. Through the glasses, I can see him. He is a big one. Ah-ooo! Ah-ooo! I am calling to him, the mating call of the female moose, my famous moose holl-air. Ah-ooo! He hears me, and he is coming. Ah-ooo!

"One mile away! Ah-ooo! Ah-ooo! A half a mile away, and he is charging. I am waiting with the gun with the dum-dum bullets. Ah-ooo!

"Five hundred yards. Ah-ooo! Ah-ooo! Ah-ooo! He is coming now. Ah-ooo!

"One hundred yards and charging. Ah-ooo! He is a BIG ONE. Ah-ooo!

"He is on top of me, and I shoot the gun!"

"What happens," Utley asked, "if the gun doesn't go off?"

"Zen," said Lecoq, "for the 54th time, I get ze shit fucked out of me."

> He is coming now. Ah-ooo!
> One hundred yards and
> charging. Ah-ooo!
> He is a BIG ONE. Ah-ooo!
> He is on top of me, and I
> shoot the gun!
> **STEVE GOODMAN**

30: One of Steve's all-time favorite jokes, "blue or otherwise," was a yarn spun by folksinger Utah Phillips about his work for the Santa Fe railway in the remote Nevada desert. The job of cook was given to the crew member who complained most about the food, and that was Phillips. Angry at the assignment, he found a giant moose turd, baked it into a pie shell and served it as dessert. One of the burliest ranchers, upon biting into it, yelped, "My God, that's moose turd pie!" But he added quickly, "Good, though." The punch line slayed Steve, who said, "It's that kind of dry humor that goes right through me." The joke appeared on a 1973 Phillips LP whose title was the punch line.

The tale drew scattered and embarrassed laughter. "You had to be there," Steve said, continuing with another lewd pun. "It was one of the great 'You had to be there in the bush' jokes."

Populating another hunting tale were two staid English gentlemen: Lord Pembroke, who had hung the stuffed head of a lion above his fireplace, and Willoughby, who asked his friend how he bagged the beast.

"It was very simple, actually," Pembroke replied. "It was 30 years ago tonight. My party and I were camped on the banks of the Zambezi, and in the morning, I woke up and got out of my mosquito netting, pulled down my trousers and nothing else, and tucked my .22 under my arm and went down to the banks of the Zambezi to bathe, take my morning bath. I was standing there knee-deep in the waters of the Zambezi with the .22 under my arm and lathered up. I had the .22 there to shoot the snakes that infest the shores of the Zambezi and like to tickle one's feet while one bathes in the morning. When all of a sudden through the bushes there appeared the head of an enormous lion, the most enormous lion I have ever seen, the lion's head you see now above the fireplace."

"No!" Willoughby said.

"Why, yes," Pembroke said. "In fact, in shock, I dropped the .22 into the Zambezi. When I picked it up and fired it at the raging, roaring lion, the charges were wet, and the gun would not go off. The lion went, 'ROOAARR!' I shat my pants!"

"Understandable, with a wet .22 and a charging, roaring lion."

"Not then, you fool. Just now, when I went, 'ROOAARR!' "

Steve's jokes at Bubba's often took musical form, such as when he sang an abortive parody of the Kris Kristofferson hit "Lovin' Her Was Easier" that Steve said Bob Dylan had taught him:

> *When I was a short-order cook*
> *she gave me a blow job while I was fryin'*
> *Lovin' her was greasier than ...*

A lengthy lead-in to a pun constituted another tune with a solitary verse:

> *I was swimmin' in the river on the island of Salaud* [31]
> *I lost my upper plate, I don't know why*
> *Won't you drop me a line if you happen to find*
> *My bridge on the River Kwai*

For college students in the crowd, Steve dropped in a couple of verses from his Chicago friend Larry Rand's "Survey of World Literature Blues":

> *Don't want a Willa Cather, no Edna St. Vincent Millay*
> *Don't want no Willa Cather, no Edna St. Vincent Millay*
> *Give me some Henry Miller, whoo-hoo*
> *And a little Hemingway*

31: "Salaud" is a guess at the spelling, based solely on Steve's pronunciation (suh-LODD). A geographical search for such an island near the Kwai in Thailand turns up empty. Steve may have made up the island's name.

I saw e.e. cummings, and I saw Ezra Pound
I saw e.e. cummings, and I saw old Ezra Pound
Let me be your Boswell, baby
Till your Dr. Johnson comes around [32]

The topper was a song that Steve and Prine had started to write as a follow-up to "You Never Even Call Me by My Name," focusing on trucks. "We didn't want to do it," Steve said, "because it'd just be another truckin' song. There's about 100 of 'em. We only got a chorus to that one." Promising to add verses later in the month, he sang the chorus, titling it facetiously, "If I Were You, I Would Have Punched Me":

It's just another truckin' song, it don't mean much to me
It's twice as young as yesterday and half as old as me
And if heartaches was commercials, we'd all be on TV
But it'd still be just another fuckin' truckin' song to me [33]

The Bubba's sets weren't all frivolity. Steve sheepishly described the trade-off of being the father of a toddler who possesses "a real attitude about everything" but "knows damn well that she doesn't have to behave when I'm around." He implored his Florida audience to embrace the impending demise of Babe Ruth's lifetime home-run title at the hands of Henry "Hammerin' Hank" Aaron of the neighboring Atlanta Braves. "He's gonna make mincemeat out of that legend," he said. "Ah, that's great, man. All the idols have feet of clay, right?" He added that the makers of Oh Henry! candy bars would start using a photo of the African-American slugger in their ads "if they've got any brains."

Steve paid equally fond tribute to two entertainers who, unbeknown to him, later would become his two most prominent professional lifesavers. He noted that when he had played two weeks earlier at Castle Creek in Austin, Willie Nelson, already a country songwriting legend, was "hard to avoid" in his hometown. Nelson appeared every night in TV commercials, inviting viewers of the local news to "follow the searchlights" to discover the new 1974 model cars at McMorris Ford. "In Texas," Steve said, "Willie Nelson isn't just like a country singer. He's sort of like soybeans. He's a commodity. He's all over the place."

Similarly, the comedian booked as the Bubba's headliner the following week drew Steve's unequivocal praise. Steve Martin, he said, "is just as sharp as they get. I don't usually stand up here and sound like a goddamn commercial, but Martin is a bitch. He's really funny. There's not that many guys you can look at 'em and say, 'That guy is really funny.' I get in free wherever I want, and I would pay to see Steve Martin work. That's the best I can say for him."

Yet another performer already had elicited in Steve such deep respect while passing through Chicago that when he stopped in at Bubba's to see Steve perform, Steve invited him to share the stage. The guest was a friend on whose first nationally distributed album Steve had played acoustic guitar at Glaser Sound in Nashville the previous spring — Jimmy Buffett. Released by ABC/Dunhill

> **I get in free wherever I want, and I would pay to see Steve Martin work. That's the best I can say for him.**
> **STEVE GOODMAN**

32: Lyrics to "Survey of World Literature Blues" ©1971 by Larry Rand, Junior Dog Music. Reprinted by permission.

33: Steve apparently never completed the composition, but Prine later inserted the line "If heartaches were commercials, we'd all be on TV" in his song "Come Back to Us Barbara Lewis Hare Krishna Beauregard" on his 1975 LP, "Common Sense."

Jimmy Buffett, shown in 1972, traded risqué puns with Steve in October 1973 at Bubba's in Coconut Grove as if the pair were "Burns & Allen 1905."
(Photo by P. Michael O'Sullivan)

in June, the LP, "A White Coat and a Pink Crustacean" (a play on the 1957 Marty Robbins hit of the same name, substituting "Crustacean" for "Carnation"), launched the laid-back beach-party image that would become Buffett's trademark. Invoking a drug joke that would identify his backup band for decades to come, Buffett already had claimed Steve as one of his honorary "coral reefers."

The half-hour Goodman/Buffett set at Bubba's was telling on several levels. On the surface, what the Coconut Grove audience saw was a pair of musicians whose loose rapport made them easy to be mistaken as brothers. Unlike the more stage-shy John Prine, Buffett matched Steve's comfortable banter line for line, and the result was, as Steve coined it, a routine akin to "Burns & Allen 1905." [34]

"Let me welcome my friend Zeke, good old Zeke-sty Nine," Steve said, embarking on a juvenile, pun-filled exchange. He bared mock horror as Buffett tuned his instrument: "You let someone draw naked women on your guitar!"

"It's a Clairol bottle, Herbal Essence," Buffett replied. "That's what it looks like, doesn't it?"

"Is that her name?" Steve said. "I went out with a girl named Herbal Essence once."

"That's Connie Lingus."

"That's Connie Lingus, huh?" Steve said. "She looks a lot like Fonda Peters. Remember her?"

"I knew her brother, Eileetcha."

"Yeah," Steve said, "and her girlfriend Edith Raw. Remember Edith? I mean, we can do these names all night."

"There's a real one," Buffett said. "When I worked in a shipyard in Mobile, there was a guy, a painter, named Willett Raynor Snow."

Recalling poorer days two years earlier in Chicago when he introduced Steve to thrift-store shopping, Buffett switched the topic to apparel.

"That shirt looks awfully familiar," he told Steve. "When I was up there, I bought those shirts. They're just khaki Navy shirts. Buy them in the Salvation Army for about a quarter apiece, so I gave him about four of 'em, and that's all I see him in."

"But you'll get to buy your own next week," Steve jabbed.

"Take you down there and get a bargain," Buffett added.

The two got around to playing music as well, splitting half a dozen songs. With Steve supplying backing vocals and guitar solos and fills, Buffett chose the conventional promotional route, singing three self-written tunes from his recent LP — the Caribbean-flavored "Cuban Crime of Passion" and a pair of quiet pieces, the serene "I Have Found Me a Home" and a poignant tribute, "Death of an Unpopular Poet" — as well as a Hank Williams standard, "You Win Again." Perhaps sensing that Buffett couldn't return the favor with equally facile accompaniment, Steve took the opposite approach, opting for standards that Buffett could field and clowning all the way.

First, Steve launched a fleeting attempt at "Side by Side," deciding at the second line, "Maybe we're ragged and funny," to halt the song. "What the hell," he told the club crowd. "You paid your money. You get to hear us fuck around." Recalling a traditional Italian song he'd learned as a high-schooler from saloon guitarist Marv Berkman at Riccardo's restaurant in Chicago, Steve turned to the familiar, bouncy Italian ditty "Hey Compare" ("Hey, Friend"). In it, the singer asks and answers how to play a lengthening list of musical instruments. Steve summoned three: the mandolin ("plink-o, plink-o"), trombone ("boom-pa, boom-pa") and saxophone ("toot-tu, toot-tu"), revving himself up to such a pitch that Buffett intervened as mock emcee to intone, "Little Stevie Goodman from Chicago, Illinois. Let's hear it for him, friends. C'mon, let's hear it for him. He came all the way here for this contest. He's contestant number one." Finally, when Steve sought a closing number, Bubba's regular Dave Cohen suggested the Roy Rogers/Sons of the Pioneers epic, "Ghost Riders in the Sky." Steve obliged, sinking his voice to a mostly reverent basso profundo.

From goofy to serious to goofy again, the set was suffused with undercurrents. It marked, as well as any moment in time can, the professional intersection of two artists — a relative beginner whose star was on the rise and for whom performing was a means to a commercial end, and one whose mid-level career had started to stagnate and for whom performing itself appeared to be its own reward. Much the same as he had dealt with Prine, Steve placed himself in a subservient role because of his regard for Buffett, ironically within a show that Steve himself was headlining. At work was a commendable generosity, a shedding of otherwise typical intensity and competitiveness, a deference to a fellow performer whom he admired. It made for a diverting and memorable evening for those present, but perhaps imperceptibly at the time, it also symbolized a difference in priorities that would propel only one of the two artists to status as a superstar.

When the week ended, Steve joined Buffett and Steve Martin as guests for a stroganoff dinner at the home of Miami musician George Blackwell and his wife, Jenny. In more private moments with Blackwell, a science enthusiast, Steve opened up about a topic that had loomed unspoken.

"At some point, they have to take me off drugs," Steve told Blackwell, explaining that his Sloan-Kettering oncologists could never be sure if his leukemia were beaten back — into remission — unless his chemotherapy were halted. For someone who had been kept alive by such constant, experimental treatment, the prospect was disquieting. "I have to stop drugs completely," Steve said, "but I'm not sure I have that kind of courage." [35]

Steve did, however, find himself conjuring up professional bravado that fall and winter, moving with Prine to break formal ties with Paul Anka by naming Al Bunetta as their sole manager. The move was hardly simple. Steve told Al Rudis of the *Chicago Sun-Times* in 1975 that Anka, who had left Buddah for United Artists, was disenchanted because "neither of us burned up the charts with our records" and felt Bunetta was mismanaging the duo. Bunetta, mean-

I have to stop drugs completely, but I'm not sure I have that kind of courage.
STEVE GOODMAN

35: Earlier in 1973, Steve used the subject of "City of New Orleans" as a metaphor in telling singer/ songwriter Bill Quateman about his leukemia. The two spoke over breakfast in a diner near Bryn Mawr, Pennsylvania, after Steve had just undergone chemotherapy in New York. "His attitude was that it was this train on its way somewhere. Sometimes it had to pull up some awful steep hills, but the train was on its way. It was this freight train, and he was pulling it. Some of the stops were shows and studios and family, and some of the stops were hospitals."

while, says he couldn't get Anka to sign papers that would pay him for his work.

One day, Anka abruptly fired Bunetta and Tom King, and legal swords were drawn. As Bunetta puts it, "Paul sued me, I sued him, and the guys (Steve and Prine) paid the legal fees. I didn't have $5 to rub together." Attorneys argued for months, "but none of it mattered," Bunetta says. "It went to arbitration, and we won, and at the same time, it kind of made me. It gave me position in the business. Hell, Anka sues you for $1 million, you're like on top of the heap in a terrible business, y'know?"

Anka says the parting reflected a lack of loyalty and says Bunetta "kind of stabbed me in the back and started his own thing and left — which was OK, but I set that whole thing up. I put Al Bunetta in business. ... There's always somebody in there looking to take advantage and form their own little thing, and that's what happened with Bunetta and them (Steve and Prine). He got their ear. He didn't want to work for me. He felt he wasn't making it as an agent, so he just formed his own little company, and away they went. But it was no skin off my nose. ... It was just another eye-opener as to the people in this industry and what they're about."

For Prine, who had just finished (with Steve's considerable help on vocals and guitar) a third Atlantic LP, "Sweet Revenge," the break with Anka came as a relief. "I just was glad to be done with him," he says. "I didn't mean him any harm. I just never quite understood the association in the first place."

By Steve's own account, the split was crucial to the musical identities of both him and his Chicago compatriot. "John and I told Paul that Al was the guy who was doing all the work, and he had no business being disgruntled with him," Steve told Al Rudis. Straining for a favorable spin, Steve added, "I'm positive that Anka meant well through the whole thing. He really was hurt that we didn't have as much in common with him as he might have thought we did at the beginning of this whole thing, either musically or psychically or what-have-you. There were these gaps. But I don't think Paul realized that they existed. It was for the best. If I saw Paul Anka on the street, man, all I'd say to him today is, 'How you doin', and thanks very much for all you did.' "

Anka says that while Steve and Prine meant well, they were "really not that sophisticated or educated" in industry finances. "I don't think it was really a question of what I was about and they were about. The overall umbrella was, I was a businessman, a music person."

Simultaneously, Steve was facing another, more visible and potentially risky parting of the ways — with Buddah Records.

The company that had built its reputation on bubblegum singles but shifted its focus to the underground FM album market found that goal elusive as other forces held sway. A wildly successful "Superfly" blaxploitation movie tie-in LP by Curtis Mayfield on Buddah's Curtom imprint, which in early 1973 hit #8 on the *Billboard* pop chart and whose title single sold more than a million copies, steered the label away from singer/songwriters and toward soundtracks. More success on Buddah's African-American front came from Bill Withers, whose

There were these gaps. But I don't think Paul realized that they existed. It was for the best. If I saw Paul Anka on the street, man, all I'd say to him today is, 'How you doin', and thanks very much for all you did.'
STEVE GOODMAN

smooth voice and sharp pen had yielded "Ain't No Sunshine" and "Lean on Me," as well as from Gladys Knight & the Pips, whom Neil Bogart had snagged from Motown. The first Knight/Pips LP on Buddah, released in mid-1973, spawned four back-to-back hits, including "Midnight Train to Georgia," a chart-topper on both white and black charts, launching the label down the road of sophisticated pop and soul.

While this change of direction proved lucrative for Buddah, the firm's corporate structure was rupturing. Bogart, the extravagant co-founder who had signed Steve, had lost interest in the firm. Dogged by his bubblegum reputation, he also smarted because his spendthrift ways ran head-on against Viewlex, Buddah's parent company, which owned three pressing plants, two tape-duplication facilities and a recording studio. Viewlex absorbed much of the revenue Bogart had generated, says the label's Northeastern promo man, Bruce Shindler. "Every time that he would make money, they would take his money and put it into their other losing things," Shindler says. "He had to get out of there and do his own thing."

By November, Bogart had left behind Steve, other artists and Buddah co-founder Art Kass — a money manager who Jude Lyons says "didn't have a clue" about the label's music — and jetted to the other coast to start a new Los Angeles-based company, Casablanca Records. [36]

"Everything was sort of goofy" at Buddah, Steve told Rudis. "They were under a considerable amount of pressure from the big corporation that was running them, so it was a buck-passing situation." Steve sensed indifference, especially after Bogart's departure. "They were all advising me to stay with it. Y'know, I mean, I smelled some bullshit."

A break was inevitable. A "Random Notes" blurb in the Feb. 28, 1974, edition of *Rolling Stone* reported that Buddah had "dropped" Steve. With affection, the item opened with "Boo, hiss," but it carelessly made a food-ographical error, misidentifying one of Steve's better-known songs and blowing its pun: "Veal Cordon Blues." The blurb also apparently blew the gist, for it was Steve who dropped Buddah. "I asked them to let me go," he later told Rudis. "We worked out an arrangement whereby they could see some participation in some future deals in return for letting me out of what was a long-term contract. It literally took us a year to get it to that point. Attorneys are wonderful things, and they speak a language all their own, and sometimes laymen don't understand it, so I didn't have the slightest idea what was going on for about a year."

Pressed to identify why Buddah couldn't make his albums commercially successful, Steve admitted chagrin over handling of the "Troubles" LP, which he and many critics felt showcased his musical essence. But he opted not to affix specific blame. "There are so many ways a record can flop," he said. "There's just so many lucky factors that can change the relative success of a recording, especially an album that doesn't have a lot of stuff on it that sounds like rock 'n' roll, things you have to work a little harder to sell in today's scheme of things."

Cutting himself adrift from Buddah at the same time as he separated from

> They were all advising me to stay with it. Y'know, I mean, I smelled some bullshit.
> **STEVE GOODMAN**

36: Bogart's Casablanca label sizzled with success, via the painted-faced, long-tongued KISS quartet and the disco-era's Donna Summer. But for Bogart, a heavy cocaine user, solvency was always a problem. "He would have hit records and lose money," says Jude Lyons. "He lost fortunes of dollars." Bogart died of cancer on May 8, 1982, at age 39.

Anka induced no small anxiety. But Steve also saw the situation in reverse. "All these people who at one stage of my career were fairly instrumental in getting it rolling and had been the big business people that I'd related to, they were all deserting the ship," he said. "It was all very disillusioning to me. It showed me how little any of this stuff meant."

Steve had little time to dwell on the abandonment. Thanks to Bunetta and Steve's own widening reputation as a performer, Steve was anything but idle. His bustling itinerary overflowed with memorable venues and pairings in late 1973 and early 1974. After a show at Wilson College in Chambersburg, Pennsylvania, Steve joined yodeling expert Bill Staines and folksinger Ray Owen in breaking college rules by staying up all night drinking whiskey and performing in the room of Staines' girlfriend in the Prentis Hall women's dormitory. Then, with her newly formed Angel Band, little-known Emmylou Harris opened a pair of shows for Steve Nov. 30 at Catholic University in Washington, D.C., returning to the stage to play encores with him.

The specificity of Steve's "Yellow Coat" left an indelible impression on Harris, both that night and during a previous show Steve had done at the Cellar Door in the same city. "Obviously, the song was so real because who has a yellow coat?" she reflects today. "It was so poignant because just by making certain references about the kid that they would babysit and the questions, you knew that there was this enormous backstory. He was such a good songwriter that he could create the scenario in your mind. You filled in the blanks."

A month later, in the wee hours of New Year's Eve at Chicago's WFMT-FM, Steve performed stellar versions of two songs with distinctly feminist leanings. The first was Michael Smith's sympathetic portrait of a troubled older loner known by teen tormentors as "Crazy Mary." Amid applause at the end, one of those in the WFMT studio, Steve's benefactor from the Quiet Knight, Richard Harding, called out, "Good man!"

Next came a "border ballad" derived from an old Scottish air and expanded in 1816 by the famed Scottish author Sir Walter Scott. Titled "Jock o' Hazeldean," the pensive waltz — about a young woman who is forced into an arranged marriage but on her wedding day elopes with her true love, Jock — came to Steve via storyteller Johnniy Morris, who had played it for Steve from an LP by a fellow Scot, Dick Gaughan. Steve's subdued, creaky-voiced, on-air introduction was as poignant as his flawless singing and playing of the song itself:

"A couple of hundred years ago, there was no such thing as liberation or anything, for men or women, for that matter," he said. "Unfortunately, marriages were decided by circumstance rather than an affinity between two people. I mean, sometimes people got married to people they didn't even like. I guess you know. So here's the story of a brave girl who broke out of all that." [37]

Two and a half weeks into the new year of 1974, Steve became the catalyst for "the musical event of any year," as journalist Phil Ceccola put it, on the first night of a Jan. 17-20 run at the Main Point in Bryn Mawr. After Trevor Veitch (guitarist for Tom Rush) and Andy Kulberg (of the Blues Project and Sea Train) opened, Steve played a full set, then brought out surprise visitor John Prine. The two played Hank Williams songs for 20 minutes, left the stage, came back with Veitch and Kulberg and welcomed another guest, blues rocker and songwriter Bonnie Raitt, for a group finale. Though they had crossed paths at the Philadelphia Folk Festival and elsewhere, it was the first time Steve, Prine and Raitt played together publicly. [38]

Steve came to the rescue of a festival comrade, 28-year-old folksinger Mimi Fariña two weeks later in Vancouver, B.C., where she had developed a bad cold while playing a five-night stint at a tiny club called the Egress. Steve, in town to open for John Prine Jan. 31 at the Queen Elizabeth Theatre, telephoned Fariña to say hello. Hearing her misgivings over having to miss work, Steve substituted for her one night, gratis.

"That was probably one of the most impressive things another performer has ever done in my life," Fariña said. "There's a camaraderie, and you really understand when somebody's sick or has laryngitis how awful that feels. You're not going to be blessed by the club owner the next time you're in town, it puts your career in some kind of jeopardy, and it can put you in sort of a panic. So knowing all that, the sensibility to reach out and care like that was most amazing." It would not be the last favor that Steve performed for Fariña.

That night, however, became memorable for Steve because of Fariña's opening act, an emerging comic with whom he had crossed paths in Florida. "The club had six people in it," Steve later told Jeff Magid, co-publisher of the L.A.-based magazine *Pro Fun*, "and there was a garbage truck out in the alley loadin' up the cans in the middle of the night. The back door was open, and the garbage truck was very much louder than he was." Four years later, the comic — Steve Martin — would become a bona-fide phenomenon and have a profound effect on Steve's career.

In another fill-in role, substituting for Fairport Convention three weeks later,

Then-little-known opener Emmylou Harris joins Steve for an encore Nov. 30, 1973, at Catholic University.
(Photo by Marc Leepson, courtesy of Michael Schreibman)

37: In the same WFMT session, Steve also provided impromptu guitar for Studs Terkel's drunken but zesty rendition of a mournful 1891 song by Charles K. Harris, "Break the News to Mother," told in the voice of a dying firefighter injured in a fire. Terkel said that when he was 5, he watched his 10-year-old brother sing the tune on street corners for a nickel.

38: Phil Ceccola, a Philadelphia writer and photographer, found an unusual market for his assessment of the Main Point show – in his "Truckin' Tunes" column for the May/June 1974 edition of *Owner Operator* magazine.

Allan Pepper, shown in the mid-1970s, eagerly booked Steve at his new Bottom Line club in Greenwich Village: "This guy really did love life."

(Photo by Peter Cunningham, http://www.wordwiseweb.com)

39: The song was announced at Notre Dame and other 1974 shows as "Hillbilly's Lament." Soon, it became "Door Number Three." In later shows, Steve said he and Buffett wrote it after lobster fishing near Buffett's Key West home, but the setting for the tune's genesis was more likely Steve's Chicago flat. Steve and Buffett also started but never finished another tune, "I'll Bet Mel Blanc's Got Money in the Bank," which cited the Blanc-voiced Daffy Duck, Porky Pig and other cartoon characters. The refrain: "If you're lying in bed, sick in the head, don't let it worry you / I'll bet Mel Blanc's got money in the bank, and maybe he'll give some to you." Meanwhile, Steve told *Rolling Stone* he was writing another TV-tinged tune, "Goodnight Mr. Peepers," about the late sitcom actor and "Hollywood Squares" comic, Wally Cox. The song never surfaced.

Steve opened for folksinger Eric Andersen in a three-day run at the Bottom Line, just eight days after the grand opening of the classy Manhattan nightspot. Proprietors Allan Pepper and Stanley Snadowsky, who had run Gerdes Folk City and booked the Village Gate, were seeking top talent for their new, 450-seat venue at New York University. "Blown away" by Steve's recent performance at Club Passim in Cambridge, Pepper had booked him as quickly as possible.

"He was a performer a guy like me kills for," Pepper says. "It was like my wife said: Steve had a smile in his voice. When you present somebody like that, your audience falls in love, and your credibility goes up. It says something about your taste." Moreover, Pepper didn't detect Steve's label woes and was relieved to find that Steve's public and private personalities were an unusually close match. "You have no idea how many performers backstage are a nightmare to be with because of their own personal problems and traumas and self-hatred and self-involvement, and it's 'me, me, me, me.' Stevie Goodman offstage was what he was onstage: a very accessible guy, a guy that you could laugh with, a guy you could hang out with. This guy really did love life."

Steve also loved a good cause, and the largest benefit concert he ever played came on March 4, 1974, at the University of Notre Dame, where he shared the stage with Bill "Oliver" Swofford, who got Steve involved, and a pair of headliners — the Nitty Gritty Dirt Band and the superstar who had diluted and claimed partial credit for "City of New Orleans," John Denver. Heavily promoted, including 10 TV news segments reported by the young Jane Pauley in Indianapolis, the show raised money to buy a building for a prison-reform program run by George Mische, known as one of the Catonsville Nine (including Daniel and Phillip Berrigan) who had burned draft files in 1968 in Maryland.

The sellout crowd of 18,000 that packed the school's basketball fieldhouse in South Bend, Indiana, just two hours east of Chicago, heard Steve — not Denver — perform "City of New Orleans." ("I get yelled at if I don't play it and yelled at if I do," Steve said.) But during an otherwise spellbinding set, Steve heard a rude reminder of Denver's pre-eminence from a guy in the audience who interrupted Steve's guitar solo in "Would You Like to Learn to Dance?" by bellowing, "Bring out John!"

A performer Steve did bring out that night — a surprise to the audience — was Jimmy Buffett, who sang a couple of songs, including one that the two played together, a country-ish sendup of Monty Hall's daytime TV game show "Let's Make a Deal."

The song had originated a few weeks prior during one of Buffett's visits to Steve's apartment in Chicago. Late one morning, the two were drinking a pitcher of piña coladas and watching the silly, long-running program when inspiration struck. "I was kind of in love with Carol Merrill (the silent, smiling, gesturing hostess) and the absurdity of the whole thing," Buffett says, and he suggested that he and Steve write a song about it. Buffett had a solitary proviso, that at least one line end with the phrase "door number three." [39] The two struggled with lyrics for 20 minutes until Steve finally blurted out, "I don't know what

Jay's got on the table," and the song "wrote itself" in just five minutes more. Its affectionate jab at the boob-tube staple easily won over the Notre Dame crowd.

The finale of the benefit, with all artists onstage, embodied the cream of the era's folk, country and pop entertainment. It began with John Prine's "Illegal Smile" (which Swofford had recorded in an unreleased demo) and evolved into a guitar-banjo face-off between Steve and the Dirt Band's John McEuen that incorporated the familiar "Dueling Banjos" theme. It continued with Denver's "Take Me Home, Country Roads," then Hank Williams' "Your Cheatin' Heart," during which Steve sang "like a cross between Louis Armstrong and B.B. King," reported Fred Graver of the Notre Dame *Observer*. Capping the proceedings was the resounding Carter family sing-along "Will the Circle Be Unbroken."

Steve's circle, of course, began with — and invariably returned to — his base of Chicago, literally and psychically. "His accent, his attitude, it was just pure Chicago," says Philadelphia harmonica player Saul Broudy. That characteristic stood out when Broudy had met Steve in the early 1970s at a benefit arranged by Paula Ballan at a drug-rehab center in Manhattan and when Steve had first invited Broudy to accompany him, during workshops at the 1973 Mariposa Folk Festival in Toronto. "It's an edge," Broudy says, "sort of a streetwise, workingman's aggressiveness."

But it was an edge softened by reality. His drive to perform stemmed from a need to "maintain my cynicism," Steve slyly told *Rolling Stone*. "I guess that's what my sense of humor is all about anyway, cynicism. I'm a pessimist. I know everything isn't all right. But that's all right. We still get up in the morning."

When he did awaken in Chicago, during breaks from touring and leukemia treatments at Sloan-Kettering, Steve focused his attention on his two families: personal and musical.

Once again, he and Nancy, their daughter Jessie having grown to toddler age, were on the move, relocating in 1973 to a larger apartment in a three-floor building on the south side of West Bittersweet Place, a tiny street just a handful of blocks northeast of Wrigley Field and a stone's throw from Lincoln Park along Lake Michigan. With tall bay windows, the sunroom facing the street was where Steve displayed his bursting guitar collection and entertained musical visitors. One of Jessie's earliest memories is sitting in a white mesh playpen in the apartment and hearing broadcasts of Cubs games. "There was always baseball," she says. "There was always someone there with long hair, and there was baseball on TV." [40]

After the Goodmans moved in, neighbors staged a summer block party that spread into the parking lot of nearby Immaculata High School, says Rusty Poehner, who lived on the north side of Bittersweet. Steve heard the commotion, grabbed a guitar, strapped on a five-pound portable amplifier (called a Pignose) and joined the gathering to perform a couple of songs. "Pretty groovy," Poehner says. "None of us had known that Steve was living in the building directly across the street," she says, "and we all had one of those moments of swelling neighborhood pride and boosterism."

Posing in 1973 with soon-to-be wife Margaret, Bill Swofford (better known by his stage and middle name, Oliver) lured Steve to perform at the 1974 prison-reform benefit at Notre Dame. Bill and Margaret became fast friends with Steve and Nancy, who helped the Swoffords find their first apartment in Chicago in 1974.

(Photo by the Pilgrim Inn, Indianapolis, courtesy of Margaret Southern)

40: Nancy's brother, Robert Pruter, recalls Steve's mania for boxing as well. The two bet on an early 1970s Muhammad Ali win over Jerry Quarry, and Pruter joined Steve and other folkies to watch Ali's Oct. 30, 1974, defeat of George Foreman in Zaire, as broadcast live in the auditorium at Roosevelt University downtown.

Steve helped boost another, more visible Chicago neighborhood at the same time as he gave a financial lift to a key family member — his father. For several years, in Elmhurst in the western suburbs, Bud had managed a Chevy dealership, which in 1972 took on the Mazda rotary-engine franchise and soon opened a dealership below 61-story Marina City, the "twin corncob" complex at the south end of Chicago's swanky Magnificent Mile. With financial help from Steve, one of the new branch's silent partners became Bud Goodman. "Steve told me that one of his greatest joys was the fact that he had made enough money that he could get his father into a Mazda dealership," says high-school friend Brad Ellis.

Two other Maine East classmates of Steve's, Jeff Lind and Dennis Scharlau, sold Mazdas at Marina City, and Bud, whose height gave him a "munchkin" appearance, was fun to work for, Lind says. "He was honest. He just had a way of talking. If I needed a deal closed and he was around and none of the managers was around, I'd say, 'Bud, come on over and help me.' He just knew the product. He'd done it his whole life."

Bud's shift to the unusual Mazda brand, popular till the firm's late 1970s financial collapse, engendered his son's pride. "Couldn't have happened to a nicer guy," Steve told his Amazingrace audience in 1973. "He's been busting his ass for 25 years selling Chevvies and stuff, always working 80 hours a week and three heart attacks. And he was shitty at selling Chevvies, too. He's much better at Mazdas." [41]

The professional parallel of father and son was not lost on Steve's musical companions in Chicago. Each was clearly in sales. What Steve was selling — and within the city folk scene's musical ethos, what he was duty-bound to sell — was entertainment. He helped tangibly extend that mission about 2 a.m. one night while leaving the Orphans music club and walking with Earl Pionke and Bill Redhed, a neighborhood friend, along Lincoln Avenue, just north of the Biograph Theater, site of the 1934 slaying of gangster John Dillinger. Pionke spotted a small sign posted in the window of a closed-up bar called the Pachyderm that read, "Establishment for Rent." He turned to Steve and Redhed and said, "Should we take a shot?"

That moment led to the launching of a landmark — a hole-in-the-wall Chicago folk-music bar and grill whose stature soon rivaled that of the Earl of Old Town a little more than a mile southeast. Eventually, there were six partners, dubbing themselves the "folk Mafia." Pionke, his Earl of Old Town burger chef Duke Nathaus and Redhed put up cash. Pionke and Nathaus set up the bar, while Redhed supplied elbow grease to make the place habitable. Ed Holstein ceased his sporadic performing to embrace the "regular job" of bartending and managing the bookings of primarily local talent. ("All folk, no boogie," he said.) With Pionke fronting cash for their shares, Fred Holstein became the house act, while Steve agreed to perform there at least twice a year.

Pionke, however, had an additional inspiration for Steve's role. The club needed a name, and Redhed, who taught English at Oakton Community Col-

41: Steve said he was about to
obtain a new car because, with his
dad as an agency manager, "I can
get one now for free, which is
about the only way you'd ever get
me to have one of them things."
But Steve also predicted his
recording of "Lincoln Park Pirates"
would result in his losing the car
someday. "I just know that
somebody's layin' for me," he said.

lege in suburban Des Plaines (and used Steve's, John Prine's and Michael Smith's lyrics in his poetry classes), assembled a list of candidates. One was "Port of Amsterdam," from a bracing Jacques Brel tune and Fred Holstein showstopper. But Pionke, knowing of the slim sales for Steve's second album and wanting to give him a lift, had just one name in mind.

"Deciding what name?" Pionke told his fellow investors. "Are you crazy? This guy's a partner. You tell me what name. You never heard a better name for a fuckin' saloon. That's the name!"

"Just like that?" Steve asked Pionke.

"Yeah, just like that. That's the fuckin' name."

Steve paused as a grin grew to an ear-to-ear smile. "Yeah," he said, "what were we thinking of?"

Thus, at 2470 North Lincoln Avenue, was born the club called Somebody Else's Troubles. [42] Gib Foster, who had created the "Troubles" LP cover and lived half a block away, was hired to carve the bar's wooden exterior sign and draw up interior graphics by replicating his original album design. His payment? "I could eat and drink there for a year," he says. "What a deal! I was over there every night."

Though it could hold only 120 at a time, Troubles (as it was known in short form) quickly became a force in revitalizing Lincoln Avenue nightlife and fueling the city's folk scene, starting with the opening weekend of March 15 and 16, 1974, when Fred Holstein opened for Steve. "Man, it was a $1 cover," Holstein said. "That joint was loaded, mobbed."

With a $5,000 up-front investment and monthly rent of only $750, "we made our money back in the first six months," Fred Holstein said. Some nights, lines streamed around the corner. "You had this neighborhood Cheers bar thing going, and the place was just a gold mine," says Larry Rand, one of the first Troubles acts. Steve, of course, was a snug fit and a potent and welcoming draw. There, says folksinger Cindy Mangsen, "It always sounded like he was smiling when he was singing."

An immediate lure was a special evening once a month throughout 1974 wherein the booked performer showed up early with the makings for dinner, prepared the meal in the saloon's kitchen and served it up before the night's first performance. The price of the dinner, two drinks and show was $6. The name: Cook & Sing.

"Steve did the first one," says folksinger Betsy Redhed, daughter of Bill, "and it turned out to be the finest of all the meals to come." On his appointed night, Wednesday, May 8, Steve and Nancy brought in 1,352 shrimp and 24 pounds of green noodles and prepared scampi in garlic butter over pasta with parmesan cheese, accompanied by salad and mini-bottles of wine. Steve made cleanup his job as well, which became an occupational hazard, says folksinger Jim Craig. While Steve scrubbed dishes in the sink behind the bar, Pionke spouted a warning.

"Hey, Steve, it's almost time for you to go on."

(Top) Gib Foster's sign for Somebody Else's Troubles, the club's storefront on Lincoln Avenue and (below) the display board for Cook & Sing nights.
(Images courtesy of Gib Foster)

42: Folksinger Utah Phillips says wags also called the club Somebody Else's Money and Somebody Else's Rubble.

"Well, give me 10 minutes," Steve replied, "so I can dry my hands out."

The scampi was a feast hard to top, although Bonnie Koloc tried with her "famous" stew. John Prine puzzled momentarily about his own contribution. "All I could make is grilled cheese, and if I made it for 100 people, they could be cold by the time I got it to the first person," Prine says, "so I thought, how about somethin' else that I really liked?" On his assigned Cook & Sing night, Prine etched a memorable contribution into the local lore by hiring White Castle to haul into Troubles countless trays bursting with 1,500 of the 7/8-ounce, 2-1/8-inch square burgers from the notorious chain. Each burger came with an order of fries, plus a bowl of Troubles cook Duke Nathaus' chili (which Prine says "would run through you like Epsom salts") and, from a local bakery, a day-old slice of apple pie into which was stuck a toothpick with a tiny U.S. flag. "The people who came were mainly liberals with money from the North Side," Prine says with a laugh, "so this might not have been their cup of tea for a dinner."

> The people who came were mainly liberals with money from the North Side, so (White Castle burgers) might not have been their cup of tea for a dinner.
> **JOHN PRINE**

Troubles became another launching pad for Steve's steely focus — offstage as well as on, as traditional folksinger Art Thieme soon experienced. In mid-1973, Thieme had traded in a long-necked Vega Tubaphone banjo for a small Martin guitar at Prager & Ridder, a second-floor music store on Wabash Avenue in the downtown Loop, but he later decided he'd made a mistake and tried to buy it back. He was dismayed to find that proprietor Eric Prager, a "notorious over-charger," had inflated the price to an exorbitant $1,200. Thieme wandered into Troubles four days before its grand opening to blow off steam about the banjo that seemed out of reach, and Steve, sitting at the bar, overheard his lament.

"How much will you pay for it?" Steve asked Thieme.

"I paid $500 for it originally," Thieme replied.

Steve got what Thieme described as "that narrow, determined look in his eye, like when there was an audience that wasn't with him."

"Well," Steve told Thieme, "get the money, and we'll do it."

Thieme withdrew $500 cash at a nearby bank branch, and he, Thieme, Fred Holstein and a couple others piled into a car and headed to the Loop. "You wait down here," Steve said as Thieme and the others walked into first-floor Rose Records. Steve went upstairs alone with the money.

Inside the music store, Steve browsed but kept coming back to the banjo. Prager quoted him a price of $1,000. Steve walked away, then came back to it, deviously telling Prager, "I'll play it onstage and mention you wherever I go if you'll cut the price." It was a lie, but one that Steve felt was justifiable. Steve offered $500, including tax, and Prager agreed. Steve walked downstairs with the banjo in a plastic bag and handed it to Thieme. "We were all just crazy about it," Thieme says. "We couldn't believe he'd done it, and we went next door to Miller's Pub to have a beer and gloat about how great it was to put one over on Eric."

Thieme marvels at Steve's galvanizing glare. "Oh, the intensity of the man.

He was just a great guy who tried to do things for folks. He'd get that look in his eyes, and you just didn't want to cross him. It wasn't a question of failing. It was just, you had to do it. It was the look in those dark eyes."

His intensity was routinely evident in a steely stare and vise-grip handshake. But it could be as powerful in relative stillness as it was in a challenging confrontation. The same month that Troubles opened, Steve made this clear following a show at the Quiet Knight by Phil Ochs.

Like others in the folk community, Steve had been disheartened by Ochs' recent decline. A brilliant composer and clear-voiced, outspoken protest singer in the 1960s, Ochs had descended into alcoholism and manic depression. Irked by what he saw as Ochs wasting his life, Steve had made him the butt of a bitter joke the previous October at Bubba's. Steve told the crowd (falsely) that he was inspired to learn "The Auctioneer," with its fast and repetitive auction calls, after Ochs and 10 others had dinner at his flat. "Someone mentioned, 'The music business has certainly gotten pharmaceutical,' and Phil Ochs says, 'Whaddya mean? Whaddya mean? Whaddya mean? Whaddya mean? Whaddya mean?' "

But probably unknown to Steve at the time of his Bubba's gig, Ochs a few weeks prior had lost the upper register of his voice during an ill-fated trip to Africa. Three strangers apparently robbed, pummeled and strangled Ochs on a Tanzanian beach, wrenching his vocal chords. When the 33-year-old was booked the following spring at the Quiet Knight, Steve and others attended with the earnest hope that he was on an upswing. "There was this comeback feel in the air," says folksinger Jack Schechtman (now Gabriel, later known as "Dean of the Obscure" for 10 years on CBC radio), who also was present, along with a visiting Arlo Guthrie.

From Ochs' first strains, however, the hopes were dashed. Backed by long-time friend Jim Glover and opening act Bob Gibson (with whom Ochs had co-written "That's the Way It's Gonna Be," a part of Steve's early repertoire and Ochs' second selection that night), Ochs was a shaky shell of his former self. Though he bounced back at the end with two timely songs excoriating Richard Nixon and the Watergate scandal, elsewhere in the show Ochs forgot lyrics, slurred words and sang off-key. "He was such a mess," Schechtman says. "He was burned out, not in good shape."

Stunned after Ochs retreated to the back room, several, including Steve, gathered for a drink at the club's bar. "Everybody was quiet and bummed," Schechtman says. In the lingering silence, Steve both sensed and seized the mood by slowly, quietly singing the sea chantey "Haul Away Joe."

"It had a 'We're pulling our way home' feel to it, like a dirge," Schechtman says. But in the hush, the chantey was anything but a showpiece. "It was not overt. It was much more discreet and sensitive," Schechtman says, "and suddenly, all these singers and musicians at the bar recognized the song and were singing along with him with a melancholy forcefulness. It almost felt like an elegy or eulogy for Ochs. It was the sense of, 'We're mourning something, but

Art Thieme, shown in 1973, was amazed by Steve's laser focus in the quest to retrieve a cherished banjo: "Oh, the intensity of the man. He was just a great guy who tried to do things for folks. He'd get that look in his eyes, and you just didn't want to cross him."

(Photo courtesy of Art Thieme)

Jack Schechtman (now Gabriel) – who witnessed Steve leading a round of "Haul Away Joe" after a poor performance by the troubled Phil Ochs on March 17, 1974, at the Quiet Knight – got a taste of Steve's intensity later that night by saying they both were "in the same place."

(Photo © Ron Schick, courtesy of Rabbi Jack Schechtman Gabriel)

43: Ochs had only glimmers of a revived spirit over the next two years and succumbed to suicide on April 9, 1976, at age 35.

we're not going to say anything because that would be very uncool.' Steve was doing something to change the energy. It was some kind of a closure for the night, because it had felt very unclosed." [43]

Later that night, trying to lend support for Steve's musical antidote to Ochs' disappointing performance, Schechtman made a comment that Steve understandably misinterpreted.

"You and I are in the same place," Schechtman said.

Steve "kind of jumped," and it was clear from his reaction that he wondered if Schechtman, too, had leukemia.

"What do you mean we're in the same place?" Steve replied.

"We are in the same place, man," Schechtman said, adding, in reference to Ochs' obvious deterioration, "Our life is always in danger."

"No, we're not in the same place," Steve said pointedly. "You have a life, and I have a life with a shadow on it."

Sometimes Steve's intensity fed a rage experienced by Steve's friends but rarely by his audiences. Close to the time that Troubles opened, Steve and Ed Holstein caught a movie at the Carnegie Theater in the Rush Street district of Chicago's Magnificent Mile and afterward stepped next door into Sweetwater, a fashionable restaurant occupying the former Mr. Kelly's nightclub. Steve was wearing Adidas athletic shoes he had just bought.

"We have a dress code," a tall maitre d' told them in a French accent, "and I will seat you when you can wear decent shoes."

Infuriated, Steve started to argue, but Holstein pleaded with him. "Steve," he said, "that guy doesn't want our money. He wants us to go. Let's go."

"No, I got my rights!" Steve spat back, then turned to the maitre d' and pitched a fit.

Holstein, frustrated, walked out. Reconsidering, he turned on his heels. Back inside, he found Steve still yelling: "These are Adidas shoes! I paid $30 for these shoes!"

The maitre d', no longer using a French accent, told Holstein, "You better get your little friend out of here, or I'm going to put him in the deep fryer."

Holstein finally persuaded Steve to leave. "He was always up for a fight," Holstein says. "It was funny, and I never found it off-putting. He was just kind of a control freak that way. We used to call him Little Caesar. He'd play up to that. He'd laugh about it."

Steve's temper flared at the ballpark as well. The Holstein brothers, Pionke, Steve and others often found their way to afternoon Cubs games at Wrigley Field (no night games because the ballpark had no lights) with sandwiches packed by Steve's Grandma Mary. Steve kept score and held court, explaining to his friends "the chess game between the pitcher and the batter and all the other subtleties," Ed Holstein says. But one day, when a larger guy in front of Steve kept standing up to cheer, Steve let him have it: "Why don't you sit down, you big asshole? I paid to see this game, too."

Al Bunetta and John Prine were Steve's companions at another game at

Wrigley, at which an umpire's call incensed Steve. He ran down the steps to the railing, citing a rule and shouting, "You had no right!" The ump halted the game momentarily, turned to Steve and briefly explained his call. Steve, realizing he was wrong, walked back up to his seat, teased by Bunetta: "Wah, wah, wah." "He had that short-guy thing," Bunetta says. "Boy, he was a terrible athlete, and he loved sports so much, but he couldn't be wrong. He was a tough, tough guy."

Baseball stadiums also could bring out the charming side of Steve's intensity, says singer/guitarist Trevor Veitch, who joined Steve for a Red Sox game at Boston's Fenway Park that year. At the outset, the two stood up to sing the national anthem, but Veitch learned that Steve had something more in mind.

"We started trying to out-harmonize each other, and right away Steve had the entire group around us, about 30 people, all improvising. With that twinkle in his eye, he was leading others and bellowing," Veitch says. "That's how powerful his personality was. It wasn't threatening. He just had this wonderful gift to make everybody warm to him." [44]

Back on the road in the spring and summer of 1974, Steve captivated audiences no matter the venue or locale. By now a circuit veteran, he took satisfaction in extending a hand to musicians not as experienced or fortunate. One show, on April 23 at Hamline University in St. Paul, Minnesota, revealed two instances of such kindness.

The opening performer, local singer Mark Henley, delivered an outstanding set, and Steve followed him to the stage, offering customary praise. But Steve went further, nailing the message home with effrontery. Glancing at Henley, who was standing in the audience nearby, he said dryly, "Next time, I open for you, asshole!"

A more tender act came shortly before the show when Steve walked up to the fieldhouse and recognized Dakota Dave Hull, an eclectic songwriter and guitarist from Minneapolis whom Steve had met at a folk festival the previous year. Hull was sitting outside, unsure he could afford the $3.50 ticket.

"Are you taken care of?" Steve asked Hull. "Let's get you on the (pass) list."

It was a moving gesture. "It made a huge impression on me," Hull says. "He didn't have to do that. He knew how lucky he was to have a song that got incredibly famous. You want to pass along that spirit of generosity." [45]

Life as a troubadour provided the chance to create many such intangibly rewarding moments. But Steve also knew that his stature as a live entertainer wouldn't last long without a simultaneous method for his new songs to be purchased and heard across the country. A successful musician continually needed to stock the commercial stream with fresh product. Steve had no regrets about his drawn-out break with Buddah, but what lay ahead?

In one sense, his relentless performing — both in Chicago and all over the country — embodied an open-ended equation. Intensity + generosity = what? Soon, Steve would find out. ♪

Steve performs April 23, 1974, at Hamline University in St. Paul, Minnesota.

(Photo © Susan Martin Robbins)

44: Sam Siegel, a Maine East High classmate, says Steve told him when they were neighbors on Bittersweet Place that one of his dreams was to sing the national anthem at Wrigley Field.

45: With equal tenderness, Steve surprised 16-year-old guitarist Tina Cammarata (now Compton) when she played "The Dutchman" while answering the phone at the Skokie branch of the Old Town School of Folk Music. "This little head pops around the door," she says, "these little hands start clapping, I look up, and it's Steve Goodman." He offered an instant accolade: "That was so pretty. You did that so nice." Steve later bid the teen and other Old Town School teachers to join him and Jethro Burns in a late-night jam at a nearby tavern. Says Cammarata: "I was the pet kid."

'I want to sing to the widest variety of people I know of'

The hippest record label in the United States was dangling for Steve Goodman the most coveted carrot a folkie singer/songwriter could receive in the disco-drenched mid-1970s — a contract. But was it really what Steve wanted? Perhaps more important, could he measure up? Was this a case of "Be careful what you wish for because you may get it"?

The heady prospect gave him pause. "You sometimes have to go away for a couple of days and just sorta figure out where the real priorities are," Steve told interviewer John Platt of Chicago's WXRT-FM. "I wanted two days by myself to make sure I was doin' the right thing."

So in April 1975, Steve motored west toward Los Angeles and took a solitary break by visiting one of the world's most awe-inspiring natural wonders, the remote and majestic Grand Canyon.

It wasn't a refuge typical for Steve, who preferred — and was hooked on — the cacophony of big-city music clubs. "I'm goofy about music. Goofy, y'hear? Nuts, goofy," he told Platt. "I go hear it all the time. I can't stand to be without it for any length of time. I would go crazy in the country listenin' to the crickets. I can't go out in the mountains too much, man. I've gotta sit around bars and hear people play or go to concerts."

But Steve also admitted, "I got my quiet moments." So before making a final decision to ink the dotted line on a contract that promised heretofore elusive musical heights, he decided to plumb some physical depths. He strode for four and a half hours down the 7-mile South Kaibab Trail and stayed overnight in one of seven bunk beds in a dorm at Phantom Ranch along the Colorado River. The next morning, he hoofed for seven and a half hours up the 9.5-mile Bright Angel Trail to the canyon's rim.

His journey into and out of "the most amazing place I ever saw" netted him a bonus for his live shows — the insight for a haunting song that beckoned from its opening line: "Run come see what this river has done." With themes environmental and spiritual ("the promised land," "for heaven's sake"), Steve hallowed "Mother Nature's masterpiece" with a lyrical one of his own. He even invoked a positive solar image ("carved the walls of Grand Canyon with the colors of the rising sun") in contrast to foreboding references in his previous

I'm goofy about music. Goofy, y'hear? Nuts, goofy.
STEVE GOODMAN

(Opposite page) With Jessie Goodman sitting onstage to his right, a slimmed-down Steve performs for Chicago's WGN-AM at the Old Town School of Folk Music on July 31, 1975, one month after the release of the LP that Steve named for his 3-year-old daughter.

(Photo courtesy of Roy Leonard)

Bob Dylan, shown Feb. 11, 1974, in Seattle during his tour with The Band, was among the high-profile artists recording for Asylum, the label Steve had in his sights.

(Photo by Clay Eals)

work. Onstage, quieting his voice to a near-whisper and using a spare, walking-paced strum, Steve conveyed a palpable reverence for the canyon, and his performance of the song never failed to send a chill up his audiences' collective spine.

When introducing his "Grand Canyon Song," though, Steve couldn't resist a tart reference to the musician with whom he had tangled over "City of New Orleans" and who had climbed to ubiquity with "Rocky Mountain High." As Steve dryly put it, "This is sort of an inverse John Denver song."

Likewise, Steve's hike also yielded him an irreverent story to share. Though on the surface the anecdote was crass, Steve couldn't have missed how it symbolized what he had been through — and still might be slogging through — to achieve music-industry success.

"I didn't know I was going to get there until I got there," Steve began the hiking tale for a later audience at San Francisco's Wolfgang's club. "I was just on an excursion and stopped at the canyon. They don't let you take a mule unless you have about a two-year reservation, so I had to walk." The steep incline and weather conditions — icy at the top and 70 degrees at the bottom — stirred Steve's concerns about safety. "I'm not exactly Nature Boy," he said. "I didn't have hiking shoes on so that I wouldn't fall into the abyss." All he had with him was a pair of English leather Clark Desert Treks. "They ain't your better basic hiking shoes," he said. So as he began his descent, he sought the guidance of a man who was passing him.

"Hey," Steve said, "how do you not fall in?"

The man's answer was blunt: "Step in the mule shit."

(Telling the story in later shows, Steve paused for a beat, then added for comic effect, "I sure hope he wasn't puttin' me on.")

Wary about the man's advice, Steve felt he had no choice, so he tried the tip. "I never thought I'd say this, but I was traipsing along saying to myself, 'Hey, man, I sure hope there's some mule shit around the next bend that I can step in.' It was a real education — and it works. It's good for traction, and you don't slide."

For his body, the hike proved a challenge. So did a nine-hour bus ride that followed, westbound to California from Flagstaff. "Everything just sort of seized up," he said. "When I got off the bus in Los Angeles, I walked like Groucho Marx for three days."

If physically bent, Steve long had been mentally prepared for making the contractual commitment. One year earlier, in early 1974, his manager, Al Bunetta, had shopped Steve to several labels, but as Bunetta says, "The truth was, nobody wanted Stevie." But Bunetta and Steve had only one label in their sights — the brainchild of industry wunderkind David Geffen, the offshoot of Elektra Records called Elektra/Asylum.

"Bunetta said all along that we were negotiating with Asylum, and that was our priority negotiating thing, and that he wasn't really serious about anything else that he was doing until he made sure that this was going to happen," Steve told Al Rudis of the *Chicago Sun-Times* in 1975. "He really wanted the Asylum deal to be a reality and worked hard on it."

Born in 1971, the year of Steve's first album, Asylum had the top three LPs on the *Billboard* Top 100 chart in March 1974, and Geffen, 31, predicted the label would gross at least $35 million by year's end. The key to his success, he told *Billboard*, was to "sign the best talent available."

And what talent! Geffen had lured the likes of his former roommate, Joni Mitchell, along with Jackson Browne, Linda Ronstadt, Carly Simon, the Eagles, gravel-voiced Tom Waits, Harry Chapin and, in the ultimate coup, Bob Dylan and The Band, whose first official album together, "Planet Waves," had sold a million copies precisely at the time that Steve's "Troubles" guest pianist had emerged for what critics had labeled the tour of the year. (Caught up in the Dylan/Band excitement, on Jan. 3, 1974, Steve rode in a limousine with Earl Pionke, the Holsteins and Larry Rand to Chicago Stadium to join 18,500 others in witnessing the rousing kickoff of the 40-show, 21-city tour.)

Geffen's public comments about his own acumen turned out to be as vague as those typical of Dylan. "I have no big secret technique for success," Geffen cryptically told *Billboard*. "I prefer to work with artists who have faith in themselves and in what we can do for them."

Backstage at a Joni Mitchell concert at Chicago's Arie Crown Theater in February 1972, Steve had met Geffen. Two years later, what snared Geffen's interest in Steve? Arlo Guthrie's inescapable version of Steve's "City of New Orleans" was an obvious factor. "My circle," Geffen says today, "knew who wrote everything." He says that he zeroed in on musicians who penned their own material, seeking out Mitchell and Jackson Browne after hearing versions of their work by Buffy Sainte-Marie and Tom Rush. "Asylum Records in the 1970s was all about singer/songwriters," Geffen says. "I thought Steve was terrific, and I thought 'City of New Orleans' was a great, great song. I was a fan."

So in June 1974, when Bunetta met with the Asylum chief in Geffen's Los Angeles office, his pitch reached receptive ears. "Geffen and Al sat there about an hour and worked out what basically is the agreement," Steve said later. But the road to signing the contract was slippery. Geffen was the epitome of intensity and bluntness. ("Geffen makes me look like Mr. Peace," Bunetta later told parodist Rich Markow.) Plus, attorneys for Bunetta and Geffen couldn't get their schedules together. Each took long vacations, and Geffen did the same. "I was the only guy who was in a hurry," Steve said.

It wasn't as if Steve were idle. His touring schedule that summer and fall — after he played guitar on Bonnie Koloc's fourth and strongest LP on the Ovation label, "You're Gonna Love Yourself in the Morning" — was back-to-back folk festivals and one-nighters all over the continent that produced indelible experiences as well as future musical material.

Foremost was Steve's appearance June 21-23 at the 14th annual Mariposa Folk Festival, held on idyllic Centre Island in Toronto Harbour. "It was beautiful, gorgeous, like Pepperland," says Al McKenney, who road-managed David

David Geffen, Asylum Records' wunderkind in 1975, was upbeat about Steve's chances at the label: "I thought Steve was terrific, and I thought 'City of New Orleans' was a great, great song. I was a fan."
(Photo by Henry Diltz)

Especially at festivals, Steve found it important to convey enthusiasm and not to worry overly about mistakes, says Anne Hills, shown in 1980. "The important part," she says, "was the jumping in and doing it."
(Photo by Art Thieme)

1: Each festival artist was paid the same $300, "a wonderful way to run a festival," said Cape Breton-born Celtic entertainer John Allan Cameron, a frequent Mariposa performer. "There certainly were no egos about how much money are you making on this and that."

2: Centre Island's boat-only access was charming but also created challenges for festival organizers. One afternoon, Steve walked up to Estelle Klein displaying a bleeding finger. Needing no reminder about his leukemia, Klein called her husband and asked him to wait at the mainland while she hustled Steve to a ferry. He was taken to Toronto's Women's College Hospital for treatment.

Bromberg. Accessible only by foot ferry and limited to 8,000 festival-goers, the island made for intimate, spontaneous performances befitting the most talented of musicians. By 1974, however, organizers had limited bookings to medium-profile artists to prevent stampedes the likes of 1972, when surprise sets by Neil Young and Joni Mitchell stirred crowd-control concerns and a visiting Bob Dylan had to be ferried away to avoid a mob in pursuit. [1]

Given his appeal and the milieu, Steve was the perfect match for Mariposa, said its booker, Estelle Klein. "I was crazy about him," she said. "I loved his brightness, his wit and his incredibly keen ear for the way people talk and what was going on around him. He had a strong sense of irony and the human condition. He had incredible electricity. As soon as he hit the stage, out it came." [2]

Equally potent was Steve's ability to create a feeling of identification, says singer/songwriter Anne Hills, who first saw Steve perform at Mariposa. "It was more important for him to put the music forward," she says. "If he flubbed, that wasn't important. The important part was the jumping in and doing it. In that way, you got the sense that he was your next-door neighbor or your best friend or your buddy down the hall who likes to just pick up the guitar and jam. There was that sense that he could walk into anybody's living room with that kind of joy and enthusiasm."

Such zest was an antidote to the "sulky, sullen, serious" folk performers of Canada, says Ontario-based singer Garnet Rogers, the then-lesser-known brother of folk artist Stan Rogers. "Steve bridged that thing between these navel-gazing singer/songwriter guys that I was hanging out with and these terrifyingly good vaudeville-style musicians who really wanted to entertain and kick it out. That was a big influence on us, seeing somebody who realized, 'I'm here to entertain.' He would try anything. It was like the circus had come to town."

Steve had sung at the 1973 Mariposa festival, and in 1974 he returned to headline an evening show with Kate and Anna McGarrigle. He also was the darling of the daytime workshops, joining that year in the provocatively named "Little Boxes (Comments on Lifestyles)," "When Does It Become a Folk Song?" and "Rednecks, White Socks and Blue Ribbon Songs (Country Classics)." But his role as a fill-in for Ramblin' Jack Elliott in a fourth workshop — with the bland name of "Improvising Lyrics" — became the most memorable. The two other musicians at this session were beat poet David Amram and guitarist Charlie Chin. Amram, a classically trained jazzman, multi-instrumentalist and symphony conductor from Manhattan, was an intense genius whom country star Marty Stuart later affectionately labeled "a planet."

Amram was the most practiced at the workshop theme, having made up songs at parties for several years. Steve's budding talents in improvisation, what some in Chicago called "make-a-song," were yet to be recognized. The two had never performed together, a dynamic that festivals loved to foster. About 5 o'clock on the morning of the workshop, while backing Canadian Indians, Greek musicians, bluegrass players, English/Irish folksingers and Morris dancers in an all-night, hotel-room picking session, they met.

"Y'know, we have a workshop today," Steve said to Amram. "What do you think we should do?"

"Well," Amram said, "we could ask the audience for some topics, I guess four topics, and we'll divide everybody up into four different sections and make up a song that rhymes. Then once we have the song, we'll get them to sing. We'll make up big-band riffs with words, feed 'em the topics back, and then on top of that, we could improvise."

Steve looked at Amram for a moment and said, "Look, I know you did stuff like that with Jack Kerouac and Dizzy Gillespie in the 1950s. I know you write symphonies and plays. But I'm a songwriter, and I take that as seriously as you do writin' a symphony or playin' jazz. Songwriting, to me, is a craft."

"I didn't mean any disrespect," Amram said. "I just know that you're a musician who can do anything because you're interested in everything."

"Well," Steve replied, "this would be a new adventure."

For another hour and a half, the two played songs for each other and retired at 7 a.m. for a few hours' rest. That afternoon, on a grassy field filled with 2,000 people, many holding umbrellas to fend off a nagging drizzle, Amram — who Steve described as "a wildman, wired for sound, as fast as they get" — started the workshop. For the finale, Amram invoked his audience-participation plan, and someone near the front of the temporary stage shouted, "*Moby Dick!*" Momentarily stunned, both Steve and Amram were game, and they plunged ahead to create a tune based on the massive 1851 novel by Herman Melville.

In jazzy, beat-poet style, Amram waxed for 15 minutes with "some of the most incredible stuff I have ever heard anybody anywhere say about anything," Steve later told WFMT-FM's Studs Terkel. "He got into the book and into the nature of man's existential struggle and talking about the 19th century and Melville and how it related to everything. It was grand." Amram recalls it more modestly as merely "sinking the big harpoon of destiny into the whale of truth. It didn't really mean anything, but it was kind of a funny image, quasi-intellectual, trying to be poetic, and it went on and on."

Listening to Amram, Steve said he was thinking, "In a minute, it is going to be my turn, and I am up the creek. It's all over now." He said he tried to summon anything he could remember about the book. "It wasn't much," he said. "All I kept seeing was ... the tattoos on Queequeg in the lithograph that was in the first copy of *Moby Dick* I ever had, and I saw Gregory Peck (who played Captain Ahab in the 1956 film) and his wooden leg." Finally, what dawned on him was the novel's first line. "So I sang, 'Call me Ishmael,' and it sort of bailed it out, and the two of us ended up having this song."

The session not only forged a bond ("friends for life," Amram says), but it also provided grist for a composition that several months later Steve polished into a rocking blues that summed up the whaling epic in just over three minutes. The title, "Moby Book," Steve later claimed, stemmed from a friend who had to deliver a grammar-school book report on the novel. The friend was so flustered that he stood up and stammered, "The name of my dick is Moby

David Amram invokes signature shtick, playing two flutes in a harmonic flourish, during the 1974 Mariposa Folk Festival held on idyllic Centre Island in Toronto Harbour.

(Photo by Shirley Gibson)

With Steve smiling at the trick, Leo Kottke rolls each of his eyes independently of the other while the musicians were backstage at an early-1970s co-billing. Kottke marveled at Steve's fortitude in the face of leukemia, "that center of him, that grown-up thing that seems to have happened early on."

(Photo by James Black, courtesy of Leo Kottke)

3: Another summertime Canadian gathering one year later, the Winnipeg Folk Festival on July 18-20, 1975, was the catalyst for an airborne meeting between Steve and Johnny Cash, who was headed to Winnipeg to play a July 18 show at Centennial Concert Hall. Aboard a plane from Chicago were festival performers, sitting in coach, and Cash's band and family in first class. "Cash had recorded 'City of New Orleans,' so everyone knew Steve, and little girl Carters kept coming back to get Steve's autograph," says Steve's harmonica player, Saul Broudy, who chatted with Cash's guitarist, Carl Perkins. At Cash's invitation, Steve and Broudy joined the Cash clan backstage before Cash's show that night, then headed to the festival the next day.

Book." Steve frequently dedicated the song to the capsulized study guides (some dubbed them "cheaters") called *Cliffs Notes* — "sort of like if *Cliffs Notes* were written by Willie Dixon."

When Steve called Amram and sang the finished "Moby Book" to him, Amram was stunned. "My gosh, man," he told Steve. "That's incredible that you could find what really had some value out of all that and be able to combine it with the lines that you did."

"Well, I cut out a lot of my stuff, too," Steve replied. "David, remember, songwriting is a craft, not an art."

None of Amram's Mariposa rap made its way into the song, but Steve gave him a co-writing credit nonetheless. "I couldn't remember a darn thing that David had written of it," Steve said, "(but) I could never have done anything with the song if he hadn't laid all of that good stuff on everybody."

The song's genesis was something hoped for by everyone attending and performing at a folk festival — one that was built into legend because Steve enshrined it. [3] "With Steve, magic happened primarily because he was wide open to doing whatever and just whizzing through," says Canadian music publicist Richard Flohil. "He didn't have reservations about being on a stage with a bunch of strangers, and he had the facility, imagination and sense of humor to willingly make an ass of himself."

A more haunting magic moment came less than three weeks after Mariposa, on July 9, following the triple billing of Megan McDonough, Steve and the closer, Leo Kottke, at the Mississippi River Festival at Southern Illinois University in Edwardsville, across the river from St. Louis. After delivering an acclaimed show for 3,000 attendees, Steve and Kottke talked of visiting a tavern in the college town, the Stagger Inn Again, because someone had told Kottke that his Capitol single of Tom T. Hall's "Pamela Brown" was on the jukebox. "That made it the second jukebox in the United States that I knew of that had me on it," Kottke says.

Kottke hesitated to go. "I'd feel sort of conspicuous," he told Steve.

"What a wuss," Steve snorted in return.

So the two ambled in, and someone dropped a quarter in the jukebox to play "Pamela Brown." By the end of the first chorus, the whole bar was singing. "I wanted to run away," Kottke says. "I couldn't handle it. I don't know why. But again, Steve wouldn't let me run away. He said, 'Fuck you. C'mon.' " The two sat in chairs, "surrounded by a bunch of drunks." Someone had a guitar, and Kottke agreed to play. He handed Steve the guitar to give him a turn, but Steve declined. So Kottke turned the tables and said, "Look, you got me in here." Finally, Steve acceded.

The next day, Kottke learned from Al Bunetta that after a concert Steve sometimes swelled up because of his leukemia treatments, and it hurt him to play guitar. "I didn't know that, and he went right ahead and did it," Kottke says. "But it's that center of him, that grown-up thing that seems to have happened early on. He was just all there. There wasn't anything left to be done."

Steve summoned the same fortitude in New York that summer when he and Bunetta were eating dinner at an Upper East Side Japanese restaurant near Sloan-Kettering. Steve excused himself to go into the restroom, and after an extended wait, Bunetta got up to investigate. He found Steve in the stall, awash in vomit and in misery. "He was all colors — yellow, green, red — and I was wiping him down, trying to get his coveralls back on so we could leave." Steve managed to issue an admonition: "Don't call an ambulance." So Bunetta phoned for a limo. The driver arrived, and as he and Bunetta walked Steve out of the restroom, a woman "looked up with fear on her face," Bunetta says. A nauseated mess, Steve pierced her disquiet with a quip: "Don't eat the fish." [4]

The same wit emerged when Steve co-headlined a high-profile benefit for social services offered by the Jane Addams Hull House in Chicago. John Prine and Arlo Guthrie (playing the Quiet Knight that weekend) also shared the stage, but because of the stunner of the day and some quick thinking, the show's cleverest moment came from Steve. It was on Sunday night, Sept. 8, one month after the Watergate-sodden Richard Nixon had resigned the presidency. The morning of the benefit, Nixon's handpicked replacement, Gerald Ford, told a national TV audience he had granted Nixon a full pardon for crimes he may have committed in office. The move was instantly unpopular, and Steve saw his chance. When he walked onstage, says singer/songwriter Thom Bishop, Steve launched into a Bill Trader song that Elvis Presley had made famous, "(Now and Then There's) A Fool Such as I." The punch line lay in the first words of the song's opening line: "Pardon me if I'm sentimental ..." [5]

It was an acerbic example of risk-taking, and a lesson for the scene's newcomers, who included Bryan Bowers, a self-taught autoharpist under Earl Pionke's wing who had been busking in Seattle for a living. After the 6-foot-4 bearded

4: Steve used wit and warmth that year in coping with a fledgling journalist prior to a show at Charlotte's Web northwest of Chicago. On a dare, Beth Austin, 16-year-old reporter for the Rockford East High *Highlights*, made Steve the subject of her first-ever interview, on a dingy backstage couch. As she pulled out a notebook, her hands quaked. "What are you shaking for?" Steve asked. "I'm not so smart." Austin ventured ahead with attempts to confirm Steve's birthdate and hometown, but Steve stopped her. "You're only asking me questions you know the answers for," he said. "Why don't you ask me something you don't already know?" A typical teen's query came to her mind: If he could be reborn as an animal, which one would he be? "I'd be a goat," Steve replied, "because they're eclectic." Austin ended the interview by asking Steve what epitaph he would like on his tombstone. After a moment's thought, he smiled as he delivered the answer: "What are you doing standing here in a graveyard when you could be out having a good time?"

5: Steve met Presley in about 1974 when Earl Pionke took Steve, the Holstein brothers and others on a gambling trip to Las Vegas. At 2 a.m., after Pionke introduced himself, The King invited the Chicago troupe to his craps table. For an hour and a half they bantered while Presley and Pionke played blackjack.

On Sunday afternoon, Aug. 25, 1974, John Prine "and the Fabulous Torpedoes" were billed for a two-hour set at the 1974 Philadelphia Folk Festival mainstage — and a big treat was that the unbilled Steve turned up to accompany Prine for much of that time. At one point (right) Steve performed a song on his own while Prine took a break with a can of beer.
(Photos by Jody Kolodzey)

and burly minstrel played a dazzling walk-on set at the University of Chicago Folk Festival, Bowers' virtuosity on the unusual instrument generated instant buzz. It was a rough-hewn talent, however, so when Bowers met Steve, in 1973 while playing a club in Denver, he did so with trepidation, because Steve's stature preceded him.

"This guy Stevie Goodman, multiple threat — sings, writes, entertains, great player, great entertainer, great human being," Bowers says. "I thought, 'Jeez, oh man, they should have drowned this guy at birth. He'll make everybody else feel bad for being alive.' And then I met him, and he was everything they said and then some."

Bowers valued Steve's empathetic tutelage, which began at the Earl of Old Town, where Steve watched Bowers play and pulled him aside for a quiet beer.

"Y'know, Bryan," Steve said, "I love what you do, but you don't have to hit a home run every time."

"What do you mean?"

"Well, I've seen you the last three nights, and you're basically goin' with all your aces," Steve said. "You don't take many chances."

"Stevie, I was a street singer six months ago. I'm scared to death to lay an egg, and I am ecstatic to have a real audience to play to and a P.A. to play through instead of playin' in traffic, so I'm tryin' to give it my best shot every night."

"Fine," Steve replied, "but you don't have to hit a home run every night. Take a few chances. Try something you're not sure of. Do your aces, too, but take some chances every night, every set."

It was "wise counsel," Bowers says, from "the best single entertainer I ever saw, and I've seen some great ones. God almighty, he wrote really good songs, he could sing like a bandit, he could play with anybody, he played his own stuff great, and he could make you laugh, make you get involved. You put all that together, it was just irresistible. Stevie's throwaway shows, the shows he wouldn't claim as a musician, were still so good that any one of us normal musicians would die for."

Bowers, who soon began sharing the stage with Steve, asked him in another private moment, this time at Somebody Else's Troubles, "What do you do when you have a bad show?"

"I don't ever have any bad shows," Steve said, poker-faced.

"Right," Bowers replied in kind. "Me either."

Both erupted in uproarious laughter, slapping each other on the back. When the two had regained composure, Bowers said, "No, what do you really do?"

"I'll tell you," Steve said, "but you've gotta tell me first."

"OK, fair enough," Bowers said. "When I have a bad show, I try not to let on to the fans who come up and say 'Oh, great show' that I knew I was out of tune or out of time or forgot a lyric. I try not to lay it on them that I didn't think I was 100 percent. And I don't let on to the club owner or the festival promoter that I did anything less. I just think to myself, 'I've gotta improve always.' Then

Bryan Bowers received perceptive advice about performing from Steve: "You don't have to hit a home run every night. ... Take some chances every night, every set."
(Photo by Paul Natkin)

Tom Dundee got a warning from Steve to beware of free drinks and the seduction of applause. Steve had such regard for Dundee that he gave the singer/songwriter the guitar on which he wrote many of his earliest songs, including "City of New Orleans."

(Photo by Art Thieme)

6: Steve admonished friend and fellow performer Harry Waller: "Remember in Woolworth's when they had the parakeets and the ladder? The bird gets to the top, the thing spins to the bottom, the bird flaps a little bit and climbs back up and gets to the next-to-the-last rung, and the thing falls. That's show business, the parakeet on the ladder."

I drive slowly and carefully all the way to the motel when I'm really in a mood to floor it and be reckless, because I'm mad and angry at myself. After I get to the motel, I go in the room, I close the door, and I lock it, and I turn the lights out, and I go into the bathroom, and I turn the light on, and I start talking to myself in the mirror."

Steve flew across the table and hugged the towering Bowers.

"I do the same thing!" Steve said. "I hate it when I have a bad show."

The key, Steve said, invariably was the forthcoming night. "The great ones always come back better than ever," he said. "When you lay an egg, you better come back stronger than ever because this ain't a right. This is a privilege."

Steve also knew the value of not taking the enterprise too seriously. Byron Roche, singer/guitarist who moved to Chicago from St. Louis, recalls Steve's typical retort when congratulated for having "made it" in the music world. "Man," Steve said, "you never make it. You just keep making it."

Tom Dundee — a Chicago singer/songwriter whose gentle missive against discouragement, "A Delicate Balance," would soon leave its mark in the hands of the Seattle-based folk duo Reilly & Maloney — heard a similarly pointed homily from Steve in the back room of the Earl of Old Town.

Steve told Dundee that someone once advised him to beware of two things. Holding up a half-empty rum and Coke, Steve rattled a solitary ice cube in the glass. "This is one," Steve said. "There'll always be a drink, and it's always free. People will buy it for you to get next to you."

Then Steve set down the drink on an old freezer case. "This is the other," he said, clapping his hands together slowly, "almost morbidly," perhaps three or four times. "The minute you believe this," he said, "you're finished." [6]

In the fall of 1974, Steve was anything but finished. His openers included a show by newly touted songwriter Wendy Waldman, who recalls the "nightmare" of following such a "warm and sweet but sidesplitting" act. "It's like, 'Oh, I love him, but don't put me there! He's gonna slaughter me, and he doesn't mean to, but I'm gonna get slaughtered.' I was nowhere near his caliber, but I loved him, and we got along really well."

Steve's "City of New Orleans" got yet another mainstream boost that fall from an unlikely source, TV's intrepid investigative reporter Geraldo Rivera, who started hosting a recurring, late-night counter-culture magazine as a rotating installment of ABC's "Wide World of Entertainment." The show took its title from the train tune's final chorus, "Good Night America." In each episode were aired recorded snippets of the song by Steve, Arlo Guthrie, John Denver, Judy Collins and others, says Marty Berman, executive producer. Rivera himself even once warbled the refrain on the air. "We loved the song. We used it all the time, in virtually every bumper," Berman says, referring to the show's fade-ins and fade-outs. "We felt like Steve wrote it just for us."

Ironically that fall, in what was the longest TV performance of his career thus far, Steve didn't get to sing "City of New Orleans." The non-opportunity came in a one-hour episode of a concert series produced by Ken Ehrlich at

Chicago public-TV station WTTW. Formerly titled "Made in Chicago," the program had been renamed "Soundstage" for the Public Broadcasting Service (PBS), which had purchased the series that September and was feeding it to the network's 240 stations across the country. The episode with Steve, filmed Nov. 11, also showcased two prominent out-of-towners: Arlo Guthrie as quasi-host and singer/songwriter Hoyt Axton. The episode was dubbed "Arlo's Gang."

With the flashiest clothing of the three, including a tan cowboy hat and blue tie-dyed jacket, Guthrie was clearly the headliner, opening with a couple of songs tweaking the recently resigned Richard Nixon, then accompanied himself on piano to sing Steve's "City." Axton, the 36-year-old songwriter ("The No No Song" for Ringo Starr, "The Pusher" for Steppenwolf and Three Dog Night's #1 hit "Joy to the World"), brought a stature rivaling that of Guthrie. His simulated shambling and brash banter ("This is as together as I ever get") nearly stole the show.

In contrast, though he received equal time during the hour, Steve was largely speechless between songs. Dressed in an olive green jacket and white shirt and wearing a short mustache and beard, Steve was oddly subdued, even on livelier tunes, looking as much at the floor and his guitar as he did the audience. Nonetheless, the TV lens conveyed Steve's warmth and vulnerability, especially on softer material. He picked with Guthrie on the railroad-themed "Boomer's Story," chipped in a guitar solo in Axton's "Boney Fingers" and sang two verses of the Bob Dylan tune "Walkin' Down the Line" and a verse of the Leadbelly closer, "Goodnight Irene." In his own mid-show set, Steve performed "Door Number Three" and "Would You Like to Learn to Dance?" The latter song stilled the crowd to silence.

Most impressive was Steve's rousing opener, the charming 1933 Billy Mayhew standard, "It's a Sin to Tell a Lie." Seemingly entranced by his guitar break, his eyes affixed themselves to the frets, and his head waggled like a bobbing-head doll. Just as his versions of "Goody Goody" and "Lady Be Good" had proved, "Sin" drew from an earlier generation's show tunes to become one of Steve's anticipated trademarks. [7] Overall, the program was a coup for the hometowner, elevating him for a highbrow national audience numbering in the millions.

On the road in 1974, Steve found inspiration to write another uptempo crowd-pleaser. While playing an Aug. 28-31 gig at the newly opened Max's Concert Club in Indianapolis, Steve stayed at the Quality Courts Motor Inn. In later concerts, Steve claimed that because the Oscar Mayer Wienermobile was parked in front of the motel, he dreamed he won the Indianapolis 500 while driving the outlandish vehicle. "No pit stops," he said dryly. "We stopped twice for mustard and relish." The dream, he said, helped inspire him to write what became the light-hearted "This Hotel Room." [8]

Borrowing from Andrew Jenkins' train song "Ben Dewberry's Final Run" and the African-American traditional ditty "Shortnin' Bread," Steve's new composition amounted to a laundry list of items found in the typical room of a motel. "I wrote down everything that was in the room, and it rhymed," he said

I wrote down everything that was in the room, and it rhymed.
STEVE GOODMAN

7: Steve sometimes combined "Sin," "Goody Goody" and "Lady Be Good" as a medley. Don Wessel, who opened for Steve at Dickinson College in Pennsylvania as part of the group Hatdance, says Steve's version of "Sin" was a revelation. "It opened up a world for us, taking a jazz standard and making it something a folkie could appreciate and love," he says. "Until that point, we were playing Neil Young and the Beatles and writing our own songs. It was like, 'You mean the stuff my dad used to listen to is cool?' Steve just stood on that bridge so strongly."

8: At times, Steve added to "This Hotel Room" a silly couplet that referenced its genesis: "Every time my feet start draggin' / I hop in the Oscar Mayer wiener wagon."

countless times in explaining the song's origin. The list built to ironic juxtapositions ("a porcelain throne and an aluminum sink," "a *Holy Bible* and a *TV Guide* / Great God almighty, it's a *TV Guide*"). It also immortalized a hucksterish remnant of 1960s Americana, the 250,000 Magic Fingers machines that for 15 minutes jiggled a motel bed's occupants to a supposedly relaxing sleep — for a price. As Steve sang, "Put in the quarter, turn out the lights / Magic Fingers make you feel all right." (Steve later told WNEW-FM's Vin Scelsa that in his travels he often found the machines to be broken. "It sounds like a wonderful idea," but "even when they work, they don't really work," Steve said. "They build you up for it, I guess — the grand setup.")

At times, Steve insinuated that the song had an alternate title, "Sanitized for Your Protection," in honor of the message on the paper loop that housekeepers slipped over a motel room's toilet seat. What elevated the tune beyond a tiny travelogue, however, was its last verse, in which the narrator had "had enough" of the room and telephoned his "baby," asking her to light a candle and place it in her window to welcome him home. A funny near-trifle thus became a love song, a pattern he would follow in later tunes to similarly touching effect.

The innocent picture painted by "This Hotel Room" notwithstanding, life as a frequent traveler was a mixed experience for Steve. He made it a rule not to skimp on fine food when touring, in part to offset the inevitable geographical disorientation. [9] "There's times I don't even know what city I'm in," Steve told Fred Holstein. Road life also offered Steve stereotypical challenges and temptations. Illegal drugs were rampant — part of the music "culture" — and Steve often smoked marijuana, sometimes securing joints from associates and those who put on his concerts and radio appearances.

Cocaine was a rare but real part of Steve's repertoire as well. One joke that made the rounds, apparently grounded in reality, was that once when Steve played the Earl of Old Town, someone passed him a note that read, "Good news: Your fly is up. Bad news: Your coke is on the floor." But fellow musicians recall that they consumed far greater quantities of hard-core drugs than did Steve. Jim Tullio, bass player who toured and recorded with Steve and found him to be "always really together," says that "back when cocaine wasn't evil," Steve almost made its ingestion into a game. On the road, Tullio says, Steve would bring out the white powder and say, "Man, I got some coke." He then would take one sniff, "the tiniest hit," and say, "Oh, this is the greatest. Here, guys," and offer it around. "He'd get it for everybody else," Tullio says. [10]

Perhaps more troubling about his road life, however, was that Steve, like other musicians, was not always sexually true to his marriage. Of his countless friends and colleagues, some knew this, but many did not, probably because it was well-hidden and sporadic. Another factor was that Steve sold faithfulness so well in his songs that few wanted to believe he would behave otherwise. Most who observed his occasional adultery are loath to identify themselves because they had such high regard for him, and spoken or not, hedged any harsh judgment of it because of his leukemia.

> **It sounds like a wonderful idea, (but) even when they work, they don't really work. They build you up for it, I guess, the grand setup.**
> **STEVE GOODMAN**

9: Besides eating well on the road, Steve insisted on paying for his accompanists' food. Lew London recalls a rare night when he reciprocated by holding Steve's guitar hostage in his car trunk. "You've treated me to probably 100 dinners, some of them pretty expensive," London told Steve. "This is the best restaurant I know of in South Jersey. If you even go for your credit card, I won't give your guitar back."

10: Steel guitarist Winnie Winston recalled that before going onstage one night during an Eastern tour, Steve sat at a table, sniffed a line of cocaine, stood up and said, "Oh, shit. What am I going to tell my kids? 'Sorry, I can't afford college. Daddy put it all up his nose.'" Then Steve laughed and shrugged, a signal to Winston that he was "an intermittent recreational user," not a junkie.

"He had an awful lot of girlfriends," said one musician who was close to Steve for many years but detached himself in some ways. "He did as much philandering as any rock star or touring guy ever did. He didn't put it in my face. I found out later. ... There's an aspect to my personality, a certain ignorance and naïveté, that really was in full force in the 'Steve Goodman, what's he doing with the ladies?' part of life."

Understandably, given his stage presence, some of "the ladies" found Steve tremendously attractive. "I remember wanting to make out with him desperately, but that was never going to be," says singer/songwriter Sally Fingerett. "He was cute, he was Jewish, oh my God, he was perfect husband material. He was a fabulously married guy. That's what made him such a catch. He was so honorable and so wonderful and so terrific. He was my Elvis. He made me weak in the knees, he really did."

Steve easily wore a "puppy-dog look" in the presence of attractive women, notes Jeff Beamsley of the Amazingrace co-op. New York folksinger Perry Barber, who says she didn't go beyond being a friend to Steve, often saw that winsomeness. "He was a little teddy bear," she says, "just very huggable, and you wanted to squeeze him and pal around with him and make everything all right for him. He was just cute. There was something very childlike and warm about him always that invited warmth from people." [11]

Steve Cohen, Steve's road manager for a year and a half, says that while he saw no evidence of straying, he noticed a "mothering instinct" directed at Steve by some women. "What were minor flirtations or could have been something more, they weren't this kind of hopped-up, drug-fueled, swinging-from-the-chandeliers, wearing-costumes-of-black-leather sexual escapades," Cohen says. "They were more of the lonely guy out on the road with someone that was being really sweet."

But multi-instrumentalist Ken Bloom, among others, insists that Steve, in contrast to many male musicians he observed in that era, didn't scavenge for women in an audience to pursue them afterward. "It was not his style," Bloom says. "At some of these gigs, there would be all of these women around, and he would do everything he could to get away. When a show was over, he really wanted a little bit of peace and quiet."

Chicago folksinger Brian Gill witnessed Steve making leading comments about women, but only as the setup for a "gotcha" punch line.

"Boy, she's a knockout," Steve confided to Gill while eyeing a waitress one night at Somebody Else's Troubles.

"Yeah, man," Gill replied, "she does look great, doesn't she?"

"But always remember this," Steve said. "The best stuff is always at home."

Still, incidents recalled by others throughout Steve's marriage point to more than mere dalliances. A radio personality remembers Steve leaving a concert with a "cute blonde" in tow. A journalist recalls Steve introducing to him two "lovely" young women whom Steve said were accompanying him to ease the suffering from his disease. "They just hold and comfort me at night when it's

Singer/songwriters Sally Fingerett and Brian Gill, an item for awhile in 1970s Chicago, were among Steve's many admirers. The feelings of Fingerett echoed those of folkscene women for the married Steve: "I remember wanting to make out with him desperately, but that was never going to be." To Gill, Steve emphasized, "Always remember this: The best stuff is always at home." (Photo by Art Thieme)

11: Barber also got a dose of Steve's humor following a painful turn of events in 1975. Trapped by a stalker, Barber had swallowed a spoon and later required surgery to remove it. Steve, who heard from mutual friend Steve Burgh about Barber's hospitalization, sent to her room a flower basket with a note: "Fork it!"

too painful for me to sleep," Steve said. A TV producer remembers groupies in Steve's dressing room during a taping. A waitress recalls Steve giving her "the leukemia look, like this might be my last night on earth." A club proprietor recounts his chagrin upon learning that Steve elected to spend two nights with the club's female cook. A singer relates that Steve once visited her apartment with others, apparently "hoping to be invited to spend the night." She wanted him to leave, but he stayed for most of the day, he admitted to her later, because "he was hoping to score. But it wasn't going to happen. For all I know, he could have been saying it to boost my ego."

Music publicist Richard Flohil also recalls "an exceedingly raunchy night on the town" with Steve and another associate. "It was one of the most memorable and silly and humorous nights I can remember, and how Steve, at all of 5-foot-2-inches, could chat three girls into a hotel room simultaneously is one of the miracles of modern life. I think that's about as far as I could go — the code of the road and all that shit."

Whatever the specifics, Steve's periodic unfaithfulness was hard on Nancy. Her brother, Robert Pruter, indelicately volunteers that Steve's attitude toward his leukemia figured in their dynamic. "Steve knew he was under a death sentence," Pruter says. "He only had so much time to live. My sister related this to me, that he was going to enjoy life to the utmost while he had those years, so he was going to fuck to the utmost. He was going to have girlfriends, he was going to have mistresses. My sister had to accept it, but I don't think she ever liked it. She would always have to be going to the doctor to get something cleared up, and the doctor would say, 'Will you tell your husband to use a condom?' "

Jessie Goodman, reflecting in her early 30s on what she's heard over the years about her dad's sexual behavior in the pre-AIDS era and her mother's steadfastness on the home front, offers an assessment that is blunt, perhaps heartbreaking: "He was a musician. It was his job to fuck around, y'know. But she thought as long as the emotional love was there that it was OK."

Observations of hundreds of cohorts and Steve's own avowals indicate that his "emotional love" for Nancy indeed was robust, unyielding and full of pride and gratitude. In a 1977 interview with *Come for to Sing*, Steve said of Nancy, "There's nothin' like her. That's the privatest stuff in the world, what I feel for her. Never felt that anywhere at anytime, before or since." [12]

Jeany Walker, Steve's would-be girlfriend in 1969 before he met Nancy, had a revealing exchange with him a dozen years later.

"My God, Steve, how did you survive being on the road all this time?" Walker asked.

"There was every possible thing always offered to me: drugs, sex, everything. It was always there offered," Steve replied. "My marriage survived that. I made it through all that."

Steve put it more strongly — with a tone as contrite as it was grateful — during a 1983 interview with NBC-TV's "First Camera." Praising Nancy's patient approach to their marriage, he said, "I've done everything I possibly could

There was every possible thing always offered to me: drugs, sex, everything. ... My marriage survived that.
STEVE GOODMAN

12: "He loved his wife more than breath," says Chet Hanson, who booked shows for Steve throughout the 1970s. Steve's depth of feeling, Hanson says, also doubled as a wicked pun: "He was always talking about the fact that he married way over his head."

over the years to blow this, and I still haven't, and so it's pretty amazing that she's as strong as she is."

In December 1974, Steve's marriage received significant fortification: Sloan-Kettering had weaned Steve from chemo and other maintenance meds, launching him into a period of dormancy called remission. "They cut me off," Steve said, "mostly because they didn't know what the hell else to do, and they couldn't really tell if there was a difference between six years and seven years of therapy." He still needed to fly to New York regularly for bone-marrow draws and other tests, but this was a new stage of his experimental treatment that all involved found hopeful. [13]

Not coincidentally, Steve and Nancy soon made a delightful discovery that offered Steve a potential future Steve hadn't let himself glimpse over the previous six years and that was to bind him to Nancy more closely than ever. The development was the very definition of unexpected: Nancy was pregnant.

Given the fears of deformed children posed by Sloan-Kettering in previous years, the news could have been ominous. But experience was already proving otherwise for other young male survivors on Ewing 8 who increasingly doubted their need to use birth control.

"One day, we checked everybody's sperm count, and people didn't have any viable sperm," says Dr. Isabel "Bonnie" Cunningham, the unit's record-keeper at the time. "We didn't know anything about sperm then, and we said, 'Oh, well, you're sterile, so it's OK.' Of course, all that means was, around the time the chemotherapy was given, momentarily the people were aspermic. Nine months later, a bunch of babies started coming along."

Today, it's well understood that certain drugs and stress can interrupt sperm production, "but that doesn't mean that two weeks later they're not going to have fabulous sperm," Cunningham says. "Once the first baby was born, somebody else had a baby, and somebody else," she says. "It turned out that the chemotherapy does not deform children. But until the first baby is born normal, you don't know these things."

Excited by the prospect of Nancy giving birth the following summer to a healthy child that he'd fathered, Steve was eager to spread the word. One of those he telephoned was Miami singer/guitarist George Blackwell. "The gun went off, and I didn't even hear it," Steve told him with glee. "I thought I'd been shootin' blanks."

The news moved quickly through the music community. "I was tremendously moved when Nancy got pregnant," says guitarist Jack McGann's companion Ann Mintz. "That was such a miracle. Everybody knew that whole story, and everybody was really thrilled for them."

Dad-to-be status held multi-faceted significance for Steve, says singer/songwriter Raun MacKinnon (now Burnham), who later accompanied Steve on recordings and in shows. Toward musical friends, Steve already had displayed "father-esque" qualities, she says, "and he felt really fortunate to express those to his immediate family." To reproduce with Nancy gave his paternalism

It turned out that the chemotherapy does not deform children. But until the first baby is born normal, you don't know these things.
DR. ISABEL 'BONNIE' CUNNINGHAM

13: Steve's hopefulness extended to advice for Lynn Barron, the daughter of his Chicago physician, Gene Handelman. When Barron, 27, was diagnosed with cancer in her right cheek, Steve and his wife Nancy visited her at Weiss hospital in Chicago before she trekked to Sloan-Kettering for surgery and radiation. "You're in the best hands," Steve said. "Some of the rooms are a little shabby, but don't worry about it. You'll be getting the best care in the world." Her treatment was successful.

Pregnancy was happy news for Steve and Nancy (right, shown in 1974), and Steve's naming of a new tune for their adopted daughter, Jessie (shown in 1974) was a prescient gift.

(Left photo by Margaret Southern, right photo courtesy of Robert Pruter)

14: Occasionally, Steve and Nancy brought Jessie downtown to Riccardo's for a late-night dinner, and when guitarist Marv Berkman and accordionist Bobby Rossi played Greek tunes from "Never on Sunday," Steve tossed Jessie onto his shoulders and danced around the restaurant. In later years, when introducing the "Jig," Steve sometimes added his two other daughters to the song's subtitle, with "Sarah's Stomp" and "Rosanna's Reel." Interestingly, in 1973 folksinger Malvina Reynolds had written "The Rigatoni Song" with Jessie in mind. The tune's lyrics included: "I know a little girl / She likes to dance and sing … She calls this thing my rigatar / … So while I play a rigatoon / we'll rig-a-jig-jig a round."

a deeper dimension, she said. "It was validation. He and Nancy loved Jessie, but you figure there were all sorts of things about him siring that kid. It meant that he was in remission."

With an ear-to-ear grin and bulging eyes, Steve told his former Lake Forest classmate Lucy Wells, "Isn't it great? We can have our own kids now!" To Wells, herself embarking on motherhood at the time, Steve's ebullience made perfect sense. "He had this absolute joy in remission in telling me that they were making babies. In the threshold of that era of feminism, these were still important things that guys could voice without someone yelling him down."

In this context, what Steve did musically was an act of prescient generosity. One afternoon near Christmas 1974, Bill Swofford sat with Steve in the front room of the Bittersweet Place flat, Swofford playing chords to a simple, major-scale song and Steve conjuring a melody. But their kids — 2-1/2-year-old Jessie and Swofford's two adopted children, Beth, 11, and Rob, 8 — were "driving them crazy," says Swofford's wife, Margaret. So Nancy and Margaret decided to take the three kids for a downtown outing. They chose an attraction Beth and Rob had never seen, the view from the 94th floor of the John Hancock Center.

When the troupe returned, Steve had fashioned a bridge for the song, and for their captive audience the two picked and strummed their creation, "a nice, two-guitar thing," as Steve put it. While the adults joked that any explanation of the song should say that it was "written while Nancy and Margaret took the kids to the top of the John," Jessie engaged in what she usually did when her dad played guitar — she danced in circles. The title thus became a natural: "Jessie's Jig," accompanied in parentheses by similarly alliterative phrases, "Rob's Romp, Beth's Bounce." [14]

By naming the song for his adopted first child, Steve thought he might include it on his first Asylum record. As he did with the two photos of her on the cover of his "Troubles" LP, he could give Jessie enduring recognition — at a time when a child he had helped conceive was about to enter the world. It amounted to a gesture of warmth and support to counter society's prejudice against adoptees.

It also fit in with a shift to a promising chapter of Steve's life. With Buddah and Paul Anka behind him and chemo at least temporarily set aside, the road ahead looked bright. Steve even had begun dieting to lose weight, laying off cognac starting Sept. 3, 1974. "I'm sick of being fat," he told Atlantic City dobro player and mandolinist Lew London. [15] Transcending the whimsy of his "Chicken Cordon Bleus," Steve, along with Nancy and the Swoffords, joined the nearby Rainbow Grocery co-op and started shunning meaty and buttery fare in favor of more veggies. Nancy, backed by her nursing courses, had "finally won him over about good eating," Margaret Swofford says, "and they got on that health bandwagon." The good vibes continued at the Earl of Old Town on the final night of 1974, [16] when Steve and Bill Swofford gave the "Jig" its public debut. With or without a contract, Steve already was making plans for recording his next album in the dormant days of January.

Once more, however, loomed the question of a producer. Without a contract, Steve had no formal guidance from Asylum, so he resumed shopping around. Because Arif Mardin at Atlantic had produced the "Troubles" LP on weekends and only as a favor, Steve felt there was "no chance" of securing his help. He asked veteran soundman Phil Ramone — for whom he had recorded a demo tape in 1971 and who had produced recent albums by Paul Simon ("There Goes Rhymin' Simon") and Michael Johnson ("There Is a Breeze") and engineered the just-released, high-selling Asylum tour LP from Bob Dylan (now back on Columbia) and The Band — but Ramone was busy. Steve joined with Steve Boone, bass player from the Lovin' Spoonful, to hire musicians and book time at a Baltimore studio, but the studio owed back rent and shut down. He considered engineer Gene Paul, son of the legendary Les Paul, for a New York session, but the price was too steep.

Steve turned to a fellow singer/songwriter whose third and most recent Asylum album was high on the *Billboard* chart, Jackson Browne, who told Steve that recording in Southern California was as expensive as in New York. "The only reason I record in Los Angeles is because I live there," Browne told Steve. "Why don't you record in Chicago?"

The question — with its implication that Steve had been caught up in a "second city" deference to the coasts — threw Steve. "I had to admit," he said, "that it made more sense than anything else anybody had said to me." So he called Paragon Recording Studios, where he'd recorded three cuts for the 1971 "Gathering at the Earl of Old Town" record, and got a deal he "couldn't refuse." He secured the engineering help of Chicago's Barry Mraz (who had produced Styx and just helmed the funk-band Ohio Players' "Fire" LP), booked the studio for 10 days in late January and early February and decided to produce and finance the project himself. "He felt he had enough experience in the studio, as both an artist and a sideman, that he could do it," said guitarist Steve Burgh.

It was an unusual step, absent upfront money from the record label. "It was

With a Limber Jack dancing wooden man made by future road manager Steve Cohen, Steve entertains Jessie and Rob Swofford (the mummy) on Halloween 1974, two months after deciding to lose weight.
(Photo by Bill "Oliver" Swofford courtesy of Margaret Southern)

15: Saul Broudy had introduced London to Steve, and the two bonded partly because London, at 5-foot-3, was only an inch taller than Steve. "Lewie," Steve said, "we gotta form an organization called Tiny Lib, and our motto is going to be, 'We're the last ones to get wet when it rains.' " London kidded back, "Yeah, but we'll be the first ones to drown."

16: On this New Year's Eve, one of Steve's openers, Charles Fleischer, arrived at the Earl dressed like a rabbit, dipping a carrot in patrons' beers and munching it. Onstage, he played "La Marseillaise," the French national anthem, on a douche bag. The wild comedian 14 years later became the title voice for the animated film "Who Framed Roger Rabbit?"

Still reeling from the loss of performing partner Homer Haynes, Jethro Burns became part of Steve's 1975 LP recording session in Chicago.

(Photo courtesy of Liz Danzig Derry)

17: A steel-guitar instruction manual that Winston and Bill Keith published in 1976 exemplified Winston's mastery and sold 30,000 copies. During the "Jig" sessions, Winston, an industrial-design professor, and Steve Burgh installed a fancy stereo system on the mantelpiece in Steve Goodman's apartment. "Honey, come in and look at this," Steve called to his wife, Nancy, who replied, "That's very nice, Stevie. Are you going to be able to reach it?" Steve looked at Winston and said, "Shit, just when I think I'm gettin' to be a good rock 'n'roll star, she knows how to stick it in pretty good."

90 percent sure that Asylum was going to buy it, but there was no contract, so we were all gambling," Steve said. "It was close. We hemmed and hawed. We sweated a little bit."

The huge cadre of players would have made anyone sweat. "I flew in guys that I really wanted to hear on it," Steve said, referring to his "Troubles" LP accompanists Burgh, Hugh McDonald and Jeff Gutcheon, as well as legendary Nashville fiddler Vassar Clements, two New Yorkers (cellist Abby Newton and singer and vocal arranger Raun MacKinnon) and a Philadelphia pair he'd met at folk festivals, Saul Broudy on harmonica and steel-guitar virtuoso Julian "Winnie" Winston. [17] Among the locals he snagged were singers Bonnie Koloc and Diane Holmes, multi-instrumentalist Ken Bloom and, for an extended session the night of Jan. 16, the seemingly ageless African-American string band of Martin, Bogan & Armstrong.

One local talent, electric guitarist Johnny Burns, was the go-between for Steve's enlistment of another musician — an Evanston resident and national legend, someone a generation older who eventually became Steve's constant musical accomplice. This newcomer to Steve's world was Burns' father, Kenneth "Jethro" Burns, the latter half of the duo Homer & Jethro.

Known for his 39-year partnership with guitarist Henry "Homer" Haynes, Burns was a humorist and musician of the most successful order. His deadpan jokes and peerless mandolin stylings, with influences ranging from country and classical to jazz and swing, were the bedrock of the pair's 35 albums and 300 singles that parodied top hits in their regular appearances on the "National Barn Dance" originating at Chicago's WLS radio and on TV shows hosted by Dean Martin and Tennessee Ernie Ford. They earned broad fame in the mid-1960s by guesting on "The Beverly Hillbillies" sitcom and creating a series of "Ooh, that's corny" spots for Kellogg's Corn Flakes. The act came to an abrupt halt, however, when Haynes, 53, died of a heart attack in August 1971, leaving Burns, 51, to ponder a potentially empty future.

"We were very worried whether he would get going, he was so depressed," Johnny Burns says. "It was terrible for him because he really lost a brother and, obviously, his career. He was so talented that he could carry on. It was just whether he had the will."

A sign of Burns' awakening came in 1974 when his son Johnny was performing as part of a house trio at the Earl of Old Town. One night, his group backed Steve during acoustic and electric sets that culminated with a walk-on from John Prine and a round of Hank Williams tunes. "My dad had come to the show with my mom," Johnny Burns says. "They came to the back room and wanted to meet Steve and John and say hi to the band." The most excited person in the tiny Star Cave was Steve.

"Oh, my God," Steve told the elder Burns, wide-eyed. "This is Jethro Burns. Homer & Jethro. I know all about your music and records. I could tell you your whole history. I saw you on the Steve Allen show. I saw you on the Johnny Carson show. I saw you on the Merv Griffin show. ..."

"He was all over my dad," Johnny Burns says. "He slammed him with his entire discography. My dad, of course, was incredibly flattered. He was a little skeptical about everything, but Dad was, of course, wrapped up in the fact that Steve was doing so many standards, right down Dad's alley."

Knowing that Burns no longer had a partner, Steve popped a question.

"Wow, if you're not doing anything some night, why don't you bring a mandolin?"

"OK," Burns said. "When?"

"Whenever."

"No," Burns said, eager for a commitment, "I need a date."

The date turned out to be Steve's LP recording sessions at Paragon, during which Burns provided mandolin licks on five songs, including a wild collaboration with Martin, Bogan & Armstrong on "Mama Don't Allow It." [18] That Steve called out the names of "Jethro" along with "Carl," "Ted" and "Howard" during the barely in-control "Mama" jam would send a clear message to the record's buyers. Those who had seen Steve in performance knew of his affection for songs of the past, but the elders' presence in the album sessions — and Steve's affectionate recognition of each — served as evidence of reverence for his roots. Here, Steve created a chance not only to play with seasoned musicians as old or older than his parents but also to pair his vocal and instrumental talents with theirs for posterity.

But while an older, folkie feel ran through the material that Steve brought to the sessions to record, the songs' themes and styles covered the musical map. This made the album as a whole — much the same as the "Troubles" LP — difficult to categorize. "You're either 'catholic' with a small 'c' in your tastes or 'eclectic,' " Steve put it years later with an almost rueful grin. "Those are the complimentary terms that are applied to what it is that I'm doing, and then the others are, 'Well, he has no focus.' " The musicality and emotional power of the selections, however, were undeniable.

Comic cuts included his old-timey "This Hotel Room," fueled by Jeff Gutcheon's barrelhouse piano and a smile-inducing bass-clarinet beat from Ken Bloom, and "Door Number Three," given a full-bore country treatment featuring Gutcheon's rolling keyboards and commanding strains of steel and fiddle by Winnie Winston and Vassar Clements. In the latter song, Steve inserted a nearly word-for-word steal from the 1965 Bob Dylan anthem "Like a Rolling Stone" that hilariously fit the tune's parody of game-show host Monty Hall: "He's not selling any alibis / when he stares into the vacuum of your eyes / and says, 'Do you wanta make a deal?' " Steve later told the British *Omaha Rainbow*, "I thought that was the funniest joke I'd come up with in years, and I'm sure it's very private, but I couldn't resist putting it on there." Dylan had given permission for the lift, to which Steve alluded tongue-in-cheek after performing the song during an interview with WXRT's John Platt. "Thanks to Bob Dylan for that last verse," Steve said. "It was nice of him to mail it in." [19]

Two other writing collaborations received vigorous treatment at the sessions:

He was all over my dad. He slammed him with his entire discography.
JOHNNY BURNS

18: "Mama Don't Allow It" was culled from two and a half hours of music that Steve recorded with Martin, Bogan & Armstrong the night of Jan. 16 at Paragon. They also ran through "Lady Be Good," "Red River Valley," "Red Red Robin," "Marie," "If I Could Be with You," "Corrina Corrina," "Sittin' on Top of the World" and "There's a Girl in the Heart of Maryland." Steve told engineer Barry Mraz, "So we spend an extra couple of hundred on tape. Just let it roll." Goofiness filled the "Mama" track, such as when Steve nudged a shivering, flu-ridden McDonald before his bass solo by saying, "Hughie, you better wake up."

19: Steve had provided guitar help on "Door Number Three" when co-writer Jimmy Buffett recorded it the previous August in Nashville for his "A1A" LP. Buffett's less effective version omitted the Dylan insert and crassly castigated Monty Hall as "you son of a bitch."

"Moby Book" and the bluegrassy "Jessie's Jig." The latter song Steve later claimed was merely a piece he used in the studio to "get the musicians to know each other," but after he heard Burns' and Clements' riffs on it, "all of a sudden that son of a bitch was cookin', so we cut it." Steve also recorded a pair of songs by artists whose work he had included on earlier LPs: Michael Smith's vividly imaged "Spoon River" waltz and a lovely, lost-love ballad by John Prine, "Blue Umbrella," both songs enriched by Abby Newton's rich harmony cello intertwined with Steve's vocal baritone. The chorus of the Prine song — reminiscent of "Yellow Coat" and drawing on a motif that Steve found increasingly potent, that of a woman who leaves a man — contained a plea resonant for someone living with leukemia: "Just give me one extra season, so I can figure out the other four."

A trio of other tunes explored all sides of the theme of faithfulness to a lover or spouse. A buoyant rendition of "It's a Sin to Tell a Lie" — which Steve had jammed on with Diz Disley and Stéphane Grappelli at the 1973 Cambridge Folk Festival, had developed later from a Fats Waller LP and had given a test run on the "Arlo's Gang" TV show — was a charmer. In it, the narrator admonishes, "Just be sure when you say I love you" because of the consequence posed in the title. Steve knew that singing and playing it solo and with passion would endear him to anyone, and the song lost none of its exuberant appeal in the recorded version. The song drew from Depression-era swing, which Steve labeled as "real heart music, so alive it just won't be denied." "Sin" became his standard show-opener, showcasing his boggling guitar work while winning over an audience. Steve didn't hesitate to send up the song's romantic lure, however, often replacing the line "If you break my heart, I'll die" with "If you break my heart, I'll break your leg." [20]

The two additional tunes turning on the same theme were Steve originals, both of which carried enduring power. In "I Can't Sleep," the narrator bemoans the departure of his beloved, having "stayed up late to watch the sunrise" because "I can't sleep when I can't sleep with you." When Steve first wrote the song, he envisioned it with a peppy, Bob Wills-style western-swing beat. But when Steve contributed guitar and vocals in late 1974 to John Prine's "Common Sense" album on Atlantic, he played "I Can't Sleep" for the LP's producer, Booker T & the MGs soul guitarist Steve Cropper. "He told me that the words were good, and I ought to slow it down," Steve said, "and he was right — at least I hope he was." The more languid version became a torch song in which the narrator wails about loneliness, backed by Bloom's lush saxophone and the "shoo-doo-be-doo" voices of MacKinnon, Koloc and Holmes. Steve later wished aloud that Ray Charles would record it. "There's a guy who would know how to sing that damn song."

A much quieter but more complex composition, "Lookin' for Trouble" ostensibly was inspired by "a friend of mine who was robbed by a woman he'd picked up in a bar. I think he was real glad that she didn't shoot him. I can understand that." Perhaps the song also drew its vision from Steve's own expe-

If you break my heart, I'll break your leg.
STEVE GOODMAN

20: Opening a show with an upbeat tune offered two pluses, Steve told Bryan Bowers. The first, Bowers said, was to quickly set a tone: "High-energy, laughter, rolling them eyes, standing on the balls of his feet, reaching up for the mike, creating tension — not tension where you felt bad, but tension where as an audience you felt like, 'All right! This guy's working for us!' " The second reason was technical. "It's like a double-check on the sound check, or it's a sound check if I didn't get a sound check," he said. "That's as loud and as exuberant as I'm going to get the whole set, and it gives the sound guy one more chance to get me dialed in."

riences on the road. It addressed a circular trio of follies: drinking, lying, then loving a woman who "was only in it for the money," which — in a clever lyrical turn — leads back to drinking. "Trouble will find you," the song warns, "in your own backyard."

Steve insisted that he wasn't out to sermonize about sin, but he allowed that a message can be more effective when set to music. "If it's got a tune to it, maybe it doesn't preach as much," he told Toronto journalist Nicholas Jennings. "I don't drink as much as I used to, but that's about all that I can say about that because I really don't want to tell anybody what to do. All that stuff's a one-way street if you can't keep it in some kind of perspective — smoking and drinking, all that stuff."

The aural effectiveness of "Lookin' for Trouble" and five of the sessions' other songs owed to the versatile harmonica of Saul Broudy. In fact, if a new star emerged from these recordings, it was he. A longtime sideman for labor folksinger Utah Phillips, Broudy had come to Steve's attention at festivals, and his mellow campfire sound — what Steve called "lonesome cowboy harp" — appealed to Steve. "Guys like Saul haven't really recorded a hell of a lot, and I had 'em play way the hell over their heads on this album," Steve said. "Spoon River" showcased a soulful Broudy solo, and his break in "Jessie's Jig" became joyous dance. But it was his sustained, minor-key mournfulness on "Lookin' for Trouble," accompanied by McDonald's bass and Steve's guitar and voice, that caught the chill of hanging by a thread. A review in the October 1975 edition of *Playboy* offered confirmation, noting "a harp accompaniment by Saul Broudy that'll break your heart."

Ironically, Broudy almost didn't play on the track. When Steve and guitarist Steve Burgh toyed with the song's arrangement, Broudy says, "they tried different things, piano, but they didn't want harmonica, so they said, 'Saul, you're off. Take a break. We're going to work on this song,' and I fell asleep under the piano. Later on, someone said, 'Maybe we should try harmonica,' and they woke me up and said, 'See what you can do on this song.' It was in C minor, and I dug out of my bag this crusty old C minor harp. I played it in one take. I only had to go over one little thing where I missed coming into the bridge, but that worked out for the best because I did a double part on the bridge. It just felt good to me, and they were visibly pleased. All the guys in the studio applauded me."

Steve's studio experience with Broudy illustrated his budding prowess as a producer. While two years earlier he had rejected the more commercially formulaic approach of Cashman & West, Steve had sung and played in enough recording sessions — his own and others' — to understand that the task was necessarily more complex than setting himself down in front of a microphone and playing as if he were onstage.

The challenge of a studio recording, Steve told the *Chicago Sun-Times'* Al Rudis, is to transform a "two-dimensional" medium into a dynamic equal to that of a life performance, hence instruments as diverse as Abby Newton's cello

The harmonica strains of Saul Broudy on Steve's "Lookin' for Trouble" recording were so soulful as to "break your heart," opined Playboy. *"Guys like Saul haven't really recorded a hell of a lot," Steve said, "and I had 'em play way the hell over their heads on this album."*

(Photo by B.L. Ochman, M. Hohner, Inc., courtesy of Saul Broudy)

Bassist Hugh McDonald found Steve as a producer to be the definition of generosity: "He was a poster child for the golden rule. If I could choose a brother, he'd be the guy."
(Photo courtesy of
Steve and Barbara Mosley)

21: At the 1973 concert, Denver claimed that recording "City" was "a lot of fun" for him and Steve. "It was kind of an exciting thing for me," he said, "because it was the first time that anybody had ever recorded one of Steve's songs, and I felt very good about that." But Denver also admitted that he'd wanted to "change it around to suit my purposes, more than anything else." In singing "City" at that show, however, Denver forgot and faked his way through a line in its first verse. RCA released the flawed performance as part of an expanded version of "An Evening with John Denver" on CD in 2001, four years after Denver's death.

and Ken Bloom's banduras. "I'm trying to paint pictures between the speakers of what the songs are about, to literally make movies out of records," he said. The approach of veteran country producer Jack Clement, as related to Steve via John Prine, was influential. "Clement doesn't even care what the damn song's about," Steve said. "It's just a concept of shooting for a sound rather than tell a story. Well, I figure if I pick the material right, the songs are going to tell stories anyhow, and now I've got to try and get them to sound like something."

Steve was a natural for the task, Steve Burgh said, because "he was able to focus so easily." Bassist Hugh McDonald goes further, noting that, unlike other producers who constantly rewrote songs in the studio or engaged in endless takes that "sucked the life" out of material, Steve exuded empathy, giving accompanists basic instructions and letting them take off.

"He was a poster child for the golden rule," McDonald says. "If I could choose a brother, he'd be the guy. I don't think there was ever a harsh word or anything but hugs and love with him. There was nobody that I had that feeling for. To this day, I would drop everything — it wouldn't matter, money has nothing to do with it — to do what was necessary for him. Beyond his talent, it was his kindness, his generosity."

Much of Steve's comfort in the recording sessions stemmed from their taking place in Chicago. Located on the fourth floor of an elevator-less building along the Magnificent Mile, the Paragon studio was a tough hoof, especially for older musicians and those hauling heavy instruments. But Steve's apartment was mere blocks, not 900 miles, away. "It was so good to be able to go to your own bed every night after working that hard," he said, "because when you make an album, you live it."

As well, Chicago provided a "different energy," said New York-based Burgh. "Chicago is a lively place, but there's something a little more down-home compared to the show-biz fascination of New York."

Nancy even stopped by with Jessie for some sessions, and Steve played with his nearly 3-year-old during breaks, says Paragon's Nancy Berek-Mraz, wife of the sessions' engineer. "He made everybody feel extremely comfortable," she says. "He was very low key and humble. He didn't walk in with this star thing at all." Instead, he would "light up the room" with his broad grin. "It was hypnotizing," she says. "You had to smile when you saw him. He always seemed so happy." The mood reflected the tenor of the sessions, she says. "It absolutely came from the heart, and you could hear it."

About the time Steve's sessions ended in Chicago, musical benefactor Arlo Guthrie finally delivered his own long-delayed message from the heart. The recipient was the star who had infuriated Guthrie by publicly claiming half the writing credit for "City of New Orleans."

In concerts, John Denver had been introducing the song with mock indignation to comic effect, noting to an audience on Aug. 14, 1973, at Colorado's Red Rocks Amphitheatre that Guthrie's version, released six months later than his, became "a giant hit record. Really ticked me off." [21]

Guthrie's wife, Jackie, finally became fed up with Arlo's carping about the blond, bespectacled superstar. "You gotta stop this," she said. "You gotta talk to the guy." Guthrie resisted, but Jackie set up an in-person meeting during a San Francisco party at the Russian Hill mansion of Werner Erhard, founder of the famed "est" encounter seminars, to which Denver was an enthusiastic adherent. Guthrie, skeptical of the scene, told a *Rolling Stone* reporter at the gathering to "leave your hat on" because he felt that he might have to leave at any moment.

Later, Guthrie says, he walked upstairs to a room in which Denver was sitting at a desk, "and I started reading him the riot act" about "City."

"Arlo," Denver said, holding up his hand, "you gotta believe me. I didn't do that."

"Well, you recorded the song," Guthrie shot back.

"Yeah, I did that," Denver replied, "but I would never steal stuff from other people. My manager did that."

"Look, it's not just stealing a song. This guy's sick," Guthrie said. "That's where the money's going. You can't take from that. You can't let the manager do that. You are the one responsible. Yeah, your manager might have done this, but you are the one."

"You're right," Denver replied. "You're absolutely right. Let's be friends. I'll take care of it. I'm going to make it right."

"John, you're on," Guthrie said.

Denver's assurance "took the pain right out of me," Guthrie says. "He was a man of his word, as far as I know, and I really admired him because it's one thing to do something stupid. It's harder to make it right."

While Guthrie never learned what Denver specifically did to "take care of it," one step Denver did take, says songwriting collaborator Bill Danoff, was to take "City of New Orleans" out of his live repertoire. "The poor thing for Steve was then that John stopped doing the song," Danoff says. "I never heard him sing it after. He was embarrassed about it."

In a sense, Steve had moved on from his anger at Denver. But at the time Guthrie settled his Denver beef in February 1975, Steve coincidentally joined another project that spelled changes in "City of New Orleans." This time it involved a pop goddess whose interpretations of trailblazing folk songs had informed Steve's fledgling repertoire 10 years prior — Judy Collins.

Collins had crossed paths with Steve at festivals but learned of "City" by hearing Guthrie's 1972 hit rendition and soon began performing it in shows of her own. "Oh, my God," she says she told herself, "I've got to record that." The song's driving melody and vivid lyrics were its selling points.

"It's the essence of popular song," she says. "He had the passport to the common, humanitarian touch, and he knew how to tell the kind of story that sticks to the ribs. It's a beautiful use of language. You see it, and it translates to just about anybody, and the melody enhances that visual power."

Collins, who grew up in Seattle, adds that though the train in "City" flows south through the Midwest, the song has "overtones of the big Super Chiefs

John Denver, shown in October 1973 in Eugene, Oregon, vowed to "make right" a festering co-writing claim for Steve's "City of New Orleans" after Arlo Guthrie confronted him.

(Photo by Clay Eals)

Judy Collins, shown in a 1977 concert, says Steve "had the common, humanitarian touch."
(Photo by Phil Saviano, Boston, MA)

22: Collins gladly would have reciprocated: "If Steve had been ready to record one of my songs, I would have played for him. It's a songwriter's responsibility. If you've got solid material being recorded by other artists and they invite you to be there, it's a big thrill because you're getting your music out to other people."

23: Indecipherably, Steve contributed to two other songs on "Judith." He was one of three guitarists on the 1932 Yip Harburg/Jay Gorney lament, "Brother, Can You Spare a Dime," and one of five singers on the Rolling Stones' "Salt of the Earth."

24: Collins' "Clowns" returned to the *Billboard* singles chart for 16 weeks in fall 1977, rising higher than in 1975, peaking at #19.

and other trains that we always think about going into the West, penetrating the pioneer regions of the country. All of us have these really yearning memories of trains and train whistles, particularly in the West."

She had quickly recorded "City " in 1973, intending to place it on her "True Stories & Other Dreams" LP, released that year. But she says she dropped it from the album to include more of her own songs. "I wanted to tuck it away and do it on an album where I didn't have as much concentration on my own writing."

Working two years later on her next LP, her 12th overall and her first under the helm of Elektra/Asylum chairman David Geffen, Collins sought Geffen's assistance to secure Atlantic's Arif Mardin as producer. She told Mardin not only that she wanted to re-record "City of New Orleans" but also that Steve should appear on the track. "I think we need to have the original here, the man who made this happen," she told Mardin. When Mardin asked Steve to participate in the sessions at A&R Studios in New York, his answer contained no reticence. "Are you kidding?" Steve said. "I'll fly in." [22]

Collins discovered that Steve was "hell on wheels on the guitar," she says. "Unbelievable player, and such a musical, sweet voice. He had one of those drop-dead voices where you can't walk away from it. And he had a wonderful kind of fey, pixie sense of humor. Very sweet natured and a pleasure to be around. I wouldn't say he was shy or withdrawn, but at the same time he was a quiet sort of guy. And then had this wry, dry sense of humor, which would have you on the floor."

The Collins version of "City" was an amalgam of Steve's and Guthrie's versions. While she used some of Guthrie's word changes and his chord "hook" in the chorus, she also sped the song back to Steve's tempo. She also added touches of her own as her silken voice sailed through the lyrics, giving the ending a triple repeat and a modified final line — "I'll be gone a million miles when the race is run" — lending the song a more optimistic tone. "It's just poetic alliteration," she says, "to get the same feeling across." Steve joined Eric Weissberg on background vocals and played guitar throughout, his most recognizable contribution coming in the recording's initial 10 seconds, which consist solely of Steve's acoustic licks. [23]

The resulting album, "Judith," released in March 1975, ranged from rock to light pop, and it soared to favor on the strength of its single, "Send in the Clowns," in which Collins brought vulnerability to the melancholy Stephen Sondheim tune from Broadway's "A Little Night Music." The single shimmered for 11 weeks in *Billboard*, rising to a high of #36, while the LP stayed in the top-100 for a whopping 34 weeks, from April through November, topping out at #24, in the process bringing Steve's "City" to a wider public and helping cement its status as a standard. [24]

That spring, Steve also leapt into a project to rescue his longtime friend, Bill Swofford, from the pop pigeonhole into which Swofford's alter ego ("Oliver") and his two 1969 pop hits had placed him. Swofford bid Steve to Minneapolis'

Sound 80 studio to produce and front money for an album intended to change his image. But the songs, mostly written by Swofford, had no hit potential, said Swofford's manager, Keith Christianson. "I tried to sell it, and it didn't work," Christianson said. "Steve knew what he was doing, he was good at what he did. The material just wasn't commercial enough to sell. It was singer/songwriter and very folkie and artsy — and when I say artsy, it was without a hook." The album, he said, was never released, and "we gave it a nice burial."

With "Judith," his own recording experiences and the Grand Canyon in mind as he rode the bus from Flagstaff to Los Angeles in early April, Steve once more weighed his own contract situation with Asylum. "I'm out of the fryin' pan and into the fire, literally," Steve reflected for WXRT's John Platt. "The music business is just so goofy every now and then, not the musicians half as much as just the nature of it."

Weighing whether to sign, Steve found it natural to fashion an analogy to the sport to which he had been devoted for as long as he could recall: "In baseball if you're a .300 hitter, you get three hits every 10 times up. It can't be helped. You get three hits every 10 times up whether they're Texas Leaguers or long doubles or what-have-you. You get your share of long ones, and you get your share of cheap ones, but they're all in the batting average, and, y'know, it's 3 for 10 for .300. And in the music business, you can be a .300 hitter if somebody says you are."

By extending him a contract, Geffen and Asylum obviously saw Steve as a musician who, in baseball parlance, could hit for average. With a new album ready to deliver, Steve decided it was time to step into the batter's box.

"It was a leap from the minor leagues," says Jerry Sharell, promotion man for Buddah from 1970 to 1973 who had joined Asylum in 1974, rising to senior vice president. "There was great believability in his talent at both labels, but in the echelons of the music business, he was joining the Tiffany of record labels. It spoke for itself."

The finalized deal was a "phenomenal" step, says Al Bunetta's former assistant Tom King. "It was brilliant. For Steve, it was a natural home, where most people were songwriters. It was a coup. It was absolutely fresh energy because the label wanted Steve to be successful. You got the impression walking into their office that it wasn't just a sales job."

The signing — plus his formal entry into remission from leukemia — gave Steve a confidence bordering on cockiness. Walking through the Asylum offices, he shouted to the former Buddah promo man, "Hey, Sharell, I bet you thought you wouldn't be seein' me again." Steve later told John Platt he was relieved that "they made me an inmate, officially."

Buzzing through a full spring itinerary, Steve landed a last-minute Saturday slot at Carnegie Hall — his third appearance in the fabled Manhattan theater — by filling in for Geoff Muldaur on May 17 as the opener for Bonnie Raitt. In contrast to his two previous Carnegie dates, this time he had a complementary musical relationship with the main act. He faced no hecklers, and, as Steve

> **In the echelons of the music business, he was joining the Tiffany of record labels.**
> **JERRY SHARELL**

Jo Ann Stepan Simich, a childhood friend of Steve's in Albany Park, shown in 1973, reconnected with Steve at Weiss Memorial Hospital upon the births of their children in 1975. When Simich said there is nothing more important than being a loving spouse and parent, Steve replied, "Well, that's old fashioned to me."

(Photo courtesy Jo Ann Stepan Simich)

Mandell recalls, "he tore that place apart." In agreement was Ian Dove of *The New York Times*, who sensed Steve's new vigor. In contrast to Raitt, Steve "appears to be constantly extending himself," Dove wrote. Singling out Steve's "Ballad of Penny Evans," the reviewer also noted that Steve "had a batch of new songs and managed to be witty and unpretentious. He is very much aware of the world around him and is able to translate it into song. ... In an overpopulated field, he stands out."

Less than a month later, as his Asylum album neared release, Steve's fatherhood took center stage. In a way, he became like the young dad Billy in "Penny Evans," because on June 11 Nancy gave birth to a daughter. Now the couple had two young girls, but unlike the war-slain Billy, Steve had just been reprieved from the medical war he had fought for more than six years.

For their new daughter's name, Steve and Nancy reached into Steve's songwriting past, when he and Ed Holstein had written what Holstein today considers a "really lousy" song. The only good thing about it, he says, was the girl's name that they started writing from. The name, Sarah, became the tune's title and the name of the Goodmans' second daughter.

Steve had joined Nancy in the delivery room for the birth at Weiss Memorial Hospital and couldn't stop beaming. Jo Ann Simich (formerly Stepan), Steve's childhood friend from Albany Park, also was at Weiss, having given birth via Caesarean section to her second child, also a girl, two days prior. Late at night, as she unsteadily walked down a hallway back to her room, a small man approached, and though she hadn't seen him since Volta school days, she soon recognized him as Steve. They greeted each other briefly but soon parted because Stepan quickly was tiring. The next day, however, Steve stopped by her room, handed her a long-stemmed rose and sat down. They talked for 20 minutes, not about old friends or Albany Park, but about life in general.

"Are you happy?" Steve asked her.

"We don't usually talk about happiness," Simich replied. "People don't ask. They're afraid to find out. Steve, I'm happy. My husband is a wonderful man. Nothing else matters."

"My wife, Nancy, just had a baby," Steve said.

"You must love her very much," she replied. "Are you happy to be a dad?"

"It's so great that you could never know."

"I'm so glad to hear that," Simich said. "It's made me sad to see some people here in the hospital not so tickled to have a baby. It really is a gift to us — and a joy. There's nothing more wonderful than loving your spouse and being a parent."

"Well," Steve said, "that's old fashioned to me."

Steve's leukemia went unspoken. Simich had no way of knowing about it, and Steve didn't disclose it. She knew he was a musician, but that was "the furthest thing from my mind," she says. "It was as simple as could be. It was as if there was something deeper that I couldn't know from facts. He just said what he said, and he meant it. It was very, very powerful."

Witnessing Sarah's birth was a transforming experience for Steve, giving him profound insights, both political and personal.

"My old lady is real tough, so I wasn't real nervous about that," Steve told Al Rudis, "but after you see a baby being born, you have a brand new respect for your mother, for openers, and for your wife, and you know why there's no Equal Rights Amendment. Men don't have to have children. ... It's staggering. If men had to have babies, it would have been ZPG (zero population growth) about the time of the Parthenon and the Greeks.

"Yeah, that's the most incredible thing, is having two children and a family and having to behave like a responsible human being. You can't stay out all night and drink and smoke dope and be whatever the self-destructive aspects of being an artist or musician, all that crap — which is all it is, these grand games you can play with yourself, to tell yourself that that's what's best for your life. But that family thing is the most important thing that ever happened to me."

If the music world needed a reminder that Steve was a father, the fact began staring record buyers in the face on Monday, June 30, the official release date for his new LP. "Jessie's Jig," the song named for his first daughter, was incorporated in the title for the album itself, "Jessie's Jig & Other Favorites." A more subtle verbal allusion appeared on the back cover and on the record itself, in the credit line for each song that Steve had written: "Red Pajamas Productions," a reference to a phrase in one of Jessie's favorite Pete Seeger children's tunes. [25]

Jessie graced the album cover visually as well, as part of a collage assembled by designer Anne Garner and complemented by a copperplate script created by Virginia Team, Garner's ex-boss at CBS Records. Anchoring the tan cover was a large, tinted black-and-white photo by Henry Diltz of a fully bearded, flower-shirted, tall-looking, much-slimmed-down, self-assured and smiling Steve. Sitting slightly tilted at the bottom, a color snapshot just one and a half inches square depicted a beach scene. Therein, bearing an expression of contentment and grasping a red, white and blue plastic float toy, knelt a swim-suited Jessie. The timing and underlying message were a perfect match.

Steve bolstered his fatherly image in a two-hour edition of WGN-AM's live "Roy Leonard Show," on July 31, 1975, at the Old Town School of Folk Music. (From left) Leonard, Fleming Brown, Bonnie Koloc, Steve, Fred Holstein, Ray Tate and Bob Gibson played, but another would-be vocalist was 3-year-old Jessie. She robustly sang "Old King Cole" off-mike while a stock report was aired. But she refused — with a "No!" — to repeat it when prompted by Steve on the air. Seven-week-old Sarah did get in an on-air wail, however. "Gotta break 'em in early," Steve cracked.

(Photo courtesy of Roy Leonard)

25: On his "American Game & Activity Songs for Children" LP, released in 1962 on Folkways, Pete Seeger sang the traditional "I Know a Little Girl," which kicked off with the verse, "I know a little girl with red pajamas, red pajamas, red pajamas. I know a little girl with red pajamas, red pajamas on."

Mike Douglas, whose syndicated afternoon talk and variety show reached six million viewers in 190 cities, gave Steve his first promotional push for the "Jessie's Jig" LP, thanks to the urging of the week's co-host, Harry Chapin.

(Photofest photo)

26: The other two songwriters fared better. A 20-ish, curly-haired, Melanie-voiced woman named Zizzie Roberts, recruited by Chapin, performed her "Song for a Smile" with a dazzling grin. "She's a hell of a lot better performer," Steve said, "so it makes it easier to come across," Pryor agreed. "I thought it was true," he told her. "I believe you." The last of the bunch, Phillies baseball organist Paul Richardson, performed an impish ditty about a Russian man lost in Siberia and forced to eat his dog. The irresistible punch line: "It's really a shame that Rover's not here because he'd really enjoy the bones." All howled, and Douglas signaled for a station break. Richardson died in 2006 from prostate cancer at age 74.

On the eve of the "Jig" release, the Asylum promo whirlwind began. Steve was in the Maryland burg of Callaway, 60 miles southeast of Washington, D.C., when a phone call bid him to a weekday TV show with an audience of six million viewers in 190 cities — the late-afternoon entertainment refuge of home-makers, "The Mike Douglas Show." Despite his middle-of-the-road image, Douglas, 49, had showcased cutting-edge artists and politicians since his show's 1961 debut, including a week in 1972 with John Lennon and Yoko Ono.

Douglas' co-host for the Monday, June 30, 1975, taping was 32-year-old Harry Chapin, whose "Cat's in the Cradle" had sored to #1 the previous December. With his brother Tom four years earlier, Chapin had witnessed Steve's guest set during the fateful Kris Kristofferson concert at the Bitter End, and Chapin invited Steve to take part in what he called an on-air songwriters workshop. Steve rented a car, made the 200-mile, overnight drive to Philadelphia and in Douglas' studio found not only the Chapins but also a comedian whose unpredictable and profane persona would spice up the proceedings, Richard Pryor.

Introduced by Chapin as "one of the finest young songwriters of Chicago," Steve sang "City of New Orleans," "I Ain't Heard You Play No Blues" and a just-written comic lament, "Unemployed." But the juice of the 90-minute show was the so-called workshop. Brought onstage were three "unknown" songwriters to debut their fledgling work, accompanying themselves on piano. Each performed a brief tune, to be judged by Steve and Pryor.

Steve had told Chapin that he "wasn't going to have anybody's blood on my hands in front of 6 million people, that even if the songs were horrible, I was going to tell the guy how much I loved him, because it didn't matter that much to me. I wasn't about to crush somebody over something as silly as a song."

The first singer, 30-ish, in square glasses, mustache and beard, identified himself as Alan Schmidt, said he loved writing pop music and shakily sang a lost-love song called "What Am I Gonna Do?" Standing over the piano, Steve and Pryor looked as if they were asking themselves the same question. The tune was, as Steve said later, "one of the two or three worst songs ever written by anybody." As Steve stared at the piano, "you could just see my face gettin' greener and greener and greener — and it wasn't your set, it was me." When Douglas sought his opinion, Steve equivocated. "Well," he said quietly, "I liked a couple of those (chord) changes. If I could play any instrument as well as that, I'd write songs that had all those chords in 'em. I sort of liked how that rolled along."

"Did you like the song, the idea?" Douglas pressed on.

"Yeah," Steve said after a pause. "I've seen people in that situation. I thought it was pretty good."

Pryor had no such restraint. He looked the singer in the eye and said, "I think you should take up plumbing." Everyone, including the singer, roared. [26]

The "Mike Douglas Show" episode, which also featured author Lula Parker Betenson, legendary outlaw Butch Cassidy's 95-year-old youngest sister (to whom Douglas sang "Raindrops Keep Fallin' on My Head"), aired nationally the following week. Meanwhile, the first review of Steve's "Jessie's Jig & Other Favorites" came in the July 5 edition of *Billboard*, which placed the LP in its "recommended" list. "Longtime folk-rock favorite comes up with a good blend of both, including some fun-filled instrumentals, some songs of Americana that he seems to do so well, some country-flavored cuts and some rock," the item read. "One of few artists who can combine equal portions of humor and sentimentality in the same LP and get away with it."

But before Asylum's promo push could fully kick in, Steve got two other unanticipated notices in the same edition. Both appeared favorable on the surface but contained irksome undercurrents.

First was a mention in the "recommended singles" list of Jimmy Buffett's latest 45, the song he had written with Steve, "Door Number Three." Steve had placed the song in the opening and most attention-getting spot on his own LP, but the simultaneous release of Buffett's version as a single shut down the potential for Asylum to give a fresh break for Steve's version. This was sealed when Buffett's rendition performed poorly, scraping the bottom of the top-100 chart for five weeks and reaching a high of only #88.

Asylum did release a single from the "Jig" LP, "It's a Sin to Tell a Lie," backed by the album's title instrumental. But it was a token effort that never charted. "It was almost a courtesy for the label to put out a single for him," says Bruce Shindler, an Asylum promotion staffer. "They weren't going to pay hundreds of thousands of dollars to get him a hit single because they knew he couldn't get a hit single. Where were you gonna get Steve Goodman played? Mass appeal makes a hit artist — relatable, mass-appeal music, and folk music is not always relatable, mass appeal. It's cerebral. The old street troubadour, that's what Steve Goodman was, and troubadours are not big in the commercial field."

More disconcerting to Steve elsewhere in the July 5 *Billboard* was the debut on the country singles chart of another of his tunes, sung by a 34-year-old who had spent most of his 20s in the Ohio State Penitentiary — David Allan Coe.

Steve was no stranger to the brash Coe, the first country artist to embrace the "outlaw" label. A year and a half earlier, Steve and Nancy had cooked Christmas dinner at their apartment for an assortment of guests: Earl Pionke, satirist Larry Rand, Rand's fiancée, African-American string-band leader Carl Martin and Coe. Steve had crossed paths with Coe, known for Tanya Tucker's version of his "Would You Lay with Me (in a Field of Stone)," and was impressed with his other songs, including "Cocaine Caroline," which Steve promoted in a Feb. 3, 1974, appearance on the Los Angeles "FolkScene" show. "He's a little strange, and people don't know quite what to make of him, but he's got some pretty good tunes," Steve told host Howard Larman. "He sticks his foot all the way down his throat two or three times a day, but he's got this enormous heart."

One instance of Coe's strangeness emerged at the Christmas 1973 gathering. Steve had called Pionke, saying he was putting Coe up for a few days and asking permission to add him to the New Year's Eve show. "I got another charity project," Steve told Pionke. "You got a few hundred? David Allan Coe just got out of jail. The guy's fuckin' busted. I met him on the road, and he can't bring his family

The old street troubadour, that's what Steve Goodman was, and troubadours are not big in the commercial field.
BRUCE SHINDLER

David Allan Coe, the ex-convict country singer/songwriter, falsely claimed in a recitation inserted in his hit version of "You Never Even Call Me by My Name" that he had a key role in inspiring Steve to write the song's triumphant final verse.
(Columbia Records promo photo)

27: Coe recognized Steve's generosity in liner notes for the "Cowboy" LP in 1974: "Thanks to Shel Silverstein, Kris Kristofferson, Steve Goodman and Leon Russell for moral support."

anywhere." Pionke agreed and came to meet Coe at the dinner (later deciding, because of Coe's dark past, to nickname him Edgar Allan Coe). Wine flowed plentifully, and after dinner, so did the music, Martin playing blues and Coe singing Hank Williams tunes. Then, Rand says, Coe embarked on an extended lecture to Martin about "what it's like to be black." Martin, like a Buddha, "slipped all the punches," Rand says. "Yeah, man, yeah," Martin replied. "I've been on the ass end of an asphalt crew before. I know what it smells like."

Steve said in later interviews that at his Christmas gathering he taught Coe not only "You Never Even Call Me by My Name" but also Michael Smith's "Crazy Mary," which Coe quickly included on his debut LP for Columbia Records in 1974, "The Mysterious Rhinestone Cowboy." [27] Coe has a different recollection, saying that Steve played him part of "You Never Even Call Me by My Name" in a back room while they and John Prine were at a Kris Kristofferson show in New Jersey. There, Coe says, came an exchange prompting Steve to write the parody's triumphant final verse. "John (Prine) and I were saying, 'Yeah, this isn't an appropriate country and western song,' and started naming the things that were left out," Coe says. "Well, Steve went back and wrote the other verse, and he called me on the phone and said, 'How about this?'"

Coe's recollection is faulty or fabricated because in concerts and interviews since December 1971, Steve had credited Chicago musician Albert Williams with the inspiration for the final verse, which Williams himself confirms. Even so, Coe carved himself a key role in the song's authorship when he sang it on his second Columbia LP, "Once Upon a Rhyme," released in summer 1975. It became the first recording of the song to include the classic, culminating verse. But some said it also showcased Coe's devil-may-care hubris at Steve's expense.

In his recording, Coe modified a lyric and added his own name: "But the only time I know I'll hear David Allan Coe / is when Jesus has his final judgment day." The topper, however, was Coe's insertion of a recitation before the final verse that spelled out a fictional hero's role for himself in its creation:

"Well, a friend of mine named Steve Goodman wrote that song, and he told me it was the perfect country and western song. I wrote him back a letter, and I told him it was not the perfect country and western song because he hadn't said anything at all about mama, or trains, or trucks, or prison, or gettin' drunk. Well, he sat down and wrote another verse to the song, and he sent it to me, and after reading it, I realized that my friend had written the perfect country and western song, and I felt obliged to include it on this album."

Kristofferson may have influenced Coe's phrasing. "He always seemed to show up in places I was doing a concert," Kristofferson says. "I'd put him on, and he'd knock 'em out every time. He had quite a voice." Most of Coe's sets consisted of self-written material, Kristofferson says, but Coe also slipped in songs of Mickey Newbury and others without crediting them. "Y'know," Kristofferson says he told Coe, "somebody out there's going to think that you're claiming that's your song, and then they're not going to believe you wrote any of those other great songs. All you got to say is, 'My good friend Mickey Newbury wrote this song,' which is the truth." Kristofferson recalls Coe "looking at me hard" in response. "Then I'm driving in the car one day, and I heard him on the radio saying, 'My good friend, Steve Goodman.' I thought, 'My God.'"

Steve said he had hoped that Porter Waggoner or another traditional country artist would record "You Never Even Call Me by My Name." But he never envisioned anyone altering it to the point of wresting away a key part of its authorship. To Steve, the Coe recitation was an unconscionable distortion, if not a lie. It stirred resentment in him similar to the ire he had directed at John Denver. "Steve was real angry about that," Coe says. "He thought that I took artistic license with the song, and he wouldn't talk to me for a long, long time."

So when the July 5 edition of *Billboard* was published, Steve couldn't be simply happy with the favorable notice for his new Asylum album. He also had to contemplate the fact that Coe's disingenuous version of "You Never Even Call Me by My Name" [28] had entered the top-100 country singles chart at #73. Over the next 13 weeks, it rose steadily, topping out at #8 for two weeks in a row. Its enduring popularity in succeeding decades as "the perfect country and western song" made it Coe's signature tune.

What Steve perceived as Coe's slight stuck like a burr. But soon, Coe says, a sage thought came to Steve from songwriter Shel Silverstein, whose hilarious, ribald songs "Three Legged Man" and "Warm and Free" Steve had performed since 1969. After Steve carped to Silverstein about Coe's recorded self-aggrandizement, Silverstein had an inaccurate but pointed reply: "Y'know, that's the first time a songwriter was ever mentioned in a song." Steve's manager, Al Bunetta, also told Steve, "Why are you pissed off? It's show business. He made it happen. He mentioned your name, so he's trying to say something, so give him a break."

Kristofferson also cooled Steve's jets, telling him, "Listen, David Allan Coe says your name on the radio once an hour, 100 times a day, all around the country. So forget all the rhinestones. That guy's doin' you a big favor."

Finally, Coe says, Steve "got the message" that Coe had enhanced Steve's stature, not stolen from it. Coe says Steve's mind also was eased by a question from Bunetta: "Do you know how many beans that's put in your pocket?" Accordingly, in intros for the song in later shows, Steve cited Coe's hit, labeling it the "full-length Technicolor version." In interviews, as with Harry Tuft of KLAK-FM in Denver, he said he was delighted with Coe. "What a nice cat." [29]

Artistic or ethical dissatisfaction aside, Steve used some of the royalties from Coe's success with "You Never Even Call Me by My Name" to needle the friend who in 1971 had helped him write it, John Prine. Steve had asked Prine a dozen times to take partial credit for creating the song, but Prine had consistently refused, saying it wasn't right to make fun of country music. When Coe's version rose high on the country chart, Steve again telephoned Prine.

"Now do you want your name on it?" Steve asked him.

"I don't want to do that," Prine said. "I'm way past the point of thinkin' maybe I was too good for the song. It's not that. It's just that if I didn't say I wanted it on there in the first place, I don't want to be an Indian giver and all of

Y'know, that's the first time a songwriter was ever mentioned in a song.
SHEL SILVERSTEIN

28: Coe altered the title of the song slightly, changing "Call" to "Called." The modification didn't affect the song's meaning. But Coe, never claiming modesty as a trait, insisted in a 1987 interview with BBC radio, "I recorded his song and started Stevie's career as a songwriter. He had much success after that."

29: Tuft told Steve on June 30, 1977, that Coe's version was "the most requested song on this station to this day." Steve replied with pride-swallowing gratitude: "I can't even believe Coe did that for me. That was a lovely gesture on his part. At the time, I certainly didn't understand it because the story wasn't the same. ... Then it hit me: 'Wait a minute. Not only is there nothin' wrong with it, but this guy is sayin' my name on the radio all around America 100 times a day by accident,' and that's just simply the loveliest thing anybody could have done."

Steve's slimmer physique is apparent as he helps Neil Adam Rosenbaum line up a pool shot March 2, 1975, in the back room of the Quiet Knight in Chicago. Neil's father, Art Rosenbaum, as well as Pete Seeger, Steve and others were playing the fourth annual benefit show for SingOut!, raising $3,000 for the magazine. Present was Marjorie Guthrie, widow of Woody Guthrie.

(Photo by Margo Newmark Rosenbaum)

Steve's slimmer physique is apparent as he helps Neil Adam Rosenbaum line up a pool shot March 2, 1975, in the back room of the Quiet Knight in Chicago. Neil's father, Art Rosenbaum, as well as Pete Seeger, Steve and others were playing the fourth annual benefit show for SingOut!, raising $3,000 for the magazine. Present was Marjorie Guthrie, widow of Woody Guthrie.

(Photo by Margo Newmark Rosenbaum)

a sudden say yes now that it's a hit. I think the song is great because of that verse, but I don't think I should change my mind right now."

"OK, fine," Steve said flatly.

Steve's reaction was puzzling. "I couldn't tell whether he was mad, or that's what he expected," Prine says. But the next day, Steve stopped at a Chicago antique store and paid some $12,000 for a wood-and-nickel Wurlitzer Victory jukebox built in 1942. With two workers from the store, Steve showed up in a pickup truck at Prine's home in Melrose Park west of Chicago, where they dropped off the jukebox. "That," Prine said later, with a laugh, "was my reward for coming up with two lines. ... I still got it in my living room. Every time I look at it, I think how stupid I am."

With the chart success of Steve's songs as recorded by Coe and Judy Collins as a backdrop in the summer of 1975, Asylum spun Steve's new album as the product of a compelling recording artist in his own right, not just as a writer of songs recorded by other singers. With his schedule packed with shows and interviews ("I'm gonna plug my new book, 'Fear of Sleeping,' " he joked in one radio appearance), the label augmented it with a high-profile promo campaign. It began with an ad that couldn't be missed by the industry — a paid photo and caption on the front page of the Aug. 23 edition of *Billboard*. Instead of the smiling visage from his album cover, however, the photo was a sober likeness that also appeared on the LP's lyric sheet, a portrait of Steve wearing a dark shirt and staring sternly into the eyes of the viewer. The grave pose belied Steve's pixieish onstage persona, but it was intended to invest him with a bit of movie-star mystery and convey the message that he was a serious musical force.

Equally provocative was the caption, which defined Steve as "one of the most compelling singers, writers and guitarists around" and attempted to set him apart from the flourishing disco trend and other superficial flash. "Steve Goodman doesn't boogie down, bump or hustle," the caption read. "Frowns on cosmic revelations. And has yet to be seen in platform shoes and space suits. He won't even sing about backstage at the Coliseum. Instead, he sings and plays with his own special verve about real people (and a few unreal ones as well) with warmth, humor and striking musical power."

Such text was not hyperbole to Vin Scelsa, deejay at New York's progressive rock WNEW-FM, who was won over on the morning after the *Billboard* ad when Steve made the first of what became four annual appearances on Scelsa's Sunday morning show. Steve charmed the equally diminutive Scelsa just a few seconds into the program by surprising him with background guitar music while Scelsa read several concert notices. Later in the show, when Scelsa plugged the airing that night of a BBC program featuring the Kinks, Steve played and sang a few lines from the British group's 1966 hit, "Sunny Afternoon." Besides a forum for songs from the "Jig" LP (Steve sang four, and Scelsa played a fifth directly from the album), their rapport produced an exchange revealing Steve's gratitude — with a hint of apprehension — about his transition to Asylum.

"Everything that they've told me has happened so far," Steve said of Asylum. "Nobody's said anything to me that was unrealistic, and it's a very pleasant situation." Steve also noted that he felt "no sour grapes" for how Buddah treated his recorded product. "It was just real hard for them to put it in the stores or anything like that," he said. "There's sort of a weird distribution setup they had, and if somebody was hot, it was easy to get their record on Buddah, and if somebody was not so hot, radio-wise or sales-wise, they just didn't press up as many, so it was just one of those unfortunate business situations."

Scelsa, a gatekeeper of the airwaves, commiserated. "It's a real hard thing," he said, "for people like yourself who make such beautiful, happy music, but music that, in a sense, is hard to put into whatever the mainstream rock 'n' roll thing is these days ... to get yourself involved with a record company that's gonna believe in what you do ... so at least you can eat."

"The shoe (also) goes on the other foot," Steve shot back. "I'm not makin' these records for playin' in the closet, either, so I'm tryin' to meet them (Asylum) somewhere, tryin' to give them something they can work with a little bit but still have it be what I do."

For that dual purpose, Steve counted his next two nights a victory. Playing at Greenwich Village's trendy Other End (the new name that Paul Colby had given the Bitter End), capacity crowds snaked around the block for two shows each night. It was as if Steve sensed he could do no wrong. Reviewers from *The New York Times* to the UK's *Melody Maker* noted a mix of musical skills and spontaneity that added up to a triumph. As Jim Fishel of *Billboard* put it, "He showed an SRO audience all there was to know about performing."

There, Steve not only pushed his new LP by accentuating his newest material, but he also mixed in all manner of standards and other tunes languishing fondly in the audience's mental firmament. He quoted from the "Beer Barrel Polka" and played the back-and-forth guitar and banjo lines of "Dueling Banjos" (which he wryly called "the ultimate playing with yourself song"). He segued from "This Hotel Room" into the Merle Travis song made famous in 1956 by

This sober likeness, an alternate pose from Steve's spring 1975 photo session with Henry Diltz, conveyed the new image that Asylum used in marketing its newly signed singer/songwriter.

(Photo by Henry Diltz)

30: "Sixteen Tons" became a regular part of Steve's repertoire, and he delighted in announcing that the song's final, tough-guy verse was his favorite: "If you see me comin' better step aside / A lot of men didn't and a lot of men died / I got one fist of iron and the other of steel / If the right one don't get ya, then the left one will."

31: Singing "Unemployed" at Troubles on March 18, 1975, Steve joked about its melodic similarity to Presley's "Too Much," citing another oldie: "We're gonna put 'Get a Job' on the flip side."

32: "Unemployed" almost had died aborning, Steve told a July 19, 1976, audience at Amazingrace. When writing it, he said, he forgot about the identically themed "Miss Beverly Jones" verse of a tune he had written four years earlier, "The I Don't Know Where I'm Goin' but I'm Goin' Nowhere in a Hurry Blues." Had he recalled the verse, "I would have gone, 'Where have I heard that?' That's what songwriters do all the time. They go, 'Where have I heard that?' "

33: Steve also solicited guitarist Charlie Chin, kitchen crew chief, but Chin refused because he felt he couldn't shirk his duties. Steve badgered Chin with praise, recalling Chin's help when Steve first played the Village in 1967, but to no avail. "I know how he feels about playing in places he's working, and I can't respect him for a minute," Steve chided. "He's entitled to be an asshole. I owe him a drink for embarrassing him like that. That's my fault, all right?" Steve later tweaked Chin in his improvised song: "I know he didn't want to play, and I can understand / But I hope Charlie Chin gets dishpan hands."

Tennessee Ernie Ford, "Sixteen Tons." [30] He introduced Leroy Van Dyke's "The Auctioneer" by slipping in a few bars of Van Dyke's "Walk on By" and trotted out a combo version of two classics he usually played separately, "Lady Be Good" and "Red, Red Robin." Stretching the bounds of audacity, when he broke a guitar string in the middle of a Hank Williams ballad, he laughed, assumed a macho pose, unbuttoned his shirt to the waist, straddled the microphone stand and belted out the 1964 Tommy Tucker classic, "Hi-Heel Sneakers."

In his Other End sets, Steve embodied the theory of his "Jig" LP — that an artist with an encyclopedic command of genres could use an impulsive versatility to succeed in an industry that fed on just the opposite. The message Steve delivered was simultaneously safe and sizzling, that he was predictably unpredictable. He even unveiled songs he'd not yet recorded, such as "Unemployed" (he had debuted it on "The Mike Douglas Show"), which resembled the tune of the Elvis Presley hit "Too Much." [31] Steve said he'd penned it "for a friend who was reading the *Chicago Tribune* want ads who has a degree in English from Northwestern." It ended with a political appeal and a strained rhyme: "Watch your step, Gerald Ford / or next election day you'll be unemployed." [32]

One of his sprawling Other End shows moved outside to Bleecker Street during its intermission. When Steve and multi-instrumentalist David Amram stepped out to chat with people standing in line, a group of buskers walked up and said, "Steve Goodman, David Amram, we really liked when you guys played together at Mariposa. We're just doing some street music tonight. Do you want to sit in with us?" The pair said, "Sure," the buskers opened their guitar cases 40 feet from the door, and before long the raggy ensemble was putting on an impromptu summer's eve show for patrons waiting to enter.

Within minutes, an agitated Paul Colby burst out of his club and stormed after Steve and Amram. "Listen," Colby spat out, "I pay you guys to play, and you stand out on the street for nothing, blocking traffic and stopping the people who are standing in line from buying tickets and going in. You're going to finish me off! If you look in these guys' guitar cases, there's not one cent in there. Everybody's having such a good time that you're stopping them from making money, too!" Unable to maintain his mock anger, Colby broke into howls, triggering laughter from the performers and those in line. A collection was taken for the street musicians, who quickly left, and Steve and Amram went back inside to play the next set.

Folded into Steve's in-the-moment persona was his proclivity for inviting musicians to the stage and instantly assessing what the unrehearsed group could handle. By the close of the second show of his first night at the Other End, Steve had summoned not only Amram on whistles and French horn, but also pianist Jeff Gutcheon, vocalist (and opening act) Raun MacKinnon, flutist Jerry Burnham, guitarists Artie Traum and Steve Burgh, harmonica player Mark Ross, violinist Larry Packer and drummer Marshal Rosenberg. [33]

The natural choice for this crew to play was a lengthy version of "Mama Don't Allow It." But what would come afterward?

"We're gonna have to make up one," Steve told the cacophonous crowd, which clearly relished the controlled chaos. For the next seven minutes, the horde onstage vamped on a blues refrain while Steve improvised nine rhymed verses that scoured the room and incorporated everything in sight, including the club's new name:

> *What's that little club, mama, Bleecker Street*
> *Used to be so bitter, now it's sweet*
> *It's the Other End, it's the Other End*
> *I can see you comin' a mile around the bend*

The names of musicians:

> *Well, nobody's losin' and everybody's winnin'*
> *When they're listenin' to the singin' of Raun MacKinnon ...*

> *The sweetest sound, and it isn't too much and*
> *The piano playing of Jeffrey Gutcheon ...*

His hometown:

> *The audiences here are the best I've known*
> *Make this Chicago boy feel right at home*

And an irresistibly risqué pun:

> *Those folks who don't like this place*
> *I've got to tell them right to their face*
> *They can kiss my other end, kiss my other end*
> *It's this little club I can see comin' round the bend*

His invention also took the form of imaginative medleys throughout 1975. In February in the H Quad Cafeteria at the Stony Brook branch of State University of New York, [34] he flowed for 10 minutes without stopping, from the fast-paced 1914 Percy Wenrich/Jack Mahoney standard "Has Anybody Seen My Gal" to Irving Berlin's 1926 hit "Blue Skies," then, dropping the tempo to a crawl, poignantly to Josh White's 1944 "One Meat Ball" and Rogers & Hart's 1937 "My Funny Valentine," then, back in a frenzy, to the culminating 1936 Matty Malneck/Johnny Mercer classic, "Goody Goody." Similarly, he closed the same show with three back-to-back Big Bill Broonzy blues tunes, "Key to the Highway," "Black, Brown & White" ("If you're black, step back") and "Long Tall Mama," then, slipping a hollow metal cylindrical slide onto his left hand's little finger, appending "I'll Fly Away" as a coda to the 12-minute mélange.

Sometimes the medleys stemmed from a request. At his spring gig at the Last Resort in Athens, Georgia, someone asked for a song by Tom Lehrer, the satirist/pianist who had inspired Steve, Stuart Gordon and other Albany Park pals in preteen days of the early 1960s. "Poisoning Pigeons in the Park" emerged from Steve without a hitch. Upon its finish, he kept strumming, gazing at the

Jerry Burnham and Raun MacKinnon, shown in a mid-1970s recording session, were part of Steve's tour de force sets Aug. 25-26, 1975, at the Other End in Greenwich Village.
(Photo courtesy of Raun and Jerry Burnham)

34: Steve played two shows Feb. 2, 1975, at Stony Brook, and Ellen Warshaw was the opener. After her first set, someone made off with her guitar. She says that Steve didn't hesitate to loan her his guitar so that she could play her second set.

ceiling and muttering absently, "Hmm, what else can I fake? Oh, I know." He continued with Lehrer's "The Elements," which listed and rhymed the first 109 chemicals on the standard periodic table and set them to the tune of "The Major-General's Song" from Gilbert & Sullivan's "Pirates of Penzance." Breathlessly, Steve completed the eight-minute medley with Lehrer's revival-survival hymn, "We Will All Go Together When We Go." Early fan Cal Burke, present for the show, found Steve's ability to summon Lehrer songs from his childhood stunning. "If I had seen God face to face when I first encountered Steve," Burke says, "this was certainly the second coming."

If I had seen God face to face when I first encountered Steve, this was certainly the second coming.
CAL BURKE

While recording the pilot installment for new "Living Room Concerts" for WLIR-FM on Long Island on Aug. 27, the day after his Other End shows, Steve wove a nearly 12-minute musical spell, playing pell-mell slide guitar on Muddy Waters' "I Can't Be Satisfied (Trouble)" then slowing and softening to "I'll Fly Away." Asked if he knew any material by country bluesman Booker T. Washington "Bukka" White, Steve, still on slide, launched into "You Don't Love Me Like You Used to Do." Midway, still strumming, he told a story about White having stayed overnight in his apartment when he opened for White in early January 1971 at the Quiet Knight in Chicago. Steve said he'd retired to his bedroom at 4 a.m., leaving White sitting on his living-room couch with a bottle of Jack Daniel's Tennessee Whiskey, and when Steve awoke at 11 a.m., he found the bottle empty and White still sitting fully dressed on the couch. "Well," Steve said White told him, "a haint (ghost) came in through the window, unscrewed the cap and drank the whiskey. I was gonna tell him that was my friend Steve's bottle, but I don't like to mess around with no dead people. And if you don't believe that one, I left the lid off, and it evaporated." Still strumming, Steve ended the 10-minute piece by moving to White's "Shake 'Em on Down," then finally, "Yes, Baby, Yes."

This medley methodology extended to Steve's own material, as he demonstrated in November in Chicago, where he improvised pastiche after pastiche during a long set at Somebody Else's Troubles. He started an eight-and-a-half-minute piece with "Chicken Cordon Bleus," sped up the tempo for a feverish instrumental ("I don't know what this is, but it sure is fast") and finally landed on Billy Edd Wheeler's "Coal Tattoo." Next, his "Lookin' for Trouble" began an 11-minute segment that included quiet, guitar-only takes on 19th century composer Edvard Grieg's "In the Hall of the Mountain King" from the play "Peer Gynt" and Kenny Ball's 1961 Dixieland hit "Midnight in Moscow" and ended with the rousing "Sixteen Tons." For Steve's nine-minute encore ("music to pay your checks by," as he put it), "It's a Sin to Tell a Lie" morphed into Brahms' Lullaby, which eased into a reflective "City of New Orleans."

While listeners found themselves riveted to Steve's extemporaneous melding of songs old and new, his medleys did have a downside, says Steve Cohen, a former Amazingrace associate who at 24 became Steve's road manager in May 1976 and observed hundreds of Steve's shows from the wings. [35] By slipping from tune to tune without a break, Cohen says, Steve denied those in the audi-

35: Steve Cohen adapted an African-American folk toy, called a Limber Jack (see photo, page 395), to sell at crafts fairs. It was a stick figure with movable arms and legs that spun and clacked when the figure was bounced on a wooden plank. In 1974, during an Amazingrace show, Steve invited Cohen onstage to contribute a noisy Limber Jack "dance" to "Mama Don't Allow It."

ence the opportunity to applaud distinct songs, particularly his own. Far better, Cohen says, for a performer to "stop, take the beat and take in that applause, that moment that you've established with that audience. I don't think he was comfortable doing that. It drove me nuts, his not letting the emotion and that connection between the audience and him bloom." At the same time that Steve revered the art of the entertainer, Cohen says, "there was almost an embarrassment over what he was able to do and the way he was able to touch a crowd."

It was a dichotomy that also manifested itself once Steve finally did conclude a song or medley. Steve often bathed in pent-up applause by shrugging slightly, scratching his head and baring a smile that hinted of bewilderment. "There was a combination of humility and self-deprecation," Cohen says, "but he also was aware of a certain manipulation. He was totally aware of what he was doing."

Steve's own explanation for his medleys was more whimsical, seasoned with a dash of mortality. "I didn't mean to be runnin' them together like that," he told a Washington, D.C., audience. "Just want to get to a few of 'em before I die. If I stop between each one of 'em, I might forget which ones I wanted to do, so I beg your indulgence."

His drive to perform invariably won out over conflicting emotions. Nowhere was this more apparent than at an outdoor, Woodstock-style show on Labor Day weekend of 1975 at Mosport Park, a racetrack northeast of Toronto. The three-day fest promoted by Getting It On Productions bid people to camp and take in music from some of the most prominent folkies in Canada (Valdy, Ray Materick) and the States (Melanie, Leon Redbone, Brewer & Shipley). Among the Sunday afternoon headliners were Steve and the act that was to follow him, Tom Rush and his band. But just as at Woodstock, the skies burst almost nonstop with rain, and high winds blew off the stage's canopy. Steve, drenched and trying to keep his guitar dry beneath an umbrella that had been hastily lashed to his mike stand, persevered as the speedway and adjacent hillside became a muddy mess. But at the end of Steve's time, Rush was as scarce as the 5,000 concertgoers, many of whom were scuttling like hermit crabs in and out of their tents in a futile effort to avoid a soaking.

Rush was on his way, barely. Rush and his band had flown to Toronto from Boston in a private plane, and Rush's limousine, his band's van and his equipment truck had gotten lost trying to find the show site. An hour late, Rush arrived, before his band and equipment. Looking out the windows of his limo, he could make out the image of a drenched Steve flailing away. As soon as Rush stepped backstage, the promoter beseeched him, "Steve wants to know how soon you can go on because his guitar is coming unglued in the rain." In the deluge, Rush took the stage sans band, singing only a few songs, including "Wasn't That a Mighty Storm," before the soundman pulled the plug. What impressed Rush most was not the woeful weather but Steve's persistence: "He literally would not leave the stage and leave the audience — what there was of them — unentertained."

Tom Rush, shown in the mid-1970s, marvels that even though he was an hour late to an outdoor festival near Toronto, Steve kept on performing in the rain until he arrived: "He literally would not leave the stage and leave the audience — what there was of them — unentertained."

(Photo courtesy of Tom Rush)

Steve's tenacity was no less steely indoors, as he demonstrated at a show he opened for John Prine on Saturday, Nov. 8, at the Saenger Theater in Mobile, Alabama. Following the sound check, Steve and Prine chatted with an elderly stage hand, who informed them that the performer who opened the Saenger in 1927 was the legendary showman who dominated the live theater stage in the early 20th century, Al Jolson. [36]

"We looked at each other, like 'Wow!'," Prine says. That night, Prine watched from the wings as Steve mixed ballads and funny songs "like he was measuring the entire crowd for a pair of pants." In the middle of Steve's final song, three guitar strings simultaneously popped. He had been playing without a guitar strap, so he dropped to one knee and laid his guitar over it to make it easier to thread new strings. "He couldn't just change 'em with it around his neck. He had to look at the guitar," Prine says. "While he was down there, he talked into the guitar mike and told 'em the story about me and him and the stage hand and that it was the same place that Al Jolson sang in 1927 — and then it hit him. He went into 'Mammy,' and it brought the house down. Then he left the stage. I'm standin' on the side of the stage, the people are standin' and applaudin', and the walls are goin' in and out."

Steve walked past Prine and said, "They're gonna love ya, Johnny."

"Thanks a lot, big guy," Prine said, shaking his head. "We might as well go home now."

Steve's bravado bolstered Prine's reception. The *Azalea City News* of Mobile described Prine that night as technically adept but distracted and slurred, in contrast to Steve's "definitely four-star" performance of "an amazingly audacious repertoire." The headline: "Goodman steals Prine's thunder."

The "Jig" LP created somewhat less thunder in late 1975. It lasted only six weeks on the Top 200 LPs chart in *Billboard*, rising to a high of only 144. Its sales approached a respectable but not phenomenal 50,000, stunted by high-profile reviews whose only substantive knock was Steve's eclecticism.

"Steve Goodman sounds like your run-of-the-mill city/country singer — at first," wrote Jim Gosa of *High Fidelity* magazine. "But with this kind of album, the more you listen, the more you hear." John Tobler, writing in the UK's *ZigZag* magazine, questioned Steve's "apparent desire to appeal to too many markets. Were he to restrict himself to maybe half the forms he uses here, the album would be a treasure." [37] *Seventeen* said the LP "paints a picture of a gentle America in this charming group of songs for all seasons," while at the other end of the magazine spectrum, Chicago-based *Playboy* called it "a scrapbook of good times and pure delight."

Critics seemed to be daring listeners to embrace the album, though its varied genres were slowing its success in the marketplace. Perhaps the most perceptive equivocation came from Stephen Holden of *Rolling Stone*, who opined that none of the LP's songs had "the classic dimensions" of "City of New Orleans" but praised them as "skillfully created modern Americana. ... The commercial modesty of 'Jessie's Jig' represents the measure of its admirable integrity."

They're gonna love ya, Johnny.
STEVE GOODMAN

36: On the night the Saenger opened, Dec. 12, 1927, the main act was the Ziegfield Follies. But Al Jolson may have played the theater not long afterward.

37: In a full-page ad in the same UK publication, which paired Steve with the country-rock Rowans, Asylum branded Steve "a musicologist of the streets."

Probing for Steve's mind-set in the face of such evaluation, Steve Lake, New York writer for the UK's *Melody Maker*, found in Steve a musician opposed to categorization and hopeful that musical barriers would crumble. Steve labeled as futile (and demeaning to Bob Dylan) the media's identification of "latter-day Dylans" such as Prine and Kris Kristofferson. "Comparisons are really unhelpful," he said. "It's become a challenge for the contemporary artist to retain his own identity in the face of the mass audience." Steve said he had found refuge in his live shows, "by limiting myself to dealing with only the people I'm facing at a particular moment, the people who paid their money and took their chances and came out of the house and sat down in the hall or club or whatever. For two hours, my obligation is to them and to the music, and that's it."

Pigeonholing that audience or that music, Steve told Neil Coppage in a mid-1975 interview for *Stereo Review*, would be abhorrent. "I'm not just singing for people between the ages of 16 and 21 with 1.2 years of college, or whatever the demographics and psychographics of it are," he said. "I want to sing to the widest variety of people I know of. I want guys who have to work for a living to listen to it, as well as college students. I just want people who like music to listen to it — and a few who don't particularly like music, because they might catch something that might brighten their day. There's enough of the ham in me to want that."

Disdain for formula was easy to express for Steve, who had been assured by David Geffen not to worry about how many copies his first Asylum LP would sell. "If it doesn't happen with this one, it'll happen with the next one," Steve said Geffen had told him. "You just make 'em, and I'll put 'em out." Such support from the label's chairman gave Steve hope about his commercial viability. "I'd love to have my record sell like Linda Ronstadt's or Orleans or any of those other people on Asylum," he told Mary Cliff of WETA-FM in Washington, D.C. "I think that's not impossible someday."

But Geffen's confidence also buoyed Steve's adherence to his musical instincts. "Anybody who tells you they aren't in this for the money in some way is giving you a lot of bull," Steve told Coppage. "Otherwise, we'd all be singin' in the closet. We're all lookin' to pay the rent with this. But there comes a point where everybody who does this for a living wants to be able to look in the mirror in the morning and say, 'Well, yesterday I didn't consciously try to cheat anybody with my music.'" To Cliff, he added that Geffen's assurance was "'about the first time I've felt I've had any kind of freedom like that to work."

One factor giving Steve's musings vitality was his visual appearance. [38] Writers noted not only his weight loss, but also his facial hair. "His small, skinny frame is given a new authority by a trim beard, which emphasizes the sharpness of his clear, brown eyes," Lake wrote, saying it signaled a "new assertiveness." The makeover had made Steve more attractive to the progressive crowd, but he also knew he didn't approximate a matinee idol. He was grateful that his label could look past that to the potential of his product. Asylum, he told Coppage, was giving the public "a chance to see somebody who looks just like themselves

> **I'm not just singing for people between the ages of 16 and 21 with 1.2 years of college, or whatever the demographics and psychographics of it are.**
> **STEVE GOODMAN**

38: Though he had slimmed down, Steve's 5-foot-2 stature continued to dog him in 1975. Patrick Goldstein recalls interviewing Emmylou Harris about her first LP for the *Chicago Sun-Times* while sitting at a crowded Chicago restaurant table with Harris and her 5-year-old daughter, along with Steve and Nancy Goodman and other musicians. When Harris stood up to leave, she asked someone to find her daughter's jacket. Goldstein picked up a tiny coat from the back of a chair, and Steve "growled with mock outrage" as he bolted from his seat and shouted, "Wait a minute, that's mine!" Later, Steve patted Goldstein on the shoulder. "Don't worry," Steve said, "everyone makes the same mistake. It's not easy going through life as an extra-small."

and sounds like themselves up there makin' all this music. ... It can only help the musician."

With prominent attention to the "Jig" LP, Steve played a teeming schedule of fall dates, including an Oct. 5 show in a Berkshire cornfield near the western Massachusetts town of Worthington. The instigator of the five-hour Sunday afternoon event was Massachusetts hometowner Arlo Guthrie. Steve's instant response to Guthrie's invitation — a benefit for a local health clinic — illustrated the friendship the two shared. "Not where or when," Steve told Guthrie, "but how do I get there?" For Marie Rhines, violinist at the benefit, Steve's appeal that day was visceral. "His voice, it came from the heart," she says. "It just made you want to cry. It just grabbed. It made me want to know him and play with him musically."

Steve's heartfelt voice also had a devilish side, as Jim Geisler soon found out. In the Georgetown neighborhood of Washington, D.C., Geisler ran the popular Cellar Door, where Steve played three sold-out shows on Saturday, Oct. 25. Geisler prided himself on moving audiences in and out of the listening room quickly to mollify D.C. police and neighbors who objected to long lines stretching down the street. Steve knew this, but between his second show and the start of his third, Steve had another purpose in mind — landing a gig for one of his Chicago brethren.

"Y'know," Steve told Geisler as the two stood in the upstairs dressing room, "I have a friend in Chicago you should really hire because this is Washington, and he does political satire."

"Right, Steve," Geisler replied quickly, walking to the door. "Look, I want an hour and 10 minutes. We gotta go. Let's go."

"No, you don't understand, Jim. You really should hire this guy," Steve said. "His name's Larry Rand. He's from Chicago. He'd work out real well here."

Agitated, Geisler said, "Steve, we'll talk about it later, next time, whatever."

Steve took off his guitar, walked to the dressing-room couch and sat down. He and Geisler could hear the customers downstairs clapping their hands, stomping their feet and shouting, "Goodman, Goodman ..." Steve looked up and said with a grin, "I don't think you heard me, Jim. I have this friend —"

Geisler shot back, "He's got a gig, OK? He's got a gig."

Steve picked up his guitar, walked downstairs and did the third show. Early the next week, Rand got a phone call from Geisler, who said, "You've got a gig. What do you do?" Rand eventually played several weeklong stints at the Cellar Door.

Both Rand and Geisler laugh at the memory 30 years later. "Jim understood that for Steve to pull a stunt like that, it must have been really important to him," Rand says. "He did have me over a barrel," says Geisler, who notes that Steve used the same technique to secure a booking for Fred Holstein. "Steve was the only one who ever held me hostage like that," Geisler says. "He had picked his moment, he knew exactly what he was doing, and you could see in his eyes his 'I gotcha!' "

> Steve was the only one who ever held me hostage like that. He had picked his moment, he knew exactly what he was doing, and you could see in his eyes his 'I gotcha!'
> **JIM GEISLER**

Such incidents put Steve into high spirits to write new songs. For subject matter, he turned to the happiest aspects of his personal life — his wife and family. In October and November, joining friend Paula Ballan and Pittsburgh-rooted singer/songwriter Patrick Chamberlain in the Manhattan apartment of guitarist Steve Burgh, he came up with a pair of tunes exploring that theme.

The first, "Can't Go Back," was a lyrical lecture from a father who warns his son to avoid the game-playing of "little girls" and to focus on staying true to a woman "who gives you good lovin'." The message, applicable to a road musician such as Steve, came wrapped in the musical style — including the grunts and "Good God, y'alls" — of a sweaty soul singer Steve revered, Wilson Pickett, with whom Steve had appeared on NBC-TV's "Midnight Special." In later concerts, Steve pumped up Pickett's role in 1962 as the voice of "I Found a Love," an R&B hit by the Falcons. "This is a song that I wrote that I was hopin' Wilson Pickett would record," Steve said. "Then again, I hope Wilson Pickett records all of 'em. I really love his singing." In performing the uptempo tune, Steve bounced on the balls of his feet, gestured wildly and stretched his voice from falsetto to the guttural, to ringing audience acclaim.

An even greater crowd pleaser but with a much quieter tone, the second song he wrote that fall was far more substantive and personal, as it directly reflected his role as a husband and father. Stemming from his poignant comment in the early summer to childhood friend Jo An Stepan Simich in her hospital room, the song was called "Old Fashioned."

Steve had sketched out the tune's affecting lyrics but had not set them to music, and Steve Burgh had written a gentle, lilting melody sans words. The words and lyrics merged when Steve and Burgh met with Chamberlain, Ballan and banjo master Stephen Wade and listened to a few Ink Spots LPs during a couple of nights at Burgh's apartment. When Burgh played the guitar piece, an excited Steve said, "I've got words for this," and it took little time for the group to give the song its final shape.

While the song's music fit the mood of a lounge act ("In my mind, I have always heard Tony Bennett singing it," Burgh said), more stirring was its lyrical sentiment. "Old Fashioned" proclaimed the virtue of true love, but instead of trumpeting it as he did in "Can't Go Back," Steve caressed it with lines such as: "The one who knows the difference between promises and passion is my old-fashioned girl." Foremost, the song addressed Steve's love for his wife, Nancy, an emotion Steve unabashedly proclaimed in many shows. But its crowning touch, extending the message to Jessie and Sarah, came in its penultimate verse with the words, "Maybe someday our daughter will be an old-fashioned girl."

Eager for feedback, Steve walked to Matt Umanov Guitars in Greenwich Village and played "Old Fashioned" for singer-actor Erik Frandsen.

"It sounds like a Hoagy Carmichael or Johnny Mercer song," Frandsen said.

"Yeah, well, I've been listening to them a lot," Steve replied.

Frandsen went on to say that in contrast to musicians inspired by Woody Guthrie, "I've always been more one of Hoagy's boys."

> **It sounds like a Hoagy Carmichael or Johnny Mercer song.**
> **ERIK FRANDSEN**

"Tell me about it," Steve said with a grin.

As with "Would You Like to Learn to Dance?," the song played especially well to women. Jamie Marks, daughter of Greenwich Village club proprietress Penny Simon, labels it as "one I can't listen to without crying." That it defined aspirations both personal and universal made it especially appealing, says Ballan. "He said it all in 'Old Fashioned.' Those are all the ways in which he wanted to see Nancy and did see Nancy," Ballan says. "Whatever else he did and didn't do, being able to go home to Nancy was his great American dream. It was his 'Father Knows Best.' "

"At that time, that was a real brave thing to write about," reflects the musical friend who had instigated the second verse of Steve's "City of New Orleans," Richard Wedler. "Everybody was looking for new freedom and consciousness, and he boiled it all down to 'the love of an old-fashioned girl.' It touched something that was very soft and loving."

Whether the two songs amounted to metaphoric flowers to Nancy for past wrongs or simply a heartfelt expression of appreciation (or both), "Can't Go Back" and "Old Fashioned" bespoke optimism.

Further brightening Steve's visibility was ABC-TV, which on Nov. 3 launched a revamped version of its "A.M. America" morning newsmagazine to compete with NBC's "Today." ABC's Bob Shanks, in charge of the overhaul, chose a name for the show that coincidentally matched the chorus phrase from Steve's most famous song: "Good Morning America." Contrary to innumerable later accounts, however, there was no connection between Steve's song and the show title. Born in Illinois and raised in Indiana, Shanks says he was inspired by a 1928 collection of Carl Sandburg poems with the same title. Shanks, a Massachusetts resident, also had been familiar with the morning show of ABC's Boston affiliate called "Good Morning New England" and figured, "If it worked for them, it'll work for us." [39]

While the match of show title and song phrase was inadvertent, it was an example of how "City of New Orleans" had permeated the culture and undergirded much of the public's perception of Steve. By this time, the song had even appeared in Screen Gems-Columbia sheet music transcribed for male/female and all-female high-school choirs by famed arranger Chuck Cassey.

The ubiquity of "City" became a repeated topic in Steve's conversations, such as during a Western tour swing when he visited Samantha Eggar and her friend Allison Caine in Eggar's Los Angeles living room. Steve listened while Caine explained the background of "Are You Lonesome Tonight?," a 1926 song written by her uncle, Lou Handman, who died in 1956 and didn't see its popularization in 1960 by Elvis Presley.

"Oh, I'd love to have a big hit like that someday," Steve said.

"Y'know, 'City of New Orleans' is a standard," Caine replied, naming Johnny Cash and others who had interpreted it on vinyl. "If they all sing your song, you're going to be fine because look what happened with our Elvis song."

They debated what constituted a standard and whether "City" qualified. In

---

Whatever else he did and didn't do, being able to go home to Nancy was his great American dream. It was his 'Father Knows Best.'
PAULA BALLAN

39: Fred Silverman, then-president of ABC Entertainment, says that it was he, instead of Bob Shanks, who originated the title for "Good Morning America." But like Shanks, Silverman says that the title had no link to Steve's "City." The phrase was "something I just improvised," he says.

the end, Steve said he simply hoped his songwriting could provide a legacy for his wife and daughters. "Things are in remission now," he said, "but you just don't know what's going to happen to us. I want to make sure that my family's going to have security."

At the same time, Steve also aimed to pay back what he saw as a debt to Memorial Sloan-Kettering Cancer Center, where he anonymously set up a fund in the name of his brother's late friend, Scott Murphy, in which to deposit much of his "City of New Orleans" earnings. "I saw him sign a whole royalty check for a quarter of a year, a three-month period, big money, right over to Sloan-Kettering," says Earl Pionke.

Eventually totaling more than $1 million, the fund targeted leukemia research and treatment. "Steve put in a lot," says Dr. Isabel "Bonnie" Cunningham. "When patients wanted to send money in honor of somebody, we frequently would suggest they put it in the Scott Murphy fund." She says that consequently, "City of New Orleans" became known as "the leukemia song" at Sloan-Kettering. "He always wanted to give something back," she says. "He was extremely generous. It was a very private thing. He never talked about it or made a big fuss. He just kept giving money in there."

In the midst of hectic touring and songwriting in late 1975, Steve was eager to take a vacation with Nancy. He set aside two weeks, Dec. 16-30, for just that, and the setting for the journey was exotic — the U.S. Virgin Islands southeast of Florida on the north edge of the Caribbean Sea.

News of a high-level shakeup at Steve's record label came one week before the trip, however. Increasingly enamored with Hollywood (and having recently fought serious illness and broken up with his paramour, Cher), David Geffen left Asylum on Dec. 9 for a film career as a vice chairman with the parent firm, Warner Communications. In a reciprocal move, Warner Brothers Records President Joe Smith ended his 14-year career at that label by shifting to the chairmanship of Asylum.

The switch spelled a less certain future for Steve because, just as with Buddah, the man who had signed him had departed, and he would have to forge a new relationship with the incoming chief. Moreover, Smith's initial public comments, reported in the Dec. 20 edition of *Billboard*, were unsettling.

Smith issued a warning undoubtedly directed at Steve and others of his mid-level ilk. "Elektra/Asylum is fortunate to have more than its share of superstars for such a small artist roster," he said. "But there are also several E/A artists just below this level of acceptance who I think could be built into huge sellers with the right kind of determined merchandising campaigns. That will be my main thrust for next year."

Was this an ominous sign or a genuine commitment of support? Just how could Steve and his music be "merchandised" for greater sales?

The questions would await the end of Steve's vacation, which promised to be a healthy getaway. Unbeknown to Steve, it also would become musically productive. In fact, Jimmy Buffett should have been there. ♪

Ten days before a family vacation in the U.S. Virgin Islands, and sporting his newly serious look for Asylum Records, Steve is billed for a solo show Dec. 6, 1975, at Hogg Auditorium at the University of Texas in Austin.

Steve ("devilish and angelic, deep and silly, fierce and tender," as described by Bonnie Raitt) performs a set in early 1977.
(Photos by Steve Cohen)

'There is no one influence?'
'Yeah, it's the hectic eclectic'

As America geared up for its bicentennial, one of its most affecting contemporary songwriters found a touchstone in a man who became the country's most revered writer one century earlier.

"I don't think anybody who lives in the United States would be telling you the truth if they didn't say that Mark Twain has affected something they wrote or something they saw," Steve Goodman told Steve Lake of London's *Melody Maker* in October 1975. "Twain's conversational sequences are the best. Nobody's ever gotten it down in the pages of a book more accurately. You can read Twain aloud today, and it's real. ... Such a strong understanding of human motivation. Twain was a musician. He had great ears. ... Twain captured the musicality of speech."

So potent were Twain's novels that they highlighted any study of American literature, Steve told John Tobler of the UK's *Omaha Rainbow* 10 months later. Students, he said, often slog through the "weighty" tomes of James Fenimore Cooper (*The Last of the Mohicans*) and Nathaniel Hawthorne (*House of the Seven Gables*, *The Scarlet Letter*) before coming up for air with the Herman Melville adventures *Billy Budd* and *Moby Dick* and being rewarded by the macabre poetry and short stories of Edgar Allan Poe. "Then there's Twain, and all of a sudden you understand. There's actually people that can write, thank God!"

Fittingly, it was a modern-day raconteur and man of letters who would spring on Steve a literary challenge.

It came from Studs Terkel, longtime WFMT-FM interviewer and author of the best-selling *Hard Times* and *Working*. From the moment Terkel had first heard Steve's three-minute musical condensation of *Moby Dick*, Terkel heralded it as a way to instill youthful appreciation of the classics. Terkel likened Steve's "Moby Book" to Woody Guthrie's "Tom Joad," which similarly summed up John Steinbeck's *The Grapes of Wrath*, and he urged Steve to go further.

"The question is, when are you going to do an album ... American classics, Goodman's interpretation?" Terkel asked Steve on the air March 13, 1975.

"I'll tell ya, Studs, there's nothing like blackmailing a fella in public on the radio into doin' something," Steve replied. "You got my arm twisted, it's behind my back, it's comin' off."

> The question is, when are you going to do an album ... American classics, Goodman's interpretation?
> **STUDS TERKEL**

Steve evaded the question at the time, but over the Chicago radio airwaves on the morning of Jan. 3, 1976, Terkel confronted him again, this time with a more tempting dare. Steve had just played New Year's Eve at the Earl of Old Town with David Amram, his brother in eclectic invention and with whom he had conjured the fledgling version of "Moby Book" a year and a half prior at the Mariposa Folk Festival. Two days after their loose, nonstop shows at the Earl (and Steve's six-minute, 18-verse tribute to 1976 during WFMT's all-night "Midnight Special"), the pair agreed to be guests on Terkel's show.

"I have this crazy, wild thought," Terkel said. "You two could put something together. It would be so astonishing. ... Suppose I gave you a challenge. If I say to you, suppose you're onstage now, same circumstances, and I said to you, *Huckleberry Finn* by Mark Twain."

Steve's eyes flared as he looked at Amram. A few awkward seconds of silence passed. "Um, words fail us," Steve finally said with a chuckle. "No, we better come up with something."

The two picked up guitars and, as they had done at Mariposa, loped into a sultry, 12-bar blues. Amram began a verbal improvisation, spouting a dozen lines about his Pennsylvania boyhood daydreams of "my favorite hooky-player Huck." Amram's lyrics were sentences crammed with syllables that spilled on top of each other quickly, and most of his lines rhymed. But they served as a mere setup for a burst of brilliance from his partner.

With just two minutes of instrumental vamping and Amram's two-and-a-half minutes of bop-style extemporizing as his only preparation, Steve created a five-minute, eight-stanza masterpiece of period detail and modern-day message, certainly laced with personal identification:

> *Huck Finn floatin' on the raft*
> *Down the Mississippi River, folks thought he was daft*
> *But he's just a good ol' boy*
> *Just a good ol' boy*
> *Tryin' to find himself a little bit of life's joy*

Retaining the "good ol' boy" refrain, Steve sailed through the epic journey — Huck's escape from a cruel father, his friendship with the black slave, Jim, and his links to Tom Sawyer, Tom's Aunt Polly and Becky Thatcher. To bring the saga to the present, Steve exalted the slow pace of Huck's time: "Twain saw what was comin' 'round the bend / Perhaps we will not see quiet times like those again." [1]

Early in Steve's portion of the song, Amram switched to pennywhistle and fife for accompaniment throughout, and the pair topped off the proceedings with another minute of gentle jamming before ending the 10-and-a-half minute suite. The result enchanted Terkel.

"And all we said was 'Huck Finn,'" Terkel marveled. "Of course, your imagination is there, the discipline is there, the giftedness is there. But it's also a freedom, isn't it?"

I have this crazy, wild thought. ... Suppose you're on stage now, same circumstances, and I said to you, *Huckleberry Finn* by Mark Twain.
STUDS TERKEL

1: The untitled Huck Finn song, apparently not copyrighted, has not been released commercially. It is available for listening as part of "The Studs Terkel Program" archive of the Chicago Historical Society. Terkel's acclaimed one-hour show aired weekdays from 1952 to 1997.

"Well," Steve replied, "besides the fact that we're kindred spirits, when you're playin' like that, Studs, for me, anyhow, it's the only time when I feel like nobody is going to tell me what I ought to do."

The improv session was more than a momentary amusement. It symbolized a surge in the middle years of the 1970s when Steve was reaching and reveling in his professional zenith. He would have later high points — new songs clever and poignant, appearances on national TV, enormous concert audiences and enriching experiences on both sides of the glass in record-company studios. But never would Steve be busier with the buzz of creativity, more in sync with societal sensibilities and so buoyant with national and international notoriety. On the home and family front, it also was a time of nesting, bolstered by his sustained remission from leukemia.

His Caribbean vacation during the last two weeks of 1975 promised to be a family-oriented break for Steve, Nancy, 3-year-old Jessie and 6-month-old Sarah, but it was possible only because Steve could mix in some work with the pleasure. It was, as he termed it later, a busman's holiday.

Jim Geisler, proprietor of the Cellar Door in Washington, D.C., had invited Steve to the island of St. Croix to perform two weekends at a 150-seat waterfront club he had just purchased and named the Foggy Bottom (the name of a D.C. neighborhood), in the King Christian Hotel in Christiansted, a tourist hub that drew visiting musicians ranging from Earl "Fatha" Hines to part-time resident Victor Borge. [2] In exchange, Geisler offered Steve and his family round-trip plane tickets and food and lodging for two weeks. For Steve and others whom Geisler engaged in a similar trade over the next two years, the attractions of the Virgin Islands — scuba diving, sailing and fishing — were a potent lure.

"My club would feed everybody, and so would every other place in town," Geisler says. "They just walked around town with the keys to the city. It was a real getaway from all of the agitation and grief of performing. Everybody who was there had this island mentality, so that people could come down and perform their music, but nobody bothered 'em. Steve could go on and perform and come offstage and go sit in the bar, and if his body language suggested that he wanted to be left alone, nobody was coming up to intrude."

But upon his arrival with Nancy and the girls, Steve found the surroundings anything but idyllic. The island was still reeling from the 1972 drug-related shootings of a dozen people on a Rockefeller family golf course, real-estate prices had plummeted and hotel occupancy had dropped to 11 percent. Marijuana traffickers disguised their cargo underwater in black plastic bales that they termed "square grouper" fish. Stories abounded of tourist abductions, and strolling through town were intimidating American eccentrics, including a gruff, sullen ogre who looked like a cross between Popeye and a pirate. Merchants labeled these locals wharf rats, and, as Geisler says, they "really were scum."

At first, the people Steve met there disturbed him, Geisler says. "He thought he'd gone to the shootout at the OK Corral or something, and he was really pissed off because he thought the island was way too rough for him to have

It's the only time when I feel like nobody is going to tell me what I ought to do.
STEVE GOODMAN

2: Across from the King Christian Hotel was another hostelry, Hotel on the Key, the basis of Herman Wouk's 1965 novel, *Don't Stop the Carnival*, and Jimmy Buffett's 1998 CD of the same name.

Nancy and the kids." By the end of the first week, however, Steve saw through their exteriors and mellowed. It didn't take long, Geisler says, for Steve to view these folks as "the quintessential halfwits and characters that you assume would run away to a Caribbean island."

The Foggy Bottom, Steve said, was a "loud drinking place," better suited to a raucous bar band than a solo folksinger. [3] But he melded into the milieu with ease, evidenced by a bold gesture witnessed by Geisler. Wandering into the club one night was a drunken hulk who called himself Jungle Prince, dressed like a native by wearing dreadlocks, loincloth, feathers and beads and "stomped his feet and hollered at people in gibberish that he made up on the spot." Steve yelled across the room to Geisler, "Jimmy, who's your friend?" and summoned Jungle Prince to the stage. "Here's this guy 6-foot-8 and Steve 5-foot-2 standing there, and he got the guy to do a song with him. It was amazing, the funniest thing."

Steve's steeliness emerged as he wrestled with the scuba experience at a diving shop 50 feet from the Foggy Bottom. Brian Friedman, a fan of Steve's and a friend of Geisler, says that Steve's obstacle was the now-antiquated diving masks. Unlike today's more panoramic headgear, the masks that were available allowed only for tunnel vision and gave some diving neophytes — including Steve — the fear of feeling shut in or enclosed. "He really had a tough time in the water with claustrophobia," Friedman says. "He did overcome it, but it took him coming back six or seven days. As long as he was willing to try, I was willing to go, and he kept coming back. I never saw anybody do that. I took thousands of people out to dive, and I don't remember anybody so persistent."

Late after one of his weekend shows, with Nancy and the girls asleep in the hotel, Steve also took his first voyage aboard a sailboat. Ex-Chicagoan John Rothchild, a day charter operator who made a living taking tourists to nearby Buck Island Reef National Monument, had heard Steve play at Amazingrace in Evanston, and he invited Steve for a moonlight ride. As the two glided around "darker than dark" Christiansted Harbor from 1 to 3 a.m. aboard the 30-foot *Sunny*, they chatted about Chicago and families. The talkative Rothchild told

3: In a later show in Atlanta, Steve said the King Christian Hotel operated as a "whorehouse" atop the Foggy Bottom club. "I didn't realize what it was until I got there. I'd be downstairs singin' in the bar, and upstairs people would be bangin' on the door where my family was: 'I got the money!' Three-thirty in the morning. Great."

Steve he had moved to St. Croix after a bad divorce, which involved a young child.

As their conversation wound down, Steve was astonished to learn that Rothchild's boat had no engine.

"So how are we gonna get back?" Steve asked.

"I'm a sailor," Rothchild replied. "That's what I do."

Rothchild explained that by keeping the boat motorless he was able to avoid having to secure a captain's license. Such logic was one of the things that made sense to Steve in a land of contradictions. He discovered that while Hess Oil operated the largest refinery in the Western Hemisphere on the island, most of the local residents — as well as emigrants sneaking onto St. Croix from Barbados, Martinique and the other French Caribbean islands — were out of work. He also found that food was shipped in from Puerto Rico because the local government had forbidden farmers to grow crops. It was an upside-down culture, its disorienting surroundings intensified by the tourist trade.

"It's like Penney's basement with palm trees," Steve later told "FolkScene" host Howard Larman. "It's real hard. Everything there is either resorts for the newly wed and the almost dead, right, or these incredible bargain-basement kinds of shack stores — literally, eight pairs of gym shoes for 34 cents. And it's tough. Rum is a buck a bottle. That's the only thing that was fairly priced on the entire island."

Upon his return to Chicago, Steve played New Year's Eve and Day at the Earl. With the bewilderment over St. Croix lingering in his mind, Steve enjoyed the freedom of improvising with David Amram. But it was short-lived. Looming was commercial reality — the need for more precise songcrafting

... and as it looked from the air. The picturesque surroundings hosted a mélange of characters and purposes that inspired Steve to write one of his most highly regarded songs, "Banana Republics."

(Photo by Brian Friedman)

during two weeks of recording sessions he had set up in late January for his second Asylum LP. The stimulus, he later told Howard Larman of "FolkScene" and John Tobler of the UK's *Omaha Rainbow*, had come from the record label. But the messenger, Steve said, was Al Bunetta, who had just transplanted his management office from New York to Wilshire Boulevard in Los Angeles, less than three miles east of the headquarters of Asylum.

"Steve," Bunetta said, "the 'Jig' was a nice album, but you know what? It didn't break any ol' national sales records, and unless you want the ol' record company to forget who the hell you are, you better make another one."

Steve said his impish reply was, "Oops."

"It's a nice album, man," Bunetta repeated. "Next."

"Al, you can't just dismiss 'em like that," Steve said.

"I know, man, but that's the way it is," Bunetta said. "If you want to play with the big kids, you have to put up with that nonsense."

"I'm not ready," Steve said.

"Well, get ready."

Steve had opted to produce the new LP with Steve Burgh's help and had completed a couple of songs, "Can't Go Back" and "Old Fashioned," from his writing sessions with Burgh the previous fall. He also had fragments of ideas for a few others, but not nearly enough material for an album. [4] Calling on a trait that always served him well, humility, Steve was not above asking for help. It was a time for putting his "money" — a belief in collaboration — where his mouth was.

Flying his musical friends into Chicago, he set to work with them — not just to play in the recording sessions, as with the "Jig" project, but also to help write the remaining tunes. One place to begin was a spoonerism that had come to him one day at 4 a.m. Inspired by his immersion in the topsy-turvy world of St. Croix, it was an amiable creation that crystallized the songwriting process and Steve's greatest aspirations: "Give me some words I can dance to and a melody that rhymes."

It was a sentiment too good to ignore. He summoned musicians to combine forces with him on the 23rd floor of the Allerton Hotel (one floor below the Tip Top Tap) along the Magnificent Mile — just three blocks north and one block west of Chicago Recording Company, where the album would be captured on tape. In Burgh's hotel room, Steve introduced the line to Burgh and a Bay Area reeds player, Jim Rothermel.

"We just started fooling around with it," Burgh recalled. "We came up with this reggae/calypso kind of groove, I came up with some little guitar things, and Steve started throwing lyrics out." The words emanated from his St. Croix experience, with references to "expatriated Americans" (the wharf rats, Jungle Prince, even Jim Geisler), including those, like John Rothchild, who "come for the sailing ... running from lovers, leaving no forward address." Burgh matched the latter line with, "Some of them are running marijuana/Some are running from the IRS." Fiddling on a flute, Rothermel gave the song some harmonic

---

The 'Jig' was a nice album, but you know what? It didn't break any ol' national sales records, and unless you want the ol' record company to forget who the hell you are, you better make another one.

AL BUNETTA

4: In his May 20 "FolkScene" interview, Steve disingenuously claimed to be a "lazy" songwriter. "I have about as much drive as the average snail," he said. "I want to go see a baseball game. I don't want to sit around and write songs." But he also noted that "the logistics of traveling just make it impossible" to efficiently compose new tunes.

direction. The finished tune revealed the emptiness and angst of U.S. visitors who look for fun in the Caribbean but end up "telling themselves the same lies that they told themselves at home." It was at once biting and poignant — and its name, Steve said, flowed naturally from United Fruit Company profiteering and U.S. political intervention in Central America, as well as the atmosphere of "The Maltese Falcon" and other exotic movies starring the scheming Sydney Greenstreet. Steve decided the title should capitalize on the colloquialism that reflected the region's most visible cash crop: "Banana Republics."

In the studio late the next night, about 3 a.m. the song came alive, in large part due to a Rothermel recorder solo that ironically cast an enchanting, dancy spell amid the sobering lyrics. Other elements, including a softly syncopated bass line by Sid Sims (replacing Hugh McDonald, who had kidney stones) and Steve's own high harmony vocals, slipped in snugly. Even Rothermel's over-dubbed arp-string synthesizer — akin to the "sweetening" from Cashman & West that Steve had rejected nearly four years prior — supplied a fitting, ethereal echo.

The result was immensely satisfying. "This was the one that in the studio we could tell was doing what it was supposed to do while we were doing it," Steve told Studs Terkel. The pianist on the cut, Jeff Gutcheon, went even further. "When we finished playing the track, it had a magical feeling to it," he says, "very special, kind of profound, because the song is very melancholy, and we played it that way. It wasn't 'Cucaracha' or anything like that. It was as sad as the song was. I remember when it was finished, it felt like we were seeing God."

Steve knew "Banana Republics" would be a highlight of the album, so there was no contesting the use of the song's key line — modified slightly — as the LP's witty, offbeat title: "Words We Can Dance To."

Moving from such a lyrical and musical high to the crafting of other songs could have been a comedown, but Steve's crew proved game. One on-the-spot creation came between sessions in the front room of Steve's apartment on Bittersweet where "Jessie's Jig" had been born. "It was a whole-nighter, just him and me hanging out one night trying not to wake the baby up," Burgh said. The idea for the song, similar to that of "Can't Go Back," was to be wary of youthful vows of love. "It's about the human condition and that things aren't always what they seem," Burgh said. "It's almost a warning: 'Danger. Stay off the third rail. The tracks may be dangerous.' [5] There's a subtlety out there, something that Steve was really good at seeing in other people." The song, recorded in the western-swing style of Bob Wills, kicked off with a delicious pun. Noting that officials "sign a piece of paper" at the moment of everyone's birth and death, Steve wrote that the truths in life can be found, "but you must read in between the lines." The last three words of the phrase became the song's title.

From the studio to Steve's apartment to the Allerton Hotel, Steve was intent that his cadre of a dozen or so musicians would get enough lines down on paper so that he could come away from the sessions with a full album. "He created a think tank and presided over it," says cornetist Peter Ecklund. The troupe tried

Jeff Gutcheon says all of the musicians who played on the 1976 recording of Steve's "Banana Republics" felt awe upon its completion: "It wasn't 'Cucaracha' or anything like that. It was as sad as the song was. I remember when it was finished, it felt like we were seeing God."

(Photo by Michael Friedman, courtesy of Jim Colgrove)

5: The so-called "third rail" of Chicago's El is the one that can electrocute anyone who comes into contact with it.

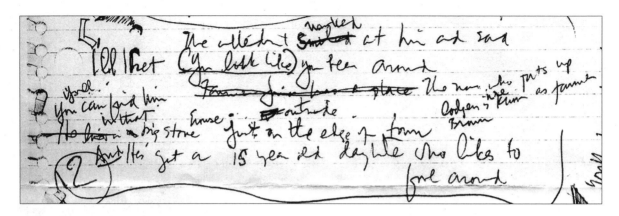

Notes taken during the songwriting session by pianist Jeff Gutcheon for the second of seven verses of "Death of a Salesman," which introduces the character of Farmer Brown and his "15-year-old daughter who likes to fool around."

(Image courtesy of Jeff Gutcheon)

6: The whiskey song had a verse written by Steve's road manager at the time, Steve Cohen, about trying to pick up a woman at a bar. The line "Well, I gave her a wink, 'Can I buy you a drink? Would you like to come on home with me?'" became part of a later song written by Steve and John Prine, "How Much Tequila Did I Drink Last Night." Cohen says the chorus of the unfinished whiskey song went: "That was just the whiskey talking, talking up the same old lies ... and I went home with *The New York Times.*"

writing a song with the theme of "It was just the whiskey talking" but couldn't get it much further than the initial concept. [6] Those assembled — including John Frigo on fiddle, Jethro Burns on mandolin, Saul Broudy on harmonica, Steve Mosley on drums and even David Amram on French horn, as well as Rothermel, Sims and Gutcheon — also put together a slinky jam on the traditional "Corrina Corrina" blues. Much like "Mama Don't Allow It," the track featured a variety of instruments in its four and a half minutes. By the end, thanks to a horn arrangement by Ecklund, it cannily assumed a Dixieland strut. But for reasons unknown, Steve opted not to include it on the "Words" LP.

The epitome of collaboration for the album came in a hotel room back at the Allerton. There, Steve gave six musicians — Burgh, Gutcheon, Rothermel, Lew London, Kenny Kosek and steel-guitar player Winnie Winston — a task equally comical and challenging, to dream up a song based on a traveling-salesman joke. They started with the typical scenario of a weary vendor who at the end of a long day stops at a gas station and gets directions to a farmer's house, where the farmer's daughter warmly greets the man and invites him to spend the night with her.

As Gutcheon took notes, the accompanists took turns serving up the plot's twists while Steve, like a circus ringmaster, sifted them into usable lyrics, sometimes shooting back choice comeback lines. At one point, Rothermel remembered the phrase "ruby lips" from the Percy Montrose campfire song "Clementine." To describe the appeal of the farmer's daughter, he suggested: "Her warm and tender ruby lips he scarcely could believe." Swift as a trigger, Steve matched the line with: "He never saw the hammer she had hidden up her sleeve." Astonishment swept the room. "He would just finish something like that," Rothermel says. "If you gave it to him, it was almost instantaneous. It was just unbelievable."

Because of the creative harmony in the room, and the fact that Steve included all six names in the song's writing credit, the tune became Burgh's favorite of his many co-writes with Steve. "We were all smoking pot and drinking beer and throwing this thing around, and it was a lot of fun because we came up with this wonderful, cohesive story from beginning to end," he said. "It even had a Stephen King punch line before we even knew about Stephen King." The punch line was reflected in the song's title — another pun, this one mordant: "Death of a Salesman."

Set to the tune of "Eight More Miles to Louisville," the 1947 Louis "Grandpa" Jones country classic, "Death of a Salesman" (or, as Steve cracked, "Willy Loman through the Gloamin' ") illustrated the range of styles that was sweeping the "Words" LP. Its seven verses bouncing along to a bluegrass beat, complete with prominent banjo by Winston, mandolin by London and fiddles by Kosek, "Death of a Salesman" joined the album's expanse of genres: the soul of "Can't Go Back," the swing of "Between the Lines," the political and personal calypso of "Banana Republics" and the romantic serenade of "Old Fashioned." And Steve wasn't done yet.

Steve opted to include a Michael Smith tune for the third LP in a row, "The Ballad of Dan Moody (Roving Cowboy)." The song's twist ending offered another touch of black humor as its conflicted protagonist inadvertently sends a posse to kill his three robbing "rodeo chums." [7] He also teamed with Gutcheon on piano, Rothermel on clarinet and Ecklund on cornet to record a slow, spare, raggy blues version of his topical plaint about joblessness, "Unemployed." [8] If all that weren't enough diversity, Steve recorded an out-and-out rocker, "Tossin' and Turnin'," the Ritchie Adams/Malou Rene party tune that Bobby Lewis made a number-one hit in 1961. With three million copies sold, it was that year's most successful single, and no doubt Steve hoped his remake 14 years later could catch similar fire. The track featured wild tenor-sax licks by Rothermel, wall-of-sound backup vocals by Raun MacKinnon and locals Diane Holmes and Mary Gaffney and what MacKinnon termed a "maniacal" electric-guitar solo by Steve, who played it "with a mad gleam in his eyes."

As Steve and his troupe reached the end of January, the pieces of the "Words" album were nearly complete. "Pressure" was Steve's one-word explanation for how the LP's final full-band song was inspired. Along with Burgh, Rothermel and Gutcheon, Steve had composed a gentle tune sans lyrics, the reverse of his usual writing process. "Five minutes before the last session," Steve told audiences later that year, "we had this great track and no words, and it was shit or get off the pot, honestly. So I sat down and wrote the son of a bitch in a hurry."

The image that came to his mind was a TV commercial for Big Brothers of America in which Ray Charles sang, "You could be a buddy to him. Why not? Couldn't you?" Quickly, Steve transformed his tune — by turns a gentle waltz and a frisky bounce — into a meditation on the exercise of discretion when falling in love with a friend whose feelings are not reciprocal. With its subtext of romantic restraint in the face of temptation ("Some things are better left unsaid"), the song became his wife's favorite song on the album, Steve said, and its title offered wise solace: "That's What Friends Are For." [9]

Steve also knew that he wanted an uncluttered closer for the LP, as was his usual practice at concerts. It had to be a piece that would settle listeners into a contemplative state, that he could sing with only his acoustic guitar and that he

Jim Post, shown in 1976, sang harmony on Steve's recording of "The Ballad of Dan Moody."
(Photo by Steve Cohen)

7: To sing the modulated reprise of the last verse, Steve brought in Jim Post, whose tenor led the tune to a ringing conclusion. "We thought we had a hit song on 'Roving Cowboy' and really worked our asses off to try to make an almost L.A./Eagle-ish production on that," Steve Burgh recalled. "We achieved what we were looking for, but the song was a little long and a little too intelligent."

8: In his recording, he removed his warning to Gerald Ford, replacing the name with a reference to "politicians." This prevented the song from becoming dated, particularly with the presidential election looming that fall.

9: Jazz solos by Jethro Burns on mandolin and 60-year-old violinist John Frigo, a former member of the Chico Marx and Jimmy Dorsey orchestras, enhanced the gentle feeling of "That's What Friends Are For." The song also benefited from the accordion of Bobby Rossi, a house musician at Riccardo's, whose late-night downtown ambience influenced Steve in his high-school years.

could mine from tradition. For that, he selected two contenders. The first was the timeless ode to unfulfilled yearning, "The Water Is Wide." The song had become newly prominent (a Pat Conroy memoir with the same title had been made into a 1974 feature film starring Jon Voight), and Steve's four-and-a-half-minute recording of it clearly came from the heart. "That song is universal," he told Win Stracke four years earlier. "Anybody who has ever been in any kind of situation involving unrequited love will understand that song. ... That's what makes that the greatest song. All the songs of unrequited love are just rewrites of 'The Water Is Wide.' "

Consciously or not, Steve turned to a song of requited love as his other potential closer, and it became the track that he chose to include on the LP. Written by William J. Hill, the tune had been popularized by a bluesman from Steve's backyard, Bill Broonzy, who had made it the most charming number in his repertoire in the decades before he died of throat cancer in 1958. More recently, Steve had heard folksinger Guy Guilbert play it for Stracke and Studs Terkel at Troubles. With an unmistakable smile in his voice and inserting an affectionate lyrical reference to "Big Bill," Steve recorded a jaunty two-minute take on "The Glory of Love."

Steve later told Terkel, who had co-produced Broonzy's final album, that no one could perform the pop standard better than Broonzy. "The thing with Bill's version of it is the driving quality that it has," Steve said. "No one's ever been able to top it." Broonzy, he said, had an incalculable influence on key folksingers Bob Gibson and Josh White, and for good reason. "He was simply a consummate musician," Steve said. "I don't think anybody had Bill's phrasing. I think Bill's vocalizing was the least regarded at the time he was living. Part of his whole shtick was his choice of material and his joy and his guitar playing." But Steve's own guitar on "The Glory of Love," along with his exuberance and overall showmanship, merited equal praise, says Hank Neuberger, who engineered and mixed the song for the LP. "He was a true acoustic guitar virtuoso," Neuberger says. "If you looked at his hands, they were the shortest, stubbiest, fattest, meatiest little non-guitar-player hands, yet he could do literally anything on an acoustic."

"The Glory of Love" rightly could be called the theme of the album. The notion of staying true to family and friends ran through half of the finished project's 10 songs, a higher percentage than on the previous year's "Jig" and his two Buddah LPs. A triumph of collaboration, the "Words" LP also illustrated Steve's ability to inspire the fast-moving cooperation of artists who by definition were driven by their own egos.

Not that every aspect proceeded smoothly. A glaring example of friction came when Steve asked David Amram, a veteran classical-music composer and conductor, to write a strings chart for his delicate charmer, "Old Fashioned."

"Write the same way for me as if you were writing a symphony," Steve told Amram, who had never arranged music for another artist. Amram responded by composing a lush, 1950s-style backdrop for a string quartet and called upon

> He was a true acoustic guitar virtuoso. If you looked at his hands, they were the shortest, stubbiest, fattest, meatiest little non-guitar-player hands, yet he could do literally anything on an acoustic.
> **HANK NEUBERGER**

a friend, Lenore Glazer, cellist for the Chicago Symphony, and three other players from that orchestra to perform it in the studio. "It was melody, harmony and counterpoint," Amram says. "I was as serious about that as I've been when I've written my symphonic and chamber music." The result pleased Amram, even though the assignment made him leery of becoming known as an arranger of others' work. "In Steve's case," he says, "I loved him so much that I did it."

But Burgh, who had come up with the music for "Old Fashioned" the previous fall, had anything but love for Amram's arrangement. He wanted to hear strings that better fit Rothermel's Charlie Parker-style sax solo in the song, not Amram's "neo-Baroque kind of sappy thing." Burgh conveyed this to Steve, who sided with Amram. "Steve got mad at me because he believed that Amram could do no wrong," Burgh said. "It put a wedge in my relationship with Steve, and it was something we never got over. We were always close friends, but somehow he would never put me and Amram together at the same time after that, and it was a real shame. I kicked and screamed, but I couldn't do anything about it." [10]

The attachment that Steve held for Amram's luxuriant arrangement stemmed in part from Steve's own vision and hope for "Old Fashioned" to be recorded and popularized by a big-name artist. Candidates he named ranged from country vocalist Ray Price to derivatives of the World War II-era African-American harmony group, the Ink Spots. Steve even told "FolkScene" host Howard Larman that he had in his sights a certain singer named Sinatra. "Great American folksingers like Frank, they could (sing it). They're the folksingers, man," Steve said. "I don't know if 100 years from now somebody'll be sittin' on their front porch snappin' their fingers and goin', 'It's witchcraft, it's witchcraft.' But I think the same way that certain actors like David Garrick (the 5-foot-4 Briton who lived from 1717 to 1779) from centuries gone by are remembered, somebody's gonna remember Sinatra. He made a dent. The guy sings good. This song doesn't have anything to do with him, but it's the kind of song that he sings good."

The generally good feelings of the "Words" LP sessions were enhanced by a quartet of concurrent bursts of national support and attention for Steve's previous work.

On Sunday, Jan. 18, just one day before the sessions began, the halftime show for Super Bowl X in Miami included an elaborate production by Up with People, the squeaky-clean dance troupe made up of 150 young adults age 18 to 25. Titled "200 Years and Just a Baby: America's Bicentennial Tribute," the patriotic program showcased "City of New Orleans." Besides seeing the Pittsburgh Steelers edge the Dallas Cowboys 21-17, the in-person crowd of 80,187 at Orange Bowl Stadium and the Nielsen-rated audience of 42.3 percent of TV households watching the CBS broadcast at home were exposed to Steve's best-known song. Eyeing the proceedings with his mother and Grandma Mary, Steve especially appreciated the view of the "City of New Orleans" choreography as broadcast from the Goodyear blimp.

"City" also began appearing on TV in more exploitive fashion, as the center-

Somebody's gonna remember Sinatra. He made a dent. The guy sings good. This song doesn't have anything to do with him, but it's the kind of song that he sings good.
STEVE GOODMAN

10: The rift over the string arrangement for "Old Fashioned" finally was resolved 24 years later when Burgh and Amram re-established contact and patched up their differences.

piece of spots by the pre-breakup Bell System. The signature phrase from the song's chorus, "Good morning, America," was a hand-in-glove fit for the Western Electric manufacturing brand of the telephone giant. Steve received no payment for the commercial use of his song because — unlike his arrangement with Asylum — Buddah Records still controlled the rights for songs issued on that label. Publicly, at least, Steve displayed no bitterness about his early contractual naivete.

"At least I didn't sign up with the John Birch Society," he told Studs Terkel. "Y'know, when you sign a deal with a record company, you get something. I wanted to make a record. Now you have to give something if you want to get something, and I gave up the administration and the publishing of those tunes."

"You gave up a good deal, y'see," Terkel replied.

"Yeah, well, but Studs, I got a good deal. I'm actually making a living playing the guitar and singing, so I'm not gonna sit here and cry to you and tell you how hard it is to do this, right?"

Terkel invoked a phrase he said had been coined by Big Bill Broonzy, "those people with dollar signs for eyes."

"Yeah, but they can't have my heart, Studs," Steve said. "They can have my signature ... and 100 years from now, it won't make any difference."

What did make a difference during the "Words" LP sessions was the just-released February 1976 edition of *Stereo Review*, which rated Steve's "Jig" LP as one of the 12 best albums of 1975. The assessment placed Steve in heady company, given that the other non-classical LPs on the list were Linda Ronstadt's "Heart Like a Wheel," Elton John's "Captain Fantastic & the Brown Dirt Cowboy," Jefferson Starship's "Red Octopus" and the Broadway cast recording of "Chicago."

One of the most upbeat songs on the "Jig" LP, "This Hotel Room," got an added boost during the "Words" sessions when it appeared that month as the closer on "Havana Daydreamin'," the latest LP of Jimmy Buffett, who still admires the song: "I thought Steve nailed it as a wonderful piece of satire about living on the road." The Buffett LP, on which Steve played guitar, also opened with another Buffett-Steve co-write, "Woman Goin' Crazy on Caroline Street." Buffett had nearly completed the tune, about a dancer-turned-prostitute in Key West, when Steve offered a few finishing lyrical touches. "It was a good chemistry, which you gotta understand doesn't happen often," Buffett says. "I was not a big collaborator in those days and still am not, but it worked very well."

All of these outside factors buoyed the crew of "Words" musicians and technicians. Burgh found the "energy level and honesty level" of the sessions higher than those of the "Jig" LP. "Artistically, it was a much greater achievement," Burgh said. "It wasn't just, 'Hey, let's just sit around and smile with Steve.' There were real guts that went into this. We weren't so innocent anymore, and it was a very intense experience."

Compounding the good feelings for everyone was the emergence of Jim Rothermel, who had backed Jesse Colin Young and Van Morrison but was new

They can't have my heart, Studs. They can have my signature ... and 100 years from now, it won't make any difference.
STEVE GOODMAN

Mimi Fariña sings at her inaugural fund-raising concert for Bread & Roses on Sept. 26, 1975. Also on the bill at the show (below, doing "You Never Even Call Me by My Name") was Steve, who the next day joined reeds player Jim Rothermel to put on the first Bread & Roses show at San Francisco County Jail.

(Photos by David Gans)

to Steve's coterie. Rothermel's mastery of countless instruments and sensitivity as an accompanist made him a prominent "voice" in the project's most distinctive tracks. It was just five months earlier that he and Steve were matched up inadvertently by a prominent Bay Area folkie — Mimi Fariña.

Known from the mid-1960s through the early 1970s primarily as Joan Baez' younger sister and folksinger Richard Fariña's widow, Fariña had emerged as solo artist in her own right. But what brought the 29-year-old to prominence in 1975 within the entertainment world was her founding of an organization dedicated to bringing free, live music to those inside the walls of prisons, nursing homes and other institutions "shut away from society." Inspired by a 1912 Irish labor poem by James Oppenheim (to be set to music by Fariña and recorded memorably by Judy Collins in 1976), Fariña named her nonprofit Bread & Roses. Her self-stated mission was equally elegant — to "use the power of performing arts to uplift the human spirit."

For a maiden Bread & Roses fund-raising show on Sept. 6, 1975, at Berkeley Community Theater, Fariña booked herself and three comrades: Steve, counterculture comedian George Carlin and *The Realist* magazine publisher and Yippie Party co-founder Paul Krassner. [11] Besides the benefit show, however, Fariña had extra duty in mind for Steve. The next day, recalling his two gigs at Sandstone prison in Minnesota, Steve became the first performer whom Fariña enlisted to perform at San Francisco County Jail.

Tagging along with a clarinet at Steve's invitation was the 33-year-old Rothermel, whose live-in partner at the time, Janis Labao, was helping Fariña to establish Bread & Roses. Rothermel had ridden along to San Francisco's airport to pick up Steve, about whom he knew nothing. That night, Rothermel caught Steve's set at the benefit, and while Rothermel was far more grounded in jazz than folk, he was captivated by Steve's take on standards like "It's a Sin to Tell a Lie" and his inventive instrumental breaks. "Some of the stuff he did I could really relate to," says Rothermel, whose thoughts swiftly turned to accompaniment. "I didn't have any doubts about my ability to play with him, and I thought it would be fun."

11: Seeking Steve out at the Bread & Roses benefit was a classmate from Maine East High and the University of Illinois, 5-foot-10 Betsy Elich (now Vandercook). "Oh, my God, Steve," she burst out upon seeing him, "you haven't grown!" Steve shot back, "And Betsy, you haven't shrunk!"

Jim Rothermel, who joined Steve in playing the "mainline" of San Francisco County Jail on Aug. 27, 1975, helped relieve tensions by accompanying the soft-shoe dance of an African-American inmate. The multi-instrumentalist later backed Steve in recording sessions and scores of concerts.

(Photo by Sherb Slack)

Such rapport came in handy for the Sunday afternoon jail gig. The destination, in the heart of the city, was the San Francisco County Jail's seventh floor, a high-security holding facility for about 400 inmates awaiting trial on murder and other felonies. They included the Zebra killers, five men on trial in connection with a six-month racially motivated crime spree involving the kidnap, rape and mutilation of 23 random victims, of whom 14 had died. Officials weren't used to bringing entertainers into such a climate. "If you were conservative, you wouldn't want to bring visitors in there, but the sheriff, Dick Hongisto, liked trying new things," says Michael Hennessey, then a sheriff's attorney who went on to be elected sheriff five years later. Fariña felt fortunate for the opportunity. "We had to pretty much beg them to let us in," she recalled 25 years later. "We told them that we would behave well and do everything they wanted us to."

Instruments in hand and escorted by a deputy, Steve and Rothermel strode with Fariña along the heavily patrolled "mainline," a narrow, bright corridor the length of a football field, with 16-man cells on each side. "They would stop in front of a cell and do a song, and then they'd walk a few more feet and do another song," Fariña said. "They were focused on walking down this corridor and playing to as many faces as they could before moving on." The inmates, raucous and angry until the duo reached their cells, were a tough audience. "You could practically cut the tension in the air," Rothermel says. But an encounter with one elderly African-American inmate punctured and dissipated the anxiety. Upon hearing the duo's lively music, the man simply said that he wanted to dance.

"This old black man had been a featured dancer back in the days of the Big Band era," Rothermel says. "He was in jail because he was a substance abuser who had gotten busted. He wasn't a violent criminal, but the other inmates knew he was there, and they started a bit of a to-do to let this guy out of his cell so he could dance to our music in the corridor."

The escorting deputy kept saying, "No way." But the inmate persisted, making a repeated and puzzling request. The inmate said he wanted some salt. "The guard," Fariña said, "didn't understand that the salt was going to make it easier for his shoes to be heard."

Eventually, Rothermel says, "the guard realized that the path of least resistance was to do that. Otherwise, people would keep making noise. So they let this guy out, and they put some salt down so he could do some soft shoe."

What followed was the stuff of magic.

"He would dance for a measure, and then Steve and Jim would sing and play for a measure, and then he would do another measure, so they were trading off," Fariña said. "He'd do rhythm. They'd give him like a rhythm solo. They'd finish a verse, and then they'd give him a little solo, and they'd start a verse. It was so nice, it was so touching, and it was so well done. It really made the place quiet. You could hear every little tap this man made, and Steve's face — talk about intense, he was grinning from ear to ear. He could not have looked happier. And he'd lean way over and watch the guy's feet, and then he'd take his four bars or whatever, and then he'd be quiet and lean over again."

This breathtaking, impromptu show, Fariña said, "was my first lesson in audience participation in an institution and how that makes the audience feel. No matter what kind of institution it is, they're away from society and feel left out and different and separated and isolated. So a wonderful way to make a room feel more complete, especially in an institutional setting, is to invite audience participation when possible — and, boy, does it work in a prison or a jail. You have to have someone who's willing to invite participation, and not all performers do that. And, too, someone who's sensitive enough to know how to make it work, when to back off, when to come back in."

Steve, she said, was "perfect" for the task. "He was a real communicator, a back-and-forth, a dialoguer and willing to hear what was out there. He liked taking that kind of risk and was good at it, and he followed through."

More brilliantly than any other incident could, the experience symbolized Bread & Roses' promising future. It also endeared Steve to the organization and vice versa. In future years, Steve played three of its annual benefit weekends, sharing the UC Berkeley Greek Theater stage with scores of the country's top names in folk and pop music. [12] In addition, the jail show bonded Steve to Rothermel, whose contributions to the "Words" LP were the first public evidence of what would become an enduring recording and onstage partnership.

While mixing the "Words" album in early spring 1976, Steve also squeezed in a handful of shows throughout the Midwest, including one — at the University of Iowa in Iowa City with John Prine — whose student-directed ad campaign was both eerie and bizarre. Instead of typical photos of the performing pair, the show's promo poster showcased an 1890s lithograph from *Harper's Weekly* depicting two obscure characters, one wearing what appeared to be Ku Klux Klan garb and holding a shotgun.

The grotesque image only made Steve laugh. "I loved that gig, man," Steve told Rick Ansorge of the *Chicago Lakes Countryside* two years later. "We were standing there in these pointed hoods with 'John Prine/Steve Goodman in Concert' underneath. So I took the poster home. When my children ask me what I do for a living, someday I'm gonna show 'em that."

This bizarre poster greeted Steve and John Prine prior to their Feb. 20, 1976, show in Iowa City. "When my children ask me what I do for a living," Steve cracked later, "someday I'm gonna show 'em that."

12: In a hotel-room jam after one of the festivals, Steve chided Fariña with a filthy pantomime version of "We Shall Overcome" that Fariña later declined to describe in detail but that takes little effort to imagine. "It was endless, he added gestures, and he wouldn't stop, and he himself was laughing throughout it, so that always helps," she said.

Steve plays during Steve Mosley's demo sessions in May 1976 in a barn in Vermont.
(Photo courtesy of Steve and Barbara Mosley)

13: As with his first album, the front-cover photo for Steve's "Words" LP was not in crisp focus. But the "appealing playful quality" of Steve's expression and pose made up for the photo's technical lapse, says designer Anne Garner. She tried to capture that quality with "quirky and energetic" lettering by Martin Donald, known for creating the same stylized script for several popular Loggins & Messina albums.

While blazing through a dozen cities in the East and South for concerts during March and April, Steve set aside a pair of multi-day intervals to play and sing on the album projects of two friends. At the Record Plant in Los Angeles, Steve played a bouncy, country-styled lead guitar for the clear-voiced Bonnie Koloc on her version of John Prine's "Clocks and Spoons," for "Close-Up," her first LP for Columbia Epic. Also on the album, her sixth overall, Koloc for the first time recorded a composition by Steve, a torch song that she softened to a quiet plea, "I Can't Sleep."

At the opposite corner of the country, in an old, high-ceilinged barn owned by folk-based Philo (now Rounder) Records in North Ferrisburgh, Vermont, Steve joined members of David Bromberg's rhythm section to contribute guitar and high harmony for six pop-styled tracks by percussionist Steve Mosley. It was merely a demo project, but Steve took it seriously, Mosley says. "He came out, paid all of his own expenses, wouldn't take a penny," he says. "We were going for a record, but he was just doing it as a friend." With styles ranging from Led Zeppelin to the Doobie Brothers, the songs — including one called "Country Day" that Steve said sounded like a corn-flakes commercial — never were released, even though their themes and production touches were clearly geared to be top-40 hits.

Steve's own "Words" LP bounded into record stores and onto the turntables of music critics and radio hosts with a splash in early April. As striking as the music inside was its visual impact. Shot by his brother David, the photos of Steve on the front and back cover and inner sleeve jettisoned the notion of an informal folkie. Instead, Steve had donned a black tuxedo with white shirt, huge white bow tie, black top hat and baton. Pinned to his lapel was a bright red carnation. Along with a mustache and beard, he retained youthfully stylish near-shoulder-length hair, but the overall message was clear. The images defined Steve as the timeless icon to which he aspired: The Entertainer.

This was no serious portrait, though. In the front-cover photo, Steve wore the electric guitar that he had used on "Tossin' and Turnin'," but the guitar was flipped upside down, obscuring the strings and leaving Steve to "strum" its wooden backside. It was a clever visual pun that mimicked the LP's heels-over-head title and was reinforced by an impish grin on Steve's face. [13] The light touch continued on the inner sleeve, where another photo showed Steve kneeling, holding the guitar front-side forward and joyfully flipping his top hat into the air, while also revealing that he had exchanged formal black shoes for a pair of white sneakers. The easy humor, however, only bolstered the depiction of a latter-day, anything-for-a-smile Al Jolson.

Full-page ads played up the persona. One, in the *Chicago Reader*, paired Steve with Asylum artist John David Souther's "Black Rose" LP, with a somber Souther also dressed in a tux. Another, in *Rolling Stone*, showed Steve seemingly tossing not only his top hat into the air but also the album itself and its cover lettering. Asylum also sent deejays black, faux-tuxedo T-shirts. It was a happy portrayal that presaged an enthusiastic reception, particularly given that the LP came just 10 months after "Jessie's Jig," a much smaller interval compared to the previous gap between albums of two and a half years. But critics, unable to pigeonhole Steve's wide-ranging package, were not so upbeat. [14]

Billboard, rarely prone to faultfinding, noted that "Words" contained "a bit of something for everyone to enjoy" and labeled it Steve's "most universally appealing LP to date." But the blurb also undercut the album's potential for mainstream acceptance by noting that Steve "already has a large cult following" — the "cult" label being hard to shake once affixed.

Cutting Steve even less slack was *Rolling Stone*. Sounding the usual plaint that Steve's albums "have never matched his live performances," the trendy magazine's Kit Rachlis denounced Steve's range of styles by saying that he "has failed to establish a durable identity as either a songwriter or interpreter. The comic material is ephemeral and the serious songs strain." With a backhand compliment, Rachlis said the "Words" LP "has more than its share of delightful moments," but "it all seems lightweight for a performer of such talent." [15]

Hometown critic Al Rudis of the *Chicago Sun-Times* suffused his review with praise, noting the album's "winning formula" and saying it was "every bit as delightful" as "Jessie's Jig." But Rudis couldn't resist implying that "Words" was not destined for success. "The reason more people haven't caught onto it is because the ingredients are rare," he wrote. "As usual, the collection is eclectic almost to extremes."

"Eclectic" quickly made its way into Steve's own vocabulary in half a dozen interviews. "There is no one influence?" Studs Terkel asked on April 30, to which Steve replied, "Yeah, it's the hectic eclectic." Three weeks later, Steve told Howard Larman of "FolkScene" that the LP had "met with mixed reaction" because of "confusion about what I'm tryin' to do. I think it's probably my fault for not honing in more on certain things. It's a hair eclectic, and some people have expressed their doubts about that side of it. But shit, I'm happy with it. ... I don't know if it all fits together in one ball when you try to put it on plastic. But it's the only way I know how to do it, so I guess I'm stuck with it. No big thing."

The album's diversity and the critical reaction to it apparently weren't dooming the initial burst of purchases for the LP, which Steve claimed was selling "better than the first three records I did put together," in an interview for a profile that ran July 19 in the *Chicago Tribune*. Still, Steve didn't harbor illusions of mass popularity. "I know there's a limited appeal for this kind of music," he said. "I mean, nothing on my records sounds like disco."

Even so, in the spring and early summer Asylum sent Steve touring nonstop to promote "Words." Helping instigate the exposure was a splashy reissue of previously released material by the competition — Steve's former label, Buddah. Fourteen of the label's current and former artists, from Paul Anka and Lena Horne to Sha Na Na and Melanie, got "The Best of" or "The Essential" treatment, each package a two-record set for the price of one. In Steve's case, Buddah merged his first two LPs, subtracted four tunes written by others ("Rainbow

The black, stenciled T-shirts with which Asylum promoted Steve's "Words We Can Dance To" LP resembled a tuxedo, complete with a red carnation and augmented with script by Martin Donald.

(Shirt courtesy of Steve Cohen, photo by Clay Eals)

14: Striking a positive chord were Richie Roberts and Bert Muirhead of the Edinburgh, Scotland-based monthly *Hot Wacks*, who rated the LP higher than recent releases by Chris Hillman, J.D. Souther, Warren Zevon and Roger McGuinn and noted Steve's uncanny ability to "write songs like they were straight from the 1930s."

15: In the face of such criticism, Steve summoned a hilarious misquote of an Illinois native son: "Abe Lincoln was right. You can't please anybody, at all, ever."

Road," "Mind Your Own Business," "So Fine" and "The Barnyard Dance") for which the label did not hold publishing rights and added the ditty Steve wrote for the 1972 presidential race, "Election sYear Rag," which had appeared only as a single. [16] With "Rag," the double-LP set finally united the two tracks that Steve had recorded with Bob Dylan. Strangely, however, and to Asylum's benefit, the Buddah set was a visual bust, featuring on the cover a dark and lethargic concert photo showing Steve with his eyes nearly closed (perhaps an attempt to convey his sensitivity) and stylized 1971 images on the inside and back.

Another Steve-related LP had a re-release later in 1976. Sales for "Gathering at the Earl of Old Town," available only at Pionke's pub, had slowed to a trickle. Stephen Powers, who in 1971 had opened a club in Rockford, Illinois, that he renamed a year later as Charlotte's Web, had started a record label, Mountain Railroad. From Bill Traut, Powers bought the 3,000 remaining copies of "Gathering," re-issuing it with a colorized cover and axing its expensive gatefold format. Steve's first official recording of "City of New Orleans," along with "Chicago Bust Rag" and "Eight Ball Blues," thus became available nationwide. Powers eventually sold nearly 15,000 copies of the 1971 Chicago folk showcase.

Earning an average of $1,000 a night while on tour in mid-1976, Steve often encountered capacity crowds and choice company. Steve was co-billed with raspy Tom Waits at Princeton University in New Jersey, and he opened for David Bromberg at Avery Fisher Hall in New York and Jesse Colin Young at the Armadillo World Headquarters in Austin, Texas. Those opening for Steve included John Hiatt at La Bastille in Houston and Charlotte's Web in Rockford, and Mimi Fariña at Milwaukee Summerfest. For two nights at the Roxy in Los Angeles, comedian Martin Mull was Steve's opener, and in the audience were singer Melissa Manchester and actress Lesley Ann Warren, along with TV producer Norman Lear, who that night offered Mull a starring role in his spin-off series "Fernwood 2Night." At the Golden Bear in Huntington Beach, California, Keith Carradine — whose song "I'm Easy," from Robert Altman's "Nashville," had just won an Oscar — showed up with plaudits.

Perhaps the zenith of crossed musical paths during this period came at the Main Point in Bryn Mawr, Pennsylvania. Warren Zevon ("Werewolves of London") was Steve's opener for three nights, and on the last of them, June 20, Steve performed for three-and-a-half hours. Joining him onstage were Zevon on drums and Zevon's accompanists, bassist Doug Haywood and ex-Fairport Convention guitarist Jerry Donahue. The crowded stage also included Chicago visitor Mike Lieber on "comb and tissue paper" kazoo, locals Lew London and Winnie Winston and the Wanamaker Lewis bluegrass band from the Cripple Creek bar down the street. "Everything was smooth, like we'd played with each other forever," says London. [17]

Near the end of the show, before Steve launched into "Mama Don't Allow It," Philly deejay Ed Sciaky sidled up and whispered in his ear the name of the singer/keyboardist whose "Piano Man" was a recent national hit and who had stopped into the club after finishing a show at the Academy of Music down-

---

Everything was smooth, like we'd played with each other forever.
LEW LONDON

16: Hoping to capitalize on the presidential election year of 1976, Buddah re-issued "Election Year Rag" as a single. But just as in 1972, it went nowhere.

17: Thanks to Steve, London was playing a brand new mandolin during the Main Point show. While recording the "Words" LP, Steve had taken note of London's worn-out instrument. Soon afterward, London received a check from Steve in payment for his participation in the sessions, but for $1,200, not the $400 he was promised. Accompanying the check was a note from Steve: "(Steve) Burgh and I went to a music store and found a really nice mandolin, and we were going to buy it for you instead of paying you, but I thought that would be presumptuous, so instead, I'm sending you this money. Go out and buy yourself a mandolin." London did so.

town. "OK, friends," Steve announced, "welcome Billy Joel. He's gonna play some piano for us now." [18] The troupe morphed into a tight and tumultuous rock ensemble on tunes ranging from "Johnny B. Goode" and "Twist & Shout" to an improvised blues in which Steve's joy shone:

I ain't had so much fun jammin' around
since I don't know when
Yeah, good people, I hope this band gets to play
one more gig one more time again

The house that the Goodmans purchased in May 1976 at 1723 Asbury Avenue in Evanston was the picture of domestic bliss.

(Illustration by Ron Crawford, 1984)

For a handful of students from Hightstown High School, 55 miles northeast of Bryn Mawr near Trenton, New Jersey, the night became an irreplaceable memory. John Bates, adviser of an after-school club focusing on concert promotion, had driven the teens to the show having promised their parents he would have them home by midnight. But as Steve repeatedly invited performers to the stage, Bates reached into his pants pocket to pull out his change. "Here's a quarter for each of you," he told the students. "Call your folks and tell them more like 3." The jam extended past 1 a.m. Driving home and talking with his students in the car, Bates found that the musician who had left the deepest impression was the evening's ringmaster. "The kids," he says, "were mesmerized by this guy."

Besides road gigs, home also beckoned for Steve that spring — a larger one for his brood that he and Nancy sought in Evanston, the college town along Chicago's northern border. At first, the two looked at rentals, including a duplex that a real-estate agent showed them on quiet Asbury Avenue. It didn't suit them, but as they turned back toward the agent's car, an elegant, three-story Queen Anne across the street caught their eye. So did its "for sale" sign.

With shingled gables, a protruding two-floor bay and a wraparound porch, the 86-year-old house at 1723 Asbury looked to be an icon of domestic contentment. [19] The three walked up to the door and gave it a knock. Artist Susan Leeb, who owned the house with her architect husband Robert, opened the door and was stunned to find one of her favorite performers and his wife asking to come inside.

As they chatted with Susan Leeb and nibbled on marinated mushrooms left over from a party the night before, the thought of living there took hold. Walking through the home, Steve and Nancy admired the remodeled kitchen and bathrooms and sweeping oak stairway, checked out the view of the tree-filled backyard from the second-floor deck and envisioned one of the four second-floor bedrooms — the large one in the front — for their daughter, Jessie.

But when they climbed to the top floor and saw its vast, 1,200 square-foot, slant-ceilinged attic, "that's what did it," says Robert Leeb. Though set up as an art studio, Steve envisioned a music room, and the Goodmans were sold. The first visitor once the deal was inked was John Prine, who showed up driving a pea-green 1951 Fordomatic Custom Club Coupe.

Financing for the May 24 purchase (just over $100,000) was a stretch, but

18: Steve's "Mama Don't Allow It" rhyme for the visiting pianist was: "Singin' out like old Jelly Roll (Morton) / Now we're gonna hear from Billy Joel."

19: After the Goodmans lived in it, the Asbury Avenue abode twice became a site on the annual House Walk of the Evanston Historical Society. The home was built in 1890-91 for Henry Hinsdale, a sugar broker, and his wife Eliza. The town of Hinsdale, 17 miles southwest of Chicago, was named for him.

Jim Craig knew the top floor of Steve's new home in Evanston symbolized a newfound contentment: "He told me how lucky that he was – and that we all were – to be musicians living in nice circumstances. He said, 'This is it. This is more than I ever dreamed of.' He couldn't believe it."

(Photo by Art Thieme)

20: Shortly afterward, when the washing machine at the Amazingrace apartment house broke down, Steve told road manager Steve Cohen to buy the concert-producing collective a new one. "That," Cohen says, "was the Steve Goodman memorial washing machine."

21: Steve's domestic bliss emerged in his latest show opener, "Abba Dabba Honeymoon," a 1914 ditty written by Arthur Fields and Walter Donovan and later popularized by Debbie Reynolds. It celebrated a silly romance between a monkey and chimp.

Steve had a ready method to generate cash. To raise a needed $3,000 to $4,000, Steve called Jeff Beamsley and asked if he could quickly book him at nearby Amazingrace. "Sure," Beamsley replied. "We can sell your shows out anytime you want." The July 19-20 concerts — two shows each night, all four of which sold out a week in advance — became known to the organizers as the "let's buy Steve a house" gig. [20]

Featuring Bob Hoban on piano and fiddle, Ken Bloom on dobro and clarinet, Mike Lieber on washboard percussion, Jim Tullio on bass, Johnny Burns on electric guitar, Jethro Burns on mandolin, Winnie Winston on steel guitar and both Saul Broudy and Peter "Madcat" Ruth on harmonica, the lengthy sets burst with spine-tingling vigor. One highlight was a 15-minute medley of "When the Saints Go Marchin' In" and "Mama Don't Allow It," the latter of which stretched to an astounding 39 eight-bar verses of stellar solos, including one verse of "silent playing" that indeed was soundless, other than chuckles from the audience. When a one-hour consolidation of the shows aired two weeks later on Chicago's WXRT-FM "Unconcert" (named for the sponsor, 7-Up, "the Uncola"), the zest of Steve and his circle of sidemen came across delightfully.

These musicians and many others sooner or later visited the Asbury Avenue home, where, befitting the source of funds for the coming monthly payments, a custom doorbell was installed to welcome visitors with the first few notes of the melody for "City of New Orleans." Lush with green plants and the smells of hearty meals (including breakfasts cooked by Steve), the house became a gathering place and its third floor a musical sanctuary. There, Steve scribbled lyrics, practiced tunes on his many guitars and listened to thousands of albums lining the walls. Tours of the house usually ended with a lengthy stay upstairs, with Steve pulling out LP after LP — everything from Steely Dan to Jackie Wilson — and repeating, "Y'gotta hear this." The room's lofty position symbolized Steve's joy at providing himself and his family a comfortable home.

"Steve was absolutely on top of the world," says Jim Craig, who with his wife and performing partner Vivian ate dinner at the Asbury home soon after the Goodmans moved in. "He and I were sitting up in that third-floor room, and he told me how lucky that he was — and that we all were — to be musicians living in nice circumstances. He said, 'This is it. This is more than I ever dreamed of.' He couldn't believe it." [21]

With Steve's furious schedule of out-of-town shows, however, life in the early days at the Asbury house wasn't entirely harmonious, illustrated by a universal story that daughter Jessie heard over the years from Steve's mom, Minnette.

"Where's my blue shirt?" Steve shouted down the stairs one day as Nancy and Jessie, then 4, were about to walk out the front door.

"Your blue shirt is in the clean laundry basket," Nancy called back, "and the iron and the ironing board are in the kitchen."

For *Chicago Tribune* reporter Lynn Van Matre, Steve alluded to such family vagaries in early July as he sat at his round oak dining table, cradling Sarah in his arms and feeding her a bottle of milk. Gesturing to Jessie and Nancy, he

In a "Heroes and Villains" workshop on June 26, 1976, at the Mariposa Folk Festival in Toronto, Steve duets with Margaret Christl while Floyd Red Crow Westerman provides accompaniment.

(Composite photo by Larry McLean)

said, "Now you see why the show-biz thing doesn't mean all that much to me. I've got this, and I wouldn't trade it for all the money in the world." [22] But he also admitted that, in a sense, he was doing just that. "These kids," he said, "I hate to leave them when I tour, but I'm not about to subject a baby to a schedule like 26 days in 15 towns. So I'm here when I'm here and gone when I'm gone. I used to feel guilty about being away, but then I figured, screw it, this is how I make my living. It's that whole leaving, out-the-door thing musicians are always writing songs about. It's true, you hate to leave. At least, I do."

Soon, once again, he was gone. After summer stops at festivals in Toronto, Milwaukee and Winnipeg, Steve flew across the Atlantic on a three-week tour of England, Belgium, the Netherlands and West Germany, starting July 24. The excursion was part of a broader strategy for Elektra/Asylum, given that others on the label — Linda Ronstadt, Warren Zevon, J.D. Souther, Tom Waits, the Cate Brothers, Andrew Gold and Jackson Browne — also embarked on European tours in 1976. But it was the first time in three years that a record company had invested in such a trip for Steve, and the performer in him couldn't wait to go. "In some ways, my music is better received in Britain," Steve told Ted Joseph of the UK's *Sounds* before the trip. "There's a real storytelling style in their traditions," he said. "You usually have a more open audience in places where the narrative tradition is strong."

Remembering him from his impressive 1972 and 1973 summer visits, the English press gave Steve buckets of ink. Instead of slighting him for his breadth of genres, the UK music papers trumpeted and celebrated it. The headline on Joseph's *Sounds* story was "Ragtime millionaire," an appealing label Steve had summoned to describe how "goofy" it was, in the midst of social and economic crises, for him to be a paid entertainer, particularly one who straddled categories. "I know I'm asking a lot of the listener, taste-wise, and I really do think about that sometimes," he said. "I'm asking somebody to give music a chance — all those different things I'm interested in."

"Eclectic troubadour," screamed a two-inch-tall headline in *Melody Maker*, whose reporter Steve Lake observed that Steve's "stance seems almost anachronistic in the 1970s. This dedication to the role of the troubadour, and quality

22: Steve later told Bill Danoff, "Kids! I never realized how selfish anybody could be. All they want us to do is give 'em stuff, give 'em stuff, give 'em stuff. Selfish little suckers, man."

(Above) Opening his summer 1976 tour of Europe, Steve joins John Prine for a concert July 24 at the July Wakes Folk Festival in Chorley, England. (Right) A week later, after a triumphant set at the Cambridge Folk Festival, Steve and his manager Al Bunetta confer eye-to-eye.

(Left photo by Roger Liptrot, right photo by Tom Sheehan)

and craftsmanship above all else, can appear almost naïve in these cynical times." But Lake gave Steve the last word. "My ambition is simply to do as much playing and performing as possible and still find time to enjoy my family," Steve said. "I know how fast the world is getting, and how everything seems to be accelerating and stuff, but I also know that if you try to keep pace, you're going to get fucked. It's going to happen. I've found my own pace, and so far as I can tell, it suits me. I don't visualize a point where I'm going to want to make any radical changes. Security is today. That other stuff is a big illusion."

In England, however, Steve lived the illusion, enjoying luxurious lodging at London's Montcalm Hotel and a Bentley limousine for shopping, all at Asylum's expense. On July 25, his 28th birthday, Steve even took visiting fiddler friend Larry Packer for a midnight-to-dawn limo ride throughout Manchester. Seized by giggles in his interview with Lake of *Melody Maker*, Steve said he felt almost guilty about such opulent treatment given low sales for his Asylum LPs. "It's my fault, man," Steve said. "I'm not fair to them. I've created a problematic situation for them by not emphasizing any one aspect of what it is that I do. But ... hehehehehehehe ... HAHAHAHA ... I don't plan to change any. I feel sincerely sorry, though, for a promo man who's got to carry one of my damn albums into a radio station, and the guy says, 'Great, what is it?' 'Uh, well, it's sort of swing-jazz-folk-blues-acoustic-electric.' I wouldn't wish that gig on anybody."

What consoled Steve, he told John Tobler of *Omaha Rainbow*, was a perception that his recordings, while not instant hits, would endure. "Ten years from now, I think that some of this stuff will hold up," he said. "Some of it's gonna wear pretty good."

Early in the tour, Steve backed up John Prine at the July Wakes Festival in Chorley and a Regents Park show in London. Later he played to raves at the Cambridge Folk Festival, with *Melody Maker* saying his shows there "justified every extravagant expectation made of him" and *Sounds* noting that he drew "the loudest and longest applause of the event." [23] He ended the excursion with a sterling set on the BBC's "In Concert," as the opener for the trendy British rock band Frankie Miller's Full House. Steve relished telling the broadcast audience of his discovery that his musical traveling-salesman joke, "Death of a Salesman," was "very English." In the States, he said, "People don't sit around and tell jokes as much as they used to. Maybe we're losing our sense of humor."

The real eye-openers of Steve's European journey, however, came when he ventured off the English island. In each of the three mainland countries he visited, Steve learned firsthand how popular his "City of New Orleans" had become — but as sung by others in native languages and with different words. "The lyrics are all changed," he told John Tobler of *Omaha Rainbow*. "Not one of them is about a train, and they were all hits, all three." His assertion apparently was two-thirds correct. In French (spoken in Belgium), Joe Dassin sang it as "Hello, Lovers." The Dutch version, by Gerard Cox, translated as "The Beautiful Summer Has Passed Already." A third version, however, rendered in German by Jack White, "Der Zug, Gennant die City of New Orleans," did stick with Steve's railroad theme and lyrics. [24]

Language also became a factor in his gigs. In Brussels, Steve sang before the famed La Monnaie opera house at the open-air Mallemunt Folk Festival, opened by Belgian rock poet Pierre Rapsat. [25] But 125 miles northeast in Amsterdam, Steve headlined an all-American show at a side-street, multi-media entertainment emporium called the Melkweg (Milky Way), with fiddler/banjoist/clogger John Hartford (author of "Gentle on My Mind") as the opening act. Another 200 and 250 miles farther northeast lay solo shows in Bremen and Hamburg, West Germany. At each stop, despite the pervasiveness of Americanized marketing and the universality of the English language, Steve's audiences contained many whose first language was indigenous. This posed a challenge for a U.S. singer whose success depended largely on comprehension of his lyrics.

Steve's solution, evident from tapes of the shows, was to slow his tempos slightly and enunciate with greater clarity. Gone was the informality of dropped consonants ("singing" and "something" instead of "singin' " and "somethin' ") and contractions ("it is" and "kind of" instead of "it's" and "kinda"). He also carefully explained idioms such as "banana republic" and "motel" ("a hotel that you can drive your car right into"). [26] The adjustments were a dash of delicacy that only added to Steve's aim-to-please charm. Confirmed by the audiences' warm reception, they aided some of the loveliest onstage work of his career.

It may not have hurt his July 30 show in Amsterdam that permeating the venue was a haze of Indian, Pakistani, Afghani, Lebanese, Moroccan, Thai and Colombian marijuana, hashish and sulfate. The rock-tinged Melkweg — "like an old Fillmore," Steve said — operated with a legal drug bazaar in its basement (hashish at $2 a gram). "It was the one place where you didn't have to smoke to smoke," Steve noted. "It was an elevating experience, to say the least."

Larry Packer, who was to play the next night at a nearby club, the Paradiso,

23: Steve's lack of pretense was in full bloom onstage at the 1976 Cambridge festival: "I was over takin' a leak in the bushes before, and I just pictured myself bein' in 'Random Notes' of the *Rolling Stone*. That's the kind of stuff that always gets in 'Random Notes' in that paper: 'Folksinger in bushes in England.' Americans love to read stuff like that. That's how we got to be 200 years old."

24: An Icelandic rock group, Brimkló, also covered "City of New Orleans" in 1976. In addition, Steve noted that an unnamed Belgian singer had covered his "Yellow Coat" in the Flemish dialect spoken in that country. The title became "Crazy Red Hat."

25: In Belgium, Steve played tourist, buying wine and lace and enjoying his room in Brussels' Hotel Bedford, where he encountered Magic Fingers with a different name: Massage Boy.

26: When Steve sang "This Hotel Room" to the Melkweg audience, he improvised a stanza that alluded to the Pulitzer Hotel, "This old hotel is my best pal / It runs right along some old canal."

as part of the Kate and Anna McGarrigle band, stood with Steve in the Melkweg balcony during Hartford's opening set. "Hartford was playing his heart out, dancing on this little platform with a pickup mike on it, doing his level best, giving his all," Packer says, "but the crowd was a couple hundred really stoned-out Amsterdam hippies just sitting there glued to the floor, not reacting in one way or another." Near the end of Hartford's set, Steve turned to Packer.

"Y'know," Steve said, "it's like these kids are on a one-way bus to the future, only they're trying to back in."

When Steve walked backstage to follow Hartford, Packer wondered how Steve would connect with this overly mellow bunch. Then, with his typically hypnotic picking on "It's a Sin to Tell a Lie," Steve burst onstage. "He wouldn't take no for an answer," Packer says. "He jumped up and down and swung his arms around, and at the end of the first song, everybody in the place was on their feet giving him a standing ovation. He destroyed them." [27]

Though he didn't let on, the one song Steve knew he had to sing was the one that worried him. "The Dutchman," the paean to an elderly couple's enduring love, was set in the very city in which he was playing. But its author, Michael Smith, had never traveled to Amsterdam, and before his own trip Steve had no idea, other than his deep regard for the composition, whether its many local allusions were mere illusions.

To find out, before the Melkweg show Steve spent two days touring Holland with the journalist and AM/FM radio personality who would broadcast Steve's concert live over the Netherlands' public VARA network, Wim Bloemendaal. Most musicians visiting from the States at the time wanted only to stick to urbanized Amsterdam, Bloemendaal says. "Then they go back home and say, 'I've been in Holland.' Steve wasn't like that. He wanted to absorb as many things of this country as he could."

In his Morris Minor Traveler, a tiny "woody" car, Bloemendaal drove Steve in and around Amsterdam, breezing by windmills, visiting a castle, browsing a second-hand bookstore, walking the walls of the fortress city of Naarden and, as referenced in the song, viewing the former Zuider Zee. (Dutch for "southern sea" and pronounced "Zider Zay," the huge bay decades earlier had been dammed and converted to a freshwater lake called the Ijsselmeer.) At Bloemendaal's request, Steve even played half a dozen songs for an informal gathering of truckers and wives in a cellar-level family restaurant. "Steve was not in a hurry," Bloemendaal says. "He took the time to do all these things." [28]

Steve found the Netherlands countryside and people as idyllic as the word pictures in Smith's song. "Amsterdam," he said, "is 700 years old and looks like an old, rundown city on some dirty old canal, and you say, 'What's so special about this place?' Except, after about three days there, it's as warm a place as there is in Europe. People are great."

"When I got here," he said, introducing "The Dutchman" at the Melkweg, "I was very curious to see if this song would hold up for me, because I liked it back in the United States. ... I thought it was one of the best songs I'd ever

He wouldn't take no for an answer. He jumped up and down and swung his arms around, and at the end of the first song, everybody in the place was on their feet.
LARRY PACKER

27: Packer accompanied Steve at the end of his show on "Johnny B. Goode" and "Tossin' and Turnin'." Hartford joined them on "The Auctioneer," "Mama Don't Allow It" ("Banjo playin' he is the best / Old John Hartford'll pass the test.") and Hank Williams' "I'm So Lonesome I Could Cry."

28: Steve was never far from his guitar. As he told Bloemendaal, "I don't think there's been two days that went by since I learned to play the guitar where I didn't play it at one time or another."

heard, and I just wanted to see whether or not Mike had been making it up, y'know, or whether or not it was real. And somehow, having never been here, he's caught this place. This song is about two old people who are old enough to remember when there was a Zuider Zee."

Before performing a delicate rendition of the tune, Steve took a step that was rare for him and audacious considering the setting. "I'm horrible at sing-alongs," he said a bit tentatively, "but if you figure out the chorus to this, I'd be honored if you'd sing it." In the middle of the song, he made an even bolder move. To teach the English lyrics to the Dutch crowd, he reviewed the chorus by speaking, not singing, its words. When the audience responded by softly singing the refrain, Steve said quietly, "That's sweet." By song's end, hearty applause and cheers engulfed the room.

"The Dutchman" didn't go over nearly as well five months later when Steve returned to play the Melkweg, says an acquaintance of Steve from the States, Joan DeFalcis (now Hauger), a Mariposa and Philadelphia festival volunteer who moved to Amsterdam in 1976 and saw Steve's Dec. 18 show there. DeFalcis revered the song's romance but found that locals resisted its images of wooden shoes and the like as antique stereotypes. "The audience was very, very cold," she says, "especially when he sang 'keeps his thumb jammed in the dam.' They laughed. It was funny to them, and I thought, 'But it's not meant to be funny.' I still saw the song as an American who'd heard it without experiencing Holland. But they seemed somewhat offended and taken aback." Steve perceived the reaction, DeFalcis says, but "consummate professional that he was, he did not bat an eye." [29]

Bloemendaal, whose radio interviews earned him a reputation in Holland similar to that of his Chicago idol, Studs Terkel, says that "The Dutchman" never offended him. He rates it "a great song" and says he has never pondered its accuracy. "Songs about a country you've never been to always have something of a dream," he says. "There's an imagination that's not completely true."

Steve's courage to perform "The Dutchman" in such a beckoning manner in Amsterdam that summer risked an emotional vulnerability that audiences rarely saw in his performances. His experience two nights later in Hamburg, however, left him vulnerable in a manner more physically frightening.

The evening started out with great promise. The European office of Warner/Elektra/Asylum put on a lavish dinner for Steve at a restaurant nearby, and because director Wim Wenders was in town filming "An American Friend" with actor Dennis Hopper, Hopper was invited to the dinner. Drugs and alcohol were plentiful, and Hopper and others eagerly imbibed. Hopper followed Steve to a 100-seat club called Onkel Pös Carnegie Hall for a midnight show and seated himself in the front row. As Steve made his way through the first few songs, an older woman in a babushka strolled table to table, selling individual red roses from a basket. "It was very European, very neat," says Steve's road manager, Steve Cohen.

In the back of the bar, however, loomed a group of rowdy inebriates. "They

Amsterdam radio personality Wim Bloemendaal, shown in the mid-1970s with idols Johann Sebastian Bach and Richard Wagner, toured Steve in and around the city and found "The Dutchman" pleasing despite its stereotypes.
(Photo by Ernst Niewenhuis, courtesy of Wim Bloemendaal)

29: After his Dec. 18 Melkweg show, DeFalcis greeted Steve, who pelted her with questions about Amsterdam. "He gave me the impression he was thinking of relocating. He asked me about the kids, safety and the schools. I guess he was concerned about violence in America. I found myself thinking, 'Is he thinking of leaving America?' I only knew of one person with a child at the time, so I couldn't give him the greatest answers."

In 1976, the Philadelphia Folk Festival billed a plethora of performers, many of whom ended up onstage with Steve for his event-closing Sunday-night show.

(Poster reprinted courtesy of Philadelphia Folk Song Society)

30: A post-show photo, printed in a booklet for the 1994 Goodman CD anthology "No Big Surprise" and circulated on the Internet, shows Steve and Hopper grinning over a pool table at Onkel Pös. One of three others closely resembles Jimmy Buffett and was identified as such in the booklet, but the Buffett-esque character actually was German jazz pianist Gottfried Böettger, says Gerd Schmerse, ex-Onkel Pös cashier.

were a little obnoxious throughout the show and weren't paying a lot of attention," Cohen says. "We didn't pay a lot of attention to them, but it was a small enough room that we could hear them being a little loud."

After some well-received livelier material, Steve opted to close with his melancholy "Yellow Coat." When he reached the song's final verse and sang the line "It's a two-day drive to New York," trouble began.

One of the drunks in back stood up and blurted, "This is Germany, not New York. We sing songs about Germany, not New York."

A seemingly somnolent Hopper leapt to his feet, turned around and glared at the heckler. "You Kraut motherfuckers!" he yelled.

Onkel Pös erupted. Chairs were shoved aside, beer glasses flew through the air, and a fight was under way. "Bedlam" is Cohen's description. On the tiny, barely elevated stage, the diminutive performer assumed he could quell the uproar. "But I looked up, and no, it was beyond that," Cohen says. "No one was paying attention to the stage anymore." The 5-foot-9 Cohen hoisted Steve with a bear hug at the waist, pulled open a nearby door, deposited Steve in the narrow closet that served as the dressing room and returned to rescue his guitar. The altercation, which brought the show to an end, lasted only a minute, but it was unsettling. In his countless club gigs, Steve wasn't immune to drunken brawls but this boorish exchange reflected international resentment that had lingered for decades. [30]

While Steve had much to sort out from his mixed European experiences, he could do it while looking fondly ahead toward one of his most welcome venues, the Philadelphia Folk Festival, held in Schwenksville, a rural town named for a German but far from any kind of pub scene.

This year, the Aug. 27-29 event heralded him as its star, and for good reason. His stage presence, encyclopedic musical knowledge and penchant for humor and improvisation had endeared him for years to festival-goers and organizers alike, and he knew that. But no one could foresee that by the end of the weekend, Steve, overconfidently rebounding on agreeable turf, would drive an arrogant wedge between officials and fans.

Cleverly titled daytime workshops — "Turn Your Radio On," " 'Twas Brillig" and "Redneck, White Sox and Blue Ribbon Beer (Country Classics)" — all featured Steve, who also emceed another workshop, "Chicago, My Home," showcasing the city whose folk scene had acquired exotic appeal for the Philly crowd. Besides introducing Chicago performers Stephen Wade, Claudia Schmidt, Jim Post, Ken Bloom, Harry Waller, Sally Fingerett, Mike Jordan, Al Day and Ed Holstein, Steve served as a down-to-earth Midwest musicologist. "There's a hell of a lot of good music in the city of Chicago," he said. "What used to be called categories — 'Well, that's jazz, that's folk' — that doesn't work anymore. That sucks. Just a musical melting pot is what it is. A lot of music came to Chicago from the South — white and black — and what happened to it when it gets there is what this is all about."

Steve also understood the complementary subtext of the Philly festival: the

overnight jam sessions in musicians' rooms at the nearby headquarters motel. Paula Ballan, architect of the festival's slate of artists during the 1970s, grasped the concept instinctively. "I would plan the party at the motel — that's what I would think of as I was booking," Ballan says. "It was who would learn the best songs from whom and what exchange of incredible creativity would be created that, if I hadn't put them together in the same time and place, would never happen. And abracadabra, magic happened."

Blues singer/songwriter Bonnie Raitt recalls one such all-night Philly song swap with David Bromberg, John Prine, her bass player Freebo and Martin, Bogan & Armstrong — and her revelation that the hub of the magic was Steve. "We were round-robining nearly every Beatles, Stones and Dylan song any of us could remember," Raitt says. "Somehow Stevie always knew all the words, all the chords and was just an irrepressible, impish jukebox of songs and energy. He literally could play anything. There's a level of musicianship that Stevie embodied that you very rarely see. He was totally a fan. That never diminished, and I'll never forget it. I will always remember him as simultaneously devilish and angelic, deep and incredibly silly, fierce and tender, the child and the father and man all mixed in. That childlike sense of enthusiasm and wonder is what we shared and what I treasured most about our friendship." [31]

Loudon Wainwright III, who witnessed several such sessions, says, "It'd start off where people would be passing the guitar, and then it became the Steve Goodman show. He would play everybody's songs, blues songs, country songs, standards, Cole Porter songs, Hank Williams songs, songs from 'South Pacific,' and all the chords, all the changes of a master guitar player. Everybody would sit back, and Steve would take us on a trip through American popular music."

Experiences such as Raitt's and Wainwright's often snowballed to produce the proverbial sum greater than its parts. "If I booked it right," Ballan says, "on Friday night the jam session at the motel would start, and by Sunday what would hit the stage would be as good onstage as what the people back at the motel heard in a room full of drugs. People who had never met each other would have been jamming and picking with a glazed, euphoric look of 'Oh my

(Right photo) Paying tribute to legendary guitarist Merle Travis, right, at the "Country Classics" workshop of the Philadelphia Folk Festival in 1976 are, from left, Gamble Rogers, Steve and Jethro Burns. *(Left photo) During the daytime workshops, a bit of the imp could be seen in Steve — and the trait crept out in full force in his festival-closing, Sunday night set.*
(Left photo by Jamie Downs, right photo by Liz Danzig Derry)

31: Though programs and archives for the Philly festival indicate no sure convergence of the artists in Bonnie Raitt's anecdote, her bass player, Freebo, places it in 1971.

David Amram, carrying a wooden flute, visits with Steve and others between daytime workshops at the 1976 Philadelphia Folk Festival.

(Photo by Jamie Downs)

32: The precise times in this section are calculated from a tape of the show and assume that a five-minute warning light was switched on at 11:55 p.m. Corroborating these calculations (including the ending time of 12:28 a.m.) are the memories of several participants who recall that Steve played about half an hour past midnight.

God, I've never made music this good,' and I could get it onto the stage."

Which is just what happened starting at 7:30 p.m. Sunday, Aug. 29, the festival's closing night, attended by nearly 7,000 paying ticket holders and more than 2,000 volunteers and backstage visitors. Ten acts played a lengthy show that was to end no later than midnight — not just according to the schedule but also by virtue of an official curfew written into the festival's agreement with the rural Upper Salford township that governed Schwenksville. Only five years earlier, the amplification of Steve's "Twelve Days of Syphilis" and other bawdy songs had triggered a township lawsuit that aimed to shut down the festival. The curfew was a part of a compromise worked out in 1972 to scuttle the suit. It recognized that people attending the festival and nearby residents who could hear its amplified music from more than five miles away needed to get some sleep before awakening to start the work week on Monday morning.

The confluence of talent and timing that night was as ominous as it was delicious, however, because the 10th and final artist on the bill was the one fully capable of bringing many of the festival's musicians to the stage in a giant collaboration — Steve Goodman.

Organizers' radar kicked in near the end of Steve's set, just nine minutes before midnight, when he led a stimulating version of "Jessie's Jig." [32] Driven by a bouncy Bo Diddley beat from Latin conga drummer Ray Mantilla and bassist Dennis Gormley, it was accented with solos from David Amram's peppery French horn, Ken Bloom's klezmer clarinet and Winnie Winston's smooth steel guitar.

When the instrumental ended at 11:54 p.m., festival organizers — including Andy Braunfeld, the festival co-chairman and legal counsel who had negotiated the curfew — anticipated just one more song. As the crowd of thousands cheered for more, Steve started to introduce Michael Smith's "Spoon River." During the intro, at 11:55 p.m., the organizers flipped a switch illuminating an onstage box with a bright red light that flashed at Steve in front of his feet. "I could see the light blinking on his pants," says Hightstown High teacher John Bates, who was standing in the audience close to the stage.

It was known as the five-minute warning light, and Steve reacted instantly.

"I was wondering why I thought I was walking around blind all weekend — this is the reason," he told the crowd with a giggle. "They're going to let us all out in the morning, too. They told us. You got the red ones, that means you get 30,000 volts, right?"

An impish gleam filled his saucer eyes as he mocked the meaning of the light: "Five minutes, Mr. Goodman, five minutes, five minutes."

Then came the step that organizers considered contemptuous but the audience found invigorating. Steve picked up from the stage a white towel that he traveled with, dramatically unfurled it and draped it over the light box. "It reminded me of a scene in some Arabian nights movie," Bloom says. "It wasn't just an offhand, casual throw. It was a serious and deliberate gesture, done with a fair bit of grace and line."

"Cover that fool up," one of Steve's accompanists said. "Yeah, that's it."

After covering the five-minute light with a white towel, Steve continues past the midnight curfew backed by (from left) Lew London, Jethro Burns, Saul Broudy and Steve Burgh.

(Photo by Liz Danzig Derry)

Those in the front rows of the audience cheered the maneuver, but a female volunteer in the wings called out, "Five minutes!"

"We'll try and keep this song under five minutes," Steve replied. "I see you."

The sidemen laughed, and Steve signaled them: "OK, I got the first verse, and then after that," he added with a laugh, "it's every man for himself."

"Spoon River" began modestly and quietly, with just Steve's voice and guitar. The calm tone of the waltz matched the mood with which Steve usually left his audiences. He sustained the song's long notes longer than usual, with a rich vocal. Volume rose steadily on the second verse as Winston on steel, Bloom on dobro, Amram on French horn and Jethro Burns on mandolin and Saul Broudy on harmonica all joined in with lush fills and solos. Still, the organizers breathed easily. Even though "Spoon River" continued past midnight, this surely would be a graceful finale. The towel bit was just for show, right?

When the audience finished applauding "Spoon River," Steve strode to his microphone at 12:03 a.m., the organizers hoping that he would bid the crowd good night. Just the opposite occurred. Steve began introducing his best-known song. "They played this on the moon and at half-time at a Super Bowl," he said nonchalantly, "so I guess in the middle of Abe Pool's farm in Schwenksville ain't so out of place."

Whereupon, at 12:04 a.m., Steve rolled into a mid-tempo version of "City of New Orleans," seasoned by Broudy's spirited high-harmony vocals and flawless solo breaks by Burns, Bloom and Winston.

Braunfeld tried to reassure a township official who was with him backstage, and he consulted with others, including stage manager David Baskin. "Steve had a connection to the audience. It was real, you could feel it," Baskin says. "You didn't get the sense that he was on one side of the proscenium arch and they were on the other. There was a real current going on there, a real connection, and he felt the connection, too."

But residents of the outlying rural areas, listening attentively for the festival's din to cease, were starting to telephone Baskin with pointed questions. "Past midnight, we were panicked," Baskin says. "We had been at the site for only five years, we had a bunch of township people who didn't love us so much and were still wary of us, and we didn't know what they were going to do."

"City of New Orleans" could have served as a fitting closer, ending at 12:09 a.m. But would Steve quit? After 30 seconds of applause, two guys in the crowd called out requests for "Turnpike Tom." Another 15 seconds later, Steve told his burgeoning band, "Yeah, let's have everybody out here." And one by one, starting at 12:10 a.m., musicians who had been standing backstage started ambling out front, with Steve's road manager, Steve Cohen, begging for time as he frantically set up additional microphones.

"Ladies and gentlemen, it has been an honor to play the Philadelphia Folk Festival with such fine musicians, and a few more are going to appear," Steve announced.

Out came New York faux trumpeter Bob Gurland.

Out came Philly-area soprano sax player Kenny Ulansey.

Out came Philadelphia keyboardist Sam Rudin, with a piano rolled out from the wings.

Out came Atlantic City mandolin/dobro player Lew London.

Out came Chicago singer Jim Post.

Out came Ontario Celtic fiddler John Allan Cameron.

Out came New York bassist Tony Markellis.

Out came "the people who taught us how to do all this shit, and I do mean taught," the seemingly ancient Chicago string-band elders Carl Martin on mandolin and Howard Armstrong on fiddle.

While the stage swelled with nearly 20 musicians and Steve thanked Cohen for squeezing mike stands into their proper positions, the backstage tension inflated like a balloon. Seconds ticked by like hours. "We were dying," says Baskin.

Shortly after 12:11 a.m., Steve's ultimate expression of musical impudence began. Electric guitarist Steve Burgh launched it with a breakneck lick that would be impossible to sustain, the crowd erupted in cheers, and Steve — with his best Louis Armstrong rasp — led the mélange in roaring into "Mama Don't Allow It." [33]

Finally, the song's flippant lyrics had found their perfect fit. "Mama" was the festival brass. Steve made this plain in the first verse: "We don't care what she don't allow. Have this festival anyhow."

The stab pierced Braunfeld. "The crowd is lovin' it, and he was lovin' it, and I'm sure it wasn't done from his point of view to be difficult, but it had us in a very bad position," he says. "There was so much adrenaline going on on the stage that it wasn't really possible to reason with anybody."

The "anybody" included not just the performing musicians but also those watching from the wings, sidelines and audience. Festival leaders, in their 15th year of providing a hallowed showcase for folk music, maintained a brisk pace by strictly limiting the length of artists' sets, thus protecting time for later acts but also acquiring the unfortunate epithet of "folk Nazis." For artists offended by such rules, therefore, each minute that Steve and his throng played overtime was a steppingstone to a catharsis. Burgh likened it to "a holy experience."

There was so much adrenaline going on on the stage that it wasn't really possible to reason with anybody.
ANDY BRAUNFELD

33: New Jersey radio host Michael Tearson, a folk musician in the 1960s who admired Steve since first seeing him in the early 1970s, says "Mama Don't Allow It" illustrated Steve's proclivity, fed by a fatal disease, for living in the moment. "That song speaks to the right now," Tearson says. "It also showed how he enjoyed being able to be a little bit disobedient. It was a metaphor for his life. That is Steve Goodman in a nutshell."

Musicians "were just incredibly pent-up," says Ann Mintz, contract producer for National Public Radio who that night was present backstage while recording the event for "Folk Festival USA." "The audience wanted more of their favorites than they got, and the performers always wanted to give the audience more than they could. They would just fight to play, and there were thousands of people screaming at them to play. They'd just get started, and then they'd get dragged off the stage. It made perfect sense that somebody finally cracked and went, 'I will not get off this stage!' For these people who have been told for all these years that they can't have as much time as they want, it was, 'Go, Steve! You tell 'em!' It was just this Dionysiac moment. It was almost sexual, that sort of pent-up release."

The "Mama" solos washed over the crowd, wave after wave. Steve called for Armstrong to solo on fiddle for a verse, then to double up on a second with Cameron. He called on Burgh for a Clapton-like solo on another two verses. Then he called on Amram for two verses on French horn. The frenetic tempo gradually settled into a chugging churning that sounded like the world's biggest kitchen Mixmaster — and the solos kept coming. Two more verses with Ulansey on sax. Two more with Broudy on harp.

Volunteers to the side pleaded with Steve to cut the song short. "Please, get the hell off!" Paula Ballan shouted from the wings. Others implored Cohen, the road manager: "You get him off, or we're going to have to pull the power."

But decibels from all directions made entreaties useless. "You're there to please the audience," Armstrong said, "and the audience keep on pluggin' and pullin' and hollerin' for you and standing up, well, what you going to do?" The answer was clear to Mantilla, the percussionist Amram brought to the festival. "It felt so good, we just kept goin', babe," he says. "By that time," Bloom adds, "there were so many people onstage and so much pandemonium. I'm sure there were some people screaming and hollering, but it's thousands of people out there raging, you've got the Mongolian cluster-fuck up there bouncing along, and everybody's playing in their little sections and stuff, so who could hear them?"

Baskin, whom Steve had given a middle-finger salute, was beside himself. "I had the township managers breathing down my neck, and there were phone calls every two seconds, 'What's going on? Why isn't the show over? You're supposed to shut down at midnight! It's 12:15!' It was a nightmare."

At 12:16 a.m., Steve called on Post for a verse of wild scat singing, and at 12:17 a.m., he called on London to solo for two verses on dobro.

The bellows from backstage finally reached Steve's ears, however. Near the end of London's first verse, at 12:18 a.m., Steve relented, cutting the instrumental solos in half. "OK, Lewie," he cut in, "everybody gets one." He called on Rudin for a one-verse piano solo. The same for Bloom on clarinet, for Winston on steel, for Burns on mandolin. Then, backed only by Mantilla's congas, Steve closed in on the final verse with a vocal. To make sure his message had been understood, he improvised, "We don't care if mama gets aloof. We're gonna raise the sky on this Schwenksville roof."

> For these people who have been told for all these years that they can't have as much time as they want, it was, 'Go, Steve! You tell 'em!' It was just this Dionysiac moment. It was almost sexual, that sort of pent-up release.
> **ANN MINTZ**

Philadelphia deejay and folk-festival host Gene Shay closed the 1976 event genially about 12:27 a.m., offering the crowd no hint of organizers' angst.

(Photo by Molly Ross)

34: That Steve bothered to correct his omission of Gurland "is just so much the kind of person that he was, in terms of being tuned in and caring about other people," Gurland says. "People in an audience pick up on a lot of stuff that they may not think they're picking up on. With Steve, audiences could sense that there was a love and humanity. It's that willingness to play on the edge and not go with what you're comfortable with that piques the electricity in a performance and allows for the magic of discovery."

After 27 orgiastic verses, the nine-minute "Mama" — an extraordinarily tight and enjoyable romp considering its chaotic assembly and the underlying anxiety — rumbled to a halt at 12:20 a.m. With cheers and shouts of "More!" raining onto the stage, Steve acknowledged the crowd: "Hope you had a nice time tonight, folks. You're the reason everybody up here was here." Then a nod to the organizers: "I want to thank the Philadelphia Folk Song Society for a nice weekend."

Then, while publicly thanking his laundry list of accompanists, Steve suddenly realized he had forgotten to call upon Gurland and the "trumpet" sounds that Gurland could create with his mouth and hands. "I'm sorry, man," Steve said. "My fault." Incredibly, Steve urged Gurland to perform on the spot: "Play it now, man. Just blow it. Let 'em know, man. Go ahead. Yeah, let's do it." While the organizers clenched their teeth, Gurland contributed a 40-second coda of aural magic, an unaccompanied blues solo on an imaginary horn. [34]

But Steve wasn't done yet. "Key of G, everybody," he told his tired troupe at 12:22 a.m., launching the one song that everyone present — attendees, organizers, musicians — realized would truly be the last, a slow waltz and traditional closer, the Huddie Ledbetter (Leadbelly) classic, "Goodnight Irene."

Steve didn't stick with the song's established words, however. Having already skewered the festival, in the second verse he gave his sword a wicked twist: "Now some people say Philadelphia is a mighty dangerous town / But, y'know, we're gonna brave those dangers when next year comes around."

At 12:24 a.m., Steve exacerbated the tension, calling on Carl Martin to play a verse on mandolin. "Friends," he announced, "Carl Martin's playin'." He knew that no one, not even the organizers, would deny the 73-year-old African-American string-band legend a departing solo.

At 12:25 a.m., Steve led an a cappella reprise of the chorus. "No instruments," he said, "just singin' now. Ready?" Vocal harmonies filled the air and rippled through the crowd, fueling yet another mystical moment.

"He had everybody in the audience — everybody — holding hands, swaying back and forth singing 'Goodnight Irene,' and I just thought, what a wonderful, lovely way to end a folk festival," says Lis Bralow, a first-time attendee who later became the event's chair of public relations. "The audience," she adds, "would never let him go."

But the clock was ticking, Steve was entering a second reprise of the chorus, and the organizers had had enough. They had to get him off the stage — "I don't think we were left with any choice," Braunfeld says — and they did so forcefully but diplomatically. At 12:26 a.m., while Steve was still singing, they sent out festival emcee and Philadelphia radio host Gene Shay. Steve gave him a crude introduction: "OK, Gene's gonna make some announcements, and we'll back him up, just like the radio, Gene. Is everybody gettin' the scale for this, Gene?"

Shay put on a genial face, revealing no angst. While everyone else kept singing and playing, in 30 quick seconds Shay thanked festival volunteers along

Steve listens while playing during the sound check for his show with Jethro Burns on Oct. 22, 1976, at Harper College in Palatine, Illinois.

(Photos by Michael Nejman)

with Steve and his musicians and dismissed the crowd with "Have a very safe trip home." But Steve had the last words, ending the festival at 12:28 a.m. by singing yet another "Irene" chorus and sputtering, "Irene, take it easy, Irene. Hey, Irene, see you around! Write if you get work!"

By that point, it was Steve who had risked putting himself out of work — at the festival itself. "They were so mad," Mintz says of the organizers. "They swore till they were blue in the face they were never going to invite him back."

No evidence exists that Steve publicly apologized or bared his feelings about the breach. But after leaving the stage, he fumed to Braunfeld and others. "Steve was not happy because he was on a roll, and he just didn't want to stop," Braunfeld says. "He was upset because he was really into the moment. He wasn't trying to hurt us." Charitably, Braunfeld adds, "It wasn't that he didn't know (about the curfew), but I don't think he understood its significance."

Braunfeld says organizers soon tried to "smooth over" conflict with the township and hoped they could ask Steve to return. "The township officials knew we were trying to get the show over," he says. "They knew it wasn't Woodstock and

A barefoot Peter "Madcat" Ruth accompanies Steve on harmonica Oct. 1, 1976, at the Power Center in Ann Arbor, Michigan.

(Photo by George Moser)

35: Today, the festival's closing Sunday concert ends at 9:30 p.m., 150 minutes earlier than the original midnight curfew.

36: Steve ended up playing a total of 110 concerts in 1976, a rate of nearly one every three days.

37: High-school senior and future radio-station program director Gary Cee told Steve after his afternoon show at Huntington, "I have all your records, even your first one." "You have my first record?" "Yeah." "That would make you *and* my mom."

that they didn't have to worry about something taking over the town."

Still, the explosive tension that Steve triggered that night ran deep. Known as an entertainer who could do no wrong onstage, he had stretched the limits far enough to disappoint insiders who had no other reason to distrust him. Decades later, though the festival survived the incident and has thrived on the Schwenksville site, and despite the legacy of Steve's magnetism, hard feelings persist. "Steve was music plus something else. I don't know what it was, but there was a light that followed him around. It was an honor to know him," Braunfeld says. "But he should have got off when we told him." [35]

Steve soon returned to the tougher reality of survival in the world of mainstream music. In the fall of 1976, despite his rose-colored summertime forecast, his "Words" LP was not selling well. The album, which lasted just four weeks on the *Billboard* Top 200 chart the previous spring and peaked at #175, was on its way to a total of just 30,000 sales, a drop of 40 percent from the 50,000 attained by the "Jig" LP. So Steve's industrious road schedule reflected the need to promote the recording. [36]

With only a few days at home in Evanston between trips, he left to play several cities and college towns in the East, did the same in the Midwest, then back to the East, back to the Midwest, again to the East, then to the Pacific Northwest, folding in Canadian stops in Toronto, Kingston, Winnipeg and Vancouver. Many shows were solitary, "An Evening with" gigs, but he also opened for John Prine and Cheech & Chong and headlined double bills whose opening acts included John Klemmer and Wendy Waldman. At each concert, he tried to leave the touch of a showman.

One opener for Steve was a three-piece East Lansing band whose name was inspired in part by "City of New Orleans," the Native Sons. A bluegrass version of "City" was part of the band's repertoire, so when the group opened for Steve at Michigan State University, Steve asked the group to return and play the song at the end of his set. Right after Steve had sung "You Never Even Call Me by My Name" while wearing a cowboy hat borrowed from the audience, he called the Native Sons to the stage, and mike stands were hastily arranged. "I had a boom mike on my banjo, and it was overextended, and it started to tip over," says band member Joel Mabus. "Steve nonchalantly reached over with his left foot and held up my mike through the last chorus — playing and standing on one foot and singing the song with the cowboy hat on. The crowd just roared."

Easily Steve's most memorable collaboration that fall resulted from a call by the same performer who had invited him the year before to "The Mike Douglas Show." Harry Chapin bid Steve and 57-year-old folk legend Pete Seeger to team with him for a pair of benefit shows on Sunday, Nov. 14, for Chapin's Performing Arts Foundation Playhouse. [37] Held at the high school in his hometown of Huntington, near the north central coast of Long Island, the two packed shows sizzled with the unique dynamic of the three social-minded musicians. Chapin's hits "Taxi" and "Cat's in the Cradle" got a warm reception, and Seeger delighted the crowd with Leadbelly's "Midnight Special" and a hilarious and in-

In an inspired teaming, Steve joins (from left) Pete Seeger and Harry Chapin Nov. 14, 1976, at Huntington (N.Y.) High School for the first of several fund-raising concerts for Chapin's arts foundation. (Photos by Geoff Parker, courtesy of Steve Cohen)

spiring feminist turn on a children's song, "There Was an Old Woman Who Swallowed a Lie" (instead of "fly"). But it was Steve who mixed acerbic whimsy with tear-inducing emotion to steal the shows.

Reflecting Democrat Jimmy Carter's victory in the presidential race a dozen days prior, Steve adjusted the last line of his "Unemployed" from a warning to a tweak: "Look what happened to Gerald Ford / Now even he is unemployed." Steve also razzed himself, noting the similarity of his "This Hotel Room" melody to that of "Shortnin' Bread." A judge had just forced ex-Beatle George Harrison to pay the Chiffons a portion of royalties for his 1970 song "My Sweet Lord" because of its resemblance to the group's "He's So Fine" hit from 1962. Steve cracked, "If the Chiffons had written 'Shortnin' Bread,' I'd be in a lot of trouble: 'My Sweet Shortnin' Bread.' "

Steve also deftly mixed seriousness with humor, not just with "The Dutchman" and "Ballad of Penny Evans," but also in introducing the gospel tune "I'll Fly Away." "This is one of those songs that proves you don't have to know anything about Jesus to like spirituals," he said, pausing a beat then adding to guffaws, "I sing it to Hare Krishnas at the airport." Vamping on slide guitar in the middle of the six-and-a-half-minute tune, Steve returned to earnestness, apologizing for his "unmitigated brass" in leading a sing-along tune in the presence of Seeger, the acknowledged master of the form.

"Forgive me, but it sure would be nice if everybody sang along on this anyhow," Steve said. "I learned how to do everything I'm doin' up here tonight from watchin' Pete Seeger, and that's no shit. Pete Seeger survivin' the blacklist made it possible for people like me and Harry to stand up here and do all this. I got a buddy who's got a copy of a tape he (Seeger) did at Northwestern University in 1957 with Big Bill Broonzy, and the FBI is in the audience — classic. We're all indebted to him, man. I think we oughta sing this for Pete." They did,

Steve joins in a Belgian radio interview with fellow American singer/songwriter Wendy Waldman during his return to Europe in December 1976.

(Photo by Steve Cohen)

loud and long, and when Steve left the nighttime show before it ended to catch a 12:30 a.m. flight, Chapin promised to bring Steve back at a future date.

Steve returned home a week later in time to watch a half-hour television documentary on Chicago's CBS affiliate, WBBM Channel 2, "Just Another Diagonal Street in Some Other Kind of Town." Focusing on the Lincoln Avenue entertainment corridor and hosted by Gene Siskel two years before his "thumbs up/thumbs down" film-review show with Roger Ebert debuted nationally, the Nov. 22 program identified Somebody Else's Troubles as "the city's most popular folk-music hangout." The focus for the Troubles segment was Steve, whom Siskel called "Chicago's own major folk artist."

Besides picking a "Lady Be Good" solo and singing "Lincoln Park Pirates," Steve was shown leading an amusingly percussive rendition of "Mama Don't Allow It" that featured Mike Lieber scraping and honking a washboard "contraption" and an open-mouthed David Amram slapping his cheeks and using his knuckles to knock on his skull — a technique called "headbone." Totaling four minutes, the footage of Steve reinforced his persona as a live act nonpareil.

Europe wanted that act to return, so for 10 days in mid-December, Steve flew back to the four countries he'd visited the previous summer, promoted by Asylum ads touting his "energy, sensitivity and humor." A solo concert in London, at the 65-year-old, 1,550-seat Victoria Palace, was "not only a splendid reminder of the golden days of the folk revival but also a superb example of how all good songs are in a sense contemporary," wrote a *New Musical Express* reviewer. Even in such a formal setting, Steve didn't hesitate to call to the stage musicians he spotted in the audience. Heather Wood and Royston Wood, two-thirds of the former Young Tradition, joined him in singing the traditional English song "The Innocent Hare" and the Cyril Tawney chantey, "Chicken on a Raft" (egg on toast).

Steve (counterclockwise from right photo, above), tunes in the dressing room before a performance for Amsterdam TV in December 1976, followed by a crossword-puzzle session aboard a ferry back to England.

(Photos by Steve Cohen)

In Belgium, where five months earlier he had entertained 5,000 people in a Brussels square, Steve put on a lengthy performance at the crowded de Beursschouwburg ("Stock Exchange Theater"), a 350-seat hall built in 1890 and designed for singers and cabaret. "The audience went crazy, they all wanted to be his friend," says Jari Demeulemeester, director of the Ancienne Belgique and booker of the show. "In my 30-plus years in show business, I've never met such a gentle and attractive person as Steve," he says. "What a creative power he had, what a presence onstage, what a wit."

Back in Chicago for his New Year's Eve show with David Amram at the Earl of Old Town, Steve embodied the wit of the cover photos of his "Words" LP. Steve and Jethro Burns conspired to wear tuxedos, but Steve went further, donning a huge top hat, white gloves and a cape, looking like a stunted, impish hippie version of Count Dracula. He also wore a disposition of delight — no doubt in part because he recently had learned that Nancy was pregnant again.

Though he had just bought a bright orange Mercedes (some friends thought

Singing oldies while wielding an electric guitar, Steve fronts the Chicago band Swingshift, including, from left, leader Ron Crick, drummer Ken Brienholt and mandolinist Jethro Burns, in a late 1976 session at Ratso's on Chicago's Lincoln Avenue. The collaboration ballooned to Steve's January 1977 touring amalgam, which he dubbed the Rolling Blunder Revue.

(Photo courtesy of Diane Holmes)

it the ugliest car they'd ever seen), Steve opted not to drive it that night to the Earl. Instead, he and Burns picked up Saul Broudy and Ken Bloom in a limo, and the snazzy troupe stopped at a blue-collar diner for pre-show burgers. "He bought dinner for everyone sitting at the counter, must have been a dozen people there," Bloom says. "They didn't know who he was, but they figured he must be something special because he pulled up in a limo wearing a tux."

Onstage at the Earl that night, Steve maintained the guise, even finger-picking "It's a Sin to Tell a Lie" with his white gloves on. "It was a real showboaty thing to do," says John Platt, then-host at WXRT-FM, "but he was able to do it and not compromise the musicianship of it."

Steve tinkered with his presentation of other recorded songs as the calendar spilled into 1977. On the icy evening of Jan. 15, Steve slotted a rare show on Chicago's South Side, at 73-year-old, 960-seat Mandel Hall at the University of Chicago. There, he preceded his Wilson Pickett-styled "Can't Go Back" with a medley of 1960s soul hits: the Delfonics' "La La Means I Love You" ("my favorite R&B song," Steve said) and Smokey Robinson's "Get Ready" ("my favorite Temps song") and "My Girl" ("my second favorite"). Steve also called opener Jim Post out to sing the high-voiced last verse of "Ballad of Dan Moody," live verification of Post's powerful contribution on the recorded track.

Instead of returning to the studio in early 1977 as he had done 12 months earlier, Steve nurtured something looser and more risky. Perhaps unbefitting a national recording artist, Steve haunted the Lincoln Avenue clubs featured in the Gene Siskel TV documentary — including Ratso's, the weeknight home of a band headed by guitarist Ron Crick called Swingshift. Diverse as Steve's own recordings, the band drew broadly from the local music scene, including Jethro Burns on mandolin, singer Diane Holmes, multi-instrumentalists Ken Bloom and Howard Levy, bassist Jim Tullio, Tom Furlong on pedal steel and saxophonist Andy Tecson, who Steve had met in Germany the previous summer.

Sitting in gave Steve the notion to recruit most of the Swingshifters, form his own band and borrow John Prine's 1975 van to play extended, free-form shows at five Illinois colleges during the snowy, sub-freezing nights of late January and early February. In tone and girth, Steve's ragtag group resembled the Rolling Thunder Revue, the unwieldy medicine-show troupe led by Bob Dylan

The Rolling Blunder lineup Feb. 5, 1977, at Northwestern University in Evanston (from left): Andy Tecson and Ken Bloom (reading music from custom "SG" stands), Steve, Jethro (barely visible) and Johnny Burns, Diane Holmes, Claudia Schmidt, Howard Levy and Jim Tullio.

(Photo courtesy of Andy Tecson)

that had toured the Northeast and South in fall 1975 and spring 1976. Steve wryly named his own experimental excursion the Rolling Blunder Revue.

The self-financed tour, which commanded Steve's full attention,[38] blended class with cacophony. Steve commissioned the construction of lighted, big-band style music stands whose logo drew from Al Jolson, "City of New Orleans" and his own initials — a top hat, a train track and the block letters "SG." The evenings began with a solo set by Steve and mushroomed into a musical mass that, much the same as the closing night of Philly, threatened to overwhelm the stage with bodies, instruments, energy and sound. Besides Bloom, Holmes, Levy, Tecson, Tullio and Burns, the crew took in Jethro Burns' son Johnny on electric guitar, bassist and washboard player Mike Lieber, drummer Angelo Varias, singer Claudia Schmidt, pianist/fiddler Bob Hoban, opening acts Jim Post to Vassar Clements and, for cameos, Bill "Oliver" Swofford and John Prine. With no established order of songs, each night's show became an adventure. "It was a whimsical thing," Holmes says. "Steve wanted to try it out and have fun with it. But he had definite ideas about the way he wanted things."

Part of the fun came from writing songs as a group in a motel room — as Steve had instigated the year before for the "Words" LP — and trying them out on the audience the next night.

The Dec. 20 death of the legendary Richard J. Daley, Chicago's "boss" mayor for the previous 21-plus years, inspired one such composition. "Steve remembered an old Irish sob-and-drink song called 'Delia's Gone,' and it was too perfect a match, with hizzoner being our Irish mayor," says Johnny Burns. "We worked best under the influence of things not legal and wine, so sitting down with a snootful and a few bowls full, Steve and I began reconstructing the song with snippets of Daley's political history." The result, "Daley's Gone," traced

38: Saul Broudy sought Steve to play on an LP he was recording that month in Baltimore. Instead, Steve supplied liner notes. Broudy, Steve wrote, was part of the "new breed of musician ... who is not impressed at all with the hyphenated hype of jazz-folk, or folk-blues, or country-rock, or any of the definitions of sound that prevent musicians from playing whatever is in their minds and hearts and hands."

Chicago Mayor Richard J. Daley observes the July 1976 Democratic National Convention at Madison Square Garden in New York City. Five months later, he was dead, and Steve soon wrote an ambivalent tribute, "Daley's Gone."

(Photo by Keith Wessel)

39: When Steve recorded "Daley's Gone" for his next album later in the year, the Bilandic verse was excised, no doubt because Steve deemed it too obscure for a national audience.

the mayor's rise from South Side "working man's" roots to his disputed role in swaying John F. Kennedy's 1960 presidential election win. Straddling criticism and commendation, the song's journalistic mien was clearest in addressing Daley's infamous sanctioning of police beatings of protesters that Steve witnessed as a college student during the Democratic National Convention. No one "could inspire more love or hate," the song said, "if you were in the park and it was 1968."

Steve said he tried to capture the city's ambivalence toward Daley. "What he did wrong, he did wrong in such a big way that there's parts of Chicago that are like Rhodesia," he said in a later interview. "He also was literally the last guy who could get that many people to jump when he talked, including a lot of smart people who knew he was good for business. A lot of people in Chicago lived real good because of this guy. He meant a lot of different things to a lot of different folks, and he got 70 percent of the popular vote every time he ran. He kept gettin' more and more popular, to where everybody knocked him and nobody ran against him. So, the guy was a heavyweight. ...

"No man is all one way or all another way. I'm not a student of politics as such, but I can tell a guy who's taking all the air out of the room when I see one, and he was one of 'em."

The final verse merged a recognition of Daley's influence with an irresistible pun at the expense of the alderman whom the city council elected to fill the remaining term, Michael Bilandic: "I guess bein' mayor of Chicago is no easy trick / It took three men to replace Daley — Michael, Bill and Dick." The college audiences in Champaign/Urbana, Carbondale, Naperville, Chicago and Evanston cheered the joke instantly. 39

Another song, a light-hearted morality tale triggered by Johnny Burns, had a wackier origin. As several in the Rolling Blunder group relaxed in a room of the Carbondale Ramada Inn after a show at Southern Illinois University's Shryock Hall, "somebody had screwed something up," prompting the younger Burns to say, "Well, if you want it done right, you've got to do it yourself." Looking up, Steve said, "Y'know, there's a song there."

Steve began to conjure a melody, then tossed lyrics back and forth with Prine. The two swept through human history to identify episodes in which famous and notorious couples — as Burns' line declared — could have assumed more responsibility for their actions. The lyrics' jest lay in who would tell whom to "do it yourself."

One scenario, inspired by Steve's recent viewing of the 1976 cinematic concoction "In Search of Noah's Ark," had God telling Noah not to give up. Another had Jesse James rejecting an idea from Billy the Kid that they exchange their names. A third had Richard Nixon telling his secretary, Rose Mary Woods, not to weep over 18 minutes of blank Watergate tape. A fourth, set at Plymouth Rock, Massachusetts, had Priscilla Mullins rejecting John Alden's proposal of marriage on behalf of his friend, Miles Standish.

Prine, who says he was trying to get out of co-writing the song, started poking at Steve, arguing that the Plymouth Rock stanza should state that the Pilgrims, not Native Americans, had invented the turkey dinner.

"Nah," Steve replied, "let's be a little more clever with the wording."

"Hey, don't talk to me about clever with words," Prine shot back. "I have an idea of what I'm doin' here."

With a straight face, Prine proposed writing each verse on a motel postcard, sending the cards to people he knew and later visiting them one at a time to collect feedback.

"No, don't do that," Steve said. "You can't do that. That's stupid!"

"No, c'mon," Prine said. "This'll be fun."

Others in the room found the late-night sparring hysterical. "We were just laughing our asses off," Tullio says. "For everything Steve pulled to the left, John pulled to the right," Johnny Burns says, "and it became funnier and funnier because John was just yanking Steve's chain, antagonizing him for the hell of it. John's nickname for him was 'Intenso' because he squeaked, he was so intense. His eyes would just burn a hole in you."

The next night, in Pfeiffer Hall at North Central College in Naperville, after Steve refined the song in the troupe's van that morning, the tune got its debut. It was a shaky version that extended seven and a half minutes, including a finish, a burst of applause and a reprise when Steve realized he had forgotten to sing the Watergate verse — and in the final chorus Steve delivered a spot-on impersonation of Nixon's voice. No one announced a name for the song, but it soon became known as "Flotilla," an oddball moniker that Prine dreamed up that had something to do with Attila the Hun.

In this alternately serious and "anything goes" atmosphere, Claudia Schmidt — a relative newcomer to the Chicago scene who like Diane Holmes was hired for the tour by Steve to provide doo-wop vocals — one night took the risk of providing what she thought would be a welcome bit of spontaneity. While Steve, in his solo set, sang his slow, romantic "Old Fashioned," she stepped out and surprised him by adding a harmony line.

Schmidt says her intent was wholly innocent, to help the tune's presentation, but Steve "let me have it" afterward. "You don't sing on that song," he commanded her. "I didn't know him that personally, and it was a song he had written for Nancy, and man, I tell you, he desecrated me," Schmidt says. "I was a mess for a little while. So I got a look at that fierce side, and it was a lonely place to be. But he blew off steam, and then he went on with things. It wasn't like he held a grudge."

Besides the personal nature of the song, what Schmidt perceived in Steve's rebuke was a sexism that many acknowledged was rampant in the folk scene, that she couldn't join Steve's "good ol' boys club" and had to stick to the role of a female backup singer. "The woman had to be the object in back," Schmidt says, even though doing so contradicted the image that Steve cultivated of welcoming improvisation. "It was a clashing of worlds," she says. "I loved Steve and loved having the total experience (of the tour), but I also loved the way he

Claudia Schmidt drew a strong rebuke from Steve for adding impromptu harmony on "Old Fashioned" during a Rolling Blunder show.

(Photo by Dan Doman)

John Prine taunted Steve in early 1977 during a Rolling Blunder Revue motel-room writing session, kidding that the group should write draft verses on postcards and mail them to friends for feedback.

(Photo by Steve Cohen)

sang 'Old Fashioned.' It also was the very thing that made him blow up at me for putting a harmony on it. It was all interconnected." [40]

The doo-wop voices of Schmidt and Holmes became prominent in the second half of each Rolling Blunder show when Steve switched to full-bore versions of the oldies "Johnny B. Goode" and "Tossin' and Turnin'." The bring-down-the-house closer was a long, raucous take on a torch song Ray Charles had popularized, Don Gibson's "I Can't Stop Loving You," with a flawless tribute to soul belter James Brown's classic routine of being overcome by torturous passion. As the song began to end, Steve knelt and started to "cry," then fell to the floor kicking and shrieking while Schmidt (in an Afro fright wig), Holmes and Johnny Burns repeated the chorus hypnotically. Cohen, the road manager, rushed to Steve, draped him with a topcoat, patted him on the back and led him offstage as the audience screamed for more. Suddenly, Steve threw down the coat, ran back and grabbed the mike to start the cycle again. "It was the funniest thing," Burns says. "We must have sung the song 15 times through before he finally got offstage because the audience was howling so much." Schmidt says the routine was Steve's way of "acting out a musical fantasy." [41]

The tour drew sellout crowds of 1,000 to 2,000 students and earned raves. The *North Central Chronicle* in Naperville termed Rolling Blunder a "smash hit." Janet Kolodzy of *The Daily Northwestern* at Northwestern University opened her review by saying, "Steve Goodman, Northwestern 'Can't Stop Loving You'."

Steve's cohorts gave him equal praise, as much for his demeanor offstage as on. More than once, there was a shortage of motel rooms, and instead of forcing others to double up, Steve elected to share with Cohen. One morning in Champaign, while the troupe readied to leave for the next town, one of the two vehicles, Prine's van, had wedged itself into the snowbound motel parking lot. "We're all barely awake, going to get coffee, and Steve's out pushing the van, getting something to put under the wheels for traction," Tullio says. "Eventually, Jethro gets in the driver's seat, and the rest of us are out pushing the damn van. It took us a half hour to get out of there, but we did. But the first guy out was Goodman: 'OK, guys.' If he were anybody else, he would be the last guy out. He was like, it's his thing, it's his show." [42]

A pair of shows Feb. 5 at Northwestern University ended the Rolling Blunder saga. The tour magnified Steve's warmth, humor and aura of humility, fortifying him as he set out on yet another concert swing through the East. His first stop, just four days later, was a Feb. 9-10 stint at the Main Point club in Bryn Mawr. There, he told his opening act, New York singer/songwriter Tom Pacheco, of his elation over the inauguration of Jimmy Carter and disclosed that he'd drafted two verses and the chorus for an uptempo song about the new president. "Steve was very up on Carter," Pacheco says. But as with "Daley's Gone," the in-progress composition also was wary, its chorus including the line, "I hope you don't change when they put you on the money." Pacheco appreciated Steve's plainspoken lyrical caution: "He was able to take important issues but write them in the vernacular of the common man."

40: Steve may have insisted on singing "Old Fashioned" solo partly because its words revealed his singular musical tastes in addition to describing his love for Nancy. The lyrics labeled Steve as "out of date and born too late to ever catch on," recognition that he wasn't headed for superstardom. This self-focus was reflected in the tune's title. In contrast, many who consider the song only a paean to Nancy recall its title incorrectly as "Old Fashioned Girl."

41: The shtick fit Cohen's view from serving as Steve's road manager for 15 months. "He lived for those two hours that he was onstage," Cohen says. "Everything else was like waiting for the dentist, just a lead-up to what he did onstage. He could have a short fuse, he could be demanding, and he had every right to be. He also had his wife and kids back home. But that connection, that communication that he made onstage, he loved that."

42: Brian Torff recalls a mid-1970s trip from New York City to a Steve show in Saratoga Springs during which Steve similarly insisted that he sit in the back seat of a jam-packed Chevy Suburban, beneath Torff's huge double bass. In the car besides Steve and Torff were David Amram, Charlie Chin and Steve Burgh. "Someone had to be underneath," Torff says. "Steve kept saying, 'Let me do it.' "

The Philadelphia Folk Festival brass stopped by on Steve's first night at the Main Point for a meeting to mend fences over his overtime stunt the previous August. The talk, says Andy Braunfeld, went well. Then, aided by David Amram, Lew London and other unbilled guests, Steve turned in a customarily riveting performance. Afterward, Laura Haynes (now Aiken), of the Philly festival's founding family, took Steve and Amram to a lengthy 2 a.m. breakfast at Minella's Main Line Diner in nearby Wayne, where Steve maintained a running commentary on his Grandma Mary and his dad. "It was unusual," Haynes says. "I had never heard him talk about his family at all." Aiken drove the pair to their hotel, and the two retired to their respective rooms. There, not long after 7 a.m., as Steve started to doze, the ring of his room phone jolted him awake.

The call was from Chicago. His father was gone.

Joseph Bayer "Bud" Goodman, the man from whom Steve had inherited his endearing humor and geniality, had suffered a fatal early-morning heart attack in the bathroom of his North Side apartment. It couldn't have been entirely a surprise, given his dad's history of coronary disease. Nonetheless, Bud's demise, at two and a half months shy of 59, hit Steve like a brick.

It was not Steve's only recent brush with the loss of someone close. Less than four months earlier, former Pittsburgh folksinger Pat Chamberlain had killed himself with a gunshot in his Manhattan apartment while on the telephone with a girlfriend who was breaking up with him. Steve had credited Chamberlain, a cerebral medical worker, for co-writing "Can't Go Back" and "Old Fashioned" and had appreciated being able to talk shop with him about leukemia.

The suicide of this singer, whose voice resembled that of James Taylor, triggered ire in the New York folk scene. "It was a wasteful, stupid, goddamn dumb thing to do," says Raun MacKinnon, who commiserated that night with Erik Frandsen at the Other End. "There was nothing sensible about it, nothing romantic, nothing artistic, nothing at all." Paula Ballan termed Chamberlain's death a wake-up call. "It almost became this bond of, 'We will not let any of us go so far down the tubes that we will let this happen to another friend again.' It was one of those real grown-up moments among a group of people who were party-hearty and living the real 1960s life, even though it was the 1970s."

Steve paid for Chamberlain's memorial service, which was held three days later on Sunday, Oct. 17, at a church near Gramercy Park in Manhattan and attended by David Amram, Saul Broudy, Stephen Wade, Patrick Sky, Paul Siebel, Jack McGann, Kenny Ulansey and other folkies. Steve flew in for the service after performing a concert the night before at the Playhouse Theater in Winnipeg, and he paid the round-trip airfare for singer/songwriter Harry Waller, transplanted from Pittsburgh to Chicago in 1975 and a friend of Chamberlain's, to attend. Steve had befriended Waller and admired his irreverent signature song, "Cockroaches on Parade," telling Los Angeles radio host Howard Larman in May 1976 that it was "one of the two or three funniest songs I ever heard."

After the Chamberlain service, Ballan pulled Waller aside to ask him how Steve was coping. "It must be hard for him," she told Waller. "It must be strange

One of the co-writers of Steve's "Old Fashioned," Patrick Chamberlain, shown at a workshop of the 1976 Philadelphia Folk Festival, committed suicide less than two months later. It was a blow for Steve, who paid for the memorial service.

(Photo by Chuck Klein)

On the plane ride home from Patrick Chamberlain's service, Harry Waller heard Steve confide his desires for an upbeat memorial for himself. He asked Waller to "pick things up a bit" and make it a party.
(Photo by Bob Friday, courtesy of Harry Waller)

43: On the same flight were Earl Pionke and a crate of frozen Sabrett's ("It's on a roll!") hot dogs. Pionke wanted to emulate New York hot-dog stands by operating one of his own outside his saloon, and only Sabrett's would do. From a Manhattan supplier, Pionke secured the case of dogs and brought it to Pete's Tavern, the 1864 restaurant frequented by writer O Henry where folkies gathered before the Chamberlain service. Steve persuaded the barkeep to ice the dogs during the service, and checked the case on his flight to Chicago. On several return trips to New York, Steve hauled more Sabrett's crates for Pionke, who sold the hot dogs in the wee hours to customers departing his bar.

for him to want to live and be fighting to live every minute of his life and to know that Pat just (gave up)."

Steve answered Ballan's query while flying with Waller back to Chicago. [43]

"Look, I don't know if you know this," he told Waller. "I'm sick. I'm gonna die before you."

Waller, who had learned of Steve's leukemia from others two months before, listened intently as Steve guessed how his own memorial service would proceed. "Look, the odds are they're going to have something for me," he told Waller. "It's gonna be at the Earl, and it's gonna be down, it's gonna be a wake." Steve predicted his friends would sing serious songs, but he sought something different from Waller. "When you get up there," he said, "do me a favor. Pick things up a little bit. Sing 'Cockroaches on Parade.' Remind 'em that it's a party."

In the midst of disillusionment over Chamberlain's suicide, Waller found Steve's upbeat admonition stunning. "But that's the way he was. He never was down. If you said something down, it'd be like, 'Harry, how could you be down?' He'd stick it to you: 'Everything's great.' Every day was a fight for him, and it was just a waste of time for him to be down."

If there ever was a time for Steve's vitality to wither, however, it was upon learning of his dad's passing, an event that Steve hadn't expected to experience. With leukemia haunting him for more than eight years, Steve had assumed he would die first — and so had his father, who likely had wrestled with the question of how he might have passed along to his son the genetic ingredients for a fatal disease. This irony pervaded Steve's thoughts as he sorted out cremation and memorial-service logistics by phone with both his brother, David, and the members of what had become his dad's new family — Norma Goodman, whom Bud had married in 1972 following his divorce from Minnette, and stepbrothers Andy Sohn, a 20-year-old New York University student, and 14-year-old Doug Sohn.

Steve later said that his father's demise sent him into "a fog" for several months. But that morning he vowed to complete his nighttime Main Point engagement without disclosing the death or calling attention to his sorrow. In the basement dressing room after the first set, however, David Amram discovered that Steve's emotions had swelled to the surface. Behind his dark hair and full beard, Steve's face had turned a pasty white.

"You don't look good," said Amram, who thought Steve's leukemia might be rearing its head. "You look terrible."

"I feel terrible."

"What can I do? What can I get you?" Amram asked. "Just stay here. Do you need a doctor?"

"No, I got a phone call this morning," Steve said. "My father just died."

Amram didn't know what to do, "so I just hugged him."

"It's OK," Steve said slowly. "It's OK."

Soon, Steve climbed the stairs, stepped back onstage and played "an incredible, beautiful, fun, energetic set," Amram says.

"That was the most amazing show I've ever heard," says Laura Haynes, who says Steve played so intensely that he snapped three or four guitar strings. Steve never divulged to the crowd the news of his father's demise, but he signaled the handful who did know — and simultaneously comforted himself — by finishing the show with a song new to his repertoire. It was a poignant Al Lewis/Vincent Rose/Larry Stock tune that had been popularized by Glenn Miller in 1940 and Fats Domino in 1956, "Blueberry Hill." The line of the song that brought tears to Haynes that night (and still does today) was, "Though we're apart, I love you still." [44]

Steve canceled concerts the next two nights at nearby Delaware County Community College and flew home, where song selection became a big factor — incredibly, the only factor — in the memorial service for Bud, scheduled for the following Monday, Valentine's Day, at Piser Memorial Chapel on Chicago's North Side. [45] There, Steve planned the event with the help of his brother and two stepbrothers. The four settled on a singular ceremony.

Family and friends arrived at the chapel to see at the front of the room a stool and a guitar. At 11 a.m., Steve strode forward, picked up the instrument, sat on the stool and said softly, "This was my father's favorite song." Already hushed, the crowd turned pin-drop silent as Steve played and sang an elegy for the gentle love to be shared at an age that neither he nor Bud would reach, Michael Smith's "The Dutchman." Except for a moment when Steve's voice cracked, it was a flawless performance. At song's end, Steve walked away, and that was it. In less than five minutes, the service was over.

"I thought it was tremendous," says Doug Sohn. "It was moving in an extremely warm way." His brother, Andy, agrees. "It was a beyond touching moment to be in that funeral chapel and for Steve to be singing that song," he says. "That was Bud's favorite song — by far, nothing close. It was the music, the melody, just the whole thing. Steve just took it to another level."

The brevity of the event also matched the suddenness of Bud's absence. "Most people get sick and die, but Bud was like boom!" Andy Sohn says. "He'd been to the doctor that week. The doctor said, 'You're great.' They'd been to a Chinese restaurant the night before, and Bud had gotten his fortune: 'You will have a long and fruitful life.' That has been our family inside joke now. God forbid anybody gets that message. I do not open up a fortune since then."

While the ephemeral service didn't agree with everyone, Andy Sohn notes that "Steve and Bud and David were never about convention. It was not going to be this rabbi who saw Bud once a year pretend like he knew him and say, 'Bud was a great father, a great car salesman,' what you usually hear at these services."

Instead, Bud Goodman went out solely with a song sung by his elder son, who, instead of playing to an audience's expectations, gave a gift to his dad. ♪

This was my father's favorite song.
STEVE GOODMAN

44: Dan Milner, who sang in the Flying Cloud, an Irish folk group, and put on more than 500 concerts at New York's Eagle Tavern, attended the Feb. 10 show and was clued in beforehand that Steve's dad had died that morning. Backstage, Milner says, Steve "paced back and forth, very deliberately looking intently downward at the floor." But onstage, he says, Steve was "masterful. It was the gutsiest show I've ever seen in folk music."

45: The tiny, paid obituary that Steve had written for the Feb. 13-14, 1977, editions of the *Chicago Tribune* conveyed warmth that his stepbrothers deeply appreciated. It described Bud as "precious husband of Norma; dear father of David and Steven; superior step daddy of Douglas and Andrew Sohn; beloved brother of Herbert; wonderful grandfather of Jessie and Sarah."

'I'm going to communicate with you if it kills me'

"You're gonna write the book, aren't you?"

Sensing that his life as a disease-threatened troubadour was a story worth telling, Steve Goodman put this question to his road manager late one night in the hallway of a hotel in the spring of 1977. "It wasn't accusatory or that he was uneasy with it," says Steve Cohen. "It was kind of revelatory to him when he said it, like he had just had an epiphany."

To Cohen, who several months later left his job with Steve, moved back to the college town of Eugene, Oregon, and wrote for an alternative weekly, the *Willamette Valley Observer*, the prospect of writing Goodman's biography — raised by the subject himself — was intriguing.

"God knows, it would have been great, if I had paid attention and gone back to my hotel room and kept a diary," Cohen says. "I didn't. I didn't at all. I never possessed that much focus. But I think he always thought that I was going to."

No matter, because Steve already had begun telling his own story via his songs. From Chicago roots ("Where Are You Goin' Mister," "City of New Orleans," "Paul Powell," "Lincoln Park Pirates," "Daley's Gone") to gratitude for his marriage ("Would You Like to Learn to Dance?" and "Old Fashioned") to joy over fatherhood ("Jessie's Jig"), Steve offered lyrical and instrumental pieces of his life's puzzle, folding into many of them pointed references to impending death.

His "Song for David" was the closest Steve had come to revealing anguish over his mortality, but it was metaphorical and intentionally masked the bearer of the emotion. With his father's death, Steve would bare his psyche much more nakedly, and the veil would lift — but not immediately. Over the next three months, Steve lost himself in a colorful palette of activity as he mulled his dad's permanent absence.

Zinging all over the continent in gigs that ranged from Montreal, Quebec, to Birmingham, Alabama ("Goodman emits joy," from *The Daily Iowan*, was a typical headline), Steve flew to Manhattan for a recording of new songs at Vanguard Records by a high-school musical hero, Tom Paxton.

The "Ramblin' Boy" had returned to New York after four years in Great Britain. He was down. "I was disgusted with the way my recording career was

(Left) Willie Nelson joins Jethro Burns in eyeing Steve, in a borrowed cowboy hat, as he mugs his way through "You Never Even Call Me by My Name" on Friday, Nov. 11, 1977, at the Austin Opry House. Later that month, Steve marveled at Nelson's walk-on. Steve told Evanston Township High School student interviewer Vicky Newberry (now Costakis) and her friend Lynne Bryan, "That's the nicest thing you can have happen to you," he said. "Down in Texas, that guy's almost like the governor of Texas."

(Photo by Scott Newton)

While Hoyt Axton and Odetta look on, Tom Paxton gives Steve a hug on Labor Day weekend of 1978 during the Bread & Roses Festival in Berkeley. Paxton was ecstatic about Steve's vocal and instrumental accompaniment for "New Songs from the Briarpatch," Paxton's domestic comeback LP in 1977. "I loved everything about what he did," Paxton says. "This is one of my favorite albums."

(Photo by Richard McCaffrey)

1: On the same New York trip, Steve also took in the March 4 premiere performance by the Philadelphia Orchestra of friend David Amram's "The Trail of Beauty." The classical piece, commissioned by conductor Eugene Ormandy, was based on American Indian music and included a passage from Chief Seattle about the native link to the land. Steve cited the concert in an interview eight months later while playing LPs of jazz clarinetist Sidney Buchet, rocker Gene Vincent, bluesman Bill Broonzy and the Scotch/Irish folk group Boys of the Lough to illustrate his wide tastes. "There's so many different kinds of music," he said.

going," he says. "I was recording in England for stupid companies and making a couple of very bad albums. That was really the bottom for me, the mid-1970s, when it came to recording." Eager to put together a fresh LP on home soil, Paxton secured a contract with Vanguard and set up a live session for March 1 at the label's 23rd Street studio, asking Steve to produce the recording. Steve declined, citing his jammed schedule. "I sure am glad," Steve said later. "I'm not far enough down the road to work (as a producer) with an artist of the stature of Tom Paxton."

But Steve did agree to be Paxton's sideman for the evening session. The result — the energetic and acerbic "New Songs from the Briarpatch" album released that summer — vindicated the choice. Steve supplied high harmony on "White Bones of Allende," "Did You Hear John Hurt?" and "There Goes the Mountain," as well as guitar embellishments for several tunes. "I loved everything about what he did," Paxton says. "I knew that his vocalizing and instrumental underpinning would be absolutely everything that was required, and it was. This is one of my favorite albums."

Later in March, after Steve took his wife, Nancy, to the Zero Mostel version of "Fiddler on the Roof" at Broadway's Winter Garden Theater,[1] he returned home to headline the taping of a local public-TV show, "Words & Music Made in Chicago." The WTTW broadcast — a half-hour program that also featured bluesman Blind John Davis, folk-rockers Aliotta Haynes Jeremiah and musical satirist Larry Rand, who also emceed — aired the following Oct. 25. Visually as well as aurally, the special cemented Steve's Chicago identity. Dressed in attire both formal and informal (a brown sports coat and blue T-shirt), he sang before a studio backdrop of the Michigan Avenue skyline and to listeners sitting in a set that resembled a pizzeria, complete with red-and-white checked tablecloths.

Midway through Steve's "Lincoln Park Pirates," the station intercut footage of what WTTW later called "a forerunner of music video." The segment showed greedy, lip-smacking, cartoon-style "pirates" prowling Lincoln Park in a tiny yellow "Yo Ho Ho Ho Towing" truck and using ropes and chains to haul away, in rapid succession, a tike's tricycle, a black-and-white border collie, an elderly woman in a wheelchair and, in a clever sight gag, a battleship in Belmont Harbor. [2] Providing a more serious complement to Steve's "Daley's Gone" later in the show was a montage of a dozen imposing photos of the late, larger-than-life mayor.

Though Steve was better known to what emcee Rand called the "white bread" public-TV viewership, Rand sought for Blind John Davis to close the show as a nod to the city's roughly 40 percent African-American population. Steve, who said he'd been promised the closing spot, couldn't agree. "Look," he told Rand, "soon I'll have a new record coming out. I don't want to close with John because you know as well as I do that if you're on camera with John, he steals the show." Eventually, the "very competitive, very intense" Steve relented, and Davis finished the program with a rollicking "Goin' to Chicago Blues." The exchange with Rand, however, illustrated what was at stake with Steve's next LP.

While his concert audiences were growing, Steve grasped the gravity of the slumping sales for his first two Asylum LPs — 50,000 for the "Jig" in 1975 and 30,000 for "Words" in 1976. "We were really alone," Steve later told Al Rudis of the *Chicago Sun-Times*. "A certain bunch of people really liked that album ('Words'), but the public said no in droves." Steve's slide also was on the radar of Joe Smith, the label's chairman, who cautiously gave Steve a green light for his next effort. "They ship a million Linda Ronstadt albums," Steve said, "so I think it's a real nice thing that Joe just didn't cut me. Y'know, this is an option album. He had to pick up my option to get this one." As a gesture of gratitude to Smith, Steve abandoned self-production. "I felt the responsibility to bring him a Steve Goodman album that he could work with," Steve said, "so I went for help."

First, Steve sought Arif Mardin, who had shepherded his "Troubles" LP in late 1972. But when popping the question to Mardin by phone, Steve empathized with the producer's response. "Look," Mardin said, "I got eight projects, and I really want to see my children sometime." So Steve turned to a veteran producer he had met during the "Troubles" sessions, New York-based Joel Dorn. With 120 albums to his credit, Dorn was a protégé of Atlantic Records co-founder Nesuhi Ertegun and had produced a sweeping scope of prominent jazz artists (Cannonball Adderley, Les McCann, Dexter Gordon, Herbie Mann) and rock and pop acts (the Allman Brothers, Leon Redbone, Don McLean, Bette Midler and Roberta Flack, including her hits "The First Time Ever I Saw Your Face" and "Killing Me Softly").

Steve perceived parallels to himself in the artists whose recordings Dorn had led to million-sellers. He was impressed that Dorn had transformed British folkie Ewan McColl's "First Time" into a mainstream hit for Flack. "Here was a guy who took something from one medium and wired it up to another and

Steve, playing during his stint on the 1977 "Made in Chicago" special on WTTW-TV, tangled with host Larry Rand over who would close the show — and for good reason. Steve knew his LP sales for Asylum were slipping. "They ship a million Linda Ronstadt albums, so I think it's a real nice thing that Joe (Smith, Asylum president) just didn't cut me," he said.

(Photo by Jon Randolph)

2: In this WTTW program, Steve kept "Lincoln Park Pirates" up to date, replacing the phrase "Daley is dozin'" with "Bilandic's been chosen," indicating the name of the new mayor. Similarly, in future years, he used the phrases "Jane Byrne's been chosen" and "(Harold) Washington's chosen."

3: Inspiration may have come from Valley Forge-area lawyer and filmmaker Hy Mayerson, who says that in one afternoon in about 1976 he loaned Steve and John Prine an early Akai video camera. The next morning, the pair brought it back, having filmed a lascivious motel-room scene of two young, voluptuous women in bed and engaging in oral sex while Steve sat nearby playing guitar. Mayerson has not shown the black-and-white film to others.

4: At the end of "Video Tape," the first verse is repeated, subtly and comically underscoring how videotape allows one to "replay all of the good parts." Steve wittily made the same point in an exchange that summer with Harry Tuft of KLAK-FM in Denver. "Are you psychic?" Tuft asked. "No, man," Steve replied with a wink. "I have incredible hindsight, though. I have an extremely well-developed sense of that stuff. In fact, sometimes I can tell what's happened to me for years."

5: Steve answered Dorn's question vaguely two years later, telling Steve North of WLIR-FM: "I got lucky, man. That one floated in. What am I gonna tell ya, that I sat around and thought about videotape for four days? Man, I gotta work, but not on that one. The good ones are always automatic, at least the first part of 'em. Then you find out if there's a way to really tell 'em to somebody. ... These things are happy accidents, is what they are. When you get a little shot of energy, it just shows up, and you're either smart enough to take out the pen and write this stuff down, or you go out and get drunk. So I was lucky that there was nobody around to get drunk with."

wasn't afraid to do it," Steve said, using a phrase — "wired up" — that had become a constant in his vocabulary. Likewise, Dorn had helped launch Midler from a cabaret entertainer at the basement-level gay Continental Baths in Manhattan to the status of a sassy pop icon. "The stuff he did with the Midler (debut) record convinced me that he knew how to work with an act that was a good live act," Steve said.

Joined by manager Al Bunetta and carrying his guitar, a hopeful Steve walked into Dorn's office in the late winter of 1977 and sang "Daley's Gone" and one other tune he had just written — a precisely conceived composition and one of Steve's favorites. Ostensibly inspired by technology [3] ("for Fred Holstein's Betamax machine," Steve said later), the song posed the delightful fantasy of being able to repeatedly experience life's joys and dodge its sorrows. In an implicit nod to his father's death and the fatal disease hanging over his own head, the song even hypothesized how gratifying it would be to "arrange to be out of town" during a visit by the grim reaper. The first verse focused on the past (via videotape), and the second verse eyed the future (via extra-sensory perception). It became the role of the third verse to carry a delicious twist — the only true romantic and realistic concept of the fantasy: "I know it will all make sense, if you love me in the present tense." [4]

The song — "Video Tape" — stunned Dorn. "It was just such a clever, fuckin' thought," Dorn said. "It was so definitively Steve, these little goofball ideas that only he could think of. Wow, you know how many times I woke up torn up in the morning? And I just thought, he did the same thing. 'You could roll it back to late last night.' Wouldn't you like to be able to do that? You think, 'Wow, how did that guy think to write a story about that?' " [5]

Such enthusiasm in a producer with a hitmaker's bag of tricks was warming, and Steve was smitten. "It looked like I had enough room to cut as much stuff as I wanted to and that all the sides of what I do would get a chance to be heard but that somebody else would take the responsibility for it," Steve said. "At a certain point, man, you just had to trust somebody, and he was the first guy who was sayin' anything that rang the right bells."

Dorn, who could not read music or play an instrument, understood and embraced the challenge embodied by Steve. "The rationale was to put him in a variety of settings and make a nice sport jacket for this one, a nice pair of slacks for that one, maybe put a nice tie, belt and shoes for the other one," Dorn said. "All of his records had sounded like some Jewish guy from Chi who went to Nashville and pretended that he was a cowboy. It didn't make it for me. It was nice, but he was a very sophisticated guy. He wasn't some fuckin', 'Hey, I'm a good old boy, even though I ain't,' which is what I thought the problem was. So what I tried to do with that record was paint a portrait of him as more than just this folkie who got lucky with one song."

What Steve had to forgo with Dorn, however, was drawing upon his former accompanists in Philadelphia and Chicago or from the David Bromberg band. "Joel wanted to give him a new sound," says violinist Larry Packer, "so he didn't want to use the musicians that Steve had been playing with." But Steve won two concessions. His musical buddies (Packer, guitarist Steve Burgh and harmonica player Saul Broudy) could back him on one of the LP's cuts (Hank Williams' "Weary Blues from Waitin' "), and they could join him, at double-scale pay, for two nights of recordings at a New York club so that Dorn could absorb the live feel of Steve's material.

Right away, for Dorn's benefit, Steve was booked into My Father's Place in Roslyn on Long Island. There, before beer-drinking college crowds on April 15 and 16, 1977, a mobile recording truck captured shows featuring Steve playing with Packer, Burgh, bassist Brian Torff, pedal-steel and banjo player Winnie Winston and mandolinist Jethro Burns. Astonishing the assemblage one night was a visit from the Manhattan author of many of the best-selling singles of the 1960s, from "Save the Last Dance for Me" to "Viva Las Vegas," the legendary Doc Pomus. "He gave Steve the Doc Pomus songbook, Steve put it on the music stand, and we played it from cover to cover," Packer says. "Steve knew all the songs, but he put it up on the stand for our benefit. That was a whole set. We played the entire Doc Pomus songbook for the composer."

With similar brashness, Steve's sessions with Dorn began a few days later in a small, third-floor studio at Regent Sound on West 57th Street near Central Park and Tiffany & Co., fueled by a stash of illegal drugs that included green Hawaiian marijuana. "We were both big potheads," Dorn said, "so before we went in, we would just smoke a bucket of reefer and start talking." Rob Mounsey, 24-year-old pianist who arranged strings for the project, says Dorn would "make this bonfire of it and light it on fire, smoking in the control room, dancing around looking for inspiration." [6]

The initial, in-studio musical inspiration came from Jethro Burns, fresh from the shows at My Father's Place. Dorn, mirroring his regard for other instrumentalists in his producing résumé, including singer/guitarist Les Paul and saxophonist Rahsaan Roland Kirk, labeled Burns a "world-class" musician. Steve escorted him to Regent Sound, and after the two toyed with a couple of Homer & Jethro parodies, Burns taught Steve a 1936 romp that had been popularized by the Mills Brothers and Al Jolson, "Is It True What They Say About Dixie?" Melodically and rhythmically, it closely resembled "It's a Sin to Tell a Lie," and with generational admiration (Burns at the time was just one year younger than Bud Goodman at his death), Steve gravitated to the song at once.

"It was the first one where anything that I was doin' was even capable of bein' on the same disk with what he had been playin' since the session started," Steve said of Burns. "This was the first one where everything wired up, where what he played gave me ideas and what I played sent him off to Mars. You could tell lookin' through the glass at the other people (in the control room) that he had woken up something. There was nothing I wanted more than to be up to any kind of level at all where I could even be playin' the same song that Jethro Burns was playing — and we hit it."

The two also dueted on a quiet love song they'd tried recording two years

> **This was the first one where everything wired up, where what he played gave me ideas and what I played sent him off to Mars.**
> **STEVE GOODMAN**

6: Steve characterized Dorn as "a wildman" in the studio who nevertheless focused on an "overview" of Steve's music. "What a pleasure to have somebody else have the responsibility," Steve told Harry Tuft of KLAK. "It's really nice to have somebody give you the old cattle prod. ... He just wanted to make a representative record."

7: "There's a Girl in the Heart of Maryland" was one of two songs for which Steve's grandfather, "Ziss" Erenburg, knew the lyrics. The other was "K-K-K-Katy," the 1918 post-World War I song written by Geoffrey O'Hara that was billed as "the Sensational Stammering Song Success Sung by the Soldiers and Sailors."

8: In 1979, for Steve North of WLIR-FM, Steve explained his ease at embracing a vintage song that might not catch on with a contemporary audience: "I know in some eternal sense how long it takes light to get to this planet from the sun. It's just stuff that you know, stuff that they taught you in grammar school, and this is really such a brief moment that we have here anyway that we might as well enjoy it and not whip the past or the near future. It just doesn't pay."

prior during the "Jig" sessions — a one-verse 1913 charmer by Ballard MacDonald and Harry Carroll, "There's a Girl in the Heart of Maryland." Steve's late grandfather, Morris "Ziss" Erenburg, long ago had taught his grandson the tune because its title paid tribute to Ziss' wife, Mary, the petite and spunky woman known by those in Chicago's folk community as Grandma Mary. 7 Over two nights that included a visit by Les Paul, Dorn let tape roll as the mandolin master and Steve played 15 to 20 unaccompanied versions of "Maryland." Each take boasted a different lilting and nostalgic solo break by Burns.

"At least you know you're not going to get a bad one," Burns deadpanned during a break.

"It's nice, though, man," Steve joked. "When it's all over, I'll have 800 Jethro Burns 'Girl in the Heart of Maryland' solos to learn."

"I'll take 'em," Burns said with a laugh.

"Right. That's really what I'm doin'," Steve said. "Get a transcription of 800 Jethro Burns 'Girl in the Heart of Maryland' solos."

"Publish a book," Dorn said.

"Right. You can just see them auctioning it off at Sotheby's," Steve added sarcastically. "Here's a hand-signed folio, 'The Annotated Jethro Burns Girl in the Heart of Maryland Solos,' recorded over two days, and Jethro Burns was chained to Regent Sound studio and whipped until he played 'Girl in the Heart of Maryland' 800 times. He was bored to tears with the fucking song after the third time."

The finished result resonated enchantment rather than boredom, and Steve's affecting vocal on the 64-year-old song echoed his self-penned sentiment in "Old Fashioned," that he was "out of date and born too late." 8

The album was not to be dominated by obscure ditties, however. Within days, Dorn brought in pianist Kenny Ascher, bassist Francesco Centeno, drummer Allan Schwartzberg, percussionist Jimmy Maelen and Eric Weissberg on pedal steel to record with Steve the basic tracks for "Video Tape." Dorn then surprised Steve with a question.

"We've got the players here," he said, "so where's the second tune for the session?"

"Well, just a minute," Steve replied.

He dug into his satchel for a sheet on which he had written only one verse for an inverted love song to his wife. In it, Steve announced to seemingly every other person, animal and object in the world his unbridled affection for Nancy but confessed that he hadn't informed her: "One of these days," the verse said, "whatever I do, I'm gonna have to find a way to tell you." [9] When Steve played it for Dorn and the musicians, giving it a driving, jump-rope rhythm, they found it to be a hilariously ironic litany. But it also was unfinished.

"So I sat down and wrote the second verse," Steve said. "I'd been thinking about it, but I just had never bothered to write any of the ideas down for it. I read it over a couple of times, and it scanned." When he came up with the line, "At the risk of repeating myself," he thought, "This sounds like a song to me now. Let's go cut it." They did, and with the addition of a Mounsey-directed sax quartet supplying backbeat honks on the lowest notes they could produce, the song became a strutting honky-tonker called "You're the Girl I Love." [10]

The sax embellishment was only one of many choreographed by Dorn. For both "Video Tape" and "Girl I Love," Dorn had Mounsey write string parts and conduct a 10-member mini-orchestra, supplying the kind of "sweetening" that Steve had rejected five years earlier from Cashman & West. For "Video Tape," Dorn also called on Eric Weissberg for a country-style steel-guitar part, and for "Girl I Love," Dorn had the rhythm section play an extended instrumental "tag," featuring a prancing piano solo by Kenny Ascher and long "oohs" by two trios, one female and one male. Dorn treated the tracks with Jethro Burns differently, opting for no additions to "Dixie" but adding to "Maryland" a delicate arrangement by a string sextet. And when Steve recorded "Daley's Gone" with only his voice and a guitar, Dorn accentuated the late mayor's Irish roots by trolling bars on First and Second avenues to find a trio of Irishmen to come to the studio and sing reverent backup vocals on the one-line chorus. [11]

"Joel's style, especially at the time, was so freewheeling," Mounsey says. "He could come up with wonderful stuff, like a movie director casting freaky little character parts. He would just throw spaghetti at the wall and see what stuck."

Dorn told Steve he was trying to give each song a distinct aural identity. What emerged was a chaotic pattern. "It was radical," Dorn said. "He'd come in, and we'd do one thing one day and another thing another day, and then I'd finish one off with 72 strings and 900 singers, and the other one was just voice and guitar. So it was odd. Anytime he sent the tapes to anybody, there was negative response."

One such critic was Steve's road manager, Steve Cohen, whose eyes rolled at what he heard in the studio. "I really thought that this was taking away from the core and soul of what Steve Goodman was," Cohen says. "They were putting this kind of gloss over it that wasn't going to appeal to anybody." But when the disappointed Cohen raised such questions in the studio, he was told, "Don't worry, you don't have experienced studio ears. When everything is added, the record will sound great."

If Steve had similar doubts, he downplayed them, at least in public. To Al

9: The words "I" and "you" were endemic to Steve's songwriting, says banjoist Stephen Wade. "His use of the second-person pronoun was a conscious decision," Wade says. "The embedded message is how he's respecting, drawing in and involving an audience, and how he's reflecting his upbringing, including whatever charms his father had."

10: In concerts, Steve enjoyed tweaking the "You're the Girl I Love" litany to see if audiences were paying attention. On June 15, 1977, at Charlotte's Web in Rockford, Illinois, Steve turned a phrase topsy-turvy by singing, "Shout it to the blind, and show it to the deaf." Two years later, at Bogart's in Cincinnati, he inserted a rhyming local reference: "Tell Charlie Brown and Peppermint Patty / Tell all the people in Cincinnati."

11: Dorn said it was his idea to find "real Irish guys" to sing on "Daley's Gone," but it was Steve who prowled the bars, telling the tall and tough-looking men inside, "I'm makin' a record. You guys want to sing on it?" But with a memory blurred by only four months, not decades, Steve recalled that Dorn was the one who did the soliciting.

Rudis of the *Chicago Sun-Times*, he later admitted that Dorn's methods initially filled him with trepidation. "I was 900 miles from home," he said, "and there were strange people in there being the judge." But Steve also said he came to understand that Dorn was imparting the craft of record production. "When it hit me that I could do somethin' different (with Dorn) and still make my music," he said, "that's when I knew the project was at least gonna have a chance."

The sporadic Dorn sessions straddled two months. Meanwhile, Jimmy Buffett surprised Steve by including on a new album, "Changes in Latitudes, Changes in Attitudes," a honey-voiced, five-minute version of Steve's "Banana Republics," with marimbas and strings (and a lyrical substitution of "ganja" for "marijuana"). The decision proved far more rewarding for Steve than Buffett's previous renditions of Steve's songs because of the wild success of the LP's first single, "Margaritaville." A paean to tropical decadence, "Margaritaville" debuted April 2 on *Billboard's* Hot 100 singles chart and stayed there for 22 weeks, peaking at #8. On the magazine's adult contemporary chart it hit #1. In ensuing decades it became Buffett's signature tune, as recognizable as "City of New Orleans."

Sales soared to more than a million for the Buffett LP, which reached #12 on the pop album chart and #2 on the country chart, and *Billboard* pegged Buffett as ABC Records' "hottest act." Buffett also inserted "Banana Republics" in his concerts that spring. Thus, the millions in Buffett's burgeoning fan base were exposed to his rendition of a Steve Goodman tune that many — including Buffett — found to be a snug fit of song and singer.

"It sounded like a song that I should have written," Buffett says. "It's a great story. It paints a real accurate vision of expatriates. For people that know them and for people that don't, it's a very vivid image. It still is, too. When you get into the most requested songs, favorites of mine or in my performances, 'Banana Republics' has got to be one of them."

Steve's skill on guitar was surging to prominence similar to that of his songwriting. Building on an ad one year earlier in *Rolling Stone* in which Steve (with the Grateful Dead's Bob Weir) endorsed Gibson guitars, the April 1977 edition of 100,000-circulation *Guitar Player* magazine ratified Steve's instrumental expertise. Managing editor Don Menn lavished him with a 3,700-word feature that stretched over seven pages. [12] Recounting Steve's choice of guitars, strings, microphones, amplifier settings, repair shops and even his antipathy for airline baggage handling ("We give them so much business, they got to treat us bad" [13]), it was largely a technical piece. But the article also fleshed out a mysterious technique that had intrigued Steve's peers and fans alike — his disappearing and reappearing flatpick.

"I devised this sleight-of-hand thing, a 'now you see it, now you don't' trick," Steve said. "I just push it (the flatpick) back with my thumb in the middle of a song. I just lock it in there and don't use it at all, and then play with my thumb and index finger, mostly. Then I slide the pick back out when I need it. I can get in and out pretty quickly, when I'm not wearing a Band-Aid. That's the only trick I have that I could say is a stylistic thing, and that's mostly because I can't

---

It sounded like a song that I should have written.
JIMMY BUFFETT

12: Asylum had sent Menn promo copies of Steve's "Jig" and "Words" albums with a note expressing caution over the dichotomy between Steve onstage and in the studio. "Goodman's recording style is significantly different from his live work," the letter from "Sam" said. "On these two LPs, you may have your share of problems picking him out of the arrangements. ... As a performer, he's continued to play solo over the years, and it's in that context that his playing comes across."

13: When Steve flew to shows, he often traveled with a replaceable guitar to avoid potential damage. Once while checking his guitar as baggage, he told singer Jay Ungar that "he didn't have time for stress and confrontation and was eliminating it whenever possible." The conversation stuck with Ungar. "I've not fully adopted Steve's approach," he says, "but I try to when I can, and it becomes more appealing as I get older."

play very well with a thumbpick. I feel like somebody's got a tourniquet on my hand when I'm wearing one of those things."

Steve also revealed in the article a glimmer of the intimacy beneath his musical passions. "I'm not all that much of a savage beast that needs soothing," he said, "but there's a certain private thing that happens when you hear something come out of an instrument that your hands are touching, even if you don't have any illusions about it. You reach a stage where you can say, 'For these five seconds, there is something I can do, and I'm just selfish enough about it to let it relax me.' At a certain level, it beats watching anybody else do something."

Buoyed by the Buffett LP and *Guitar Player* profile, Steve maintained a full plate of appearances that spring. He took on university shows in Missoula, where he played softball with the snowy mountains in the background, and in Grand Forks, where he opened for Robert Klein and joked with the Jewish comedian about the challenge of observing Passover in North Dakota. He recorded a second Easter appearance on Vin Scelsa's WNEW-FM show,[14] played a co-billing with Leon Redbone in Royal Oak, Michigan, and joined the New Riders of the Purple Sage and Flying Burrito Brothers for a May Day concert at the Washington University quadrangle in St. Louis. From there, Steve headed south. It was there that the fog began to lift as his feelings jelled about the death of his father.

Steve's thoughts of Bud Goodman already had surfaced sporadically onstage. At the Boarding House in San Francisco on March 9, his encore included a subdued explanation of a song title — that when he, as a high-school senior, wanted to purchase a used car, his dad warned him away from buying "Somebody Else's Troubles." Then he began a solemn version of the composition by saying, "This is my old man's song."

The sentence contained a prophetic phrase. Shows scheduled for Steve on May 4 in Baton Rouge and May 5 in Little Rock were canceled because of poor ticket sales. But Steve was already headed to Louisiana, where he stopped at Lafayette General Hospital for a leukemia-related blood test on his way to Texas for a string of concerts in Dallas, Austin and Houston.[15] And late at night in Lafayette apparently was when and where Steve shed his first tears over Bud Goodman's death.

Audiences in the spring of 1977 saw Steve's dexterity on slide guitar (the metal tube on the pinky finger of his left hand) as he played a lively version of the spiritual, "I'll Fly Away."
(Photos by Steve Cohen)

14: Scelsa told Steve that "Flotilla" ("If you want it done right, you've got to do it yourself") "is a great song. That's gotta become like an underground hit single." Steve replied, "Right, it'll be played only in caves, right? I can see it now. It'll hit the *Cave Billboard*." It's likely that "Flotilla" was recorded during the Dorn sessions, given that it was a staple of Steve's shows throughout 1977, but the delightful litany of lesson-learners has not been officially released.

15: On Steve's Texas swing, his opener was country songwriter Steve Young, who says he "was really strung out, drunk and on drugs all the time." Young says Steve counseled him with compassion. "He very gently was trying to issue me a warning," Young says, "and it got through to me." Young says he quit drinking two years later.

The next day, he stepped inside a phone booth and dialed the number for John Prine. "I got one," Steve told him. It was Steve's practice to call Prine when he'd written a song, whether completed or just a verse or two, and "I got one" was the tip-off. "He would just drop the phone and start singin' into it, whether he had a guitar or not," Prine says. On this occasion, Steve had started a composition, and "he sang it to me a cappella," Prine says. It was a tribute to his father. The title was "My Old Man."

"Geez, that song," Prine says with a sigh. "I loved it from the get-go."

With concrete detail bolstering his unguarded grief, "My Old Man" let Steve expose emotion that was — in a men's-club musical world and in a 1970s society that was not yet suffused with socially acceptable male vulnerability — decidedly untraditional.

To write "My Old Man" was, for Steve, a catharsis, both exhausting and freeing. "Everything just lifted the night that song got (completed)," he said. After performing his Texas gigs, he flew back home to Chicago, then on to New York. There, after claiming to have stayed up for three straight nights, he finally finished the song. On a brisk afternoon in mid-May, he grabbed a guitar and walked into a tiny back room at third-floor Regent Sound. Present were Saul Broudy and Steve Burgh, there to record what Joel Dorn called a "front porch" rendition of "Weary Blues," along with Dorn and his engineer, Vince McGarry. Steve got out his guitar and perched on a chair near a microphone.

"Turn the mike on and don't say nothin'," Steve said. "Just roll the tape."

Steve strummed softly then began singing even more softly.

"Wait a minute," McGarry said, climbing out of his control-room chair and walking into the performance area. "The mike isn't picking you up." McGarry adjusted the microphone to within a breath of Steve's mouth, returned to the control room and motioned for Steve to start again.

For the next four minutes and nine seconds, Dorn, McGarry, Burgh and Broudy sat rapt as Steve sang them the finished song. In it, Steve told his dad's life story, but remarkably he related each stage directly or indirectly to himself. One passage, depicting Bud's stint as a World War II pilot and first marriage, ended with "Not long after that, he was my old man." Another stanza told of fights in which Steve and his brother incited Bud's rage and then "tuned him out." Yet another section used gentle humor to describe Bud as an auto dealer — "He could look you in the eye and sell you a car" — and with the substitution of "song" for "car," Steve could have been describing himself. In the final verse, after recounting Bud's fatal heart attack at age 58, Steve bared his sorrow: "For the first time since he died, late last night I cried / I wondered when I was gonna do that for my old man."

Throughout, Steve's voice cracked, sometimes wavering, sometimes whispering. Then he was done.

"I almost cried after that," McGarry says. "That was pretty powerful. We got one take on it, at that moment."

"Everybody was sitting there freaked out," Broudy says. "We turned around

Geez, that song, I loved it from the get-go.
JOHN PRINE

to each other and didn't know what to say. Will this translate, will this work on a record? This is a magic moment, but sometimes it just doesn't translate."

Dorn, who had lost his own father nine years earlier, found himself uncharacteristically speechless. "I can't really explain the uniqueness of the moment," he said. "Steve had a dark side and a very intense side. He just walked in, and he got it out of his system." Of more than 1,000 recording sessions with a full spectrum of artists, Dorn said, "That's one of the half a dozen or dozen most memorable moments I've ever had."

With the microphone so close, Steve's voice on the playback sounded as if he were inside the listener's ear. It was the very definition of intimate.

The only thing marring the performance was a pause in the middle of the last verse, at precisely the point in the lyrics in which Steve was about to admit that he had cried. He simply "broke up," Broudy says. He kept strumming softly but couldn't get out the words. A measure went by, then a second and a third. During the fourth, he emitted a barely audible "Mm" and moistened his lips as he tried to compose himself. Then, at the end of the sixth measure, he resumed the song.

"It was almost a clunker, which normally wouldn't have made it to a master (tape)," McGarry says. "But the performance was just so good. It was just right there. It was as emotional as could be."

Steve later said that a second run-through would have been impossible. "That's take one and take last," he told Al Rudis. "I just went in there and sang it, and somethin' aired out there." Steve viewed the extended gap near the end philosophically. "We're human, that's how it goes," he said. "That's the way the eggs look sometimes. Sometimes they have little spots on them. I can't help it. I can't help thinkin' that Venus had a couple of pimples, y'know. I'm not making any comparisons. I'm just sayin' that anything that's really good to me has something about it that's just a little askance so that you can see the rest of it."

Dorn embraced the flaw and decided to preserve it sensitively, calling upon his guru of classical accompaniment, William S. Fischer. The African-American session arranger had assembled the strings for Dorn-produced tracks by Roberta Flack and Bette Midler, and he wrote and conducted the string backing for Steve's "There's a Girl in the Heart of Maryland." The composer of four operas, Fischer found "My Old Man" a fitting challenge. "I had the expertise to accompany words," he says, "especially if there was action and if the music had to accompany gloom and doom."

Except for Steve's four-bar guitar intro, Fischer's strings ran the entire length of "My Old Man," never dominating it. In fact, the delicate strains were engineered to feel gently connected to Steve's vocal but also recessed, as if the sextet were playing quietly in the next room with a slight echo. It was one case, everyone agreed, in which the "sweetening" was genuinely sweet. Steve found a typically disarming way to explain it. The strings, he said, were added "just so there'd be something else to listen to while a guy tells a story like that, and then to have it (the arrangement) be as sympathetic to the situation, Fischer's a special guy."

I can't help thinkin' that Venus had a couple of pimples. ... Anything that's really good to me has something about it that's just a little askance so that you can see the rest of it.
STEVE GOODMAN

Of all the songs Steve recorded with Dorn that spring, "My Old Man" clearly emerged from Steve's gut. "Not every song can come from that place," Steve told Al Rudis. "There's just so many times that you can go to the bottom like that. That don't mean I don't feel that somewhere in me all of the time. There's just so many times it can come out, and who'd want to live with a guy who was sayin' stuff like that 24 hours a day?"

Because Steve reveled in his role as a father and father-to-be, some thought he was well situated to fete his own dad in a song. Others, upon first hearing "My Old Man," sized it up as an affectionate wish for how he would want his children to view him after his own death. But Steve didn't explore those theories publicly. Instead, he said that the song's message was literal and straightforward — the inevitability of grief, and the value of tears.

"I don't expect to ever completely get over it, missin' someone I loved that much," Steve told Rudis. "Y'know, it was the only one of those I had, and that's how it is." [16]

"I really didn't know how to deal with him just ducking out," Steve told Jack Hurst of the *Chicago Tribune* three years later. "You know for sure that you didn't hear all that somebody said to you, and your chances of getting to hear it again are severely reduced when they die. That's really what that song's about."

As Steve performed "My Old Man" in concerts, usually late in a show, the message reduced audiences to silence, and countless tears welled. Steve's Lake Forest College classmate Sidney James (now Kistin) attributed this effect to how the song reflected his Jewish roots. "He talked so specifically and lovingly about a normal life for a normal man," she says. "In Jewish tradition, there is the celebration of daily life, and there are prayers for just about everything, like 'Thank you for letting me tie my shoes today,' and he had that kind of moment-to-moment appreciation."

Ray Frank, who helped shape Steve's previously most revealing composition, "Song for David," says that "My Old Man" gripped listeners because its specificity produced an identification that was universal. "You hear a very compassionate portrait of his father," Frank says, "but you hear more than just compassion. You get the emotion of this lost life, and that had a real ring of truth. It was this glimmer of recognition, 'Yeah, that's the way it really happens.' It's a perfectly done story song, a portrait that with such concision points to so much about a person's life and what that life meant to somebody else. The genius is that you feel that way about your old man, I feel that way about my old man, and everybody does. He was able to talk about the conflicts between them as well as appreciate him. What genius!"

Specificity and universality were the hallmark of another partially written musical obituary that Steve brought to the studio — not about the death of a person but rather the swift evaporation of the 1900s. As Steve later told concert audiences, a calendar from an auto insurance company inspired the song. "This particular calendar had a 77 after the 19," he said, "and it struck me that the date was a whole lot later than I thought it was. Y'know, it's seven short of (the

---

It's a perfectly done story song, a portrait that with such concision points to so much about a person's life and what that life meant to somebody else. The genius is that you feel that way about your old man, I feel that way about my old man, and everybody does.

RAY FRANK

16: Later in 1977 at Somebody Else's Troubles, Steve consoled Chicago publicist Marianne Jasin over the death of her father. "There's something to be grateful for that you had your father," he told her. "There's a lot of people who grow up and don't even know what it's like to have a father."

Orwellian year of) 1984 and 23 away from the millennium." The message, he said sardonically, was, "Your time is up."

But the ever-faster pace of life, prompted by technological advances, was no laughing matter, Steve lamented in an interview with Emily Friedman, editor of the Chicago folk-music magazine *Come for to Sing*. [17] "It's very hard for me to even sit down with a book," he said. "Reading used to be a diversion, and now people have to visually assimilate so much information during the course of a day that they simply don't want to do it on their time off. Everything speeded up so much. ... The human race has got to take the rap. It wasn't the apes, and it wasn't the machines. They were invented. They didn't ask to be here." In an interview with Larry Kelp of the *Oakland Tribune*, Steve added, "There's just so much happening so rapidly all the time, and thanks to electronic media covering it, there's no way you can do anything but just observe and gape."

What resulted from these trenchant thoughts was the beginning of a lyrical feast — a composition stuffed with details that defined the decades from 1899, "when everybody sang 'Auld Lang Syne'," to the present moment, when linoleum floors, petroleum jelly and two world wars had gotten "stuck in the revolving doors." The smorgasbord of images was balanced by a sing-along chorus set to a gospel tune that Hudie Ledbetter (Leadbelly) had adapted as "The Meeting at the Building Soon Be Over." In Steve's hands, the chorus — and the song's title — became "The Twentieth Century Is Almost Over."

Steve had written only two verses for the song, however, and didn't know how to proceed further, so he invited a Chicago friend to the studio. "He sang me what he had," recalls John Prine, "and I said, 'Well, sure, I could contribute somethin' to that.' We got to goin' on it, and it rolled along pretty good." Prine wrote a third verse with a presciently environmental theme — colder winters, hotter summers, dried-up wishing wells and an embarrassed Mother Earth caught "making love to the man in the moon." He and Steve went out for lunch and together came up with the triumphant final stanza, with Father Time impatiently tapping his toes and the Judgment Day looming in the rear-view mirror. The result, as Al Rudis later apprised Steve, was a clever cross between a slice-of-life and a jolly doomsday — and it became the first officially credited co-write for Steve and Prine.

"Twentieth Century" had an unmistakable air of mortality — of the unmerciful passage of time and the obvious lesson to not waste it. [18] The message became crystallized in what Joel Dorn considered the best line of the song — and of any Steve Goodman song: "Everybody's waiting for something to happen / Tell me if it happens to you."

"I say that twice a month," Dorn said in 2000, seven years before his death. "How much more clever could you get? If you asked me to define what Steve did with words that set him apart, it would be that line. It's just so surreal and evocative. It had nothing to do with the 20th century. That line was just one of the great lines of 20th-century literature. It's just so singular."

The key lay in the phrase "waiting for something to happen," Dorn said.

Your time is up.
STEVE GOODMAN

17: The name of *Come for to Sing* magazine came from the lyrics of the traditional song "Cotton-Eyed Joe." The legendary Bob Gibson also made famous his own tune, "I Come for to Sing."

18: Two years later, Steve cryptically cited his leukemia in telling journalist Shaun Kelly why he wrote "Twentieth Century" with 23 years of the century still left. "You never know if you are going to be around for such an event," Steve said of the century's end. "You could drop dead at any moment. There have been so many crazy things that have happened this century, despicable, head-scratching things. That said, everything that I have ever loved in this world also existed during this time. When the clock strikes midnight (before) Jan. 1, 2000, there will be a lot to say goodbye to then, don't you think?" Kelly recounted his chat with Steve in the Dec. 17, 1999, *Greenwich Times/Stamford Advocate*.

Steve recorded "The Twentieth Century Is Almost Over" with (above) Pete Seeger after fleshing out the song (above right) with John Prine, and producer Joel Dorn looking on.
(Photos by Emilio Rodriguez, from the *SingOut!* Resource Center)

19: The song's "waiting for something to happen" line could have been inspired by the Hank Williams/Bob Gazzaway country classic "Just Waitin'," which consists of a litany of characters (old maids, crooners, burglars, farmer's daughters, hitchhikers, city slickers) waiting for various things to happen. Self-mockingly, it concludes with the line, "Honey, I'm just waitin' for you."

"What he's talking about is the something that, first of all, doesn't happen, and, second of all, doesn't exist, and third of all, who gives a shit anyway, and, fourth of all, what are you talking about? Go out and have a sandwich. Do something. Throw a ball. Buy some Chicklets. Do anything. But stop fuckin' waiting around for whatever it is you're waiting around for, man. Pretty soon, they're going to drop the fuckin' door, and you're not going to be able to get out." [19]

While the verses tended toward the existential, the song's "all over this world" chorus and melody were flush with tradition, which led Steve to seek backing vocals and banjo from the era's pre-eminent folk hero, Pete Seeger. "I wrote the song with him in mind," Steve said, "but he's such a busy guy that, though I've known him for years, we'd never really had time to talk." But their co-billing at the Chapin fund-raiser the previous November had forged an indelible bond.

"He just called me up and said, 'I've written a song. Would you come and help me record it?' " says Seeger, who didn't hesitate to drive from his home 60 miles north in Peekskill to help out. Steve was "one of those surprise geniuses," he says. "This kid out of Chicago would show up with a few absolutely magical songs. But that's the wonderful thing about life. We never know when or where genius is going to pop up. He had a subtlety that hardly anybody else had. Steve Goodman could be incisive, at the same time very gentle and humorous. He was one of the most genuine human beings I ever knew."

In the studio, Seeger "knew just what to play," Steve said. "It was two takes and we had it." Meanwhile, Dorn, who had worked with Seeger while producing Don McLean's "Homeless Brother" LP in 1974, took the folkie sing-along cue and decided that what the chorus of "Twentieth Century" needed besides Steve's guitar and Seeger's banjo was voices — lots of them.

"Y'know that Coke commercial, 'I'd like to teach the world to sing,' remember how that built? Can you get the sense of the camera pulling back? That's all I wanted to do," Dorn said. "I wanted to make that feel like the whole world was singing." Prine stuck around to vocalize on the track, and Steve summoned friends Heather Wood, of Manhattan, and Bill "Oliver" Swofford, who flew in from Georgia. Dorn also enlisted the three Irish singers from "Daley's Gone," plus four others. "I added layer after layer after layer," Dorn said. "It's just fuckin' 'Hootenanny.' I tried to make it sound like there were 10,000 people."

At times, it may have seemed to Steve that the album would have nearly that many styles. In all, he and Dorn recorded 17 or 18 songs that spanned the musical map, including several that didn't make the final cut. One was a Latin-tinged, ahead-of-its-time celebration of sexual diversity, "Men Who Love Women Who Love Men." Steve created the tune, he said, while observing the "varied and sundry types" emerging from the Port Authority Bus Terminal as he patronized a pizza stand at the corner of Manhattan's then-tawdry 42nd Street and Eighth Avenue and walked to a theater where he joked that he saw a double bill of "Debbie Does Everybody" and "Tell Them Johnny Wadd Was Here." Taking inventory of the ways people make love (with their own gender, for pay, with machines, in a crowd), the song threw up its hands and concluded with a wink: "It's so hard to know what to do, when you don't know who you're talking to."

After having written half a dozen Chicago-based songs, it had been past time for Steve to pen a tune drawn from the city that because of its show-biz focus and Sloan-Kettering had become his second home. So he paid tribute to the Big Apple as he introduced "Men Who Love Women Who Love Men" to audiences that spring. "If you think people are the most interesting thing there is to see in the world — seriously, if you think that that's one of the things that really makes it tick, is just observing other folks, and very benignly, too, with a considerable amount of love, if you just like lookin' at people, New York is a trip," he said in Wichita. "Whew! They got a whole lot of different types there, of sizes, shapes, races, persuasions. I'm tellin' ya, it's a hell of a place. Can't breathe, but it's a hell of a thing to see." [20]

Another track recorded that spring but absent from the resulting album was Steve's pensive "Grand Canyon Song," to which Dorn appended a gospel choir that didn't "wire up right" for Steve. A studio recording of Shel Silverstein's goofy road romp, "Three Legged Man," with cheek slapping by Steve Mosley, also didn't make the album. Nor did a new romantic trifle by Steve, "Just Lucky I Guess," which he envisioned as R&B sung in a country style, akin to Ray Charles. Holding genuine promise was yet another new song, "Laid Back," a mid-tempo rocker based on the rhythm and chord structure of Chuck Berry's "Memphis." With a strain of Steve's folkie cleverness, the tune also had pop-hit earmarks: an engaging vocal, a syncopated "hook" in the chorus and a theme of unrequited lust — a guy who's tired of being "laid back" by a girl who is leading him on but won't commit. But mysteriously, it, too, was a reject. [21]

The sweep of styles in Steve's sessions with Dorn reached to soul, with a recording that did make the album — a Smokey Robinson tune that 19-year-old Mary Wells had made a #1 R&B hit and top-10 pop hit for Motown in 1962, "Two Lovers." Dorn had seen Steve and his bandmates play it at My Father's Place and suggested it as a "dark, night-clubby" track for the album. "It wouldn't

**New York is a trip. Whew! They got a whole lot of different types there, of sizes, shapes, races, persuasions. ... Can't breathe, but it's a hell of a thing to see.
STEVE GOODMAN**

20: Steve's lengthy onstage explanations sometimes played poorly, such as at the Wichita show, at which Steve opened for Pure Prairie League and which drew a rowdy crowd. During Steve's intro of "Twentieth Century," a woman shouted, "Who cares?" Steve replied, "Well, shit, lady, I did."

21: Sadly, Steve's "Laid Back" has never been officially released. Other songs recorded with Dorn — "Men Who Love Women Who Love Men," "Grand Canyon Song" and "Three Legged Man" — turned up in other incarnations on later LPs.

Malvina Reynolds' quickly written slam of a sexist jurist, "The Judge Said," drew the interest of Steve, who produced and played on a 45-rpm single that was packaged with a recall petition.

(Photo by Alejandro Stuart, courtesy of Nancy Schimmel)

22: Steve liked that Mounsey's tremolos and trills faded in and out on "Two Lovers." "Mounsey did this cool thing," Steve said. "He made it sound like a million buzzing bees. It's like all the bees come out of the flowers at the same time and then go back."

just be a one-guy or one-guitar version of it," Dorn told Steve. "We could try to make a real record of it."

What appealed to Steve about "Two Lovers" was its culminating twist. In most of the tune, the narrator tells of having two lovers, one good and one bad, but they actually are one person's split personality. "That song's like playin' Liar's Poker, for God's sake," Steve said. "Here's a guy lookin' the girl right in the eye, or it's a girl lookin' a guy right in the eye, and sayin', 'You're both of them.' ... I enjoy hearin' therapy songs like that."

But while Steve was enamored with the song's lyrics, Dorn focused on achieving a pop sound. Yet another rhythm section — Leon Pendarvis and Rob Mounsey on piano, Cliff Morris and John Tropea on guitars, Will Lee on bass, Gary Mure on drums and Errol Bennett on percussion — along with a five-member choir and a 12-member orchestra transformed "Two Lovers" into a keyboard-and-strings-based cut that, while pretty, retained little of Steve's persona beyond his own reverent voice. [22] It was only at the song's end, during the last 20 seconds of fadeout, that a wistful pennywhistle solo by David Amram injected a Steve-like spark.

While pushing his envelope to pop, Steve came up with an intriguing name for the new LP, "Say It in Private," a line from his "You're the Girl I Love" litany. It reflected the irony inherent in the business of manufacturing art for the masses. It also was a signal that Dorn's puckish producing had gotten under Steve's skin, and Steve soon seized such a chance of his own. It emerged politically on Friday, May 27, in a college town 100 miles northwest of Chicago.

That night, 76-year-old folksinger Malvina Reynolds — best known for writing the satire of society's homogenization "Little Boxes" (popularized in 1964 by Pete Seeger) and the environmental "What Have They Done to the Rain?" (made a hit in 1965 by the Searchers) and co-writing "Turn Around" (the Kodak theme song) — played a concert with Rosalie Sorrels in Madison, Wisconsin. There, feminists were abuzz about a county judge who two days earlier had sentenced to only a year's probation a 15-year-old boy who had pleaded guilty in the three-member gang rape of a 16-year-old girl in the back stairway of a local high school. It was not the sentence but the judge's remarks that stirred a firestorm. The judge, Archie Simonson, called rape a "normal" reaction, given the "sexually permissive" female clothing in the liberal city dominated by the University of Wisconsin. His antiquated comments swelled with irony when it was reported that the victim had been dressed in corduroy pants, a turtleneck sweater and an outer blouse.

"I'm trying to say to women, 'Stop teasing'," Simonson told the *Capital Times* that Friday morning. "There should be a restoration of modesty in dress, and the elimination from the community of the sexual gratification business. Whether the women like it or not, they are sex objects."

Calls sounded for the judge's resignation, and the story quickly went national. Simonson even appeared on NBC "Today" and Phil Donahue's syndicated TV talk show. The morning after her concert, Reynolds, whose songwriting had swung radically leftward in recent years, responded instantly in her own way, writing a tune called "The Judge Said," whose lyrics were printed in the May 28 edition of the *Capital Times*. With a chorus proclaiming "We're going to screw the judge" and a melody set to the tune of "When Johnny Comes Marching Home," the song became a battle cry for Simonson's ouster.

It's unclear who contacted whom, but a few days later Steve jumped at the chance to produce a recording of Reynolds singing "The Judge Said" in Chicago. The connection was unsurprising, given that for years Steve had admired and shared festival stages with Reynolds, who had written an affectionate 1975 children's song, "If You Were Little," in Steve's honor. Reynolds, he said later, had been a sporadic visitor to his home in Evanston "to play grandmother" to his girls. ("Tremendous woman," Steve said while introducing her at one show, and Reynolds responded with an affectionate Yiddish label, "my boychik.") On quick notice, Steve gathered five male musician friends (Howard Levy, Sid Sims, Angelo Varias, Bob Hoban and Jethro Burns) for a late-night session at Chicago Recording Company. Five female backup singers linked to Reynolds (Kathrine Barber, Sally Fingerett, Lee Hartz, Amanda Tucker and Reynolds' daughter, Nancy Schimmel) showed up as well. While Steve played guitar, the combination of Levy's harmonica, Hoban's violin, Burns' mandolin and Varias' snare created the haunting aural picture of a limping fife-and-drum troupe from the Revolutionary War.

Tension arose at the session because of a gender clash. "Here they're letting Steve do the production on it, and there were some women who were strident feminists at the time," Varias says. "They didn't like the idea of bringing in all these males to tell women how to do the piece." But Schimmel, who taught summer school in Madison, says her mother merely wanted the song to get out quickly and was grateful for help regardless of gender. "She just didn't know the kind of people that Steve knew and that loved Steve and were happy to come out and do something for her," Schimmel says. "That was the feeling of the evening, 'Oh, here we are all together. Let's make music.' "

So that her recording could bolster Wisconsin's first-ever judicial recall, Reynolds had a single made of "The Judge Said," backed by another track recorded at the Chicago session, "Young Moon," a parent's song to a girl that Reynolds intended as a tribute to Steve's daughters. [23] Reynolds mailed the 45 to those who received her *Sporadic Times* newsletter, and she inserted in the sleeve a recall petition. How many petitions were submitted to the Dane County election department via Reynolds' single is unknown, but the recall effort easily made the ballot. To the satisfaction of Reynolds and tens of thousands of Madison residents, Simonson was soundly booted from office in September and replaced by family attorney Moria Krueger, the county's first elected woman judge.

Steve's further forays into the recordings of others in mid-1977 were hardly as political but reflected a flowering of product in the Chicago folk scene. He joined Jim Post [24] for a Post-arranged a cappella trio treatment of the traditional "Walkin' in Jerusalem" on the first LP of autoharpist Bryan Bowers, "The View

23: The Steve-produced recording of "The Judge Said" was included in a posthumous Reynolds LP, "Mama Lion," in 1980, but "Young Moon" was never released on an album or CD. Steve later told an audience that Reynolds wrote "Young Moon" for her daughter, Nancy Schimmel, but Schimmel says she's sure her mom penned it with Steve's daughters in mind.

24: Post says that after he sang on Steve's recording of "The Ballad of Dan Moody (Roving Cowboy)" in 1976, he wanted Steve to reciprocate for an LP of his. Steve, however, was a session no-show, "which really hurt my feelings." Later, Post says, he summoned his Texas gospel roots by teaching Bowers "Walkin' in Jerusalem." Bowers recorded the tune with Post on high harmony. Post took the tape to Steve's house and played it for him. "Man, that needs a baritone," Steve said. "Yeah," Post said, "I thought so, too." "Well, I needed to do that with you." "Yeah, you did, but you didn't show up the last time I asked you to come and record with me." "Hell," Steve said, "re-record it. I'll pay for it." Thus, "Walkin' in Jerusalem" was recorded as a trio.

Emily Friedman, editor of Come
for to Sing *magazine.*
(Photo by Larry Rand)

25: Joan Baez added to Steve's
1977 presence in the record bins.
For her new "Blowin' Away" LP,
Baez recorded his "Yellow Coat,"
which she had heard at Quad
studio in Nashville when Steve
recorded it in 1971. But Joel
McNally of the *Winnipeg Free
Press* panned Baez' version: "In
concert, with a minimum of
accompaniment, it knocks out an
audience. Somehow it got
cluttered all up on the record."

26: Part of Steve's family focus
was that he and Nancy, whose
mother was a Quaker, were paid
members of the Northside
Meeting of Friends, says NPR
commentator Scott Simon, who
spent his formative and young-
adult years in Chicago. Steve and
Nancy attended sporadically to
take part in silent Quaker worship.
After one meeting, Steve and
Simon "talked about the Cubs as
an antidote to religion," says
Simon, who provided a brief
account in his acclaimed 2000
sports memoir, *Home and Away.*

from Home," recorded at Chicago's Acme Studios on the independent label
Flying Fish. Another debut album at the same studio and on the same label, by
multi-instrumentalist Ken Bloom, drew on Steve's vocals for three Bloom tunes,
"Ephraim Ed George," "The Great War" and "Pilgrim's Progress" along with
Wendy Waldman's "The Eagle and the Owl." [25]

A debut production on the home front also pervaded Steve's thoughts as
spring slipped into summer. "I'd like to sing a song for Nancy Goodman, who
is infanticipating in Chicago," he told an audience on June 24 at the Orpheum
Theatre in Wichita during an introduction to "Old Fashioned." In mock conversation with himself, he continued: "So, 'Yeah, what're you doin' *here*, asshole?'
'Yeah, right.' Not till July, anyhow. I'll be home by July first. I made her promise
not to have this child till I got there."

The stork kept the pact, and the Goodmans' third daughter, Rosanna, arrived on Wednesday, July 13. To those in Steve's musical world, the birth renewed respect for him as a dad and for his steady pursuit of a career to support
his kids. Steve Cohen recalls "some little kid screaming who was driving me
nuts" on a flight between gigs and Steve countering the agitation by saying,
"That's just the sweetest sound you'll ever hear." Cohen says the remark irritated those like himself who reveled in the no-strings, touring lifestyle, but it
also reflected "a real strong need to provide for the family because he realized he
wasn't going to be around forever." Likewise, Claudia Schmidt found Steve's
fatherhood courageous in the face of his leukemia. "It was a sign of how big his
heart was," she says. "It's a moment of extreme decision one way or another.
Am I going to expand or contract? He definitely expanded around it."

For Steve, however, Rosanna's arrival sparked even deeper feelings of connection and commitment, as he expressed four days later in a wide-ranging
interview with *Come for to Sing* editor Emily Friedman in the third-floor music
room of the Goodmans' Evanston home. "This is a real good year for me," he
said, "because I figured out I can't do everything. That's not a surrender. It's a
decision, the complete end of innocence. I can't go out every night and play in
a concert and be a father to three girls and be a husband to Nancy — and be on
this album or do that, or produce 'em, too, and try and handle all the travel
arrangements, and be the publisher, and all this stuff. This is the year I found
out. I can't do it all. Can't do it."

In contrast to his equivocal comments of previous years, Steve named as his
first priority his family. [26] "That's the one right on top," he said, "and the others
vie for position behind it. Every now and then, the music one really comes up
there and takes a run at it. But (family) is far and away the champion. ... I do
have some responsibilities here (at home). Some people have made some incredible promises to me. I'm wired up to that, so I don't mind being frustrated a little. Otherwise, I'd just go out and play." (In a later interview with
John Rockwell of *The New York Times*, he added, "I have my family. They understand they're living with a maniac. I'm blessed, man.")

Steve even took note of his links to John Prine in expressing wistfulness for

a closer tie to his sole sibling. "I pray that someday I'll know my own brother as well as I know John, OK? I don't love David any less for saying that. I love him more. I can't find him sometimes, y'know. Great guy." (David later reflected, "We had our fights, our rivalries. We went our separate ways.")

In part, Steve's feelings were a response to weariness brought on by a succession of draining events — the death of his father, the creation of his fifth album and the birth of his third child — that, on the surface, at least, had little to do with his leukemia. "No wonder I look like I've been sittin' under a punch press," the near-29-year-old joked. "That's how I got to be 5-foot-2. I was 9-foot-4 until I started doin' this shit. My legs are like erasers. They're just startin' to wear away." More seriously, he added, "I sleep with both eyes open, and not 'cause I'm lookin' for anything. It's because it requires a certain amount of energy to close 'em, and I refuse to use that. I'm so out of it I don't even think to close 'em. The mechanism that closes the eyes, it's out. It's on the blink." [27]

Fledgling Chicago singer/songwriter Andrew Calhoun got a glimpse of Steve's fatigue when he gave Steve a ride from Troubles to the Earl of Old Town. Frustrated at an inability to advance from open-mike sessions to paid gigs, Calhoun asked Steve, "So how does someone get work?"

"Well," Steve said, "how old are you?"

"I'm 19."

"Well, that's how old I was when I started to get work," Steve replied wearily. "Don't be in such a fuckin' hurry."

But Calhoun already knew that Steve hadn't practiced what he was preaching. "He was in a hurry," Calhoun says. "He was driven."

Steve was driven more toward his family, however, than in previous summers. Though Steve opened for Pure Prairie League in Wichita and Jerry Jeff

Accompanied by bassist Jim Tullio and Larry Rand on kazoo, Steve performs a 25-minute set during the annual benefit show for Come for to Sing *magazine on June 19, 1977, at Somebody Else's Troubles. Looking on at left is Harry Waller.*

(Photos by Jim Polaski)

27: This was no isolated claim. Nine months earlier, Steve told Toronto journalist Nicholas Jennings, "A lot of the time, I can sleep sitting up. I can be wide awake but not be movin'. I guess I don't sleep very much, out cold, but I can sit still for hours and go off into another world. I never really learned how to meditate, but what I'm doin' must be a cousin of it. I could probably get a lot more out of it if I studied."

Walker in Phoenix [28] and did solo shows in Vancouver and Victoria, B.C., his midyear concert schedule was comparatively slim. Bypassing the 1977 festival circuit, he stayed closer to home than he had in years past, freeing time to attend to his kids' concerns, including a traditional rite of passage for 5-year-old Jessie.

"She lost a tooth the other night," Steve told Emily Friedman, "and when I took it out of her mouth, I went, 'Oh, here,' but I dropped it, and it was gone. It was on this rug, and it's the same color as the tooth. Still haven't found it." To compensate, Steve scribbled a note for Jessie to slip under her pillow to explain the absent tooth to the tooth fairy. "I drew a picture of a tooth on it, and I wrote, 'Please accept this,' and an arrow with the word 'tooth.' I asked Jessie to endorse it, to sign her name. Supposedly, it's a big thing for a little kid, that the faster they can read and write, the better off their protoplasm is, right?"

Jessie took to the task, but not without serious consideration. "You could just see her mind working," Steve said, imagining her thought process: "First, this guy wants me to believe there's a tooth fairy. Second, if there is a tooth fairy, he's gonna give me money for my teeth, or somethin' under my pillow if I leave it under the pillow. Three, if there is a tooth fairy, and if he does leave money under the pillow if you leave him the tooth, he can get in and out of the room quietly. Fourth, the tooth fairy will accept this piece of paper instead of a tooth."

Skepticism engulfed Jessie's face. Steve said she had to be thinking, "The tooth fairy is a schmuck!" Even so, Jessie cooperated with her father's plan. But she signed the note in an unusual fashion: After J and E, she wrote the numeral 9, then a squiggle, then I and E.

"Jessie," Steve said, "what's that squiggle after the 9?"

"It's a nose," she said.

"A nose?" Steve asked, pointing at his own nose.

"A nose," she said.

Steve swelled with pride at his daughter's willingness to creatively challenge the conventions of writing. "She signed J-E-9-Nose-I-E. The S's became a 9 and a nose. That's some remarkable stuff. And she drew the 9. It wasn't that she was tryin' to make an S and it became a 9. Smart kid. She's got it wired. I just hold a box with a wire and stick comin' out of it (a guitar), but my kid spells her name J-E-9-Nose-I-E."

The summer was not without risky moments with Jessie. Family filled the Goodman home at the time of Rosanna's birth, as did friends such as Paula Ballan from New York and steel-guitarist Winnie Winston and his girlfriend, Amy Burnham, both of Philadelphia. The roomy house pulsed with activity, Winston recalled. "Grandma Mary was something else," he said. "She challenged everybody to do pushups, and she was beating everybody. She was a rough little lady." In the hubbub, Ballan, Winston and Burnham offered to take Jessie to the Carnegie Theater on Chicago's Rush Street strip to see Walt Disney's animated "Fantasia" during the first reissue since its 1940 release. Steve drove the four into the city, planning to pick them up later.

Smart kid. She's got it wired. I just hold a box with a wire and stick comin' out of it (a guitar), but my kid spells her name J-E-9-Nose-I-E.
STEVE GOODMAN

28: Walker startled Steve at the close of Steve's opening set by walking onstage during "You Never Even Call Me by My Name" and chiming in on its chorus. Afterward, Steve told the audience, "That was really lovely of Walker to do that. What a sweet cat." But inside, Steve was "pissed," says road manager Steve Cohen, because his pacing was violated. "There was always that protocol of who can come onstage and calling them up. Steve wasn't asking. Jerry just ambled up, and it was awkward."

After the movie ended and Steve had arrived for the pickup, "Paula and Amy went into the ladies room to smoke a J," Winston said. "They came out, gave it to me in a little matchbox, and Stevie and I went into the men's room to have a toke or two. Just as we walked out of the toilet cubicle, the door of the men's room opens, and there's a Chicago motorcycle policeman walking into the bathroom." Steve bolted, but Winston stayed behind, washed his hands, nodded to the cop and walked out.

When all were out on the sidewalk, Ballan was flush with relief. "Jesus," she said, "we knew you guys were in there, and this cop walks in and walks straight up to the bathroom, and we thought, 'Oh shit.' I saw the headline: Folksinger arrested smoking dope while at 'Fantasia' with his little girl." [29]

Though he thought he had finished the LP with Dorn, Steve encountered on Aug. 6 a fantasia of the three-minute variety. It was in the unlikely setting of a tour bus. He had borrowed the vehicle from John Prine, who was playing a full-band gig in Central Park, and he rode it to Washington, D.C., where he opened for Dickie Betts (Allman Brothers Band) at Carter Barron Amphitheatre. Along for the ride was a duo that formed the rhythm hub of Crackin', a seven-piece San Francisco-based rock/R&B/disco combo. The two were drummer Peter Bunetta — Al's brother and Steve's connection to the group — and bassist Rick Chudacoff. On the bus, Chudacoff kept playing a hypnotic set of chord changes, and Steve dared himself to write matching words before the bus arrived in the nation's capital. The lyrics that Steve conjured were equally ethereal, describing being drawn to a potential lover's "magnetic field," almost as would a stalker. "You better watch out," the chorus warned, "if you don't want me around all the time."

The result, "I'm Attracted to You," was a slow, pulsing come-on tune that emulated the sensuous, jazzy appeal of Boz Scaggs. Excited about the song's potential as a single, Steve, Chudacoff and Peter Bunetta rushed into Regent Sound upon their return to Manhattan to "stop the presses" and add it to the album. Dorn at once envisioned it as "a great little pop track" and added a Scott Hamilton sax solo, a Rob Mounsey string section and a choir headed by Kenny Vance for the recurring line, "You better watch out."

The track's tone was such a departure from the others Steve had recorded with Dorn that Steve felt it had to be the LP's opening song. "There was just no other place to put it on the disk," Steve told Al Rudis, "because once you've established any other kind of feeling on the record, this is a digression from it. But it opens the album in a way that, once you get used to it, then it's just a nice thing to have there, and it's a good introduction that this is going to be a little bit different than some of the other albums."

Steve was speaking of the aural effect. But visually, "Say It in Private" was also "a little bit different." Steve's huge, deep-set eyes — easily his most compelling facial feature — fell into deep shadows as they gazed in early October from the cover of the new album. The image was nothing if not a shock.

Instead of conveying the persona of a musician, the cover depicted a replica

We thought, 'Oh shit.' I saw the headline: Folksinger arrested smoking dope while at 'Fantasia' with his little girl.
PAULA BALLAN

29: Steve's adoration for his girls was a high point for journalists who came to the Evanston home. In November 1977, when Evanston Township High School student Vicky Newberry (now Costakis) and her friend Lynne Bryan arrived for an interview, screams and babbling often dotted the conversation. At one point, 2-1/2-year-old Sarah walked in to announce that soon the family would be heading to a Chinese restaurant. "You're all dressed up to go dreaming," Steve told Sarah, who replied, "Gonna get Chinese. You get some, too. You get some, and you get some, and you get some, and you can have some, and they can have some, and they can have some." Steve answered, "Everybody's gonna have some, huh? That's very nice of you." Then Steve told the interviewers, "That's a very sharing young lady. ... She's a heart surgeon."

of the famed 1793 painting "The Death of Marat" by French revolutionary Jacques-Louis David. The grisly original image showed David's close friend, Jean-Paul Marat, stabbed in the chest and dying, his lifeless right hand clutching a quill pen, his left hand grasping a petition from his female assassin and his red blood dripping into the tub in which he soothed a chronic skin disease. On Steve's album cover, however, the sagging, closed-eyed head of Marat gave way to that of a murky but smiling Steve, as if he were enjoying an antique bath. ("At least they took the blood off the towel," said Steve's wife, Nancy.) Instead of a petition, Steve's left hand held a sheet of lyrics handwritten with the quill pen: "Say it real quiet, say it out loud, say it in private, say it in a crowd. ..." Steve's leukemia was not public by any means, but here was his new LP, modeled on a classic painting that invoked death at its most gruesome.

"I was just using it as a base of a surrealistic twist on the mood of it all," says Tony Lane, art director for the album and for Elektra/Asylum who thought of using J.L. David's painting. [30] "It was tongue-in-cheek and tragic and moody and all of these layers of feelings, more of a mosaic of emotions in a curious way, which you have license to do with album covers." Lane, who had no idea that Steve suffered from a fatal disease, revered his music but had only the record's title and lyrics to work with. "Steve loved the idea," he said. "The concept, on a literal level, was that at a time in the past in your own private bathroom, you could be writing your novel while sitting in the tub all day. I just felt in the gut that this was right and was just pulling loose references to relationship and privacy and writing."

Steve's sense of humor emerged on the flip side of the LP cover, which showed the identical scene but without Steve. "He'd gotten up out of the tub," Lane says. "It's a one-two punch, that's all."

To Joel Dorn, the treatment was a travesty. "I saw that cover and, man, I wanted to strangle somebody," he said. "It was a dumb, fuckin' cover for that record. I loved (the phrase) 'Say It in Private.' Great title because it's a great line from a song. But that cover was the work of somebody who was well trained in the art of nothing. It didn't relate to anything."

It amounted to high art laid low — or just plain low art. Either way, Asylum played up the visual and verbal theme by plying distributors, deejays and the press with custom notepads so that they could "Say It in Private." The label also bought full-page ads in *Billboard* and *Rolling Stone*. "Steve Goodman is well known for the things he has said in public," said one. "Now, here's a chance to hear what he has to say in private." [31]

What the critics said was split. Typically, *Billboard* and *Variety* fawned over the album, and John Rockwell of *The New York Times* said it was "so good that he may finally begin to win the attention for himself that he's long deserved." The *Illinois Entertainer* cited the record's "fresh pop infusion" and "that quality of universality that we occasionally overlook because he is also so much our own." Praise ran from the national ("very trendy eclecticism, craftsmanship turned loose on a catalog of trivia," by Noel Coppage of *Stereo Review*) to the

I saw that cover and, man, I wanted to strangle somebody.
JOEL DORN

30: As art director for *Rolling Stone*, Tony Lane used a similar approach when the magazine discovered Patty Hearst's whereabouts on a Pennsylvania farm. Lane redid Andrew Wyeth's "Christina's World," depicting Hearst crawling up the hill.

31: In private, Steve upbraided Asylum publicist Art Fein for including in an October 1977 press bio the notion that Arlo Guthrie's "City of New Orleans" chord changes had "irked some Goodman fans." Fein was trying to lend Steve individuality. But for Steve, loyalty and gratitude were more important. "He took me to task in the office, mildly but crossly, and said that Arlo had done him a huge service, that he loved Arlo, and that this (reference) was not right," Fein says. The statement was excised from a revised press bio that was issued the next month.

Freeze frame: If Steve could have preserved favorite moments, he might have picked these that Jim Shea captured in about 1980. (Above) He poses for potential album-cover images, and (below) his wife, Nancy, and children (from left) Jessie, Sarah and Rosanna mug in a Los Angeles recording studio.

Red-ribbon day: Steve (top, foreground) marks graduation from Volta Elementary School in 1961 with (clockwise from Steve) Cary Lerman, Chuck Zis, Alan Rosenfeld, Tony Mackin, Rick Eisenstaedt and Rodney Zolt. (Photo from Lore Eisenstaedt.)

Beah heah: In late 1966, Steve (right photo, center) reunites with high-school buddies (clockwise from upper left) Jeff Lind, Tom Heston, Herb Johnson, Paul Niesen, Chuck Branick, Bob Pottinger and Bill MacKay. (Photo from Paul Niesen.)

Backyard band: Steve (above, center) fronts the Impalas on an evening in July 1966, reflecting his continued link with the high-school group in college years. Others performing at this anniversary party for the parents of keyboardist Paul Gryglas were (from left) guitarist Kent Cerrone, Casey Kenzel on tambourine, drummer Frank Guignon (partly hidden) and Gryglas. With the band, Steve also recorded a 45-rpm single of "Shotgun" and "House of the Rising Sun." (Photo courtesy of Paul Gryglas/DuGrant.)

Audience of one: Greenwich Village club manager Penny Simon's 8-month-old son, Eddie, is enthralled by Steve as he plays guitar in her apartment in the summer of 1969 while in town for treatment at Sloan-Kettering. (Photo by Penny Simon.)

Ganging Chad: (Right) Fiddler/pianist Bob Hoban joins Steve in his breakout opening stint for Chad Mitchell in late 1969 at Punchinello's in Chicago. (Photo by Chad Mitchell, courtesy of Bob Hoban.)

Learning to dance: At a Feb. 6, 1970, reception at the Earl of Old Town after his wedding earlier in the day, Steve performs as family friend Kay Lind looks on, then poses with Nancy and a wedding cake and with his father, Joseph Goodman, and high-school friend Cathy Lind. (Photos courtesy Cathy Lind Edler.)

Journey in song: The City of New Orleans, shown heading south from Chicago on April 24, 1971, was the mode of transit Steve and Nancy chose for visiting Nancy's grandmother in Mattoon two months after their wedding, and it was on that ride that Steve finalized his most famous and enduring tune. (Photo by James I. Jeffery, postcard image courtesy of Audio-Visual Designs, Herkimer, New York, http://www.audiovisualdesigns.com.)

Making the scene: For an April 13, 1973, special called "They Kept the Faith," Chicago's WTTW-TV re-created a club environment and engaged a who's who of local folk acts, whom Steve led in a finale of Paul Clayton's standard, "Gotta Travel On." Accompanying him (from left) are Ginni Clemmens, John Prine, Jim Post (partly hidden), Bonnie Koloc, Ed Holstein, Earl Pionke, Tom Dundee, Wally Friedrich, Fred Holstein and Bryan Bowers. Afterward (right photo), Post talks with Steve, Clemmens and Dundee talk with others, and Fred Holstein listens. (Photos by Jon Randolph.)

Night life: The clubs most influential in Steve's life — and in the Chicago folk scene of the 1970s — were (below left) the Earl of Old Town at North Avenue and Wells Street and Somebody Else's Troubles on Lincoln Avenue. (Photos by Art Thieme.)

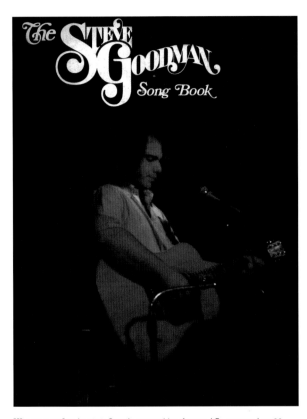

His own write: In 1973, Steve's songwriting for two LPs spawned an 80-page songbook that is long out of print (Cimino Publications Inc., New York).

Dual devotion: Recognizing the delicate and enduring love story told in Steve's version of Michael Smith's "The Dutchman," Buddah Records issued the 45-rpm single in a charming picture sleeve. (Art by Glen Christensen.)

Pair of jeans: Buddah linked two acts in 1971 for Japanese record-buyers.

Rutabaga rhumba: Fiddler/painter Howard Armstrong's delightful vision of Carl Martin's "The Barnyard Dance (The Vegetable Song)" became the cover image for the first LP by the African American string band Martin Bogan & Armstrong, on Flying Fish Records. Steve brought the group to prominence after a dormancy of several decades and adopted the album's title tune as a staple of his performances. He later wrote a ballad, "You Better Get It While You Can," in tribute to Martin. (Howard Armstrong artwork printed by permission of Barbara Ward Armstrong, http://www.sweetoldsong.org.)

Joyous jig: For Steve and Nancy, the adoption of Jessie (right, 1972, and above, 1974) represented bold optimism and marked the start of a growing family. (Photos courtesy of Margaret Southern.)

In the swing: At a Wilmette-Glenview park in 1976 (from left): Nancy, Steve and Ruthie Rudis, with kids Sarah and Jessie Goodman and Rachel Rudis. (Photo by Al Rudis.)

Halloween 1974: (from left) Beth & Rob Swofford, Nancy & Jessie Goodman, Margaret Swofford (who supplied the photo).

The eyes of music: In the first months of Steve's treatment for leukemia in 1969, folk impresario Paula Ballan of New York (shown with Steve in about 1976 in Central Park) became Steve's fast friend. Her fifth-floor Upper East Side apartment, a half block from Sloan-Kettering Cancer Center, served as not only a hostel and gathering place for traveling musicians but also a hip refuge in which Steve could stave off the unappetizing effects of chemotherapy. (Photo by Chuck Klein.)

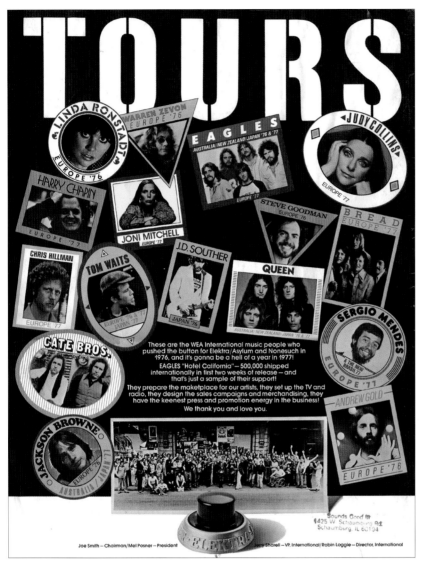

The big leagues: In 1975, Steve signed with the country's hottest label, Elektra/Asylum Records, and immediately was in heady company, as played out in this 1976 poster advertising the roster's European tours. (Poster courtesy of Kathy Shedd.)

Prine in tow: Steve was no stranger to England, however, following his impromptu appearance at the 1972 Cambridge Folk Festival with a return in 1973 (below) with friend John Prine, shown in front of their hotel. (Photo by Harvey Andrews.)

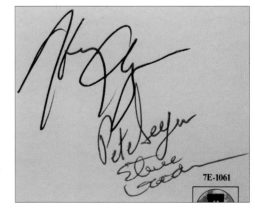

Up for the Count: The tuxedoed Steve — looking every inch an impish version of Dracula — poses with Jethro and Lois "Gussie" Burns at the Burns home in Evanston before heading into Chicago for his New Year's Eve 1976 show at the Earl of Old Town. (Photo from Johnny Burns.)

Trusty trio: Steve joined Pete Seeger to co-headline with Harry Chapin two shows Nov. 14, 1976, to benefit Chapin's arts foundation in Huntington on Long Island. (Right) A fan, Fil Feit, managed to get all three to autograph Steve's "Words We Can Dance To" album, released earlier that year. (LP detail courtesy Fil Feit.)

Surveying his scene: The darling of the 1976 Philadelphia Folk Festival, Steve strolls the grounds (above). For the "'Twas Brillig" workshop Sunday afternoon, Steve (right, center) awed (from left) Ken Eidson, Jethro Burns, Gamble Rogers, Johnniy Morris, road manager Steve Cohen and (in hat) Ken Bloom. (Photos by Chuck Klein.) Closing the festival nine hours later, Steve (below, center) bid nearly 20 musicians to the main stage — including (from left) Lew London, Jethro Burns, Saul Broudy, Steve Burgh, Dennis Gormley, Ray Mantilla, David Amram, Winnie Winston and Ken Bloom — and went a half hour overtime, angering festival leaders. (Photo by Bob Yahn.)

Back, but bound: Two years later, in 1978, Philly bid Steve's return but made sure he closed the Friday-night show, not the festival-ending Sunday concert. He joined (above, from left) Howard Armstrong, Carl Martin and Ted Bogan at a workshop, mimicking their play-behind-the-head shtick. (Photos by Molly Ross.) During his nighttime show, Steve jammed on guitars both electric (below) and acoustic and enlisted saxophonist Ken Bloom (left) and (bottom, from left) Lew London and David Amram. (Photos by Barry Sagotsky.)

Cold comfort: Touring chilly Alaska in January 1978, Steve immersed himself in the outdoors (above), and from the stage in Anchorage and Juneau (right) read Robert Service's icy epic poem, "The Cremation of Sam McGee." (Photos by Geoff Feiler.)

Perfect pair: From head gear to instruments, Steve was an apt opener for more than 200 Steve Martin shows, including (series below) May 8-14, 1978, in Cherry Hill, New Jersey. (Photos by Marianna Samero, courtesy of Scott Atkinson.)

Glitz galore: Steve (left) adopted brighter garb for a Martin opener July 29, 1979, at Maple Leaf Gardens in Toronto. (Photo by Bert Dickie, via Shawn Irwin.) The marquee of Las Vegas' ritzy Riviera (above) shouts their June 12-25, 1980, co-billing.

Warm to the touch: For his successful first stint with Steve Martin (right, April 4, 1978, in Dallas), Steve's tie reveals that a tropical clime was on his mind. (Photo by Homer Martin, courtesy of Steve Martin.) During a late-spring break in the Martin dates, Steve took "a rich man's vacation" in Acapulco, Mexico. Steve held his youngest, Rosanna, after a dip in the Princess Hotel pool (above), and enjoyed a meal with (clockwise) Nancy, Rosanna, Paula Ballan (along as a nanny), Jessie and Sarah. (Photos courtesy of Paula Ballan.)

Tropical compadres: Steve drops in for a guest set during a concert by Jimmy Buffett in 1978. Steve had befriended Buffett before the latter's 1977 rise to fame with the hit "Margaritaville." Steve led the writing of what many believe to be the ultimate Buffet song, "Banana Republics," which Buffett also recorded in 1977. (Photo by Kathy Shedd.)

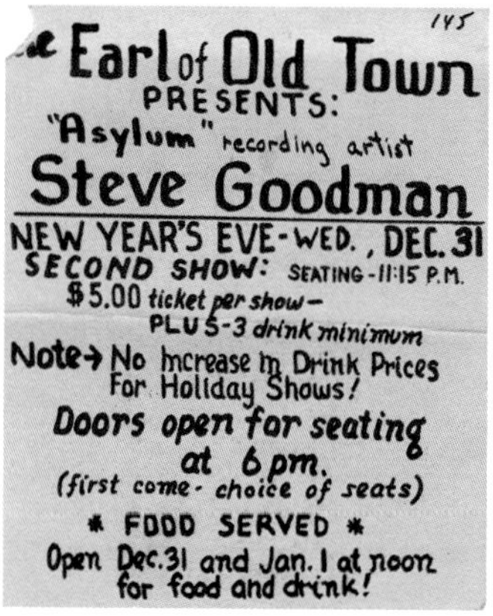

Dependable bill: Steve headlined every New Year's Eve show at the Earl of Old Town from 1970 through 1981, including in 1975 (ticket courtesy of Chris Farrell) and, with Jethro Burns, in 1978 (photo courtesy of Johnny Burns).

Ring it in on the air: An inevitable, inseparable part of Chicago's New Year's Eve ritual was the live, all-night "Midnight Special" show and party at WFMT-FM. After headlining three sets at the Earl of Old Town, Steve ventured in the wee hours of the fledgling year to the station's studio, where he led a troupe of musicians in a marathon, one-time-only New Year's-themed ditty and often an extended version of "Mama Don't Allow It." Steve jams (right) with fiddler Randy Sabien and singers Jim Post (hidden) and Tom Dundee on New Year's Eve 1980, and he performs solo (above) the next year at 4:50 a.m. (Photos by Art Thieme.)

Opening lyric from New Year's Eve 1975: "Well, look at you, look at me, here we are at WFMT / And it's New Year's Eve, it's New Year's Eve / It's New Year's Eve, so what's new?"

Lucky strike: In the empty grandstand of Wrigley Field, Steve performs his recently written "A Dying Cub Fan's Last Request" for a Bob Sirott story on WBBM-TV at the tail end of the baseball work stoppage in late July 1981. It became the only time Steve played the song at Wrigley, because in future years General Manager Dallas Green barred the lovingly mocking epic from the ballpark. The ban led WGN exec Dan Fabian to commission Steve to write a wholly upbeat theme song. The result was "Go, Cubs, Go." (Video capture courtesy of Bob Sirott and Jessica Kaplan.)

Stevie's jig: (Right) Steve and his wife, Nancy, dance at the Manhattan wedding of Steve & Jamie Burgh on Feb. 26, 1983. Steve served as best man for his friend and longtime musical collaborator. (Photo courtesy of Steve Burgh.)

Tight trio: (Above) Steve and John Prine join Maria Muldaur April 4, 1982, at the El Mocambo in Toronto. (Photo by Jane Harbury, via Shirley Gibson.)

Wedding witness: (Left) Beneath a Jewish chuppah, Steve beams as friend and multi-instrumentalist David Amram and Lora Lee Ecobelli wed on Jan. 7, 1979, at Temple Israel in New York City. (Photo courtesy of David Amram.)

No gum: With every Red Pajamas LP, buyers got a custom baseball card showing Steve in a softball windup and "stats" on the back. (Card courtesy of Roy Leonard.)

BIG LEAGUE CARDS

**STEVE GOODMAN
RED PAJAMAS** 1984

Bounce-back busker: For his live Red Pajamas LP, coming after recovery from relapse in 1983, Steve envisioned a sly front cover of "Live at Carnegie Hall" (left photo by Jack Wilding) and back cover of "and Points West" (right photo by Jim Shea). Steve dropped the concept after he and Shea discovered the Artistic Hair barbershop (see p. 618).

Cash with a kick: Helping Steve resume performing in early 1983 was Johnny Cash, who added Steve and Jethro Burns to his show. (Photo below in Watertown, South Dakota, May 8, 1983, by John Redlinger, via Elwood & Dorothy Brugman.) Two days earlier, in Bloomington, Minnesota, singing "You Never Even Call Me by My Name" in a hat from the audience, Steve cracked, "All I need now are Johnny Cash's boots." Mere seconds later, a grinning 6-foot-2 Cash, in stocking feet, strode onstage and set his tall boots in front of Steve (right), to the delight of Cash's guitarist Marty Stuart and the audience. With help, the 5-foot-2 Steve donned the boots, which rose past his knees. (Photos at right by Pat Katz.)

Onstage in 1983: Steve was busier than ever in his second remission, joined by John McEuen of the Nitty Gritty Dirt Band Aug. 15 at Red Rocks, Colorado (left photo courtesy of Chuck Morris), backed by David Amram on piano, vamping while Steve changes a broken string, June 23 at the Lone Star Cafe in New York City (above photo by Marlene Rosol) and co-headlining the Harbor Moon Festival (in a Chicago White Sox hat) with Jay Leno Sept. 25 in at the Highlands Ski Area in Tilton, New Hampshire (right photo by Laurie McCarthy).

Mama allows: In Steve's second-to-last booked show, a June 21, 1984, benefit at Haverford College near Bryn Mawr, Pennsylvania, Steve (above, second from left) jams on "Mama Don't Allow It" with a stageful of musicians (from left) David Buskin, Saul Broudy, Bonnie Raitt, Tom Rush, David Bromberg, Jim Hale and Robin Batteau. (Photo by Molly Ross.)

Final frame: On May 26, 1984, Steve – in cowboy hat, reflective sunglasses and a Johnny Cash tour jacket – and friend Harry Waller stand in front of Steve's Grandma Mary's apartment building. They wore brave smiles for a snapshot that Steve's brother, David, took and gave Waller as a keepsake. The trio then headed to O'Hare International Airport. It was Steve's last hour in Chicago and became part of a song Waller wrote about Steve, "Why Did He Have to Leave?" (Photo courtesy of Harry Waller.)

Tribute troupe: Posing (above from left) at the Jan. 26, 1985, Steve tribute at Arie Crown Theatre in Chicago are (rear row) John Bainey, Tom Radtke, Jim Rothermel, Harry Waller, David Amram, Don Stiernberg, (standing row) David Young, John Perrot, Jethro Burns, Ray Nordstrand, Bryan Bowers, Paula Ballan, John Hartford, Jim Tullio, Bonnie Koloc, Diane Holmes, Ellen Germaine, Peter Bunetta, Billy Prine, Bonnie Raitt, Angelo Varias, Arlo Guthrie, Neil Serroka, Steve Burgh, Ed Holstein, Hank Neuberger, David Bromberg (partly hidden), Roy Leonard, Johnny Lee Schell, Nancy Bromberg, (seated row in middle) Howard Levy (holding foot), Hugh McDonald, Jeff Hanna, Jackson Browne, Jimmie Fadden, John McEuen, Bob Hoban, (seated on floor) Corky Siegel, Ashley Mendel, Richie Havens, David Goodman, Maple Byrne, Dan Einstein, Al Bunetta, John Prine, Garry Fish, Fred Holstein. (Photo by Jim Shea.)

In the family: Steve's ebullient Grandma Mary Erenburg (above) grins on New Year's Eve 1989 or 1990 during the WFMT-FM "Midnight Special." (Photo courtesy of Chris Farrell.) Steve's mom, Minnette Goodman, and manager, Al Bunetta, hug (left) at the May 14, 2006, Tom Dundee tribute at the Old Town School of Folk Music, in front of a poster for a Nov. 13, 1997, tribute to Steve. (Photo by Jef Jaisun.) A street sign (far left) denotes two blocks of Chicago's Lincoln Avenue named for Steve. (Art Thieme photo.)

international ("a mature achievement ... a real masterpiece," by Paolo Filipponi, of the Italian music magazine *Mucchio Selvaggio*).

The downside, however, was dismal. Several critics, including those close to home, accused Steve of betraying his audience. "Fans of Steve Goodman are in for a surprise, if not shock," wrote the *Chicago Sun-Times*' Al Rudis, normally one of Steve's biggest boosters. Rudis wrote that Steve was "risking the displeasure of those who would like him to stick to folk-style music. What is he going to say if accused of selling out?" A review by Greg Easterling in *The Daily Illini*, the student paper at the University of Illinois, which Steve attended in 1965-67, chimed in by calling the LP "half a hit" whose strings were "ludicrous sounding and definitely an unwelcome intrusion."

Most scathing were the notices from England, where Steve had built a reputation as a folk star. "Another Goodman goes down," punned the London-based *Melody Maker*, whose Colin Irwin called the album "a bummer of the first degree" describing a homogenization of Steve's persona. "For a long time he's been one of the more rewarding sons of Woody Guthrie, managing to maintain vast sincerity in an abused area of music, but this time around, the soul of Woody seems to have been sacrificed for a rather meek indulgence in sentiment," Irwin wrote. "In the past, his records haven't done him full justice, but this one is offensive for the way it submerges his instantly distinguishable vocal style in a welter of strings." Linnet Evans of *Sounds* likewise said the album's "hack" production consigned it for Sunday afternoon airplay on the BBC's middle-of-the-road Radio Solent. "Little Stevie remains a fine, urbane, decorous singer," Evans wrote, "but the personality promised in (his) early years has, like time itself, slipped away." The LP's "essentially hollow core" also nagged at Patrick Humphries of *New Musical Express*. "It's not a bad album, but its effect is about as lasting as a tin of Pacific air."

The number and breadth of the reviews spoke to Asylum's promotional resolve, and the vigor of critical disappointment ironically reflected a depth of regard for Steve's musical skills and showmanship. The biggest rap stemmed from the album's plunge into studio refinement at the very time that fans yearned for a more authentic, "Steve-like" sound. Not surprisingly, interviewers and fans had been pushing Steve for a "live" album for years.

But a "live" LP usually amounts to "nonsense," Steve had told "FolkScene" in 1976. "You (the listeners) are not there. You're at home, looking at these speakers," he said. "Live albums are always going to be unsatisfactory because there's no visual dimension to them. Sometimes they capture a certain energy you just never get in the studio ... but I feel bad about goin' to a record store and payin' X number of dollars to hear 2,000 people clap for eight minutes, say, out of 30. If I could ever do a live album where all that extraneous stuff before and after was electronically removed so that you wouldn't have to put up with that at home, then OK, I'd do it."

In July 1977, when Emily Friedman of *Come for to Sing* pressed for an answer to why he hadn't released a "live" recording, Steve was more blunt. "I've got to

> **Little Stevie remains a fine, urbane, decorous singer, but the personality promised in (his) early years has, like time itself, slipped away.**
> **LINNET EVANS**
> *SOUNDS*

be honest with you," he said. "Everybody thinks it's a problem but me, OK?" While admitting that "I just haven't been able to make one (album) that did the same thing that I do live," Steve also described what he viewed as the impossibility of the task. "You can't see a record," he said. "I think the only reason that what I do live goes over well live is because I'm not playin' for blind people."

Dogging Steve further was Al Rudis, who prodded him on whether "Say It in Private" was a "radical departure" from "the good old stuff" of his folk roots. Steve equivocated but finally became testy. "Anybody who listens to the whole album and thinks that is gonna have to really need to discuss it with themselves, because I'm not gonna have any answers for 'em," he said. "I haven't gone anywhere. This is just something else I've learned how to do, and hopefully, I'll do it better next time. ... I'm not embarrassed by any of this stuff, and when people ask why we did it, it's really because we like to hear that kind of music sometimes. I, fortunately or unfortunately, can't listen to one kind of record seven days a week."

When Steve invoked a "sense of craft" that he was trying to bring to his songs and records, Rudis smelled a ruse. "A craftsman, really, is a guy who has all the skills and can turn out one fine bookshelf after another," Rudis said, "but it's not like an artist. When people start saying, 'I like the craft of writing songs,' to me that says, 'I don't really have anything to say anymore. Now it's just a craft. Now I just can put together these songs.'"

"The great artists get up and do it every day, the great ones," Steve countered, "and so us laymen, we can get up and do it every day, too, and be organized about it as a craft. ... It's all I can do to be the Steve Goodman that I am right now, and if that means that I think that part of it is a craft, well, shit, then I'll have to stand by that. You're welcome to call me on it all you want, but that don't mean when you go down there and knock out reviews that you don't think that part of it — an ability to do things with words to say what you feel — is a craft. I think a guy who makes good shoes is a guy who makes good shoes, and you don't have to hang 'em up on a wall to look at 'em. It's how they feel on your feet."

All the talk became academic, however, when Steve got back out on the road that fall to promote the album by doing what he did best — entertain audiences. This began with his most riveting and classy national exposure to date, a slot on the young but influential PBS-TV show taped in the Texas state capital, "Austin City Limits." In its third season as a showcase for country acts that were based in or had performed frequently in Austin, the show by virtue of its association with "outlaw" artist Willie Nelson had taken on a hip image that stretched far beyond the boundaries of its music. To extend its geographical reach and appeal to fans of "progressive" songwriters, for its first three installments that season the show booked Michael Murphy ("Wildfire" and "Geronimo's Cadillac"), Steve and John Prine, in that order — each receiving a generous, full-hour treatment, in contrast to the half-hour stints accorded other acts in the first two years.

> **You can't see a record. I think the only reason that what I do live goes over well live is because I'm not playin' for blind people.**
> **STEVE GOODMAN**

Taped Sept. 8 in the round before 300 young adults in Austin's KLRN Studio 6A, the show became an ideal platform for Steve's mesmerizing persona. Though it paid Steve a scale fee of only $250, the show's real value was that in a few months (and in repeats years later) it would reach millions of viewers. It was "what you call your basic career-saver," Steve said later.

True to his well-groomed upbringing, Steve's physical appearance that night indicated that he understood the opportunity. He donned garb stylish for the late 1970s: an open-neck, wide-collared red-and-white checked shirt beneath a blue sports coat and pants — essentially a leisure suit, plus purple tennis shoes impishly covering his feet. And as he walked onstage, Steve's not-quite-shoulder-length hair had been blown dry and was neatly combed.

But as Steve careened through his set — especially a boisterous string of "Twentieth Century," "Chicken Cordon Bleus," "This Hotel Room" and "Can't Go Back" — his sculpted look quickly disintegrated. Waggling his mane almost uncontrollably, jogging in place, bouncing on the balls of his feet and waving his arms, pointing his index finger and punching the air with his fists, Steve resembled a cross between a prizefighter and a revivalist and ended up a sweaty, tangled mess. "I'm sure these people on the sides ... you won't know what it is, but it's the aroma of perspiration meetin' up with dry-cleaning fluid," he cracked. "It's a special kind of smell. It just comes around every now and then when it's the last thing you need." In a near-whisper that matched a faint blues vamp on the guitar, he added a rueful rhyme: "Carbon tet (tetrachloride), carbon tet, you're all wet, carbon tet." [32]

Through the dishevelment, Steve's personality shone like the sun. Back and forth, he morphed from a human pogo stick to a fragile vase ("Old Fashioned," "The Dutchman"), his voice darting from a commanding rasp to an aching hush. He worked each prop to its extreme, slipping a proffered white carnation between the strings at the end of his guitar neck and trying with little success to keep a borrowed, oversized cowboy hat from covering his eyes. ("What a lid!" he clucked in the middle of "You Never Even Call Me by My Name.") Cheered back for an encore, he strapped on his guitar and shrugged. "I know how loose that was," he said. "They're obviously gonna have to get the scissors out for this set, so it don't matter now. You try to concentrate, you get in trouble." At that very moment, his guitar strap snapped, his guitar dropped, and he caught the instrument just before it hit the stage, whereupon he snatched it by the neck, upended it and pretended to bash his head with the guitar body. The audience roared at the engaging self-deprecation. [33]

"He was an absolutely one-man show," says Terry Lickona, then an assistant producer for the series. "He projected this air of sweetness and innocence but also with a wink in his eye."

For Steve, "Austin City Limits" was nothing less than a triumph. It was as if he were addressing the doubts of many. This, the show said, was stagecraft. This was the real Steve, the "live" Steve, who had never left.

Nor, really, had Steve's dad, who was a character in both song ("My Old

They're obviously gonna have to get the scissors out for this set.
STEVE GOODMAN

32: Returning to Austin for a show at the Armadillo on a sweltering summer evening, Steve wore a swimsuit instead of pants. With his guitar covering the trunks, to the audience he appeared to be nude below his waist. Midshow, he called to the stage Jethro Burns, who spotted around Steve's feet a huge ring of sweat.

33: Producers edited the show with a wink to their medium. Steve opened with "Red Red Robin," but the aired show began with "Video Tape." Producers also kept Steve's final encore, a slide-guitar version of the theme from the popular teen show from Steve's youth, "American Bandstand." Thus, the program was bookended by TV-related songs. (Other trimmed tunes were "You're the Girl I Love," "Daley's Gone" and a request, "Winter Wonderland," through which Steve endearingly stumbled as the audience "fed" him lyrics.)

Man") and word as Steve toured that fall. With the distance of time and a musical vehicle to cement his dad's reputation, Steve felt comfortable embellishing it onstage with sardonic shots. [34] In a two-night run at the Bottom Line in Greenwich Village, he deadpanned, "His middle name was Bayer, B-a-y-e-r. There's nobody else in the family with anything even resembling that name. His mother said that she named him for aspirin. She said she had her reasons."

Steve lamented that his dad never fully shook the desire for his son to earn his keep in a more respectable way. "It's funny that your father will look at you and tell you your whole life that you're wasting your time, you're not accomplishing anything, this and that — y'know, the middle-class values and all that stuff," Steve told Toronto journalist Nicholas Jennings. But Steve had perceived a glimmer of appreciation when Bud flew to New York in April 1976 to see his son's opener for David Bromberg at Avery Fisher Hall. "It was a pretty nice thing," Steve said. "I guess it hit him that this (music career) is keeping me off the street."

The appreciation, however, didn't keep Steve from telling his Bottom Line audiences that Bud had bypassed the entire Avery Fisher show, "disappearing" during the sound check with the 18-year-old girlfriend of his steel-guitar player, Winnie Winston. "They just split," Steve said. "Nobody saw 'em."

While Steve's elfin eye rolling implicated the May-December pair with sexual innuendo, the outing with Bud Goodman couldn't have been more innocent, says Winston's girlfriend, Amy Burnham (now Pollien). "It was a nice evening," she says, "and for a couple of hours we just walked up and down the streets. We were selling each other cars, choosing Lincoln Continentals and ancient Dodges that were abandoned and Jeeps and what you find in New York. I would convince him to buy the white station wagon, and he convinced me to buy the first SUV I ever saw. Then we went to a coffee shop and had coffee and pie while Bud charmed three or four waitresses. We talked about his experiences in the war and my experiences in the protest movement and just had a wonderful time and got back to the concert to find that people had really missed us." [35]

It was during his four Bottom Line shows on Oct. 10-11 that Steve not only sang "My Old Man" but also, in an apparent gesture of equality, unveiled a sentimental song about his mother's side of the family. He had written the tune 14 hours before the first show and handed the lyric sheet to his stepbrother, NYU student Andy Sohn, for safekeeping. [36] Midway through the show, Sohn slipped the paper back to Steve, who unfolded it in an apparent daze. "The bag under the right eye is from this song," he said. "About 6 in the morning this came in." Titled "Old Smoothies," the sweeping waltz, which captured the flow and feel of skating, recalled Steve's youth when his grandparents, "Ziss" and Mary Erenburg, took him to see the Ice Capades at Chicago Stadium. The "smoothies" were an elderly pair of skaters who would "spin on the frozen spray." But Steve also sang of their complement — the escorts next to him in the stands, Ziss smiling and taking the hand of Mary, tears welling in her eyes.

Steve's Bottom Line concerts were in other ways extraordinary. Three days

---

It's funny that your father will look at you and tell you your whole life that you're wasting your time.
STEVE GOODMAN

34: Art Curtis, a Maine East High classmate of Steve's, recalls Steve introducing "My Old Man" at a 1978 or 1979 Ravinia Festival concert near Chicago by saying, "I never knew a man who could tell bigger lies with a straight face than my father." It was, Curtis says, "a very left-handed compliment."

35: Steve told Winston that his dad once sold him a station wagon that was a lemon. "It's a good car, Stevie," Bud had said. "You'll love it. I'll give you a good price on it." But Steve told Winston that the car was "in the shop all the time. My own dad did this to me."

36: After his father's death, Steve maintained strong relationships with stepbrothers Andy and Doug Sohn, inviting them to club dates and recording sessions. "I've taken to heart his high-spiritedness and the notion that you've just got to live life," Andy says. "It's been a huge inspiration for me with my family and kids."

earlier, John Rockwell had topped his *New York Times* column, "The Pop Life," with a flattering profile of Steve, helping to pack the house, and WNEW-FM simulcast the early show of Oct. 10, bringing the proceedings to millions of listeners in Manhattan and beyond. Steve started each of his sets solo, then was joined, one by one, by Jethro Burns on mandolin, Saul Broudy on harmonica, Winnie Winston on steel guitar and Steve Burgh on electric guitar. Fiddlers Larry Packer and Tex Logan also turned up for the Oct. 11 shows, as did John Prine. The hype, the crowds, his new material and his accompanists all energized Steve. [37] Mary McCaslin, who with Jim Ringer opened all four shows, says Ringer later marveled that it was the first time he had seen someone "do an entire performance standing on his toes."

For Rob Mounsey, who had supplied piano and string charts for the "Say It in Private" LP, the Bottom Line shows were a first exposure to Steve outside the studio — and he was astounded. "He sprints out to see how fast he can get to the microphone, starts banging on the guitar and singing 'Red, Red Robin,' just himself and the guitar, and he sings it as fast as he can sing it. The audience just immediately loves him. You gotta love this guy. He puts out everything. He puts out 1,000 percent energy. He could do no wrong after that. He's got everybody in the palm of his hand."

It was an enduring lesson for Mounsey. "Studio work can become distancing and academic. You can get reductionistic about what you're doing with all these details, and you're forgetting about an audience," he says. "But when I saw Steve at the Bottom Line, it made me remember that music is communication. Otherwise, there really is no point. When he came out like that — 'We're going to communicate or else. I'm going to communicate with you if it kills me, and damn it, you're going to like it, no matter what I have to do' — it just made you love him. You couldn't help yourself."

Even a potentially rude detour to baseball couldn't mar the Bottom Line crowd's admiration. It even may have enhanced his appeal.

Led by sluggers Reggie Jackson, Graig Nettles and Thurmon Munson, the hometown Yankees had just edged the Kansas City Royals for the right to return to the World Series, and the first game, against the Los Angeles Dodgers, was set for the night of Oct. 11 at Yankee Stadium. It was a classic match-up, and, as Winston recalled, "Steve was just kicking himself because he couldn't be there."

His time to go on for the Bottom Line's early show came about an hour into the game, a tight contest that was headed for extra innings. So Steve lugged to the stage a 12-inch black-and-white TV set and positioned it so it was visible to him and part of the audience. "I'm sorry, but the World Series is on, and I can't be there, so I'll just have to keep my eye on it," he said with a grin. "You'll have to excuse me, but I can't not watch this game."

The partisan crowd voiced its approval, and early in his show, between songs, Steve turned up the volume and updated the audience with the score (New York eventually won, 4-3 in 12 innings). Steve's audacious TV-set shtick remains

> **When I saw Steve at the Bottom Line, it made me remember that music is communication. Otherwise, there really is no point.**
> **ROB MOUNSEY**

37: The Bottom Line shows were so exhilarating that one night Steve, David Amram and Larry Packer walked to nearby Bleecker Street and played from 3 to 5:30 a.m. near the steps of the Bitter End. "Finally," Packer says, "the street-sweeping machines came and sprayed water all over us, and we had to move."

indelible for those present that night, including Larry Wadalavage, who regarded it as "incredibly ballsy and selfless." [38]

For Steve himself, the most endearing part of his Bottom Line shows may have been his collaboration with the father figure of Jethro Burns. The gig was among the first of more than 30 that Steve played with Burns through January — Steve's first long-term tour with the man he revered as a musical master. No doubt aware of the dad/son symbolism, Steve introduced Burns after playing "My Old Man," drawing whoops from the crowd. "This is a world-class player," Steve said, "and it's an honor to be anywhere in the vicinity of this dude."

Once Burns was onstage, the two tore into an instrumental duet or two and threw in a parody that Burns had honed during his Homer & Jethro days. Then, for the rest of the set, Burns supplied expert fills and solos for songs that benefited from his mandolin, including "Spoon River," "City of New Orleans," "The Dutchman" and "Jessie's Jig." Their cornball chemistry and respect — demonstrated by their patter before playing Burns' "Don't Let the Stars Get in Your Eyeballs" [39] — was palpable.

"Let's do a Homer & Jethro song," Steve said to Burns. "This is the only one I know well enough to even take a passing shot at. Is it still in G?"

"Yeah, let's do it in G," Burns replied.

"All right," Steve said.

After a beat, Burns said, "Where's G?"

The crowd groaned.

"She's out back changin' the strings," Steve said.

"She's out there," Burns replied. "I got a definite maybe from her."

More faintly, the crowd groaned again.

"Is this how these jokes used to go over when you did 'em back then?" Steve asked, and the audience erupted with laughter.

"No sir," Burns deadpanned. "Sometimes they flopped." [40]

The laughter and groans soon turned to awestruck applause as Burns' jazzy licks entwined with Steve's speedy guitar.

"The way I feel about when he plays is so special," Steve told Al Rudis. "There's just a few guys that are that good. I have three daughters, and maybe someday I'll have grandchildren, and somebody'll tell them that their grandfather played with Jethro Burns. I mean, he's a special guy." Steve later told Larry Kelp of the *Oakland Tribune*, "It's so nice to see a younger audience react to Jethro. Without him, there's no David Grisman. He and Bill Monroe changed the way mandolin was played. Otherwise it might still be stereotyped, like in Italian commercials."

Of course, notes Bob Hoban, Steve's slapstick collaborator at Punchinello's, it was in Steve's interest to idolize Burns. "Steve was in hog heaven," Hoban says. "If Steve wasn't the finest player, he recognized that it was great playing with the finest. Steve was being Jack Benny. He knew the audience would remember Steve Goodman, not the cast."

Burns tried to rebuild his career by recruiting a replacement for his late

---

38: Steve was keenly attuned to pennant races, though the Cubs rarely contended — and when they did, they eventually collapsed. Journalist Steve Weitzman joined Steve at Shea Stadium on Sept. 20, 1976, for a Mets/Pirates game. Weitzman was a huge fan of the Pirates, whose late-inning surge gave them a 4-3 lead that was keeping their National League playoff hopes alive. In the bottom of the ninth, however, rookie Lee Mazzilli, called up just two weeks earlier, pinch-hit a walk-off homer, his second big-league round-tripper, to win the game for the Mets 5-4. Weitzman was "stunned and speechless," he says. But Steve, wizened by years of Cub losses, whacked Weitzman on the shoulder and elicited a grin by saying, "September baseball is a motherfucker."

39: Perry Como made Slim Willet's "Don't Let the Stars Get in Your Eyes" a hit in 1953, setting up the song for a Homer & Jethro parody.

40: Another shared joke penetrated the core of their enterprise. "Ask me what the secret of show business is," Jethro would say. Steve would respond, "What's the —" and before Steve could get out the question, Burns would interject, "Timing." Burns' son, Johnny, says Steve "would do that every chance he got, no matter how funny it wasn't. People wouldn't get it and would say 'What?' and he would do it over and over again."

partner, Homer Haynes — and with Ken Eidson, of Glenview, he secured bookings for several years as "The New Homer & Jethro." But Eidson, a teacher, wasn't willing to travel as often as Burns, so the duo's success was limited. Burns also had begun offering mandolin lessons in his home, stayed connected with brother-in-law and ace Nashville guitarist Chet Atkins and even recorded a self-titled solo album in 1977 for Flying Fish, backed by Vassar Clements on fiddle, his son Johnny on guitar and nine other top Chicago musicians.

But none of these activities compared with the satisfaction of performing with Steve. In comments shocking for someone who had performed thousands of shows and produced 35 albums and 300 singles in a 39-year career with Haynes, Burns placed his association with Steve on a higher pedestal.

"I've enjoyed this Steve Goodman tour better than anything I've done in show business," Burns told Michael R. Brown of the *Chicago Reader* in mid-December. "I'm getting to play to a young audience, Goodman's fans. It's a kick to go out and play and have them dig and know and appreciate what I'm playing. In fact, it's embarrassing because I've never had anybody appreciate my playing. All my life I've played clubs to wealthy, sophisticated people who kind of go 'Ho hum. That was nice.' But these young people come to dig the music. And I like being around Goodman. He's some kind of champion. He gives more credit to other musicians than any superstar I've ever worked with. When he brings you on, you're not a sideman or a warm-up. He brings you on as a star."

While Steve and Burns both lived in Evanston and shared musical talent, storytelling skill and offbeat humor, their differences also made them click, says Burns' eventual protégé, Don Stiernberg. "What was beautiful about it was that they just were themselves," Stiernberg says. "I don't think either one tried to adapt his style to the other one. It just meshed organically. It was good music, but what people got more was like a conversation between these two talents." [41]

"You couldn't talk about two more different people," says Steve Cohen, who was immersed in the dynamic. "Jethro had done it already. He had raised kids already. It was a nice thing for Jethro, semi-retired, to still be able to play and keep current, and he was happy to be a side person. And Jethro just always deferred. If there was conflict — missing the schedule, missed a bus, miss a

41: Stiernberg, playing as part of Jethro Burns' quartet, walked into a comic bit in the early 1980s when the group opened for Steve at Harper College northwest of Chicago. Steve asked the 6-foot-2 Stiernberg to join him on Bill Monroe's "Love, Please Come Home." Onstage, Steve told him, "Just lean over and sing harmony in my mike." When Stiernberg bent over to do so, Steve looked up at him, getting a few laughs, then crouched and sang into his much lower guitar mike. Miming a baseball catcher, Steve said, "One's a fastball, two's a curve. ..." It brought down the house.

42: Other musicians learned from Burns, who once told Winnie Winston how he'd silenced a heckler during a Homer & Jethro booking in Las Vegas. "You, out there," Burns said, "where'd you come from?" "We're from Palm Beach, California." "Oh, did you drive out?" "Yeah." "You having a good time?" "Oh, we're having a wonderful time." "You have any kids?" "No." "So, you just left the house?" "Yeah." "What makes you think you turned the stove off?" The heckler and his wife came up afterward and said, "You've ruined our vacation." "That's OK," Burns replied, "you ruined our set."

43: The two-show Nov. 1, 1977, Atlanta gig itself was a challenge. Opener Tim Bays says Steve had a cold, operating on antibiotics and three hours of sleep and facing a 5 a.m. flight the next day. Steve performed a stellar first set, thinking it was simulcast on WKLS-FM, but discovered that the second show would be simulcast instead. He apologized to the audience for needing to repeat songs and turned in a hoarse but well-received performance. At 2 a.m. as Steve packed up in the dressing room, "a young woman who was generously overserved entered in tears, saying how much she loved Steve's music and hated herself," Bays says. Steve sat and talked with the suicidal woman "until she somewhat sobered up and got past the self-destructive ideation, just in time to leave for his flight with no sleep whatsoever."

44: Steve also may have derived the line from the fact that in 1977 his road manager, Steve Cohen, dated a woman named Lisa Lombardo, who claimed to be the bandleader's niece.

plane, this guy didn't get onstage — nothing mattered. He was unflappable, where Steve was very flappable. Jethro never had that urban intensity that Steve had, and he was the perfect foil because everything just rolled right off his back. It was the earlier version of 'Whatever. Just get up there and play.' " [42]

Perhaps because of Burns' laissez-faire influence, a schedule foul-up for the two in Atlanta resulted not in fury but in facetiousness. Pulling up to the Great Southeast Music Hall and finding the lights dark and the parking lot empty, Steve and Burns quickly concluded they'd arrived on the wrong night. It was fertile inspiration for Steve to write a tribute to futility, and it drew guffaws from audiences that fall, notably its refrain (and title): "There's No Business Like Show Business When There's No Business." [43] The tune's first line, "There's no place around here looks like the place, so this must be the place," was even a lift from "We Want Our Mummy," a 1939 short film by the Three Stooges.

As they traversed the South (including an Austin Opry House show with Willie Nelson and David Amram as walk-on guests) and into the Midwest and West in early November, Steve grew close to Burns beyond their music. Don Stiernberg says Steve especially appreciated Burns' approach to his leukemia. "You hear a lot of people say, 'I know how you feel,' but nobody knows how you feel except you," Burns told Steve. "I'm not going to tell you anything about that. I'll just tell you that whatever you need from me, you let me know."

On their tour, Steve also sharpened intros to his newer songs. For instance, after learning of the Nov. 5 death of Guy Lombardo, Steve linked the famed New Year's Eve maestro to "Twentieth Century." He told audiences that he and John Prine had penned the tune "for the late Guy Lombardo's band, to give 'em somethin' to sing at the end of the century." In future years, Steve went further, saying that as the new millennium "gets closer and closer, I just can't wait to cash the royalty check when they record it, y'know. Might as well dream." [44] It was an inside joke, for the public didn't know of Steve's leukemia and that his demise would likely come well before the century's completion.

There was no hint of Steve's disease when he and Burns snagged a 30-minute slot on the Nov. 16 edition of "90 Minutes Live," a popular TV show that aired throughout Canada. The evening program was hosted by Peter Gzowski, who built fame in coming decades as the engaging interviewer of CBC Radio's "Morningside." True to the "live" format, Steve and Burns supplied plenty of seemingly off-the-cuff moments to delight the studio audience and viewers at home. During "City of New Orleans," Burns' instrumental dexterity contrasted with an oddly bored expression, but when he broke his mandolin pick during a solo, in a split second he pulled from his coat pocket a replacement, dropping only a couple of beats before continuing. From Gzowski, Steve borrowed a black cowboy hat that — like the one in his "Austin City Limits" taping — kept settling uncomfortably over his eyes. With practiced verbal and visual slapstick, he and Burns supplied an entertaining version of "Don't Let the Stars Get in Your Eyeballs," which was transcended by Steve's touching solo performance of "My Old Man," after which tears appeared to well in his eyes.

Steve's undeniable stage appeal prompted critics to seek imaginative ways to describe him. Rose Marie Lattanze, in the *Glassboro Whit*, a New Jersey college newspaper, said that in concert Steve was "looking like Paul Simon and acting like Michael J. Pollard, with that perpetual grin on his face." On the other coast, David L. Wilson led his review in the *Orange County Register* by writing, "Imagine Will Rogers with a Gibson guitar instead of a lariat."

But it was a West Coast swing from British Columbia to California that gave writers a choice angle on Steve's height — fueled by Steve himself. The seven-show stint called for Steve and Burns to open for the quirky singer/songwriter Randy Newman, who had just scored his first pop hit, "Short People," a tongue-in-cheek novelty song that was sweeping the airwaves and eventually would reach #2 on the *Billboard* Hot 100 and sell more than a million copies. With its nasty yet catchy refrain of "Short people got no reason to live," it was a pointed satire of "small"-minded prejudice of all kinds. But it stirred ire among those who, whether or not they understood the joke, found it insensitive and inflammatory.

For his "Short People" tour, Randy Newman engaged as his opening act the ultimate short person — Steve, who told audiences, "I'm gonna get a pair of stilts for the gig."
(Photo courtesy of Gary Norris)

Not 5-foot-2 Steve, however. "Short People" gave him a vehicle to banter about his own challenged stature. "I'm gonna get a pair of stilts for the gig," he told a San Francisco audience three days before the tour. Later, Steve said that Newman "was telling everybody he was an equal opportunity employer."

Joking aside, Steve's respect for the success of Newman's incisive songwriting was immense, particularly given the domination of the pop charts in 1977 by mindless disco (epitomized by the 25 million-selling "Saturday Night Fever" two-LP soundtrack). "Randy is where Stephen Foster meets Victor Borge," Steve told Larry Kelp of the *Oakland Tribune*. "It's great to see him have a hit record and be so popular now with music where lyrics are the thing."

Newman — long before his career veered into film composing (the province of his famous uncles Alfred and Lionel) — was a brilliant, stay-at-home lyricist for whom the word "reclusive" could have been coined, says his manager at the time, Elliott Abbott. "The only way to get Randy out was to tell him you had a great person to open for him," he says. "You needed a bomb to get him out of his house. He didn't want to leave. He liked where he was, and he felt there was no point to work."

Steve's persona as "just one of the happiest people I ever met" played a key role, Abbott says, in inducing Newman to tour in support of "Short People" and the million-selling LP on which it appeared, "Little Criminals." Newman had never seen Steve perform, but he trusted Abbott's assessment because a dozen years earlier Abbott (under his previous last name of Engelhart) had played drums in Steve's Sammy house band at the University of Illinois, the Juicy Fruits. "With Randy being as crotchety as he used to be, we had to be pretty careful who we put out on the road with him, but you just couldn't not love Steve Goodman. This is a guy who always had a smile on his face. You couldn't feel bad if you were around him. He was magic."

Newman eventually agreed. But along with his audiences he soon discov-

Steve Cohen, shown preparing the stage at a 1976 Goodman show at Harper College in Palatine, Illinois, one year later slammed the "Say It in Private" LP in a review, violating his former boss' sense of loyalty.

(Photo by Michael Nejman)

45: Michael Levin — who had sung and played a few songs with Steve as a would-be pledge at the University of Illinois in 1967 and, 10 years later as a sales and promotion staffer for KZAM-FM, saw the Seattle stop of Steve's tour with Newman — sizes up the artists' complementary charm: "Steve was full of personality, and Randy was just the opposite. He had anti-charisma, which was part of his appeal. Steve was all about charisma and joy."

ered the sharp contrast between his staid act and Steve's. While the onstage picture of Newman was that of a self-absorbed musician sitting with bowed head and darkened glasses behind a grand piano, Steve resembled an electrified marionette. [45]

"Pop music hasn't produced many natural performers, but he was one," Newman says. "I don't think I stood up in my performing history, but he was bouncing all over the place. He was a hell of a performer. I was lucky to get someone as good as he was. But I'll tell you, I felt a little twinge, like how can I follow this? It worried me that he was too entertaining to follow. But the better the opening act, the better it is for you. It's very rare in pop music where someone does any sort of comedic content. Both he and I had quite a bit of it. We were doing the same sort of things, making the audience laugh and then getting them completely quiet with a ballad. It was a good pairing. It was rare. (Jim) Croce (also) opened for me, and he was the same kind of guy. Steve was actually like Bette Midler, who is one of the best performers. He liked it up there."

When the Newman tour reached the University of Oregon's McArthur Court on Nov. 20, Steve reconnected with his former road manager, Steve Cohen, who had resigned the previous summer and moved back to Eugene to begin a more settled life. Invited backstage, Cohen encountered "Saturday Night Live" comedian John Belushi, a graduate of Chicago's Second City comedy troupe, who was in the college town for the filming of the crass movie comedy "*National Lampoon's* Animal House." Wandering around in a stupor, Belushi left an unsavory impression. "There's nobody home," Cohen sadly told Steve, who replied, "You got that wired." The exchange was "a nice little bond," Cohen says. "It was a realization that I knew exactly what he was thinking, and no one else would have said that to him." An amateur harmonica player, Cohen was further pleased when Steve later invited him onstage to play a solo in "Jessie's Jig." Hours later, however, the good feelings soured.

After the show, Steve, Burns and others retreated to Cohen's house in West Eugene for a late-night song swap. Soon after arriving, Steve went into the bathroom, where he found a copy of that week's *Willamette Valley Observer*. In it was a glowing preview of Steve's opening set by Cohen, who wrote, "His ability to make an audience identify with him is fantastic. He's incapable of doing a bad show." Cohen also labeled Burns "the world's best mandolin player, bar none."

But the bulk of the article detailed Cohen's deep disappointment with Steve's "Say It in Private" LP, particularly the "cottony symphonic overkill" of its production. "Joel Dorn," Cohen wrote, "proves once again that 'more can be less.' The album suffers from a 'constructed' quality, where added orchestration and vocals sound like additions, rather than integral parts of a whole. It's the difference between making an album and making music. There is a compressed and muted tone to the production that results in a dry sound and stilted feeling."

Emerging from the bathroom, Steve was furious, and he fumed. "I was trying to strike out on my own," Cohen says, "and I was probably trying to say something and make my mark." Steve, however, considered the printed slam an act of disloyalty. "I really meant what I said," Cohen says. "I thought the album sucked, but I still thought he was a great live performer, and part of me wanted to push him to do something different. But forget it, he was not happy." From then on, Cohen had little contact with his former boss.

Steve and Burns were the picture of loony loyalty as they breezed through a notable broadcast the following month — a Dec. 4 slot as guest deejays for the offbeat and delightfully non-prescription "Dr. Demento Show," aired on KMET-FM in Los Angeles and syndicated across the nation. On the air since 1970 (and still airing today), the popular Sunday evening program showcased a panorama of oddball and obscure hits of the past. The zany parodies of Homer & Jethro fit this format, of course, but host Barry Hansen also felt he had a kooky kinship with Steve. Called upon to spin his favorite oldies, Steve obliged with a voice reminiscent of his high-school radio stint and a passel of rarities that pleased "the good doctor." They ranged from the rockers "Who Slapped John?" by Gene Vincent and the Blue Caps and "Somethin' Else" by Eddie Cochran, to the soul-styled "Mm-mm-mm" by Major Lance and "Who's Loving You?" by Smokey Robinson, all of which were capped by the sublime radio paean, Mark Dinning's "Top 40 News, Weather and Sports."

In the midst of such hip nostalgia, one other request from Steve sprang strictly from the middle of the road — and soon bolstered his own stage act. Painting the fantasy of living with a lover in an isolated paradise, it was a song by Nick Acquaviva and Ted Varnick, "In the Middle of an Island," which Tony Bennett had made a #9 hit in 1957. "I think that anybody who stands inside a travel agency could appreciate this," Steve said. "This is just the other side of the wall." After Hansen aired Bennett's campy version, complete with Hawaiian guitar and ukulele, Steve asked the host for a tape of the "terrific little song" so he could learn the words. Steve later worked up a speedy rendition as an upbeat opener for his shows. [46]

The topper of the "Dr. Demento" appearance came when Hansen served up a straight line for an exchange proving that Steve could joke about the demise of his father — and anyone. While playing a couple of cuts from the "Say It in Private" LP, Hansen said, "It's one of my favorite albums of the year, and I josh you not." He then took note of a thematic thread running through the final three songs on the LP's second side: "Daley's Gone," "My Old Man" and "The Twentieth Century Is Almost Over."

"It's the only album," Hansen said, "that has three obituaries in a row to close out the album, but it leaves you feeling happy."

Steve's classic answer, uttered instantly, broke up the coterie listening in the KMET studio: "There's more to the newspaper than the sports page."

It was a quintessential Chicago retort: direct, profound and tinged with dry wit. Steve brought these qualities back to his hometown for his by-now-legendary New Year's Eve show at the Earl of Old Town. With David Amram returning as his opener, Steve also had bookings at the Earl for Dec. 30 and Jan. 1, but

Dr. Demento, aka Barry Hansen, hosting Steve on his radio program Dec. 4, 1977, had an astute observation about the "Say It in Private" LP: "It's the only album that has three obituaries in a row to close out the album, but it leaves you feeling happy." But Steve supplied an instantly classic punch line.

(Photo courtesy of Barry Hansen)

46: When opening shows with "In the Middle of an Island," Steve appended two of his own songs as so-called "island music": "Banana Republics" for St. Croix and "Men Who Love Women Who Love Men" for New York's Manhattan.

Bette Midler – shown at the Roxy in L.A. two weeks before showing up at Steve's New Year's Eve show at the Earl of Old Town – belts out a tune. Midler dueted with Steve on the closer, "Goodnight Irene."

(Photo by Bob Scott, courtesy of Darrell Redmond)

47: At his post-Earl gig on WFMT's live New Year's edition of the "Midnight Special," Steve sang impromptu couplets that used wordplay and nostalgia to express optimism for 1978: "I know the coming 12 months will be great / because my favorite records are 78s / The hole comes out of the same place in both sides / and everything about them was made with a whole lot of pride / And round they went a little bit too fast / recording the music that was made in the past / But I think they get just one more whack / In '78, the 78s will be back."

Dec. 31 was *the* night. [47] It was even recorded for later broadcast on WXRT-FM. Despite freezing temperatures and huge drifts of snow, a crowd packed the tiny club at North and Wells. Steve several times acknowledged the chill, playing early in his set an instrumental version of "Winter Wonderland" and later inserting an irresistible couplet in "This Hotel Room":

> *There is no finer place, I do believe*
> *than the Earl of Old Town on a snowy New Year's Eve*

Such warming touches were part of Steve's usual unexpected fare. Not even Steve, however, could have predicted the showstopper who walked into the Earl out of the blue.

Well after 2 a.m., the typical pastiche of accompanists called from the audience — Amram, Ken Bloom, Brian Torff, Roland Hicks, Bonnie Koloc, Claudia Schmidt, Howard Levy, Saul Broudy, Jethro Burns and Winnie Winston, 10 in all, overflowing the postage-stamp stage — took shape for 22 verses of "Mama Don't Allow It." Before the song began, however, the phone behind the bar rang, and Earl Pionke picked it up.

"This is your old girlfriend," said the voice on the other end.

Pionke recognized the voice from years gone by. It was the sassy singing sensation who had just wrapped up the final set of a 10-night stand at Park West, the 750-seat theater just one-half mile north of the Earl — Bette Midler.

The two jousted with bawdy banter for a minute or so before Midler asked, "Hey, you think you could get me into that little fuckin' dump of yours?"

"You got any energy left?"

"Fuck you," Midler said. "Fit me in. Hold those fuckers up. I want to be on that stage. I'll be there in a cab in 10 minutes."

Wearing a flesh-tone body suit and a "Happy New Year" banner, the 5-foot-1 dazzler walked into the club and up to Steve, who didn't miss a beat. He told the crowd about how she had opened for comic Mort Sahl in 1968 at Mr. Kelly's nightclub on Rush Street, singing from charts she had brought from the Continental Baths in Manhattan.

"She tore us all up," Steve said. "We used to sit at the back table, her and Koloc and me and Ed Holstein at 4 in the morning until she got done at Kelly's. … We'll sing 'Goodnight Irene' to end the new year. Would you make Bette Midler welcome, folks?"

With a hoarse but hearty voice, Midler sang a verse and offered harmony on the "Irene" choruses. An impromptu verse by Steve sealed his appreciation:

> *Well, I know that Bette worked two sets tonight*
> *and the 10 nights that went before*
> *But it was so sweet of her to come up here and sing with us*
> *and welcome this New Year's once more*

At least one of Steve's accompanists that night — Torff, the bassist — worried about the apparent effect on Steve of the night's freeze. "I sensed that he wasn't well, even though he wouldn't talk about his illness," Torff says. "He wore about two or three coats. He had on a winter coat, and then he seemed like he was wearing another winter coat three or four sizes bigger so that he could put it over the other coat. When I saw that, I realized that something was going on. Not that I knew him well enough to even ask him, but he would not talk about it. It was not something that he wanted to publicly acknowledge. But it scared me."

Still, the fact that Steve had lived through another New Year's Eve and was approaching his 30th birthday held a personal significance to which many others his age hardly gave a thought. Without revealing his disease, Steve indicated that his predominant public emotion was gratitude.

"I'm having the time of my life right now," he told Larry Kelp of the *Oakland Tribune* in an article printed five days into 1978. "It's so exciting. My wife had our third daughter this (past) summer, I've got a new album out and Jethro Burns is performing with me." When Kelp told him it was rare to converse with "a creative talent who isn't depressed or frustrated," Steve replied, "You have Nancy Goodman to thank for that. In fact, my personal life is so good and interesting that if the rest of the world hit me in the head, the blow would roll off."

Steve's sunny side [48] masked what was becoming a familiar commercial blow. Despite Asylum's promotional blizzard, his "Say It in Private" LP was fizzling instead of sizzling. It never charted in *Billboard* and was headed toward domestic sales of fewer than 30,000 copies, a slight dip from the sales for his 1976 "Words" LP and 40 percent below that of the 1975 "Jig."

Such stagnation was no surprise to Joel Dorn. "Asylum hated the record I made with Steve," he says. "Al (Bunetta) hated it. You have no idea how much everybody hated this record. I don't think Steve was nuts about it until later." Dorn said the recurring complaint from Asylum about the LP was that besides the absence of an obvious single, it seemed scattered, that "there was no connection from cut to cut, which I had done on purpose."

Dorn played the finished product for Jerry Sharell, the label's senior VP for creative services, artist development and promotion. "As soon as he heard it, I could see that look," Dorn said. "I knew this record was dead in the fuckin' water, man. You get that perfunctory stuff where they start saying, 'Wow, that's a great drum sound' or something that means, 'Would you like to take my sister to the prom? I'll give you $50.' It didn't kill me because it happened to me a lot in that period. I was making a lot of records nobody liked from the record company but which have stood the test of time." Dorn went so far as to say that "Say It in Private" is the album that most effectively defined Steve. "In the big picture, this tells you more about him than his other ones," he said. "That doesn't mean I'm saying it's better. But I set out to paint a picture."

To Steve, of course, the "test of time" was a luxury. But Dorn's enthusiasm and methods had rubbed off. He had experienced other producers working with him and his material. He had produced two of his own albums, albeit with

Steve drew this coffee-stained sketch for singer/songwriter Willie Nininger. Consciously or not, the dizzy image reflected low sales for Steve's latest LP, which producer Joel Dorn quickly sensed "was dead in the fuckin' water, man."
(Image courtesy of Willie Nininger)

48: Steve's ebullience shone prior to a Dec. 3, 1977, show in Old Cabell Hall at the University of Virginia. During sound check, the opener – Willie Nininger, who had penned "I'm Proud to be a Moose" for TV's Captain Kangaroo – was playing "City of New Orleans" then spotted Steve and Burns in the balcony. "We were just warming up with that song," Nininger told Steve. "Of course, we're not going to do it in our show." Steve replied, "Oh, it sounded good. I think you should do it." Nininger answered, "There's no way I'm going to do your most famous song when I'm opening for you. I think it'd cause a revolt in the audience." Steve said, "Then why don't you come up and do it with me at the end of my show?" Nininger and his band got two encores and joined Steve and Burns for a half hour of closing songs and encores. "It was magical," Nininger says, "one of the best shows we did in our life."

the aid of experienced musicians and engineers, and he had produced the Malvina Reynolds single. The public perception of him, if anything, was as a songwriter and performing artist. But after working with Dorn, Steve started seeing an equally satisfying future for himself in producing the records of others — what M.G. Maples, reporter for the *Illinois Entertainer*, identified as "the whole different world of professional listening, which is performing's flip side."

"Steve always wanted to be a record producer," says Steve's neighbor, multi-instrumentalist Howard Levy, for whom Steve played countless LPs in his third-floor music room in Evanston. With each track, Steve kept up a running patter: "Listen to what those guys were doing. Listen to that. Listen to the background vocals in there. Listen to this. Listen to that."

Producing others' music in the least intrusive manner possible continued to be Steve's path. Squeezing sessions close to home at Chicago's Curtom Studios between dates on his fall 1977 tour, he directed the recording and mixing of the third album on Flying Fish by the elderly African-American trio he had worshipped and played with for years — Martin, Bogan & Armstrong. Instead of imagining elaborate ways to "sweeten" or otherwise enhance the trio's charming, old-time tunes, Steve saw his job as essentially to capture their musicianship and charm. "This is no archive record," Steve later wrote in the LP's liner notes, "just the latest news from string-band music's resident good-time experts."

The "news" ranged from traditional tunes such as "Jamaica Farewell" and the salacious "Ice Cream Freezer Blues" to originals such as Howard Armstrong's tender and evocative "Streets of Old Chicago" — and all of the tracks reflected an approach both spare and spontaneous. "Steve was very thorough," says project engineer Fred Breitberg, who had assisted on Steve's jingle sessions in 1969. "He really knew the group, he knew what their capabilities were, and he knew what was important to bring out of them. He didn't overproduce. He didn't want to hear it hyped up. He wanted to hear the pure musical thing as if he was in the room with them, and with Martin, Bogan & Armstrong, you got what you got."

The only accompanists — in addition to Steve on acoustic guitar and Howard Armstrong's bassist son Tom ("Rap"), who had joined the trio's act — were bassist Jim Tullio and Howard Levy, who musically maneuvered himself into a live studio take that made it onto the album. Steve had told Levy, "I'm going to have you overdub vibes and harmonica on 'Jamaica Farewell,'" but Levy pleaded, "I don't want to just overdub. Man, I want to play with those guys." Levy saw his chance at the end of a session when everyone was packing up instruments. He sat down at Curtom's Steinway piano, "and I started playing some blues, just laid out my most soulful vibe, and Carl Martin walked over and started singing 'Mm-mm,' singing along with me, and then started singing, 'I've got this naggin' woman,' and Steve heard it." Steve told Breitberg, the engineer, "Freddy, this is really happening. Bring some mikes in right now. Mike that piano, and get a mike on Carl." Thus became Martin's "Nagging Woman Blues."

Steve was very thorough. He really knew the group, he knew what their capabilities were, and he knew what was important to bring out of them.
FRED BREITBERG

The standout of the LP, which became its title, was the sentimental tune written by Billy Rose, Mort Dixon and Ray Henderson and featured in the Ziegfield Follies of 1923, "That Old Gang of Mine." With Armstrong's gentle fiddle, Ted Bogan's wailing vocal and "chunk-chunk" guitar and Martin's nostalgic recitation in the middle, the song became the trio's definitive ensemble piece. Capturing the theme visually, Armstrong used marking pens to draw a colorful nighttime street-corner scene for the album's cover. For the back cover, Steve's brother David supplied a photo portrait of three childhood chums who were easy to imagine as the trio's youthful "gang."

While Flying Fish owner Bruce Kaplan's overall aim was to document American musical history, Tullio says that Steve was a singular advocate for Martin, Bogan & Armstrong. "That's a great legacy of Steve's," Tullio says. "I don't think that record would have been made if Steve didn't champion for it. During that period of time, that was not cool. To be a folkie was way passé, and the folkies didn't really have any reality in the pop world or the modern world musically, but Goodman had his hand in both. He knew every old record, and he just revered that music and knew its brilliance. And these guys were of the status of Jelly Roll Morton and Scott Joplin. They were unsung heroes, and Steve was always for the underdog."

Steve's support for the trio was as practical as it was musical. "If you're playing or working for somebody," Armstrong said, "you want to know how your work is accepted. Next thing you want to know is how the pay's coming in, and we didn't have to wait no two or three weeks for our check or borrow money or anything like that. Steve would back it up. We always considered him as part of the group, and whatever he did for us he was doing for himself, roughly speaking, and so we appreciated it."

Such integrity was a quality that Steve and many others admired in one of his Troubles co-founders, the soft-spoken English teacher Bill Redhed, who died suddenly on Christmas Eve 1977. The song Steve chose to sing at Redhed's funeral service was a Red Hayes/Jack Rhodes country classic, "Satisfied Mind." The lyrics' quiet esteem for friendship over wealth had deep impact for Chicago bassist Mike Dunbar, whose band, named Redhead (a play on the name of Redhed's daughter Betsy, vocalist for the group), was about to break up. "I was getting success-driven," Dunbar says, "and after hearing Steve do that song, I realized that success was something that came or went. I decided I was just going to forget about success and work on art. It changed my life."

Steve soon would have a life-changing effect on another musician — his longtime friend John Prine, who had left Atlantic Records and signed with Steve's label, Asylum. Prine had spent the summer of 1977 in Nashville playing new songs and filling up "boxes and boxes of tape" with producer Jack Clement. But they spent their $50,000 budget and "didn't have anything at the end that we could really build a record on," says Prine, who was in the midst of a crisis both personal and creative, as he and his wife, Ann Carole, were going through a divorce. "I was pretty despondent over the whole thing. I just had no

> **During that period of time, ... to be a folkie was way passé, and the folkies didn't really have any reality in the pop world or the modern world musically, but Goodman had his hand in both.**
> **JIM TULLIO**

energy whatsoever. I thought, geez, I thought I made this record. I put every-thing I had into it, and I didn't know what to do about it." In Hollywood, he consulted a dozen producers who had worked with artists from Tom Waits to Sam Cooke to Bobby Darin. He even talked with the famed Phil Spector and wrote a couple of songs with him. But Prine says that "none of it really made sense to me."

Into the breach stepped Steve. "He could see I was goin' nowhere," Prine says. Steve suggested working with Joel Dorn, and Prine did record two tracks with Dorn in New York. Steve also took Prine to Los Angeles and recorded a couple of songs with Ry Cooder. Still no luck, however. "It wasn't happenin' for me," Prine says. Finally, Steve suggested himself.

"Listen," Steve told Prine, "why don't we just stay in Chicago? I'll get all Chicago guys. All you gotta do is show up every day. Just come down to the studio. I won't ask you to do anything that you wouldn't like. I won't ask you to do anything dumb or stupid. Just do what I ask you to do, and I can give you a really good record."

Prine, who felt "emotionally gone," relented. "I didn't want to do anything," he says. "I was goin' through all kinds of changes, and he saw that I was lost. He knew he loved the songs, and he knew that I loved the songs, but I was just spent. I thought, 'Well, I'll go down and listen to my friend.' He just guided me through it."

It became Steve's first project of 1978 and would boil on his musical front burner for the better part of three months. But before he delved seriously into producing Prine's LP, he and Jethro Burns were headed for a place where the clime was colder than Chicago and that Steve had never seen — Alaska. [49]

Despite temperatures 10 to 20 degrees below freezing, Steve saw his mid-January week in the 49th state as an adventure. The promoter, Goodtime Pro-ductions, had brought up Prine and Taj Mahal for successful concerts, so Steve held at bay his apprehensions about frigid weather and flew to Anchorage and Juneau during the region's coldest season. He even learned two Alaska songs to sing there: "Saginaw, Michigan," a Klondike ballad popularized by Lefty Frizzell in 1964, and "North to Alaska," known for the Johnny Horton version in the 1960 John Wayne movie of the same name.

The concerts — benefits for the Alaska Public Interest Research Group and the Southeast Alaska Conservation Council — did not break even, says co-owner Geoff Feiler, who with his partner was investing funds earned during construction of the Alaska Pipeline, the controversial, two-year project that had ended the previous spring. "The shows were definitely heavily promoted," Feiler says, "but Steve just wasn't well-enough known." For Steve, however, the trip was far more rewarding for his immersion in the novel surroundings, indoor and outdoor.

The night before their Jan. 15 Anchorage show, Feiler took Steve and Burns to the Warehouse, a former church converted to a nonsmoking, acoustic-music club, to see a folk/bluegrass troupe called Dr. Schultz, the Last Frontier Band,

I was lost. He knew he loved the songs, and he knew that I loved the songs, but I was just spent. I thought, 'Well, I'll go down and listen to my friend.' He just guided me through it.
JOHN PRINE

49: The only other time Burns had traveled to Alaska was for USO shows as part of Homer & Jethro.

Organizers of Steve's January 1978 tour of Alaska with Jethro Burns created this caricature (based on his expression on the "Words" LP) for posters to promote the shows. (Left) The day of his Anchorage concert, Steve sampled a replica of the Iditarod Trail by taking a one-hour dogsled ride for three miles in nearby Eagle River. (Left photo by Geoff Feiler, poster image courtesy of Johnny Burns)

named for pharmacist Don "Doc" Schultz. During a break, the band's lead guitarist, Loren Arment, gently invited Steve and Burns to join them onstage. The two shot back, almost in unison, "God, I thought you'd never ask!" With borrowed instruments, the two performed a set that ranged from raucous tunes to quieter material such as "The Dutchman." "People were transfixed and crying when Steve sang that," says Pat Rickert, co-owner of the Warehouse. "He was an adorable little imp. He had incredible ability, but it was more than that. There was an empathy for life."

During their concert the next night at West High School, Steve and Burns invited the Schultz band onstage for the finale, Steve leading the assemblage on the obscure gospel tune "Somebody Touched Me." The Schultz band's bassist, Goodwin Trent, says the pair of visiting "stars" quickly dismantled the band's initial timidity. "It was a wonderful experience for those two very talented guys to play music with us and still have their head screwed on straight as far as relating to other human beings." [50] Schultz, whose group had earned fame as the official band of the Iditarod sled-dog race, goes further. Playing with Steve and Burns, he says, surpassed anything in his experience. Steve's deference and desire to play in the keys and style of his band "taught me music, friendship and, most important, how to be humble, that we are not the only persons, onstage or not, who share this universe."

The day of the show, Schultz band manager John Speer helped Steve sample a replica of the 1,150-mile Iditarod Trail by arranging a one-hour dogsled ride in Eagle River, east of Anchorage. Wrapped in a hooded parka and led by a musher,

50: Trent today lives in Tacoma, Washington, and when he attends Friday night temple service and says the Kaddish prayer for those no longer living, he always remembers Steve. "He's one of the few people other than my family that I think of then," he says. "There are a lot of musicians who pass away, but few of them really affect you, and certainly Steve Goodman was one of those."

Jethro Burns and Steve crack each other up while performing Jan. 16, 1978, at Juneau-Douglas Auditorium.

(Photos by Geoff Feiler)

51: Steve's ride in the Alaskan snow paralleled his decision back in Chicago to record three radio spots for John Deere snowmobiles that aired in the winter of 1977-78. He told interviewers he did the ads at the behest of "a very dear friend who bailed me out of a couple of scrapes. ... I'd do anything for the guy." He didn't identify the friend, who remains unknown. In a bouncy 6/8 jig, the jingles' jaunty, upbeat lyrics celebrated the Wisconsin firm's new recreational products: the Little John Spitfire, the Liquifire and the Cyclone. Typical was this verse: "Of all the trail performance sleds a man can hope to drive / There's nothin's half so handsome, and there's nothin' so alive." The jingles ended with the catch phrase: "Hey, nothin' runs like a Deere." The firm, which had begun selling snowmobiles in 1972, gave up the product in 1984, opting to concentrate on farm machinery.

Steve slid along three miles of a snowy practice run. Steve, huddled in the basket of his sled, wore a gleaming grin. [51]

The chilly excursion invigorated Steve, who added an extraordinary closing element to his shows that night in Anchorage and the next night in Juneau — and it wasn't a song. Setting his guitar on a stand to the side, Steve picked up and opened a 735-page, 57-year-old hardcover book, *The Collected Poems of Robert Service*, and read aloud one of his favorite pieces of writing — the celebrated Sourdough's most famous work, "The Cremation of Sam McGee."

The 15-verse narrative, inspired by Service's eight years in the Yukon at the turn of the 20th century, reeked of black humor. In it, the narrator describes a request by McGee, a former Southerner who prospects for gold in the Yukon and foretells his frozen death. McGee's request, based on an "awful dread of the icy grave that pains," is to be cremated. The narrator complies, setting McGee's corpse afire inside a broken-up wooden boat. Suspecting after a time that his friend is "cooked," the narrator peeks inside to find a shocking scene:

> *And there sat Sam, looking cool and calm,*
> *in the heart of the furnace roar.*
> *And he wore a smile you could see a mile,*
> *and he said: "Please close the door.*
> *It's fine in here, but I greatly fear*
> *you'll let in the cold and storm.*
> *Since I left Plumtree, down in Tennessee*
> *it's the first time I've been warm.*

The poem's sensory narrative, its flawless rhythm and rhymes and especially its "gotcha" ending fit Steve's sensibilities exquisitely. He likely had been exposed to the classic in high school or college, and to his Alaskan audiences it made sense for him to invoke the masterwork of a writer they claimed as their own. But no one present — excepting Burns and Steve's new road manager, Tim Messer — knew of the poem's personal relevance, given Steve's leukemia.

The creative wrinkles that Steve brought to the Alaskan expedition gave him outlets for expression that helped him persevere in Chicago with John Prine's LP project. A similar break was a return engagement for Steve on Jan. 22 at Huntington High School on Long Island with Harry Chapin and Pete Seeger. Yet another outlet was the Jan. 30 taping of a WTTW-TV "Soundstage" special, "David Amram & Friends," for which Steve sang Amram's "Summer Nights and Winter Rain" and helped with a typical Amram make-a-song from topics tossed out by the studio audience. "Man, that little cat's beautiful," another guest, Dizzy Gillespie, told Amram afterward. "He can sure play and sing his ass off."

Steve persevered with the Prine sessions at Chicago Recording Company, but they were no breeze. While Steve was "overwhelmed with excitement," he also was constantly on edge to obey Prine's working style, says Hank Neuberger, project engineer. "Steve really found his production method, and it was entirely about serving the song," he says. "Once he had a rhythm track, he would take a lot of time to embellish it with a little embroidery to try and make the songs come alive. But if it got away from the song, if Prine was uncomfortable, he'd dial it back, throw it away and try it another style. So there was tremendous sensitivity that makes it the most sympathetic production John ever got."

Half the songs Prine brought to the sessions fairly screamed for sympathy, given that they referenced or hinted at his divorce or feelings of pointlessness. This didn't escape Steve's notice, says Howard Levy, who contributed piano and accordion on a pair of songs. Levy recalls Steve telling Prine, "I want you to write something a little more cheerful for this album, because these songs are so depressing you're going to have to give out a razor blade with each record."

In many ways, Steve's intensity inundated the sessions. "That studio with Steve in it was never big enough," says Johnny Burns, electric guitarist on several tracks. "He was like a pingpong ball in a microwave. Absolute energy. Total chaos, this karmic chaos." He invited suggestions, says drummer Tom Radtke, and quickly determined whether they fit. "He didn't make you feel like you had screwed up or you were wasting his time," he says. "It was nice give and take." But Steve's focus nevertheless was riveting. "You could see the wheels turning," says singer Diane Holmes. "You couldn't ignore him," says autoharpist Tyler Wilson. "It was a whole other side of Steve," says fiddler Dave Prine, John's older brother. "To me, Steve was always the lovable, funny guy who made you laugh no matter what was going on. But all of a sudden he went into this heavy-duty producer mode. He could be a tyrant when he got into it. Boy, you put him in charge, and his Napoleon hat came out."

Steve's passion was matched by Prine's, to the point where the two broke into a wee-hours, post-session argument about the recording in the back corner of the Earl of Old Town — oddly enough, while folksinger Jeff Jones performed Prine's gentle "Hello in There." At one point, Steve grabbed Prine by the shoulders, and Prine shouted back, "Goddamn it, I don't want to do it that way! Why can't you fuckin' understand!" The tiff was getting louder by the minute. "You

> **All of a sudden he went into this heavy-duty producer mode. He could be a tyrant when he got into it. Boy, you put him in charge, and his Napoleon hat came out.**
> **DAVE PRINE**

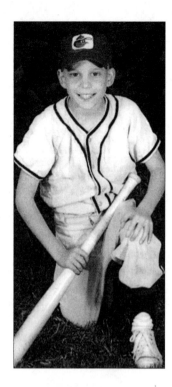

Leukemia patient Alan Brin's connection with Steve was instant, says Alan's mother, Marcia: "I said to Steve, 'I'd like to introduce you to my son. You and he have something in common.' He saw Alan's bald head, and Steve knew immediately what I meant."
(Photo courtesy of
Marcia and Harvey Brin)

52: The Chicago musicians Steve recruited for the Prine LP became the hub for the Famous Potatoes, Prine's touring backup band in the late 1970s and early 1980s.

could just see the eight people in the Earl torn between watching Jeff sing and watching these two folk icons kill each other," says Johnny Burns. Finally, doorman Gus Johns quieted the pair, and Prine said, "Oh, sorry. We're just working out something here."

Softening the intensity was the constellation of accompanists whom Steve assembled, ranging from a dozen Chicagoans [52] to the Bay Area's Jim Rothermel, who supplied delightful pennywhistle, saxophone and clarinet solos and touches throughout, and Los Angeles heartthrob Jackson Browne, who sang backup on one song. "Even though Steve had so many people coming in and out working on different stuff, he had a vision for how he heard it coming together," Radtke says. "It just seemed to have a nice direction and a flow." Part of the direction came from Steve's constant consultation with Joel Dorn, a connection that Steve kept secret from all concerned, even Prine. "I was the sounding board on that album," Dorn said. "We talked every night on the phone, and he played me everything he did, but we kept it quiet because I was such a persona non grata."

The finished product — highlighted by the upbeat and highly listenable "Fish & Whistle" and "That's the Way That the World Goes Round" — reflected the collaboration and vision. "At night, I'd go home not thinkin' that we had anything from the studio," Prine says, "but when Steve mixed the whole thing and played it for me, here he gave me a beautiful record. Steve didn't have to prove his friendship to me, but that's where he came through." Steve agreed. "Absolutely the best work I've done yet," Steve said a year later in an interview with CBS Radio music commentator Peter O.E. Bekker. "Fortunately, John brought fabulous performances. A friendship can be on the line, and at least I didn't screw up John's stuff."

It couldn't have hurt that Steve had extended a hand of generosity during the Prine sessions to a pint-sized leukemia patient from the northwest suburb of Morton Grove. On the evening of Dec. 29, 1977, Marla Brin, a 17-year-old fan of Steve, persuaded her mother to take her and her younger brother to the new Niles branch of Laury's Discount Records, where Steve was signing copies of "Say It in Private." While the public did not know of Steve's leukemia, Marla had learned of it through the grapevine, so his disease was of special interest to her 9-year-old brother, Alan, who was receiving treatment at Children's Memorial Hospital on Chicago's North Side. It didn't take long for Alan's and Marla's mother, Marcia, to send the signal.

"I got Steve's attention for just a minute, and Alan was bald and wearing a baseball cap," Marcia Brin says. "I said to Steve, 'I'd like to introduce you to my son. You and he have something in common.' He saw Alan's bald head, and Steve knew immediately what I meant. So Alan and I waited until after the crowd thinned out, and then Steve talked to Alan, and we just connected. Alan was a very open little boy. He was not the least bit shy. He would speak to anybody. By the time we left the record store, he was sitting on Steve's lap, and they were the best of friends."

This led to an invitation by Steve for Alan and his family to visit one of the

Prine sessions. "They allowed us to come into the engineer's room and check out the equipment," Marcia Brin says. "Alan was pushing the buttons."

Shortly after the visit, in April 1978, Alan's leukemia relapsed, and he flew to Seattle for a bone-marrow transplant (sister Marla was the marrow donor) at the Fred Hutchinson Cancer Research Center. Steve telephoned Alan there to offer encouragement, which impressed Marcia Brin: "We couldn't get over how nice Steve was."

Hope for Alan's survival, however, soon ran out. [53] His death from post-transplant CMV pneumonia on June 18 came as a blow — not unlike the severity of the metaphorical setbacks Prine sang of in what became his LP's title song. Describing "being brought down to zero" and trapped in "your very own chain of sorrow," the tune became "Bruised Orange." Prine says he chose the word "orange" because he likes the colors of autumn and Halloween, and he ate oranges "by the dozen" as a child. "It just came up as somethin' that's really sweet and delicate and gettin' bruised just by bein' mishandled," he says. In short, the orange symbolized the human heart.

For Steve, oranges held a similar meaning, as more of a life force. Though his leukemia was not active, Steve understood that vigilance was a necessity. Like many millions, Steve knew of the longstanding advice of Nobel Prize-winning scientist and peace activist Linus Pauling that high doses of Vitamin C (ascorbic acid) helped fight colds and other ailments. In 1976, Pauling co-authored a well-publicized follow-up study extending his counsel to cancer. In findings later debunked, Pauling said that cancer patients treated with mega-doses of C survived three to four times longer than those who did not ingest such supplements. Steve sought the Vitamin C offered by oranges in the hope of keeping his disease in remission.

"He devoured oranges," says Tyler Wilson's wife Joan, "because he was told that it was something he could do besides medication." Howard Levy says the breakfasts that Steve prepared for visitors to his Evanston home always included fresh-squeezed orange juice. "He was way big into oranges," adds Jim Tullio. "If he didn't have another orange, he'd sit there and just chew on the skins." [54]

Steve also took his penchant for oranges on the road. Vince McGarry, engineer for the "Say It in Private" LP in Manhattan, says that to each session Steve brought three oranges and "chowed down" on them. Steve's standard concert rider — the contract provision spelling out items to be provided backstage — included oranges and orange and grapefruit juice. Barbara Kushner, wife of singer/songwriter and show promoter Roland Kushner, recalls a New York show in which Steve had a three-pound bag of oranges in the dressing room. "He had a little suitcase, and he had all this stuff that he was injecting into the oranges," Kushner says. "It was holistic vitamin things. Somebody had set him up with all this stuff. He sat there methodically pushing these concoctions into the oranges and then eating them."

Soon, a different and felicitous kind of fuel would be injected into Steve's professional life — something "wild and crazy." ♩

He was way big into oranges. If he didn't have another orange, he'd sit there and just chew on the skins.
JIM TULLIO

53: Six months after Alan's death, Marcia and husband Harvey Brin started a chapter of the Leukemia Research Foundation in their son's name that has raised more than $4 million. CMV pneumonia is no longer automatically fatal for leukemia patients. Steve's next LP, "High and Outside," released in February 1979, was dedicated to Alan's memory.

54: "I think Steve liked peelin' 'em more than eatin' 'em," Prine says. "He used to peel 'em the same way that George Burns would use a cigar. Steve would peel it, and he'd stop peelin' it and make his point, and then he'd sit down and look down at the orange and start peelin' it again."

The tone of Steve's 1978-80 tours with "the Beatles of comedy," Steve Martin, is reflected in this backstage pass and Mount Rushmore-themed tour sweatshirt — complete with Washington wearing a through-the-head arrow, Jefferson sporting rabbit ears, Roosevelt donning funny-nose glasses and Lincoln modeling balloon headgear.

(Photo by Clay Eals, sweatshirt design by Maple Byrne, sweatshirt and backstage pass courtesy of Jack Lapp)

'This place is on fire, and I know the music has to reflect that'

On death row, a stay of execution can feel like a rebirth, a chance to lead a more inspired and meaningful life. Steve Goodman's life already abounded with activity and significance in the late 1970s. What took awhile to sink in was his pardon.

Like everyone, Steve faced major sorrows (the loss of his dad, declining album sales) and found corresponding joys (new fatherhood, a plunge into record production). Unlike most others, however, the fatal disease of leukemia dogged him endlessly. The remission that had begun in late 1974 did not supply instant relief. "It was always a very cautious thing," says John Prine. "It took him a long time to think he was in remission, to actually think that he'd be around for a good, long time. He was very skeptical." But as his remission gradually became more believable and real, it provided Steve "a physical reprieve and a spiritual release," recalled his wife, Nancy. "He had more energy and control over his life than ever." [1]

A sure sign was Steve's guitar playing, which by spring 1978 had become ferocious. Onstage, the evidence was inescapable. More than ever, he was breaking guitar strings.

Like flat tires for a bicyclist, broken strings for a touring guitarist are an inescapable hazard of the road. More than most musicians, Steve faced this. Though he re-strung his guitar before every show, he broke strings repeatedly. [2] "It was his gorilla guitar technique," says saxophonist Andy Tecson. "He was just so intense. His level of energy and commitment to the audience and music was so extreme that he was always pushing it a little bit, giving it everything he had. If that meant breaking a guitar string, he did it."

Steve knew that what mattered was not the breaking of the string itself. Rather, it was how he would respond.

Some singer/guitarists simply try to keep strumming with a diminished sound. Others halt their song, and their mood shifts to awkward embarrassment as they stumble through an apology while reaching for another guitar and tuning it or fishing around for a new string to replace the broken one. But Steve instinctively knew that the trick was not to let the momentum and charm of his act collapse. Instead of putting his show on hold, he was primed to persevere.

It was his gorilla guitar technique.
ANDY TECSON

1: Nancy Goodman's reflection on Steve's late 1970s state of mind came in her liner notes to the 1988 compilation album, "The Best of the Asylum Years Vol. 1."

2: When Steve changed strings, he saved them for his economical harmonica accompanist Saul Broudy, who also played guitar. Broudy called them DOGS (day-old Goodman strings). Steve's road manager, Steve Cohen, also sent one-show-use strings to a fellow Amazingracer, Danny Einbender. "They were just broken in," Einbender says. "They were ready after one playing, if you ask me."

If a string broke at the close of a song, Steve's answer was to jive his way through a crowd-pleasing final phrase. During his Long Island shows with Pete Seeger and Harry Chapin on Nov. 22, 1976, a string snapped as he came to the end of one of his earliest compositions, so he morphed its final words into: "He had the I don't know where I'm goin' but I'm goin' backstage to change the guitar-string blu-u-ues." At the Boarding House in San Francisco on March 9, 1977, a string sprang during the final line of Steve's encore, which he quickly augmented. "Just as long as baby's out there bustin' somebody else's strings and bubbles," he sang, "everything is gonna be all ri-i-i-ght."

More often, however, string breaks happened mid-song and mid-set. Steve's initial solution was to keep a tuned guitar in reserve. If a string snapped during a lyrical section, he continued singing the words loudly off-mike as he grabbed the second guitar, returning to the mike and seamlessly sustaining the song. If the break came during an instrumental section, as during "You Never Even Call Me by My Name" on April 3, 1977, in Grand Forks, he kept the song alive by singing the guitar part while dashing for the backup guitar. This show-must-go-on tactic delighted audiences unfailingly.

"It's self-defense," Steve told Rick Ansorge of the *Chicago Lakes Countryside*, during his Feb. 22-24, 1978, run at Harry Hope's in Cary, Illinois, and after a first show in which four strings had broken. "I just refuse to let it mess anything up," he said. "You don't have time to think up there. 'Cause if you think about it, it's disastrous. You just keep going." Grinning, he added, "I learned that from, ah, Yogi Bear." Frustration lurked beneath his humor, however. "I have not developed a light enough touch that also gives the sound I like to hear on the guitar," Steve admitted, "so I'm about ready to go in the cave and relearn to hold the pick or something."

Instead of tempering his guitar technique, however, Steve found himself testing his talent for improvisation. A rigorous trial came during his quartet of shows with Jethro Burns on March 3-4, 1978, at the Mariah Coffeehouse at Michigan State University in East Lansing.

By any measure, the Mariah engagement was a virtuoso collection of performances for Steve, who breezily bared the breadth of his repertoire. In each of his four shows, he played more than 22 songs, inserting medleys of fondly recalled tunes and giving them fresh affection. In the early show on March 3, he strolled through the Joe Turner shouter "Shake, Rattle and Roll" and segued to another 1950s classic, the Chords' doo-wop "Sh-boom," noting it was written "before the white guys stole it." In the late show, he turned from "That Old Gang of Mine" to oldies "Blue Suede Shoes" and "I Think We're Alone Now." In the first show the next night, he linked two gospel tunes, "I Saw the Light" and the frenetic "I'm Saved," to the sardonic English music-hall ballad "Lunatic Asylum" and "the best hangover song I ever heard," the a cappella "On a Monday Morning." He saved the most extensive medley for the final show: Gene Vincent's "Lotta Lovin'," Roy Orbison's "Dream Baby," the Temptations' "Don't Look Back" and "My Girl," culminating with a raucous "Hang on Sloopy."

The magic was in more than the medleys, however. Steve slyly referenced the disco-dance craze by using brief versions of the Bee Gees' "Stayin' Alive" (in reverential falsetto) and "How Deep Is Your Love" to introduce "Would You Like to Learn to Dance?" Similarly, he and Burns vamped through Rossini's "William Tell Overture" and the "Dueling Banjos" theme before launching into "Jessie's Jig." Steve experimented with a gentle guitar line for his usually a cappella "Ballad of Penny Evans." He also trotted out two John Prine songs from the "Bruised Orange" LP he was producing and debuted a quiet one of his own — a wry meditation on interconnectedness inspired by best-selling *Roots* author Alex Haley's "Tonight Show" presentation of Johnny Carson's genealogy back to the year 1521 — called "Family Tree." ("As the leaves grow higher and higher, we must be on the lookout for a forest fire.") [3]

But as panoramic as were his Mariah shows, Steve could not avoid breaking strings. In fact, the first popped string came during the first show's first song, "In the Middle of an Island." Grabbing his replacement guitar and finishing the tune, he kidded, "Things are falling apart all around us, even as we stand here." The next night, at the end of his first show, a string snapped during "Rocky Top," and he left Burns to fill with mandolin for a few bars as he found his second guitar. "Jethro Burns on the mandolin, folks," Steve said dryly afterward. "Didn't break a thing."

Midway through his final show, however, his backup strategy backfired. Finishing "Does Your Chewing Gum Lose Its Flavor (on the Bedpost Overnight)?" with a flourish, Steve heard the telltale "sproing." As he lurched for his backup guitar, he chanted the bouncy, mantra-like Leadbelly blues, "Take This Hammer (Carry It to the Captain)," and eventually returned to the microphone strumming on the replacement. But just two minutes and five verses into "Hammer," a string broke on the backup. All Steve had left was his voice:

> *Oh well-a, well-a, sing a cappella*
> *Well-a, well-a, sing a cappella*
> *Well-a, well-a, sing a cappella*
> *Both guitars are gone, both guitars are gone*

Steve vamped through two more ad-lib verses about how the spotlight was making him perspire, then extracted himself by bringing Burns to the stage, which bought him a minute or so to replace the broken strings. Escaping a major faux pas, he emerged with his showmanship intact. But he also knew he needed to devise a more foolproof scheme to keep broken strings from breaking his show. The discovery dawned on Steve at the time that he needed it the most.

The time came on (or soon after) the first night that he opened for nothing less than a show-biz phenomenon — the likes of which today's America, with its widening and compartmentalized media, probably will never see again. He was relatively young, 32, but gray-streaked hair gave him an air of maturity. His material was wacky, but a short haircut and white suit gave him a straight-laced look. He was a stand-up comic but also a talented musician. By early 1978, he

Things are falling apart all around us, even as we stand here.
STEVE GOODMAN

3: Of the origin of "Family Tree," Steve told Larry Kelp of the *Oakland Tribune*, "All of a sudden I've got three kids. So this is it. And I wonder, what can I say to kids who are, like, 15 and 16? Maybe to tell them to look at pictures and films of past generations and look at the faces of people who came out of that, because we're all part of their protoplasm, the family of man." The song was released 28 years later in 2006, on the posthumous "Live at the Earl of Old Town" CD.

For John McEuen, whose
brother Bill managed Steve
Martin and who twice opened
for Martin, the gig was a nervy
challenge. "They didn't want
just anybody to fill that slot and
do lousy," he says. "They were
trying to make it a good show,
and the slot was open to
anyone who could survive."
(Photo by Alan Messer,
courtesy of Chuck Morris)

had tilted toward the counterculture, having hosted "Saturday Night Live" four times, but he also had appealed to the mainstream, having appeared 20 times as a comic or guest host for "The Tonight Show with Johnny Carson." He straddled so many strata that he had become the definition of "household word." His name, too, was Steve — Steve Martin.

From teen-age jobs at the Disneyland magic shop and Knott's Berry Farm, Martin had worked his way into writing for "The Smothers Brothers Comedy Hour" and other TV shows. Often appearing in on-screen skits or playing the banjo, he also built an early-1970s following in clubs and by opening for the Nitty Gritty Dirt Band and the Carpenters. Mocking himself and the concept of entertainment became his game. As Martin later reflected, his secret was to play a character who "assumed that everything he said was brilliant" and "had total confidence, with nothing to back it up."

Reinforced by a 1976 "On Location" concert film aired 15 times on the newly national satellite cable network Home Box Office, Martin's celebrity swelled. His debut album, "Let's Get Small," [4] became a hit in the fall of 1977, by which time Martin had exploded. For a mostly youthful demographic, he had become the nation's comic relief — the Carter-era antidote for the gravity that lingered from the Watergate scandal and the Vietnam War. He headlined in college-town arenas normally reserved for rock bands, outdrawing such acts as Fleetwood Mac while embedding in the nation's consciousness the satiric/ironic exclamations "I've got happy feet," "I am a wild and crazy guy" and especially "Excu-u-use me!" Many in his sold-out audiences of 10,000 to 20,000 wore the goofy headgear for which Martin had become known — an arrow through the temples, rubber-nose glasses, bunny ears and animals made from sausage-shaped balloons. Because of his ubiquity, Martin's concerts were not opportunities for discovery so much as they were cacophonous festivals of adoration. Fans' jaws ached afterward from riotous laughter.

Martin's arena shows, however, ran barely an hour. To bolster an illusion of substance, to accommodate latecomers and to provide an intermission to sell T-shirts and other merchandise, Martin needed an opening act. "If you don't have that intermission, it's not like going to a show," says the Nitty Gritty Dirt Band's John McEuen, whose brother Bill managed Martin. "But they didn't want just anybody to fill that slot and do lousy. They were trying to make it a good show, and the slot was open to anyone who could survive."

Finding a match wasn't a simple matter, says Martin's road manager, Kenneth "Maple" Byrne. It couldn't be another comedian who would conflict with Martin's act. A musical act wouldn't be home free, either. "People knew they were coming to a comedy concert, and music was kind of a back seat," Byrne says. Martin did play banjo, "but he didn't do as much of that on TV as he did in concert," Byrne says. "For people who just saw him on TV, it was a prop." Still, a musical act was the best bet for an opener — but not a band, which would be too loud and whose equipment would take too long to dismantle during intermission. "One person was logically all you could do," Byrne says.

4: Sales of "Let's Get Small" mirrored the comic's rise to fame. The LP was released in September 1975, but it didn't hit the *Billboard* LP chart until fall 1977, peaking at #10 on Nov. 26 and Dec. 3.

"It had to be a single act — a single act that could handle that crowd."

The challenge, Martin says, was formidable. "My audience at that point would be the worst for any performer to go in front of," he says. "I'm not criticizing the audience. It was just a tough crowd. This was when the crowds were enormous, and they were really there to see me. It was a very hard spot to fill. I'm not saying there weren't plenty of people who wanted to do it. But there weren't many people who could."

John McEuen tried it a couple of times, as did singer/songwriter Megan McDonough and autoharpist Bryan Bowers. "I died in front of that crowd," Bowers says. "I got ate up and spit out." The mainstay opener in late 1977 and early 1978 became former Lovin' Spoonful sparkplug John Sebastian, who had returned to the charts with his theme for the TV show "Welcome Back, Kotter."

"During that year," Sebastian says, "the white suit and bunny-ears, crazy-guy thing sprung, and by the end of the year it was a pop-concert vibe, an hysterical fan trip. It was a terrific opportunity and one that you could make work for you, but you had to make sure that your time was filled with information. You couldn't slow down and get introspective or you'd lose 'em." Sebastian has no complaints about his run with Martin — "I can't exactly make it out to be the Romans and the lions," he says — but he allows that more than once he was booed by the rabid, "We want Steve!" crowds. "But I got 'em," he says. "That's just being patient. You have to show your stuff in the midst of a boo or two or a bottle cap or two, and if you do that, the tide of the audience will turn."

Patience didn't always save Sebastian, however. The booing wouldn't stop when he opened for Martin in Minneapolis, says guitarist Don Venne, who attended the show. When the din became unbearable, Martin walked onstage and, with controlled anger, told the crowd, "If you don't stop this, I'm not gonna do a show. This is my friend, and I've asked him to be here, and you need to respect what he's doing." Then Martin walked offstage, and Sebastian finished his set to a more respectful reception.

"There were times when it didn't work, and sometimes it was really bad," says John McEuen, who became the catalyst for an enduring solution. Lunching with Martin's booking agent, Marty Klein, McEuen told him, "Look, you know you're having a problem getting an opening act that can do the job. In my 12 short years in this business, there's only one guy who can hit the consciousness of Steve's audience, keep them entertained, be funny, go over and probably get an encore occasionally."

That guy was Steve Goodman.

Klein agreed to ask Martin to give Steve a try for a few dates. Martin was amenable. "I knew who he was," Martin says. "I knew he wrote 'City of New Orleans,' but I didn't know him much. I was just in a fog those days."

Steve had been planning with Nancy to set aside family time after his tours with Burns and album sessions with Prine. "We'd been working five nights a week in the studio and moonlighting on weekends playing the guitar," he told

John Sebastian persevered through his opening gigs for Steve Martin by demonstrating patience "in the midst of a boo or two or a bottle cap or two."
(Photo by Catherine Sebastian)

Carol Wallace of the *Philadelphia Daily News*. "I was just about fried." But the sudden chance to join Martin — in the early spring, just when PBS-TV affiliates across the nation were broadcasting the Steve Goodman episode of "Austin City Limits" that was recorded the previous fall, as well as his "Soundstage" concert with David Amram — couldn't have been timed better.

Still, Steve was reticent. When he first heard of the gig from Al Bunetta, it was by phone at Somebody Else's Troubles. There, Steve told Harry Waller, "I don't think it's a good idea." But it didn't take long for Steve to change his mind. "This was a don't-miss kind of thing," he said of opening for Martin. "This guy is like the Beatles of comedy. I knew I'd never get a chance to do anything like this again. It really fell out of the sky. It was a break."

His break began at Texas Tech University in Lubbock on Friday, March 31, 1978, the first night of an 11-day, 15-show tour of the southwestern and southeastern United States, undertaken in a Silver Eagle charter bus leased from the Dirt Band. Furnished with hand-built teakwood couches, a settee and full galley, the spacious vehicle sported eight plush bunks. On board, however, were just four people: the two performers, road manager Byrne and the driver, Jack Lapp, a 28-year-old Vietnam vet from New Jersey who piloted the bus for 400 to 700 miles each day between gigs, from Texas to New Mexico, Missouri, Tennessee, Georgia and back to Texas.

Three days into the trip, Steve carved a self-image for his fellow passengers that fit the tour's tone. The afternoon after an April 2 show in El Paso, Steve crossed the U.S. border into Juarez and returned with a gigantic black sombrero with tiny mirrors attached to its band. Later, while driving the bus east on Interstate 10 toward Dallas, Lapp pulled into a rest stop for water. "The air conditioning had gone out," Lapp says. "We were out in the desert, and it was hotter than hell." Steve grabbed his guitar, donned the broad-brimmed hat, jumped out of the bus, climbed atop a picnic table and serenaded nearby truckers with a Dave Kirby song that country star Charley Pride had popularized eight years prior, "Is Anybody Going to San Antone?" Lapp's April 3 diary entry completed the balmy picture: "Sitting in a rest area with a cool breeze in west

Texas desert, Steve G playing excellent old cowboy tunes wearing sombrero. Made up tune about sitting there playing. Very enjoyable."

On the same day, *Newsweek* hit the newsstands with a cover story certifying Martin's fame. His legs splayed at the knees, his arms stretched diagonally and his face radiating with a loony, toothy grin, the color photo of the white-suited goof was accompanied by large, yellow lettering proclaiming "Comedy's New Face." The nation's hottest star was on tour, and Steve Goodman was along for the ride.

To open for Martin, Steve didn't overhaul his typical set so much as refine it to fit the 30 to 40 minutes he would get with an impatient crowd. Upbeat material — "the loudest, fastest songs I could find" — prevailed. "The Auctioneer" was a must. So were "City of New Orleans," "Chicken Cordon Bleus" and "You Never Even Call Me by My Name," including the cowboy-hat shtick and imitations of country instruments. For his first tune, Steve stuck with singing a good-time standard from a previous generation — usually "Red, Red Robin" — and launching it with an engaging, frenetic acoustic-guitar solo that he began playing the moment he hit the stage.

The immediate difference between Steve and the other openers was clear to Byrne. "Just being good wasn't the criterion," he says. "It was getting 'em with the first song, and he did." Pat Baumgarten, Martin's business manager, also saw the contrast. "McEuen and Sebastian were softer," he says. "With Goodman, there was something in his mind that he had to prove to the audience, that he had to win them over."

Nor did Steve's grip on an audience escape the eye of Martin. "In 30 seconds, as soon as they heard the sound of Steve's guitar, he would have them, and they would be quiet and be listening," he says. "He just had a presence."

To Martin, an accomplished banjo player, Steve's guitar was an invaluable catalyst. "The sound of his guitar was so uplifting," Martin says. "It was kind of simple, done without artifice. Authoritative, confident, really melodic, good chords. He did like to bang on it, but he had a beautiful sound. It was never just noise. It was pure music, and people loved it. He turned them around instantly. It was amazing to see. I loved it. People loved him when they heard it, and they were hearing it for the first time. Most songs or performers they have to get used to, but they really, really liked him. People liked him instantly."

Critics noticed. "With only his guitar, Goodman was magic, converting the Martin lunatics in the audience to the point where they begged him back for an encore," wrote Pete Oppel of the *Dallas Morning News*. "Those familiar with the Martin lunatic fringe know this is no mean trick."

Perhaps ironically, the audience's affinity for Steve didn't stem from fame. Sebastian, well known for his stoned, ingratiating appearance in the 1970 film "Woodstock," had a name with cachet. An announcer could say, "Please welcome John Sebastian" and trigger recognition. Steve, however, despite five albums, national TV exposure and status in the music world, had little renown with the masses — and certainly with most of those pouring into Martin's shows.

> **It was pure music, and people loved it. He turned them around instantly. It was amazing to see. I loved it. People loved him when they heard it, and they were hearing it for the first time.**
> **STEVE MARTIN**

A complicating factor was that he shared the headliner's first name. So he opted for no one to announce his sets and instead let his guitar make the intro.

Ron Crick, who had led the Chicago band Swingshift a year and a half prior, saw the strategy play out during the Martin tour's April 9 stop at Hofheinz Arena in Houston. "The fieldhouse is packed with people with arrows in their heads, and I'm waiting for Steve, waiting for the intro," Crick says. "The lights come down, and Steve walks out, no intro, unassuming, almost looks like he was a roadie, and all of a sudden he starts playing. It took him a couple of seconds for people to kick in, and he won them over."

Steve clued in Crick when the two met at a club later that night.

"What's with the no-intro?" Crick asked.

"Ron, think about it," Steve replied, imitating the effect that an announcer's introduction would have:

"Ladies and gentlemen, here's Steve —"

Instantly the crowd would whoop, whistle, scream.

" — Goodman!"

Just as instantly, the crowd would deflate: "Ohhhh."

"He didn't want to put himself in that situation," Crick says, "and I thought that was pretty slick. I thought it was a great, humble way to enter. You're already the underdog as an opening act, much less opening for Steve Martin and all that craziness, but he pulled it off."

Steve later claimed not to expect anything from Martin's audiences, given that the opposite was true. "It's to my advantage that they're not expecting anything from me," he said. "Then I can get an honest reading of what's happening. If something's not working, I have to figure out what to do."

Steve's impact in the Southern states soon cinched the impression in the minds of everyone — including Martin — that Steve was the comic's ideal counterpart. As *The Washington Post* noted, "Martin may have found the perfect opening act in Steve Goodman, a fine songwriter whose lyrics and performance reflect what (novelist and screenwriter) Thomas McGuane called reversible brain damage." As a result, Steve was invited back for tour after tour with Martin, crisscrossing the continent while Martin's goofy, million-selling hit "King Tut" (capitalizing on a national museum tour of treasures from the ancient Egyptian King Tutankhamun) reached #17 on the *Billboard* Hot 100. The continuing gig with Martin became Steve's dominant career thread for two years through mid-1980 as he racked up an astounding total of more than 200 such show-openers that extended to the end of Martin's stand-up comedy career. [5] Martin knew that in Steve he had found a kindred professional soul.

"The greatest thing about Steve was his nature," Martin says. "He was a happy, up guy. He did not assault the audience. They weren't exhausted by the time I got onstage. It was a perfect match. He was a single act, I was a single act, both playing acoustic instruments. I like economy, and I don't mean financial. He was one guy with a guitar. It was easy. It was simple. And it was somehow in the spirit of my show, too, which was just clean."

> **The greatest thing about Steve was his nature. He was a happy, up guy. He did not assault the audience. They weren't exhausted by the time I got onstage. It was a perfect match.**
> **STEVE MARTIN**

5: The only interruption of Steve's streak of Martin openers came Oct. 11, 1978, at New York City's Carnegie Hall. There, Steve gave way to the Blues Brothers – Dan Aykroyd and John Belushi, the wildly successful "Saturday Night Live" graduates of Second City – Belushi from the improv club across the street from Chicago's Earl of Old Town and Aykroyd from its Toronto offshoot.

Drawing Martin's admiration was Steve's attention to eccentric detail, such as the red or green tennis shoes that accompanied his otherwise conventional shirt-and-sport-coat attire. "People really warmed to the tennis shoes since they were so unpretentious," Martin says. Steve's between-song patter — almost that of a comic himself — also found Martin's favor. "He was wry," Martin says. "It had to be a delicate kind of comedy to be compatible with me. It couldn't be hit-'em-over-the-head, because I was going to do that. He just was charming." Perhaps most of all, Martin was relieved by Steve's mastery of the unwieldy crowds. "I have a sympathy for performers, and I hate it if they're having a hard time," he says, "so I was glad that he could control them and actually entertain them."

Steve held other tangible benefits for Martin's tours, including his flexibility. "He was a low-maintenance kind of act," Baumgarten says. "He was the kind of guy if you got in a jam, you could call him and he'd try to get to places. He'd try to make it work, and he liked to work."

The eagerness made sense because the Martin tours, with their bulging audiences and glitzy stature, held rewards for Steve both financial and intangible. "I got to play to more people in the last month and a half than I did in two years," he told Wallace of the *Philadelphia Daily News* in May 1978. "It really is the luckiest thing that's ever happened to me, in that I'm getting to go out there and see all kinds of people who never heard these songs — and they seem to be enjoying themselves."

"That was the best thing that ever happened to Steve," says his manager, Al Bunetta, who joined Steve at many of the Martin dates. "For (more than) two years we toured and made great money." The remuneration was not insignificant. In 1978, the Martin tours were grossing $45,000 to $95,000 per show, from which Martin was becoming a millionaire with each two- to four-week stretch. By comparison, Steve's own monetary rewards were minor league, but he earned between $1,000 and $2,000 per set, a notable take for steady work as an opener. (Steve later told Scottish storyteller Johnniy Morris, "If I made what Steve Martin makes in a year, I could pay you $500,000 a year just to answer my phone.")

The singular success of Steve's pairing with Martin — what wags called (and Steve confirmed) "throwing a Christian to the lions" — confounded some of Steve's colleagues. "That should never have happened," says Tom Rush's guitarist, Trevor Veitch. "On paper, it didn't compute. That was taking your life in your hands."

If Steve braced for the enormity of the task, he rarely let on. "I'm not used to walking out onstage and seeing arrows," he told Wallace of the *Daily News*, "but I know why they're out there, and I think it's great." To Baumgarten, the business manager, Steve appeared "absolutely fearless" in his opening role.

But Chuck Morris, Denver promoter who booked the Martin tour for a show 15 miles west at Red Rocks Park on June 17, 1978, discovered otherwise. Just before the lights dimmed, Morris and Steve sat at the side of the stage

> **That should never have happened. On paper, it didn't compute. That was taking your life in your hands.**
> **TREVOR VEITCH**

Denver concert promoter Chuck Morris was surprised to find Steve shaking nervously before his Steve Martin opening set for a crowd of 18,000 at Red Rocks Park. "He never realized how good he was," Morris says. "It probably made him great because he was always on his toes."

(Photo courtesy of Chuck Morris)

gazing at the 18,000 people filling the amphitheater. "There were about 1,000 people in front with balloons on their heads screaming for Steve, and it wasn't Stevie Goodman," Morris says. "They had the phony glasses with the big nose, and it was nuts. Stevie was shaking, man. I was a good friend by then and was saying, 'Don't worry.' He never realized how good he was. It probably made him great because he was always on his toes. But he was so scared to go out, and he went out there and destroyed the place. He had the place in stitches."

Oddly, the expanse of the arenas and other massive settings diminished any perception of Steve's short stature and capitalized on his talent. "He spoke directly to people," John McEuen says. "You could see his eyes from 30, 50 rows away. He had a smile that hit the back of the room. He was loud. He wasn't an introverted, soft, folk-music singer. He was vibrant with life, and he put that through the mike and his body movements. Once you get 10 rows away, it doesn't matter how big somebody is. They all kind of look the same. He was also the James Cagney of guitar playing: 'Take this, you dirty rat.' Cagney wasn't very tall, either, but you never doubted his attitude. It was Steve's attitude that got the music across."

Steve's aggressiveness also resulted in broken guitar strings. Before Martin's demanding crowds, he said later, such a lapse gave him a feeling of "terror." Snapping a string in Columbia, Missouri, during his eighth Martin opener, Steve even resorted to the trick he had improvised three years earlier in Mobile, Alabama, singing "Mammy" into his guitar mike.

Soon, however, Steve devised a new way to cope with the challenge. He seemed to take a cue from Martin, whose act included ridiculous magic tricks (with a dime, hardly visible to those in the fifth row, let alone the 50th) and fits of hysteria (gyrating wildly around the stage, or grabbing the mike to enjoy a feigned electrical shock). Steve's broken-string solution also invoked magic and hysteria, but it was something that apparently few — if any — performers have ever replicated. It was the definition of audacity:

When a string broke, Steve kept singing. But instead of continuing the song, he improvised rhyming lyrics for a new one on the spot, in the same key and rhythm as the interrupted tune. Meanwhile, road-manager Byrne rushed onstage and fanned an assortment of six new strings within Steve's reach. Steve picked out the correct replacement and strung it through its proper peg on the guitar and wound it up — never missing a beat of his improvised song. The words of the made-up tune addressed how he had broken a string, what he was doing to fix it and anything else he happened to observe at the moment, delivered with self-deprecation and laughter. Once he got the string in place and tuned, Steve seamlessly segued to the original song, resuming at the same point he had interrupted it, and he finished the tune to thunderous applause.

"That's two diverse, opposite things, to entertain an audience and do a technical procedure," says jazz violinist Randy Sabien, who saw Steve pull it off several times. "That's like a dentist filling a cavity and tuning a car at the same time. Or changing your pants while doing heart surgery."

Virtuoso shtick, it also was rich with risk and suspense. Could Steve keep making up lyrics that rhymed until he finished the re-stringing and tuning? Under pressure, would he draw a blank? Audiences, on edge, were rapt. "Every second or third night, this thing would happen," says Chicago recording engineer Hank Neuberger. "The crowd would go nuts because you never see anyone do that." [6]

Its appeal wasn't lost on Steve Martin. "That was almost a regular bit," he says. "In fact, when a string didn't break, we were losing a bit out of his show." When it did occur, Martin shrewdly capitalized on it in his own set. "Didn't you love that Steve Goodman?" Martin would tell the audience. Holding up the snapped string, Martin would add mischievously, "Did he pull that phony broken guitar-string trick on all of you guys?"

Martin's tongue-in-cheek implication — along with the unfailing success of Steve's masterstroke — eventually spurred Steve's musician friends and fans to speculation. Some wondered if Steve purposely strummed his strings so hard that one would snap. Others suspected he used old strings or filed them to make them break more easily. Some surmised the routine was a brash contrivance that Steve employed to show off his gift for improvisation. But others, citing the intense difficulty of such a tour de force, couldn't imagine anyone — Steve included — intentionally inciting such a dilemma.

"I'd like to clear that up," says road-manager Byrne. "Goodman changed strings, or I changed strings for him, every show," he says, quashing the notion that Steve consciously played with used or defective strings. "If he did two shows a night, he changed them between shows." Byrne does say that the shtick was contrived to the extent that Steve could have simply switched to a backup guitar. "But what he did was better than picking up another guitar and finishing the song," he says. "He definitely didn't want a second guitar, so if that's the contrived part of it, I will cop to that. He definitely had in mind that if a string broke, he could handle it. But did he break strings on purpose? I don't believe that. He joked onstage about his 'delicate, birdlike technique,' but it wasn't like there was anything wrong with the guitar or his technique. It was just something that was going to happen. If he really wanted to break strings, he wouldn't have changed them every show."

Steve's strings generally snapped during louder tunes like "You Never Even Call Me by My Name" and not "the subtler stuff," Byrne says. The more upbeat or funny the song, the more effectively he could respond to a broken string with ad-libs. "He took some pride in being able to do that, and well he should have," Byrne says. "He obviously knew that it went over. You couldn't not be aware of that. It served the show, and it served the material. It helps if you have songs that can stop and start like that. Most people don't have that kind of material and couldn't carry it out and not just have things completely fall apart, which is an important thing. The momentum is obviously the whole crux."

The stunt quickly set Steve apart from other performers, many who today marvel at what they consider unattainable showmanship. "For most of us," says

> Didn't you love that Steve Goodman? Did he pull that phony broken guitar-string trick on all of you guys?
> **STEVE MARTIN**

6: Los Angeles attorney and Goodman fan David Schulman aptly pegs Steve's broken-string shtick as a mix of two roles from early Yiddish theater: the badchan (the emcee or jester) and the tummler (the organizer who pulls things together). Both personas, he says, draw on "the Yiddish capacity to laugh and go on in the face of tragedy."

Louisiana oilman Tony Andress befriended Steve during the Martin/Goodman tours, finding himself drawn to Steve's song about his father: "You can't listen to a song like 'My Old Man' and not understand that there was something good running in this guy."

(Photo courtesy of Tony Andress)

7: The oilman also revered Steve's "You Never Even Call Me by My Name," particularly when Steve borrowed a cowboy hat from the audience. "It'd be about four sizes too big for him, and he could just about spin around inside of it, and the hat would never move."

guitarist Trevor Veitch, "if you broke a string onstage, it was a minor tragedy. Everything would grind to a halt. For him, a broken string was an opportunity, like 'Oh, boy, I broke a string, here we go!' " Folksinger Mark Ross, a friend since 1967 days in New York, opts for a baseball metaphor. A string break for Steve, he says, "was like your designated hitter or relief pitcher. You keep him sitting on the bench until you need him. The opportunity arises, and there it is."

Steve embraced other risks while opening for Martin. In one of four shows April 4-5, 1978, at the Music Hall in Dallas, Steve sang his quiet tribute to Nancy, "Old Fashioned," a move he likened to an ancient parable. "It's like there are two doors on the stage, and if you play one song, a beautiful lady will walk out, and if you play the other, you get the tiger," Steve told *Times-Herald* reporter Sean Mitchell. "When I played 'Old Fashioned' last night, I knew the tiger was coming, but I thought, what the hell, somebody's going to be listening."

Another non-"wild and crazy" move was to lace many of his sets with his most vulnerable and aching song, "My Old Man." Its power reduced even the rowdiest of Martin's audiences to near-silence. "That was great, fabulous," Martin says. "We all loved that song. It was a beauty. It was poignant and lyrical, so direct. Sentimental without being corny."

"My Old Man" also ensnared a wealthy friend of Martin's, oilman Tony Andress, who owned a Louisiana-based refinery with offices in eight states and had met Martin when he hired him in mid-1977 to perform at a company party in Abilene. Andress flew his private plane to more than 50 of Martin's shows and soon met his opening act backstage. For Andress, "My Old Man" was a moving bonus. "Pretty soon," Martin says, "Tony was waiting for that song more than he was my show."

"The song was kind of a bond between us," Andress says of Steve. "A lot of times he'd get emotional with it, and I could feel and understand what it meant to him. It meant the same to me about my father, who was still alive then, and it touched me about my children's needs."

Before each show Andress attended, he asked Steve to perform "My Old Man" for him privately, and Steve did so. "It got to where he'd just come in and say, 'OK, sit down. I'm ready to do it again.' You can't listen to a song like 'My Old Man' and not understand that there was something good running in this guy." 7

The link to Andress went beyond a single song. It exemplified a trait that many found in Steve. "He was just so down-to-earth," Andress says. "No one had any reason to be talking with me or visiting with me. I represented nothing — a guy in the oil business who didn't have a clue. Steve quickly sought me out and wanted to know everything about me: 'Tell me what you're doing.' I'm sitting there interested more in being into him, but I can't hardly do it because he's such a neat person that he's wanting to know me. We did a lot of talking. He wasn't all wrapped up in himself. He knew there was a lot more to life than

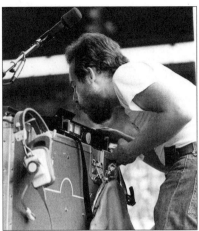

The role of road manager Maple Byrne was crucial on the Steve Martin/Steve Goodman tours, whether he was (upper left) testing the output cord for Martin's banjo (with Martin rearing back in mock alarm) or (above) testing the onstage cassette deck used for sound effects and music cues. The crowds drawn by the Martin phenomenon — as during the 1979 New York State Fair in Syracuse (left) — were vocal and seemed to extend forever.

(Photos by Bill Thompson)

Steve, who often sat playing guitar in the jump seat of the tour bus during all-night trips between shows, marveled with driver Jack Lapp late on May 3, 1978, when the two spotted the Aurora Borealis, as shown in this drawing from the time. When Lapp slowed the bus at a toll booth, however, the toll taker shrieked, thinking Steve's guitar was a shotgun.

(1978 illustration by Jack Lapp)

'what my last song did.' He knew that other people have something a little significant he could learn from. Some of those (entertainers) won't even acknowledge that you're around, but he was very different, a thoughtful person in every regard. His mind ran deep."

Steve noticed in Martin a similar intelligence, but it took awhile. The two generally separated once they had reached a city. Martin, shielded in limos, often visited art museums incognito. "Steve Martin was basically untouchable, unless you were the mayor's daughter and had a personal connection," says Lapp, the bus driver. "He was royalty, and the rest of us were the leftovers, the working people." In contrast, Steve frequented cafés, bars and other public areas largely unnoticed. After shows, he engaged in late-night jams with a local rock band in El Paso and a country group in Albuquerque. In Binghamton, New York, he played the last few songs of a late set at SUNY with Bonnie Raitt.

Where the performing pair came to know each other was on the bus. "Steve Martin loved the bus because it gave him a privacy area," Lapp says. There, in contrast to the raucous stereotype of a mobile party, the foursome listened to recorded music while Lapp drove and the others talked, read newspapers, played cards or chess and slept. "Stevie G," as he was sometimes called, worked crossword puzzles, checked Cubs box scores and scribbled in a notebook of half-written songs. [8]

For long stretches, solitude reigned. At times, marijuana was passed around, but discreetly out of respect to the headliner, who only occasionally feigned smoking it. "He's a quiet, strong-willed guy," Steve said of Martin in a radio interview. "He can't do what he does onstage 24 hours a day. Nobody can." Lapp adds, "People would have imagined that he was the wild and crazy guy, but he wasn't. It was all an act."

"We got along," Byrne says, "which was very important because it was a courtesy to bring the opening act on the bus. It made sense, it was efficient, but if we hadn't gotten along, it would have been rough. They both were making enough that they could have done their own travel, but it made sense to do it the way we did it, to just roll in with four people and roll out with the dough."

Martin can't recall if Steve's leukemia was an open topic on the bus. "I might have known all along, but it was in remission," he says. "You want to sweep that stuff under the rug. But he never made you feel sorry for him, ever. He made you feel (so) relaxed that you didn't even think about it. If it's not bothering him, then it's not bothering me."

While Martin recalls a few instrumental jams with Steve, most of Steve's on-bus guitar playing came in the still of the night. Steve perched with his guitar on the front stoop (or "jump seat") next to Lapp and softly played song after song — oldies, baseball tunes, his own compositions — as the miles rolled by. He often told Lapp how he missed Nancy and his daughters and wished he were home. Yet Steve also made the bus into a home of sorts, documenting its journey in fanciful sketches on the cardboard shirt-backs left from regular stops at dry-cleaners. [9]

8: An occasional addition to the bus was Lapp's companion, Debbie Nystrom, who kept the refrigerator stocked, tidied up the galley and served as a low-profile flight attendant. "I tried to make it a refuge," she says. Because of Steve's leukemia-related nausea, Nystrom often brought him 7-Up and crackers. Particularly soothing, she says, were her handmade oatmeal cookies.

9: In one sketch, Steve drew the bus in profile as if it were a pair of funny-nose glasses, the wheels serving as lenses. In another, Steve showed the bus rolling through a Texas town that sported a variety of wacky storefronts: "The Fried Food Autograph Restaurant," "Heart Break Hotel: No TV, No Phone," "Clothes: Paternity Suits a Specialty," "College of Drugs: Classes in (1) Mindlessness, (2) Idiot Wisecracks," "Reverb Gym: 4 Shows Tonight!" One business offering banjos, books, swimming and tennis was "Closed." Signs along the thoroughfare read, "Road to Ruin" and (with a straight-ahead arrow) "Poverty."

10: "Truck Drivin' Man," a hit for Terry Fell in 1954 and a three-chord country standard ever since, was a staple when Steve jammed with musicians with whom he hadn't rehearsed. In shows broadcast on the radio, he slyly labeled the song a "feces-kicker."

11: Martin, Byrne, Lapp and Elias say it is possible that while riding on the bus Steve contributed stray lines or ideas that Martin used in his act or in "The Jerk." But they recall no specifics. "Nobody was really afraid to put in their two cents' worth," Byrne says, "but it was kind of a foreign field to us."

One overnight trek, eastbound along the New York State Thruway from Niagara Falls to Hartford, Connecticut, was both magical and maniacal. While Martin and Byrne slept, Steve ceased his guitar playing as he and Lapp got a lengthy view of the Aurora Borealis, the rarely seen dancing sheets of color that some call the Northern Lights. The two were marveling at such visual fortune as Lapp slowed the bus to stop at a tollbooth. When Lapp opened his sliding-glass window to pay the toll, the woman in the booth shrieked at Steve's guitar. "She thought he had a shotgun in his hands and was pointing it at her and we were going to rob her," Lapp says. "Then she saw what it was, and she laughed."

Steve's picking was such a fixture on the bus that in one overnight stint Byrne held the bus' CB-radio mike so that Steve could sing and play "Truck Drivin' Man" [10] for the airwaves. When Steve finished the song, a message came back from a nearby trucker: "That's a purty good rendition there, good buddy, but where the hell did ya learn to play and sing and drive all at the same time?"

The CB radio also had more practical purposes, including early one morning on the Pennsylvania Turnpike when the bus' clearance lights had sent a short into the fuel gauge, making it appear the bus was holding a quarter of a tank more diesel fuel than it actually had. When the tank emptied, the bus sputtered to a stop. Lapp pulled it over and used the CB to hail a trucker who picked him up and drove him to a truck stop for fuel. Martin, Steve and Byrne were left sleeping in the bus for the two hours that Lapp was gone. "Here I left the biggest star sitting on the side of the road, no engine running," Lapp says. Later, after Lapp had gotten the bus moving again, Steve asked him, "Did we stop last night?" Lapp said yes but was embarrassed to disclose the reason. "I got air in my fuel line somehow," he finally told Steve. A week later, Steve figured out the joke. He came up to Lapp, pointed at him and said, "Oh, I get it, air in the fuel line."

For two weeks in September and October of 1978, while Martin's second LP rose to #2 in *Billboard*, the population of the bus grew by 50 percent. Riding along were Al Bunetta and comedy writer Michael Elias, whom Martin had invited along to collaborate with him on stage bits, TV sketches and the script for what became Martin's first film, "The Jerk." [11] Steve marveled at the discipline he saw in Martin during this stretch.

"He's one of the hardest-working people I've ever met," Steve told Philadelphia radio host Gene Shay. "This guy would be doing two shows a night and writing his TV special on the bus in between. I ain't never saw anybody go 24 hours a day at it like that. It's pretty amazing. I wish the guy gets a nice time-out for himself because he's a really good guy. He's just been working his behind off for three years." In an interview with DeKalb radio host Bill Munger in 1980, Steve marveled at Martin's indefatigability. "I was always amazed at not only his energy and his stamina, but just at his perseverance and his ability to not let the audience suffer for the way he was feelin'," Steve said. "That's not an easy gig, the one he has."

Elias, who saw every Martin/Goodman show in that two-week stretch, experienced his own awe at Steve's own resilience as an opener. "Every night, he would come out, and he would end up where they were absolutely enthralled," Elias says. "It was one of the most heroic show-business acts I'd ever seen."

In a sense, Martin had two opening acts. After the initial Goodman set and the intermission, the house lights dimmed, but instead of Martin walking onstage, the audience saw a film on a giant screen. It was a seven-minute, one-joke romp starring Buck Henry, Teri Garr and, in the title role, an addled Martin as "The Absent-Minded Waiter." In the Oscar-nominated short, directed by Carl Gottlieb, Henry escorts Garr to dinner at a fancy restaurant where everything goes wrong, thanks to Martin's feeble memory. Garr's frustration boils but is finally doused when Henry pays for the meal with a $100 bill and Martin supplies Henry with $10,000 cash as change. Audiences roared at Henry's vindication. "The film was guaranteed funny," Elias says, "and Steve (Martin) would come out as the film was ending. He didn't have to worry about getting his first laugh. He already got it." Steve Goodman would not forget the impact of such a film.

Steve's connection with Martin in 1978-80 was constant but not continuous. Breaks of several weeks opened up between legs of the tour, and Steve was far from idle. After a couple of stints on the road with Martin, he made good on a promise to devote time to his family and took Nancy and the three girls, along with Paula Ballan as a nanny, on a late spring 1978 vacation in Acapulco. "He decided that he really wanted to have a rich man's vacation," Ballan says. Their base in Mexico's premier tourist city, the Princess Hotel, filled the bill, with its 15-floor Aztec pyramid-shaped tower, pools and gardens featuring swans, flamingos and tropical birds.

New songs reflected Steve's family focus. Besides "Family Tree," Steve had penned and begun performing "Hand It to You," a bouncy tribute to domestic bliss whose title credited Nancy for his happiness. Typically, he threw wry wordplay into the final verse, in which he noted that when he receives his paycheck, "I've got to hand it to you." [12]

Steve's musical family also beckoned him after the sudden March 17 death at age 77 of Berkeley folksinger Malvina Reynolds. Enough musicians to fill a four-day festival offered to perform at a May 18 memorial concert and political benefit. But organizers narrowed the one-night slate to 10 artists, including Pete Seeger, Country Joe McDonald, Rosalie Sorrels and Steve. The invitation stirred Steve's gratitude, [13] and because the show fell between his Martin trips he could accept. But for Steve, the tribute, befitting the range of Reynolds' constituencies, turned into a nightmare.

In unseasonable 80-degree weather, an overflow crowd of 3,500 trickled through a single entry to Berkeley Community Theater, and the concert, plagued by delayed set-ups and confusion typical of a one-time event, started late and proceeded in fits and spurts until nearly midnight. The Reynolds fans present ranged from devotees of her songs of nonconformity ("Bury Me in My Overalls") and not-so-simple children's tunes ("Magic Penny") to environmentalists

Michael Elias, co-writer of "The Jerk" who rode on the Martin/ Goodman tour bus for two weeks, was amazed by Steve's success as an opener: "It was one of the most heroic show-business acts I'd ever seen."
(Photo courtesy of Michael Elias)

12: Steve decided that one verse of "Hand It to You" that he performed in mid-1978 was too raw for the studio version he recorded later that year. The verse: "She got the big smile, she got the big blue eyes / I better watch my step 'cause she's twice my size / She let me drink a little wine, she let me smoke a little grass / But if I get out of line, she'll kick my ass."

13: In a brief statement in the concert program, Steve noted that his three girls "fondly remember" Reynolds, who Steve said "was on fire. Her work still is."

Like others, Rosalie Sorrels, who sang at the Malvina Reynolds memorial show, was bothered by the hissing and booing during Steve's "Old Fashioned," which she saw as a fitting tribute to Reynolds: "She was, in fact, old fashioned."
(Photo by Art Thieme)

14: Some recall that Steve stopped in the middle of "Old Fashioned" and segued to "Men Who Love Women Who Love Men." But this is unlikely, given the preponderance of other recollections. Also, had that happened, Larry Kelp would have mentioned it in his *Oakland Tribune* review. The show was taped, evidenced by the airing of portions on NPR's "Folk Festival USA," but a recording that includes the end of Steve's set has not surfaced, making verification of the incident difficult.

("God Bless the Grass") and radical feminists ("We Don't Need the Men"). Though all leaned left, they were divided by ideological crevasses. "All of these disparate people claimed Malvina as their own," says Barbara Millikan, who attended the show, "but there were definitely factions in the crowd who had no use for each other." This became obvious before the end of Steve's set.

He opened mordantly but suitably with a respectful crack: "Hard to have a proper funeral for an improper person like Malvina Reynolds." Accompanied by reeds player Jim Rothermel, Steve sang Reynolds' quiet, gentle, minor-key "Young Moon," along with boisterous versions of his "City of New Orleans" and "Twentieth Century." Then he closed with a tender composition that Reynolds had admired and that addressed the heart behind her activism. But the song — "Old Fashioned," with its four mentions of the phrase "old fashioned girl" — infuriated those who found the phrase repressive and insulting.

First came streams of hisses. Then others booed those who were hissing. Less than half of the crowd was booing or hissing, but the disruption was obtrusive. Startlingly, a song of passion that usually moved audiences to silence and tears was instead diverting attention from Steve and fomenting a war of reactions. Rothermel gamely added a tenor-sax line to Steve's guitar and vocal, but while the two soldiered to the song's conclusion, the experience came as a jolt.

"I'm really sorry you thought I was preachin'," Steve said with some confusion as he addressed the crowd in what Larry Kelp of the *Oakland Tribune* described as a hurt voice. "That's sure not why I did that song."

"It was unnerving," Rothermel says. "To me, the song was a wonderful sentiment — a love song to his wife where he says, 'I only hope that our daughter can grow up to be like you.' But to the militant feminists in the audience, all they heard was 'old fashioned,' and they weren't going for it. I would think that if Malvina Reynolds were there, she would have loved the song. But these people weren't relating to Malvina Reynolds or Steve Goodman. They suddenly went for their own cause."

In part, Steve and Rothermel were confused because they couldn't detect the different purposes behind the boos and hisses. "We thought maybe they were booing us," he says. "After the fact, I realized why they had done that. But more power to Steve. He finished the song. He didn't stop singing." [14]

Some insist they saw Steve leaving the stage in tears. Others dispute that. Regardless, the incident shook him up. "He was pretty shattered," says Faith Petric, who was among several performers that night who felt shocked and ashamed. Country Joe McDonald, next on the program, told the crowd, "We're trying to have a memorial here. Can't you keep that stuff at home?"

To Rosalie Sorrels, Reynolds' former performing partner who for decades has kept her songs alive in concerts and recordings, Steve's "Old Fashioned" should have been seen as a perfect homage to Reynolds. "She was, in fact, old fashioned," Sorrels says. "She was married for years. She may have been a Socialist and a member of the Communist Party, but she was old fashioned in all kinds of ways. She had no criteria for your politics except that you be kind and

helpful to people. One of the reasons she liked Steve was that he was not political. He was just a really good human being with no agenda in that sense. She
never thought everybody had to think the same thing. She would just like it if
they would think at all."

Privately, the incident clearly bothered Steve. His manager, Al Bunetta, who
attended the tribute, was a merciless tease while driving him back to their hotel.
"Hey, Steve — s-s-s, s-s-s," Bunetta said over and over with an uproarious laugh.
Other times, Steve tried to push the hissing under the rug. Larry Hanks, who
sang at the memorial, bumped into Steve later and reminded him of it. "Oh,
God, don't mention that," Steve said. "It's a terrible memory."

But in public, it became light-hearted stage material. Less than three weeks
after the tribute, Steve played to a similarly sized audience of 3,000 from the
revolving stage of the Forum, an outdoor theater at Ontario Place along the
Toronto waterfront. There, he referenced the incident and introduced "Old
Fashioned" by referencing a rock hit by the Animals to crack a pun. "I sang this
song there, and it was roundly misunderstood in Berkeley. So here we are in the
round, and oh, Lord, please don't let me be misunderstood." With that prelude,
"Old Fashioned" drew resounding applause from the more mainstream audience, and Steve basked in it, using his typical line after a quiet tune, "Thanks
for lettin' me sing that, folks." [15]

At the show's opening, the rotating stage at Ontario Place fueled Steve's

*With the 1,815-foot CN Tower,
the world's tallest freestanding
structure, as a backdrop (upper
right), Steve performs for 3,000
on June 6, 1978, on the rotating
stage of the open-air Forum at
Ontario Place in Toronto.*
(Photo by Terry Murray)

15: The Reynolds-show hissing
echoed jovially during Steve's
1983 interview with David Gans of
Record magazine. "I certainly
didn't mean to make any kind of
political statement. ... I was so
surprised that I didn't have time to
feel awful. Berkeley is forgiven,
OK? I think Malvina would have
laughed. ... There are days when
the bear eats you. You can't let
that stuff win."

Tom Colwell, backed by Steve while playing at Dirty Dan's on Chicago's Lincoln Avenue, marvels, "I do not remember music like that ever coming out of my guitar, before or since."
(Photo courtesy of Tom Colwell)

16: During the Forum sound check, he had asked how fast the stage could revolve. Technicians obligingly set the stage spinning as Steve jogged in the opposite direction to stay in the same place. The Forum was razed to make way for a new theater in late 1994.

17: One of Steve's made-up verses for "Mama Don't Allow It" at the 1978 Philly festival addressed the nagging rain: "We don't care if mama gets pissed. Now we gotta play it in the mist."

18: For a 1997 reunion of the Amazingrace founders, a T-shirt was produced with the names of 150 acts that had played the coffeehouse. Steve was the only performer listed with the appendage "and Friends."

humor in a way that would have suggested to feminists that Steve needed sensitivity training. Wearing a satiny, royal-blue bomber jacket with yellow sleeves and a naked, pink woman embroidered on the back, he raced onstage and bobbed into "Red, Red Robin." He stopped in the first verse, turned to the audience behind him and asked, "Do her tits bounce? I don't know." [16]

Surprisingly, given a calendar peppered with Steve Martin dates, Steve flung himself fully into the summer festivals that he had shunned the year before. He starred in Pete Seeger's first Great Hudson River Revival north of New York City on June 18, played four workshops (hosting one) and a concert at Mariposa in Toronto the weekend of June 23-25, popped in at Ravinia north of Chicago July 19, headlined at Philly on Aug. 25 (bringing six other musicians to the stage in a rain-sodden, nighttime show Friday, [17] not the festival closer on Sunday) and joined a panoramic lineup for Mimi Fariña's Bread & Roses Festival in Berkeley on Sept. 4.

The Chicago-area club scene also enticed Steve on otherwise unoccupied nights. In July, he contributed three songs to a final-night send-off for the Amazingrace coffeehouse in Evanston. [18] At other times that summer, he preferred to drift into clubs more anonymously.

One evening he walked into Dirty Dan's, a few doors from Somebody Else's Troubles, and sat at the bar listening to a set by bassist Mike Lieber and a Seattle visitor, Tom Colwell. Lieber told Colwell to invite Steve to the stage but noted that Steve didn't want others in the club to know that he was present. So when Steve assented, Colwell introduced him (and drew a laugh from Lieber) by using the impromptu name of "Joe Steel." Loaning Steve a six-string guitar, Colwell launched into "City of New Orleans" on his 12-string, with Steve harmonizing on the chorus. Steve accompanied Colwell and Lieber on a few more songs, "and I do not remember music like that ever coming out of my guitar, before or since," Colwell says. "He was adding a lot of wonderful stuff, noodling around back there, and it was just a real joy — a warm flush of 'Oh, wow. Here I am making music with Steve Goodman and sounding better for it.' "

Into his blur of formal and impromptu shows Steve squeezed a vacation in Hawaii, which he had not seen since he and Nancy spent his jingle money and impulsively flew there seven and a half years prior. The impetus was a July 2, 1978, show that he opened for Steve Martin at Honolulu's Neal Blaisdell Arena. But Steve was determined not to hoard the earnings from his Martin dates. Joined by manager Al Bunetta and road manager Maple Byrne, Steve extended his stay in Hawaii and was escorted around the islands by a man Steve hadn't seen since shortly after his leukemia diagnosis in January 1969 — his former Sloan-Kettering roommate, Jack Goldberg.

Goldberg, who had lived in Honolulu for a year, met the group at the airport after learning of the concert. He served as an insider's guide to restaurants, snorkeling in Hanauma Bay and other unpublicized spots for the visitors, who were billeted at the posh Kahala Hilton, an isolated, 10-floor beachfront hotel known as a celebrity hideaway. Steve always picked up the tab during their outings, and this stirred Goldberg's guilt. Near the end of the week, while looking at clothes in the Hilton's men's store, Steve tried on a silky Malibu shirt selling for a pricey $55.

"Goldberg," Steve said, "you like these shirts?"

"Yeah, they're beautiful," Goldberg replied. "What's not to like?"

"They got one that'll fit you?" Steve said to his portly friend.

"Oh, I'm sure they do."

"Go ahead, try one on," Steve said. "Let me see how it looks on you." When Goldberg did so, Steve said, "Hey, it looks great. You got it."

"Steve, I can't take this shirt," Goldberg said. "This is a $55 shirt. This is just too much."

"I want you to understand something," Steve told him. "I've always dreamt of being able to come back to Hawaii, and I've never been able to afford to take this kind of a vacation. So I made a deal with myself that whatever money I could attribute to the time that I was spending in Hawaii that I've earned for this portion of my tour, I was going to spend it all here and have as good a time as possible. So we could do this one of two ways: You can either take that shirt and have a good time, or you can just be a miserable son of a bitch and refuse my hospitality."

Goldberg took the shirt, which became a keepsake.

Steve's recent studio work resulted in a variety of musical gifts for the public in 1978. In April, Flying Fish issued "That Old Gang of Mine," an album by Martin, Bogan & the Armstrongs consisting of songs Steve had produced the previous fall and a couple of leftover tracks the group had made during the 1975 sessions for Steve's "Jessie's Jig" LP. Though not widely distributed or advertised, "That Old Gang of Mine" bore intrinsic stature because of Steve's involvement.

Of much greater impact the next month was the debut of the Steve-produced "Bruised Orange" album by John Prine. With both artists now on Asylum, the label capitalized on their identity as songwriters. In a full-page ad for "Bruised Orange" in *Billboard*, a collage of fake 45s inscribed with the names of 39 artists who had recorded Steve's and Prine's compositions encircled a photo of the pair. "If you think John Prine and Steve Goodman write great songs," the headline said, "you're in great company."

Critics pronounced "Orange" a return to top form for Prine and gave Steve much of the credit. "Goodman has made this one of Prine's most listenable albums," wrote the *Chicago Sun-Times*' Al Rudis. "He shines the light on Prine's jokes by understating the music." In *Billboard*, "Orange" reached only #116 on the pop-album chart, but the magazine cited Steve's creation of a "tantalizing sound" for Prine. By year's end, the LP had sold 125,000 copies, more than twice the sales figures for any of Steve's albums, and it had prompted a pile of accolades, the highest coming from *Time* magazine, which named it one of 1978's 10 best.

Steve at times joined Prine to tour on behalf of the album — and in one

Steve's opener for Steve Martin on July 2, 1978, in Honolulu became the impetus for a welcome vacation: "I made a deal with myself," he told friend Jack Goldberg, "that whatever money I could attribute to the time that I was spending in Hawaii that I've earned for this portion of my tour, I was going to spend it all here and have as good a time as possible."

On the heels of her success in Woody Allen's film "Annie Hall" (the Rolling Stone *cover is from June 30, 1977), Diane Keaton recorded half a dozen vocal demos for producer Kenny Vance, including Steve's "I'm Attracted to You." But Keaton never finished the project, and the tracks remain unreleased.*

instance it could have triggered his instant demise. Prine, backed by his Famous Potatoes band, also was billed with the New Grass Revival in a college auditorium in Illinois, and the troupe was "smashed, toasted," says guitarist Johnny Burns. While Steve did a solo set, Burns and two members of the Revival, Sam Bush and Curtis Burch, sneaked into the loading space beneath the stage. There, they found a trap door and figured out that Steve was standing on it. They hatched the loony idea of opening the door, and Burns and Bush climbed onto a chair, reaching up to pull out the pins.

"What're you doing!" boomed a voice from behind. It was road manager Tim Messer.

"Wouldn't it be great if Steve came crashing through there?" Bush said. "He'd love this!"

"He's right above us, and if we can get the pin loose, the door will open," Burns said.

"And he'll fall and kill himself," Messer said. "He's 10 feet off the ground!"

Sheepishly, Burns and Bush looked at each other. They vaguely recall that they were planning to catch Steve, and they later realized that the falling trap door would have "creamed" them and thwarted their rescue of Steve.

More on their minds in the moment, however, was the inherent humor. "It could have been a very exciting moment in Steve's life," Burns says. "We thought it would be a funny joke to see this little guy disappear all of a sudden, like 'Wow, that was great. How'd you do that?' "

Burns says he told Messer, "Steve would love this, even if he did break his leg. He'd think this was big stuff." Fortunately, no one, including Steve, had a chance to find out.

Besides restoring Prine to favor, "Bruised Orange" also embedded Steve's producing prowess in the minds of others. One was Alice Playten, the 5-foot actress and singer who had met Steve in 1973 when she earned fame and an Obie Award on Broadway for her portrayal of Mick Jagger in a *National Lampoon* revue, "Lemmings." Steve's supervision of "Orange," Playten says, "really affected me. I thought it was one of the most perfectly beautiful albums. Each song was structured so beautifully. Knowing that he and John were friends, I thought he got a portrait of someone. It just popped for me. I really, really heard it." The night of Steve's May 14 show at the Roxy in L.A., Playten asked him to produce a demo session of hers for Warner Brothers. Steve was "extremely agreeable," the session was projected for fall 1979, and Playten was jazzed. "I wanted to be around someone who understood how less was more."

Those who didn't blink saw ephemeral contributions by Steve to other recordings in 1978. Bob Gibson, trying a comeback with ex-partner Hamilton Camp, released a Flying Fish album, "Homemade Music," with a Steve song that undoubtedly held meaning for the drug-afflicted troubadour, "Lookin' for Trouble." On Jimmy Buffett's new "Son of a Son of a Sailor" LP, Steve sang harmony on the title track. Then came a glancing but potentially pivotal connection with one of the year's hottest female celebs, Diane Keaton.

Emerging from mid-level fame, Keaton had won the Academy Award for best actress in April for her ditsy performance as the title character of Woody Allen's 1977 comedy "Annie Hall." In the film, which was named best picture, Keaton's quirky wardrobe of men's vests, neckties, baggy pants and fedora hats had set off a fashion craze. But even more surprising, "Annie Hall" revealed Keaton as a talented singer who could croon the standards "It Had to Be You" and "Seems Like Old Times" with a voice both smooth and alluring. Keaton seemed poised to branch into a music career.

Soon after her Oscar win, New York vocal arranger Kenny Vance received a call to produce a demo session for Keaton. The year prior, Vance had arranged vocals for Steve's "I'm Attracted to You," and Vance suggested the song to Keaton as one of half a dozen tracks for her to record at RCA Studios. (Others included Steely Dan's "Oh Wow, It's You Again" and Al Green's "I'm Still in Love with You.") Keaton, who had just broken up with Woody Allen in favor of actor Warren Beatty, arrived at the studio and, with Beatty present and the lights turned off, sang each song. [19]

Her take on "I'm Attracted to You" was stunning. Vance had slowed the tempo slightly from the pace of Steve's version, and the quiet backing came from a bass, a drum and the glowing bell tones of a celeste. Keaton, who had memorized the song's words, sang them with a sultry vulnerability. "She had a tremendous feel for lyrics," Vance says. Her treatment made clear that Steve's ethereal composition was suited to the voice and persona of a woman.

Keaton and Beatty soon left for the Soviet Union to scout locations for "Reds," Beatty's epic in which they both would star. "I'll be back in about three months," Keaton told Vance, "and we'll finish the album." But three months stretched into three years on "Reds," and Keaton never returned to the project. The demo tracks, which survive today, have never been released. Her version of "I'm Attracted to You" swelled with potential as a pop hit that may have opened new doors for Steve. Sadly, it remains only an intriguing "What if?" [20]

A brush with a different kind of greatness that year became a reality, but only because Steve willed it to happen. Bob Hoban, Steve's off-and-on musical partner since 1969, had produced in 1976 a Flying Fish LP of show tunes and standards that featured a Hoban idol, swing violinist Joe Venuti. [21] To produce a second such album, Hoban had booked two days in June 1978 at Chicago's Curtom Studios. The career of Venuti, 74, had stretched to the Roaring Twenties, and he was revered as the first successful improvisational violinist. Steve, who with Harry Waller had seen a Venuti show in Toronto, ached to rub shoulders with him and made that clear to Hoban.

But Hoban felt torn because he already had booked a swing rhythm section for the session. "I just couldn't see where Steve would fit," he says. "Nothing was going to jell or blend." Hoban stalled, but Steve kept phoning him at the studio. Midway through the second day, Hoban relented and invited Steve to the session. It was against Hoban's better judgment. Steve was a fine improviser on guitar but a relative foreigner to jazz. Besides, Venuti was in a foul mood —

19: Vance says that Warren Beatty entered the studio when it was dark. A musician spilled coffee on him and started wiping his pants before looking up and realizing it was Beatty.

20: "I'm Attracted to You" had another would-be brush with greatness in 1981. Gene Chandler (real name: Eugene Dixon), the African American soul stylist whose "Duke of Earl" hit #1 in 1962, released Steve's song of seduction on his "Here's to Love" LP for the 20th Century label. The tune was released as a single but died. "It came out and went right back in," Steve told an Atlanta audience that year. "So I actually have a record of Gene Chandler singin' this thing at home, right? I used to go see him at the Regal Theater in Chicago, watch him sing 'Duke of Earl.' In 1963-64, I used to go and see him all the time down there. I always knew it was possible that in America one of your heroes could cut one of your songs. What a deal, right? I thought that was the best thing that had happened in years."

21: The 1976 LP, " 'S Wonderful: 4 Giants of Swing," featured Venuti, Jethro Burns, Eldon Shamblin and Curley Chalker.

Steve badgered his way into playing acoustic guitar for what turned out to be the last song recorded by famed swing violinist Joe Venuti.

(Photo © Walt Disney Productions, courtesy of Paul Anastasio and Catherine Alexander)

he hadn't told anyone, but he was in the painful throes of terminal cancer. "He was arguing over everything, mad at the world," Hoban says, "and now we're going to introduce somebody whom he's never met or probably ever heard of, and he's going to shit in his pants. I mean, it would have taken Louis Armstrong raised from the dead to walk in the door for him to smile."

Hoban approached Venuti: "Joe, a guy I got coming in is Steve Goodman."

"Who the hell? Good for you," Venuti answered. "Does he deliver pizza? C'mon, let's get this shit cut."

Steve drove to Curtom with Jethro Burns (who had been part of Hoban's 1976 Venuti project) in time to record one last track. Hoban introduced Steve to Venuti, who replied, "Aw, fuck on that. Cut whatever you're gonna cut." Steve suggested "Honeysuckle Rose," the bouncy Fats Waller tune. "Let's just fuckin' play it," Venuti spat out.

So they did. Midway, Steve played a spare and bluesy solo, throwing in an off-kilter riff on a racetrack trumpeter's herald. But with double-time solos by Burns, bassist John Vany and Venuti, the four-minute song ended with a flourish. There was just one problem. Venuti's last run climbed a scale that never reached the final note. "Venuti quit playing, said 'That's it' and packed up," Hoban says. (Later, Hoban and engineer Fred Breitberg tried to spin the final note a full tone higher on the tape, but to no avail. "It's a quarter-step flat," Hoban says, "but who gives a shit?") As Venuti returned his violin to its case, Steve approached him.

"Thank you very much, Mr. Venuti," Steve said.

"Yeah, yeah," Venuti replied. "Who's driving me? C'mon, let's go."

Steve sidled up to Hoban and said quietly, "You weren't going to call me here."

"Yeah."

"If I were you, I wouldn't have called me here."

Two months later, on Aug. 14, Venuti succumbed. So the Curtom session became his last, and "Honeysuckle Rose" the final recording of his 50-year career. For Steve, the session, released on LP in early 1979, stirred a dichotomy of emotions. "Steve was sweating bullets," Hoban says, but his nervousness was exceeded only by a compulsion to make music with a master. "Steve would have loved to be in there for 25 hours. He was the only person who could have bluffed his way through it, but it was the roughest session in his life."

The delicious pressure of experiences with Venuti, Steve Martin and the like demanded a diversion. Steve's perennial answer lay inside one of his cherished symbols of home, Wrigley Field.

His lifelong passion for baseball had taken root in many locales. Steve carried a mitt with him on road trips, playing catch with musicians and road crews and organizing them to play softball games on the lawn of The Ark coffeehouse in Ann Arbor and the Commons in Cambridge before shows at Club Passim. Steve was the catcher, and Bonnie Raitt's guitarist, Freebo, was the pitcher in one such contest, whose players included singer/guitarist Chris Smither and

Raitt herself. Steve also caught countless major-league games on radio and TV and pored over box scores and standings. In New York and other cities, Steve was a fixture at big-league stadiums, and he made it a practice to arrive early in remote towns where he had concerts so that he could take in a few innings of farm-team ball. Once, when he and Al Bunetta were driving to a Washington, D.C.-area venue for a show, they came upon a ballpark in Virginia. Steve pulled their rental car to a stop at the side of the road. His explanation was simple: "There's this player I want to see, man."

But the biggest lure for Steve's diamond devotion was his hometown team, the Cubs, and in the summer of 1978 he sought to inculcate his oldest child. Just as his grandfather and father had done with him, Steve wanted Jessie to appreciate the communal joys of the Friendly Confines of Wrigley. That summer, despite the acquisition of slugger Dave Kingman, the Cubs as a team were nothing special. But a fan favorite was ex-Yankee Bobby Murcer, whose trademark since 1973 was a rocking chair in which he relaxed in the clubhouse. It was an amiable image for a 6-year-old to grasp, so Steve helped Jessie assemble a poster that read, "Hit a Homer, Bobby," accompanied by Jessie's drawing of a rocking chair. When Steve took her to Wrigley Field, they sat in the bleachers above right field, where Murcer played, and they snared his attention with the sign.

The bleachers became Steve's haunt on many afternoons and early evenings that season. While the Cubs cruised to a typically mediocre 79-83 record and a third-place finish in the NL East, Steve found a musical method in the face of diamond ennui to boost the team and the spirits of other fans. He brought a mini-concert to the ballpark.

Strapping a battery-operated Pignose portable amplifier to his waist and carrying a three-quarter-sized guitar, Steve led a troupe of musicians — including Bob Hoban on fiddle and mandolin, Jim Tullio on kazoo and Angelo Varias and Gus Johns with tambourines and other shakers — to a perch in the front rows above right field. The bunch showed up an hour or two early, stretched over a dozen seats and performed country and bluegrass standards while fans filed in during batting practice. [22] The overlook afforded maximum exposure to the setting sun and the game and assured a minimal disruption of concession sales above. More important, the locale let the group sing and play to Murcer. "We called ourselves Murcer's Marauders," Hoban says. "He loved country music, and he'd smile and clap his hands. One time, he even said, 'Keep going.'" Mike Leonard of NBC "Today" says the 32-year-old Murcer "would tip his hat to Steve, and it was this concert of a great folksinger to an aging outfielder."

Their show didn't let up once the game began. Between innings and during rallies, Steve and gang improvised songs, chants and other snippets that were transmitted to nearby fans by Steve's coffee-can-sized amp. "If the Cubs were batting and got somebody on and there was some potential, we'd strike up and do something, and the bleachers would be applauding along," Hoban says. "Some people were really into it," Varias says, "and others were just watching

Bobby Murcer, the Chicago Cubs' newly acquired rightfielder, was the object of affection for Steve and 6-year-old daughter Jessie, who made a "Hit a Homer, Bobby!" sign and displayed it from the bleachers of Wrigley Field. Steve and other musicians called themselves Murcer's Marauders.

(Chicago Cubs photo, courtesy of Lefty Blasco)

22: Attendance was sparse, in stark contrast to the hip Wrigleyville scene of decades later in which games routinely sold out.

Fred Holstein, shown in 1978 at Somebody Else's Troubles, got a pleasant shock when a contingent led by Steve showed up on June 6 of that year for Holstein's album-release gig at Kenny's Castaways in New York's Greenwich Village.

(Photo by Marianne Jasin)

the game and amused by what Steve was doing. It wasn't like a concert, where everybody was paying attention, but Steve would stand up and sing something to be funny, and people all laughed. They were amenable to things that were more quirky."

With Cubs' buttons, flags and a Gilligan-style sailor's hat, Steve was easy to spot, and he fielded requests for songs or autographs. But nearby fans also respected his desire to focus on the game. Those in his section were not the notorious bunch that came to be known as the Bleacher Bums, whose antics were portrayed in a play by the same name that had opened the previous summer in Chicago and who typically congregated in left field. "Those were the hard-core guys, the guys who would be very vicious to players, swearing a lot and throwing stuff on the field," Varias says. "In right/right-center, it was more the artists' den. It was a little more genteel."

But only a little. Steve's conversation at the stadium was "the very natural guy talk," Varias says. "It was never the beauty or imagery of baseball. It was stuff about different players and abilities, and 'Fuckin' Cubs, they're gonna break our hearts again.' "

Steve's serenades at Wrigley perfectly merged his passions for music and baseball. Given the Cubs' perennial misery, it was fitting that Steve's command performance in that milieu took place in the rain.

With guitar, amplifier and full Cubs garb, Steve joined Tullio at the Evanston El station one afternoon and headed south under cloudy skies. "He looked like a typical tourist fan, the guy you wouldn't want to sit next to," Tullio says. Shortly after the pair arrived at Wrigley, walked inside and met up with Hoban and Varias, the sky opened up. In the downpour, Tullio stuffed Steve's guitar under his coat, "and everyone ran under the bleachers," Tullio says. "Someone says, 'Hey, there's Steve Goodman,' and Steve decides to give a concert." Standing on stairs in an archway, and in competition with the recorded music on the stadium's scratchy loudspeakers, the four pulled out their instruments and the mini-amp. Out came "Take Me Out to the Ball Game," "City of New Orleans" and other standards, played for soaked fans who called out requests. "We were under the bleachers, so the echo was amazing," Tullio says. "It was jammed, and once people started hearing it, more and more came back. He did an hour-and-a-half show, and nobody left." For Varias, Steve's expression told the whole story: "His eyes glistened because it was like a real concert. It was pretty cool."

Another Wrigley buddy, mentor Fred Holstein, reached the out-of-town big leagues that summer, and Steve was there to pay respects. Holstein was booked for a June 6-8 run at the Kenny's Castaways club in Greenwich Village, on the strength of his first LP, released on the tiny Philo label in December. Unbeknown to Holstein, a Chicago contingent, including Steve, flew to New York for his opening and crouched in the balcony when he walked onstage.

Launching into his typical opener, Utah Phillips' "I Remember Loving You," Holstein heard harmony from above. It was the voices of Steve along with Martha Redhed, widow of Somebody Else's Troubles co-owner Bill Redhed. The show of support moved Holstein to tears. As he crudely put it, "I dropped my load." Steve borrowed a guitar and backed Holstein for the rest of his set. Later on the balmy night, the Chicagoans celebrated by riding the free Staten Island ferry, with Steve leading a sing-along on Woody Guthrie's "Roll On, Columbia."

Beckoning from California that year was another project to bring out Steve's musical moxie. His manager's brother, Peter Bunetta, lured Steve to the session, organized by a pair of producer/writers, Michael Olmstead and Peter Derge. Combing the industry, Olmstead and Derge had assembled a mélange of artists — including Joy of Cooking singer Terry Garthwaite and guitarists Jeff Baxter of Steely Dan and Wah Wah Watson of Motown — to record an album for kids. Based on an animated character originated at a cheerleading camp run by Olmstead, the LP was called "The GoGo the Blue Gorilla Show." Its cover, illustrated by famed sci-fi artist George Barr, took on the appearance of a TV-series soundtrack, which was the intention. "It was supposed to be the 'Ed Sullivan Show' of the animals," says Rick Chudacoff, bassist on the album. "The idea was to first do the LP and then sell it as a TV show."

Ranging from rock to country to punk, the 11 songs each matched a jungle cartoon character, from Tammy Turtle and Mouse the Cat to Burpy the Frog and Smelly the Skunk. The producers tapped Steve for the role of Ollie Otter, who — in waltz tempo, joined by an accordion and with the refrain of "You Otta Be an Otter" — sang a message of undersea environmentalism:

> *The water's polluted with oil and all kinds of muck*
> *Sometimes when I'm bored and I swim to the shore I get stuck*
> *What am I to do? Water that was blue*
> *Is now just a sick ugly grey — yuck!*

Though Steve didn't pen the song, its images and wordplay snugly fit his persona, and he sang it with verve. "Our kids loved it. His kids loved it," says Jim Tullio. "He was very into that project and tried to help it as much as he could. Every cut on that record is really good, with great artists."

But while Steve's otter tune was a standout, the cartoon collaboration went nowhere. Few copies of the LPs were pressed and printed, and whatever promotion that was undertaken failed to light a fire. Al Bunetta even got into the act, bringing it to the attention of Neil Bogart, but the former Buddah chief wasn't interested. Bogart's response was, "If you don't have Mickey Mouse, you've got nothing." [23]

Though these projects and pastimes marshaled Steve's energy in mid-1978, so did attention from close friends whose connection extended to cancer. One was Richard Harding, owner of the Quiet Knight, the site seven years earlier of the two most significant turning points in Steve's career (Arlo Guthrie hearing "City of New Orleans" and Kris Kristofferson leading Steve to Paul Anka). Harding's son John, a 25-year-old Chicago firefighter, had been diagnosed with testicular cancer at Illinois Masonic Hospital, which did not specialize in treating the disease. "I was scared shitless," John Harding says, and his dad advised

You Otta Be An Otter

Wailing about undersea muck, Steve sang the role of the environmentally conscious Ollie Otter for the children's LP, "The GoGo the Blue Gorilla Show."

(Illustration by George Barr, LP © Michael Olmstead and Peter Derge)

23: Though the Palo Alto Children's Theatre mounted productions of "Go Go" in 1992 and 2005, the "Go Go" LP has not been reissued in any form. Today stray copies of the album occasionally turn up on eBay, and it remains a mere curiosity.

talking with Steve. Based on Steve's referral, John was "welcomed with open arms" at Sloan-Kettering and in three weeks underwent surgery that cured him. What John appreciated most in Steve was his directness.

"The guy lived under the threat of death constantly and knew what I was going through," John says. "When we talked about this, he zeroed right in on me with those dark eyes, and it was no bullshit. I was really young, and I couldn't talk to anybody about it because they couldn't relate. 'Yeah, you have cancer, you might die. That's a drag. Did you hear that the Cubs won yesterday?' But Steve took it seriously and helped me out."

John Harding's dad puts it more bluntly. Wide-eyed, Richard Harding mists up and says hoarsely, "I owe my son's life to Steve Goodman."

Cancer also struck a Maine East High friend of Steve's the same year. Brad Ellis, who had started chemo and radiation for Hodgkin's lymphoma in his groin, learned that Steve was playing the Harry Hope's ski lodge in Cary, northwest of Chicago near Ellis' home, so he decided to attend with Maine East friend Jerry Needelman. When the two visited with Steve, Ellis broke the news about his disease. "He literally cried," Ellis says. "It was instantaneous. Didn't even take a moment for it to sink in. The tears just started running down his face. My pain instantly became his."

"Steve," Ellis told him, trying to offer comfort, "I'm not facing what you're facing. The kind of stuff I've got is very curable. My doctor says there's a 90 percent chance of a complete cure. I don't have to deal with the shit you're dealing with."

Through tears, Steve nevertheless replied, "You can't let this stop you."

"You know me," Ellis joked, parroting a line he had learned from his father. "If I can't take it with me, I'm not going."

Steve's message was dead serious, however, and in the last half of 1978 he heeded it himself by planning his next album on Asylum. With leftovers from "Say It in Private" and new songs he had written, Steve had amassed enough material for the core of a new LP. He also had resumed collaborating with old friend Steve Burgh, and the two looked forward to recording a promising ditty they were writing about the foolhardiness of best-laid plans. "It sure looked good on paper, but it wasn't so hot in reality" was the song's refrain and would-be title. "We had a verse about how this couple got the *Kama Sutra* out, and they got all tangled up, and the paramedics had to come out and untangle them," Burgh said. Steve even sought the help of witty songwriter/poet Shel Silverstein on the tune, but it never was finished. "It was wonderful," Burgh said. "It would have been a good, funny Steve Goodman song." [24]

Momentarily, Steve sidestepped a return to the studio. Relenting to the calls of critics and fans for a live album, he arranged for a sound truck to be present outside the Earl of Old Town Aug. 15-16 to record a pair of midweek shows with David Amram, Corky Siegel, Jethro Burns and Hugh McDonald. Billed as "New Year's in August with Steve Goodman and Friends," the summer sets also raised funds for a Chicago organization treating children's disabilities.

I couldn't talk to anybody about it because they couldn't relate. 'Yeah, you have cancer, you might die. That's a drag. Did you hear that the Cubs won yesterday?' But Steve took it seriously and helped me out.
JOHN HARDING

24: Steve and Burgh also contemplated writing another song, "Is Anybody Home?," which Burgh said was "about being out of touch, on the road, away from the people you love." The composition that they did finish, "One Bite of the Apple," which examined the temptations of infatuation, appeared on Steve's next LP. Originally, "Apple" was a gentle chord progression to which Steve whistled a melody and gave the title "Whistler's Mother-in-Law" when he performed it on the New Year's Eve 1976 edition of WFMT-FM's "Midnight Special."

Newer compositions that Steve taped at the Earl included "Men Who Love Women Who Love Men," "Family Tree," "Hand It to You," "Old Smoothies" and a sly commentary on the entertainment business, "What Have You Done for Me Lately?" (Steve had written the chorus for "Lately" and solicited help from Shel Silverstein, who mailed Steve a verse depicting a man's rescue of a drowning woman. After her revival, she pops the title question.) Steve also taped a variety of others' songs, from "In the Middle of an Island" and "My Funny Valentine" to "Roll On, Columbia" and "I'll Fly Away." As a bonus, he threw in an improvisation about the Chicago Cubs to the New Orleans-style tune of "When the Saints" ("I want to be in the bleachers / When the Cubs go marchin' in"). The performances were strong, but the presence of elaborate recording equipment and a primed crowd made for an artificial feel, and Steve was unconvinced. No matter how galvanizing he was onstage, the studio environment was intriguing him most. [25]

His experiences with "Say It in Private" and "Bruised Orange" "turned around how I think about sound," Steve told Peter O.E. Bekker of WCBS-AM. The resulting confidence convinced him that he could return to his "Jig" and "Words" role and produce his next album himself. So between Steve Martin openers and other gigs and with the help of engineer Hank Neuberger, he spent the last six months of 1978 darting in and out of Chicago Recording Co. laying down tracks and mixing them for his next LP. Such studio work was increasingly crucial to Steve. As he told Bekker the following April, Steve had convinced himself that shaping his music for public consumption was as important — if not more so — than creating the songs themselves.

"What I really tried to concentrate on" in the late 1978 studio sessions, he said, "was what happens to the song after it leaves your pen and your guitar. I felt very limited by the art of songwriting. Songwriting had to become something that could grow. The songs had to have life. You don't just write 'em and then leave 'em alone. These songs are for people to hear, y'know? They're not for a place in a museum. They're kinetic. They have energy."

Songs, he explained, face a cacophony of competition. "The general noise level in the world is up so much in the last 20 years that it defies credulity. The amount of sound that people have to listen to every day, just bells ringin', telephones, buzzers, new electronic noises, the whir of air conditioners — sounds that were not there (before) that people deal with, that really affect how people think." Such influences, he said, triggered the "sound revolution" that resulted in the phenomenon of "Saturday Night Fever" and other disco hits. "It's sound that got people out for disco. I promise you that that's what it was. It wasn't that people were waiting for that beat, 'cause at a certain point it's (all) 1-2-3-4. It's the sound."

The key task for a musician is to "get a handle on what's goin' on in the street," he said. "The recording studio can be the greatest tool in the world, or it can be an ivory tower, and you have to be really careful that you don't get in there and you start listenin' only to the sounds that you make. You have to go

The songs had to have life. You don't just write 'em and then leave 'em alone. These songs are for people to hear, y'know? They're not for a place in a museum. They're kinetic.
STEVE GOODMAN

25: Nine months later, Steve North of WLIR asked Steve to compare live performing with studio recording. "That's like askin' me what's the difference between an apple and an orange," Steve replied. "They both grow on trees, and they're both fruit, and ... they're both good for you. That's really where it stops, though."

out in the world. ... Sounds are street noises. They're the tones, the actual frequency of sound waves of all the various musical instruments that are available to work with. ... There's 200 thousand billion quadzillion things you can do with sound, and these days that's the big challenge, to take the song and turn it into sound."

Steve likened the task to hitting a moving target. "It's such a kinetic world right now," he said. "This place is on fire, and I know the music has to reflect that. The second you record somethin', it's already too late."

The songs that Steve recorded that fall ran his customary gamut, from a rocker, a bouncy shuffle, a quiet love song and a bossa nova to a lazy blues, a teeny-bop trifle and a reggae-esque groove.

The audacity of "Men Who Love Women Who Love Men" was augmented by a Dixieland strut, complete with a "When the Saints" brass herald and popping handclaps on the backbeat. "We wanted to make it like an anthem, like a parade, like 'Seventy-six Trombones' but for this generation," says drummer Peter Bunetta. Steve's trademark wordplay also surfaced in "Luxury's Lap," which tweaked the insatiably wealthy ("All of that green just makes them blue") and bore the unstated backdrop that Steve had written most of the tune during a non-luxurious ride from Evanston to Chicago on an El train.

But the sound that Steve shaped for them all — backed by the Crackin' rhythm section of Rick Chudacoff and Peter Bunetta [26] and augmented by a constellation of instruments, synthesizers, strings and ubiquitous "sha-la" and "oo-oo" backup singers — bore an unmistakable sheen.

"That was a very good time for Steve," says engineer Neuberger. "He really loved his writing, and he was very proud of his ability to produce his own records. He had this great little band that he put together, and they really rocked. They had a great groove going on. It wasn't folk music. To Steve, it sounded like radio music, pop music. I really thought he came alive for that."

To others, however, the recordings were blanketed in an aural gloss that was unlike the spare arrangements of "Bruised Orange" and that distanced the words and music — and Steve himself — from the listener. "He was deliberately trying to put what I call a sun tan on the music," says Jim Rothermel, who contributed saxophone, flute and clarinet to several tracks. "He was trying to give it that quality that would reach people who wouldn't normally relate to his music. It was probably a good intent, but at the same time he really sacrificed a lot of who he was."

That Steve was exchanging his persona for a pop sound mirrored a trend in the clubs of his home city. "The great Chicago folk boom is finished," wrote Eliot Wald earlier that year in the *Chicago Reader*. Wald traced the transformation of formerly folk enclaves into havens for jazz, blues, pop and punk rock or to spaces with "For Rent" signs hanging in the windows. Only Somebody Else's Troubles and a "slipping" Earl of Old Town were holding the torch. [27] Wald said less-known singer/songwriters and other acoustic musicians loosely grouped as "folk" were finding it difficult to land gigs. Indeed, Earl Pionke announced in

---

To Steve, it sounded like radio music, pop music. I really thought he came alive for that.
HANK NEUBERGER

26: Steve was so happy with the work of Rick Chudacoff and Peter Bunetta that he credited them, along with engineer Hank Neuberger, as assistant producers.

27: Steve wasn't an absentee from Troubles. On an open-mike night at the club in early 1979, Irish dulcimer player Wade Hampton Miller played "City of New Orleans," not seeing that Steve was present. "When I saw him, I just about crapped," Miller says. "But he had this big grin on his face and said, 'Hey, great job, man. I like your version. I've never seen anyone playing a dulcimer standing up. How do you balance it on that strap, and how did you get it to sound like a train?' So I'm showing him how I mute the strings with my palm, and we're talking about pickups and preamps like the couple of happy little gearheads we both were. It was like I'd known him all my life."

September 1978 that Troubles would cut its music to weekends only. (The shift began in mid-1979, and the Troubles name bit the dust in December 1980, when Pionke changed it to a rhyming pun: Earl's Drink Inn on Lincoln.)

"John Travolta is the enemy," the Wald article quoted comic songwriter Larry Rand. "Between 'Saturday Night Fever' and the bad weather, the folk clubs have been hurt badly."

The rise of disco was only natural following the Vietnam War, as stated in the article by traditional folksinger Art Thieme. "After every war, there's a period of boogie: the Gay '90s, the Roaring '20s, '50s rock and disco in the '70s," he said. "People don't want to be serious, sit still and listen to sad songs. They want to have a good time."

Steve's Dec. 29, 1978, appearance with Bonnie Koloc on WGN-AM's Roy Leonard show symbolized the shift — and foretold an unintentional abandonment of his core audience. The chat started harmlessly enough with Steve's characteristic blurring of the definition of folk music.

"Really, all it is is whatever people are singing," he said. "Old Marvin Gaye songs, they're folk music."

But Leonard pressed for Steve's assessment of the disco craze and received an answer that made lemonade of a lemon.

"I really like it," Steve said of disco. "I know that's gonna sound like so much sacrilege, but I think anytime that there's a lot of dance music in the air, it's just good for music, and disco music gave the whole business such a wonderful kick in the butt that I think it's a good thing. ... I don't like anything that gets to be where it's the only thing goin' on, but I don't think disco music has excluded the rest of the spectrum of popular taste."

"Well," replied Leonard, no fan of disco, "next week I'll probably have 'City of New Orleans' disco."

"Oh yeah," Steve said, playing along, "we're thinking of re-cuttin' everything disco, all right? Just thinking of it."

"Just think about it for a long while, will you please, Steve?" Leonard said with a laugh. "As a matter of fact, think about it for a long, long while." [28]

Steve redeemed himself when Leonard, noting that a minute and a half remained in the radio show, asked him to "do some picking." In a nod to New Year's Eve just two days away, Steve responded with a jaunty, folkie guitar version of "Auld Lang Syne."

For 43 seconds, the Steve of old was back. ♪

> **I don't like anything that gets to be where it's the only thing goin' on, but I don't think disco music has excluded the rest of the spectrum of popular taste.**
> **STEVE GOODMAN**

28: Four months later, interviewed by Jeff Magid of the L.A. music magazine *Pro Fun*, Steve defended disco because "everybody's the star, everybody gets up and dances." He also said the craze had a precedent in the Roaring Twenties. "Flappers wanted to hear the Charleston, and all the Dixieland players must have been sittin' around goin', 'What is this thing called the Charleston?'"

Steve tips his visitor's hardhat while touring a Commonwealth Edison nuclear plant in Zion, 30 miles north of Chicago, after writing the theme music for the WMAQ-TV documentary "In Our Nuclear Backyard." The program, which called for a halt to the construction of new nuclear-power plants, aired June 28, 1979.

(Photo by Dillon Smith)

'He couldn't play to his audience because they wouldn't let him'

One new song commanded Steve's thoughts in early 1979. On the surface, it was just another in a long string of his romantic commentaries. But it soon took on multiple meanings. Its title: "The One That Got Away."

A dispiriting application of the tune took shape soon after Steve rang in the New Year at the Earl of Old Town with the full complement of Martin, Bogan & the Armstrongs (with Howard's son Tom on bass). The first musician of the venerable string band's billing — the member of the group to whom Steve was closest, the hard-living Carl Martin — died four months later, on May 10, at age 73. In an interview a few weeks before Martin's passing, Steve summed him up as "the most charming guy since Louis Armstrong, the only guy who can get away with singing 'Hello Dolly' these days." [1] The loss, keenly felt by Steve, was that of a seemingly ageless mentor and three generations of musical memory.

"The One That Got Away" was easily the standout composition of the songs Steve had recorded the previous fall for his new album. [2] Written in late 1977, the tune cleverly depicted "two old middle-aged men" in a bar bragging of their romantic near-conquests and "two old middle-aged girls" in a beauty salon doing likewise. The scenarios set up a pitch for the value of commitment — that love practiced "with your fingers crossed" results only in dreams of "the one that got away."

Not only did the song's theme fit Steve's personal life and professional persona, it also had potential commercial appeal, particularly for baby boomers settling into adulthood. The lyrics matched intelligence and maturity with gentle humor ("bendin' each other's ears and bendin' their elbows, too") and youthful wordplay ("rock 'n' roll Romeos and their jukebox Juliets"). Perhaps most important to Steve was the song's sound. Its amiable, country-rock arrangement supported a hummable, melodic hook and Eagles-style harmonies.

Still, something was missing. "I couldn't quite figure out what was wrong," Steve said, "and then it hit me. It's a song about men and women, and there better be a woman's voice singin' on this thing."

That insight yielded what became perhaps the song's greatest asset. The woman he found to sing the complementary lead vocal was a waitress he and John Prine had met in 1973 at the Egress in Vancouver, B.C. — Nicolette Larson.

The death of musical mentor Carl Martin saddened Steve, who called him "the most charming guy since Louis Armstrong."

(Photo by P. Michael O'Sullivan)

1: Jazz/pop virtuoso Louis Armstrong had died eight and a half years earlier, in July 1971.

2: Steve had debuted a formative version of "The One That Got Away" — including references to *Cosmopolitan*, horoscopes and "wipin' away a tear" — during the New Year's Eve 1977 edition of WFMT-FM's "Midnight Special."

Nicolette Larson provided an edgy harmony vocal on Steve's recording of his standout composition, "The One That Got Away." But Larson's quick ascendence as a solo artist soon spelled a roadblock for the song's commercial fate.

(Warner Brothers photo, courtesy of Linda Larson)

Since then, this friend of Linda Ronstadt had parlayed an aching edge in her voice into ace backup singing on tours by Hoyt Axton and Commander Cody and on albums by Emmylou Harris and Neil Young. "She was always willing to sing: anywhere, anytime and for any reason," says Larson's manager, Derek Sutton. Even so, when Steve snagged the 5-foot-2 charmer via Harris for the female part on "The One That Got Away," she was unknown to the masses.

But Larson was not to be obscure for long. While Steve finished recording his album in the fall of 1978, Larson's harmony vocals zoomed to prominence on Young's mellow "Comes a Time" LP, which entered the *Billboard* pop-LP chart on Oct. 21 and stayed there for the next 30 weeks, peaking at #7 and selling more than 500,000 copies. Not even a month later, Larson's own stunning debut LP, "Nicolette," exploded upon its release, hitting the *Billboard* chart on Nov. 18, staying for 37 weeks, peaking at #15 and also selling 500,000-plus. Her first single from the album, a disco-ish version of Young's "Lotta Love," leapt onto the *Billboard* Hot 100 chart on Nov. 25 and stayed for 19 weeks, peaking at #8. Overnight, Larson was the definition of a hot property, commercially and critically. *Rolling Stone* even named her the best female singer of 1978.

All of this would have seemed to work in Steve's favor. Maybe, with the help of Larson's voice, "The One That Got Away" finally would put him on the mainstream map as a recording artist. A seeming omen of such impending success occurred when Steve and engineer Hank Neuberger flew to Los Angeles to record Larson's vocal.

On the plane, the conversation between Steve and Neuberger centered on Bruce Springsteen, whose music Neuberger revered but Steve had discounted as more hype than substance. But Springsteen's "Darkness on the Edge of Town" LP had been released the previous June, and Steve was impressed by one of its tracks, the rocker's loud and angry rant against his father, "Adam Raised a Cain."

"I'm starting to hear it," Steve told Neuberger. "I get it now. I've got the 'Darkness' album. It's really good. The songwriting is really important. I start to see what you're talking about."

Neuberger explained that Springsteen typically explored the "Adam" theme further onstage by recalling incidents of discord with his dad. "It's obviously an important thing to him," he said.

The two were still chatting about Springsteen at 1 a.m. as they checked into the Sunset Marquis Hotel in West Hollywood. While they waited at the reservation desk, the front door flew open, and in walked none other than Springsteen. Wearing a white T-shirt with rolled-up sleeves, he had a stunning brunette on one arm and held in his other arm a supermarket bag with a loaf of Wonder bread and a six-pack of Coca-Cola. Steve crossed the lobby to meet the superstar.

"Bruce Springsteen, I just want to introduce myself. I'm Steve Goodman, and I really like your songwriting."

"Steve Goodman?" Springsteen replied. "That song about your old man — great song!" Then he walked off.

The compliment stupefied Steve. "He was on Cloud 9 for the rest of the week," says Neuberger, who notes that Steve's "My Old Man" had been out for only about a year. "For Springsteen to know about it and also be obsessed with his own father and writing about that, Steve was just floating."

Little did Steve know that he was about to sink. As Steve and Elektra/Asylum prepared for a Feb. 20, 1979, release of his new album, they also anticipated issuing "The One That Got Away" as a single — not as a courtesy, the way that Steve's 45s had been released before, but with the full intention of making it a hit. Blocking the doorway, however, was Elektra/Asylum's parent company and Nicolette Larson's label, Warner Brothers. Buoyed by her success with "Lotta Love," Warners refused to allow Steve's single to be released until Larson's second 45, "Rhumba Girl," climbed in the *Billboard* chart to #30 or higher — which never happened. It was, as the *Los Angeles Times* later characterized it, a feud within the corporate family.

"This kind of overexposure could jeopardize Nicolette's career," Warners promo director Russ Thyret told Patrick Goldstein of the *Times*. "I don't want there to be any confusion among radio programmers — or listeners — as to what the new Nicolette Larson single is. It's the timing that bothers me."

Curiously, no one at Warners was talking about Steve's career. The Warners brass felt they had to choose between Steve and Larson, and they picked the hot newcomer, infuriating the subordinate label Asylum. "It would be different if this were between competitive companies like Warners and CBS," said Asylum promo director Ken Buttice. "But what aggravates me is that we're in the same family. I don't think another Nicolette song on the radio would hurt at all."

Al Bunetta was so irate that he decided to fly to Cannes in the south of France to the annual MIDEM music-industry conference attended by Elektra/Asylum president Joe Smith and Warners president Mo Ostin. Steve, hearing of Bunetta's plan, showed up on his doorstep at 7 a.m. and said, "I can't go back to Chicago because it's snowing, so I'm gonna go to France with you." Once the two arrived in Cannes, Bunetta — "like a stalker," he says — cornered Smith and Ostin. "You guys," Bunetta says he told them, "this is the one shot that this guy has with this record. You mean to tell me you're going to hold it up? Well, you guys can kiss my ass, and you're both phony."

Thwarted in the in-person showdown, Steve and Bunetta stayed on to enjoy a vacation in France and Italy. The defeat seemed to bring out Steve's feistiness. As they rubbernecked through St. Peter's Basilica in Rome, Steve carried on a running narration about the ancient artwork. They passed a tourist group and its guide, and Bunetta said, "Steve, you just told me something about the mosaic period. This guy's saying something different." Steve replied, "Fuck him. He doesn't know," and walked over to pick an argument with the guide.

Back in the States, Asylum released Steve's new album without a corresponding single but maintained its pressure on the Warners chief, Mo Ostin. In late March, Ostin relented, but only a bit. He OK'd issuing "The One That Got Away" as a 45 on the condition that Asylum not mention Nicolette Larson's

Hank Neuberger found that a chance encounter with Bruce Springsteen — and the rock superstar's praise of "My Old Man" — was an omen for Steve. "For Springsteen to know about it and also be obsessed with his own father and writing about that, Steve was just floating."

(Photo by Emily Neuberger)

Duet vocalist Nicolette Larson's name was nowhere to be found on Steve's 45-rpm single of "The One That Got Away," which was exactly the way that Larson's label, Warner Brothers, the parent company of Steve's label, Asylum, wanted it.

(Image courtesy of Norm Siegel)

name in advertising. "It's a struggle," an anonymous Asylum source told Goldstein of the *Los Angeles Times*. "Warners really destroyed our momentum. We're having trouble building a radio base." *Record World* raised hopes by picking the single as "sleeper of the week," but that's exactly what the 45 did — slept — as it eventually and sadly proved true to its title.

The album may have been equally doomed. Steve's sixth LP, it was the first whose title did not derive from a song title or lyrics therein. Originally, it was to be named for the song "Luxury's Lap," but the album instead took on a visual and verbal pun, "High and Outside." Set at night, the cover's trick image looked from inside an upper-floor apartment through two windows to a big-city skyline. Glaring back through one of the windows was Steve, literally "high and outside." [3] The back cover, from the reverse angle, showed a smiling and seemingly floating Steve as he walked away. It was "a breath of fresh air, so to speak," says Ron Coro, who designed the cover and constructed an elaborate set (and snared a flying pigeon) so that photos by Ethan Russell could create the illusion. "The idea," Coro says, with unintentional irony, "was to fool the consumer into thinking that Steve was walking on solid ground until you turn to the back."

Steve was pictured in a white dinner jacket (like John Travolta's in "Saturday Night Fever") along with a red shirt and dark tie. His hair, clipped to collar-length, was carefully combed back, no lock out of place. Coro asked Steve to wear the formal garb to provide "an elegant touch," but the result was markedly different from the wink-wink tuxedo that Steve had donned for the "Words" LP two years prior. Besides their visual pun, the "High and Outside" cover photos, including one on the inner sleeve, conveyed an image as slick as the songs inside — and the critics noticed.

"Pity the poor, white, male singer/songwriter," wrote *The New York Times'* John Rockwell, a consistent booster of Steve. "Disco reigns right now, which means ... (that) earnest, guitar-strumming, sensitively sincere singer/composers in a folk idiom are about at the very bottom of the hierarchy of hip. Yet indefatigably, stubbornly, they keep putting out records." Steve's "High and Outside," Rockwell said in terms that danced around the album's unsubtle strain toward the mainstream, "seems about his most convincing bid so far for commercial acceptance. That doesn't mean he's sold out in some craven way. It just means that the confidence of his approach and the diversity of the styles he assays seem very promising in terms of potential FM airplay and, eventually, sales." The only song Rockwell cited was Steve's "delightful duet" with Nicolette Larson. Alluding to "some relatively weak material," Rockwell nevertheless rated the album "a charmer."

A harsher appraisal might have been expected from *Rolling Stone*, but the take by reviewer Tom Carson was sweet, if backhanded. He termed the album "a touch less idiosyncratic and more straightforwardly MOR (middle of the road) than usual. Though this year's clone, Nicolette Larson, wanders in for one cut to juice things up a bit, much of the material settles into a quiet, familiar groove. ... For me, the artist's unerring decency and solid craftsmanship can be quite infectiously lulling in the age of high-powered corporate rock. Within his limits, Steve Goodman's a modest little master." [4]

To promote "High and Outside," Steve and Al Bunetta won a victory of sorts with Asylum, persuading the label to back a tour that served as partial consolation for the flap that removed Nicolette Larson's name from the LP's publicity. It was a milestone, Steve's first industry-financed tour with a full band. Pleasing Steve, the band was the backbone of "High and Outside": bassist Rick Chudacoff and drummer Peter Bunetta, along with reeds player Jim Rothermel and vocalist/percussionist Arno Lucas. Steve also secured Jim Ehinger — a pianist for Martha Reeves and Yvonne Elliman — through Chudacoff and Bunetta. But he still needed a female voice for "The One That Got Away" because Nicolette Larson was touring on her own, backed by Little Feat. He offered the role to Raun MacKinnon, but she couldn't leave a full-time job for six weeks. Eventually, Steve found such a singer via Ehinger, whose new wife headed a Los Angeles rock band under her own name and years later became known as film actress Amy Madigan.

"They wanted a female singer, and they really only needed it for the one song," Ehinger says. "Amy could play a little keyboards, too, and that didn't hurt. They figured that since we were married, they weren't going to pay her anything. It was going to be two for the price of one." Ehinger asked Steve, "You wanted two for one, but how about two for two, or at least two for one and three-quarters?"

An agreement was struck, and the tour was on. It had to wait a month for the return of Chudacoff, Bunetta and Ehinger, who were backing Maria Muldaur on shows in Australia and Japan. In the meantime, Steve earned an accolade from an improbable icon — the nation's best-known symbol of popular classical music.

It stemmed from a star-studded tribute to the murdered Chilean musician Victor Jara held March 2 at the venerated 2,800-seat Beacon Theatre in Manhattan. Steve was billed along with Tom Paxton and Josh White Jr. as the U.S. musical performers to complement Quilapayun, a seven-man Chilean folk group. Actors Jon Voight, Lee Grant and Max Gail ("Barney Miller") emceed and did readings. Two days later, *The New York Times*' Robert Palmer labeled it a "leaden" evening, with Steve the lone exception. After starting his pre-intermission segment with a crack ("It's about time somebody did some irrelevant material"), Steve snagged a rave from Palmer. "It was left to Mr. Goodman, whose set touched on human-rights issues but was almost completely irrelevant to Chile, to demonstrate once again that the best advertisement for humanism is often a finely crafted song, sensitively played and spiritedly, even boisterously, sung."

An even bolder endorsement awaited Steve in the moments following his set, which he ended with "The Twentieth Century Is Almost Over." [5] He left the stage to applause and skipped up the backstage steps to the dressing room. With the ovation still ringing, an even louder, rapid-fire stomp-stomp-stomp

For me, the artist's unerring decency and solid craftsmanship can be quite infectiously lulling in the age of high-powered corporate rock. Within his limits, Steve Goodman's a modest little master.
TOM CARSON
ROLLING STONE

4: *People Weekly* labeled "High and Outside" a "pick." Pegging Steve as "a sardonic, folk-tinged composer of the Randy Newman school," the magazine said he "pleasantly handles this selection of mostly his own material."

5: Steve said he was honored when he learned in late 1979 that Johnny Cash had recorded "Twentieth Century" for a forthcoming rockabilly LP. "I hope it doesn't sound too much like those Standard Oil ads he used to do," Steve cracked, "but I'm glad he did it anyway. Good guy."

Leonard Bernstein was so taken by Steve's set during a March 2, 1979, tribute to Victor Jara at Manhattan's Beacon Theatre that he boomed out a desire to write songs with Steve.

(Photo © Pierre Voslinsky, Leonard Bernstein Office, courtesy of the Milken Archive of American Jewish Music)

6: At My Father's Place in Roslyn, New York, Steve realized in the middle of one of his solo songs, "This Hotel Room," that he had mixed up its stanzas. To the crowd's delight, he improvised: "I know a short attention span is the mummy's curse / But I think I sang the verses in reverse."

7: The April 28, 1979, tour stop, at the Bayou in Washington, D.C., became the basis for a posthumous CD, "Live Wire," issued by Red Pajamas in 2000. Unfortunately, the cover photos for the CD were taken during a May 26, 1983, show at Park West in Chicago, when Steve looked markedly different.

noise approached from the stairway, swelling with each stomp. "Someone was running really hard," says Doug Yeager, the manager of Paxton and the younger White. Finally, the mystery man ran into the room, panting. It was one of the evening's speakers, the charismatic Leonard Bernstein.

"Where is he? Where is he?" Bernstein roared. "Who wrote that song? I want to write songs with him!" The emphysemic 61-year-old ran over to shake Steve's hand. The two never ended up collaborating, but at an uncertain time for Steve, plaudits from the longtime conductor of the New York Philharmonic and composer of "West Side Story" were uncommonly gratifying.

Steve's full-band tour kicked off April 16 at Michigan State University, streaming into clubs in 19 cities throughout the East, Midwest and West and playing one or two shows a night. Asylum advertised most of the slate in *Rolling Stone*, and shows on Long Island and in Cincinnati and Washington, D.C., were simulcast on FM radio.

The shows were an adjustment for Steve. Though for years he had defined his act by impulsiveness and improvisation, out of courtesy to his touring accompanists he had to work with a fixed set list. Likewise, he had to pay closer attention within each song itself. "He was so used to playing by himself that he couldn't just stick in an extra bar before the bridge or wait a second before he went to the chorus," Ehinger says. "He never got used to the idea that if he changed things spontaneously, there were five other people. It kept happening. Nothing drastic. It was kind of fun, actually. But you always had to be prepared."

Despite that challenge, "High and Outside" couldn't have received a more energetic push. In contrast to the LP's polished and distant studio sessions, and with the presence of live audiences, the shows cooked. "I gotta hear this kinda music right now," Steve told Marianne Meyer of the New Jersey-based *Aquarian*. "We gotta pump a good time." Upbeat tunes like "Men Who Love Women Who Love Men" and "Hand It to You" came alive, and reworked versions of quieter material such as "The Dutchman" and "Would You Like to Learn to Dance?" ("I wrote this just in time for the disco craze about nine years ago," Steve cracked) were all the more effective. "We really want to show that we can play dynamics, that we know how quiet it's supposed to feel, and when it's up, how loud it's supposed to be," Steve said. "It's not just a matter of volume. From day one of rehearsal, we knew that the ballads were gonna be hotter than the hot tunes, 'cause there ain't no way I'm gonna be Rod Stewart."

Throughout the shows, Steve often played electric guitar, and he reserved a spot in the middle for a smattering of acoustic solo tunes. [6] The big question — how "The One That Got Away" would play — was answered decisively by Madigan, whose throaty voice, fuller and deeper than Nicolette Larson's, proved a rich complement to Steve's. Overall, the tour filled its venues, and a schedule that had begun with three weeks of dates expanded to five. The packed audiences roared their approval. [7]

The accompanists fondly recall the tour because of the comfort and respect extended them by Steve. "He was a great pied piper," says Peter Bunetta. "He was tremendous at leading and great at not dictating. He nurtured, he didn't control."

"The energy we shared onstage was unbelievable, and the experience was definitely one of the more enjoyable ones in my life," adds Arno Lucas, an African-American who became "a victim of forced busing to achieve music" in Steve's introduction of him onstage. "He didn't act like a star," Lucas says. "Some of the people I've worked with, the star thing is ever present, and it sucks. They tend to forget why they started doing it in the first place, and the things that really mean something to them are not the things that made them people who could harness the magic. But Steve wasn't one of those guys. We all rode on the bus together. We'd sit down and hang for hours and laugh and scream. It was as good as it gets, in terms of hanging with a person who is ultimately the boss. He'd be the last guy if there was something to eat. He'd never want to go first. He was a very generous guy."

At tour's end, Steve tendered extra payments to his band mates, which astonished other musicians. "There was money left over, so Steve gave everybody a bonus," says guitarist Charlie Chin. "I had never heard of that being done before. What usually happens is, you figure the cost of the guys that you're carrying, then at the end of the trip if you've got extra money, well, you keep it."

Generosity and attentive audiences, however, didn't translate to album purchases. "High and Outside" ended up with only 15,000 sales, just half of what his two previous LPs, "Private" and "Words," had sold, and less than a third of the figures for his first Asylum LP, "Jessie's Jig."

His slide with the label was steepening, which Steve admitted with disarming embarrassment. "I must be in arrears to the record company for God knows what," he told the *Aquarian*. "(But) those kind of pressures can't really affect the music. You can only be what you're gonna be. If it feels right, that's what counts." Steve told Peter O.E. Bekker of WCBS of his gratitude. "Asylum's been sponsorin' us in the studio for four years," he said. "I think they've been great with me, man, because I ain't exactly pullin' my weight compared to Linda Ronstadt or Queen or somebody like that. I really think it's nice of 'em that they're keepin' me around."

The trend, however, was ominous. "You gotta realize that the big band at the time was Steely Dan, this clinically sounding music," says Steve's friend and bassist Jim Tullio, who had carved a career in producing jingles. "Some of the tracks (on "High and Outside") I loved, but some of them were too thought-out, too intellectual, too calculated. The emotion was not there. If Goodman had anything, he had this emotional base, which made him great, but he was trying to be Steely Dan. It's like, 'Steve, it's not you.' "

It wasn't as if Steve were shielded from the disconnect. Breaking the bad news privately was one of his most prominent and consistent champions, New York radio host Vin Scelsa.

Scelsa had hosted four interview shows with Steve on progressive-rock

> **If Goodman had anything, he had this emotional base, which made him great, but he was trying to be Steely Dan. It's like, 'Steve, it's not you.'**
> **JIM TULLIO**

During the March 22, 1978, taping of Vin Scelsa's show for WNEW-FM, this happy threesome — David Amram on flute, Scelsa on alto sax and Steve on guitar — painted a picture of comradeship. But just a year later, Scelsa found that his musical tastes, and those of his audience, had changed. So he opted not to play Steve's new "corny, stylized, old-fashioned, crooner kind of album" on the air.

(Photo courtesy of Vin Scelsa)

WNEW-FM from 1975 to 1978 and was the only deejay at the station consistently playing Steve's records. They had shared a diminutive stature and a love of on-air banter. In the fourth of their "Easter" collaborations (so named because of proximity to the holiday), Scelsa asked Steve to sing "Easter Parade," and Steve initially responded with a piece of improvised Christmas silliness, "Rudolph the Easter Reindeer." Scelsa had learned "Easter Parade" on his little-used Selmer alto sax and intended to back Steve on the Irving Berlin tune on the air. But before they got to the song, Steve (along with second guest David Amram) induced Scelsa to honk a fitful sax solo on "Mama Don't Allow It." The playful rapport left the impression that the two were inseparable comrades.

By 1979, however, Scelsa's tastes had shifted to the harsh, trendy punk-rock movement that encompassed Patti Smith, the Ramones, the Clash, Elvis Costello, Graham Parker and the Talking Heads. "In the middle of all this came 'High and Outside,' and it was the exact antithesis of the direction that I was going in on the radio," Scelsa says. "I felt it was sort of a corny, stylized, old-fashioned, crooner kind of album, so I never played it."

In touch with Asylum promo staff in New York, Steve learned of his LP's disappearance from Scelsa's WNEW turntable. One night, he phoned the deejay. "Let's not mince words," he said. "How come you're not playin' my record, man?"

"This is really hard for me to say," Scelsa replied, "but I don't like it that much, and it doesn't fit in with what I'm doing."

The two talked further, Scelsa says. "I could tell he was hurt, because he was moving in a different direction, and I just was not willing or interested in going in that direction with him. He was OK with it. He understood. It was hard for me to get it out, and it made me look at myself and think, 'Am I being a hypocrite here? I'm supporting all this other music, but why can't I continue to support my friend's music, too?' Today, I recognize it was totally stupid on my part and that certainly I could have figured out a way to make it fit, but back then it was just a hard choice I had to make." Sadly, it was Scelsa's last conversation with Steve.

While the unfolkie polish of "High and Outside" was meeting with rejection, Steve needed a refuge. So when he played a June 21-23 stint at the Hot Tin Roof on Martha's Vineyard island, south of Massachusetts' Cape Cod, he brought along Nancy and the three girls, all hosted by Hot Tin Roof founding partner Carly Simon. Oldest daughter Jessie, 7, found the Simon spread a paradise. "She had this huge barbecue cookout," she says. "There were trash cans full of seafood. John Belushi was there. They couldn't get me out of the pool." Steve found his own tranquil diversion, thanks to folk and blues singer Geoff Muldaur, also an island resident. "I took him fishing for striped bass in Menemsha Creek," Muldaur says. "It was a quiet, starry night, and we were drifting with the outgoing tide. He got onto a 20-pounder and brought it in. I've never seen a guy so happy."

Another distraction — and a means to vent frustration — became softball, on summertime Sundays on a lakeside diamond at Loyola Park in the Rogers Park neighborhood of Chicago's far North Side near Evanston. The "Great Folkie Softball Games," as its participants called them, began at 11 a.m. and ran through the afternoon — sometimes co-ed, sometimes all guys. The players included Bob Hoban, Howard Levy, Tom Piekarski, Jim and Vivian Craig, Jim Tullio, Harry Waller, Mary Gaffney, Chris Farrell, Mike Jordan, Tom Dundee, Johnny Burns, Angelo Varias and Mike Lieber. Most saw the sessions as an easygoing release. They played for fun, sometimes stopping balls with their feet to keep from jamming their fingers and forfeiting a musical gig.

Not so Steve, however.

For Steve, softball unleashed intensity bordering on the fearsome. His favorite position was shortstop, a spot where he could be in the flow of most plays. (No one recalls if he chose it as a pun on his height.) But the place his competitive juices gushed was on the basepaths, exemplified by the second game of a doubleheader that still grips the memories of its players. Early in the game, sprinting from first to second on a sure double-play ball, Steve was an easy out, but Varias, at short, took his time throwing to Hoban, who couldn't peg the ball to first in time to complete the twin killing. Unimpressed as he walked off the field, Steve spat at Hoban, "Why don't you peel it and eat it, you big ape?"

The more visceral play came late in the game, a nail-biter with a lone run separating the teams. Again on base, Steve took off on a hit and soon was rounding third in a blaze. Someone threw the ball to Piekarski, the third-baseman, who fired it home to Hoban, who had switched to catcher. The ball arrived just before Steve did. "It was dead on the money," Hoban says, "and Goodman was

I took him fishing for striped bass in Menemsha Creek. It was a quiet, starry night, and we were drifting with the outgoing tide. He got onto a 20-pounder and brought it in. I've never seen a guy so happy.
GEOFF MULDAUR

Singer/songwriter Tom Dundee found a clue to Steve's persona when daring him at a Bay Area nude beach to shed his clothes and frolic in the surf.

(Photo from Tom Dundee LP, "A Delicate Balance," Freckle Records, by permission of Jack Burg)

dead out." But Steve steamed along and barreled into Hoban, Pete Rose-style, knocking him over and forcing the ball out of his mitt. Hoban was dazed as Steve shouted, "You dropped the ball, asshole!" Enraged, Hoban lurched to his feet and took a swing at Steve, "as hard as I could," he says, "but it didn't put him in the lake."

Steve had acquired an athletic build and demeanor to match his passion for the game. His daughter, Jessie, says that on the floor of their Evanston home, her dad did 100 push-ups at a time, sometimes with her younger sisters Sarah and Rosanna sitting on his back. Lieber, one of the folkie softball players, who today coaches baseball, says Steve's greater physical strength translated to agility on the field. "He made up for his height with quickness," Lieber says. "There was no wasted motion. Beautiful, smooth, just the way he approached the ball. At short, he could cover a lot of ground. He was off with the ball, that eye/body coordination. The reflexes were really quick. He could see a trajectory. He was there. He didn't make easy catches look hard. He made hard catches look easy."

But the crash that Steve induced at home plate alarmed another player, Levy, who yelled at him across the diamond, "Jesus Christ, man, it's just a game! Steve! Geez!" Levy shakes his head at the memory. "He was playing real ferociously, and it turned me off because it was the other side of Steve," he says. "As nice as Steve was, he was that fierce, because the fierce thing is what gets you where you're going."

Another of the Rogers Park softball players, Tom Dundee, witnessed an equally fierce Steve off the diamond and 2,000 miles west. After playing concerts at different venues in San Francisco, the two met, and Dundee drove Steve to nearby Marin County to take in the coastal phenomenon of a nude beach. Steve was reluctant, but Dundee insisted. Once they arrived, Dundee dared Steve to shed his clothes and partake of the ocean. Steve declined, so Dundee disrobed, left Steve behind and ran out to frolic in the chilly Pacific surf. After getting his fill of the waves, Dundee started walking back in toward the land. Soon, the sight before him was a stunner. It was Steve, striding toward him, naked. As the two met, Dundee towered over Steve by a foot. Steve's eyes were wide, and he wore a rueful grin. What Steve said, Dundee never forgot. To him, it was Steve's encyclopedic character encapsulated in a sentence:

"Every time I swore I'd never do something, some motherfucker taller than me did it, and so I had to do it, too."

The two scurried out to the surf. For 15 minutes, they laughed and cavorted, as Dundee said, like a couple of kids: "I was swimmin' like a child with Steve Goodman, who was a child of God."

His performance schedule dotted with Steve Martin openers in 1979, Steve also trained his tenacity on side projects, including an October demo session at the Record Plant in Los Angeles for ex-"Lemmings" singer Alice Playten. "Yellis" (as Steve called her in his Chicago inflection) wanted to stay away from what she regarded as stereotypical "victimized girl songs." So with the Crackin' core of Rick Chudacoff, Peter Bunetta and Arno Lucas, Steve oversaw the recording of a trio of tunes showcasing Playten's powerful voice, which careened from raspy to seductive. In Steve's hands, the Nick Lowe shouter, "I Knew the Bride When She Used to Rock 'n' Roll," got an almost impossibly frenetic, punkish tempo, matched flawlessly by Playten's driving vocal. Another selection, slower and in the new-wave mold, "Daddy, Daddy, Walk My Way," drew on tight backup vocals by Bonnie Raitt, Amy Madigan and Rosemary Butler. Opened by a bluesy guitar line by Steve, the third composition was a slinky and infectious Maria Muldaur-style, Bobby Charles love song, "Good Place Now," which boasted the note-perfect harmonica strains of John Sebastian. The song was, as Steve put it, "like what would happen if Billie Holiday sang country."

The Playten tracks spanned commercial genres, and Steve's production of them matched the sound of other successful music of the time. Despite the tracks' polish and hit potential, however, they never surfaced publicly. [8]

Intriguingly, Steve added a new dimension to his professional persona in 1979 without really seeking it. He merely answered a series of invitations from a refreshing new realm — the world of TV and radio producers on a search for someone to write and perform musical commentary on current affairs. This swath of offers began in the place that knew him best, Chicago.

"The Good Gang Express" became Steve's first foray into theme writing for television. Hosted by African-American newsman Warner Saunders, it was a children's program produced by WBBM-TV, the CBS affiliate, that celebrated racial diversity without bludgeoning it. In the half-hour show, Saunders drove a bright orange van (the "Express" of the show's title), carrying a mixed group of eight children, ages 7 to 13, to hands-on activities and sites in Chicago, from the Lincoln Park Zoo and a local farm to the studio of a mime at St. Nicholas Theater and Evanston's Robert Crown skating center. Producer Gail Sikevitz hired Steve to write the sprightly theme song, whose lyrics underscored the show's goal, to "Let the good times roll till the sun goes down / With a carload of kids from all over town." Sitting with Steve in the kitchen of his Evanston home on a Sunday morning, Sikevitz marveled at how fast the tune tumbled out of him.

"I explained the concept," Sikevitz says, "and he started picking out notes and chords and just wrote it." While Steve fashioned the tune, his youngest daughter Rosanna, not quite 2, burst into view. "She was a tiny thing with lovely, curly hair, and she had escaped from a diaper. She ran through the kitchen naked and ran into the backyard filled with flowers and grass, and she just twirled with abandon and joy as he played."

With Steve's song playing at the opening and close of the show and in the "bumpers" before commercials, "Good Gang" got great local reviews, but only two episodes of the labor-intensive program aired, on March 3 and April 28. Still, it won a 1979 Chicago Emmy for children's programming.

Steve tackled a more ominous topic when asked by a friend of Sikevitz, producer Dillon Smith of WMAQ-TV, Chicago's NBC affiliate, to write the theme for a half-hour documentary on nuclear power. The March 28 meltdown

Singer/actress Alice Playten sought for Steve to oversee a Los Angeles recording session in 1979, and Steve produced three tracks for Playten that were never released.

(Photo courtesy of Alice Playten)

8: It was about this time that in Evanston, Steve also produced the recording of a road song written and performed by Harry Waller, "Ride on the Prairie." In addition, Steve had produced demo tracks in mid-1978 for Tom Dundee.

of a reactor core at Three Mile Island in Pennsylvania, had made tangible the nation's fears about nuclear energy. Smith, the station's editorial commentator, decided a local special should alert Chicagoans to the dominant role played by five such plants within an hour of the city, including the two Commonwealth Edison nuclear plants in Zion, 30 miles north. But Smith also was determined to go further — and did so, appearing on camera at the end of the program calling for a halt to the construction of new nuclear plants.

"I thought that I'd like to make this a little more show-biz because it was going to be awfully dry," Smith said. "I wanted to add some fun to it. I knew some people who could do a musical theme, but I was looking for somebody with personality and a touch that only Steve had. So I called Steve and said, 'Hey, I need a song. I don't have much money.' It wasn't like we were going to make any money on the show. I said I could pay him $300. He said, 'That's OK, fine.' "

Smith supplied the show's title — "In Our Nuclear Backyard," based on the nuclear plants' proximity — and Steve wrote a matching song that laid out facts chillingly but without moralizing. "Mothers and fathers and husbands and wives / Are leading their radiological lives ... Oh, how their need for this power has grown / Along with the chances of perils unknown / When they live in a world that is accident prone." A refrain rang throughout: "Right in our own backyard." Like Sikevitz, Smith was awed by Steve's writing speed. "Let's see," Steve told him dryly, "I think it took about 25 minutes, but I had a couple of phone calls. But still it took a little longer than 'City of New Orleans.' "

Steve's involvement with "Backyard" didn't end with writing and recording the song for its use in the special's opening, wrap-up and bumpers. When Smith mentioned in passing that he was driving to one of the Commonwealth Edison plants to film stand-up shots outside, Steve said, "That sounds like fun. Could I go?" Smith obtained a security clearance for Steve, and the pair toured the facility. Inside, Smith shot a photo of Steve wearing a hardhat, and the station's publicists put it to good use. On the Sunday before the special's Thursday, June 28, airdate, the photo, cropped to a portrait, ran in the TV section of the *Chicago Sun-Times*. "It made it as if Steve was the star of the show," Smith said, "but that was OK because we needed Steve because he was so popular in Chicago." 9 The evening that "Backyard" aired, Steve joined others who worked on the special to view it at Smith's condo. There, Steve gave Smith a wickedly suitable gift — a hardhat for protection against Skylab, the space station that fell to Earth just two weeks later in sparsely populated sections of Australia.

A topic less scientific and closer to Steve's heart became his next TV writing assignment — parenthood. WMAQ profiled Family Focus, a Chicago agency devoted to answering the tough questions of new mothers and fathers. Narrated by actor Tony Franciosa, the 30-minute special, "A Permanent Condition," consisted mostly of interviews with parents and ended with a quote from Khalil Gibran, author of *The Prophet*. Sandra Weir, producer, hired Steve to compose the theme, and he responded with "Homo Sapiens," a gentle and

Let's see, I think it took about 25 minutes, but I had a couple of phone calls. But still it took a little longer than 'City of New Orleans.'
STEVE GOODMAN

9: Steve performed "In Our Nuclear Backyard" three weeks later at the Ravinia Festival in Highland Park, just 15 miles south of the Commonwealth Edison plant. Thereafter, the song was never again played or recorded by Steve or aired on WMAQ.

deceptively simple tune. Assuring parents that they "will never feel ready to take in all of the love and responsibility," the song asked them not to set expectations for their kids but rather to instill a sense of right and wrong and family belonging.

"His children were small at the time, and he was very much into the whole thing," says Bonnie Remsberg, family-planning professor at the University of Chicago who wrote the script. What impressed Remsberg more was learning that Steve was taking his personal reproductive role one crucial step further. Shortly before the Aug. 28, 1979, airdate for "A Permanent Condition," she visited with Steve at Somebody Else's Troubles, and because she, too, lived in Evanston, she offered to give him a ride home. Before they left, and in front of several others at the club, Steve raised a delicate topic in a manner that was decidedly offhand.

"I've been spending the day investigating birth control," Steve said.

"Oh, really," Remsberg said. ("Men just didn't talk like that in those days," she says. "Not a whole lot of 'em do now, but they sure as hell didn't then.")

"Yeah, I just checked out having a vasectomy," Steve said.

"Really?"

"Yeah, I've decided that it's time," he said. "It's been Nancy's responsibility, and I've decided it's time for me to take responsibility."

Remsberg remains stunned by Steve's disarming frankness. "We weren't particularly close, and I wasn't a confidante," she says. Vasectomy "certainly was the right thing to do and the responsible thing to do, but the fact that he even made the announcement, I was just inordinately impressed."

Another way Steve took parental responsibility was to bring music into his children's schools, starting with 7-year-old Jessie, who in fall 1979 was a second-grader at the private Baker Demonstration School at the National College of Education in Evanston. There, teacher MaryJo Cally guided students in creating a story about what it would be like for them to stay overnight at the school, wearing pajamas and ordering pizza.

She invited Steve to take it a step further by setting the story to music, as he had done with several stuffed-animal stories the children had written. The result — a cassette recording by Steve with the theme of "We're gonna have a party tonight" — was part of a presentation to parents at an assembly. "The kids all wore their pajamas and carried their stuffed animals onstage," Cally says. "It was a creative-writing experience that Steve enhanced a lot. We had a blast."

Steve's connection with Cally deepened when he gave her a copy of the "GoGo the Blue Gorilla" LP, which she often played in class. Steve also chaperoned field trips to museums, including a trek to the Chicago Historical Society to see an exhibit on the Great Chicago Fire of 1871 and the mythic bucket-kick of Mrs. O'Leary's cow. When a guard shushed excited children as they climbed a stairway, Steve replied, "Hey, man, take it easy," and when a boy who was enthralled by a talk leaned on a fire door, setting off alarm bells, Steve led the

I just checked out having a vasectomy. ... It's been Nancy's responsibility, and I've decided it's time for me to take responsibility.
STEVE GOODMAN

group to another room. "C'mon, children," he said, "let's move on, let's move on." His rapport with the kids was exceeded only by the obvious regard in which Jessie held him. "He was her hero," Cally says. "There was no doubt about it. He walked into school, and it had nothing to do with his notoriety. It had to do with his being her dad."

Doing well in school was part of what Steve instilled in Jessie. Once, while working on homework for Cally, her dad told her that a B grade was not good enough. "That's just above average," he said. "You have to try harder." Her father's songwriting also seeped into the consciousness of Jessie, who, in 1979 upon the death of her pet hamster, named Sweety Bun, made up a tune and warbled it over the phone to Steve, who was in Los Angeles. Sung to "O Tannenbaum," the German Christmas carol, the song's only lyrics were, "Oh, Sweety Bun, oh, Sweety Bun, you're such a lovely hamster."

Vivid in Jessie's early memories is her father's unfailing open-door policy. Often, she says, Steve came home at 4 or 5 a.m. with a musical friend or two in tow. "Nancy," he would say, "this is so-and-so. Could you cook up something now?" The policy continued even when Steve was out of town. "He would call from the road, and people would stay with us left and right, complete strangers we didn't know, just a musician he met at a bar who needed a place to stay." Other times, the middle-of-the-night calls would be for sharing new song lyrics or jokes he'd just heard. At 3 a.m., Jessie would hear the phone ring and her mother answer it.

"Guess what?" Steve would say. "Two guys walk into a bar —"

Nancy would interrupt. "I've heard this one before," she'd say.

"No, no, no," Steve would answer, "it's the Cincinnati version."

And he would relate the joke in a new way that never failed to trigger laughter. "He was so funny," Jessie says. "He had jokes that he would tell over and over. Every joke, he told it 50 times."

That fall, Steve's music and humor impressed not just his family in Evanston but also those with instant access to ears all over the country. National Public Radio, whose "Folk Festival USA" show had frequently broadcast Steve's Philly performances, hired him to supply musical commentary for the network's popular afternoon show "All Things Considered." Steve's role, a hand-in-glove fit, was to fashion songs that poked at the issues of the day, in the same manner that NPR already had employed folksy Florida songwriter and storyteller Gamble Rogers. Exposure to the educated listeners of NPR's 220 stations promised to be a plum. In contrast to the vagaries of studio "sound" and hitmaking, this assignment played to Steve's established strengths of quick writing and observational wit.

But the first of what he called his "newspaper songs" for NPR was infused with the blackest humor possible — or, as Steve put it, "right there on the edge, on the razor blade of you either laugh or throw up." The tune addressed the devastating crash of an American Airlines DC-10 jet shortly after its May 25, 1979, takeoff from Chicago's O'Hare field. Killing all of the plane's 258 passengers and 13 crew, it shocked the nation and became the worst accidental single-aircraft disaster in U.S. history (remaining so until the 9/11 attacks of 2001).

Long accustomed to air travel, Steve was stunned by the calamity, and his musical response, written at the San Francisco airport, was bitter. His song merged two folk techniques: a lengthy narrative and a repeated phrase. The result was the seven-verse "Ballad of Flight 191," whose sarcastic mantra, "They know everything about it," was heard no fewer than 36 times, plus six more times in extended fashion: "They know everything about it but why / That plane fell out of the sky." The verses detailed the abortive trip, including the separation of one of the jet's engines from its wing and the tragic aftermath. The final stanza revealed a void that Steve, living with a fatal disease, found most galling: "You can still get a ride on a DC-10. ... They were gone for awhile, but they're back again. ... They make one or two technological advances. ... You pay your money and you take your chances."

"Flight 191" roiled with anger similar to the fury Steve had expressed seven years earlier in "Ballad of Penny Evans." But the emotion was more cynical, and its third-person approach lacked a sympathetic protagonist. Instead of blanketing its venom in grief, "Flight 191" amounted to a harangue.

Steve knew the tune's bite was risky. "This ain't exactly what you call your pop record," he told Philadelphia radio host Gene Shay. Explaining the song at San Francisco's Great American Music Hall, he said, "There hasn't been a real good ambulance-chasing song in awhile. I don't think there's a need for such songs, but there hasn't been a good one since the Titanic or the Reuben James."

In all, Steve, backed by Jethro Burns, recorded 11 topical songs for NPR's "All Things Considered" weekend producer Deborah Amos and NPR Chicago bureau chief Scott Simon in Studs Terkel's studio at WFMT-FM on Michigan Avenue. [10] In addition to "Flight 191," the network aired four of Steve's songs to accompany stories that fall: "Daley's Gone" (Sept. 25, Chicago patronage), "Unemployed" (Oct. 10, teachers' right to organize), "Twentieth Century" (Oct. 28, leaders of yesteryear) and "Election Year Rag" (Oct. 31, John Connally and the milk-fund scandal). [11] But Steve's role as a topical commentator for NPR went no further.

The next month, Steve's songs had another bid to hit the nation's public airwaves, not for radio but for TV. The connection came via an editor of the *National Lampoon*, Sean Kelly. The two had been brought together, strangely enough, by a different plane crash. Kelly — like Steve, a baseball fanatic (their wives labeled them "baseball homos") — had been irked by what he considered overkill and maudlin reportage of the Aug. 2, 1979, death of Yankees catcher Thurman Munson in the crash landing in Akron, Ohio, of a small jet that Munson had piloted. In response, Kelly wrote a parody called "Who's Catching for the Yankees in Heaven Tonight?" and phoned Alice Playten to read her its lyrics. "You have to call Steve Goodman," she said, "because he's a baseball freak." Once Steve heard the words, he told Kelly, "You are one sick human being. I'm not writing music to this. We'll both get killed."

There hasn't been a real good ambulance-chasing song ... since the Titanic or the Reuben James.
STEVE GOODMAN

10: Steve's racy humor was in full tilt after the NPR taping session in Chicago. He, Simon and Amos caught a late dinner at Moe's Corned Beef Cellar on Rush Street, where Steve passed along to Amos a line he'd picked up: "If God had not wanted man to eat pussy, he would not have made it look like a taco."

11: NPR also may have secured Steve's songs for its new daybreak program, "Morning Edition," which debuted Nov. 5, 1979. *The Washington Post* reported Nov. 4 that he was slated as a "regular commentator." But of more than two dozen NPR sources, no one recalls Steve's involvement with the a.m. show, and run sheets do not reflect use of any of his songs. Likely, Steve's songs were aired only on "All Things Considered."

Soon, Kelly recruited Steve for the cast of a fledgling show for the Public Broadcasting System. Eyeing the success of NBC's four-year-old "Saturday Night Live," PBS planned a series with similar satire — but with the twist of taping shows at college campuses. To get a pilot under way, PBS plugged into the *National Lampoon* network, hiring Kelly as head writer. [12] The pilot, "Good Grief America," was filmed Tuesday evening, Nov. 13, 1979, in 78-year-old Woolsey Hall at Yale University in New Haven, Connecticut. It featured comic Gary Goodrow, "Animal House" actor Jamie Widdoes, PBS analyst (now CNN host) Jeff Greenfield and Shelley Barre of the comedy group The Proposition.

Steve sang several topical tunes that night, including the encore, "Men Who Love Women Who Love Men." He rolled out a new takeoff on a Temptations hit, "Ain't Too Proud to Beg," that tweaked the $1.5 billion federal loan guarantee that ailing auto giant Chrysler had pleaded for and that President Carter and Congress approved that fall. Scoffing at company spokesman Joe Garagiola's TV ads for rebates, the tune concluded ruefully that "Uncle Sam got to carry the load."

The most wicked of Steve's new musical tracts, however, was a talking blues that capitalized on a crisis that had ignited just nine days earlier. Employing bitter puns, the song skewered the Nov. 4 takeover of the U.S. Embassy in Tehran by Iranian militants who seized 66 Americans (52 of whom were held hostage through the remaining 14 months of the Carter presidency). The lyrics exuded caustic humor: "I called the ayatollah on the telephone. He said, 'How the hell did you get through to me?' I said, 'It was Yankee ingenuity. I told the operator, make it Persian to Persian.' He said, 'What?' I told him, 'It was a joke: How many Iranians does it take to screw up the world?' "

To those familiar with Steve's music, an even more startling experience at Yale was to hear him sing the pilot's title song. Steve willingly poked fun at his most famous composition by changing the iconic lyrics of its chorus to "Good grief, America, where are you?"

PBS, which set aside $14,500 for the project, had told *The New York Times* that it hoped to air the pilot nationally in late November. But that was before the show took place. Widely advertised at Yale ("We're putting the sophomoric back into college humor — and the freshmen, juniors, seniors and grad students should be there, too!" shouted an ad in the *Yale Daily News*), the free event at 8 p.m. drew only 700 students to the 3,000-seat hall. Worse, only 100 stayed to the end. Boos, hisses and shouts of "Boring!" rang out.

Sheila Wellehan, writing in the student paper, called it a flop whose material, culled partly from student ideas, was largely "cheap shots at women, gays and political leaders." The nadir of the night, Wellehan said, was a skit showing Pierre Trudeau, the recently defeated Canadian prime minister, receiving a late-night phone call from his estranged wife, Margaret, who said she was at Studio 54 in New York City with Massachusetts Sen. Edward M. "Teddy" Kennedy. Summoning the memory of Kennedy's infamous Chappaquiddick scandal of 10 years earlier, Trudeau told Margaret, "Ask him to give you a ride home."

There was laughter in the crowd, but it wasn't really the 'Saturday Night Live' type of 'Wow,' which is what they were shooting for.
JAY WHITSETT

12: Steve later skewered Kelly and his *Lampoon* link with vicious affection: "My kind of guy: no taste at all, and no shame, either. What a rag that is. They don't care what they do — all the way from 'Shoot This Dog' and all that stuff. He's a sort of a sick kind of guy."

WE'RE PUTTING THE SOPHOMORIC BACK INTO COLLEGE HUMOR.

AND THE FRESHMEN, JUNIORS, SENIORS AND GRAD STUDENTS SHOULD BE THERE TOO!

It's a public television show with a difference. You.

"Good Grief America" is a free-form sequence of irreverent blackouts, spontaneous one-liners, outrageous parodies, put-downs and put-ons. An anthology of side-splitting songs, skits and satire. The best of college humor.

The players? The cast includes Jaime Widdoes from **Animal House**. Singer Steve Goodman. Gary Goodrow, Sean Kelley and Elaine Psihountas from the off-Broadway smash **National Lampoon's Lemmings**. Shelley Barre from **Grease**. And comic Jeff Greenfield.

"Good Grief America" is the pilot program of a proposed new public television series. A realistic, honest, witty, silly and laugh-filled appraisal of America. And we want you there. Participating.

Connecticut Public Television will videotape "Good Grief America" before a live audience at Woolsey Hall on Tuesday, November 13 at 8 p.m. Tickets are free. In fact, there aren't any tickets. Just come. Laugh. And tell your friends.

GOOD GRIEF AMERICA

TONIGHT AT 8 WOOLSEY HALL

A production of ⊕ Connecticut Public Television

With the taping of a pilot program for "Good Grief, America," Steve — singing a parody of his most famous song — was in on the ground floor of a PBS-TV comedy show that aimed to rival the popularity of NBC-TV's "Saturday Night Live." But the pilot was grounded before it had a chance to air, the victim of hasty preparation and jokes that fell flat for an audience of students at Yale.

(Ad from the Nov. 13, 1979, *Yale Daily News*, reprinted by permission)

The performers, says Jay Whitsett, the pilot's associate producer for Connecticut Public Television, "were really upbeat, and they thought they were creating something that was cutting edge. But somehow when it all came together at Yale, there was laughter in the crowd, but it wasn't really the 'Saturday Night Live' type of 'Wow,' which is what they were shooting for." Several PBS staff who flew in from Alexandria, Virginia, to see the taping were not impressed. "Pretty much every skit that came out, they didn't laugh," says Whitsett, who was seated directly in front of the PBSers. "They were very, very excited when they came in and were anxious to see it, but they didn't think it was funny. When they left, I could see it in their body language."

Banjoist and folk historian Stephen Wade, shown in 1976, found Steve's "Flight 191" to be a humorless travesty, "one of the worst songs he ever wrote."
(Photo by Jamie Downs)

"I basically strangled it in its crib," says Barry Chase, PBS director of news and public affairs programming. "It wasn't a close call. It didn't really advance the art much beyond 'Saturday Night Live.' It was reasonably literate and clever in some respects, but it wasn't terribly funny."

Steve, who provided the musical and comedic "glue" between skits, was the pilot's only true standout. The *Yale Daily News'* Wellehan said Steve's "folk singing and guitar work brightened an otherwise dismal show." Whitsett says, "If there was a bright spot, it was him. The other folks were talented, but I don't think the material was that rich for them as an ensemble." An underlying factor was that the PBS of 1979, says Sean Kelly, was schizophrenic about its desires for such a prickly program. "We did a pretty funny show," Kelly says, "but a couple of weeks went by, and we didn't hear anything from the PBS guys. They were afraid that some of the stuff was a little edgy. Finally, they got back to us, and they said they'd been reviewing the tapes, and they realized it was perfectly acceptable. The problem was, by then it was dated."

Thus, Steve's second venture into public broadcasting died as quietly as his first. Though he kept breathing life into his "newspaper songs" in concerts over the next 12 months, he grew increasingly harsh in presenting "Flight 191," the first and most scathing of the batch. In one show, Steve ruefully skewered the flight as "nonstop: Chicago to almost Chicago." In another, he simply said, "God, that upset me. Shit." Emily Friedman, *Come for to Sing* editor, says, "He was seething." The song — and Steve's uncharacteristic acidity — grated on hometown musical friends who were touched most directly by the tragedy.

"It didn't work here because there were so many people from here who died," says Ed Holstein. "It was well-intentioned, but nobody was quite sure what his point was. It was very ambiguous. But at least he would try stuff. He wasn't ever an offensive guy. Every time he did something, it was with a good heart. He really was a curious guy, and he wanted to write about interesting things. He had a very topical sense. He would have been a terrific reporter. His mind knew how to work that way. A year or two later, that song might have worked, but it was just too soon."

"That song was one of the worst songs he ever wrote," says Stephen Wade, the native Chicagoan whose long-running, one-man revue "Banjo Dancing" opened at the city's Body Politic theater on Lincoln Avenue one week before the crash. "That damn DC-10 song was a true failure of songwriting on his part, which was very rare. It wasn't funny. I told him to stop performing it, and others did, too."

Eventually, bowing to such beefs or because it was no longer timely, Steve grounded "Flight 191" from his shows and never released the song. [13]

One last abortive tryst with public broadcasting in 1979 teamed Steve with three musical comedy colleagues from his past, Warren Leming, Nate Herman and Bob Hoban. The trio concocted a multi-episode satire for radio called "The Unhistory of Rock 'n' Roll," its segments poking fun at blues, rockabilly and other genres. With interest from NPR and a potential sponsorship from 7-Up

13: At least eight of Steve's performances of "Flight 191," along with his "Ain't Too Proud to Beg" parody and his talking blues about the Iran hostage crisis, survive on tapes of his shows from November 1979 through December 1980.

("the Uncola"), they recorded demos at Curtis Mayfield's studio in Chicago. Singing two of the songs was Steve.

In one, written by Herman, Steve impersonated the late Elvis Presley in mocking The King's 1970 request to then-President Nixon to become a federal drug agent. ("I just want to be a G-man / Through eternity, your G-man.") The other was a Hoban-written, off-color imitation of Marty Robbins, spoofing his "El Paso" hit with "El Forward Paso," in which a Texas college football coach employs Rosa, a cheerleader, in the locker room at halftime to inspirational effect. ("Those boys got back on the gridiron, passing and punting as never before / Rosa had taken 11 sad losers and shown each one of them just how to score.") The series died aborning, however, and never was aired.

Other purely upbeat developments sustained Steve in 1979.

In another collaboration with Sean Kelly, he wrote the music for a set of wacky Kelly lyrics that ridiculed a quartet of prevalent pop styles: punk, reggae, the posturing of Bruce Springsteen ("I'm a close approximation of an uptown imitation of a white boy's simulation of a black man's blues" [14]) and ABBA-style disco ("Is the best part of our 45 the hole?"). In an arrangement totaling less than four minutes, Steve made each of the song's four sections sound like the music it was satirizing. Given that these styles had grown more fashionable than any of Steve's own records, in his concerts Steve took devilish delight in performing the sendup, which was titled "What Were You Expecting — Rock 'n' Roll?" The tune became the only music on *National Lampoon*'s spoken-word comedy LP, "The White Album," released in 1980. Steve served as the track's producer. [15]

Two guest slots on hugely popular TV shows — one in Canada, and one in the United States — also gave Steve a boost at the end of the decade.

John Allan Cameron, the Cape Breton-born Celtic fiddler, guitarist and singer who hosted a weekly variety program for the Canadian Broadcasting Corporation, brought Steve onto an episode that aired Friday evening, July 13, 1979. The two had befriended each other at summer festivals, and Cameron aimed to provide viewers a healthy dose of Steve between the show's comedy sketches. "I wanted people to see the real Steve Goodman, and we didn't have a heck of a lot of time," he said. The 30-minute program, taped three weeks earlier at Mount Saint Vincent University's Seton Auditorium in Halifax, included a quartet of sections featuring Steve. He performed "City of New Orleans" (backed by a band and a trio of female singers), picked a breakneck, 30-second guitar solo on "Turkey in the Straw" ("something American as apple pie," Cameron said) while Cameron step-danced, and dueted with Cameron on "Twentieth Century" (cut off by the closing credits). [16]

Most meaningful to Cameron, however, was a segment in which he, on violin, and Steve, on guitar, jammed on a sprightly fiddle tune for a mere 60 seconds. "That little thing we did on fiddle and guitar was totally off the cuff," Cameron said. "It was unrehearsed, and that's one of the things I learned from Steve, to be more unpredictable so that the audience doesn't know what's going

14: Ironically, some accused Steve of perpetrating that very "simulation." At a late 1970s festival in Illinois, singer/ songwriter Jim Kanas witnessed the dismay of octogenarian folksinger Nimrod Workman, who noted the formulaic chording of the young guitarists around him. "Oh," he said, "you guys play pretty-boy blues like Steve Goodman." Workman, who had a cameo in the film "Coal Miner's Daughter," died in 1994 at age 99.

15: The name of the *National Lampoon* "White Album" was a parody of the 1968 Beatles double-LP known by the same name. The backdrop of the Lampoon LP was white and included a sketch of studio musicians in Ku Klux Klan sheets. The real reason for the name, however, was its reference to cocaine, said Steve Burgh, who played guitar on "What Were You Expecting – Rock 'n' Roll?" "It was the peak of the white-powder era," he said, "and those guys at the Lampoon were into it as much as anybody else."

16: Cameron began the show by singing Shel Silverstein's "Three Legged Man," which Cameron said Steve had taught him during a 55-minute long-distance call. Steve had told him, "You've been bugging me about this song for about two and a half years. It's my dime. Here it is." After Cameron related the story, Steve added, "Thank you for this engagement, so I can pay my phone bill."

John Allan Cameron hosted Steve more graciously on his 1979 Canadian TV show than Steve fared later that year on the L.A.-based "Tonight Show."

(Photo by John R. Rowlands)

17: The day after the Cameron show aired, Steve connected with another prominent Canadian, opening for Gordon Lightfoot at the July 13-15 National Maritime Heritage Festival at Fort Adams State Park in Newport, Rhode Island. Shaun Kelly (no relation to the *National Lampoon* editor) recalls it as uniquely affecting. Because the stage was only a few hundred yards from the ocean, Steve ran through chanteys and other sailing songs, including John Denver's hit, "Calypso." When he broke two strings mid-"Somebody Else's Troubles," he said, "Now what can I play with only four strings?" and launched into Johnny Rivers' "Mountain of Love." When he joined Lightfoot for the headliner's first song, "The Wreck of the Edmund Fitzgerald," spotlights lit their guitars as fog rolled across the pair during the opening chords. To the crowd, Steve whispered, "This is cool."

to happen next. When you become predictable, you become an oddness. You've got to take a risk." [17]

Steve's other TV appearance that fall, on "The Tonight Show," certainly qualified as a risk. In the United States, he had earned prominence on the "Soundstage" and "Austin City Limits" programs for PBS and had become a frequent presence in a range of Chicago TV programs. But the famed late-night talk show hosted by comic icon Johnny Carson was the big ticket — a mainstream audience of nearly six million households. In conjunction with an Oct. 25, 1979, gig at the Golden Bear in Huntington Beach, Steve snagged a "Tonight Show" guest slot for the night before, and he was ready. He rented a black tuxedo with big black bow tie (like his image on the "Words" LP, sans top hat), and he prepared to sing his latest album's edgiest song, "Men Who Love Women Who Love Men." No doubt he felt the goofy hymn to sexual diversity would resonate in the Hollywood milieu.

Many other performers whom Steve had helped or who had opened for him in years past had landed repeated and successful shots on Carson's 90-minute program. Hopes ran high that Steve's music and wit would leave an impressive mark. Bit by bit, however, the significance of the opportunity dissolved.

Carson was absent, replaced by a guest host, the then-lesser known, 32-year-old comedian David Letterman, assuring a smaller viewing audience. The night's guest list was lengthy: the magician Stan Kramien, comedian George Gobel, singer Diahann Carroll, who sang a Kurt Weill medley, and comic (and frequent guest host) Jay Leno, whose standup routine included balloon gags. In lengthy chats with Letterman, Gobel read a poem and joked about Mother-in-Law Day, Carroll discussed cartoons, cooking, candlelight dinners and pickpockets, and Leno talked of his recent move and sidewalk blowers. As the clock ticked and ticked, Steve waited backstage.

Finally, with less than three minutes of the show's airtime remaining, Steve was introduced. "My next guest is a singer/composer who wrote the smash hit 'City of New Orleans,' " Letterman said. After a plug for Steve's Golden Bear show and displaying the "High and Outside" LP, Letterman said, "It's a real pleasure to have him with us tonight. Would you please welcome Steve Goodman."

Heavy, orange-print curtains parted in the middle, and as the studio audience applauded, the tuxedoed Steve strode onstage carrying a guitar. To the uninitiated, he probably looked like any other singer, but those familiar with Steve's down-to-earth demeanor could see his distress. Gamely trying to hide his agitation, Steve wore a forced smile, his eyes glassy as those of a deer in the headlights. "Thanks, folks," he said as he began to strum. "I dedicate this to Jay (Leno) and his balloon lovers." Then he launched into "Men Who Love Women" in a tempo nothing short of frenetic. It was a note-perfect performance, and he rolled and widened his eyes during the funniest lines, but it felt like a race — because it was. He needed to finish the song before his time was up, and it was no easy task. Singing all four verses and four renditions of the chorus while maintaining a frozen smile and glazed stare, Steve squeezed a song that had run three-and-a-half minutes on his LP into exactly two.

Strumming the final chord with a flourish and bowing quickly while the studio audience cheered, Steve turned to his right to glean whether he would be invited over to talk. Seeing no such bid from Letterman, he turned his fixed grin back to the audience, swung his left arm into the air as if to say, "That's all, folks," then put his left hand into his pants pocket. Letterman signaled for a final commercial.

"It was a disaster," says singer Raun MacKinnon, who watched anxiously with her husband, flutist Jerry Burnham. "Talk about flops. We felt very bad. His slot got pushed to the end. He told us later he had the option to do it or not to do it, and he thought it was probably the only chance he was going to get, so he did it. But he was totally in a panic. It was a huge opportunity, it kind of got squandered, and it was not his fault. He was put in an insurmountable performing situation. He used to lecture me about how you've got to play to your audience, and then he got into a situation where he couldn't play to his audience because they wouldn't let him."

The experience exemplified how Steve and other top folksingers never fully connected with the mainstream, says Emily Friedman, editor of *Come for to Sing*. "None of those in acoustic music were ever able to figure out how you go big-time," she says. "In my cynicism, I think it's because the people in this milieu are too good, because if you're very good, you're eccentric, and if you're eccentric, you're not pabulum, and if you're not pabulum, they can't sell 20 million of your work. You have to be nondenominational, whereas Stevie was every kind of denomination."

The folk/acoustic music scene continued to plummet both nationally and in Chicago on the cusp of the 1980s. "Where have all the players gone?" a *Chicago Reader* headline pleaded on Dec. 12. "The amazing thing is how thoroughly the folk scene that was thriving four or five years ago has vanished," said the story. "Two years ago, a *Reader* writer commented that the folk scene was fading, and half a dozen singer/songwriters cornered him in a Korean restaurant to tell him he was wrong. Today, not one of those singers works regularly in Chicago." Especially souring was "the Goodman-Prine-Koloc generation of singers, who might as well live in L.A. for all the direct influence they have here," the article said. "For awhile, it looked like the city was on the verge of developing a long-term performing and writing community that we could enjoy over the long haul, that could bring some continuity and the benefits of experience to the younger performers. It seemed like the sort of fringe benefit that ought to be part of city life. Well, it's gone. Better luck to us all next time."

The death knell was premature, however, given sporadic evidence of the folk scene's vitality. No better example emerged than a Nov. 4, 1979, benefit in Chicago for Michael Cooney, the longtime itinerant songster from Toronto who had shunned commercial success but was an acclaimed festival singer facile with humor as well as guitar, banjo and concertina. That month, the uninsured

Michael Cooney, who suffered a severe brain injury in an auto collision, was the beneficiary of a Nov. 4, 1979, fund-raising concert, for which Steve was a headliner. With sardonic humor, Steve opened his first set with "Somebody Else's Troubles."
(Photo courtesy of Michael Cooney)

Notorious Cubs slugger Dave Kingman was the subject of both a WMAQ-TV special and a Steve-written theme song commissioned by the station. In the tune lay the seeds of more universal baseball themes that Steve yearned to explore.

(Photo from AU Sports Memorabilia)

18: The benefit, which included unbilled performances from Jethro Burns, Corky Siegel and Bob Gibson, raised $10,000 for Cooney and was one of many events that let him pay his hospital bills. Cooney recovered and performs today, his humor intact: "It's not true that they removed three-quarters of my brain and now all I can play is New Age music."

19: The song, with the straightforward title of "Dave Kingman," was never released by Steve — or anyone — on record.

Cooney underwent brain surgery in Providence, Rhode Island, to remove a blood pool that had formed in his skull following a head-on auto collision with a drunken driver three months earlier in eastern Connecticut.

Emily Friedman organized the two-show benefit, for which she quickly secured Pete Seeger, Art Thieme and Cindy Mangsen, with emcees Ed Holstein and Studs Terkel. She also solicited Steve with a letter, but Steve reserved his reply — and gallows humor — for an in-person encounter. A few days later, as Steve walked up to her, Friedman waggled her index finger at him.

"For Cooney? Of course," Steve said. "Besides, I've got an angle on this."

"What's that?" Friedman said.

"He's gonna owe me for the rest of his life."

Steve's sardonic tone continued at the benefit, held at Stages Music Hall, a former ballroom-dance theater on Clark Street. Introduced by Terkel as "a bard in the old tradition and the new tradition," Steve told the packed crowd, "This is great of you all to show up. I'll tell ya, if any of you are ever in jail and you have one dime, what you oughta do is call Michael Cooney." He opened his first set with a song tailor-made for a fund-raiser to help someone recovering from life-threatening surgery: "Somebody Else's Troubles." [18]

Rolling Stone had a warning of its own for Steve's musical troubles. In the first-ever attempt to catalogue and rate the LPs of the rock era, the magazine on Dec. 1, 1979, published the 631-page *Rolling Stone Record Guide*, and in it Steve's album ratings were lukewarm. Only one of his releases received a ranking as high as three stars, the 1976 "Essential" compilation of Steve's first two Buddah LPs. Reviewer Ariel Swartley labeled him "the perfect master of the latter-day urban folk scene" but pointed to a cloudy horizon. "Goodman confuses taste with style and substitutes the accepted values of a small community for a personal voice," she wrote. "He's deservedly a cult figure selling small subtleties and limited perfections, though his cult may not be willing to follow him through the strings and studio singers he's using now."

A Chicago sports figure who also had professional troubles that fall was the temperamental Cubs outfielder Dave Kingman, who was coming off a career year with 48 homers and 115 RBI but making a notorious name for himself as an anti-social loner whose bursts of anger stirred enmity. WMAQ-TV found Kingman such an intriguing character that it produced a one-hour documentary, "Dave Kingman: From Out of Left Field," that aired the first week of the 1980 season, on April 5. For the theme song, the NBC affiliate turned to its own designated hitter — Steve.

Because of his baseball mania, Steve warmed instantly to the task. His country-rock tune, backed by a piano-dominated rhythm section and sporting an infectious melody reminiscent of the 1978 Kenny Rogers hit "The Gambler," took a sympathetic approach to the 6-foot-6 slugger. It called him "the home-run hero of the national pastime," lamented that Kingman "can't understand why they won't leave him alone" and concluded with the hope that in the off-season "his time is his own." [19]

At the close of the 1970s, Steve (shown at the 1974 Mariposa Folk Festival in Toronto) had his sights set on commercial success — and a new West Coast home that would improve his odds.

(Photo by Sue Kozin)

Ever gregarious, Steve was not known in Chicago for Kingman-style yearnings for privacy. But unknown to many, he did have his sights set elsewhere. The members of Crackin', who had backed him on tour and his most recent recordings, were based in Los Angeles. So was Al Bunetta, who had moved there from New York four years earlier. So, too, was the headquarters for Asylum Records. It had long been conventional wisdom that to achieve national success, a Chicago musician had to leave town for one of "the coasts." In his residences, songwriting topics and much of his recording and TV work, Steve for years had assiduously — even proudly — bucked that tide. But with his album sales in freefall, Steve knew that his future niche would lie in connecting with others who could bring his songs to prominence. While his periodic cancer treatments were in New York, his key musical contacts were situated in or near Hollywood.

The time drew nigh for a career move. California was calling. ♪

While posing in a baseball jacket for the camera's "Hot Spot" (the title of his fifth and last LP for Asylum), Steve Goodman couldn't help playfully warding off a light meter with his eyes. Reflecting his strained quest for pop/mainstream success in 1980, these are alternative images from the photo session that resulted in the album's front- and back-cover imagery.
(Photos by Jim Shea)

'I hope to continue this search for what is called pop'

Bewilderment, sadness, anger — kicking in were the earmarks of grief. To friends and fans, the prospect that Steve Goodman would abandon the Chicago area was as likely as the Statue of Liberty walking away from New York harbor. They were stunned.

Emblematic of the reaction was bassist and jingle producer Jim Tullio, Steve's neighbor in Evanston who, largely at Steve's behest, had moved to Chicago from New York in 1974 and had stayed put instead of moving to Los Angeles in 1975. Tullio had set down roots in the hub of the Midwest and felt betrayed by his beloved colleague's imminent departure. "I was pissed," Tullio says.

"Of anybody who lives in Chicago, why the hell would you leave?" Tullio implored Steve. "You're the biggest Chicago advocate here. You're an icon in this town."

Further boggling the mind was Steve's destination — Southern California, the home of Hollywood, Disneyland and all things superficial and stereotypically foreign to Carl Sandburg's City of the Big Shoulders. Why was Steve going from grit to glitz?

Steve's public answer centered on his career. "I knew more phone numbers in (area code) 213 than I did in 312, and that wasn't anybody's fault here," he almost kiddingly told Roy Leonard of Chicago's WGN radio. [1] "We wouldn't have left for any reasons other than it just got to the point where if I wanted to find out where I was going to be working next, I had to call Los Angeles. And when all the numbers in 212 in New York started movin' out there, too, I knew I was in trouble."

Jack Hurst of the *Chicago Tribune* elicited a more thoughtful defense. "Chicago continually produces real good musicians of all different types. It's a wonderful area," Steve told him, "but the focus of the music business is on either of the coasts. I don't want to imply that there isn't a music business in Chicago, but the focus of the big picture for the United States appears to be someplace else.

"There aren't three or four major labels competing for artists and record sales in Chicago. So sometimes you've got to leave Chicago to find out if any of the stuff you're doing is any good. You just want to know one time if somebody

> I don't want to imply that there isn't a music business in Chicago, but the focus of the big picture for the United States appears to be someplace else.
> **STEVE GOODMAN**

1: Steve had been signaling this sentiment for years. For instance, he told Jim Bates of the *Columbia Missourian* "Vibrations" magazine in April 1978, "What people don't realize is that the musicians who make it out of Chicago do so because they maintain good contacts on the coasts."

besides you likes it. I don't know why, really. You just want to see what else is going on. It's a curiosity thing."

Steve's musical curiosity extended from the aural to the visual because of his brushes with local and national TV and his exposure to Steve Martin's transition to moviemaking — and all signs pointed west, he told Asia Locke of the New Jersey-based *Aquarian*. "Los Angeles is the show-biz center now," he said 10 months after the move. "With the film companies and television and now videocassettes, it keeps spreading out. There are more musicians out here, and more music is getting made out here." Steve also had told Chicago singer/songwriter Michael Smith ("The Dutchman"), "I want to get close to the movie thing, get close to what's happening, and I want to be there when the deals are happening." [2]

Colleagues in Chicago knew also of Steve's hope that California could re-ignite industry interest in his ability as a studio producer, despite the silence that followed the critical acclaim for his work on John Prine's 1978 "Bruised Orange." When Harry Waller tried to give kudos for the Prine LP to Steve, he responded with sarcasm: "It was such a great record John never asked me to do another one." Howard Levy also sensed Steve's disquiet. "He got bitter because he really expected to get more credit as a record producer for the job he did with John," Levy says. "He single-handedly rescued John's career with 'Bruised Orange,' and he was disappointed that the world didn't flock to his door to produce albums. No one ever called." The void played a role in Steve's move, Levy says. "After awhile, this place (Chicago) is a self-contained universe," he says. "You could be very talented, and everyone here could love you to death, but in terms of national sales, what did it translate into for Steve?"

As the 1980s began, Prine himself moved to Nashville, seeking a greater circle of collaborators and a closer proximity to country music. The third member of Chicago's so-called holy trinity, Bonnie Koloc, also had moved — to New York, where she eventually joined a Broadway show. [3] Steve's relocation to California followed the same logic, and for more than a year his colleagues in Los Angeles had encouraged Steve to uproot himself, as drummer/producer Peter Bunetta said, "just to be around the right place at the right time, to get involved in things."

But when Steve talked with other friends, his rationale for pulling up stakes had nothing to do with music. It was all about his three girls and an awareness of his mortality. He told Tullio, "Man, I just want to be out by the ocean with my kids with the time I have left." Corky Siegel, Chicago harmonica player and blues-band leader, found Steve "really excited" when he visited Steve after the move. "Corky, look at this," Steve said. "I'm a few blocks from the ocean, and here we are in California, and the weather's good out here, and I really wanted this for the kids." His enthusiasm made Siegel a believer that music was not the key motive. "It was definitely for the kids," Siegel says. "That was the big, big, big, big, big reason."

Besides career and family, Steve's personal viability also was a factor. For

2: Steve's attraction to L.A. wheeling and dealing emerged in a joke he played on the Beach Boys' disoriented founder, Brian Wilson, during a March 1, 1980, Eagles/Roy Orbison concert at the Inglewood Forum. With guitarist John O'Kennedy, Steve snagged seats near the stage and in front of the bathrobe-clad Wilson, whom Steve had never met. "Hey, man," Steve told Wilson, "I had such a good time at our session the other day. If you want me to come back and redo any of those solos, I'd be glad to." Wilson stared back in a daze, but Steve kept on. "Listen," Steve continued, "I just found out I got a record deal." Finally, Wilson responded. "Oh, really? That's cool, man." "Yeah, I just signed with Columbia Records. I buy four records a month and get 12 for free."

3: Koloc won awards starring as Mrs. Kate Macauley in Joseph Papp's Off Broadway musical, "The Human Comedy," which finally reached Broadway in April 1984. Bucking the leaving-Chicago trend in 1980 was David Bromberg, who moved from New York to Chicago within a week of when Steve left for California. But Bromberg's move proved the same point in reverse because he was curtailing his performing and recording to delve into building violins.

fighting leukemia, Steve knew that year-round sunshine would be better than Chicago's bitter winters. "The move had a lot to do with his health," says his daughter, Jessie. "His circulation had become pretty bad because of all the intravenous stuff, and I know he was looking forward to warmer weather."

Not insignificant, in Steve's view, was the fact that Los Angeles hosted two major-league baseball teams. While Steve still scorned the Los Angeles Dodgers for abandoning Brooklyn and serving for decades as a Cubs nemesis, the newer California Angels, playing in Anaheim, were appealing because their benevolent owner was a famous singing cowboy. "The Angels would be easy to adopt," he said later. "Gene Autry plays guitar and sings good, the things I try to do." Steve could remain a Cub fan forever, but in L.A., as he had enjoyed in Chicago, he would have two nearby venues for viewing big-league ball.

With these motivations swirling in his psyche, Steve's move west started getting specific during his trip to California to perform Oct. 24, 1979, on "The Tonight Show." Meeting him the following night for his performance at the Golden Bear in Huntington Beach was Liz Redfearn (now Forrester), the wife of Steve Redfearn, Emmylou Harris' longtime road manager who also had roadied during Steve's spring 1979 full-band tour to promote "High and Outside." Steve stayed at the Redfearns' apartment, situated an hour south of L.A. and less than a block from the Pacific Ocean in an Orange County burg of 25,000 by the name of Seal Beach. Steve later said the overnight visit left a deep impression: "I said, 'God, what a boring place!' Except I notice that I fell asleep right away."

With Nancy, Steve returned to Southern California in November, and for the better part of a week, he said, the two scouted residences "within an hour-and-20-minute radius of Hollywood's studios, record-company offices and all that nonsense." Relatively tiny Seal Beach — with a reputation for good schools, a 50-shop Main Street and a Coney Island-style heritage evidenced by a 73-year-old, six-block-long pier jutting over the surf — came into greater focus. "Nancy didn't want to leave Chicago," Forrester says. "She was an East Coast-type girl. She wanted to go to New York. She wasn't crazy about Seal Beach, but she would follow Steve anywhere."

To settle in a city encircled by the gated, 541-acre, 1962-vintage Leisure World retirement community on the north, the mysterious, 4,069-acre, World War II-era U.S. Naval Weapons Station to the east and oil derricks looming offshore might have seemed incongruous for a hip, 31-year-old musician bred in Chicago. But Seal Beach also possessed a vigilantly small-town feel and stone's-throw access to a mile of white, sandy beach. Combined with its proximity to the entertainment world and two busy airports, the appeal was undeniable. As Steve explained to Jackson Browne, "I can live anywhere. If I'm going to be traveling so much, I'm going to live someplace that I like being." [4]

Steve eyed a dwelling being built at 312 Eighth Street, whose house number matched Chicago's area code. One of two town houses on a former single-family lot, it was positioned a half block south of Pacific Coast Highway 1 and two blocks north of the ocean pier. Three doors south and across Electric Av-

I said, 'God, what a boring place!' Except I notice that I fell asleep right away.
STEVE GOODMAN

4: That Steve didn't feel compelled to stay in Chicago made sense to Browne. "He was connected eternally to those people and felt he didn't have to be there the whole time," Browne says. Besides, he says, Steve could remain gregarious regardless of locale. "He was the guy who could walk into any town and get up a neighborhood sandlot game."

The Goodmans' home in Seal Beach, as it looked in 2000.
(Photo by Clay Eals)

5: Steve's rationalization didn't wash with Michael Smith. "I did not understand why he moved there," he says. "The Seal Beach house was a yodel from the next house, and you could hardly walk in between them. Evanston was a beautiful, old, monstrous house on a shady, quiet street. If I could live in that house, I would never fucking leave. You could carry me out. ... Instead, there's this place with the oil derricks on the beach. It was just awful. It was a soulless, empty place." But at least Southern California didn't have to wrestle with the title creatures of Harry Waller's "Cockroaches on Parade." Introducing the song in October 1981 at Hop Singh's in Marina del Ray, Steve said its origin sprang from the abrupt Chicago seasonal changes: "A certain day happens in the fall, and the temperature drops just 30 degrees that day, and it really doesn't warm up until spring, and all of the animals with exoskeletons come inside."

enue were the Seal Beach library and, nearing its grand opening, the Red Car Museum, inside a 1925 electric railcar. Across the back alley were picture-framer and fast friend Jim Moore among other friendly merchants whose storefronts dotted palm-tree-lined Main Street. Steve called the environs "kid heaven."

The house had four levels, with three bedrooms, two baths, three decks, a garage and an interior stairway that zigzagged from bottom to top. Encased in stucco, the 2,150-square-foot structure was topped by a Spanish red-tile roof. In contrast to the stately, vintage girth of the Goodmans' Evanston home, this new home was barely wider than the length of a typical car. In today's parlance it would be called a skinny house. "Everybody out there lives in houses made out of papier-mache," Steve told WGN's Roy Leonard. "Everything is half the size and costs twice as much." Steve told steel guitarist Winnie Winston that he didn't like the house's cinched-up interior, but for Jack Hurst of the *Tribune* Steve said that the "little bitty" structure wasn't bothersome. "It's a different lifestyle," he said. "You're outdoors a lot more." [5]

With Nancy's assent, the home purchase was closed. "It was bang-bang," Forrester says. "They had to put the house back in Evanston on the market, and Nancy had to go back and wrap all that stuff up and get the kids." Steve also attended a going-away party at the Earl of Old Town, at which friends performed his songs, says bartender Roger Surbaugh. Bonnie Koloc sang a sendup of "Eight Ball Blues," while Steve and John Prine dueted on "Paul Powell."

The actual move took place in April 1980. Steve left Chicago first, driving west — making stops in the Arches and Grand Canyon national parks and in Las Vegas — with daughter Jessie in his bright orange Mercedes sedan. (Steve later told Winnie Winston, "I never had a Mercedes, so why not? I figured if I wanted one, I might as well have one. This one was there, and nobody wanted it, so that's my car. Do you believe I'm driving around in a Mercedes? Me?")

Boggled by how his "City of New Orleans" royalties had let him move to Southern California, Steve soon had visitors, including former Sloan-Kettering roommate Jack Goldberg. When Goldberg pulled up at 312 Eighth Street, greeting him outside was Steve, "giggling like a little child."

"What the hell's so funny?" Goldberg asked as he stepped out of his car.

"Goldberg," he said, pointing to the house, "that was one fucking song! One song built that fucking house!"

Such absurdity played itself out in other aspects of life in bilingual L.A. "When I got to move out west," Steve told a Minneapolis concert audience that fall, "my friends told me that if I wanted to order any food in restaurants or get my laundry done, I would have to learn how to talk backwards." With the same sentiment, Steve greeted Michael Smith, whom he flew west so the two could write songs together. After Steve picked up Smith at the Los Angeles airport, and while they inched along in a traffic jam while heading south on the San Diego Freeway to Steve's home, Steve told him, "It's all backwards out here." The concept for a song quickly took root.

Back in Evanston and not long before Steve's move, Smith and Steve had composed a tune based on the 1958 killing spree of 19-year-old Charles Starkweather and 14-year-old Caril Fugate that had been dramatized in the 1973 film "Badlands," starring Martin Sheen and Sissy Spacek. Called "Danger," the song omitted the couple's names and avoided mentioning their killings and focused instead on their nighttime quest for risky thrills.

This collaboration — a first for Steve and Smith — followed what became a pattern for the two writers. First, Steve challenged Smith to come up with a topic. "He made it clear that that was my job," Smith says. "When he walked into the room, there was this kind of electricity, this energy, and you felt like you had to meet it, and how you met it was, you were creative." Once the topic was set, Steve often fleshed out and finished the tune in one session. "In general, he would write most of a song," Smith says. "I would come up with the first line. Then he was running, and I was assisting. That's the way I was brought in, like a football game. There was a quickness."

So when Smith and Steve sat stuck in the California traffic, [6] Smith threw out the germ for a tune. "Let's do a song about 'The Name Game,' " Smith said, referring to the Shirley Ellis 1965 soul novelty hit, in which Ellis transformed first names into upbeat rhymes — a ditty that schoolkids throughout the country chanted incessantly in the mid-1960s. Building on Steve's "It's all backwards out here" comment, Smith added, "How about if people talked backwards?" Steve enlarged the idea, Smith says. "He said talking backwards will be something we do that people will admire you for, that if you did it, then people would think you are hot stuff."

From that grew one of Steve's most entertaining songs, officially dubbed "Sdrawkcab Klat (Talk Backwards)." It was a catchy tune whose impact depended on a precise reading of simple and complex phrases as if their letters were in reverse order. Filled with wordplay, the lyrics swelled to a preposterously logical conclusion, predicting a new constitutional right to "reverse elocution" and the rise of TV shows "captioned for the forward-impaired." [7]

The fledgling song found its potency when Steve sang it. "When we would write," Smith says, "he would stand up and perform the song. There was a lot of sitting opposite with the legal pads, but once things got rolling and sometimes right away, he would literally perform and do facial things for you." So when Steve sang to Smith that talking backwards could help a man win over his date ("See if that doesn't take off the chill"), a wry look crossed his face. "It was conspiratorial," Smith says, "like he was giving you this little advice that no one knew — confidentially, talk backwards. And I would fall down, it was so fucking funny, just that look. It was a privilege to see it. It was so bizarre. It took the song to a different plane. It was a funny idea to advise people to talk backwards, but when you actually saw someone who advised you to talk backwards, it was hilarious."

The co-written "Talk Backwards" — which Steve later claimed was inspired by the babble he heard from the rewinding of tapes in language labs during his years at Maine East High and the University of Illinois — was an indication

> **He said talking backwards will be something we do that people will admire you for, that if you did it, then people would think you are hot stuff.**
> **MICHAEL SMITH**

6: "It's been hard to write songs about L.A.," Steve told his Hop Singh's crowd in 1981. "I haven't quite figured it out." Then, to the tune of "Rock Island Line," he sardonically began to sing, "Y'know, the Santa Ana Freeway is a mighty good road. …"

7: One of the lines that Steve spoke in reverse in the lyrics to "Talk Backwards" was lifted from a classic parody by Homer & Jethro: "Your teeth are like stars. They come out at night."

that Steve hadn't left his trademark wit in Chicago. What's more, in Smith he had found a kindred partner because, as with Steve, Smith's songwriting ran from the touching ("The Dutchman") to the twisted. Smith says their joint work style also resembled the creative sparring of John Lennon and Paul McCartney. "I definitely was in competition with Steve to some degree to reassure myself that I was in the same plane," he says.

"Stevie said to me, 'You know, there are only a few people who do what we do.' He wasn't talking about folk music. He was talking about a specific thing that goes on when you write a song that's clever. Like the line (from "My Old Man"), 'He could look you in the eye and sell you a car.' That line is like me. That's the way we wrote, both the same. We were both willing to put things that are poignant and humorous next to each other. It was like the blender. It was like 'Oh, I have an orange. Let me throw that in the blender and see what happens.' He was the blender. He would just shake it up and come up with something."

> ## It was like 'Oh, I have an orange. Let me throw that in the blender and see what happens.' He was the blender. He would just shake it up and come up with something.
> **MICHAEL SMITH**

The two got "all shook up" in another collaboration in which Smith told Steve, "Let's write a song about Elvis imitators." In the nearly three years since Elvis Presley had died at 42 of a drug overdose and heart disease, impersonators of The King had sprung up and sparked frequent press coverage. "Now it's like your local dentist, your local Elvis imitator," Smith says, "but at that time, it was novel to even refer to an Elvis imitator."

The idea for the song was not to ridicule the mimics but to salute them affectionately. [8] "Those guys who did the Elvis imitating were always a little dorky, but Steve and I felt they were very sincere," Smith says. "They love Elvis and immerse themselves in his every attribute. I understand where that comes from. If I could look like that and be an Elvis imitator, goddamn I would." The tune, in the voice of an impersonator, detailed Presley's clothing, hair and mannerisms and seamlessly cited a half-dozen of his song titles, leading to choice zingers: "Imitating Elvis is the only way / I can make it through my imitation day," and "I was imitating him before he died."

Both "Elvis Imitators" and "Talk Backwards" soon found their way to recordings and Steve's stage shows. But such irreverence did not prevail in Steve's overall musical output in 1980. Instead, he forged a direction that aimed for safety but was fraught with risk. It was triggered by his teaming with a new, California-based collaborator.

Steve's favored rhythm section at the time, Peter Bunetta and Rick Chudacoff, had left Crackin' and branched into producing other artists, including an early-1970s friend from upstate New York, soft-rock singer/songwriter Robbie Dupree, who had moved to L.A. and begun recording with the pair. Dupree's debut album, released on Elektra in early 1980, spawned a Dupree-Chudacoff co-write, "Steal Away," which rode the *Billboard* Top 100 for 23 weeks and peaked at #6. A follow-up Dupree single, "Hot Rod Hearts," which peaked at #15, was co-written by a composer and keyboardist who already had recorded two LPs on Warner Brothers and had co-written the 1979 Michael Johnson hit "This

8: For his Hop Singh's audience in Marina del Ray in October 1981, Steve imagined it would be a "nice job" to be a Presley imitator: "A job like that, you know you've hit it. They play a lot of music from '2001,' and you have to throw a cape on and do a dead guy's act." During a March 1982 show in Michigan, Steve noted Presley's uniqueness: "That won't be back, whatever he was doin'. That was so unusual that people are still tryin' to get it." In a return visit July 24, 1983, to the Dr. Demento show, Steve likened Elvis mimicry to a growth industry. "We live in an ersatz world," he said. "It's just a matter of time before we get imitations of everything."

Night Won't Last Forever" — Bill LaBounty. The thought of everyone in this "musical family," as Peter Bunetta put it, was to help the newly arrived Steve accomplish something he had never achieved, a hit single and album in his own name. The catalyst was to be LaBounty.

"This guy is really wound up," LaBounty thought at their first meeting and writing session at his hideaway A-frame on Lake Arrowhead, 90 miles east of Los Angeles in the San Bernardino Mountains. Instantly, Steve threw out lines like "Pain is my old friend" and "Death is my girlfriend" that stunned LaBounty. "Lyrically, I thought, 'This is gonna be fun,' but I didn't take what he was saying seriously like it was autobiographical." Then Steve told him about his leukemia. "I'm living on borrowed time," Steve said. "I don't like to waste time on bullshit."

Bill LaBounty, Steve's new-found songwriting partner in 1980, says Steve wanted "everything," including a hit.
(Photo by Dion Ogust)

The two clicked, partly because of their reciprocal tastes. Steve revered LaBounty's jazz and R&B influences, from Louis Armstrong and Bing Crosby to Ray Charles and Marvin Gaye, and gravitated to LaBounty's style, which was "more derivative from the overall sound of the music and not the lyric." The pair also shared a hunger for success. "I wanted desperately to get a hit, and Steve wanted everything," LaBounty says. "He felt awful about it. He thought that should be one of the things he should get done before he died, because that was what his career was, and he thought, 'Everybody wants me to do this. I need to do it. People love what I do.' "

Their connection was sealed when, on a lunch outing, Steve took LaBounty along to Elektra/Asylum in Hollywood, where Steve had an appointment with an A&R (artist and repertoire) VP who had just moved from the East Coast and whom Steve had never met. Somewhat experienced in dealing with record labels, LaBounty was puzzled that once they arrived at the E/A lobby, Steve invited him into the VP's office to witness what typically was a private meeting.

Inside the VP's office, the topic turned to one of Steve's demo tracks whose instrumentation included acoustic guitar, dobro and steel guitar. The VP told Steve, "You gotta take this steel off, man. This is disco."

Steve glared at the VP for a moment and said, "So, you're from the East Coast, huh?"

"Yeah."

"So, what's the biggest chance you've ever taken?"

The VP fidgeted and couldn't come up with an answer.

"Well," Steve said, "have you ever taken any chance in your life on anything?"

The VP became visibly irritated, not just at what Steve was asking him but also by being put on the spot in front of LaBounty.

"Y'know what?" Steve finally said with a tone both disarming and serious, "I don't really give a fuck about what you think is commercial or disco or anything. This is my music. This means everything to me."

LaBounty was astonished. "That was Steve Goodman to me," he says. "I had never looked at it that way, that it's your life. I would just be thinking, 'Give me the deal. Where do I sign?' After that meeting, anything Steve Goodman said, I wanted to know about and be involved with. It transcended my career or the music business or anything. Even though he was intense and sometimes hard to be around, I was always thrilled when I'd hear from him because he was so real to me."

Coming back to L.A. from out-of-town shows, Steve often retreated to Lake Arrowhead for a day or two to write with LaBounty instead of heading home to Seal Beach. "He had this beautiful family," LaBounty says, "but it broke his heart to have to go and see his family and love them like any normal person would. He would rather have been almost anywhere else, on a stage or in a studio, than to see what he was going to be leaving behind." For Steve, Lake Arrowhead became a refuge. "Sometimes, we'd go out to eat and dance and flirt with girls at a bar near there. He'd say, 'You come down into Seal Beach and stay,' but it was sort of half-hearted. I could tell he really kind of dug comin' up there and just hangin' out."

Their talks often strayed to deep issues, including once when LaBounty had returned from a troubled family visit. Recalling his own anger over parental pressure to become a doctor, Steve had curt advice.

"I'm gonna tell you something that's gonna save you thousands of dollars in analysis," he said.

"What's that?" LaBounty asked.

"Forgive your father."

LaBounty thought to himself, "I ain't gonna forgive my father. *You* forgive your father." Later, LaBounty says he realized, "It doesn't matter whether you want to forgive your father or not. You have to, to survive on a certain level. Steve already knew that. He was way down the line in terms of karma."

Straining LaBounty's patience, cocaine use was part of their sessions and lasted until early in the morning. "Steve liked to party," he says. "He let me know: 'You can call me a drug freak or whatever, but I have to cram a lot of stuff in.' I couldn't keep up with him. He used to make me nervous, drive me crazy, because I would try it at first, and God knows I played around too much with the coke, but at one point I remember sayin', 'I've gotta stop doin' this.' But Steve was still going. He was stronger than a fuckin' bull, and he would party all night. It'd be 3 in the morning, and I'd say, 'Look, I gotta go to bed.' I'd go and get in bed, and I'd hear him out there making popcorn in the air popper, and popcorn would be all over the floor. Then around 5:30 or 6 while the sun was coming up, he'd come and sit on the edge of my bed, and go, 'Ah, check this! Ah! Ah!' He'd play through a line, and I'd tell myself I'm glad the weekend's over because this insane motherfucker's gonna leave and I can rest for a little while."

Such excess reeked in a line that Steve told LaBounty he wanted to expand into a song. Strumming hard on the guitar, "he'd break and sing, 'Hit bottom, and the bottom falls out.' Then he'd be back in his groove again." The song with the sharp refrain was never completed, however.

Another tune, which the two did finish, grazed the same theme. "Bobby

> **It broke his heart to have to go and see his family and love them like any normal person would. He would rather have been almost anywhere else, on a stage or in a studio, than to see what he was going to be leaving behind.**
> **BILL LaBOUNTY**

The sound and spirit of bassist Rick "Cheese" Chudacoff (left) and drummer Peter Bunetta (right) drew such respect from Steve that they not only served as the rhythm section for his late 1970s recordings but also co-produced the forthcoming LP, "Hot Spot."
(Photo by Jim Shea)

Don't Stop," modeled on Steve's old friend Bob Hoban, described a bar pianist who played all manner of old songs to satisfy "the broken-hearted lovers and losers who are cryin' tonight." The song, however, betrayed a severe lack of originality. Though it had a pulsing, disco-tinged beat instead of a rolling waltz, it closely matched Billy Joel's "Piano Man" hit of six years before. "It's kind of a Billy Joel-type thing," LaBounty says, "but it was really Steve. I mean, he'd been in those places."

LaBounty also shared with Steve a tentative love song he had written with Nashville composer Michael Garvin called "Sometimes Love Forgets." Inspired by an interracial relationship, the lyrics spoke vaguely of lovers in "two different worlds, too far apart," one pleading to the other not to "let go yet." During this time, Steve also finished five other compositions: "Still Trying to Care," "Hit and Run Lover" (assisted by Michael Smith), "Trust Me," "Part of Your Life" (assisted by Harry Waller) and "Can't Find My Heart." Three bore Steve's familiar "she done him wrong" theme, but all five were indistinct and banal. With this satchel of tunes, however, Steve felt ready to hit the recording studio.

Awaiting him there were Peter Bunetta and Rick Chudacoff, as well as veteran engineer Gary Brandt, whose credits ranged from Gordon Lightfoot's popular 1970 album, "If You Could Read My Mind," to a self-titled 1979 LP by the funk artist Prince. (Steve later referred to Bunetta, Chudacoff and Brandt as "a nice Nairobi Trio," an affectionate nod to the Ernie Kovacs TV sketches that inspired him as a child.) The setting to cut the tracks was Brandt's small, converted home in North Hollywood, dubbed Alpha Studios. 9 Bringing in guitarists Brian Ray (Etta James' band) and Jeff "Skunk" Baxter (Steely Dan, Doobie Brothers), keyboardist Bill Elliott and a half dozen others, Bunetta, Chudacoff and Brandt were primed to pump out hits for Steve — and the style was unequivocally pop.

The troubles in Steve's Alpha sessions were multi-faceted. First, the lyrics, lacking narrative threads, offered only vague romantic advice and consolation. While the tempos and dynamics covered a broad range, the instrumentation essentially copied overly familiar ground. Ray's guitar on "Danger" 10 sounded like that of George Harrison, and on "Trust Me" it resembled the lines of Stephen

9: At Gary Brandt's home studio, Steve recorded his vocals in the foyer of the bathroom. For the *Philadelphia Inquirer*, Steve later cracked, "You don't walk out on the street with a high-tone attitude after you've been singing in the bathroom all day."

10: Before recording "Danger" for the LP, Steve sought advice from *National Lampoon* editor Sean Kelly, who embellished the lyrics' sense of doom with the line, "Out beyond the edge of / Fingers on the ledge above / Danger."

Stills. Jim Rothermel's sax sound on "Hit and Run Lover" recalled the Phil Woods sax line in Billy Joel's "Just the Way You Are." Moreover, strings arranged by Bill Elliott blanketed nearly every song with a slick sheen. On most of the tracks, Steve played acoustic guitar, but the glossy glut of other sounds buried it. [11] Throughout, it was clear that Steve was simply trying to be someone other than himself.

"He knew that it was a little bit of a sellout," Chudacoff says. "He didn't feel dishonest about it, but he wanted to have success in the business, and he saw his numbers going down. He had a pop consciousness in his head, so it was not totally out of character, just a stretch."

Peter Bunetta says the polish that he and Chudacoff brought to the songs reflected Steve's "What have I got to lose?" mentality. Besides, he says, the sessions had value that went beyond commercial. "We became even closer friends," Bunetta says. "He showed us more of what a true artist he was by not being indifferent to our vision."

In one key instance during the Alpha sessions, Steve's authentic vision held sway with his collaborators. Their recording of "Talk Backwards" was classic Steve. With Jim Rothermel re-creating a big-band sax section on clarinet and tenor sax, Peter Bunetta bouncing brushes off a reel-to-reel tape box, three sets of hands snapping their fingers and Steve picking a jaunty acoustic guitar, the two-and-a-half-minute track became a toe-tapping, smile-inducing tour de force. Unfortunately, it was the lone exception.

Nowhere was Steve's distinctiveness more rapidly nearing exile than with a song on which all involved had placed most of their hopes. "Sometimes Love Forgets" had been written for one voice, but LaBounty and Steve realized that its verses could be divvied up for two, and the potential was ripe for a male-female duet. Such pop couplings had been the recent rage (or gimmick), with "Whenever I Call You Friend" by Kenny Loggins and Fleetwood Mac's Stevie Nicks hitting #5 in mid-1978 and the ubiquitous "You Don't Bring Me Flowers" by Neil Diamond and Barbra Streisand topping the charts six months later. Steve himself had tried it with Nicolette Larson on "The One That Got Away" in 1979, and only record-label politics had kept it from a shot at similar success. For a duet partner on "Sometimes Love Forgets," Steve turned to another singer who was no stranger to vocal teaming, Phoebe Snow.

With a powerful, dark-hued contralto that scatted and soared over several octaves, the New Jersey-based Snow (real last name: Laub) was known for her 1974 debut jazz-pop hit and LP "Poetry Man" and for dueting with Paul Simon on the gospel-tinged "Gone at Last," which had risen to #23 in 1975. Steve had known of Snow since his early days with David Bromberg and Steve Burgh. What touched Snow about Steve when the two met in 1979 in Chicago was his attentiveness, particularly given her difficult decision to raise her autistic daughter, Valerie, by herself.

"I had a very big self-esteem problem," Snow says. "I would always be uptight about some craziness, and he would be there, t-h-e-r-e. That was one of

---

He knew that it was a little bit of a sellout. ... He had a pop consciousness in his head, so it was not totally out of character, just a stretch.
RICK CHUDACOFF

11: With no small irony, given that his guitar was largely inaudible, Steve later pegged the resulting album as "the first time anyone got close to making an acoustic guitar Motown record."

the most luminescent parts of his personality. I was blown away by him."

Snow discovered this vividly during a second swing through Chicago, where she was sitting "in some crappy motel room" about 10 at night and sobbing about "some kind of grief." Steve had told her to call him if she ever needed to, so she picked up the phone.

"You don't sound so good," Steve told her.

"No, no," Snow said, "I'm fine."

"What do you want? What do you need? Can I get you anything?"

"Oh, I'm OK."

"C'mon."

Finally, Snow said with a whimper, "There's no QuikChek, not even a 7-Eleven. There's nothing around here. I just wanted some popcorn."

Within the hour, Steve arrived at her motel room with a brimming paper bag of popcorn that Nancy had just popped on the stove.

"Here, is this enough?" he asked. He sat in a chair and said, "Now, you talk, and I'll listen."

"You don't want to hear what I have to say!"

"Yes, I do. Go ahead."

Snow finally blurted out her problem, and when she was done, Steve said, "Well, let's solve this thing."

"Oh, you can't solve it," she said, and she shifted the topic, complaining about her constant battle to drop a nagging 10 or 15 pounds of weight.

"Oh yeah?" Steve said. "Well, you want to know how fat I was? Eat the damn popcorn!"

So when Steve and manager Al Bunetta called Snow and asked her to duet on "Sometimes Love Forgets," she quickly agreed. "They were really thinking this was going to be a commercial, mainstream thing," Snow says, particularly for the older, CHR (contemporary hit radio) market that took to the Loggins/Nicks and Diamond/Streisand pairings.

When Snow and Steve recorded their vocals together in a New York studio, "it was a love fest," Snow says. "Every time I did a vocal take, Steve would be beside himself with excitement: 'God, that was so good. Oh, my God, that sounded so good.' He was one of the most validating people I ever knew. Lots of hugs. If there was a good take, you hug. It was a great, great day, and we both thought that as mainstream and commercial and overtly CHR as it was, we loved it. We thought, 'Jesus, maybe this will do really well.' We had our dreams and fantasies about it."

Amid the euphoria, however, lurked a prophetic vibe. "I noticed that Steve's vocals were very reserved," Snow says. "They didn't have that high-spiritedness that his live stuff did and the earlier albums did, and I thought, 'He's holding back. Why is he holding back so much?' Maybe it was in deference to the whole tone of the song and being commercial and thinking, 'I better not get too left of center here. We better just stick to the beaten path of this melody.' So I thought, 'Yeah, OK, I'm going to hold back, too.' It was all implied and never stated, but

Phoebe Snow, who found solace in telephone calls with Steve, says he was "one of the most validating people I ever knew. Lots of hugs. If there was a good take, you hug."

(Photo courtesy of Phoebe Snow)

Steve beams at Jethro Burns during a dazzling mandolin solo by the latter at the "No Nukes Under the Sun" concert April 3, 1980, in the college town of DeKalb, west of Chicago.

(Photo courtesy of Jim Kanas)

12: In "Sometimes Love Forgets," Snow let loose her gifted voice only briefly, soaring to a high note during what she sarcastically labels "the all-important fade, where everybody has to grandstand and be obnoxious." But even then, her vocal gymnastics were timid compared to a similar ending to her "Gone at Last" duet with Paul Simon.

13: After the DeKalb sound check, singer/songwriter Jim Kanas implored Steve and Jethro Burns to join him at the Axe in Hand guitar shop, where they jammed on "The Devil's Dream" and other bluegrass tunes. After buying a guitar, Steve thanked Kanas for the prod. "Steve knew damn well what I wanted to do," Kanas says. "He knew that I wanted to say that I'd played with Steve Goodman. It was a gift. He wanted to help me as a student. There was zero arrogance, zero baggage."

we made it real sweet and mellow. You can tell by the performances that we were just really reserved." [12]

The result was a tepid track in which Snow didn't sustain notes in showcase spots and Steve's voice was likewise subdued. It didn't bode well for the album to come. But during the months that the LP was finalized, Steve took comfort where he had long proved his success — on the stage.

An immediate result of his mid-April move to Seal Beach was that Steve landed many more concert bookings in Los Angeles, San Diego and elsewhere in Southern California. One of his first gigs in the sunnier clime, an anti-nuclear-power benefit, mirrored one of his last Midwestern shows before the move. The cause matched the theme he had written for a Chicago TV documentary the year before, but the difference between the two events illustrated the breadth of his celebrity-laden new world:

◆ On April 3, he was the headliner for a No Nukes Under the Sun benefit at the Egyptian Theater in DeKalb, a college town 65 miles west of Chicago. [13]

◆ On May 25, after his relocation, he was just one cog in a much larger, longer rally at the Hollywood Bowl, called Survival Sunday III.

Befitting L.A.'s role as a national media center, the Survival Sunday roster encompassed musicians Graham Nash and Mary Travers and activists Dr. Helen Caldicott, Bella Abzug, Ron Kovic and Winona LaDuke. Steve's written entry in the program booklet was both terse and direct: "It does no good to blame the energy companies for ruining the environment if we continue to let them." But he couldn't let the solemn occasion pass without a poke at his newly adopted base. As reported by *Los Angeles Times* columnist Patrick Goldstein, Steve finished his Survival Sunday set with a crack that contained more truth than its

More nattily dressed than at the Illinois no-nukes show, Steve dons a white coat to perform April 27, 1980, at the eighth annual 49er Banjo, Fiddle & Guitar Festival at Cal State Long Beach. The occasion didn't command complete formality, as Steve wore tennis shoes and invited his youngest daughter, nearly-3-year-old Rosanna, to cavort onstage. (Photos by Tom Shaw, courtesy of the Long Beach Press-Telegram)

sarcasm let on: "I wish I could stay longer, but I'm in a cocaine pyramid in Redondo Beach and tonight's my night." [14]

With President Carter vulnerable in the fall election, Steve could understand that playing at such events was important. Steve also began to consider writing an anti-nuclear song of his own. "You can't be too sincere, if you really admit it, about something like the end of the world," he told David Gans of *Record* magazine. "Anybody who lines up on the human side of that issue is OK with me."

But Steve also told Jack Hurst of the *Chicago Tribune* of the uneasiness he felt that year in the role of an entertainer spouting about politics. "It's unpopular to have opinions like this," he said. "I agree that the Soviet Union shouldn't push people around. I don't think they're such nice guys. But it's ridiculous to put a man on the moon and then say we have to go to war over oil. Put a tenth of the energy they put into putting a man on the moon into finding a substitute for the internal combustion engine, and the deed would be done. But Congress is a marketplace. ... But if you say that stuff out loud, it's like, 'Who the hell is *he* to say that?' "

Far less political were Steve's openers for Steve Martin, which had persisted since 1978 but dwindled in 1980 when the comic's success with his first feature film, "The Jerk," spurred him to create another. Martin's final standup shows, all with Steve in tow, came that summer in runs of 10 days and two weeks at the Riviera in Las Vegas and a one-week stint at Resorts International in Atlantic

14: In the middle of a club show later that year, another musician playing with Steve inadvertently dropped a packet of cocaine onstage. Steve saw it but kept focusing his gaze forward, then segued into an improvised blues with the theme of "Busted."

City. These sets before two-drink-minimum crowds netted him helpful visibility, such as a squib by *Las Vegas Review* columnist Charles Supin: "Getting my vote for one of the best opening acts this year is Steve Goodman." But the casino shows also were fiercely challenging, says one of Steve's folkie sidemen, Lew London, who lived near Atlantic City and witnessed one of the last Steve/Steve pairings.

"Casinos are not fun," he says. "I've seen Eddie Murphy bomb at a casino. My wife went to see Tony Bennett, and the audience walked out before his encore. They want to gamble, they want to hang, and half of them are there conked, so they're not a good audience, by nature. But Steve slayed them, and when Steve Martin came up onstage, they were ready. He had truly warmed them up, and I had a new sense of respect for how outstanding he could be. It's one thing playing for a crowd of people in a concert in a nice hall, but casino audiences are the worst, just the worst." [15]

The casino environment also was fertile ground for laughter, which engineer Gary Brandt discovered when he, Peter Bunetta and Rick Chudacoff drove with Steve from L.A. to Nevada to see one of his Vegas openers. Unschooled in gambling, Brandt picked up a numbered Keno ball and asked Steve, "What's this?"

"OK, I'll show you what the deal is there," Steve replied. "You got a dollar?"

"Yeah, I got a dollar," Brandt said, pulling a bill from his wallet.

"Give it to me," Steve said, yanking the greenback from Brandt and stuffing it in his own pocket. With a grin, Steve said, "That's it!" [16]

With similar sleight of hand, Steve embraced the international gamble of pleasing Dutch-, French- and German-speaking audiences attending festivals Aug. 22-24, 1980, in the Belgian cities of Brussels, Heusden-Zolder and Beveren-Waas. Billed with the Tennessee-based Red Clay Ramblers, "Britain's First Lady of Folk" Julie Felix, the Italian/Jewish-steeped Ensemble Havadia and groups from Holland and Scotland, Steve left a formidable impression. Reviewing the Heusden-Zolder event, *Vooruit*, a Belgian Socialist newspaper, marveled at how Steve, "sweating and standing on the tips of his toes," sang while replacing a broken guitar string in the middle of "City of New Orleans." The paper also noted that Steve played three encores, each time asking the next act, the Red Clay Ramblers, for permission. Concluded *Vooruit*: "Very good, sympathetic, fraternal and not cocky. Everybody agreed."

The trio of Belgian festivals let Steve and Nancy enjoy a short vacation in Europe, and Steve was in good shape for the trip. "I was amazed because I had heard that he'd been sick," says Mike Craver, keyboardist for the Red Clay Ramblers, who visited with Steve and Nancy in a motel room while Steve gushed over a guitar he'd just purchased there. "He was the picture of health and even kind of pumped up, like he'd been going to the gym."

Back in the States, Steve brought this buff look to his old hometown, at the Ravinia Festival in Highland Park and Charlotte's Web in nearby Rockford. He also played Chicago Fest at Navy Pier, where, with bassist Steve Rodby, drum-

---

Very good, sympathetic, fraternal and not cocky. Everybody agreed.
VOORUIT
BELGIUM

15: At dinner in Atlantic City before a show, Steve told Lew London that he and Steve Martin had hopped a ride together in a tourist pushcart along the town's famed boardwalk.

16: Steve returned to Nevada Dec. 11-19, 1980, to perform two-a-night casino shows at Harrah's in Reno opening for the Nitty Gritty Dirt Band, which was riding "American Dream," a pop hit written by Rodney Crowell. "It was really hard to follow that guy," says the Dirt Band's Jeff Hanna. "He really pushed us — by himself."

mer Tom Radke and electric guitarist Elliott Randall, he underscored his return with "Sweet Home Chicago" and raced through a rocking "Mama Don't Allow It," lyrically coaxing an impromptu juggler of fire sticks to cease his risky maneuvers. "Steve was the orator," says Randall, a frequent visitor to Chicago for jingle work, "and our purpose was simply to be the grass that he laid on. It was magic."

Joining Steve for these gigs and others in the summer of 1980 were Jethro Burns and Jim Rothermel, and their in-joke name became the Power Trio — a play on the ear-deafening guitar/bass/drums bands tagged with that label. "The understanding was that what we lacked in loudness we made up for in musical ability and experience," Rothermel says. The rapport and virtuosity of the three seemed effortless as they spurred each other to new heights. Burns breezed through impossibly speedy solos on mandolin [17] while Rothermel embodied a clinic on versatility with his backing and breaks on clarinet, saxophones, harmonica, whistles and flute.

In this milieu, Steve summoned songs from all stages of his career and pulled out surprises, such as an incongruous bluegrass version of the poignant title tune from the 1966 film "Alfie." But the only selections he performed from his pending LP were two co-writes with Michael Smith: the edgy "Danger" and the irresistible "Talk Backwards." He ignored the rest of the pop compositions as if he were sheepish about their impending release and instinctively knew his audiences wouldn't accept them. Instead, further deepening the gap between his recordings and shows, he trotted out in-progress versions of two comic story songs that were more typically Steve.

One, about a teenage boy's soon-to-be aborted romance with a girl who lives in a motor home, featured Steve's trademark wordplay: "She tells me she loves me, but I know it can't last / Because she's a girl with a portable past." It had started out as a jazz-blues takeoff on Billie Holiday's "God Bless the Child," says Harry Waller, who had given the tune a funny phrase that poked fun at a mobile, bargain-basement lifestyle: "The furniture is genuine Naugahyde." Steve, however, converted the song to a country-western feel to fit its theme, as he told one crowd, "for the government loan program to veterans that sprays all these guys with Agent Orange and then lets 'em buy trailers." Its title: "God Bless Our Mobile Home." [18]

The other fledgling effort, which played well in boozy clubs, had a fast, thumping beat "like an Anacin commercial," Steve said. It was a litany of ludicrously exaggerated effects from an alcohol binge called "How Much Tequila (Did I Drink Last Night)?" [19] (To finish the song, Steve six months later found the perfect collaborator — the musical partner whom he routinely had rescued onstage after many a bender, John Prine. They finished the tune in a Pacific Northwest motel room. Lines such as "I drank so much that my hair got drunk" came from Prine, who says with a laugh, "I never could get my hair right.")

In fall 1980, Steve also sought out much younger audiences, asking his daughter Jessie's teacher, Ann Schmitz at McGaugh Elementary in Seal Beach, if he

Steve was the orator, and our purpose was simply to be the grass that he laid on. It was magic.
ELLIOTT RANDALL

17: Steve's regard for Burns' skills hit print in 1980 in liner notes he penned for the Flying Fish LP "Jethro Burns Live," recorded at Amazingrace in Evanston. Noting their tours "from Miami in August to Juneau in January," Steve wrote, "I never once heard him play or say anything that wasn't the very thing that everyone else in the room wished they had played or said. How he did it is his secret and our reward."

18: Singer/songwriter Roy Book Binder clued Steve in three years later that the proper term for what the song described was "motor home," in which Book Binder toured, not "mobile home," which Steve used in the title and chorus. By then, Steve said, it was too late to change the wording.

19: When the song drew cheers, Steve quipped, "I see we all went to separate schools together."

could stop in and perform for her third-graders. "I didn't know who he was," Schmitz says. "He was Jessie's daddy, that's all I knew, and I said sure." Steve stopped by one day and played for 40 minutes, engendering a not-unfamiliar reaction. "He was fantastic, and the kids were spellbound," Schmitz says. "I was absolutely in rapture with his performance and the charm of that music, and I didn't want him to leave." Schmitz, 5-foot-4, ran to the classroom door and blocked it, saying, "Don't go, don't go, don't go."

Asylum would have loved a similar response to Steve's new LP when it was released in mid-October — and in appearance, at least, the label tried to make it marketable to the masses. Borrowing from the pensive but piercing persona of Asylum's Andrew Gold (pop hits "Lonely Boy" and "Thank You for Being a Friend"), art director Ron Coro had photographer Jim Shea pose Steve in a black T-shirt and blue baseball jacket with shiny gold sleeves, standing in three-quarter profile and staring intently into the lens. Cropped to show only his head and upper body, the image "was photographed strictly for recognition purposes," Coro says. "Steve was so small on the last cover ('High and Outside') that we went the other way with a simple shoot using a red gloss background and a 'hot' spotlight." The LP's title fell naturally from the shoot: "Hot Spot."

Steve's Mona Lisa countenance in the photo made it hard to understand the intended meaning. Seen at a glance, the album's front cover conveyed a macho, commanding stare. But examined a few moments more, Steve's expression seemed slightly pained or at least aware of the game, as if his eyes were saying, "Do I have to do this?" A more genuine approach would have showcased the photo that filled the back cover — in the same setting and lighting, Steve's head angled back, wincing and grinning at the pretense.

The record inside put Steve in a "hot spot" with Asylum, starting with its obvious lack of substance. Though Steve's four previous Asylum LPs had 10 songs and averaged 18 minutes a side, "Hot Spot" had only nine tunes, the sides averaging 16-1/2 minutes. More than the math, the problem lay in the music itself. Whereas Steve's previous LPs were eclectic, each a patchwork quilt of engaging genre samples, this one was a dull blanket with only one bright square, "Talk Backwards." Positioned as the last track, this glimmer of the "real" Steve was buried by the album's oppressive blandness.

But critics were in a charitable mood, perhaps influenced by the devastating Dec. 8, 1980, murder of John Lennon. As the calendar flipped to 1981, they used their review space not to critique Steve's record so much as to hope that it finally would help him turn the commercial corner. Larry Kelp of the *Oakland Tribune* labeled the album "as slick and pop-oriented as they come," adding, "It may just have the right sound to get some radio airplay and score him a hit record." *Cash Box* called the LP "commercially accessible MOR (middle of the road) pop and rhythmic rock."

The magazine that had named Steve's folk-oriented "Jessie's Jig" LP one of the 12 best of 1975 strained to praise his latest. "Goodman has not written any of those funny little social commentaries he used to," said Noel Coppage of *Stereo*

> **Goodman has not written any of those funny little social commentaries he used to. ... The backing and production are a little slick, but they do give good equipment something to do.**
> **NOEL COPPAGE**
> *STEREO REVIEW*

Review. "He's written the kind of thing (Boz) Scaggs might sing — but just about everything here has well-crafted lyrics and a real tune. And there's a morning-radio duet with Phoebe Snow ... that's nice to have on when you're shaving or driving to work or something. The backing and production are a little slick, but they do give good equipment something to do. ... The more of an indoors-type person you are, the better you'll like this album."

One of the few writers not to pull punches was Johnny Cash expert Patrick Carr, who in *Country Music* magazine praised Steve's past work but excoriated the new LP as representative of the "vague, smoggy and ultimately soporific" music produced in the "recording mills" of Los Angeles. "The musicians don't care, the producers are too mellow, the artists had a boring day, and the guiding light is often far too commercial: Let's do some love songs boys, let's banish the bass player, let's not be offensive, let's aim for Kansas and hope it sells."

To counter such criticism, direct and implied, Steve wore a game face. For a Jan. 16, 1981, article, he told Jack Lloyd of the *Philadelphia Inquirer* that he refused to be "defensive" about seeking a hit. Sadly, Steve also started saying things about "Hot Spot" that he knew weren't true. "It comes closer to the values on my second album, 'Somebody Else's Troubles,' than anything I've done since," he said. "I'm proud of it, and I don't see where the viewpoints have changed that much. There are some story songs, songs about relationships and the one novelty song." With similar deception, 10 days later Steve told Peter Bekker of WCBS New York, "I hope to continue this search for what is called pop ... because it turns out the slicker records I make, the more they sound like folk records somehow." [20]

Asylum, continuing its policy of courtesy singles for Steve, issued "Sometimes Love Forgets" then "Bobby Don't Stop" as 45s, and Steve insisted that the LP as a whole was gaining a foothold. "I was told that it would be a slow work record, that it would take time to warm up, and for once, those guys at the record company, they were right," Goodman told Asia Locke in the Feb. 25, 1981, *Aquarian*. "It's really gratifying. It's being picked up by stations that haven't played me before. It's not tearing up the charts or anything, but it's getting played."

What charmed Steve's interviewers was the same quality that won over his live audiences — beneath the self-deprecation and sarcasm, an unrelenting positive attitude. "I see guys in the studios working hard on a sound," he said in the *Aquarian*, "and every now and then, someone really breaks through. If you're good, it will happen. I really believe that. If I didn't believe that, I'd get a job." Similar hope emerged when Steve explained to Bekker the value of group rehearsals before laying down studio tracks. "If everybody really is prepared when they get there, there is the chance for the inspiration. That's all you can ask for in this life is your shot, and you bring everything you've got to it."

Reality also snaked into Steve's comments, however. As he wryly said to Bekker in passing, "There aren't any Brink's trucks behind hearses."

Making up for the journalistic equivocation over "Hot Spot" was the occa-

Every now and then, someone really breaks through. If you're good, it will happen. I really believe that. If I didn't believe that, I'd get a job.
STEVE GOODMAN

20: Steve later confided to writer David McGee that he knew the slick tracks on "High and Outside" and "Hot Spot" weren't his best work. "I was trying to stay on the label, I was trying to stay in the game," Steve said. "I thought there were good songs on there that sounded a lot better in concert than they do on that record. I can do them better onstage than the way they're produced on those records. Some of those songs I'll never play, but we're taking our shot because we're getting pressure to make a record that radio will play."

Ron Crick, with whose band, Swingshift, Steve had played four years earlier, was astonished to see Steve attempt a duet with a woman in the audience at Rockefeller's in Houston. "He's got balls to do this," Crick thought to himself. "This could really bomb."

(Photo courtesy of Ron Crick)

21: Cathi and Stuart Norton, of the Indiana R&B band Nightshift, were part of a similar risk Steve took at the turn of the decade at a club in Bloomington, Indiana. Steve insisted that the two join him for a final pop song, assuring them they would know its lyrics. But they didn't, a fact that soon became obvious. Midway, Steve put his arm around Cathi and sang, "And we'll learn the words to / 'Let It Be Me.' " The reaction was immediate. "The audience exploded with laughter, as did we," Cathi says.

sional, delicious vindication — such as on Sunday night, Nov. 23, 1980, in the Heights district of north Houston, during a sold-out show in a 350-seat music club and former bank called Rockefeller's. Not only did Steve's Texan fans encircle him on the main floor, but they also surrounded him above, leaning on railings from a second floor framed by classic pillars just a dozen feet over the stage. The venue was the definition of intimacy, and early in the show, as Steve noodled between songs and thought aloud about what he would play next, a female voice called to him from on high.

" 'Sometimes Love Forgets,' " she cried out.

It astonished him to hear a request for a tune that had been in release for only five weeks.

"Yeah, that's good," Steve replied dismissively. "I'll sing both parts of a duet."

A few in the audience chuckled, but the woman persisted.

"I know it," said the voice in the balcony.

Steve briefly looked upward and to his left to find a face to match the voice, but the search was futile. "All right," he finally said. Then he began the song's guitar introduction.

The crowd quieted and tensed. Was he really planning to duet with an unseen stranger? Ex-Swingshift leader Ron Crick, who had opened for Steve that night and was sitting in the front row, thought to himself, "He's got balls to do this. This could really bomb."

Steve sang the first half of the opening verse, then played guitar as the woman started to sing the verse's second half from the balcony. So far, so good. But hearing her vocal range, Steve sensed a faux pas in the making — the woman's voice would not easily reach the high harmony in the chorus. He halted the song before the chorus, adjusted the capo on his guitar neck to a lower key, then started over. "And she nailed it with him," Crick says. "It was the most magical thing I had ever seen in my life. The place exploded. It was just going crazy."

The woman, an unseen Juliet to Steve's Romeo, "did not want to steal the limelight, did not care if she was seen, did not want anything other than to hear that song," Crick says, "and if she could hear it that night and help in the effort to have others hear it by participating in the performance, well, that's what could happen, and she was letting Steve know it." But it was Steve who had taken the bigger risk. "He was like a lifesaver, a band leader and a songwriter and producer, just doing it all on the fly," Crick says, "and afterward, he just looked up and waved." [21]

Such isolated moments, rare and energizing for any performer, did not translate into commercial viability. "Hot Spot" may have propelled Steve onto a few pop-radio playlists. But it continued his steady slide on Asylum — from sales of 50,000-plus, 30,000-plus, fewer than 30,000 and 15,000-plus for his first four LPs to a downright chilly total for the fifth album of only a little more than 10,000.

Steve kept touring to promote "Hot Spot" in early 1981, though he usually performed only "Bobby Don't Stop" and "Talk Backwards" from it. His ex-

tended trips deepened pressures on the home front, apparently sending Nancy over the boiling point. "She got angry at me and at the kids, some dumb thing I was doing or saying or the kids were doing or saying," he told Lake Forest College friend Lucy Wells at a Jan. 21 show at the Paradise in Boston. "She took the charge card, she went to New York City, she spent the weekend going to galleries and nice restaurants, she bought a whole lot of stuff, and she got on the plane and came back, and it cost me a lot of money." Not that Steve begrudged her the spree or took marriage lightly. While dedicating "The Dutchman" to Wells' parents that night, he told the club audience, "There are some people here who are smarter than the rest of us. They've been married 40 years."

Family clearly was not far from his mind while he was on the road. Greeting former Chicago friend Jeany Walker Feb. 6 at a co-billing with John Prine in Portland, Oregon, Steve took quick note of her bulging abdomen, evidence that she was pregnant with her third daughter. Stories about his own three girls spilled out. "Ah, Walker, you're in there now," he said. "When you have three kids, you might as well have 1,000."

During this time, several tangential ventures served as welcome distractions. Influenced by Jethro Burns and the late Carl Martin and taught by road manager Maple Byrne, Steve learned the basics of the mandola — slightly larger and lower-pitched than a mandolin, "like a viola is to a violin," he said. When he opened for John Prine, this allowed Steve to use the instrument as an alternative to guitar during his end-of-show backing for songs such as Prine's country-ish "Paradise."

Invited by Sean Kelly, who worked as a writer during the sub-par 1980-81 season of NBC-TV's "Saturday Night Live," Steve visited the set of the hip late-night show, where Kelly introduced him to other writers. To a one, they were in awe, Kelly says. "Not *the* Steve Goodman?" they asked. Leslie Fuller, a former Chicagoan, was so pumped by Steve's presence that she walked into producer Jean Doumanian's office to ask that he be given the next episode's musical slot. "Steve Goodman's here," Fuller said. "He can make up a song about anything. That might be fun to do on our show." But the idea went nowhere.

Perhaps the biggest distraction came on Feb. 1, 1981. Nearly 10 years after the

Steve clowns with a mandolin during a photo session. Taught by Maple Byrne, he learned how to play the instrument's larger relative, the mandola. "The mandola sounds great in the car," he told an Atlanta audience in 1984. "Perfect for the car. In fact, that's where it should be recorded. I think next time we record the mandola, we'll just mike the inside of the car because this thing always sounds good in the car for some reason. It's good for 'Sea of Love.' "

(Photos by Jim Shea)

22: The most recent "City of New
Orleans" covers were on a 1979
comeback album by C.W. McCall
(real name: William Fries), known
for his 1975 trucker hit "Convoy,"
and on an uncredited, Tennessee-
based LP commemorating the
May 5, 1980, centennial of the
Chattanooga Choo Choo train.

23: During one of the Bottom Line
shows, Steve started his cowboy-
hat routine for "You Never Even
Call Me by My Name," but sent
forward to the stage was a
motorcycle helmet. Steve donned
it and reeled off a 10-minute
medley of biker oldies beginning
with "Born to Be Wild" and ending
with three "dead-girl songs," as he
termed them: "Teen Angel," "Tell
Laura I Love Her" and "(Laurie)
Strange Things Happen." The
medley was included on the 1994
anthology, "No Big Surprise."

deadly crash that prompted Amtrak to abandon the City of New Orleans name for its north-south railroad line in favor of "Panama Limited," Amtrak reverted to the original name. The move was based on the enduring popularity of Steve's song of the same name, reflected by versions that had been recorded by more than 30 artists in the past nine years. [22] Taking the cue, writers who interviewed Steve on the road made queries about "City of New Orleans" a regular occurrence. Just as he had done beginning in 1972, Steve repeatedly expressed his gratitude to Arlo Guthrie. Both a blessing and a curse, the "City" topic deflected hard questions about "Hot Spot," but it also embedded Steve's persona in the increasingly distant past.

A conspicuous example was *Rolling Stone*, which, backed by Miller beer, launched a syndicated radio feature called "The Rolling Stone Magazine Rock Revue." In a segment of less than two minutes that was taped in early 1981 and aired nationwide in July, the program couldn't resist "City of New Orleans." A snippet of Guthrie's version of the "City" chorus began the segment, followed by a male announcer who intoned, "You've heard this song millions of times, but do you know who wrote it? ... The tune is more famous than Steve, but he told *Rolling Stone* magazine that he doesn't mind." Steve's calm voice addressed the familiar topic with a fresh analogy. "There are several photographs, for instance, and paintings that I admire, and I might not necessarily want to know the guys that took the photo or made the painting, but I'm very happy to know their work and see what they saw, just for a moment," he said. After praising Guthrie's version of "City," Steve ended humbly with a truism: "You really just always have to do your best and just let what happens happen."

"City" also had worked its way into the musical consciousness of pop superstar Paul Simon. The *Boston Globe*'s Steve Morse had noted that Simon's recent single, "Ace in the Hole" — with its chorus line of "Where you been so long? Don't you know me? I'm your ace in the hole" — was "a subtle reworking of parts of Steve Goodman's 'City of New Orleans.' "

Simon was intrigued enough by Steve to attend one of his Jan. 23-24, 1981, shows at the Bottom Line in New York. [23] Afterward, he invited Steve to his apartment for wine and a chat. As diminutive as Steve, Simon had built himself into a star of movies and TV as well as music, and he offered Steve some advice. "You're great, man," Simon said. "Your act is great, your songs, everything's great. But the one thing you don't do is, you don't show enough of your sexuality onstage." Steve said he fell apart laughing. He later told his "Say It in Private" LP producer Joel Dorn, "Can you imagine a 5-foot-2 guy who looks like I look bein' sexy? What the fuck was he talking about?"

The best advice for Steve, which he understood all too well, even if he didn't admit it publicly, was not to keep chasing the elusive mantle of pop success but to mine the wellspring of his own experiences and yearnings. Songwriting — "the one part of me that I want to last," he had told John Denver nearly 10 years prior — was the key. That approach had resulted in "City of New Orleans" and so many other exceptional, if lesser-known, compositions.

The tangible turning point came late Friday night, March 13, three or four hours after Steve had finished two shows at the Bogart's club in Cincinnati and had fallen asleep in a motel room. In the wee hours of Saturday morning, he bolted upright in bed. The muse, as he fondly labeled it when he wrote "City of New Orleans," had returned. It was time for another musical milestone to spill out. This time, the topic — which had ignited his passion since before he could remember — was baseball.

Steve later said the song emerged that night "out of a dream." He said he wrote three-quarters of it upon awakening and finished it at dinner. The impression he left was that it sprang forth in less than a day's time, virtually at once. But as with "City of New Orleans," the real story was more complex.

Since early childhood, Steve's life had been imbued with baseball, and particularly the hapless Chicago Cubs. His emotions bounced from anguish ("Being a Cub fan is like being a Jew because long periods of suffering are involved," notes Carolyn Purdy-Gordon, wife of Steve's childhood friend Stuart Gordon) to anger ("The Cubs are a shit organization," Steve had told folksinger Chris Farrell). What few realized, however, was that Steve's desire to write a song about the national pastime had run deep for more than a decade, and his attempts had been frequent and futile.

Mocking himself with diamond lingo, Steve told his audience on Oct. 2, 1973, at Bubba's in South Miami that he had been trying to pen a song about baseball since 1969. "I get about three-quarters of the way through it, and then I walk somebody and take myself out," he said. "I never get to finish the damn thing. It's true. I get about three-quarters of the way through it, and then I'm struggling, it's a hot afternoon, and I'm lookin' to the bench, and the manager comes out and yanks me. I get pinch-hit for all the time."

Not infrequently, baseball fueled his onstage improvisations, such as the weekend of Oct. 31-Nov. 2, 1975, at Club Passim in Cambridge when he made up a song about the sixth game of the World Series two weeks prior. The 7-6 Boston win over Cincinnati was feted as the best-played Series game ever. Red Sox rightfielder Dwight Evans supplied one of its many highlights in the 11th inning with an acrobatic, game-saving catch of a Joe Morgan fly followed by a quick throw to first base to double up Ken Griffey. In his song, Steve delighted his Beantown crowd by rhyming the name of Evans with a phrase about him snaring "a ball hit to the heavens." [24]

Steve trained his baseball sights homeward in August 1978, improvising at the Earl of Old Town a Cubs song to the tune of "When the Saints Go Marchin' In." Its 10 verses shrewdly commented on the team's slugger, Dave Kingman, and ace reliever, Bruce Sutter, as well as Bill Veeck, owner of the "inept" White Sox of the South Side. Steve's made-up lyrics also aired his fervent hope for a World Series between the Cubs and White Sox but crassly pointed out, "The chances of that are as good as that of me pissin' on the moon."

"Dave Kingman," which Steve composed on assignment for Chicago's WMAQ-TV in early 1980, also pricked Steve's baseball longings. While the

I never get to finish the damn thing. It's true. I get about three-quarters of the way through it, and then I'm struggling, it's a hot afternoon, and I'm lookin' to the bench, and the manager comes out and yanks me.
STEVE GOODMAN

24: Steve's improvisation at Passim inspired Howie Newman, a Boston folksinger who mailed Steve demo cassettes and in 1976 recorded a baseball novelty single, "Blasted in the Bleachers." When Newman gave Steve a copy of his "Blasted" 45, Steve insisted on paying Newman its $1 sale price. Later, Newman told Steve that while he had sold 600 copies of the single, he lost $700 on the project. "You didn't lose $700," Steve shot back. "You paid $700 for an education." Newman eventually followed Steve's lead by writing baseball songs, issuing CDs and singing several of Steve's tunes.

On the same January 1981 eastern swing during which he played the Bijou Café in Philadelphia (above), Steve had a sardonic chat about baseball with New York radio journalist Peter Bekker. A month and a half later was born "A Dying Cub Fan's Last Request."

(Photo by Tom Reynolds)

chorus and first two verses of the tune focused on the cranky Cubs slugger, Steve also slipped in hints of a more generalized song about the team, including a reference to Kingman's homers landing outside Wrigley Field on nearby Waveland Avenue. Tellingly, the song's final verse was a lament for "the fans in Chicago who have waited so long for a winner to cheer" and for "the city that's so tired of sayin' 'Wait till next year'."

Likewise, in his Jan. 26, 1981, interview with Peter Bekker for WCBS in New York, Steve tied his fervor for baseball to his resignation over the Cubs' perennial failure. "I require the Chicago Cubs to win sometime during my life," he said, "but I must admit, I despair having this requirement filled during my lifetime." Acknowledging the hypocrisy of a descending musician criticizing a losing baseball team, he added, "They (the Cubs) could say the same thing about my band. I'm sayin' if you interviewed the Chicago Cubs about my music, you would get the same thing."

When Bekker tried to sympathize by noting his own St. Louis roots, Steve jumped in with a correction. "Now, you guys won a baseball championship during the lifetime of most Americans here," he said, alluding to the champion St. Louis Cardinals of 1967. "The Chicago Cubs won the pennant the same year that World War II ended. I thought that in some way that that was symbolic, that that was the last time. Now, I must admit that if they are ever again going to use nuclear weapons in wars, if that's the next time the Cubs win, I hope the Cubs never win, OK? Because those were the two things that happened that year — the Cubs won the National League pennant, and people destroyed each other a lot. I don't think they're tied up, either, but those are really the two major events of that year, somehow."

"Well," Bekker replied, "they were both unprecedented."

"Yes," Steve said, "and, my God, I hope one of 'em's repeatable. I know which one that is."

A month and a half after the Bekker interview came Steve's "dream," late the night of March 13. His reservoir of motivation and effort resulted in what many consider the most evocative baseball song ever written. It was an ironic homage to the Cubs, but it also was a meditation on mortality and futility that underscored the countless and eloquent essays making the case for baseball as a metaphor for American life. It was, as Steve titled it, "A Dying Cub Fan's Last Request."

The song's narrative hook was that of a terminally ill "old Cub fan" spelling out to friends his explicit vision of the perfect "doubleheader funeral" — an elaborate cremation at Wrigley Field that invoked two dozen details and phrases familiar to Cubs enthusiasts and diamond fans of any stripe. Peppering the lyrics were Frosty Malts and crushed paper beer cups, "bleacher bums" and pigeons beneath the El tracks, Hall-of-Famer Ernie Banks' buoyant "Let's play two" and a live organ rendition of "Na Na Hey Hey Goodbye." Permeated with dry humor, the words built to a conclusion that relied on an irresistibly spiritual pun while also referencing the big-league team just 18 minutes away from his

Seal Beach home. In the song's instantly classic punch line, the dying man assured his friends that he soon would be using "season's tickets to watch the Angels" but added, "You, the living, you're stuck here with the Cubs, so it's me that feels sorry for you."

For those close to Steve, the song would swell with worrisome symbolism because it could be seen as referencing his "dying" recording career or, more directly and poignantly, his fatal disease. But because Steve's leukemia was still a secret to the masses and because the lyrics were cast in third person and labeled the protagonist as elderly, the song could stand on its own without triggering unwanted inferences. On its face, the tune linked Steve and its main character in only one way that was obvious — both were long-suffering fans of the Cubs. It was a theme that could spark widespread empathy from baseball devotees who anguished during sustained failure and rooted in vain for the underdog.

While appealingly contemporary, "Dying Cub Fan" was hardly original. It borrowed from the form and content of an English ballad originating in the 18th century, "The Unfortunate Rake." Endlessly modified, performed and recorded by African-American jazz artists as "St. James Infirmary" and by folk and country musicians as "Streets of Laredo," the ballad carried an enduring motif. In each rendition, a rueful or mournful man foreshadowed his demise by issuing a litany of instructions for how his body was to be dressed and paraded through town. In more recent times, the song had morphed into other prominent versions. It became the quiet title theme of the 1973 baseball film "Bang the Drum Slowly," in which a mentally impaired catcher played by Robert DeNiro faced a terminal disease. It also formed the basis of Willie McTell's "Dyin' Crapshooter's Blues," which David Bromberg learned from Erik Frandsen in Greenwich Village and included on his raucous 1976 album, "How Late'll Ya Play Til?"

"Dying Cub Fan" built on established influences in other ways as well. It was a talking blues, a storytelling format that Bob Dylan, Phil Ochs and other folkies had popularized for youthful audiences. Its theme drew from *The Year the Yankees Lost the Pennant*, the 1954 Douglas Wallop novel that celebrated the mythical, devil-inspired rise of the lowly Washington Senators to league champs and that was transformed into the 1955 Broadway musical and 1958 film "Damn Yankees!" It's also possible that for the culminating line in the "Dying Cub Fan" chorus, Steve had absorbed in his childhood a phrase coined by *Mad* magazine in 1961, "the doormat of the National League." [25]

Notwithstanding its many sources, or perhaps because of them, "A Dying Cub Fan's Last Request" was a work of down-to-earth genius. That it had touched a nerve was verified when Steve debuted it in a pair of shows in Chicago with Jethro Burns on Saturday, March 14, mere hours after he finished writing it. His reasoning for bringing out such a major work so quickly was almost incidental, he said later. "I wanted to have something fresh to sing to my family and friends there, much less anybody who had to get in to see us play," he told Yardena Arar, L.A.-based writer for The Associated Press. "With the baseball season coming up, it came to me that that might be a good idea."

I wanted to have something fresh to sing to my family and friends there, much less anybody who had to get in to see us play. With the baseball season coming up, it came to me that that might be a good idea.
STEVE GOODMAN

25: In "Sing Along with *Mad*," a 20-page bonus section of the 1961 collection *More Trash from Mad #4*, appeared a parody to the tune of "How Are Things in Glocca Morra?" called "How Are Things in Philadelphia?" The satirical lyrics mocked the ineptness of the Phillies, and the song was subtitled: "A tribute to the doormat of the National League."

26: Wigginton's experience interviewing Steve at his Seal Beach home mirrored that of those who had visited Steve in his third-floor sanctuary in Evanston. For an hour and a half, Wigginton says, "he must have pulled out 40 albums. He would play a bit of a cut, get excited by it, draw a connection to the next song he just had to play for me, find the next song and before the first was done the second was on the turntable. The whole time we talked was interspersed with him pulling the arm up on the turntable, grabbing his guitar and playing a bit of something else. He was this lovely, sweet man, fascinated by music – all music."

27: Burns loved the Cubs but had no illusions about their prowess. Ed Stiernberg, who photographed the Park West show, heard Burns say, "The Cubs are so bad that they ought to move to the Philippines, where they could be called the Manila Folders." In 1982, Burns recorded a corollary to Steve's "Dying Cub Fan," a poem called "Mandolin Picker's Epitaph," for his "Tea for One" LP on the Kaleidoscope label. His ideal gravestone marker: "He wasn't funny, and he couldn't sing. He didn't prove a doggone thing. But boy, that S.O.B. could play."

28: In the early 1980s, Roy Leonard flew west to broadcast his live, Oscars-related WGN show from Beverly Hills. One of his guests was Steve, who drove an hour from Seal Beach to arrive at 7 a.m. During a 1983 show in Rockford, Illinois, Steve said that over the years WGN had provided "the heart and soul of any airplay I get in the world."

But the song's unveiling at 750-seat Park West was anything but nonchalant. Steve had hurriedly arranged for video images of Cubs games that were nearly four times his size to appear behind him as he played the tune. "They have an 18-foot screen behind the stage, so we hooked up the machine, and when we got to the second chorus they cued in the footage," Steve later told Mark Wigginton of the *Long Beach Press-Telegram*. [26] "It is the first time I've ever gotten a standing, booing ovation. People were standing and clapping and booing at the same time." Steve said he didn't know why until he turned around to glimpse the larger-than-life footage — which depicted the tempestuous Dave Kingman, who two weeks prior had been traded to the New York Mets, hitting a homer as a Cub.

Still in Chicago two mornings later, Steve performed it at about a quarter to noon on the WGN-AM "Roy Leonard Show," reading the lengthy lyrics from scraps of paper and relying on Burns for instrumental embellishment. [27] At seven minutes and 15 seconds, it was more than twice the length of most songs heard on the radio. As the pair completed the epic tune, their host convulsed into giddy laughter. "This program will never be the same," Leonard said. "That's a gem, Steve."

The WGN phone lines lit up. "I want that record," said the first caller, a middle-aged woman named Delores.

"Honest?" Leonard asked. "Would you rush out to buy it if it came out on a record?"

"Yes! I'm one of the nuts that believes."

"Oh, Delores," Steve said, "I'm glad you liked it."

"Well, you're a Cub fan, aren't you, Steve?" Leonard said. "Really, legitimately?"

"Yeah, to the bone," Steve said. "I like the White Sox, too. I'm a Chicago sports fan. I've lived (nearly) my whole life here and suffered with these teams."

The caller invoked a mélange of Chicago football, baseball and hockey organizations: "You mean you believe in the miracle that one day the Bears will win, the pennant (World Series) will be between the Sox and the Cubs, and the Stanley (Cup) trophy will be with the (Black)Hawks?"

"Well, yeah," Steve said, "and besides that, when I was a kid, I used to go watch Loyola win a national basketball tournament (in 1963). So there's every reason to think some other school around here might do that someday, too."

Identically passionate calls kept on coming long after Steve and Burns left the radio studio. The seed for the song had been sewn in the perfect medium because WGN long had been the Cubs' flagship station. Equally apt was that the song's first broadcast was on the show of Roy Leonard, who had worked in radio since 1951, launched his WGN show in 1967 and welcomed visits by Steve since 1972. [28] For the Midwestern metropolitan audience of eight million people, Leonard was the number-one voice of friendly credibility — and one of Steve's most ardent champions.

"The guy had the greatest sense of humor of any human being I've ever met," Leonard says. "That's what made him so charming. He never had an entourage. He just walked in, like the mailman, only he had a guitar on his back instead of the mail. He was one of the most genuine people I ever met, so self-effacing, so down-to-earth. He knew what he did was good. I don't know that he really knew how good he was, but he enjoyed doing it so much, it wouldn't make any difference. When he came in, he would always say, 'What do you want me to do?' That was it. He never asked to have something said or read or played. It was always, 'What can I do for you?' He had a natural feeling for what should be said and done. It was like having a beer together in a bar. He never had to put on a persona other than what he was. He looked at you, and you would like him immediately."

WGN listeners embraced "Dying Cub Fan" with equal immediacy as Leonard replayed it in response to requests in the weeks ahead. But other circumstances beyond Steve's control also gave the song life. On Feb. 25, the big-league players had voted in favor of a work stoppage to take effect May 29, and the prospect of the majors' first midseason strike filled the newspapers and stoked water-cooler chats nationwide. What's more, the reliably inept Cubs got off to one of their worst starts, going 2-13 in April and 8-20 in May, triggering a lengthy (five minutes and 10 seconds) segment on the May 31 edition of the ABC-TV Evening News. Along with pictures of the Great Chicago Fire of 1871 and the Cubs' 1945 National League pennant, as well as a sound bite from Ernie Banks, [29] the nationally broadcast story showed Steve wearing a Cubs hat and jacket and singing and playing portions of "Dying Cub Fan" from the playground bleachers at his daughter Jessie's school in Seal Beach.

But while Steve's Cub song grew wings, his Asylum recording career was in freefall. Despite his public optimism, [30] Steve knew it. Late one night after a show in Philadelphia that he had opened for John Prine, Steve summoned Prine, Al Bunetta and his two concert-booking agents, Elizabeth Rush (now Marsden) and George Carroll, to his hotel room. The mood was foreboding. "There was a lot of pressure on about why Steve was not doing well," says Marsden, who says that she and Carroll were expecting a rant about how their bookings were not adequately boosting sales for Steve's "Hot Spot" LP. Though they thought the album sub-par, they also felt that it wasn't yet the right time to convey that opinion to Steve. They were prepared to "be mensches and go, 'Fine, whatever,' to take it and shut up."

Steve, however, had a surprise in store. "OK, you guys," he said as everyone pulled up chairs. "I called you here because of the lack of success that's happening with this record. I just wanted to really let you know, person to person, how I feel about it. I think that you guys did everything that you could do, and I just really want to thank you because I know you put a tremendous effort into this above and beyond. Y'know, the bottom line is, I didn't deliver you a good record, and I just want to say I'm sorry."

The admission was dumbfounding. "We sat there looking at him blank, going, 'What's the punch line here?' We could not imagine an artist saying this,

WGN-AM radio host Roy Leonard found that Steve's down-to-earth approach to his "Dying Cub Fan" song exemplified his endearing unpretentiousness: "He never had to put on a persona other than what he was."
(Photo courtesy of WGN Radio 720)

29: Coincidentally, Ernie Banks had just released a recording of his own, a spoken-word piece set to a disco beat called "Teamwork." A benefit for Boys Clubs, the recording's refrain was "Teamwork: It's workin' for me."

30: Steve told Associated Press writer Mary Campbell, "I can read and see. I know there are starving children. And I know the inane ways we spend our time and the inane things we talk about. But you better have some optimism because that really appears to be the prime motivating factor of life."

Joe Smith, Elektra/Asylum president, found it "agonizing" in 1980 to drop Steve, "one of the good guys," from the hip label: "He wanted a hit record, I know, but when we had a mandate from corporate headquarters to cut costs, Steve was one of the victims."
(Photo courtesy of Joe Smith)

31: Prine says he came to feel constricted by Asylum and knew he would have felt the same at another label: "That's when I really did some soul-searchin' and figured out how can I continue doin' this for a livin' and not have to deal with these people, because they had absolutely nothin' to do with what I do."

but the reality is that that was true. That was not a hit record," Marsden says. "But Stevie doing that was just Stevie. It was the classiest thing. Even if we had screwed up, he probably would have said the same thing because he was just such a nice guy and so well grounded in the realities of the business. With his illness, he had a good set of priorities about life. The failure of a record that people, for whatever reasons, had thought was going to be a big hit was important to him, but not important enough to compromise any values or to lose perspective. That was rare."

What was not rare, in the late spring of 1981, was Asylum's decision to drop Steve from the label. Kenny Batiste, head of A&R at Elektra, called Al Bunetta into his office one morning to deliver the news — and the same axe also fell for John Prine, who, after "Bruised Orange," had recorded two more albums for Asylum. [31] "They got rid of my whole roster in one five-minute morning," Bunetta says. "They said, 'We don't want your guys in.' They said it in a nice way, but at the end of the day, that's what it was." The decision "crushed" Bunetta, particularly in the case of Steve. "I knew it, but I couldn't tell Stevie because him being sick, what am I gonna do? Go back and say, 'Hey, and y'know what else? You don't have a label anymore.' " Instead, Bunetta says that he told Steve, "We're not doin' this anymore. We're gonna make our own stuff, because they don't get what we're doin', and John wants out, too."

For Elektra/Asylum president Joe Smith, the decision was tough. "It was one of those downturns in the record business," he says. "We weren't making any money, and we had to cut costs. We were signing black artists and trying to get a little more rock 'n' roll into the company with the Cars and other bands. We had this roster of singer/songwriters. We had four tough, independent women: Carly (Simon) and Joni (Mitchell) and Judy (Collins) and Linda (Ronstadt). We had Jackson (Browne) and the whole Jackson crowd: J.D. Souther and Warren Zevon. Somewhere, we had to cut.

"It was an agonizing thing. I didn't personally get involved in it too much. I OK'd what A&R marketing and promotion people said. They said Steve had taken a shot with a few records and was not showing any perceptible gain. People loved Stevie Goodman, and I could see the affection from the crowd. But if he filled a club one night, those were all the people in that town that wanted to see him. He could play the next night, and there'd be nobody there. So the feeling was that there was not a broad audience that we could tap. He wanted a hit record, I know, but when we had a mandate from corporate headquarters to cut costs, Steve was one of the victims. We felt very badly about it because he was one of the good guys."

More blunt is Jerry Sharell, who worked as a promoter at Asylum since shifting from Buddah in 1973: "With all due respect to Steve's talent and to Al Bunetta, five albums is a lot of albums to be going through with very little success. It's a hard thing to say, and no artist wants to hear it, but there comes a time when you have to let the man go somewhere else because we haven't been able to do it for him." Stage success was admirable, he says, but in the music business of the early 1980s, "you were really only as good as your record."

Asylum's rejection had to have hurt Steve deeply — and may have intensified his leukemia, says singer/songwriter Wendy Waldman, who had shared the stage with him several times. "It was tragic and needless," she says. "The commercial machine, for some of us, was really lethal. It was dangerous, especially in those days where everyone around you defined you by whether you had a damned record deal."

That summer, Steve stomached the rebuff, at least publicly, with grace and humor. [32] In baseball parlance, he cracked to Perry M. Lamek of the *Milwaukee Sentinel*, "I think I'll be re-signed in the free-agent draft. Maybe I can record for the Cleveland Indians. The Brewers don't need anyone, do they?" More seriously, he expressed no regrets about bringing an increasingly pop — and less successful — sound to his LPs. "You have to feel an obligation to put on them only what you really believe in. You take your lumps if they don't sell, but that way you never have to apologize." Besides, he added sardonically, "The first time you ever take a dime for playing music in public, you're in *show business* up to your ears."

Sometimes, Steve's response to Asylum's rejection resembled that of a Pollyanna hiding unspoken resentment. "I think it's just a question of timing," he told Leland Rucker of the *Kansas City Star*. "These guys (Asylum) are tryin' to make a living, so I can't fault them. ... It's not gonna change my music because it appears to be goin' over well enough live. I feel like I'm just spoiled, as long as I keep comin' up with something that's entertaining, that audiences appear to enjoy. ... In a way, it's a break for me to be unsigned right now. I have to look at it that way because this is the kind of music we make."

While being cast adrift pegged him in the eyes of some as a "cult artist," Steve slyly disavowed the tag. "Charles Manson had a cult following," he told Rucker. "I don't want to have a cult following, if that's what it means. Not my department." But like a deft politician, Steve also implicitly admitted a desire to part ways with the slick pop sound he had embraced: "I do know that what has worked, as such, for me over the years is some small situations, sound-wise, based around acoustic instruments, so I'm tryin' to put together a string-band project. I'm lookin' to get back in the studio before the end of the year."

Actually, he already had done so. WGN's Roy Leonard had kept Steve apprised about the giddy calls to the station about "Dying Cub Fan" and had forwarded to him fan letters begging for copies of it. In response, Steve flew Jethro Burns to Los Angeles to add his mandolin to a studio version of the song that brought the ballpark to listeners' ears. It opened with crowd cheers before fading into Steve's subdued recitation and soft guitar strums and Burns' gently dancy mandolin. On the first run through the chorus, the crowd noise morphed into a swaying clap on each backbeat. During the second run, the crowd cheered again, and echoed voices chimed in. The effect was as if Steve was performing the song at Wrigley Field and everyone was inspired to sing.

For this version, Steve polished the lyrics, inserting four "he said" attribu-

The commercial machine, for some of us, was really lethal. It was dangerous, especially in those days where everyone around you defined you by whether you had a damned record deal.
WENDY WALDMAN

32: Steve's warmth emerged during a gig in Atlanta, where he reunited with Tom Hayward from long-gone Bistro days. Hayward's wife Sandy, who had shared her antibiotics when Steve had colds in the early 1970s, suffered from stomach cancer. Steve gave the Haywards custom T-shirts stating, "1981 Annual Steve Goodman Summer Tour." On Sandy's shirt was "Chief Pharmacist." Eight months later, she died.

Steve's "Red Pajama Records" 45-rpm single for "A Dying Cub Fan's Last Request" came closely on the heels of Asylum Records letting him go.

(Photo courtesy of Alan "Chip" Pruzik)

tions to enhance the message that the dying Cub fan of the song was a fictional character and not him. He also sped the tune's tempo slightly and excised a couple of lines referring to Ernie Banks, Cubs broadcaster Jack Brickhouse and ex-Cubs manager Leo Durocher. This resulted in a length of six and a half minutes, which was 45 seconds shorter than the version he had played on the air for Roy Leonard but still twice the length of most radio songs.

"Dying Cub Fan" was pressed as a single that featured on the flip side a sprightly Steve-Jethro rendition of the classic "Take Me Out to the Ball Game." The latter tune included a hilarious lyrical amendment to a home fan's hopes for victory. In place of "If they don't win, it's a shame," Steve sang, "If they don't win, what else is new?"

It was the first sales product of the newly independent Steve, and the name printed at the top of the 45's label took its cue from the song-credit line he had used since 1975, "Red Pajama Records," giving more prominence to a favorite children's song of his daughters. The appellation "was almost under the heading of a joke," says Dan Einstein, an assistant whom Al Bunetta hired that summer. "That was his, 'Hey, gotta put a name on it.' "

Not many copies of the single were printed, but quite a few were mailed to radio stations, with mixed success, says Bobbi Cowan, a publicist whom Bunetta hired to promote the song. "Dying Cub Fan," while inherently endearing, had several liabilities. "I couldn't get it on the radio," says the Los Angeles-based Cowan. "It was too long, he was a folkie that most people out here had never heard of, and the Cubs, who cared about them?" Cowan was able to secure valuable media interviews, however.

One was with a friend from Steve's Albany Park childhood, Bob Sirott, an entertainment/lifestyle reporter for Chicago's CBS-TV affiliate, WBBM Channel 2. Recorded in the final week of July for airing on the evening news prior to Steve's Friday, July 31, set at Chicago Fest, the Sirott piece was unique for its setting. It became the only known and recorded instance in which Steve performed "Dying Cub Fan" inside Wrigley Field. Wearing a Cubs hat and jacket, Steve played the song over and over while sitting in the grandstand on the third-base side. Sirott's cameraman filmed Steve with various pans and zooms, even shooting him from the right-field bleachers 400 feet away.

The Friendly Confines, however, were empty, owing to the midseason baseball strike, which had begun June 12 and was to end July 31. Questioned by Sirott, Steve regarded the work stoppage with a rueful grin. "I can't believe they did this," Steve said. Referring to the Chicago Black Sox gambling scandal three generations prior, he said, "I think the strike is the worst thing that's happened since the game was fixed in 1919." Sirott noted that Steve's single might fare better without a strike, and Steve agreed, kidding that he would record a Spanish version and sell it during winter ball in Puerto Rico. "But this is an eminently survivable casualty," Steve told Sirott. "It's just a little idiot song about the Cubs and about what it feels like to actually love the sport." [33]

Back in California, the song also caught the interest of 27-year-old Roy

33: Fueling Chicago interest in "Dying Cub Fan" was recent news that the Wrigley family, the Cubs' owner since 1915, had sold the team to the Tribune Company, publisher of the *Chicago Tribune* and owner of WGN radio and TV. When Roy Leonard raised this with Steve on July 31, Steve cracked, "Well, that settles that. We can get objective reporting now."

In late July 1981, near the end of major-league baseball's first in-season work stoppage, Steve is interviewed in an empty Wrigley Field by a friend from his childhood in Albany Park, Bob Sirott, for WBBM. The topic was Steve's "little idiot song about the Cubs," but he also addressed the strike, which he termed "the worst thing that's happened since the game was fixed in 1919."
(Video capture courtesy of Bob Sirott and Jessica Kaplan)

Firestone, the sports journalist and entertainer immortalized in the 1996 film "Jerry Maguire" who in 1981 was just one year into hosting his first cable sports-talk show, the Santa Monica-based "UpClose" for the USA Network. While in college, the Florida native had appeared on a bill with Steve as a standup comic in the early 1970s at south Miami's Flick Coffeehouse, where he was exposed to Steve's facility with the genre of blues — into which "Dying Cub Fan" snugly fit. "George Will once said the Cubs fan is about 70 percent baseball fan and 30 percent scar tissue," Firestone says, "and I think that's what that song is about." Firestone says Steve considered "Dying Cub Fan" a novelty tune, but Firestone, who has listened to the song more than 100 times, told Steve it was much more. "The song was humorous, but it also had a tone of knowledge to it," he says. "He had a great blues sort of a trill in his voice, this technical ability to convey the irony of the song. He combined the musicality and the lyrics." [34]

At times during 1981, it seemed that for Steve nothing was more compelling than baseball. [35] He rushed band members to his upstairs hotel room a few hours before he was to open for John Prine on Saturday, June 6, in Columbia, Maryland. The reason for the frenzy was that Dodgers rookie Fernando Valenzuela's first pitching appearance at Wrigley Field was the televised Game of the Week. The troupe missed viewing the phenom, as Chicago had knocked him out in the fourth inning en route to a rare, 11-5 victory. But they did catch the debut of gangly, red-haired catcher Jody Davis, who eventually became connected to Steve in a way neither anticipated.

"Dying Cub Fan" quickly reached the nationally syndicated Dr. Demento radio show, which first aired the song Aug. 23. Soon, the Emil Verban Society — named for an obscure 1940s second-baseman, and subtitled the "Chicago Cubs Fan Club of Washington, D.C." — inducted Steve into its phantom club

34: For KCBS-TV in Los Angeles, Firestone re-interviewed Steve in 1983 upon the release of a live version of "Dying Cub Fan" on LP and after Steve had gone public about his leukemia. "He talked about how laughter is more important than money and an official position of success. The more laughs you've had, the greater life you live."

35: Steve's sports mania was not confined to baseball, as illustrated Sept. 16, 1981, when he played Kansas City's Uptown Theatre. Opening act Darrell Lea says Steve couldn't wait for the morning paper for news about the evening's welterweight fight in Las Vegas between Sugar Ray Leonard and Thomas Hearns. From the theater, Steve called the *Kansas City Star* sports desk to find out the victor (Leonard, in a TKO).

Reflecting baseball's dominant role in Steve's life, Steve and photographer Jim Shea celebrate the first-place finish of their fantasy-league Ponce Lions team with a champagne sudsing in the Goodman kitchen in Seal Beach.

(Photo courtesy of Jim Shea)

36: Started in 1975, the by-invitation-only Emil Verban Society topped out at 700 members. It still holds meetings every two years, says founder Bruce Ladd, of Chapel Hill, North Carolina.

as member # 114. He was in esteemed company. The roster included senators, congressmen and even a former Cubs announcer and current White House resident, Ronald Reagan. While attending Steve's Nov. 11 show at the Bayou in D.C., some 40 of the Verbanites officially welcomed him to their ranks. [36]

But much as Steve had cemented publicly his passion for baseball with "Dying Cub Fan," he hardly limited himself to that persona, particularly given that his being dropped by Asylum meant that his livelihood depended on show dates more than ever before. Not atypically, in 1981 he was racking up stage moments both peerless and perilous.

At Pete Seeger's Clearwater Revival on Sunday, June 21, one of several festivals he played that summer and fall, Steve encountered a relatively new aspect of folk concerts — a sign-language interpreter for the hard of hearing. The interpreter for Steve's set was Sal Perreira, a 27-year-old who had learned sign language in high school but didn't know Steve's music and was not a folk fan.

"It was more of a get-my-face-out-in-public kind of thing and advertise my-self," he says. "It sounded like a fun way to spend the day." It was an unknowing underestimation.

In the performers' tent before the set, Steve gave Perreira a rundown of his songs and their content. But when Steve got to "Talk Backwards," a skeptical look filled Perreira's face. "We're going to be talking backwards," Steve said, and Perreira replied, "OK, I'll give it a shot." Perreira assumed Steve would be merely reversing words in a sentence.

"Well, here's the test for Sal," Steve said onstage as he began the song, and Perreira discovered that the task was much more complex — that Steve was singing words as if they were *spelled* backwards. As the gibberish began, Perreira froze. "I looked over at him, and I dropped my persona of trying to reflect his attitude," he says. "You're supposed to try to convey the character and spirit of the message, but I just dropped everything I was doing. I was stunned, and we both cracked up. I couldn't sign anything because I had no idea what he was talking about. Nothing can be signed like that. It was a cute little scenario that was totally spontaneous. I just loved it."

So did the audience. "Everybody was hysterical," says Philadelphia Folk Festival stalwart Laura Haynes (now Aiken). "It was an absolutely wonderful interplay. Most of the time, the interpreter is just an adjunct that everybody tries to ignore. So when you see that somebody is actually talking to them and including them in the performance, it was a triple whammy. It was a great song, a great performer and a really great interpreter."

Steve may have wished he'd had an interpreter a month later at a memorial concert for Harry Chapin. The antsy, passionate singer/songwriter and hunger activist, with whom Steve had performed several times, had died July 16 after he swerved his Volkswagen in front of a flatbed tractor-trailer that rear-ended the car and exploded its gas tank on the Long Island Expressway. The instant demise of the strapping and vibrant 38-year-old came as a shock to millions. For Steve, it also meant the loss of a heartfelt champion.

Two years earlier, in August 1979, Chapin had hosted a two-hour "Star Special" on BBC radio in London, spinning his favorite discs. Of 16 acts that Chapin selected, he played two or more songs by only four: the Beatles, Bob Dylan, Don McLean and Steve. "Of all the performers in America ... who can go out with a guitar and entertain an audience, without a band, without all the accoutrements, without superstar status around them, Steve Goodman is the man," Chapin said. "Unbelievable performer. ... Steve is about 5-foot-2 inches tall, but by God, the energy, the energy, the energy." The two Steve songs Chapin chose to air were "City of New Orleans" and what he called a companion to his "Cat's in the Cradle" for its father-son theme, "My Old Man." "Oh boy," Chapin said, "it's a box of Kleenex there and a towel. Great song. You know, you write a song like that, it's got to stay innocent and simple, and by God, he did it." [37]

Chapin's July 23, 1981, memorial service was anything but simple. One of a dozen listed musicians and speakers, including three from Congress, Steve chose

I was stunned, and we both cracked up. I couldn't sign anything because I had no idea what he was talking about. Nothing can be signed like that.
SAL PERREIRA
interpreter

37: Chapin and Steve had recorded for the same label, Elektra/Asylum, but there is little reason to believe that the connection influenced his effusiveness for Steve.

Michael Cooney takes a break with Steve during the 1981 Winnipeg Folk Festival. Cooney had recovered from his 1979 auto accident and was grateful to Steve and others for singing at benefits for his medical care.

(Photo by Jim Polaski)

38: Buffett's version of "Elvis Imitators" surfaced on his four-CD box set "Boats, Beaches, Bars & Ballads" in 1992, "against a lot of people's better judgment," according to Buffett's liner notes. "So far," he wrote, "I have not heard from Elvis, so I don't know if he likes it or not, but I wouldn't be surprised if he's seen at one of our shows this summer."

to perform "The Twentieth Century Is Almost Over." He no doubt thought the song's quirky summary of the 1900s would be a good fit for the 1,000 mourners who filled Grace Episcopal Church in Brooklyn Heights. By the first sing-along chorus, says Harry's brother, Tom Chapin, "What started out as a funeral turned into a celebration. It just literally lifted the room."

Steve winced, however, when he got to words in the final verse: "The Judgment Day is getting nearer / There it is in the rear-view mirror." Later, Steve called Al Bunetta. "I made such a blunder," Steve told him. "I was singing, 'There it is in the rear-view mirror,' and that's when he died, when he didn't look in the rear-view mirror." It would not be the last time that Chapin's death haunted Steve.

Bolstering Steve's spirits the next month, country/folk star Emmylou Harris not only arranged for Steve to open for her at an outdoor afternoon show Aug. 16 at the Parkwest resort east of Salt Lake City. She also asked him to fill in for her Hot Band's lead guitarist Frank Reckard, who had missed a plane connection to the ski-slope site. The surprise highlight came while Steve helped Harris perform Chuck Berry's "You Never Can Tell" (a country hit for her in 1977) for the encore. Steve delighted the audience of 6,000 by resurrecting from his college-era shows Berry's center-stage signature — a duck walk.

"You never knew what Steve was gonna do," Harris says, "but this time he was really taking advantage of having the drums and bass. Obviously, he wasn't Frank Reckard, and he never pretended to be a lead guitar player, but with sheer heart and soul and energy, he replaced the lead-guitar part. Just his presence got us all through it, because Steve exuded joy."

Collaborations with another prominent performer in 1981 gave Steve a boost in the wake of his departure from Asylum — and the connection came in a Nevada casino. When Jimmy Buffett played Caesar's Palace in Lake Tahoe, Steve stopped by and played "Elvis Imitators" for Buffett, who embraced the ditty for his stage show. ("I'm an Elvis fan of all the Elvises," he says.) Buffett also hurried to record it in Nashville, backed by the original Jordanaires, the gospel quartet that sang on nearly every Elvis Presley record in the 1950s and 1960s. "Thank you very much, ladies and gentlemen," Buffett began the track, in a velvet voice. "I'd like to do this next song especially for you and for The King." Though it was true to the Presley sound, Buffett saw the recording as merely "a joke," and it was released only as an MCA single and with no fanfare. "Because the engineers didn't want their names on it" and in keeping with his frequent spoofs, Buffett listed himself and his band as "Freddie and the Fishsticks." Without marketing or the Buffett identity, the single "disappeared," as Steve put it, and bypassed the mainstream. [38]

Two other songs partly written by Steve had more immediate staying power because Buffett recorded them in the fall of 1981 for his "Somewhere over China" LP, released in January 1982. "It's Midnight and I'm Not Famous Yet" was a tale that Buffett had started about casino gambling. After losing $40 in bets at Caesar's Palace, Steve helped Buffett finish the tune. Filled with amusing rhymes (Lester

On Chuck Berry's "You Never Can Tell," Steve, in sunglasses, does the duck walk while filling in on lead guitar for a delighted Emmylou Harris and her Hot Band on Aug. 16, 1981, at the Parkwest ski resort east of Salt Lake City. Other accompanists, from left, were Wayne Goodwin (in back of Steve), fiddle; Barry Tashian, guitar; Mike Bowden (back to camera), bass; along with Steve Fishell in the foreground on pedal steel.

(Photo by Tracy Gershon)

Polyester and "someone we know / hits a keno") and jargon, the otherwise sad song let Steve rattle off a carefully enunciated intro detailing his weekend with Buffett. "We went to the casino and studied the crap table," Steve said at an October 1981 show in Appleton, Wisconsin. "On the felt, they had stuff like 3-2 for 32 hop. If the 3-2 comes up, it's 30 to 1, and yo, that's a bet on the 11. So you'd hear people goin', 'Hard 4, hard 6, buck for the boys, 10-dollar yo, 32 hop, round the horn. Roll 'em.' It's a nice way to divest yourself of any loose money you might have floating around." For an Atlanta audience, Steve added, "There are no clocks or windows in these places, so it's always midnight."

Melancholy also infused "Where's the Party," a tune Steve had written with Bill LaBounty about "your average lonely guy on the street" who had stopped by LaBounty's home and spilled out his life story. ("Every now and then somebody does that, and you get two or three songs out of it," Steve said at a later club show, "and you hope that you can change it enough so that he won't understand that it's him if he happens to be wherever you're singin' it.") "Buffett needs a song like this," Steve told LaBounty. Buffett liked it but felt it needed a musical bridge, so he and Steve wrote one, and it wound up on Buffett's LP.

The phrase "Where's the Party" conveyed the stereotypical essence of Southern California, and Steve could not keep Hollywood vernacular from drifting into his conversation. Hence his lingo in clueing in Leland Rucker of the *Kansas City Star* in late August 1981 about his recent writing: "Next week, I have to go play the songs for these guys, and if they buy 'em, OK. But I got the meeting, y'know what I'm sayin'? I just take a meeting and play my stuff."

"These guys" were film execs, and Steve's "stuff" was aimed at the movies. The previous year, he had tried pitching an original song that narrowly missed inclusion in the soundtrack of the Kurt Russell comedy "Used Cars." More recently, he had worked up "Six Pack," for a film of the same name starring Kenny Rogers as a has-been race-car driver whose fortunes are rescued by six orphans who become his pit crew. The tune described the heartwarming scenario, but laced within the lyrics was a metaphor for Steve's own drive to perform. "A racin' man is all I ever want to be," went one line, "until the day that checkered flag comes down for me." Another line was more introspective: "Every race is harder than the one before, and it makes me wonder what it is that drives a man to drive until he can't no more." Whatever its virtues, producers of the movie, released in August 1982, opted for a theme less literally tied to the film's plot, Rogers' co-written hit "Love Will Turn You Around."

Inspired by his proximity to both Hollywood and the ocean, Steve jumped at the chance to pitch a tune for another film in production — a beach movie. "I've always wanted to do a song called 'Don't Get Sand in It'," he said while visiting his *National Lampoon* friend Sean Kelly in New York. The flick fell through, but Steve pushed ahead with a recording of the song, which emerged in July 1982 on an obscure Rhino LP, "The History of Surf Music 1980-1982, Vol. 3: The Revival."

Ostensibly, "Sand in It" was a lighthearted, Beach Boys-style rocker, but what Steve actually had in mind was an off-color joke that recalled the bedding of girls on the beach during his high-school Young Life trip to Miami. With Kelly's help, Steve came up with a litany of objects — all rhyming with "sand" — that he didn't want to get "in it." The punch line lay in the unidentified pronoun "it," which referenced a man's and woman's private parts. The litany included "contraband," "a baby grand" and "members of the band." But when it became more explicit with "gland" and "expand," Steve's wife put on the brakes. "Nancy convinced Steve that it wasn't going to help his career to go onstage and perform this stuff," Kelly says. "She insisted that the lyrics be cleaned up considerably." The finished song did retain a clue to its racy meaning, however, with a perfect pun in one of its last lines: "Don't you know that it would be a pity / If you get your little nitty gritty." [39]

Steve fared better in hawking his work to the movies when he reunited with comic-turned-actor Steve Martin, along with the director of Martin's "The Jerk," Carl Reiner. In October 1981, [40] the *Los Angeles Times* reported that Steve had written the title song for Martin's second feature-film venture with Reiner. The title, whose mordant humor appealed to Steve, was "Dead Men Don't Wear Plaid." Reiner, an admirer of Steve's "totally original" opening acts for Martin, says Steve was the perfect songwriting fit for the black-and-white sendup of 1940s detective films, which incorporated dozens of classic clips. "I thought he was so special," Reiner says. "He worked very hard to do what I thought was a brilliant lyric to 'Dead Men Don't Wear Plaid.' He had two verses or quatrains of all the things dead men don't do: 'Dead men don't do this, don't do that, and dead men don't wear plaid.' It was hilarious, hysterical."

But Reiner later decided he needed to establish a film-noir tone for "Dead

---

Nancy convinced Steve that it wasn't going to help his career to go onstage and perform this stuff.
SEAN KELLY

39: "Steve knew all the words to every stupid, smutty camp song in the world," says Sean Kelly, "and not just the words but all the variations." Kelly had given Steve the two-volume 1968 reference work, *The Rationale of the Dirty Joke*, by folklorist Gershon Legman, who examined the psychology of humor. "You would think Christmas morning had broken," Kelly says. "Steve had no interest in the Freudian analysis of these jokes, but he was really amazed to see them all in one place." Legman died in 1999.

40: Martin, without Reiner, had just completed a bittersweet cinematic tribute to 1930s Hollywood musicals, "Pennies from Heaven." Among the film's songs were two standards that Steve had long embraced in the recording studio and onstage: "It's a Sin to Tell a Lie" and "The Glory of Love."

Steve Martin and Carl Reiner tangle in the film "Dead Men Don't Wear Plaid," for which Martin's longest-lasting opening act — Steve Goodman — wrote the film's original, unused title music, as well as "Dead Men's Bolero," a ditty consisting of items from a Mexican restaurant menu.

(Universal Pictures/Photofest photo)

Men," so he excised Steve's title song. Instead, Reiner used a dramatic, classical overture written by the 74-year-old legendary Hungarian film composer Miklós Rózsa that played ominously while the opening credits appeared over a stormy nighttime skyline. But all of Steve's work wasn't left on the proverbial cutting-room floor. For a mid-movie sequence set in the Spanish-speaking coastal country of Peru, Steve took on a much more difficult writing challenge, and what he came up with — as farcical as his title song — did make the cut.

The parody drew its inspiration from a goofy episode Feb. 4, 1981, at an Arizona restaurant. The day after Steve's co-billing with John Prine at Dooley's in Tempe, promoter Danny Zelisko had steered the two to a Mexican eatery on Indian School Road. Road manager Maple Byrne drove them in a rented station wagon to the restaurant, where they discovered a line of customers waiting to get in. While Byrne locked up the car, Steve and Prine walked toward the entrance, and a manager who recognized the pair ran out to greet them. "We closed down the restaurant to see your show last night," the manager said. "We have a table for you inside."

After a fine meal, Steve turned to Byrne and said, "OK, go get the instruments out of the car." Byrne retrieved a mandola and a guitar, Steve donned a sombrero hanging on the wall, and he and Prine entertained diners like a Mariachi band, improvising "Hasta lumbago," "I love my rancho grande" and other nonsensical Spanish phrases. "It was anything they could think of that had that texture to it," Byrne says. They knew they had struck a chord when waiters and waitresses gave them the restaurant T-shirts off their backs and an elderly woman reached up to Prine's pocket and inserted a dollar bill.

Steve took the identical approach to create his song for the "Dead Men" film. He matched Spanish words for food to words mouthed by 26-year-old Ava Gardner singing in a cantina in footage from "The Bribe," a 1949 detective film. "It was such a funny idea," Reiner says. "That was all Steve's doing. He

The new-look Steve wowed an "Austin City Limits" fund-raising audience on Jan. 17, 1982.

(Photo by Scott Newton)

41: Steve did play "Dead Men's Bolero" live at least once, on May 27, 1982, at the Bayou in Washington, D.C., shortly after "Dead Men Don't Wear Plaid" was released to moviehouses. At the same show, Steve performed a song stringing together the names of obscure major-league baseball players, including Jose Valdivielso, infielder in 1955-61 for the Washington Senators.

42: *Chicago Sun-Times* columnist Ron Rapoport similarly says matter-of-factly that Steve actually suffered from two diseases, the non-medical malady being "a belief that getting out of Chicago and moving to the entertainment center of Los Angeles would be better for his career."

just said, 'Let me play with that.' We didn't tell him what to do. He just did it." The lilting tune, which in "Dead Men" was sung by a woman whose voice was synchronized as if it were Gardner's, was heard primarily in the background while Steve Martin talked with Reni Santoni and the glamorous Gardner flitted in and out. Mostly, the lyrics catalogued a typical Mexican restaurant menu. But Steve also threw in the occasional gag, such as "mariposas de amor," which literally means "butterflies of love" but is more commonly understood as "the crabs."

When the movie was released in May 1982, Steve received a few press plugs plus distinctive recognition in the credits. His was the final name listed, along with the name of the song — a joke in itself, "Dead Men's Bolero," referring to the seemingly endless litany of food items, which if eaten together would induce anyone's demise. The title also alluded to Maurice Ravel's hypnotic "Bolero," which had leapt to prominence in the 1979 Bo Derek film, "10." But Steve's song, the only one of his compositions ever to appear in a Hollywood feature film, was largely indecipherable and all too easy to miss. "We couldn't use it louder than the dialogue," Reiner says. "That was the problem." [41]

The real problem, surmised longtime musical ally David Amram, was that Steve was seeking film work at all. Amram, who visited Steve in Seal Beach during this period, found him overly mired in the movies. It was a disappointment for a close friend who regarded Steve alongside Chicago's literary greats. "Steve could have been like Studs Terkel, Nelson Algren or Carl Sandburg if he hadn't moved to California trying to give his music to 400 lawyers," Amram says. "Steve was too good for that. He already had something he had built." [42]

What Steve had built, and what he reverted to in the winter and spring of 1982, was his base of folk and country-tinged music — a combination that Willie Nelson, Kenny Rogers and other prominent genre-straddlers were bringing into the mainstream. While Steve was making little headway on the big screen, he was allowed to bring his musical base quite effectively to the pervasive box in America's living rooms. When PBS wanted the crew of "Austin City Limits" to stage a marathon concert that member stations could use as a pledge-drive fundraiser, Austin station KLRN enlisted more than two-dozen big-name country acts, from Tammy Wynette to the Texas Playboys. Also signed up for the show's standard union wage of $254.70 were two folk artists whose music bordered on country and whose previous stints on the program had drawn raves — John Prine and Steve.

For the show, performed in the round on Jan. 17 in Austin, edited down to three hours and aired repeatedly as a "Down Home Country Music" special on PBS stations starting in March, Steve received a generous half hour. For 22 minutes, he performed three tunes by himself and three more with Jethro Burns. For another eight minutes, he backed Prine on two tunes. But this was a Steve whom few had seen before.

True, the informality of his duds — a bright blue shirt, light-blue jeans and green sneakers — was familiar. Before New Year's Day, however, Steve had trimmed his hair considerably from its previous shoulder-length shag and had shaved off his mustache and beard, a constant presence since 1975. Cleared away was his scruffy halo in favor of a look that more effectively exposed the cherubic, ironic and impish expressions that crossed his face repeatedly onstage. The effect was enhanced by a new "Austin City Limits" filming style that focused more exclusively on performers (and less on the audience) and made use of a handheld camera to achieve tight close-ups.

As a result, viewers across America were exposed to Steve on TV more intimately than ever before. Steve responded with a set that mixed the best of his new songs with solid chestnuts. From upbeat crowd-pleasers ("Talk Backwards," "Elvis Imitators") to achingly quiet, tear-wellers ("The Dutchman" and a collaboration with Bill LaBounty about "a guy who flunked a one-night stand," called "I Just Keep Falling in Love"), Steve captured the studio crowd of 400, and no doubt the millions watching at home.

His comradely pairing with Prine on Prine's sentimental "Souvenirs" was a kick, but the undeniable highlight of Steve's segment of the PBS show was the pure joy that emanated from him and the father figure of Burns. It was a quality that had to be seen as well as heard to be fully comprehended. Expertly captured on video, the delight on Steve's face as he repeatedly looked back at Burns and admired the accompanist's flying-fingers mandolin solo during "City of New Orleans" bore a shine that was solar. In a career of stellar stage shows, this one rated at or near the top. [43]

At every turn on the road, Steve seemed to make connections with his past. During a two-night run at the Birchmere in Alexandria, Virginia, he tried out a just-drafted tune that he said was inspired by John Prine's "Dear Abby" but actually hearkened to his risqué tunesmithing more than 10 years prior at the Philadelphia Folk Festival. Titled "Letter to the Penthouse Forum," it was merely a repeated blues pattern in the background that supported a spoken story whose justification seemed to be to stuff in a maximum number of puns about sex. Hence, it depicted Steve and a friend (Dick Gozinya in one version, Stupendous Dork in another) "boning up" for a college algebra exam before visiting "Herbie's Tumble Inn." There, sitting at the bar were female Siamese twins, who — in the song's most wicked wordplay — asked Steve and his friend, "Won't you join us?"

Sometimes, Steve's acid tongue spelled trouble similar to the kind invited by his childhood pranks in Albany Park. When he and Prine flew to Saskatchewan for a gig in Saskatoon, the two waited at baggage claim while road manager Garry Fish fetched a rental car. As Prine leaned against a post, a Royal Canadian Mounted Police officer walked up and started talking.

Seeing this, Steve walked over and said, "What's the matter, Johnny? Dudley Do-Right givin' you a hard time?"

Steve was invoking the name of a cartoon Mountie from the 1960s who was so witless that the character at one point had been banned from Canadian TV. The Mountie talking to Prine was not pleased.

What's the matter, Johnny? Dudley Do-Right givin' you a hard time?
STEVE GOODMAN

43: "He commanded the room," says Jeff Peterson, "Austin City Limits" audio engineer at the time. "Everyone had total allegiance." Part of Steve's appeal came from deadpan asides that broke up the studio crowd. Gesturing to those behind him "in the round," he summoned a pun: "Steve, it's good to see your back in Austin." When the audience waited 15 seconds for him to tune for "The Dutchman," he mumbled, "Time is money, money is time, time is tape." He added, "Stop tuning. Can't tune, anyway. No sense tryin'." Introducing the traditional South American tune "Tico Tico," which he performed with Burns, he said, "Here's a little instrumental we can all sing."

"I need you to come with me right now," the Mountie told Prine, "and bring your little friend with you."

In the RCMP airport office, the Mountie "proceeded to just screw with us for well over an hour," Prine says.

When Fish located the pair in the office, Steve piped up in a loud voice, "Dudley Do-Right's got a bug up his butt."

It was not a smart thing to repeat. Steve "finally caught on that the more he was gonna open his mouth about it, the guy was gonna just detain us that much longer," Prine says. Eventually the pair made it to their sound check. [44]

Steve was reminded of humor of a similar stripe — the Second City troupe across the street from the Earl of Old Town — when the nation learned March 5, 1982, of the drug-related death of Second City alumnus and "Saturday Night Live" star John Belushi. That night, at the Paramount Theatre in Austin, Steve and Prine dedicated Prine's wistful "Souvenirs" to Belushi. (To Ray Goettsch, co-proprietor of the Harry Hope's music club in Cary, northwest of Chicago, the dedication made sense. Goettsch likened Steve's magnetism to that of Belushi. "You were drawn to him," Goettsch says, "because you thought you were going to have fun.")

Fun was the prescription a month later, after Steve and Prine [45] played Convocation Hall at the University of Toronto. The two settled in a few blocks west at the El Mocambo Tavern for a late blues set fronted by a singer who had dueted with Steve 10 years earlier on his "Troubles" LP, Maria Muldaur. Later, in Prine's room at the nearby Sutton Place Hotel, the three continued the reunion. Muldaur, who had deepened her religious convictions and released her first all-gospel LP for a Christian label, was reluctant to imbibe, says Jane Harbury, longtime manager of Toronto's Riverboat club, who also was present. But after Prine began singing blasphemous songs and he and Steve badgered her to drink, eventually she relented.

"Honey, we just partied all night long," Muldaur says. "The whiskey and wine were flowing, and so were the stories. They had their guitars out and were singing songs, and the sun came up, and we were still partying." Her elation was tinged, however, with an ominous feeling about Steve. "I knew he was sick, and I thought, 'God, what spirit!' He just had such a positive spirit. He was like a little light when he came into a room. He was always, always positive and so sweet, and I'll remember that night always because I knew in the back of my mind, 'I wonder when I'll see him again or if he'll be feeling this good the next time I see him.'"

Steve renewed fond ties in early May when he ventured a few miles south of his home to catch a show by Leo Kottke at the Golden Bear in Huntington Beach. There, he became enamored of the opening act, L.A. songwriter J. Fred Knobloch, and between shows Steve invited him to his house for a stab at crafting a song.

Two days later, while Nancy was away and the girls were in school, and over marijuana and shots of Aquavit, the pair created a neighborhood ruckus. Blar-

44: Garry Fish never regretted working as road manager for both Prine and Steve, even though he was paid only to be Prine's roadie. Eventually, Steve got wind of the situation. "Each night he shoved a $50 or $100 bill in my pocket," Fish says. "I kept saying no, but he wouldn't let me refuse. I would have done the job anyway."

45: The frequent Steve/Prine pairing often prompted comparisons. Renée Doruyter, in the Feb. 6, 1981, *Vancouver Province*, wrote, "Where Prine's cheerier moments smacked of a Gahan Wilson cartoon, Goodman came across with the infectious warmth of a Paddington bear." Bill Kent wrote in the Feb. 1, 1982, *Philadelphia Inquirer*, "Prine tends to frame his sardonic, wistful lyrics in country and rock ballads. Goodman leans more toward Woody Guthrie and *Mad* magazine." Ben Elder, who profiled Steve for *Acoustic Guitar* magazine, later observed, "John's heroic appeal comes from long hours of introspective contemplation, whereas Steve is the Ultimate Fireworks Show. Shock and ha."

ing on the TV were the California Angels and the newly acquired Reggie Jackson, who were playing the slugger's former team, the New York Yankees. At the same time, Steve was "wanking away" on a Gibson Melody Maker electric guitar connected to a Fender Champ amplifier. The din was so loud that police arrived to ask them to tone it down. But out of the session came a tune melodically similar to the ubiquitous Bobby Hebb hit from 1966, "Sunny," and whose lyrics bore an intriguing twist: "You can marry anytime you want, but a lover is forever." Completion of the song, however, was put on hold.

Possibly Steve's most fulfilling reconnection with the past that spring came when he agreed to be the on-camera host for a Chicago TV tribute to the home-town saloon that had given him his start in 1967. As if it were a talisman, Steve wore his blue "Down Home Country Music" shirt for the taping of the half-hour documentary for WMAQ-TV, which marked the 20th anniversary of the Earl of Old Town. It was an episode of "Warner and You," a program that aired Saturday evenings (and repeated Sunday mornings) hosted by Warner Saunders that routinely interviewed guests from the Ku Klux Klan's David Duke to philanthropist W. Clement Stone. This installment was entirely lighthearted, featuring an interview with Earl Pionke, as well as singing and commentary by Bob Gibson and Bonnie Koloc. Steve performed portions of "City of New Orleans" and "A Dying Cub Fan's Last Request" and narrated the saga of the "streetwise" club owner who had launched him. "Big old neighborhood guy with a lot of class," Steve said. "He ran a school for us singers here. ... A few of us graduated, but we all come back and play these class reunions." [46]

As Pionke neared his 50th birthday in mid-June, Steve expressed his gratitude by engineering a meeting he had long dreamed of between Pionke and Dr. Tim Gee, the Sloan-Kettering oncologist who had supervised Steve's leukemia treatment since his diagnosis in 1969. Midway through a dinner with Pionke and Gee in Manhattan, Steve turned to Gee and offered a stunning summary of his appreciation. "Dr. Gee, you're the guy that keeps me alive," he said. "There's no way I could thank you, but I want to thank you in front of this very special person, Earl, here. Y'know, I got good parents, really good parents, but Earl taught me something that didn't come through my parents. Earl taught me that when you get it, pass it all around, and the sooner the better. You got the fuckin' watermelon? Six guys eat that motherfucker. You come across fortune from a song? Spread it. Do it. Do your good acts. You keep me alive, and this guy taught me how to spread life. I cannot compliment him in any better way."

One artist who had spread life for Steve was 50-year-old country legend Johnny Cash. After initially spurning "City of New Orleans" while focused on his "Gospel Road" project in late 1971, Cash had recorded his own version in 1973 and 1975, and it became a staple of his concerts for years to come. In 1980, Cash also had recorded Steve's and Prine's "The Twentieth Century Is Almost Over" for his "Rockabilly Blues" LP. With his wife June, Cash had seen Steve open several times for Steve Martin and counted himself an admirer. So while it was a major gesture, it was not entirely a surprise that the Cashes featured Steve

Songwriter J. Fred Knobloch met Steve at the Golden Bear in Huntington Beach, and soon the two were at work on a tune with an intriguing punch line: "You can marry anytime you want, but a lover is forever."
(Photo by Jim Messer, courtesy of J. Fred Knobloch)

46: Filled with music, the "Warner and You" episode about the Earl's 20th anniversary included audio snippets of recordings by Jim Post and Ed and Fred Holstein and video snippets of performances by Mike Jordan, Betsy Redhed, Tom Dundee and Charlie Koster.

and Prine as their musical guests during a Sunday, June 20, 1982, benefit concert at the John F. Kennedy Center for the Performing Arts in the nation's capital. A capacity audience of 2,400 attended the black-tie affair, and dignitaries in the $100 main-floor seats included Democrats "Tip" O'Neill of Massachusetts, who was House speaker, and Sen. Robert Byrd of West Virginia, who played fiddle onstage during one Cash tune.

Steve warmed to the concert's beneficiary, the Vince Lombardi Cancer Research Center at Georgetown University. But he also knew the Home Box Office cable-TV channel was taping the show for national broadcast. For such a vast potential exposure, the Cashes showcased their extensive retinue, which included songwriter and then-son-in-law Rodney Crowell ("Louisiana in the Broad Daylight") and future country superstars Vince Gill on guitar and Marty Stuart on mandolin. But HBO cameras confirmed that of all the performers in the 80-minute presentation, Steve stole the show.

Cash introduced Steve by divulging his embarrassment over passing up the chance to be the first prominent singer to put "City of New Orleans" on the musical map. "It's one of the classic railroad songs of the age," he said, "and this man is one of the classic writers." As Steve walked onstage with a close-cropped haircut and in a black tuxedo, his eyes bore a twinkle that penetrated the hall. While he eventually performed "City," he started by donning a white cowboy hat he had borrowed from Cash and launched into another early song that lampooned every other country tune played that night, his and Prine's "You Never Even Call Me by My Name." In peak form, Steve aurally and visually mimicked a swath of instruments and performers — including Cash's trademark habit of continually adjusting his guitar high on his chest. At his every comic line and gesture, the crowd roared as they did for no other.

"That audience just melted," Prine says. "He had 'em right in the proverbial palm of his hand."

As any entertainer would hope to convey, Steve looked to be in the full flush of health during the Cash show. But trouble lurked beneath the veneer. While his guitar hid the fact, he had started to put on weight. In addition, for several months fatigue plagued him. He had begun to lose feeling in the bottom of his right foot. Getting up flights of steps had become an ordeal. But after seven and a half years of remission, Steve didn't attribute the symptoms to leukemia. He surmised he was having back or kidney problems. "I thought I was out of the woods and looked for all kinds of other things." He told Richard Kreck of the *Denver Post*, "I tried to blame it on everything else, from old age to overindulgence. But I wasn't indulging that much, and I wasn't all that fucking old."

Prine, with whom Steve toured that spring, had seen his partner's confidence gradually build after years of stopping in at hospitals on the road every Thursday to get his blood tested. "His cell counts would be under what any human was supposed to have, and (the hospitals) would want to keep him," Prine says. "He had to always explain, especially if he went to a place that didn't know that much about it. They'd come back scratchin' their heads and go, 'You

> **I thought I was out of the woods and looked for all kinds of other things. I tried to blame it on everything else, from old age to overindulgence.**
> **STEVE GOODMAN**

shouldn't even be walking around.' And Steve would go, 'Oh, let me see the papers. There you go. Oh, that's good. That's good. You should have seen two months ago.' He just had to call his doctors in New York and give 'em a report."

By the time the two performed in the June 20 Cash show, Prine says, Steve had shed his wariness. "That was just about the time that he was getting ready to think that maybe he might be around for a good, long while."

Soon he would find out exactly the opposite. Riding to Philadelphia in a tiny Fiat with Stephen Wade and Wade's girlfriend and plinking on Wade's banjo, Steve instantly went into agony. "The pain came into his back, and it was just awful," Wade says. "It knocked the tar out of him. I knew this was really bad, whatever the hell this was." They stopped the car, got out for awhile, and then resumed the trip to a hotel, where Steve quickly fell asleep. In Philadelphia, Steve opened for Peter, Paul & Mary on Friday, June 25, at Mann Music Center. [47] Steve also visited the Philly home of producer Joel Dorn, arm-wrestling Dorn's son, Mike, 14, and only barely winning the contest. Afterward, he told Dorn, "My leg feels funny, and I should never have any trouble beating a 14-year-old kid."

The same weekend, Steve joined 18 other acts at the ninth annual Telluride Bluegrass Festival in Colorado. [48] But fatigue and periodic pain were plaguing Steve, says Sam Bush of the New Grass Revival. "He was feeling pretty sluggish up there in the mountains," Bush says. "He figured it was the altitude."

Steve was about to reconnect with the worst part of his past. On Friday, July 16, one year to the day after the sudden death of Harry Chapin, Steve was billed with Pete Seeger and others to play a "Remember When the Music" tribute to Chapin at Pier 84 in New York City. Chapin's widow, Sandy, had sent Steve a written invitation, and Chapin's brother Tom recalls Steve telephoning to ask if he could bring along Jethro Burns, which he did. But just one day before the show, feeling "horrible," Steve checked into Memorial Sloan-Kettering Cancer Center.

A spinal tap revealed he was no longer in remission. The medical term was relapse. In layman's terms, his leukemia, as deadly as ever, was back. This time, it was no secret. ♫

47: Peter, Paul & Mary had recorded Steve's "Would You Like to Learn to Dance?" in October 1981 for an LP, "Such Is Love," that was released in 1983.

48: At a post-festival gathering at a hunting camp and a hot springs in nearby Dunton, Steve's impishness emerged. For Sam Bush of the New Grass Revival, Tim O'Brien of Hot Rize and others, he played a Blair Maclean parody of the Hank Snow and Johnny Cash novelty hit "I've Been Everywhere," called "I've Seen Pubic Hair."

Clearly visible, as Steve performs for his 5-year-old daughter Rosanna's kindergarten class, is the bump on his scalp that covered the device that delivered medicine to his spinal cord. Steve played for the classes of all three of his daughters on an early June day in 1983 at McGaugh Elementary School in Seal Beach.

(Photo by Bill Hodge, courtesy of the *Long Beach Press-Telegram*)

'You're dead, you're alive, you're dead, you're alive ...'

Few people so early in life rack up the breadth and depth of printed accolades as had Steve Goodman. By mid-1982, more than 1,000 newspaper and magazine articles had anticipated and trailed Steve's travels in North America and Europe and had kept the world apprised of his music. But in late July came headlines that Steve long had dreaded. Everywhere at once, nestled in the celebrity blurbs and often accompanied by a happy mug shot, the refrain was stark.

In *The Sun* of Bremerton, Washington, a small city in which Steve had never performed, the headline was "Leukemia returns."

In the giant tabloid of his hometown, the *Chicago Sun-Times*, it rang out even louder: "Goodman leukemia returns."

It was an odd phrase, given that none of the papers had reported Steve's disease since its onset in 1969. The new headlines seemed to convey that the mainstream public already knew of both him and his condition when, for the most part, the opposite was true. Though active on the national stage, Steve was hardly a household word. Moreover, out of respect to Steve, who did not want to be recognized for his malady, hundreds of family members, musicians and other friends had kept an informal pact to stay mum. Even the handful of media types who had known of or suspected Steve's leukemia had kept the info under wraps.

But when Steve missed the widely advertised July 16, 1982, memorial concert for Harry Chapin in New York (John Prine was Steve's last-minute replacement), plus a July 18 booking at Manhattan's Lone Star Café, they were the only times in anyone's memory — including Steve's — that illness had kept him from delivering a scheduled performance. [1] Emmylou Harris made a passing, onstage reference to his relapse at a July 23 show at the Ravinia Festival north of Chicago, and the newspaper blurbs ran two days later. Notoriety was inevitable. Kicking in was a timeworn journalistic principle: Tragedy grabs readers.

Steve's relapse even merited a blip on the 10-month-old TV celebrity show "Entertainment Tonight." It was a rueful irony. "I'd been doing what I do for 15 years," Steve later told Jack Hurst of the *Chicago Tribune*, "and I never made 'Entertainment Tonight.' I had to get sick as a dog to do that."

Coverage of his relapse was as vague as it was brief. Louisa Anderson of

> I'd been doing what I do for 15 years, and I never made 'Entertainment Tonight.' I had to get sick as a dog to do that.
> **STEVE GOODMAN**

1: Regulars at Steve's shows had often seen him consume cough drops — and jokingly crackle the wrappers within hearing distance of the microphone.

Dr. Isabel Cunningham, who had tracked Steve since she was a record-keeper at Sloan-Kettering in 1969, says the Ommaya reservoir in his skull in 1982 was easier to cope with than one might expect: "Nobody likes the idea of having something in their head, but it's no pain, it's nothing. Bam-bam, you're done. Spinal fluid comes out, you put the medication in and get out."

(Photo courtesy of

Dr. Isabel Cunningham)

2: Before his relapse, Steve had told Sean Kelly, "If this thing comes back, I'm going to let it take me. I'm not going to go through that chemo shit again." To explain, Steve told a joke about cannibals who planned to fillet a victim and make a canoe of his skin. As his last wish, the man asked for a fork. With it, he repeatedly stabbed himself and said, "Try making a canoe out of me now!" Kelly says Steve "didn't want doctors to make a canoe out of him again. Of course, when it came back, he changed his mind."

Sloan-Kettering said only that Steve's condition was stable and that "his prognosis for recovery is excellent." Obscured were the severity of his setback and the necessity for treatment and recuperation that likely would run through the remainder of 1982.

Despite the rarity of Steve having survived acute lymphoblastic leukemia for 13-plus years after diagnosis, the reason for his relapse was not complex. The relatively few leukemia cells that had lain dormant in Steve's bone marrow during his seven-and-a-half-year remission had awakened and found a new home — his spinal cord. He also had developed meningitis. This was not an unusual progression for ALL, but it also was not a development that oncologists routinely prevented then, as they do today, with a spinal tap.

How to treat Steve's relapse also was straightforward, if grisly. [2] In his chest and near his heart, Sloan-Kettering doctors implanted a Broviac catheter — a silicon tube allowing a syringe to deliver chemo drugs directly to his bloodstream — that bypassed the need for repeated and difficult intravenous injections in Steve's over-poked veins. The catheter was sewn to his chest skin and held in place by a cuff, so that when Steve wore a shirt, it was covered and called no attention to itself.

The catheter wasn't all that Steve needed to stay alive. For chemo to reach the spinal fluid that circulated throughout his brain and spinal canal, doctors pursued a separate portal in his skull. They needed to embed beneath his scalp an Ommaya reservoir, a plastic, dome-shaped device that had been introduced in the late 1960s. "It's like a squished Ping-Pong ball with a little straw on the end," says Dr. Isabel (Bonnie) Cunningham, who by 1982 had become an oncology fellow at Sloan-Kettering and was helping treat Steve. "It's put in through a teeny hole in the skull, and the end of the straw sits in the ventricle where the spinal fluid is made." Its medical benefit was clear. "If you lie the person down, that little Ping-Pong ball fills up with spinal fluid, so it's a direct shot," Cunningham says. "Nobody likes the idea of having something in their head, but it's no pain, it's nothing. Bam-bam, you're done. Spinal fluid comes out, you put the medication in and get out."

As anyone might, Steve worried about the effect of a medical gadget rooted next to his brain. He called Bill LaBounty, with whom he had been working up a song about romantic hypocrisy. Eventually known as "In Real Life," the tune's refrain lamented how "people say one thing and then they do another." When Steve reached LaBounty, he said, "You're gonna have to finish the bridge to that song 'cause they're puttin' a pipe in my head."

"What do you mean they're puttin' a pipe in your head?"

"Never mind," Steve replied. "You don't want to know."

After the surgery, however, Steve felt comfortable enough with the Ommaya reservoir to sardonically christen it a "turkey baster." Once Steve resumed chemo, the apparatus was as evident as it was effective. Like 1969, Steve again lost all of his thinning hair, and the corresponding bulb formed a new and recognizable mound that protruded slightly right-of-center atop his cranial landscape.

Treatment, including spinal taps and whole-brain radiation, was extensive. But while it supplied hope for another remission, it could not counter the basic message of his relapse. From talks with Sloan-Kettering oncologists and his own observation of "the class of 1969," Steve knew that second remissions ran much shorter. As his first remission had worn on, he had been lulled into thinking that he might avoid a premature demise. But now the scenario was back to an early end, looming (as he had once written and often sung) "in the rear-view mirror." [3] He was running out of time.

Facing him again were the emotional questions of impending death. This time, much more was at stake. At 34, an age not even half as old as most people expect to reach, Steve had built an enviable family, a rich network of friends and musical colleagues and a career as a sterling entertainer. His songwriting, singing and guitar playing had had incalculable impact on hundreds of peers, including many who had surpassed him in the public consciousness. Could he, in the remaining sands of his hourglass, reach the elusive mantles of wide public recognition and commercial success, if not for his own sake, then for that of his wife and daughters? If so, what songs could he write, or what musicians could he inspire, to achieve that end? At home, in what ways could he further cement his bond with Nancy and nurture Jessie, Sarah and Rosanna? Could he reconnect with many of his countless comrades and fans? If so, how best could he tell them goodbye?

Moreover, how would all of that be colored by the fact that his leukemia was now public? Steve had much to think about as he remained at Sloan-Kettering. While he contemplated his cosmos, the TV supplied bittersweet reminders of previous health. "Johnny Cash America," the show on which Steve had guested spectacularly at the Kennedy Center in Washington, D.C., got its first national broadcast Sunday, Aug. 15, on HBO. Within the week, it was aired three more times. One week later, PBS stations in Los Angeles, Washington, D.C., Chicago and other cities across the country rebroadcast the "Down Home Country Music" fund-raising special that featured Steve's joyful pairing with Jethro Burns. The next month in Chicago, the Steve-hosted WMAQ episode of "Warner and You" that feted the Earl of Old Town also had an encore showing.

The irony was unavoidable. In the taped images flowing into America's living rooms, Steve appeared to be alive, well and in top form. In reality, he was in a hospital bed fending off death.

Fortunately, a stream of callers and visitors understood that contact could rebuild his vitality. Initially, though, the contact was rugged. Some, like Howard Levy, tried by phone to joke with Steve, but "he was really low, really zonked." Phoebe Snow, who stopped by Steve's room, found him both fatigued and furious. "Do you believe this fucking thing came back?" he spat at her. "I have so much to do." When Snow tried to update him on her mother's failing health and her autistic daughter, the understanding that Steve had extended her previously had vanished. "Yeah, yeah, yeah, but look at this crap I have to put up with," he shot back. Snow says the anger frightened her to the point of think-

Yeah, yeah, yeah, but look at this crap I have to put up with.
STEVE GOODMAN

3: The rear-view mirror reference from "The Twentieth Century Is Almost Over" popped up later after a jam session that Steve attended in the Laurel Canyon woodshop of ex-Chicagoan Richard Wedler. When Wedler and Steve stepped outside to say goodbye, they noted words on a car's rear-view mirror — "Objects In Mirror Closer Than They Appear" — and decided the phrase was worthy of a song. But neither of them developed the concept.

Recording engineer Gary Brandt was among Steve's visitors at Sloan-Kettering, and instead of weary complaints, Steve picked up a guitar and played him "Elvis Imitators" — while wearing a rubber Elvis Presley head mask.

(Photo by Jim Shea)

ing, "Why don't I just shut up because all I'm doing is pissing him off?"

The outrage that Steve felt about his diagnosis in 1969 had returned with his relapse. His fury was so deep that for a couple of weeks he considered chucking his performing career. He later recalled telling himself, "This is a signal. I undoubtedly should stay off the road. There's something about the way that I'm living that is messing me up." The thought didn't last long, however. "It hit me that it's the only damn thing I know how to do."

Slowly re-emerging were Steve's equilibrium and dry wit. One factor was "a humbling amount of mail — enough to make you wonder what happens when somebody like Dolly Parton goes to the hospital." Also aiding his recovery was the poking of those close to him, including Al Bunetta's mother, Mary, whose homemade cookies, called tassies, were among Steve's favorite foods. Once, when Steve called her and started complaining about his chemo, Mary Bunetta interrupted him. "Steve," she said, "only the living take this medicine."

One of Al Bunetta's tasks was to disclose the relapse to those close to Steve, including some, like Phoenix promoter Danny Zelisko, a friend who shared Maine East High roots and a baseball mania with Steve but who had not been aware of Steve's leukemia. After Bunetta called Zelisko with the news, Zelisko picked up the phone and called Steve to commiserate, but when his tears welled and he began to whimper, he was stopped by Steve's sarcasm: "What the hell are *you* cryin' for? I'm the one that's dyin'."

Bunetta himself witnessed the gradual revival of Steve's spirits while challenging him with an implicit question.

"Stevie, I don't know how you can deal with all of this stuff," Bunetta said. "It's amazing, I can't fathom it."

"Al, do me a favor," Steve answered. "If anything happens, feel sorry for me for a day, feel sorry for yourself two days, and then get it on."

Evidence began to sprout that Steve was moving on, using the language of his profession. Hollywood studio owner Gary Brandt, who had flown to New York to visit Robbie Dupree, dropped in at Sloan-Kettering and located Steve sitting up in bed in a four-person ward.

"Man, how you doin'?" Brandt said.

"I gotta tell ya," Steve said, "if you ever have this problem, this is the place to go. Wait, I gotta show you something."

He reached over and picked up a rubber head mask in the likeness of Elvis Presley, pulled it over his head, grabbed a guitar and played "Elvis Imitators," breaking up Brandt and the other patients.

Lee Grills, at whose Rochester pizza parlor Steve had been inspired 10 years before to write the anti-war "Ballad of Penny Evans," found Steve lying in bed with an elasticized piece of plastic covering his scalp.

"Steve, how ya doin', buddy?" he said. "What's with the shower cap?"

Pulling back the cap to reveal his Ommaya reservoir, Steve said with a smile, "Man, if you're 70 years old and they tell you you're having brain surgery, tell 'em you're going to Hawaii."

Then he asked Grills to hand him a mandola that stood at the side of his bed. Flat on his back and too weak to sit up, Steve rested the instrument on his belly and began strumming song after song.

Steve was likewise prone when producer Hank Neuberger visited from Chicago. Referring to the May 11, 1981, death of reggae's biggest star, Steve told him with a glint, "This is the room Bob Marley had at this hospital. Bob never made it out of here." Steve then played his mandola for Neuberger, introducing a song he had just written.

For more than two years, since his move to Southern California, where he lived two miles from a Navy nuclear-weapons station, Steve had pondered writing a broadside against nuclear power. With the help of New Yorker Sean Kelly, he had come up with one, an uptempo acoustic rocker called "Watchin' Joey Glow." [4] Like so many of his songs, this one employed a wicked wit to tweak mortality. Set in an underground shelter after the world has been permeated with fallout, it depicted a "post-nuclear nuclear family" that included an irradiated boy with an "incandescent" smile, a none-too-subtle reference to Steve himself. The ditty — a "Dr. Strangelove song," says Kelly — satirized the bleakness and pointed up the absurd advantages of a tyke who could transform a leg of lamb into a roast by hugging it and personify a well-lit Christmas tree. Steve likened the lyrics to the black humor of the Woodstock-era anti-war anthem of Country Joe & the Fish. "From what I can see, this (anti-nuclear) movement does not have a 'Feel Like I'm Fixin' to Die Rag,' " he said later onstage. "This is sort of like a Willie Nelson bomb song." [5]

But he wasn't as assured about the tune — or any of his compositions — when talking with Neuberger from his hospital bed. Steve brought a broad grin to Neuberger's face when he played "Watchin' Joey Glow," and Neuberger said, "That's great. It's so funny, so clever, so insightful."

"Nah," Steve said, "it's just something I made up. It's not a real song."

The statement befuddled Neuberger. "What do you mean, it's not a real song?"

"Well, it's just this topical stuff that I do. It's not real songwriting."

"I don't buy that," Neuberger said. "What about 'Penny Evans'?"

Steve's reply bared the sentiment of a songwriter who hesitantly dared to hope his work would outlive him in the voices of others.

"Maybe if a woman sang it, it would work," Steve said. "Maybe if a woman sang it, it'd be a real song."

While Steve was recapturing his repartee and humility, he also was gaining stamina. From Sloan-Kettering, he appeared by phone on Roy Leonard's radio show in Chicago. From his bed, Steve also sang and played guitar for a film the cancer center was putting together for other patients. And just as he had felt in 1969, Steve yearned to break free of the hospital confines.

With the assent of his doctors, Steve visited the Greenwich Village apartment of David Amram, where Steve's friend Sean Kelly also had alighted. Kelly cherished and railed against what he regarded as Steve's childlike personality,

From what I can see, this (anti-nuclear) movement does not have a 'Feel Like I'm Fixin' to Die Rag.' This is sort of like a Willie Nelson bomb song.
STEVE GOODMAN

4: Though Steve never said so, it's plausible that he drew the structure for "Watchin' Joey Glow" from a sentimental song about parenthood called "Watching Scotty Grow," written by Mac Davis and made #1 adult-contemporary hit in 1971 by pop crooner Bobby Goldsboro.

5: In another onstage introduction of the song, Steve said, "Hopefully, we can get this to Ernest Tubb, and he can sing it at Survival Sunday. The guy looks like he's seen the end of the world."

New Grass Revival founder and leader Sam Bush got pointed advice when Steve learned by phone of Bush's bout with cancer. "Some people," Steve said, "will tell you that chemotherapy's been killin' me ... but go on and take the medicine, and let that be your life-insurance policy."

(Photo courtesy of Sam Bush)

and away from the hospital it came to the fore. Steve demanded instant attention, which at times made him "the most unbelievable pain in the ass on the planet Earth," Kelly says. "It's endearing and possibly a big part of creativity, but it can also make you wish 'Would you just fuck off for about 10 minutes now, because I'd just like to finish this.' When you add that Steve was the oldest son in a Jewish family and was extremely talented and very tiny and then got sick, the wonder of it was that he wasn't the biggest egoist since Nietzsche. And in fact, he wasn't. But he couldn't wait. He wasn't patient."

One unauthorized excursion stoked Steve's passion for baseball. The accomplice was the Seal Beach road manager who had triggered Steve's move to the coastal community, Steve Redfearn. The two diamond fans had shared season's tickets for the California Angels, so when Redfearn flew to New York to visit his friend, their talk inevitably turned to the national pastime.

"This could be the last night we're able to see each other," Steve told Redfearn. "Where do you want to go?"

"Yankee Stadium," Redfearn answered. "No doubt."

Redfearn hired a limo, sneaked Steve down a freight elevator and motored him to his hotel room, where Steve "put on some of my clothes, which he looked ridiculous in." The limo took the pair to Yankee Stadium in time for a game. "We spent more time outside the park than inside, just walking around talking, watching the kids play basketball across the street," Redfearn told the *Orange County Register* in 1984, "and just like Goodman, he was immediately over there talking to the kids." The two bought $200 worth of T-shirts for Steve's daughters, Redfearn's son and friends. When they got to their seats, Steve had worn himself out. In the sixth inning, he fell asleep on Redfearn's shoulder.

Steve's gradual recovery enhanced his confidence in chemo to the point of endorsing the procedure for peers such as New Grass Revival mandolinist/fiddler Sam Bush, who was diagnosed that November with testicular cancer. Oncologists were urging light-dose chemo, but Bush was wary.

"Hey, Sammy, chemo ain't cute, man, but you can do it," Steve told Bush by phone. "Some people will tell you that chemotherapy's been killin' me, but I've taken it for 14 years. Man, those doctors, they don't know how it feels. They're just the drug dealers. They don't take the stuff, they just sell it. But go on and take the medicine, and let that be your life-insurance policy."

Bush took Steve's advice, undergoing two surgeries and six weeks of chemo, and was back on the road in January.

As Steve's strength swelled that fall, he flew home to Seal Beach, securing blood work at UCLA Medical Center and returning periodically to New York for checkups. In California, Steve resumed a semblance of normalcy, using his baldness to hilarious advantage by donning a tux at Halloween and walking the neighborhood dressed as Daddy Warbucks to Jessie's Little Orphan Annie.

Steve also hooked up with musical friends, including some — like his former colleague at Asylum, Jackson Browne — who had missed the summer headlines. When Steve stopped by Browne's studio in downtown Los Angeles to say hello, his nearly hairless head, with fuzz that had just started to re-grow, announced the long-delayed news. Steve was typically friendly and cheerful, but in a sober moment he disclosed to Browne a grim forecast tinged with a phrase coined by the 1950s Beat poet Lord Buckley.

"I've got a few more options here," Steve said, "but after that, if that doesn't work out, it's gonna be Nathan Shakin'.'"

Browne was stunned. But Steve punctured the stillness by playing for Browne "A Dying Cub Fan's Last Request," a gesture that the million-selling performer grasped instantly. "It was very poignant to be hearing this hilarious song about mortality from a guy that was at the same time letting me know about his disease," Browne says. "He had a way of getting out of that moment. As a performer, he had spent his life going from a really poignant moment to a hilarious moment. He could take it back and forth. He got us out of there. But he was a very sensitive guy, and he was not going to leave you sitting there."

Nor did Steve intend to let himself or his audiences stagnate. Without a record label, he depended mostly on performing for his livelihood. But whether he could perform a full set, and if so, how often, remained an open question. Even if he could get back out on the road, he had no fresh product to aid his promotion. His latest LP for Asylum, the tepid "Hot Spot," was more than two years old, and only one of its tracks, the hilarious "Talk Backwards," had become a mainstay of his repertoire.

These dicey circumstances led Steve to a pair of crucial decisions. The first — common today but unheard of at the time — was that he would form his own company, to be called Red Pajamas Records as a nod to his daughters. ("All of this is for them anyhow," Steve said later.) Second, in a step that Steve had resisted for years, Red Pajamas' debut LP would be a collection of live recordings from the previous decade.

"I noticed that there weren't seven or eight record companies lined up outside my house with wheelbarrows full of money asking me to record," Steve told Rip Rense of the *Los Angeles Herald Examiner*. "There were so many people who cared, and people seemed to be responding more to songs at live gigs than my recordings, so I sort of felt an obligation to respond." To Sam Sutherland of *Billboard*, Steve admitted that he had given up on a slick studio sound in favor of spotlighting his rapport with an audience. "I figured I better put exactly what I felt on the record and not try to chase somebody else's idea of what's good or commercial," he said. Ultimately, the reality of the clock also steered his thoughts, Steve told Patrick Goldstein of the *Los Angeles Times*. "I figured I'd just do this myself and see what happens," he said. "I guess a lot of other people would want to wait and see if they could get another record contract, but I just don't have the time."

While getting blood work one afternoon at UCLA Medical Center, Steve announced his plan to Al Bunetta and assistant Dan Einstein. "We both looked at him cross-eyed," Einstein says. "I don't think Al had any of the energy or the thought to say, 'Yeah, let's go for it.' It was, 'Are you fucking kidding?' But with

Jackson Browne was shocked by Steve's hairless head but was heartened when Steve played him "A Dying Cub Fan's Last Request" to break the seriousness: "He was a very sensitive guy, and he was not going to leave you sitting there."
(Photo courtesy of Alyssa Archambault)

An alternative photo for what became the "Artistic Hair" LP.

(Photo by Jim Shea)

6: Of the timeless ode "The Water Is Wide," Steve told Robert K. Oermann of the Nashville *Tennessean,* "You don't have to be ill or religious to appreciate a song like that. ... I'm moved by it, but tears would keep me from getting to the end of the performance. Besides, right now I'm healthy, so everything's cookin'."

Steve in such a vulnerable position, what could you do? You couldn't do anything but say 'Sure' and figure it out later." Only a few independent record labels, such as Flying Fish and Rounder, were surviving in the face of the conglomerates in the early 1980s, so "it wasn't a popular decision," Einstein says. "None of us had ever done this before, so it was definitely a learn-while-you-earn situation. And we did."

On weekends, Einstein pored over 70 hours of live Steve tapes, including some that Bunetta had confiscated from audience members who had tried to record Steve's concerts on the sly. "There was a closet full of tape, reel-to-reel, cassettes, a loose collection of things that had been taken from radio shows and sound checks or were pulled from live shows," Einstein says. "Nobody had ever done anything with 'em other than stash 'em away." Einstein had been only vaguely familiar with Steve's work, so he brought fresh perspective. Friday afternoons, he and Bunetta hauled a reel-to-reel player to Steve's living room, where, bolstered by Nancy's cooking, they sifted the material, evaluating it more on performance quality than technical sound. "I don't think there was a whole lot of pretense or thought put into it," Einstein says. "It was let's just do it. We have this collection of stuff. It doesn't cost us anything. It's basically a free record, and the performances are amazing, so why not?"

What emerged was a string of pearls. Taken from shows in Chicago, New York, Philadelphia, Berkeley and Appleton, Wisconsin, the collection was dominated by tracks that had not appeared on his Buddah or Asylum LPs. They ranged from a bluesy guitar showcase ("East St. Louis Tweedle-Dee") to a wild sing-along (Carl Martin's "Let's Give a Party," assisted by Jethro Burns and David Amram), from a kooky crowd favorite (Shel Silverstein's "Three Legged Man") to a hushed, traditional metaphor for mortality ("The Water Is Wide," again with Amram). [6] It also featured animated versions of previously issued staples ("City of New Orleans," "Old Fashioned" and "Chicken Cordon Bleus").

The aggregation relied heavily on TV appearances, tapping "Austin City Limits" for four songs that Steve had never released: "Elvis Imitators" and "Tico Tico" from the 1982 episode and a pair of outtakes from the 1977 show, "Red Red Robin" and a response to an audience request for "Winter Wonderland" that illuminated Steve's facility with ad-libs and rhyme. ("It's kind of absurd / when you don't know the words / to sing walkin' in a winter wonderland.") The album closer, from HBO's "Johnny Cash America," was Steve's tour de force rendition of "You Never Even Call Me by My Name." It would be the first time for Steve's complete version of the country parody to appear on vinyl, unadulterated by David Allan Coe's self-aggrandizing recitation. It also would be the first time it included a proper co-writing credit for John Prine.

No date or venue was identified for each song, lending the assortment a timeless and universal quality. Each side of the LP amounted to a mini-concert that could have been performed anywhere. Best of all, the album stripped away the studio trappings of his previous releases and revealed Steve as crowds experienced him. As he slyly characterized it in liner notes, the package delivered "a

Chapter Seventeen: 'You're dead, you're alive, you're dead, you're alive ...'

619

pretty fair representation of what I expect from myself at a concert: a few surprises, a few favorites, some laughs and some quiet moments during which the audience can reflect on the fact that they had to pay for this."

Underscoring the sweeping scope of the material but poking fun at his lack of celebrity and invoking a pun, Steve concocted a trenchant album title — "Steve Goodman: Alive at Carnegie Hall and Points West" — and a corresponding visual concept for its cover. On the front of the LP would be a photo of him busking with an open guitar case in front of the prestigious Manhattan venue at which he had performed three times. The backside would complete the joke, with Steve standing in front of San Francisco's Golden Gate Bridge, a symbol of the West.

To execute this visual farce, Steve called on Jim Shea, who had photographed his "Hot Spot" LP cover. [7] With Shea, Steve traveled in late 1982 to New York and San Francisco to pose for the needed photos. After the latter shoot, the two headed downtown to partake of an egg dish, "Joe's Special," at the legendary Original Joe's in San Francisco's Tenderloin district. Around the corner, at 169 Eddy Street, they spotted an empty, rundown barbershop, and on the front window was painted an intriguing name. Shea told Steve to stand beneath the sign. Steve, wearing sunglasses and a dark pea coat in the chilly air, removed the brown woolen hat that had covered his nearly bald head, leaned against the window, crossed his legs and flashed a grin while Shea shot three photos. In those few seconds were the seeds of a radically different concept.

Artistic Hair was the name displayed on the barbershop window, [8] and there, in Shea's photos, stood a beaming Steve, his Ommaya bump clearly visible. In his "chemo cut," Steve embodied a visit to life's ultimate barber. "We got the proofs back, and we all started screaming," Einstein says. "We said, 'Steve, here it is, Artistic Hair. Let's stop right there.'"

Einstein called the barbershop to secure permission for the name and image. When the owner came to the phone, Einstein started to explain: "We're starting a record label. We want to use a picture that we took of your shop." The response was swift. "Yeah, great," the owner said, then hung up.

The LP cover became a visual nod and reassurance — not just that Steve had leukemia, but also that he was bearing and baring it with a laugh. It was disease with drollery, mortality with mockery, woe with wit. It was what many had long known as the unabashed Goodman style. [9]

But without an established company's distribution and marketing machinations, how would the self-financed album get into the hands of listeners? "Steve's idea," Einstein says, "was that if people are going to buy it, they can pay for it. In other words, we were not going to get into the whole game of the record business. His thing was, it's a C.O.D. label. So if a record store wants it, they pay for it, cash on the barrelhead. And if his fans want it, sell it by mail order or at shows. He was way ahead of his time."

In contrast to today's milieu, in which performers routinely vend CDs via the Internet and after shows, in the early 1980s it would have been considered

His thing was, it's a C.O.D. label.
DAN EINSTEIN

7: Steve had prevailed on Shea to give his brother David an entrée to photography. "He willed it," says Shea, who notes that David worked the O'Hare airport loading docks in Chicago before signing on as Shea's assistant in L.A. In an online interview at a 1997 tribute concert for his brother, David wrote that Steve "kept me out of the music business because he said music is a dirty business."

8: While "Artistic Hair" was the name painted on the window, the full name of the business, listed in the 1983 Yellow Pages, was Artistic Haircutting. Its proprietor was Irvin Lefko.

9: An example was etched between the innermost rings of the second side of the "Artistic Hair" vinyl, where a turntable's tone arm never reaches. An impish "in" joke cited Steve's lead oncologist at Sloan-Kettering, Tim Gee, and Steve's recovery from relapse: "Dr. Gee — Whoopee!"

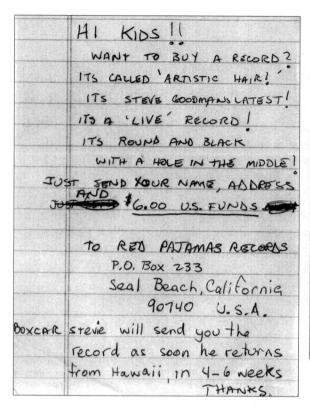

The handmade nature of Steve's new record label is reflected in the text he drafted for a sales flier (left) and the finished flier itself.

(Materials courtesy of Maple Byrne)

unseemly for a singer to be his own point-of-purchase salesman. "Steve wasn't real comfortable with selling his own product off the stage," Einstein says. The question, he says, became "Who's the midget who comes out at halftime and tells you to go into the lobby and buy it?" As Steve, Bunetta and Einstein tinkered with this notion, an idea was born: "Let's get other people to tell the story." Who better than the phalanx of celebrities Steve had befriended over the past dozen years? Also, lodged in Steve's memory was "The Absent-Minded Waiter," the seven-minute film Steve Martin had played before each of his live shows — and that had triggered audience laughter before Martin set foot onstage. The solution was clear. Create a brief movie to "introduce" both Steve and his new live LP at each of his upcoming shows. The vehicle was to be satire.

"Faint praise is how I would refer to it," says comic singer/songwriter Martin Mull, tapped to be the on-screen narrator. "At first blush, it sounds like we're praising someone. At second blush, it's a dish."

Mull, 39, was a spot-on choice as the central disher, having shared the stage several times with Steve and written a song with him. After a 1979 co-billing near Detroit, the two had retired to a Holiday Inn and come up with "Talk Dirty to Me," a self-mocking blues about an aging (and declining) male libido that necessitates the singer's title plea to his lover. Though Mull performed the ditty in October 1980 on a Smothers Brothers TV special, neither Steve nor Mull recorded it. Like Steve, Mull had lost his record contract because of declining sales in the 1970s. "There was," as Mull put it, "a mandate by the American people to get me out of the music business, and I succumbed." By early 1983, Mull had become better known as a star of TV (faux talk-show host Barth Gimble of "Fernwood 2Night") and films ("FM," "Serial"), and readily believable in Steve's intro film as a smarmy host.

Perhaps Mull's most genuine qualification was his regard for Steve, honed in the mid- to late 1970s when he trailed Steve on the club circuit. "There was this legendary presence, like an aura that he left," Mull says. "He was smart, he was impish, and he had a leprechaun's way onstage. But it was never smart-aleck or disrespectful or down the nose at anyone, even though he had the right to be down the nose at half the singer/songwriters who couldn't sing, couldn't write and couldn't play — and he could do all of those things in spades."

For the shoot, Al Bunetta enlisted a veteran cinematographer from TV ("Laugh-In," "Kojak") and movies ("Superman"), Bob Collins. In a van, Steve, Dan Einstein and Collins drove to L.A. locales and completed the shoot in one day. Mull's segment was shot last because it had to tie in blurbs from the other celebs, each of whom created a distinctive dig: Jackson Browne ("Steve Goodman, who's he?"), Jimmy Buffett and Bonnie Raitt (discussing, supposedly seriously, how much they were to be paid for the bit), Carl Reiner (likening Steve to a Muppet) and the comedian for whom Steve had opened more than 200 times, Steve Martin (recalling Steve as "a tall woman"). When the crew arrived at Mull's house to shoot his overarching segment, Steve conferred with him for a few minutes. Then Mull sat at his dining-room table and improvised his unscripted part as a drippingly insincere huckster.

All of the luminaries recall jumping at the opportunity to help Steve. "It was a Good Samaritan thing," Reiner says. "We knew his condition, and we just wanted anything that would perpetuate his memory." [10] Collins, then 48, had not known Steve prior to the project but quickly adopted the same sentiment. The single day he spent with Steve and the others burns so brightly in his memory that when he speaks of it, tears well up. "I relished every second of it," says Collins, who teaches moviemaking at the North Carolina School of the Arts. "I've shot millions of films, and I can't think of anything that struck me more in my heart than workin' on that thing with Stevie. He attracted people to help and cooperate with him and sing with him. He was the most beloved individual I know of in the industry."

While the new LP and intro film were finalized, those in the industry who revered Steve conjured up ways to help get him back on his musical feet — not with charity or seeming make-work but bona fide tasks. Among the first came from someone whom Steve had not met: Tom Bocci, music production director for Walt Disney Studios.

Disney was working up the pilot for a TV Western comedy series based on its 1975 and 1979 "Apple Dumpling Gang" movies. Depicting the life of a frontier gambler who had won two children in a card game, the series was called "Gun Shy." [11] Bocci — who had snagged Toronto-area singer Stan Rogers to

Martin Mull embodied "faint praise" as the host of a short film that introduced Steve's "Artistic Hair" LP to audiences. (Photo from Capricorn Records, courtesy of Martin Mull)

10: Steve later told Jack Hurst of the *Chicago Tribune* that when he asked Carl Reiner to do the bit, Steve dryly told the better-known funnyman, "If you ever need anything like this for your career, please feel free to call me up."

11: Steve himself was gun shy, as folksinger Mark Ross discovered Feb. 22, 1983, at the Wilma Theatre in Missoula. "There was a little bit of trouble around town, and I was packing a gun, just to protect myself," Ross says. "I showed up backstage and gave Steve a hug." Steve felt a lump and asked Ross, "What's that?" "A gun," Ross replied. "Get the hell out of here with that thing. Don't come back with that." Ross stashed the gun at his flat and returned to the theater.

pen two songs for the Canadian Pavilion at Walt Disney World in Florida —
had long admired Steve's musical storytelling. [12] Unaware of Steve's disease, Bocci
called Al Bunetta to hire Steve to write the "Gun Shy" theme. Bunetta agreed
that a creative assignment would fuel Steve's spirits and asked Bocci to call Steve
at Sloan-Kettering. When Bocci told Steve that "Gun Shy" took place in an
1869 California gold-mining burg, piquing Steve's interest was the town's name.

"Quake City" was the musical result. From his hospital bed, Steve composed and, backing himself on mandola, recorded on a cassette a song that
bared the gambler's affection for his hometown. In words that served the show
and mirrored the topic on Steve's mind, the chorus ended: "I know when I die
I will go to Quake City. It's a little bit of heaven right here on earth." In January
1983, Steve mailed Bocci the cassette with a handwritten note: "Obviously my
time is limited, but here's the demo. Hope you can use it." The tune appeared
in the pilot, but the pilot never aired. Still, Bocci says, the pilot helped sell the
series to CBS-TV, which ran six half-hour episodes from March 15 to April 19.

A far better known benefactor than Bocci stepped into the breach at the
same time Steve composed "Quake City" — Johnny Cash. The country legend,
minus his wife June, who was undergoing an especially arduous hysterectomy
at the Mayo Clinic in Minnesota, showcased Steve with his entourage for mid-
January shows in the Oregon cities of Salem and Eugene. It was, as Steve said,
"my first 'job' job" of the year. Steve was billed as a special guest and came
onstage midway through Cash's show, singing three or four songs. It was a chance
to "work myself back into shape gradually" for which Steve was deeply grateful.
"He's one of my heroes anyway, but he's 51 years old, and he gets out there, does
his show," Steve later told WGN's Roy Leonard. "He's a special man, and he
gave me my chance. He was fabulous." [13]

By month's end, Steve could resume being a headliner. On Thursday, Jan.
27, opened by Bryan Bowers, Steve played a midsize venue that was his hallmark — the 1907-era, 450-seat Great American Music Hall in San Francisco. In
most every way, it was an archetypal show. He stepped onstage wearing a small
cap, and as if he were boldly announcing his return, he began with a crucial
shift: "City of New Orleans" was his opener. Throughout the 80-minute set, he
mixed in other dependable pieces with new and unheard tunes, at the end bringing onstage Bay Area mandolin virtuosos David Grisman and Mike Marshall
(the latter on violin) to jam on standards by Hank Williams and Bob Wills.

His newer material echoed genres that Steve had mastered. Notable was
"California Promises," another poignant woman-done-the-man-wrong song,
but it gained depth from a simple simile. The song likened the woman's devious
vow — "I will never love another / Wait for me till I return" — to the insincere
pledges that people in the entertainment industry were notorious for breaking
every day. [14] Steve's intro for the tune gained a droll bite from the day's top news
story, a storm that had raked the Southern California coast and destroyed the
Seal Beach Pier just two blocks from his home. "This song is for a guy waiting
for his girl," he said. "She's standing on the pier, and the pier gets washed away."

12: On June 2, 1983, Stan Rogers died horrifically from smoke inhalation when the Toronto-bound plane that he boarded in Austin following the Kerrville Folk Festival caught fire and had to land in Cincinnati. Eight days later during a show at Austin's Soap Creek Saloon, Steve dedicated "The Dutchman" to Rogers.

13: During Cash's Jan. 21 stop at the Hult Center in Eugene, Oregon, famed rock photographer Jim Marshall captured Steve. Wearing a woolen tam, white shirt and dark sports coat, his hands gripping the top of a chair that he straddled, Steve riveted Marshall's lens with plaintive eyes and a Mona Lisa near-smile. "Hey, Jimmy," Steve told Marshall, "I know you're not taking pictures of me because of the way I look, but it's OK, man. I'd like to be in your book someday." Marshall replied, "If you're not in the book, there won't be a book." The photo was one of 124 in Marshall's 2000 tome, Not Fade Away.

14: "California Promises" originated with a slippery vow – "Steve, we'll be over in a little while" – that others frequently made on the phone. Steve told writer David Gans he learned that in California, "a little while might be next week. In Chicago, someone says they'll be over in a little while and you'd better go upstairs and wash your face 'cause that's the doorbell ringin', not your headache."

With a backup vocal by Rita Coolidge, "California Promises" made its way that September to Jimmy Buffett's next LP, "One Particular Harbor." [15] But another song that Steve debuted Jan. 27 in San Francisco not only failed to reach vinyl but also vanished from his shows soon thereafter. It was a narrative that traced an unusual homeless man named Joseph Cruz, a 55-year-old Navy veteran whose saga had triggered splashy segments on New York TV news while Steve lay in his hospital bed the previous summer. Cruz' enigmatic existence beneath the tram that crossed the East River Drive fascinated Steve.

"He was a sober fellow," Steve said. "He wasn't a wino, he wasn't begging, and people would bring him stuff. He lived on the lane divider, he had a lawn chair, and the city couldn't stand it because I guess the winter before someone had frozen to death, and so they had to get him off the street. He refused to go to the men's shelter because he didn't like how it smelled, and he didn't want to live with his daughter. Why, I don't know. But they took him off to the nut house, even though he was as lucid as the next guy."

In his song, Steve used the Spanish version of Cruz' first name (José) and told his story in compassionate, even romantic terms. "José's little island is a one-man traffic jam," Steve sang, "beneath the sun and the moon and stars and the Roosevelt Island tram." Noting that a judge would not condone Cruz' "public privacy," Steve ended the tune with downcast sympathy: "The welfare Boy Scouts know that you can't help someone cross the street when they just don't want to go." Cruz thus joined a long line of down-to-earth, real and fictional characters — including Beverly Jones, Turnpike Tom, Penny Evans, expatriated Americans, his father, even Michael Smith's Dutchman — to populate Steve's musical universe. It wouldn't be the last time he would summon lyrical images of a man on the street.

No words were spoken during the San Francisco show about Steve's leukemia. The only instance that came close was during his intro of "You Never Even Call Me by My Name," when Steve doffed his cap to try on a cowboy hat he had coaxed from the audience. A guy near the stage took note of Steve's nearly bald dome.

"Are you tryin' to look like Paul Simon?" the man shouted.

"No, man," Steve replied, not missing a beat. "He has a lot more hair than I do."

The brief exchange, after which Steve continued the intro, resembled a shrug. In fact, the whole show felt nearly like old times, including hearty and sustained applause after every song, at which Steve typically scoffed. "I don't really have a following outside the city of Chicago," he said. "It's just that they used to have eight million people there, and a few of 'em moved. That's how I get to play all these gigs."

The real test of Steve's new strategy came three weeks later, when Steve headed for the Pacific Northwest to open five mid-February shows for John Prine. In Vancouver, B.C., Spokane, Portland, Seattle and Missoula, Steve charmed audiences not only with his performances [16] but also with the Martin Mull intro

15: Steve brought "California Promises" to Buffett shortly after the two wrote "Frank & Lola," a rollicking trifle about a bickering couple on a second honeymoon. "I heard he was in a leukemia ward in New York," Buffett told the *Coconut Telegraph* fanzine in October 1986. "I was in a cab callin' all the hospitals — they wouldn't give me any information — and I thought, goddamn, I'm gonna find out where he is. And I went to a friend's house to make more phone calls, and there was Goodman sittin' on the bed. And I said, 'God, I thought you were dead already,' and he said naw, he had just gotten out. So we sat up and drank a couple bottles of champagne and started the song right there. Then he had to go back in, and I thought the best thing for him was to get his mind off this shit. So we wrote the rest over the telephone. And that's the last time we wrote together. But goddamn, could he get on the phone. He was heavy into working on the song." Buffett recorded "Frank & Lola" for his "Last Mango in Paris" LP, released in June 1985.

16: Steve's opener for Prine in Seattle got an atypically vicious review, from *The Seattle Times*' Paul de Barros, who ignored the Opera House audience's acclaim and the heart behind Steve's jest. "It would be hard to imagine a more repellent performer," de Barros wrote. "His tasteless topical songs, a clever form of extended sick joke, ridiculed women and handicapped persons and referred to subjects such as nuclear holocaust with careless stupidity. His snickering, schoolboy irreverence, far from exposing anything about ourselves or the world, merely fell back on itself with a smug, hollow ring."

film and the availability of a new LP. He charged $6 per album, $2.98 lower than the list price found in record stores. Starting a new pattern, he stayed after each show to meet buyers and inscribe the LPs. In Seattle, with the help of road manager Maple Byrne, he sold 70 copies. In Portland, the sales totaled 119. Steve was on his way to becoming what he facetiously called a "mogul." [17]

Steve's tour with Prine yielded another co-write, "If She Were You," a country-ish, lost-love plaint on which the pair later dueted in a demo recording. "It's about a fella who calls his girl up from the pay phone of a bar where he's been talking to another woman, and he's not real sure of himself," Steve said during a concert. "If we could get this to George Jones, we'd be in business."

Prine also tagged along (as did David Allan Coe) on March 11 while Steve taped a segment for one of the first episodes of "Bobby Bare & Friends: Songwriter's Showcase," for the fledgling cable-TV network TNN (The Nashville Network). A pop and country star known for his 1963 version of Mel Tillis' and Danny Dill's "Detroit City," the laid-back Bare had befriended Steve in 1970s Chicago on late nights at the Earl of Old Town after playing the Quiet Knight. For this installment of his new show, Bare, then 47, combined segments with Don Schlitz ("The Gambler"), Paul Craft ("Drop Kick Me, Jesus, Through the Goal Posts of Life") and Steve for an hourlong examination of "the masters of the tongue-in-cheek songwriting skill."

When Steve walked into the Bullet Studios in Nashville for the taping, his cropped hair and Ommaya reservoir startled Bare, who was accustomed to Steve's scruffy beard and shoulder-length shag. "It was a real shocker to see somebody that full of energy and magic with their head shaved off and that thing in it, whatever it was," Bare says, "but he didn't make a big deal of it at all."

Steve didn't need to, for the TV camera did it for him, especially in close-ups that exposed his shiny, bumpy pate while Bare, in a low-key drawl, interviewed him in a control room. The two touched on the origins of "City of New Orleans," "You Never Even Call Me by My Name" and "Talk Backwards" (all of which Steve performed on the show), his discovery by Kris Kristofferson and Paul Anka, the meaning behind his Red Pajamas logo, and the breadth of tunesmiths in Chicago. ("Willie Dixon is probably the most prolific great

17: Steve's grandmother, Mary Erenburg, bought 100 copies of "Artistic Hair." "Gram, what's with you?" Steve asked. "I'm the lucky one," she replied. "I'll pay for them, and I'll sell them."

songwriter that pop music has seen," Steve said. "He can make 'Pitch a wang dang doodle all night long' come out good.") Steve's leukemia was not a focus, but Bare did point out the "Artistic Hair" LP cover with his new "do." The 20-minute segment, which aired nationally in the fall, was a further step by Steve to bring the visual element of his cancer into the public eye.

The coming of spring meant a return to New York every three to six weeks for checkups and low-dose chemo at Sloan-Kettering, as well as a string of guest slots crisscrossing the Florida panhandle with Johnny Cash. [18] During this five-show stint in early March, Cash's wife, June, deepened her connection with Steve. The two commiserated at the Cashes' Florida home, north of Tampa on the central Gulf Coast, Steve about his leukemia and June about the wrenching complications from her hysterectomy, including a staph infection, a second operation, a stint in intensive care and depression that left her at 94 pounds. "I had a hole that wouldn't heal in my stomach. My friend, Steve Goodman, had a hole in his head and his chest, where he applied medicines daily," she wrote sadly in *From the Heart*, her 1987 memoir. "We sat on the dock and soaked up the sun. ... We waited for the holes in our bodies to heal."

Steve had little time to wait, however. He spanned the country with solo shows, a Kenny Rankin co-bill and openers for Kenny Loggins (with a visit to a Dodgers spring-training game in Vero Beach, Florida) and Leo Kottke. [19] The oddest pairing came April 25, with Bob Seger. Weeks beforehand, the raw-voiced rocker's show at 14,870-seat Veterans Memorial Coliseum in Phoenix had been sold out. The opener was to be Michael Bolton, on the cusp of morphing into a pop crooner. But Bolton had abruptly abandoned the Seger tour, unbeknown to Phoenix promoter Danny Zelisko. About 9 a.m. the day of the show, Zelisko got on the phone with Seger's manager, Punch Andrews.

"So who do we have opening tonight?" Andrews asked.

"I thought you were bringin' the opener with you," Zelisko said.

"Oh, no," Andrews said. "Bolton left the tour."

"Well, you don't have an opener," Zelisko replied.

"We gotta have an opener," Andrews said. "Seger ain't gonna do the whole show himself."

Zelisko cut the talk short, hung up, thought for a moment and called Andrews back. "Why don't we have Steve Goodman?" he asked.

"That little folkie guy?" said Andrews, taken aback. "Just him? There's 15,000 people comin'."

"Yeah, he'll be great," Zelisko said. "Don't worry about it."

Zelisko located Steve at home in Seal Beach, where he had just returned after getting chemo at UCLA Medical Center. "Oh, goddamnit," Steve said, "I just left L.A., but I'll turn around and go back to L.A. and fly over."

It had been nearly four years since Steve had played such an immense arena, and even then it was for Steve Martin's wacky, arrow-in-the-head fans, not a hard-core rock crowd. Moreover, "Phoenix was notorious for trashing any front act," says Gary Montgomery, executive director for the Arizona State Fair and

18: When the Cashes sought for Steve to open for them later in the spring, Steve wanted to bring the mischievous Jethro Burns along and asked Cash if he knew Burns. In a story that record-store worker Mike Saccoliti heard at separate times from Steve and Cash protégé Marty Stuart, Cash replied that he had last encountered Burns at an O'Hare International Airport men's room. Cash, who was not comfortable in public restrooms, and Burns were standing at adjoining urinals when Burns leaned over and uttered a deadpan remark. Steve said the crack was "My, what a pretty peter you have!" (Stuart remembered the line as "That is the prettiest one of those I have ever seen.") Steve said later that when Cash related the story to him, he felt relief, telling himself, "Whew, he knows Jethro."

19: Steve joined Kottke for three encores Aug. 13 at the Oscar Mayer Theatre in Madison, Wisconsin, and when the two tuned, Steve broke into the "Dueling Banjos" theme. Kottke responded with a riff from TV's "The Outer Limits."

Steve beams, along with Bob Seger (center) and promoter Danny Zelisko, shortly before Steve's last-minute opening set for the raw-voiced rocker at 14,870-seat Veterans Memorial Coliseum in Phoenix.

(Photo by Lissa Wales, courtesy of Danny Zelisko and Tom McKay)

Coliseum. (Soulful British singer Robert Palmer once had to leave the Coliseum stage while opening for high-voltage Heart when a glass bottle thrown by a fan struck Palmer in the mouth.) The prospect of Steve facing a throng gathered for Seger's deafening "Old Time Rock 'n' Roll" was worrisome.

But Phoenix embraced Steve "and gave me one of the best moments of my career," Montgomery says. "Five minutes into his set, he had a rabid crowd eating out of his hand." [20] If there were doubts about Steve's recovery from relapse, he dispelled them that night. In full fettle, Steve was back.

Music scribes across the continent knew it — and celebrated. Steve had given them a new live LP and a seemingly everywhere-at-once road schedule to write about. But Steve's biggest news hook was the notion that he was living on a thread. Instead of shying from the topic, Steve found a rationale to embrace it. "He never said this out loud, at least to me," Dan Einstein says, "but I think he thought, 'If I can help somebody else get through this, then maybe my going public would be a positive thing.' Being a patient of Sloan-Kettering for so many years, he saw a lot more on the inside than most people did, and he had to have been affected by that. So I think that even if it was subconscious, he was doing something that he thought might help somebody else."

Steve's take on his disease, reflected in dozens of interviews in 1983, was laced with his dry wit. "I can't complain," he told Sam Sutherland of *Billboard*, "and it wouldn't do any good if I did." He downplayed the rarity of his ALL, preferring to address cancer more generally. "This illness thing is not my career, but I understand the responsibility it engenders," he told Jonathan Takiff of the *Philadelphia Daily News*. "There's a lot of misplaced hysteria about cancer. Did you know that one out of four people in this country have some kind of oncological experience, even if it's just getting a small piece of skin removed? If you're in a room with three other people and none of them has cancer, maybe it's time for you to go see the doctor."

His plight, he noted, was not unique in the music milieu. "The reason I had kept a low profile about it for so long was that I didn't want any favors, didn't want to have to explain my special set of circumstances," he told Jack Hurst of

20: Near the end of his Phoenix set, Steve summoned Zelisko and bid him to "Have a seat" on the Coliseum stage. "I'm gonna play Danny's favorite song," Steve said, launching into "A Dying Cub Fan's Last Request." As Steve played, Zelisko gradually "died" and by song's end lay prone, to the delight of the crowd, which gave Steve two standing ovations. "Steve kicked this audience's ass," Zelisko says. "None of them knew he was sick, I'm sure."

the *Chicago Tribune*. "Everybody has a set of special circumstances. There are musicians on the road who are diabetics. I know a couple of musicians who are epileptics. Yet you never hear about those things. This is slightly more life-and-death, but I couldn't see dragging it around as part of my press kit."

Steve's verbal gymnastics sometimes played out jarringly. While a one-inch-tall *Winnipeg Sun* headline shouted, "Goodman's cancer back under control," Steve's first quote in the Morley Walker story was: "I'll answer questions about it, but I refuse to trade on it." Referring to famed Canadian bone-cancer victim and amputee who doggedly completed 3,339 miles of a cross-country fund-raising run in 1980 before succumbing to lung cancer, Steve added, "I don't see myself as another Terry Fox or anything. There are a lot of brave people out there who don't get their names in the newspaper, and I'm really no different."

Endearingly, Steve also exalted the deeds of his oncologists. "My songs aren't gonna change the world or cure anything, but I don't think my life has been worthless, either," he told Robert K. Oermann for the Nashville *Tennessean* and *USA Today*. "I have a rating system, and I just think the life-saving research guys are maybe a notch higher on my totem pole than an entertainer is."

When Oermann pressed Steve on whether leukemia had given him spiritual insight, Steve remained the humble Everyman. "I come from a Jewish family, and my wife's dad is a preacher. We've evolved our own non-secular way of dealing with eternity," he said. "Look, we all face the same odds. You run the same chance I do. You could be run over crossing the street this afternoon. I'm comfortable with gallows humor. I had it long before, and I find I'm still comfortable with that point of view. All this is just a reminder that we only have so long here. It just means be productive while you can."

The productivity illustrated by "Artistic Hair" drew unqualified raves. [21] *People Weekly*, accompanying its review with a photo of Steve performing in a cowboy hat, called the album "delectable." *The Washington Post* labeled it "a telling vinyl portrait of one of the most essentially good-natured songwriters and performers to emerge from the early 1970s folk boom." Dave Hoekstra of the *Chicago Sun-Times* said it "captures the unique effervescence of a Goodman concert." Jack Hurst of the *Chicago Tribune* called it "arguably Goodman's best LP." Patrick Goldstein of the *Los Angeles Times* said it highlighted how Steve's songs "find a ray of humor in almost any circumstance." Alanna Nash — the first journalist authorized to view the remains of Elvis Presley in 1977, and who later wrote two award-winning books on The King — wrote glowingly in *Stereo Review* that Steve's "delightful" album honored his "old zany, skeptical self."

Even more gratifying than the praise, each of the reviews listed the LP's price (which because of venue surcharges jumped to $7 in mid-April) along with the Seal Beach post-office box from which it could be ordered. The original pressing was 2,500 copies, but post-concert sales were steady (from 37 to 191, averaging 79 a night), and mail orders flowed into Seal Beach at a rate of 15 to 20 a day. By mid-March, Steve had sold 1,000 copies and considered pressing another batch and assembling a Volume II. "This whole thing has made me very happy,"

In an interview, Steve, shown May 11, 1983, playing the Rainbow Music Hall in Denver, revealed a spiritual side of his mortality: "I come from a Jewish family, and my wife's dad is a preacher. We've evolved our own non-secular way of dealing with eternity."
(Photo by Gina Jett)

21: Amid sterling press coverage, Steve still encountered an occasional blunder. Stephen Holden, in an otherwise laudatory review of Steve's June 23 shows at Manhattan's Lone Star Café, wrote in *The New York Times* that Steve had performed "Arlo Guthrie's 'City of New Orleans.' " Nine days later, *The Times* printed a correction.

Flanked by Jethro Burns (left) and Jim Rothermel and backed by bassist Jeff Czech on May 26, 1983, at Park West in Chicago, Steve roars through a culminating "Mama Don't Allow It," only to find that ...

22: Einstein wasn't able to share with the public one aspect of that "love." When Einstein drove Steve through Florida that spring, Steve punned, "We should do an album called 'Don't Cut the Bluegrass,' " made up of bluegrass versions of songs "that shouldn't ever be done bluegrass." It was the seed of an idea that never was executed — an all-instrumental Steve LP. "If only we had recorded more of just him playing," Einstein says with a sigh. "His playing was unbelievable. I don't think even a lot of his fans realized how great a picker he was, just a dynamic acoustic guitar player."

he told Patrick Goldstein, "because it's convinced me that there's still a place for me in the music business where I can make the kind of music I love. So far, the record is simply a nice acorn, but if it grows into a big old tree, that would be nice, too. Right now it's just great being out there playing my songs."

Demand for the LP on the road became delightfully unpredictable, says Dan Einstein. "I'd get a phone call Friday night at midnight or 1 in the morning saying we'd sold 100 or 150 more than we thought we would. So I'd run to LAX in the middle of the night with three cases and try to overnight 'em. I got to know those guys at Air Express pretty well. We didn't care what the cost was at a certain point because you wanted to spread the love." [22]

Steve clearly wanted to do the same. From the first moments of his mid-1983 shows, Steve displayed the confidence and humility that put audiences at ease. After the Martin Mull intro film played, Steve walked out and with a nod to the screen ("Thanks, Martin") re-established his self-deprecating persona as if he had never been gone. As he cracked to Dave Hoekstra in the *Illinois Entertainer*, "I like what I do, and it beats working behind an elephant in the circus."

Some of his driest humor came on swings through his Midwestern homeland, including an April 16 visit to WGN-AM in Chicago. "He's lookin' pretty good," host Roy Leonard told listeners. "I like your new hairdo, by the way."

"Thank you, Roy," Steve said. "I'm lucky to have any. Some of it's growin' back. The doctor said he can't do anything about male-pattern baldness. I can't imagine why."

"Turn around and face the other way," Leonard said, "because you know where it's growing back real great is right in the back."

"Really?"

"It's absolutely super."

"Maybe I'll have it transplanted to my shoulders or something."

Three weeks later, when Steve and Jethro Burns opened for the Johnny Cash

Chapter Seventeen: 'You're dead, you're alive, you're dead, you're alive ...'

629

... he has broken a guitar string. Midsong, while Burns, Czech and Rothermel vamp, Steve improvises lyrics and changes the string, ending the extended tune (left) with a flourish — and, in the process, breaking up Burns and Rothermel.

(Photos by Ed Stiernberg)

show May 4-7 at the Carlton Dinner Theatre in Bloomington, Minnesota, Steve pulled off a hilarious physical feat. During the Friday night, May 6, concert, he solicited a cowboy hat from the audience for "You Never Even Call Me by My Name." After receiving and donning a hat adorned with a stylish feather, Steve pushed the envelope. "All I need now are Johnny Cash's boots," he said. Mere seconds later, Cash, in stocking feet, strode onstage and set his tall, brown boots in front of Steve. With a roll of his eyes, Steve shucked his own boots and tried to don the Cash-sized stompers. He struggled because the footwear of the 6-foot-2 icon reached so high on his legs that they locked his knees. Cash's costumer, grandmotherly Goldie Adcock, rushed out and laced up the boots, and Steve performed the country parody with incongruous attire. [23]

In the Minneapolis area, Steve and Burns doubled up and played a trio of

23: At two other Carlton shows, Steve arranged to have a local friend, Michael Simmonds (also 6-foot-2), attend in hat and boots so that Steve could similarly borrow the too-big attire. The first time, however, Simmonds was sitting in the balcony. When Steve called his name, it took him awhile to reach the stage. Steve stalled for time by joking that Simmonds must have stopped at the restroom. Next time, Steve secured tickets for Simmonds on the main floor.

Michael Smith, shown in the mid-1980s, collaborated with Steve in 1983 on a litany of late-night mail-order products, called "Vegematic."

(Photo by Art Thieme)

24: By the end of the Chicago show, on May 26, 1983, at Park West, Steve had called Jethro Burns, Jim Rothermel, Jeff Czech, Corky Siegel and Don Stiernberg to the stage. He closed with an audacious 13-minute medley, caressing five pop and soul hits — "Havin' a Party," "You Really Got a Hold on Me," "Talk to Me," "Lover's Question" and "My Girl" — before closing with the Bill Monroe bluegrass classic, "Love, Please Come Home."

lunch gigs, at Supervalu, a shopping-mall design firm; at 3-M (Minnesota Mining and Manufacturing), and at Stillwater Prison. The trigger for the third show, Steve delighted in telling a Chicago audience [24] later that month, was an inmate claiming to be Bob Dylan's cousin, Steve Zimmerman. "He called me up and said, 'Well, listen, I'm callin' you from prison,' and he wasn't just visiting."

The day after the Stillwater concert, the Cash motorcade rolled to Watertown, South Dakota, for a topsy-turvy, three-hour fund-raiser for diabetes research during which — with no advance notice of the switch — Cash and crew played as the opener for Steve and Burns. Transportation logistics, says Cash manager Lou Robin, prompted the flip-flop.

On the Cash bus that month, Steve played a new John Prine song for the troupe: "Unwed Fathers," depicting teenage mothers who are driven "under cover" and the babies' fathers who "can't be bothered." It brought the entourage to a hush. "We were goin' down the interstate when he was singin'," says Marty Stuart, Cash's mandolinist and backup vocalist, "and it was almost like the trees stood still, and nobody moved, and nobody breathed. His performance was so captivating, and the song was just beyond words. It was like one of those endings to an incredible book or movie where everybody's cryin' and just kinda shakes their head and walks off. That was the most eloquent moment I ever experienced with Steve."

The relentless evenings on the road, both before and after his relapse, became the inspiration for a song with a wittier bite than "This Hotel Room" that Steve finalized and began playing that spring. Instead of detailing the commonplace items found in a typical motel, he catalogued the stranger-than-fiction products hawked in the interminable commercials aired on late-night TV — from the Pocket Fisherman and the Ginsu Knife to a Minute Mender and the Seal-a-Meal food-storage system. The thread for the tune was an ill-fated man who falls asleep watching TV and dreams he has phoned in orders for each of the useless items. "Four to six weeks later," the deliveries start crowding him out of his home.

Steve began writing the screed against materialism and advertising with Michael Smith in Chicago, crafted it further in the living room of Greenwich Village guitar merchant Matt Umanov, recorded a demo tape in Hollywood and mailed it to Shel Silverstein with an aural plea for guidance. "Dear Shel — help," Steve intoned, explaining the song's core: "The stuff just keeps coming. It's like Mickey and the Sorcerer's Apprentice. The water keeps comin', OK? And I don't quite know how to express that. Guy pinches himself, and it doesn't matter whether he's asleep or awake by that point. It's just that he's in a scrape. So you tell me what to do with that, OK?"

Silverstein got partial writing credit for the song, even though Steve retained the wording he had sent Silverstein: "Parcel post in the pantry, Federal Express in the hall, COD to the ceiling but I just couldn't pay for it all." He also added a verse urging listeners to "rip the telephone out of the wall" to avoid such mail-order misery. But Steve was still unsure about the song's irreverent reference,

Chapter Seventeen: 'You're dead, you're alive, you're dead, you're alive ...'

631

urged by Michael Smith, to a chain of theme parks called Six Flags.

"I had seen an article in *The New Yorker* saying that Oral Roberts University was known as Six Flags over Jesus," says Smith, who with Steve tried to incorporate such blasphemy in the song. In the original lyrics, the last item in the litany of products was "an all-expenses-paid weekend for three at Six Flags over Jesus." But Smith says others told Steve that the phrase was "too scary" and that his fans wouldn't accept it. Steve changed it to "Six Flags over Burbank," an alteration that Smith says robbed the song of its bite. "It was kind of bloodless," Smith says. "When he said he had to change it, I thought, 'Of course, that's what you do when you're big-time.' "

At first, Steve considered calling the song "The Man Who Had Too Many 800 Numbers," but he settled on a one-word title that spotlighted the name of late-night TV's plastic slicer/dicer/chopper, the "Vegematic." In concerts, he introduced the tune's narrator as "one of the nameless, blameless millions that fall asleep every night to the tune of the Turner Broadcasting System." Like "This Hotel Room," the ditty stirred instant recognition and became a reliable crowd-pleaser.

Even more affecting that spring was his use of a two-year-old song to stir the ultimate human identification — that of mortality. "A Dying Cub Fan's Last Request" took on obvious new significance with public awareness of Steve's disease. Because his hair had grown back into short, curly locks by late spring and summer, he could joke about his near-baldness on the "Artistic Hair" LP cover: "Now that I have more hair, we've been thinking about giving out Magic Markers with the album so people can draw it back in." But his receding hairline still exposed his Ommaya reservoir bump, visible evidence of his plight. Accordingly, the "Dying Cub Fan" fantasy of planning a perfect funeral was all the more comprehensible and urgent.

Still, when presenting the song in shows, Steve trained his focus on the Cubs, not himself. He performed the epic with renewed vigor, donning a blue Cubs hat and occasionally — in a reversal of his usual cowboy-hat shtick — flinging it into the crowd afterward. [25] He also wrung every bit of affectionate acerbity he could muster from the plight of the second-division, second-rate team.

In his "Dying Cub Fan" intros, Steve directed his eye-rolling to what he saw as the Cubs' self-destructive player transactions, including a trade for Dodgers third-baseman Ron Cey. "They signed a 35-year-old third-baseman to a five-year contract," Steve said. "They're gonna have to get him a cane and dog to lead him out to third base. About the middle of the third year of that contract, I figure Ron Cey will be just about done, just about cooked. Wait'll he discovers Chicago pizza." [26]

At other times, he pointed out the outcome of the day's Cubs game. A loss proved his overall point, while a rare win indicated that "they're tryin' to make me look bad." Steve also couldn't resist taking on the team's play-by-play announcers, a natural target given that since high school he had pictured himself in that role.

Steve, shown Aug. 14, 1983, at Red Rocks Amphitheatre west of Denver, dons a Cubs hat to play his baseball epic, "A Dying Cub Fan's Last Request."
(Photo by Claudia Engel)

25: When Steve pitched a Cubs hat into the crowd on Dec. 1, 1983, at Orchestra Hall in Minneapolis, Colin Isaacson snagged it and after the show asked Steve to inscribe it. On the underside of the brim Steve wrote: "Nice catch."

26: Steve was nearly right about Cey, who had four solid years for the Cubs until playing his last season, 1987, for the Oakland A's.

During his April 30, 1983, show at McCabe's, Steve mugged like a country singer and imitated a violin during "You Never Even Call Me by My Name." Between shows, he forged a visual pun, mugging with one of his biggest fans.
(Photos by David Gans)

Invoking a pun on the Japanese vulgarity for suicide, Steve told a crowd at Rockefeller's in Houston, "The Cubs, a special ball club. Harry Caray is their broadcaster this year. Does that tell you somethin'? That's the guy's name." Caray, a shameless booster who had announced for the South Side White Sox and St. Louis Cardinals, was a particular butt of Steve's imitation and jest. "Harry puts the accent on the first syllable of every sentence," Steve noted during a show at McCabe's Guitar Shop in Santa Monica. "He always has these mono-syllabic words: '*He* struck him out.' '*Ohhh*, for the long one.' "

Caray's predecessor, Jack Brickhouse, whose tenure with the Cubs stretched to the 1940s, didn't escape Steve's teasing observations. "He'd make some fabulous bloopers," Steve said. "Now, these are magic. Brickhouse would say stuff like, 'Ball, strike, no, uh, no, no, no, ball, strike, no, ball.' And he'd be sittin' in Wrigley Field, and he'd say, 'That's amazing. The last time that happened was when Atlanta played Houston here.' Classic Jack. He's a wonderful guy, though."

For shows in a big-league city, Steve tried to arrive a day early to see a game. Such visits gave him fresh stage material. In Houston, he tweaked the team's musical supplication to its beer sponsor, Stroh's. "They don't play those damn records at Wrigley Field," Steve said. "The people in Chicago would shoot that guy." He talked of watching a game in Minneapolis under the inflated roof of the Hubert H. Humphrey Metrodome, named for the former vice president and U.S. senator who had disappointed anti-war activists during his 1968 presidential run but had been lionized for his liberalism before his 1978 death from bladder cancer. This time, Steve's vignette was more sentimental than sarcastic. "The guy sittin' next to me looks over at me, and he says, 'Y'know, it figures they named it for a politician. The damn thing's held up with hot air.' He actually said that. I said, 'C'mon, man, that guy's from your state.' "

In singing "Dying Cub Fan" itself, Steve directed further attention to the baseball diamond by referencing specific Cubs. In his original line, "Have one of 'em drop a routine fly," he routinely replaced "one of 'em" with the name of a current player — second-baseman Ryne Sandberg or outfielder Keith Moreland — or a former one, such as catcher Harry Chiti.

But occasionally Steve couldn't help slipping into the tune's lethal theme. "I don't know if I could survive if the Cubs won," he said at Soap Creek Saloon in Austin, Texas. "It'd be a coronary event, I tell ya."

Genuine wackiness was sometimes what it took to direct both the audience's and Steve's attention away from death and toward what he had long considered his true calling — to provide pure entertainment. Just such an instance jumped up and nearly slapped Steve in the face on Saturday, July 9, during the 10th annual Winnipeg Folk Festival. It was Steve's fourth appearance at the yearly event, and after joining in an afternoon "What's a Good Song?" workshop, he and Jethro Burns were nearing the end of their evening mainstage show when onto the stage burst a human fireball.

Two nights earlier, in the lobby of the festival hotel, Burns was jamming with a coterie of guitar and fiddle players when a bearded, wild-haired 34-year-old approached carrying a handful of spoons. His stage name was Artis the Spoonman. He had appeared on TV's "The Gong Show" and since 1974 had made a living as a soloist and sideman for everyone from folkies to Frank Zappa. Mitch Podolak, Winnipeg music director, had invited Artis to the 1983 festival, and in the hotel lobby Artis asked Burns if he could play along. "Just don't play louder than me," Burns replied. The admonition became futile given Artis' free-form banging of spoons all over his body. Looking on, Steve labeled Artis for onlookers as "the Buddy Rich of Pluto." Three songs later, Burns leaned over to Artis and said, "You're playing louder than me." Mortified, Artis left. The next day, walking in back of the mainstage, Artis came upon Steve and Burns, and Steve told Artis, "You'll have to join me onstage tomorrow."

The opportunity emerged during Steve's typical closer with a half-dozen accompanists, "Mama Don't Allow It." At song's end, Steve cued Artis, who sprang onto the stage, beating spoons frenetically all over his arms, legs and face, windmilling his arms, prancing in bare feet and wildly gyrating his head and full mane of hair. A spellbinding blur, Artis rattled his utensils so quickly that they sounded like an out-of-control typewriter. "I was all over the stage, in full delight," he says. "I just took that moment and wrung it for all that was in it. I was doing a Steven Tyler (Aerosmith singer), tongue out of my mouth, ahhh!" While the audience screamed its approval, Steve, in the background, bent down near his mandola, which lay flat on the stage, and carefully slid it out of the reach of Artis' leaping legs. While he and Burns kept time with soft strumming, Steve just shook his head and let a grin wash over his face. [27]

It was a riveting, transcendent moment for all who saw it. But it also was fleeting. Plainly visible afterward was the evidence of Steve's inevitable decline.

"He was obviously in really bad shape," says Canadian publicist Richard Flohil, who had stood beside the stage with John Hartford. "Our eyes were

Artis the Spoonman, shown in 1983, became the aural and visual highlight of Steve's "Mama Don't Allow It" jam at the 1983 Winnipeg Folk Festival. "I just took that moment," Artis says, "and wrung it for all that was in it."
(Photo courtesy of Artis the Spoonman)

27: Based today in Seattle, Artis sports a shaven head or short haircut and plays spoons in a style that is still idiosyncratically wild.

glued to the guy. He'd done this incredibly high-energy performance, standing up for a full-hour set, which was rare for festivals. If he wasn't in pain, he was really pushing his energies to the absolute limit. He had put so much into that set, but it was more than that. It was almost like, 'Check this. You're not going to see this again, and it's as good as I possibly could ever deliver.' When he walked off the stage, he was absolutely, utterly, completely drained. I was figuring, 'This guy hasn't got much longer.' He looked so fucking awful."

The dichotomy that Flohil and others in the music world glimpsed only occasionally was experienced nonstop by Steve's household on the days he was home. A roller coaster of emotions ran continuously in and around the Goodman residence in Seal Beach — and it was a full house because Steve's doting Grandma Mary had flown in for an extended stay, and his mom, the equally attentive Minnette, was a frequent visitor.

"You don't pay attention to the difficult times. You enjoy the good ones," Minnette said in an interview later that year. "The bummer was watching Nancy hand over her kids to me so that she could stay with him in New York, or knowing that he needed to see his kids to tell them how tough things really were. But he takes all of this and works his ass off and produces like few people I know." [28]

"On a difficult day when he was really feeling bad or scared or whatever," Nancy said, "he could still make that joke somewhere along the line, and that's wonderful. That's the true treasure of him."

The home-front highs were cheery, especially for the three girls, who witnessed their dad's countless jokes and a revolving door of musicians and other friends, along with Steve's constant guitar playing and singing. Jessie Goodman says the home at times was a kid heaven. In the living room, with the backing of a soul-music tape, Steve often did a spot-on imitation of James Brown. When Marvin Gaye performed his unorthodox version of the national anthem for the Feb. 13, 1983, NBA All-Star Game at The Forum in nearby Inglewood, Steve turned up the volume on the house's big-screen TV to earsplitting level. When the "Star Wars" sequel "Return of the Jedi" opened in late May, Steve "dragged us out of bed," says Jessie, for its 9:30 a.m. screening. He told the girls, "We have to see the first one."

The in-home, kitchen-table business of stuffing Steve's "Artistic Hair" LP into cardboard flats, addressing, labeling and sealing the packages and wheeling them in a shopping cart across the alley and one block down Main Street to the Seal Beach post office held a fascination for the girls. The three also swelled with pride on a June morning when Steve visited their schools to perform mini-shows in their classrooms. In Rosanna's kindergarten class at McGaugh Elementary, Steve reeled off the sing-alongs "The Green Green Grass Grows All Around," Tom Paxton's "Going to the Zoo" and "I've Been Working on the Railroad" before Rosanna asked for "Elvis Imitators," a request that Steve gladly filled, eliciting squeals from the 5-year-olds. In second-grader Sarah's class, she bid him to sing his goofy "Talk Backwards" and the Jimmy Driftwood race-horse

28: In the same interview, for NBC "First Camera," Minnette also cited Steve's childhood affection for singing in the temple choir: "He had a beautiful voice as a child. I'm not sure it's beautiful now, but it really was then." In a November 2006 interview for Chicago's WBEZ-FM, Minnette said Steve's temple singing led to his love for music, which in turn fed his cheery attitude and respect for others: "He was an all-right guy. If you were his friend, there wasn't anything he wouldn't do for you. He could be a pain in the tush, OK? He really could. But he did care about people."

ditty "Tennessee Stud," [29] and for Jessie and other fifth-graders he performed a truncated (and likely sanitized) "Dying Cub Fan" along with the Harry Waller gross-out favorite, "Cockroaches on Parade."

Steve brought Sarah and Rosanna along to his return appearance July 24 on the L.A.-based Dr. Demento Show on KMET-FM, with the girls trying out the host's bells, duck calls and train whistles. Sarah even proffered an endearing but bittersweet on-air greeting: "Hi, Mommy! Hi, Grandma! Hi, Daddy — oh, you're right here."

From the road as well, Steve's daughters felt his presence, such as when a blue trunk arrived from New York bearing brand-new versions of the year's hottest toy, the Cabbage Patch Kids. The soft-skinned, pudgy dolls, with individualized "adoption" papers, were such a rage that they became nearly impossible to find. With the help of Manhattan friend Marilyn Quine, who had known Steve since his days of playing The Ark in Ann Arbor and the Philadelphia Folk Festival in the early 1970s, Steve tracked down a trio of the rarities. The two scurried to Woolworth's to buy the trunk for shipping them home. "I don't know many guys who would do that," Quine says. "He never turned to me or anybody else and said, 'Please take care of this.' He really took care of things himself." The dolls made such an impression that Jessie can still describe their names and hairstyles.

As uplifting as were the highs, the lows were demoralizing. "He wasn't always thinking straight when he had the Ommaya reservoir thing in his head, so there was a lot of ugliness," Jessie says, and one of her dad's fixations was on body weight. Steve sporadically limited his diet to fish, plain popcorn, oranges and seltzer, and he expected Jessie, who had started to get plump during puberty, to exercise similar restraint. "He was a disciplinarian," she says. "His fa-

29: Asked by one of Sarah's classmates, "How fast can you play?" Steve responded, "How fast can you listen?"

ther drove him crazy about his weight, and he said kids used to make fun of him. So he wrote out about 10 of these cardboard lists of what I could eat and what I couldn't eat. He got really nuts about it, and it was an ongoing control thing." Such pressure, along with the shunning by Southern Californians "when you're short, chubby, dark haired and your last name is Goodman," added up to considerable tension for Steve's eldest daughter. [30]

Steve's strain extended to all three girls, says Robert Pruter, brother of Nancy Goodman. "He was yelling and screaming at the kids," Pruter says. "He was like a maniac, and Nancy had to explain, 'It's not your father. It's his illness.' "

While Steve raved about Nancy's cooking and showered her with gifts, arguments were frequent. "I remember them fighting all times of day and night," says Jessie, 11 at the time. She recalls her dad's painful admission that "his career, his music, came first, then baseball, then his family and friends. That's just the order it was." Once, in the middle of the night, Jessie awakened to the sound of strife, and she wandered into the living room to find her dad getting ready to sleep on the couch.

"What does this mean?" Jessie recalls asking him. "You're gonna get a divorce?"

"No, no, no, no," Steve said. "Husbands and wives, they fight. It just happens. If you don't fight with people, it means you don't necessarily care or you don't love them."

A thorn between Steve and Nancy stemmed from her suppressed and long-delayed desire to complete a nursing degree and go back to work outside the home in the medical field. Given that their girls were in school, Nancy felt she could resume nursing classes. It was a prospect that Steve did not embrace. "He was not happy," Jessie says, "because who was going to deal with everything?" It also was an implicit and pointed indication that life could and would go on without him.

The underlying angst boiled over, Jessie says, when the couple consulted a therapist at Nancy's behest. In a counseling session that Jessie learned of later, Nancy asked Steve if he would support her re-enrollment in nursing school.

"Oh, well, I guess so," he replied, "since you've been on vacation for 15 years."

"Steve, vacation?" Nancy shot back. "You think vacation is raising your three kids and you, running your record company, running your house, and you view it as vacation?"

"Yeah, vacation," he deadpanned, "with damn good pay."

The arrogant cynicism of Steve's retort apparently reflected only the bitter half of his feelings on the topic, however. Jessie discovered this at an after-school softball practice at McGaugh Elementary. Her dad, dressed in a Cubs jacket, jeans and sandals, had just awakened, and he ran up to her with an envelope in his hand and pulled her off the field.

"Jessie, come here, come here," he said, happily waving the envelope, which he had opened. Inside was a letter notifying Nancy that she had passed tests to allow her to be admitted to a local nursing school. "Don't tell her I opened the

You think vacation is raising your three kids and you, running your record company, running your house?
NANCY GOODMAN

30: Fourteen years later, when Jessie secured details about her birth parents, she took some solace in her weight struggles. "My biological parents are Puerto Rican and Italian," she says. "They're short, they're chunky, they're always gonna be that."

envelope, but look, your mom's gonna be a nurse. Look how smart she is!"

"But that's for Mom," Jessie said. "That's not for you."

"So?" Steve said. "So what? We'll just close it up and act like we don't know. Look, it doesn't look like it's open, right?"

That evening, when Nancy came home and found the letter, the first thing out of her mouth was, "This envelope's been opened." Steve said nothing and just grinned at Jessie.

Years later, Jessie came to terms with her dad's mixed feelings about her mom's resumption of medical training. "He really was proud of her," she says. "It was, 'You're taking attention away from me and my life, and I'm sick, and I need this, and my kids, and me, me, me, me, me.' Yet deep inside, it was, 'Look, look, look at how smart your mom is.' " [31]

The turmoil in the Goodman household spilled out vividly in the 1983-84 school year during a conference Sarah's third-grade teacher had with Steve and Nancy. For the teacher, Cathy Turley (now Shaw), in her fourth year of teaching, it was a window to extraordinary insight.

The topic, at least initially, was Sarah, whom Turley had found to be a creative, poised "little light" in the classroom. "She had this twinkle in her eyes, which never went down." But Sarah also possessed a streak of mischief and was "always on the edge."

One day, just when Turley got her rambunctious class of 30 settled down, Sarah raised her hand and cracked a joke, breaking the calm. "It just took the air out of my sails," Turley says. "It was that complete feeling of 'Oh, my God — again.' I didn't yell, but I did say, 'Sarah, it was a good joke, but the timing wasn't there.' " It was enough of an incident that Turley decided to raise it with Sarah's parents.

Turley had dealt primarily with Nancy, and in the conference she was meeting Steve for the first time. She knew nothing about him or his music. "I didn't even own a record player, and I doubt if I had anything other than a transistor radio in my apartment." Though Steve's and Nancy's relative physical stature reminded her of Sonny & Cher, Turley regarded them like any other parents and got right to her point about Sarah.

"She's a neat kid," Turley told the pair, "but if she keeps cracking jokes at the wrong time, she could find herself in a bit of trouble."

Leaning back in his chair, legs crossed, Steve looked at Turley as if to size her up a bit. "Well," he said, "I guess I should tell you this," and he filled her in on his leukemia. "Y'know, there are a lot of serious things in this world, and there are a lot of serious events in our lives," he said. "At our house, we have to look at them with a lot of humor. You can't take it too seriously. It's called life. We're training Sarah to laugh at stuff, laugh at the serious stuff, and she's doing it."

The explanation shook Turley to her toes. "It was so perfect," she says. "It gave me a perspective and a total insight. I could just literally see: cancer, family decisions, three kids. Time slows down in a blip, and you can see it all. He was very clear in his picture, in what he was saying."

> **Y'know, there are a lot of serious things in this world. ... At our house, we have to look at them with a lot of humor. You can't take it too seriously. It's called life.**
> **STEVE GOODMAN**

31: Starting an encore set late on June 9, 1983, at Rockefeller's in Houston, Steve incorporated his pride for Nancy's return to nursing. "My wife went back to school, and she came home the other day and said two words to me that I haven't heard in 18 years: 'lab partner.' So now," he said. "everything from here on out is an elective. ... For those of you that have to get up in the morning, none of these songs are required."

Gallows humor prevailed when Steve posed on June 21, 1983, for photos for People Weekly. *Shown in this alternative image, Steve picked a tune on octave mandolin while he lay across railroad tracks leading nowhere. Beyond the fence was the U.S. Naval Weapons Station.*

(Photo by Neal Preston)

32: Turley later bought a Goofy hat at Walt Disney World and used it in her class as an incentive. Students had to "pay" her coupons to wear the hat and tell jokes. Sarah Goodman, she said, "opened the door for a lot of kids after her to crack jokes at the wrong time and not get nailed."

When Turley pointed out that Sarah had become more focused in recent weeks, Steve and Nancy explained that they had enrolled her in a Saturday drama class in nearby Irvine. The workshop drew on Sarah's creativity but also imparted responsibility in the same fashion as did Steve's career. "If she doesn't remember her lines, she doesn't go onstage," Steve said. "If she doesn't remember to get the props out, she isn't in the show."

The half-hour conversation overhauled Turley's approach to her profession. "That was a life message," she says. "From that day on, my teaching space changed. I had to really look at how I talked with kids. How seriously are you taking it? You've got to get your perspective going and lighten up a little bit — and learn about your child and give them permission to create. I talk about that every time I see a parent: 'What is your child doing after school? It's not just sports. Are they doing art? Are they in drama?' It was a huge lesson for me." [32]

Lessons from Steve's fatal disease soon were to spread to millions. His story had become too compelling to ignore.

People Weekly, the nine-year-old celebrity magazine ensconced at supermarket counters, dispatched staff writer Susan Champlin to Seal Beach on June 21 to conduct an interview focusing on the details of Steve's leukemia. Champlin, unfamiliar with Steve's music, shaped his comments into a 1,800-word, first-person story, with Steve's name in the byline, as was customary for the magazine's "Coping" section. Champlin says she was leery of delving into a topic normally

For People Weekly, *Steve injected medicines into the Brouviac catheter in his chest, but the magazine did not run the self-injection photo.*

(Photo by Neal Preston)

considered private, but Steve's humor and self-deprecation "made it easy, made the thing work." When Steve turned a cliché on its ear — "I went through the 'Why me?' stage, but then I got to 'Why not me?' " — Champlin knew she was in the presence of a singular personality. "He was the first person I ever heard say that," she says. "It was emblematic of his entire approach."

Though Steve didn't sugarcoat his prognosis ("They don't throw the word 'cure' around much"), he conveyed grace and gratitude, crediting his family for bravery and strength. Baseball metaphors for his plight sneaked in occasionally (Nancy "handled it like it was some pop fly"), and the culminating bywords combined raillery and resilience: "If you can't laugh at it, then it becomes bigger than you and you're in trouble," Steve said. "We haven't won yet. The game is still on. But it's great to be in the game."

Photos shot for the piece by Neal Preston intriguingly reflected the same themes. He captured Steve sitting at his kitchen table and using a syringe to inject himself with medicine, holding Cubs and White Sox schedules and wearing a Cubs hat while mugging in front of a torn "W.F." (Wrigley Field) banner. The two Preston images that saw print got more to the heart of Steve's message. One was traditional, showing Nancy and the three girls snuggling in a chair with Steve spreading his arms around them from behind. The other, which ran as the lead photo, was visual humor from the gallows.

Its setting was a set of railroad tracks that led to the Navy's nuclear-weapons

Dr. Tim Gee, Steve's lead oncologist since his diagnosis in 1969, played a major role in Steve's segment on NBC "First Camera," in footage shot at Sloan-Kettering Cancer Center.
(Photo courtesy of
Dr. Isabel Cunningham)

station next to the boulevard running from the San Diego Freeway into Seal Beach. There, lying prone across the tracks with his legs crossed, plucking his octave mandolin (bouzouki) and bearing a bright grin, was Steve. The gag was clearly on him. The rails reinforced his most famous song, "City of New Orleans," but Steve also was in the perfect position for a train to run him down. As if the point weren't obvious enough, across the tracks in the distance stood a locked, anchor-fence gate topped with barbed wire. Bolstering the "in" joke, behind the fence lay a military base whose only business was destruction. It was clear that if a train were barreling along, its journey soon would end.

Equally prominent national attention came that summer from NBC-TV, which was launching its ninth attempt in 14 years to create a magazine show to rival CBS-TV's ratings giant "60 Minutes." The new show, aired on Sunday nights, was called "First Camera," and one of its producers, Lisa Freed, was a fan of Steve's. Freed thought of Steve as the focus of a segment after she read an article disclosing his leukemia and detailing his home-based record business. "I'm not somebody who loves doing celebrity profiles," Freed says, "and he was sort of the antithesis of it."

Steve's saga was a tough sell, and Freed felt accomplished when she convinced higher-ups that he was a worthy topic. "First Camera," she says, "was a little quirky and probably mistakenly was not going after the huge stories that magazine shows go after today." [33] Over lunch at Il Cortile in Manhattan's Little Italy, Freed told Steve that the only way her bosses would let her do the segment was if he "opened his life" on film. With a shrug, Steve assented, Freed says. "He really made you believe that he didn't look at it as a great tragedy."

The "First Camera" crew followed Steve exhaustively. Settings included a Cubs game at Wrigley Field, a raucous performance with Jethro Burns at Chicago Fest (with snippets of "City of New Orleans" and "Chicken Cordon Bleus"), a Hollywood recording studio ("California Promises"), a solo show in Vail, Colorado ("Elvis Imitators"), his kitchen table, the Seal Beach post office, a local airport (where he kissed his daughters goodbye before climbing onto a small plane) and the Acropolis luncheonette in New York. Along the way, the crew interviewed Steve and the women shaping his life: Nancy, his mother, Minnette, and Grandma Mary.

The most grueling footage came during his treatment at Sloan-Kettering. As Steve lay on his stomach on a table in a small exam room, he clenched a tooth guard and winced while Dr. Timothy Gee and staff withdrew marrow from his pelvis. While Steve was sitting up, a nurse gave him an injection through his chest catheter, and while he lay on his back and a tissue covered his head, Gee shot medicine into the Ommaya reservoir in his scalp. (At one point, Gee gave Steve a playful pat on the rear. Steve zinged back, "You do this for a living?")

Long before today's "ER" dramas, these were unusually vivid visuals for TV and for the crew itself. "The cameraman walked out of that practically as white as a ghost," Freed says. "His mother had died of cancer, and he'd already gone through the whole process."

33: Low ratings forced the cancellation of NBC's "First Camera" less than a year after its launch, on April 1, 1984.

Steve's reflections on his disease were as captivating as the footage. "There's nothing like having to deal with a problem to get you out of yourself," he said. "You have to just be objective suddenly and take care of business — or roll over, and I don't have that in my personality."

Some of Steve's more wrenching comments didn't make it into the finished segment, especially exchanges in which host Lloyd Dobbins asked if anger over leukemia had fueled his musical career. "I guess there is some kind of rage underneath all these jokes, some internal boiling going on," Steve said, "but I tried to use that energy and that anger to deal with the situation. I'm told I was a decent patient, but I know in my heart I was not a really good patient. The meaning of the word 'patient' becomes very clear to you when you have to wait in hospitals for things to happen, and I was not patient."

Still, Steve said he had learned to avoid complaining, because gripes would turn away audiences and be intolerable to those close to him. "The other thing is, Lloyd, if you walk around the pediatric wards of any of these places I've been in, you really can't feel sorry for yourself. You know, I've had my fun."

Dobbins tried digging more deeply with a familiar question: "Still, there would be a temptation to say, 'Why me, God?' "

"Well, yeah," Steve replied, "but since I know I'm not gonna get an answer, I don't worry about it too much. Oh, I ask the question a couple of times a year, you know."

"No answer yet?"

"No, the line's busy," Steve said, invoking spiritual jest. "I've been put on hold."

While *People Weekly* and "First Camera" assembled their stories in the late summer and early fall, Steve was anything but on hold. [34] Even while getting chemo at Sloan-Kettering, he couldn't stay still for long. On a late Friday afternoon in August, when hospital staff met in the fourth-floor outpatient lounge for weekly "Liver Rounds" (beer, wine and hors d'ouevres), Steve was the guest star in a rock band of oncologists and nurses called the L-17s, named for the current leukemia treatment protocol. Leading a set of oldies, Steve was the proverbial life of the party, playing a borrowed Wurlitzer stereo electric guitar and throwing in zingers to keep the mood light. He encouraged the crowd of 100 to "take a little pause for the cause, a blast for the cast," and in the middle of Tommy Tucker's classic "Hi-Heel Sneakers," he modified a verse to fit the oncological setting:

Put on your hi-heel sneakers
Wear that wig hat on your head
Well, the chemo knocked your hair out,
and I'm sure you're gonna knock 'em dead

The only song of his own that he sang was "You Never Even Call Me by My Name," which he introduced by noting the impossibility of fitting every country/western cliché into one song: "You can see how chemotherapy has ruined

Lisa Freed, producer of the NBC-TV "First Camera" segment on Steve, found his attitude toward his disease to be disarming: "He really made you believe that he didn't look at it as a great tragedy." (Photo courtesy of Lisa Freed)

34: A frequent Manhattan hangout spot for Steve during this time was Matt Umanov Guitars in the Village. Mike Saccoliti, who had seen Steve in concert a dozen times and worked nearby, discovered Steve sitting at the store counter one afternoon. Saccoliti quietly mentioned to a friend who worked at the store, Candice Smith, that Steve once had performed the obscure "My Brooklyn Love Song" (by Ramez Idreiss and George Tibbles, from the 1948 film "If You Knew Susie") during a show. Smith turned to Steve and asked if he recalled the tune. Steve grabbed a guitar, took the pair to the back of the store and sang it. Saccoliti thanked Steve and told him he was a Brooklyn native. "Well," Steve replied, "dis bud's for you."

Manhattan friend Marilyn Quine, who had fought bone cancer as a child, witnessed Steve's superstition about rubber bands signifying good luck. "If he found a rubber band on the floor," she says, "he'd put it around his wrist right away." Soon, in support, Quine was doing the same thing.

(Photo courtesy of Marilyn Quine)

my mind." Instructing his band mates to "lean into the mike" like a typical country act, he cracked, "It's great to tell doctors what to do for a change," adding quickly, "That was a cheap shot. I apologize."

More potent than his banter, says intern and L-17s keyboardist Dr. Lee Schwartzberg, was the fact that Steve was playing at all. "He had gotten treatment that day around lunchtime, and about 5 o'clock when we were setting up, he seemed very puny," Schwartzberg says. "But as soon as we got out there and started playing, he sort of lit up. He went from being someone who had literally gotten sick from chemotherapy hours before to someone who made the room his, the way he always did."

Steve didn't always mask his angst with performance, says family friend Marilyn Quine, who had a bond with Steve partly because she had battled youthful bone cancer in one knee and who babysat Steve's daughters when Nancy brought them to New York to visit. Quine left Sloan-Kettering one weekday afternoon with Steve after he had received a blood transfusion and had a particularly discouraging talk with his doctors. Slowly walking uphill along East 68th Street toward busy First Avenue, Steve started rocking back and forth.

"You're dead, you're alive," he said, punctuating each sentence with a stomp on the sidewalk. "You're dead, you're alive, you're dead, you're alive. ..."

"It was the first anger I'd ever seen in him," Quine says. "I didn't look at it as feeling sorry for himself, but it was realizing that this could be it. It was the only time I ever saw him do the equivalent of throw your arms up in the air and say, 'Oh, my God, it's me.' "

Leavening the melancholy was a superstition that Steve had adopted, a compulsive attachment to rubber bands. "If he found a rubber band on the floor, it was good luck," Quine says. "He'd put it around his wrist right away. Rubber bands became a big thing." Quine herself began wearing them as a form of support. "If I found a rubber band, it went around my wrist until it broke or took itself off."

Steve's most absorbing support that summer and fall, as always, came from music. He opened for Judy Collins at L.A.'s Universal Amphitheatre and for the Nitty Gritty Dirt Band at Red Rocks in Colorado, co-headlined (with Jay Leno and others) the Harbor Moon Folk Festival in Tilton, New Hampshire, and finished a revision of his "Good Gang Express" song for use by NBC in a nationally televised children's afternoon show, "Kidstown USA." With sales of his "Artistic Hair" LP shooting past the 2,500 break-even point and reaching 7,500, Steve also fit in sessions at the WFMT-FM studio in Chicago, Studio by the Pond near Nashville and Gary Brandt's Alpha Studios in Hollywood to prepare a second album to sell by mail order and on the road.

For the second album, Steve orchestrated a mix of concert tunes (recorded much more professionally than the live cuts on "Artistic Hair") and lightly produced studio tracks, three of which drew on backing from pals Rick Chudacoff and Peter Bunetta. The idea was to let those who saw Steve in concert take home a recording of newer material they had just heard him perform plus older songs that he hadn't released on LP. [35] Standouts among the album's dozen offerings included a live version of "Dying Cub Fan" (immortalizing Keith Moreland as the player to "drop a routine fly") and the smile-inducing "Take Me Out to the Ballgame" that Steve had recorded in 1981 with Jethro Burns. In this collection, lean arrangements of "Old Smoothies," "Grand Canyon Song," "Vegematic," "How Much Tequila," [36] "California Promises" and "Watchin' Joey Glow" made their recorded debut. So did two duets: a bouncy instrumental (with Steve on mandola and Jim Rothermel on recorder) called "If Jethro Were Here" and a first-take vocal pairing of Steve and John Prine on Prine's chestnut, "Souvenirs."

The latter track, which Prine had written in 1970 before he met Steve, unwittingly had become a wistful accounting of their friendship. For the recording, Steve imitated Prine's sandpaper voice ("My wife calls me the Zelig of folk music," Steve cracked), and their vocals and guitars melded as if they were brothers. "It was a natural for us," Prine says. "He had this way of playin' that made it sound like I could really play, like it was comin' out of my guitar. That's kinda what he did with everything that he did, onstage, offstage, through a lot of different situations. He would work his butt off to do his best, and if he liked you, he would shine that light on you. He was not at all anywhere close to a selfish person, even unconsciously."

In Steve's self-mocking vision, the tunes he had gathered for the new LP resembled the mélange of Vegematic-style items he had been mocking in song. For an album title and visual theme, he turned to "Artistic Hair" photographer Jim Shea for inspiration, and they found a fitting metaphor in the gigantic sales of cheap paintings hawked in L.A.'s airport hotels with such slogans as, "You can afford art for $69!" Shea recalled seeing store after store of tawdry lawn statues during a recent trip to Mexico, and since Steve's home was just a two-hour drive from Tijuana, the two headed south to find a photo backdrop. They settled on an outdoor stand filled with figurines: lions, parrots, ducks, pigs, monkeys, rams, nymphs, gunslingers and even W.C. Fields. His octave mandolin propped against his right leg, Steve stood grinning amid this array of animal and human faces, and the LP cover and title were born: "Affordable Art." [37]

His hair had lengthened to a wispy curl, and while his Ommaya reservoir bump didn't jump out, it was clearly visible. "It was like a war wound," Shea says. "It wasn't that he was proud of it, but it was almost like a punk-rock aesthetic: 'This is me. Take it or leave it.' " More remarkable was the large pair of sunglasses that would obscure Steve's most riveting facial feature for the second album in a row. "The sunglasses were just a prop, but they added a certain cool factor, the Ray Charles thing," says Shea, who was glad that Steve wanted to wear the shades. "His eyes were so intense, they were distracting almost. It was like he was looking right through you."

Both of Steve's major media pieces — and his galvanizing gaze — hit the nation in the fall of 1983. The *People Weekly* profile, straddling four pages, ran in the Oct. 3 edition, whose cover stories trumpeted Bobby Kennedy Jr.'s heroin

In the version of "Dying Cub Fan" that Steve placed on his second Red Pajamas LP, he immortalized Keith Moreland as the Cub to "drop a routine fly."
(Photo by Stephen Green for the Chicago Cubs)

35: At Steve's request, the president of Elektra/Asylum, Mel Posner, contributed Steve's original recording of "Talk Backwards" for use on the LP.

36: The credits for "How Much Tequila" listed a slide guitarist: "Rick N. Backer." It was a pun on the brand name of an electric guitar given fame by the Beatles. The actual guitarist was Steve.

37: Coincidentally, Chicago had its own "Affordable Art" shop, on North Avenue three doors west of Wells Street, near the Earl of Old Town, says Steve's Lake Forest College classmate Bob Gross.

abuse and the first crowning of an African-American, Vanessa Williams, as Miss America. The impressive treatment was heartening to Steve, except for a refusal by editors to print an address from which readers could order his LPs. Susan Champlin had to break the news that *People* had a policy against printing such promo info in their "Coping" stories. Steve's retort was incisive: "But this is how I cope!"

Meanwhile, the NBC "First Camera" segment, called "You Can't Keep a Goodman Down," [38] filled one third of an hour that also reported on a Miami Dolphins offensive lineman and the bureaucratic morass faced by residents of Guam. It ran on Sunday, Nov. 20, the same night that ABC-TV aired its landmark nuclear-bomb drama, "The Day After," and one week before TNN broadcast the "Bobby Bare & Friends" episode that featured Steve. [39]

Among those happiest to see the conspicuous coverage were Steve's doctors at Sloan-Kettering. "We had wanted him to go public, mainly because he'd done well," says Dr. Monroe Dowling. "We wanted to let people understand that his leukemia wasn't basically a death sentence."

Precisely when the public was getting its most intimate look at Steve's life, the road was revealing hints of his demise. Set to open for John Prine on Oct. 7 at Southern Illinois University in Carbondale and on Oct. 8 at Sangamon State University in the Illinois capital of Springfield, Steve missed both shows. "It's embarrassing when that happens, and that can't be helped," he said later. "It's certainly not foreseeable or avoidable, I guess. But for the most part I've been very, very lucky." A day-of-show ad in the SIU paper announced his absence as "due to illness." Filling in were Michael Johnson at SIU and Leo Kottke at Sangamon, and ticket refunds were offered to anyone dissatisfied. For each crowd, Prine gave an optimistic report on his friend: "He's feeling a lot better and wanted me to tell you hello," he said at Sangamon, "and he's sorry he couldn't make it."

While getting treatment at Sloan-Kettering, Steve found time for a gesture that those who knew him regarded as endearingly typical. The brother of Steve's longtime Philadelphia Folk Festival friend Laura Haynes (now Aiken) had died Oct. 2 of suicide. Steve, in his hospital room, learned this from Saul Broudy, picked up the phone and reached Haynes while her family's rabbi was leading a session of remembrances. "I can't tell you what that meant to me," she says. "He called to comfort me when my brother had taken his life, and he was fighting to keep his own. He was so caring that way. It's a mitzvah, doing good things for other people, and mitzvahs are what make all of us better people."

Steve also found time that fall to perform a musical mitzvah for the Nitty Gritty Dirt Band. The scatological "Don't Get Sand in It" already had appeared earlier that year as a throwaway Dirt Band 45. (While the band was recording it, one of its members called Steve at Sean Kelly's home in New York and said, "We want to ask you a question. Is this a dirty song?" [40]) The Dirt Band's manager, Chuck Morris, wanted to capitalize on his group's home state and instigate a more heartwarming and better-selling single. So from the South Carolina shores

---

We had wanted him to go public, mainly because he'd done well. We wanted to let people understand that his leukemia wasn't basically a death sentence.
DR. MONROE DOWLING

38: Eight months earlier, the *Los Angeles Times* had used the same phrase as the headline for a column on Steve.

39: Because the Nov. 20 edition of "First Camera" was pre-empted at the last minute in the East, the segment on Steve was rebroadcast as part of a different episode Sunday, Dec. 18.

40: The next spring, telling an Atlanta audience why he wrote "Don't Get Sand in It," Steve slipped in a couple of racy puns: "One day it just came over me. It's sort of like the boy's got it in him, and it's gotta come out, right?"

Chapter Seventeen: 'You're dead, you're alive, you're dead, you're alive ...'

645

of Myrtle Beach, where the band was playing, Morris called Steve in Seal Beach and asked him to write a Colorado-based Christmas song, "something to tug at the heartstrings." The catch was that Morris wanted the band to record it in Nashville two days hence.

"You're out of your fuckin' mind, but maybe I'll try for five minutes," Steve replied. "I've gotta get permission from my rabbi first."

The next day, the Dirt Band motored west, and when the bus hit a truck stop for gas, singer/multi-instrumentalist Jimmy Ibbotson found a pay phone and called Steve. "I've got the first verse," Steve said, singing and playing the fledgling lyrics and notes over the phone while Ibbotson scribbled down the words and chords. The bus stopped 150 miles later, and Ibbotson called again. "I got another verse," Steve said. Another 200 miles passed. "Call me back in a few hours," Steve said. Two hours later, another stop. "I got the chorus coming!" Between stops, Ibbotson and the other band members were learning the tune, and by the time they reached Nashville, the song was done, and the Nitty Grittys could play it. They recorded "Colorado Christmas," with high harmony by Emmylou Harris, and a 45 was released in time for the holidays. It rose to only #93 on the *Billboard* country chart in late December, but it's been a regional and seasonal hit ever since. [41]

The song's effect, Ibbotson says, lay in its arousal of universal emotions in one-to-one fashion, the same as Steve's stage appeal. Ibbotson cites a line in which the narrator, recalling his boyhood, says, "The carolers on the hillsides sang their songs of Christmas joy / Well, I always thought they sang 'em just for me." The line is a stunner, Ibbotson says. "If that doesn't make the story of Christmas personal, I don't know what could," he says. "We all feel that way."

Steve had rebounded from chemo enough for NBC-TV to shed light that fall on another of Steve's poignant songs — one that *People Weekly* and "First Camera" had largely ignored. Mike Leonard, Chicago correspondent for the early-morning "Today" show (and no relation to WGN's Roy Leonard), had become aware of "A Dying Cub Fan's Last Request" at the same time that the Cubs had typically lumbered to the end of the 1983 season in fifth place in the NL East. Leonard thought that while the World Series played out between the Baltimore Orioles and Philadelphia Phillies, it would be a warming gesture for Cub followers — and baseball fans across the nation — to hear Steve sing his musical lament from Wrigley Field. "I just made up a story so we could air the song," Leonard says. "I thought the song had to get heard by people, and the 'Today' show's a pretty good audience. Great works of art often don't get seen, and I had at least enough power and control to shift that song to the view of a larger group of people."

To film the story on Oct. 15 for airing three days later, Steve agreed to fly to Chicago. But there was one catch. The Cubs — led by Dallas Green, the ex-pitcher and manager who as the team's general manager was invoking the slogan "Building a New Tradition" — wouldn't let Leonard film Steve singing "Dying Cub Fan" inside Wrigley. "Anything that was in the past, Dallas wanted

Great works of art often don't get seen, and I had at least enough power and control to shift that song to the view of a larger group of people.
MIKE LEONARD

41: The Nitty Gritty Dirt Band re-recorded the song in 1997, with Alison Krauss singing the Emmylou Harris harmony.

no part of because the Cubs had been losers," says Chuck Swirsky, then-WGN sports director. "He was trying to cleanse the despair of the franchise from previous regimes." Citing a phrase from "Dying Cub Fan," Dan Fabian, then-WGN program director, adds, "It was the 'doormat of the National League' that just flipped him."

"We didn't need any more negativity than we already had," says Green, now an executive for the Philadelphia Phillies. "We were trying to climb over that. It took us awhile to have people understand that it wasn't fair to the Cub fans and to the people that worked for the Cubs to be labeled losers."

Mike Leonard came up with an end-run around Green's objection, however. He secured the use of an apartment rooftop across Waveland Avenue that looked over the left-field stands into Wrigley, and he shot the piece from there. With the nearly deserted ballpark as the backdrop, Steve sang the song in the fall chill. Much of the time, the brim from the large Cubs hat he was wearing obscured his eyes and face. "It was a bit of a sad scene because he was a dying Cub fan, literally, and the field was empty," Leonard says.

Hank Neuberger, who with his wife drove Steve to the shoot, found the setting "incredibly poignant" at the time. "Of course, today you realize, my God, he looks like death," Neuberger says. "The Cub hat is swimming on his head, and he looks so frail."

But Steve persisted in an accompanying interview, grinning broadly, denying that the song was autobiographical ("I didn't perceive myself as this old guy") and mustering joke after joke about the appeal of his ill-fated team. "I love baseball more than I love the Cubs, but the reason I love baseball is the Cubs," he told Leonard. "The Cubs are a team that need parents or something. They need someone to help them. Kids see that, I think, at an early age. ... You sort of know they're going to field a team. You just never really know how."

While in Chicago, Steve dropped in at the Earl of Old Town, which was about to field a new lineup. Folk music was no longer thriving at the place where Steve had gotten his true start. Owner Earl Pionke, who had dropped weeknight entertainment during the previous six months, had just signed partnership papers to convert his club to a new musical fare and name, B.L.U.E.S. at the Earl. He considered it a better choice than turning the Earl into a "brass and glass" singles bar.

"Earl, I don't believe it," Steve told Pionke. "I'm proud of you. You finally got off your dead ass." But Steve also sealed a longstanding reservation. "You're gonna have blues here seven nights a week? Well, you tell them one night a year on New Year's Eve there's going to be a young folkie named Steve Goodman."

Steve got back on the road that fall with a solo show in San Francisco, warm-up sets for Prine in a weekend jaunt to Calgary and Edmonton and a pair of swings through the Midwest as the opener for Prine and comic George Carlin. A makeup show Dec. 9 at Southern Illinois University also had pegged Steve as the opener, but the main act, Leo Kottke, had something else in mind. Kottke, who had felt stymied by similar billings with Steve, was simply fed up.

"There were a lot of people who just wouldn't follow him, because there was nobody and has not been anybody, at least who was carrying a guitar, who could run a crowd the way he did," Kottke says. "The curve started, it shot up and out there, and he never dropped the ball. You could not turn away from him when he was up there, and it was murder to follow him because he used them up. There just was no audience left. You had to go out and be patient until it was over with. That's about all you could do."

Kottke, who had raised this beef with Steve to no avail at previous pairings, buttonholed him during the afternoon sound check at SIU and asked to flip-flop their sets. "Look," Kottke said bluntly, "just close it."

"Nah, you're the headliner," Steve said. "You're selling more tickets."

"Well, fuck it," Kottke shot back. "They don't care. Why should we care? It doesn't matter. You're just too much. It's hard to get up after that."

Steve paused, and the gleam in his eye grew brighter. "Well," he finally said, "why don't we have a referee come in, and we'll flip a coin."

It was shtick that Kottke couldn't resist. So for a crowd of 800, walking onto the Shryock Auditorium stage were Steve, Kottke and an NCAA referee, in a traditional black striped shirt. As reported by the SIU student newspaper, the *Daily Egyptian*, Kottke won the coin flip and opened the show. He also joined Steve at the end for a guitar jam and a duet on his lone hit, "Pamela Brown."

Unknown to most in the audience but transparent to Kottke was a sign of Steve's continuing health crisis.

"He delivered this perfect set, had them falling apart, the music was beautiful, people were crying and laughing," Kottke says, "but from chemo he'd entirely lost the use of one joint in his index finger. To bend this thing at a 90-degree angle was impossible, and the joint just plain collapsed when he fretted with it. In other words, he really couldn't play, and who knows what kind of pain there was. He played anyhow, obviously barely flopping along with that finger. You would hear the finger now and then, but you knew what he intended — and still he killed 'em. It was murder, as always. He could get music out of a turnip."

Steve's stamina, however, was turning volatile, and as 1983 wound to a close, his voice sometimes resembled the proverbial vegetable.

He did squeeze out a guest slot — with Mimi Fariña, Jennifer Warnes and the duo of David Buskin & Robin Batteau — on Dec. 27-28 for Tom Rush's third annual holiday concerts in Boston's Symphony Hall. He sang "Watchin' Joey Glow" and "Old Smoothies" solo, then bid Rush's band to join him on "City of New Orleans" — and the accompanists scooted onstage for the opportunity. Though Steve dominated a post-show party with his Flatiron mandola (he "picked and sang us all into the ground," Rush wrote later), Steve's endurance soon began to sag.

In Chicago four days later, Steve kept his reaffirmed commitment to Earl Pionke — and satisfied the expectations of his hometown fans — by playing two New Year's Eve sets at the renamed B.L.U.E.S. at the Earl. Mandolinist

When Earl Pionke announced plans to revitalize and rename his Earl of Old Town club as B.L.U.E.S. at the Earl, he got an earful from Steve: "I'm proud of you. You finally got off your dead ass." But Steve also insisted he was not about to skip out on his annual gig on New Year's Eve.

(Photo by Larry Rand)

For Steve's portion of Tom Rush's December 1983 holiday show, held at Boston's wreath-ringed Symphony Hall, filling the stage were (clockwise from Steve), Rush; Irwin Fisch (behind Rush), piano; Eric Lilljequist, Dean Adrien and David Buskin, vocals; Wells Kelly, drums; Paul Guzzone, electric bass; Marshal Rosenberg, percussion; and Robin Batteau, violin.
(Photo by Frank Siteman)

Stuart Rosenberg says Steve went from being "really frail, void of energy, pale as a ghost, not a pretty sight" in the Star Cave back room to an unworldly stage presence.

"It was like somebody opened a valve on a gas tank," Rosenberg says. "All of a sudden, he inflated with energy, and he pounced onto the stage like a Superball. He hit the stage rocking, just beaming joy and energy and whimsy and communicating that incredibly endearing, slightly mischievous thing that made every person in the room lean into him and gave an hour and 20 minutes that just got better and better and smokier and hotter and cooler and more fabulous and more party. It was dazzling."

As he had done for more than a decade, Steve trouped to WFMT-FM that night to play on the early-morning New Year's "Midnight Special." But the indefatigable image he projected in previous years was now a mere shadow. His tempos languished, his strumming faded in and out, and his voice descended to a low croak. His fatigue was palpable. But his will was both resilient and resolute — and the five songs that he played could not have more accurately epitomized his life in music.

With no accompaniment but his guitar, Steve started with a pair of new tunes. The first was a just-written tribute to Carl Martin, Steve's musical mentor who had died in 1979, and to Martin's string band compatriots Ted Bogan and Howard Armstrong. "He was like a grandfather to me," Steve told the several dozen in the WFMT studio and the untold thousands of radio listeners throughout Chicagoland. "He was about the best guy I ever met."

Steve had given the song its debut mere hours earlier at the Earl, with bassist Mike Lindauer holding up five pages of yellow legal paper on which Steve had scrawled the lyrics. His words encapsulated Martin's life by describing the mandolinist's leadership of a mid-1970s "all-night blow-out jam" similar to the one Steve was leading at that very moment. The crowd hushed as Steve rasped the tune's pointed, bittersweet refrain (and title): "You Better Get It While You Can." [42] Steve presented it as Martin's earthy homily, but on this night Steve was not merely the messenger. He embodied both the lesson and its teacher.

His next musical discourse encompassed gratitude and goofiness, in a form he was known for mastering — improvisation. As he had done in previous New Year's broadcasts, Steve unveiled a freewheeling song to ring in the year, to be sung at this time and setting and no other. His 1984 installment had five verses and a chorus, some of which he had worked out earlier and some that emerged on the fly. Though he didn't mention his recovery from relapse the year prior, it was expressly implied in lyrics that revealed his regret for not having attended the Jan. 1, 1983, show and instead sending a proxy tape. He added, with no little poignancy:

> I'm glad to be back in the studio
> with all of the friends in town
> And I hope to come back at the end of the year
> when '85 rolls around

Then came an unplanned instant that revealed Steve's gift for on-the-spot invention. He sang:

> There's lots of great musicians in Chicago
> and some of 'em play right here
> And some of 'em you never get to see
> because there's reasons that aren't clear

Right after the word "clear," from the background intruded an audible, metallic clap that might have thrown another musician. But with no pause and keeping with his gentle rhythm, Steve persevered, eyeing the clock on the wall and letting his listeners know what had just happened:

> And sometimes they drop their beer cans
> in the middle of a sensitive song
> But at 4:26 in the morning
> you can't say that was wrong

It was another fleeting flash of Goodman magic, and the studio audience whooped and applauded its approval. Steve pressed on with lyrical appreciation

---

He was like a grandfather to me. He was about the best guy I ever met.
STEVE GOODMAN

42: That Steve was raised in a Jewish home intensifies the song's homage, says L.A. attorney David Schulman. "I don't think it's a coincidence that Steve could see an old black man who is operating in his tradition — the musical entertainment comedic tradition — and not be intimidated but instead deeply love that man. The relationship between Jews and blacks throughout the 20th century is a mixed bag, troubled and marvelous, but it's a special relationship."

Ray Nordstrand, shown chatting with Steve at the July 9, 1983, Winnipeg Folk Festival, was paid tribute in Steve's frog-voiced presentation of a one-time-only song on New Year's Eve 1983 at Nordstrand's WFMT-FM in Chicago.

(Photo by Juel Ulven)

43: Enthusiasm for "Affordable Art" was so great that footage for a second intro film was shot in Martin Mull's backyard. In it, Steve, playing a down-and-out songwriter, hid in the leaves as Mull kicked him and a dog urinated on him. The film, however, was never finished.

to WFMT's Ray Nordstrand and Rich Warren for letting him record tracks at the station for his "Affordable Art" LP ("a little homemade record"). His final verse wrenched the emotions from laughter to tears:

> *Now this old studio got a real high*
> *ceilin' and a wooden floor*
> *It's just the kind of place for acoustic guitars*
> *and basses that start to snore*
>
> *So Ray and Rich, I'll seeya around*
> *when the next time comes to record*
> *And for WFMT I'd just*
> *like to say thank the Lord*

Next came a leisurely, undulating version of "Mama Don't Allow It," with visiting Saul Broudy on harmonica, Rich Markow on the jug, Larry Rand on "imitation saxophone" (kazoo), Jim Polaski on mandolin, Mike Lindauer on fretless bass and Kathy Kelly on spoons. Steve opened the jam with, "Open the windows and close the doors / Play the first tune of 1984," but for much of the song he was a recessed presence. On his final tune, the inevitable "City of New Orleans," weariness pervaded Steve's voice, and others in the studio took notice. Their lusty harmonies, instrumental solos and handclaps masked the fact that Steve was just plain worn out.

The passion and pathos of the wee-hours music had been both stunning and revealing. It also became the first of many signals in 1984 that Steve was bidding farewell. Steve continued to abound with activity — and with the zeal of the dying Cub fan of his song, "who knew his time was short." But it came in sporadic bursts, extreme intensity followed by extended rest. He found fortification in the reviews that poured in at the year's outset for "Affordable Art."

"A spirited and lovely album chock full of little gems," wrote Richard Harrington of *The Washington Post.* "Gourmet," chimed in *Billboard.* "Likely his best," said Larry Kelp of the *Oakland Tribune*, giving it four stars. "His most modest and most likable album," wrote Robert Christgau of the *Village Voice*: ("True, he's too sentimental when he's serious," Christgau added. "Even when he's funny, he's too sentimental. His natural lyricism is a palliative, though.") Finally, Dave Hoekstra of the *Chicago Sun-Times* labeled the album, and Steve's music in general, "the most fun you can have with your pants on." [43]

Going further was Larry Rand in the *Chicago Reader*. "Goodman is my Man of the Year in Folk," Rand wrote, rating "Artistic Hair" and "Affordable Art" as not only Steve's two best LPs but also among 1983's finest. "Goodman's survival is one of the year's miracles. ... The humiliations and tribulations of show business must seem trivial and merely absurd next to Goodman's medical ordeal. He is a heroic figure."

The 35-year-old hero hadn't lost his gift for self-effacing metaphor, however. That much was clear in an interview with David Gans of *Record* magazine, in

Chapter Seventeen: 'You're dead, you're alive, you're dead, you're alive ...'

651

which Steve likened each of his previous LPs to an eclectic supermarket sack. "Inside, there's a roll of paper towels, a can of chili, three oranges, four chicken legs," he said. "You look at it as a whole, and it's a shopping bag full of groceries. But if you just take things out one at a time — that's the one that's going to tell everybody what's in the rest of the bag? You might be in trouble. The reason 'Affordable Art' works better than some of the other records is that it looks like I went shopping to make one meal. I invited some friends over, and I knew just what I was going to cook, different things, course by course."

With the tasty new LP came a new price, $8, but when sold at concerts, Steve's albums now were augmented by a simulated baseball card depicting him in baseball hat and glove, gripping a softball. The idea came from Emmylou Harris' road manager, Phil Kaufman, whose business card looked like a baseball card. "He saw that and liked it," Kaufman says. The back of the card even had its own tongue-in-cheek statistics, written by Steve: "Shows played: 1,011. Shows stolen: all but one. Strings broken: 14,638. Records released: 9. Records broken: all. Records stolen: N.A. Played for Buddah Records 1971-74, Asylum Records 1975-81, Red Pajamas 1983-84. (Spent half of 1982 on disabled list.)"

Steve embarked on an ambitious road schedule for the winter and spring of 1984, but the stops were not always for performances. In New York for leukemia treatment, Steve also was a guest Jan. 5 at an unusual 53rd birthday gathering for actor Robert Duvall. "Tender Mercies," in which Duvall played a washed-up country singer, had been released the previous March, and he was three months away from winning a best-actor Oscar. In Duvall's apartment, once owned by famed opera tenor Enrico Caruso, Steve (and two other Steves, Burgh and Mandell) sang and played country songs with June Carter Cash while actors Harry Dean Stanton and John Savage (who had played Sloan-Kettering leukemia patient Eric Lund in a TV movie eight years earlier) looked on. [44]

It was Steve's link to June Carter Cash that had brought him to the Duvall party. The connection also prompted Steve during the same month to drive Nancy and his daughters two hours east of Seal Beach to the Betty Ford Center in Rancho Mirage to touch base with June and her husband Johnny, who was undergoing six weeks of alcohol and drug treatment. There, Steve sang and played guitar for the Man in Black, who considered Steve's visit an important element in his rehabilitation. (Three months later, when Steve guested on a Cash show April 29 at the Anaheim Convention Center, Cash introduced Steve by saying, "I love this little man. He is a great talent and one of the greatest people I've ever known." Steve wryly dismissed the compliment: "Thank you, John. You said that just the way I wrote it. Y'never know what a guy will do for a backstage pass.")

Steve aided another friend in January — John Prine, who flew to Los Angeles so that Steve could produce at Gary Brandt's Alpha Studios the recordings of two new Prine songs, "Take a Look at My Heart" and "People Puttin' People Down." The latter track made it onto Prine's next LP, "Aimless Love," which Prine released in late 1984 on a new label that he named after a Buddy Holly hit,

The reason 'Affordable Art' works better than some of the other records is that it looks like I went shopping to make one meal. I invited some friends over, and I knew just what I was going to cook, different things, course by course.
STEVE GOODMAN

44: Not many days afterward, when Al Bunetta and his wife, Dawn, were visiting Steve in Seal Beach, a knock came at the door. It was Robert Duvall. "Hey, does Steve Goodman live here?" Duvall had brought his guitar to swap songs with Steve, who played for Duvall a selection of Prine tunes.

Raun MacKinnon, shown in 1976, got a glimpse of Steve's beneath-the-surface anger in February 1984. On the sidewalk outside the club, Steve castigated a seller of cutout LPs for taking money from his family. She had never seen Steve so irate. "How dare you do this to me!" Steve screamed at the vendor. "I have children to support! I've got babies!"

(Photo by Susan Spelman, courtesy of Raun MacKinnon Burnham)

Oh Boy Records. The entrepreneurial example, Prine says, came from Steve's Red Pajamas venture. "Because Al (Bunetta) and Dan Einstein had been able to help Stevie with that, I knew that we could do the same with Oh Boy."

The Red Pajamas LPs meant more than artistic independence to Steve. He saw them as financial sustenance for him and his family at a time of high medical expense and into an uncertain future. As he had joked for David Gans, during his relapse Steve had been thinking, "Are we gonna sell one of the cars or a kid or something?" These feelings led to an incident in Greenwich Village that unglued him.

When Steve played four shows Feb. 3-4 at the Bottom Line, all seemed well. These were "up" nights, and during one set, he drew a table of Hollywood luminaries: Robert Duvall, plus the duo of Glenn Close and Jeremy Irons, who were starring in the Tony Award-winning "The Real Thing" at Broadway's Plymouth Theatre. An exchange with a woman in the audience illustrated the gusto.

"We love you, don't go away," the woman shouted.

Steve shot back, "Nobody's dyin' here."

Between sets, however, singer and friend Raun MacKinnon hustled backstage to tell Steve that he had competition for his wares on the street — a "wussy opportunist" who had snagged a stash of Steve's old LPs from a New Jersey distributor and was peddling them for $15 apiece.

"Do you know there's a guy selling your records out in front of the club?" MacKinnon asked. "Is he one of your people?"

"God, no," Steve said.

He shot outside to confront the "runty" seller, fury in his eyes:

"How dare you do this to me! I have children to support! I've got babies! I've got to make a living, and you're taking the money out of my mouth!"

The vendor didn't budge, but the club's co-owner, Allan Pepper, who recognized the man from other nights on which he had sold the remaindered LPs of other artists, persuaded him to leave.

Such street sales, Pepper says, weren't uncommon in an era when most performers considered it "cheesy" to hawk their own albums during gigs and, on the advice of their labels, left such selling to record stores. But that didn't mollify Steve's rage. Neither Pepper nor MacKinnon had ever seen Steve so angry. "This was not the guy I knew," Pepper says. "He really lost it." The explanation, Pepper says upon reflection, was mortality closing in. "What was going through his mind, if he knew the end was near, was that he wanted to give the guy hell for getting money that should come to him."

To the same end in early 1984, Steve conducted a relentless campaign to collaborate on compositions that would outlive him. "City of New Orleans" certainly fell into that category. It had even given rise to a question in the trendy new board game Trivial Pursuit. ("How many sacks of mail on the City of New Orleans?" The answer: 25.) But it wasn't enough. As he told Robert K. Oermann of the Nashville *Tennessean*, "The more I work, the better I feel, because I'm not exactly the world's leader in song copyrights." Steve welcomed artist after artist to his Seal Beach home, and the visitors became engulfed in creative projects, with varying degrees of completion:

◆ Matthew Wilder, whose bouncy, synthesizer-drenched "Break My Stride" had reached #5 on the *Billboard* Hot 100 in late summer 1983, was produced by Rick Chudacoff and Peter Bunetta, and Bunetta introduced Wilder, 31, to Steve. For Wilder's follow-up LP, the two wrote "Scandal," about an extramarital affair. The idea was Wilder's, but Steve conjured the title. "It was to his benefit to be collaborating with an artist currently on the radio," Wilder says. "He had an understandable, cynical viewpoint about the 1980s-style music that was on the airwaves, myself included, but he was generous and kind enough to let me in and be a part of it." "Scandal" became an also-ran cut on Wilder's "Bouncin' Off the Walls" LP, which flopped on its release that fall. Still, the musicians had clicked, partly because they shared a diminutive height but mostly due to Steve's talent. "Like a really good chess player," Wilder says, "from the start of a song he could see the endgame." Such clarity informed Steve's outlook on leukemia. "He was very brave and somewhat cavalier about it," Wilder says. "He had a real fighter's instinct. He really wasn't about to give in."

◆ David Grisman, whose self-developed "Dawg" mandolin style and collaborations with Stéphane Grappelli and Jerry Garcia had brought him fame, got to know Steve via Jethro Burns. Grisman, 39, hosted Steve at his San Francisco home one afternoon at Steve's behest. "I've got all these melodies," Grisman told him. "Just write words to one." Nothing jumped out of the one-day session, but Steve eventually incorporated some of Grisman's ideas in an upbeat rant he'd written in 1981 about mechanized communication, "Telephone Answering Tape." [45] Steve was "just a really upbeat ball of energy," Grisman says. "He was a little guy with a large presence and just a real sweetheart."

◆ Another mandolinist, Bob Tangrea, who had played a street-corner singer in the 1976 Oscar-winning film "Rocky," had met Steve via folk traditionalist John Herald. Steve invited Tangrea, 33, to sing backup vocals on "How Much Tequila," and the two spent hours at Steve's house working on a song Steve had started, "Fire Escape," about a man lamenting a lost romance while sitting on an outdoor landing in an inner-city barrio. They finished the mournful tune, but it was never recorded. "Steve was very up," Tangrea says, "and just looking to play music and write."

◆ Jim Geisler, whose Foggy Bottom club on St. Croix island inspired Steve's "Banana Republics," came for dinner at Steve's home and wound up sketching out the plot line for a film. As dreamed up by satirist Larry Rand, with whom Steve had been talking and who also had performed at the Foggy Bottom, the movie would focus on two hapless U.S. expatriates who open a music club in the Caribbean. The pair would stumble upon a rich family's scam to lower the islands' real-estate prices. "Steve had a bunch of ideas for this character that he was going to play, the nightclub singer," says Geisler, who still has the notes from his brainstorm session with Steve. But the film never came to pass.

Matthew Wilder, who collaborated with Steve on "Scandal," admired his co-writer's craft. "Like a really good chess player," Wilder says, "from the start of a song he could see the endgame."
(Photo by Randy Nichols, courtesy of Matthew Wilder)

45: Of the increasingly ubiquotous answering machines, Steve told an Atlanta audience, "I hate those things. I don't know why I do. I guess I'll have to go get analyzed just to figure out why I hate telephone answering tapes. It's bad enough havin' to talk to whoever it is you felt you had to call, much less havin' to talk to their damn machine. That's what it is, something like that."

◆ The New Edition, the African-American teenage Jackson Five-like pop quintet (a forerunner of New Kids on the Block and featuring Bobby Brown, future husband of Whitney Houston), was seeking material for a debut LP on MCA. Rick Chudacoff, Peter Bunetta and Arno Lucas had come up with a candidate, with "shoo-be-doo-wop" flourishes, but needed help with the lyrics. After a writing session with Steve, the formulaic love song became "Maryann," an also-ran cut on the New Edition's wildly successful, self-titled album, which that fall topped the *Billboard* R&B chart, spawned two #1 R&B hits and rose to #6 on the pop-LP chart.

◆ Marty Stuart, the country superstar who in 1984 was a sideman for Johnny Cash (and had married his daughter Cindy), had secured Steve to produce solo demo tracks for him, in the first-ever sessions at Nashville's now-revered Treasure Isle studio. Stuart also bunked at Steve's Seal Beach home, where the two co-wrote a pair of songs. "Do You Really Want My Lovin'?" appeared on Stuart's self-titled rockabilly LP in 1986, but "It Just Don't Pay (to Know What You Don't Know)," drawn from a Goodman expression, never was recorded. Steve, a "free thinker" in Stuart's estimation, was a dominant force. Cribbing from a witticism attributed to novelty songwriter Roger Miller, Stuart says, "Writing with Steve Goodman was kinda like co-painting with Picasso." [46]

The co-writers who may have received the most undiluted dose of Steve's persona in 1984 were Jimmy Ibbotson and Jeff Hanna of the Nitty Gritty Dirt Band. The two were eager for a two-day session that Chuck Morris had arranged for them with Steve, for whom "Let's make up a song" was a consistent expression. "I loved that," Hanna says. "It was a great way of defusing the importance of writing a song."

The work began after the visitors' plane arrived at L.A. airport and Ibbotson picked up a phone. "I put on my radio deejay voice and was pretty excited about seeing him and said, 'We're up in *Holly*wood!' That sort of stuck with him." It was the seed of their first jointly written song, the tale of a tender, young woman who arrives in the film capital to start a career but turns on her heels after finding she will succeed only if she sheds her clothes. In an outcome both vivid and symbolic, the woman (and the song title) became the "Face on the Cutting Room Floor." The three also came up with a lightweight character study of a not-so-innocent female, a motorcyclist they enshrined as the "Queen of the Road." But more striking than the songs themselves was Steve's stern resolve to get them done.

As they sat around coffee cups, cassette tapes, legal pads and a tape recorder on a long kitchen table and looked out a back window to the alley, the trio engaged in what Hanna termed "call-and-response" writing. One threw out a thought or a line, and the other two critiqued it. Steve's bursts were rapid-fire. "His ideas grew like Chia Pets," Hanna says, citing the novelty planters hawked on TV. Throughout, Steve strummed a Flatiron mandola and became a firm arbiter. Sometimes when Hanna or Ibbotson insisted on a line, Steve simply said, "No." Soon, Ibbotson was ready for a respite.

Writing with Steve Goodman was kinda like co-painting with Picasso.
MARTY STUART

46: John Hartford, invited by Stuart to play on the session, saw a side of Steve he had never witnessed. "Something about his guitar or the microphone didn't please him, and he got so goddamned mad, I thought he was going to fall off the stool," Hartford recalled in 2000. "He just totally, totally lost it. On the way home, I thought, 'That might be where some of the cancer came from.' I very consciously worked on not being that kind of guy because I had a terrible case of anger, a man at war with himself." Hartford died June 4, 2001, at age 63, after fighting non-Hodgkin's lymphoma for 15-plus years.

"OK, Stevie, great, we got a couple words," Ibbotson said. "Let's get high."

"Whatever you have to do, but I'm busy," Steve said. "We're writin' here, Ibby! Focus! Settle down!"

Frustration set in, and Steve looked ever more weary.

"Listen, man," Ibbotson said. "There's an ocean right down the block. I gotta take a break. I gotta walk down the road."

"OK," Steve said, "but hurry back because I really think we've really got this thing."

Ibbotson got up, then stopped in his tracks. "Let's go walk along the beach and write," he said.

"No, we're here," Steve said. "We've got our stuff. Now, c'mon. This is what happens now (in the song). What happens again? What about this?"

They went back to work, but Ibbotson eventually returned to angling for a break. That's when Steve invoked his disease.

"Look," Steve said, "I know it's gonna get me. I don't have the luxury you guys do to go off and smoke a doobie and rent a surfboard. We're only here for a couple days. Let's make the most of it."

His admonition stilled the air.

"Y'know, guys, this might be the last song I ever write," Steve added. "Let's make sure we get it finished. Let's make sure we get it demo'ed. Let's make sure we like it. Let's make sure we're ready tomorrow to start something else. This may be our last day on Earth."

Finally, after more work, Steve eased the tension by turning to a sport he had taken up fiercely.

"All right," he said, "you guys want to take a break. We'll go to the health club. I'm playin' racquetball these days."

"Well," Ibbotson said with hesitation, "we really don't play too much."

"Don't worry," Steve said. "I'll stand the both of you, two against one."

To Ibbotson, the proposition sounded bizarre. "I figured, OK, two healthy guys against this guy who's pretty close to death's door," he says. "He cleaned our clocks. He showed great energy. He shut us out. He knew all the angles. He played us for fools."

In racquetball, however, lay a tangible clue to Steve's urgency. His prowess notwithstanding, while on the courts Steve was starting to notice numbness in his right foot, just as he had before his July 1982 relapse. He also experienced fevers and mouth sores. He reported this to his doctors, but relapse was not the prognosis. Instead, after evaluating a low white blood-cell count and pulling another painful bone-marrow sample from his pelvis, Steve's oncologists had a forecast that was far worse. A new, surprising and more devastating type of leukemia had taken root — myelodysplasia. ♪

Steve's songwriting sessions in Seal Beach with Nitty Gritty Dirt Band members Jimmy Ibbotson (top) and Jeff Hanna revealed Steve's intense desire to make use of every moment.

(Photos courtesy of Chuck Morris)

Supported by a board that would have been airbrushed out later, Steve strikes a playful pose for a potential cover image for his "Santa Ana Winds" LP in spring 1984. To reinforce the desert theme of the album's title song, photographer Jim Shea drove Steve 70 miles northeast of Seal Beach to El Mirage Lake Bed, whose dry, cracked, mosaic of clay seemed endless. Also packing powerful symbolism, however, was the sunset.

(Photo by Jim Shea)

'You just don't understand — I've gotta do this'

The 15 years of radiation, chemotherapy and maintenance drugs that had kept Steve Goodman alive had taken a heavy toll. Much of his bone marrow had been beaten up and burned out, had turned to scar tissue and could no longer efficiently churn out normal cells.

"That occurs sometimes when these diseases transform, either from the disease or from the drugs," says one of Steve's Sloan-Kettering oncologists, Dr. Monroe Dowling. "It's a dire consequence of the disease because somehow or other, you've got to figure out how to get the bone marrow to start functioning again, and you have to get it to start functioning in such a fashion so that it's not going to function abnormally. You want it to function normally. Well, that's easier said than done."

The preferred treatment for myelodysplasia was what might be called super-chemotherapy — a transplant of Steve's bone marrow. Soon, Steve's destination would be Seattle and the nine-year-old Fred Hutchinson Cancer Research Center, the world's leader in transplantation and whose director of medical oncology, Dr. E. Donnall Thomas, would receive a Nobel Prize six years later for his (and his wife Dottie's) life's work in originating the procedure. In the time prior to the transplant, Steve would receive regular transfusions of his blood.

Steve's chances of surviving a transplant were slim. Some said they were 15 percent, some said much lower. "We all knew that it was very, very, very, very high risk, and so did Steve," says another of Steve's Sloan-Kettering oncologists, Dr. Isabel (Bonnie) Cunningham. "Steve always knew he was dying because he was a guy with a death sentence that keeps getting postponed. He never thought he didn't have a fatal disease. He used to say that he didn't mind dying because he thought he'd lived a whole lifetime in the years he'd been given. He had all these children, he had his wife, he traveled around the world, and he thought that each year was just putting it off a little longer."

What he couldn't put off was bolstering his songwriting legacy — and a prime opportunity came via his favorite sport. The general manager of the Chicago Cubs, Dallas Green, was determined to bring wins and a winning spirit to Wrigley Field. Meanwhile, Dan Fabian, program director for WGN, which broadcast the team's games, was desperate to replace the team's stale Mitch Miller

> You've got to figure out how to get the bone marrow to start functioning again. ... Well, that's easier said than done.
> **DR. MONROE DOWLING**

> OLD MAN ^WINTER ~~HAS~~ GONE AWAY
> ~~[crossed out]~~
> AND THE CUBS ARE PLAYING BALL TODAY
> HEY CHICAGO WHAT DO YOU SAY —
> THE CUBS ARE GOING ALL THE WAY

Dan Fabian, program director for WGN radio, devised a way for Steve to be allowed to perform at Wrigley Field — by commissioning Steve to write a new Cubs theme song. Above right, in Steve's hand, is a verse for "Go, Cubs, Go" that he drafted and then rejected, scribbled on cardboard.

(Photo courtesy of WGN Radio 720, cardboard courtesy of Maple Byrne)

theme song, "It's a Beautiful Day for a Ball Game." Fabian, an "unrepentant folkie," was dismayed by Green's ire for Steve's "A Dying Cub Fan's Last Request" but also hopeful that Steve could be the solution to his dilemma. When Steve was in Chicago and appeared on WGN's "Roy Leonard Show," Fabian pulled him aside during a break and popped the question: Would he like to write the Cubs' new theme song?

"Yeah, I'd love to do it," Steve said. When the radio show was over, Steve "literally bounced" into Fabian's office. "It's gonna be an anthem," he said. A week later, Steve called Fabian from Seal Beach and said, "I've got something I think you'll like." In early March, while the Cubs were on their way to compiling a miserable spring-training record of 7-20, Steve was back in Chicago leading a session of stalwarts to record the song — a rocker with a Bo Diddley beat and an infectious refrain (and title) tailored for raucous fans, "Go, Cubs, Go."

With optimism at odds with his own health outlook, Steve poured into the tune a litany of upbeat phrases — "You better get ready for a brand new day," "This is the year, and the Cubs are real" — that delighted the management of the team and WGN. The song, in whole and in snippets for commercials, was aired on the Cubs' opening-day broadcast and for every game thereafter. "That had some juice to it," says Dallas Green. "The moment you heard it, it was electrifying," says Chuck Swirsky, WGN's sports director. Part of the song's appeal lay in aural immediacy, as produced in Studio A at Chicago Recording Co. by Hank Neuberger, veteran of three of Steve's Asylum LPs. A roaring lead-guitar line by Johnny Burns (Jethro's son) kicked off "Go, Cubs, Go," followed by the keyboards of Pat Leonard (future musical director for the Jackson brothers and producer of Madonna, Pink Floyd and Jewel), a backup choir of Steve's friends and Steve's own strong, engaging vocal. This was not the drone of a loser or victim of any kind.

Yet for all its exuberance, the song was merely the alter ego of "Dying Cub Fan," which in its fatalism was as devoted and affectionate as "Go, Cubs, Go" was in its blind faith. Those who could hear both tunes in their mind found the pairing delicious. "Steve really understood what the fiber of being a Cub fan was all about," says Cubs executive John McDonough, who became the team's director of sales and marketing in 1983. "Instead of being overwrought with pain, he seemed to say, 'I'm gonna put a lighter spin on this because I'm going through what millions are going through. They're gonna win eventually, but let's have some fun with it in the meantime.' He might have been the first guy to kind of tell everybody, 'Look, it's OK that you can laugh at this a little bit, and it's gonna get better.' It was almost like he was the therapist."

While in town that month, Steve provided welcome therapy for his long-time musical friends, the Holstein brothers. Three years prior, Ed, Fred and Alan Holstein had opened their own music club one door south of the fading Somebody Else's Troubles and christened it Holsteins. More spacious than Troubles or the Earl of Old Town, Holsteins quickly became the premier folk venue on Chicago's North Side. On Friday, March 2, 1984, Mike Cross began a two-night run at the club, but by the end of his first night, Cross had lost his voice and was "croaking." The next day he reported this to Ed Holstein, who said, "Steve Goodman is in town to do the Cubs commercial. Maybe we can get him to fill in."

A "croaking" Mike Cross, shown in 1982, had to bow out of a March 3, 1984, show at Holsteins in Chicago. Steve, who happened to be in town, became the surprise fill-in.
(Photo by Art Thieme)

Holstein tracked down Steve at the home of backup singer, LP production coordinator and former Earl of Old Town waitress Mary Gaffney, where Steve was a guest for dinner. "Well," Steve said to Holstein, "don't tell Al (Bunetta) about this, but I'll do it." Relieved, Cross flew home to North Carolina, and Holstein put a hand-lettered sign in the front window: "Tonight: Steve Goodman." Typical of the response was cab driver and filmmaker Loretta Smith, who in years past had given Steve many rides home to Evanston. Walking by Holsteins in the early evening and spotting the notice, she instantly understood that it would be a rare chance to see Steve play in a small venue. She bolted inside and got on the pay phone to spread the word.

That night, the club was jammed with Chicago compatriots. But the Steve they saw was not the Steve they had known. "He looked rough," says Larry Rand. "He was sunken, a little emaciated and lined up funny in his spine." [1] Rand was prepared for an intense show because of a conversation the two had beforehand. "At first, it seemed, 'Steve's being unusually friendly,' but then, just the way he was relating to me, it was like, 'Let's make this quality time,' and there was no doubt why we were making it quality time." Onstage, Steve brightened, and in two shows he unveiled new tunes such as "Face on the Cutting Room Floor" and solicited requests for old ones — referring to people in the audience by name, Rand says, as if sending personal farewells. "It wasn't like 'What would you like to hear?' It was 'Larry, what do you want to hear? Joe, what do you want to hear?' This was direct-connection stuff."

While Steve's voice was clear, his guitar playing was "there one minute and gone the next," Rand says. "Because it was there some of the time, I don't think the nonmusician audience understood how much of it wasn't there." But technical proficiency didn't matter, Rand says, because of the emotions that hung in the room. "The fact that he survived the set was extraordinary, he was so frail," Rand says. "He was literally saying goodbye to many of us whom he had known for years. It was beyond any and all criticism, and the vision of him on that stage playing through the pain and dread still haunts me."

The poignancy didn't end with the shows. At 2:30 a.m., well after Holsteins

1: Al Bunetta reflects upon Steve's sickly appearance in his final months: "I'm so happy that Stevie was here pre-AIDS because the way he looked sometimes, he didn't need that."

had closed, Steve asked Loretta Smith to drive him and Mary Gaffney to his Grandma Mary's home on West Bittersweet Place, where he was staying. Steve was so weak that Smith and Gaffney had to help him up to the fifth-floor apartment. Hearing his key in the lock, Grandma Mary came to the door in her nightgown, and the foursome stayed up talking the rest of the night. Steve pulled out a 5x7-inch photo his brother David had taken of Grandma Mary, his mother, Minnette, his wife, Nancy, and his three daughters. He held up the photo and pointed to the image of Nancy.

"This woman's a crapshooter," he said over and over. "The doctors told her never to try to have a baby, and she went ahead and did it. People told her not to marry me, and she went ahead and did it."

Smith and Gaffney left at dawn. Before stretching out to sleep on his grandmother's couch, Steve stayed up awhile longer with her. In reference to the just-departed females, he said, "I'm leaving these two young women to you. These are your adopted granddaughters. I want you to stay in touch with them after I'm gone, and I want you to embrace them as surrogate grandchildren."

It was an indirect way for Steve to assure his grandmother of later companionship from his generation. Step by step, he was preparing for the inevitable.

The preparation continued in Atlanta on March 21 at the 400-seat Moonshadow Saloon. [2] Opener Tim Bays had brought along an unfinished song, and before their show he asked Steve in the dressing room to help him finish it. "We feverishly knocked out a last verse just as I rushed out to do my set," Bays says. Steve watched as Bays sang the brand-new tune as his closer. Walking offstage, Bays told Steve, "Man, I just had to try it!"

"Figured you would," Steve replied. "That's how it is with new songs."

Bays thanked Steve for the help and said he would register the composition as a co-write.

"No thanks," Steve said. "You can mention me if you want, but the song is all yours."

By staying an extra day in Atlanta, Steve gently let go of a friend and performing peer. Phoebe Snow, who had not seen her "Sometimes Love Forgets" duet partner for more than a year, caught a glimpse of Steve backstage while finishing her first set. "He looked very dissipated, he was extremely thin and very tired-looking, and his hair, the pattern didn't look like a traditional male baldness, and I thought, 'Right, right, Sloan-Kettering. Oh, shit.' " During the intermission, Snow asked him to join her onstage for a pair of songs during her second show. The two settled on a "Rockin' Robin" duet, but Steve also soloed on "My Old Man," at Snow's request. "It was so beautiful," she says. "I was thinking I wasn't going to be able to finish my show, I was so overcome."

As Steve exited to applause and Snow returned to the stage, she told him, "Don't leave. Just don't leave. I want to talk to you after. I want to know what's going on."

"Well," Steve said softly, "I'll try."

Her intent, she says, was to reciprocate for the many times that he had lis-

---

This woman's a crapshooter. The doctors told her never to try to have a baby, and she went ahead and did it. People told her not to marry me, and she went ahead and did it.
STEVE GOODMAN

2: The impression Steve left publicly about his disease was optimistic to the point of inaccuracy. "The prognosis is OK. I seem to be in pretty good shape," he told Russ Devault of the *Atlanta Journal/Constitution* prior to his Moonshadow show. For the aptly headlined article ("He's upbeat, not beat"), Steve devised a charming way to put into context his 15-year, post-diagnosis survival and his lack of a musical hit. "Everybody's always coming up and asking me when my big break is going to get here," he said. "Well, it did already. I've had my big break, and I'm enjoying it."

tened to her vent about the strain of coping with her daughter and mother. "I was so excited when the show was over because I thought, 'I am going to be there for him like he was there for me, and we're going to have the most meaningful conversation we've ever had,' so I got all pumped up."

But as Snow came backstage, her road manager handed her a paper plate. On it, Steve had scribbled a pep talk: "Dear Phoebe, I really tried to stay, but I got a little tired. You were incredible tonight. I've never heard you singing so beautifully. Keep up the good work. I'll talk to you soon."

The note was reassuring, but it became their last contact. For Steve and others close to him, it was to be a season of "lasts":

◆ A last show March 31 at the University of Michigan in Ann Arbor, where in the dressing room Steve roared with laughter at opener O.J. Anderson's just-written parody of "Michael, Row the Boat Ashore," "If I Had a Hammer" and other campfire standards. The ditty, called "Folk Rap," later would become a staple for the Limeliters. "He was falling off his chair," Anderson says. "He was rolling around and turning red. He said, 'That's the greatest thing I've ever heard.' It was the best response he could have given me. He had such integrity and dignity." After his show in 700-seat Lydia Mendelssohn Theatre, however, Steve was so tired that he couldn't walk. David Siglin, manager of The Ark, and road manager Maple Byrne used a fireman's carry to lift Steve upstairs to sign autographs for fans.

◆ A last visit to Alaska, a six-day, seven-show tour with John Prine in early April during which Steve got some unexpected airplay on KRKN-FM in Anchorage that recalled the bleeping he'd experienced 11 years earlier in Chicago with "Lincoln Park Pirates." When Steve's car pulled up to the station for an interview, host J.D. Chandler had just finished airing "Vegematic," a risky choice given a phrase in the culminating verse: "And all that shit was here." Chandler edited it by whispering "shhh" over the offending word, and Steve walked into the studio with a grin. "He just loved it," Chandler says. During the live interview, Steve improvised a song about KRKN and Anchorage and, to Chandler's relief, discussed his leukemia. "He was surprisingly upbeat about it," Chandler says. "I felt uncomfortable bringing it up, but he made me feel a whole lot better about it. He had that way about him, very accessible and full of joy even in the face of death. I got the feeling that it wasn't real, that it couldn't happen to him."

◆ A last tribute to mentor Jethro Burns, whom Minneapolis-based KTCA-TV had decided to enshrine in a one-hour special. It was sparked by a documentary the station had aired in January, focusing on the 1983 Winnipeg Folk Festival and called "Festival of Friends." In it were included stage and interview clips of Steve and Burns. [3] "There was such cool camaraderie between the two of them," says producer Kathryn Riley. "You just knew there was a story there." KTCA filmed the bulk of the Burns special on April 11 by taping a studio concert in which Burns performed with his own band and three guests: his son Johnny, guitar legend (and brother-in-law) Chet Atkins and Steve. In addition

> I was so excited when the show was over because I thought, 'I am going to be there for him like he was there for me, and we're going to have the most meaningful conversation we've ever had.'
> **PHOEBE SNOW**

3: In the "Festival of Friends" documentary, Steve and Burns were shown playing "Is It True What They Say About Dixie?" It also included nearly a minute of Artis the Spoonman's spellbinding contribution to Steve's "Mama Don't Allow It."

The obvious rapport between Steve and Jethro Burns at the 1983 Winnipeg Folk Festival (above) gave Minneapolis-based KTCA-TV the inspiration to produce a one-hour special in April 1984. The show's title was "Jethro & Friends."

(Photos by Juel Ulven)

to an all-comers jam on "Sweet Georgia Brown" at the end of the show, time limits allowed Steve and Burns to pair up unaccompanied on only two songs — indelible but polar opposites.

One was a wry blues that Steve had started writing 12 days earlier while flying from Texas to Arizona after a two-day, four-show stint at Soap Creek Saloon in Austin. "Somebody at the bar was trying to drag Stevie off to Willie Nelson's hot tub," says road manager Maple Byrne. "He was convinced that it was gonna get around that he'd ended up in Willie's hot tub, so he demurred on that." The next morning, after only three hours of sleep and while the two walked the aisle inside their plane, Byrne asked Steve, "Well, how's the hot-tub refugee feeling this morning?" It was a potent question. "Of course," Byrne says, "those brown eyes lit up, and the legal pad came out, and that was a fruitful flight, even in our sleep-deprived condition." In the dressing room at the Burns taping in Minneapolis five minutes before the show, Steve finished the song, which was a send-up of Hollywood decadence. It was so new that Steve taped the handwritten lyrics onto the monitor speaker in front of him for reference. "Hot Tub Refugee" sent the audience into howls at the end of every pun-drenched line.

Steve's other selection, an equally inspired choice (about "two people who are older than you," Steve told Burns on camera), was "The Dutchman." The poignancy of the 64-year-old mandolinist accompanying the gaunt, 35-year-old singer/songwriter on Michael Smith's ode to mortality and devotion was unmistakable. With a solemn face and closed eyes, Burns picked as if in a trance, while Steve sang with a smile as brilliant as the glow of his Ommaya-reservoir bump in the studio lights.

The most moving portion of the program, titled "Jethro & Friends," was offstage, however. It was a 15-minute prelude, for which the musicians had assembled two nights earlier in the basement unit of a duplex rented by KTCA staffer Marian Moore. There the troupe gathered on a couch and chairs around a television for a surprise — 1950s and 1960s kinescope footage of Homer & Jethro appearances in Kellogg's Corn Flakes commercials and on TV variety shows hosted by Tennessee Ernie Ford and Dean Martin. Burns had not seen the clips since their original air dates, and as he watched them, over his face crept a wistful mist. By focusing on reflections of Burns from the TV screen, cameraman Peter Brownscombe superbly captured the largely suppressed emotions of the mandolinist's 39-year partnership with Henry "Homer" Haynes.

But a different, present-tense partnership also played out on the couch. Flanking Burns with equal intimacy were his son Johnny on his left and Steve on his right. For Marian Moore, whose job was to interview the troupe for voiceover comments about Burns, the affection was too strong to ignore. In a separate interview with Johnny, she asked, "How do you feel seeing your father relating like he does with Steve?" Unwittingly, Moore touched a nerve, for as a child Johnny had felt abandoned by his father's constant Homer & Jethro touring. Johnny shot back, "How would you feel if your father found somebody else to sort of fill your footsteps?" Hearing his retort, Moore, whose own father, an Episcopalian bishop, was often away from home in her youth, started crying.

The exchange didn't make it into the finished program, but it reflected the bond forged by Steve and Burns. It was a connection that, on balance, Johnny Burns did not resent.

"My dad's celebrity was at the cost of some of his family, and growing up relatively alone, I got used to it," Johnny says. "But when I saw my dad's (fatherly) feelings come out with somebody else, I was glad because Steve needed a dad, he was a friend of mine, and there's nothing that you'd like better than to have your parents like your friends. But with Steve, it was a little bit of a twinge for me. I was so worried about my dad, seeing him go down into the abyss after Homer died, and then to see Steve, who I was working with, pull him out. It was like, 'Wow, this is OK. This is a good thing.' The trade-off was almost worth it. Part of me would rather have had my dad, but Steve's a pretty good guy to trust with your old man. It could have been a lot worse. There was a purity to the whole thing. Everybody liked everybody else so much." [4]

Part of Johnny Burns' twinge was the knowledge of Steve's pending demise. But pressing on between transfusions, which could not continue indefinitely because of the high risk of lethal infection, Steve still had work to do. From mid-April to late May, he took on only a pair of close-to-home gigs — a benefit for ailing Scottish folksinger Dick Gaughan at McCabe's Guitar Shop in Santa Monica, and a final guest slot with Johnny Cash at the Anaheim Convention Center — so that he could focus on recording one more self-produced LP.

When Steve approached Gary Brandt to use his Hollywood studio for the album, Brandt was flush with other projects.

"I don't know how I'm gonna have time, Steve, with all this stuff I'm doing here," Brandt said.

"You just don't understand, you don't get it," Steve repeatedly pleaded. "I've gotta do this."

Brandt says he finally "got it." He made the time for the project and was glad he did. "Steve was singing incredibly well, better than on any of his other albums," Brandt says. "It was almost like, 'This is it. This is gonna be my best work.' Man, he was just perfect."

Steve's collaborations and own writing had given him a collection of songs to preserve on vinyl, and to pull off the project he called on a mix of lesser-known musical friends (such as virtuoso Jim Rothermel on saxes, recorders and harmonicas) and celebrities. Emmylou Harris stopped in ("tripped all over herself to do it," says her guitarist Steve Fishell) to harmonize and provide a spoken part on "Fourteen Days," Steve's story of an embittered romance resulting in suicide in Seattle — a nod to the life-or-death procedure that he soon would face 1,100 miles north. [5] Kris Kristofferson also visited the studio to try a lead vocal on "Face on the Cutting Room Floor," a cut for which Steve ended up singing lead, and to supply a guttural "putt-putt" chant for the motorcycle ditty "Queen of the Road." With arch sarcasm, Kristofferson intoned at the end of

The trade-off was almost worth it. Part of me would rather have had my dad, but Steve's a pretty good guy to trust with your old man.
JOHNNY BURNS

4: Johnny's younger sister, Terry King, says that while Johnny at times performed and recorded with their famous dad, he created his own separation, largely because his rock focus clashed with the jazz roots of their father. "Dad adored John and was very proud of him," King says, "but John kept Dad at a distance."

5: Maine East High friend Willie Riser recalls a phone call with Steve, who was in Seattle for a blood transfusion — possibly during a layover between the Alaska tour and the "Jethro & Friends" taping in Minneapolis. "Y'know, Seattle's a really cool town, enlightened, beautiful," Steve said with a laugh. "This wouldn't be a bad place to die."

the track, "That's art." Steve retained the utterance in the finished product. [6]

Such breeziness pervaded the sessions. "It was magic," says Chuck Fiore, longtime bassist for Billy Vera and the Beaters. "On a normal record date, you spend three hours on one song, but with Steve's stuff, it just came out all at once: 'Yeah, this is it. That's a keeper. Yeah, first take. Let's go onto the next song. Really? Yeah. That's great. OK, final? That's OK with me.' It was the best record I ever played on."

"Completely lighthearted" is how Fishell recalls the collective mood. "There was no pessimism about Stevie's situation," he says. "We were aware of it, but we kind of shut it out. We knew he was very sick, but we didn't know that it was as bad as it was, so there wasn't this feeling of like, 'Oh, this is it.' It was more like, 'Wow, Stevie's really sick, but he really wants to make a record, and that's incredible that he's got the energy to do it, so let's get in there and do what we can.' "

"Sometimes it was difficult," says Kevin Wells, British drummer who played on many of the cuts. "He was having a hard time with his health, but you never knew it because he'd give you that little frowning, half-sneaky smile and was just way into the music. The health was secondary."

The title of the LP, "Santa Ana Winds," came from one of its songs, a jazzy bouncer that Steve had started writing March 3 in Chicago with Mary Gaffney and singer/songwriter Mike Jordan and had finished on his front porch in Seal Beach. At the tune's base was a failed romance and the desire to "let my feelings go" and "feel that jet stream flow" from the notoriously toasty gusts that blew west from the Santa Ana desert into the Los Angeles basin. [7] WGN host Roy Leonard later hailed the track as the ultimate "early-morning wakeup song." In an extended version that didn't make the LP, Fiore says Steve imitated an unctuous emcee, "as if he were in a Knights of Columbus dance that he was introducing. It was the funniest thing, and we were all laughing in the background."

Closing the LP, however, was the tune whose advice Steve knew could truly wrap up his life, "You Better Get It While You Can." Its lesson ("If you wait too long, it'll all be gone") also had universal relevance. Likewise, the song's presentation — just Steve's voice and guitar, backed by a gentle Jethro Burns mandolin and recorded at the WFMT studio in Chicago — stood out with singular intimacy. In ways both literal and metaphoric, it felt like Steve was coming full circle.

Underscoring the project's urgency was the impression created by the LP cover, photographed by Jim Shea. He absorbed the desert theme of the title song and drove Steve 70 miles northeast of Seal Beach to El Mirage Lake Bed, whose dry, cracked, clay mosaic seemed to stretch forever. With a purple sunset glowing behind him, Steve propped a guitar against the ground, stood and, sans sunglasses, stared almost beatifically, not at the camera but into the distance. The wide, low angle of Shea's lens gave Steve a vertical stature far beyond his frame, so that no one viewing the image would imagine he was 5-foot-2.

"I never thought of him as short," Shea says. "He was bigger than life, as tall

---

He was having a hard time with his health, but you never knew it because he'd give you that little frowning, half-sneaky smile and was just way into the music.
KEVIN WELLS

6: In these sessions, Steve also re-recorded "The One That Got Away," singing both the male and female parts, perhaps in an attempt to resurrect the song given its burial by Asylum in the wake of duet partner Nicolette Larson's solo success in 1978-79.

7: Steve joined more than 15 musicians who have enshrined the hot gusts lyrically. Others included the the Doors ("L.A. Woman," 1971), Debby Boone ("California," 1978), Beach Boys ("Santa Ana Winds," 1980) and Randy Newman ("I Love L.A.," 1983). The songs drew renewed attention during the devastating, wind-driven Southern California fires of October 2007.

as a lumberjack. But it was that John Wayne-John Ford kind of low angle to make him look bigger."

Shea also used a low shutter speed, which created a ghostly blur along the edge of Steve's clothes and hair. Shea says that while he didn't intend it in the moment, the overall result became "an obscure reference to his passing."

One of Steve's oncologists went further upon seeing the image. "It sent shivers down my spine," says Dr. Lee Schwartzberg, "It was eerie. This was a cover of a guy who's looking beyond."

While this album image would not convey jest, Steve couldn't escape a giddy absurdity in its creation. The day that he was to pose for the LP cover, Steve had just bought, paid for and driven off a car lot a new, $14,000 white Toyota minivan. On his way to Shea's studio, he drove by Nudie's Rodeo Tailors, the renowned North Hollywood outlet for rhinestone cowboy suits. In one window of the expansive Western storefront, Steve spotted a tan, country-style shirt curiously adorned on the breast with a pair of double-ended arrows. He pulled over the minivan, left the keys in the ignition, walked inside and bought the shirt that he ended up wearing in the desert photo.

During the few minutes he was gone, however, someone made off with the minivan. When Steve reported the theft to police, he was bereft of information. "It doesn't have a license plate yet," he said. "It doesn't have insurance yet." Police told him, "You're talkin' about a car that doesn't exist." He had to accept the loss as permanent, and soon it became a huge joke. Walking into Shea's studio and wearing his Nudie's purchase, Steve dryly greeted the photographer by saying, "This is my $14,000 shirt."

The loss was far more than financial, for lying on the front seat of the minivan had been a khaki travel bag that Steve had slung over his shoulder and carried with him everywhere. Inside were lyric notebooks, medications, photos, a Walkman, an address book — and the written drafts for a trio of children's stories that had grown out of characters and narratives he had improvised with his daughters at bedtime.

The set of tales was a project that Nancy was encouraging Steve to finish. Having admired a "Cockroaches on Parade" booklet drawn by Harry Waller, Steve enlisted the Chicago songwriter and painter to create illustrations for his kids' stories. But in his flash of automotive inattention, the groundwork for this creative legacy vanished.

The names and personalities of the characters live on in the memories of Waller and Jessie Goodman, who had jotted down pieces of the stories herself. Short Sharon was 6 inches tall, a version of Thumbelina who used magic shoes to climb down drainpipes and solve crimes at night, including a case of missing jewels that were stolen by the Lincoln Park Pirates and hidden on Tom the Tugboat. Rita Leggs, "with two 'g's' because her legs were so long," wore pigtails and glasses and swam on a swim team. Polly the Plant could make water and heal people. Movie the Cat was a silver tabby with jade-green eyes that made films. The name of the final character, who wore a red jogging suit, was inspired

The "Santa Ana Winds" album cover (alternate image above) "sent shivers down my spine," says Dr. Lee Schwartzberg, one of Steve's oncologists. "It was eerie. This was a cover of a guy who's looking beyond."

(Photo by Jim Shea)

Harry Waller's renderings of characters dreamed up by Steve and his three daughters included (from left) Movie the Cat, Short Sharon, Tom the Tugboat and others whose names remain lost to bygone memories. The plan that Steve had to write a children's storybook ended when his minivan and a khaki travel bag containing the draft stories were stolen from the parking lot of Nudie's Rodeo Tailors in North Hollywood.

(Illustrations by Harry Waller)

by Abbott & Costello's baseball-based "Who's on First?" routine, I Don't Know Jones. The imaginary dialogue was familiarly circular:

"What's your name?"

"I Don't Know Jones."

"I don't know Jones, either. What's your name?"

"No, it's I Don't Know Jones."

In late May, during a trip to Chicago (preceded by a masterful solo show at Kansas City's Parody Hall in which he unveiled a cautionary ballad about a Canadian homeless man, William Kemp), Steve re-conferred with Waller. Sketches prepared by Waller to salvage the children's stories project revved him up. "Yeah, I like these," Steve said. "Sunglasses, and make his chin go out. ... Yeah, this, man. Yeah, this, this is it. This is it. ... Yeah, the tugboats, man. Stick with those. We got those. Perfect, those. ... Don't worry about Short Sharon. I've got a whole plan figured out now. I'll write it down. I'll have it to you in a couple of weeks. ... I'm gonna be back."

Using his Grandma Mary's couch as a home base, Steve covered a lot of ground in his five-day homecoming trip to Chicago. He performed at the opera house in the northwest suburb of Woodstock, where he ran into Mark Nowakowski, who hadn't seen Steve in the 19 years since he helped run the Y Coffeehouse and college-bound Steve played there. When Nowakowski said, "Hello, Steve, I knew you way back when," Steve instantly shot back, "Whatever happened to the Y?" Nowakowski's jaw dropped at the instant recognition, and with a twinkle, Steve pointed his hand as if it were a pistol and pulled his index finger back like "Bang, gotcha!" The exchange reminded Nowakowski of a "Turnpike Tom" line: "I had just been had in a sanitary way by the outlaw with the fastest sense of humor."

Steve also played two shows at Park West, where he had debuted "Dying Cub Fan" three years earlier. There, he did a favor for NBC "Today" correspondent Mike Leonard, whose daughter was in kindergarten and was among several children Leonard was profiling as part of the future high-school class of 2000. As a complement for the piece, Leonard wanted to film Steve performing

"The Twentieth Century Is Almost Over." Steve obliged and played it while a cameraman recorded it mid-concert.

"Hey, Mike, was that OK?" Steve shouted afterward to Leonard, who was standing in the back of the packed theater.

"Yeah," Leonard answered.

"You want me to play it again?"

"No, that's fine."

"People were looking around and wondering what the hell was going on, because he didn't say anything about why he was singing the song," Leonard says, "but I thought it was generous of him to say that in the middle of a set."

Few wanted to believe that night that Steve himself was "almost over," but the evidence was clear to Harry Waller, who saw piles of oranges in Steve's dressing room and observed Steve reeling onstage. "It was a great show, but in the last 30 minutes he was dragging," Waller says. "He was having trouble talking and playing. It was the first time I saw him that he was winded. The last 20 minutes onstage, I was thinking, 'Oh, God, he's gonna drop over,' but he just kept on going. That's really when I realized he was on his way out."

Keeping Steve energized during the Chicago trip was the performance of his favorite baseball team. When he hit town, the Cubs were 23-15 on the season and atop the National League East — and his "Go, Cubs, Go" had become the ballpark and radio anthem he had envisioned. Steve celebrated May 24 with a pilgrimage to Wrigley Field. After a morning appearance on Roy Leonard's show at WGN radio, he joined Leonard for a doubleheader against the Atlanta Braves. While the Cubs executed a twin killing, Steve fielded a couple of key chances to promote his authorship of the theme song.

In the middle of the fifth inning of the first game, while groundskeepers smoothed the infield, the Cubs had Steve perform "Go, Cubs, Go" from the aisle behind home plate. Road manager Maple Byrne and Hank Neuberger, co-producer of Steve's "Go, Cubs, Go," who also accompanied Steve that day, say that even though Steve sang and played a guitar into a microphone, few among the 24,500 in attendance heard his performance. "Steve was announced by the PA announcer very perfunctorily," Neuberger says. "They had him stand where the Dixieland players stand, where no one even knew where he was. It was kind of a downer." Steve's second chance to pump "Go, Cubs, Go," this time for the TV audience watching from home, was sitting in for a half inning or so with Harry Caray as part of the play-by-play broadcast. [8]

The morning of Steve's departure, Harry Waller joined him and road manager Maple Byrne for a scrambled-eggs breakfast at Grandma Mary's at Bittersweet Place. There, Steve eagerly played Waller a tape of his in-progress LP. The track with the ominous reference to suicide in Seattle, "Fourteen Days," filled Steve's patter. "Y'gotta hear the song with Emmylou," he implored Waller. "Y'gotta hear it. Wait, wait, wait. Forget these. Hear this one. Hear this one. Y'gotta hear this one." In the inflated fervor of the moment, he added, "It's the greatest thing I've ever written."

They had him stand where the Dixieland players stand, where no one even knew where he was. It was kind of a downer.
HANK NEUBERGER

8: Apparently, no recordings or documents survive to verify Steve playing "Go, Cubs, Go" in the Wrigley Field stands or guesting on Harry Caray's broadcast. WGN and Cubs sources do not recall either instance, but they say that each was possible. Hank Neuberger insists that the in-the-stands performance took place, and Chicago folksinger Rich Ingle firmly recalls Steve's TV appearance with Caray, which also was referenced later in the year in the *Kansas City Star*.

Floating atop a baby-blue plastic air mattress in the swimming pool of Phoenix friend and promoter Danny Zelisko, Steve hilariously lip-synchs on June 2, 1984, to a rough-mix tape of his just-recorded dig at California culture, "Hot Tub Refugee," diving into the drink at the song's close.

(Video captures by Jay Roberts from home movie courtesy of Danny Zelisko)

Steve's brother David showed up to drive Steve to O'Hare, and Waller went along for the ride. Before they hopped in the car, David pulled out a Felix the Cat version of a Polaroid camera, snapped Steve and Waller, who stood shoulder to elbow, and gave Waller the photo. In it, Steve, wearing reflective sunglasses, a white cowboy hat and a shiny, black Johnny Cash tour jacket, gripped a yellow Penny Lane record-store bag. Waller held a rolled set of drawings. Their easy smiles belied — or fought off — their awareness that they were beginning what possibly was Steve's last hour in Chicago.

The route to the airport was mildly meandering because Steve asked David to cruise past several touchstones of his early life. As they circled Wrigley Field, Steve reminisced about gaining free admission to countless games thanks to his great uncle, newspaperman Harry Romanoff. Riding past his childhood home in Albany Park, Steve talked of playing softball outside his backyard at Eugene Field Park. By the time they reached O'Hare, all that was left were good-byes and "a little hug." Then Steve was off to L.A.

In Seal Beach, the McGaugh Elementary media teacher for Steve's three girls, Lois Cohn, had asked him to emcee and sing a song or two at the 30th-anniversary student video festival of the state's Media and Library Educators Association in June at USC. Steve warmly declined. "Oh, if only I could," he said, "but I'm much too ill to do that anymore."

Steve did perform in June, but his shows were few and full of emotion. When promoter Danny Zelisko threw a party on June 2 to celebrate 10 years in the business, Steve flew to Phoenix for the bash. Steve performed for 250 of Zelisko's associates at the Jockey Club, but a more unusual and private spectacle unfolded that afternoon in the swimming pool at Zelisko's home. There, in an echo of his 1971 appearance in London on "Country Meets Folk," Steve floated on a long, baby-blue plastic air mattress and, with a tape of his in-progress LP blaring from poolside speakers, lip-synched "Hot Tub Refugee" and three other tunes. Gesturing grandly during instrumental breaks, he played air piano and clarinet while Zelisko caught the antics on film.

After the dip and before heading to the evening party, Steve reached to pick an orange off a nearby tree and fell, fully clothed, into the pool. He and Zelisko drove off to buy fresh tennis shoes to replace his sopping green sneakers. "Here, you keep 'em," Steve told Zelisko with a self-mocking grin. "They'll be worth something someday."

Steve (lower left) joined an all-star folk show June 21, 1984, to benefit the shuttered Main Point north of Philadelphia. Posing in Roberts Hall of Haverford College were (clockwise from Steve) Tom Rush, David Buskin, emcee and co-producer Gene Shay, proprietor Jeanette Campbell, Bonnie Raitt, David Bromberg, Campbell's daughter, Susan Campbell (who, next to her mother's club, ran a pottery and music store called Beside the Point), and Robin Batteau.

(Photo by Molly Ross)

Three weeks later, Steve flew to Philadelphia to join an all-star folk lineup in a benefit to pay tax debts for the proprietress of the closed Main Point in Bryn Mawr — the club at which Steve had learned of his father's death seven years earlier. The June 21 show at nearby Haverford College also showcased Tom Rush, David Bromberg, Bonnie Raitt, and David Buskin & Robin Batteau and was emceed by Philly Folk Festival stalwart Gene Shay. But it was Steve who provided the capacity crowd at Marshall Auditorium with the simplest and most profound greeting: "Nice to be here. Nice to be anywhere." He also supplied a blunt explanation of why he couldn't miss the show: "Jeanette Campbell used to hire me every nine months or so, and you just can't let the IRS do this shit to blind widows, y'know, so we all got together here to beat those guys."

In a 35-minute set, Steve sang seven songs, told stories about the performers and saluted Paula Ballan and other friends in the audience. Especially stirring was his "Face on the Cutting Room Floor," which, like his "Dying Cub Fan," was ostensibly about a fictional character and not himself. But no one listening to his intro could miss the correlation: "This is a song about a young woman who goes to California to become a movie star. That's never happened to anybody you know, right? Two hundred times a day such events occur. The girl in this song escapes. Good news." The best "news," however, came at the show's end — at an all-comers jam on "Mama Don't Allow It" and "Jambalaya" that included Saul Broudy and rivaled the climaxes of Steve's New Year's Eve shows at the Earl of Old Town.

With unintended synchronicity, the performance that became Steve's last booked gig was the first-ever Bridgeton Folk Festival, held one hour south of Philly in southern New Jersey. Steve was the sole national act for the June 23 event, which inaugurated Bridgeton's new Sunset Lake Amphitheater.

The June 23, 1984, debut of the Bridgeton (N.J.) Folk Festival became Steve's last scheduled performance, and he typically regaled the Sunset Lake Amphitheater crowd with his cowboy-hat closer, "You Never Even Call Me by My Name." His encore (below) became the last "Mama Don't Allow It" he would perform. Steve called to the stage the previous band, Whilden's Wagon, including bassist Eric Waltman (left) and guitarist Fred Whilden.

(Photos © Sherrie Buzby/ The Bridgeton Evening News)

His Saturday in the town of 20,000 didn't lack for challenges. Eating lunch at Benjamin's Restaurant downtown, he had dietary limits, and he told festival founder Bob Rose that the 80-degree early summer heat was wearying. But he also displayed typical charm, posing for photos at the Rose family's bookstore and stopping in front of a jeweler's window to watch TV coverage of the Cubs' extra-innings bout with St. Louis at Wrigley Field. [9]

Before Steve's 6:45 p.m. show at the amphitheater, where Whilden's Wagon, a bluegrass/swing quartet, had just finished a set, Ernie Trionfo was disassembling his steel guitar to move it offstage when from behind came a sharp voice: "Where do you think you're goin' with that stuff?"

Trionfo turned to find himself staring at one of his musical heroes, a big-eyed, grinning Steve. "I'm just packing up my gear," Trionfo said.

"Nah, leave it up," Steve said. "I'm gonna call you guys up during my set."

Trionfo, who had seen three of Steve's shows, including a Steve Martin opener in Atlantic City, was dumbstruck. "My heart stopped," he said, and the other three — guitarist Fred Whilden, bassist Eric Waltman and fiddler Rob Ward — felt similarly flush. "We were like the proverbial kids in the candy store."

Though gaunt and pale, Steve opened his show with "Somebody Else's Troubles" and delivered a vibrant, "mesmerizing" set, Trionfo says, before bringing back the local quartet to accompany him for "You Never Even Call Me by My Name" and participate in his trademark encore of "Mama Don't Allow It." While it was — and still is — unusual for a headliner to invite locals to be part of the headliner's act, for Steve it had remained standard practice. "It showed us his incredible generosity of spirit," Trionfo says. But none of the four suspected they would be the last musicians ever to perform on a stage with Steve.

Capping the proceedings was a pre-Independence Day fireworks spectacle that Steve and nearly 1,000 attendees watched as it cascaded over Bridgeton's Piney Point and marked the sunset of Steve's performing career.

While in the East, Steve had a culminating conversation with his early benefactor, Earl Pionke, whom he had bid to New York for the occasion. "Earl, I don't have a chance," he told Pionke over dinner, adding that he was undergoing a transplant because of "how they kept me cheatin' the devil." Steve said he felt it important to tell Pionke to his face that Pionke couldn't remain the godfather of his daughters because of Steve's Jewish roots and Pionke's Catholic background (or what Pionke called his own "blithe spirit"). "This has to be official," Steve said. "Like I said, I'm not going to make this thing, and I want us to be straight." Pionke took the pronouncement in stride. "We made our peace with that," he says. "We celebrated two days and had a great time."

In the Big Apple, Steve also shrugged off a major-league thrill to honor a little-league friendship. He telephoned folksinger Perry Barber, who had nurtured an interest in baseball three years earlier by becoming a paid umpire.

"I have tickets to see Dwight Gooden pitch at Shea Stadium," Steve said, knowing that Barber and everyone else in New York was aware of the rookie phenomenon. "Wanna come?"

> **I'm not going to make this thing, and I want us to be straight.**
> **STEVE GOODMAN**

9: Ryne Sandberg's two game-tying homers off Bruce Sutter led to the Cubs' 12-11 win over the Cardinals and gave the star second-baseman a new nickname, "Kid Natural." On Steve's "Go, Cubs, Go" 45-rpm single that was released later that summer, a shouted "Kid Natural" is clearly audible in the fadeout.

The Babe Ruth-level umpiring of singing friend Perry Barber proved more compelling for Steve to witness in June 1984 than a game at Shea Stadium featuring New York Mets rookie phenom Dwight Gooden.

(Photo courtesy of Perry Barber)

10: In part, WGN took its inspiration from two 1969 45s featuring players' voices: "Pennant Fever" (a take-off on the Peggy Lee hit "Fever") sung by Billy Williams, Ron Santo, Don Kessinger, Randy Hundley, Nate Oliver, Gene Oliver and Willie Smith, and "Bleacher Bums" sung by Ernie Banks, Santo and Ferguson Jenkins. Lyrics of the latter song were based on announcer Jack Brickhouse's home-run call: "Hey-key, holy mackerel, no doubt about it, the Cubs are on their way!" Later in the 1984 season, Moreland, a country-music fan, and other Cubs recorded "Men in Blue," a single that sold 74,000 copies and raised $80,000 for spina-bifida research.

Barber's answer would have been yes, but she already had agreed to umpire a Babe Ruth-level game of 14-year-olds on a sandlot above the Great Kills garbage dump on Staten Island. So with regrets, she declined.

Steve's reply, given his condition, was both hearty and heartbreaking.

"Well, y'know what?" Steve said. "I can see Dwight Gooden pitch another time. I want to come and see your ballgame."

The two rode with Barber's umpiring partner to the game via the Staten Island ferry. Sitting on the sidelines, Steve was an attentive observer. More than once Barber heard his encouragement: "Good call, ump!"

Other performing opportunities soon beckoned, but Steve's health woes had taken center stage. The Los Angeles Dodgers asked him to do something he had pined for but never had done — sing the national anthem before a Cubs game. The chance came June 30, before a Saturday night Chicago-L.A. game at Dodger Stadium. But Steve, in treatment, had to cancel. The Toronto *Globe and Mail* had trumpeted that Steve would play the 1984 Mariposa Folk Festival in mid-July, but that booking also was called off. John McEuen of the Nitty Gritty Dirt Band gamely had advertised Steve as part of his fourth annual Rocky Mountain Opry on Aug. 25 in Denver but made sure to use the word "may."

Transfusions, other treatment and preparation for a transplant in Seattle filled Steve's July, but the month also swelled with musical encouragement.

In Chicago, the Cubs cruised to 18-10 for the month, sparking legitimate hopes for a World Series bid. Likewise, local ardor soared for Steve's "Go, Cubs, Go," which was played endlessly on WGN and at Wrigley Field. WGN was proceeding with a plan to bring to Hank Neuberger's studio five popular Cubs players — ace pinch-hitter Thad Bosley, goofball reserve outfielder Jay Johnstone, catcher Jody Davis, leftfielder Gary "Sarge" Matthews and Keith Moreland, the rightfielder infamously mentioned in Steve's "Dying Cub Fan" — to overdub backing vocals for the tune's catchy refrain. The idea was to press "Go, Cubs, Go" into thousands of 45-rpm singles that WGN could promote with a unique identifier: "Steve Goodman with the Chicago Cubs Chorus." Each copy would sell for $1.50, and proceeds would go to the station's Neediest Kids Fund. [10]

Unknown to Steve, his more fatalistic Cubs song was picking up notice in the team's clubhouse. New York public-access TV host and *Sport* magazine columnist Havelock Hewes was interviewing the power-hitting Moreland. Hewes was preparing a program forecasting "The Inevitable Collapse" of the Cubs and wanted to know Moreland's feelings about being singled out as someone who would "drop a routine fly."

The redheaded Moreland, a longtime fan of Steve's country-tinged material, told Hewes he was both "tickled" and honored. In fact, Steve had asked Moreland's permission before pressing into vinyl the version of the song that mentioned his name, and he had readily agreed.

"You know," Hewes told Moreland, "he actually is dying of leukemia."

Moreland blanched, nabbed a ball from a clubhouse staffer, signed it, got other Cubs to sign it and handed it to Hewes.

Recording backup vocals on "Go, Cubs, Go" at Chicago Recording Company in July 1984 are Cub players (from left) Thad Bosley, Jay Johnstone, Jody Davis, Gary Matthews and Keith Moreland.
(Photo by Renee Tondelli, courtesy of John Tondelli)

"You've got to get this ball to him," Moreland said. [11]

Raising his right palm, Hewes replied, "I swear I will."

Equally heartening as the Cubs were to Steve in July was the nationwide release of the 40th LP of Willie Nelson. Steve had known since the previous October that Nelson — by then, an icon of country and pop songwriting, albums, TV and the movies — had booked time at the well-known Nashville studio of Lincoln "Chips" Moman and recorded "City of New Orleans." [12] "That, to me, is about as good as you can do," a beaming Steve had said to NBC's Mike Leonard. But until the summer of 1984, Steve didn't know when or how the track would be released.

The result couldn't have been more spectacular. The grizzled and chiseled profile of the 51-year-old Nelson rose from a mountain landscape like a statue as he stared resolutely right-to-left, in a stunning illustration by Bill Imhoff. Anyone picking up the album couldn't miss Nelson's crimson bandana into which a white feather was tucked, all against an Indian red sky. To follow Nelson's eyes was to turn the album over, where the sky separated into pink and linen stripes that became an outstretched bird's wing. The horizon line merged into rail tracks, and a locomotive faded into view, roaring leftward as it became the stark-white head of an open-mouthed bald eagle, the entire enterprise barreling into a swath of stars on a blue background. The colors and symbols — the mountains, the train, the eagle, the elements of the American flag, the intensity — all merged into an arresting, evocative image that reflected the song title that Nelson had chosen as the LP's name, "City of New Orleans."

Inside, the music made even a stronger impression. "City" was the lead track, just 12 seconds shy of five minutes in length, its arrangement arousing a feeling of majesty. Nelson, who had first heard and been drawn to the song by the version recorded in 1973 by country star Sammi Smith, had a mental image of it

11: The .975 lifetime fielding percentage of Keith Moreland, who played first base, third base and catcher as well as outfield, did not merit ridicule. But Moreland was the right player for Steve to kid in the song, insists drummer Angelo Varias. "That was a knowledgeable wink," Varias says. "Lots of Cubs have dropped routine flies, but Moreland would be the perfect person to encapsulate that sense because he was a big, stocky guy and looked clumsy in almost everything he did."

12: Nelson had wakened Steve with a 3 a.m. phone call to impart the news about the recording, Steve later told singer/songwriter Jim Post. "Kid, I did it," Nelson said, "and I think it's the best thing I've ever done." There was no small irony in Nelson having placed an overnight call to someone who had made countless such calls to others, but Steve was irked. "What possesses people, what gets them so mixed up," Steve said, "that they don't know what time of day it is when they're calling?"

The artwork for and promotion of Willie Nelson's "City of New Orleans" LP fit the singer's view of the song. "It's one of those anthems," Nelson says. "Universal. ... It's a great patriotic song, to me, and it's a very Native American song."

(1984 Columbia Records billboard)

13: "It's the best outsider anthem anyone has ever written for America," says Darcie Sanders, co-founder of the Amazingrace Cooperative in Evanston. "For people coming of age in the 1960s and 1970s, that's how we all felt. We were the native sons and daughters, but maybe America didn't know us or recognize us. ... Who has not felt that their life is disappearing? It's the questioning, the trying to get closer, and yet the train is speeding away, the sense of the lost moment. That's how a whole generation felt about their relationship with America and themselves as Americans."

14: Steve observed his 36th in unexpected style. The past winter, he had invited countless people, including actor Robert Duvall, to what he thought would be a birthday bash. When the date arrived, however, Steve was weak and in bed. Duvall phoned Steve from the airport: "I've come out here for the birthday party. How do I get to Seal Beach?" Steve jumped out of bed, told Nancy to call friends, ran to a wine store and ordered out for food in time for Duvall's arrival.

distinct from other interpretations, particularly Arlo Guthrie's lament. Nelson did use Guthrie's slightly altered lyrics, which 30 other artists also had adopted, but he also imagined a more inspirational tempo and tone. "I heard a faster version, more of a happier song," Nelson says.

Just as with Charlie McCoy on Steve's original and "Toots" Thielemans on John Denver's remake, harmonica was a key element in Nelson's "City of New Orleans." But in the hands of Nelson's mouth harpist Mickey Raphael the instrument went further, becoming the song's pulse. Matching Raphael's syncopated throb, Nelson's smooth, nasal voice and stuttering lead guitar pulled the words and melody along the metaphorical track as if born to the task.

The producer, Moman, "crazy about trains," had revered Guthrie's 1972 hit version of the song and suggested it, reasoning that enough time had elapsed to record a new version. "The whole band, Willie and everybody, caught the spirit of the song," Moman says. "Another day, it might have been a ballad, but that particular day, everybody's spirit had a lot to do with the way it came out."

What Steve wanted "Go, Cubs, Go" to become for the Chicago Cubs, Nelson wanted "City of New Orleans" to become for an entire nation.

"It's an anthem," Nelson says with no equivocation. "It means probably something different to everybody who hears it, but it's one of those anthems. Universal. It doesn't matter what country we're in, they want to hear that. It's a great patriotic song, to me, and it's a very Native American song. It just feels that way: 'Don't you know me, I'm your native son?' And the greatest line in there, other than 'I'm your native son,' is 'Good morning, America, how are you?' It's a very positive statement." [13]

For Steve, eyeing a marrow transplant in Seattle as he marked his 36th birthday, [14] the timing of Nelson's LP was a gift. Columbia Records issued "City of New Orleans" as a single, and it began to climb the country charts. Ironically, however, Nelson says the juxtaposition of his recording of "City" and the severest test of Steve's health was entirely coincidental. "I didn't even know he was that sick," he says. "I didn't even think about it. I just was doing the song."

At Arlo Guthrie's home, the phone rang.

"Arlo, congratulations."

"What?"

"This is me, Steve Goodman."

It was the first time the two had talked in years.

"Steve," Guthrie said with a laugh, "how you doing?"

"Congratulations, we've got a hit."

"What do you mean, we got a hit?"

"Willie recorded our song."

"Willie?"

"Willie Nelson. He recorded 'City of New Orleans.' "

"What are you calling me for?" Guthrie asked. "It's your song."

"Yeah," said Steve, his wit intact, "he didn't record it my way, either."

Guthrie, weary of playing "City" night after night, occasionally had excised the song from his shows. ("Buy the record," he had joked to one fan shouting a request from a Penn State audience in about 1980.) But Guthrie found Steve's call funny and sweet. He suggested something they had never done before.

"Why don't we go on tour together?" Guthrie asked Steve. "Why don't we just do a whole tour?"

It would be the first time that both the writer and the initial popularizer of "City of New Orleans" would appear in a multi-show engagement.

"Y'know what? I've been thinkin' of that, too," Steve said. "I've just got to go into the hospital, and I've gotta do some stuff. I don't know if I'm gettin' out or not, but if I do, let's go on tour together."

They agreed to set agents to work lining up bookings. [15] "We really wanted to do it," Guthrie says. "I thought it would be so great. We would play together and do all that fun stuff." But even more important was the fact that Steve and Guthrie were talking at all. There had been no avoidance of each other. Their lives merely had resembled passing ships. "We renewed what little friendship we had," Guthrie says. "I felt as close to this guy as I do to any of my family members, having only met him a few times, and so it wasn't any big deal to let all of that time go by and have nothing get lost. It felt just like family."

For those in Steve's closest circle, however, the family feeling often forced a deeper honesty that didn't allow for long-range plans.

In early August, when Steve flew back to Los Angeles after what became his final treatment at Sloan-Kettering, Al Bunetta picked him up at the airport. Steve looked like "a skeleton," and Bunetta was glad he'd had the foresight in the 85-degree heat to bring him a bottle of cold seltzer water. They climbed into Bunetta's car. The news from New York had been certain. The transplant in Seattle was a go. The marrow donor was to be his brother, David, improving the chances for success over a transplant with an unrelated donor. But the outlook was still bleak. Steve was quiet for a moment, then spoke.

"Y'know, on the plane, I sat next to a little guy in a checkered suit," Steve said. "I didn't say a word to the guy the whole trip. I just didn't feel like talkin' to anybody. I think I was really angry. And when the plane touched ground, the man turned to me and said, 'Y'know, buddy, the problem with the world today

ARLO GUTHRIE
With
SHENANDOAH
Special Guest Star
STEVE GOODMAN
AUGUST 28

Arlo Guthrie's charm, wit, and talent have made him a popular entertainer the world over. Son of the lengendary Woody Guthrie, troubadour of the common man in the 30's and 40's, Arlo has been greatly influenced by his father's creative genius and has demonstrated, eloquently, his own gift for combing politics and song in the Guthrie tradition. Arlo's first album, released in 1967, zoomed him into stardom with the epic-ballad "Alice's Restuarant." It was the first popular anti-war song that combined both the political and humourous qualities that have become Arlo's trademark. In 1969 he starred in the major motion picture of that same name, directed by Arthur Penn for United Artists. Arlo Guthrie's best known tunes: "Mr. Customs Man" and "City of New Orleans" demonstrate his wholesome accoustical sound that has achieved popular acclaim for him. He has recorded fourteen albums for Warner Brothers, including a double album, Arlo Guthrie and Pete Seeger: Precious Friend. When not touring the United States or Europe he is a frequent guest on television talk shows. His home state has honored him by making Arlo's song "Massachusetts" the official folk song of that state.

STEVE GOODMAN
Steve Goodman's music reflects a medley of influences. He likes rock 'n' roll as a youngster, and picked up the guitar for the first time at the age of 13. Incorporating far-flung influences and merging them with a keenly perceptive wit, good-humor and fleet-

A page of the August 1984 program of the Westbury, New York, Music Fair indicates the contemplated, double-billed summer tour of Steve and Arlo Guthrie that never occurred.

15: Because it was to include David Bromberg as well, the series of bookings was to be called "Menage a Tour." Guthrie and Bromberg ended up touring with John Sebastian on the West Coast and Doc Watson in the East.

is people buy things they don't need that they can't afford to please people they don't even know.' He got up and walked off the plane, and I felt so bad that I didn't say anything to him."

The usually talkative Bunetta kept his eyes on the freeway. Steve spoke again.

"Y'know, my doctor says I'm not going to make Christmas."

Bunetta didn't know what to say. Then he spotted the Goodyear blimp descending not far from the freeway. He thought it might deflect Steve's thoughts.

"Y'know, I've never seen the Goodyear blimp land," Bunetta said.

"I haven't either," Steve said.

Bunetta slowed his car and pulled it to the shoulder, and they watched the airship — from which images of the Up with People halftime performance of "City of New Orleans" were broadcast during the 1976 Super Bowl — ease to the ground. It was diverting, perhaps symbolic. It colored how Steve depicted for Bunetta the slim odds he faced in Seattle:

"It's like goin' up on a tall building and jumpin' off into a wet sponge."

Bunetta finally found some words: "Fuck 'em. What do they know?"

Steve knew he was scheduled to fly to Seattle on Wednesday, Aug. 15. The day before, he had spent eight hours at Long Beach Memorial Hospital getting a blood transfusion. As Bunetta understood it, "He wasn't making blood anymore, so his blood would only last a few days." While he ate dinner at home at about 7:45 that night, the phone rang.

It was Steve Redfearn, the friend who had lured Steve to Seal Beach and who ran the Pacific Amphitheatre at Orange County Fairgrounds, 15 miles away in Costa Mesa. Nearly 11,000 pop fans were pouring into the outdoor venue for a nostalgic show of 1940s standards by ex-country rocker Linda Ronstadt and a 43-piece orchestra conducted by Nelson Riddle. The concert's opening act, comedian Ronn Lucas, was to go on in 15 minutes. But Lucas had not arrived.

And he was not going to arrive. Lucas, the opener for Ronstadt's national tour, knew about Ronstadt's six dates later that month at L.A.'s Universal Amphitheatre, but he had not been told about the Aug. 14 Costa Mesa date and thought he had the night off. After a full day at Disneyland with his fiancée, Lucas returned home to Santa Monica, 50 miles from the concert, to find an urgent message from his agent. "I would not have made it in the rush-hour traffic," he says. "Maybe if I could have gotten a helicopter. ..."

Redfearn needed a fill-in. Now. "This is no pressure," he told Steve. "Pretend it's not me calling. But I thought you'd hate me if you found out I didn't call you. Do you want to get in the car and open for Linda?"

Friends drove Steve to Costa Mesa, and Steve tuned his guitar along the way. When he arrived, he walked onstage nearly an hour after the scheduled showtime and launched into his set with an ironic quip: "I knew that moving to Orange County would pay off." He sang seven or eight songs that included "City of New Orleans," "You Never Even Call Me by My Name" and the California-tweaking "Hot Tub Refugee." In 30 minutes, the one-man band had wowed yet another enormous audience. Few present suspected it would be his final show.

That night, Al Bunetta was at home commiserating with a couple of friends over Steve's departure for Seattle just hours away. "I was crying," Bunetta says. "I was booking this tour for Stevie that I knew he would never do." The phone rang, and it was Steve, ebullient. "It was like he was all better," Bunetta says.

"Al, what a great night," Steve said. "Look, I did something I shouldn't have done. But Redfearn called me, and I had to go play it, and it worked out real well, man, and I did a great job. I had to use a stool, but they liked me, and I made some more friends. And I knocked on Linda Ronstadt's door, and she wanted me to do the rest of the tour, and I said, 'Linda, I don't think that's gonna happen.' "

"Yeah, Stevie, that's great," Bunetta said.

Steve gave one more indication of his future, or lack thereof.

"I'll tell ya what else I did," he said. "I signed (endorsed) the check 'Al Bunetta.' So hey, I'll seeya later. Bye." [16]

The next day, Dan Einstein met Steve and Nancy at L.A. International so that Steve could OK proofs of the "Santa Ana Winds" LP cover. Then the couple flew to Seattle. There, Steve and Nancy received full use of a refuge away from the public — the three-story Victorian home of autoharpist Bryan Bowers and his wife, dubbed "Bowers Towers." In a stroke of synchronicity, the dwelling in the quiet Madrona neighborhood overlooked the same panorama of Lake Washington and Mount Rainier as in the back-cover photo of Bowers' first LP, "The View from Home," on which Steve had sung "Walkin' in Jerusalem."

"You can come, bring whoever you want, if you need a quiet place," said Bowers, who had called Steve from a long summer tour. "Nobody will know where you are, so you can be out of the limelight to have some calm."

Steve called back half an hour later. "Is it OK if we bring my mom and my brother and John Prine and Al Bunetta, our manager?"

"Absolutely," Bowers said.

In return, Steve asked Bowers to fill in for him at several imminent performances with David Bromberg in Utah and environs. Bowers was stunned:

"Stevie, you don't have to throw me dates because I'm giving you a house."

"I can't do 'em," Steve cut in with a reply. "I want you to have 'em. Shut up and take the dates."

When Bowers returned to his home in Seattle, on Aug. 18, his birthday, the entourage that Steve had described on the phone had taken up residence at his home — and Steve had at the ready a birthday gift for him, a pocket cassette recorder. "Here's this guy getting ready to get his blood changed with his brother," Bowers says, "and he's still trying to help, do something nice."

Though Bowers used the recorder for years, it eventually got away from him on the road, but the memory of the day he received it lingers indelibly. "I revered the thought that he took the time, facing what he was facing, to go out and buy me a little birthday present. I'll revere it the rest of my life."

Bowers and his wife were to leave town on a delayed vacation with friends, so his time with Steve was transient. Bowers arranged a breakfast for Steve at the

It worked out real well, man, and I did a great job. I had to use a stool, but they liked me, and I made some more friends.
STEVE GOODMAN

16: The check for Steve's fill-in set was for $3,600, says Ronn Lucas, who says he was forced to pay it out of his $6,000-a-week salary. His agent reimbursed him for half.

Dill Piccolo restaurant in Seattle's Central Area with Tom Dundee, a Chicago singer/songwriter who had moved west several years prior. Dundee, a produce truck driver, could stop in for only about 17 minutes, and as he was about to leave, Steve saw him to the door to deliver a can't-miss message of poignancy.

"Tom, I want to show you somethin'," Steve said, reaching into his pocket and pulling out a 5x7 of his wife, Nancy, his mother, Minnette, his Grandma Mary and his daughters, Jessie, Sarah and Rosanna. It was the same photo he had shown Loretta Smith and Mary Gaffney six months earlier in Chicago.

"Wow, Steve," Dundee said.

"Yeah," Steve said, "four generations of Goodman women." Pointing a stubby index finger at Nancy's face, he added, "That's the one I'm worried about."

Dundee hugged and kissed Steve, then bolted to his produce truck. The exchange "broke my heart," Dundee says. It was the last time he saw Steve.

Not long afterward, Bowers dropped Steve and his clan at McCormick's seafood restaurant in downtown Seattle for an abrupt farewell. On the Fourth Avenue sidewalk, Bowers hugged the others. Then the musical Mutt & Jeff eyed each other.

"I'll seeya, man," Steve said.

"I'll seeya, Stevie," Bowers replied.

He reached out, and Steve hugged him. "I knew I'd never see him again," Bowers says. "He knew. I know he knew I'd never see him again. He was trying to put the bright face on it. But he knew it was over. And I drove away, and I was all choked up. Everybody else was babbling in the car, and I was Adam's apple up in my throat. I could hardly talk."

Three days later, on Tuesday, Aug. 21, Steve was admitted to Room 8055 at University of Washington Hospital, a research-based institution sprawling along the north bank of the ship canal connecting freshwater Lake Washington with saltwater Puget Sound. Steve didn't lack for distractions as he prepared to undergo his transplant under a Fred Hutchinson Cancer Research Center protocol. Willie Nelson's "City of New Orleans" single, on a steep ascent, had just entered the *Billboard* country chart at #55, and the corresponding LP already had reached #17. Steve also learned that the one-hour "Jethro & Friends" special was getting its first two airings that week on KTCA-TV in Minneapolis.

Gifts started arriving from friends in the music world. The Nitty Gritty Dirt Band sent more than 100 balloons that filled Steve's hospital room, and Steve took them to the pediatric floor and handed them to children who were patients. Folksinger Jim Post recalls a more astonishing gesture from Steve Martin, who sent Steve a blank checkbook. [17] Steve had musical gifts of his own for the hospital oncologists and nurses, sitting on his bed with his guitar and playing tunes that could be heard up and down the eighth-floor hallway. "For someone of his stature," says Dr. Martin Tallman, an oncology fellow and Steve's hands-on physician at the UW, "he was quite unpretentious."

The impression Steve left was of down-to-earth amiability, says Dr. Alex Fefer, Steve's attending physician, who had been part of the original, five-mem-

> **I knew I'd never see him again. ... I drove away, and I was all choked up. Everybody else was babbling in the car, and I was Adam's apple up in my throat.**
> **BRYAN BOWERS**

17: Steve Martin does not recall the checkbook gift but doesn't disavow it. "Could be," he says. "I don't know. People tell me things all the time that they say I've done that I don't recall."

ber Hutch transplant team when it formed in mid-1968. "Steve was not angry at the world, but he was not faux happy, either," Fefer says. "He was realistic and somewhat resigned but not depressed. He was just a regular guy."

Back in Steve's hometown, the Cubs, riding a five-game winning streak the day of Steve's hospitalization, were leading the NL East by five games and heading toward a 20-10 record for August. Steve not only studied the standings but also learned of the release of "Go, Cubs, Go" as a single. Fans were snapping up copies so briskly that the raucous ditty was well on the way to more than 60,000 total sales over the next three years — ironically, a figure that Steve hadn't attained with any of his LPs. "I think 'Go, Cubs, Go' mirrored where that ball club was," says Chuck Swirsky, WGN sports director. "If anything emphasized or paralleled the year and the personality of that club, it was that song."

The Cubs — and Steve — were even stirring national interest, meriting a two-and-a-half-minute story Aug. 30 on the NBC Evening News about whether the team could make it to the World Series. Incorporated in the story was footage of Steve singing and playing "A Dying Cub Fan's Last Request."

Like Margaret in "The Dutchman," Steve's wife was a constant presence in Seattle while Steve received pre-transplant chemotherapy and radiation. "Nancy was stayin' at the hospital," says John Prine. "She never left his side. She even slept there." The only times Nancy left were for occasional breaks or during visits by others, including Minnette and David Goodman, Al Bunetta and Prine, and during Steve's countless phone calls to everyone from benefactor Paul Anka to accompanist and co-writer Arno Lucas to high-school friend Brad Ellis.

"Harry, I'm dyin'," he told Harry Waller by phone.

"What? C'mon, man," Waller replied. "What are you talking about?"

"No, this is it. I'm goin'. It's gonna be real soon."

Waller was speechless, admittedly an unusual state for him. Eventually, he told Steve, "Look, man, only the good die young. You and I are gonna be like 100, so buck up there."

"Look, I know," Steve said. "I'm just gettin' weaker, and there's nothin' they can do. I just know it's gonna happen real soon."

Steve was not as glum in talking with Dr. Bonnie Cunningham. Saying goodbye in so many words, he thanked her for all she had done since his first visits to Sloan-Kettering in 1969. "He told me he loved me, and he hung up the phone," she says. "He always said nice things when he hung up the phone."

Arlo Guthrie knew he might be saying goodbye to Steve, "so I wanted to make sure that he understood that I really loved him and he had changed my life." Though their talked-of tour had fallen through, the two bantered about setting up another. "We had these plans we were making in the face of what really seemed to me to be a 50-50 shot," Guthrie says. "I figured he stood as much chance of getting out of there as he did of not." Even so, Guthrie knew he needed to be ready for Steve's demise. "It was one of those sad milestones in your life, and you realize it's maybe a milestone for you, but it might be a headstone for somebody else."

> **I think 'Go, Cubs, Go' mirrored where that ball club was. If anything emphasized or paralleled the year and the personality of that club, it was that song.**
> **CHUCK SWIRSKY**

To some, Steve talked music, as with Jethro Burns and banjoist Stephen Wade, both of whom heard Steve sing them a fledgling work of drollery, "Coffee Just Makes Me Sleepy." To others, Steve's M.O. was wisecracks along with a rosy, no-big-deal update, as with ex-Lake Forest College classmate Lucy Wells.

"Hey, Luce!" he greeted Wells. "So, what are the jokes on the East Coast?"

"Steve," she said, "you coming to town? Where are you calling from?"

"No, no, had this thing lined up with Arlo Guthrie, but I guess I'm gonna cancel it," Steve said. "I'm out here in Seattle. My brother's lettin' me have some of his bone marrow."

When he called David Amram in New York City, Steve regaled him with a version of his news that was upbeat to the point of evasion.

"Well, I'm out here, and I've got my guitar, and I'm in my pajamas and playin' for some of the patients," Steve said. "I'm doin' pretty well. I'm gettin' a pretty good response from the crowd. What're you doin'?"

Amram said he was working on a film script with Floyd Red Crow Westerman, a country singer and Native American activist with whom Steve had shared the Mariposa Folk Festival stage. Steve asked to speak with him.

"Steve, be strong," Westerman told Steve. "Know that the Great Spirit is watching over you. We're going to say prayers for you and your family to recover and to live for a long, long time."

Westerman looked at Amram sadly, shook his head and handed the receiver back to Amram. Steve told him, "What a guy. I'll call you in a few days."

He never did. Instead, he underwent the transplant, which was preceded by a week of total body radiation (termed "the nuclear bomb" by Fefer) and two days of chemo. The oncologists knew his chances of surviving the operation were slim to none but gamely moved ahead.

"The rationale," says Dr. Marilyn Croghan, a resident at the UW Medical School, "was that he's going to die of this disease, so why not try something, even though that something has not worked and we have no scientific basis to suggest that it will work." Fefer adds, "He was not at all a good candidate for transplant. It's just that there were really no other options."

The day of Steve's transplant was Friday, Aug. 31. In the aftermath, complications ensued in his kidneys and liver. Weakened and bedridden from the procedures, he still used the phone to contact the outside world. But in the face of death, Steve could not find professional contentment.

It wasn't as if clues of songwritng success were absent. While *People Weekly* had pegged Willie Nelson's version of "City of New Orleans" as "on the listless side, especially for a train song," it nevertheless was rising quickly on the country charts. It had reached #32 as a single and #8 as an album by the weekend of Steve's transplant. As well, the Nitty Gritty Dirt Band had recorded "Face on the Cutting Room Floor" and placed it on the flip side of another ascending country single, "I Love Only You." [18]

In spite of their popularity, however, these records also blatantly reminded Steve that he would never have a hit of his own. "Well, maybe I'll get a Grammy

---

The rationale was that he's going to die of this disease, so why not try something, even though that something has not worked and we have no scientific basis to suggest that it will work.
DR. MARILYN CROGHAN

18: Similarly that year, the Nitty Gritty Dirt Band had recorded Steve's "Video Tape," a 1977 song whose depth Steve acknowledged during his March 21 show at the Moonshadow Saloon in Atlanta: "Every now and then, I write these songs before it's a good time to write 'em. Nobody understands 'em for a few seasons. It's not because I'm so smart. It's because I'm so dumb." The Dirt Band placed "Video Tape" on the flip side of a 45, "Long Hard Road (The Sharecropper's Dream)." Later, the Dirt Band's version of Steve's "Colorado Christmas" took off on Canadian country-music stations, says Jeff Hanna. "Everywhere we went in Canada, people knew the song like it was a radio hit," he says.

Award after I die," Steve muttered sarcastically from his hospital bed. At one point, Robert Pruter, Steve's brother-in-law, remembers Steve spitting out a bitter sentiment about Nelson's "City" success: "This is what Willie Nelson gets. What do I get?"

Nonetheless, Steve managed to keep making a little music for bedside audiences. They included a Chicago compatriot, Jim Post.

On the bill for Seattle's 14th annual Bumbershoot Festival over Labor Day weekend, Post initially mistook Steve's brother, David, for Steve when David picked him up at Sea-Tac airport. The high-voiced and unpredictable Post often had served as Steve's foil in their early performing days, when the two forged their friendship by goading each other to heights of improvisation and charm. When David brought Post to Steve's eighth-floor hospital room, the same driven dynamic held sway.

Listless and connected by tubes and wires to machines, Steve asked David to open his closet and pull out a guitar, one that Post long ago had loaned Steve permanently. "That's Jim's guitar, by the way," Steve told David. "A lot of good songs came out of that guitar, and there's a lot more songs in it." He asked Post to play for him, and Post obliged with a few tunes, including Monty Python's "The Galaxy" merged with "Lighten Up," a spiritual meditation on the infinitely expanding universe that Post had just written and recorded for a new LP. "You don't know the answer, and neither do I," Post sang, "so, meanwhile let's just all lighten up." But the normally unabashed Post found his serenade a struggle. "Those were the two or three hardest songs I ever sang," he says.

Perking up a little, Steve said, "Here, I'll play you one," and reached for the guitar. "Face on the Cutting Room Floor" was the gentle result. "I'll play you another one," he said. It was "Fourteen Days."

"He got up in bed, and with the guitar in his hand he was a little more alive, but still very weak," Post says. "His hands were cramping up so bad, and he had a hard time playing." But he persevered. Post thought to himself, with affection, "Just like Goodman to try to one-up me again."

The morning of Sept. 7, *Chicago Tribune* columnists Skip Myslenski and Linda Kay mentioned Steve's transplant and cheered him on, ending a blurb with, "Go, Steve, Go." Back in Seattle, Steve continued his post-transplant phone calls. With 12-year-old daughter Jessie, diet was a topic. "Are you drinking eight glasses of water a day?" he asked. "You better write it down and make sure you don't eat this and don't eat that." With school starting, he also urged her, "Do your homework."

To Steve Fishell of Emmylou Harris' band, however, Steve seemed to be taking Post's "lighten up" advice. Fishell, who had just returned from Australia, didn't think this phone call to Steve would be his last, "but I knew he wasn't doing well. He sounded very dopey and drugged up and sleepy." Fishell struggled to find the right words to say.

"Man, I hope you're feeling better," Fishell said. "I sure hope you're doin' OK. I was thinking about you when I was away —"

Those were the two or three hardest songs I ever sang.
JIM POST

"Hey," Steve cut him off, "did you hear the one about. ..."

The joke was a prurient pun that paired the Japanese car model Mitsubishi with the phrase "itchy pussy."

Fishell found it hard to believe that in his own way Steve was trying to console him. "I'm thinkin' that's the last thing this guy's gonna say, some hysterical 'guy joke,' but he was just trying to stun me with humor so that I'd lighten up a little bit and be myself in an otherwise really difficult moment," Fishell says. "I remember thinking, 'This guy is unbelievable. He's not goin' out without a laugh.' I could never have told a joke in that conversation. To retain his sense of humor after having gone through such a terrible event and probably realizing that the tunnel was closing in on him, to laugh all the way to the end, I envy that so much. Even in the most depressing of circumstances, to maintain your sense of humor is a gift."

Fishell was among many who called to express affection and appreciation to their formerly energetic friend. Foremost were Ray Nordstrand of the "Midnight Special" and the Holstein brothers, who telephoned Steve for several nights in a row from the pay phone in the rear of the Holsteins club on Chicago's Lincoln Avenue. The topic — the Cubs' steady march to the NL East pennant — was familiar and diverting, but "it was hard to talk about the Cubs when he was in such bad shape," Nordstrand said. "We were all telling him that he'd come through and were hoping for the best, but he refused to say anything that would make you feel sorry for him. There was no pity stuff. He wouldn't allow that, and it kept things positive and hopeful, for him and everybody else."

The afternoon of Sept. 12, Nordstrand, Fred Holstein and visiting folksinger Utah Phillips saw the Cubs slam Montreal 11-5 at Wrigley Field. While paying for a beer, Holstein caught a ball off the bat of Expos catcher Gary Carter. That night, Holstein got on the pay phone and told Steve his news. But a weary Steve, eating Chinese food, turned the conversation to a matter of the heart.

"Freddie," he said, "I love you."

"I love you, too, man."

Over the next day or so, Steve's condition worsened, to the point where he couldn't use his bowels without pain or difficulty. This led to one of his last utterances, as related by Nancy to Jessie: "I just wish I could take one good shit." [19] If ever a farewell line could encapsulate Steve's irreverence, that was it.

Suffering from veno occlusive disease (blockage of the small veins of the liver), Steve fell into a coma on Friday, Sept. 14, his body kept alive by machines. Tubes in Steve's mouth and nose maintained rhythmic breathing and other vital signs. John Prine had left. Minnette had flown south to Seal Beach to stay with Jessie, Sarah and Rosanna. Al Bunetta departed as well. "It was just so anticlimactic," he says. "When Stevie wasn't breathing on his own anymore, I didn't even know him. All I kept thinking of was, it shouldn't be happening. It's finally here, the day we've all dreaded, him especially."

Nancy remained at the hospital to monitor her husband's care, confer with doctors about the maintenance of life support and greet the occasional visitor.

> When Stevie wasn't breathing on his own anymore, I didn't even know him. All I kept thinking of was, it shouldn't be happening. It's finally here, the day we've all dreaded, him especially.
> **AL BUNETTA**

19: Nancy told *National Lampoon* editor Sean Kelly that Steve mumbled a similar phrase while in his coma: "Mommy, can I have just a little piece of toilet."

One of the last was actually a trio: onetime protégé Jimmy Buffett, his guitarist Josh Leo and photographer Jim Shea. Buffett chartered a jet for him and Leo to fly north, while Shea had flown in separately from L.A. Buffett and Leo did not know what to expect. When they walked into Steve's room and saw him, as Leo puts it, "tubed to the max," the only sound was the apparatus pushing air into and out of Steve's chest. The scene pierced Buffett. "It hit me very hard," he says. "I'd never seen anybody like that." Leo adds, "It just stopped us cold."

Buffett says he knew Steve wouldn't want them to remain upset. "We got our guitars out," Leo says. "Buffett just started talkin' to Steve like he was right there awake, and we started playin' songs." Leo doesn't recall which ones. "We were just playin' stuff. We probably played some of his (Steve's) stuff." At one point, Buffett said, "I just wrote this song, and I'll play it for you." When Buffett finished, Shea says, "all the bells and whistles next to Steve's bed went off." Buffett said under his breath, "I guess he didn't like my song."

It was one last moment of humor. The next day, Thursday, Sept. 20, at 2:45 p.m., with Nancy and David by Steve's side, the end that had been diagnosed, anticipated and thwarted for nearly 16 years finally arrived. After persuading David that it finally was time, Nancy made the agonizing decision to pull the plug. And like the "old Cub fan" of his song, 36-year-old Steve slipped away.

* * *

Not long afterward, the phone rang at the Goodman home in Seal Beach. Minnette, who had been preparing dinner, answered it. Nancy was calling to say that Steve had died. The three girls were home from school, and Jessie watched as Minnette gripped the receiver. "Her hands were as red as her fingernails," Jessie says. After Minnette hung up, she told Jessie, "You have to do your homework." She turned back to the kitchen and resumed cooking. At dinner, Minnette bravely but evasively told her grandchildren, "Someone very special is coming home tonight. You're going to be very happy to see them." The girls, of course, thought it would be their mom and dad.

Late that night, after the girls had gone to bed, Jessie awoke to the smell of cigarettes, which startled her because Steve didn't allow smoking inside the house. "Oh, Dad's gonna be pissed," Jessie thought. As she stirred from her bed, her bedroom door opened, and her mother turned on the light. Nancy noticed posters of rock bands and actors that Jessie had tacked up on her walls during the Seattle ordeal. "Oh, your room really looks like a teenager's now," Nancy said, then told Jessie that her dad was gone.

Her sisters, Sarah and Rosanna, remained asleep as Jessie joined the adults. Al Bunetta (who had been in David Geffen's office that afternoon when he learned of Steve's death), his wife Dawn and Minnette sat rather silently, just smoking. Jessie curled up on a couch next to Minnette, who was still dressed in her nightgown. Her words to her granddaughter stuck with Jessie decades later: "It isn't right. It isn't fair. But while we're here, everyone has to earn their star, and your dad certainly did."

In Seattle, Steve's brother and marrow donor, David, hadn't found an evening

> **It isn't right. It isn't fair. But while we're here, everyone has to earn their star, and your dad certainly did.**
> **MINNETTE GOODMAN**

flight, so he called Tom Dundee. "I can't get a plane till 7 in the morning. I know nobody in Seattle, but I got your phone number," David told Dundee. "Will you hang out with me tonight?" Dundee took him to the ragtag 24-hour Dog House restaurant near Seattle Center for a burger and organ music from local legend Dick Dickerson. Then they headed downtown to the 211 Club, a second-floor professional pool parlor where, over a pitcher of beer apiece, they began a game that echoed one of Steve's first compositions — Eight Ball.

After the two sank the solid and striped balls, the game was down to the eight, an easy shot in the corner pocket. It was Dundee's turn. He tried hard to sink it, but it rattled in the corner just shy of the pocket — in Dundee's parlance, "tit-tit-tit-tit-tit-fuck-you." David looked up with dark, saucer eyes like Steve's and said something that Dundee felt defined the Goodman family's toughness: "Tom, you don't have to give me a break just 'cause my brother died." Then David sank the eight. Twenty years later, Dundee reflected on the impact of David's steeliness: "You've never been hit in your nuts like that."

Word of Steve's passing fanned out quickly that day and had a similar effect. Al Bunetta held up a plane's takeoff so that John Prine could step outside briefly and receive his call. "I knew it was comin', but it still hit me like a train," Prine says. He returned to his plane seat and shared the news with two passengers who flanked him. "They didn't know Steve or I from Adam, but I had to talk to somebody," Prine says. "They couldn't have been nicer. They understood that I'd lost a friend."

Fred Holstein "freaked" when he heard. "I went bananas," he said. "I got stupid. I went to a restaurant and unloaded on a friend. I got nuts. I got rude and real, real drunk. It hit me like a cold shovel."

David Amram was playing to a full house at Holsteins in Chicago and learned of Steve's death from Ed Holstein between sets. Amram recalled how Steve had learned of his father's death seven years earlier at the Main Point in Bryn Mawr, and he tried to summon the same focused attention. He returned to the stage and dedicated a song to Steve. "We have to rejoice in his life and his strength and what he did in a short time that most people would never do if they lived to be 100," Amram said. Later, in his hotel room, Amram fell into tears before pulling himself together and returning to Holsteins, where the crowd was in a funk. "It was almost the way it was when John F. Kennedy died," he says. "There was a real feeling of loss and sadness. They wanted it not to be true, and they wanted the time to go back and reverse itself and change the outcome, but they couldn't. They were realizing this extraordinary person wasn't here."

Paula Ballan was hosting three friends in her fifth-floor Manhattan flat, and that night a black wren flew in through her window. "We couldn't get this bird out," she says. "It was flapping and bumping into pictures and lampshades. We decided to go to sleep and let it figure its way out. We didn't want to hurt it. So we turned off the lights and went to bed and left the window open. We woke in the morning to a phone call. The bird was gone, and Steve was dead."

Bryan Bowers experienced something equally eerie. He was playing autoharp during an evening tempest of rain, thunder and lightning at the Colorado Chautauqua in Boulder, but later, after he had gone to sleep, he awoke to a calm, clear, blue sky. As he closed his eyes and wondered why he had awakened, he heard Steve's voice shout, "Bowers!" The next morning, he flew to Nashville and learned that Steve had died the afternoon before. "I'm not a loony tune," Bowers says. "I'm as straight arrow as you can get, but what I heard in the middle of the night wasn't like desperation or despair. It was exuberance. He was saying goodbye."

The morning after, from coverage in newspapers and on radio and TV, many others learned of Steve's passing.

Vin Scelsa of WNEW-FM was up early, getting exercise about 6 a.m. on a walk through his New Jersey neighborhood and listening to a portable radio when he heard the news. He stopped, and a few feet away from him stood a deer, frozen in Scelsa's presence. "It was a complete shock," Scelsa says. "I didn't even know that Steve had gone into relapse. I looked at the deer and started crying."

Steve Burgh heard at 7 a.m. via a phone call from his mother. Burgh — who had written, produced and performed music with Steve throughout the 1970s and at whose 1983 wedding Steve had served as best man — brooded all day. That evening, he went for a walk in Manhattan and bumped into another Steve, pop singer/songwriter Steve Forbert, whose LPs he had produced. In front of 10 others, Burgh said, he slammed Forbert against a post and punched him in the face, shouting, "Steve Goodman's dead, and I'm stuck with you!" It surprised Burgh because, as he said later, "I don't hit people." [20]

Befitting his profession, Roy Leonard, Steve's longtime champion at Chicago's WGN-AM, found words of comfort when others could not. "We all want to say something," he told listeners. "The whole thing is so sudden. ... I have so many happy, funny memories of Steve, but I'm terribly sad, as we all are. I'm glad that he doesn't have to suffer anymore because it's been a real tough period for Steve the last couple of years. But he never asked for sympathy. ... Oh, I hope he's smilin' somewhere. I really do. ... God must be awfully lonely up in heaven and needs some laughs."

Dr. Rick Eisenstaedt, who had been bar-mitzvahed with Steve, was jogging and listening on a Walkman to NPR when he heard. "An incredible tragedy," he thought. Laura Haynes (now Aiken) of the Philadelphia Folk Festival also heard the news on NPR as she was driving to work on an expressway. "That just killed me," she says. "I lost it at work. They sent me home." Sally Fingerett was driving on Interstate 81 in the Pocono Mountains of eastern Pennsylvania when she, too, heard via NPR. "I just pulled over and cried," she says. In Phoenix, singer/songwriter Jamie Anderson, who was running reports in a computer room when she heard it via radio, burst into tears. Sidney James Kistin, Steve's Lake Forest College friend, was taking her children to preschool in rural New Mexico only to find the director of the school sobbing. "I'm so sorry," Kistin said, "can I help you?" The director replied, "I just heard that Steve Goodman died."

Oh, I hope he's smilin' somewhere. I really do. ... God must be awfully lonely up in heaven and needs some laughs.
ROY LEONARD

20: Forbert doesn't remember the encounter with Burgh, but he respects Goodman's musical impact, citing his range from "I'm My Own Grandpa" to the "true classic" of "City of New Orleans."

Marc Horowitz, who accompanied Steve at his first billed Bitter End gig, was driving along the West Side highway into Manhattan and heard it on his car radio. "I just completely lost it," he says. "My eyes filled with tears, and I couldn't see the road, so I pulled over to the curb to stop for a minute. I hadn't expected it to hit me as hard as it did because we weren't terribly close. But it was a terrible thing. It was a defining moment in my existence."

Howard Primer, who toured Chicago's South Side blues clubs with Steve in high school, was living 70 miles from Seattle and working in state government in Olympia at the time of Steve's transplant and decline. A friend had told him that Steve wanted to see him, and Primer tried several times to reach Steve by phone, but his calls weren't put through. He finally drove to Seattle, but when he reached the eighth floor at UW Hospital, he was told that Steve had died the day before. "I was so torn up," he says. "I had wanted to go back and be once again the two guys that never had dates. I was trying to find my way in life, building a new business and finding my morality again, which had been lost on behalf of my career. Hearing that he had died was absolutely devastating."

Al Ierardi, the butt of an affectionate joke by Steve in spring 1973 at the Earl of Old Town, was in his car and listening to the radio while queued up at a McDonald's drive-up window in Champaign, Illinois. Hearing the news, he pulled out of the line, parked and wept for a few minutes.

Jack Decker, who taught Steve his first guitar chords in high school, thought of his late wife, Joyce, to whom he had been married for eight years. She had succumbed to leukemia three weeks after her diagnosis in 1973. "Thinking of Steve was like thinking of my wife who passed away," he says. "It broke my heart when he died, sort of like getting stuck in the side by a needle."

Tom Rush heard while at Blue Jay Recording Studio in Carlisle, Massachusetts, supervising the final mix of Steve's performance of "City of New Orleans" at Rush's holiday concert the previous December in Boston. The track was for a live LP. "It was hard to believe," he says. "I mean, there he was on the speakers at that very moment, singing his heart out, alive as anybody I'd ever heard, right there in the room with us." [21]

Greg Trafidlo, fellow open-mike performer at the Fickle Pickle in Steve's high-school days, had finished an opening set with the Bass Mountain Bluegrass Boys at a club in Roanoke, Virginia, when headliner Mike Cross delivered the news to everyone in the room. "A good friend of ours who brought a lot of light in the world," Cross said sadly, "has gone elsewhere to spread sunshine."

Norm Siegel, bassist, was running the sound for a band named Freewheel at Woody's Jazz Kitchen in Chicago when his ex-wife informed him. "I went all to pieces," he says.

The news reached Gib Foster, who designed the "Somebody Else's Troubles" LP cover, during a stint filling in at Louisiana State Tech University for a graphic-design teacher who had died. Two nights after Steve's death, Foster was attending a party at the home of art professor Peter Jones, and the radio was tuned via cable to WFMT-FM in Chicago. Shortly after 9 p.m., Jones told Foster, "Hey,

> **A good friend of ours who brought a lot of light in the world has gone elsewhere to spread sunshine.**
> **MIKE CROSS**

21: Tom Rush played "City of New Orleans" as the closer to his Symphony Hall concerts Dec. 27-29, 1984, as a tribute to Steve.

they're dedicating the whole 'Midnight Special' to Steve Goodman." Foster replied, "Well, that's great. Turn it up." As they drank, talked and listened to the music, Jones had a somber realization. "Gib, this is a memorial for Steve Goodman," he said. "Oh, no," said Foster, who soon left the party.

On the afternoon of the next day came the wedding of mandolinist Don Stiernberg. His mentor and Steve's beloved performing partner, Jethro Burns, was in attendance, as was Johnny Frigo, who had played bass and violin on Steve's "Words" LP and whose quartet was to provide music for the reception. "Can you imagine?" Stiernberg says. "Here I am getting married, and I've got Jethro, my hero, and Johnny, my hero, both in the same room. We gathered around the piano for a second, and Johnny put his hand on Jethro and said, 'Hey, I've got to tell you. I'm really sorry about Steve.'"

Brian Gill, who had been driving north on Sheridan Road in Chicago when radio host Studs Terkel imparted the news, had a vivid dream four nights later. In it, Steve took him by the hand, and the two flew euphorically like Supermen over a mountain ridge and into a dell. There, they sat across a campfire, and Steve conveyed to Gill a "You can do it, too" message. "I was so happy that he had come to see me because I was yearning for him," Gill says. "Hell, wouldn't it be a gas if all of us had this dream, all of us back there in the old days?"

Word spread quickly in the newspapers of Great Britain, and when it reached Harvey Andrews, who had first been bowled over by Steve at the 1973 Cambridge Folk Festival, he thought of the greater context of the era's deceased folk songwriters. "There was Goodman, there was Phil Ochs, Harry Chapin and Stan Rogers, and we lost them all in their 30s," he says. "As a genre, it had the heart torn out of it. It was as if a plane went down with Clark Gable, James Stewart, Humphrey Bogart and Jimmy Cagney on it."

Jeany Walker, who in 1969 had improvised dances to Steve's music at the Earl of Old Town, was living in a cabin on rural Vashon Island near Seattle. It took several weeks for news of Steve's death to reach her. "The kids were asleep, and my oldest daughter was up, so I could leave for a little bit, and I went into town to get a cup of coffee and get the Sunday paper. I got in the car and was driving into town, and without thinking I turned on the radio, and it was playing 'City of New Orleans.' At the end, the announcer said, 'That song was played by Steve Goodman, who died last month in Seattle.' That was the only time that radio ever worked. For months, I couldn't hear a note of music without just crying, and I couldn't dance at all. I could not move to any music. I was devastated."

If Steve's demise did not make sense, the cascade of visceral responses did. As noted by Howard Berkman, Steve's high-school musical mentor, competitor and friend, "I don't think anybody who was close to Steve could ever really deal with it right because you can't really associate Steve with dead. Steve you associate with really alive, like a fuckin' nuclear pile, like life just burning out of somebody, just burning through his skin from the inside, like a special effect in a science-fiction movie. He was a driven guy. He was on fire." ♪

I was so happy that he had come to see me because I was yearning for him. Hell, wouldn't it be a gas if all of us had this dream, all of us back there in the old days?
BRIAN GILL

On Oct. 2, 1984, just 12 days after Steve died, iconic Wrigley Field celebrates the Cubs' status as divisional champs.
(Photo by Kasey Ignarski)

'The big bang in the little shape ... this really vivid, burning coal'

If ever a life story could be depicted in nine seconds, it came close to happening in the sunny but brisk air of Tuesday, Oct. 2, 1984, in Chicago's North Side baseball cathedral.

A crowd of 36,282 filled every seat at Wrigley Field to witness the first game of the National League playoffs between the Cubs and the San Diego Padres. Hope was rampant. If the Cubbies could win just three playoff games, they would enter the World Series for the first time in 39 agonizing years.

Fans were riding the twin sentiments of the man who had written the ironic valentine "A Dying Cub Fan's Last Request" and the catchy mantra "Go, Cubs, Go." In fact, when the Cubs had clinched the NL East Division title on Sept. 24 in Pittsburgh, hundreds of tanked-up loyalists back in the Windy City took to Lincoln Avenue in front of the Ultimate Sports Bar and Grill to bellow again and again the latter tune's hopeful refrain: "Hey, Chicago, whaddya say, the Cubs are gonna win today." On the same night, thousands of carousers convened outside Wrigley Field, over and over chanting "Go, Cubs, Go!"

But having died in Seattle just four days before the clincher, Steve Goodman couldn't join in his hometown's revelry.

Steve would have been the definitive choice to sing the national anthem for the Oct. 2 playoff game, but the Cubs came up with an inspired pinch-hitter, Jimmy Buffett. His stats were impressive: Buffett had written five songs with Steve, recorded another four of Steve's tunes (notably "Banana Republics," arguably the ultimate Buffett song) and enlisted Steve as a sideman on four of his albums. Long before Buffett had become a celebrity, he was Steve's comrade, and while Buffett had cultivated a party image rooted in the Caribbean, for his favorite city he had adopted Chicago.

The Cubs' choice was bittersweet, however, and as Buffett strode out of the home dugout that afternoon, wearing a blue blazer, open-necked yellow shirt and teardrop sunglasses, he knew it.

It was Steve who had befriended the up-and-coming singer, had supplied a couch as gratis lodging, had introduced Buffett to the afternoon joys of no-lights Wrigley Field and had fronted Buffett $50 for train fare to a Denver gig. As Buffett soared past him in the musical world, it was Steve who had sung

> Hey, Chicago, whaddya say, the Cubs are gonna win today.
> **FANS AT THE ULTIMATE SPORTS BAR AND GRILL**

(Near-left photo) Outside 70-year-old Wrigley Field on the night of Sept. 24, 1984, ecstatic fans celebrate the Cubs' clinching of the National League East Division title. (Far-right photo and below) Eight days later, on Oct. 2, 1984, Steve's compatriot Jimmy Buffett sings the national anthem "for Steve Goodman" to launch the NL playoffs at the Friendly Confines.

(Video images thanks to Dave Hoekstra. Image of fans courtesy of WGN-TV. Major League Baseball ® footage of Buffett used with permission of Major League Baseball Properties, Inc. Pre-game photo of Wrigley Field by Kasey Ignarski.)

Buffett's praises countless times onstage. In conventional, music-industry success, Buffett the protégé had vastly eclipsed Steve the mentor.

And on this afternoon, while Buffett was present, Steve was gone.

"At this time," the PA announcer intoned at 1:16 p.m., "we ask that you please rise and join in the singing of our national anthem, as sung by the popular recording star, Jimmy Buffett."

Cheers and applause rippled through the 70-year-old ballpark in recognition of Buffett's name. He stepped to the microphone and looked up to his right, at the stands above third base.

"This," he said, in a stately tone and with an infinitesimal pause, "is for Steve Goodman."

He turned his gaze to the grandstand straight ahead, leaned a few inches closer to the mike and opened his mouth in the shape of an "o." But the fans had heard Steve's name, and their cheers surged louder than before. Buffett stopped and grinned, happy, even grateful, to be upstaged by his absent friend. Then he briefly bowed his head, lifted it, leaned in again and began the anthem.

For the curly-haired singer, those nine seconds — the time between the moment that he was announced and the moment that he began singing — were profound. "To walk into that was like going to church," he says. "That was where I said goodbye to Steve Goodman. It was much better than being in the hospital, let me tell you."

Closer to his home, Buffett had performed the national anthem at a Florida football game or two, but for this occasion at Wrigley, he knew the stakes were much higher. "This was kind of like the eulogy, Chicago's goodbye to Steve Goodman." He had realized the potential before the game, and he began intently singing the song, listening to the lyrics and practicing. The night before, he had checked into Chicago's plush, circa 1928 Whitehall Hotel near the Magnificent Mile. "Everybody was kind of celebrating and wanted to go out, and I said, 'No, I can't. I've got to be on the money for this thing tomorrow.' So I went to bed and got up early in the morning, and I was showering and everything, and I'm singing the national anthem in the shower and all morning long."

To his surprise, Buffett found that he already had an audience. "I walked out of my hotel room about the same time the guy in the room next to me came out of his door, and he looked at me with this look of fear in his eye, like, 'Who is this whacko super-patriot who sings the national anthem every morning?' I looked at him and said, 'It's OK, I'm doing it at the ballgame,' and as I walked past him, he said, 'Boy.' Goodman would have loved that — me working that diligently, and some guy thinking about some whacko, militia guy going to blow up the town."

What Buffett did do for Steve's town was deliver a nearly Steve-perfect moment to honor a hero. Buffett sang "The Star-Spangled Banner" traditionally and forthrightly, with only a tiny lyrical lapse and a couple of minor melodic modifications. [1] The respectful treatment boded well for the Cubs, who went on to trounce the Padres 13-0 and prevailed the next day as well.

But when the series shifted to San Diego, the Padres bounced back to win three straight, denying the Cubs a World Series berth and preserving the eerie accuracy of Steve's "Dying Cub Fan" lyrics. ("The last time the Cubs won a National League pennant was the year we dropped the bomb on Japan.") The "Go" of the Cubs came to a screeching stop.

A similar dichotomy of celebration and sadness permeated a trove of tributes to Steve immediately after his Sept. 20 death. [2] While Steve's body was cremated and a private service was held three days later at his Seal Beach home, obituaries erupted from the nation's press. They emerged first from Seattle and Chicago (where it was front-page news) and fanned out to *The New York Times*, the *Los Angeles Times* and all points in between, eventually reaching national magazines such as *SingOut!*, *Goldmine* and *Rolling Stone*. [3]

Given the Cubs' unusual ascent, some of the headlines employed the timely diamond theme ("Funny how you can date a life with baseball," "Blues being played for ultimate Cub fan"). But at least one essay leapfrogged the easy link and angrily skewered the "corporate cowardice" that had failed to fully promote Steve's artistry. "Woe be to those who are called to achievement at a time when gestures and posturing mean more than God-given talent applied honestly in service to humanity," wrote David McGee in *Record* magazine. Quoting Steve's

> **This was kind of like the eulogy, Chicago's goodbye to Steve Goodman.**
> **JIMMY BUFFETT**

1: After Buffett sang the 80-second anthem, Steve got a nod from Don Drysdale, the former Dodgers pitcher who had just been inducted into the Hall of Fame in Cooperstown and was anchoring ABC-TV's coverage: "So, our national anthem sung by Jimmy Buffett, of course dedicated to Steve Goodman, a songwriter here in Chicago who passed away just prior to the club's '84 Eastern Division championship."

2: The Leukemia Research Foundation of Chicago even dedicated its Oct. 14 bike-a-thon in Elk Grove to Steve.

3: The *Rolling Stone* obituary appeared in the magazine's Nov. 8, 1984, edition, which featured Steve Martin on the cover. Neither the Martin profile nor the obituary mentioned Steve's remarkable run of 200 openers for Martin.

The catalyst 13 years earlier for Steve's leap to the national stage, Kris Kristofferson, pauses midsong during the star-studded tribute to Steve held Nov. 3, 1984, at Pacific Amphitheatre in Costa Mesa.
(Photo by Anne Dowie)

4: Two months after Steve's death, his broadcasting friend from the Netherlands, Wim Bloemendaal, aired a two-hour tribute on the public VARA network with music and interviews with John Prine, David Amram, Tom Paxton, Jethro Burns and banjo player Bill Keith.

"City of New Orleans," McGee closed his review of Steve's career by noting, "The steel rail still ain't heard the news."

Befitting Steve's profession, broadcast media also aired special shows that featured his myriad recordings and rare, unreleased tapes. In Chicago, a WFMT-FM "Midnight Special" tribute ran more than four hours, Roy Leonard devoted one of his WGN-AM morning shows to Steve, and the local public-TV station, WTTW, aired a half-hour of "Soundstage" and "Made in Chicago" clips. Elsewhere, Steve's aural eulogists included the legendary Oscar Brand on his WNYC-AM "Folksong Festival" in New York; Bill Munger on his nationally syndicated WNIU-FM "Song Bag" from DeKalb, Illinois; Gene Shay and Ed Sciaky jointly on WHYY-FM and WIOQ-FM in Philadelphia; and Leilani McCoy with guest Tom Dundee on KEZX-FM in Seattle. 4

The tone of these written and broadcast pieces [5] was both somber and sparkling, writers and announcers agreeing that Steve would not want morbidity to befoul the enjoyment of music, his or others'. "Let's keep it light," wrote Don McLeese, pop-music critic for the *Chicago Sun-Times*. "The music of few other performers was as consistently life-affirming." Several journalists even revealed their personal affection for Steve's music and Steve himself. "I don't usually carry out public mourning practices in this space," wrote Martin Keller in the Minneapolis *Nightlines*, "but Goodman's death hit home more than the deaths of some far greater musicians who've left behind their vinyl sides."

Musicians still very much alive who fell into the so-called "greater" category in 1984 and had collaborated with Steve over the years jumped at the chance to pay tribute to him — in a Nov. 3 show that organizer Steve Redfearn already had started planning while his friend's transplant was under way in Seattle. Redfearn secured free use of the facility that he managed, the Pacific Amphitheatre in Costa Mesa, the final venue Steve had played, as the last-minute opener for Linda Ronstadt. Redfearn worked with Al Bunetta to convene a lineup of stars that they hoped against hope would also include Steve. "This was something I would do whether he pulled through or not," Redfearn told the *Los Angeles Times* one week before the event. "It would be great if Steve could have been there to perform."

The lineup that took shape boggled the musical mind: Kris Kristofferson, Jackson Browne, Jimmy Buffett, Emmylou Harris and her Hot Band, Jethro Burns, Randy Newman, John Prine, George Carlin, Rosanne Cash and Rodney Crowell, David Amram, and J.D. Souther, along with emcee Martin Mull. The jaw-dropping closer was Willie Nelson, whose "City of New Orleans" album reached #1 on the *Billboard* country LP chart nine days after Steve's death and settled into that spot for what would become an astounding 12 straight weeks. ("Getting Willie was like getting the pope," says Buffett accompanist Steve Fishell.) Performers and staff donated their time, and "everybody has really been pitching in," Redfearn said the week before the event. Browne, Harris and Mull recorded radio promo spots. Souther even asked to sweep the stage and set up equipment.

The day of the show, Saturday, Nov. 3, was the exact date Nelson's "City of New Orleans" reached #1 on the *Billboard* country singles chart, and when the music began at 6 p.m., a coterie of accompanists ("The Bleacher Bums," including Peter Bunetta and Rick Chudacoff) had gathered. Unbilled luminaries included Booker T. Jones ("Green Onions"), crooner Rita Coolidge (Kristofferson's ex) and the Eagles' Timothy B. Schmit. [6] For the next five and a half hours, the 18,000 who filled the amphitheatre not only witnessed a unique spectacle but also contributed, with their $20 and $10 admissions, a total of $150,000 to leukemia research, split between Memorial Sloan-Kettering Cancer Center in New York and the University of Washington School of Medicine in Seattle.

Only one sixth of the nearly 60 songs performed were written by or directly

Let's keep it light.
DON McLEESE
CHICAGO SUN-TIMES

5: Jethro Burns' praise for Steve was heard nationally via UPI radio. "His 'City of New Orleans' will be around as long as there's a music industry," Burns told UPI correspondent Ginny Kosola. "He was just the best writer/ entertainer you're gonna see."

6: Missing was Bryan Bowers, who on the night of the concert played a Steve tribute of his own at Hightstown High School in New Jersey. Teacher John Bates' students had produced shows at the school by Gamble Rogers, Michael Cooney and others in the years since Bates had herded his class to Steve's memorable show (with drop-in Billy Joel) in 1976 at the Main Point. Bates' current students were hoping to book Steve for a fall 1984 show at the school. Instead, they snagged Bowers, who played a selection of Goodman songs on his autoharps. "The kids completely lost it," Bates says. "It was so amazing a catharsis. It all came full circle."

related to Steve, but the mix fit the perception held by everyone of what would have been Steve's wish — including Mull, the gently sarcastic emcee who was forced to ad lib at length between acts and backstage couldn't stop weeping. [7] "The last thing in the world he would want would be for us to sit here and extol his virtues and his songwriting prowess and fill out our Kleenex," Mull told the crowd. "What he really would like is for all of us to just have a terrific time and, as you young people put it so beautifully, 'boogie' in his honor."

Highlights laced the mini-sets throughout the evening, and as Todd Everett of the *Los Angeles Herald Examiner* reported, "the more Goodman was in their minds, the more effective were their performances." Possibly the most touching piece came from Buffett, who offered a warm, acoustic version of "Banana Republics," joined by steel-drum master Robert Greenidge, whose brightly tropical solo and backup work "ricocheted over the crowded, moonlit hillside," noted *San Francisco Examiner* critic Philip Elwood. An unusual boy-girl duet by Prine and Harris on Prine's "Souvenirs" added poignancy, as did Browne's elegiac "For a Dancer" and a trio of new songs by Kristofferson that bore harsh, spiritual themes. David Amram's pennywhistle danced through "The Water Is Wide" and entwined with Jim Rothermel's clarinet and soprano saxophone and Jethro Burns' mandolin in "It's a Sin to Tell a Lie" and "Jessie's Jig."

Under-the-radar connections to Steve were evident for those who could perceive them. Mull trotted out the erotic blues for the aging male that he'd written with Steve, "Talk Dirty to Me." Johnny Cash's daughter, Rosanne, quietly dedicated "Looking for a Corner" to Steve's three daughters, while Prine likewise played "Fish & Whistle" at the request of Jessie, oldest of the three. Newman banged out his satiric "Short People," a reminder of the hit he was riding when 5-foot-2 Steve was his opener in 1977. And Harris started her set with the Hank Snow standard "I'm Movin' On," which had been cited in December 1972 by Apollo 17 astronaut Harrison Schmitt after a recording of "City of New Orleans" awakened him in orbit. [8]

But such inside references were lost on many in the near-capacity crowd, which seemed far more familiar with the stars than with Steve. That gap was repaired midshow when a 20-minute collection of film clips (assembled by the photographer of Steve's final four LP covers, Jim Shea) depicted Steve performing "Talk Backwards," "City of New Orleans" (several versions edited together), "You're the Girl I Love" and "You Never Even Call Me by My Name." The compilation revealed Steve's captivating stage presence for the uninitiated, but for those who knew him, it was hard to bear, particularly when Steve cinematically morphed from his shaggy, bearded persona to his chemo cut. "I bawled like a baby," says Chudacoff. Still, the screening had a salutary effect. Steve on celluloid triggered the evening's only total standing ovation, and reviewers noted that he had "stolen his own show."

What should have been the night's high point — closer Willie Nelson and his Texas-based band, flown in at his own expense — instead became, for many, an endurance test. As a nighttime chill set in, Nelson opened with what Tim

> The last thing in the world he would want would be for us to sit here and extol his virtues and his songwriting prowess and fill out our Kleenex.
> **MARTIN MULL**

7: "It was one of the most difficult things I've ever had to do," Mull says. "It was like if you had an extended draft physical at the Department of Motor Vehicles."

8: Another obscure touch lay inside the eight-page concert program, which referenced Steve's intolerance to cold by including the Robert Service classic "The Cremation of Sam McGee." Few knew Steve had read the poem from the stage in 1978 in Alaska.

Grobaty of the *Long Beach Press-Telegram* called a "startlingly dispirited version" of "City of New Orleans," slurring or forgetting a few of the words. Then, as Grobaty noted, Nelson "descended into an abbreviated version of his tiresome regular set." Willie's troupe ran through a drawn-out succession of a dozen songs before rallying others onstage for a trio of gospel tunes: "Will the Circle Be Unbroken," "Amazing Grace" and "Uncloudy Day." Grobaty opined that the spiritual finale came too late because Nelson's 50-minute set "had broken the thread" focusing on Steve.

The entire show was an endurance test for Steve's widow, Nancy, who was a reluctant participant backstage and awash in an emotional swirl. "She was crisp about the boundaries, like 'I don't want to hear it, don't get soppy on me,' and I respected that," says Rosanne Cash. "She was very together, and she was protecting herself because if she had let down and let everyone's grief come into her, she would have never survived the night. That was a long night." [9]

After years of supporting Steve's career and treatment, Nancy finally could step away from the road show to receive the care for herself and her daughters that she had forgone for so long and that neighbors in Seal Beach were willing to give. An interview with Nancy published in *The Journal* of Seal Beach three days before the tribute show supplied a glimpse of her state of mind. She told reporter Catherine Cate that she found Seal Beach "a very special place, especially when you are engulfed in so much pain and sorrow. This is a town where people look out for each other. They really care. There have been so many kindnesses; merchants who allowed us to run tabs because it simplified the financial logistics, especially while I was out of town with Steve, people who look out for the girls. … There is absolutely no way I can ever thank everyone for all they have done for us."

Nancy also saluted the "mom and pop" venture that Steve's career had spawned in the last year and a half of his life. She spoke fondly of "our own little garage business" of selling Steve's Red Pajamas LPs.

Indeed, almost lost in the avalanche of print and broadcast obituaries and preparations for the tribute concert was the release of Steve's "Santa Ana Winds" album, which took place the very week of his death. As 1985 approached, word that Steve's final project was available trickled out in small, easy-to-miss reviews. Dave Hoekstra of the *Chicago Sun-Times* labeled the LP a "brilliant" survey of "all of Goodman's musical directions," Robert K. Oermann of the Nashville *Tennessean* wrote that it was "full of affection, absurdist humor and unbridled joy," and Dan Forte of *Guitar Player* magazine called it "the best studio effort of his 10-album career."

Steve himself wrote the best reviews, however, having composed witty liner notes for each of the LP's songs and wielding an irresistible pun in his final dedication to Nancy and his daughters, "who have me down cold." [10]

The album reviews and all-star tribute stood as successes on their own, but back in Steve's old hometown of Chicago, a visceral sensation had been surging since his death. Jimmy Buffett's nod to Steve at the Cubs' first playoff game just

This is a town where people look out for each other.
NANCY GOODMAN

9: In contrast, Steve's mother, Minnette, was upbeat and gregarious backstage. "She was very exuberant about appreciating the music she was hearing and complimenting me," says "Bleacher Bum" Rick Vito. "I'm sure it was a mixture of emotion for her, but she was very sweet and smiling." Vito says that he had been straining for something to tell her, but "she made it easy." Vito wound up saying, "Well, that's where your son got his sweetness."

10: Steve's song annotations were deceptively offhand. Of the sax part on "The Big Rock Candy Mountain," Steve referenced a jazz legend: "No, that's not the late, great Art Pepper — it's Jim Rothermel, a versatile and under-recorded player. He's also a valued friend." Rothermel sees a deeper message beyond the praise: "It's his way of kicking me in the butt and saying, 'I'm going to leave now, but you better keep going, and you'd better do right.'"

wasn't enough. Record producer Hank Neuberger, who hadn't attended the California concert, picked up a phone to call Al Bunetta.

"You just can't believe the intense, pent-up feeling for Steve that exists in Chicago," Neuberger told Bunetta. "People want to come together and have a little catharsis about this. We have to come up with something."

Bunetta hesitated, reeling from the enormity of Steve's departure and the marathon in Costa Mesa. But Neuberger persisted.

"Al, you're just not going to believe it," he said. "This just has to be done. There's too much need for this."

In late November, Bunetta flew to Chicago to meet with Neuberger and Arny Granat, who with his partner Jerry Michaelson at Jam Productions had promoted Steve's Chicago shows at the Auditorium Theatre and Park West since 1977. Their initial discussion in Granat's apartment was brief, and the conclusion was inevitable. Chicago needed its own tribute to its native son.

The only true challenge was identifying the venue. The show in sunny Southern California had drawn 18,000, but Chicago's notoriously frigid and snowy winter was nigh. Steve's ideal solo venue had been 750-seat Park West, but Granat wanted to roll the dice. "Well, I don't know if we can fill it," he said, "but maybe we should try the Arie Crown Theater. It's about 4,300 seats." Bunetta blanched, but Granat oozed confidence. "I think it'll work," he said. "Let's just try it."

Granat's belief stemmed in part from loyalty and gratitude, illustrated by a vignette from three years earlier that he and Bunetta related to Neuberger. On the near-freezing night of Nov. 6, 1981, Steve had played a Granat-promoted show at Chicago's Park West that captivated those who attended. Backstage afterward, Steve asked Bunetta, "How did everybody do?"

"It was great," Bunetta replied. "You killed. Everybody loved it."

"No," Steve said, "how did Arny and Jerry do?"

"Well, they took a little hit tonight," Bunetta said. "The weather was bad, and the turnout wasn't quite what they expected. They took a little hit."

"They've promoted me for years," Steve said. "I can't let that happen. Let's give 'em some money back."

"What do you mean?" Bunetta asked.

"Well," Steve said, "they guaranteed the show, and they paid us, but we didn't do what we were supposed to do, which is bring people out. Let's give 'em some money back."

Steve walked over to Granat, put about $2,000 in his hand and said, "You've got to have this money."

"What are you talking about?" Granat said. "I don't want this. You know I guaranteed your show."

"No, no, no," Steve said. "We're in this together. I don't want you to get hurt tonight."

Granat, who for 15 years had promoted 300 to 400 events a year, was stupefied. "That's the only guy that *ever* did that," he told Neuberger.

"Steve had integrity with a capital 'i.' He *was* integrity," Granat reflects. "In my 25 years, he was the only artist that actually offered money back and I didn't have to come in on kneepads — and I would have had to come in on kneepads just to talk to him eye to eye," he says with a laugh. "In this business, loyalty is not commonplace. You cherish it. It's what I built my reputation and business on, and with Goodman, you could take it to the bank, in every sense."

So the group in Granat's apartment set the tribute at Arie Crown, for Saturday evening, Jan. 26, 1985. Assisted by Maple Byrne and Dan Einstein, they secured a slate that, like the California production, had its share of Goodman-related stars. Topping the bill were Arlo Guthrie, the Nitty Gritty Dirt Band, Phoebe Snow, John Hartford, David Bromberg, Bonnie Raitt and Bryan Bowers, plus repeaters from the Costa Mesa show: John Prine, Jethro Burns and David Amram. It was a less intensely high-powered array of artists, however, because it also took in vaunted locals Ed and Fred Holstein, Michael Smith, Bonnie Koloc and Harry Waller, none of whom possessed national stature but gave the lineup a rich Chicago flavor and context. Bearing the same low-profile mix was the backup band — Steve Burgh, Johnny Burns, Jim Rothermel, Bob Hoban, Howard Levy, Hugh McDonald and Tom Radtke (with musical director Jim Tullio) — and for the tribute they were dubbed "the Lincoln Park Pirates." Regional radio favorites Roy Leonard of WGN and Ray Nordstrand of WFMT were tapped as emcees, and just as in California, the show became a fund-raiser for leukemia research.

Bandied about by organizers were the names of Bob Dylan, Robert Duvall, Bill Murray and Steve Martin, but those were the "more implausible" possibilities, says Byrne. Besides, the package of committed artists was quite appealing. Shortly after New Year's, Granat ran an ad in the Chicago papers. The *Tribune* ran a three-inch story Jan. 4. The $20 tickets went on sale Jan. 7, and Granat's hunch proved prescient. All 4,500 seats sold in four hours.

Pre-concert buzz was fanned by lengthy Goodman retrospectives in the *Tribune* and *Sun-Times*. Even the replacement of Phoebe Snow, who had a schedule conflict, with Richie Havens (famous from "Woodstock" but bearing no real connection to Steve) failed to dull the enthusiasm. Musicians agreed to fly in one and two days early for rehearsals at Chicago Recording Co. [11] Well before the 7 p.m. start time on the bitterly cold evening of Jan. 26, crowds swarmed to Arie Crown Theater. Situated on the South Side next to Lake Michigan, the theater was part of enormous McCormick Place, the convention center that Steve had noted in "Daley's Gone" had been rebuilt by the legendary late mayor after a 1967 fire.

Like the California show, this one exceeded five hours, but rehearsals and smooth equipment changes kept the pace brisk. The sincerity of emcees Leonard and Nordstrand lent the event warmth, and musical highlights dazzled the crowd like fireworks.

Led by Johnny Burns, the "Lincoln Park Pirates" donned bright-blue Cubs hats to launch the show with boisterous versions of "Take Me Out to the Ball

In this business, loyalty is not commonplace. You cherish it. It's what I built my reputation and business on, and with Goodman, you could take it to the bank, in every sense.
ARNY GRANAT

11: The day before the tribute, a local TV reporter asked Arlo Guthrie, "Do you think that if it's possible for Steve to be there, his spirit will find a way?" Before Guthrie could respond, Johnny Burns stuck his face before the camera and said, "Not if the Bulls are in town!" Many fell apart laughing in recognition. Burns says he was not exaggerating: "If Steve had a choice of playing (music) with these guys or watching Michael (Jordan) play, 'Sorry, gonna be down at the (Chicago) Stadium, can't make it tonight.' God forbid if the Cubs had been there."

Game" and "Go, Cubs, Go." Waller, as he had promised Steve following Patrick Chamberlain's suicide in 1976, brought out what he called "the Chicago national anthem," his "Cockroaches on Parade." Bowers sang and strummed a poignant "Satisfied Mind" (echoing Steve's rendition at Somebody Else's Troubles co-founder Bill Redhed's funeral seven years earlier). Hartford sang, played banjo and clogged on plywood to his "Gentle on My Mind." Bonnie Koloc's clear voice soared on Steve's "I Can't Sleep." Michael Smith supplied a slow, stately version of the song that Steve had made Smith's signature, "The Dutchman," restoring the lyrics Steve had changed and inducing a theater-wide hush.

The event not even half over, emcee Leonard gushed about the musicianship ("Isn't this the best 20 bucks you ever spent?"), but Jethro Burns sent emotions even higher. Before the 20-minute film of Steve's concert clips was shown, Burns stepped onstage, cementing the audience's affection for the honoree. Tilting at his reputation for deadpan one-liners, Burns preceded his swing set with an accolade of stunning earnestness. "If I would say God and Steve Goodman, I would give Goodman top billing," Burns said, adding, "If that's sacrilegious, I don't give a damn."

The awe-inspiring moments never let up. Amram delighted with his whistles on "The Water Is Wide." Bromberg sang a note- and nearly word-perfect "A Dying Cub Fan's Last Request," aided by his wife, Nancy, and three other backup singers. [12] ("That," he said later, "was a lot of words to learn." The sentiment of his low-key approach to the song was a welcome antidote to his companion piece, an angry, screeching and unsuitable blues titled "I Will Not Be Your Fool.") Guthrie, the original popularizer of "City of New Orleans," obliged with a vigorous version of his hit. Prine, in recognition of his long and close friendship with Steve, closed the show. Earlier he had hauntingly dueted with Raitt on his "Angel from Montgomery," but he saved his most startling contribution for last — "My Old Man," a rare instance of publicly performing one of Steve's songs. "I hope Minnette and Grandma Mary and Nancy and David will kinda forgive me for takin' liberties with this song," Prine told the audience, but his version, backed by both Levy and Rothermel on recorder, was both reverent and exquisite. The only thing that topped it was a full ensemble vamp on "Mama Don't Allow It."

In different ways, the tribute became a catharsis. "It was one of the loveliest nights I've ever spent anywhere," said Fred Holstein, who performed Bob Franke's "Thanksgiving Eve" (with the lyric, "Love till you love it away"). "It was a celebration for this guy, and everybody left their egos at the door. Everybody was high off each other, hugging each other and kissing. No attitudes at all." But for some, it tapped so deeply into their love for Steve as to be agonizing. Steve Burgh, who flew in from New York and played electric guitar on many songs, called it "a loving nightmare. We were all there to honor Steve, but the fact that he wasn't there was so painful. It was like being hit over the head with a hammer continuously for two days."

The mixing of local artists with national stars raised questions about the

---

If I would say God and Steve Goodman, I would give Goodman top billing. If that's sacrilegious, I don't give a damn.
JETHRO BURNS

12: The other "Dying Cub Fan" harmonizers were Diane Holmes, Ellen Germaine and Bonnie Herman. Some rolled their eyes at Bromberg trying a song they felt was uniquely identified with Steve. "It's possible that performing that song was not tactful," he says. "It hit pretty close to the mark." But Bromberg, who had moved to Chicago in 1980 to de-emphasize his stage shows and to learn violinmaking, did publicly perform "Dying Cub Fan" at least one more time, on Jan. 23, 1987, at Holsteins.

omission of dozens of other Chicago-based and Goodman-related folkies such as Art Thieme and Bob Gibson. Nonetheless, fans in the audience embraced the show as their own. For the *Tribune*, Ron Blumenfeld of Skokie recalled "being towed away by the 'Lincoln Park Pirates' when it only cost $30." John Orzechowski also was glad to see Steve get his due. "Goodman had poor success," he said. "He was kind of like the old Cubs. He had a lot of hits but never a lot of runs."

* * *

The ball that was inscribed by Keith Moreland (fainter signature in the center) and other 1984 Cubs, and which Havelock Hewes intended to deliver to Steve before he died, became the keepsake of singer-umpire Perry Barber, who muses: "It is the repository of all the lost hopes of the universe, Pandora's box in the form of a sphere."

(Photo by Clay Eals)

The concert tributes to Steve were far from the final evidence that his music and spirit would endure. Rather, they were just the beginning — harbingers of seemingly endless reverberations as the years and decades wore on.

The first clue came a month after the Arie Crown show, on Feb. 26 in Los Angeles, where Steve snagged something in death that had eluded him while he was alive — a Grammy Award. His "City of New Orleans" was recognized as the previous year's "best country song." Though he had written it in 1970 and recorded it in 1971, his classic train tune was eligible because of Willie Nelson's chart-topping 1984 version. John Prine and Steve's middle daughter, Sarah, accepted the award. "Thank you for recording my dad's song," the 9-year-old told the star-studded crowd, including Grammy winners Tina Turner, Cyndi Lauper and Prince. In a bulletin-board display at McGaugh school in Seal Beach, teachers saluted Sarah and her 7-year-old sister, Rosanna, who "looked great up onstage dancing with Prince and many other musicians."

Two months later, Havelock Hewes, in the "Finish Line" column of the April edition of *Sport* magazine, tried to expiate his guilt over never having delivered to Steve the signed Cubs baseball given him in mid-1984 by Keith Moreland. "Perhaps it is better to be a disgrace publicly than to live knee-deep in private shame," Hewes wrote. Moreland had handed Hewes the ball to give to Steve like "a doctor prescribing penicillin for a sick child." But Hewes kept putting off delivery of the prescription, reasoning that "Steve would rather get the ball as a token of solace after the Cubs had folded." But it was Steve, not the Cubs, who had folded first. In his column, Hewes left readers hanging about what he would do with the ball.

Steve's friend, New York folksinger-turned-umpire Perry Barber, who later became the fifth woman to work as an ump in pro baseball, devoured Hewes' column and wrote him an impassioned letter. Hewes decided to give her the ball, and after he secured Moreland's blessing, the signed orb was hers. "Perry shared some of the feeling of being a baseball fan with teams that have come up short," Hewes says, "so the idea of something that reflects lost hopes was probably the most poignant thing that she could receive." Barber cherishes it as a sentimental symbol of the potential lost with Steve's death at 36. "It is the repository of all the lost hopes of the universe," she says, "Pandora's box in the form of a sphere." [13]

Arlo Guthrie, who for years had been telling his story of meeting Steve at the Quiet Knight in 1971, started dedicating his performances of "City of New

13: Perry Barber umpires for the independent Atlantic League and for major-league spring-training and exhibition games.

Orleans" to Steve after his death. While performing on Aug. 4, 1985, at the Newport Folk Festival in Rhode Island, Guthrie also connected with an emotional comrade who had sung harmony on Steve's first LP. As Guthrie introduced "City," Newport veteran Joan Baez rushed onstage in tears to sing harmony. Afterward, she was still crying. "The memory of Steve is vivid," Baez told a reporter. "He was such a lovely guy. I was either going to cry or sing, so I decided to sing."

Not a month and a half later, at the first Farm Aid benefit concert on Sept. 22, 1985, Guthrie traded verses with Willie Nelson on "City of New Orleans" for 80,000 people filling Memorial Stadium at the University of Illinois in Champaign, the home of Steve's first abortive attempt at college 20 years earlier. The landmark event, including the Nelson-Guthrie duet, reached millions of cable-TV viewers via The Nashville Network.

In late fall of that year, Al Bunetta and Hank Neuberger released a double-LP digest of the Arie Crown performances, titled "Tribute to Steve Goodman." The Red Pajamas album was miserly for a two-fer set, averaging fewer than five songs per side, and it upended the show's original flow and momentum, notably sprinkling John Prine into three separate spots rather than presenting him contiguously. It also reflected a few unfortunate choices, such as the inclusion of David Bromberg's egocentric "I Will Not Be Your Fool" instead of his generous rendition of "Dying Cub Fan." In fact, of the album's 19 tracks, only six were songs that Steve had written or co-written, and only three others were tunes that he had recorded or frequently performed — a conspicuous paucity for a tribute project.

On the plus side, however, the album was lavishly illustrated (32 photos of Steve and 25 from the show), and its emotional song intros and slate of artists transformed it into a sum greater than its parts. Quickly it picked up sterling reviews. "Totally tasteful, with not a morbid or maudlin moment anywhere," wrote Al Rudis in the *Long Beach Press-Telegram*. Going further was Robert C. Trussell of the *Kansas City Star*: "You may have heard of the resurgence of folk music — who said it ever really left? — and here is an opportunity to sample what it's all about."

Grammy Award voters agreed. For the period of Oct. 1, 1985, through Sept. 30, 1986, the first year for which the Recording Academy divided its folk classification into "best traditional" and "best contemporary," the Goodman tribute album won in the latter category, which was announced in the annual ceremony held Feb. 24, 1987. The honor helped nudge Bunetta to gather musicians to fill out stray demo tracks left behind by Steve and assemble what became his first posthumous LP, "Unfinished Business." Released six months later, in August 1987, the album was curiously faceless, with no artwork on the front cover and only a tiny dressing-room photo of Steve on the back. But a lyric sheet inside included a brief poem by Nancy Goodman that both lamented and saluted "the unfinished business of a life of love and hoping."

The LP's 10 tracks ranged from spacey ("Whispering Man," co-written with

> He was such a lovely guy. I was either going to cry or sing, so I decided to sing.
> **JOAN BAEZ**

Michael Smith) to racy ("Don't Get Sand in It"). On this LP, though, the gems were the more serious selections: Steve's own take on "Colorado Christmas," a live solo version of "The Dutchman" and two of his wife Nancy's favorites, a duet with Jethro Burns on "A Fool Such as I" and the Rogers & Hart standard "My Funny Valentine." [14] These were a fine setup for the album's masterpiece, Steve's poignant co-write with Bill LaBounty, "In Real Life," whose words ached with lost opportunity. "It's the world that isn't fair," Steve sang. "People say one thing, and then they do another. ... It happens all the time in real life." The emotions of the somber songs had appeal of their own, but they also drew on the sobering sentiment three years after his death that Steve was no longer present.

For some, however, the opposite illusion had a powerful pull. Jim Tullio, who produced the tracks "In Real Life" and "Colorado Christmas" at Chicago's Streeterville Studios, worked while Steve's mom, Minnette, chose to sit by his side. "Steve would be talking to the engineer on tape," Tullio says. "He'd be playing the guitar, then he'd tell a joke to the engineer, and I tell ya, we must have heard this thing 400 times, back and forth, by overdubbing this and mixing that, and every time it got me. The song would be over, and Steve would say, 'Hey man, I got one for you,' typical Steve, and it was like he was there." Tears constantly welled in Minnette's eyes. [15]

Like the tribute album, "Unfinished Business" struck a chord with Grammy voters. For the second straight year, and the third time in four years, a project in Steve's name had secured a Grammy. The LP won for "best contemporary folk recording," and in a pre-recorded ceremony, Nancy, the girls, Al Bunetta and Tullio stepped up to the dais to receive the award from Judy Collins, with Sarah delivering a brief speech.

The occasion was bittersweet for sardonic singer/songwriter Loudon Wainwright III. In both the ceremonies for 1986 and 1987, albums by Wainwright — first "I'm Alright" and then "More Love Songs" — were up for Grammys, in the same category as Steve's albums. "Both times I got beat, both times by Steve Goodman, and I'm pissed off about that," Wainwright says with a wry grin. "So as far as I'm concerned, he is still alive. That son of a bitch, he must have been laughing at me." [16]

* * *

If he were observing from an otherworldly locale, Steve Goodman would have found much to laugh and smile about in the two-plus decades following his death. His influence as a songwriter and performer did not evaporate in his absence. To a striking degree, his reach branched like the arms of a mammoth tree.

"City of New Orleans," of course, became the touchstone. Through the end of 2007, at least 39 artists recorded new versions of the song after Willie Nelson's 1984 rendition topped the *Billboard* country charts — as many as the 39 variations that were released in Steve's lifetime. As confirmation of the power and ubiquity of Arlo Guthrie's 1972 version, nearly all of the post-1984 recordings of "City" employed Guthrie's word and chord changes.

14: The recording of "My Funny Valentine" came from an unlikely source. Secretly, Steve had sung it into the answering machine on Bunetta's office desk, removed the cassette and tossed it into a drawer. Later, Bunetta found the tape. "That's the most beautifully sung song I've ever heard," says Chicago radio producer Mary Gaffney. "I could hear qualities a cantor would have."

15: Steve's spirit moved Minnette more tangibly as well. One night, after attending a birthday party on Chicago's North Side, she walked to the lot where she had parked her car, only to find it had been hauled away by Lincoln Towing. She told a Chicago newspaper reporter, "Maybe it's just my kid's way of saying, 'Hi, Mom!' "

16: Wainwright, who hasn't snagged a Grammy bid since, is still haunted by his competitor's stagecraft. "Steve was kind of a one-man wrecking crew," he says. "He was like Sugar Ray Robinson. Pound for pound, he was the hardest hitter, and although he had this big grin on his face, he was vicious. He would get out there like a little Jack Russell and just shake the audience until there wasn't really anything left. If you did have the misfortune to follow him, you were in deep shit."

Prominent singers included country star (and Earl Scruggs' son) Randy Scruggs, who traded vocals with John Prine on "City" for Scruggs' 1998 CD, "Crown of Jewels." It has been the only instance, other than the live version of "My Old Man" on the Chicago tribute album, in which Prine has recorded a song by Steve. [17] Guthrie himself also re-recorded "City" in unconventional fashion — in polka rhythm with Jimmy Sturr and his acclaimed, 11-piece polka band on its 2002 CD, "Top of the World," which won a 2003 Grammy for best polka recording. Sturr had met Guthrie when both performed at the 2000 Farm Aid in Manassas, Virginia, and after the 9/11 terrorist attack, Sturr enlisted Guthrie to "do something a little patriotic," selecting "City" and "This Land Is Your Land" by Guthrie's father, Woody. "Arlo has such a great style," Sturr says. "I think of him as the East Coast Willie Nelson."

Also trying their hand at "City" were lesser-known artists such as New Orleans pianist David Roe, who with his wife, Laura, eerily survived a fiery, March 15, 1999, crash of the City of New Orleans train. Roe and his "Royal Rounders and Friends" dedicated their "Angel of New Orleans" CD to the rescue workers who saved their lives. Another interpreter was the steel guitarist who often accompanied Steve on record and in concert, New Zealand homeopathist Winnie Winston, who, before his own death from cancer in 2005, recorded a version of "City" that appeared on a posthumous CD, "Misty Morn."

While most of these musicians found Guthrie's "City of New Orleans" template irresistible, one holdout was Brian Gill, who in 2006 released his true-to-Steve version on a self-produced CD, "Playin' Favorites." Gill, born and raised in Kankakee, felt indelibly linked to the train that ran through his hometown and to Steve's song about it. Gill's years of informal tutelage with Steve in Chicago inspired him to write 75 songs, one of which, "Daddy Smoked His Life Away," became the theme for the American Cancer Society's Great American Smokeout in 1988. As Gill later moved to Las Vegas, Nashville and his present home of Moscow, Idaho, his performances in clubs and on radio and TV often included "City," with Steve's original lyrics and chords intact. "I've always played it the way he showed me," Gill says. "Steve had the purest love of a great song, and a great song is absolutely immobilizing."

Just in time, John Denver finally recognized this. In 1997, he assembled "All Aboard!," a delightful children's CD of 14 train songs that included, as the project's final tune, a new recording of "City of New Orleans" that concurred with Arlo Guthrie's version and not the cloying, sanitized one Denver had released 26 years earlier. Restored to the song were Steve's full writing credit, his references to Memphis and the Mississippi River and his phrases "old black men" [18] and "the disappearing railroad blues." It was an upbeat, triumphant track, textured with dobro, fiddle and harmonica and anchored by the 53-year-old Denver's rich, mature voice. The recording had a heartbreaking coda, however. Just 47 days after its Aug. 26, 1997, release, Denver died in a plane crash, producing an unintended but synchronous result. The righted "City" became the final Denver track issued in his lifetime. [19]

Arlo has such a great style. I think of him as the East Coast Willie Nelson.
JIMMY STURR

17: Prine allows that someday he may record a CD of Steve's songs: "I'd love to do it, but I gotta figure out how. I'd like it to be a special album, y'know, not just a standard tribute thing."

18: Longtime Chicago folksinger Art Thieme would love to release a live version of "City" that he sang one week after Steve's death. But he mangled a phrase, singing "graveyards full of old black men," instead of "freight yards," so he opted not to release the tape. "It was a slip of the tongue," he says, "but I just can't fill those graveyards with black men." Thieme, now of Peru, Illinois, and wrestling with multiple sclerosis, is no longer able to perform.

19: Following his death, Denver's "All Aboard!" CD found a spot on the *Billboard* Top 200 chart for just one week at #165 on Nov. 1, 1997, before disappearing.

"It's one of those songs that can be done by so many different artists in so many different ways," says Judy Collins, who re-recorded a version of "City" drenched with steel guitar, piano and her soaring soprano in 2000 for her "Live at Wolf Trap" CD, DVD and PBS-TV show. "It just is a spellbinding song."

New England folksinger Charlie King found the "City" theme and melody so compelling that it became a model for a song he wrote to rally commuters to protest a proposed cut in funding for the Shore Line East train connecting the cities of New London and New Haven. Echoing the fate of Steve's signature song, King wrote, "Good morning, Connecticut, how are you? Don't you know us, we are here to stay?" [20]

"City of New Orleans" even transcended the musical world to the realm of visual art. Aneta Sperber, a quilter and photographer from Bloomington, Indiana, "covered" the song with a creation of her own — a 78-by-84-inch, queen-size quilt that used photo transfers of train images. Begun in 1988, when Sperber was 46, finished in the mid-1990s and occasionally displayed publicly since then, "Railroad Crossing" was inspired by Steve's "City," especially the "disappearin' railroad blues." Sensitive to "the corporate and governmental transportation decisions that all but destroyed the railroads of this country," Sperber embedded her images so that they would be "very hard to find, as if they are disappearing," the longtime Midwesterner says. "There are trains that you can barely see in the quilt, and there are trains that are much more obvious — all the stages of becoming and going." [21]

There was no mistaking the trains in another form of visual art, the scratchboard watercolors that graced *The Train They Call the City of New Orleans*, a 32-page, hardcover children's picture book created by noted illustrator Michael McCurdy and published in 2003. Accompanied by the song's lyrics (including Guthrie's "steel" instead of "steam"), the muted and detailed images traced the train's trek from snowy, industrial Chicago through Midwestern farming towns and Mississippi bayous to New Orleans. The book was re-released a year later with a CD in which Tom Chapin, a singer who witnessed Steve's Bitter End debut in May 1971, spoke and sang the lyrics, and the project snagged a Grammy in 2005 for "best spoken word album for children."

"City" found its way into the eyes and ears of children and adults in a more insidious fashion in 1998, when Steve's most popular song became enveloped in the American consumerism that he often skewered. Makers of Ex-Lax were seeking a way to depict the exhilaration that a customer would experience upon awakening after ingesting the laxative the night before. Imagining an attractive woman in a nightgown sitting up in bed, her arms outstretched in elation, ad agency gurus thought of "City" and its chorus: "Good morning, America, how are you?" In the world of TV spots, it was a perfect subliminal fit — a commercial message for an audience of baby boomers driven by a nostalgic, popular song.

But would it respect the memory of Steve? Al Bunetta, who had finally retrieved from Buddah Records the "City of New Orleans" publishing rights for

> **There are trains that you can barely see in the quilt, and there are trains that are much more obvious — all the stages of becoming and going.**
> **ANETA SPERBER**

20: Jim Willey, mayor of Elburn, a far-west suburb of Chicago, penned a similar rewrite of the "City" lyrics on his Internet blog in February 2007, commemorating the Metra commuter train serving his city, the Village of Elburn: "It'll be gone eighty-eight miles when the trip is done." Six months later, before the Baltimore Regional Transit Board, Art Cohen, sang rewritten "City" lyrics to seek a boost in transit funds. His take-off was called "The Region of Old Excuses."

21: Saturated reds, greens and greys filled Sperber's creation. Her grandmother, Flora McMannis of Ohio, assisted her with it.

the benefit of Steve's family, worried over the Ex-Lax overture and telephoned Steve's widow, Nancy.

"I've got good news and bad news," Bunetta said.

"What's the good news?" she said.

"This ad agency wants to use 'City of New Orleans' in a commercial."

"Well, it's not *War and Peace*," Nancy replied. "Go for it. What's the bad news?"

"The bad news is, it's Ex-Lax."

Nancy burst into laughter. "That's pretty ironic," she said. "Steve was so constipated from all the chemo treatments. Don't you remember how he used to say, 'Man, if I could have one good dump, I'd live forever'?"

So for the use of six key words of the "City" chorus for a full year, a six-figure deal was struck. The resulting TV spot, with the woman awakening joyfully, aired day and night, all but inescapable. It was a financial boon for Nancy, who with her daughters had moved to New York in 1987 and five years later had married Manhattan literary agent Craig Tenney and settled down in Brooklyn Heights to pursue a career as a nurse practitioner. [22] A pleased Bunetta characterized the deal for Canadian publicist Richard Flohil: "That's the house paid for, three kids through college, done."

Jessie Goodman, who was 26 when she first learned of her mother's Ex-Lax conversation with Bunetta, later was contacted by friends and others who were incredulous over the use of her dad's most beloved song for a crass purpose. "Steve would be rolling over in his grave" was a common plaint. "What, are you kidding?" Jessie replied. "He'd be sitting here laughing his ass off, going, 'Yeah, OK, no problem.' "

Richard Wedler, who had prodded Steve to write the second verse of "City," agrees that Steve "would have loved it." In fact, he says, Steve probably would have uttered the ultimate irony: "Hey, no shit!"

Perhaps unsurprisingly, Arlo Guthrie received complaint letters with a "Why did you sell out?" message over the Ex-Lax spot, a reflection of his close identification with "City" in the public consciousness. "I am still a train guy to a lot of people," he says. "They'll show up with their railroad hats at the shows, the old guys." But the misperception that he had written the song had pitfalls as well as plums — and in a memorable cross-country journey that took place years after Steve's death, he witnessed both.

The Burlington Northern Railway, consolidated from three lines in 1970 and operating across the northern Midwest and West over the next 25 years, contacted Guthrie by telephone. "Arlo, we want you to write a song about Burlington Northern," an official told him. "We're going to give you your own train. You're going to have your own car with your own private chef."

The invitation instantly reminded Guthrie of when the Bonneville Power Administration had hired his dad in 1941 to be driven through Oregon and Washington for a month to write songs to promote the cheap public power resulting from the construction of hydroelectric dams. That trip had spawned

That's pretty ironic. Steve was so constipated from all the chemo treatments. Don't you remember how he used to say, 'Man, if I could have one good dump, I'd live forever'?
NANCY GOODMAN TENNEY

22: "She wanted to have her own life, and she didn't want to be anyplace where she would have been Steve Goodman's wife," says Robert Pruter of his sister Nancy's move to New York. "She wanted to be her own entity, and she didn't want all this baggage."

"Roll On, Columbia" and dozens of other classic Woody Guthrie tunes. Arlo Guthrie readily accepted the BN offer, flew to Chicago and boarded a BN train heading west through the scenic Dakotas and partway into Montana, where a BN official hopped aboard.

"Arlo," said the official, "we're so thrilled to have you on the train."

"I'm really thrilled to be here," Guthrie replied.

"We want you to write a song for Burlington Northern that all the employees at Burlington Northern can sing."

"I would love to be able to do that for you," Guthrie said.

"If you can write us a song just like you wrote 'City of New Orleans,' we'll be thrilled."

Guthrie says he didn't know how to respond, given that he already had traveled a fair distance in the private car.

But he decided to tell the truth: "Y'know, I didn't write 'City of New Orleans.' I only sang 'City of New Orleans.' "

Thud.

"Oh," replied the dumbfounded official.

Guthrie told the official he was looking forward to seeing the gargantuan strip mines and Big Bertha shovels of western Montana so that he might create a workingman's song similar to those of his father. The official quickly arranged to drop off Guthrie near West Yellowstone.

There, Guthrie composed "one of the better songs I've ever written," about a mineworker who got sick and died on the job and whose grave is marked by plastic flowers. "There's a white picket fence around the grave of Mike McGilvray, who had come from Massachusetts for to work upon the grade," his song began. But Guthrie says it was not a composition that BN wanted to sponsor.

"They wanted me to write a propaganda tune, which was a shame because I could have written a great song for them," he says. "They didn't understand the difference. You have to be able to have freedom, like my dad when he wrote the songs for the Bonneville Power Administration. They gave him a chauffeur and said, 'Go anywhere you want.' And he did, and he wrote great songs for them that are still being sung today."

Guthrie says his strip-mining song still needs a couple more verses, and someday he may finish it. More precious to him than the tune, however, is the irony of its genesis.

"It's one of those Steve Goodman moments," Guthrie says, "when something that was totally attributable to him got passed on to me for no good reason, even though I was perfectly capable of writing a decent song for them myself. Goodman would have got a big kick out of that." [23]

Soon enough, Guthrie became embroiled in a more substantive connection to "City of New Orleans" and its significance. Over the years, he had immersed himself in efforts to preserve rail lines, joining then-President Carter's son Chip in 1979 in riding Amtrak's Montrealer passenger train to a Washington, D.C., rally to stave off its cancellation. Twenty-five years later, in June 2005, Guthrie

Y'know, I didn't write 'City of New Orleans.' I only sang 'City of New Orleans.'
ARLO GUTHRIE

23: In spite of the inaccurate perception of the song's author, Burlington Northern's zeal for "City of New Orleans" reflects the view of Ellis Paul, singer/ songwriter from Charlottesville, Virginia, who says Steve's lyrics hold a deeply American appeal. "It's a universal perspective, even though he is speaking from a train's perspective. It's a song about American manifest destiny and the glory of travel and the freedom of being a human being in a free society. It's more than a train. It's about America. He's talking, really, about more than 300 million people, and he did it beautifully. You cannot listen to that song without feeling like we're lucky to be where we are."

Arlo Guthrie, shown in 2004 at the Oklahoma festival named for his father, gave "City of New Orleans" new life following Hurricane Katrina.

(Photo by Jim Dirden)

24: Shortly after Katrina, Australian folk-festival leader Keith McKenry used "City" as the basis for a take-off that spread via the Internet: "Good morning, America, where are you? ... There'll be thousands of us dead ere day is done." Indiana songwriter Peter Weisz penned a similar plaint, "The Pity of New Orleans." Seven months later, on April 14, 2006, the online *Grist* summoned the tune's original title in castigating the lack of large-scale recycling in Katrina cleanup: "The Train Wreck They Call the City of New Orleans."

announced he might stage a similar protest to save the City of New Orleans and 17 other long-distance rail lines from an extinction threatened by Congress. Diverting attention from that cause two months later, however, was the infamous Hurricane Katrina, which devastated New Orleans and other cities along the north-central Gulf Coast.

"After we sent our money into the Red Cross, like everyone else I was sitting around, glued to the television and horrified at what was going on," Guthrie told reporters. "I saw a little banner, a ticker creeping across the screen, saying the City of New Orleans (train) is resuming service to New Orleans. And I thought, 'Why don't we get on that train and do some fund-raisers, on the way down from Chicago?' I wanted to do something that only I could do, and it seemed like this was a thing where I could help in some way that would be unique and a lot of fun and would actually do some good."

His seven-show tour, from Dec. 5 to 17, kicked off at the Vic Theatre, a few steps around the corner from the site of the former Quiet Knight, where Guthrie had first heard Steve play "City of New Orleans" for him in March 1971. For the tour's final concert, at the legendary Tipitina's in New Orleans, Guthrie teamed with the musician who had sent "City" to the top of the country charts while Steve underwent his transplant, Willie Nelson. Beneficiaries of the $140,000 raised by the tour were the severely damaged music venues of New Orleans, whose plight was given prominent attention by national press covering Guthrie. All along, however, the backdrop was the spirit of the song — an insight that informed the singer's approach.

"Anybody who saw the aftermath of 9/11, when the planes were grounded and traffic was at a standstill, the only things running were trains," Guthrie told Dave Hoekstra of the *Chicago Sun-Times*. "It didn't make any sense to me why we wouldn't afford ourselves as a country every opportunity to keep goods and services and people moving." [24]

For Steve's widow, Nancy Tenney, the song was having a salutary effect both concrete and intangible. Royalties from "City of New Orleans," she told Hoekstra in December 2005, were "still taking care of the girls" (Jessie, then 33, Sarah, 30, and Rosanna, 28). But the impact, she said, went far beyond financial. "It is the most incredible legacy, the pride of that. Here was a guy (Steve) who wanted everything and knew he was only going to have a certain amount of time to get it," she said. "To have somebody like Arlo Guthrie recognize that early on was amazing."

U.S. Sen. Hillary Clinton, Steve's classmate from Maine East High School days, confirms the tune's lasting appeal. "I really think 'City of New Orleans' is one of the great songs that came out of my generation," she says. "I love that song, and I think that Steve's passion and narrative storytelling ability just struck a chord with so many people."

But Steve's musical legacy has billowed out far beyond "City of New Orleans." In the more than two decades since the issuance of the 1985 Chicago tribute album, 52 artists have recorded an eye-opening 24 other songs written or co-written by Steve. [25] Of those compositions, two — the torchy blues "A Lover Is Forever" and the cautionary "Lookin' for Trouble" — were the clear favorites. "Forever" triggered recorded interpretations by nine artists, while "Trouble" clocked in with eight.

"A Lover Is Forever," which germinated in a raucous session with Fred Knobloch at Steve's home in 1982, came together nearly a decade later in the hands of Knobloch, who gave its melody a mood of melancholy jazz, reminiscent of Julie London's classic take on "Cry Me a River." Knobloch built the song on Steve's key line — "You can marry anytime you like, but a lover is forever" — and began singing it around Nashville in the early 1990s. In quick succession came recordings by Rosanne Cash ("The twistedness and the beauty of that line kinda sums Steve up, doesn't it?" she says), Etta James and country superstar Trisha Yearwood. The Yearwood version, closing her sixth LP, "Everybody Knows," is definitive, aided by a spare strings trio and the haunting harmonica of Kirk "Jelly Roll" Johnson. It remains the most affecting Goodman song that Steve apparently never recorded himself.

"Lookin' for Trouble," which spotlights a circular trilogy of temptations — drinking, lying and womanizing — appealed personally to African-American folksinger Josh White Jr., the son of a musical hero of Steve's who died in 1969 at age 54. "I'm an alcoholic," says the junior White, "so I know what drinking can do, and I know I'm a liar. I've been a liar all my life. We who drink are in those situations with people." Besides sensing the song's intrinsic value, he also wanted to honor Steve. "I don't care if only one copy is sold," he says. "In my mind, I've honored him by recording it."

Diane Taraz, who also recorded "Trouble," sees it as capturing "the rueful sense of futility we all struggle with in our everyday lives." Her version, "probably the most intense vocal I've ever recorded," is darker than Steve's original, in contrast to the ironic subtext of Steve's voice. "Even when I'm singing a happy song I often have a cry in my voice — the exact opposite of Steve," Taraz says. "Even on sad songs, Steve always had a smile in his voice. You could just hear him keeping things in perspective, ready to break into a big smile and have a good laugh at the big joke of life."

One of Steve's other songs, "The Ballad of Penny Evans," was recorded five times from 1985 on. Three others, "Banana Republics," "Frank and Lola" and "The Twentieth Century Is Almost Over," each drew three recorded interpretations. Three more Steve compositions, "I Can't Sleep," "I Just Keep Falling in Love" and "You Never Even Call Me by My Name," were each recorded twice. Easily the most politically provocative of these tracks was the version of "Penny Evans" recorded by brash and unpredictable singer/songwriter Michelle Shocked.

An East Texas native who ranges from gospel to big-band swing, Shocked learned "Penny Evans" on her childhood front porch from her father's circle of folksinging friends. She welcomed its female viewpoint on war ("it puts a very personal face on a very public experience") and began singing it in her mid-20s while touring with Billy Bragg in the late 1980s, as a complement to Bragg's

Josh White Jr., shown in 2000 at the Clearwater Revival in New York, sought to honor Steve by recording a version of his "Lookin' for Trouble."
(Photo by Clay Eals)

25: Not included in those totals are reissues of others' versions of Steve-written songs that originally were released before his death. Also not included are tracks on a tribute CD released in June 2006 by Steve's youngest daughter, Rosanna. The CD featured "City of New Orleans" and 11 other tunes written or co-written by Steve as performed by 10 of Rosanna's musical friends. The project included versions of six songs not recorded by anyone other than Steve. (See "On the Record" section for details.)

Michelle Shocked, who has embraced "Ballad of Penny Evans," sings July 4, 2002, in Steamboat Springs, Colorado.
(Photo by Larry Fox, <larry-fox.com>)

26: Two artists have updated the song's lyrics. Christy Martin of the Mountain View, California, duo Four Shillings Short advanced the protagonist's age to 61 and wrote a new last line: "Now they say the war is over, but another has begun." (Jacquie Manning of the Cary, Illinois, duo Small Potatoes regularly performs this version.) The ex-husband of famed singer/ songwriter Joni Mitchell, Chuck Mitchell of Keokuk, Iowa, penned his own update in 2006 and issued it as a CD single. His Penny Evans is "a widow of that Iraq War they said would soon be won," and, "The mission's been accomplished, the line drawn in the sand."

27: The Highwaymen's prancing "Twentieth Century" track, driven by a bouncy organ, played loose with the lyrics and even omitted the song's third verse.

male anti-war song, "Tender Comrade." Her strident rendition of "Penny Evans" — a cappella like Steve's — often came as a final encore, and she released live versions on a 1988 extended-play album, a 1990 video, a 1992 Newport Folk Festival CD and an expanded version of her "Short Sharp Shocked" CD in 2003.

The enduring power that "Penny Evans" wields apart from Steve was realized in Shocked's embrace of it, given that she never saw Steve perform or heard his recording of the song. With the onset of the Persian Gulf War in 1991, Shocked and her audiences realized that the song transcended the specifics of Vietnam 20 years before. Twelve years later, when the United States launched the post-9/11 war in Iraq, Shocked discovered that "Penny Evans" resonated deeply among Europeans. "They don't really hear a lot about Americans being against the Bush administration policies," she said in 2003. "They kind of get the sense that we're all marching in lockstep. So the song becomes really liberating." [26] Shocked allows that "Penny Evans" eventually may become identified as much with her as it was with Steve, but she also honors its creator. "Among my dad and his friends, Steve Goodman's songs were a standard. He was the songwriter's songwriter."

Doug Supernaw, a rising country singer/songwriter of the early 1990s, obviously felt the same way. He managed to enlist four legends of the genre — Merle Haggard, Charley Pride, Waylon Jennings and David Allan Coe — to join him in singing Steve's and John Prine's "You Never Even Call Me by My Name" on his 1994 CD, "Deep Thoughts from a Shallow Mind." The choices were deliciously apt, as the first three were named in the original lyrics for the song (and in Supernaw's version sang those very phrases) and Coe, in a self-aggrandizing version, was the one who 19 years earlier had lifted the tune to #8 on the *Billboard* country chart. Commendably, Supernaw's midsong recitation correctly credited Steve for the song's authorship and not Coe, and the track overall was an interpretation that was both respectful and fun. But the big names didn't ensure success for the Supernaw CD, which received tepid reviews, and the all-star single rode the *Billboard* chart for just seven weeks, topping out at #60.

With a similar quartet of country songwriting icons, a far more successful CD was the setting for the earliest and most prominent of three recordings of "The Twentieth Century Is Almost Over" made after Steve's death. It was the debut release of the Highwaymen: Willie Nelson, Johnny Cash, Kris Kristofferson and Waylon Jennings, and Nelson and Cash traded lead vocals on "Twentieth Century." [27] The 1985 album spawned two hit singles and reached #1 on the *Billboard* country chart, remaining in the top 75 country LPs for an astounding 14 months. That the group included one of Steve's songs in the project was no accident, says Kristofferson, who notes that all four were Steve's fans. Particularly striking was the regard for Steve held by Cash and Nelson, whom Kristofferson likens to "the guys up on Rushmore. They stand for the country."

The end-of-the-century song, presciently written in 1977 by Steve and John

Prine, also turned up, with Nancy Tenney's assent, in a Mount Rushmore-like TV commercial. The classy 60-second spot, airing in late 1999 on NBC's "Friends," Fox's "Ally McBeal" and many cable stations, traced the history of Mercedes-Benz automobiles, a bright orange edition of which Steve once owned. The intent, said the Merkley Newman Harty ad agency, was to "highlight over 100 years of innovation and heritage from the world's oldest automobile manufacturer." Creative director Andy Hirsch, who had first heard "Twentieth Century" in the late 1980s, knew it would be a perfect fit. "It was so eclectic and engaging that I filed it in the back of my head for use at some later date," he said. "With the end of the century fast approaching, I figured it was now or never." [28]

The phrase "now or never" also fit the approach that Al Bunetta and Nancy Tenney took to Steve's own recordings in the years following his death. After the Grammy-winning "Unfinished Business" LP of 1987, Bunetta repackaged Steve's 1975-80 Asylum recordings and released two "best of" LPs, with 10 tracks each, in 1988 and 1989. Each was a hodgepodge with little continuity or emotional cohesion.

Five years later, however, in 1994, came a landmark package to make up for the lapse — a two-CD anthology titled "No Big Surprise" (a line from Steve's song "In Real Life"). It consisted of 23 studio tracks and 19 live recordings, more than half of which (24) had not been previously released. Coming a decade after Steve died, the Red Pajamas collection let the CD-buying public hear for the first time a cornucopia of Steve's aural gems, many of them stripped down from their studio overproduction to just Steve and his guitar. Rarities abounded: a charming 1968 jingle for Red Ball Jets tennis shoes, a 1979 remnant from one of Steve's onstage broken-string improvisations and a 1983 rendition of Michael Smith's "Wonderful World of Sex" in which Steve forgot the last verse and filled in with his own. ("Michael Smith would be embarrassed if he knew / This is the one song of his that I blew.")

Thoughtfully assembled, "No Big Surprise" began auspiciously with Steve's underrated musical admonition to read "Between the Lines," and it ended even more effectively with a studio version of Herman Hupfeld's "Casablanca" film theme, "As Time Goes By." In the latter tune, Steve alternated between delicate romanticism and rampant hilarity, straddling singing styles from 1940s Jerry Colonna to 1950s doo-wop and slipping in zingers ("Yes, the world will always welcome lovers — thank goodness," and "Moonlight and love songs, never out of date / Hearts full of passion, the other songs can wait"). The symbiotically aching tenderness and semantic sendups of Steve Goodman, along with his affection for the classics, all were encapsulated in this song — whose theme, not incidentally, was the passage of time that Steve no longer had.

The music, however, was only part of the package. A 36-page, CD-sized booklet held a heartfelt, anecdote-filled, 2,000-word essay written by Nancy Tenney (and assisted by her husband, Craig), a shorter remembrance by Al Bunetta [29] and testimonials by Johnny Cash, Steve Martin, Bette Midler, Rob-

> **With the end of the century fast approaching, I figured it was now or never.**
> **ANDY HIRSCH**

28: "Twentieth Century" was the basis for a contest by *Chicago Tribune* columnist Eric Zorn, who asked readers to write a verse to cover the final 23 years of the 1900s. The winner saluted "Calvin & Hobbes," the nicotine patch and TV's "Survivor." The song also was one of several Goodman tunes embraced by "filk" musicians — those who create original folk tunes or write new words to existing ones, with a science-fiction or fantasy bent. Before the 2000 election results were finalized, Los Angeles filker Barry Gold sang his wife Lee's takeoff to the "Twentieth Century" tune, called "Election 2000 Hasn't All Been Counted." Later, Lee Gold wrote a follow-up, "The Twenty-First Century Is Just Beginning."

29: Bunetta had taken John Prine's cue from a decade earlier and in late 1992 moved his office to Nashville from Los Angeles.

ert Duvall and a dozen other celebrities. Laced throughout were 26 photos, including part of Steve's original, handwritten lyric sheet for "City of New Orleans" and an iconic shot of preschool-aged Steve astride a young bear in Chicago's Lincoln Park — a Cub fan atop a real-life cub. On the cover, a photo reflected the serenity of the song that Steve arguably had given his most endearing interpretation over the years. In the 1976 scene, bathed in sepia, Steve watched and listened while an elderly Amsterdam resident fished in a canal and held aloft his left index finger as if to make a point. It was Steve taking a lesson from "The Dutchman."

In some cases, photo captions were missing or inaccurate, and song annotations were sketchy, but the package was an overall ear- and eye-opener, the first recorded product to reflect the stature that fans and critics felt Steve deserved. Chicago reviewers Dan Kening of the *Tribune* and Dave Hoekstra of the *Sun-Times* gave the anthology four stars, Hoekstra calling it "a passionate representation of Goodman's unique versatility." The pastiche reflected "a song chest that illuminated (Steve's) love of life, even in the face of death," said *Billboard*. "Most of the material, some of it more than 20 years old," wrote Alanna Nash in *Stereo Review*, "sounds perfectly fresh and quintessentially American." Robert Christgau of the *Village Voice* called the anthology Steve's first great album and zeroed in on its "irresistible" live cuts, saying they proved Steve not only enjoyed himself but also consummated his quest "to induce us to enjoy ourselves as well."

Like Steve himself, "No Big Surprise" was a tough act to follow. But Bunetta tore into the task, releasing in 1996 "The Easter Tapes," a consolidation of Steve's four mid-1970s shows with host Vin Scelsa on WNEW-FM, with David Amram supplying flutes and percussion on seven of the CD's 20 tracks. Bunetta followed up in 2000 with "Live Wire," a slightly realigned version of Steve's full-band show from April 28, 1979, at the Bayou in Washington, D.C. [30] In the first years of the new century, Bunetta also secured the requisite rights and released all of Steve's Buddah and Asylum LPs on CD. In September 2006, Bunetta released another live CD edited from Steve's Aug. 15-16, 1978, shows at the Chicago club where he got his true start, "Live at the Earl of Old Town." [31]

The topper of Steve's posthumous releases, however, came in early 2003 when Bunetta assembled an array of video footage for a two-hour DVD. Though it provided no narration and only a few dates for context, it was a singular feat — the first chance most people had in two decades to simultaneously see and hear Steve at his best, onstage. Eighteen of the film's 20 musical tracks came from Steve's 1977 and 1982 appearances on "Austin City Limits." The other two were Steve's 1983 rendition of "A Dying Cub Fan's Last Request" for NBC "Today" (along with most of his interview with Mike Leonard) and a 1978 studio performance of "You're the Girl I Love." It was the long-delayed realization of a project that Bunetta had first planned to release for Christmas 1995, and he arranged for interviews of Kris Kristofferson, John Prine and Nancy Tenney to be filmed in the spring of that year at the Bitter End in New York. Clips from that foot-

---

Most of the material, some of it more than 20 years old, sounds perfectly fresh and quintessentially American.
ALANNA NASH
STEREO REVIEW

30: Inexplicably, the photos on the front and back cover of "Live Wire" did not depict Steve's then-shaggy hair and full mustache and beard. Instead, the uncredited images (taken by Ed Stiernberg) showed a shorthaired, post-relapse Steve restringing his guitar and playing it (and a mandola) on May 26, 1983, at Chicago's Park West.

31: This CD began charmingly with an intro by Earl Pionke: "Well, folks, I believe this thunderous applause is probably not for me, so without further waiting, let's bring out the guy you all came to see here and enjoy, our own Steve Goodman!" The spoken bit came not from the 1978 shows, however, but was recorded anew in 2006 by producer Jim Tullio.

age, as well as later interviews with Arlo Guthrie, Marty Stuart and Bunetta himself were included as a bonus. [32]

The DVD was a stunner, and *SingOut!* reviewer Michael Tearson captured the catharsis. "Every second here is just brilliant, absolutely essential stuff," he wrote. "But that doesn't surprise me. I never saw a Steve Goodman set that was anything less. ... I may still feel cheated that Steve Goodman isn't walking around the planet and playing and writing anymore, but this DVD sure helps ease that perpetual ache."

Soothing that sting in the years following Steve's death were 35 LP and CD compilations that included performances by Steve of 15 songs drawn from his own albums. Fifteen of the collections — with names ranging from "America Forever" to "Mystery Train" — featured "City of New Orleans." Steve's "Banana Republics" figured in three compilations, while his version of "The Dutchman" appeared in two. Baseball samplers drew heavily from Steve's diamond songs, with "A Dying Cub Fan's Last Request" in four projects, "Go, Cubs, Go" in two and "Take Me Out to the Ball Game" in one.

Steve's tunes kept turning up in all manner of media, including uses on television ranging from the surreal to the silly to the serious. Fans of the cult "X Files" spinoff "Millennium" heard Steve singing "Danger" inconspicuously in the background of a dark barroom scene in the fourth episode ("The Judge," aired Nov. 22, 1996) of the Fox series' first season.

Mainstream TV fans in the mid-1990s also got a dose of Steve — most of them not knowing it because he was not named — while watching ABC's phenomenal "America's Funniest Home Videos." A Chicago couple won $100,000 for a video titled "Baby Sings the Blues," in which a father sang to his infant son Steve's ditty "I Ain't Heard You Play No Blues." After each time the word "baby" turned up in the dad's singing, the infant squealed, "Baby!" The epitome of cuteness, it handily nabbed the prize.

Viewers of TNN's "Nashville Now" show on Aug. 13, 1990, saw June Carter Cash recite her brief chapter on Steve and their mutual endurance of pain from her 1987 memoir, *From the Heart.* Her husband Johnny called the piece "a sad, very poignant thing that I like very much." As June read it, in the background Steve's "City of New Orleans" was picked slowly on guitar, and a young woman used melancholy "oo-oo" tones to sing its melody.

From the Heart was far from the only book that delved into Steve's life and music after his death. Steve turned up prominently from the mid-1980s to the mid-2000s in histories of the music scenes in New York's Greenwich Village and Austin, Texas; in biographies of artists ranging from Bob Dylan and Bob Gibson to Johnny Cash and Jimmy Buffett; and in a handful of "who's whos" of folk and Jewish musicians.

A weighty 2003 compendium, *Stars of David: Rock 'n' Roll's Jewish Stories*, interpreted Steve's life in the context in which he was raised but that he rarely embraced publicly as an adult. "Goodman had lived as if the great sage Hillel was constantly by his side reminding him that the essence of Judaism was abid-

> **Every second here is just brilliant, absolutely essential stuff. But that doesn't surprise me. I never saw a Steve Goodman set that was anything less.**
> **MICHAEL TEARSON**
> *SINGOUT!*

32: Bunetta's inclusion as an interviewee on the DVD was partly a reflection of his loyalty. "I just feel very comfortable being loyal," he says. "We all need to be loyal. You can be an asshole, you can be whatever you want to be, as long as at the end of the day you're loyal. And that's why I gravitated toward John (Prine) and Steve. Two out of two? I mean, what did I do right, y'know?"

ing by the golden rule, and the rest just commentary," wrote Scott Benarde. "Though he was forced to live with a fatal disease, he preferred to brighten others' lives rather than complain about his own. ... Steve Goodman was a good man in the truest sense of the word."

Focusing on the legacy of Steve's recordings, *The Guinness Encyclopedia of Popular Music*, released in 1992 and edited by Colin Larkin, also set the stage for an extended appreciation of his work. "It is highly likely that the largely excellent catalogue of this notable performer will be re-evaluated in the future," the book concluded. "While he may not be aware of the posthumous praise he has received, few would regard it as less than well deserved."

Print recognition of that theme unfolded further in the May 1997 edition of *Acoustic Guitar* magazine, with the headline of Ben Elder's 11-page profile of Steve drawing from one of Steve's best-crafted songs, "The One That Got Away." Steve snared a passing reference in Jonathan Lethem's critically praised Brooklyn-based novel, *The Fortress of Solitude*, released in 2003. And of 46 songs reprinted with full words and lead sheets in the 50th anniversary edition of *SingOut!* in 2001, Steve was the sole songwriter to merit the inclusion of two: "City of New Orleans" and "Vegematic."

Almost every week, Steve turned up in news stories and on Internet sites in ways as diverse as his songs. A *Chicago Sun-Times* interview with Texas singer/novelist (and future candidate for governor of Texas) Kinky Friedman referenced a 1997 dinner he had with then-President Clinton, a fan of Steve's who made him the first topic of conversation. An Internet site for the Cloudbuster Hootenanny Songbook, a set of tunes for hang-glider enthusiasts, supplied gliding-related lyrics for Steve's "Video Tape" and "Daley's Gone." [33] An Associated Press feature quoted Steve's "This Hotel Room" in detailing the history and fitful survival of the mechanical motel-bed massager called Magic Fingers.

Sometimes the references were more substantive and wrenching. In a 2003 column in the *Orange County Weekly*, Jim Washburn apologized for labeling Steve a "perennial opening act" in his *Orange County Register* review of the 1984 Linda Ronstadt show that became Steve's last. "People can drop dead at any time, and that's no reason to gild their talents," Washburn wrote, "but it should make us more cognizant of what we write and whether we do it to be truthful or because being snide might make you look cool."

Steve even became the focus of a 3,000-word research paper by Barbara Ellingsen for a music-history class at Elmhurst College near Chicago. Her composition, completed in 2000, argued that Steve deserves public recognition equal to that of folk legend Woody Guthrie. "The genre that Guthrie popularized, Goodman refined and perfected," wrote Ellingsen, who backs up her belief with action. An elementary teacher in Oak Lawn on Chicago's South Side, she regularly plays for her students Steve's recordings of "City of New Orleans," "Go, Cubs, Go" and "The Water Is Wide."

Chicagoan Toby Gibson in 1995 launched an extensive Internet site, the Steve Goodman Scrapbook, which for the first time let fans chat in a concen-

---

People can drop dead at any time, and that's no reason to gild their talents, but it should make us more cognizant of what we write and whether we do it to be truthful or because being snide might make you look cool.
JIM WASHBURN
ORANGE COUNTY WEEKLY

33: The melody of another Steve song, "Lincoln Park Pirates," acquired new lyrics in February 2007 when 52 men raised $70,000 for a Chicago chapter of the Leukemia Research Foundation during a Colorado ski trip. To the "Pirates" tune, David Gassel wrote "The LRF Skiers" (with a hearty chorus of "Way, hey, schussing away ..."). Backed by guitarist Richard Ruderman, the group sang the song at the farewell dinner, not knowing until later that the boy in whose honor the chapter was founded – Alan Brin of Morton Grove – had met Steve in early 1979 and attended a recording session Steve was helming for John Prine's "Bruised Orange" LP. See pages 510-511.

trated fashion about Steve. Seven years later, John Epstein of Holyoke, Massachusetts, founded the online Steve Goodman Preservation Society, devoting himself to safeguarding and distributing unofficial recordings of Steve's myriad concert and radio performances.

Upon the deaths of many notables — Lincoln Towing's Ross Cascio in 1987, Jethro Burns in 1989, Fred Holstein in 2004, Ray Nordstrand in 2005 and Tom Dundee in 2006 — Steve figured prominently in the obituaries. His name also was oft-invoked during a 2000 tribute to Nordstrand (dubbed "Nordstock") and in memorial concerts for Holstein, Nordstrand and Dundee, all presented at Chicago's Old Town School of Folk Music, the institution that had given 14-year-old Steve some of his earliest guitar lessons in 1962.

But Steve himself also was the focus of tribute shows staged in later years. [34] The most elaborate one was a Nov. 13, 1997, benefit for the 40-year-old Old Town School's expansion to a 40,000-square-foot former library in Chicago's Lincoln Square/Ravenswood neighborhood. [35] The week of the glitzy musical homage, organizer Al Bunetta along with Steve's mom, widow and three daughters presided over the city's ceremonial renaming of a two-block portion of Lincoln Avenue, close to the new school site, as Steve Goodman Way.

The concert took place at a Chicago landmark, the 84-year-old, 4,200-seat downtown circus palace, Medinah Temple. It echoed the Chicago and Costa Mesa tributes of 13 years prior, with Arlo Guthrie, John Prine, Jackson Browne and Emmylou Harris among the headliners, along with a re-screening of Steve performance footage that left the audience in tears. "It makes me so sad, I can't stand it," whispered one woman. But ticket prices for the show were steep, ranging from $35 to $250 (raising nearly $500,000 for the Old Town School), and instead of incorporating a dollop of local musicians as was done in 1985, the eight-act slate was purely national in stature. An odd element, given the occasion and setting, was that half of the artists — Iris DeMent, Lyle Lovett, Kathy Mattea and Todd Snider [36] — had no historical connection to Steve.

Still, the evening summoned long-simmering emotions. Filmed salutes by Kris Kristofferson and movie critic Roger Ebert opened the show along with the Steve footage. Co-emcee Roy Leonard read a heart-tugging telegram from Johnny Cash and pointed out the presence of Steve's mother, widow and three daughters. Each performer sang a Steve song, with Harris interpreting "Yellow Coat," the song that had touched her a dozen years prior. Prine went one better, tackling "You Never Even Call Me by My Name" and then "My Old Man," telling the audience he had often absorbed the title as "My Old Pal." The most riveting moments of the night, however, came from an 85-year-old Chicago legend.

Studs Terkel, who had hosted Steve four times on his WFMT radio show in the 1970s, held the crowd in the semicircular arena spellbound with an overflowing oration. Dressed in a three-piece suit and holding a paper cup, the co-emcee labeled Steve "a cockeyed wonder" and likened his simplicity and punch to those of actor Spencer Tracy and prizefighter Joe Louis. "Steve sang a lyric to

The cover of the 1997 tribute program depicted a youthful Steve atop a Chicago cub.

34: A stage musical, "Somebody Else's Troubles," had its first public reading April 30, 2007, at Theatre Building Chicago. The two-act, 90-minute show, scripted by Judy Freed and directed by Allan Chambers, incorporated 14 Goodman songs. Jacquie Manning and Rich Prezioso (the duo Small Potatoes), Peter Oyloe, Christine Conley and Kevin Cassidy made up the cast, which traced the road romance of Beverly Jones and her friend Fred of Steve's "The I Don't Know Where I'm Goin' but I'm Goin' Nowhere in a Hurry Blues."

35: Coincidentally, the library building that would newly house the Old Town School of Folk Music was situated practically next door to a former home of Lincoln Towing, made infamous by Steve's "Lincoln Park Pirates."

36: Ten years later, Snider used in his promo materials a quote from Prine: "Hardest act to follow since Steve Goodman."

Saul Broudy, Steve's harmonica accompanist and backup vocalist, and his companion and future wife, Coleen Boyd, pause in the lobby of the new Birchmere in Alexandria, Virginia, during the World Folk Music Association tribute to Steve held Jan. 15-16, 1999.

(Photo by Clay Eals)

37: Terkel's salute appeared in an 86-minute DVD of the 1997 show, "Larger Than Life: A Celebration of Steve Goodman and His Music," produced by John Anderson and released by Al Bunetta in fall 2007. Besides the eight Steve songs performed during the show, the DVD includes footage of Steve's family celebrating the Steve Goodman Way dedication and interviews of Arlo Guthrie, Jackson Browne and Lyle Lovett. A portion of proceeds will go to the Old Town School of Folk Music.

a song, that was it," Terkel said. "You were captured by it." He toasted Steve's ability to "sing 'The Dutchman' as though it were the only song in the world. ... He was radiant like one of those 1,000-watt incandescent bulbs that lights up a darkened room."

Where Terkel soared, however, was in linking Steve to the roots of his songwriting. "Out of this crazy, goofy, wild, corrupt, rotten, yet creative and hopeful town, Chicago, came our bard," Terkel said. "Whenever I hear that song 'My Kind of Town, Chicago Is,' I hear the voice of Frank Sinatra. What the hell does he know about Chicago? ... Who else could write the 'Lincoln Park Pirates,' laughing at the little crooks in our town who make the town the crazy town it is. Who else could write 'A Dying Cub Fan's Last Request'? It was Steve facing his ultimate adversity, saying there's one thing worse than death — being a Cub fan forever and ever and ever. And who else could sing a song and write a song about his old man? It wasn't about Steve's father, but all our fathers. And, of course, who else could write a song about a train? ... Steve Goodman's train, City of New Orleans, was not about a city of New Orleans, not even about the train. It was about all the trains bound for glory."

The repudiation of Sinatra and recognition of Steve's locally inspired craft brought repeated roars of approval from the audience. Delivered by Chicago's best-known raconteur 13 years after Steve's death, it became what some considered the troubadour's ideal eulogy. [37]

Fourteen months later, the World Folk Music Association seized a timely hook for another Steve tribute, naming its 14th annual benefit festival on Jan. 15-16, 1999, "The Twentieth Century Is Almost Over." Though held in Alexandria, Virginia, at the 500-seat Birchmere, the billing for the sold-out event, attended by Steve's mom, Minnette, proved far more Chicago-centric than the glitzy 1997 show at Medinah Temple. Onstage the first night (the one devoted solely to Steve) was a choice assortment of artists based in or frequently playing in Chicago, and all had been Steve's compadres: Michael Smith, Anne Hills, Jim Post, Bonnie Koloc, Saul Broudy and Tom Paxton. Each performed at least one song written by or associated with Steve, with Smith and Hills soloing or collaborating on eight. The closer, Post, took note of Steve's improvisational stagecraft.

"Oh, the thrills he gave to us and our lives," Post said, "especially when he went wandering off on places, and he would look at his hand and the guitar like, 'Do they belong together? Where does this chord progression go that I started playing?' And then he'd come back with some brilliant thing that made us all sort of shudder at his greatness."

The only hitch came at the end, when, after a Post-led ensemble take on "City of New Orleans," the musicians couldn't respond to audience requests for "Twentieth Century" because none of them knew the words. In the next night's follow-up show, they corrected the slight and performed the festival's theme tune, reading lyrics from a photocopied sheet.

Ensuing years produced further musical tributes to Steve around the country, [38] and the 20th anniversary of his death spurred three of significance. The first and most hand-in-glove came on Sept. 19, 2004, emceed by Tom Dundee at Lucille's, the former Somebody Else's Troubles club on Chicago's Lincoln Avenue. The marathon featured locals Ed·Holstein, Harry Waller, Al Day, Corky Siegel, Mick Scott, Barbara Barrow (wife and singing partner of Michael Smith), Chris Farrell, Norm Siegel, Jim Tullio and Howard Levy soloing and backing each other up on the very stage from which Steve had played so often in the 1970s. The evening couldn't have been more moving, with Steve's mother, Minnette, and brother, David, club owner Earl Pionke and 100 others enjoying 37 songs, 24 of which were written by or associated with Steve.

As if to channel the honoree, Dundee set the tone with doses of brashness and sensitivity. Introducing "You Never Even Call Me by My Name," he lacerated the maker of its hit rendition. "It's amazing that the version of the song that most people outside of Chicago know was by David Allan Coe, who added that total bullshit line about how he prompted Steve Goodman to write the last verse," Dundee said. "But we all know that Steve Goodman had more talent in his pudgy little finger than David Allan Coe has in his bloated, hillbilly ass."

Dundee's tender side emerged when he excised from his version of "Somebody Else's Troubles" Steve's final verse about an undertaker. Also, during an instrumental break in his version of "Would You Like to Learn to Dance?" and while his accompanists kept playing, Dundee lay down his guitar, bid Minnette to her feet and gently swayed with her for a few seconds. As she sat back down, Minnette wiped a tear from her cheek, Dundee kissed her twice, and he returned to the stage to finish the song.

Two months later, many of the same musicians trouped to the Old Town School of Folk Music for a more formal tribute that also highlighted the school's teachers as performers. [39] Remarkably, every one of the more than 30 songs played at the Nov. 26 event was written by or associated with Steve. They included a little-heard burlesque blast from Steve's distant (1969) past — "Heavily into Jesus," reprised by Nate Herman, co-founder of Wilderness Road, the folk-rock group that had evolved from Second City.

Sandwiched between the two Chicago-based tributes was one on Oct. 2 at The Presbyterian Church in Chatham, New Jersey, that featured Steve's East Coast musical coterie: Steve Burgh, Saul Broudy, Dennis Gormley, Erik Frandsen, Perry Barber, Heather Wood, Leslie Berman and Paula Ballan. [40] Selections ranged from comic to caustic, and with the Iraq war raging and the Bush-Kerry election looming a month away, "Election Year Rag" and "The Ballad of Penny Evans" took on added meaning. Raising $2,500 for leukemia research by their attendance were 190 fans, including, in the front row, Steve's widow, Nancy Tenney (and her husband, Craig), and youngest daughter, Rosanna.

For Nancy, the tribute marked a rare return to the music scene she had long left behind. As she reflected in 2005, her emotions about her 14-year marriage to Steve were still mixed.

"That was an incredible time in my life, but it was also a very, very difficult

38: Small-scale tributes to Steve abounded. In Alaska, part of the Anchorage Folk Festival on Jan. 28, 2001, was devoted to Steve songs. A gathering on Oct. 28, 2001, north of Seattle on Guemes Island featured Bryan Bowers, Saul Broudy and Jeff Gutcheon. An outdoor festival June 19, 2004, at Park Ridge Public Library, near Steve's high-school home of Niles, Illinois, featured Bradley Ditto, Jim Post and Peter "Madcat" Ruth. Post also staged a tribute to Steve and to Stan Rogers, "The Best Damn Songs Most People Never Heard," that ran in February and March 1993 in Skokie. Plus, folksinger Ian Woofenden hosted Steve sing-alongs in 1998, 2005 and 2007 at the Northwest Folklife Festival in Seattle.

39: Performers at the Nov. 26, 2004, tribute included John Brennan, Steve Dawson, Al Day, Tom Dundee, Chris Farrell, Nate Herman, Ed Holstein, Randy Lee, George Levison, Steve Levitt, Julie Macarus, Michael Miles, Bill Paige, Jim Polaski, Byron Roche, Norm Siegel, Barb Silverman, Mick Scott, Don Stiernberg and Harry Waller.

40: Joining in at the Oct. 2, 2004, tribute were latter-day interpreters Mike Agranoff, Stratton Doyle, Jesse Lew, Laurie MacAllister, Eric Schwartz and George Wurzbach.

Rosanna Goodman – shown applauding with her mother Nancy at an Oct. 2, 2004, tribute to Steve in New Jersey – says she wanted her multi-artist "My Old Man" CD, issued in summer 2006, to "be young."
(Photo by Jody Kolodzey)

41: Her dad's baseball mania is also part of Rosanna Goodman, who appeared briefly in a Chicago Cubs TV documentary aired in September 2006 on HBO.

42: The LP by Jaisun – known as a blues photographer and for his 1969 novelty hit "Friendly Neighborhood Narco Agent" – was called "Midnight Invitation." Recorded in Denmark, it included a song to honor Jaisun's singing companion, Alex Campbell, called "99 Years on the Road," a reference to the ages of Jaisun, then 39, and the ailing Campbell, 60. Jaisun later realized he had inadvertently appropriated the bouncy bass line of "City of New Orleans" for the tune.

time," she told Dave Hoekstra of the *Chicago Sun-Times*. "Some things are hard to revisit, some things are great. But Steve was an incredibly intense, fascinating person to be around. So it was also very, very magical."

Soon after the New Jersey tribute, Rosanna Goodman began recording her own tribute to her father. Rosanna, a Brooklyn musician and RCA video producer, snared 10 friends and musical acts from her late-20s age group and laid down a dozen interpretations of Steve's songs, released on CD in June 2006 as "My Old Man: A Tribute to Steve Goodman." The CD, Rosanna proudly says, also inspired her mother to begin assembling a book of her father's friends' memories.

Rosanna, who sang her CD's title track with no lyrical changes, took care in announcing the project to say it was for her sisters Jesse (present-day spelling), a pet groomer in Staten Island, and Sarah, a social worker in Los Angeles. But she also zeroed in on a goal. "I wanted the record to be young," Rosanna told Dave Hoekstra. "I wanted musicians who maybe don't know my father's music and have a kinship with each other to get to know the music — and they did."

Her headstrong approach hasn't surprised Al Bunetta, who manages the distribution of Rosanna's CD and all of Steve's Red Pajamas products. "Rosanna, she's her dad," Bunetta says. "She looks like Stevie. She's got that streak Stevie had, that work ethic, that tenacity. She's her dad." [41]

* * *

Beyond organized events and recorded versions of his songs, there exist little-known indications of Steve's legacy that are even more passionate and personal.

Quietly and without any coordinated effort, eight musicians or musical acts dedicated albums to Steve soon after his death: Jimmy Buffett, David Allan Coe, Tom Dundee, Bela Fleck, Stefan Grossman, Jef Jaisun, [42] Eddie Walker and the Nitty Gritty Dirt Band.

Even more extraordinary, more than two dozen artists paid individualized homage by writing, performing and recording tribute songs to Steve or songs mentioning him prominently. Nowhere, until now (see discography), have these compositions been catalogued in one place. Some reside unnoticed on commercial LPs and CDs, while others linger on unreleased demo tapes. For the most part, the stature of their creators has eluded the mainstream. But their emotions and messages remain sturdy and stirring.

Overarching the tribute tracks are the twin themes of mortality and loss, and the songs tackle that territory from varying angles. Roland Kushner of Bethlehem, Pennsylvania, embedded it in a sequel to Steve's "Ballad of Penny Evans," titled "Penny Evans' Daughters." In Kushner's hands, the three girls are grown up and having to explain their father's death to children of their own:

It's a lesson, it's a struggle,
it's an honor earned each year
The raising of a family
standing strong and fighting fear

(From right) Buddy Mondlock and Jessica Anne Baron, half of the Chicago group Double Date, each wrote tribute songs to Steve shortly after his death. The other two members joining in a whimsical pose on a park bench in a promo photo from 1984 are Laura Wasserman (now Hall) and Mike Lindauer.

(Photo courtesy of Mike Lindauer)

Some of the songs approached Steve's absence metaphorically, including "Gather at the River" by ex-Chicago folkie Don Lange of Dundee, Oregon:

> *Little magician cast a spell*
> *as bright as any sun*
> *The measure of his magic no tongue could tell*
> *But he fell prey to a demon in his blood*
> *He ran a good race, a little too slow*
> *We'll meet again at the end of the road*

Seattle photographer and guitarist Jef Jaisun found his simile by looking to the sky, in "Flying with the Angels": [43]

> *He's flying with the angels, high above*
> *Flying with the angels, singing out for love*

Jessica Anne Baron of Del Mar, California, also embraced an astronomical approach. As part of the band Double Date, she had gained prominence in the Chicago folk scene about the time that Steve departed it for Seal Beach. In "Light Up the Sky," her chorus likened Steve to the elusive lights of the night: [44]

> *Long after the stars go out, long after they die*
> *Long after the stars go out, they light up the sky*

Baron's musical partner in Double Date, Buddy Mondlock, who opened for Steve at his New Year's Eve 1980 show at the Earl of Old Town, took a complementary tack in his "No Choice." Originally inspired by Vincent van Gogh, Mondlock expanded his topic to songwriters. He wrote of the inevitability of the life that captured them, ending each of his seven verses and chorus with the phrase, "He never really had no choice." One verse specifically addressed Steve:

> *And they all talked about him when he died*
> *They smiled and they theorized*
> *But when he was through they'd laughed and cried*
> *And he never really had no choice*

43: Jaisun wrote the song Sept. 21, 1984, the day after Steve died, and he performed it that night on Seattle's KEZX-FM with Tom Dundee on harmony vocals and harmonica and host Leilani McCoy on backup vocals.

44: The "star" metaphor is echoed by an observation by folksinger Marty Peifer: "Steve burned a little brighter because he knew he wasn't going to burn longer."

In "Heroes," Steve Hopkins of Austin, Texas, employed irony to sum up Steve's songwriting:

> *He could paint the prettiest pictures*
> *and all he used was words*

In "Richer for the Time," Toronto's Norm Hacking dwelled on Steve's enduring impact:

> *Feeling richer for the time we all sing together*
> *Stayin' up late till the bitter end*
> *And whatever is lost in the winter frost*
> *Lives on in our hearts like the song of a friend*

Brian Gill, in his "Song for Steve," chose plainspoken description, citing his "scuffling days" in which he donated blood to earn $5 for the cover charge for Steve's shows at the Quiet Knight club in Chicago. "You knew he had the real stuff when he looked you in the eye," Gill sang. His devotion to Steve suffused the deceptively simple, anthemic chorus:

> *I sing his tunes every now and then*
> *Just so you won't forget*
> *A good friend is dead and gone*
> *But his song ain't over yet*

Several compositions emulated Steve's storytelling style to leave a vivid impression. Eddie Walker of North East England first became enthralled by Steve during the 1972 Cambridge Folk Festival, and the story of his enchantment flowed throughout his "Song for Steve Goodman." In performances, Walker turns the tune into a 10-minute tour de force, segueing into a rollicking version of "City of New Orleans," signaled by his chorus:

> *Here comes that train song again*
> *So damn good I wish that it would never end*
> *But like that railroad era, you're lost and gone, my friend*
> *Just like all those railroad men who were heroes just like you*

Like Walker, a songwriter from Carmel, Indiana, Peter Weisz, seized on Steve's impromptu 1972 Cambridge Folk Festival sets, describing him as "a matzo ball in bib overalls" in his gentle waltz, "The Man with the Golden Tune." Weisz ended his saga nearly a dozen years later:

> *We roared when he sang the Vegematic song*
> *Then he put his blue Cubbies hat to his breast*
> *I had to turn away when he started to play*
> *"A Dying Cub Fan's Last Request"*

Harry Waller, a Chicagoan since 1974, also used imagery to pinpoint the awe he felt in the presence of Steve. Book-ending his four verses were the day he met Steve on Lincoln Avenue and the day 10 years later when he bid Steve a final goodbye at O'Hare airport. In between were details laced with wordplay:

Every time he walked right in
He'd be wearin' that silly grin
And tell you the worst joke you just heard

Waller's chorus, however, ached with an unanswerable plea:

Chicago's never been so cold
Like the day that I was told
It was all over for my friend Steve

Every day I sit and cry
Every day I ask myself why
Why did he have to leave?

More tribute tunes remain to be written, including one from the pen of Steve's closest musical partner, John Prine. So says Nashville musician Keith Sykes, who knew Steve well and has written with and produced recordings of Prine. "I just know that there's one that's coming," Sykes says.

Prine himself allows the possibility. "When I'm writin' about somethin' that personal, I kinda trust that over a period of time it'll come out," Prine says. "I trust my instincts more than my conscious efforts. In other words, I trust my gut more than I trust myself, and if I was writin' a song about Stevie, I'd sure like it to come straight from the gut."

For Marilyn Quine, who had joined in Steve's rubber-band superstition during his final year, the gut was the source for a poem that spilled out of her after his death:

Little big man
Alone on stage
Huge guitar
slung across your chest.

Little big man
Dwarfed by a hospital bed
Slender IV tubes
attached to your arms.

Public cowboy
Captivating crowds
Private soldier
fighting death.

I miss you.

> **I trust my gut more than I trust myself, and if I was writin' a song about Stevie, I'd sure like it to come straight from the gut.**
> **JOHN PRINE**

Tom Paxton also painted a poetic picture [45] but in sardonic style:

> *Chicago Shorty would write you a song,*
> *Then he'd play the damned thing all night long,*
> *Make you coffee, fry you an egg,*
> *Tickle your funny bone, pull your leg,*
> *Talk your head off, laugh at your jokes,*
> *Kiss your sister and charm your folks,*
> *Lend you his house, lend you his car,*
> *Give you the strings from his last guitar.*
> *Stevie'd let you name the place,*
> *Meet your plane and carry your case.*
> *Chicago Shorty lived his life,*
> *Loved his children, loved his wife.*
> *He was a joy for me to know,*
> *And I miss the little bastard so.*

* * *

Tom Paxton, shown backed by Steve in about 1980, wrote a witty paean to "Chicago Shorty." (Photo by Jim Shea)

45: Reprinted by permission.

46: At a Feb. 17, 2007, show in Lexington, Prine played the tune on a guitar owned by Steve because the one he usually used "broke its neck in Kalamazoo."

47: Coe told the BBC in 1987: "A lot of people come to me and say, 'It's a shame Steve died,' and I say, 'It's a great thing that Stevie lived for 15 more years.' People also say, 'It must be a bitch knowin' you're gonna die,' and I say, 'Y'mean no one's told you yet?' "

48: In a two-disc DVD compilation of the shows, released by Buffett in 2006, Buffett added a third nod to Steve — footage of the concert setup backed by audio of Steve's version of "Go, Cubs, Go."

Of course, tributes to Steve Goodman are not limited to sporadic special events or one-time-only recordings or writings. They take place literally every day or night, and in all corners of the continent and beyond.

In every one of his 50 to 75 shows a year, Prine dedicates his "Souvenirs" to Steve. [46] Similarly, "City of New Orleans" is a fixture in the concerts of Arlo Guthrie, who is on the road for more than 75 percent of each year, and Willie Nelson, who tours with his band constantly. During Nelson's musical marathons, "City" becomes a celebration. Each time his band gets to the "Good morning, America" chorus, the house lights flash, and the crowd roars.

Likewise, "You Never Even Call Me by My Name" is a staple for David Allan Coe, who averages four performances a week. During the recitation, he routinely mentions Steve and sings a snippet of "City of New Orleans" in a lecture about the importance of songwriters. But he notes that the reach of the country parody, via his own version, is not confined to stage shows. "My niece used to work for Lone Star Steak House, and she told me, 'Uncle David, they play your song four times a day, and every time they do, we have to stop what we're doing and twirl our towels and sing with you.' It's the most-played song on jukeboxes, and it's #4 on karaoke. It's timeless." [47]

Jimmy Buffett, who quoted the lyrics of "Banana Republics" in his 1999 best-selling memoir *A Pirate Looks at Fifty*, rarely fails to include a Steve-written song in each of his frequent performances. On Labor Day weekend of 2005, when Buffett played the first two concerts ever performed in Chicago's 92-year-old Wrigley Field, he doubled the ante. For 39,000 fans, he sang Steve's "Banana Republics," dedicating it to Minnette and David Goodman, who were in the ballpark. After dark, he moved to the empty right-field bleachers with only an acoustic guitar (and the acoustic-guitar backing of Mac McAnally) to perform an encore of "City of New Orleans." [48]

Film actor Jeff Daniels ("The Purple Rose of Cairo"), who doubles as a folk musician and runs a live theater in his hometown of Chelsea, Michigan, counts Steve's humor and storytelling as an early influence. "I saw him at the Bottom Line walking out with just a guitar and with comedy and then doing a 180, making you cry," he told Mark Brown of the *Rocky Mountain News* in late 2006. "There's a structure to what he's doing, and I was too young to really understand. But I was interested in it." Emulating Steve, Daniels composed and regularly performs a baseball lament, "The Lifelong Tiger Fan Blues."

Even ageless rocker Neil Young is said to have adopted the opening melody of Steve's "City of New Orleans" for the rant he began singing onstage in 2006, "Let's Impeach the President."

But the day-to-day influence and exposure of Steve's music goes beyond the shows of celebrities. From coast to coast, performers who lack mainstream stature but ply stages with talent give grateful nods to Steve.

David Roth of Orleans, Massachusetts, who met Steve in Alaska in 1978, often incorporates in his shows "The Dutchman" and "Would You Like to Learn to Dance?" Greg Trafidlo of Salem, Virginia, intentionally sings his "Seafood Shop Shantyman's Song" in the same "way-hey" meter as Steve's "Lincoln Park Pirates." Mike Strobel of Rochester, New York, includes a Steve song in every show he plays. "City of New Orleans" is the signature song of George Swanson of Southwest Harbor, Maine. Jamie Anderson of Durham, North Carolina, teaches songwriting by using Steve's "This Hotel Room" as an example of how a tune can be written about anything. London-based guitarist-producer Elliott Randall is one of many who promote Steve's songs at MySpace.com and on other Internet blogs.

David Gans, the Oakland-based host of radio's "Grateful Dead Hour" for more than 20 years, chafes at being pigeonholed as a performing Deadhead and often sings Steve's "Elvis Imitators" as a form of therapy. "It's a perfect song to make light of my own travail," he says. "It's a wry commentary on being presumed to be a Grateful Dead cover artist. Plus, it's a hilarious song. I use it to satirize my own bizarre situation in life."

Don Oja-Dunaway of St. Augustine, Florida, inserts "City of New Orleans" in every set — in Steve's fast tempo, "like I was on the train. Every time I sing it, I get excited because I can see all that stuff." Farther south on the Florida coast, in Delray Beach, "City" is one of Rod MacDonald's most-requested songs.

In hundreds of shows a year, Ray Owen of Gettysburg, Pennsylvania, often sings a Steve staple, "The Barnyard Dance," with a new verse incorporating extra fruits and veggies. Similarly, he extends "Vegematic" with a litany of faux celebrity TV spots. Owen imitates the voices of Neil Young singing of a Sara Lee cinnamon swirl (to the tune of "Cinnamon Girl"), James Taylor becoming a candy man ("Handy Man"), and Bob Dylan, on a health kick, selling "joggin' on to the spa" ("Knockin' on Heaven's Door").

Lois Scott and her Plum Loco Band, based in the Pittsburgh suburb of White Oak, sings "You Never Even Call Me by My Name" in her every show, stem-

For Grateful Dead expert and singer/songwriter David Gans, "Elvis Imitators" serves as a hilarious form of therapy.
(Photo by Stuart Steinhardt)

For singer Lois Scott, shown in 2005 and who performs in and around Pittsburgh, Steve's "You Never Even Call Me by My Name" saved a bar set and has become a staple of her shows.
(Photo by Kevin Stiffler)

A fund-raising circle named for Steve greets concert-goers at The Ark, Ann Arbor, Michigan.
(Photo by Clay Eals)

ming from a 1980 incident at the Red Top biker bar in the burg of New Alexandria. Rowdy patrons, irked with the repertoire of Scott's then-band, Back Up and Push, admonished her to sing some "cool tunes — or else," she says. "I went into the bathroom and on toilet paper wrote down every word that I could remember to 'You don't have to call me darlin', darlin'.' I came out of the bathroom and ran over a quick arrangement with the band." When she and her band performed the tune, one biker kicked her monitor, bellowing, "Do it again!" She sang it three more times, and at night's end, three bikers, including the one who had kicked the monitor, helped carry the band's equipment to its van. "It saved our lives," says Scott, who in her rendition correctly references Steve as the song's author and personalizes it by substituting Dolly Parton and Minnie Pearl for the male country singers therein.

Fred Rubin, TV writer and cinema professor from Los Angeles, performs with famed rock photographer Henry Diltz in a band called Loose Gravel, and Steve's "Men Who Love Women Who Love Men" is their perennial opener. "It just gets the audience nuts," Rubin says.

Likewise, Ernie Trionfo and Eric Waltman — who played with Steve in Bridgeton, his last scheduled gig — anchor a New Jersey band, the Snake Brothers, and due to their brush with Steve, they still perform "It's a Sin to Tell a Lie," "You Never Even Call Me by My Name" and "Mama Don't Allow It."

Two musical acts in California's south Bay Area make Steve's music a vivid presence. Brian Kramer performs a half-hour, Steve-style show in the San Bruno schools, and the Flying Other Brothers often fit "City of New Orleans" into a mix of Grateful Dead and psychedelic rock tunes in 75 shows a year. The Brothers' version of Steve's classic prompted Independence Day 2005 revelers in the town of Arcata to dance in the city plaza, noted the local *Times-Standard*, "with the smell of barbecue chicken mixing well with the smell of incense."

At the Bluebird Café, the famed Nashville singer/songwriters' haven, a large 1976 portrait of Steve by photographer Robert Corwin oversees shows. In Ann Arbor, Michigan, Steve's visage greets visitors to The Ark coffeehouse, where the nonprofit concert club, which has operated in several local sites since 1965, salutes a Steve Goodman Circle of donors of $25,000 or more. Likewise, in Steve's birth city, the Old Town School of Folk Music maintains a Steve Goodman Scholarship Fund, set up at the 1997 tribute as part of its endowment.

Chicago native Mary Morris, a prolific Brooklyn author (*Nothing to Declare: Memoirs of a Woman Traveling Alone*) who saw Steve perform several times and reveres "City of New Orleans," often thinks of him at her readings. "Gee, Steve Goodman would get this crowd going," she tells herself. "These people are a bunch of duds. I've gotta get something happening here."

Similarly, until his death on Nov. 25, 2007, Toronto singer/songwriter Norm Hacking focused on Steve's view "that it's a privilege to get up and do this, and this might be the last time I ever have the privilege." He first summoned the thought in 1989 for a crowd of 1,000 at the Great Canadian Theatre Company in Ottawa: "Smack dab in the middle of my set, I got a standing ovation. The

Duncan Jennings, 13, (left) and Callam Jennings, 16, practice guitar chords in 2003, a reflection of having been raised on Steve's music by their father, Toronto journalist and former Riverboat club manager Nicholas Jennings, who in his sons' infancy used "City of New Orleans" to sing them to sleep.

(Photo by Carol Hay)

whole theater was standing. I didn't know what to do. This had never happened before. Every time I said, 'Thank you,' five voices yelled, 'No, thank you.' I had gotten an energy surge from that thought, and it seemed to affect everybody."

Browning Porter of Charlottesville, Virginia, struck by a line in Steve's and Michael Smith's "Talk Backwards" ("Amaze your friends when you start to rap"), had youths in mind when he created a hip-hop version, "Rapping Backwards." He and partner Jeff Romano in the band Nickeltown perform it every show.

The reach of Steve's music to both young and old is confirmed by WFUV-FM folk host Dennis Elsas of New York, who regularly spins Steve's version of "The Dutchman" and relishes the response. "Every time I play it, there's a phone call or e-mail that says, 'What was that?' Of all his songs, it just has that poignancy," Elsas says. "It's what we call an 'Oh wow' song, like, 'Oh wow, I can't believe they're playing that again. I haven't heard that in so long.' But for the younger audience, or just the audience that never heard it before, it also strikes a chord enough so that people will say, 'Who's that? How do I get that?' It still has that timeless quality."

Often, as with all forms of culture, youthful reverence for Steve's music comes from elders' inculcation. Case in point: Canadian journalist Nicholas Jennings, a dishwasher-turned-manager at the old Riverboat in Toronto. During the infancy of his two sons in the late 1980s and early 1990s, Jennings played guitar and sang them to sleep with "City of New Orleans" and Woody Guthrie's "Hobo's Lullaby" (the title of the Arlo Guthrie album that included his hit version of "City"). Today, the two teens, Callam and Duncan, also play guitar and are budding musicians who know the lyrics to several of Steve's songs. As a bonus, the younger son, Duncan, is huge fan of trains.

Vermont college student Cassi Nelson, whose father raised her on Steve's comic songs when she was a grade-schooler, recalls early-teen days when she heard Steve's version of "The Dutchman" on the CD player in her parents' car. "I cried and cried, and my dad started joking that I was turning into a typical woman," she says, "but something really got to me. The fact that the wife takes care of her husband even though he's so old, them walking home, and him waving at the ships — I was so taken with it. I have listened to it so many times that there must be a hole forming from the laser in the CD."

Jessica Mocarski felt the same while planning her wedding in 2002 in Racine, Wisconsin. For years as a child, she had listened to Steve's songs, played on the family car stereo by her father, Tim. As she reached her late teens, "I Can't Sleep" — with its arresting refrain, "I can't sleep when I can't sleep with you" — appealed to her. When the 22-year-old introduced it to her fiancé, Darrell Borkowski, a fan of 1980s metal rock, she was surprised that he, too, was drawn. For the first dance at their wedding reception, Steve's recording played while the couple looked into each other's eyes and sang along with every word.

* * *

In sheer numbers, the largest enduring tribute to Steve Goodman plays out before tens of millions each year in the hub of America's heartland.

It's true that "Go, Cubs, Go" is no longer the Chicago Cubs theme song, WGN having replaced it in 1987 with "Here Come the Cubs," recorded by the Beach Boys to the tune of their 1965 hit "Barbara Ann." [49] Ensuing years have seen newer theme songs, including four between 1999 and 2006.

But Steve's Cubs tune never left the Friendly Confines or the airwaves of Chicagoland. "Go, Cubs, Go" has remained a familiar aural presence at Wrigley, where sellout crowds of 41,000 gather 81 times each year. WGN-AM still uses snips of the song between commercials and the play-by-play, reaching a million listeners 162 days a year. It became a phenomenon in 2007, roaring over stadium loudspeakers upon the last out of every home win, and when the Cubs won the National League Central, Illinois Lt. Gov. Pat Quinn proclaimed Oct. 5 as Steve Goodman Day. [50] (A day later, a loss ended their World Series quest.)

Perhaps fittingly, Steve's other Cubs song, the more complex "A Dying Cub Fan's Last Request," is still persona non grata at Wrigley. That's because in contrast to its rah-rah younger brother, it remains eerily accurate. Despite valiant tries in 1989, 1998 and 2007 and a near-miss in 2003, the Cubbies still haven't won an NL pennant "since the year we dropped the bomb on Japan." [51]

"Dying Cub Fan" continues to captivate Steve's most prominent high-school classmate, Sen. Hillary Clinton. "As a Cubs fan, I know what a big part the Cubs played in my growing up, and they are just relentlessly disappointing. Y'know, they just break your heart every year. The song is so true to Steve, but it also captures the feelings of so many of us who remember going to Wrigley Field and the arguments in the hallway about the Cubs versus the Sox." [52]

One person who often hears about "Dying Cub Fan" is Keith Moreland, the rightfielder whom the song immortalizes for dropping "a routine fly." The gratitude of Moreland — a play-by-play man for University of Texas football who often graces Cub fan events in Chicago — swells with each year. The tune, he says, reflects Steve's sportswriter-like grasp of reality. "You can hear the emotion of every Cub fan that's been around since 1945," he says. "Steve knew life, and he knew the picture, and to have a person who is dying write a song about the dying love of the Cubs, I am thrilled to have my name mentioned in it."

49: WGN's Dan Fabian, who had asked Steve to write "Go, Cubs, Go," used loopy logic to defend what he admitted was a "silly" switch to the Beach Boys in 1987: "The Cubs are the closest thing we have to an ocean in Chicago."

50: Organizing the day's ceremony at the James Thompson Center in Chicago was Elizabeth Austin, Quinn's communications director, who had interviewed Goodman in 1974 in Rockford (see page 385).

51: A St. Louis sports columnist slammed the home Cardinals for playing Steve's recording of "Dying Cub Fan" over the Busch Stadium sound system while the Cubs stretched on the field before a Cards/Cubs game on June 22, 2004. "It's time for Cardinals fans to drop the arrogant pose and face up to the truth," wrote Bernie Miklasz of the *Post-Dispatch*. "You don't have the Cubs to kick around anymore." By year's end, however, Chicago languished in third place while St. Louis had won the NL Central title.

52: Art Thieme, a folksinger who specialized in traditional songs and pun-filled jokes, penned a parody of the classic "As Time Goes By" in 2005, after the Chicago White Sox won the World Series. The first verse: "You must remember this / A curse is still a curse / And the Cubs are still the Cubs / Fundamentals should be applied / As time goes by." The last verse: "The Cubs blew it again / Again and then again / Again and then again / Again and then again / And time goes by."

"Dying Cub Fan" also begged the question of the unseen physical legacy of Steve himself, or what was left of him after cremation. For its "old Cub fan," the song outlined an elaborate funeral at Wrigley, culminating in a bonfire at home plate. The resulting ashes would "blow in a beautiful snow" over the left-field wall to their "final resting place out on Waveland Avenue." No such ceremony took place for Steve. But his ashes did round a few bases.

In a little brown box and shipped apparently at Steve's behest, the ashes arrived in the fall of 1984 at the Wilshire Boulevard office of Al Bunetta. Steve's longtime manager wasn't present, however, and Tracy Gershon, who did administrative work for Bunetta, signed for the package. "All of a sudden, I realized what it was," Gershon says. "It was pretty unnerving. I'd never sat there with a box of ashes. It could have been anything, but I saw it was from a funeral home, and I realized they were Steve's ashes. I kind of freaked out."

Tracy Gershon, who worked for Al Bunetta, thought of a wicked prank when she signed for a box of Steve's ashes: "Al! I got Stevie's ashes delivered, and there was a leak, and Stevie's all over the office!"
(Photo courtesy of the Gershon family)

After a few anxious moments, a question leapt to Gershon's mind: "What would Stevie want me to do with these?" Quickly, she thought of a plan.

Bunetta at the time was rarely seen without a lit cigarette. "He was a huge smoker," Gershon says, "and he used to let his ashes in his ashtray just pile up." She decided to pick up Bunetta's ashtray and sprinkle its contents all over his office. "I don't know what possessed me to do this," she says. "I think I was channeling Steve Goodman at the time."

When Bunetta returned to the office, Gershon ("I'm a good actress") put on a convincing act of desperation. "Al! Al!" she screamed. "Stevie's ashes were delivered, and there was a leak, and Stevie's all over the office!"

Shock filled Bunetta's visage. He froze. Then he looked around the room and shouted, "Get the Dust Buster! Get the broom! Get something!"

For an excruciating five minutes, Gershon prolonged the charade. Then she burst out laughing and told Bunetta the truth. Bunetta, too, roared with laughter. It was as if, to cap their years of back-and-forth pranks, Steve had dealt Bunetta the final punch line: "Gotcha!"

Fast-forward to spring 1988. With the city's permission and to the ire of traditionalists, the Cubs finally were installing lights at Wrigley Field. Steve's brother, David, who had started work as a photo assistant for *Playboy* magazine, obtained a film canister's worth of Steve's ashes from Bunetta in L.A. Five days before the Cubs' April 15 home opener, David placed a phone call to Chicago. Picking up the phone was Steve's singer/songwriter/artist friend, Harry Waller.

Bunetta had told David he tried to organize an ash-sprinkling ceremony at Wrigley but was rebuffed. David thought it was worth another shot. "I'm coming to town in three days," David told Waller. "I've got some ashes. Steve wants to be put in Wrigley Field, and I think you're the guy who can get us in there."

Warily, Waller agreed. Friends at a music club that night steered him to the phone number of a groundskeeper at Wrigley, and the next day he made the call. Waller gave a quick rundown on Steve and explained his request.

The groundskeeper listened, incredulous. "You can't do that," he said. "There's no way in hell you're gonna do that."

David Goodman, shown in 1998, conspired with Harry Waller in April 1988 to grant his brother's musical wish and set some of Steve's ashes free in the breeze over the left-field wall of Wrigley Field.

(Photo courtesy of Chris Farrell)

Waller gave it his all. "Look, this is his dying request, for God's sakes. He meant so much to Chicago. There's got to be someone there I can talk to."

He was put on hold for five minutes, then another voice came on the line. Waller made the same pitch.

"No, that's a felony," the voice said. "We can't let you come in here with ashes. It's not a graveyard. You're crazy."

Waller started considering Plan B. He and David had said that if they couldn't get inside Wrigley, at night they would set up a long ladder outside the stadium and fling the ashes in. But Waller finally got through to a third voice.

"Hi, I'm Harry Waller."

"Harry Waller, songwriter?"

"Yeah, I'm calling about Steve Goodman."

"Steve Goodman? I'm a big Steve Goodman fan. What's up, Harry?"

Once more, Waller detailed the request.

"Look, I know you're not going to let this go," the voice said, "so here's the deal. If you call tomorrow, talk to this guy, and that's your last shot."

Waller made the call about 10 a.m. Wednesday, April 13, and repeated his request. "Is there a way we can just get in? We're not going to make a big deal. Nobody will know we're there."

"Yeah, yeah, yeah. Come over this afternoon. I'll get you in. I'll have your name waiting at the gate. We're working on the grounds, but they'll get me."

David picked Waller up in a Cadillac he had rented at O'Hare airport and showed him the film canister. "Y'know Harry," he said, "we either have Steve's heart and we're putting his heart in Wrigley Field, or we're putting his asshole in there, one or the other. Either way, we've got some of him."

The two arrived at Wrigley and were let in. Finding Waller's contact, David rewarded him with an advance copy of *Playboy* with a $20 bill in the foldout.

"So," the staffer asked, "where do you want to put him?"

"He wants to be by home plate," Waller said.

The three walked through the stadium, which was awash with activity, workers raking the grounds and welding the light standards — a plethora of people present to witness a potential act of illegality. David and Waller looked at each other and for the first time opened the film canister. Instead of fine powder, they discovered the contents were mostly small chunks of bone.

"It's probably not a good idea to sprinkle bones where they're going to slide into home plate," David said.

"Well," Waller said, "where else do you want to put him?"

"In the Cub song, you've got to sprinkle his ashes in left field," David replied, "so that they waft over into Waveland Avenue."

The two hiked to the left-field bleachers. When they reached the ivy-covered fence, they stopped. David said a few words, lustily sang the "Dying Cub Fan" chorus, then poured out the contents of the canister. In the swirling breeze, remnants of Steve drifted onto the outfield's warning track, into the hedge and — as Chicago winds soon would insure — over the wall to Waveland Avenue.

Not long afterward, Steve's widow, Nancy, and his daughters trouped to Cooperstown, New York, home of the National Baseball Hall of Fame. There, at home plate of Doubleday Field, they sprinkled the rest of the troubadour's remains. "We snuck over a gate at night," daughter Rosanna told Andy Pulliam of the suburban Chicago Internet radio station 104.9/The Edge in November 2006. "He's there. ... That's where legends go."

Thus, as he presaged in song, Steve finally had a "doubleheader funeral."

* * *

Chicago bassist Norm "Mad Dog" Siegel, shown performing in May 2006 at Bill's Blues Bar in Evanston, says Steve tugged at all manner of emotions, but "mostly he'd make you laugh."
(Photo by David Hartman, courtesy of Norm Siegel)

To sum up anyone's life is a tough task. In Steve's case, many have tried, with profundity and punch.

"He was volcanic," says Claudia Schmidt. "I never saw him do anything remotely tepid. It was over the top, all the time."

"He didn't do glitz," says Steve Martin. "He was of another time."

"He was an unsung hero," says Howard Berkman. "He put some things down that nobody will improve on. He was like Georgia O'Keefe, Winslow Homer, Ernest Hemingway. He just hit it."

"He was unbearably cute," says Wendy Waldman. "He was tiny and fierce and funny and wicked. He was wonderfully physical and spatial. He was a real clown. You couldn't stay really serious in one of his sets. You were defenseless."

"He could be a biting, caustic little boy, but he had a lot of heart," says Norm "Mad Dog" Siegel. "He could make you laugh, and he could tug at you and make you cry. Mostly, he'd make you laugh."

"He showed you his clay feet all the time," says Josh White Jr.

"He seemed to be more entertained than entertaining, and that, of course, is tremendously entertaining," says Geoff Harpham.

"He was a singing fire hydrant," says Trevor Veitch. "He would have loved that, and he would have written a great song about it."

"He was a little bit nuts when he was performing," says Raun MacKinnon Burnham. "He had these crazy eyes, this slightly Rabelaisian look."

"He could be funny even before he did anything funny," says Andrew Calhoun. "He had this mad energy. He could just stand there and be funny."

"He was something out of the ordinary, and yet he was in the ordinary," says Oscar Brand. "He was everybody."

"He was the big bang in the little shape," says Tom Paxton. "His universe was always expanding to include, include, include, rather than to subtract, subtract, subtract. His circle kept growing larger and larger."

"He transcended all that folk scene," says David Amram. "He was much more than that — jazz, classical music, politics, baseball. He appreciated all of the progressive ways of thinking, but he also tried to be a real person and wasn't Mr. Achtung of Political Correctness. He played for cowboys, right-wingers, shit-kickers. He saw the soulfulness in everybody. He didn't see it in terms of left wing or right wing or the good guys and the bad guys. He saw the world as one place where everyone could get together."

"He was this really vivid, burning coal," says John Prine.

Chicago singer/songwriter Al Day says Steve's use of the word "rowboat" in "When My Rowboat Comes In" was a humble way of "speaking to the catalog of his material and his whole career."

(Photo by Tanya Tucka)

"He was the go-to guy if you wanted to get grounded," says Gary Brandt. "No one else was as to the point and understood the way something should be."

"He had a way of becoming your old, best friend," says Joel Mabus. "He could have been the most popular politician of all time. He had that Bill Clinton look-you-in-the-eye-and-seduce-you kind of thing, naturally."

"It sounds so simplistic to say, but when I think of Steve, even now, I just get a big smile on my face," says Sen. Hillary Rodham Clinton.

"He was too real, a magnet of God's love from above," said Steve Burgh. "I never saw a guy who had so many people so legitimately close to him."

"He was like a Gabriel," says Richard Stock. "He was like an angel who came down and played guitar instead of trumpet."

"There was a spiritual dimension that let him transform his own special suffering into other people's joy," says Rabbi Jack Schechtman Gabriel.

"There is a godliness and divinity to suffering, and he was a teacher in many ways," says Phoebe Snow. "Listen to his words, the words of somebody who was wise beyond his life span."

"He was a healer, a medicine man, a shaman, a mystic, and he never took himself too seriously," says John Bates. "It's so maddening to know he belongs here and how much we need him. Where is his replacement? Where is the Kelly Girl, where is the temp service who sends in the next Steve Goodman? Where the hell is the next Steve Goodman? There isn't one."

* * *

Steve himself invoked what may endure as his own best reckoning. To use a Goodman phrase, it was "no big surprise" that it came in a song. Not "City of New Orleans" or any of his other widely known compositions. It wasn't even a tune that he was known to sing publicly. The trigger to write it came while he sat on the couch of a Colorado friend, Jane Hansen (now Lang), and sang "Row, Row, Row Your Boat" with her two children, Jerry and Julie, on his lap. He recorded it 13 months before his death, on Aug. 23-24, 1983, and it snuggled unobtrusively at the end of the first side of his "Affordable Art" LP.

It was called "When My Rowboat Comes In."

The title and theme flowed from an ancient phrase, "When my ship comes home," a reference to seagoing vessels that carried fortunes from foreign lands. The expression embedded itself in pop culture in innumerable instances, including a speech by Mr. Potter in the 1946 film "It's a Wonderful Life." Bob Dylan, in one of his earliest and most optimistic clarion calls, capitalized on the clause in his 1964 David & Goliath song, "When the Ship Comes In." [53]

Steve's substitution of "rowboat" for "ship" was a typically self-slighting joke. But it was more than mere jest, says Chicago songwriter Al Day, who sang the song at the Nov. 26, 2004, Old Town School tribute to Steve. "He's looking at himself," Day says. "He's looking at what he is without being particularly grandiose, speaking to the catalog of his material and his whole career."

The "rowboat" reference had become an occasional, deceptively incidental presence in Steve's descriptions of himself on radio and in the newspapers:

53: Dylan's inspiration for the song apparently was quite mundane. He wrote it after being denied a room at a hotel.

◆ Back in 1973, Steve had used it when New York radio host Alison Steele asked him about his "discovery" by Kris Kristofferson and Paul Anka. "Yeah," he said, "my rowboat came in."

◆ In 1981, he used it when telling *Kansas City Star* reporter Leland Rucker that he would love to tour again with a full band but only if he had enough financial backing to keep from leaving his wife and three daughters high and dry: "If our rowboat came in and all of a sudden there were just pots of money layin' around, I'd blow some of it on a band in a minute."

In 1983, the phrase flowered into a composition that summoned the stormy elements of weather — clouds, rain, lightning, thunder and a "smoky sky" — to represent life's trials. But in the tranquillity of dawn, the song beckoned another key symbol. It was one that in previous compositions had tormented Steve as he feared its disappearance in his life. Here, it brought him peace.

Showcased in the chorus, the symbol was the sun. "When the sun comes out on the other side," Steve sang, "everything will be all right when we go rowin'."

In this calming image, the sun no longer represented a formidable adversary or agent of doom. Instead, the sun could "come out on the other side" much as his music could live on without him. Whatever the ways that he had strained for commercial success or compromised his family and home life, this irreverent elf had lived out his destiny. The musical milieu was his extended family, his real home was onstage, and there, for many, he *was* the sun.

The song's gentle recording featured Marty Stuart's spine-tingling mandolin and warm harmonies by Nashville vocalists Sharon and Cheryl White. Right away, those who carefully listened to the track sensed its meaning and power.

When Jane Harbury, former manager of the Riverboat in Toronto, received "Affordable Art" in the mail from Steve, she played "When My Rowboat Comes In." Immediately, she picked up the phone to call him.

"This sounds awfully personal," she said.

"Yeah, you got it," Steve replied. "You nailed it."

When Jimmy Ibbotson of the Nitty Gritty Dirt Band heard the song, he got chills. "There was just so much love in there about making this journey and getting to the end of it with the one you love," Ibbotson says. "He shamed me into staying with my wife a little longer than I might have. I mean, that's what he would do. He would open up people's hearts. He would reawaken this spirit of wonder and joy that apparently he felt all the time."

Philadelphia Inquirer critic Steven X. Rea called it "a wonderfully odd, beautiful song, ripe for plucking by some savvy, hit-making recording artist. ... (It) deserves to be a hit along the lines of Goodman's 'City of New Orleans.' "

But for Don Schultz, who with his Last Frontier Band shared stages in Alaska with Steve in 1978, the song transcended commercialism. Schultz regards "Rowboat" as "one of Steve's remarkable creations that arose from his lifelong fantasy of all good things finally happening to all good people."

The song was a satisfying signal. Steve had surmounted his own last frontier. His race with the sun was finally over. ♪

He would open up people's hearts. He would reawaken this spirit of wonder and joy that apparently he felt all the time.
JIMMY IBBOTSON

Discs, videos, books and sites

DISCS

This is an attempt to compile a comprehensive list of Steve Goodman's recorded and unrecorded audio musical contributions.

In cases in which an LP is listed but no corresponding CD re-release, it is possible that a CD issued at a later date can be located on the Internet.

Scores of compilation CDs not listed here contain Goodman songs recorded by other artists, particularly versions of "City of New Orleans" by Arlo Guthrie, Johnny Cash and Willie Nelson and "You Never Even Call Me by My Name" by David Allan Coe. To find these CDs, the best bet for up-to-date info is via the All Music Guide, http://www.allmusic.com, and other Internet sites.

Listings are chronological within categories. (**G**) denotes Grammy winner.

STEVE GOODMAN'S LP/CD RECORDINGS

(Most recordings in this category are available on CD at **Oh Boy Records**, 33 Music Square West, Suite 102B, Nashville, TN 37203-6607. Phone: 615-742-1250. Toll-free phone: 800-521-2112. E-mail: ohboy@ohboy.com. Internet site: **http://www.ohboy.com**. Individual track info can be found there and at other sites.)

"Steve Goodman," LP, 12 tracks, **1971**, Buddah Records, BDS 5096. Early version had gatefold cover. Later version eliminated gatefold (and lyrics). Released on CD, 1999, Buddah Records, with two bonus tracks. Guitar, vocals.

"Somebody Else's Troubles," LP, 11 tracks, **1972**, Buddah Records, BDS 5121. Released on CD, 1999, Buddah Records, with two bonus tracks. Guitar, vocals.

"Jessie's Jig & Other Favorites," LP, 10 tracks, **1975**, Asylum Records, 7E-1037. Producer, guitar, vocals.

"The Essential ... Steve Goodman," two LPs, 20 tracks, **1976**, Buddah Records, BDS 5665-2. Combo of first two Buddah LPs, minus four songs written by others, plus "Election Year Rag." Repackaged as "City of New Orleans" in Germany and Yugoslavia, Buddah SOKOJ 6.28428. Released on CD, 1992, Unidisc. Variation: "City of New Orleans," two CDs, Pair PCD-2-1233. Guitar, vocals.

"Words We Can Dance To," LP, 10 tracks, **1976**, Asylum Records, 7E-1061. Producer, guitar, vocals.

"Say It in Private," LP, 10 tracks, **1977**, Asylum Records, 7E-1118. Guitar, vocals.

"High & Outside," LP, 10 tracks **1979**, Asylum Records, 6E-174. Producer, guitar, vocals.

"Hot Spot," LP, 9 tracks, **1980**, Asylum Records, 6E-297. Guitar, vocals.

"Artistic Hair," LP, 12 tracks, **1983**, Red Pajamas Records, RPJ-001. Producer, guitar, vocals.

"Affordable Art," LP, 12 tracks, **1983**, Red Pajamas Records, RPJ-002. Producer, guitar, mandola, vocals.

"Santa Ana Winds," LP, 10 tracks, **1984**, Red Pajamas Records, RPJ-003. Producer, guitar, vocals.

"Unfinished Business" (**G**), LP, 10 tracks, **1987**, Red Pajamas Records, RPJ-005. Guitar, vocals.

"The Best of the Asylum Years Vol. 1," LP, 11 tracks, **1988**, Red Pajamas Records, RPJ-006. Producer, guitar, vocals.

"The Best of the Asylum Years Vol. 2," LP, 12 tracks, **1989**, Red Pajamas Records, RPJ-007. Producer, guitar, vocals.

"The Original Steve Goodman," selections from first two Buddah LPs, CD, **1989**, Buddah Records SCD-4923. Guitar, vocals.

"No Big Surprise: The Steve Goodman Anthology," two CDs, 42 tracks, **1994**, Red Pajamas Records, RPJ-008. Producer, guitar, mandola, vocals.

"The Easter Tapes," CD, 19 tracks, **1996**, Red Pajamas Records, RPJ-009. Guitar, vocals.

"Live Wire," CD, 17 tracks, **2000**, Red Pajamas Records, RPJ-015. Guitar, vocals.

"Steve Goodman Live at the Earl of Old Town," CD, 17 tracks, **2006**, Red Pajamas Records, RPJ-017. Guitar, vocals.

STEVE GOODMAN'S 45-RPM SINGLE RECORDINGS

"City of New Orleans," b/w "Mind Your Own Business," **1971**, Buddah 180. Other versions: b/w same (mono/stereo), 1972, Buddah 270; b/w same, 1984, Buddah BG 28; b/w same Collectable B3528; b/w "Would You Like to Learn to Dance?," Radio Active Gold RD 66; b/w "Would You Like to Learn to Dance?," 1984, Buddah BG 28. Guitar, vocals.

"The I Don't Know Where I'm Goin' but I'm Goin' Nowhere in a Hurry Blues," b/w same (mono/stereo), **1972**, Buddah 232 or 2011126. Another version b/w "Turnpike Tom." Guitar, vocals.

"Election Year Rag," b/w same (mono/stereo), **1972**, Buddah 326. Other versions b/w "Somebody Else's Troubles"; b/w same (mono/stereo), 1976, Buddah 541; b/w "City of New Orleans," picture sleeve, "Original version ... with Bob Dylan on piano," Buddah 37 004, Germany. Guitar, vocals.

"The Dutchman" (by Michael Smith), b/w "Song for David," **1973**, BDA 348, picture sleeve. Guitar, vocals.

"Somebody Else's Troubles," b/w same (mono/stereo), **1973**, BDA-369. Guitar, vocals.

"It's a Sin to Tell a Lie," b/w same (mono/stereo), **1975**, Asylum 45284. Another version b/w "Jessie's Jig," Asylum EK 45284. Producer, guitar, vocals.

"Blue Umbrella," b/w "Jessie's Jig," **1975**, Asylum AYM551. Producer, guitar, vocals.

"Can't Go Back," b/w same (mono/stereo), **1976**, Asylum 45331. Another version b/w "Between the Lines," Asylum EK 45331. Producer, guitar, vocals.

"Death of a Salesman," b/w "Unemployed," **1976**, UK version, Asylum K13055. Producer, guitar, vocals.

"Video Tape," b/w same (mono/stereo), **1977**, Asylum E-45481. Another version b/w "My Old Man." Guitar, vocals.

"The One That Got Away," b/w same (mono/stereo), **1979**, Asylum, 46012. Another version b/w "Luxury's Lap," Asylum EK 46012. Producer, guitar, vocals.

"Men Who Love Women Who Love Men," b/w same (mono/stereo), **1979**, Asylum E-46522. Another version b/w "The One That Got Away," Asylum, EK 46522. Producer, guitar, vocals.

"Sometimes Love Forgets" with Phoebe Snow, b/w same (mono/ stereo), **1980**, Asylum 47069. UK version: K12509. Guitar, vocals.

"Bobby Don't Stop" (co-write: Goodman, Bill LaBounty), b/w same (mono/stereo), **1981**, Asylum E-47107. Guitar, vocals.

"A Dying Cub Fan's Last Request" 6:28, b/w "Take Me Out to the Ball Game" 2:58, **1981**, Red Pajama Records, RP-1001. Guitar, vocals. Accompanied by Jethro Burns. Early version, different from the one on LPs and CDs.

"Go, Cubs, Go" (with the Chicago Cubs Chorus) b/w same (mono/ stereo), **1984**, WGN 784, proceeds to Neediest Kids Fund. Co-producer, guitar, vocals.

"In Real Life" (co-write: Goodman, Bill LaBounty), **1987**, Red Pajamas Records. Guitar, vocals.

STEVE GOODMAN'S RECORDINGS IN LP/CD COMPILATIONS

"Give Joy to the World ... with Music," two-LP set, October **1977**, Warner-Elektra-Atlantic Records, WEA SMP-4, includes Goodman's version of "Two Lovers" (by Smokey Robinson).

The Dr. Demento Show, host Barry Hansen, radio shows on LP, cassette and CD: Aug. 23, **1981**, April 1, 1991, April 6-7, 1996, April 9, 2000, "A Dying Cub Fan's Last Request."; Sept. 9, 1984, "Talk Backwards"; Oct. 29 and Nov. 4, 1984, "The Ballad of Carl Martin (You Better Get It While You Can)"; May 3, 1998, "Chicken Cordon Bleus"; April 9 and Oct. 1, 1989, "Vegematic"; Aug. 8, 1999, "The I Ain't Heard You Play No Blues"; Jan. 1, 2000, "Lincoln Park Pirates."

Steve's daughter, Jessie, makes a home recording of her dad in about 1980 in the Goodman kitchen in Seal Beach.
(Photo by Jim Shea)

"The History of Surf Music 1980-1982, Vol. 3: The Revival," LP, July 20, **1982**, Rhino RNLP 054, includes "Don't Get Sand in It" (co-write: Goodman, Sean Kelly). Liner notes: "He spent his formative years in the Windy City but is currently part of the Surf 'n Sand set in Seal Beach."

"Cubs Party Album and Rally Starter," cassette, **1987**, WGN Radio, includes "Go, Cubs, Go."

"Folked Again: The Best of Mountain Railroad," LP, **1987**, Mountain Railroad, includes "Chicago Bust Rag" (written by Greg Hildebrand).

"Storytellers: Singers and Songwriters," CD, **1987**, Warner Special Products, 9-27615-2, includes "Banana Republics" (co-write: Goodman, Steve Burgh, Jim Rothermel). Also includes Arlo Guthrie's version of "City of New Orleans."

"Baseball's Greatest Hits," CD, **1989**, Rhino, includes "A Dying Cub Fan's Last Request."

"70's Greatest Rock Hits, Vol. 15: Singers/Songwriters," CD, **1992**, Priority 53706, includes "City of New Orleans."

"Folk Song America: A 20th Century Revival," four CDs, Feb. 1, **1994**, Smithsonian Folkways 464, includes "City of New Orleans."

"The Ballads of Madison County," CD, **1993**, includes "The Dutchman."

"The Buddah Box," three CDs, **1993**, includes "City of New Orleans."

"The Coach Collection," CD, **1994**, includes "Chicken Cordon Bleus."

New Country magazine, CD, March **1995**, includes "You Never Even Call Me by My Name."

"Troubadours of the Folk Era Vol. 4," CD, **1995**, Rhino 71843, includes "City of New Orleans."

New Country magazine, "Summer Travel" CD, summer **1995**, includes "City of New Orleans."

"Mellow Rock Hits of the '70s," CD, **1996**, Rhino 72519, includes "Banana Republics."

"Wacky Classics of the '70s," two CDs, **1996**, Time/Life Warner Special Products, includes "The I Don't Know Where I'm Goin' but I'm Goin' Nowhere in a Hurry Blues."

"Folk Favorites of the '60s and '70s," **1996**, Reader's Digest, four CDs, includes "City of New Orleans."

"Mystery Train: Classic Railroad Songs Vol. 2," CD, March 11, **1997**, Rounder 1129, includes "City of New Orleans."

"Chicago Cubs Greatest Hits Vol. 1," CD, **1998**, includes "Go, Cubs, Go."

"America Forever: 20 Great Patriotic Favorites," CD, **1998**, includes "City of New Orleans."

"Soft Rock Classics," three CDs, Oct. 27, **1998**, Rhino 75549, includes "Banana Republics" (co-write: Goodman, Steve Burgh, Jim Rothermel).

"Have a Buddhaful Day," CD, **1999**, Buddha 1, includes "City of New Orleans."

"Timekeepers," CD, November **1999**, Minnesota Public Radio, includes "The Twentieth Century Is Almost Over" (co-write: Goodman, John Prine).

"Chicago," CD, **2000**, Virgin Mega Music, EMI-Capitol 30073-0-0, includes "A Dying Cub Fan's Last Request."

"Singin' with Emmylou," CD, **2000**, includes, as the final track, "Fourteen Days."

"Keepers Railroad Tracks," October **2003**, Minnesota Public Radio, includes "City of New Orleans."

"Real Folk," three CDs, **2003**, BMG 982, includes "City of New Orleans."

"The Ultimate Singer/Songwriter Collection," two CDs, **2003**, Realm/Warner Brothers Special Products 3620, includes "City of New Orleans."

"Great American Train Songs," CD, 2003, Green Hill Productions, includes "City of New Orleans."

"Bouncin' a Little: Another Story of Swing," Japan, CD, **2003**, includes "It's a Sin to Tell a Lie."

"Diamond Cuts: Volume XII, Seventh Inning Stretch," CD, **2004**, part of nine-volume set, includes "A Dying Cub Fan's Last Request."

"The Folk Scene," **2004**, BMG Special Products, two CDs, includes "City of New Orleans."

"Mariposa 2005," CD, **2005**, Mariposa Folk Foundation, MAR2005, includes "Old Fashioned."

"The Best of the Land of Nod Store Music, Vol. 1," CD, Oct. 11, **2005**, Land of Nod, Ryko Distribution, includes "Take Me Out to the Ballgame."

"The Great American Baseball Box," four-CD set, Oct. 18, **2005**, label Shout!, distributed by Sony, includes "A Dying Cub Fan's Last Request."

"Elvis Mania Volume 7," CD, **2006**, Silly Records, SR8026, includes "Elvis Imitators."

"Old Town School of Folk Music Songbook Volume 4," CD, November **2007**, Bloodshot Records, OTS4, includes live version of "City of New Orleans."

"30 Years of Great Folk Hits," year uncertain, Reader's Digest, two CDs and bonus CD, includes "The Dutchman."

"Lonesome Whistle Railroad Classics," CD, year uncertain, Cumberland Records.

STEVE GOODMAN'S CONTRIBUTIONS TO OTHERS' LP/CD RECORDINGS

Vocal on "Old Man River" for Maine East High School's "Musically Speaking," two LPs, **1964**, Delta Records, live recording of Mainspring 1964, sold as fund-raiser for school.

Guitar, vocals on "Shotgun," b/w "House of the Rising Sun," for Impalas' 45-rpm single, **1965**.

Guitar, vocals on "There Is a Meeting," "I'm a Drifter," "If I Had My Way," "You've Lost That Lovin' Feeling," "Stormy Monday," "Cherry Berry," "Good Times," "Mighty Mississippi" and "The First Time Ever I Saw Your Face" for demo tape of trio including Bill Wencel and Lycurus Mitchell, **1967**.

Vocals on Bill "Oliver" Swofford's unreleased studio tracks, **1971**.

Guitar, vocals on "Eight-Ball," "Chicago Bust Rag" (by Greg Hildebrand), "City of New Orleans" for "Gathering at the Earl of Old Town," sampler LP, **1971**, Dunwich, 670, duotone gatefold cover. Re-released with color cover minus gatefold in 1976 by Mountain Railroad, MR 670.

Guitar, vocal on "Paradise" and guitar on "Flashback Blues" for John Prine's "John Prine," LP, **1971**, Atlantic SD 8296.

Vocal (as "Turnpike Tom") on "Friends with You" for John Denver's "Aerie," LP, **1971**, RCA LSP-4607.

Guitar, vocals on seven tracks for John Prine's "Diamonds in the Rough," LP, **1972**, Atlantic SD 7240.

Vocals on "As Long as I Love" and "I Can't Control Myself," unreleased tracks by Doris Abrahams, May **1973**.

Guitar, vocals on nine tracks for John Prine's "Sweet Revenge," LP, **1973**, Atlantic 7274.

Guitar for Jimmy Buffett's "A White Sport Coat and a Pink Crustacean," LP, **1973**, ABC Records, DSX 50150.

Guitar for Bonnie Koloc's "You're Gonna Love Yourself in the Morning," LP, **1974**, Ovation OVQD/14-38. Also, "a special thanks to Steve Goodman."

Guitar for Jimmy Buffett's "A-1-A," LP, **1974**, ABC Records, DSD 50183.

Guitar, vocals on three tracks, notably "City of New Orleans," for Judy Collins' "Judith," LP, **1975**, Elektra 7E-1032.

Guitar, vocals on six tracks for John Prine's "Common Sense," LP, **1975**, Atlantic SD 18127.

Guitar for Jimmy Buffett's "Havana Daydreamin'," LP, **1975**, MCA Records 37023.

Guitar on "Clocks and Spoons" for Bonnie Koloc's "Close-Up," LP, **1976**, Epic 34184.

Vocals, guitar on six unreleased demo tracks by Steve Mosley, **1976**.

Guitar, vocals for John Prine's "Prime Prine," LP, **1976**, Atlantic 18202.

Producer, guitar for Malvina Reynolds' "The Judge Said," b/w "Young Moon," 45-rpm single, **1977**, Sporadic Times CS-54, Berkeley. Both tracks also released on Reynolds' "Mama Lion," posthumous LP, 1980, Cassandra Records, CR 050, Berkeley, CA. "The Judge Said" also released on Reynolds' "Ear to the Ground: Topical Songs 1960-1978," CD, 2000, Smithsonian Folkways Recordings.

Guitar, vocal on "Old Fashioned" for "Mariposa 1976," two LPs, **1977**, Mariposa Folk Festival, Toronto, Ontario, MSH-239.

Guitar, vocals for Tom Paxton's "New Songs from the Briarpatch," LP, **1977**, Vanguard VSD 79395, and on CD, "Tom Paxton: Best of the Vanguard Years," June 20, 2000, Vanguard 79561.

Vocal on "Walkin' in Jerusalem" for Bryan Bowers' "The View from Home," LP, **1977**, Flying Fish, FF-037.

Vocals on four tracks for Ken Bloom's "Ken Bloom," LP, **1978**, Flying Fish, FF-051.

Overall producer plus guitar, vocals on five tracks for Martin, Bogan & the Armstrongs' "That Old Gang of Mine," LP, **1978**, Flying Fish, FF-056. Released on CD, 1992, Flying Fish.

Overall producer plus guitar, vocals on seven tracks for John Prine's "Bruised Orange," LP, **1978**, Asylum 6E-139.

Vocal (as Ollie Otter) on "You Otta Be an Otter" for "The GoGo the Blue Gorilla Show," children's LP, **1978**, Blue Gorilla Records, BG 2301, Mountain View, CA.

Vocal on "Son of a Son of a Sailor" for Jimmy Buffett's "Son of a Son of a Sailor," LP, **1978**, ABC Records AA-1046.

Guitar on "Honeysuckle Rose" for "Joe Venuti in Chicago, 1978," LP, **1979**, Flying Fish, FF-70077. Released on CD, 1993.

Producer, guitar for "I Knew the Bride When She Used to Rock 'n' Roll," "Daddy, Daddy, Walk My Way," "Good Place Now" unreleased demo tracks by Alice Playten, October **1979**.

Producer for "Ride on the Prairie," demo track by Harry Waller, **1979**.

Producer for demo tracks by Tom Dundee, **1979**.

Vocal on "G-Man," "El Forward Paso," unreleased studio tracks with Bob Hoban, **1979**.

Producer, co-writer (with Sean Kelly), "What Were You Expecting – Rock 'n' Roll?" for "National Lampoon White Album," LP, **1980**, Label 21, Jem Records, 212002, also on CD, 2004, Uproar 3848.

Guitar, vocals on "City of New Orleans" for Tom Rush's "Late Night Radio," LP, **1984**, Night Light Recordings, Hillsboro, NH, HS-48011.

Producer of "People Puttin' People Down" for John Prine's "Aimless Love," **1984**, Oh Boy 002, and on CD, 1990, OBR-002CD.

Co-writer, arranger for "One Last Chance" for Tom Dundee's "Right Lane Man," LP, **1985**, Flyte Records, Seattle, WA.

Guitar, vocal on "Souvenirs" for John Prine's "John Prine Live," two LPs, **1988**, taken from duet for "Down Home Country Music" TV special, Jan. 17, 1982, Oh Boy Records.

Producer, guitar, vocals for tracks in John Prine's "Great Days: the John Prine Anthology," two CDs, Aug. 17, **1993**, Rhino 71400.

Guitar, vocals on "City of New Orleans" and "Goodnight Irene" for "Philadelphia Folk Festival: 40th Anniversary," three CDs, Sept. 25, **2001**, Sliced Bread.

Guitar, vocals on six tracks (recorded in 1976 at Amazingrace, Evanston, IL) for Bonnie Koloc's "Timeless," CD, **2004**.

OTHERS' RECORDINGS OF 'CITY OF NEW ORLEANS' ON LP/CD

John Denver on "Aerie," LP, **1971**, song credited as "by Steve Goodman and John Denver," RCA, LSP-4607, on "Aerie" CD, 1997, and on several Denver compilations. Also, a live version from Aug. 14, 1973, at Red Rocks, appeared on "An Evening with John Denver (Expanded)," remastered CD, March 2001.

Arlo Guthrie on "Hobo's Lullaby," LP, **1972**, Reprise Records, MS 2060, and on many other Guthrie compilations, live CDs and other compilations, including "Together in Concert" (with Pete Seeger), two LPs, 1975, Reprise 2214.

Seldom Scene on "The Seldom Scene Act 1," LP, **1972**, Rebel SLP 1511 and on "Recorded Live at the Cellar Door," double LP, 1975, Rebel SLP 1547/48, recorded Dec. 27-28, 1974. Also on "The Best of the Seldom Scene Vol. 1," CD, 1996, Rebel 1101.

Kirk Felix on "For My Friends," LP, **1972**, Coward Records RI3555.

Joe Dassin, on "Joe," LP, **1972**, CBS, France. (Lyrics changed to "Salut Les Amoureux," meaning "Hello, Lovers.") On several later LP and CD compilations.

Johnny Cash on "Johnny Cash & His Woman," LP, **1973**, Columbia KC 32443, and on many other Cash compilations and live CDs.

Country Gentlemen on "Country Gentleman," LP, **1973**, Vanguard, VSD 79331 (stereo), VSQ 40021 (quadraphonic), on "The Country Gentlemen Featuring Ricky Skaggs," LP and CD, 1987, Vanguard 73123, and on "The Complete Vanguard Recordings," CD, Feb. 5, 2002, Vanguard 79711.

Lynn Anderson on "Keep Me in Mind," LP, **1973**, Columbia KC 32078.

Chet Atkins on "Superpickers," LP, **1973**, RCA APL-1, 0327. Released on CD, "Picks on the Hits/ Superpickers," Nov. 24, 1998, One Way 35126.

Theodore Bikel on "For the Young: A Fabulous Flight through Folksongland," LP, **1973**, Peter Pan, 151, Orange Blossom series. Reissued in 1976 as "Hit American Folk Songs" in the "Bicentennial Series" of Peter Pan.

Brothers Four on "Live in Japan," two LPs, Oct. 10, **1973**, Sony CBS SOPJ 56-57, Quadraphonic, recorded at Tokyo's Kosei-Nenkin Hall.

Bluegrass Alliance on "Tall Grass," LP, July **1973**, Bridges, BG 27001.

Henson Cargill on "This Is Cargill Country," LP, **1973**, Atlantic SD 7279.

Sammi Smith on "The Toast of 45," LP, **1973**, Mega, M31-1021, on "The Rainbow in Daddy's Eyes," LP, 1974, Mega, on "Sammi/ Zodiac," LP, 1976, ZLP-5000, and on CD, "The Best of Sammi Smith," Aug. 22, 1996, Varese 5574.

Hank Snow on "Sings Grand Ol' Opry Favorites, LP, **1973**, RCA. Also on "All About Trains," LP, 1975, RCA ANL 1-1052, and on "The Singing Ranger Vol. 4," nine CDs, April 4, 1995, Bear Family.

Mac Wiseman on "Concert Favorites," LP, **1973**, RCA LSA 154 UK.

Steve Bledsoe on "You're the Greatest Woman I've Known," LP, **1974**, Super Star, SSLP-1002, Nashville, TN.

Gerard Cox on "Die Goeie Ouwe Tijd," LP, **1974**, The Netherlands, Columbia 80462. Song converted to "The Beautiful Summer Has Passed Already."

Steve introduces "You Never Even Call Me by My Name" on July 12, 1981, at the Winnipeg Folk Festival.

(Photo by Jim Polaski)

Hopeton Lewis on "The Dynamic Hopeton Lewis," LP, **1974**, Jamaica, Dynamic Records, DY-3342.

Redwood on "Up Country," compilation LP, **1974**, BBC Records, Rec 179.

Cathie Stewart on "Springhill," LP, **1974**, Canadian Talent Library CEL 1908.

Judy Collins on "Judith," LP, **1975**, Elektra 7E-1032, and on other Collins compilations.

Folklore (Pauline Sloan, Paul Sloan, Pat Campbell, Brendan Sands, Frank Lennon) on "First of the Folklore," LP, **1975**, Homespun Records, HRL 104.

Jerry Reed on "Mind Your Love," LP, **1975**, RCA APL-1, 0787.

James Durst on "In Concert," cassette, **1976**, recorded at Barrington High School, Barrington, IL.

Jancis Harvey on "A Portrait of Jancis Harvey," LP, **1976**, Westwood Recordings, Wales, MCPS WRS 107.

Johnny Cash on "Destination Victoria Station," LP, **1976**, Columbia Special Products, P13043, VS 150. Sold at Victoria Station restaurant chain.

Jack Hudson on "McTavish's Kitchen," two compilation LPs, **1976**, Canon Records, Scotland.

Limeliters on "Reunion Vol. 1," LP, **1976**, Brass Dolphin.

Brimkló on "Rock 'n' roll öll mín bestu ár," LP, **1976**, Geimsteinn GS 100, Iceland.

Jack Grochmal on "Wabash Cannonball," compilation LP, **1977**, National Geographic, 07796.

The Stonemans on "On the Road," LP, **1977**, CMH Records, 6219.

André Van Duin on "Het Is Weer Voorbij Die Mooie Zom," LP, **1977**, Ne 0523.

Marlene Powell on "A Country Girl with a Country Song," LP, **1978**, Cambrian (UK), SCLP 637.

Matthew & the Mandarins on self-titled LP, **1978**, EMI Records, EMGS 5016, Singapore.

Patrick O'Sullivan and Lina Jeong on "Don't Let Me Be Misunderstood," LP, **1978**, Salisbury Labs SALS D2D 002.

The Cumberlands on "The Cumberlands Live," LP, recorded Dec. 9, 1978, released February **1979**. Also on "The Best of the Cumberlands," LP, 1980.

C.W. McCall on "C.W. McCall & Co.," LP, **1979**, Polydor PD-1-6190.

Unidentified musicians on "Chattanooga Choo-Choo Centennial," LP, **1980**, Terminal Station, Chattanooga, TN.

Karel Gott ("The Golden Voice of Prague") on "Country Album," LP, **1982**, Czechoslovakia, Supraphon, 1113 3088.

*Backed by (from left)
keyboardist Howard Levy,
vocalist Bonnie Koloc,
bassist John Baney and
mandolinist Jethro Burns,
Steve jams on the Chicago
Fest stage in August 1983
at Navy Pier.*

(Photo courtesy of Howard Levy)

Clam Chowder on "For Here or to Go," LP, **1982**. Folk/filk group, Indigo Hound Audio Labs, Delta, PA.

Willie Nelson on "City of New Orleans," LP, **1984**, FC 39145, and on many other Nelson compilations and live CDs, including "Farm Aid Vol. 1," two CDs, Sept. 12, 2000, Redline 75003.

Arlo Guthrie on "HARP (Holly Near, Arlo Guthrie, Ronnie Gilbert, Pete Seeger)," LP, **1985**, Redwood Records, Oakland, CA, live recording from Sept. 17, 1984, at the Universal Amphitheatre, Los Angeles. Expanded and re-released as "HARP: A Time to Sing," CD, Sept. 25, 2001, Appleseed Recordings.

Arlo Guthrie on "Tribute to Steve Goodman" (**G**), two LPs, **1985**, Red Pajamas Records, RPJ-004.

David W. Cook and Reinterpretation Jazz Band on "Whence Came Jazz?," cassette, Nov. 1 **1985**, RJB-1985, with new words and arrangement.

Richard Clayderman on "Romantic America," LP, **1988**, Columbia FC 44211. Released on "Love American Style," CD, 1996, Quality 6753.

Modern Folk Quartet on "Bambo," CD, **1990**, PCCY-00061, Japan.

Glenn Yarbrough & the Limeliters on "Joy Across the Land," CD, **1993**, GNP Crescendo 2219, and other Yarbrough compilations.

Willie Nininger on "American Groove," CD, **1994**, Switzerland.

Lewis Grizzard on "One Last Time," CD, **1994**, Southern Tracks Records, Atlanta, GA.

Skip Haynes on "Chicago Songs," CD, Sept. 16, **1996**, Quicksilver Records, Reseda, CA.

John Denver on "All Aboard," cassette and CD, **1997**, Sony Music, new version of song conforming more closely to Goodman's original words.

Jeff Turner & the Nashville Connections, part of "Train Songs Medley" on "For You, Vol. 2," CD, **1997**, K-Tel International, Switzerland.

Paul & Margie on "40 Most Popular American Folk Songs," two CDs, Jan. 27, **1998**, ARC 1431.

Mark Dvorak on "The Streets of Old Chicago," CD, **1998**, Depot Recordings.

Randy Scruggs (with John Prine sharing vocals) on "Crown of Jewels," CD, July 14, **1998**, Warner Brothers/WEA, 46930.

Lena Teigen on "Melodie d'Amour: The Romantic Sound of Lena Teigen," CD, Sept. 15, **1998**, Prism 226.

Greg Schindel on "Train Singer," CD, **1998**, Schindel Music.

Allegra on "Fifteen," CD, **1999**, Sub City 8.

Joe Brown on "On a Day Like This," CD, April 19, **1999**, Round Tower Music, RTM CD92, UK.

George Gaines Swanson on "City of New Orleans," CD/cassette, **1999**, Old Times Records.

Mike Fedel on "I Miss Your Smile," CD, **1999**, in memory of drunken-driving victim Amy Elizabeth Eridon Fedel, Ann Arbor, MI.

Cynthia Crane on "The Secret Life of a W.A.S.P.," CD, Jan. 1, **2000**, Original Cast Record, 9211.

Johnny Cash, live version, on "The Highwaymen" compilation, two CDs, **2000**, Goldies, Netherlands, GLD25380.

Judy Collins on "Live at Wolf Trap," CD, **2000**, Wildflower Records, recorded June 18, 2000, at Wolf Trap Foundation for the Performing Arts, Vienna, VA.

The Broadway Kids on "Sing America," CD, Aug. 22, **2000**, Lightyear 54367.

David Roe with the Royal Rounders and Friends on "Angel of New Orleans," CD, **2000**, Orchard 7667.

The Big Wu on "Live 3/13/98," three CDs, May **2001**, recorded at Cedar Cultural Centre, Minneapolis, MN.

Rob Oxford on "Americana ... Trains, Trains and More," CD, **2001**.

Jimmy Sturr Band (with Arlo Guthrie on lead vocal) on "Top of the World" (**G**), CD, **2002**, Rounder Select.

Charlie Waller and the Country Gentlemen on "45 Years of Memories," CD, **2002**, Pinecastle 1121.

Dave Kelly on "Resting My Bones," CD, Feb. 11, **2002**, Hypertension, HPP 1209, UK.

John Boutte & Uptown Okra on "Carry Me Home," CD, **2003**.

Rig the Jig on "Passing Through," CD, **2004**, Toucan Cove 50668.

Winnie Winston on "Misty Morn," CD, **2005** (posthumous), Gwyneth Evans, 54A Collins Avenue, Tawa, Wellington 6006, New Zealand.

Steve "Doc" Wood on "The Golden Vanity," CD, January **2005**, Neoga Records, North Kingstown, RI.

Brian Gill on "Playin' Favorites," CD, **2006**, BrianGillMusic.com.

Lizzie West & the White Buffalo on "I Pledge Allegiance to Myself," CD, April 18, **2006**, Appleseed Records B000EMGAG2.

Luther Wright & the Wrongs on "My Old Man: A Tribute to Steve Goodman," CD, June 7, **2006**, Red Pajamas Records RPJ-016.

Cathy Cowette on "Songs for a Winter's Night," CD, Dec. 13, **2006**, CathyCowette.com.

Sam Bush, Stewart Duncan, Ronnie McCourey, David Grier, Richard Bailey and Denis Crouch, on "The Lonesome Whistle Classics," CD, year uncertain, Cumberland Records, B0002K1RSW.

Smokey River Boys on "Songs of the West," three CDs, year uncertain.

Smoky Mountain Heritage on "Smoky Mountain Hymns," year uncertain.

Michael McCloud on "Gretastits," CD, year uncertain, Key West, FL.

OTHERS' RECORDINGS OF 'CITY OF NEW ORLEANS' AS 45-RPM SINGLE

John Denver, flip side of "Everyday," **1972**, RCA 74-0647.

Arlo Guthrie, b/w "Days Are Short," **1972**, Reprise, REP 14202. Domestic picture sleeve with "Hobo's Lullaby" LP cover photo. (In France, picture sleeve showed Guthrie smoking a cigarette and playing guitar.)

Bluegrass Alliance, b/w "Sugar Daddy," **1972**, Bridges.

Hopeton Lewis, b/w "The Wind Cries Mary," **1973**, Dragon, DRA 1001, UK.

Sammi Smith, flip side of "Don't Blow No Smoke on Me," **1973**, MEGA 615-0 118.

Jack White, "Der Zug, Genannt die City of New Orleans," b/w "Hey Girl, Was Ist Geschehn," **1973**, Telefunken U56252, Germany.

Jerry Reed, flip side of "The Telephone," **1975**, RCA 10325.

Willie Nelson (**G**), **1984**, Columbia 38-04568.

OTHERS' RECORDINGS OF STEVE GOODMAN SONGS OTHER THAN 'CITY OF NEW ORLEANS'

Bill "Oliver" Swofford, "Eight Ball Blues," unreleased studio tracks, **1971**.

Jackie DeShannon, "Would You Like to Learn to Dance?" for "Jackie," LP, **1972**, Atlantic SD 7231, and on expanded "Jackie Plus," CD, Jan. 1, 2004, Rhino Handmade 7832.

Jimmy Buffett, "Door Number Three" (co-write: Goodman and Buffett) for "A1A," LP, **1974**, ABC Dunhill DSD 50183.

David Allan Coe, "You Never Even Called Me by My Name" (original title was in present tense, co-write: Goodman, John Prine) for "Once Upon a Rhyme," LP, **1975**, Columbia Records, 3-10159. Track also released on "For the Record: The First 10 Years," two LPs, 1984, Columbia, and on other Coe compilations and live CDs.

Iain MacKintosh, "The Ballad of Penny Evans" for "Encore," LP, Scotland, **1975**, Dara Records MPA 010. Also on "Songs for Peace," LP, Scotland, 1983, FolkFreak FF 4010.

Jimmy Buffett, "Woman Goin' Crazy on Caroline Street" (co-write: Buffett, Goodman) and "This Hotel Room" for "Havana Daydreamin'," LP, January **1976**, MCA Records 37023. "This Hotel Room" also on "Live in Las Vegas," CD, Oct. 7, 2003, Mailboat 2102, and "Live in Cincinnati, OH," CD, Jan. 13, 2004, Mailboat 2106.

Bonnie Koloc, "I Can't Sleep" for "Close-Up," LP, **1976**, Epic 34184.

Katy Moffatt, "I Can't Sleep" for "Katy," LP, **1976**, Columbia 34172, and on CD re-release, "Katy/Kissin' in the California Sun," Oct. 22, 2002, Westside 920.

Joan Baez, "Yellow Coat" for "Blowin' Away," LP, **1977**, Columbia Portrait 34697, and on CD, 1990, Columbia 34697.

Jimmy Buffett, "Banana Republics" (co-write: Goodman, Steve Burgh, Jim Rothermel) for "Changes in Latitudes, Changes in Attitudes," LP, **1977**, ABC Records, AB-990. Also on CD, "All the Great Hits," Sept. 22, 1998, Prism Leisure 3420.

Bob Gibson & Hamilton Camp, "Lookin' for Trouble" for "Homemade Music," LP, **1978**, Mountain Railroad, MR-52781.

Steve Young, "I Can't Sleep" for "No Place to Hide," LP, **1978**, RCA 12510. Also on "Renegade Picker/No Place to Hide," CD, 2005, BMG International 187473.

Diane Keaton, "I'm Attracted to You" (co-write: Goodman, Rick Chudacoff), unreleased studio track, **1978-79**.

Gene Chandler, "I'm Attracted to You" (co-write: Goodman, Rick Chudadoff) for "Here's to Love," LP, **1980**, 20th Century, 397357.

Lucio Dalla & Francesco De Gregori, "Banana Republic" (original is plural "Republics," co-write: Goodman, Steve Burgh, Jim Rothermel) for "Banana Republic," LP, **1979**, Italy, RCA PD 74839.

Big Twist & the Mellow Fellows, "(It Would Be) You and Me" (co-write: Peter Bunetta, Rick Chudacoff, Goodman, Hank Neuberger) for "Big Twist & the Mellow Fellows," LP, **1980**, Flying Fish, FF-229. Released on CD, 1992, FF-90229.

Johnny Cash, "The Twentieth Century Is Almost Over" (co-write: Goodman, John Prine) for "Rockabilly Blues," LP, **1980**, Columbia, and on CD, 1999, Koch 7979.

Jimmy Buffett, "Where's the Party?" (co-write: Buffett, Goodman, Bill LaBounty) and "It's Midnight and I'm Not Famous Yet" (co-write: Buffett, Goodman) for "Somewhere over China," LP, **1981**, MCA Records 5285. "It's Midnight and I'm Not Famous Yet" also appeared on "Live in Las Vegas," CD, Oct. 7, 2003, Mailboat 2102.

Robbie Dupree, "In Real Life" (co-write: Goodman, Bill LaBounty) for unreleased LP, **1982**, and for "Carried Away," CD, 1987, Capitol 71360. Live version titled "Real Life" recorded Sept. 18-19, 1998, appeared on "Live: All Night Long," CD, April 1, 2000, Orchard 2808. Both versions contain a verse written by Dupree.

Sharon Bradley, "The Ballad of Penny Evans" for "Hello in There," LP, **1982**, Pan 111, The Netherlands.

Nitty Gritty Dirt Band, "Don't Get Sand in It" (co-write: Goodman, Sean Kelly) for "Let's Go," LP and cassette, June **1983**, Liberty 51146.

Nitty Gritty Dirt Band, "Colorado Christmas" for "A Christmas Tradition," compilation LP, **1983**. Released on their own "Christmas Album," CD, Oct. 7, 1997, Rising Tide 53048.

Peter, Paul & Mary, "Would You Like to Learn to Dance?" for "Such Is Love," CD, **1983**, recorded October 1981, Peter, Paul & Mary label, and on CD, 1998, Warner Brothers 47084.

Jimmy Buffett, "California Promises" for "One Particular Harbor," LP, September **1983**, MCA 25061. Also released on "Boats, Beaches, Bars & Ballads," four CDs, May 1992, MCAD4-10613, and on "Biloxi," CD, 1998, Premium Music, 17420.

New Edition, "Maryann" (co-write: Rick Chudacoff, Goodman, Arno Lucas) for "New Edition," LP, **1984**, MCAD-31028. Later released on CD.

Nitty Gritty Dirt Band, "Face on the Cutting Room Floor" (co-write: Goodman, Jeff Hanna, Jimmy Ibbotson) and "Video Tape" for "Plain Dirt Fashion," LP, **1984**, Warner Brothers 25113, and on "Plain Dirt Fashion/Partners, Brothers & Friends," CD, Jan. 27, 2004, Wounded Bird 5113. "Face on the Cutting Room Floor" appeared on "More Great Dirt: The Best of the Nitty Gritty Dirt Band Vol. II," LP, 1989, Warner Brothers 1-25830, and on "Live Two Five" (live version), CD, July 8, 1991, Liberty 93128.

Matthew Wilder, "Scandal" (co-write: Wilder, Goodman) for "Bouncin' Off the Walls," LP, **1984**, Columbia Private I, P.I. 04617. Also on CD, "18 Original Classics," 1999, Collectables Records, Narberth, PA.

Bonnie Koloc, "I Can't Sleep"; Nitty Gritty Dirt Band, "Face on the Cutting Room Floor" (co-write: Goodman, Jeff Hanna, Jimmy Ibbotson); Ed Holstein, "Blues That Steve Taught Me" (co-write: Goodman, Ed Holstein); John Prine, "My Old Man"; Jim Rothermel, "California Promises," for "Tribute to Steve Goodman" (**G**), two LPs, **1985**, Red Pajamas Records, RPJ-004.

Julia Ecklar & Catherine Cook, "The Ballad of Penny Evans" for "Brandywine," cassette, February **1985**, Off Centaur Publications, OCP-38, filk music.

Jimmy Buffett, "Frank and Lola" (co-write: Buffett, Goodman) for "Last Mango in Paris," LP, June **1985**, MCA, and on "Boats, Beaches, Bars & Ballads," four CDs, May 1992, MCAD4-10613.

Nitty Gritty Dirt Band, "Queen of the Road" (co-write: Goodman, Jeff Hanna, Jimmy Ibbotson) for "Partners, Brothers & Friends," LP, **1985**, Warner Brothers 4-25304, and on "Plain Dirt Fashion/ Partners, Brothers & Friends," CD, Jan. 27, 2004, Wounded Bird 5113.

Nicolette Larson, "I Just Keep Falling in Love" (co-write: Goodman, Bill LaBounty) for "...Say When," LP, **1985**, MCA 5556.

Highwaymen (Johnny Cash, Waylon Jennings, Kris Kristofferson, Willie Nelson), "The Twentieth Century Is Almost Over" (co-write: Goodman, John Prine) for "Highwayman," CD, **1985**, Columbia 40056, and on "Highwayman Super Hits," CD, May 2, 1999, Sony 69797.

Gene Parsons and Meridian Green, "Lookin' for Trouble" for "Birds of a Feather," LP, **1988**, Sierra Records 6004, and on CD, 1992, StringBender Records. Also a live version on "Live from Caspar," CD, 2001, StringBender 003.

Michelle Shocked, "The Ballad of Penny Evans" for "Anchorage," live EP from Glastonbury, **1988**, London Records, LONT 193, ZPMSC 11651/52. Another live track of same song recorded March 31, 1989, at Berklee Performance Center, Boston, appears on "Turn of the Decade: Ben & Jerry's Newport Folk Festival," CD, March 23, 1992, Red House Records, RHR CD-36. Also on "Short Sharp Shocked (Expanded)," CD, 2003, Mighty Sound 1004.

Iain MacKintosh, "My Old Man" for "Gentle Persuasion," LP, Scotland, **1988**, Greentrax TRAX 014.

John Prine, "If She Were You" (co-write: Goodman, Prine) for "German Afternoons," LP, cassette and CD, **1990**, Oh Boy 003.

Marty Stuart, "Do You Really Want My Lovin'?" (co-write: Stuart, Goodman) for "Marty Stuart," LP, **1992**, Columbia, CK-52960, and on several later CDs.

Ana Belen, "Banana Republics" (co-write: Goodman, Steve Burgh, Jim Rothermel) for "Con Las Manos Llenas," CD, **1993**, Alex 3422. Also on "Mucho Mas Que Dos," CD, 1999, BMG International 21179.

Etta James, "A Lover Is Forever" (co-write: Goodman, Fred Knobloch) for "How Strong Is a Woman: The Island Sessions," CD, **1993**, 4th & Broadway, 444056.

Andy Antipin, "The Twentieth Century Is Almost Over" (co-write: Goodman and John Prine) for "Café Philippe," CD, **1994**, Eclectic Synergy, AVL-93142.

Catfish Hodge, "Unemployed" for "Catfish Blues," CD, **1994**, Wild Cat/Uni 9201.

Gene Chandler, "I'm Attracted to You" (co-write: Goodman, Rick Chudacoff) for "Rainbow '80: A Golden Classics Edition," CD, Aug. 26, **1994**, Collectables 5140, and on "'80/Here's to Love, from the Windy City," CD, June 22, 1999, Westside 607.

Doug Supernaw, "You Never Even Call Me by My Name" (co-write: Goodman, John Prine), accompanied by Merle Haggard, Charley Pride, Waylon Jennings, David Allan Coe, for "Deep Thoughts from a Shallow Mind," CD, **1994**, BMG.

Roger Martin, "You Never Even Call Me by My Name" (co-write: Goodman, John Prine) for "Back from the Dead," CD, Oct. 10, **1995**, Cleveland Int'l 1011.

Rosanne Cash, "A Lover Is Forever" (co-write: Goodman, Fred Knobloch), live recording from 1991, Coach House, San Juan Capistrano, for "Retrospective," CD, **1995**, Columbia.

Jim Hoehn & Kevin Mulvenna, "Banana Republics" (co-write: Goodman, Steve Burgh, Jim Rothermel) for "Live at RACAfest," CD, **1996**, Milwaukee, WI.

Diane Taraz, "Lookin' for Trouble" for "Gathered Safely In," CD, Sept. 24, **1996**, Beacon 10143.

Petty Booka, "Colorado Christmas" for "Christmas Is Everywhere," CD, Nov. 21, **1996**, BNTN-018.

Trisha Yearwood, "A Lover Is Forever" (co-write: Goodman, Fred Knobloch) for "Everybody Knows," CD, **1996**, MCA-11477.

Jamie Hartford, "Lookin' for Trouble" for "What About Yes," CD, Dec. 9, **1997**, Paladin 24693.

Pepe Castillo, "Banana Republics" (co-write: Goodman, Steve Burgh, Jim Rothermel) for "Banana Land," CD, April 21, **1998**, M.I.L. Multimedia 8529.

Josh Kadish & Randy Rush, "Chicken Cordon Bleus" (co-write: Goodman, Paula Ballan, Toni Mandel) for Middle-Aged Guy with a Guitar, **1998**, Portland, OR.

Katy Moffatt, "I Just Keep Falling in Love" for "Angel Town," CD, **1998**, HMG 3004.

Mollie O'Brien, "Looking for Trouble" (original title omits the "g") for "Big Red Sun," CD, Aug. 18, **1998**, Sugar Hill Records 3885.

Ruth Brown, "A Lover Is Forever" (co-write: Goodman, Fred Knobloch) for "A Good Day for the Blues," CD, March 2, **1999**, Bullseye Blues and Jazz, 619613.

Kathy Mar, "The Twentieth Century Is Almost Over" (co-write: Goodman, John Prine) for "My Favorite Sings," CD, May **1999**, Prometheus Music.

Anne Hills & Michael Smith, "Danger" (co-write: Goodman, Smith, Sean Kelly) for "Paradise Lost & Found," CD, Aug. 24, **1999**, Redwing 5406. CD also includes "The Dutchman" and "Spoon River," both by Smith.

Fred Knobloch, "A Lover Is Forever" (co-write: Goodman, Knobloch) for "Songwriters on Beale St.," CD, Nov. 2 **1999**, Syren 211966.

Jim Stevens, "Lookin' for Trouble" for "Playing Favorites," CD, **1999**, Slimpicker Productions, SLMPKR001.

Jelly Roll Johnson, "A Lover Is Forever" (co-write: Goodman, Fred Knobloch) for "Jelly Roll Johnson and a Few Close Friends," CD, **2000**, American Originals 3004.

Fred Knobloch & Jelly Roll Johnson, "A Lover Is Forever" (co-write: Goodman, Knobloch) recorded live April 27, 2000, for "Live at the Bluebird Café," CD, Sept. 12, **2000**, American Originals 4003.

Josh White Jr., "Don't Go Looking for Trouble" (original title "Lookin' for Trouble") for "Cortelia Clark," CD, **2000**, Silverwolf Records.

Joe Ferry & Brian Knox, "Frank & Lola" (co-write: Jimmy Buffett, Goodman) for "The Reggae Tribute to Jimmy Buffett," CD, **2001**, Snake Machine 2802.

The Living Room Kings, "Rapping Backwards" (partially rewritten version of "Talk Backwards," co-write: Goodman, Michael Smith) for "King of My Living Room," CD, **2001**, Charlottesville, VA.

David Gans, "Elvis Imitators" (co-write: Goodman, Michael Smith) for "Solo Acoustic," CD, **2001**, Perfectible Recordings, PERF-03, Oakland, CA, recorded live 1999-2000.

T.R. Ritchie, "Grand Canyon Song" for "River of Song: An Anthology of River Songs," CD, March 6, **2001**, Orchard 0030.

Charlie King & Karen Brandow, "The One That Got Away" and "The Ballad of Penny Evans" for "I Struck Gold," CD, **2001**, Appleseed APR 1050, West Chester, PA.

Blues Rockets, "Frank & Lola" (co-write: Jimmy Buffett, Goodman) for "The Blues Tribute to Jimmy Buffett," CD, **2002**, Snake Machine 2806.

Hikora, "A Lover Is Forever" (co-write: Goodman, Fred Knobloch) for "My Foolish Heart," CD, **2002**, Tara 6550.

Tim Vana, "I Can't Sleep" for "River of the Plains," CD, **2002**, TV Recordings.

Mose Scarlett, "Don't Go Lookin' for Trouble" (original title "Lookin' for Trouble") for "Precious Seconds," CD, **2002**, Borealis Records BCD 146.

Kris Gannon "Lookin' for Trouble" for "Songs I Wish I'd Written," CD, **2002**, Kueblar Records 2002, San Francisco, CA. LP also includes Michael Smith's "The Dutchman."

Cynthia Kaay Bennett, "A Lover Is Forever" (co-write: Goodman, Fred Knobloch) for "Wish I Knew," CD, Dec. 16, **2003**, Orchard 803135.

Bonnie Koloc, "I Can't Sleep" for "Timeless," two live CDs, **2004**.

Danny Gotham, "My Old Man" for "Luzerne," CD, **2004**, dannygotham.com.

Pat Flynn, "Lookin' for Trouble" for "reVision," CD, **2006**, patflynnmusic.com.

David Roth, "Would You Like to Learn to Dance?," for "More Pearls," CD, **2006**, Stockfisch Records. CD also includes "The Dutchman," by Michael Smith.

Rosanna Goodman, "My Old Man"; Ana Egge, "Old Fashioned" (co-write: Goodman, Paula Ballan, Steve Burgh, Patrick Chamberlain); Matt Keating & Emily Spray, "Danger" (co-write: Goodman, Michael Smith, Sean Kelly); Crescent & Frost, "If She Were You" (co-write: Goodman, John Prine); Chris Brown, "Yellow Coat"; Chris Brown & Kate Fenner, "The Ballad of Penny Evans"; Luther Wright & the Wrongs, "Jessie's Jig"; Tony Scherr, "Just Lucky I Guess"; Kate Fenner, "I Just Keep Falling in Love" (co-write: Goodman, Bill LaBounty); Anna Hovhannessian, "A Lover Is Forever" (co-write: Goodman, Fred Knobloch); Teddy Kumpel, "Watchin' Joey Glow" (co-write: Goodman, Sean Kelly), for "My Old Man," CD, June 7, **2006**, Red Pajamas Records, RPJ-016.

Jen Sygit, "The Ballad of Penny Evans," duet with Rachael Davis, for "Leaving Marshall St.," CD, Sept. 28, **2006**, Earthwork Music #1201.

Chuck Mitchell, "The Ballad of Penny Evans (Iraq, 2006)," CD single, **2006**, csmitchell7@earthlink.net.

Mike Felten, "Paul Powell," for "Tossin' It Away," CD, May **2007**, Landfill Records 2005.

Steve (right) feigns drunkenness at the May 13, 1960, bar mitzvah of Barry Ellegant (center) with friend Joel Robbins.

(Photo courtesy of Benyomin Ellegant)

OTHERS' 45-RPM SINGLE RECORDINGS OF STEVE GOODMAN SONGS OTHER THAN 'CITY OF NEW ORLEANS'

Jimmy Buffett, "Door Number Three" (co-write: Goodman, Buffett), b/w "Dallas," **1974**, ABC Dunhill 12113.

David Allan Coe, "You Never Even Called Me by My Name" (original title is in present tense, co-write: Goodman, John Prine), **1975**, Columbia Records.

Gene Chandler, "I'm Attracted to You" (co-write: Goodman, Rick Chudadoff) 20th Century.

Jimmy Buffett (as Freddie & the Fishsticks, featuring the Jordanaires), "Elvis Imitator" (original title is plural, co-write: Goodman, Michael Smith), b/w same, **1981**, MCA-51224, and on "Boats, Beaches, Bars & Ballads," four CDs, 1992, MCAD4-10613.

Nitty Gritty Dirt Band, "Colorado Christmas," b/w "Mr. Bojangles," **1983**, Liberty 1513.

Nitty Gritty Dirt Band, "Video Tape," flip side of "Long Hard Road (The Sharecropper's Dream)," April **1984**, Warner Brothers Records 7-29282.

Nitty Gritty Dirt Band, "Face on the Cutting Room Floor," flip side of "I Love Only You," fall **1984**, Warner Brothers Records 7-29203.

Willie Nelson, "City of New Orleans" (**G**), 4:48, b/w 4:10 version, **1984**, Columbia Records.

Nitty Gritty Dirt Band, "Queen of the Road," flip side of "Modern Day Romance," May **1985**, Warner Brothers Records 7-29027.

Jimmy Buffett, "Frank & Lola" (co-write: Buffett, Goodman), flip side of "If the Phone Doesn't Ring, It's Me," **1985**, MCA-5600.

OTHERS' RECORDINGS WITH STEVE GOODMAN LINER NOTES

Saul Broudy, "Travels with Broudy," LP and cassette, **1977**, Adelphi Records, Silver Spring, MD.

Martin, Bogan & the Armstrongs, "That Old Gang of Mine," LP, **1978**, Flying Fish, FF-056.

Jethro Burns, "Jethro Burns LIVE," LP, **1980**, Flying Fish, FF-072.

Michael Smith, "There," CD, **2000**, Bird Avenue; 2002, Wind River Records. (Liner notes by Minnette Goodman: "What do you say to convey the many sides of this gentle, deep and talented author? Just keep writing, Michael.")

OTHERS' SONGS AND POETRY WRITTEN IN TRIBUTE TO STEVE GOODMAN OR MENTIONING HIM

Malvina Reynolds, "If You Were Little," written in **1975**, released posthumously on "Mama Lion," LP, 1980, Cassandra Records, Berkeley, California.

Perry Barber, "Love Can Do That," unreleased demo, about **1975**.

Wendy Waldman, "Love Is the Only Goal" for "Strange Company," LP, **1978**, Warner Brothers, BSK 3178. Written for Steve Goodman and John Prine.

Don Lange, "Keeper of the Flame," about the demise of the Chicago folk scene, written in **1982**, unreleased demo.

Brian Gill, "Song for Steve" and "I Had a Dream," unreleased demos, **1984**.

Jef Jaisun, "Flying with the Angels," unreleased demo, **1984**.

Harry Waller, "Why Did He Have to Leave?," unreleased demo, **1984**.

Jessica Anne Baron, "Light Up the Sky," written in **1984**, unreleased demo, 2006.

Peter Weisz, "The Man with the Golden Tune," written in **1984**, unreleased demo with guitar, vocals by Tim Brickley, 2006.

Jim Gary, "Another Good Man Is Gone," **1984**, unreleased demo, Brornsongs, Elmhurst, Illinois, jimgary.com.

Perry Barber, "Mr. Right Left," unreleased demo, about **1985**.

Stefan Grossman, "Lament for a Goodman" for "Shining Shadows," LP, **1985**, Shanachie Records 95002.

Jeff Gutcheon, "Another Train," unreleased live track, **1985**, incorporates "City of New Orleans" lyrics.

Tom Paxton, "For Steve Goodman," poem, **1985**.

Eddie Walker, "Song for Steve Goodman" for "Picking My Way," LP and cassette, April **1985**, Ragged Records, RAGR003, UK.

Don Lange, "Gather at the River," written in **1985**, unreleased demo.

James Durst & Ferne Bork, "Light Up the Sky" (written by Jessica Anne Baron) for "Light Up the Sky," LP, **1987**.

Chris Farrell, "Old Town, Old Friend," written in **1986**, unreleased demo. Lyric pairs "Good morning, America" with "Goodnight Irene."

Norm Hacking, "Richer for the Time," written in 1985, for "Stubborn Ghost," LP, **1988**. Released on "Skysongs" CD, 2001. Backup vocal on "Richer" by Michael Smith.

Reuben "Lounge Lizard" Morgan, "Life Down on the Bistro," for "Remember Friends," CD, **1990**, re-released on "No Worries," CD, 2006.

Steve Hopkins, "Heroes," cassette, **1990**. Released on CD, "Just Another Day in Paradox," 1999.

John Wesley Harding (Wes Stace), "Phil Ochs, Bob Dylan, Steve Goodman, David Blue & Me" for "It Happened One Night," CD, **1991**, Rhino, from live recording Nov. 5, 1988, at Strand on the Green, London.

Pierce Pettis, "This Is for Lena's Café," unreleased live track, Oct. 27, **1991**, the Left Bank Café, Blue Hill, ME.

Toby Gibson, "The Late Steve Goodman Blues" (to the tune of John Prine's "The Late John Garfield Blues"), unreleased song, **1997**, displayed on Gibson's Internet site, the Steve Goodman Scrapbook.

Moss Bliss, "Our Old Steve" (to the tune of "My Old Man"), unreleased song, **1998**.

Buddy Mondlock, "No Choice" for "Poetic Justice," CD, **1998**.

Jimmy Buffett, "Prince of Tides" for "Hot Water," CD, **1998**. Lyrics mention Goodman among "such good friends to me."

Roland Kushner, "Penny Evans' Daughters," written in 1999, for "527" CD, July **2000**, BMI.

Blind Lemming Chiffon, "Life is a Beautiful Thing" (to the tune of "You Better Get It While You Can"), unreleased song, **2001**.

Sunset Johnson, "Musical Lady," written by Johnson and Jill Hobbs in **2002**, unreleased demo, UK. Lyric: "... the genius of Steve Goodman and his Monday morning rail."

Andrew Calhoun, "Goin' Down to See John Prine," for "Tiger Tattoo," CD, **2003**, Waterbug Records. Lyric: "When Goodman brought Kristofferson to score John his big break ..."

Arlo Guthrie, "My Old Friend," recorded in June 2004 concert for "Live in Sydney" 2-CD set, **2005**, Rising Son #1125. Written in tribute to his father's peers and his own.

Bill Hartwell, "The Best Friend I Never Knew (for Steve Goodman)," for "Better Than Never," CD, **2007**, billhartwell.com.

OTHERS' RECORDINGS DEDICATED TO STEVE GOODMAN

David Allan Coe, "The Mysterious Rhinestone Cowboy," LP, **1974**, Columbia, KC 32934. Gives "special thanks" to Goodman, Shel Silverstein, Kris Kristofferson and Leon Russell for "moral support" on debut album.

Don Lange and Doug Freeman, "Freeman & Lange," LP, **1975**, Flying Fish, FF-011. "Special thanks to Steve (A Little Is A Lot) Goodman."

Bela Fleck with the New Grass Revival, "Deviation," LP, **1984**, Rounder Records 37719.

Tom Dundee, "Right Lane Man," LP, **1985**, Flyte Records, Seattle, WA.

Stefan Grossman, "Shining Shadows," LP, **1985**, Shanachie Records, Ho-Ho-Kus, NJ, Shanachie 95002.

David Allan Coe, "Darlin', Darlin'," LP, **1985**, Columbia PCT-39617.

Jef Jaisun, "Midnight Invitation," LP, **1985**, Fix-n-Mix FMX 185, Denmark.

Jimmy Buffett, "Last Mango in Paris," LP, **1985**, MCA R2933.

Eddie Walker, "Picking My Way," LP and cassette, **1985**, Ragged Records, RAGR003, UK.

Nitty Gritty Dirt Band, "Partners, Brothers & Friends," LP, **1985**, Warner Brothers 4-25304.

Joe Bethancourt, "Who Fears the Devil? The Songs of Silver John," CD, **1994**, Random Factors 1008. Goodman mentioned among "all the wandering Bards out there who are keeping the music alive."

VIDEOS

Listings are chronological within categories.

STEVE GOODMAN ON VHS/DVD

"Dead Men's Bolero," dubbed as voice of Ava Gardner in "Dead Men Don't Wear Plaid," feature film, **1982**. Directed by Carl Reiner and starring Steve Martin.

"LIVE from Austin City Limits and More," VHS/DVD, Feb. 18, **2003**, Red Pajamas Records, RPJ-500, includes most of Goodman's two "Austin City Limits" performances, his NBC "Today" interview and performance from 1983, and a 1978 studio performance of "You're the Girl I Love," plus interviews with six sources.

STEVE GOODMAN'S TV APPEARANCES

Unknown show title, WTTW-TV, Chicago, IL, possibly in **1967-68**, Sunday morning show.

"Where Has All the Music Gone" episode of "Made in Chicago," WTTW-TV, Chicago, IL, probably in **1972**. Hosted by George Carlin. Other guests Bonnie Koloc and Fred Holstein.

"The David Frost Show," syndicated, taped in December 1971, aired Jan. 3 and 5, **1972**. Song: "City of New Orleans." Another episode aired March 1, 1972. Songs: "Eight Ball Blues" and "Yellow Coat." A third episode aired June 28, 1972.

"Take a Giant Step," WNBC-TV, New York, NY, recorded and aired live April 29, **1972**, 60 min. Songs: "The I Don't Know Where I'm Goin' but I'm Goin' Nowhere in a Hurry Blues," "Mind Your Own Business" and "I Bid You Goodnight." Second guest: Barbara Walters.

"The Old Grey Whistle Test," BBC-TV, London, taped May 1972, aired June 6, **1972**, with interview and "City of New Orleans."

"One of a Kind," KCET-TV, Los Angeles, CA, 30 min., taped Dec. 6, 1972, first aired Feb. 18, **1973**. Seven songs.

"The Ian Tyson Show," CBC-TV, Canada, 30 min., taped Jan. 19, 1973, aired 9:30 p.m. April 17, **1973**. Other guests: Sylvia Tyson, George Hamilton IV.

Unidentified show, Los Angeles, CA, 60 min., recorded in **1973**, shown only in Sweden. Four songs. Other guests: Lori Lieberman and Swedish singer Tomas Ledin.

"They Kept the Faith," WTTW-TV, Channel 11, Chicago, IL, taped in March 1973 at Arie Crown Theater, aired April 13, **1973**. Other guests: Fred Holstein, John Prine, Ginni Clemmens, Jim Post, Bonnie Koloc, Ed Holstein, Bryan Bowers, Tom Dundee, Wally Pillich, Earl Pionke.

"Made in Chicago," WTTW-TV, Channel 11, Chicago, IL, aired Friday, June 18, **1973**, four-and-a-half hours. Other guests: John Prine, Holstein brothers, Earl Pionke, Curtis Mayfield, Jerry Butler, Barbara Mason, Gene Chandler, Gordon Lightfoot.

"The Midnight Special," ABC-TV, Los Angeles, CA, aired July 20 (actually 1 a.m. July 21), **1973**. Songs: "Somebody Else's Troubles" and "Would You Like to Learn to Dance?" Other guests: Joan Baez (host) Black Oak Arkansas, Bloodstone, Mimi Fariña, Wilson Pickett, Pointer Sisters.

Unidentified show, recorded July 27 or 28, **1973**, in Sweden with John Prine.

Steve (left) accompanies mentor and folk legend Bob Gibson at the 1973 Philadelphia Folk Festival. The two also appeared in a March 1982 WBBM-TV documentary that celebrated the 20th anniversary of the Earl of Old Town.

(Photo by Steve Ramm)

"The Old Grey Whistle Test," BBC-TV, London, aired July 31, **1973**. Songs: "Chicken Cordon Bleus," "Would You Like to Learn to Dance?"

"Chicago Camera," WMAQ-TV, Channel 5, Chicago, IL, aired 1 p.m. Nov. 17, **1974**, from Earl of Old Town. Other guests: Fred Holstein and host Jerry G. Bishop.

"Soundstage: Arlo's Gang," WTTW-TV, Chicago, IL, taped Nov. 11, 1974, first aired Nov. 25, **1974**, 60 min. "It's a Sin to Tell a Lie," "Door Number Three" and "Would You Like to Learn to Dance?," plus accompaniment on others. Host Arlo Guthrie, other guest Hoyt Axton.

"The Mike Douglas Show," syndicated, Philadelphia, PA, taped July 1, 1975, aired July 8, **1975**. Three songs. Guest host: Harry Chapin. Other guests: Richard Pryor, Lula Parker Betenson, Charlie Callas and Tom Chapin.

"Superstars of Rock," WFLD-TV, Channel 32, Chicago, aired 9 p.m. Aug. 2, **1975**. Other guests: Tower of Power, Olivia Newton-John, Delbert & Glen.

"Philadelphia Folk Festival," PBS-TV, aired Aug. 20, **1975**. Other guests John Prine, Tom Rush, Don Reno and the Tennessee Cutups, Deadly Nightshade, Norman Blake.

"Just Another Diagonal Street in Some Other Kind of Town," WBBM-TV, Chicago, IL, aired Nov. 22, **1976**, 30 min., documentary on Lincoln Avenue businesses and nightlife. Portions of three songs. Host: Gene Siskel. Others shown: Doug Kershaw, Junior Wells, Saul Broudy, Mike Lieber, David Amram, Ed Holstein, Ray Nordstrand, Earl Pionke.

"The Old Grey Whistle Test," BBC-TV, London, aired Dec. 14, **1976**. Song: "Banana Republics" from 1976 Cambridge Folk Festival.

Unidentified show, taped Dec. 16, **1976**, Munich, Germany.

"Janis Ian & Friends," for HBO or PBS, Los Angeles, taped July 20, **1977**, air date unknown. Other guests: Taj Mahal, Buffy St. Marie, and Dave Van Ronk.

"Words and Music in Chicago," WTTW-TV, Chicago, IL, taped March 1977, aired fall **1977**, date uncertain, 30 min. Songs: "Daley's Gone" and "Lincoln Park Pirates." Other guests: Blind John Davis, Aliotta Haynes Jeremiah and Larry Rand.

"90 Minutes Live," CBC-TV, aired Nov. 16, **1977**, with Jethro Burns, 30-minute segment. Five songs.

"Austin City Limits," KLRN-TV, Austin, TX, recorded Sept. 8, 1977, aired March 4 and April 8, **1978**, 60 min. Thirteen songs.

"Soundstage: David Amram & Friends," WTTW-TV, Chicago, IL, recorded Jan. 30, 1978, aired April 15 and 20, **1978**, 60 min. Song: "Summer Nights and Winter Rain," backup on others. Host: David Amram. Other guests: Jethro Burns, Dizzy Gillespie, Bonnie Koloc.

"The Good Gang Express," WBBM-TV, Chicago, IL, two 30-minute episodes, **1979**. Theme song for children's show. Host Warner Saunders.

"The John Allan Cameron Show," Halifax, Nova Scotia, Canada, CBC-TV, taped June 24, 1979, first aired July 13, **1979**, 30 min. Four songs.

"In Our Nuclear Backyard," WMAQ-TV, Chicago, IL, aired June 28, **1979**, 30 min. Theme song for documentary.

"A Permanent Condition," WMAQ-TV, Chicago, IL, aired Aug. 28, **1979**, 30 min. Theme song for documentary.

"The Tonight Show," NBC-TV, Los Angeles, CA, aired Oct. 24, **1979**. Song: "Men Who Love Women Who Love Men." Guest host: David Letterman. Other guests: George Gobel, Diahann Carroll, Jay Leno.

"Dave Kingman: From Out of Left Field," WMAQ-TV, Channel 5, NBC, Chicago, IL., Chicago, IL, aired April 5, **1980**. Theme song for documentary.

"ABC Evening News" segment on Chicago Cubs, May 31, **1981**, 5:10 min. Song: "A Dying Cub Fan's Last Request." Reporter: Dick Schaap.

WBBM-TV news segment on baseball strike and "A Dying Cub Fan's Last Request," Chicago, IL, sometime July 26-30, **1981**. Reporter: Bob Sirott.

Episode on 20th anniversary of Earl of Old Town for "Warner and You," WBBM-TV, Chicago, IL, March **1982**, 30 min. Songs: "A Dying Cub Fan's Last Request" and "City of New Orleans," plus narration. Host: Warner Saunders. Others shown: Earl Pionke, Bob Gibson, Bonnie Koloc, Tom Dundee, Betsy Redhed, Mike Jordan, Charlie Koster.

"Down Home Country Music," KLRN-TV, Austin, TX, recorded Jan. 17, **1982**, aired later in year, 30 min., fund-raiser for PBS-TV by crew of "Austin City Limits." Seven songs. Other guests: Jethro Burns, John Prine.

"Johnny Cash America," HBO-TV, Kennedy Center, Washington, D.C., taped June 20, 1982, first aired Aug. 15, **1982**, 120 min. Songs: "You Never Even Call Me by My Name" and "City of New Orleans," backup vocals. Other performers: June Carter Cash, John Prine, Rodney Crowell, Marty Stuart.

"Bobby Bare & Friends," TNN-TV, aired March 12, **1983**, 20-minute segment of 60-minute show. "You Never Even Call Me by My Name," "Talk Backwards" and "City of New Orleans," plus interview.

NBC "Today" segment, recorded Oct. 15, **1983**, aired soon thereafter, filmed on walkup outside left field of Wrigley Field, Chicago, IL. Interview, song: "A Dying Cub Fan's Last Request." Reporter: Mike Leonard.

"You Can't Keep a Goodman Down" episode for "First Camera," NBC-TV magazine, recorded summer 1983, aired Nov. 20 and Dec. 18, **1983**, 20 min. Portions of four songs. Reporter: Lloyd Dobbins. Producer: Lisa Freed.

"Festival of Friends" documentary on July 9-10, 1983, Winnipeg Folk Festival, KTCA-TV, Minneapolis, MN, aired Jan. 30, **1984**, 60 min. Interview, portions of two songs.

"Jethro & Friends" documentary on Jethro Burns, KTCA-TV, Minneapolis, MN, filmed April 9-11, 1984, aired Aug. 22, **1984**, 60 min. Songs: "Hot Tub Refugee" and "The Dutchman," plus accompaniment on "Sweet Georgia Brown." Other guests: Chet Atkins, Don Stiernberg, Johnny Burns.

"NBC Evening News" segment on Chicago Cubs, Aug. 30, **1984**, 2:20 min. Portion of "A Dying Cub Fan's Last Request." Reporters: Mike Leonard.

"Made in Chicago," tribute, WTTW-TV, Chicago, IL, aired late September **1984**, 30 min. Seven songs from 1974, 1977, 1978.

"Tribute to Steve Goodman," KLRN-TV, Austin, TX, **1985**, 30 min. Seven songs from 1978, 1982 "Austin City Limits" shows.

"NBC Evening News" segment on Chicago Cubs, aired Oct. 5, **1989**, 2:40 min. Song: "A Dying Cub Fan's Last Request." Reporter: Mike Leonard.

"Behind the Music: Harry Chapin," VH1-TV, **2001**, Goodman shown in brief documentary footage.

OTHER STEVE GOODMAN-RELATED TV OR VIDEO/DVD

Johnny Cash, "City of New Orleans" for "Ridin' the Rails: The Great American Train Song," VHS, **1974**. Sings same song on "Hee Haw" TV show, aired April 16, 1974, and sold via TimeLife.

Martin Mull-hosted concert intro video, **1983**, viewable at http://www.stevegoodman.net.

Jimmy Buffett, "The Star Spangled Banner," dedicated to Goodman, Game One of National League Division Series, WGN-TV, Chicago, IL, broadcast live Oct. 2, **1984**, Chicago Cubs vs. San Diego Padres, Wrigley Field.

Nitty Gritty Dirt Band, "Face on the Cutting Room Floor" (co-write: Goodman, Jeff Hanna, Jimmy Ibbotson) for "Austin City Limits," **1985**, also included on "Twenty Years of Dirt," VHS, 1991, Warner Reprise Video.

Jimmy Buffett, "Door Number Three" (co-write: Goodman, Buffett) for "Deal," VHS, **1985**, Active Home Video, documentary on TV's "Let's Make a Deal," used Buffett's version of song.

Willie Nelson and Arlo Guthrie, "City of New Orleans" for "Farm Aid 1985," aired Sept. 22, **1985**.

Jimmy Buffett, "Door Number Three" (co-write: Goodman, Buffett) for "Live by the Bay," VHS, March **1986**, MCA 80332.

The Highwaymen, "City of New Orleans" for "Highwaymen Live!," VHS, **1990**, 19V 49055, 25 songs, interviews, 98 min. Willie Nelson is lead singer.

Michelle Shocked, "The Ballad of Penny Evans" for "The Captain Swing Revue," VHS, **1990**, PolyGram PMV 081977, recorded Dec. 12, 1989, at the Apollo Theatre, Oxford, England.

June Carter Cash, "Nashville Now," TNN-TV, aired Aug. 13, **1990**, reading of a brief chapter on Goodman from her memoir, *From the Heart*, as "City of New Orleans" played in background.

Rosanne Cash, "A Lover Is Forever" for "Interiors Live," **1991**, Sony Music Video Enterprises, 19V-49078, 19 songs, 80 min.

"The I Ain't Heard You Play No Blues," basis for prize-winning segment, "Baby Sings the Blues," on ABC-TV's "America's Funniest Home Videos," originally aired in **1990-97**, date uncertain, with frequent repeats.

"Danger" (co-write: Goodman, Michael Smith) played in background of "The Judge" episode of "Millennium," Fox-TV, **1996**.

Steve poses for his first Asylum LP in spring 1975.

(Photo by Henry Diltz)

Bonnie Koloc, Jim Post, Jim Hirsch, many others, as well as Minnette and David Goodman in audience, "City of New Orleans" finale to "Old Town Reunited," WTTW-TV, Chicago, IL, aired Sept. 20, **1998**, concert at new site of Old Town School of Folk Music.

Anne Hills, Michael Smith, Bonnie Koloc, Jim Post, Tom Paxton, Saul Broudy, others, "Steve Goodman Tribute: The Twentieth Century is Almost Over," World Folk Music Association benefit festival, recorded Jan. 15, **1999**, VHS, available at WFMA Internet site.

Jimmy Buffett, "Live from Wrigley Field," DVD, **2006**. "Banana Republics" and "City of New Orleans," performed by Buffett and band on Labor Day weekend 2005. Goodman's version of "Go, Cubs, Go" is played over footage of the concert set-up.

Arlo Guthrie, John Prine, Emmylou Harris, Jackson Browne, Iris DeMent, Lyle Lovett, Todd Snider, "Larger Than Life: A Celebration of Steve Goodman and His Music," DVD, **2007**, Oh Boy Records. Performances from Nov. 13, 1997, tribute concert at Medinah Temple, Chicago. A portion of proceeds goes to the Old Town School of Folk Music.

BOOKS

The listings are chronological.

Songs of American Sailormen, Joanna C. Colcord, W.W. Norton and Co., New York, NY, enlarged and revised edition, **1938**. Includes "The Flying Cloud." Former edition, *Roll and Go, Songs of American Sailormen*, 1924, Bobbs-Merrill Co., Indianapolis, IN.

Chicago: The Second City, A.J. Liebling, Alfred A. Knopf, New York, NY, LC catalog card number: 52-8506, 143p, **1952**.

Aerie, John Denver, Cherry Lane Music, piano/vocal songbook with guitar frames for all songs on "Aerie" LP, including Denver's modified version of "City of New Orleans," 48p, **1971**.

The Steve Goodman Song Book, Steve Goodman, Buddah Music/Turnpike Tom Music, distributed by Cimino, piano arrangements, chord symbols and guitar frames for all songs written by Goodman on first two LPs, eight pages of photos, poster, 80p, **1973**.

Ten Years of Folk: a History of the Cambridge Folk Festival, Ken Woollard and Elizabeth Twinem, Grand Old Opry, England, 96p, **1974**.

The Improbable Rise of Redneck Rock, Jan Reid, photos by Melinda Wickman, Heidelberg Publishers, Austin, TX, ISBN 0-913-20604-0, 342p, **1974**.

City of New Orleans, choral arrangement by Chuck Cassey; Screen Gems-Columbia Publications, Miami, Florida, 12p, **1975**.

The Folk Music Sourcebook, Larry Sandberg and Dick Weissman, Alfred A. Knopf, New York, ISBN 0-394-49684-1, 276p, **1976**.

Folk Music: More than a Song, Kristin Baggelaar and Donald Milton, Thomas Y. Crowell, Co., New York, NY, ISBN 0-690-01159-8, 418p, **1976**.

For what time I am in this world: Stories from Mariposa, Bill Usher and Linda Page-Harpa, Peter Martin Associates Ltd, Toronto, Canada, ISBN 0-88778-167-5, 228p, **1977**.

The Rolling Stone Record Guide, edited by Dave Marsh, Random House, New York, ISBN 0-394-73535-8, 631p, Dec. 1, **1979**, and later editions.

Steve Martin: An Unauthorized Biography, Marsha Daly, Signet, New York, 202p, **1980**.

Steve Martin: The Unauthorized Biography, Greg Lenburg, Randy Skretvedt and Jeff Lenburg, St. Martin's Press, New York, ISBN 0-312-76189-9, **1980**.

You're So Cold I'm Turnin' Blue/ Martha Hume's Guide to the Greatest in Country Music, Martha Hume, The Viking Press/Penguin Books, New York, ISBN 014006348X, 202p, **1982**.

The Folk Festival Book: The Stories of the Winnipeg Folk Festival, Steve Johnson and Sheldon Oberman, Turnstone Press, Winnipeg, Canada, ISBN 0-88801-085-0, 138p, **1984**.

Hoot! A 25-Year History of the Greenwich Village Music Scene, Robbie Woliver, St. Martin's Press, New York, ISBN 0-312-10995-4, 258p, **1986**.

Great Jews in Music, Darryl Lyman, Jonathan David Publishers, Middle Village, NY, ISBN 0-824-60315-X, 326p, **1986**.

No Direction Home: The Life and Music of Bob Dylan, Robert Shelton, Beech Tree Books, William Morrow, New York, NY, ISBN 0-688-05045-X, 573p, **1986**.

Austin City Limits: The Story Behind Television's Most Popular Country Music Program, Clifford Endres, U of Texas Press, Austin, ISBN 0-292-70378-3, 136p, **1987**.

From the Heart: The Intimate Memoirs of a Woman of Courage and Faith, June Carter Cash, Prentice Hall Press, New York, ISBN 0-135-30767-8, 244p, **1987**.

Bob Dylan: Behind the Shades, Clinton Heylin, Summit Books, New York, NY, ISBN 0-671-73894-1, 498p, **1991**.

The Guinness Encyclopedia of Popular Music: Volume 2, Colin Larkin, Guinness Publishing, ISBN: B000G-HF8K-O, **1992**.

Steve on the WTTW-TV program "Made in Chicago," probably 1972.

(Photo by Jon Randolph)

Thirty Years of the Cambridge Folk Festival, Dave Laing and Richard Newman, Music Maker Books, Cambs, England, 162p, **1994**.

Singer-Songwriters: Pop Music's Performer-Composers from A to Zevon, Dave DiMartino, *Billboard* Hit Makers Series, Billboard Books, New York, NY, ISBN: 0-8230-7629-6, 320p, **1994**.

All Music Guide to the Blues, Michael Erlewine, Vladimir Bogdanov, Chris Woodstra, Cub Koda, Miller Freeman Books, San Francisco, CA, ISBN 0-87930-424-3, 423p, **1996**.

Jimmy Buffett: The Man from Margaritaville Revealed, Steve Ing, St. Martin's Griffin, New York, ISBN 0-312-16875-6, 364p, **1996**.

Chicago Days: 150 Defining Moments in the Life of a Great City, the staff of the *Chicago Tribune*, edited by Stevenson Swanson, Cantigny First Division Foundation, Wheaton, IL, ISBN 1-890093-04-1, 276p, **1997**.

Jackie 'The Joke Man' Martling's Disgustingly Dirty Joke Book, Jackie Martling, Simon & Schuster, New York, NY, ISBN 0-684-84677-2, 224p, **1997**.

Not Fade Away: The Rock & Roll Photography of Jim Marshall, David Fahey, editor, Little, Brown and Co., New York, NY, ISBN 0-8212-2362-3, 130p, **1997**.

MusicHound Folk: The Essential Album Guide, Neal Walters and Brian Mansfield, Visible Ink Press, Detroit, MI, ISBN 1-5789037-X, 1,030p, **1998**.

Paul Powell of Illinois: A Lifelong Democrat, Robert E. Harley, Southern Illinois University Press, Carbondale, IL, ISBN: 08093-2272-2, 229p, **1999**.

Gonna Sing My Head Off, Kathleen Krull, editor, Alfred A. Knopf, ISBN 0-3948199-1-8, 145p, **1992**. Details for 62 songs, including "City of New Orleans." Incorrectly states Goodman wrote "City" during 1972 Muskie campaign trip. (But it does include the Steve staple "Mama Don't Allow It.") Reissued in 2003 as *I Hear America Singing* with 23-song CD that doesn't include "City."

Bob Gibson: I Come for to Sing, Bob Gibson and Carole Bender, Folk Era, Naperville, IL, ISBN 0-9614594-1-7, 410p plus CD, **1999**.

Home and Away: Memoir of a Fan, Scott Simon, Hyperion, New York, ISBN 0-7868-6415-X, 368p, **2000**.

Night Moves: Pop Music in the Late '70s, Don Breithaupt and Jeff Breithaupt, St. Martin's Griffin, New York, ISBN 0312198213, 218p, **2000**.

A Johnny Cash Chronicle: I've Been Everywhere, Peter Lewry, Helter Skelter Publishing, London, ISBN 1-900924-22-6, 256p, **2001**.

Folk and Blues: The Encyclopedia, Irwin Stambler and Lyndon Stambler, Thomas Dunne Books, St. Martin's Press, New York, ISBN 0-312-20057-9, 793p, **2001**.

How Bluegrass Music Destroyed My Life, John Fahey, Drag City, Chicago, ISBN 0-9656183-2-3, **2001**.

The Bitter End: Hanging Out at America's Nightclub, Paul Colby with Martin Fitzpatrick, Cooper Square Press, New York, ISBN 0-8154-1206-1, 233p, **2002**.

Rainbow Quest: The Folk Music Revival & American Society, 1940-1970, Ronald D. Cohen, University of Massachusetts Press, Amherst and Boston, MA, ISBN 1-55849-348-4, 365p, **2002**.

The Virgin Encyclopedia of 70s Music, editor Colin Larkin, Virgin Publishing, ISBN 1852279478, 544p, **2002**.

Stars of David: Rock 'n' Roll's Jewish Stories, Scott R. Benarde, Brandeis University Press, ISBN 1584653035, 375p, **2003**.

The Train They Call the City of New Orleans, Steve Goodman, illustrated by Michael McCurdy, G.P. Putnam's Sons, New York, ISBN 0-399-23853-0, 32p, **2003**. Re-released in 2004 with CD by Tom Chapin. **(G)**

Rock and Roll Year by Year, Luke Crampton and Dafydd Rees, DK Publishing, ISBN 0756613345, 600p, **2005**.

Born Standing Up, Steve Martin, Scribner, New York, ISBN 1416553649, 224p, **2007**. Includes full-page Bubba's flyer promoting Martin, Steve Goodman, Michael Smith and Barbara Barrow.

INTERNET FAN SITES

The Steve Goodman Scrapbook, http://www.cobo.org/goodman/. Visitors can subscribe to the Chi-Shorty e-mail discussion list.

The Steve Goodman Preservation Society, http://www.folkblues .com/goodman/, http:// launch.groups.yahoo.com/group/ stevegoodman/. Visitors can subscribe to notifications about concert tapes.

A village in the thousands

No project is the work of merely one person. An African proverb affirms this, and Steve's most famous high-school classmate, Hillary Rodham Clinton, enshrined it a decade ago in pop culture: *"It takes a village."*

This book's village numbers in the thousands, and I am fortunate to be able to thank more than **2,200** of them by name. Some, however, must go nameless. They include countless librarians and archivists (who do "save the world," in both senses of the phrase) and the anonymous folks who decades ago tape-recorded and duplicated hundreds of Steve Goodman concerts and interviews, both in person and off the radio. The Internet – from Google and the All Music Guide to countless individual sites – also has been invaluable.

Top among the named must be publisher **Jack David** and others associated with ECW Press, including Mary Bowness, Crissy Boylan, Rachel Brooks, Robyn Burnett, David Caron, Tania Craan, Dallas Harrison, Amy Jacobson, Kulsum Merchant, Meghan Newton and publicist **Simon Ware**. Another bulwark of support has been my family, including my wife, **Meg Eals**, my daughter and son-in-law, **Karey and Jesse Bacon**, and my mom, **Virginia Eals**, before strokes sapped her lucidity. Our cat, **Dozen**, supplied loyal and sometimes vocal company throughout.

I have tried to account for all who aided this project, but I may have omitted some names. If so, in advance I humbly apologize.

INTERVIEWEES

The names listed here total **1,087**. Of those, several went above and beyond to champion this project or otherwise give it viability:

David Amram
Paula Ballan (if the project has a singular angel, she's the one)
Perry Barber
Howard Berkman
Saul Broudy (my first source)
Al Bunetta
Ken "Maple" Byrne
Sen. Hillary Rodham Clinton
Steve Cohen
Dr. Isabel Cunningham
John Epstein
Chris Farrell
Gib Foster
David Gans
Brian Gill
Jesse Goodman
Stuart Gordon
Bob Gross
Jeff Gutcheon
Arlo Guthrie
Dave Hoekstra
Gina Jett (awesome cover photo)
Roland & Barbara Kushner
Jack Lapp
Roz & Howard Larman
Roy Leonard
Tracy Leonard
Jude Lyons
Steve Martin
David McGee
Terry Murray
Ray Nordstrand
Patrick Michael O'Sullivan
Earl Pionke
Jim Polaski
John Prine
Marilyn Quine
Larry Rand
Jon Randolph
Ron Rosoff
Marlene Rosol
Jim Rothermel
Al Rudis

Barry Sagotsky
David Schulman
Jim Shea
Bob Sirott
Loretta Smith
Margaret Southern
Studs Terkel
Art Thieme (photos at http://rudegnu.com/art_thieme.html)
Harry Waller
Rich Warren

Below are the rest, an amalgam of those I interviewed in person, by phone and via e-mail. Many also shared valuable materials.

A

Mary Golden Abbate, Elliot Abbott, Doris Abrahams, Gaylen Adams, Noah Adams, Ami Adler, Mike Agranoff, Laura Haynes Aiken, Michael Aisner, Joseph & Mary Ann Ales, Blaine Allan, Bill Allen, Jamie Anderson, Jim Anderson, John Anderson, O.J. Anderson, Tony Andress, Harvey Andrews, Paul Anka, Rick Ansorge, Howard Armstrong, Rebecca Armstrong, Artis the Spoonman, Brian Augustyn, Elizabeth Austin

B

Jack Baker, Marcia Baker, Steve Baker, John Bambach, Ron Banion, Liz Bardar, Bobby Bare, Jessica Anne Baron, George Barr, Doug Barram, Lynn Barron, Heidi Barton, David Baskin, John Bassette, John Bates, Pat Baumgarten, Tim Bays, Jeff Beamsley, Ira Becker, Steve Begor, John Benda, Michael Bender, Kenneth Bennett, Dr. William Benz, Nancy Berek-Mraz, Bob Berg, Kathie Berg, Marv Berkman, Leslie Berman, Marty Berman, Scott Berman, Jerry Bernstein, Thom Bishop, Linda Black, George Blackwell, Mike Blair, Sharon Blair, Mark Bliesener, Wim & Sharon Bloemendaal, Ken Bloom, Ron

Blumenfeld, Jay Blunk, Marla Bovar Boarini, Tom Bocci, Ron Bohannon Sr. & Jr., Barbara Bonner, Roy Book Binder, Charlene Bos, John Bowen, Bryan Bowers, Kate Ertel Bowers, Dick Boyell, Jane Stracke Bradbury, Susan Moestue Bradford-Smith, Lis Bralow, Laura Jean Campo Bramer, Oscar Brand, Gary Brandt, Steve Brandt, Chuck Branick, Jim Brankin, Andy Braunfeld, Lin Brehmer, Fred Breitberg, Henry Brenghause, Lee Brenkman, Bob Brewer, Michael Brewer, Harvey & Marcia Brin, Marla Brin, Chuck Brockman, Bert Brodsky, David Bromberg, Bruce Brookoff, Joe Brown, Phil Brown, Ruth Brown, Jackson Browne, Elwood & Dorothy Brugman, Edwin Brys, Jim Buchheit, Jimmy Buffett, Ron Buffington, Peter Bunetta, Jack Burg, Kathleen Rogers Burgess, Steve Burgh, Cal Burke, Don Burnham, Jerry & Raun MacKinnon Burnham, Shari Lewis Burnham, Johnny Burns, Sam Bush, David Buskin, Ted Butterman

C

Dennis Cahill, Greg Cahill, Steve Cahill, Allison Caine, Andrew Calhoun, Terry Callier, MaryJo Cally, John Allan Cameron, Val Camiletti, Paul Carlson, Dick Carter, Bruce Carver, Rosanne Cash, Chuck Cassey, George Castle, Gary Cee, Kent Cerrone, Susan Champlin, J.D. Chandler, Len Chandler, Tom Chapin, Barry Chase, Charlie Chin, Keith Christianson, Rick Chudacoff, Michael Churchman, Susan Ciriello, Dr. Bayard "Barney" Clarkson, Gina Clement, Ginni Clemmens, Mary Cliff, Dave Cline, David Allan Coe, Michael Cogan, Andy Cohen, Dave Cohen, Larry Cohen, Ron Cohen, Lois Cohn, Paul Colby, John Coleman, Bob Collins, Judy Collins, Cerphe

Colwell, Tom Colwell, Tina Cammarata Compton, Michael Conlon, Tom Connely, Ry Cooder, Jack Coombe, Michael Cooney, Mort Cooperman, Ron Coro, Nancy Covey, Bobbi Cowan, Bob Craddock, Jim & Vivian Craig, Scott Craig, Mike Craver, Colleen Creedon, Ron Crick, Gary Cristall, Ingrid Croce, Dr. Marilyn Croghan, Mike Cross, Lee Cupp, David Curran, Art Curtis, Bob Cycon, Jeff Czech

D

Dan Daley, Bill Danoff, Danny Davenport, Jimmy Davenport, Lindsay Davis, Ron Davitt, Al Day, Jack Decker, Roger Deitz, Jari Demeulemeester, Jim Dernehl, Liz Danzig Derry, Jackie DeShannon, Les Detterbeck, Justin Devereaux, Jim Dickinson, Dave Dillman, Gerry Dionne, Jim DiOrio, Bradley Ditto, Tim Dixon, Ross Dolloff, Joel Dorn, Dr. Monroe Dowling, Irma Dunaway, Mike Dunbar, Tom Dundee, Robbie Dupree, James Durst, Judy Dyke

E

Greg Easterling, Betsy Ebeling, Roger Ebert, Peter Ecklund, Cathy Lind Edler, Samantha Eggar, Jim Ehinger, Ken Ehrlich, Gene Eichelberger, Dan Einbender, Dan Einstein, Dr. Rick Eisenstaedt, Ben Elder, Michael Elias, Benyomin "Barry" Ellegant, Barbara Ellingsen, Brad Ellis, Dennis Elsas, Dale Englehardt, Bob & Claudia Engel, Michael "Eppie" Epstein, Mark Erenburg, Pat Erenburg, Steven Erenburg, Pam Glaser Espana, Phil Marcus Esser

F

Dan Fabian, Joe Fagan, Susan Fahey, Mimi Fariña, Harriet Farkas, Dr. Alexander Fefer, Geoff Feiler, Art Fein, Nancy Felixson, Bernie Fiedler, Howard Fields, Joe Fields, Sally Fingerett, Chuck Fiore, Roy Firestone, William S. Fischer, Garry Fish, Steve Fishell, Jim Fisher, Frank Fitzmaurice, Charles Fleischer, Jim Fleming, Richard Flohil, Steve Forbert, Pete Fornatale, Liz Ouderkirk Forrester, Jim Fox, Andy "Flash" Frances, Erik Frandsen, Ray Frank, Volmar "Chip" Franz, Freebo, Lisa Freed, Jim Freitag, Brian Friedman, Emily Friedman, John Frigo, Donnie Fritts, David Fry

Steve rocks out on electric guitar during a Canadian gig in the mid-1970s.

(Photo by Charles Seton)

G

Jack Schechtman Gabriel, Mary Gaffney, Frye Gaillard, Glenn Galen, Jane Kamman Galler, Jonathan Galloway, Jerri Gallup, Gary Gand, Dennis Gardner, Anne Garner, Pat Garvey, Dick Gaughan, David Geffen, Jim Geisler, Dedre Gentner, Paul Geremia, Ellen Germaine, Tracy Gershon, Tom Ghent, Ron Giannetti, Scott Gibbs, Kay Gibbs-Novy, Lorna Gladstone, Jim Glover, Ray Goettsch, Anita Gold, Lee Gold, Alan Goldberg, Jack Goldberg, Gary Goldstein, Patrick Goldstein, Jeff Gordon, Dennis Gormley, Arlynn Gottlieb, Carl Gottlieb, Bob Graham, Arny Granat, Archie Green, Bob Green, Dallas Green, Meridian Green, Rosey Grier, Tom & Jackie Anderson Griesemer, Lee Grills, David Grisman, Stefan Grossman, Paul Gryglas/DuGrant, Frank Guignon, Guy Guilbert, Francis "Spike" Gummere, Barbara Gunger, Bob Gurland, Charles Gutfeld

H

Norm Hacking, Jack Haffercamp, Dr. Joel Hagedorn, Jack Hakim, Jim Hale, Frank Hall, Laura Hall, Roy Hallberg, Frank Hamilton, Natalie Handelman, Larry Hanks, Jeff Hanna, Barry Hansen (Dr. Demento), Randy Hansen, Rick

Hansen, Chet Hanson, Jane Harbury, John Harding, John Wesley Harding (Wes Stace), Richard Harding, France Harper, Geoff Harpham, Chris Harris, Emmylou Harris, Larry Harris, Doug Harrison, John Hartford, Katie Webb Hartwell, Jancis Harvey, Joan DeFalcis Hauger, Richie Havens, Ed Hawes, Tom Hayward, Doug Haywood, Dr. Clark Heath, Paul Hecht, John Heenan, Sherry Heiden, Kevin Hennessey, Nate Herman, Havelock Hewes, Joe Hickerson, Bill Hicks, Greg Hildebrand, Anne Hills, Jim Hirsch, Marty Hirsch, Bob Hoban, John Hockett, John Holder, Bill Holland, Diane Holmes, Alan Holstein, Ed Holstein, Fred Holstein, Dennis Holton, Steve Holton, Keith Holzman, Steve Hopkins, Steve Horelick, Marc Horowitz, Ken Horseman, Michael Hosek, Bernard Hoskin, Bill "Gus" & Karen "Ruby" Howard, Roy Howarth, John Howson, Johnno Hulbert, Ralph Hughes, Dakota Dave Hull, Link Hullar

I-J

Angela Iacchetta, Janis Ian, Jimmy Ibbotson, Al Ierardi, Richard Ingle, Bob Ingram, Bob Isaacson, Colin Isaacson, Ron Isaacson, Dr. Robert Israel, Dan Jaffe, Jef Jaisun, Marianne Jasin, Ella Jenkins, Nicholas Jennings, Debbie Jett, Gus Johns, Herb Johnson, Sunset Johnson, Bob Johnston, Danny Johnston, Eric Jones, Roger Jones, Barbara Jonesi, Mark Josephs

K

Michael Kamen, Pete Kaminsky, Jim Kanas, Dr. Norman Kanter, Benjamin Kanters, Judy Karzen, Phil Kaufman, Dave Kelly, Jak Kelly, Sean Kelly, Shaun Kelly, Larry Kelp, Pat Kenny, Jay Kernis, Ron Kickasola, Louis Killen, Charlie King, Terry Burns King, Tom King, Betty Kippels, Sidney James Kistin, Joe Klee, Al Klein, Chuck Klein, Estelle Klein, Michael Klenfner, Gary Klott, Mal Klugman, J. Fred Knobloch, Rick Kogan, Kenny Kosek, Leo Kottke, Sue & Brian Kozin, Lynda Marks Kraar, Brian Kramer, Linda Hirsch Krawczyk, Benjamin Krepack, Kris Kristofferson, Tom Krumm, Ken Kruss, Bill Kubeczko, Marc Kuhn, Phyllis & Paul Kurland

L

Bill LaBounty, Carol Laciny, John LaCloche, Bruce Ladd, Randy Lamson, Ted Landphair, Tony Lane, Jane Hansen Lang, Don Lange, Patti Latour, Alan Lawson, Doyle Lawson, Darrell Lea, Patti Nunn Leary, Tomas Ledin, Robert & Susan Leeb, Warren Leming, Patricia Lenahan, Josh Leo, Mike Leonard, Sam Leopold, Cary Lerman, Michael Levin, Howard Levy, Dick Lewis, Nancy Lewis, Rick Lewis, Sydney Lewis, Wanamaker Lewis, Barry Lewison, Terry Lickona, Mike Lieber, Allan Lieberman, Lori Lieberman, Gordon Lightfoot, Jeff Lind, Mike Lindauer, Gregory Lindeman, William C. "Buzzy" Linhart, Michael Litt, Shirley Litt, Jim Lloyd, Russ Locke, Paula Lockheart, Lew London, Augustino Loprinzi, Eudice Lorge, Michael Lorge, Tom Lovejoy, Gene Lubin, Arno Lucas, Ronn Lucas

M

Joel Mabus, Rod MacDonald, Bill MacKay, Tony Mackin, Bob & Kee Malesky, Steve & Terry Mandell, Cindy Mangsen, Ray Mantilla, Jo Mapes, Kathy Mar, Arif Mardin, Rich Markow, Jamie Marks, Elizabeth Rush Marsden, Vicki Marti, Jackie Martling, Bobby Mason, Seth Mason, Rita Matulef, Judith Maute, Ira Mayer, Hy Mayerson, Bill McCarter, Bob McCarthy, Mary McCaslin, Cathal McConnell, Mary Ann Wambach McCrary, Michael McCurdy, Hugh McDonald, Country Joe McDonald, John McDonough, Megon (formerly Megan) McDonough, John McEuen, William E. McEuen, Vince McGarry, Alvin McGovern, Al McKenney, Keith McKenry, Keith McKie, John McLaughlin, Ralph McTell, Renee Rinka Means, Gary Mechanic, Lewis Merenstein, Dan Michaels, Lynn Pankau Miller, Michael Miller, Oscar Miller, Wade Hampton Miller, Barbara Millikan, Dan Milner, Dennis Minogue (Terry Cashman), Ann Mintz, George Mische, Chad Mitchell, Chuck Mitchell, Tim Mocarski, Hardye Simons Moel, Katy Moffatt, Bud Molin, Lincoln "Chips" Moman, Buddy Mondlock, Gary Montgomery, Mick Montgomery, Jym Mooney, Jim Moore, Joe & JoAnn Moore, Marian Moore, Keith Moreland, Reuben Morgan,

Chuck Morris, Johnniy Morris, Kenton Morris, Mary Morris, Linda "Mori" Morrison, George Moser, Steve & Barbara Mosley, Mark Moss, Rob Mounsey, Doug Moyes, Geoff Muldaur, Maria Muldaur, Martin Mull, Kevin Mulvenna, Bill Munger, Ellen Press Murdoch

N

Kristi Nebel, Jerry Needelman, Rick Neeley, Peter Neff, Michael Nejman, Cassi Nelson, Willie Nelson, Jim Netter, Hank Neuberger, David "Fathead" Newman, Howie Newman, Randy Newman, Abby Newton, Steve Nider, Paul Niesen, Mike Nilles, Willie Nininger, Cathi Norton, Mary Muehleisen Nowak, Lois Scott Novakovich, Mark Nowakowski, Betty & Herb Nudelman, Debbie Nystrom

O

Barry Oberman, Tim O'Brien, Sonny Ochs, Robert K. Oermann, Charlie Offer, Don Oja-Dunaway, Danny O'Keefe, John O'Kennedy, Milt Okun, Eddie O'Laughlin, Lindon Spooner Oldham, Scott O'Malley, John Orzechowski, Fred Oster, Ray Owen

P

Tom Pacheco, Larry Packer, Bob Patterson, Ellis Paul, Terry Paul, Tom Paxton, Terry & Lenora Pearl, Myrna Pedersen, Marty Peifer, Norm Pellegrini, Gayle Pemberton, Robin Pendergrast, Allan Pepper, Sal Perreira, Chuck Perrin, Mitch Perry, Jim Peterik, Jeff Peterson, Faith Petric, Bruce "Utah" Phillips, Tom Picardo (Tommy West), Tom Pickles, Simeon "Wally" Pillich, Irene Pinn, Janet Planet, Joel Platt, John Platt, Alice Playten, Mitch Podolak, Wally Podrazik, Rusty Poehner, Ruth Pohlman, Ethel Polk, Neal Pollack, Amy Burnham Pollien, Browning Porter, John Posniak, Jim Post, Bob Pottinger, Stephen Powers, Paul Prappas, Howard Primer, Dave Prine, Robert Pruter, Carolyn Purdy-Gordon, Norbert Putnam, "Stretch" & Teresa Pyott

Q-R

Bill Quateman, Tom Radtke, Bonnie Raitt, Bill Rall, Elliott Randall, Mickey Raphael, Ron Rapoport, Maggie Ratchford, Thurl Ravenscroft, Martha & Betsy

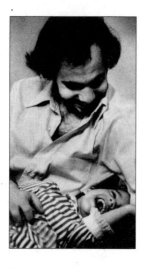

Steve gives his daughter Jessie a mid-1970s tickle.

(Photo courtesy of Gib Foster)

Redhed, Carl Reiner, Mark Reishus, Bonnie Remsberg, Marie Rhines, Ronnie Rice, Bob Rich, Fred Rickert, Pat Rickert, Rolando Rico, Bob Riek, Tom Riesenmy, Kathryn Riley, Willie Riser, Roy Ritzmann, Dan Roan, Sally Bourdeau Roberts, Barb Pritchard Robbins, Susan Martin Robbins, Byron Roche, Jeff Rochman, Garnet Rogers, Nancy Rogers, Mike Rohm, Dr. Herbert "Chip" Rollins, Steven Romanoski, Ron Rooks, Sid Root, Bob Rose, Jon Rose, David Rosen, Stuart Rosenberg, Alan Rosenfeld, Marshall Rosenthal, Dr. Larry Ross, Mark Ross, Molly Ross, David Roth, John Rothchild, Dave Rowe, Fred Rubin, Leland Rucker, Catherine Rude, Sam Rudin, Bob Rusch, Tom Rush, Peter "Madcat" Ruth, Gary Ryan, Joan Ryan

S

Glenn Sabatka, Randy Sabien, Mike Saccoliti, Josephine Sage, Nancy Sage, Beth Cohn Sair, Darcie Sanders, Ben Sandmel, Mike Sangiacomo, Meryl Saverslak, Beth Scalet, Dennis & Sandy Scharlau, George Scarola, Vin Scelsa, Shawn Schey, Nancy Schimmel, Paul Schlesinger, Claudia Schmidt, Harrison "Jack" Schmitt, Ann Schmitz, Susan Miller Schneider, Mick Scott (Herbert Scarpelli), Mike

Schreibman, Don Schultz, Jim Schwall, Ed Schwartz, Sue Ellen Lorge Schwartz, Dr. Lee Schwartzberg, Steve Schwarz, Ed Sciaky, Virginia Riser Scott, John Sebastian, Pete Seeger, Ron Shaffer, Linda Shamest, Ed Shane, Bob Shanks, Jan Stein Shapiro, Larry Shapiro, Jerry Sharell, Billy Joe Shaver, Allan Shaw, Cathy Turley Shaw, Gene Shay, Kathy Shedd, George Shepard, Steve Sher, Wendy Sheridan, Bruce Shindler, Michelle Shocked, Paul Siebel, Mark "Corky" Siegel, Norm Siegel, Sam Siegel, Les Siemieniuk, David & Linda Siglin, Gail Sikevitz, Fred Silverman, Ira Silverman, Jo Ann Stepan Simich, Michael Simmonds, Al Simmons, Carly Simon, Penny Simon, Scott Simon, Dick Simpson, Sid Sims, Bob Skilton, Patrick Sky, Candice Smith, Dillon Smith, Joe Smith, Michael Smith, Rand Smith, Jewel Fay "Sammi" Smith, Jim Smoak, Stanley Snadowsky, John Snider, Phoebe Snow, Andy Sohn, Doug Sohn, Dr. Herb Sohn, Patricia Domzalski Solans, Rosalie Sorrels, Dave Spaulding, Anita Sperber, George Spink, MaryAnne Erde Spinner, Doug Stacey, Jim Staahl, Bill Staines, James Lee Stanley, Sukie Askew Stanley, Burt Stein, Lee Stein, Peter Steinberg, Paul Stern, Jim Stevens, Kris Erik Stevens, Barb Nicker Stewart, Don Stiernberg, Ed Stiernberg, Richard Stock, Chuck Stolberg, Terry Stoodley, Terry Straker, Don Strandell, Eileen Alonso Stratton, Len Strazewski, Mike Strobel, Marty Stuart, Jimmy Sturr, Joe Sundwall, Roger Surbaugh, Bill Sutton, Derek Sutton, George Gaines Swanson, Neesa Sweet, Scott Swinney, Chuck Swirsky, Beth Swofford, Rob Swofford, Keith Sykes

T

Fletcher Taft, Jonathan Takiff, Dr. Martin Tallman, Bob Tangrea, Jeff Taras, Diane Taraz, Lyle Tartak, Ray Tate, Cyril Tawney, Keith Taylor, Mike Taylor, Michael Tearson, Andy Tecson, Harold Thom, Russ Thyret, Terry Tiz, John Tobler, Neil Tolciss, Lily Tomlin, John Tondelli, Brian Torff, Steve Trachtman, Greg Trafidlo, Jim Trattner, Artie Traum, Bill Traut, Bill Travis, Goodwin Trent, Ernie Trionfo, Harry Tuft, Jim Tullio, Rick Turner, Scott Turner

U-V

Ken Ulansey, Juel Ulven, Matt Umanov, Jay Ungar, Georgia Kariotis Valos, Tim Vana, Kenny Vance, Betsy Elich Vandercook, Phil Van Huesen, Ivan Van Laningham, Melvin Van Peebles, Angelo Varias, Trevor Veitch, Don Venne, Jim Videbeck, Rick Vito, Roger Voegele

W

Larry Wadalavage, Stephen Wade, Loudon Wainwright III, Eliot Wald, Wendy Waldman, Eddie Walker, Jeany Walker, Jerry Jeff Walker, Morris Walker, Ed & Dana Ward, Herb Ward, Lenny Waronker, Carrie Ann Warner, Ellen Warshaw, Doc Watson, Jack Watters, Charlotte Webb, Pat Webb, Richard Wedler, Hart Weichselbaum, Suzanne Weil, Daniel Weinberg, Ron Weindruch, Ron Weisner, Eric Weissberg, Peter Weisz, Steve Weitzman, Bob Welland, Barbara Wells, Kevin Wells, Lucy Wells, Bill Wencel, Donna Wender, Don Wessel, Steve Westman, Jerry Wexler, Bill Whamond, Gary B. White, Josh White Jr., Laura Freedman White, Susan White, Vernon White, Ken Whiteley, Jay Whitsett, Mark Wigginton, Matthew Wilder, Bucky Wilkin, Albert Williams, Flawn Williams, Mason Williams, Robert Williams, David Wilson, Linda Wilson, Tyler & Joan Wilson, Jesse Winchester, Julian "Winnie" Winston, Phillis "Toxie" Wirtz Witwicki, Heather Wood, Janette Ferdinand Woods, Joan Woollard, Dai Woosnam

X-Y-Z

Elliott Yablun, Bob Yahn, Arnie Yarber, Doug Yeager, Gene Yellin, Steve Young, Dolly Zander, Arnie Zarber, Danny Zelisko, Paul Zollo, Dr. Rodney Zolt, Bill Zorn, Ed Zuckerman, Irving Zummer

THOSE ASSISTING IN OTHER WAYS

Countless photographers, librarians, professional and amateur archivists, gatekeepers, transcribers, administrative assistants and others provided materials, enhanced my research and offered invaluable support.

The names listed here total **1,137**, including my conscientious compatriot, **Ian Woofenden**. Others deserving special note are:

Alyssa Archambault
Laura Barnard
and **Karen Barnes**
(Seattle Public Library's infinitely patient, interlibrary-loan duo)
Kathy Bremner
Sherrie Buzby
Mary Ann Fisher ("Ah, Goodman people, y'know")
Shirley Gibson
Siobhan O'Sullivan Harvey
Valerie Magee (ace webmaster)
Richard McCaffrey
Gary Norris
Joe Novak (audio engineer and preservationist extraordinaire)
Brett Paine
John Rieber
Gary Snyderman
Ilene Waterstone

Here are the names of others whom I can identify:

A

Jeremy Abbott, Alan Ackerman, Nicholas Adams, Martha Adcock, Zack Adcock, Jim Addie, Vic Aderhold, Rachel Adler, Catherine Alexander, Mary Alfieri, Tom Alger, Blaine Allan, Sandra Allen, Dan Amato, Deborah Amos, Paul Anastasio, David Anderson, Forrest Anderson, Ian Anderson, Janine Anderson, Tara Anderson, Paul Ansell, Steve Anzaldi, Dr. Fred Appelbaum, Kristen Applequist, Yardena Arar, Rich Archbold, Elaine Ardia, Warren Argo, Barbara Ward Armstrong, Jennifer Armstrong, Lori Arthur, Matt Asendorf, Doug Ashford, Robert Askren, Rachel Athey, Jonathan Atkin, Scott Atkinson, Barb Chaffer Authier, Nina Avramides

B

Sahar Baba, Jonathan Baer, Joan Baez, Jim Baggett, Kenny Baker, Patricia Bakunas, Martin & Sally Baker, Mariella Bakken, Irene Balogh, Andy Balterman, Rick Bannerot, Ellen Barkon, Paul Barnaby, Crispin Bartlett, Robert Barnett, James Bates, Martha Kelly Bates, Robin Batteau, Lois Baum, Dave Baxter, Jason Baxter, Patricia Beaber, David Beadle, Christopher Beam, Greg Bechtloff, Joachim Becker, John & Janice Weeks Becker, Michelle Bega, Peter O.E. Bekker, Gary Belich, Penelope Bell, Steve Benbow, Carole Bender, Dave Bendett, Mary & Ray Benischeck, Mary Bennett, Don Benson, Jim Beplat, Barbara Berg, Andrea Berger, Valerie Berger, Art Berggrin, Al Bergstein, Helene Berinsky, Jennie Berkson, Brian Bernardoni, Chuck Berman, Freddy Berowski, Joelle Bertolet, Alex Bevan, Sue Betz, Doug Bicknese, Betsy Biehn, Joel Bierig, Ray Bierl, Dan Billings, Leon Billings, Jeremy Birnbaum, Jerry Bishop, Bob Bittner, Bill Black, Wayne Blagdon, Dana Blakeslee, Lefty Blasco, Frank Blau, Andrew Blauner, Jim Blauvelt, Moss Bliss, Tim Blixt, Charles Blottin, Dick Boak, Krista Boehnert, Richard Boehmcke, Scot Bolsinger, Joe Bonomo, Els Boonen, Ruthane Bopp, Sherry Bowen, Don Bradshaw, Paul Brady, John Braheny, Chuck Brandt, Kelly Braun, Lori Brayer, Jon Bream, Doug Breckenridge, Irene Breedlove, Dan Brewer, Tim Brickley, Bryn Bridenthal, Heather Briston, Dana Britten-Stein, Simon Bronner, John Brown, Steve Brown, Mike Brubaker, Rhonda Brunn, Kerri Brusca, Charlie Bryant, Dona Bubelis, Gail Buchalter, Curtis Burch, April Burcham, Reeda Buresh, Jamie Burgh, Victor Burgos, Kimberly Butler, Paul Button

C

Brian Cahill, Don Caldwell, Hamilton Camp, Chad Campbell, Jeff Campbell, Fred Campeau, Barbara Cansino, Mike Canzoneri, Michael Cardozo, Robert Carleton, Terry Carlin, Sam Carman, Caroline Carney, Patrick Carr, Janelle Carroll, Gordon Carter, Jeanette Casey, Catherine Cate, Marty Cavanaugh, Phil Ceccola, Flora Schwartz Chamberlain, Jim Charlton, Amy Chen, Mark Chester, Blind Lemming Chiffon, Barbara Chouinard, Brad Chrisman, Margaret Christl, Michael Churchman, Laura Cifelli, Paul Cioe, Jim Clark, Susan Clark, Mike Clayton, Cree Clover, Elisabeth Cnobloch, Peter Coan, Wes Coates, Paul Cobley, Barbara Cohen Cochran, Ron Coden, Gordon Cohn, Ron Cohn, Robert Coleburn, Jim Colgrove, Janice Collins, Ned Comstock, Neal Conan, Bill Conlin, Mike Conlon, Mike Connelly, Scott Constans, Matt Cook, Joe Cornejo, Jan Cornish, Phyllis "Pat" O'Sullivan Corona, Amber Corrin, Lu Cortese, Warren Cosford, Vicky Newberry Costakis, Christopher Costanza, Erma Couden, Kevin Courrier, Geoff Cox, Jennifer Craig, Midge Cranor, Lucinda Crawford, Ron Crawford, Don Crawley, Martin Cribb, Geoff Crimmins, James Cruce, Linda Cubbidge, Brent Cunliffe, Peter Cunningham, Barbara Curtin, Bob Curtis, Jim Cypher, Andrew Czernek

D

Kristina Daily, Maryanne Dalzell, Michael Damsky, Leonard David, Marv David, Chris Darling, Michael Darnton, Martha Davidson, Marta Dawes, John deGraaf, Steve Deitelbaum, Roger Deitz, Chris DeJohn, Linda Delaford, John Delgatto, Katherine dePaul, Karen Dereszynski, Jed Derry, Doug Desmarais, John Devine Jr., Polly Diaz, Amy Dickerson, Bert Dickie, Henry Diltz, Jim Dirden, Kitty Donohoe, Nora Dornan, Mary Claire Dougherty, Jean Doumanian, Anne Dowie, Kate Downing, Jamie Downs, Bob Drew, Dru Druzianich, Beth Dube, Alec Dubro, Frank Dudgeon, Reid Duffy, Charlyne Dunbar, Mac Dunlop, Mark Dvorak, Steve Dyck

E

Larry Eagle, Dave Eals, Doug & Denise Eals, Michael Ebner, Dan Edelson, David Adam Edelstein, Gordon Edes, Allen Eichhorn, Mary Eidson, Bill Eidson, Pam Eisenberg, Lore Eisenstaedt, Bob Elliot, Neenah Ellis, Dave Emlen, Judy Englander, Dan Epstein, Kristen Erenburg, Amy & Josh Escobedo, Dave Eskenazi, Gwyneth Evans, Laura Evans, Todd Everett

F

Lola Falana, Lee Faulhaber, Jackie Feare, Mike Fearn, Cassie Fedrick, Barry Feinstein, Fil Feit, Cliff Feldman, Nancy Feldman, Mike Felten, Teresa Ferguson, Donna Fields, Stephanie Fields, Andrew Fignar, Ben Finkelstein, Terry Finn, Timothy Finn, Christine Firth, Terry Fish, Frank Fitzmaurice, Kelly Flint, Pat Flynn, Joella Foulds, Rex Fowler, Barbara Fox, Larry Fox, Emil Fray, Linda Freitag, Janice Frey, Marissa Fugate, Doug Fuhrmann

G

Mark Gager, Jim Gary, Linda Gainer, Monique Garcia, Betty Gard, Dave Gardner, Matt Gardner, Adam Garfinkle, Bill Garrett, Danny Garrett, Mickey Garvey, Josep A. Gaspar, Frank Gatyas, Mitch Gawlik, Cathy Genovese, Scott Gibbs, Toby Gibson, David Gilbert, Barbara Gilblair, Kristen Gilkeson, Jody Gill, Charlie Gillett, Rita Gillis, Artis Gilmore, Kathy Ginter, Priscilla Giraldo, Jessica Girlando, Sarah Mae Glass, Howard Glazer, Holly Gleason, Carole Goad, Clive Godden, David Godine, Audrey Gold, Eli Goldberg, Rochelle Goldstein, Bridget Gonzales, Allan Goodrich, Elizabeth Goodrich, Deana Gorbet, Ken Gorka, Sarah Gorres, David Goss, Danny Gotham, Harold & Laura Grams, Matt Gray, Mike Gray, Beverly Green, Stephen & Meg Green, Ken Greengrass, Gail Grieb, Emmy Lou Griffin, Steve Grills, Karolyn Grimes, Tim Grobaty, Maryrose Grossman, Bob Gruen, George Gruhn, Jackie Guidry, Ania Gunderson, David Gutcheon, Annie Guthrie, Jackie Guthrie

H

Gary Haber, Herbert Hadad, Chuck Haddix, Boyd Hagen, Dennis Halbin, Donna Halper, Tom Hambright, Dick Hanchette, Kelly Hancock, Beryl Handler, Bill Haney, Liane Hansen, Andy Hanson, Bruce Hanson, Tom Hardin, Mark Hare, Richard Harris, Roy Harris, Candy Hart, Ed Hartig, David Hartman, Bradford Harvey, Jill Hattersley, Rebecca Hauger, Frank Haulgren, David Hausam, Carol Hay, Susan Hayes, John Hazelton, Lee Hazen, Pat Heath, Sandy Heberer, Terry Heckler, Hurricane Heeran, Jeff Heiman,

Steve. interviewed in 1980-81 in Seal Beach.

(Photo by Tom Shaw, courtesy of the *Long Beach Press-Telegram*)

Christina Heliker, Mitch Heller, Matt Hemmingsen, Don Hendershot, Tony Hendra, Kevin Hennessey, Mark Hertzberg, Cheryl Hertzer, Marjorie Hess, Bob Hiebert, Trina Higgins, Joy Hildebrand, Roberta Hilliger, Joey Hinkle, Doug Hinman, Larry Hinman, Roger Hinman, Joan Hipp, John Hockett, Fenton Hollander, Dan Holmes, Len Holsclaw, Patrick Hopkins, Keith Housewright, Kate Howe, Marian Hubler, Rob Hudson, John Hughes, Hester Huiting, Krystal Hunt

I-J

Carmen Ifkovits, Tadd Igarashi, Kazimer "Kasey" Ignarski, Les Irvin, Shawn Irwin, Ralph Jaccodine, Robin Jacob, Stuart Jacobson, Raymond Janicek, Cheryl Johansson, Eric Johnson, Wilbur & Dorothy Johnson, Andy Jones, Ron Jones, Raissa Jose, John Joyner

K

Danny Kahn, Susanne Kalweit, Arnie Kamen, Jenny Kane, Kathy Kane, Terry Kane, Andy Kaplan, Diane Kaplan, Jessica Kaplan, Amy Karatz, Mason Katz, Pat Katz, Lynn Kear, Paul Kehoe, James Kelly, Susan Kempin, Cheryl Kendrick, John Kennamer, Steve Kerber, Cathy Kerr, Sue Kessell, Galene Kessin, Joyce Ketterer,

Greg Kihn, Michael Kilduff, Barbara King, Heather King, Karen King, Larry King, Doug Kirby, Mark Kirchmeier, Jim Kirk, Marty Kistin, Michelle Klein, Chuck Knapp, Bill Knight, Jerome Knill, Peter Knobler, Jeff Kocar, Spider John Koerner, Charlotte Kolczynski, Jody Kolodzey, Janet Kolodzy, David Koppel, Rob Koppelman, Ginny Kosola, Michael Krieger, Steve Kronen, Marc Kuhn, George Kupczak

L

Gary Laga, Leon Lamal, Deborah Lamberton, Lesli Larson, Linda Larson, John Leader, Seth! Leary, Lisa Leclair, Don Lee, Margaret Lee, Sharen Lee, Shu-Lin Lee, Marc Leepson, Anne Leibold, Mary Leonard, Perry & Ronnie Leonard, Tim Leonard, John Leonardini, Sue Leventhal, June Levin, Bruce Levine, Mark Leviton, Sherrie Levy, Donna Lewis, Rick Lewis, Peter Lewry, Claudia Libowitz, Joyce Lieberman, Hal Lifson, Alana Lines, Roger Liptrot, Marilyn Knapp Litt, Maria Llambias, Chuck Loebbaka, Stephen Logowitz, John Long, Veronica Lopez, Sandy Lord, Suzanne Eggleston Lovejoy, Paul Lovelace, Brian Lucas, Nigel Luckhurst, Larry Luddecke, Sidney Lund, Carol Lyke, Andy Lyman, John Lynch, Arlene Lynes, Peter Lysy

M

Cyril MacInnes, Brownie Macintosh, Chris Macke, Colby Maddox, Dave Maenza, Jimmy Magahern, Jeff Magid, Karen Magnifico, Bill Mahin, Elizabeth Mahoney, Gregory Malcolm, Bob & Kee Malesky, Jim Maley, Howard Mandelbaum, Jacquie Manning, Pamela Manning, Ken Marcus, Richard Marcus, Dianne Mariano, George Marinelli, Tony Markellis, Andy Markley, Dave Marsden, Kenneth Marshall, Anna Martin, Christy Martin, Sharlene A. Martin, Rita Martinez, Dave Marzullo, Akida Mashaka, Ray Materick, Bill May, Tom May, Elizabeth Mazur, Paolo Mazzanti, Anthony McAndrew, Jim McArdle, Patrick McCallister, Laurie McCarthy, Bill McCloud, Deborah McColl, Charlie McCoy, Leilani McCoy, Shawn McCrohan, Judy McCulloh, Terry McCune, Laura McElroy, Barbara McGlothern, Rick McGrath, Katey McGuckin, Roger McGuinn, Tom McKay, Bill McKee, Michelle McKenzie-Voigt, Brian McKim, Ben McLane, Jim McLaughlin, Alison Chapman McLean, Larry McLean, Andrew McLennan, Carol McMenamin, Norris McNamara, Jan McTaggart, Rob Medina, Rafael Medoff, Bruce Mehlenbacher, Frits Meijer, Jan Meisenhelter, Debbie Meister, Tab Melton, Ashley Mendel, Toni Mendell, Don Menn, George Merlis, Rick Merrill, Max Merritt, Henry Mietkiewicz, Art Miller, Buddy Miller, Matt Miller, Paul Mills, Sarah Mishkin, Christine Mitchell, Gary & Paula Mitchell, John Moe, Hajara Mohiuddeen, Bud Molin, Gabriel Moliterno, Dan Molvar, Jane Monkfield, Merle Monroe, Jean Montiel, Mike Morrow, Terry Moses, Natalie Mosier, Andrea Moss, Steven Moss, Julia Mucci, Cynthia Mullens, Ceil Muller, Scott Munn, Colleen Murdock, Joann Murdock, Katy Murphy, Mike Murphy, Tracy Murray, Lissa Muscatine, Tom Musick, Jim Musselman, James Musser, Margot Myers

N

Roger Naber, Skip Naft, Michael Nash, Ellen Nassberg, Brian Nation, Paul Natkin, Ilko Nechev, Margie Needelman, Tim Neely, Paula Kamman Nelson, Sue Schmied Nelson, Bill Nestos, Roger Neville-Neil, David

Newland, Tim Newport, Scott Newton, Rob Neyer, Don Nicoll, Alan Niester, Eric Nitschke, Rolf Nölle, Steve North, Kristen Nyitray, Suzanne Nyren

O

Peter O'Brien, Russel O'Brien, Mary Joan O'Connell, Dan O'Connor, Rosemary Tobin O'Connor, Tim O'Connor, David Oesterreich, Dion Ogust, Greg O'Haver, Audrey O'Kelley, Keith Olesen, Earl Oliver, Ron Olson, Pat O'Neil, Dennis O'Neill, Joan Orr, Stuart Ortiz, Charles Osgood, Chloe Ottenhoff, Bren Overholt

P

Susan Painter, Marlene Palmer, Kevin Papa, Mike Paquin, Malcolm Paramor, Gail Parker, Gary Parker, Kenneth R. Parker, Ron Parker, Steve Parker, Rachel Parkman, Jeanne Passin, Sam Pathy, Larry Pattis, Gena Paul, Eden Juron Pearlman, Abe Peck, Marla Pendergrast, Chris Penton, Linda Wolf Pepper, Rhonda Perkins, Diana Park, Chuck Perrin, Scott Perschke, Alan Peters, Dr. Rex Peters, Diana Franzusoff Peterson, Jenny Peterson, Pierce Pettis, Renee Phelan, Patti Phelps, Roger Piantadosi, Roger Piegza, Rich Pilling, Richard Pinney, Sue Pittak, Dick Pleasants, Anne Polaski, Alex Polaski, David Ponak, Sarah Poontong, James & Sandra Porteous, Craig Porter, Dr. Jerome Posner, Nicole Porter, Jayme Powers, Ron Pownall, Eric Predoehl, Gary Pressy, Neal Preston, Josh Preston, Barbara Price, Scott Price, Dale Primer, Mino Profumo, Nicole Proulx, Alan "Chip" Pruzik, Chuck Pulin, Andy Pulliam, Michael Putland, Mark Pynes

Q-R

Jane Quinn, Millie Rahn, Steve Ramm, Xeno Linhart Rasmusson, Steve Rathe, Steve Redfearn, Darrell Redmond, Moshe "Morry" Reem, Philippe Reines, Ted Reynolds, Tom Reynolds, Bruce Reznick, Don Rhodes, Bob Ribokas, Betty Richards, John Richardson, Ken Richardson, Arthur Richman, Libby Riddles, Bob Riesman, Gary Riskin, Shelley Waitsman Riskin, T.R. Ritchie, Alan Ritter, Travis Rivers, Jay Rizick, Susan Michaelson Roads, Dan

Roan, Jay Roberts, John Roberts, Hazel Robertson, Lou Robin, Gail Robinson, Jim Robinson, Lee Robinson, Rob Robinson, Shauna Brown Rolland, Alan Rommelfanger, John Rook, Herb Root, Jeff Rosen, Margo Newmark Rosenbaum, Jack Rosenberg, Steve Rosenberg, Ted Ross, Pat Rothenberg, John R. Rowlands, David Rudkin, Roger Russell, Marla Ryan, Honey Ryan, Tom Ryan, Linda Dillon Rydman

S

Carla Sacks, Kathy Kloss Saffer, Felice Berkman Sage, Michael Salsburg, Marianna Samero, Holly Sammons, Helen Sanders, Pat Sandona, Warner Saunders, Paul Savedow, Phil Saviano, Steve Sawyer, Ben Schafer, Ralph Schatz, Gail Scheible, Beth Scher, Steve Scher, Ron Schick, Scott Schillo, Suzanne Schindler, Fredie Beth Rolsky Schmutte, Jessica Schneider, Marc Schneider, Steve Schneider, Gerd Schmerse, Jerome Schneidman, Mike Schreibman, Michael Schumacher, Steve & Pam Schuster, Eric Schusterman, Andy Schwartz, Allan Schwartzberg, Sharon Schwartzberg, Dave Sciarra, Rich Seafield, Catherine Sebastian, Kevin Seeley, Joel Selvin, Charles Seton, Can Sertoglu, Audrey Shannon, Dan Sharon, Reenie Shea, Tom Sheehan, Lynn Sheeran, David Sheffield, Sue Sheftel, Scott Sheldon, Nick Shelton, Jane Shepherd, Stan Shiebert, Mark Shields, Moe Shore, Kay Shortridge, Debbie Siegel, Doug Siegel, Holly Siegel, Larry Siegel, Jon Sievert, Steven Silver, Art Silverman, John Sincock, Frank Siteman, David Skover, Bob Slack, Sandy Slater, Martha Smiglis, Bee Smith, Daniel Smith, Doug Smith, Lucy Smith, Robert Smith, Sandy Smolen, James Snow, Robert Soffian, Matt Sohn, Evan Soldinger, Bonnie Somers, Dom Soto, Jeff Sotzing, Terry Sparks, Glenn Spatola, Dan Spatucci, Mark Spector, Susan Spelman, Ingrid Speros, Matt Spiece, Keely Stahl, Susan Stamberg, Lyndon Stambler, Paul Stamler, Bob Stane, Randy Starks, Wayne Starling, Charlie Steadham, Billy Stephens, Will Stephens, Abby Sternberg, Bob Stevens, Dick Stewart, Myra Stiernberg, Kevin Stiffler, Michael Stiver, Alan

Steve and John Prine await their turn during a workshop at the 1976 Mariposa Folk Festival.

(Photo courtesy of Diane Holmes)

Stoker, John Stoll, Steve Stone, Lee Strassberg, Allen Streicker, Pegge Strella, Joe Striegler, Alice Stuart, Robert Sullivan, Melissa Summerfield, Joe Suo, John Swann, Ernie Swanson, Ariel Swartley, Lucy Swenson, Kim Swofford, Peggy Swofford, Jen Sygit

T

Josh Talley, Becky Tanner, Michael Tapes, Angelina Tarallo, John Taylor, Maria Leilani Taylor, Robert Tebbetts, Terry Teigen, Terry Tenopir, Carol "Dutchy" Thieme, Faye Thompson, Marina Terzi, Lynn Thitchener, Kenn Thomas, Bill Thompson, Mike Thorne, Donnie & Zane Thornley, D.D. Thornton, Tracy Tingley, Sallie Tisdale, Gordon Todd, Lana Toliver, Jimmy Tomasello, Wayne Tomkowaik, Faye Tomlinson, Renee Tondelli, Manno Toshikazu, Happy Traum, Chandler Travis, Lorett Treese, Neal Trilling, Celeste Troon, Debra Trowbridge, Michael Trujillo, Tanya Tucka, Terry Tucker,

Walter Tunis, Tanisha Turner, Terry Tveraas, Paul Tyler, Wendy Tyner, Ian Tyson, Vera Tzoneva.

U-V

Arthur Usherson, Gale Vaccaro, Carla Vail, Hans van den Hoek, Burda Vandeborne, Frank Vandepitte, Chuck VanderVennet, Jerry VanderWood, Leroy & Gladys Van Dyke, Jacques van Gool, Matt Van Hattem, Heidi Van Heel, James Van Hise, Lynn Van Matre, Gene Vano, Robert Vardill, Carla Veil, Jamie Vavonese, Milton Vedder, Anna Vidal, Tamara Vidos, Eugene Vigil, Mark Volatile, William Vollmar, Bob Vorwald, Jerry Vovcsko

W

Norm Wahl, Lissa Wales, Morley Walker, Janet Wall, Nancy Wallace, Peter Wallace, Duncan Walls, Jim Walsh, Kristi Walsh, Susan Besaw Walsh, Christine Walters, Eric Waltman, Christopher Ward, Steven Ward, Anita Pedersen Warren, Denny Warrick, Jim

Washburn, Tom Wasserman, Rich Watton, Jim Watson, Weasel, Ralph Weinberg, Mike Weindruch, Roger Weiner, Sarah Weinman, Miller & Ann Bell Weisman, Steve Weiss, Dick Weissman, Pete Weldon, Sam Welker, Keith Wessel, Richard "Wes" Westerfield, Jessica Whetman, Clive Whichelow, Sara Whitehead, Diane Bloomgarden Whiteley, Kathi Whitley, Frank Whittaker, Robert Wiard, Jack Wilding, Tim Wiles, Tom Wilk, Mary Ann Williard, Don Willis, Diane Willman, Beverly Williams, Tom Wilmeth, Dick Wilson, Paul Wilson, Jesse Winchester, David Winter, Jeff Winter, Kim Witherspoon, David Witz, Dave Wohl, Robert Wolf, Laura Woliver, Garrett Wollman, Ray Wolverton, Sharon Woodhouse, Jodie Wright, Jill Wylly, Bob Wynne

X-Y-Z

Judy Yacko, Mark Young, Jeff Yurkoski, Jay & Mary Zacharias, Paul Zaich, Anne Zald, Bruce Zalman, Jan Zauha, Mark Zegan, Mel Zerman, Eve Zibart, Dr. John Zielinski, Arleen Zimmerle, Sally Zito, Tom Zito, Eric Zorn, Toby Zwikel

INSTITUTIONS, ORGANIZATIONS

Especially helpful: the Chicago Historical Society; the online archives of the *Chicago Tribune*, *The New York Times* and many other newspapers; the Museum of Broadcast Communications in Chicago; the Museum of Television & Radio in New York City; the National Aeronautics and Space Administration; the Old Town School of Folk Music; Seattle Public Library; the *SingOut!* Resource Center; the University of Illinois at Chicago Special Collection; and the Harold Washington Library Center in Chicago.

An inscription by Steve on his "Artistic Hair" LP.

(Image courtesy of Chris Farrell)

Elektra/Asylum promotes Steve's new "Words" LP in at the Roxy in L.A., 1976.

(Poster courtesy of Steve Cohen)

A train motif inspired by "City of New Orleans" dwarfs Steve in this 1976 Eugene, Oregon, poster.

(Poster courtesy of Steve Cohen)

With Steve as a senior, the caption for this Maine East High Lens photo read: "Those frosh are getting bigger every year."

Steve tunes at June 1973 Culpepper festival in Warrenton, Virginia.

(Photo by Andrew Czernek)

*A flyer plugs Steve's show
Aug. 2, 1976, in Hamburg.*

(Flyer courtesy of Steve Cohen)

Steve's Survival Sunday III portrait, May 5, 1980, Hollywood Bowl, Calif.

(Image courtesy of Loretta Smith)

Steve holds John Klemmer in his fingers in this Sept. 18, 1976, poster from SUNY, Buffalo, New York.

(Poster courtesy of Steve Cohen)

Performers at the Oct. 2, 2004, tribute in New Jersey (from left): Erik Frandsen, Mike Agranoff, Steve Burgh, Dennis Gormley, Heather Wood, Perry Barber, Saul Broudy, Laurie MacAllister, Leslie Berman (holding Steve's first LP), Eric Schwartz, Stratton Doyle, George Wurzbach and Jesse Lew.

(Photo by Barry Sagotsky)

Mock fiddle during "You Never Even Call Me by My Name" at Dooley's, Tempe, Arizona, Feb. 2, 1981.

(Photo by Ben Elder)

Q

R

New Year's Eve 1976, Earl of Old Town, Chicago.

(Photo by Liz Danzig Derry)

*At the Lone Star Café,
June 23, 1983, New York.*

(Photo by Marlene Rosol)

Steve plays the Bridgeton, N.J., Folk Festival on June 23, 1984, less than three months before his death.

(Photo © Sherrie Buzby/ *The Bridgeton Evening News*)

The Al Jolson-like image of "The Entertainer" was the theme in this Bogart's poster, 1976, Cincinnati.

(Poster courtesy of Steve Cohen)

2. Norm Hacking

(Photo by Shirley Gibson)

3. Jessica Anne Baron

(Photo courtesy of Gayle Mitchell)

4. John Wesley Harding

(Photo by Susan San Giovanni)

5. Pierce Pettis

(Photo by Amy Dickerson, www.amydickerson.com)

6. Buddy Mondlock

(Photo by Karen Will Rogers)

CD TRACKS 1–9

1. SONG FOR STEVE (3:19)

Brian Gill, Moscow, Idaho

This affecting one-man, one-guitar piece is by a heart-on-sleeve stalwart of the 1970s Chicago folk scene. Written wholly for Steve, it contains a ringing refrain that sums up this collection: "His song ain't over yet."

Contact: briangillmusic@hotmail.com
http://www.briangillmusic.com

2. RICHER FOR THE TIME (2:44)

Norm Hacking, Toronto, Ontario, Canada

The lone Canadian contribution, by a long-heralded Toronto folkie, this song uses gentle production and a sing-along chorus to turn the specific into the universal.

From the CD, "Skysongs … A Writer's Collection," 2001, 3FLAM2002, SOCAN.
Contact: info@normhacking.com
http://www.normhacking.com

3. LIGHT UP THE SKY (5:07)

Jessica Anne Baron, Del Mar, California

Though Steve is unnamed, he is this song's sole inspiration. Its powerful metaphor — an extinguished star that is still burning — applies to everyone. Plaintive piano complements a swirl of voices that dares you not to harmonize.

Contact: jess.gitc@sbcglobal.net
http://www.guitarsintheclassroom.com

4. PHIL OCHS, BOB DYLAN, STEVE GOODMAN, DAVID BLUE AND ME (4:32)

John Wesley Harding (Wes Stace), Brooklyn, New York

This poignant vision of the author's ritual inspiration appears here in a previously unreleased version.

© 2006 Plangent Visions Music, Inc. (ASCAP). Recorded Nov. 30, 2003, Eckmann Arena, Ringwood, New Jersey. Original version is from the CD, "It Happened One Night," Appleseed APR CD 1083.
Contact: jwh@armory.com
http://www.johnwesleyharding.com

5. THIS IS FOR LENA'S CAFÉ (4:19)

Pierce Pettis, Mentone, Alabama

Fittingly a live recording, this is an aching tale of the Saratoga Springs, New York, music club called Caffè Lena, the kind that was Steve's staple in his early years.
Contact: slap@hiwaay.net
http://www.piercepettis.com

6. NO CHOICE (3:36)

Buddy Mondlock, Nashville, Tennessee

Without naming him, this anthemic song is specific to Steve, particularly its final verse, but it applies to the destiny in all of us — including how this biography came to be written and published.

From the CD "Poetic Justice," 1999. © 1985 by Fire of Change Music (ASCAP), © ℗ 1998 by Buddy Mondlock.
Contact: buddymon@aol.com
http://www.buddymondlock.com

7. PENNY EVANS' DAUGHTERS (3:02)

Roland Kushner, Bethlehem, Pennsylvania

This reverent a cappella sequel to Steve's own a cappella "Ballad of Penny Evans" is based on a traditional sea chantey popularized by Lou Killen. Kushner's echoed voice symbolizes the voices that came before.

From the CD entitled "527," © ℗ BMI, Roland Kushner, 2000.
Contact: music@rjkushner.com
http://www.rolandkushnermusic.com

8. OLD TOWN, OLD FRIEND (2:52)

Chris Farrell, Chicago, Illinois

From another Chicago stalwart, this country-tinged track salutes the Old Town scene and cleverly merges Steve's "City of New Orleans" chorus ("Good morning, America") with Hudie ("Leadbelly") Ledbetter's best-known song ("Goodnight Irene").

Farrell on vocal and acoustic guitar, Victor Sanders on bass and electric guitar.
Contact: chrisbfarrell@hotmail.com
http://www.chrisfarrellweb.com

9. FLYING WITH THE ANGELS (4:14)

Jef Jaisun, Seattle, Washington

In this track recorded the night after Steve's death, Jaisun's pained voice cries out with hopeful sentiment, backed by the harmony of Steve's friend Tom Dundee and a barely heard Leilani McCoy. Dundee's quiet harmonica provides pensive counterpoint.

Contact: jef@jaisunphoto.com
http://www.jaisunphoto.com

7. Roland Kushner

(Photo by Bruce S. Putchat)

8. Chris Farrell

(Photo by David Sheffield)

9. Jef Jaisun

(Photo by Margie Paez)

10. Greg Hildebrand, 1990s

(Photo by Christine Gilchrist)

11. Steve Hopkins

(Photo by Susan
Michaelson Roads)

CD TRACKS 10–15

10. OFFICER RIGONI TO THE RESCUE, OR HOW THE PEOPLE OF THE STATE OF ILLINOIS SAVED ME FROM MYSELF (2:09)

Greg Hildebrand, Minhamite, Victoria, Australia

Technically not a tribute song, this was written the year before Steve "arrived" at the Earl of Old Town. But Steve enshrined it as "Chicago Bust Rag" on the first LP in which he participated ("Gathering at the Earl of Old Town," 1971), so its very presence here constitutes a tribute to Steve. Here is the seldom-heard original version, by the author himself, based on the traditional tune of "Stagger Lee."

Contact: jessoffel@hotmail.com

11. HEROES (5:06)

Steve Hopkins, Austin, Texas

This musician's homage to Buddy Holly, John Lennon and Harry Chapin culminates with a verse about Steve. Hopkins hails from Austin, a city with a rich music scene in which Steve had a strong following.

From the CD "Just Another Day in Paradox,"
© Steve Hopkins, MAYDEWS Music, 1999 (BMI).
Contact: shopkins@austin.rr.com
http://www.stevehopkinsmusic.com

12. THE MAN WITH THE GOLDEN TUNE (4:18)

Words and music by Peter Weisz, Carmel, Indiana / Vocals and instrumentals by Tim Brickley, Indianapolis, Indiana

This expertly executed narrative catches Steve at three stops along his musical journey: the 1972 Cambridge Folk Festival, a 1980 opener for Steve Martin and in 1983 at the Hummingbird in Indianapolis.

Contact: peter@peterweisz.com
http://www.peterweisz.com
info@timbrickley.com
http://www.timbrickley.com

13. GATHER AT THE RIVER (4:50)

Don Lange, Dundee, Oregon

This moving tribute starts out 100 years ago, sneaks into the Steve-inspired verse of "little magician" and then drives home the connection to Steve with the destination of the Mississippi River, the "City of New Orleans." Lange is a former Chicago folkie who runs a winery near Portland.

© 2006 Barking Spider Music (BMI), administered by Bug Music, all rights reserved, used by permission.
Contact: donlange@europa.com
http://www.donlange.com

14. LIFE DOWN ON THE BISTRO (4:16)

Reuben "Lounge Lizard" Morgan, Daytona Beach, Florida

This salute to a long-gone music club in Atlanta, Georgia, comes in a samba-esque tempo and with full instrumentation, linking Steve to peers Jimmy Buffett and Gamble Rogers.

From the CD "No Worries," 2006.
Contact: cooljams@hotmail.com
http://www.tiptopwebsite.com/loungelizard

15. SONG FOR STEVE GOODMAN (5:27)

Eddie Walker, Brookfield, Middlesbrough, United Kingdom

This epic story song from England was recorded at the 2003 Cambridge Folk Festival, a few hundred yards from the scene described in the first verse. Walker's warmth, admiration and eye for detail emulate those qualities in Steve himself. His chorus also conveys the departure of both Steve and the passenger train. And in every concert, as in this one, Walker ends the song by segueing to "City of New Orleans," never deviating from Steve's original words.

Original version on the LP "Picking My Way," 1985, Ragged Records, RAGR003.
Contact: eddie.walker13@ntlworld.com
http://www.eddiewalker.net

12. Peter Weisz

(Photo courtesy of Peter Weisz)

13. Don Lange

(Photo courtesy of Don Lange)

14. Reuben Morgan

(Photo by Mason Katz)

15. Eddie Walker, 1985

(Photo by Studio Tristan)

16. Harry Waller, late 1970s

(Photo by Paul Natkin)

CD TRACKS 16–19

16. WHY DID HE HAVE TO LEAVE? (3:21)

Harry Waller, Chicago, Illinois

A ringing ballad by a longtime Chicago folkie, this mini-biography of a friendship sports a strong narrative, specific references, a driving guitar melody, an emotional vocal and even a couple of jokes.

© Roach-Hound Publishing (BMI). **Contact**: hwalle001@yahoo.com

17. I HAD A DREAM (3:35)

Brian Gill, Moscow, Idaho

This ethereal tale poses an answer to the question posed by Harry Waller's song, and because it is by the same musician who created the opening track, it fits as the other vocal bookend for the CD. Gill recently arrived in Idaho by way of Chicago, Las Vegas and Nashville, and the 23-year-old dream expressed in this tune inspires him to this day.

Contact: briangillmusic@hotmail.com http://www.briangillmusic.com

18. THE DUTCHMAN (2:43)

Jay Haynes, piano, Villanova, Pennsylvania

Given most prominence by Steve, this ode to love and aging (by Michael Smith) is lovely in any version, but especially on solo piano. Jay Haynes was the son of a founding family of the Philadelphia Folk Festival, at which Steve starred. Haynes, who recorded this at a family gathering in 1979 before leaving for Army duty at Fort Dix, committed suicide in 1983, a year before Steve's death. His arrangement, moving gently between 4/4 and 3/4 time, can be enjoyed by those with no knowledge of Steve and the song's lyrical themes. But for those familiar with both Steve and the song, it can wring tears of reconciliation.

Song © Michael Peter Smith, Chicago, Ill., Bird Avenue Publishing (ASCAP), 1969. **Contact**: http://www.michaelsmithmusic.com

19. STEVE GOODMAN AUDIO CLIPS (6:13)

In April 1975, John Platt (then of WXRT-FM in Chicago, now of WFUV-FM in New York) drew from Steve some of the most intriguing interview comments of his career. Here, Steve reveals his musical philosophy and affection but with a wink that bares the folly of taking it all too seriously.

Thanks to John Platt, to former WXRT executive vice president Seth Mason, to WXRT host Lin Brehmer and especially to Michael Damsky, WXRT vice president and general manager, for his authorization that allowed these excerpts to be included. **Contact**: WXRT-FM, Chicago, Illinois http://www.wxrt.com

18. Jay Haynes, 1978

(Photo by Kristen Gilkeson, courtesy of Mary and Ray Benischeck)

**CD engineer:
Joe Novak**
jnovak@aol.com

Total time: 75:53

'A good friend is dead and gone, but his song ain't over yet'

Brian Gill wrote tracks 1 and 17 of the accompanying CD.
(Photo by Geoff Crimmins of the *Moscow-Pullman Daily News*)

See details on all 19 of the CD tracks on the previous three pages, 775-777.

Words, music and all aspects of performance on these tracks are by the songwriters, and all tracks are previously unreleased, except as noted.

Implicit in Steve Goodman's life is the powerful notion that music can change individuals and the world — and it doesn't stop when we die. As singer/songwriter Brian Gill phrases it, Steve's "song ain't over yet."

In tune with that notion, this biography would not seem complete without a CD that presents a hefty sampling of songs written after Steve's death that pay tribute to him or mention him significantly.

When I set out in the late 1990s to research and write this book, I had no vision for such a musical appendage. But as I interviewed sources and was referred repeatedly to others, gradually the existence of these compositions — born independently of each other — penetrated my consciousness. Somewhere along the way, the concept for the CD was born. My final tally of such tunes is more than two dozen (see pages 737-738 of "On the Record"), and I'm overjoyed to include so many of them on the disc affixed to the inside back cover.

The CD, nearly 76 minutes long, provides musical evidence of how Steve's spirit continues to inspire others across three continents — in all corners of the United States as well as in Canada, England and Australia. Even more warming, however, is that, following Steve's example, the CD sheds light on deserving artists whose recordings often fall outside the spotlight. With obvious affection for Steve, these musicians donated their tracks to this project. I am grateful beyond words for their generosity.

The songs' styles and tempos range all over the musical map, but they address the common and compelling themes of mortality, loss, grief and, most of all, appreciation for life and the relentless passage of time.

Arranged like one of Steve's concerts (and aided by the expert engineering of Joe Novak), the CD begins with a couple of rousers, then darts between loud and soft, upbeat and somber, riding an arc that finishes with a quiet instrumental so that the crowd can leave for home with a warm glow.

At the end is a spoken-word bonus in which Steve himself weighs in with observations both charming and humble. It's a welcome slice of his personality to savor, both for newcomers and for those who have not heard him speak in far too long. Then again, Steve's own songs "speak" to us every day. ♪

Clay Eals